Cost Management

A Strategic Emphasis

SAS Activity-Based Costing (ABC) Software Integration

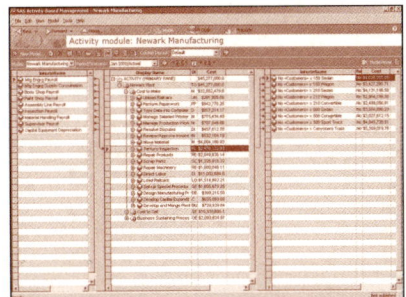

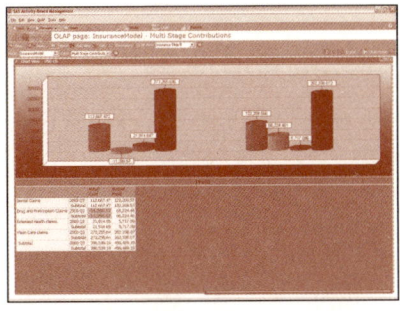

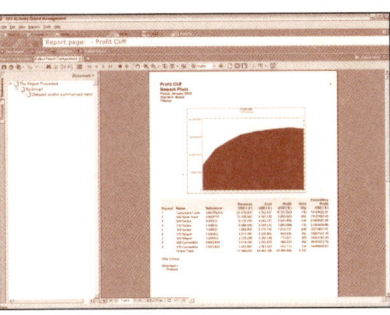

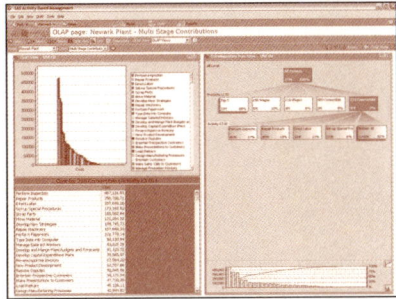

Activity-Based Costing (ABC) is a cost accounting method used by leading firms to accurately determine the costs of their product lines, service lines, distribution channels, and customers. SAS's Activity-Based Costing (ABC) Software is then used to identify the firm's most profitable products and customers, their inefficient operations, and their most effective and ineffective management methods.

The increasing complexity of manufacturing and service operations, together with increasingly competitive business conditions, has caused many organizations to adopt improved cost accounting systems, such as ABC costing. These organizations typically use software such as SAS Institute's ABC system to perform the data organizing and calculations required by ABC. Blocher/Stout/Cokins' learning resources includes SAS ABC software, together with class-tested case materials and tutorials that utilize the SAS ABC software.

The SAS ABC software (formerly called OROS) maintains and processes information about the activities within a company. OROS Quick, a simplified version of the fully functional software, includes all the steps of developing an ABC system, including:

- Creating the necessary files of information about cost resources, activities, and cost objects
- Creating the cost driver assignments
- Data entry
- Calculating ABC costs
- Comparing ABC costs to traditional cost calculations

The OROS Quick software and a related tutorial are available for download at **www.mhhe.com/blocher5e,** the Online Learning Center (OLC) that accompanies Blocher/Stout/Cokins *Cost Management: A Strategic Emphasis,* 5e. The software and tutorial are designed for those new to ABC as well as the more experienced user.

The Blocher/Stout/Cokins *Cases & Readings Manual* and OLC include three short cases that can be used with the tutorial and software to build a simplified ABC model. The objective of each case and tutorial is to illustrate how a comprehensive ABC software system such as SAS can be used. While the cases are greatly simplified, the software is capable of running large scale, complex applications. In this way, the cases provide insight into actual applications of ABC that go well beyond the typical textbook examples. Additional cases will be added to the OLC as they become available.

Cost Management

A Strategic Emphasis

Fifth Edition

Edward J. Blocher

University of North Carolina at Chapel Hill
Kenan-Flagler Business School

David E. Stout

Youngstown State University
Williamson College of Business Administration

Gary Cokins

Strategist, Performance Management Solutions
SAS/Worldwide Strategy

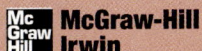
McGraw-Hill
Irwin

McGraw-Hill
Irwin

COST MANAGEMENT: A STRATEGIC EMPHASIS

Published by McGraw-Hill/Irwin, a business unit of The McGraw-Hill Companies, Inc., 1221 Avenue of the Americas, New York, NY, 10020. Copyright © 2010, 2008, 2005, 2002, 1999 by The McGraw-Hill Companies, Inc. All rights reserved. No part of this publication may be reproduced or distributed in any form or by any means, or stored in a database or retrieval system, without the prior written consent of The McGraw-Hill Companies, Inc., including, but not limited to, in any network or other electronic storage or transmission, or broadcast for distance learning.

Some ancillaries, including electronic and print components, may not be available to customers outside the United States.

This book is printed on acid-free paper.

2 3 4 5 6 7 8 9 0 DOW/DOW 0

ISBN 978-0-07-352694-2
MHID 0-07-352694-0

Vice president and editor-in-chief: *Brent Gordon*
Editorial director: *Stewart Mattson*
Executive editor: *Richard T. Hercher, Jr.*
Editorial coordinator: *Rebecca Mann*
Marketing manager: *Kathleen Klehr*
Senior project manager: *Bruce Gin*
Production supervisor: *Michael McCormick*
Designer: *Matt Diamond*
Senior media project manager: *Greg Bates*
Cover design: *Jenny El-Shamy*
Interior design: *Matt Diamond*
Typeface: *10/12 Times Roman*
Compositor: *Laserwords Private Limited*
Printer: *R. R. Donnelley*

Library of Congress Cataloging-in-Publication Data

Blocher, Edward.
    Cost management : a strategic emphasis / Edward J. Blocher, David E. Stout, Gary Cokins.—5th ed.
      p. cm.
    Includes index.
    ISBN-13: 978-0-07-352694-2 (alk. paper)
    ISBN-10: 0-07-352694-0 (alk. paper)
    1. Cost accounting. 2. Managerial accounting. I. Stout, David Edward. II. Cokins, Gary. III. Title.
HF5686.C8B559 2010
658.15'52—dc22   2009015756

www.mhhe.com

We dedicate this edition . . .

To my wife, Sandy, and our sons, Joseph and David

Ed Blocher

To my wife, Anne, and our sons, David and Kevin

David E. Stout

To my wife, Pam Tower, and my mentor, Robert A. Bonsack—a true craftsman in the field of cost management

Gary Cokins

Special Dedication:

In recognition of the significant influence he has had on management accounting, and in particular on our thinking about strategic cost management, we dedicate this edition to the memory of Professor John K. Shank.

Meet the Authors

Edward J. Blocher is professor of accounting at the Kenan-Flagler Business School at the University of North Carolina at Chapel Hill. His undergraduate degree (economics) is from Rice University, his MBA from Tulane University, and his Ph.D. from the University of Texas at Austin. Professor Blocher presents regularly on strategic cost management at the national meetings of both the American Accounting Association (AAA) and the Institute of Management Accountants (IMA).

While he is involved in a number of accounting organizations, Professor Blocher has been most continually active in the IMA, where he is now a trustee of the Foundation for Applied Research (FAR). He is a certified management accountant (CMA), has taught review courses for the CMA exam, and has served on the IMA's national education committee. Professor Blocher is also the author or co-author of several articles in management accounting and in other areas of accounting and has served as associate editor and reviewer for a number of accounting journals. Recently he published an article in *Issues in Accounting Education* (February 2009) on the topic of teaching strategic cost management.

Putting research and teaching into practice is important to Professor Blocher, who has worked closely with other firms and organizations in developing products, publications, and teaching materials. He was a member of the task force for the IMA that developed a new definition of management accounting in 2008. He currently serves as the chair of academic research proposals for the IMA's FAR program. Also, he has provided expert testimony and has consulted with a number of organizations, including Blue Cross and Blue Shield of North Carolina, the American Institute of CPAs, Grant Thornton, and the State of North Carolina, among others.

David E. Stout is the John S. and Doris M. Andrews Professor of Accounting, Williamson College of Business Administration, Youngstown State University. Previously, he held the position of the John M. Cooney Professor of Accounting, School of Business, Villanova University. David earned his Ph.D. in accounting (1982) from the Katz Graduate School of Business, University of Pittsburgh and teaches in the cost/managerial accounting area. He served previously as editor of *Issues in Accounting Education* and serves currently as senior associate editor of the *Journal of Accounting Education* and as a member of the editorial board of each of the following journals: *Issues in Accounting Education; Journal of International Accounting, Auditing & Taxation; China Finance and Accounting Review; International Journal of Management Education; IMA Educational Case Journal;* and, *Management Accounting Quarterly/Strategic Finance.* In addition, he serves as a member of the editorial advisory board of *Accounting Education: An International Journal.* Professor Stout has published over 75 articles in numerous professional and academic journals including *Advances in Accounting Education, Issues in Accounting Education,* the *Journal of Accounting Education, The Accounting Educators' Journal, Advances in International Accounting, Behavioral Research in Accounting (BRIA), The CPA Journal, Educational and Psychological Measurement, Management Accounting, Management Accounting Quarterly, Financial Practice and Education, Strategic Finance,* and *Advances in Accounting.* David is past president of the Teaching, Learning & Curriculum (TLC) Section of the AAA, past president of the Academy of Business Education (ABE), and past president of the Ohio Region, American Accounting Association (AAA). In 2007, he was the recipient of the R. Lee Brummet Award for Distinguished Accounting Educators, Institute of Management Accountants (IMA), and the Ohio Outstanding Accounting Educator Award, which is cosponsored by the Ohio Society of CPAs and the AAA's Ohio Region. In 2008, David received the Distinguished Achievement in Accounting Education Award from the AICPA, and the Distinguished Service Award for Educators given by the IMA. Also in 2008, David was inducted into the Hall of Honor, TLC Section of the AAA and was selected by *Ohio Magazine* as one of Ohio's Outstanding College and University Teachers.

Gary Cokins is a global product marketing manager involved with performance-management solutions with SAS, a leading provider of business analytics software. Gary is an internationally recognized expert, speaker, and author in advanced cost management and performance-improvement systems. He received a BS degree in industrial engineering/operations research (with honors) from Cornell University in 1971 and an MBA from Northwestern University's Kellogg School of Management in 1974. Gary began his career as a strategic planner with FMC Corporation and then served as a financial controller and operations manager. In 1981 he began his management consulting career with Deloitte Consulting and continued with KPMG Peat Marwick. He then headed the National Cost Management Consulting Services for Electronic Data Systems (EDS). Gary was the lead author of the acclaimed *A Manager's Primer on ABC Costing,* published by the IMA. He also has two successful books in *Activity-Based Costing and Performance Management.* Gary participates and serves on professional society committees including: The Consortium for Advanced Management–International (CAM-I), the Supply Chain Council, the IMA, and the International Federation of Accountants (IFAC). He is also a member of *Journal of Cost Management* Editorial Advisory Board.

The Author Team: Selected to provide a leading book in cost management based on leadership in teaching experience, commitment to learning, and up-to-date knowledge of real-world management accounting practices.

Blocher/Stout/Cokins:

Welcome to Students:

We have written this book to help you understand the role of cost management in helping an organization succeed. Unlike many books that aim to teach you *about* accounting, we aim to show you how an important area of accounting, cost management, is *used* by managers to help organizations achieve their goals.

An important aspect of cost management in our text is the strategic focus. By strategy we mean the long-term plan the organization has developed to compete successfully. Most organizations strive to achieve a competitive edge through the execution of a specific strategy. For some firms it is low cost, and for others it might be high quality, customer service, or some unique feature or attribute of its product or service. We know in these competitive times that an organization does not succeed by being ordinary. In contrast, it develops a strategy that will set it apart from competitors and ensure its attractiveness to customers and other stakeholders into the future. The role of cost management is to help management of the organization attain and maintain success through strategy implementation. Thus, for every major topic covered in our text there is a larger issue, which is: "How does this organization compete? What type of cost-management information does it need?" We do ***not*** cover a cost-management method simply to become proficient at it. We want you to know why, when, and how the technique is used to help the organization succeed.

A strategic understanding of cost management is so important that many senior financial managers are coming back to school to learn more about strategy, competitive analysis, and new cost-management techniques. Knowing how to do the accounting alone, no matter how well you do it, is by itself no longer sufficient. Cost management with a strategic emphasis is one way to enhance your career and to add value to your employer, whatever type of organization it might be.

Key Text Features that Integrate the Strategy Emphasis

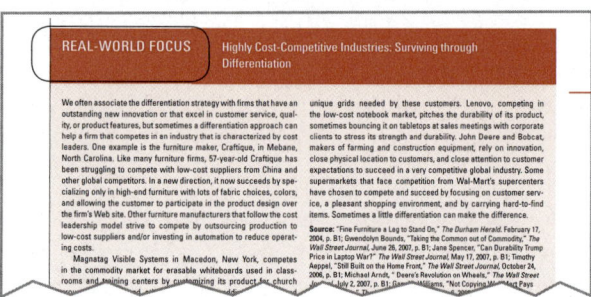

Real-World Focus *Cost Management,* 5e, explains how accounting systems can add value to the organization. The **Real-World Focus** boxes throughout the text take real organizations and demonstrate strategy in action and the role that cost management plays in supporting the organization's strategy.

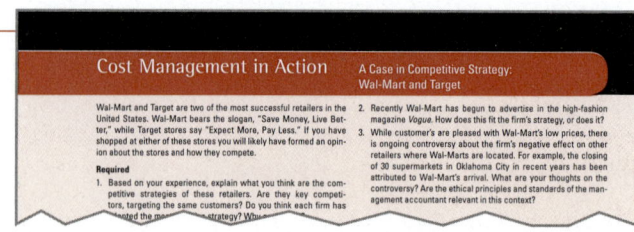

To augment this coverage, the Blocher team encourages students to further explore real-world companies through **Cost Management in Action** boxes that appear throughout the text. This feature poses important questions that make students think critically about the relationship between cost management and management strategy. At the end of each chapter, the authors then supply their comments for the **Cost Management in Action** boxes.

Problem Material The Blocher team has taken great care to develop assignment material that effectively reinforces concepts, procedures, and strategic issues presented in each chapter. In addition, each chapter has one or more end-of-chapter assignments that focus on an international context or a service (i.e., nonmanufacturing) setting. Other end-of-chapter assignments require the use of Excel or the consideration of ethical issues to the topic at hand. All such assignments are marked appropriately for easy identification, as follows:

 Strategy    International   Service   Ethics    Excel

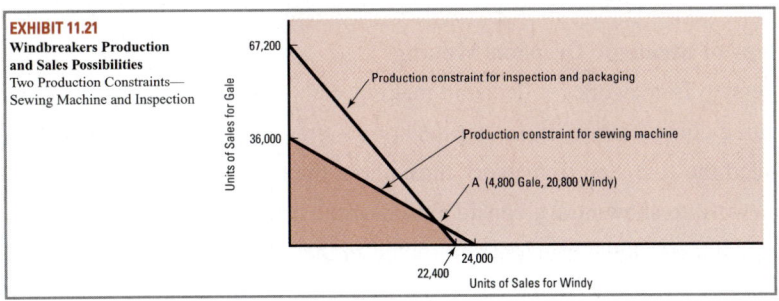

EXHIBIT 11.21
Windbreakers Production and Sales Possibilities
Two Production Constraints—Sewing Machine and Inspection

Text Illustrations Clear and concise exhibits help illustrate basic and complicated topics throughout the book.

Excel Solutions Manual Introduced for the fourth edition, the *Excel Solutions Manual* is revised and updated. This supplement consists of an Excel workbook for each chapter and comes in two versions: one for the instructor, the other for students. Each workbook provides for the instructor the solution to *every* exercise and problem in the chapter, each in its own worksheet in the workbook. Each solution has three components: background information, data, and solution/model-building. The Excel solutions provide the basis for the instructor to both guide students through the use of Excel in solving problems, and a useful tool for generating new problems.

The *Excel Solutions Manual* also has a student version that differs from the instructor's version in only one respect: worked-out solutions are available for only half of end-of-chapter exercises and problems. The remaining problems (without solutions) can be used for Excel assignments. In other respects the student version of the manual is identical to the instructor version. Because all pertinent information for each exercise and problem, including background information and data, is included in each worksheet, the *Excel Solutions Manual* is very easy to use.

Cases and Reading Manual

The supplemental *Cases and Readings Manual,* available in electronic form, challenges students to think about and use cost-management information in a real-world setting. The longer articles provide a basis for more comprehensive and in-depth discussions about the role of *cost management* in helping an organization successfully execute its strategy. We have found the *Cases and Readings Manual* to be particularly useful for upper-level undergraduate courses and for MBA course offerings.

Tegrity Campus: Lectures 24/7

Tegrity Campus is a service that makes class time available 24/7 by automatically capturing every lecture in a searchable format for students to review when they study and complete assignments. With a simple one-click start-and-stop process, you capture all computer screens and corresponding audio. Students can replay any part of any class with easy-to-use browser-based viewing on a PC or Mac.

Educators know that the more students can see, hear, and experience class resources, the better they learn. In fact, studies prove it. With Tegrity Campus, students quickly recall key moments by using Tegrity Campus's unique search feature. This search helps students efficiently find what they need, when they need it, across an entire semester of class recordings. Help turn all your students' study time into learning moments immediately supported by your lecture.

To learn more about Tegrity watch a 2-minute Flash demo at **http://tegritycampus.mhhe.com**.

Assurance of Learning Ready

Many educational institutions today are focused on the notion of assurance of learning, an important element of some accreditation standards. *Cost Management* is designed specifically to help support your assurance of learning initiatives with a simple, yet powerful solution.

Test bank questions for *Cost Management* map to a specific chapter learning outcome/objective listed in the text. You can use our test bank software, EZ Test and EZ Test Online to easily query for learning outcomes/objectives that directly relate to the learning objectives for your course. You can then use the reporting features of EZ Test to aggregate student results in similar fashion, making the collection and presentation of data simple and easy.

AACSB Statement

The McGraw-Hill Companies is a proud corporate member of AACSB International. Understanding the importance and value of AACSB accreditation, *Cost Management,* 5e recognizes the guidelines detailed in the AACSB standards by connecting selected questions in the test bank to the six general knowledge and skill areas in the AACSB standards.

The statements contained in *Cost Management,* 5e are provided only as a guide for the users of this textbook. The AACSB leaves content coverage and assessment within the purview of individual schools, the mission of the school, and the faculty.

New Framework to Integrate Strategy: The Five Steps of Strategic Decision Making

The first edition of *Cost Management* introduced a five-step framework for decision making with a strategic emphasis. The framework shows that each decision starts and ends with a consideration of the organization's strategy. To extend and integrate the strategic emphasis, the fifth edition has included the five-step framework throughout the text. In all but a few chapters there is a short section that uses the five-step framework to show how a consideration of the organization's strategy plays a key role in making the decision that will address the business-related problems presented in that chapter.

The Current Economic Recession Increases the Importance of Reviewing and Executing Strategy

The current economic recession is addressed in the text, both in the chapters and in the end-of-chapter exercises and problems. The recession requires firms to place an even greater emphasis on executing their strategy. Moreover, the economic difficulties may require a firm to review and modify its strategy to compete more effectively in the changed economic conditions.

Online Supplement for Assignments, Exams, and More...

A new learning supplement, **Practice4Performance (P4P),** is available for use with the fifth edition. P4P was developed by Professor Paul Goldwater at the University of Central Florida. **P4P** is the 2008 winner of the American Accounting Association's *Jim Bulloch Award for Innovations in Management Accounting Education.* **P4P** does the following for the instructor:

- Provides a library of over 3,000 questions that are updated with new data each time the system is accessed by the student; detailed solutions are included for each question.

- Simulates scenarios–**P4P** has the ability to create randomized, multistep analytical problems that vary significantly with each iteration, saving instructors valuable time in creating their own materials.

- Provides partial credit on multiple-choice questions as a built-in option that decreases the points awarded per question as the number of attempts increases.

- Has live tracking of all statistics related to student practice sessions, homework, quizzes, and exams.

- Provides flexibility in how to structure and schedule quizzes and exams—the number of questions, difficulty level of questions, types of questions (e.g., qualitative- or calculation-based), and learning objectives addressed are all within the control of the instructor.

- Administers assignments, grading, and interaction through P4P-integrated communication features such as online document posting, class/individual announcements, and message boards.

Excel Tutorials

Free to adopters of the fifth edition is a set of Excel tutorials, one for each chapter. This new resource provides a context-based means for students to hone their Excel skills. In many cases, the Excel tutorial is linked to the demonstration problem included at the end of the chapter. The tutorials cover a wide variety of Excel topics, from elementary to the intermediate level, and some at the advanced level. The tutorials are an easy way for students to learn more about Excel without having to ask the instructor.

New Chapter Organization and Parts Introductions

The new edition has reorganized the parts and sequence of chapters to follow the sequence used by many of our adopters. Thus, the process-costing and cost-allocation chapters were moved up, and capital budgeting is now included as a chapter in the section on planning and decision making. These two changes permit a more streamlined presentation. There are now four major parts to the text: Part One, introduction to strategy, cost management, and cost systems;

Cost Management?

Part Two, planning and decision making; Part Three, operational-level control; and Part Four, management-level control. A new feature of the text is the inclusion of an introduction to each of the four parts to explain the learning objectives of the chapters in that part. Briefly, the objective of Part One is to introduce foundational concepts, including strategy, strategy implementation, and product-costing systems. The coverage of cost systems begins with job costing and is followed by ABC, process costing, and joint product costing/cost allocation. Part Two, planning and decision making, begins with cost estimation, since planning and decision making are guided by knowledge of cost drivers and cost behavior. Covered in Part Two is short-term profit-planning (CVP), budgeting, decision making, capital budgeting, target costing, the theory of constraints, and pricing. Parts Three and Four study performance measurement: Part Three looks at this issue from the perspective of those who manage operations on a day-to-day basis, while Part Four examines performance evaluation at a higher level: business-unit managers who have responsibility for divisions, product lines, or manufacturing plants, and whose units are evaluated as cost centers, profit centers, or investment centers.

Integration of Important Topics throughout the Text

Key topic areas for the course are integrated across the chapters. As noted above, strategy is integrated throughout the text. In addition, accounting for "lean" is included in four chapters as it relates to the subject matter of that chapter. Similarly, time-driven activity-based costing (TDABC) is covered in the ABC chapter and also in the chapter on budgeting. ABC appears in most of the chapters in Part Two, as it has a key role in planning and decision making. Nonfinancial performance measures and the balanced scorecard (BSC) are introduced in Part One and then covered as part of operational and management control chapters included in Parts Three and Four. Resource consumption accounting (RCA) is covered both in Chapter 5 and again in Chapter 15. The topic of capacity resource planning is covered in Chapters 10 and 15. These are just examples of the efforts the authors have made to integrate key topics throughout the text.

Important Changes in Each Chapter of the Fifth Edition

Part One: Introduction to Strategy, Cost Management, and Cost Systems

Chapter 1: Cost Management and Strategy

- Inclusion of the IMA's new (2008) definition of *management accounting* and linkage of the definition to the objectives of the text. The new definition stresses the role cost management has in helping an organization develop and implement its strategy.
- Complete reorganization to show more clearly the elements of the contemporary business environment and the management accountant's response to the new business environment; new terms added include *lean accounting, business intelligence,* the *strategy map, enterprise sustainability,* and *enterprise risk management.*

- Enhanced coverage of the role of cost management in the global economy and in the current economic recession.
- New Real-World Focus (RWF) examples throughout the chapter, including surveys of current practice.

Chapter 2: Implementing Strategy: The Value Chain, the Balanced Scorecard, and the Strategy Map

- New Real-World Focus (RWF) examples, including surveys of current practice.
- Expanded coverage of the strategy map with an entirely new illustration and including new exercise material.
- Increased coverage of sustainability.
- Enhanced material on implementation issues associated with the balanced scorecard (BSC).

- New exercises and problems with an emphasis on strategy and the value chain.

Chapter 3: Basic Cost Management Concepts

- New Real-World Focus (RWF) examples.
- New exercises and problems.
- Shortened, more clarified presentation in the chapter.

Chapter 4: Job Costing

- New Real-World Focus (RWF) examples.
- Replacement of old ledger-based exhibits with new exhibits based on job-costing software.

- Shortened, more clarified presentation of the chapter.
- New exercises and problems with a focus on service industries.

Chapter 5: Activity-Based Costing (ABC) and Customer Profitability Analysis

- New coverage of resource consumption accounting (RCA) and lean accounting.
- New Real-World Focus (RWF) examples, including surveys of current practice.
- Expanded coverage of time-driven ABC (TDABC).
- Expanded coverage of customer lifetime value, introduction of the concept of customer equity, and discussion of strategy implementation for customer profitability analysis.
- New exercises and problems focusing on strategy, the cost of capacity, resource consumption cost drivers, and ethics.

Chapter 6: Process Costing

- Revised coverage of *backflush costing* with a new illustration and associated end-of-chapter assignment material.
- New problem material with a focus on sustainability.

Chapter 7: Cost Allocation: Departments, Joint Products, and By-Products

- New Real-World Focus (RWF) examples.
- New assignment material with a focus on service companies.
- Revision to clarify the relationship between departmental cost allocation and the costing methods used elsewhere in the text.
- Complete rewrite of Exhibits 7-10, 7-11, and 7-12 to clarify these exhibits.

Part Two: Planning and Decision Making

Chapter 8: Cost Estimation

- Several new Real-World Focus (RWF) boxes featuring examples from *Freakonomics* (Steven D. Levitt and Stephen J. Dubner) and *Super Crunchers* (Ian Ayres).
- New self-study problem and exercise on nonlinear regression.
- Improved exhibits to illustrate the use of Excel for regression analysis.
- New exercises and problems with a focus on research using the Internet.

Chapter 9: Profit Planning: Cost–Volume–Profit Analysis

- New Real-World Focus (RWF) examples, including one in a global context and another that focuses on the analysis of automobile fuel efficiency.
- New section on the use of value streams and lean accounting for short-term profit-planning.
- Revision and extension of the section on ABC-based CVP analysis.
- New problems and examples with an emphasis on strategy and service organizations.

Chapter 10: Strategy and the Master Budget

- New discussion of "what-if"/ sensitivity analysis and related end-of-chapter Excel-based exercises and problems.
- Use of the statement of cash flow format for preparation of cash budgets.
- Extension of activity-based budgeting (ABB) to time-driven activity-based budgeting (TDABC) and related discussion of capacity resource-planning issues.
- Expanded discussion of incentive issues regarding budgeting systems, including the "Beyond Budgeting"

controversy, alternative incentive-compensation schemes, and the use of rolling financial forecasts.
- Increased number of service-based and strategy-related end-of-chapter exercises and problems.

Chapter 11: Decision Making with a Strategic Emphasis

- Updated Real-World Focus (RWF) examples.
- New section on the use of value stream management and lean accounting in decision making.
- New exercises and problems with a special focus on strategy.

Chapter 12: Strategy and the Analysis of Capital Investments

- Discussion of the modified internal rate of return (MIRR) evaluation criterion.
- For equipment-replacement type decisions, presentation of alternative formats for structuring the analysis: total cash flows vs. analysis of differential cash flows.
- Coverage of the topic of real options as a means of dealing with uncertainty in the analysis of capital budgeting projects.
- Inclusion of additional strategy-related end-of-chapter assignments.
- Addition of new Real-World Focus (RWF) items.

Chapter 13: Cost Planning for the Product Life Cycle: Target Costing, Theory of Constraints (TOC), and Strategic Pricing

- New coverage of analytical pricing methods, including illustrations.
- New and updated Real-World Focus (RWF) examples throughout the chapter.
- New exercises and problems with a focus on strategy and on service industries, including an example of a TOC application in a restaurant.

Part Three: Operational-Level Control

Chapter 14: Operational Performance Measurement: Sales and Direct-Cost Variances, and the Role of Nonfinancial Performance Measures

- Reorientation of chapter contents to focus initially on the use of flexible budgets and standard costs for short-term financial control.
- Inclusion of additional strategy-related end-of-chapter assignments.
- New section, and related assignment material, regarding just-in-time (JIT) manufacturing.
- New section regarding the use of nonfinancial performance indicators and linkage to an organization's balanced scorecard (BSC).
- Five new Real-World Focus (RWF) items.

Chapter 15: Operational Performance Measurement: Indirect-Cost Variances and Resource-Capacity Planning

- Inclusion of *Statement of Financial Standards No. 151:* "Inventory Costs—An Amendment of ARB No. 43, Chapter 4" (www.fasb .org/pdf/aop_FAS151.pdf).
- New discussion regarding capacity resource planning and the role of ABC data for managing resource-capacity spending.
- New discussion regarding earnings-management opportunities (under absorption costing) based on choice of denominator volume level.
- New discussion regarding both variable and short-term fixed-cost components in batch-level support costs tracked by ABC systems.
- Five totally new end-of-chapter problems, including three covering strategy, one service-context

problem, and one ethics-related problem.
- Inclusion (Appendix) of the expected value of perfect information (EVPI) within the context of the variance-investigation decision under uncertainty.

Chapter 16: Operational Performance Measurement: Further Analysis of Productivity and Sales

- New Real-World Focus (RWF) examples, updated for recent survey data.
- New section on lean manufacturing with related exercise material.
- Greater emphasis on strategy, including a five-step example illustrating the role of market variances in strategy implementation.
- New end-of-chapter material with a focus on the current economic recession.

Chapter 17: The Management and Control of Quality

- Expanded discussion of "lean" as a strategy, as well as cost-system design issues associated with lean manufacturing.
- Inclusion of five new Real-World Focus (RWF) items.
- Seven totally new end-of-chapter exercises, plus two new research-based end-of-chapter problems.
- Inclusion of more strategy-related end-of-chapter assignments.

Part Four: Management-Level Control

Chapter 18: Strategic Performance Measurement: Cost Centers, Profit Centers, and the Balanced Scorecard (BSC)

- New and updated Real-World Focus (RWF) examples, including surveys from practice.

- New section covering accounting for lean, including a related end-of-chapter exercise.
- New problems with a focus on strategy, globalization, and ethics.
- Shortened, improved, and more focused coverage of the implementation of the balanced scorecard (BSC) for performance measurement.

Chapter 19: Strategic Performance Measurement: Investment Centers

- New discussion regarding strategic issues associated with the use of ROI as a financial-performance indicator.
- Expanded discussion of estimating EVA® NOPAT and EVA® Capital, using both the financing approach and the operating approach.
- Presentation and discussion of a general transfer pricing rule, including implementation issues associated with this rule.
- Ten totally new end-of-chapter exercises and problems, including assignments related to strategic considerations, service-sector applications, the use of Excel, and international operations.
- Two new Real-World Focus (RWF) items in the body of the chapter, one dealing with transfer-pricing issues, the other dealing with estimating human capital ROI.

Chapter 20: Management Compensation, Business Analysis, and Business Valuation

- New and updated Real-World Focus (RWF) examples, including updated surveys from practice and examples that include the effect of the current economic recession on compensation, business analysis, and business valuation.
- New problem material with a focus on strategy and value creation.

Supplements

For Instructors...

Instructor's Resource CD-ROM (ISBN 007724351X): Contains all essential course supplements such as the Instructor's Resource Manual, Solutions Manual–Word format (both student and instructor versions), Test Bank (Word format), EZ Test Bank, PowerPoint® Presentations, and Excel Solutions Manual (both student and instructor versions). All instructor supplements are prepared by the authors.

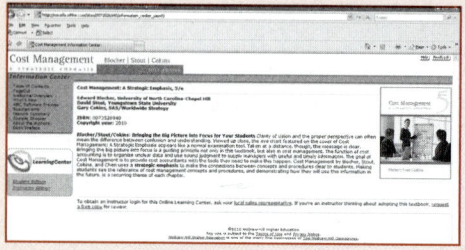

Online Learning Center (OLC): www.mhhe.com/blocher5e. The Instructor Edition of the *Cost Management: A Strategic Emphasis, 5e* OLC is password-protected and another convenient place for instructors to access course supplements. Resources for professors include: the Instructor and Student Solutions Manual (in both Word and Excel formats), teaching notes for the casebook, links to professional resources, sample syllabi, text updates, and the set of Excel tutorials.

Practice4Performance (P4P) (ISBN 0077997557 for book and P4P access card): A new learning supplement, **Practice4Performance (P4P),** is an online assignment and exam manager. It provides over 3,000 questions that are updated with new data on each student session with the system. This is a great system to use with large sections, and where the instructor wants to provide the students with the incentive to improve their performance in the course by "practicing for performance." The system not only administers student practice sessions, assignments, and exams (including automatic grading of all sessions, assignments and exams), but also provides student and instructor interaction features such as online document posting, class/individual announcements, and message boards. It is a complete solution for easy management of assignments and exams, and a great incentive for students to try practice questions in addition to those assigned.

For Students...

Cases and Readings for use with *Cost Management: A Strategic Emphasis, 5e:* This manual contains cases and articles covering a variety of important topics. The case scenarios put students in situations that allow them to think strategically and to apply concepts they've learned in the course. Key readings have been chosen to give students more background into the evolution of strategic cost management topics as well as to contemporary controversies in the field.

Online Learning Center (OLC): www.mhhe.com/blocher5e. The Student Edition of the *Cost Management: A Strategic Emphasis,* 5e OLC contains many tools designed to help students study, including: the Cases and Readings Manual, check figures, text updates, links to professional resources, chapter overviews, chapter objectives, multiple-choice quizzes, Excel tutorials, Present Value tables, and PowerPoint® presentations.

SAS Software: SAS's Activity-Based Costing (ABC) software is used worldwide for performance management functions and analysis. *Cost Management* incorporates SAS Software in its ABC case material to prepare students for calculating ABC costs, creating cost-driver assignments, and organizing cost information using real-world software. Visit the Blocher OLC today to learn more!

Acknowledgments

Our Sincerest Thanks . . .

In writing this book, we were fortunate to have received extensive feedback from a number of accounting educators. We want to thank our colleagues for their careful and complete review of our work. The comments that we received were invaluable in helping us to shape the manuscript. We believe that this collaborative development process helped us to create a text that will truly meet the needs of today's students and instructors. We are sincerely grateful to the following individuals for their participation in the process:

Reviewers for 5e:

Wagdy Abdallah, *Seton Hall University*

Nas Ahadiat, *California State Polytechnic University-Pomona*

Wede E. Brownell, *University of Central Oklahoma*

Jeffrey Cohen, *Boston College*

Cheryl Corke, *Genesee Community College*

Joe Dowd, *Eastern Washington University*

Rafik Elias, *California State University-Los Angeles*

James M. Emig, *Villanova University*

Sidney Ewer, *Missouri State University*

Michael Flores, *Wichita State University*

Sanjay Gupta, *Valdosta State University*

Betty Harper, *Middle Tennessee State University*

Jeannie Harrington, *Middle Tennessee State University*

Todd Jensen, *California State University-Sacramento*

Larry N. Killough, *Virginia Polytechnic Institute*

Leslie Kren, *University of Wisconsin–Milwaukee*

Joetta Malone, *Strayer University*

Man C. Maloo, *Towson University*

Linda Marquis, *Northern Kentucky University*

John McGowan, *St. Louis University*

Michael Morris, *University of Notre Dame*

Ann Murphy, *Metropolitan State College of Denver*

Lisa Owens, *Clemson University*

Martha L. Sale, *Sam Houston State University*

Marsha Scheidt, *University of Tennessee–Chattanooga*

Kenneth P. Sinclair, *Lehigh University*

Shiv Sharma, *Robert Morris University*

Rich White, *Florida Metro University*

Previous Edition Reviewers:

Vidya N. Awasthi, *Seattle University*

K. R. Balachandran, *New York University*

Mohamed E. Bayou, *School of Management, University of Michigan–Dearborn*

Marvin L. Bouillon, *Iowa State University*

Wayne Bremser, *Villanova University*

Bea Chiang, *The College of New Jersey*

Dennis Caplan, *Oregon State University*

Alan B. Czyzewski, *Indiana State University*

Robert J. DePasquale, *Saint Vincent College*

Robert W. Duron, *Chadron State College*

David Eichelberger, *Austin Peay State University*

Jerry W. Ferry, *University of North Alabama*

Michael Flores, *Wichita State University*

Jay D. Forsyth, *Central Washington University*

Mike Grayson, *Jackson State University*

Olen L. Greer, *Southwest Missouri State University*

Donald C. Gribbin, *Southern Illinois University*

Judith A. Harris, *Nova Southeastern University*

Aleecia Hibbets, *University of Louisiana–Monroe*

Jay Holmen, *University of Wisconsin–Eau Claire*

Linda Holmes, *University of Wisconsin–Whitewater*

Norma C. Holter, *Towson University*

David R. Honodel, *University of Denver*

Bambi Hora, *University of Central Oklahoma*

Paul Juras, *Wake Forest University*

Sanford R. Kahn, *University of Cincinnati*

Larry N. Killough, *Virginia Polytechnic Institute and State University*

Mehmet C. Kocakulah, *University of Southern Indiana*

Laura Jean Kreissl, *University of Wisconsin–Parkside*

Sandra S. Lang, *McKendree College*

Randall E. LaSalle, *West Chester University of Pennsylvania*

Dan Law, *Gonzaga University*

Stephen Makar, *University of Wisconsin–Oshkosh*

Brian L. McGuire, *University of Southern Indiana*

Laurie B. McWhorter, *Mississippi State University*

Yaw M. Mensah, *Rutgers University*

Cheryl E. Mitchem, *Virginia State University*

Jennifer Niece, *Assumption College*

Margaret O'Reilly-Allen, *Rider University*

Chei M. Paik, *George Washington University*

Hugh Pforsich, *University of Idaho*

Shirley Polejewski, *University of St. Thomas*

Jenice Prather-Kinsey, *University of Missouri–Columbia*

Dennis Shanholtzer, *Metropolitan Slate University*

Kenneth P. Sinclair, *Lehigh University*

John L. Stancil, *Florida Southern College*

Ronald A. Stunda, *Birmingham–Southern College*

Jerry Thorne, *North Carolina A&T State University*

We also want to recognize the special efforts of:

Michael Garner

Scott Stier

Jaime Kudary

Finally, we are most appreciative of the outstanding assistance and support provided by the professionals of McGraw-Hill/Irwin: Stewart Mattson, our editorial director, and Dick Hercher, Executive Editor, for their guidance; our developmental editor, Rebecca Mann, for her invaluable suggestions; Sankha Basu, our marketing manager, for his significant promotional efforts; Bruce Gin, our project manager, for his attention to detail; Matt Diamond, for the outstanding presentation of the text; and Gregory Bates, our media project manager, for his technical expertise in delivering our multimedia material. An added thanks to Beth Woods and Ilene Leopold Persoff for their significant contributions to the accuracy of our text.

Ed Blocher

David E. Stout

Gary Cokins

Brief Contents

Contents

PART THREE
OPERATIONAL-LEVEL CONTROL   589

PART ONE

Introduction to Strategy, Cost Management, and Cost Systems

The objective of the first seven chapters is to introduce the strategic approach to cost management and to cover the basic concepts of cost accounting systems.

Chapter 1 is an introduction to cost management—how companies plan for success and the management accountant's role in implementing strategy. The chapter includes coverage of the Institute of Management Accountants newly revised definition of management accounting. It is also an introduction to the current environment of business including contemporary management techniques and professional responsibilities.

Chapter 2 focuses on some of the principal means that organizations use to implement strategy. The chapter introduces a strategic management system known as the *balanced scorecard (BSC)*, the strategy map, and the value chain, and shows how these tools can be used to help the organization implement its strategy. These tools are foundational tools that appear throughout the text; this is why they are covered in this early chapter.

Chapter 3 defines the key terms that management accountants use to describe product cost systems and cost information for planning, decision making, and control. This terminology is important for both accountants and managers alike. The chapter also introduces the differences in management accounting between service, manufacturing, and merchandising companies.

Chapters 4–7 cover costing systems and their role in strategy implementation.

Chapter 4 provides an introduction to costing systems by defining the elements of cost and how these elements are combined to determine the cost of a *cost object* (e.g., product or service). The chapter assumes a volume-based approach for allocating indirect costs to cost objects. There are a number of variations on this basic cost system, each of which is designed to fit a particular manufacturing or service environment. These variations are explained in Chapters 5, 6, and 7. Standard costing is considered primarily a control tool and is included in Part Three, Operational-Level Control.

Chapter 5 covers a strategically important advance in product costing called activity-based costing (ABC). Rather than using the volume-based approach (explained in Chapter 4), the ABC approach incorporates the details of all the activities that are needed to provide the product or service. The result is much more accurate, and therefore more strategically useful, cost information regarding the resource demands of an organization's outputs.

Chapter 6 introduces process costing, a costing system that is applicable for firms that have relatively homogeneous products passing through similar processing steps, often in a continuous flow. Commodity-based industries are of this nature: food processing, chemical, and consumer products firms.

Chapter 7 covers cost-allocation issues associated with costing systems—departmental cost allocation and joint cost allocation. The chapter begins with an overview of the objectives and strategic role of cost allocation and then shows how departmental costs and joint costs are allocated to products.

CHAPTER ONE

Cost Management and Strategy

After studying this chapter you should be able to . . .

1. Explain the use of cost management information in each of the four functions of management and in different types of organizations, with emphasis on the strategic management function
2. Explain the contemporary business environment and how it has influenced cost management
3. Explain the contemporary management techniques and how they are used in cost management to respond to the contemporary business environment
4. Explain the different types of competitive strategies
5. Describe the professional environment of the management accountant, including professional organizations and professional certifications
6. Understand the principles and rules of professional ethics and explain how to apply them

Talk about a success story! Wal-Mart has grown from its first discount store in 1962 to become the world's largest company, with almost $400 billion in sales. It has achieved this through clear day-to-day attention to accomplishing its business strategy and to living up to its motto of "Save Money—Live Better." Wal-Mart achieves success through extensive use of technology and aggressive efforts to grow the business globally. And the environment is very competitive! A key competitor, Target, with a different strategy and a different motto ("Expect More, Pay Less") is challenging Wal-Mart with aggressive new advertising campaigns and new stores. During the 2004–2006 period, Target was outpacing Wal-Mart in sales growth and stock price growth. This reversed in the 2006–2008 period, as the global economic outlook weakened for many consumers and the low-cost strategy of Wal-Mart has been more success-ful. Now Target is facing the heat of increased competition from Wal-Mart.[1] The stakes are high and the competition is fierce. Imagine yourself as a manager for one of these companies; how would you help your company be more competitive?

This book is about how managers use cost management to build a successful company as those at Wal-Mart and Target have done. Everyone wants to be a winner, and so it is in busi-ness and accounting. We are interested in how the management accountant can play a key role in making a firm or organization successful. Now you might be asking, Don't we have to know what you mean by *success?* Absolutely! A firm must define clearly what it means by success in its mission statement. Then it must develop a road map to accomplish that mission, which we call *strategy.* Briefly, strategy is a plan to achieve competitive success. In Wal-Mart's case, the mission is to achieve customer value, and the strategy involves the extensive use of technology to reduce cost, a management structure that welcomes change, and a con-stant focus on customer service. For Target, the competitive focus is promise of value through brand recognition, customer service, store location, differentiated offerings, quality, fashion, and price.

Because we are interested in how the management accountant can help a company be suc-cessful, we take a strategic approach throughout the book, beginning with an introduction to

---

[1] Same-store sales were up 5% for Wal-Mart in the third quarter of 2008, while same store sales at Target were down by 0.4%. Karen Talley and Ann Zimmerman, "Wal-Mart Forecasts Gains as Rivals Stumble," *The Wall Street Journal,* February 18, 2009, p. B1; Ann Zimmerman, "Target's Profit Continues to Slide," *The Wall Street Journal,* November 18, 2008, p. B1.

strategy in this chapter. The key idea is that success comes from developing and implementing an effective strategy aided by management accounting methods. These management accounting methods are covered in this text chapter by chapter; we include them in the text because we know they have helped companies succeed.

LEARNING OBJECTIVE 1

Explain the use of cost management information in each of the four functions of management and in different types of organizations, with emphasis on the strategic management function.

The most successful man in life is the man who has the best information.

Benjamin Disraeli, a 19th-century prime minister of England

As Disraeli knew in the 19th century, having the best information is the key to success. In today's business environment, the development and use of cost management information have important strategic roles in an organization's success.

Management Accounting and the Role of Cost Management

Cost management information is developed and used to implement the organization's strategy. It consists of financial information about costs and revenues and nonfinancial information about customer retention, productivity, quality, and other key success factors for the organization.

Cost management is the development and use of cost management information.

Management accounting is a profession that involves partnering in management decision making, devising planning and performance management systems, and providing expertise in financial reporting and control to assist management in the formulation and implementation of an organization's strategy.

Management accountants are the accounting and finance professionals who develop and use cost management information to assist in implementing the organization's strategy. **Cost management information** consists of financial information about costs and revenues, and nonfinancial information about customer retention, productivity, quality, and other key success factors for the organization. **Cost management** is the development and use of cost management information.

The strategic role of the management accountant in an organization is explained in the definition of management accounting provided by the Institute of Management Accountants (IMA). Relevant additional information on the definition can be found in the Statement on Management Accounting: *Definition of Management Accounting* on the IMA's Web site, www.imanet.org/publications_statements.asp.

Management accounting is a profession that involves partnering in management decision making, devising planning and performance management systems, and providing expertise in financial reporting and control to assist management in the formulation and implementation of an organization's strategy.

Management accountants use their unique expertise (decision making, planning, performance management, and more), working with the organization's managers, to help the organization succeed in formulating and implementing its strategy. Cost management information is developed and used within the organization's information value chain, from stage 1 through stage 5 as shown below:

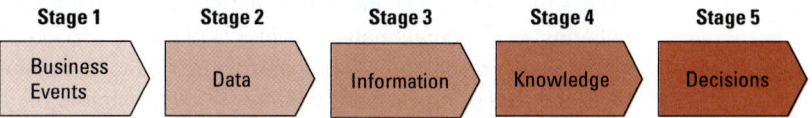

At lower stages of the value chain, management accountants gather and summarize data (stage 2) from business events (stage 1) and then transform the data to information (stage 3) through analysis and use of the management accountant's expertise. At stage 4 the information is combined with other information about the organization's strategy and competitive environment to produce actionable knowledge. At stage 5 management accountants use this knowledge to participate with management teams in making strategic decisions that advance the organization's strategy.

In a typical organization (illustrated in Exhibit 1.1) management accountants report to the controller, a key accounting professional in the firm. The controller, assisted by management accountants, has a wide range of responsibilities, including cost management, financial reporting, maintaining financial information systems, and other reporting functions. The chief financial officer (CFO) has the overall responsibility for the financial function; the treasurer manages investor and creditor relationships, and the chief information officer (CIO) manages the firm's use of information technology, including computer systems and communications.

EXHIBIT 1.1

A Typical Organization Chart Showing the Functions of the Controller

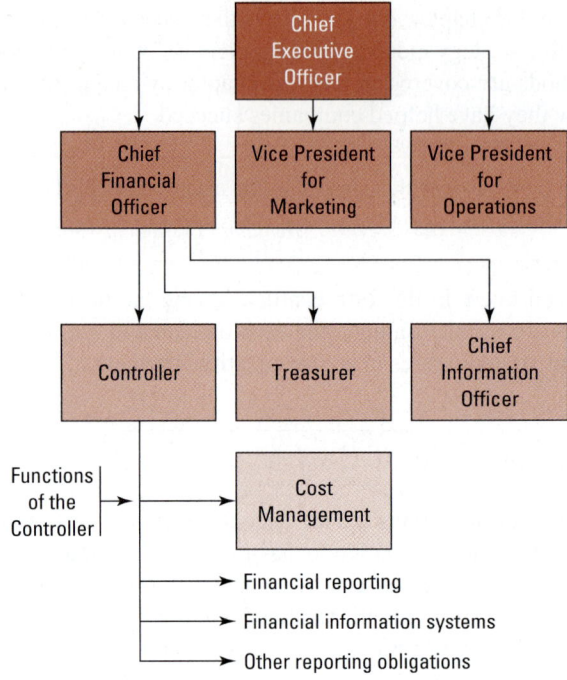

In contrast to the cost management function, the financial reporting function involves preparing financial statements for *external users* such as investors and government regulators. These financial accounting reports require compliance with certain external requirements. Cost management information is developed for use *within* the firm to facilitate management and is not required to meet those requirements. The main focus of cost management information therefore must be *usefulness* and *timeliness;* the focus of financial reports must be *accuracy* and *compliance* with reporting requirements. However, strict adherence to accuracy can compromise the usefulness and timeliness of the information. The function of the financial systems department is to develop and maintain the financial reporting system and related systems such as payroll, financial security systems, and tax preparation. The challenge for the controller is to reconcile these different and potentially conflicting roles.

The Four Functions of Management

The management accountant develops cost management information for the CFO, other managers, and employee teams to use to manage the firm and make the firm more competitive and successful. Cost management information is provided for each of the four major management functions: (1) strategic management, (2) planning and decision making, (3) management and operational control, and (4) preparation of financial statements. (See Exhibit 1.2.) The most important function is **strategic management,** which is the development and implementation

Strategic management is the development and implementation of a sustainable competitive position.

EXHIBIT 1.2

Cost Management Information Is Needed for Each of the Four Management Functions

1. **Strategic Management.** Cost management information is needed to make sound strategic decisions regarding choice of products, manufacturing methods, marketing techniques and channels, assessing customer profitability and other long-term issues.
2. **Planning and Decision Making.** Cost management information is needed to support recurring decisions regarding replacing equipment, managing cash flow, budgeting raw materials purchases, scheduling production, and pricing.
3. **Management and Operational Control.** Cost management information is needed to provide a fair and effective basis for identifying inefficient operations and to reward and motivate the most effective managers.
4. **Preparation of Financial Statements.** Cost management information is needed to provide accurate accounting for inventory and other assets, in compliance with reporting requirements, for the preparation of financial reports and for use in the three other management functions.

Our unique approach in this book is to demonstrate cost management from a strategic emphasis. Every cost management method we cover is linked to the firm's strategy, that is, how the method helps the firm to be successful. Why emphasize the strategic approach? Managers tell us why . . .

A 2008 survey of 250 chief executive officers by the public accounting firm Ernst & Young indicated that more than 84% agreed or strongly agreed with the statement, "The Chief Financial Officer (CFO) in our company is seen as a business partner of the CEO." Similarly, a 2005 IBM Corporation study of 900 CFOs found that most agreed that the most important areas for the CFO were "measuring and monitoring business performance" and "partnering with the organization to identify and execute growth strategies." Furthermore, the IBM study showed a significant decrease over the last 10 years in the attention CFOs paid to basic accounting transactions, with a corresponding large increase in the attention devoted to "decision support and performance management."

A 2003 survey of 1,995 members of the Institute of Management Accountants (the IMA is an international professional organization for management accountants) reported "Cost management plays a significant role at companies; 81% of all respondents reported that cost management was important to their organization's overall strategic goals." Further, the survey reported, "Second, the role of management accountants has changed, and they're being increasingly perceived as business partners who focus on key strategic issues well beyond the boundaries of traditional finance. This was evidenced by the result that 56% of the respondents agreed that contributing to core strategic issues was a high priority for management accounting."

The 2003 survey validates the findings of a 1999 survey of 300 members of the IMA that showed the accountants viewed themselves as broad finance professionals whose most important work activities included long-term strategic planning, financial and economic analysis, customer and product profitability, computer systems and operations, and process improvement

The Society of the Management Accountants of Canada has developed a competency framework for certified management accountants in Canada, which has the following introduction:

Certified Management Accountants (CMAs) do more than just measure value—they create it. As the leaders in management accounting, CMAs apply a unique mix of financial expertise, strategic insight, innovative thinking and a collaborative approach to help grow successful businesses.

These results show an important shift in the management accounting profession to strategic analysis, cost management information, and nonfinancial as well as financial information. This represents a move away from financial reporting only. One might say that management accounting has changed its focus to "growing the beans" instead of just "counting the beans."

- The principal journal for the profession, *Management Accounting,* changed its name to *Strategic Finance* in April 1999. As noted in the above surveys, managers now view accountants in the cost management function as finance professionals having an integral, strategic role in a firm's management. The work of accountants, no longer scorekeepers only, is better described as "strategic finance."

- The American Institute of Certified Public Accountants (AICPA), another key professional organization for accountants, has also recognized the change in the profession. The AICPA uses the term *new finance* to refer to the growing focus on strategy and "business partnership" for accountants who work within firms.

- The business press generally has set new and more strategic expectations for accountants. An example is the recent *Business Week* article, "Up From Bean Counter: The Role of the CFO Is Expanding to Strategist, Venture Capitalist, and Chief Negotiator." The title tells it all!

Sources: "Competency Map of the CMA Profession," The Society of Management Accountants of Canada, www.cma-canada.org; Ashish Garg, Debashis Gosh, James Hudick, and Chuen Nowacki, "Roles and Practices in Management Accounting Today," *Strategic Finance,* July 2003, pp. 30–35; AICPA Web site (www.aicpa.org), "Center for Excellence in Financial Management"; Marcia Vickers, "Up From Bean Counter: The Role of the CFO Is Expanding to Strategist, Venture Capitalist, and Chief Negotiator," *BusinessWeek,* August 28, 2000, pp. 119–120; Ernst & Young, *What's Next for the CFO? Where Ambition Meets Reality,* 2008, www.ey.com/Global/assets.nsf/Estonia_E/CFO_report/$file/CFO%20report.pdf; IBM Corporation, *The Agile CFO: Acting on Business Insight,* 2005, www-935.ibm.com/services/us/imc/pdf/ge510-6239-agile-cfo-full.pdf; Gary Siegel, James E. Sorensen, and Sandra Richtermeyer, "Are You a Business Partner? Parts 1 and 2," *Strategic Finance,* September and October 2003.

Planning and decision making involve budgeting and profit planning, cash flow management, and other decisions related to operations.

Operational control takes place when mid-level managers monitor the activities of operating-level managers and employees.

Management control is the evaluation of mid-level managers by upper-level managers.

of a sustainable competitive position in which the firm's competitive advantage provides continued success. A strategy is a set of goals and specific action plans that, if achieved, provide the desired competitive advantage. Strategic management involves identifying and implementing these goals and action plans. Next, management is responsible for **planning and decision making,** which involve budgeting and profit planning, cash flow management, and other decisions related to the firm's operations, such as deciding when to lease or buy a facility, when to repair or replace a piece of equipment, when to change a marketing plan, and when to begin development of a new product.

The third area of responsibility, control, consists of two functions, operational control and management control. **Operational control** takes place when mid-level managers (e.g., site managers, product managers, regional managers) monitor the activities of operating-level managers and employees (e.g., production supervisors and various department heads). In contrast, **management control** is the evaluation of mid-level managers by upper-level managers (the controller or the CFO).

Preparation of financial statements

requires management to comply with the financial reporting requirements of regulatory agencies.

In the fourth function, **preparation of financial statements,** management complies with the reporting requirements of relevant groups (such as the Financial Accounting Standards Board) and relevant federal government authorities (for example, the Internal Revenue Service and the Securities and Exchange Commission). The financial statement preparation role has recently received a renewed focus as countries throughout the world have adopted International Financial Reporting Standards (IFRS), and the United States is expected to adopt these standards by 2014. The financial statement information also serves the other three management functions, because this information is often an important part of planning and decision making, control, and strategic management.[2]

The first three management functions are covered in this text. Strategic management and the design of the costs systems upon which strategic decisions rely is covered in Part One. Part Two covers planning and decision making, Part Three covers operational control, and Part Four covers management control. Financial reporting is covered in other accounting texts.

Strategic Management and the Strategic Emphasis in Cost Management

Effective strategic management is critical to the success of the firm or organization and is thus a pervasive theme of this book. The growing pressures of economic recession, global competition, technological innovation, and changes in business processes have made cost management much more critical and dynamic than ever before. Managers must think *competitively;* doing so requires a strategy.

Strategic thinking involves anticipating changes; products, services, and operating processes are designed to accommodate expected changes in customer demands. Flexibility is important. The ability to make fast changes is critical as a result of the demand of the new management concepts of e-commerce, speed-to-market, and flexible manufacturing. Product life cycles—the time from the introduction of a new product to its removal from the market—is expected to become shorter and shorter. Success in the recent past days or months is no longer a measure of ultimate success; the manager must be "driving" the firm by using the windshield, not the rear-view mirror.

The strategic emphasis also requires creative and integrative thinking, that is, the ability to identify and solve problems from a cross-functional view. The business functions are often identified as marketing, production, finance, and accounting/controllership. Instead of viewing a problem as a production problem, a marketing problem, or a finance and accounting problem, cross-functional teams view it from an integrative approach that combines skills from all functions simultaneously. The integrative approach is necessary in a dynamic and competitive environment. The firm's attention is focused on satisfying the customers' needs; all of the firm's resources, *from all functions,* are directed to that goal.

Types of Organizations

Cost management information is useful in all organizations: business firms, governmental units, and not-for-profit organizations. Business firms are usually categorized by industry, the main categories being merchandising, manufacturing, and service. Merchandising firms purchase goods for resale. Merchandisers that sell to other merchandisers are called *wholesalers;* those selling directly to consumers are called *retailers.* Examples of merchandising firms are the large retailers, such as Wal-Mart, Target, and Amazon.com.

Manufacturing firms use raw materials, labor, and manufacturing facilities and equipment to produce products. They sell these products to merchandising firms or to other manufacturers as raw materials to make other products. Examples of manufacturers are Ford, General Electric, and Cisco Systems.

Service firms provide a service to customers that offers convenience, freedom, safety, or comfort. Common services include transportation, health care, financial services (banking, insurance, accounting), personal services (physical training, hair styling), and legal services. In the United States, service industries are growing at a much faster rate than manufacturing or merchandising, in part because of the increased demand for leisure and convenience and society's increased complexity and need for information.

---

[2] The professional groups and the accountant's professional responsibility are identified and explained at the end of this chapter. See also, "The Diverse Roles of Professional Accountants in Business," International Federation of Accountants, November 2004 (www.ifac.org).

Governmental and not-for-profit organizations provide services, much like the firms in service industries. However, these organizations provide the services for which no direct relationship exists between the amount paid and the services provided. Instead, both the nature of these services and the customers that receive them are determined by government or philanthropic organizations. The resources are provided by governmental units and/or charities. The services provided by these organizations are often called *public goods* to indicate that no typical market exists for them. Public goods have a number of unique characteristics, such as the impracticality of limiting consumption to a single customer (clean water and police and fire protection are provided for *all* residents).

Most firms and organizations use cost management information. For example, manufacturing firms use it to manage production costs. Similarly, retail firms such as Wal-Mart use cost management information to manage stocking, distribution, and customer service. Firms in the service industries, such as those providing financial services or other professional services, use cost management information to identify the most profitable services and to manage the costs of providing those services.

Cost management information is used in a wide variety of ways. Whatever the business, a firm must know the cost of new products or services, the cost of making improvements in existing products or services, and the cost of finding a new way to produce the products or provide the services. Cost management information is used to determine prices, to change product or service offerings to improve profitability, to update manufacturing facilities in a timely fashion, and to determine new marketing methods or distribution channels. For example, manufacturers such as Toyota study the cost implications of design options for each new product. The design study includes analysis of projected manufacturing costs as well as costs to be incurred after the product is completed, which include service and warranty costs. Service and warranty costs are often called *downstream costs* because they occur after manufacturing. By analyzing both manufacturing and downstream costs, Toyota is able to determine whether product enhancements might cause manufacturing and downstream costs to be out of line with expected increases in customer value and revenue for that feature.

Both large and small firms in all types of industries use cost management information. A firm's degree of reliance on cost management depends on the nature of its competitive strategy. Many firms compete on the basis of being the low-cost provider of the industry's goods or services; for these firms, cost management is critical. Other firms, such as cosmetics, fashion, and pharmaceutical firms, compete on the basis of product leadership, in which the unusual or innovative features of the product make the firm successful. For these firms, the critical management concern is maintaining product leadership through product development and marketing. The role of cost management is to support the firm's strategy by providing the information managers need to succeed in their product development and marketing efforts, such as the expected cost of adding a new product feature, the defect rate of a new part, or the reliability of a new manufacturing process.

Not-for-profit and governmental organizations also must have a strategy to accomplish their mission and satisfy their constituents. Historically, governmental units and not-for-profit agencies have tended to focus on their responsibility to spend in approved ways rather than to spend in efficient and effective ways. Increasingly, however, these types of organizations are using cost management for efficient and effective use of their financial resources.

The Contemporary Business Environment

LEARNING OBJECTIVE 2

Explain the contemporary business environment and how it has influenced cost management.

Many changes in the business environment in recent years have caused significant modifications in cost management practices. The primary changes are (1) increase in global competition; (2) lean manufacturing; (3) advances in information technologies, the Internet, and e-commerce; (4) greater focus on the customer; (5) new forms of management organization; and (6) changes in the social, political, and cultural environment of business. The current global economic recession that started in late 2007 will surely have a significant effect on each of these six changes. It is likely there will be an even greater rate of change in each of these six areas as firms search for new ways to compete and governmental regulations adapt to the difficult economic times.

The following table indicates the percentage of sales coming from outside the home market for the listed companies.

	1993	2007
General Electric	16.5%	50%
Wal-Mart	0.0	22.3
McDonald's	46.9	65.3

Source: Company annual reports.

The Global Business Environment

A key development that drives the extensive changes in the contemporary business environment is the growth of international markets and trade due to the rise of economies throughout the world and the decline of trade barriers. Businesses and not-for-profit organizations, as well as consumers and regulators, are all significantly affected by the rapid growth of economic interdependence and increased competition from other countries. The North American Free Trade Agreement (NAFTA), the Central America Free Trade Agreement (CAFTA), the World Trade Organization (WTO), the European Union (EU), and the growing number of alliances among large multinational firms clearly indicate that the opportunities for growth and profitability lie in global markets. Most consumers benefit as low-cost, high-quality goods are traded worldwide. Managers and business owners know the importance of pursuing sales and operating activities in foreign countries, and investors benefit from the increased opportunities for investment in foreign firms.

The increasing competitiveness of the global business environment means that firms increasingly need cost management information to be competitive. Firms need financial and nonfinancial information about doing business and competing effectively in other countries.

> The winning companies in the global competition will be those companies that can put together the best of research, engineering, design, manufacturing, distribution—wherever they can get it, anywhere in the world—and the best of each of these will not come from one country or from one continent.
>
> *Jack Welch, former CEO of General Electric*

Lean Manufacturing

To remain competitive in the face of the increased global competition, firms around the world are adopting new manufacturing technologies. These include just-in-time inventory methods to reduce the cost and waste of maintaining large levels of raw materials and unfinished product. Also, many firms are adopting the lean methods applied in Japanese manufacturing that have produced significant cost and quality improvements through the use of quality teams and statistical quality control. Other manufacturing changes include flexible manufacturing techniques developed to reduce setup times and allow fast turnaround of customer orders. A key competitive edge in what is called *speed-to-market* is the ability to deliver the product or service faster than the competition.

Use of Information Technology, the Internet, and Enterprise Resource Management

Perhaps the most fundamental of all business changes in recent years has been the increasing use of information technology, the Internet, and performance management systems. This *new economy* is reflected in the rapid growth of Internet-based firms (companies such as Amazon, eBay, and Google); the increased use of the Internet for communications, sales, and business data processing; and the use of enterprise management systems. These technologies have fostered the growing strategic focus in cost management by reducing the time required for processing transactions and by expanding the individual manager's access to information within the firm, the industry, and the business environment around the world.

Focus on the Customer

A key change in the business environment is increased *consumer expectation* for product functionality and quality. The result has been a shorter product life cycle, as firms seek to add new features and new products as quickly as possible, thereby increasing the overall intensity of competition.

In past years, a business typically succeeded by focusing on only a relatively small number of products with limited features and by organizing production into long, low-cost, and high-volume production runs aided by assembly-line automation. The new business process focuses instead on customer satisfaction. Producing value for the customer changes the orientation of managers from low-cost production of large quantities to *quality, service, timeliness of delivery, and the ability to respond to the customer's desire for specific features.* Today many of the critical success factors (discussed later) are customer oriented. Cost management practices are also changing; cost management reports now include specific measures of customer preferences and customer satisfaction.

Management Organization

Management organization is changing in response to the changes in technology, marketing, and manufacturing processes. Because of the focus on customer satisfaction and value, the emphasis has shifted from financial and profit-based measures of performance to customer-related, nonfinancial performance measures such as quality, time to delivery, and service. Similarly, the hierarchical command-and-control type of organization is being replaced by a more flexible organizational form that encourages teamwork and coordination among business functions. In response to these changes, cost management practices are also changing to include reports that are useful to cross-functional teams of managers; the reports reflect the multifunctional roles of these teams and include a variety of operating and financial information: product quality, unit cost, customer satisfaction, and production bottlenecks, for example. The changes in manufacturing, marketing, and management in organizations are summarized in Exhibit 1.3.

EXHIBIT 1.3 **Comparison of Prior and Contemporary Business Environments**

Manufacturing	Prior Business Environment	Contemporary Business Environment
Basis of competition	Economies of scale, standardization	Quality, functionality, customer satisfaction
Manufacturing process	High volume, long production runs, significant levels of in-process and finished inventory; this is called the "push" approach	Low volume, short production runs, focus on reducing inventory levels and other non-value-added activities and costs; this is called the "pull" approach
Manufacturing technology	Assembly line automation, isolated technology applications	Robotics, flexible manufacturing systems, integrated technology applications connected by networks
Required labor skills	Machine-paced, low-level skills	Individually and team-paced, high-level skills
Emphasis on quality	Acceptance of a normal or usual amount of waste	Goal of zero defects
Marketing		
Products	Relatively few variations, long product life cycles	Large number of variations, short product life cycles
Markets	Largely domestic	Global
Management Organization		
Type of information recorded and reported	Almost exclusively financial data	Financial and operating data, the firm's strategic success factors
Management organizational structure	Hierarchical, command and control	Network-based organization forms, teamwork focus—employee has more responsibility and control, coaching rather than command and control
Management focus	Emphasis on the short term, short-term performance measures and compensation, concern for sustaining the current stock price, short tenure and high mobility of top managers	Emphasis on the long term, focus on critical success factors, commitment to the long-term success of the firm, including shareholder value

Social, Political, and Cultural Considerations

In addition to changes in the business environment, significant changes have taken place in the social, political, and cultural environments that affect business. Although the nature and extent of these changes vary a great deal from country to country, they include a more ethnically and racially diverse workforce, and a renewed sense of ethical responsibility among managers and employees.

The new business environment requires firms to be flexible and adaptable and to place greater responsibility in the hands of a more highly skilled workforce. Additionally, the changes tend to focus the firm on factors *outside* the production of its product or provision of its service to the ultimate consumer and the global society in which the consumer lives.

The Strategic Focus of Cost Management

The competitive firm incorporates the emerging and anticipated changes in the contemporary environment of business into its business planning and practices. The competitive firm is customer driven, uses advanced manufacturing and information technologies when appropriate, anticipates the effect of changes in regulatory requirements and customer tastes, and recognizes its complex social, political, and cultural environment. Guided by strategic thinking, the management accountant focuses on the factors that make the company successful rather than relying only on costs and other financial measures. We are reminded of the story of the Scottish farmer who had prize sheep to take to market. When asked why his sheep were always superior to those of his neighbors, the farmer responded, "While they're weighing their sheep, I'm fattening mine." Similarly, cost management focuses not on the measurement per se but on the *identification of those measures that are critical* to the firm's success. Robert Kaplan's classification of the stages of the development of cost management systems describes this shift in focus:[3]

Stage 1. Cost management systems are basic transaction reporting systems.

Stage 2. As they develop into the second stage, cost management systems focus on external financial reporting. The objective is reliable financial reports; accordingly, the usefulness for cost management is limited.

Stage 3. Cost management systems track key operating data and develop more accurate and relevant cost information for decision making; cost management information is developed.

Stage 4. Strategically relevant cost management information is an integral part of the system.

The first two stages of cost system development focus on the management accountant's measurement and reporting role, and the third stage shifts to operational control. In the fourth stage, the ultimate goal, the management accountant is an integral part of management, not a reporter but a full business partner, working on management teams to implement the firm's strategy. This requires the identification of the firm's critical success factors and the use of analytical, forward-looking decision support. **Critical success factors (CSFs)** are measures of those aspects of the firm's performance essential to its competitive advantage and, therefore, to its success. Many of these critical success factors are financial, but many are nonfinancial. The CSFs for any given firm depend on the nature of the competition it faces.

Critical success factors (CSFs)
are measures of those aspects of the firm's performance that are essential to its competitive advantage and, therefore, to its success.

Contemporary Management Techniques: The Management Accountant's Response to the Contemporary Business Environment

LEARNING OBJECTIVE 3

Explain the contemporary management techniques and how they are used in cost management to respond to the contemporary business environment.

Management accountants, guided by a strategic focus, have responded to the six changes in the contemporary business environment with 13 methods that are useful in implementing strategy in these dynamic times. The first six methods focus directly on strategy implementation—the balanced scorecard/strategy map, value chain, activity-based costing, business intelligence, target costing, and life-cycle costing. The next seven methods help to achieve

[3] Robert S. Kaplan, "The Four-Stage Model of Cost System Design," *Management Accounting*, February 1990, pp. 22–26.

strategy implementation through a focus on process improvement—benchmarking, business process improvement, total quality management, lean accounting, the theory of constraints, enterprise sustainability, and enterprise risk management. Each of these methods is covered in one or more of the chapters of the text.

The Balanced Scorecard (BSC) and Strategy Map

Strategic information using critical success factors provides a road map for the firm to use to chart its competitive course and serves as a benchmark for competitive success. Financial measures such as profitability reflect only a partial, and frequently only a short-term, measure of the firm's progress. Without strategic information, the firm is likely to stray from its competitive course and to make strategically wrong product decisions, for example, choosing the wrong products or the wrong marketing and distribution methods.

To emphasize the importance of using strategic information, *both financial and nonfinancial,* accounting reports of a firm's performance are now often based on critical success factors in four different perspectives. One perspective is financial; the other three are nonfinancial:

1. **Financial performance.** Measures of profitability and market value, among others, as indicators of how well the firm satisfies its owners and shareholders.
2. **Customer satisfaction.** Measures of quality, service, and low cost, among others, as indicators of how well the firm satisfies its customers.
3. **Internal processes.** Measures of the efficiency and effectiveness with which the firm produces the product or service.
4. **Learning and growth.** Measures of the firm's ability to develop and utilize human resources to meet its strategic goals now and into the future.

An accounting report based on the four perspectives is called a **balanced scorecard.** The concept of balance captures the intent of broad coverage, financial and nonfinancial, of all factors that contribute to the firm's success in achieving its strategic goals. The balanced scorecard provides a basis for a more complete analysis than is possible with financial data alone. The use of the balanced scorecard is thus a critical ingredient of the overall approach that firms take to become and remain competitive. An example of a balanced scorecard is shown in Exhibit 1.4.

The **strategy map** is a method, based on the balanced scorecard, that links the four perspectives in a cause-and-effect diagram. For many companies, high achievement in the learning and growth perspective contributes directly to higher achievement in the internal process

The **balanced scorecard** is an accounting report that includes the firm's critical success factors in four areas: (1) financial performance, (2) customer satisfaction, (3) internal processes, and (4) learning and growth.

The **strategy map** is a method, based on the balanced scorecard, which links the four perspectives in a cause-and-effect diagram.

EXHIBIT 1.4
Financial and Nonfinancial Measures of Success
Critical Success Factors

Financial Measures of Success	Nonfinancial Measures of Success
Sales growth	**Customer**
Earnings growth	Market share and growth in market share
Dividend growth	Customer service (e.g., based on number of complaints)
Bond and credit ratings	On-time delivery
Cash flow	Customer satisfaction (customer survey)
Increase in stock price	Brand recognition (growth in market share)
	Internal Processes
	High product quality
	High manufacturing productivity
	Cycle time
	Product yield and reduction in waste
	Learning and Growth
	Competence of managers (education attained)
	Morale and firmwide culture (employee survey)
	Education and training (training hours)
	Innovation: number of new products

perspective, which in turn causes greater achievement in the customer satisfaction perspective, which then produces the desired financial performance. The strategy map is therefore a useful means in understanding how improvement in certain critical success factors contributes to other goals and to the ultimate financial results.

The Value Chain

The **value chain** is an analysis tool organizations use to identify the specific steps required to provide a competitive product or service to the customer. In particular, an analysis of the firm's value chain helps management discover which steps or activities are not competitive, where costs can be reduced, or which activity should be outsourced. Also, management can use the analysis to find ways to increase value for the customer at one or more steps of the value chain. For example, companies such as General Electric, IBM, and Harley-Davidson have found greater overall profits by moving downstream in the value chain to place a greater emphasis on high-value services and less emphasis on lower-margin manufactured products. A key idea of the value-chain analysis is that the firm should carefully study each step in its operations, to determine how each step contributes to the firm's profits and competitiveness.

Activity-Based Costing and Management

Many firms have found that they can improve planning, product costing, operational control, and management control by using **activity analysis** to develop a detailed description of the specific activities performed in the firm's operations. The activity analysis provides the basis for activity-based costing and activity-based management. **Activity-based costing (ABC)** is used to improve the accuracy of cost analysis by improving the tracing of costs to products or to individual customers. **Activity-based management (ABM)** uses activity analysis and activity-based costing to help managers improve the value of products and services, and to increase the organization's competitiveness. ABC and ABM are key strategic tools for many firms, especially those with complex operations, or diversity of products and services.

Business Intelligence

Business intelligence (also called *business analytics* or *predictive analytics*) is an approach to strategy implementation in which the management accountant uses data to understand and analyze business performance. Business intelligence (BI) often uses statistical methods such as regression or correlation analysis to predict consumer behavior, to measure customer satisfaction, or to develop models for setting prices, among other uses. BI is best suited for companies that have a distinctive capability which can be derived from measurable critical success factors. BI is similar to the BSC because it focuses on critical success factors; the difference is that BI uses analytical tools to develop predictive models of core business processes.

Target Costing

Target costing is a method that has resulted directly from the intensely competitive markets in many industries. **Target costing** determines the desired cost for a product on the basis of a given competitive price, such that the product will earn a desired profit. Cost is thus determined by price. The firm using target costing must often adopt strict cost reduction measures or redesign the product or manufacturing process to meet the market price and remain profitable.

Target costing forces the firm to become more competitive, and, like benchmarking, it is a common strategic form of analysis in intensely competitive industries where even small price differences attract consumers to the lower-priced product. The camera manufacturing industry is a good example of an industry where target costing is used. Camera manufacturers such as Minolta know the market price for each line of camera they manufacture, so they redesign the product (add/delete features, use less expensive parts and materials) and redesign the production process to get the manufacturing cost down to the predetermined target cost. The automobile industry also uses target costing.

Life-Cycle Costing

Life-cycle costing is a method to identify and monitor the costs of a product throughout its life cycle. The life cycle consists of all steps from product design and purchase of raw materials to delivery and service of the finished product. The steps include (1) research

---

The **value chain** is an analysis tool firms use to identify the specific steps required to provide a product or service to the customer.

Activity analysis is used to develop a detailed description of the specific activities performed in the firm's operations.

Activity-based costing (ABC) is used to improve the accuracy of cost analysis by improving the tracing of costs to products or to individual customers.

Activity-based management (ABM) uses activity analysis and activity-based costing to help managers improve the value of products and services, and to increase the organization's competitiveness.

Business Intelligence is an approach to strategy implementation in which the management accountant uses data to understand and analyze business performance.

Target costing determines the desired cost for a product on the basis of a given competitive price so that the product will earn a desired profit.

Life-cycle costing is a method used to identify and monitor the costs of a product throughout its life cycle.

and development; (2) product design, including prototyping, target costing, and testing; (3) manufacturing, inspecting, packaging, and warehousing; (4) marketing, promotion, and distribution; and (5) sales and service. Cost management has traditionally focused only on costs incurred at the third step, manufacturing. Thinking strategically, management accountants now manage the product's full life cycle of costs, including upstream and downstream costs as well as manufacturing costs. This expanded focus means careful attention to product design, since design decisions lock in most subsequent life-cycle costs.

Benchmarking

Benchmarking is a process by which a firm identifies its critical success factors, studies the best practices of other firms (or other business units within a firm) for achieving these critical success factors, and then implements improvements in the firm's processes to match or beat the performance of those competitors. Benchmarking was first implemented by Xerox Corporation in the late 1970s. Today many firms use benchmarking. Some firms are recognized as leaders, and therefore benchmarks, in selected areas—for example, Nordstrom in retailing, Ritz-Carlton Hotels in service, Toyota in manufacturing, Apple Computer in innovation, among others.

Benchmarking efforts are facilitated today by cooperative networks of noncompeting firms that exchange benchmarking information. For example, the International Benchmarking Clearinghouse (www.apqc.org) and the International Organization for Standardization (ISO) (www.iso.org) assist firms in strategic benchmarking.

Business Process Improvement

Whether you think you can or whether you think you can't—you're right.

Henry Ford

Henry Ford realized that the right attitude is important to success. That belief is what continuous improvement is all about. **Business process improvement (BPI)** is a management method by which managers and workers commit to a program of continuous improvement in quality and other critical success factors. Continuous improvement is very often associated with benchmarking and total quality management as firms seek to identify other firms as models to learn how to improve their critical success factors. While BPI is an incremental method, business process reengineering (BPR) is more radical. BPR is a method for creating competitive advantage in which a firm reorganizes its operating and management functions, often with the result that positions are modified, combined, or eliminated.

Total Quality Management

Total quality management (TQM) is a method by which management develops policies and practices to ensure that the firm's products and services exceed customers' expectations. This approach includes increased product functionality, reliability, durability, and serviceability. Cost management is used to analyze the cost consequences of different design choices for TQM and to measure and report the many aspects of quality including, for example, production breakdowns and production defects, wasted labor or raw materials, the number of service calls, and the nature of complaints, warranty costs, and product recalls.

Lean Accounting

Lean accounting uses value streams to measure the financial benefits of a firm's progress in implementing lean manufacturing. Lean accounting places the firm's products and services into value streams, each of which is a group of related products or services. For example, a company manufacturing consumer electronics might have two groups of products (and two value streams)—digital cameras and video cameras—with several models in each group. Accounting for value streams can help the firm to better understand the profitability of its process improvements and product groups, which leads to better decision making.

The Theory of Constraints

The **theory of constraints (TOC)** is used to help firms effectively improve a very important critical success factor: cycle time, the rate at which raw materials are converted to finished

Benchmarking is a process by which a firm identifies its critical success factors, studies the best practices of other firms (or other business units within a firm) for achieving these critical success factors, and then implements improvements in the firm's processes to match or beat the performance of those competitors.

Business process improvement is a management method by which managers and workers commit to a program of continuous improvement in quality and other critical success factors.

Total quality management (TQM) is a technique by which management develops policies and practices to ensure that the firm's products and services exceed customers' expectations.

Lean accounting uses value streams to measure the financial benefits of a firm's progress in implementing lean manufacturing.

The **theory of constraints (TOC)** is used to help firms effectively improve the rate at which raw materials are converted to finished products.

products. The TOC helps identify and eliminate bottlenecks—places where partially completed products tend to accumulate as they wait to be processed in the production process. In the competitive global marketplace common to most industries, the ability to be faster than competitors is often a critical success factor. Many managers argue that the focus on speed in the TOC approach is crucial. They consider speed in product development, product delivery, and manufacturing to be paramount as global competitors find ever-higher customer expectations for rapid product development and prompt delivery.

Enterprise Sustainability

> **Enterprise Sustainability** means the balancing of the company's short- and long-term goals in all three dimensions of performance—social, environmental, and financial.

Enterprise sustainability means the balancing of the organization's short- and long-term goals in all three dimensions of performance—social, environmental, and financial. We view it in the broad sense to include identifying and implementing ways to reduce cost and increase revenue as well as to maintain compliance with social and environmental regulations and expectations. This can be accomplished through technological innovation and new product development as well as common-sense measures to improve the social and environmental impacts of the company's operations. Ford Motor saves money through improvements in its storm water draining system at it River Rouge, Michigan plant; other leaders in sustainability include Toyota and Honda motor companies, McDonald's, and Wal-Mart, among many others. The Dow Jones Sustainability Indexes (www.sustainability-indexes.com/07_htmle/sustainability/corpsustainability. html) identify and rank companies according to their sustainability performance.

Enterprise Risk Management

> **Enterprise risk management** is a framework and process that firms use to manage the risks that could negatively or positively affect the company's competitiveness and success.

Enterprise risk management is a framework and process that organizations use to manage the risks that could negatively or positively affect the company's competitiveness and success. Risk is considered broadly to include (1) hazards such as fire or flood, (2) financial risks due to foreign currency fluctuations, commodity price fluctuations, and changes in interest rates, (3) operating risk related to customers, products, or employees, and (4) strategic risk related to top management decisions about the firm's strategy and implementation thereof.

How a Firm Succeeds: The Competitive Strategy

> If you do not know where you are going, you will probably get there.
>
> *Anonymous*

EXHIBIT 1.5
Mission Statements of Selected Companies

Ford Motor Company (ford.com)

Provide personal mobility for people around the world.

IBM (ibm.com)

To lead in the creation, development, and manufacture of the industry's most advanced information technologies, and to translate these into value for our customers.

Google (google.com)

To organize the world's information and make it universally accessible and useful.

United Parcel Service (ups.com)

Your world synchronized.

Walt Disney (disney.com)

To make people happy.

Merck (merck.com)

To preserve and improve human life.

Sara Lee (saralee.com)

Simply delight you . . . every day.

EXHIBIT 1.6

Sara Lee Corporate Strategy

Source: Sara Lee Corporation (saralee.com and 2008 annual report).

The company is focused on building sustainable, profitable growth over the long term by achieving share leadership in its core categories: innovating around its core products and product categories; expanding into high opportunity geographic markets and strategic joint venture/partnerships; delivering superior quality and value to our customers; and driving operating efficiencies.

- **Focusing on innovation, execution and performance.** As a branded consumer goods company, we know successful new products are a key driver of Sara Lee's success.
- **Building big brands in big markets.** Sara Lee has a strong portfolio of big and growing brands that compete in large consumer markets around the world.
- **Fostering a new culture.** Living and breathing our values every day, our people around the world work as teams, act with integrity, are inclusive, use the imagination and, most important of all, have the passion to excel.

A **strategy** is a plan for using resources to achieve sustainable goals within a competitive environment.

LEARNING OBJECTIVE 4

Explain the different types of competitive strategies.

A firm succeeds by implementing a **strategy,** that is, a plan for using resources to achieve sustainable goals within a competitive environment. Finding a strategy begins with determining the purpose and long-range direction, and therefore the mission, of the company. Exhibit 1.5 lists excerpts from the mission statements of several companies. The mission is developed into specific performance objectives, which are then implemented by specific corporate strategies, that is, specific actions to achieve the objectives that will fulfill the mission. See the Sara Lee corporate strategy in Exhibit 1.6. Note that Sara Lee's broad mission statement is explained in terms of more specific objectives, which are in turn operationalized through specific corporate strategies.

Firms also are beginning to use cost management to support their strategic goals. Cost management has shifted away from a focus on the stewardship role, that is, product costing and financial reporting. The new focus is on a management-facilitating role: developing cost and other information to support the management of the firm and the achievement of its strategic goals (Exhibit 1.7).

Without strategic information, the firm is likely to stray from its competitive course, to make strategically wrong manufacturing and marketing decisions: to choose the wrong products or the wrong customers. Some of the consequences of a lack of strategic information are shown in Exhibit 1.8.

Developing a Competitive Strategy

In developing a sustainable competitive position, each firm purposefully or as a result of market forces arrives at one of the two competitive strategies: cost leadership or differentiation.[4]

EXHIBIT 1.7

Cost Management Focus in Prior and Contemporary Business Environments

	Prior Business Environment	**Contemporary Business Environment**
Cost management focus	Financial reporting and cost analysis; common emphasis on standardization and standard costs; the accountant as financial accounting expert and financial scorekeeper	Cost management as a tool for the development and implementation of business strategy; the accountant as business partner

[4] This section is adapted from Michael Porter, *Competitive Advantage*, The Free Press, 1985. The Porter concept of strategy is widely used. See for example, Michael E. Porter, "The Five Forces that Shape Strategy," *Harvard Business Review,* January 2008, pp. 79–93. Porter makes the point that strategy is even more important in times of broad economic crisis, in his article, "Why America Needs an Economic Strategy," *BusinessWeek,* November 10, 2008, pp39–42. There are many articles and books on strategy. For another important view on strategy, see John K. Shank and Vijay Govindarajan, *Cost Management,* The Free Press, 1993; Robert S. Kaplan and David P. Norton, *Strategy Maps,* Harvard Business School Press, 2007; and Robert S. Kaplan and David P. Norton, "Mastering the Management System," *Harvard Business Review,* January 2008, pp 63–77. A recent framework for strategy is the resource-based view of the organization, as explained by David J. Collis and Cynthia A. Montgomery, "Competing on Resources," *Harvard Business Review,* July–August, 2008, pp 140–150.

- Decision making based on intuition instead of accurate cost information
- Lack of clarity about direction and goals
- Lack of a clear and favorable perception of the firm by customers and suppliers
- Incorrect investment decisions; choosing products, markets, or manufacturing processes inconsistent with strategic goals
- Inability to effectively benchmark competitors, resulting in lack of knowledge about more effective competitive strategies
- Failure to identify most profitable products, customers, and markets

Cost Leadership

Cost leadership
is a strategy in which a firm outperforms competitors in producing products or services at the lowest cost.

Cost leadership is a strategy in which a firm outperforms competitors in producing products or services at the lowest cost. The cost leader makes sustainable profits at lower prices, thereby limiting the growth of competition in the industry through its success at reducing price and undermining the profitability of competitors, which must meet the firm's low price. The cost leader normally has a relatively large market share and tends to avoid niche or segment markets by using the price advantage to attract a large portion of the broad market. While most firms make strong efforts to reduce costs, the cost leader may focus almost exclusively on cost reduction, thereby ensuring a significant cost and price advantage in the market.

Cost advantages usually result from productivity in the manufacturing process, in distribution, or in overall administration. For example, technological innovation in the manufacturing process and labor savings from overseas production are common routes to competitive productivity. Firms known to be successful at cost leadership are typically very large manufacturers and retailers, such as Wal-Mart, Texas Instruments, and Dell.

A potential weakness of the cost leadership strategy is the tendency to cut costs in a way that undermines demand for the product or service, for example, by deleting key features. The cost leader remains competitive only so long as the consumer sees that the product or service is (at least nearly) equivalent to competing products that cost somewhat more.

Differentiation

Differentiation
is a competitive strategy in which a firm succeeds by developing and maintaining a unique value for the product or service as perceived by consumers.

The **differentiation** strategy is implemented by creating a product or service that is unique in some important way, usually higher quality, customer service product features, or innovation. Sometimes a differentiation strategy is called *product leadership* to refer to the innovation and features in the product. In other cases the strategy might be called a *customer-focused* or *customer-solution* strategy, to indicate that the organization succeeds on some dimension(s) of customer service. This perception allows the firm to charge higher prices and outperform the competition in profits without reducing costs significantly. Most industries, including, consumer electronics, and clothing, have differentiated firms. The appeal of differentiation is especially strong for product lines for which the perception of quality and image is important, as in cosmetics, jewelry, and automobiles. Tiffany, Bentley, Rolex, Maytag, and BMW are good examples of firms that have a differentiation strategy.

A weakness of the differentiation strategy is the firm's tendency to undermine its strength by attempting to lower costs or by ignoring the necessity of having a continual and aggressive marketing plan to reinforce the differentiation. If the consumer begins to believe that the difference is not significant, lower-cost rival products will appear more attractive.

Other Strategic Issues

A firm succeeds, then, by adopting and effectively implementing one of the strategies explained earlier (and summarized in Exhibit 1.9). Recognize that although one strategy is generally dominant, a firm is most likely to work hard at process improvement throughout the firm, whether cost leader or differentiator, and on occasion to employ both of the strategies at the same time. However, a firm following both strategies is likely to succeed only if it achieves one of them significantly. A firm that does not achieve at least one strategy is not likely to be successful. This situation is what Michael Porter calls "getting stuck in the middle." A firm that is stuck in the middle is not able to sustain a competitive advantage. For example, giant retailer Kmart/Sears has been stuck in the middle between trying to compete with Wal-Mart

A commodity is a product or service that is difficult to differentiate and, as a result, becomes a natural for cost leadership competition. Examples include building materials, many consumer electronics products, and many of the things we buy in supermarkets. Thomas L. Friedman, award-winning columnist and author, has addressed the issue of commodities in the current business environment in his book, *The World Is Flat*. One reason the "world is flat" is because any product or service that is a commodity will find its low-cost supply anywhere in the world—wherever there is the lowest cost. Commenting on India's growth in outsourcing work from other countries, Friedman notes that the portion of work that can be digitized is a good candidate for outsourcing. He provides examples from the accounting profession (tax return preparation), the legal profession (paralegal), and journalism (press releases, company reports); these activities are being outsourced to the low-cost supplier. The accountant or journalist instead provides value-adding services to the customer (such as tax planning, financial analysis, and news analysis). Some parts of the work are in effect "commoditized."

Other examples of commodities include personal computers (PCs), cell phones, and airlines. The PC industry has seen sales rise while profits fall. Dell manages to maintain its growth in profits and sales by moving successfully into new markets (China) and product lines (television sets and digital music players).

As in the PC industry, where prices have fallen as product performance has risen, prices and cost competition have increased in the cell phone industry as new manufacturers have entered the market and regulatory changes in the United States make it easier for users to switch providers.

The airline industry continues to move in the direction of the low-cost carriers, as shown by the trend by the carriers to charge for once-free items such as pillows, meals, and headsets.

Alan Blinder, economist and well-known advisor to banks and governments, estimates that almost 2 million accounting and bookkeeping jobs are currently "highly offshorable"; similarly, almost 400,000 computer programmer jobs, and 300,000 data entry jobs could be lost, leading the list of many other occupations.

What about a possible slowdown in globalization? The global economic recession that started in 2007 has had its effect on the trend to globalization. As economies suffer, views on trade and employment are changing. *The Economist* reports that while in 2002 78% of Americans were positive about foreign trade, in 2007, that number had shrunk to 59%. And a July 2008 survey showed a significant number of Americans saw foreign trade as a threat, and not an opportunity.

Sources: Thomas L. Friedman, *The World Is Flat: A Brief History of the Twenty-First Century* (New York: Farrar, Straus, and Giroux, 2005); "Less Friendly Skies," *BusinessWeek*, July 11, 2005, p. 16; "Pricing Pressure Squeezes Cellphone Makers World-Wide," *The Wall Street Journal*, January 15, 2005, p. B1; "For Dell, Success in China Tells Tale of Maturing Market," *The Wall Street Journal*, July 5, 2005, p. 1; Pete Engardio, "The Future of Outsourcing," *BusinessWeek*, January 30, 2006, pp. 50–64; David Wessel and Bob Davis, "Pain from Free Trade Spurs Second Thoughts," *The Wall Street Journal*, March 28, 2007, p. 1; Pete Engardio, "Let's Offshore the Lawyers," *BusinessWeek*, September 18, 2006, pp 42–43; Suzanne Barlyn, "Call My Lawyer . . . In India," Time, April 14, 2008; Justin Scheck, "Forecast Clouds Dell's Results," *The Wall Street Journal*, November 30, 2007, p. B3; "Globalization: Turning their Back on the World," *The Economist*, February 21, 2009, pp 59–61.

on cost and price, and with style-conscious Target on differentiation. Some have suggested that Kmart/Sears might find success by abandoning the suburban locations where Target and Wal-Mart are strong and instead focusing on their many urban locations where they offer convenience to the urban shopper.

Developing a competitive strategy is the first step for a successful business. The critical next step is to implement that strategy, and this is where the management accountant comes in. The management accountant works to implement strategy as a part of the management team, by contributing the management accountant's specific expertise (cost management methods). We cover these methods in each of the chapters as we go through the text. Our focus in each chapter, then, will be to show how the method we are covering in that chapter

EXHIBIT 1.9

Distinctive Aspects of the Two Competitive Strategies

Aspect	Cost Leadership	Differentiation
Strategic target	Broad cross section of the market	Focused section of the market
Basis of competitive advantage	Lowest cost in the industry	Unique product or service
Product line	Limited selection	Wide variety, differentiating features
Production emphasis	Lowest possible cost with high quality and essential product features	Innovation in differentiating products
Marketing emphasis	Low price	Premium price and innovative, differentiating features

We often associate the differentiation strategy with firms that have an outstanding new innovation or that excel in customer service, quality, or product features, but sometimes a differentiation approach can help a firm that competes in an industry that is characterized by cost leaders. One example is the furniture maker, Craftique, in Mebane, North Carolina. Like many furniture firms, 57-year-old Craftique has been struggling to compete with low-cost suppliers from China and other global competitors. In a new direction, it now succeeds by specializing only in high-end furniture with lots of fabric choices, colors, and allowing the customer to participate in the product design over the firm's Web site. Other furniture manufacturers that follow the cost leadership model strive to compete by outsourcing production to low-cost suppliers and/or investing in automation to reduce operating costs.

Magnatag Visible Systems in Macedon, New York, competes in the commodity market for erasable whiteboards used in classrooms and training centers by customizing its product for church groups, hospitals, and other organizations—adding graphics and unique grids needed by these customers. Lenovo, competing in the low-cost notebook market, pitches the durability of its product, sometimes bouncing it on tabletops at sales meetings with corporate clients to stress its strength and durability. John Deere and Bobcat, makers of farming and construction equipment, rely on innovation, close physical location to customers, and close attention to customer expectations to succeed in a very competitive global industry. Some supermarkets that face competition from Wal-Mart's supercenters have chosen to compete and succeed by focusing on customer service, a pleasant shopping environment, and by carrying hard-to-find items. Sometimes a little differentiation can make the difference.

Source: "Fine Furniture a Leg to Stand On," *The Durham Herald.* February 17, 2004, p. B1; Gwendolyn Bounds, "Taking the Common out of Commodity," *The Wall Street Journal*, June 26, 2007, p. B1; Jane Spencer, "Can Durability Trump Price in Laptop War?" *The Wall Street Journal*, May 17, 2007, p. B1; Timothy Aeppel, "Still Built on the Home Front," *The Wall Street Journal*, October 24, 2006, p. B1; Michael Arndt, " Deere's Revolution on Wheels," *The Wall Street Journal*, July 2, 2007, p. B1; Gary McWilliams, "Not Copying Wal-Mart Pays Off for Grocers," *The Wall Street Journal*, June 6, 2007, p. B1.

is used in implementing strategy. We will use the following five-step framework to show how the method demonstrated in the chapter can be used to help the organization achieve its strategy by solving a particular problem.

The Five Steps for Strategic Decision Making

The five steps for decision making with a strategic emphasis are listed below, together with a short illustration of how the steps could be used by Wal-Mart to help the company deal with the problem of rising fuel prices that affect the cost of the firm's use of trucks to deliver products from Wal-Mart's warehouses to its retail stores.

The first step is to determine the strategic issues surrounding the problem, because the solution of any problem must fit the organization's strategy. A good decision is one that makes the organization more competitive and successful. By starting with the strategic issues, we ensure that the decision fits the organization's strategic goals.

1. **Determine the strategic issues surrounding the problem.** Fuel costs are critical to Wal-Mart because it competes on low cost and low prices. So this problem will get close management attention. In contrast, the effect of a rise in fuel prices will likely not be as critical for a differentiated company, such as a high-end retailer like Nordstrom.

2. **Identify the alternative actions.** In one alternative, Wal-Mart considers the use of smaller and more fuel-efficient trucks together with a relocation of its warehouses, to reduce travel time and fuel usage. Another option would be to outsource all of Wal-Mart's delivery needs to other trucking firms.

3. **Obtain information and conduct analyses of the alternatives.** Wal-Mart collects relevant cost information and calculates the expected cost of each alternative and finds that the use of other truckers would provide significantly lower total fuel cost. Considering the problem strategically, Wal-Mart projects on the one hand that it can more effectively compete with Target by providing more rapid delivery of fast-moving items to its stores, and that this could be accomplished with the use of smaller trucks. On the other hand, Wal-Mart also knows that it competes on cost and that lower cost is critical to its success.

4. **Based on strategy and analysis, choose and implement the desired alternative.** After considering the options, Wal-Mart chooses to outsource the delivery function to other

trucking firms, in order to maintain or perhaps improve its low cost position. In contrast, a high-end retailer such as Nordstrom might have chosen the option with more rapid delivery and higher cost, because its strategy is based on quality of product and customer satisfaction. Knowing the strategic context for the decision can make a big difference!

5. **Provide an ongoing evaluation of the effectiveness of implementation in step 4.** To provide an ongoing review of delivery costs, Wal-Mart top management instructs operational managers in the firm to present an updated review of the decision to top management once every quarter. In this way, changes in costs or strategic objectives will be reviewed on a regular basis.

Look for these five steps for the topics in the chapters ahead.

The Professional Environment of Cost Management

LEARNING OBJECTIVE 5

Describe the professional environment of the management accountant, including professional organizations and professional certifications.

Personally, I'm always ready to learn, although I do not always like being taught.

Winston Churchill

If I had eight hours to chop down a tree, I would spend six sharpening my axe.

Abraham Lincoln

Winston Churchill, the former prime minister of the United Kingdom, and Abraham Lincoln, the 16th president of the United States, understood the importance of continuous learning. Their words apply equally well to the management accountant. Management accountants must continuously improve their technical and other skills and maintain a constant high level of professionalism, integrity, and objectivity about their work. Many professional organizations, such as the Institute of Management Accountants (IMA) and the American Institute of Certified Public Accountants (AICPA), encourage their members to earn relevant professional certifications, participate in professional development programs, and continually reflect on the professional ethics they bring to their work.

Professional Organizations

The professional environment of the management accountant is influenced by two types of organizations: one that sets guidelines and regulations regarding management accounting practices and one that promotes the professionalism and competence of management accountants.

The first group of organizations includes a number of federal agencies, such as the Internal Revenue Service, which sets product costing guidelines for tax purposes, and the Federal Trade Commission (FTC), which, to foster competitive practices and protect trade, restricts pricing practices and requires that prices in most circumstances be justified on the basis of cost. In addition, the Securities and Exchange Commission (SEC) provides guidance, rules, and regulations regarding financial reporting.

The role of the SEC was recently strengthened by the Sarbanes-Oxley Act of 2002 which created the Public Company Accounting Oversight Board (PCAOB) to establish rules for "auditing, quality control, ethics, independence, and other professional standards relating to the preparation of audit reports for issuers." Of particular importance to management accountants is that the SEC, in implementing the act, now requires each public company to disclose in its annual report whether it has a code of ethics covering its chief financial executives, including high-level management accountants such as the controller.

In the private sector, the Financial Accounting Standards Board (FASB), an independent organization, and the AICPA supply additional guidance regarding financial reporting practices. The AICPA also provides educational opportunities in the form of newsletters, magazines, professional development seminars, and technical meetings for management accountants.

Congress established the Cost Accounting Standards Board (CASB) in 1970 (Public Law 91–379), which operates under the Office of Federal Procurement Policy "to make, promulgate, amend and rescind cost accounting standards and interpretations thereof designed to achieve uniformity and consistency in the cost accounting standards governing measurement, assignment, and allocation of cost to contracts with the United States federal government." The CASB's objective is to achieve uniformity and consistency in the cost accounting standards used by government suppliers to reduce the incidence of fraud and abuse. Twenty standards cover a broad range of issues in cost accounting.

In addition, to enhance cost accounting standards and financial reporting by federal governmental entities, Congress established in 1990 the Federal Accounting Standards Advisory Board. The FASAB publishes reports and documents on cost accounting concepts and standards that are comparable to those used in business firms.

Another group of organizations supports the growth and professionalism of management accounting practice. The Institute of Management Accountants (IMA) is the principal organization devoted primarily to management accountants in the United States. The IMA provides journals, newsletters, research reports, management accounting practice reports, professional development seminars, and technical meetings that serve the broad purpose of providing continuing education opportunities for management accountants. An especially important service of the IMA is its 35 Statements on Management Accounting (SMAs) which cover a broad range of practice areas for the management accountant: leadership strategies and ethics (4 statements), technology (1), strategic cost management (9), business performance management (14), governance, risk, and compliance (2), and the practice of management accounting (5). In the United Kingdom, the Chartered Institute of Management Accountants (CIMA) performs a similar role, as does the Society of Management Accountants (SMA) in Canada, the Spanish Management Accounting Association, the French Accounting Association, and the Institutes of Chartered Accountants in Ireland, Australia, Scotland, and India. Similar organizations are present in most other countries around the world.

In areas related to the management accounting function, the Financial Executives International (FEI) provides services much like those provided by the IMA for financial managers, including controllers and treasurers.

Because one of the management control responsibilities of the management accountant is to develop effective systems to detect and prevent errors and fraud in the accounting records, the management accountant commonly has strong ties to the control-oriented organizations such as the Institute of Internal Auditors (IIA).

Even if you're on the right track, you'll get run over if you just sit there.

Will Rogers

Wal-Mart and Target are two of the most successful retailers in the United States. Wal-Mart bears the slogan, "Save Money, Live Better," while Target stores say "Expect More, Pay Less." If you have shopped at either of these stores you will likely have formed an opinion about the stores and how they compete.

Required

1. Based on your experience, explain what you think are the competitive strategies of these retailers. Are they key competitors, targeting the same customers? Do you think each firm has adopted the most effective strategy? Why or why not?

2. Recently Wal-Mart has begun to advertise in the high-fashion magazine *Vogue.* How does this fit the firm's strategy, or does it?

3. While customer's are pleased with Wal-Mart's low prices, there is ongoing controversy about the firm's negative effect on other retailers where Wal-Marts are located. For example, the closing of 30 supermarkets in Oklahoma City in recent years has been attributed to Wal-Mart's arrival. What are your thoughts on the controversy? Are the ethical principles and standards of the management accountant relevant in this context?

Professional Certifications

The role of professional certification programs is to provide a distinct measure of experience, training, and performance capability for the management accountant. Certification is one way in which the management accountant shows professional achievement and stature. Two types of certification are relevant for management accountants. The first is the Certified Management Accountant (CMA) designation administered by the Institute of Management Accountants, which is achieved by passing a qualifying exam and satisfying certain background and experience requirements. The exam has four parts: (1) business analysis, including global business, financial statement analysis, and economics; (2) management accounting and reporting; (3) strategic management; and (4) business applications (the applications of topics in parts 1 through 3, plus ethics, behavioral issues, and organizational issues). The material required for part (2) of the exam is covered throughout this book; portions of parts (1), (3), and (4) are also covered.

The second certification is the Certified Public Accountant (CPA) designation. Like the CMA, the CPA is earned by passing a qualifying exam, which the AICPA prepares and grades, and by satisfying certain background, education, and experience requirements. Unlike the CMA, which is an international designation, the CPA certificate is awarded and monitored in the United States by each state and territorial jurisdiction which has its own set of criteria. While the CPA designation is critical for those accountants who practice auditing, the CMA is widely viewed as the most relevant for those dealing with cost management issues. Many countries have certificates that are similar to the CPA and CMA, and many management accountants have both the CMA and the CPA certification.

Professional Ethics

LEARNING OBJECTIVE 6

Understand the principles and rules of professional ethics and explain how to apply them.

Ethics is an important aspect of the management accountant's work and profession. Professional ethics can be summed up as the commitment of the management accountant to provide a useful service for management. This commitment means that the management accountant has the competence, integrity, confidentiality, and credibility to serve management effectively.

The IMA Statement of Ethical Professional Practice

The ethical behavior of the management accountant is guided by the code of ethics of the Institute of Management Accountants (IMA). The IMA code of ethics specifies *minimum* standards of behavior that are intended to guide the management accountant and to inspire a very high overall level of professionalism. By complying with these standards, management accountants enhance their profession and facilitate the development of a trusting relationship in which managers and others can confidently rely on their work.

The IMA statement of ethical professional practice contains four main standards: (1) competence, (2) confidentiality, (3) integrity, and (4) credibility (Exhibit 1.10). The standard of competence requires the management accountant to develop and maintain the skills necessary for her or his area of practice and to continually reassess the adequacy of those skills as their

EXHIBIT 1.10
Institute of Management Accountants Code of Ethics

Source: www.imanet.org

1. Competence

Each member has a responsibility to:
1. Maintain an appropriate level of professional expertise by continually developing knowledge and skills.
2. Perform professional duties in accordance with relevant laws, regulations, and technical standards.
3. Provide decision support information and recommendations that are accurate, clear, concise, and timely.
4. Recognize and communicate professional limitations or other constraints that would preclude responsible judgment or successful performance of an activity.

2. Confidentiality

Each member has a responsibility to:
1. Keep information confidential except when disclosure is authorized or legally required.
2. Inform all relevant parties regarding appropriate use of confidential information. Monitor subordinates' activities to ensure compliance.
3. Refrain from using confidential information for unethical or illegal advantage.

3. Integrity

Each member has a responsibility to:
1. Mitigate actual conflicts of interest. Regularly communicate with business associates to avoid apparent conflicts of interest. Advise all parties of any potential conflicts.
2. Refrain from engaging in any conduct that would prejudice carrying out duties ethically.
3. Abstain from engaging in or supporting any activity that might discredit the profession.

4. Credibility

Each member has a responsibility to:
1. Communicate information fairly and objectively.
2. Disclose all relevant information that could reasonably be expected to influence an intended user's understanding of the reports, analyses, or recommendations.
3. Disclose delays or deficiencies in information, timeliness, processing, or internal controls in conformance with organization policy and/or applicable law.

firm grows and becomes more complex. The standard of confidentiality requires adherence to the firm's policies regarding communication of data to protect its trade secrets and other confidential information. Integrity refers to behaving in a professional manner (e.g., refraining from activities that would discredit the profession, such as unfair hiring practices) and to avoiding conflicts of interest (e.g., not accepting a gift from a supplier or customer). Finally, credibility refers to the need to maintain impartial judgment (e.g., not developing analyses to support a decision that the management accountant knows is not correct). The guiding principles behind these standards are honesty, fairness, objectivity, and responsibility. IMA members are expected to behave in accordance with these principles and standards.

How to Apply the Code of Ethics

Handling situations in which an ethical issue arises can be very challenging and frustrating. To effectively resolve an ethical issue, it is crucial to understand the firm's business and strategy. Determining whether a particular action is ethical requires an understanding of the business context to understand the intent of the act—is it for a business purpose or is it intended to mislead or disguise fraud? An example is Sherron Watkins, an Enron Corporation employee, who is credited with bringing that firm's 2001 accounting fraud to light. She wrote a letter to the CEO about financial accounting practices at Enron that did not appear to fit the firm's business or strategy. In contrast, Betty Vinson at first rejected and then agreed to make false accounting entries that were part of the accounting scandal at WorldCom in 2001–2002. As noted by the U.S. attorney prosecuting the case against Ms. Vinson, ". . . just following orders" is not an excuse for breaking the law.[5] The IMA has suggested guidance for resolving ethical issues, shown in Exhibit 1.11

---

[5] Susan Pulliam, "A Staffer Ordered to Commit Fraud Balked, Then Caved," *The Wall Street Journal*, June 23, 2003, p. A1.

EXHIBIT 1.11

IMA Guidance on Resolving Ethical Conflicts

Source: Institute of Management Accountants' Web site www.imanet.org

---

Resolution of Ethical Conflict

In applying the Standards of Ethical Professional Practice, you may encounter problems identifying unethical behavior or resolving an ethical conflict. When faced with ethical issues, you should follow your organization's established policies on the resolution of such conflict. If these policies do not resolve the ethical conflict, you should consider the following courses of action:

1. Discuss the issue with your immediate supervisor except when it appears that the supervisor is involved. In that case, present the issue to the next level. If you cannot achieve a satisfactory resolution, submit the issue to the next management level. If your immediate superior is the chief executive officer or equivalent, the acceptable reviewing authority may be a group such as the audit committee, executive committee, board of directors, board of trustees, or owners. Contact with levels above the immediate superior should be initiated only with your superior's knowledge, assuming he or she is not involved. Communication of such problems to authorities or individuals not employed or engaged by the organization is not considered appropriate, unless you believe there is a clear violation of the law.
2. Clarify relevant ethical issues by initiating a confidential discussion with an IMA Ethics Counselor or other impartial advisor to obtain a better understanding of possible courses of action.
3. Consult your own attorney as to legal obligations and rights concerning the ethical conflict.

Summary

The central theme of this book is that cost management information includes all the information that managers need to manage effectively to lead their firms to competitive success. Cost management information includes both financial and nonfinancial information critical to the firm's success. The specific role of cost management in the firm differs depending on the firm's competitive strategy, its type of industry and organization (manufacturing firm, service firm, merchandising firm, not-for-profit organization, or governmental organization), and the management function to which cost management is applied (the functions are strategic management, planning and decision making, management and operational control, and preparation of financial statements).

Changes in the business environment have altered the nature of competition and the types of techniques managers use to succeed in their businesses. These changes include (1) an increase in global competition; (2) lean manufacturing; (3) advances in information technologies, the Internet, and enterprise resource management; (4) a greater focus on the customer; (5) new forms of management organization; and (6) changes in the social, political, and cultural environment of business.

Management accountants have responded to the above six changes in the contemporary business environment with 13 methods that are useful in implementing strategy in these dynamic times. The first six methods focus directly on strategy implementation—the balanced scorecard/strategy map, value chain, activity-based costing, business intelligence, target costing, and life-cycle costing. The next seven methods focus on strategy implementation through a focus on process improvement—benchmarking, business process improvement, total quality management, lean accounting, the theory of constraints, enterprise sustainability, and enterprise risk management.

To apply new management methods effectively, it is crucial that the management accountant understand the firm's strategy. Strategy is the set of plans and policies that a firm employs to develop a sustainable competitive advantage. Using Michael Porter's framework, a firm can compete effectively either as a cost leader or through differentiation.

A variety of professional organizations supports management accounting, including the Institute of Management Accountants (IMA), the American Institute of Certified Public Accountants (AICPA), the Financial Executives International (FEI), and The International Federation of Accountants (IFAC), among others. Several relevant certification programs recognize competence and experience in management accounting; they include the Certified Management Accountant (CMA) and the Certified Public Accountant (CPA).

The management accountant is responsible to the firm and to the public for maintaining a high standard of performance and ethical responsibility, as set forth in the IMA Statement of Ethical Professional Practice. The professional ethics standards of the management accountant include competence, confidentiality, integrity, and credibility.

Key Terms

activity analysis, *12*
activity-based costing (ABC), *12*
activity-based management
(ABM), *12*
balanced scorecard, *11*
benchmarking, *13*
business intelligence, *12*
business process
improvement, *13*
cost leadership, *16*
cost management, *3*
cost management information, *3*

critical success factors
(CSFs), *10*
differentiation, *16*
enterprise risk management *14*
enterprise sustainability *14*
lean accounting *13*
life-cycle costing, *12*
management accounting, *3*
management control, *5*
operational control, *5*
planning and decision
making, *5*

preparation of financial
statements, *6*
strategic management, *4*
strategy, *15*
strategy map *11*
target costing, *12*
theory of constraints
(TOC), *13*
total quality management
(TQM), *13*
value chain, *12*

Comments on Cost Management in Action

A Case in Competitive Strategy: Wal-Mart and Target

These questions are intended for open discussion and expression of differences of opinion. Here we have a proforma of some thoughts on these competitive issues, combined with some of the most recent news reports available at the time of publication.

1. Most would argue that Wal-Mart is a cost leader because of its focus on low prices. Its operating efficiencies and persistent pursuit of low costs from its suppliers help Wal-Mart to achieve these low prices; the slogan says it all about that firm, "Save Money, Live Better."

   Target also values low prices, but competes somewhat differently. As the company Web site states, the firm has a "promise of differentiation and value" and "upscale, fashion forward." Moreover, the Target financial report to the SEC (10K) states that, for Target, the competitive focus is "brand recognition, customer service, store location, differentiated offerings, value, quality, fashion, price, advertising, depth of selection, and credit availability." These statements point to a differentiated firm, even though low price is an element of the contribution. Another difference is that Target's advertising budget is somewhat larger, at 3% of sales, relative to 1% at Wal-Mart.

   Perhaps another indicator: where do the richest 10% of Americans shop? For these wealthy Americans, Home Depot, Target, and Costco are the three most popular retailers (Costco is another low-cost retailer, with fewer customers—and a different customer base).

	Men	Women
Target	46%	61%
Home Depot	69	60
Costco	46	54

   At the time of this writing, April 2009, Wal-Mart has had a stock price decline of 11% over April 2008, while Target's stock priced has fallen by 27% in the same period. Why? A major reason is that the decline in the economy and customer expectations during this period drew more cost-conscious shoppers to Wal-Mart, while in contrast, the upscale message of Target is losing traction. Further, a Citigroup study found that, while Target's prices are within 1–3% of Wal-Mart, 87% surveyed shoppers said they shopped at Wal-Mart because it is the cheapest. The conundrum for Target at this time of economic decline is that shoppers place a much higher value on the reputation of Target over Wal-Mart. A study reported by *BusinessWeek* in July 2007 indicated that if Wal-Mart had the reputation among shoppers that Target had, Wal-Mart's stock price would increase by an estimated 5%.

2. The decision to advertise in *Vogue* shows Wal-Mart's intent to change customer expectations, and to get the message out to consumers that Wal-Mart has quality fashion products. The initial ad piece appeared in the September 2005 issue of *Vogue.* In mid-2005, Wal-Mart selected John Fleming to head up marketing; Mr. Fleming previously led the firm's online business and is also a 19-year veteran of Target Corp. The question is, can Wal-Mart manage to be arguably the world's best cost leader, and show some style at the same time?

3. The controversy over Wal-Mart's competitive and labor practices has drawn a lot of comment in the press, and opinions are divided. One line of argument would say that, as for any large business, Wal-Mart must compete in an increasingly competitive global economy, while others would say that their values are in conflict with this type of competition. The role of the management accountant in this context is to help the firm succeed, and to do so in an ethical manner, as set out in the IMA principles and standards—competence, integrity, confidentiality, and credibility.

Source: "Can Wal-Mart Fit Into a White Hat," *BusinessWeek,* October 3, 2005, pp. 94–96; "Wal-Mart's Fashion Fade," *The Wall Street Journal,* July 2, 2004, p. B1; "Wal-Mart Sets Out to Prove It's in Vogue," *The Wall Street Journal,* August 25, 2005, p. B1; "Where do the rich Shop?" *BusinessWeek,* May 24, 2004, p. 13; "Corporate Scandals Hit Home: Reputations of Big Companies Tumble," *The Wall Street Journal,* February 19, 2004, p. B1; Gary McWilliams, "Customers Trade Down as Economic Angst Grows," *The Wall Street Journal,* July 11, 2008, p. 1; Ann Zimmerman, "As Message Misses Mark, Target's Profit Drops," *The Wall Street Journal,* February 27, 2008, p. B1; Jennifer Reingold, "How Target Does It," *Fortune,* March 31, 2008, pp. 74–86; Pete Engardio and Michael Arndt, "What Price Reputation?" *BusinessWeek,* July 9, 2007, pp. 70–79; Gary McWilliams, "Credit Card Ills, Weak Sales Hurt Target," *The Wall Street Journal,* August 20, 2008. p. B3. Also, the firms' Web sites: Wal-Mart at www. wal-mart.com and Target at www.target.com

Self–Study Problem

(For solution, please turn to the end of the chapter.)

Strategy: An Ethical Issue

Frank Sills, the CEO and founder of ENVIRO-WEAR, is facing the first big challenge of his young company. Frank began the company on the principle of environmental consciousness in the manufacture of sports and recreation wear. His idea was to develop clothing that would appeal to active people who were concerned about quality, about waste in manufacturing and packaging, and the environmental impact of the manufacture of the goods they purchased. Starting with a small shop in Zebulon, North Carolina, Frank was able to develop his small business through strategic alliances with mail-order merchandisers, and by effective public relations about his environmentally concerned processes. A special advantage for the young firm was Frank's knowledge of accounting and his prior experience as a CPA in a major public accounting firm and as a controller (and CMA) of a small manufacturing firm.

ENVIRO-WEAR had reached $25,000,000 in sales in its sixth year, when a disastrous set of events put the firm and its prospects in a tail spin. One of the key sales managers was overheard by a news reporter telling jokes about the poor quality of the firm's clothing, and the news of it spread quickly. Also, rumors (largely unfounded) spread at the same time that the firm was not really as environmentally conscious in its manufacturing and packaging as it claimed. The result was an immediate falloff in sales, and some retailers were returning the goods.

Frank intends to fire the manager and deny publicly any association with the manager's comments, as well as to defend the firm's environmental record.

Required

1. On the basis of Porter's analysis of strategic competitive advantage, what type of competitive strategy has ENVIRO-WEAR followed? What type of strategy should it follow in the future?

2. What are the ethical issues involved in the case, and how would you resolve them?

Questions

1-1 Give four examples of firms you believe would be significant users of cost management information and explain why.

1-2 Give three examples of firms you believe would *not* be significant users of cost management information and explain why.

1-3 What does the term *cost management* mean? Who in the typical firm or organization is responsible for cost management?

1-4 Name three professional cost management organizations and explain their roles and objectives.

1-5 What type of professional certification is most relevant for the management accountant and why?

1-6 List the four functions of management. Explain what type of cost management information is appropriate for each.

1-7 Which is the most important function of management? Explain why.

1-8 Identify the different types of business firms and other organizations that use cost management information, and explain how the information is used.

1-9 Name a firm or organization you know of that you are reasonably sure uses cost management and explain why it does so. Does it use cost leadership or differentiation, and why?

1-10 As firms move to the Internet for sales and customer service, how do you expect their competitive strategies will change?

1-11 As firms move to the Internet for sales and customer service, how do you expect their need for cost management information will change?

1-12 What are some factors in the contemporary business environment that are causing changes in business firms and other organizations? How are the changes affecting the way those firms and organizations use cost management information?

1-13 Contrast past and present business environments with regard to the following aspects: basis of competition, manufacturing processes and manufacturing technology, required labor skills, emphasis on quality, number of products, number of markets, types of cost management information needed, management organizational structure, and management focus.

1-14 Name the 13 contemporary management techniques and describe each briefly.

Brief Exercises

1-15   Identify what you think is a very successful firm and explain why. How did it become successful?

1-16   Do you think there is value to the firm and to its shareholders of a strong ethical climate in the firm?

    a.   Why or why not?

    b.   A recent survey showed that 29 percent of teenagers in the United States believe that "one has to bend the rules to succeed" in business. Comment on this result and discuss the implications.

1-17   In 2004 the drug VIOXX was removed from the market by the pharmaceutical giant, Merck & Co. The drug was used to relieve arthritis pain and was especially beneficial for patients who needed a medication that was easy on the stomach. But research reports showed there was a risk of strokes and heart attacks after taking VIOXX for 18 months. Evaluate Merck's decision on business and ethics grounds.

1-18   What would you consider to be the strategy of the Coca-Cola company, cost leadership or differentiation, and why?

1-19   What is a commodity? Give some examples of what you consider to be commodities and explain whether you think the company making the commodity product or service is a cost leader or a differentiator and why.

1-20   Take as an example the bank where you have your account(s) and say whether you think it is a cost leader or a differentiator and why.

1-21   Consider the three broad categories of firms: manufacturers, retailers, and service firms. Give an example of a cost leader and a differentiator in each of the three categories. Do there tend to be more cost leaders relative to differentiators in one or more of these categories?

1-22   Michael Porter argues a firm cannot be at the same time a cost leader and a differentiator. Do you think a firm could be a cost leader and then become a differentiator, or vice versa?

1-23   What is the difference between strategy and planning?

Exercises

1-24   **Strategy, Real Estate Services**   As a management accountant in a small real estate services firm, you have become aware of a strategic initiative in your firm to promote its services to a new class of customers. Currently, most of your firm's customers lease space in large office buildings where they might occupy three or more floors of the building. Your firm provides maintenance, security, and cleaning services for the office space leased by these customers. The strategic initiative you have discovered is to seek out smaller firms that occupy as small a space as a few thousand square feet. You know that most of these smaller firms are now serviced in a haphazard manner, with part-time help for which turnover is very high; some of the smaller office buildings might not employ security of any kind. You expect that the demand for your company's services among firms of this smaller size will be good, but you are worried about the profitability of these new customers. In fact, although you cannot prove it with hard numbers, you are sure that this new strategy will cause big losses for your firm. You have not been consulted about this new strategy by the firm's owners because you are not viewed as part of the management decision-making team. You would like very much, however, to be more involved in the company's strategy development and decision making.

Required   What should you do or say about this new strategic initiative?

1-25   **Risk Management, Enterprise Sustainability, and Lean Accounting**   Jane Englehard is a feature writer for *National Business Weekly.* Her assignment is to develop a feature article on enterprise risk management. Her editor has asked her to research the available literature, including the Institute of Management Accountants Statements on Management Accounting (SMAs; www.imanet.org/publications_statements.asp.), and to write an informative article that would be useful to those who are not familiar with the topic. Note that the download of an SMA is free but it does require a login with your name, address, and e-mail address (you may enter your university or college where it indicates "company").

Required

1.   What are some of the key points that Jane should integrate into her article on enterprise risk management? What are the main ideas she would want to communicate in her article?

2.   Same as (1) above, but assume Jane's topic is enterprise sustainability.

3.   Same as (1) above, but assume Jane's topic is lean accounting.

Problems

1-26   **Contemporary Management Techniques**   Tim Johnson is a news reporter and feature writer for *The Wall Street Review,* an important daily newspaper for financial managers. Tim's assignment is to develop a feature article on target costing, including interviews with chief financial officers and operating managers. Tim has a generous travel budget for research into company history, operations, and market analysis for the firms he selects for the article.

Required

1. Tim has asked you to recommend industries and firms that would be good candidates for the article. What would you advise? Explain your recommendations.

2. Assume that Tim's assignment is a feature article on life-cycle costing. Answer as you did for requirement 1.

3. Assume that Tim's assignment is a feature article on the theory of constraints. Answer as you did for requirement 1.

1-27   Professional Organizations and Certification   Ian Walsh has just been hired as a management accountant for a large manufacturing firm near his hometown of Canton, Ohio. The firm manufactures a wide variety of plastic products for the automobile industry, the packaging industry, and other customers. At least initially, Ian's principal assignments have been to develop product costs for new product lines. His cost accounting professor has suggested to Ian that he begin to consider professional organizations and professional certifications that will help him in his career.

Required   Which organizations and certifications would you suggest for Ian, and why?

1-28   Balanced Scorecard   Johnson Industrial Controls, Inc. (JIC), is a large manufacturer of specialized instruments used in automated manufacturing plants. JIC has grown steadily over the past several years on the strength of technological innovation in its key product lines. The firm now employs 3,500 production employees and 450 staff and management personnel in six large plants located across the United States. In the past few years, the growth of sales and profits has declined sharply, because of the entrance into the market of new competitors. As part of a recent strategic planning effort, JIC identified its key competitive strengths and weaknesses. JIC management believe that the critical strengths are in the quality of the product and that the weakness in recent years has been in customer service, particularly in meeting scheduled deliveries. The failure to meet promised delivery dates can be quite costly to JIC's customers, because it is likely to delay the construction or upgrading of the customers' plants and therefore delay the customers' production and sales.

JIC's management believes that the adoption of the balanced scorecard for internal reporting might help the firm become more competitive.

Required

1. Explain how the balanced scorecard might help a firm like JIC.

2. Develop a brief balanced scorecard for JIC. Give some examples of the items that might be included in each of these four parts of the scorecard: (a) customer satisfaction, (b) financial performance, (c) manufacturing and business processes, and (d) human resources.

1-29   Banking, Strategy, Skills   A large U.S.–based commercial bank with global operations recently initiated a new program for recruiting recent college graduates into the financial function of the bank. These new hires will initially be involved in a variety of financial functions, including transactions processing, control, risk management, business performance reporting, new business analysis, and financial analysis. Recognizing that they are competing with many other banks for the relatively small number of qualified graduates, the firm has assigned you to develop a skills statement to be used in college recruiting as well as an in-house training program for new hires. You have some old training manuals and recruiting guides to assist you, but your boss advises you not to use them but to start with a fresh page. The reason for developing new materials is that the bank recently reorganized based on new management methods.

Required

1. Briefly explain 8 to 10 critical success factors for this bank. Consider how a bank of this size remains competitive and successful.

2. Develop a one-page outline of the skills statement and training program that your boss requested. Be brief and specific about the proper job description of a new employee in the finance area of the bank. What is the role of professional ethics, if any, in the job description? *Hint:* Use a balanced scorecard approach.

1-30   Consulting, Skills   A consulting firm offering a broad range of services will soon visit your college to recruit graduates. This firm has more than 20,000 professional staff in 275 offices of 11 different countries. Most of its clients are large corporations in a variety of different industries. Because of the opportunity for the experience and travel, you are very interested in getting a job with this firm. You have an interview in two weeks, and you're planning to do some research about the firm and the job to be as well prepared as you can be for the interview.

Required   Write a brief, one-half page statement of what you think the job description for this employer is. What skills would you need to succeed as a consultant in this firm?

1-31 Activity Analysis in a Bank   Mesa Financial is a small bank located in west Texas. As a small bank, Mesa has a rather limited range of services: mortgage loans, installment (mostly auto) loans, commercial loans, checking and savings accounts, and certificates of deposit. Mesa's management has learned that activity analysis could be used to study the efficiency of the bank's operations.

Required

1. Explain how activity analysis might help a bank like Mesa.

2. Give six to eight examples of activities you would expect to identify in Mesa's operations.

1-32 Ethics, Product Quality   HighTech, Inc., manufactures computer chips and components. HighTech has just introduced a new version of its memory chip, which is far faster than the previous version. Because of high product demand for the new chip, the testing process has been thorough but hurried. As the firm's chief of operations, you discover after the chip has been on the market for a few months and is selling very well that it has a minor fault that will cause hard-to-discover failures in certain, very unusual circumstances.

Required   Now that you know of the chip's faults, what should you disclose and to whom should you disclose it?

1-33 Strategy: Selling Electronics   Samsung, the large Korean manufacturer of electronics, has just developed a new 80-inch plasma TV. The TV is expected to retail in the range of $50,000. Normally, Samsung sells its TVs and other electronics in Big Box retailers such as Best Buy. In this case, Samsung is thinking of choosing a different means to retail the product.

Required   What retail store or stores, or what method would you suggest Samsung should use in selling its new TV?

1-34 Strategy; Calvin Klein   For many, the name Calvin Klein (CK) is synonymous with high-fashion clothing and accessories, super models, and fashion shows. It has an image of quality and style. In reality, a significant amount of CK products are sold by discount retailers such as Costco. How can this be? The answer is that 69-year-old designer Calvin Klein licensed Warnaco Group and other manufacturers to produce his products. Under this arrangement, CK receives a royalty based on Warnaco's sales. As it turns out, Warnaco found that it could be more successful with the brand through a broad strategy involving a number of retailers, including discounters.

Required   What type of strategy (cost leadership or differentiation) is Calvin Klein following at this time? Comment on how effective you think the relationship with Warnaco is likely to be.

1-35 Strategy; BMW   In 2003 the premier auto manufacturer, BMW, introduced a new compact SUV (the X3) in an effort to grab a greater share of the overall luxury car market. Because its own resources were pretty well tapped out by a large number of new vehicles BMW had already introduced, the automaker decided to have the new SUV built by the parts manufacturer, Magma International, based in Toronto. The vehicles would be manufactured by Magma in an Austrian plant.

Required   Comment on the strategic issues surrounding BMW's introduction of this new SUV. Do you think the company made the right decisions? Why or why not?

1-36 Strategy; Innovation   One common measure of a firm's efforts in innovation is the amount the firm spends on research and development and capital spending (new plant and equipment) relative to other expenditures. Based on 2004 information for U.S. firms in the Standard and Poor's 500 stock index, innovation measured in this way differs significantly among industries. The highest rates of innovation are in software and services, semiconductors, drugs, biotech, and technology hardware. Somewhat lower levels of innovation are seen in the food and beverage, consumer goods, household products, and automobile industries.

Required

1. Comment on the differences observed above from a strategic point of view.

2. When compared to large non-U.S. firms in the Standard and Poor's database, the highest innovators have a similar rate of innovation in the U.S. and non-U.S. firms for the household products industry and the food and beverage industry. However, the rate of innovation is somewhat higher for non-U.S. firms in the auto industry and consumer goods industry, but somewhat higher in the United States for firms in the software and services, drug, biotech, and semiconductor industries. Comment on these differences from strategic and global competitive points of view.

1-37 Strategy; Analyzing a Commodity Business   SanDisk Corp, the Sunnyvale, California, firm, is the world's largest manufacturer of removable memory disks used in digital cameras, cell phones, music players, and game consoles. Like many electronic components of this type, the business is very cyclical and price competitive. Most analysts view the product as a commodity, and thus vulnerable to global low-cost competition. SanDisk has adopted a new strategy to attempt to distinguish itself based on innovation and increased advertising. The firm has developed waterproof memory cards and cards with a security feature—the owner's fingerprint is needed to operate the device.

Required   What type of strategy did SanDisk follow at this time? What strategy was intended in SanDisk's new plans? Comment on how successful you think the new strategy would be.

1-38 Ethics; The WorldCom Scandal   The story of the telecom giant WorldCom came to a sad turn in 2002 as the firm filed for bankruptcy, with some of the managers facing criminal charges for fraud. In 2000 a severe slump in the telecom business led to pressures within WorldCom to reduce expenses and improve the financial statements to meet investor expectations. On orders from top managers, accountants within the firm created fraudulent financial statements, ultimately resulting in an $11 billion fraud. The fraud was detected as a result of an inquiry by the SEC, which led an internal auditor within WorldCom to start an investigation that uncovered the fraud in 2002. The successor firm, MCI (which had previously merged with WorldCom and is now part of Verizon), under the leadership of new top management, formed the office of chief ethics officer who had the responsibility for MCI's policy of training all MCI's U.S.-based employees, an ethics hotline, an ethics pledge signed by the firm's top 100 executives, and a company code of ethics, among other responsibilities.

Required   What should be the role of an ethics officer? To whom should the ethics officer report within the organization? Do you think MCI had a good plan for ensuring ethical behavior within the firm? How would you change the MCI ethics policy, if at all?

1-39 Ethics; Who, What, and Where?; Use of Internet   Occupational fraud is defined by the Association of Certified Fraud Examiners (ACFE) as "the use of one's occupation for personal enrichment through the deliberate misuse or misapplication of the employing organization's resources or assets". This means that the perpetrator of the fraud steals assets from the employer, in contrast to financial fraud in which the firm's financial statements are misrepresented. For example, the Enron case is a case of financial fraud, while the theft of the company's inventory by an employee would be occupational fraud. The ACFE completed a study of 508 cases of occupational fraud reported in 2004 (www. acfe.com/documents/2004RttN.pdf). The study shows some distinct patterns to these fraud cases.

Required   Go to the ACFE link shown above and review the study to determine the following.

1. Are first time offenders more likely or less likely to commit fraud?
2. Most frauds are detected by audit, revealed by the perpetrator, or exposed by a tip from another employee?
3. Does or does not a fraud hot line which employees can use to report suspected fraud help in reducing the cost of fraud?
4. Is the cost of fraud higher in small companies or larger companies?
5. Is age or gender of the perpetrator associated with the cost of fraud?
6. What do these results tell you about the incidence of fraud and how a company can best protect itself from occupational fraud?

1-40 Strategy; Auto Tire Manufacturing   Michelin, the 118-year-old French manufacturer of tires, is a worldwide leader in tire sales. But there are plenty of challenges. One is the growth of low-cost tire producers in Southeast Asia and elsewhere. Michelin knows that most tire buyers are shopping primarily for price, viewing tires primarily as a commodity. This is true even though the problems with Firestone and other tire makers in recent years have brought consumer attention to tire safety. To help differentiate his firm's product, Edouard Michelin (Michelin's former CEO) pushed development of technologically advanced tires that, for example, provide blowout protection and are more suited for high-performance use.

Required   Is the auto tire a commodity? Would you consider Michelin to be a cost leader or a differentiator, and why?

1-41 Strategy; Brand Value   Each year, *BusinessWeek* reports the 100 top brands in the world. The leading brands are determined from a calculation by Interbrand Corp, an independent rater. The calculation is based on an analysis to determine what portion of the firm's sales and earnings can be credited to the firm's brand. For 2007 (reported in the September 29, 2008, issue), the top 10 brands were, in order:

Coca-Cola
IBM
Microsoft
GE

Nokia

Toyota

Intel

McDonald's

Disney

Google

In 2009, *BusinessWeek* (April 20, 2009) also reported a survey by the Boston Consulting Group of 2,700 senior executives to determine the world's most innovative companies. The top 10 in order are:

Apple

Google

Toyota

Microsoft

Nintendo

IBM

Hewlett-Packard

Research in Motion

Nokia

Wal-Mart

Required   Which of the above firms would you classify as a cost leader and which would you classify as a differentiator, and why?

1-42   **Strategy and Balance Scorecard; Customer Service**   In its ranking of firms on the basis of customer service, *BusinessWeek (March 2, 2009)* collaborated with J.D. Power & Associates (a global marketing information firm that conducts independent surveys of customer satisfaction; *BusinessWeek* and J.D. Power are both owned by McGraw-Hill Companies) to develop a list of the top companies. The ranking was based in part on ratings by J.D. Power and also by a survey of 5,000 readers of *BusinessWeek*. The top 10 firms are listed in order:

1. Amazon.com
2. USAA, an insurance firm for military personnel
3. Jaguar
4. Lexus
5. The Ritz-Carlton
6. Publix Supermarkets
7. Zappos.com, online retail
8. Hewlett-Packard
9. T. Rowe Price, brokerage
10. Ace Hardware

Required   Which of the above firms would you classify as a cost leader and which as a differentiator, and why?

1-43   **Ethics, Product Quality**   Green Acres, Inc., is a large U.S.-based multinational producer of canned fruits and vegetables. While Green Acres has a reputation of traditionally using only organic suppliers for its fruits and vegetables, it has recently experimented with produce from farmers known to have genetically modified crops. These genetically modified fruits and vegetables are often cheaper than their organic counterparts because farmers are able to achieve greater yields than with organic crops, and they have provided the firm with a way to cut its production costs. As Green Acres' chief of operations, the firm's marketing researchers have informed you that consumers continue to view Green Acres' products as organic despite the fact that Green Acres has never placed the word *organic* on its product labels. Moreover, the marketing researchers have discovered that Green Acres' sales and profits have dramatically increased due to this misperception in the wake of debates over the health and environmental consequences of genetically modified organisms.

Required   Now that you know of your consumers' misperception about your product, should you disclose your use of genetically modified crops to the public?

1-44   **Strategy; Discounting, Differentiating, and Contract Manufacturing**   Contract manufacturing refers to a process in which one company, the contract manufacturer, produces the same or very similar products for other manufacturers or retailers. As an example, headquartered in Singapore, Flextronics is a large electronics manufacturing services company providing design, engineering, and manufacturing services to automotive, computing, consumer digital, industrial, and health care product companies. Microsoft is one of Flextronics' customers, among many others. Another example is High Tech Company (HTC), a Taiwan-based company that manufacturers cell phones and other products for the consumer electronics industry. Acer is another Taiwan-based computer manufacturer, the fourth largest in the world, but not a well-known brand. To change that image, Acer purchased Gateway Computer in October 2007 and is shedding its contract manufacturing business. Both HTC and Acer are now embarked on a strategy to gain brand recognition and to move away from the contract manufacturing business.

In a related instance, Menu Food, Inc of Ontario, Canada, a contract manufacturer, produces pet food for Procter and Gamble (Iams brand), Colgate-Palmolive (Science Diet brand), and Wal-Mart (the O'Roy brand). While Menu Food says it has 1,300 recipes, it may be hard to distinguish one product from another except for the branding due to advertising and promotion by the manufacturers and retailers who purchase the product from Menu and for differing prices.

In a final example, fashion products and fashion apparel by such well-known designers as Martha Stewart, Isaac Mizrahi, and Vera Wang are appearing in discount retail stores. Vera Wang has developed a line of clothing for Kohl's, Martha Stewart for K-Mart, and (until recently) Mizrahi for Target.

Required   For each of these cases of contract manufacturing, consider the strategic and competitive implications of the buyer-seller arrangement.

1. For the Taiwan-based companies HTC and Acer
2. For Menu Food
3. For Vera Wang and Martha Stewart

1-45   **Learning about Different Professional Organizations; Using the Internet**   There are a number of professional organizations throughout the world that represent the interests of the management accountant professional, providing educational materials and other services to the management accountant. A partial list of some of these organizations is provided below.

Institute of Management Accounting: www.imanet.org/

Society of Management Accountants (Canada) www.cma-Canada.org/

Chartered Institute of Management Accountants (UK): www.cimaglobal.com

American Institute of Certified Public Accountants: www.aicpa.org/index.htm

Financial Executives International: www.financialexecutives.org

Required   In 200 words or less, explain how the different organizations support the profession of management accountant, that is, the nature and extent of the publications they offer, educational programs, and other services. Use specific examples that you notice in reviewing the Web sites.

1-46   **Current Economic Information; Use of the Internet**   There are a number of sources of economic and demographic information that can assist the management accountant. The information includes financial information such as interest rates, employment, income, international trade, output of goods and services, consumer price levels, and market values of stocks and bonds. The management accountant uses this information to better understand the environment in which his or her firm competes. For example, when interest rates are moving up (or down) rapidly, the management accountant will want to consider the effect of the interest cost changes on his or her analysis and recommendations regarding managing cash flow, introducing new products, improving or expanding production facilities, and so on. There are many sources for this information; two useful sources are shown below:

White House Summary of Statistical Information: www.whitehouse.gov/fsbr/esbr.html

New York Stock Exchange: www.nyse.com

Required

Review *only* the White House statistics for international, output, and production statistics. Comment on the current state of the economy that you see in these statistics, in 200 words or less.

1-47   **Different Professional Certification Programs**   There are several professional certificate programs that are of interest to management accountants. Each certificate is awarded based on the results of a comprehensive exam plus other education and experience requirements. Perhaps the best known is the CPA which is administered by each of the 50 states and five other jurisdictions in the United States. The CPA certificate represents achievement of a broad knowledge of the accounting profession, including auditing, tax accounting, and governmental accounting, among others. Information about the CPA is available at the American Institute of Certified Public Accountants (AICPA) Web site.

The Institute of Management Accountants (IMA) has a professional certification program leading to the Certificate in Management Accounting (CMA). The CMA exam has a framework similar to that of the CPA exam except that its focus is on broad business knowledge, strategy implementation, and competence in management accounting, rather than taxation and auditing.

American Institute of Certified Public Accountants: www.aicpa.org/index.htm

Institute of Management Accounting: www.imanet.org/

Required Review the AICPA and IMA Web sites and, in 200 words or less, explain how the two certificate programs differ, and which certificate program (if any) might be most appropriate for you given your current career interests. Use specific examples that you notice in reviewing the Web sites.

Solution to Self-Study Problem

An Ethical Problem

1. ENVIRO-WEAR's strategy to this point is best described as the differentiation strategy, wherein Frank has been able to succeed by differentiating his product as environmentally sound. This has appealed to a sufficient number of customers of sports wear, and ENVIRO-WEAR has grown accordingly. However, given the unfortunate jokes made by the sales manager and the rumors, the differentiation strategy is unlikely to continue to work, since the offense of the jokes and the disclosure of some discrepancies in the manufacturing methods will undermine the appeal of environmentally sound manufacturing. Frank will have to work quickly to maintain differentiation, perhaps through a quick response that effectively shows the firm's commitment to quality and environmental issues. Failing that, Frank should quickly decide what change in strategy will be necessary for his firm to survive and continue to succeed. Frank should consider a new strategy, perhaps based on cost leadership. The cost leadership strategy would bring Frank into competition with different types of firms, and the question for Frank would be whether his firm could successfully compete in that type of market.

2. There are a number of ethical issues in the case, which are especially important to Frank as a CMA and a CPA with previous experience in public accounting practice where ethics are very important. Frank should try to identify and understand the different options and the ethical aspects of the consequences of those options. For example, should Frank deny all charges against the company? Should he undertake an investigation to determine what his other sales managers think (do they have the same view as the offensive sales manager)? Do the manufacturing processes of the firm really live up to the claimed quality and environmental standards? It seems the relevant ethical issue requires communicating unfavorable as well as favorable information and disclosing fully all relevant information that could reasonably be expected to influence a consumer's understanding of the situation. To disguise or mislead consumers and others would be in conflict with the professional standards Frank is very familiar with.

   Also at issue is whether it is appropriate to fire the offensive sales manager. Most would probably agree that the firing is appropriate, since the sales manager has publicly put himself at odds with the strategic goals of the firm. However, others might want to consider the consequences of the firing and its fairness to the employee.

CHAPTER TWO

Implementing Strategy:
The Value Chain, the Balanced Scorecard, and the Strategy Map

After studying this chapter, you should be able to . . .

1. Explain how to implement a competitive strategy by using Strengths-Weaknesses-Opportunities-Threats (SWOT) Analysis
2. Explain how to implement a competitive strategy by focusing on the execution of goals
3. Explain how to implement a competitive strategy using value-chain analysis
4. Explain how to implement a competitive strategy using the balanced scorecard
5. Explain how to expand the balanced scorecard by integrating sustainability

Amazon.com typifies successful competition in the new economy far more than many firms. Some would say that Amazon invented the Internet retailing business model that all other dot-coms are struggling to copy. Amazon understands well the strategy (i.e., business model) of developing and maintaining customer loyalty, which is the key to success in retail e-business, and implements it effectively.

Speaking of Jeff Bezos, the founder and CEO of Amazon.com, Robert Hof of *Business-Week* writes:

> "Jeff Bezos . . . was one of the few dot-com leaders to understand that sweating the details of Internet technologies would make all the difference. Amazon wasn't the first store on the Web. But Bezos beat rivals in inventing or rolling out new Internet technologies that made shopping online faster, easier, and more personal than traditional retail. He offered customized recommendations based on other buyers' purchases, let people buy an item with just one mouse click, and created personalized storefronts for each customer."[1]

The amazing thing about Amazon is that it created such a successful strategy for e-commerce at a time when there was no model to use as a guide. As Hof suggests, Amazon's success appears to come from its ability to deliver excellent customer service with very low prices. It has differentiated itself through efficient and error-free operating systems that provide reliable, convenient service. Amazon's operations are so efficient that it is now performing the e-tail order-taking and order-filling services for several other retailers, including the retail giant, Target; these services provide highly profitable fees to Amazon.com. Another growing service area is the sale of used merchandise. The great news for Amazon is that these new services provide fat margins, from 45 to 85 percent, far higher than e-tail sales.[2] How did Amazon implement this strategy? By careful planning and disciplined execution.

---

[1] Robert D. Hof, "Jeff Bezos: The Wizard of Retailing," *BusinessWeek,* December 20, 2004.
[2] "Now Comes the Flood," *BusinessWeek,* August 8, 2005.

Firms choose to compete by either cost leadership or differentiation, as explained in Chapter 1. This chapter considers the various means for implementing that competitive strategy: (1) SWOT analysis, (2) focus on execution, (3) value-chain analysis, and (4) the balanced scorecard and the strategy map.

The chapter concludes with an introduction to enterprise sustainability, which we present as an extension of the balanced scorecard. The value chain, balanced scorecard, and strategy map are foundational concepts that will appear again throughout the remaining chapters.

If you don't set goals, you can't regret not reaching them.

Yogi Berra

Strengths-Weaknesses-Opportunities-Threats (SWOT) Analysis

SWOT analysis

is a systematic procedure for identifying a firm's critical success factors: its internal strengths and weaknesses and its external opportunities and threats.

Skills or competencies that the firm employs especially well are called **core competencies.**

LEARNING OBJECTIVE 1

Explain how to implement a competitive strategy by using Strengths-Weaknesses-Opportunities-Threats (SWOT) Analysis.

One of the first steps in implementing strategy is to identify the critical success factors that the firm must focus on to be successful. **SWOT analysis** is a systematic procedure for identifying a firm's critical success factors: its *internal* strengths and weaknesses and its *external* opportunities and threats. Strengths are skills and resources that the firm has more abundantly than other firms. Skills or competencies that the firm employs especially well are called **core competencies.** The concept of core competencies is important because it points to areas of significant competitive advantage for the firm; core competencies can be used as the building blocks of the firm's overall strategy. In contrast, weaknesses represent a lack of important skills or competencies relative to the presence of those resources in competing firms.

Strengths and weaknesses are most easily identified by looking inside the firm at its specific resources:

- **Product lines.** Are the firm's products and services innovative? Are the product and service offerings too wide or too narrow? Are there important and distinctive technological advances?
- **Management.** What is the level of experience and competence?
- **Research and development.** Is the firm ahead of or behind competitors? What is the outlook for important new products and services?
- **Operations.** How competitive, flexible, productive, and technologically advanced are the current operations? What plans are there for improvements in facilities and processes?
- **Marketing.** How effective is the overall marketing approach, including promotion, selling, and advertising?
- **Strategy.** How clearly defined, communicated, and effectively implemented is corporate strategy?

Opportunities and threats are identified by looking outside the firm. Opportunities are important favorable situations in the firm's environment. Demographic trends, changes in regulatory matters, and technological changes in the industry might provide significant advantages or disadvantages for the firm. For example, the gradual aging of the U.S. population represents an advantage for firms that specialize in products and services for the elderly. In contrast, threats are major unfavorable situations in the firm's environment. These might include the entrance of new competitors or competing products, unfavorable changes in government regulations, and technological change that is unfavorable to the firm.

Opportunities and threats can be identified most easily by analyzing the industry and the firm's competitors:[3]

- **Barriers to entry.** Do certain factors, such as capital requirements, economies of scale, product differentiation, and access to selected distribution channels, protect the firm from

---

[3] The five forces of industry competition are adapted from Michael E. Porter, "The Five Competitive Forces that Shape Strategy," *Harvard Business Review,* January 2008, pp. 79–93.

newcomers? Do other factors, including the cost of buyer switching or government regulations and licensing restrictions restrict competition?

- **Intensity of rivalry among competitors.** Intense rivalry can be the result of high entry barriers, specialized assets (and therefore limited flexibility for a firm in the industry), rapid product innovation, slow growth in total market demand, or significant overcapacity in the industry. How intense is the overall industry rivalry facing the firm?

- **Pressure from substitute products.** Will the presence of readily substitutable products increase the intensity level of the firm's competition?

- **Bargaining power of customers.** The greater the bargaining power of the firm's customers, the greater the level of competition facing the firm. Bargaining power of customers is likely higher if switching costs are relatively low and if the products are not differentiated.

- **Bargaining power of suppliers.** The greater the bargaining power of a firm's suppliers, the greater the overall level of competition facing the firm. The bargaining power of suppliers is higher when a few large firms dominate the group of suppliers and when these suppliers have other good outlets for their products.

SWOT analysis guides the strategic analysis by focusing attention on the strengths, weaknesses, opportunities, and threats critical to the company's success. By carefully identifying the critical success factors in this way, executives and managers can discover differences in viewpoints. For example, what some managers might view as a strength others might view as a weakness. SWOT analysis therefore also serves as a means for obtaining greater understanding and perhaps consensus among managers regarding the factors that are crucial to the firm's success.

A final step in the SWOT analysis is to identify quantitative measures for the critical success factors (CSFs). Critical success factors are sometimes called *value propositions,* that is, the CSF represents the critical process in the firm that delivers value to the customer. At this final step the firm converts, for example, the CSF of customer service to a quantitative measure such as number of customer complaints, or a customer satisfaction score.

Identifying critical processes and developing measures for the CSFs involves a careful study of the firm's business processes. Product development, manufacturing, marketing, management, and financial functions are investigated to determine in which specific ways these functions contribute to the firm's success. The objective at this step is to determine the

EXHIBIT 2.1
Measuring Critical Success Factors

Critical Success Factor	How to Measure the CSF
Financial Factors	
• Profitability	Earnings from operations, earnings trend
• Liquidity	Cash flow, trend in cash flow, interest coverage, asset turnover, inventory turnover, receivables turnover
• Sales	Level of sales in critical product groups, sales trend, percent of sales from new products, sales forecast accuracy
• Market value	Share price
Customer Factors	
• Customer satisfaction	Customer returns and complaints, customer survey
• Dealer and distributor	Coverage and strength of dealer and distributor channel relationships; e.g., number of dealers per state or region
• Marketing and selling	Trends in sales performance, training, market research activities; measured in hours or dollars
• Timeliness of delivery	On-time delivery performance, time from order to customer receipt
• Quality	Customer complaints, warranty expense
Internal Business Processes	
• Quality	Number of defects, number of returns, customer survey, amount of scrap, amount of rework, field service reports, warranty claims, vendor quality defects
• Productivity	Cycle time (from raw materials to finished product); labor efficiency; machine efficiency; amount of waste, rework, and scrap
• Flexibility	Setup time, cycle time
• Equipment readiness	Downtime, operator experience, machine capacity, maintenance activities
• Safety	Number of accidents, effects of accidents
Learning and Growth	
• Product innovation	Number of design changes, number of new patents or copyrights, skills of research and development staff
• Timeliness of new product	Number of days over or under the announced ship date
• Skill development	Number of training hours, amount of skill performance improvement
• Employee morale	Employee turnover, number of complaints, employee survey
• Competence	Rate of turnover, training, experience, adaptability, financial and operating performance measures
Other	
• Governmental and community relations	Number of violations, community service activities

specific measures that will allow the firm to monitor its progress toward achieving its strategic goals. Exhibit 2.1 lists sample CSFs and ways in which they might be measured.

Execution

> It is very hard to develop a unique strategy, and even harder, should you develop one, to keep it proprietary. Sometimes a company does have a unique cost advantage or a unique patented position. Brand position can also be a powerful competitive position—a special advantage that competitors strive to match. However, these advantages are rarely permanent barriers to others. . . . So, execution is really the critical part of a successful strategy. Getting it done, getting it done right, getting it done better than the next person is far more important than dreaming up new visions of the future.
>
> *Louis V. Gerstner, Jr.*

Source: Louis V. Gerstner, Jr., *Who Says Elephants Can't Dance?* (New York: Harper Business, 2002), pp. 229–230.

LEARNING OBJECTIVE 2

Explain how to implement a competitive strategy by focusing on the execution of goals.

Lou Gerstner is credited with the remarkable success of IBM in the 1990s. He became CEO of IBM at a very troubled time for the company. He rejected the notion that he could save the company with some high vision, but instead he determined that the company needed to focus on execution. This meant determining the critical success factors and putting in place the processes to develop, achieve, and regularly inspect these processes. At IBM this meant a focus on the customer: beginning with a careful understanding of the customer's needs, then working on "faster cycle times, faster delivery times, and a higher quality of service." The service focus has served IBM well as its profits have grown to $10.5 billion in 2007 compared to the $8 billion loss in 1993, the year Gerstner took over at IBM. Current IBM CEO, Samuel J. Palmisano, continues Gerstner's focus on execution. When referring to an earnings shortfall in the first quarter of 2005, he noted that the company had trouble closing deals at the end of the quarter, and "we attribute most of that to our (lack of) execution." IBM's stock fell sharply in the first quarter of 2005 but recovered quickly and has been increasing ever since.

Effective execution requires a concise statement of strategy that is clearly communicated within the organization. It requires a business process approach to management, in which the CSFs are clearly identified, communicated, and acted upon. It means aligning strategy with action, or as the saying goes, "plan your work and then work your plan."

The nature of the types of CSFs that the manager executes depend, of course, on the type of strategy. For cost leadership firms, the CSFs are likely to relate to operational performance and quality, while differentiated firms are more likely to focus on the customer or innovation. Exhibit 2.2 summarizes the differences between the two types of competition, the nature of the required skills and resources, and the focus of efforts in execution. Also, while most topics we cover in the text are applicable to executing strategy for both cost leadership and differentiated firms, the topics in Part Three (Operational Control) are particularly relevant for the cost leadership firm, while those in Part Two (Planning and Decision Making) are useful for both types of firms.

Looking more closely at differentiated firms, the key CSFs and execution issues are in marketing and product development—developing customer loyalty and brand recognition, emphasizing superior and unique products, and developing and using detailed and timely information about customer needs and behavior. This is where the marketing and product development functions within the firm provide leadership, and the management accountants support these efforts by gathering, analyzing, and reporting the relevant information. Firms that excel in the execution of these functions include Coca-Cola, Microsoft, and IBM which have been the top three global brands for the last seven years.[4]

Both cost leadership and differentiation firms also can improve on execution through benchmarking and total quality improvement. The Malcolm Baldrige National Quality Program (U.S. Department of Commerce; www.quality.nist.gov) sets forth improvement criteria and awards firms that excel on these criteria. The criteria include a wide variety of business functions,

EXHIBIT 2.2

Effects of Competitive Strategy on Required Resources and Execution

Strategy	Required Resources	Execution
Cost leadership	• Substantial capital investment and access to capital • Process engineering skills • Intense supervision of labor • Products designed for ease of manufacturing	• Tight cost control • Frequent, detailed control reports • Structured organization and policies • Incentives based on meeting strict quantitative targets
Differentiation	• Strong marketing capability • Product engineering • Corporate reputation for quality or technological leadership • Long tradition in the industry or unique skills drawn from other businesses	• Strong coordination among functions: research, product development, manufacturing, and marketing

[4] "The 100 Top Brands," *BusinessWeek*, September 29, 2008.

including leadership, strategic planning, marketing, information and analysis, human resources, process management, and business results. Another resource for benchmarking is the International Organization for Standardization, a network of national standards institutes from 145 countries (www.iso.org).

Value-Chain Analysis

LEARNING OBJECTIVE 3

Explain how to implement a competitive strategy using value-chain analysis.

Because execution is so important in implementing strategy, managers must know how the firm's strategy and its CSFs are implemented *in each and every phase of the firm's operations.* In other words, managers must implement their firm's strategy at the detail level of operations. This sequence of activities must include all the steps necessary to satisfy customers. Value-chain analysis is a means to reach this detail level of analysis.[5]

Value-chain analysis is a strategic analysis tool used to better understand the firm's competitive advantage, to identify where value to customers can be increased or costs reduced, and to better understand the firm's linkages with suppliers, customers, and other firms in the industry. The activities include all steps necessary to provide a competitive product or service to the customer. For a manufacturer, this starts with product development and new product testing, then to raw materials purchases and manufacturing, and finally sales and service. For a service firm, the activities begin with the concept of the service and its design, purpose, and demand and then moves to the set of activities that provide the service to create a satisfied customer. Although the value chains are sometimes more difficult to describe for a service firm or a not-for-profit organization the approach is applied in all types of organizations. An organization might break its operations into dozens or hundreds of activities; in this chapter, it is sufficient to limit the analysis to no more than six to eight activities.

The term *value chain* is used because each activity is intended to add value to the product or service for the customer. Management can better understand the firm's competitive advantage and strategy by separating its operations according to activity. If the firm succeeds by cost leadership, for example, management should determine whether each individual activity in the value chain is consistent with that overall strategy. A careful consideration of each activity should also identify those activities in which the firm is most and least competitive.

The value chain can be thought of as three main phases, in sequence: (1) upstream, (2) operations, and (3) downstream. The *upstream phase* includes product development and the firm's linkages with suppliers; *operations* refers to the manufacturing operations or, for a retailer or service firm, the operations involved in providing the product or service; the *downstream phase* refers to linkages with customers, including delivery, service, and other related activities. Some have referred to the analysis of the upstream phase as *supply chain management* and to the analysis of the downstream phase as *customer relationship management.*

The determination of which part or parts of the value chain an organization should occupy is a strategic analysis based on the consideration of comparative advantage for the individual firm, that is, where the firm can best provide value to the ultimate consumer at the lowest possible cost. For example, some firms in the computer-manufacturing industry focus on the manufacture of chips (Texas Instruments) while others primarily manufacture processors (Intel), hard drives (Seagate), or monitors (Sony). Some manufacturers (Hewlett-Packard, Apple) combine purchased and manufactured components to manufacture the complete computer; others (Dell) depend primarily on purchased components. In the sport-shoe industry, Reebok manufactures its shoes and sells them to large retailers; Nike concentrates on design, sales, and promotion, contracting out all manufacturing. In effect, each firm establishes itself in one or more parts of the value chain on the basis of a strategic analysis of its competitive advantage.

Value activities
are activities that firms in the industry must perform in the process of designing, manufacturing, and providing customer service.

Value-chain analysis has two steps:

Step 1. *Identify the Value-Chain Activities.* The firm identifies the specific **value activities** that firms in the industry must perform in the processes of designing, manufacturing, and providing customer service. For example, see the value chain for the computer-manufacturing industry in Exhibit 2.3.

---

[5] This section is based on John K. Shank and Vijay Govindarajan, *Cost Management* (New York: The Free Press, 1993). See also the Institute of Management Accountants Statement on Management Accounting, "Value Chain Analysis for Assessing Competitive Advantage," Institute of Management Accountants, (www.imanet.org/publications_statements.asp).

EXHIBIT 2.3
Value Chain for the Computer Manufacturing Industry

Step in the Value Chain	Activities	Expected Output of Activities
Step 1: Design	Performing research and development	Completed product design
Step 2: Raw materials acquisition	Purchasing, receiving, and stocking	Various parts and metals
Step 3: Materials assembled into components	Converting raw materials into components and parts used to manufacture the computer	Desired components and parts
Step 4: Intermediate assembly	Converting, assembling, finishing, testing, and grading	Boards, higher-level components
Step 5: Computer manufacturing	Final assembling, packaging, and shipping the final product	Completed computers
Step 6: Wholesaling, warehousing, and distribution	Moving products to retail locations and warehouses, as needed	Rail, truck, and air shipments
Step 7: Retail sales	Making retail sale	Cash receipts
Step 8: Customer service	Processing returns, inquiries, and repairs	Serviced and restocked computers

The development of a value chain depends on the type of industry. For example, the focus in a service industry is on operations and on advertising and promotion rather than on raw materials and manufacturing. An example of a service industry value chain is shown in self-study problem 1 at the end of the chapter.

Step 2. *Develop a Competitive Advantage by Reducing Cost or Adding Value.* In this step, the firm determines the nature of its current and potential competitive advantage by studying the value activities and cost drivers identified earlier. In doing so, the firm must consider the following:

1. **Identify competitive advantage (cost leadership or differentiation).** The analysis of value activities can help management better understand the firm's strategic competitive advantage and its proper positioning in the overall industry value chain. For example, IBM, Boeing, General Electric, and other firms have increased emphasis on services for their customers, as many of these services are more profitable than the sale of their basic products.

2. **Identify opportunities for added value.** The analysis of value activities can help identify activities in which the firm can add significant value for the customer. For example, food-processing plants and packaging plants are now commonly located near their largest customers to provide faster and cheaper delivery. Similarly, large retailers such as Wal-Mart use computer-based technology to coordinate with suppliers to efficiently and quickly restock each of its stores. In banking, ATMs (automated teller machines) were introduced to provide improved customer service and to reduce processing costs. Banks have begun to develop on-line computer technologies to further enhance customer service and to provide an opportunity to reduce processing costs further.

3. **Identify opportunities for reduced cost.** A study of its value activities can help a firm determine those parts of the value chain for which it is *not* competitive. For example, firms in the electronics business, such as Flextronics International Ltd. and Sanmina-SCI, have become large suppliers of parts and subassemblies for computer manufacturers and other electronics manufacturers such as Hewlett-Packard, Sony, Apple and Microsoft, among others. The brand-name manufacturers have found that outsourcing some of the manufacturing to firms such as Flextronics reduces total cost and can improve speed, quality, and competitiveness.

Value-Chain Analysis in Computer Manufacturing

The computer industry provides an opportunity to show value-chain analysis in action. The Computer Intelligence Company (CIC) manufactures computers for small businesses. CIC has an excellent reputation for customer service, product innovation, and quality. CIC is able to compete with the larger manufacturers of computers because it designs the product specially for each customer and has superior service. CIC has a growing list of customers

The passage of the North American Free Trade Agreement (NAFTA) in 1997 and reduced restrictions on international trade through the World Trade Organization (WTO) have created many opportunities as well as obstacles for global companies. Identify one or two of the strategic issues for companies like Boeing in the United States or automakers throughout the world as a result of these changes in the global business environment.

(Refer to Comments on Cost Management in Action at end of chapter)

who are willing to pay a small premium for these advantages. The manufacturing process consists primarily of assembling components purchased from various electronics firms plus a small amount of metalworking and finishing. The manufacturing operations cost $250 per unit. The purchased parts cost CIC $500, of which $300 is for parts that CIC could manufacture in its existing facility for $190 in materials for each unit plus an investment in labor and equipment that would cost $55,000 per month. CIC is considering whether to make or continue to buy these parts.

CIC can contract out to another firm, JBM Enterprises, the marketing, distributing, and servicing of its units. This would save CIC $175,000 in monthly materials and labor costs. The cost of the contract would be $130 per machine sold for the average of 600 units sold per month. CIC uses value-chain analysis to study the effect of these options on its strategy and costs. The analysis is summarized in Exhibit 2.4.

The Five Steps of Strategic Decision Making for CIC Manufacturing

1. **Determine the strategic issues surrounding the problem.** CIC competes as a differentiator based on customer service, product innovation, and reliability; customers pay more for the product as a result.

2. **Identify the alternative actions.** CIC faces two decisions, the first of which is whether to make or buy certain parts, which CIC currently buys for $300 but could manufacture for $190 per unit plus an additional $55,000 monthly cost.

The second decision is whether to continue marketing, distributing, and serving its products or to outsource that set of activities to JBM enterprises for $130 per unit sold and save $175,000 per month in materials and labor costs.

3. **Obtain information and conduct analyses of the alternatives.** First decision: CIC calculates that the monthly cost to buy is $180,000 (= 600 × $300) while the monthly cost

EXHIBIT 2.4
Value-Chain Analysis for CIC Manufacturing Company

Value Activity	Option 1: Continue Current Operations	Option 2: Manufacture Components and Contract Out Marketing, Distributing, and Servicing Functions
Acquiring raw materials	CIC is not involved at this step in the value chain.	CIC is not involved at this step in the value chain.
Manufacturing computer chips and other parts	CIC is not involved at this step in the value chain; the cost of these parts is $200 to CIC.	CIC is not involved at this step in the value chain; the cost of these parts is $200 to CIC.
Manufacturing components, some of which CIC can make	CIC purchases $300 of parts for each unit.	CIC manufactures these parts for $190 per unit plus monthly costs of $55,000.
Assembling	CIC's costs are $250.	CIC's costs are $250.
Marketing, distributing, and servicing	CIC's costs are $175,000 per month.	CIC contracts out servicing to JBM Enterprises for $130 per unit sold.

FLEXTRONICS INTERNATIONAL, INC

Flextronics is a large international contract manufacturer of electronics products. Contract manufacturers like Flextronics, which is headquartered in Singapore, provide electronics manufacturing services to automotive, industrial, medical, and technology companies. In 2004 the firm purchased a majority stake in the award-winning design firm, Frog Design (the firm that designed the Apple computer, the Macintosh). Flextronics' strategy with this acquisition is to expand its contract manufacturing business by including upstream activities such as design—designing both the electronic components, and the look and feel of the product. The latter type of design is where Frog Design excels. Flextronics will be able to provide greater value to customers since it can take the customer's job from start to finish—design through delivery, saving time and cost for the customer. The firm's purchase of Nortel's manufacturing operations in 2006 and the purchase of Solectron (a competing contract manufacturer) in 2008 have helped to solidify Flextronics' strategy as the complete solution for those seeking electronics contract manufacturing—it provides integrated services to design, build, ship, and service the product.

GOING DOWNSTREAM WHERE THE PROFITS ARE

Many manufacturers of expensive equipment and autos also have a finance unit. The finance unit is a downstream activity that provides the customer access to the needed funds, once the purchasing decision has been made. Looking ahead, the finance units of these corporations are facing the difficult times of the 2008 liquidity crisis and recession. For example, in 2008 Target Corp. reported sharply lower profits from its credit card business due in part to write-offs of bad debts.

Finance Unit Profit as a % of Total Profit		
	2004	**2007**
Ford Motor	103%*	*
General Electric	49%	46%
Deere	22%	19%
Caterpillar	19%	13%

*In 2004, Ford's finance unit earnings exceeded total company earnings because of losses in the automotive segment; in 2007, the finance unit earned $1.2 billion, not enough to make up for the loss in the automotive segment of $5 billion. All information is taken from company annual reports.

LOUIS VUITTON MOVES DOWN THE VALUE CHAIN

Because lower-cost rivals have gotten new fashion trends to the showroom faster than Louis Vuitton (the luxury fashion manufacturer) and taken sales from the company, Louis Vuitton has chosen to totally revamp its manufacturing process to be more in line with the flexible, fast, processes of other industries such as electronics manufacturing. Instead of design, the focus is now on making sure the product is available promptly to retailers. Strategically, the company has revamped its value chain.

Gary McWilliams, "Credit Card Ills, Weak Sales Hurt Target," *The Wall Street Journal,* August 20, 2008, p. B3; Christina Passariello, "Louis Vuitton Tries Modern Methods on Factory Lines," *The Wall Street Journal,* October 9, 2006, p. 1.

---

to manufacture the part is only $169,000 (= [600 × $190] + $55,000); thus making the part saves $11,000 per month.

Second decision: CIC calculates that the monthly cost of the contract with JBM enterprises would be $78,000 (= 600 × $130) per month. This is a $97,000 saving over the in-house cost of $175,000 per month.

4. **Based on strategy and analysis, choose and implement the desired alternative.** First decision: As a differentiator based on product quality and innovation, CIC considers the importance of the quality of the part in question and decides to manufacture the part. Note that while this would save CIC $11,000 per month, the key reason for the decision is to control the quality of the part and thereby improve overall quality and to support the firm's differentiation strategy. Note, however, that if CIC believes that the supplier can provide the part at a higher level of quality than can CIC, the better strategy is reversed; it is now better to continue to buy, even if the costs are higher, in order to support quality, a critical success factor.

Second decision: As a differentiator based on customer service, CIC considers the continued high level of service from in-house personnel as critical to the company's success and continues to maintain these personnel, even if it means the loss of monthly savings of $97,000.

5. **Provide an ongoing evaluation of the effectiveness of implementation in Step 4.** Management of CIC realize that the quality of the product and of customer service is critical to the company's success. So, CIC will continue to review the quality of product and service provided internally. If the quality of the part purchased outside or the service provided internally is inferior then a change would be desirable.

The Balanced Scorecard and Strategy Map

The balanced scorecard (BSC) and strategy map, introduced in Chapter 1, are key tools for the implementation of strategy. The BSC implements strategy by providing a comprehensive performance measurement tool that reflects the measures critical for the success of the firm's strategy and thereby provides a means for aligning the performance measurement in the firm to the firm's strategy. Thus, managers and employers within the firm have the awareness of the firm's CSFs (through the balanced scorecard) and an incentive to achieve these CSFs in moving the firm forward to its strategic goals. The strategy map is also used to implement strategy, but in contrast to the focus on performance measurement in the BSC, the main role of the strategy map is to develop and communicate strategy throughout the organization. The strategy map links the perspectives of the BSC in a causal framework that shows systematically how the organization can succeed by achieving specific critical success factors in the learning and growth perspective, thereby leading to desired performance in internal processes, and thus to desired performance in the customer perspective and finally to the ultimate goal, financial performance and, for a public firm, shareholder value. In sum, the BSC provides the structure of performance measures and the strategy map provides the road map the firm can use to execute the strategy.

The Balanced Scorecard

Prior to the wide use of the BSC in the late 1990s, firms tended to focus only on financial measures of performance, and as a result, some of their critical nonfinancial measures were not sufficiently monitored and achieved. In effect, the BSC enables the firm to employ a strategy-centered performance measurement system, one that focuses managers' attention on critical success factors, and rewards them for achieving these critical factors.

Now a rapidly increasing number of firms, not-for-profit organizations, and governmental units use the BSC to assist them in implementing strategy. A recent survey of 193 global organizations shows the adoption rate of the balanced scorecard is 50 percent. As noted in Chapter 1 the balanced scorecard consists of four perspectives, or groupings of critical success factors: (1) the *financial perspective* includes financial performance measures such as operating income and cash flow; (2) the *customer perspective* includes measures of customer satisfaction; (3) the *internal process perspective* includes measures of productivity and speed, among others; and (4) *learning and growth* includes such measures as employee training hours and the number of new patents or new products. The BSC provides five key potential benefits:

Benefits of the BSC

- A means for tracking progress toward achievement of strategic goals.
- A means for implementing strategy by drawing managers' attention to strategically relevant critical success factors, and rewarding them for achievement of these factors.
- A framework firms can use to achieve a desired organizational change in strategy, by drawing attention to and rewarding achievement on factors that are part of a new strategy. The BSC makes the nature and direction of the desired change clear to all.
- A fair and objective basis for firms to use in determining each manager's compensation and advancement.
- A framework that coordinates efforts within the firm to achieve critical success factors. BSC enables managers to see how their activity contributes to the success of others and motivates teamwork.

Implementing the BSC

To be implemented effectively, the balanced scorecard should:

- Have the strong support of top management.
- Accurately reflect the organization's strategy.
- Communicate the organization's strategy clearly to all managers and employees, who understand and accept the scorecard.
- Have a process that reviews and modifies the scorecard as the organization's strategy and resources change.

- Be linked to reward and compensation systems; managers and employees have clear incentives linked to the scorecard.
- Include processes for assuring the accuracy and reliability of the information in the scorecard.
- Ensure that the relevant portions of the scorecard are readily accessible to those responsible for the measures, and that the information is also secure, available only to those authorized to have the information.[6]

Because of its emphasis on performance measurement, we will again cover the BSC when we cover operational control (Part Three) and management control (Part Four) in later chapters.

The Balanced Scorecard Reflects Strategy

The BSC can be viewed as a two-way street. Since it is designed to help implement strategy, it also should reflect strategy. One should be able to infer a firm's strategy by a careful study of the firm's BSC. For example, consider the BSC of an electronics manufacturer shown in Exhibit 2.5. Does this firm follow a cost leadership strategy or a differentiation strategy, and why?

EXHIBIT 2.5   **The Balanced Scorecard for an Electronics Firm**

Source: Chee W. Chow, Kamal M. Haddad, James W. Williamson, "Applying the Balanced Scorecard to Small Companies," *Management Accounting,* August 1997, pp. 21–27.

	Measures
Customer Perspective	
Quality	Own quality relative to industry standards; number of defects; delivered product quality
Price	Own price relative to competitive market price; sales volume; customer willingness to pay
Delivery	Actual versus planned; number of on-time deliveries
Shipments	Sales growth; number of customers that make up 90 percent of shipments
New products	Number of new products; rate of technology improvements; percent of sales from products introduced in last two years
Support	Response time; customer satisfaction surveys
Internal Capabilities	
Efficiency of manufacturing	Cycle time; lead time; manufacturing overhead cost/quarter; rate of increase in use of automation
New product introduction	Rate of new product introduction/quarter
New product success	New products' quarterly sales; number of orders
Sales penetration	Actual sales versus plan; increases in number of $1 million customers each quarter
New businesses	Number of new businesses each year
Innovation	
Technology leadership	Product performance compared to competition; number of new products with patented technology in them
Cost leadership	Manufacturing overhead per quarter as a percent of sales; rate of decrease in cost of quality per quarter
Market leadership	Market share in all major markets; number of systems developed to meet customer requests and requirements
Research and development	Number of new products; number of patents
Financial Perspective	
Sales	Annual growth in sales and profits
Cost of sales	Extent it remains flat or decreases each year
Profitability	Return on total capital employed
Liquidity	Cash flows
Employees and Community Perspective	
Competitive benefits and salaries	Salaries compared to norm in local area
Opportunity	Individual contribution; personal satisfaction in job
Citizenship	Company contributions to community and the institutions that support the environment

[6] The above is based on information from: Robert S. Kaplan and David P. Norton, *Strategy Maps* (Boston: Harvard Business School Press, 2007); Raef Lawson, Toby Hatch, and Denis Desroches, *Scorecard Best Practices,* (New York: Wiley, 2008).

Exhibit 2.5 shows that the electronics firm places the customer perspective at the top of the scorecard. Also, while price is mentioned, note that the emphasis is on customer satisfaction, through quality, innovation, and service. A strong theme through the entire scorecard is the importance of innovation and new products. This seems to fit pretty well a firm that succeeds through differentiation based on quality and innovation, and the scorecard reflects that. Cost control is mentioned in the innovation perspective, but as supportive of the differentiation strategy, rather than in conflict with it. Note also the inclusion of an "employees and community" perspective that reflects this firm's strategic emphasis and desire to achieve in these areas.

Timing, Cause-and-Effect, and Leading Measures in the BSC

Another look at the BSC for the electronics firm in Exhibit 2.5 will reveal that some of the measures are likely to be taken daily or weekly (sales or number of defects) and some monthly or less frequently (cash flow, return on total capital). So, the BSC is not a single document that is presented on a given weekly or monthly cycle, but the measures will be updated on their appropriate time line. Also, some of these measures are known to have a cause-and-effect relationship with other measures, for example improved quality should increase sales and customer satisfaction. So, some measures are in effect "leading indicators" of what will happen to other measures in later periods. The insights to be gained from understanding these cause-and-effect relationships are captured in the strategy map.

The Strategy Map

A **strategy map** is a cause-and-effect diagram of the relationships among the BSC perspectives.

While the electronics firm in Exhibit 2.5 placed the customer perspective at the top of the BSC to show its priority, it is also possible to create a strategy map by linking the perspectives in the order they contribute to the overall success of the firm. A **strategy map** is a cause-and-effect diagram of the relationships among the BSC perspectives. Managers use it to show how the achievement of goals in each perspective affect the achievement of goals in other perspectives, and finally the overall success of the firm.

For most firms, the ultimate goal is stated in financial performance, and for public firms in particular, in shareholder value. So, the financial perspective of the BSC is the target in the strategy map. The other BSC perspectives contribute to financial performance in a predictable, cause-and-effect way. For many firms, the learning and growth perspective is the base upon which the firm's success is built. The reason is that learning and growth—resulting in great products and great employees—drives performance in the internal processes perspective and also the customer perspective. Similarly, great performance in the internal processes perspective drives performance in the customer perspective; better operations mean more satisfied customers. Finally, satisfied customers lead directly to improved financial performance.

An Illustration of the Strategy Map: The Martin & Carlson Co.

To illustrate how the strategy map and the balanced scorecard can be used to implement strategy, we take an example, Martin & Carlson Co., a manufacturer of high-end furniture. Janet Martin and Jack Carlson, both highly skilled in woodworking, started a small business in Graham, North Carolina, in 1984 to produce handmade furniture. First customers were friends and acquaintances; because of the very high quality and distinctive style of their furniture, the list of customers grew quickly, and Jack and Janet moved into larger space and hired and trained additional woodworking employees. At present the company has grown to become a nationally recognized manufacturer with annual sales of $200 million. Because of their distinctive brand, Jack and Janet have never experienced price competition, but in recent years the costs of the commodities they require, including fuel, have risen sharply, and it has become more difficult to maintain their profitable growth. A consultant has been called in to help them assess their strategy going forward.

The assessment began with the consideration of the firm's mission and strategy. Owning a privately held business, Janet and Jack felt that their strategy should reflect their personal values as well as the need to provide a successful business. The consultant took them through the sequence of steps. First, determine the mission of the company and its competitive strategy (see Chapter 1 for coverage of mission and strategy). Second, use SWOT analysis and value-chain analysis to further develop the strategy. Third, determine a balanced scorecard

EXHIBIT 2.6

A Strategy Map for Martin & Carlson

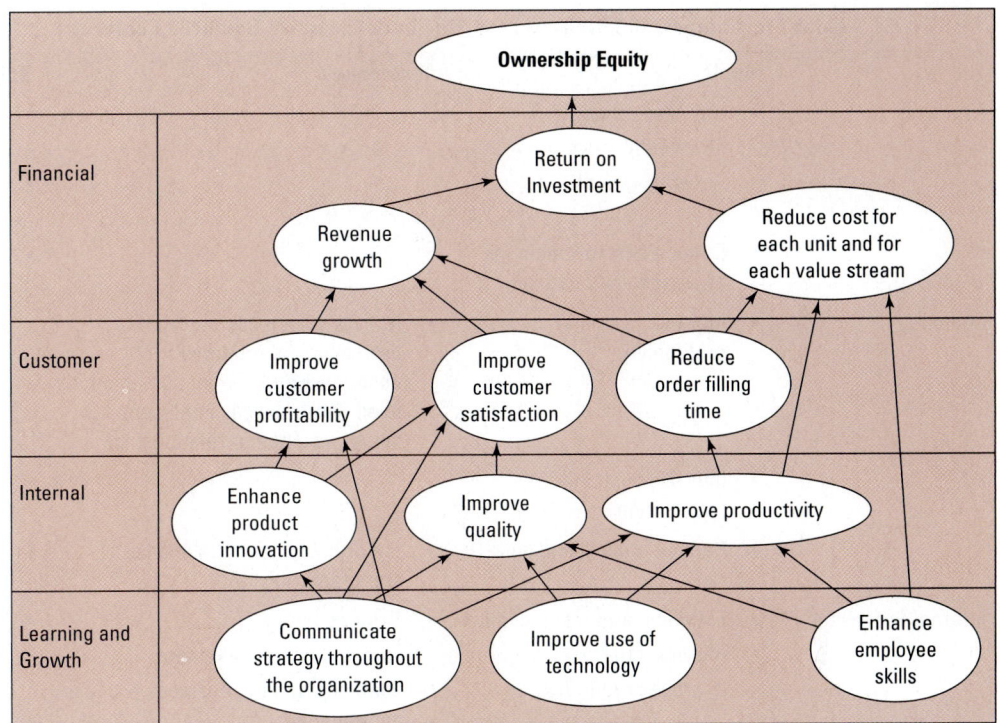

and strategy map for the company, which would require identifying and linking goals, management techniques, and critical success factors.

In the first step, Jack and Janet chose their firm's mission, based on personal values, values they knew were shared by their employees: "To be the highest-rated brand in crafted furniture." The strategy then followed: to differentiate the firm based on innovation, style, quality, and customer service (with an emphasis on short lead time, the time from receipt of an order to delivery of the customer's order). They chose as the firm's tagline, "To delight with our product, and impress with our speed."

The second step (SWOT and value chain) provided further insights which are reflected in the BSC and strategy map. The third step was to develop the strategy map, shown in Exhibit 2.6. The financial goals are revenue growth, cost reduction, and increased return on investment (which would be achieved by the revenue growth and cost reduction). Similarly, goals were set for the other three perspectives of the BSC, being careful to ensure that the goals were consistent with the firm's mission and strategy. Note how the goals are linked to show the causal relationships among the goals. For example, improved customer satisfaction (a customer goal) should positively affect revenue growth (a financial goal). The strategy map is a key tool for Janet and Jack to better understand their road to success and, importantly, a way to communicate to their employees where and how the firm needs to perform to achieve the firm's strategy and mission.

The next step was to determine how to achieve and to measure these goals. The techniques, shown in the middle column of Exhibit 2.7, are the contemporary management techniques covered in Chapter 1. They are tried and true tools for achieving the goals. The final step was to determine the measures that, when achieved, would show progress on the desired goals. For brevity, we have a small number of measures here, though in practice there may be 100 or more measures. Also, the strategy map and scorecard could be integrated with the concepts of lean accounting or enterprise risk management, which we have not attempted here. These measures are what constitute the BSC for the company.[7] Janet and Jack now have the tools

[7] "Lean Enterprise Fundamentals," Statement on Management Accounting (www.imanet.org/publications_statements.asp); Mark Beasley, Al Chen, Karen Nunez, and Lorraine Wright, "Working Hand in Hand: Balanced Scorecards and Enterprise Risk Management," *Strategic Finance*, March 2006, pp. 49–54; Mark L. Frigo, "When Strategy and ERM Meet," *Strategic Finance*, January 2008, pp. 45–49.

EXHIBIT 2.7 Goals, Techniques, and Measures for Martin & Carlson's Balanced Scorecard

	Goals	Techniques	Balanced Scorecard: Measures
Financial	• Increase return on investment		• Return on investment
	• Revenue growth		• Percentage increase in sales, by product line
	• Reduce cost for each unit and each value stream		• Cost per unit, by product line
Customer	• Improve customer profitability	• Activity-based costing used to determine the profitability of customers and distribution channels, used with business intelligence to manage customer relationships	• Customer profitability by distribution channel and customer groups
	• Improve customer satisfaction		• Survey customer satisfaction
	• Reduce order-filling time	• Theory of constraints and lean manufacturing	• Lead time, the time between when the order is received and delivered
Internal Processes	• Enhance product innovation	• Target costing	• Number of profitable new products or product features
	• Improve quality	• Total quality management	• Number of defects detected
	• Improve productivity	• Lean accounting, business process improvement	• Inventory level, process speed
Learning and Growth	• Communicate strategy throughout the organization	• Strategy map and balanced scorecard	• Percentage of employees trained on the firm's strategy map
	• Improve use of technology	• Business intelligence, enterprise risk management	• Number of business risks discovered and analyzed
	• Enhance employee skills		• Training hours in skill development

they need to understand their strategy, to communicate it to employees, and to measure performance to strategic success. What would happen if they had not developed these strategic tools? The answer is shown in Exhibit 1.8 on page 16.

Expanding the Balanced Scorecard and Strategy Map: Sustainability

> Sustainable growth seeks to make more of the world's people our customers—and to do so by developing markets that promote and sustain economic prosperity, social equity, and environmental integrity.
>
> *Charles O. Holliday, Jr, CEO of DuPont*

Sustainability means the balancing of short- and long-term goals in all three dimensions of the company's performance—social, economic, and environmental.

LEARNING OBJECTIVE 5

Explain how to expand the balanced scorecard by integrating sustainability.

The growing concerns worldwide about global warming, volatile gasoline prices, high commodity prices, and corporate social and environmental responsibility have created new expectations that organizations adopt the triple bottom line—social, economic, and environmental performance (or, "people, planet, and profits"). The triple bottom line has come to be known as **sustainability,** that is, the balancing of short- and long-term goals in all three dimensions of performance. Economic performance is measured in traditional ways, while social performance relates to the health and safety of employees and other stakeholders. The environmental dimension refers to the impact of the firm's operations on the environment.

Many companies manage sustainability in a strategic manner, through sustainability reports to shareholders. Some, such as Nike and Ford Motor Co., integrate sustainability into their balanced scorecards, both as a separate perspective and as additional measures in the internal process, customer, or learning and growth perspectives. Business intelligence firms such as IBM, Oracle, and SAS Institute offer sustainability scorecard software (a screen shot of the SAS software is shown in Exhibit 2.8). The following shows why and how a number of global organizations are adapting to the challenge of sustainability.

EXHIBIT 2.8

SAS Corporate Responsibility Scorecard

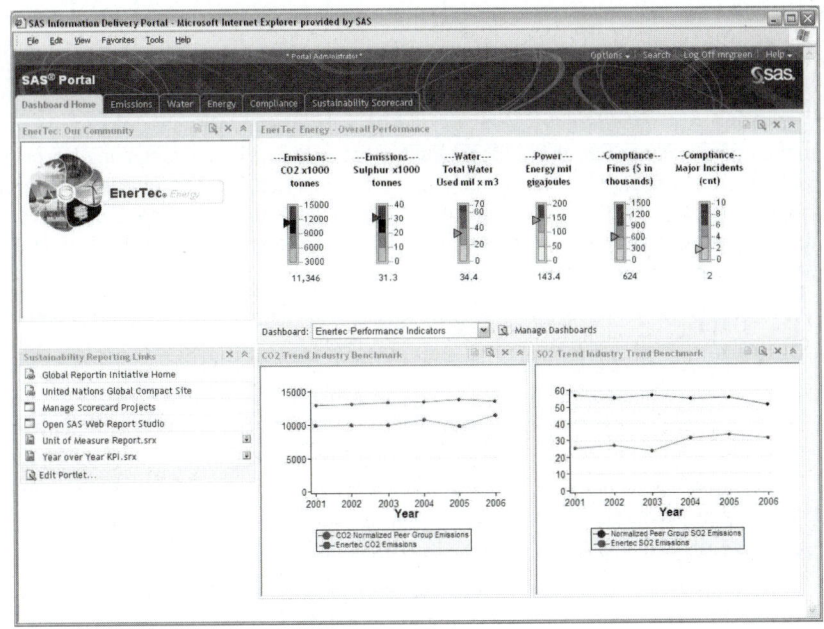

Indicators of the Concern about Sustainability

The concern for sustainability has many dimensions. One is global warming which was highlighted by former vice president Al Gore's documentary, *An Inconvenient Truth*—a responsibility for all organizations and consumers; this dimension views sustainability as a "green issue." Others concern labor, health, and safety issues in corporations around the world, and these issues would place sustainability as a part of enterprise risk management.

Corporations are under pressure from regulators and shareholders to adopt sustainable practices. Being rated on sustainability, for example by the Dow Jones Sustainability Index (www.sustainability-indexes.com), places additional pressure on companies. Some companies, including Toyota and Wal-Mart, have adopted sustainability to improve profits. As a result of these developments, recent surveys show that the majority of chief executives see sustainability as playing a key role in their corporate strategy. College students do as well; a recent survey showed that 80 percent would prefer to work for a "green" company.[8]

How Companies Have Responded

In 2005, a survey of 250 of the world's largest global companies showed that 52 percent prepared environmental and social responsibility reports, as compared to 35 percent in 2001.

The five reasons most often given by the survey respondents for choosing to report on corporate responsibility were (1) economic considerations, (2) ethical considerations, (3) innovation and learning, (4) employee motivation, and (5) risk management or risk reduction. Many of the respondents felt that responsibility reporting would lead to business opportunities, reduced risk, an enhanced ethical reputation, and greater ease in employing skilled workers.

The industries that had more than 80 percent of their companies adopting corporate responsibility reporting included the auto industry, oil and gas, finance and insurance, and electronics

---

[8] Marc J. Epstein, *Making Sustainability Work: Best Practices in Managing and Measuring Corporate Social, Environmental and Economic Impacts* (San Francisco: Berrett Koehler Publishers, 2008); Joann Lublin, "Environmentalism Sprouts Up on Corporate Boards," *The Wall Street Journal*, August, 11, 2008; Tamara Bekefi and Marc J. Epstein, "Transforming Social and Environmental Risks into Opportunities," *Strategic Finance*, March 2008, pp. 42–47; Stephanie Rosenbloom and Michael Barbaro, "Green-Light Specials, Now at Wal-Mart," *The New Your Times*, January 25, 2009, Business Section, p 1; Yuliya Chernova and Sari Krieger, "How to Go Green in Hard Times," *The Wall Street Journal*, February 9, 2009, p. R1. See also, Thomas L. Friedman, *Hot, Flat and Crowded*, (New York: Farrar, Strauss and Giroux 2007).

Patagonia, maker of clothing and gear for the outdoors enthusiast, is known for its focus on environmental issues in its manufacturing and company strategy. As an example of its commitment to the environment, the company studies the environmental impact of planned new products. One new product, a wool shirt, would be made from wool from New Zealand, processed in a factory in Japan, sewn in Los Angeles, and then packaged in Reno for distribution to retail locations worldwide. Patagonia figured the following would be the impact on the environment for a single shirt:

Miles traveled	16,280
Pounds of carbon emitted	47
Waste generated (oz)	9 (for a 7 oz shirt)
Energy consumption (megajoules)	89 (This is enough electric power for an average household for 20 hours.)

Patagonia verdict: not sustainable; the product was not produced

Source: *National Geographic Adventures,* February 2008, p. 40; www.Patagonia.com.

and computers. These industries are leading the way in corporate environmental and social responsibility. For example, two firms frequently mentioned in corporate responsibility include Toyota and Ford from the auto industry. Toyota rates highly for its hybrid gas–electric vehicles and its efforts to promote environmental management systems and waste reduction efforts. Ford is included because of its efforts in developing hybrid cars, fuel economy, and vehicle safety. Other recognized companies include General Electric which works on reducing the emissions of the jet engines it produces and on developing solar energy. Home Depot is recognized for its community service—allowing employees time off to participate in important community activities.[9]

Sustainability Measures for the Balanced Scorecard

Environmental performance indicators (EPIs) are the CSFs in a sustainability perspective; they are defined in three categories by the World Resources Institute (www.wri.org):

1. Operational indicators measure potential stresses to the environment; for example, fossil fuel use, toxic and nontoxic waste, and pollutants.
2. Management indicators measure efforts to reduce environmental effects; for example, hours of environmental training.
3. Environmental condition indicators measure environmental quality; for example, ambient air pollution concentrations.

Social performance indicators (SPIs) include:

- Working conditions indicators that measure worker safety and opportunity: for example, training hours and number of injuries.
- Community involvement indicators that measure the firm's outreach to the local and broader community: for example, employee volunteering and participation in Habitat for Humanity
- Philanthropy indicators that measure the direct contribution by the firm and its employees to charitable organizations

The role of the management accountant, in developing the sustainability perspective of the BSC, is to make these EPIs and SPIs an integral part of management decision making, not only for regulatory compliance but also for product design, purchasing, strategic planning, and other management functions. As for the BSC, there are a number of implementation issues, including measurement problems and confidentiality issues. For example, the Global

[9] *KPMG International Corporate Responsibility Reporting 2005,* University of Amsterdam.

Reporting Initiative (www.globalreporting.org), an independent global institution in partnership with the United Nations and other groups, has a goal of developing generally accepted standards for sustainability reporting.

Summary

This chapter has discussed the four cost management resources for implementing strategy: SWOT analysis, a focus on execution, value-chain analysis, and the balanced scorecard and the strategy map. The first, SWOT analysis, helps management to implement strategy by providing a system and structure in which to identify the organization's critical success factors. The second, execution, is a management focus on making priorities and achieving these CSFs. The third, value-chain analysis, helps management to implement strategy by breaking the organization down into a sequence of value-providing activities; management can identify the CSFs at each step in the value chain and ask the question, How do we add value at this step in the value chain? The final step, the balanced scorecard and strategy map, provides a means to collect, report, and analyze the CSFs; the BSC helps management to measure progress to strategic goals and to align employees' performance efforts, incentives, and rewards to these strategy goals.

An important supplement to the balanced scorecard, or in the form of a separate report, is the organization's performance in the area of sustainability. Because of global warming, increases in commodity prices, and other factors, expectations for corporate social and environmental responsibility has increased significantly in recent years.

Key Terms

core competencies, *34*	sustainability, *46*	value activities, *38*
strategy map, *44*	SWOT analysis, *34*	

Comments on Cost Management in Action

In addition to changes in trade restrictions, fluctuations in currency have had a large effect on global competitors. The fall of the U.S. dollar relative to most currencies in recent years has created an opportunity for increased exports for U.S.-based multinational companies. The changes have also caused non-U.S. manufacturers such as BMW and VW to locate plants in the United States where the cost of doing business is relatively low due to the rise in the Euro and relatively high wage costs in parts of Europe. For example, a recent study of the cost of doing business in selected countries shows the United States to have an advantage relative to many countries (the survey did not include China and other Asian countries nor the recent rise in the U.S. dollar):

Country	Cost of Doing Business (relative to U.S. at 100%)
Mexico	79.5
Canada	99.4
U.S.	100.0
Australia	100.2
France	103.6
Britain	107.1
Netherlands	107.3
Italy	107.9
Japan	114.3
Germany	116.8

Other issues concern the degree of global integration—multinational companies operating simultaneously in many countries. Just as BMW and VW locate plants in the United States for strategic reasons, U.S.-based manufacturers such as Boeing use parts made overseas (in one Boeing plane, 70 percent of the parts are sourced from non-U.S. suppliers).

Some companies deal with global competition by becoming more competitive. For example, the tire maker Bridgestone Firestone, to achieve cost advantage in its U.S. plants, focuses on developing employee skills. In one North Carolina plant, applicants for the local tire plant must complete a series of specialized courses at the nearby community college. Another way to succeed is to pursue differentiation, as at Pendleton

Woolen Mills in Portland, Oregon. The mill, built in 1910, is one of the last functioning woolen mills in the U.S. Pendleton succeeds by specializing in upscale fabrics, such as vintage baseball uniforms and commemorative blankets and dance shawls for Native American Tribes.

Source: "KPMG Competitive Alternatives 2008," *BusinessWeek,* April 14, 2008, p. 6; "Globalization Bites Boeing," *BusinessWeek,* March 24, 2008, p. 32; Edward Taylor, "Automakers Shift to Offset Effects of Soaring Euro," *The Wall Street Journal,* February 28, 2008, p. a13; "A Tale of Survival," *Time,* December 2004, p. A16; "Manufacturing Lessons," *The Raleigh News & Observer,* January 28, 2007, p. E1; "A Bigger World," *The Economist,* September 20, 2008, pp. 3–14.

Self-Study Problems
(For solutions, please turn to the end of the chapter.)

1. Value-Chain Analysis

The Waynesboro Bulls is a Class-AA baseball team and farm club for the Atlanta Braves. The Bulls' league consists of eight teams that are all located within a 150-mile radius of Waynesboro. The Bulls ranked sixth of eight last year, but have high hopes for the coming season in part because of the acquisition at the end of the last season of a great new pitcher, Wing Powers. Wing had the next to best ERA last season. Wing is also a popular player, seen frequently in the community, using his humor and occasionally outrageous behavior to develop a local fan club called the "Wingers." None of the other players come close to Wing in popularity. Head Coach Bud Brown, a 15-year veteran of the Bulls, is optimistic for the coming season, noting the team's luck has "got to change." The Bulls have only 2 winning seasons in the last 10 years. The Waynesboro baseball park is somewhat typical of AA parks, though somewhat older and a bit smaller. It serves a variety of sodas and beers and nachos to its fans on game days. Also in a 150-mile radius of Waynesboro are 3 NASCAR venues, 2 outdoor concert venues, 12 colleges with competitive sports teams, 1 major league football team, 1 major league basketball team, but no major league baseball team.

Jack Smith, a consultant for the Waynesboro Bulls has been asked to complete a value-chain analysis of the franchise with a particular focus on a comparison with a nearby competing team, the Durham Buffaloes. Jack has been able to collect selected cost data as follows for each of the six steps in the value chain. Single-ticket prices range from $4.50 to $8.00, and average paying attendance is approximately 2,200 for Waynesboro and 3,400 for Durham.

Average Cost per Person at Scheduled Games

Waynesboro Bulls	Activities in the Value Chain	Durham Buffaloes
$0.45	Advertising and general promotion expenses	$0.50
0.28	Ticket sales: At local sporting goods stores and the ballpark	0.25
0.65	Ballpark operations	0.80
0.23	Management compensation	0.18
0.95	Players' salaries	1.05
0.20	Game-day operations: security, special entertainment, and game-day promotions	0.65
$2.76	Total Cost	$3.43

Required   Analyze the value chain to help Jack better understand the nature of the competition between the Bulls and the Buffaloes and to identify opportunities for adding value and/or reducing cost at each activity.

2. SWOT Analysis

Required   Refer to the information in Self-Study question 1, regarding the Waynesboro Bulls. Prepare a SWOT analysis for the Bulls.

3. The Balanced Scorecard

Required   Refer to the information in Self-Study question 1, regarding the Waynesboro Bulls. Prepare a balanced scorecard for the Bulls.

Questions

2-1   Identify and explain the two types of competitive strategy.

2-2   Identify three or four well-known firms that succeed through cost leadership.

2-3   Identify three or four well-known firms that succeed through product differentiation.

2-4   How are the four strategic resources—SWOT analysis, execution, the value chain, and the balanced scorecard—linked in a comprehensive strategic analysis?

2-5 What is a strategy map and how is it used?

2-6 What is SWOT analysis? For what is it used?

2-7 What is the role of the management accountant regarding nonfinancial performance measures such as delivery speed and customer satisfaction?

2-8 What is a critical success factor? What is its role in strategic management and in cost management?

2-9 Identify four or five potential critical success factors for a manufacturer of industrial chemicals. Explain why you consider those factors critical for the firm to be successful.

2-10 Identify four or five potential critical success factors for a large savings and loan institution.

2-11 Identify four or five potential critical success factors for a small chain of retail jewelry stores.

2-12 Identify four or five potential critical success factors for a large retail discount store that features a broad range of consumer merchandise.

2-13 Identify four or five potential critical success factors for an auto-repair shop.

2-14 What is a balanced scorecard? What is its primary objective?

2-15 Contrast using the balanced scorecard with using only financial measures of success.

2-16 What is sustainability and what does it mean for a business?

2-17 Explain the uses of value-chain analysis.

Brief Exercises

2-18 Think of an example of a firm that succeeds on cost leadership and give some examples of its strengths and weaknesses that would be included in a SWOT analysis.

2-19 Think of an example of a firm that succeeds on differentiation and give some examples of its strengths and weaknesses that would be included in a SWOT analysis.

2-20 What industries do you think are most suited for the value-chain analysis and why?

2-21 How would you explain the relationship between value-chain analysis and the use of the balanced scorecard for a firm that uses both? You can use a hospital as an example.

2-22 Suppose you are a large firm in a service business and you think that by acquiring a certain competing firm, you can generate growth and profits at a greater rate for the combined firm. You have asked some financial analysts to study the proposed acquisition/merger. Do you think value-chain analysis would be useful to them? Why or why not?

2-23 Consider the question in 2-22 above. How would your answer differ if the firm were a manufacturer?

2-24 What are some of the key issues to consider in effectively implementing a balanced scorecard?

2-25 How many measures are usually on the balanced scorecard?

2-26 1. Consider a commodity business such as building materials, many types of food products, and many types of electronics products. A good example of a commodity is gasoline. Are these companies likely to compete on cost leadership or differentiation, and why?

2. Consider professional service firms such a law firms, accounting firms, and medical practices. Are these firms likely to compete on cost leadership or differentiation, and why?

2-27 Many would argue that the TV manufacturing business has become largely a commodity business, and competition is based on price, with many good brands offered at low prices at retailers such as Wal-Mart. The manufacturers of TVs are said to have a barrier to entry from other potential competitors because the existing manufacturers (Phillips, Sony, Samsung, etc.) have spent huge sums to develop their brands and manufacturing facilities. In recent years there has been a large growth in the number of contract manufacturers (such as Flextronics) that manufacture TVs for the large firms. How does this affect the competition within the industry? Are there now new opportunities for smaller manufacturers of TVs?

Exercises

2-28 **Special Order, Strategy** Joel Deaine, CEO of Deaine Enterprises, Inc. (DEI), is considering a special offer to manufacture a new line of women's clothing for a large department store chain. DEI has specialized in designer women's clothing sold in small, upscale retail clothing stores throughout the country. To protect the very elite brand image, DEI has not sold clothing to the large department stores. The current offer, however, might be too good to turn down. The department store is willing to commit to a large order, which would be very profitable to DEI, and the order would be renewed automatically for two more years, presumably to continue after that point.

Required Analyze the choice Joel faces based on a competitive analysis.

2-29 **Strategy, Auto Parts** In the mid-1990s, a large retailer of auto parts, Best Parts, Inc. (BPI), was looking for ways to invest an accumulation of excess cash. BPI's success was built on a carefully developed inventory control system that guaranteed the availability of a desired part on demand 99 percent of the time and within one business day for the remaining 1 percent. The speed and quality of service set BPI apart from other parts dealers, and the business continued to grow.

On the advice of close friends and consultants, BPI's owner and CEO decided to invest a significant portion of the excess cash in a small chain of gift and craft stores in shopping malls.

Required Determine BPI's competitive strategy (cost leadership or differentiation) in the auto-parts business. Assess whether this competitive advantage will or will not facilitate success in the new venture.

2-30 **Ethics; Sustainability**

Like myself, perhaps you love a good cup of coffee. Suppose that you do, and you have the following information about the company that makes the coffee you are considering. You are selecting a pound bag of coffee and you can choose to pay anywhere from $5 to $15 for the bag of coffee. In each of these cases, we mean ethical standards to refer to business practices and labor relations; an example of an unethical business practice would be price fixing, and an example of unethical labor relations would be discrimination in hiring practices.

Required: Report the dollar figure asked for in each part of the four cases, and for each case, explain briefly your rationale for the price differences.

Case A: How much would you pay for the bag of coffee if (a) you know with certainty the company has high ethical standards, (b) you know with certainty the company has low ethical standards, and (c) you do not know anything about the company's ethical standards?

Case B: Similar to Case A, except that you only know what the company says about its ethical standards; however, you have for some time had high expectations that the company has high standards. How much would you pay for the bag of coffee if (a) you now find out with certainty the company has high ethical standards, or (b) you now find out with certainty the company has low ethical standards?

Case C: Same as Case B, except that you have for some time had low expectations that the company has high ethical standards. How much would you pay for the bag of coffee if (a) you now find out with certainty the company has high ethical standards, or (b) you now find out with certainty the company has low ethical standards?

Now suppose that with your cup of coffee you like to relax in a comfortable all-cotton shirt. You have the option to purchase a 100 percent organic cotton shirt, a 50 percent organic shirt, a 25 percent organic, or a totally nonorganic shirt. Organic production is more environmentally safe, using no toxic dyes and no harmful cleaning or processing materials.

Case D: What price would you pay for the cotton shirt, from a low of $15 to a high of $30?

1. For the 100% organic shirt
2. For the 50% organic shirt
3. For the 25% organic shirt
4. For the nonorganic shirt
5. How much would you pay if you had no idea how much organic content was in the shirt?

Problems 2-31 **Strategy, Balanced Scorecard, Health Care** Consumers, employers, and governments at all levels are very concerned about the rising costs of health care. As a result, health-care systems nationwide are experiencing an ongoing demand to improve the efficiency of their operations. The health-care industry faces significant challenges due to changing patient needs, reduced reimbursement, and the fierce competitive environment. The industry is experiencing consolidations through systemwide mergers and acquisitions as a way to reduce operating costs. Patients and payors are demanding a one-stop shopping approach. While improving operations is necessary, the quality of the health care delivered must not be jeopardized. The Medical University of Greenbelt is feeling the impact of the increasing penetration of its market by managed-care companies. As a result, management has been asked to develop a strategic plan to ensure that its funding sources will continue to meet the demands of its patients.

Because it is an academic medical center, the Medical University of Greenbelt's mission encompasses three components: clinical care, education, and research. Management must consider these competing objectives in the proposed plan:

Required

1. What should the Medical University of Greenbelt's strategy emphasize?
2. Do you think a balanced scorecard could help ensure the success of the Medical University of Greenbelt? What advantages does a balanced scorecard have over a traditional approach?

3. Determine four or five critical success factors for each of the four areas within the balanced scorecard. Remember that in addition to patients, its employees, suppliers/distributors, other training entities, community, and payors are considered customers.

4. What types of challenges will management face in implementing a balanced scorecard? How can employee buy-in be increased?

2-32   Strategic Positioning   Fowler's Farm is a 1,000-acre dairy and tobacco farm located in southern Virginia. Jack Fowler, the owner, has been farming since 1982. He initially purchased 235 acres and has made the following purchases since then: 300 acres in 1985, 150 acres in 1988, dairy equipment and buildings worth $350,000 in 1988, and 315 acres in 1998. The cost of farmland has inflated over the years so that, although Jack has a total investment of $1,850,000, the land's current market value is $2,650,000. The current net book value of his buildings and equipment is $300,000, with an estimated replacement cost of $1,250,000. Current price pressures on farm commodities have affected Fowler's Farm as well as others across the country. Jack has watched as many of his neighbors either have quit farming or have been consolidated into larger, more profitable farms.

Fowler's Farm consists of three different operating segments: dairy farming, tobacco, and corn and other crops intended for livestock feed. The dairy farm consists of 198 milk-producing cows that are grazed on 250 acres of farmland. The crop farm consists of the remaining acreage that covers several types of terrain and has several types of soil. Some of the land is high and hilly, some of it is low and claylike, and the rest is humus-rich soil. Jack determines the fertilizer mix for the type of soil and type of crop to be planted by rules of thumb based on his experience.

The farm equipment used consists of automated milking equipment, six tractors, two tandem-axle grain bed trucks, and numerous discs, plows, wagons, and assorted tractor and hand tools. The farm has three equipment storage barns, an equipment maintenance shed, and a 90,000-bushel grain elevator/drier. The equipment and buildings have an estimated market value of $1,500,000.

Jack employs five full-time farmhands, a mechanic, and a bookkeeper and has contracted part-time accounting/tax assistance with a local CPA firm in Pittsboro. All employees are salaried; the farmhands and the bookkeeper make $25,000 a year, and the mechanic makes $32,000 annually. The CPA contract costs $15,000 a year.

In 2010, the farm produced 256,000 gallons of raw milk, 23,000 bushels of tobacco, and 75,300 bushels of corn. Jack sells the tobacco by contract and auction at the end of the harvest. The revenue in 2010 was $1,345,000, providing Jack a net income after taxes of $233,500.

Jack's daughter Kelly has just returned from college. She knows that the farm is a good business but believes that the use of proper operating procedures and cost management systems could increase profitability and improve efficiency, allowing her father to have more leisure time. She also knows that her father has always run the farm from his experience and rules of thumb and is wary of scientific concepts and management principles. For example, he has little understanding of the accounting procedures of the farm, has not participated in the process, and has adopted few, if any, methods to maintain control over inventories and equipment. He has trusted his employees to maintain the farm appropriately without using any accounting or operating procedures over inventories or equipment, preventive maintenance schedules, or scientific application of crop rotation or livestock management.

Required   Identify and describe briefly the competitive strategy for Fowler's Farm and explain your choice.

2-33 SWOT Analysis

Required   Develop a SWOT analysis for Fowler's Farm based on Problem 2-32. The analysis should include two to three items in each category: strengths, weaknesses, opportunities, and threats.

2-34 Value-Chain Analysis

Required   Develop a value chain of six to nine activities for Fowler's Farm based on Problem 2-32.

2-35 The Balanced Scorecard

Required   Develop a balanced scorecard with three or more groups of CSFs for Fowler's Farm based on Problem 2-32. Explain your choice of groups and identify four to five CSFs in each group. Make sure that your CSFs are quantitative and can be measured.

2-36   Strategic Positioning   Tartan Corporation has been manufacturing high-quality home lighting systems for more than 90 years. The company's first products in the 1920s—the classic line—were high-quality floor lamps and table lamps made of the highest-quality materials with features that other manufacturers did not attempt: multiple switches, adjustable heights, and stained glass. In the 1950s and 1960s, the company introduced a number of new products that were in demand at the time, including track lighting and lava lamps, which became the company's Modern line. In keeping with its brand image, Tartan ensured that these new products also met the highest standards of quality in the industry. A new customer style emerged in the 1960s and 1970s, which resulted in another new line of products, Contemporary. It was followed in more recent years by two new product lines, Margaret Stewart and Western.

Jess Jones, the company's chief financial officer, had become concerned about the performance of some of the product lines in recent years. Although total sales were growing at an acceptable rate, approximately 10 percent per year, the sales mix was changing significantly, as shown in the following product line sales report. Jess was particularly concerned about the Classic line because of its sharp drop in sales and its high costs. Because of the high level of craftsmanship required for the Classic line, it always had higher than average costs for labor and materials. Furthermore, attracting and retaining the highly skilled workers necessary for this product line were becoming more and more difficult. The workers in the Classic line in 2010 were likely to be older and very loyal employees who were paid well because of their skill and seniority. These workers displayed the highest level of workmanship in the company and, some would argue, in the entire industry. Few newer employees seemed eager to learn the skills required in this product line.

Moreover, manufacturing capacity was experiencing an increasing strain. The sharper than expected increase in sales for the Western styles had created a backlog of orders for them, and plant managers had been scrambling to find the plant capacity to meet the demand. Some plant supervisors suggested shutting down the Classic line to make capacity for the Western line. Some managers of the Margaret Stewart line argued the same thing. However, eliminating the Classic line would make obsolete about $233,000 worth of raw materials inventory that is used only in the manufacture of Classic line products.

Tom Richter, the firm's sales manager, acknowledged that sales of the Classic line were more and more difficult to find and that demand for the new styles was increasing. He also noted that the sales of these products reflected significant regional differences. The Western line was popular in the south and west, and the Contemporary, Modern, and Stewart styles were popular nationally. The Classic line tended to have strong support only in the northeast states. In some sales districts in these states, Classic sales represent a relatively high proportion of total sales.

Kelly Arnold, the firm's CEO, is aware of these concerns and has decided to set up a task force to consider the firm's options and strategy in regard to these problems.

Product Line Sales Report

	Classic	Contemporary	Margaret Stewart	Modern	Western
2007	20%	33%	5%	40%	2%
2008	16	35	11	34	4
2009	14	33	14	33	6
2010	9	31	18	31	11

Required Describe Tartan's competitive strategy. On the basis of this competitive strategy, what recommendation would you make to the task force?

2-37 SWOT Analysis

Required Develop a SWOT analysis for Tartan Corporation based on Problem 2-36. The analysis should include two to three items in each category: strengths, weaknesses, opportunities, and threats.

2-38 Value-Chain Analysis

Required Develop a value chain of six to eight items for Tartan Corporation described in Problem 2-36. Why would the value chain be useful to a firm like Tartan?

2-39 The Balanced Scorecard

Required Develop a balanced scorecard with three or more groups of CSFs for Tartan Corporation described in Problem 2-36. Explain your choice of groups and identify four to five CSFs in each group. Make sure that your CSFs are quantitative and can be measured.

2-40 Strategy Map

Required Based on your analysis of Tartan Manufacturing Company, create a strategy map for the company.

2-41 The following are critical success factors for Dell Inc.
- Product manufacturing time.
- Customer perception of order-taking convenience and accuracy.
- Revenue growth.
- Selling expense to sales ratio.
- Number of new manufacturing processes developed.
- Order processing time.
- Raw materials inventory.
- Training dollars per employee.
- Number of emerging technologies evaluated.
- Customer retention.
- Manufacturing defects.
- Number of new manufacturing processes under development.
- Customer satisfaction with speed of service.
- Gross margin.
- Operating cost ratio.

Required
1. Using the four BSC perspectives of learning and growth, internal processes, customer, and financial, sort these CSFs into the appropriate perspective.
2. Create a simple strategy map for Dell Inc.

2-42 **Strategic Analysis** Jim Hargreave's lifelong hobby is racing small sailboats. Jim has been successful both at the sport and in the design of new equipment to be used on small sailboats to make them easier to sail and more effective in racing. Jim is now thinking about starting an Internet business in his garage to sell products he favors as well as some he has designed himself. He plans to contract out most of the manufacturing for the parts and equipment to machine shops and other small manufacturers in his area.

Required Develop a strategic analysis for Jim's new business plan. What should be his competitive position; that is, how should he choose to compete in the existing market for sailboat supplies and equipment? How is he likely to use cost management information in building his business?

2-43 **Strategic Analysis** Consider the following companies, each of which is your consulting client:
1. Performance Bicycles, a company that supplies bicycles, parts, and bicycling equipment and clothing from its Web site.
2. The Oxford Omni, a downtown hotel that primarily serves convention and business travelers.
3. The Orange County Public Health Clinic, which is supported by tax revenues of Orange County and public donations.
4. The Harley-Davidson motorcycle company.
5. The Merck pharmaceutical company.
6. St. Sebastian's College, a small, private liberal arts college.

Required Determine each client's competitive strategy and related critical success factors.

2-44 **Strategic Analysis, the Camera Industry** Olympus, Kodak, Canon, and other firms in the market for low-cost cameras have experienced significant changes in recent years. The rate of introduction of new products has increased significantly. Entirely new products, such as the digital camera, are coming down in cost, so they are likely to be a factor in the low-cost segment of the market in the coming years. Additionally, product life cycles have fallen from several years to several months. The new products in this market are introduced at the same price as the products they replace, but the new products have some significant advances in functionality. Thus, there are price points at which the customer expects to purchase a camera of a given functionality. In effect, the camera manufacturers compete to supply distinctive and therefore competitive functionality at the same cost as that of the previous models.

The manufacturing process for Olympus, one of the key firms in the industry, is representative of the others. Olympus makes extensive use of suppliers for components of the camera. Working closely with the suppliers, not only in a supplier's manufacturing process but also in the supplier's design of the parts, ensures the quality of the parts. Each supplier is, in effect, part of a team that includes the other suppliers and Olympus's own design and manufacturing operations.

Required

1. How does this type of competition differ from the Michael Porter framework of cost leadership and differentiation?

2. Develop a value chain for Olympus camera company. What are the opportunities for cost reduction and/ or value enhancement for Olympus?

2-45 Strategic Analysis, the Balanced Scorecard, and Value-Chain Analysis; the Packaging Industry
Dana Packaging Company is a large producer of paper and coated-paper containers with sales worldwide. The market for Dana's products has become very competitive in recent years because of the entrance of two large European competitors. In response, Dana has decided to enter new markets where the competition is less severe. The new markets are principally the high end of the packaging business for products that require more technological sophistication and better materials. Food and consumer products companies use these more advanced products to enhance the appeal of their high-end products. In particular, more sturdy, more colorful, more attractive, and better-sealing packaging has some appeal in the gourmet food business, especially in coffees, baked goods, and some dairy products. As a consequence of the shift, Dana has had to reorient its factory to produce the smaller batches of product associated with this new line of business. This change has required additional training for plant personnel and some upgrading of factory equipment to reduce setup time.

Dana's manufacturing process begins with pulp paper, which it produces in its own mills around the world. Some of the pulp material is purchased from recycling operators when price and availability are favorable. The pulp paper is then converted into paperboard, which is produced at Dana's own plants or purchased at times from outside vendors. In most cases, the paperboard plants are located near the pulp mills. At this point in the manufacturing process, the paperboard might be coated with a plastic material, a special embossing, or some other feature. This process is done at separate plants owned by Dana. On occasion, but infrequently when Dana's plants are very busy, the coating and embossing process is outsourced to other manufacturers. The final step in the process is filling the containers with the food product or consumer product. This step is done exclusively at Dana-owned plants. Dana has tried to maintain a high reputation for the quality of the filling process, stressing safety, cleanliness, and low cost to its customers.

Required

1. Describe Dana Company's new strategic competitive position.

2. Develop a value chain for Dana. What are its opportunities for cost reduction and/or value enhancement?

3. Dana's management is considering the use of a balanced scorecard for the firm. For each of the four areas within the balanced scorecard, list two or three examples of measurable critical success factors that should be included.

2-46 Strategy Requirements under the Baldrige National Quality Program The Baldrige National Quality Program was established by the U.S. Congress in 1987 to promote quality awareness and to enhance the competitiveness of U.S. businesses. The program is under the National Institute of Standards and Technology (NIST), a nonregulatory federal agency within the Commerce Department, and is administered by the American Society for Quality (www.asq.org/) under contract to the NIST. The program has seven categories of performance criteria including leadership, strategic planning, customer focus, information and analysis, human resources, process management, and business results. The last category, business results, includes four parts: customer-focused results, financial and market results, human resources results, and organizational effectiveness results. Recipients of the prestigious Malcolm Baldrige National Quality Award are recognized annually for the firms' achievements in meeting these performance criteria.

Required

1. Go to the NIST Web site that shows the Baldrige Program's Criteria for Performance Excellence (www. quality.nist.gov/Business_Criteria.htm) and review the performance criteria. Comment on the degree to which the program stresses strategy development and strategy implementation.

2. How would you compare the process within a firm to develop a balanced scorecard versus developing the performance measures to compete in the Baldrige program?

2-47 Value Chain: The Oil and Gas Industry; Internet Research
The oil and gas industry is often in the news these days as consumers look for ways to deal with the large increases in fuel prices in recent years. Some concerns have been expressed about the profits of

these firms. We will use the value chain to study the industry and find out where the profits are. At a relatively high level, the value chain of the oil and gas industry would look like the following.

1	Exploration: Oil and natural gas leasing; purchasing rights to explore, drill, and extract crude oil and natural gas from privately or publicly owned land
2	Drilling
3	Oil and gas equipment and services
4	Transport of unrefined oil and unprocessed gas: oil and gas pipelines
5	Oil and gas refining
6	Oil and gas marketing
7	Transport of refined product to retailer or distributor; oil and gas pipelines; trucks
8	Purchase and use by customer

Step one of the value chain is to identify the land where oil and/or gas are likely to be present, followed by drilling to obtain the product, and then additional steps until the product is delivered to the customer, usually in a convenience store or a retail outlet of one of the large integrated oil firms such as Exxon Mobil or BP. The 2007 movie, *There Will be Blood,* shows a dramatic view of the process involving these steps in the early days of the oil industry.

Steps one and two are often combined into what is called a *sector* for oil and gas exploration and drilling. Also, refining and marketing are often combined into a sector, oil and gas refining and marketing. Thus, there are four sectors:

1. Oil and gas drilling and exploration.
2. Oil and gas equipment and services.
3. Oil and gas pipelines.
4. Oil and gas refining and marketing.

There are a number of companies that operate in just one of the sectors. Some operate in two or more. There is also a fifth group of companies, integrated oil and gas producers, that operates throughout the value chain.

In addition to the four sectors, there are the last two steps in the value chain that involve delivery and purchase of product. The delivery of the product to the customer is often by truck, but could also be by pipeline. Integrated oil and gas producers are involved in these last steps as well as independent truckers and distributors.

Required   Go to the Yahoo link biz.yahoo.com/p/1conameu.html and research the four sectors of the industry.
1. For each of the four sectors, determine (a) the size of the sector as measured by the number of firms in the sector and the total market cap of the sector (this is the value of all of the outstanding shares of a firm at the date you do the research, for all firms in the sector), (b) the profitability of the sector, as measured by return on equity (ROE: ROE is earnings divided by total shareholder equity), and net profit margin (profit to sales) of the sector. Put the information in a table so that you can readily compare the sectors on the four measures. Interpret the table of measures in terms of where the profits are in the oil and gas industry. Which part of the industry would a company like to be in and why?

2. What are some of the critical success factors for each of the first seven steps in the value chain for this industry?

2-48 **Strategy; Critical Success Factors; Martial Arts Training**   Martial Arts of Cincinnati (MAC) provides karate training and practice services in three locations in Cincinnati, Ohio. MAC is known for its quality of training and has grown rapidly in recent years due to its solid reputation and the growing interest in martial arts, particularly karate. George Moody, the owner of MAC, is a retired police officer who has been training and teaching martial arts for almost 20 years. He has a plan to grow his business to 10 locations in the Cincinnati area in the coming 5 to 10 years. George thinks that by careful attention to customer service, and by choosing his locations wisely, he can achieve this goal. He plans to locate his new studios in strip malls where rental costs are relatively low. This way he can keep his prices down, perhaps lower than other competitors, and thereby attract more customers.

George has developed a list of indicators that he uses to manage the business. The indicators are targeted to George's two key concerns—sales growth and teacher performance.

Sales Indicators

Number of introductory lessons
Number of new students
Number of students attending classes
Total Number of enrolled students
Class Size by teacher and age group

The first four indicators are obtained on a daily basis, while the last is obtained weekly

---

Teacher performance indicators (for each teacher)

Number of classes taught
Average number of students per class
Average retention percentage
Student progress in martial arts skills

The first three of these indicators are obtained weekly, while the last one is obtained monthly.

Required

1. How would you describe George's competitive strategy?
2. George has listed some of his CSFs. Critically review these indicators, and explain which CSFs you would add, or change, and why.

2-49 **Balanced Scorecard and Strategy: Food Ingredients Company** The balanced scorecard for a small food-ingredients company is shown below. The information is based on an actual company, and detailed information about its operations and strategy is confidential. You may assume that the firm's products and services are used by a diverse set of customers, including different types of food processors (Kraft, Heinz, Unilever, . . .), restaurant chains, bakeries, supermarkets, and the like. The company is located in a large city.

BALANCED SCORECARD FOR A FOOD INGREDIENTS COMPANY

Goals	Scorecard Measures
Financial Perspective	
Capture an increasing share of industry growth	Company growth versus industry growth
Secure the base business while remaining the preferred supplier to our customers	Volume trend by line of business; revenue trend by line of business; gross margin
Expand aggressively in global markets	Ratio of North American sales to international sales
Commercialize a continuous stream of profitable new ingredients and services	Percentage of sales from products launched within the past five years; gross profit from new products
Customer Perspective	
Become the lowest-cost supplier	Total cost of using our products and services relative to total cost of using competitive products and services
Tailor products and services to meet local needs	
Expand those products and services that meet customers' needs better than competitors	Percent of products in R & D pipeline that are being test-marketed by our customers
Customer satisfaction	Customer survey
Internal Perspective	
Maintain lowest cost base in the industry	Our total costs relative to number one competitor; inventory turnover; plant utilization

(Continued)

Maintain consistent, predictable production processes	First-pass success rate
Continue to improve distribution efficiency	Percentage of perfect orders
Build capability to screen and identify profitable products and services	Change in customer profitability
Integrate acquisitions and alliances efficiently	Revenues per sales dollar

Learning and Growth Perspective

Link the overall strategy to reward and recognition system	Net income per dollar of variable pay
Foster a culture that supports innovation and growth	Annual preparedness assessment; quarterly report

Source: Chee W. Chow, Kamal M. Haddad, and James W. Williamson, "Applying the Balanced Scorecard to Small Companies," *Management Accounting,* August 1997, pp. 21–27.

Required   Based on the information provided, determine what you think is the competitive strategy of the company. Does the balanced scorecard shown above reflect this strategy? Why or why not?

2-50   Strategic Positioning: The Airline Industry

Required   Since 9/11/01, the airline industry has struggled with increased security-related costs and a decline in the number of passengers. Which airlines do you believe are most competitive right now, and why? Describe the nature of the competition in the airline industry right now and into the future.

2-51   Value-Chain Analysis

Required   Develop a value chain for the airline industry. Identify areas in which any given airline might find a cost advantage by modifying the value chain in some way. Similarly, identify areas of the value chain in which the airline might be able to develop additional value for the airline customer. For example, consider ways the ticketing operation might be reconfigured for either cost or value-added advantage.

2-52   Value-Chain Analysis
Sheldon Radio manufactures yacht radios, navigational equipment, and depth-sounding and related equipment from a small plant near New Bern, North Carolina. One of Sheldon's most popular products, making up 40 percent of its revenues and 35 percent of its profits, is a marine radio, model VF4500, which is installed on many of the new large boats produced in the United States. Production and sales average 500 units per month. Sheldon has achieved its success in the market through excellent customer service and product reliability. The manufacturing process consists primarily of the assembly of components purchased from various electronics firms plus a small amount of metalworking and finishing. The manufacturing operations cost $110 per unit. The purchased parts cost Sheldon $250, of which $130 is for parts that Sheldon could manufacture in its existing facility for $80 in materials for each unit plus an investment in labor and equipment that would cost $35,000 per month.

Sheldon is considering outsourcing the marketing, distributing, and servicing for its units to another North Carolina firm, Brashear Enterprises. This would save Sheldon $125,000 in monthly materials and labor costs. The cost of the contract would be $105 per radio.

Required
1. Prepare a value-chain analysis for Sheldon to assist in deciding whether to purchase or manufacture the parts and whether to contract out the marketing, distributing, and servicing of the units.
2. Should Sheldon (a) continue to purchase the parts or manufacture them and (b) continue to provide the marketing, distributing, and servicing or outsource these activities to Brashear? Explain your answer.

2-53   Strategy, Ethics
The tire business is becoming increasingly competitive as new manufacturers from Southeast Asia and elsewhere enter the global marketplace. At the same time, customer expectations for performance, tread life, and safety continue to increase. An increasing variety of vehicles, from the small and innovative gas/electric vehicles to the large SUVs, place more demands on tire designers and on tire manufacturing flexibility. Established brands such as Goodyear and Firestone must look to new ways to compete and maintain profitability.

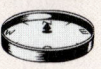

Required
1. Is the competitive strategy of a global tire maker cost leadership or differentiation? Explain your answer.
2. What are the ethical issues, if any, for tire manufacturers?

2-54 Strategy, Value Chain In the late 1990s, the bicycle maker Cannondale Corp. faced a variety of key strategic issues. One was the firm's continued dependence on Shimano Inc. of Japan to supply many parts for its bikes, particularly the derailleur, brakes, and crankset. A particularly troublesome aspect of this situation was that Shimano's high-quality and highly innovative parts were relatively expensive. Cannondale wished to reduce its dependency on these outsourced parts. A second issue was the increasing competition from Trek Bicycle Corp. and Specialized Bicycle Components Inc. for bicycles in the upper-end range of the market where Cannondale competed. Cannondale had built a successful business on the basis of high quality and innovative products. Its customers were bicyclists who expected the highest quality and most advanced features. Industry analysts predicted consolidation in the industry for manufacturers that use Shimano parts but cannot differentiate their products effectively; these bicycle makers will likely be forced to compete on price.

Required

1. Consider the use of Shimano parts as one aspect of the value chain for Cannondale. Describe Cannondale's current strategy. How should this strategy change, if at all, to compete effectively with Trek and Specialized?

2. Should Cannondale continue to outsource Shimano parts? Why or why not?

2-55 Value Chain; Harley-Davidson Harley-Davidson Inc. (HD) is one of the most recognized brands worldwide. The motorcycle manufacturer has one of the most loyal owner groups of any company. Unfortunately, the firm's success has come at a price. New customers are sometimes frustrated at long waiting lists for a new bike, and other potential new customers say they are turned off at the enthusiasm of some of the current owners. The average age of a Harley rider has risen from 35 in 1987 to nearly 47 in 2006. Harley has a *Wild Bunch* reputation that drives some customers away, and a "this is for a different generation" effect on some potential younger customers. Other potential customers are simply intimidated at the idea of riding a 400+ pound Harley-Davidson. To deal with these concerns, and to try to encourage new owners, HD developed the Rider's Edge program in which anyone who could pass the Motorcycle Safety Foundation's written test and driving test would be eligible for instructions on how to ride a Harley. The instructions are provided by local dealers.

Required Where does this program fit in the Harley-Davidson value chain? From a value chain perspective, how does the Rider's Edge program at Harley-Davidson support the firm's strategy?

2-56 The Balanced Scorecard; Strategy Map; Banking Carlos Aguilar, a CMA and consultant in Los Angeles, has been asked to help develop a balanced scorecard for a local medium-sized commercial bank. Carlos is familiar with the area around the bank and he knows that the bank has succeeded in part because of good community ties and customer service. The bank managers also realize that employee morale is an important factor in the success of the bank.

Required

1. Carlos has asked you to help him in the initial phases of this project. Specifically, he has asked you to identify the balanced scorecard perspectives you would use for this bank, and a short list of four to five critical success factors that you would include in each perspective.

2. Also, he is interested in knowing how the concept of a strategy map might be applicable for this client. Prepare a brief report for Carlos.

3. Explain how the balanced scorecard for a bank could be linked to an incentive compensation plan for the managers and employees of the bank.

2-57 Value Chain; Multiple Industries Generally, the value chains involved in providing a given product or service can be from multiple industries that can be interconnected in complex ways. One example is the auto industry where the primary consumer, the purchaser of an auto, is served by many different industries. The figure below shows five industries that support the auto purchaser directly: the manufacturer of the auto, the bank or financial institution that finances the loan for the car buyer, the insurance company, auto repair, and at some point, a company that purchases the car and resells it. The arrows show the links of service in this multiple industry value chain.

The value chain for the manufacturer is shown in the center column, and the steps in the chain are shown as design, purchase of materials, purchase of components (brake systems, seats, dashboard, carpeting, etc), assembly, and delivery to the auto dealer. To the right of the figure we show one of the suppliers of components for the auto manufacturer, and auto parts manufacturer that provides brake systems. This manufacturer also requires supplies from other companies, which in turn require parts or materials from other companies. So there are two or more levels, or "tiers," to the supply chain for the manufacturer. A thorough understanding of the value chain for the auto industry requires consideration of the full complexity of all the different suppliers and industries involved.

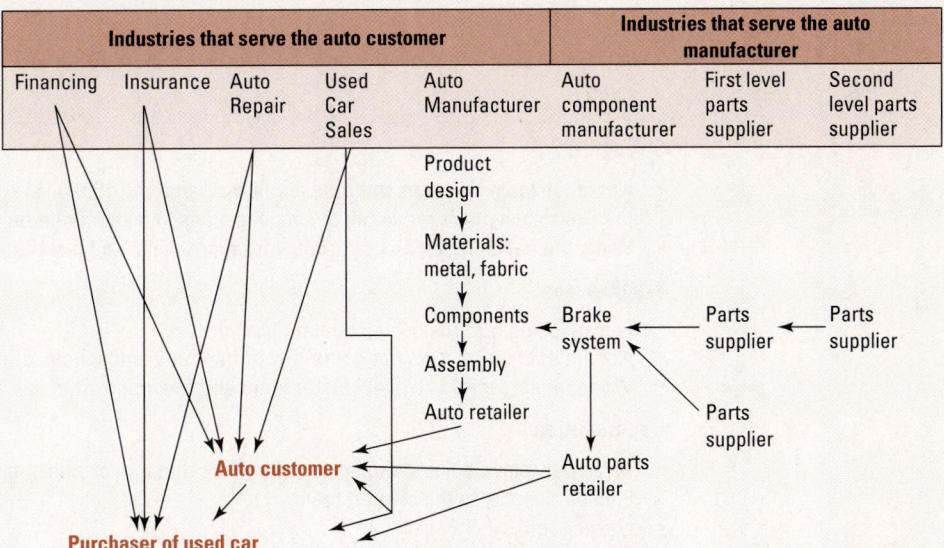

Required Using the above figure as a guide, create a multiple-industry value chain for a boat manufacturer, including financing, repair, used sales, and parts suppliers.

2-58 Follow-up to 2-57; Value Chain for Financing Auto Purchases

Required Consider the comprehensive value chain in Problem 2-57 and complete a value chain for the financing portion of the value chain only. Use a value chain with four to six steps, beginning with the application for a loan by the car buyer and ending with the car buyer completing the loan and purchase.

2-59 Foreign Currency Exchange Rates

The Web site shown below provides historical information on the exchange rates of currencies used throughout the world. Review the changes in exchange rates for the last few years.

www.federalreserve.gov/releases/H10/hist/

Required (choose 1, 2, or 3):
1. Which Asian countries have experienced changing exchange rates relative to the U.S. dollar in the recent few years, and what are the implications of this trend for global companies such as Amazon.com or General Electric?
2. Most European countries now use the euro as the currency for international exchange. Study the recent trends in the euro and determine the implications of this trend for global companies such as Wal-Mart.
3. Which North American countries (other than the U.S.) have experienced changing exchange rates relative to the U.S. dollar in the recent year, and what are the implications of this trend for global companies such as Ford Motor Company?

Solutions to Self-Study Problems

1. Value-Chain Analysis

The cost figures Jack has assembled suggest that the two teams' operations are generally quite similar, as expected in AA baseball. However, an important difference is the amount the Durham team spends on game-day operations, more than three times that of the Waynesboro Bulls. That difference has, in part, built a loyal set of fans in Durham where gate receipts average more than twice that of Waynesboro ($28,500 versus $12,350). The Buffaloes appear to have found an effective way to compete by drawing attendance to special game-day events and promotions.

To begin to compete more effectively and profitably, Waynesboro might consider additional value-added services, such as game-day activities similar to those offered in Durham. Waynesboro's costs per person are somewhat lower than Durham's, but its cost savings are probably not enough to offset the loss in revenues.

On the cost side, the comparison with Durham shows little immediate promise for cost reduction; Waynesboro spends on the average less than Durham in every category except ticket sales and management compensation. Perhaps this also indicates that instead of reducing costs, Waynesboro should spend *more* on fan development. The next step in Jack's analysis might be to survey Waynesboro fans to determine the level of satisfaction and to identify desired services that are not currently provided.

2. SWOT Analysis

Avid baseball fans will probably improve greatly on these solutions.

Strengths:

- Not much local competition for baseball; note that the 150-mile radius is probably irrelevant anyway as the Bulls' customers are local; the main issue is local competition.
- Wing, the new pitcher; an opportunity for more wins, and increased fan interest.

Weaknesses:

- Lots of losing records, which hinders fan interest.
- Not much to offer by way of game-day promotions and special attractions.
- What appears might be a lackluster team and coaching staff.

Opportunities:

- More new players like Wing, especially those that can create some fan excitement; it seems there is little personality to the current team.
- New coach.
- Improve the baseball park; add some improvements, such as better parking, seats, etc.
- Increase the quality and variety of food and beverages beyond soda, beer, and nachos.
- Lower the ticket prices; offer free tickets to those who have attended a certain number of games.
- Offer special promotions, in which groups (employees of a given company; those over 65, etc.) get a free or low-price admission.

Threats:

- Only the closest of the other venues (NASCAR, outdoor concerts, etc) would be a threat to this basically local audience.

---

3. The Balanced Scorecard

While the key to growth and profitability is probably increasing fan interest, this will probably come about most directly through improvements in operations and personnel. Here is a partial list of examples.

Operations (at the Bulls' park, and on travel days):

- Cleanliness of park and restrooms as measured by a survey of fans or regular review by management.
- Parking, measured by number of complaints.
- Timeliness and comfort for players and coaching staff on away-days; player and staff survey.

Personnel (coaching and players):

- Players' performance statistics.
- Average player salary (benchmark to other teams).
- Average player age.
- Player satisfaction as measured by multiple question survey.

Customers (the ticket buying fans):

- Survey of customer satisfaction.
- Number of paying customers to number of free admissions.

Financial:

- Ticket sales revenue.
- Revenue; food and beverages.
- Other revenue (parking, etc).
- Ballpark maintenance cost, by category.
- Travel costs for away games.

CHAPTER THREE

Basic Cost Management Concepts

After studying this chapter, you should be able to . . .

1. Understand the strategic role of basic cost management concepts
2. Explain the cost driver concepts at the activity, volume, structural, and executional levels
3. Explain the cost concepts used in product and service costing
4. Demonstrate how costs flow through the accounts
5. Prepare an income statement for both a manufacturing firm and a merchandising firm

LEARNING OBJECTIVE 1

Understand the strategic role of basic cost management concepts.

As we will see in this chapter, irrespective of their competitive strategy, successful firms find that they need to apply cost management effectively and, in doing so, to understand the key concepts and terms of cost management. We begin with an example firm that illustrates the importance of understanding the complexity of a firm's operations—the number and diversity of its products, production processes and locations, distribution networks, and types of customers. Complexity on any of these dimensions will have consequences for costs, and the management accountant has developed the necessary vocabulary to identify and describe these effects.

A good example of a firm that deals effectively with complexity is Procter & Gamble (P&G), one of the world's leading consumer products companies, maker of such well-known products as Tide detergent and Crest toothpaste. P&G has achieved success through product excellence and continuous improvement. One key area of continuous improvement is the firm's emphasis on cost reduction through product and process simplification. To accomplish this, P&G uses a concept that we study in this chapter: the influence of product and process complexity on overall costs. In the early 1990s, P&G had as many as 50 different varieties of some of its brands, including different size containers, and flavors. In addition to variety, the number of trade promotions, discounts, rebates, and coupons that affected P&G's net price were complex. The high complexity in products and pricing increased manufacturing costs, inventory holding costs, selling and distribution costs, customer service costs, administrative and accounting costs, and other operating costs. Over a period of five years, P&G reduced its product variety by one-half, and its profits surged. At the same time, P&G improved its supply chain—the process of managing its suppliers—to reduce supply chain cost and to improve product quality and product innovation.

The importance of product simplification to P&G is also reflected by its recent strategic decision not to complete a merger with the drug makers American Home Products Corp. and Warner-Lambert Co. At first glance, the marriage of these three powerful firms might seem to offer a good way to achieve market dominance and economies of scale. On second thought, however, would P&G's capabilities in developing and marketing consumer brands such as Tide detergent be a competitive advantage in developing and marketing drugs? The technologies and expertise from product development to product marketing and distribution are quite different. Moreover, P&G has established an enviable reputation as a consumer-goods company, but it does not have a reputation as a health-focused company (as, for example, does Johnson & Johnson). The firm is not likely to maintain a dual image. In fact, a successful strategy normally requires a single focused image in the marketplace, and the merger would dilute and confuse P&G's already excellent reputation as a consumer-products company. Again, simplicity and clarity of strategy produce winners.

Costs, Cost Drivers, Cost Objects, and Cost Assignment

LEARNING OBJECTIVE 2

Explain the cost driver concepts at the activity, volume, structural, and executional levels.

A cost

is incurred when a resource is used for some purpose.

Cost pools

are the meaningful groups into which costs are often collected.

A cost driver

is any factor that causes a change in the cost of an activity.

A cost object

is any product, service, customer, activity, or organizational unit to which costs are assigned for some management purpose.

A value stream

is a group of related products.

Cost assignment

is the process of assigning costs to cost pools or from cost pools to cost objects.

A direct cost

can be conveniently and economically traced directly to a cost pool or a cost object.

An indirect cost

has *no* convenient or economical trace from the cost to the cost pool or from the cost pool to the cost object.

A critical first step in achieving a competitive advantage is to identify the key costs and cost drivers in the firm or organization.

A firm incurs a **cost** when it uses a resource for some purpose. For example, a company producing kitchen appliances uses certain resources, the costs of materials (such as sheet metal and bolts for the enclosure), costs of manufacturing labor, and other costs. Often costs are assigned into meaningful groups called **cost pools.** Costs can be grouped in many different ways, including by type of cost (labor costs in one pool, material costs in another), by source (department 1, department 2), or by responsibility (manager 1, manager 2). For example, an assembly department or a product engineering department might be treated as a cost pool.

A **cost driver** is any factor that has the effect of changing the amount of total cost. For a firm that competes on the basis of cost leadership, management of the key cost drivers is essential. For example, to achieve its low-cost leadership in manufacturing, P&G carefully watches the design and manufacturing factors that drive the costs of its products. It makes design improvements when necessary, and the manufacturing plants are designed and automated for the highest efficiency in using materials, labor, and equipment. For firms that are not cost leaders, the management of cost drivers may not be so critical, but attention to the key cost drivers contributes directly to the firm's success. For example, because an important cost driver for retailers is loss and damage to merchandise, most retailers establish careful procedures for handling, displaying, and storing their merchandise.

A **cost object** is any product, service, customer, activity, or organizational unit to which costs are assigned. Products, services, and customers are generally cost objects; manufacturing departments are considered either cost pools or cost objects, depending on whether management's main focus is on the costs for the products or for the manufacturing departments. The concept of cost objects is a broad concept. It includes products, groups of products (called **value streams**), services, projects, and departments; it can also apply to customers or vendors, among many other possibilities. Cost objects play a key role in decision making, performance measurement, and strategy implementation, as well as financial statement preparation and tax preparation.

Cost Assignment and Cost Allocation: Direct and Indirect Costs

Cost assignment is the process of assigning resource costs to cost pools and then from cost pools to cost objects. There are two types of assignment—direct tracing and allocation. Direct tracing is used for assigning direct costs and allocation is used for indirect costs. Any cost is either a direct or indirect cost, relative to the cost pool or cost object. A **direct cost** can be conveniently and economically traced directly to a cost pool or a cost object. For example, the cost of materials required for a particular product is a direct cost because it can be traced directly to the product.

In a manufacturing company, the materials cost is accumulated in cost pools (manufacturing departments) and then is traced to each product manufactured, which is the cost object. Similarly, an airline's cost of preparing a passenger's meal is a direct cost that can be traced to each passenger. For a direct cost, the cost driver is the number of units of that object, for example, the number of cartons of Tide produced by P&G, or the number of passengers on Flight 617 for Delta Airlines. Total direct cost increases directly in proportion to the number of cartons or passengers.

In contrast, there is no convenient or economical way to trace an **indirect cost** from the cost to the cost pool or from the cost pool to the cost object. The cost of supervising manufacturing employees and the cost of handling materials are good examples of costs that generally cannot be traced to individual products and therefore are considered indirect costs. Similarly, the cost of fueling an aircraft is an indirect cost when the cost object is the individual airline customer since the aircraft's use of fuel cannot be traced directly to that customer. In contrast, if the cost object for the airline is the flight, the cost of fuel is a direct cost that can be traced directly to the aircraft's use of fuel for that flight.

Since indirect costs cannot be traced to the cost pool or cost object, the assignment for indirect costs is made by using cost drivers. For example, if the cost driver for materials handling

EXHIBIT 3.1
Relationships between Costs, Cost Pools, and Cost Objects, in Appliance Manufacturing

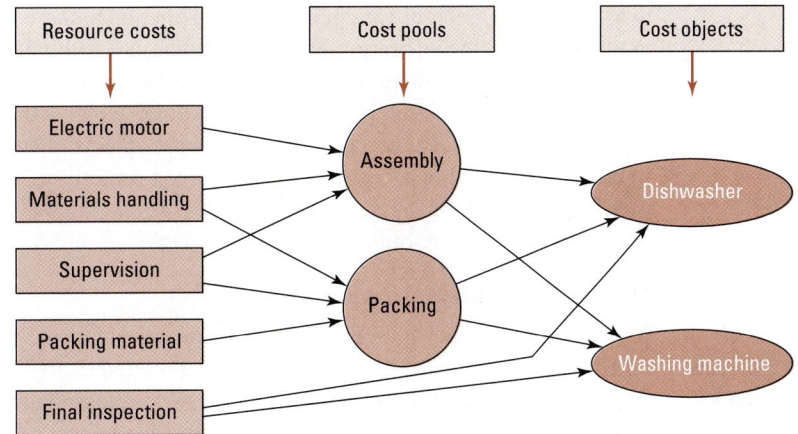

cost is the number of parts, the total cost of materials handling can be assigned to each product on the basis of its total number of parts relative to the total number of parts in all other products. The result is that costs are assigned to the cost pool or cost object that caused the cost in a manner that is fairly representative of the way the cost is incurred. For example, a product with a large number of parts should bear a larger portion of the cost of materials handling than a product with fewer parts. Similarly, a department with a large number of employees should bear a large portion of the cost of supervision provided for all departments.

The assignment of indirect costs to cost pools and cost objects is called **cost allocation,** a form of cost assignment in which direct tracing is not economically feasible, so cost drivers are used instead. The cost drivers used to allocate costs are often called **allocation bases.** The relationships between costs, cost pools, cost objects, and cost drivers in appliance manufacturing are illustrated in Exhibit 3.1 and Exhibit 3.2. This simplified example includes two cost objects (dishwasher, washing machine), two cost pools (assembly department, packing department), and five cost resources (electric motor, materials handling, supervision, packing material, and final product inspection). The electric motor is traced to the assembly department and from there directly to the two products, assuming for simplicity that the same motor is used in both appliances. Similarly, the packing material is traced directly to the packing department and from there directly to the two products. Each finished product, dishwasher or washing machine, is inspected, so the cost of final inspection is traced directly to each of the two products. The two indirect costs, supervision and materials handling, are allocated to the

Cost allocation
is the assignment of indirect costs to cost pools and cost objects.

Allocation bases
are the cost drivers used to allocate costs.

EXHIBIT 3.2
Selected Examples of Costs, Cost Pools, Cost Objects, and Cost Drivers in Appliance Manufacturing

The Flow of Cost Assignment

Resource Cost	Cost Driver	Cost Pool	Cost Driver	Cost Object
Direct Costs				
Electric motor	Direct trace	Assembly department	Direct trace	Dishwasher and washing machine
Packing material	Direct trace	Packing department	Direct trace	Dishwasher and washing machine
Final inspection	Direct trace		→	Dishwasher and washing machine
Indirect Costs				
Supervision	Allocation base: Number of employees in the department	Assembly and packing departments	Allocation base: Direct labor hours for each product	Dishwasher and washing machine
Materials handling	Allocation base: Weight of materials	Assembly and packing departments	Allocation base: Number of parts in the product	Dishwasher and washing machine

two cost pools (assembly and packing departments) and are then allocated from the cost pools to the products (the allocation bases are shown in Exhibit 3.2).

Exhibit 3.2 illustrates the differences between direct and indirect costs and the different types of cost drivers for each. The direct costs—motor, packing material, and final inspection—are traced directly to the final cost objects, the dishwasher and washing machine. In contrast, the indirect costs cannot be traced directly to the products and instead are allocated to the products using an allocation base. The details of the allocation of indirect costs are not explained here but are covered in Chapters 4 and 5.

Direct and Indirect Materials Costs

Direct materials cost includes the cost of materials in the product or other cost object (less purchase discounts but including freight and related charges) and usually a reasonable allowance for scrap and defective units (e.g., if a part is stamped from strip steel, the material lost in the stamping is ordinarily included as part of the product's direct materials).

On the other hand, the cost of materials used in manufacturing that are not part of the finished product is **indirect materials cost.** Examples include supplies used by manufacturing employees, such as rags and small tools, or materials required by the machines, such as lubricant. For convenience and economic feasibility, direct materials that are a very small part of materials cost, such as glue and nails, are often not traced to each product but are included instead in indirect materials.

Direct and Indirect Labor Costs

Direct labor cost includes the labor used to manufacture the product or to provide the service plus some portion of non-value-added time that is normal and unavoidable, such as coffee breaks and personal time. Other types of nonproductive labor that are discretionary and planned, such as downtime, payroll taxes, fringe benefits (vacation, etc.), and training usually are included not as direct labor but as indirect labor.

Indirect labor costs include supervision, quality control, inspection, purchasing and receiving, materials handling, janitorial labor, downtime, training, and cleanup. Note that an element of labor can sometimes be both direct and indirect, depending on the cost object; for example, labor for the maintenance and repair of equipment might be direct to the manufacturing department where the equipment is located but indirect to the products manufactured in that department.

Although these examples of direct and indirect costs are from a manufacturing setting, the concepts also apply to service companies. For example, in a restaurant where the cost object is each meal served, the food and food preparation costs are direct costs, but the costs of purchasing, handling, and storing food items are indirect costs. Similarly, in professional services firms such as law firms or accounting firms, the professional labor and materials costs for providing client service are direct costs, but the costs of research materials, nonprofessional support staff, and training are indirect costs. An example of cost drivers at a service company, Pennsylvania Blue Shield, is shown in Exhibit 3.3.

Other Indirect Costs

In addition to labor and materials, other types of indirect costs are necessary to manufacture the product or provide the service. They include the costs of facilities, the equipment used to

---

Direct materials cost includes the cost of the materials in the product and a reasonable allowance for scrap and defective units.

Indirect materials cost refers to the cost of materials used in manufacturing that are not physically part of the finished product.

Direct labor cost includes the labor used to manufacture the product or to provide the service.

Indirect labor cost includes supervision, quality control, inspection, purchasing and receiving, and other manufacturing support costs.

EXHIBIT 3.3
Resource Costs, Cost Pools, Cost Objects, and Cost Drivers at Pennsylvania Blue Shield

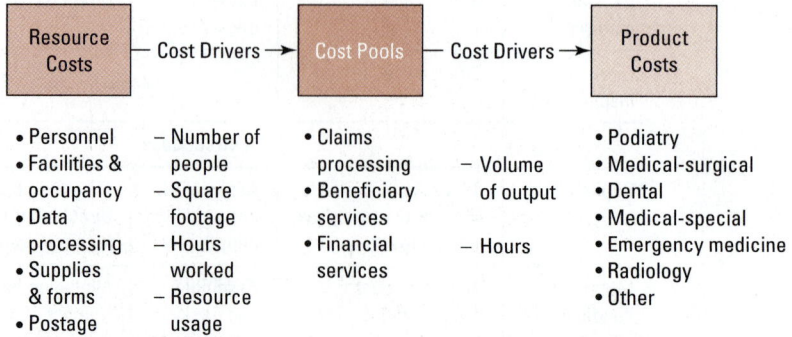

manufacture the product or provide the service, and any other support equipment, such as that used for materials handling.

All indirect costs—for indirect materials, indirect labor, and other indirect items—are commonly combined into a cost pool called **overhead.** In a manufacturing firm, it is called **factory overhead.**

The three types of costs—direct materials, direct labor, and overhead—are sometimes combined for simplicity and convenience. Direct materials and direct labor are sometimes considered together and called **prime costs.** Similarly, direct labor and overhead are often combined into a single amount called **conversion cost.** The labor component of total manufacturing costs for many firms that have highly automated operations is relatively low, and these firms often choose to place their strategic focus on materials and facilities/overhead costs by combining labor costs with overhead.

> All indirect costs are commonly combined into a single cost pool called **overhead** or, in a manufacturing firm, **factory overhead.**
>
> **Prime costs**
> refer to direct materials and direct labor that are combined into a single amount.
>
> **Conversion cost**
> refers to direct labor and overhead combined into a single amount.

Cost Drivers and Cost Behavior

Cost drivers provide two important roles for the management accountant: (1) enabling the assignment of costs to cost objects, as we saw in the above discussion and in Exhibits 3.1 and 3.2, and (2) explaining cost behavior, how total costs change as the cost driver changes. Generally, the increase in a cost driver will cause an increase in total cost. Occasionally, the relationship is inverse; for example, assume the cost driver is temperature, then in the colder times of the year, increases in this cost driver will decrease total heating cost. Cost drivers can be used to provide both the cost assignment and cost behavior roles at the same time. In the remainder of this section, we focus on the cost behavior role of cost drivers.

Most firms, especially those following the cost leadership strategy, use cost management to maintain or improve their competitive position. Cost management requires a good understanding of how the total cost of a cost object changes as the cost drivers change. The four types of cost drivers are activity-based, volume-based, structural, and executional. Activity-based cost drivers are developed at a detailed level of operations and are associated with a given manufacturing activity (or activity in providing a service), such as machine setup, product inspection, materials handling, or packaging. In contrast, volume-based cost drivers are developed at an aggregate level, such as an output level for the number of units produced. Structural and executional cost drivers involve strategic and operational decisions that affect the relationship between these cost drivers and total cost.

Activity-Based Cost Drivers

Activity-based cost drivers are identified by using activity analysis—a detailed description of the specific activities performed in the firm's operations. The activity analysis includes each step in manufacturing the product or in providing the service. For each activity, a cost driver is determined to explain how the costs incurred for that activity change. Example activities and cost drivers for a bank are illustrated in Exhibit 3.4. The total cost to the bank is affected by changes in the cost drivers for each activity.

The detailed description of the firm's activities helps the firm achieve its strategic objectives by enabling it to develop more accurate costs for its products and services. The activity analysis also helps improve operational and management control in the firm since performance at the detailed level can be monitored and evaluated, for example, by (1) identifying which activities are contributing value to the customer and which are not and (2) focusing

EXHIBIT 3.4
Bank Activities and Cost Drivers

Activity	Cost Drivers
Provide ATM service	Number of ATM transactions; number of customers
Provide cashier service	Number of customers
Open and close customer accounts	Number of accounts opened or closed
Advise customers on banking services	Number of customers
Prepare applications for new loans	Number of loan applications prepared
Process loan applications	Number of loan applications processed
Prepare approved loans and disburse funds	Number of loans approved
Mail customer statements	Number of accounts by customer type and size

EXHIBIT 3.5
Total Cost over a Wide Range of Output

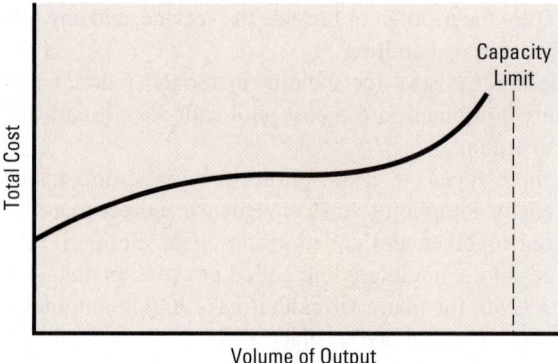

attention on those activities that are most costly or that differ from expectations. Activity-based costing and activity-based management are explained in Chapter 5.

Volume-Based Cost Drivers

Many types of costs are volume-based, that is, the cost driver is the amount produced or quantity of service provided. Management accountants commonly call this volume, or volume of output, or simply output. Good examples of volume-based costs are direct materials cost and direct labor cost—these costs increase with each unit of the volume of output. Note that the three cost drivers—the output of complete units, the quantity (in pounds, etc.) of direct materials, and the hours of direct labor—are all volume-based cost drivers and are proportional to each other.

The total of a volume-based cost increases at the rate of increase in volume, and over short ranges of output, the relationship is approximately linear. Over a very broad range of output, say, from output of zero up to plant capacity and beyond, the relationship between volume of output and cost tends to be nonlinear. As illustrated in Exhibit 3.5, at low values for the cost driver, costs increase at a decreasing rate, due in part to factors such as more efficient use of resources and higher productivity through learning. The pattern of increasing costs at a decreasing rate is often referred to as *increasing marginal productivity,* which means that the inputs are used more productively or more efficiently as manufacturing output increases.

At higher levels of the cost driver, costs begin to increase at an increasing rate, due in part to inefficiency associated with operating nearer the limit of capacity; the less efficient resources are now being used, overtime may be required, and so on. This cost behavior in the higher levels of the cost driver is said to satisfy the *law of diminishing marginal productivity.*

The nonlinear cost relationships depicted in Exhibit 3.5 present some difficulties in estimating costs and in calculating total costs since linear, algebraic relationships cannot be used. Fortunately, we are often interested in only a relatively small range of activity for the cost driver. For example, we might know in a certain instance that the *volume-based* cost driver will fall somewhere between 3,500 and 3,600 units of product output. We observe that within this range, the total cost curve is approximately linear. The range of the cost driver in which the actual value of the cost driver is expected to fall and for which the relationship to total cost is assumed to be approximately linear is called the **relevant range.**

This simplification process is illustrated in Exhibit 3.6 and Exhibit 3.7. Exhibit 3.6 shows the curved actual total cost line and the relevant range of 3,500 to 3,600 units; Exhibit 3.7 shows the linear approximation of actual total cost; within the relevant range, the behavior of total cost approximates that shown in Exhibit 3.6. Note that the cost line above 3,600 and below 3,500 in Exhibit 3.7 is a dotted line to indicate that this portion of the line is not used to approximate total cost because it is outside the relevant range. Chapter 8 shows the process management accountant's use for estimating the cost curves shown in these exhibits.

Fixed and Variable Costs

Total cost is made up of variable costs and fixed costs. **Variable cost** is the change in total cost associated with each change in the quantity of the cost driver. The cost driver can be activity-based or volume-based, though typically management accountants in practice use the term

Relevant range
is the range of the cost driver in which the actual value of the cost driver is expected to fall and for which the relationship to total cost is assumed to be approximately linear.

Variable cost
is the change in total cost associated with each change in the quantity of the cost driver.

EXHIBIT 3.6 **Total Cost and the Relevant Range**

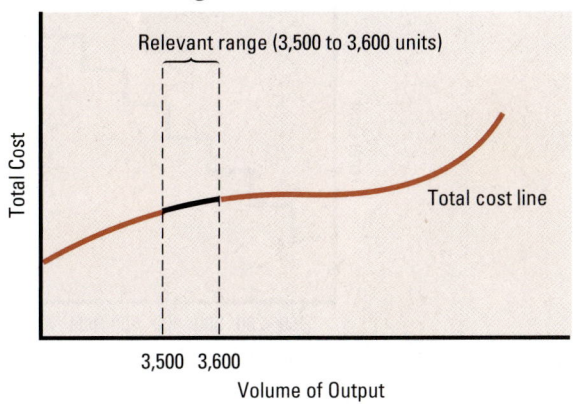

EXHIBIT 3.7 **Linear Approximation for Actual Cost Behavior, within the Relevant Range**

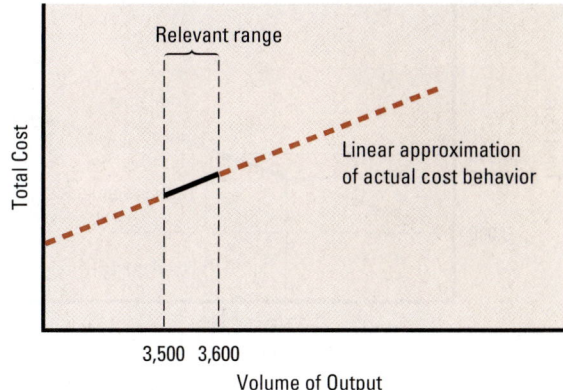

Fixed cost
is the portion of the total cost that does not change with a change in the quantity of the cost driver within the relevant range.

Mixed cost
is the term used to refer to total cost when total cost includes both variable and fixed cost components.

variable costs in connection with volume-based cost drivers. Common examples of variable costs are costs of direct materials and direct labor. In contrast, **fixed cost** is that portion of the total cost that does not change with output within the relevant range. *Total* fixed costs and *unit* variable costs are expected to remain approximately constant within the relevant range. Fixed cost is illustrated as the horizontal dashed line at $3,000 in Exhibit 3.8. Variable cost is $1 per unit, total cost is the upward-sloping line, and total variable cost is the difference between total cost and fixed cost. Total cost of $6,500 at 3,500 units is made up of fixed cost ($3,000) plus total variable cost (3,500 × $1 = $3,500); similarly, total cost at 3,600 units is $6,600 ($3,000 fixed cost plus 3,600 × $1 = $3,600 variable cost).

Fixed costs include many indirect costs, especially facility costs (depreciation or rent, insurance, taxes on the plant building), production supervisors' salaries, and other manufacturing support costs that do not change with the number of units produced. However, some indirect costs are variable since they change with the number of units produced. An example is lubricant for machines. The term **mixed cost** is used to refer to total cost that includes costs for both variable and fixed components as illustrated.

The determination of whether a cost is variable depends on the nature of the cost object. In manufacturing firms, the cost object is typically the product. In service firms, however, the cost object is often difficult to define because the service can have a number of qualitative as well as quantitative dimensions. Let's develop cost objects for one type of service firm, a hospital, which could use a number of measures of output including the number of patients served, the number successfully treated, and so on. However, a common approach in hospitals is to use the number of patient-days since this measure most closely matches the way the hospital incurs costs.

It has sometimes been said that all costs are variable in the long run; that is, with enough time, any cost can be changed. While it is true that many fixed costs do change over time (for example, the cost of rent might increase from year to year), that does not mean these costs are variable. A variable cost is a cost for which *total costs change with changes in the volume of output.* Fixed costs are defined for a period of time rather than in relationship to volume of output, and it is assumed that fixed costs will not change during this period of time which is usually taken to be a year. For example, rent is a fixed cost that is normally the same amount *per year* and does not vary with volume. Strategically, especially for a cost leader type of firm, the important point is that both fixed and variable costs can be managed, but variable costs are managed in the very short term, as each unit is produced, while fixed costs are managed over a period of time. Some fixed costs cannot be changed for a relatively long period of time (for example, depreciation on the plant building) while others can be changed more quickly (for example, equipment with a one-year lease).

To summarize, when we want to understand the cost behavior of a certain cost object (for example, in order to predict total cost), we have to have clearly in mind the following three questions: (1) what is the cost driver (or cost drivers if there are two or more) for this cost object; (2) what is the relevant range of the cost driver for which we are developing the cost estimate; and (3) what time horizon are we using for fixed costs (usually one year is used)?

EXHIBIT 3.8   **Total Cost, Total Variable Cost, and Fixed Cost**

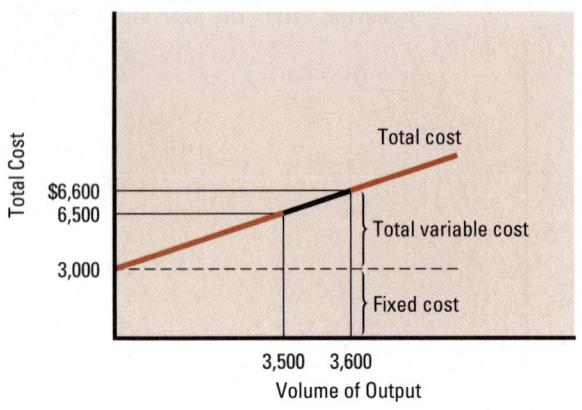

EXHIBIT 3.9   **A Step Cost**

Step Costs

A cost is said to be a **step cost** when it varies with the cost driver but in steps.

A cost is said to be a **step cost** when it varies with the cost driver but does so in steps (Exhibit 3.9). Step costs are characteristic of certain clerical tasks, such as order filling and claims processing. For example, if a warehouse clerk can fill 100 orders in a day, 10 clerks will be needed to process approximately 1,000 orders; as demand exceeds 1,000 orders, an eleventh clerk must be added. The steps correspond to specific levels of the cost driver for which an additional clerk is required; in effect, each step corresponds to one additional clerk. The steps will be relatively narrow if clerks are added for relatively small increases in the cost driver; the steps will be wider for large increases.

Unit Cost and Marginal Cost

Unit cost (or **average cost**) is the total manufacturing cost (materials, labor, and overhead) divided by the number of units of output.

Unit cost (or **average cost**) is the total manufacturing cost (materials, labor, and overhead) divided by the number of units of output. It is a useful concept in setting prices and in evaluating product profitability, but it can be subject to some misleading interpretations. To properly interpret unit cost, we must distinguish *unit variable* costs, which do not change as output changes, from *unit fixed costs,* which do change as output changes. See Exhibit 3.10. For example, a driver's cost per mile is likely lower for a person who drives a car for 20,000 miles/year than it is for a person who drives a car for only 5,000 miles/year because the fixed costs are spread over more miles. These relationships are illustrated graphically in Exhibit 3.11. The management accountant is careful in using the terms *average cost* and *unit cost* because of the potential for misleading interpretations.

Capacity vs. Usage of Costs

It is important to distinguish between costs that provide capacity for operations (e.g., plant building and equipment) and costs that are consumed during operations (e.g., direct materials and labor). The former are fixed costs, while the latter are variable costs. In practice, the management accountant uses care in making the distinctions because sometimes capacity-type costs are treated as variable costs. For example, compare the cost of two types of direct labor employees who work in the assembly of a product: one is a salaried worker who is paid by the month and another a worker paid by the hour. The former is a capacity (fixed) cost, while the latter is a variable cost. While both workers might be considered direct labor because they work in product assembly, if volume of output falls and the salaried worker is idle, the total cost of labor does not change, while the total cost of labor would fall for a wage worker who has fewer hours. On the other hand, effective managers try to schedule production and

EXHIBIT 3.10
Illustration of Fixed Cost and Variable Cost per Unit

	Fixed Cost		Variable Cost	
Units of output	10,000	20,000	10,000	20,000
Per unit	$ 10	$ 5	$ 8	$ 8
Total	$100,000	$100,000	$80,000	$160,000

EXHIBIT 3.11
Average Variable Cost and Average Fixed Cost

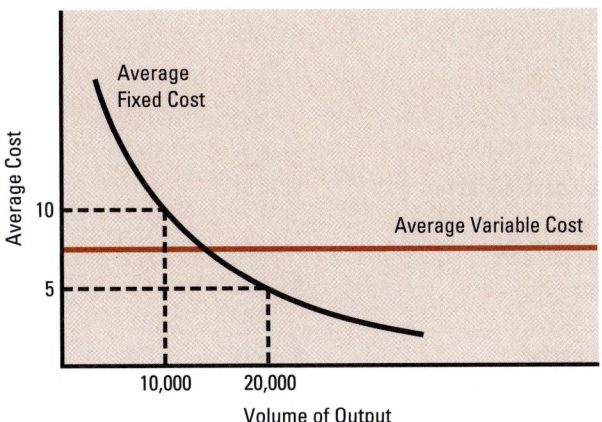

labor carefully by using part-time help and by other means, so that no workers are idle; then, all assembly work can be considered a direct and variable cost. When idle time is present, some management accountants measure the cost of the unused capacity. Note that the cost of unused capacity would potentially apply to many types of fixed costs.

Structural and Executional Cost Drivers

Structural cost drivers are strategic in nature and involve plans and decisions that have a long-term effect with regard to issues such as scale, experience, technology, and complexity.

Structural and executional cost drivers are used to facilitate strategic decision making. **Structural cost drivers** are strategic in nature because they involve decisions that have long-term effects on the firm's total costs. Here are four examples of structural decisions.

1. Scale. Larger firms have lower overall costs as a result of economies of scale. For example, a retail firm such as Wal-Mart or Target must determine how many new stores to open in a given year to achieve its strategic objectives and compete effectively as a retailer.

2. Experience. Firms having employees with greater manufacturing and sales experience will likely have lower development, manufacturing, and distribution costs. For example, a manufacturer such as Hewlett-Packard uses existing manufacturing methods as much as possible for new products to reduce the time and cost necessary for workers to become proficient at manufacturing the new product.

71

The following data is provided by the U.S. Department of Agriculture (USDA) regarding the cost of soybean production in the U.S. Heartland (Minnesota, Iowa, South Dakota, Indiana, and Illinois and parts of Ohio, Missouri, Nebraska, and Kentucky) and the Mato Grosso region in western Brazil. The data is used to analyze the cost competitiveness of soybean production in the United States and Brazil.

REQUIRED:

1. What can you learn from the information below about the cost competitiveness of the United States and Brazil in soybean production?

2. Critically evaluate the cost information.

Source: Data from U.S. Department of Agriculture (USDA), Economic Research Service (Refer to Comments on Cost Management in Action at end of Chapter.)

Cost per Acre and per Bushel of Soybeans		
	U.S. Heartland	**Brazil's Mato Grosso**
Variable costs (per acre)		
Seed	$ 19.77	$ 11.23
Fertilizers	8.22	44.95
Chemicals	27.31	39.97
Machinery	20.19	18.22
Labor	1.29	5.58
Other	1.81	12.11
Total variable costs	$ 78.59	$132.06
Fixed costs (per acre)		
Equipment depreciation	$ 47.99	$ 8.97
Land costs (rental rate)	87.96	5.84
Taxes, insurance	6.97	.55
Farm overhead	13.40	14.65
Total fixed costs	$156.32	$ 30.01
Total production cost (per acre)	**$234.91**	**$162.07**
Total cost per bushel		
Average yield per acre	46.00	41.65
Variable costs	$ 1.71	$ 3.17
Fixed costs	3.40	.72
Total costs per bushel	**$ 5.11**	**$ 3.89**

3. Technology. New technologies can reduce design, manufacturing, distribution, and customer service costs significantly. For example, manufacturers such as Procter & Gamble use computer technology to monitor the quantities of its products that its customers (typically, large retailers) have on hand so that it can promptly restock these products as needed.

4. Complexity. How many different products does the firm have? As noted in the opening discussion of Procter & Gamble, firms with many products have higher costs of scheduling and managing the production process, as well as the upstream costs of product development and the downstream costs of distribution and service. In particular, the current economic recession has caused firms to trim their brand offerings; for example, in 2009 Kraft Foods dropped its South Beach entrees and is pulling Handi-Snack puddings from the U.S. market.

Strategic analyses using structural cost drivers help the firm improve its competitive position. These analyses include value-chain analysis and activity-based management. Value-chain analysis can help the firm assess the long-term consequences of its current or planned commitment to a structural cost driver. For example, the growth in size and capability of parts manufacturers for automakers should cause the automakers to reassess whether they should outsource the manufacture of certain parts.

Executional cost drivers
are factors the firm can manage in the short term to reduce costs, such as workforce involvement, design of the production process, and supplier relationships.

Executional cost drivers are factors the firm can manage in short-term, operational decision making to reduce costs. They include the following:

1. Workforce empowerment. Are the employees dedicated to continual improvement and quality? This workforce commitment will lower costs. Firms with strong employee relationships, such as Federal Express, can reduce operating costs significantly.

2. Design of the production process. Speeding up the flow of product through the firm can reduce costs. Innovators in manufacturing technology, such as Motorola and Allen-Bradley, can reduce manufacturing costs significantly.

3. Supplier relationships. Can the cost, quality, or delivery of materials and purchased parts be improved to reduce overall costs? Wal-Mart and Toyota, among other firms, maintain a low-cost advantage partially by agreements with their suppliers that they will provide products or parts that meet the companies' explicit requirements as to their quality, timeliness of delivery, and other features.

Plant managers study executional cost drivers to find ways to reduce costs. Such studies are done as a part of operational control, which is covered in Part Three.

Cost Concepts for Product and Service Costing

LEARNING OBJECTIVE 3

Explain the cost concepts used in product and service costing.

Accurate information about the cost of products and services is important in each management function: strategic management, planning and decision making, management and operational control, and financial statement preparation. Cost accounting systems differ significantly between firms that manufacture products and merchandising firms that resell those products. Merchandising firms include both retailers, which sell the final product to the consumer, and wholesalers, which distribute the product to retailers. Service firms often have little or no inventory, so their costing systems are relatively simple. Costing systems are introduced here and covered in detail in the remaining chapters of Part One. First, we have to define product costs.

Product Costs and Period Costs

Product inventory for both manufacturing and merchandising firms is treated as an asset on their balance sheets. As long as the inventory has market value, it is considered an asset until the inventory is sold; then the cost of the inventory is transferred to the income statement as **cost of goods sold.** It is helpful in understanding product costs for a manufacturer to consider the value chain. The value chain of a manufacturer begins with the upstream activities of design, product development, and new product testing and then moves to manufacturing, followed by the downstream activities of distribution, sales, and customer service. The costs of the upstream and downstream activities are *not* product costs.

Cost of goods sold
is the cost of the product transferred to the income statement when inventory is sold.

Product costs for a manufacturing firm include *only* the costs necessary to complete the product at the manufacturing step in the value chain:

Product costs
for a manufacturing firm include *only* the costs necessary to complete the product: direct materials, direct labor, and factory overhead.

1. Direct materials. The materials used to manufacture the product, which become a physical part of it.
2. Direct labor. The labor used to manufacture the product.
3. Factory overhead. The indirect costs for materials, labor, and facilities used to support the manufacturing process.

Product costs for a merchandising firm include the cost to purchase the product plus the transportation costs paid by the retailer or wholesaler to get the product to the location from which it will be sold or distributed.

Period costs
are all nonproduct expenditures for managing the firm and selling the product.

All other costs for managing the firm and selling the product are not product costs. They are expensed in the period in which they are incurred; for that reason, they are also called **period costs.** Period costs (nonproduct costs) include the general, selling, and administrative costs that are necessary for the management of the company but are *not* involved directly or indirectly in the manufacturing process (or, for a retailer, in the purchase of the products for resale). Advertising costs, data processing costs, and executive and staff salaries are good examples of period costs. In a manufacturing or a merchandising firm, period costs are also sometimes referred to as *operating expenses* or *selling and administrative expenses.* In a service firm, these costs are

EXHIBIT 3.12
Furniture Manufacturing Costs: Variable/Fixed, Direct/Indirect, and Product/Period Costs

The manufacture of dining table sets is used to provide examples of costs for each cost concept: variable/fixed, direct/indirect, and product/period. The furniture manufacturer for these dining table sets has organized its manufacturing by product line: dining table sets, upholstered chairs, sofas, bedroom furniture, end tables, and outdoor furniture. Each product line has its own manufacturing team although much of the equipment in the plant is shared among product lines (e.g., multiple product lines use the table saws). The company owns its retail sales outlets, each of which offers all of the firm's products. The cost object in this illustration is the *product line* for dining table sets (*not* each dining set produced).

Variable/Fixed, Direct/Indirect, and Product/Period Costs for the Product Line, Dining Table Sets

	Product Cost		Period (Nonproduct) Cost
	Direct	**Indirect**	
Variable	Wood and fabric	Power for table saws	Sales commissions for sales
Fixed	Salary of manufacturing supervisor for dining table sets	Depreciation on table saws used for all product lines	Insurance and depreciation on company-owned sales outlets

Note: This illustration is based on the *cost object*, the product line for dining table *sets*. The examples would not change if we had chosen instead to have the cost object be *each set* manufactured except that the manufacturing supervisor's salary would no longer be a direct fixed product cost. It would become an *indirect* fixed product cost because the salary can be traced to the product line but not to each table set manufactured.

LEARNING OBJECTIVE 4
Demonstrate how costs flow through the accounts.

often referred to as *operating expenses*. Exhibit 3.12 summarizes the previous sections with an illustration showing examples of variable and fixed, direct and indirect, and product and period costs for a furniture manufacturer.

Manufacturing, Merchandising, and Service Costing

The cost flows in manufacturing, retail, and service firms are illustrated in Exhibits 3.13, 3.14, 3.15A, and 3.15B. The left-hand side of Exhibit 3.13 presents a graphic representation of the flows of costs for a manufacturing firm. The first step of the manufacturing process is to purchase materials. The second step involves adding the three cost elements—materials used, labor, and overhead—to work in process. In the third step, as production is completed, the production costs that have been accumulating in the Work-in-Process account are transferred to the Finished Goods Inventory account and from there to the Cost of Goods Sold account when the products are sold.

In the merchandising firm, shown on the right-hand side of Exhibit 3.13, the process is somewhat simpler. It purchases merchandise and places it in the Product Inventory account. When sold, it is transferred to the Cost of Goods Sold account. The merchandising and manufacturing firms in Exhibit 3.13 are shown side by side to emphasize the difference: The merchandising firm purchases inventory but the manufacturing firm manufactures inventory using materials, labor, and overhead.

Materials Inventory
is the cost of the supply of materials used in the manufacturing process or to provide the service.

Work-in-Process Inventory
contains all costs put into the manufacture of products that are started but not complete at the financial statement date.

Finished Goods Inventory
is the cost of goods that are ready for sale.

Manufacturing firms use three inventory accounts: (1) **Materials Inventory,** where the cost of the supply of materials used in the manufacturing process is kept; (2) **Work-in-Process Inventory,** which contains all costs put into the manufacture of products that are started but not complete at the financial statement date; and (3) **Finished Goods Inventory,** which holds the cost of goods that are ready for sale. Each account has its own beginning and ending balances.

An inventory formula relates the inventory accounts, as follows:

$$\text{Beginning Inventory} + \text{Cost added} = \text{Cost transferred out} + \text{Ending Inventory}$$

The terms *cost added* and *cost transferred out* have different meanings, depending on which inventory account is being considered:

Inventory Account	Cost Added	Cost Transferred Out
Materials Inventory	Purchases of materials	Cost of materials used in production
Work-in-Process Inventory	1. Cost of materials used	Cost of goods manufactured, for products completed this period
	2. Labor cost	
	3. Overhead cost	
Finished Goods Inventory	Costs of goods manufactured	Cost of goods sold

EXHIBIT 3.13
Cost Flows in Manufacturing and Merchandising Firms

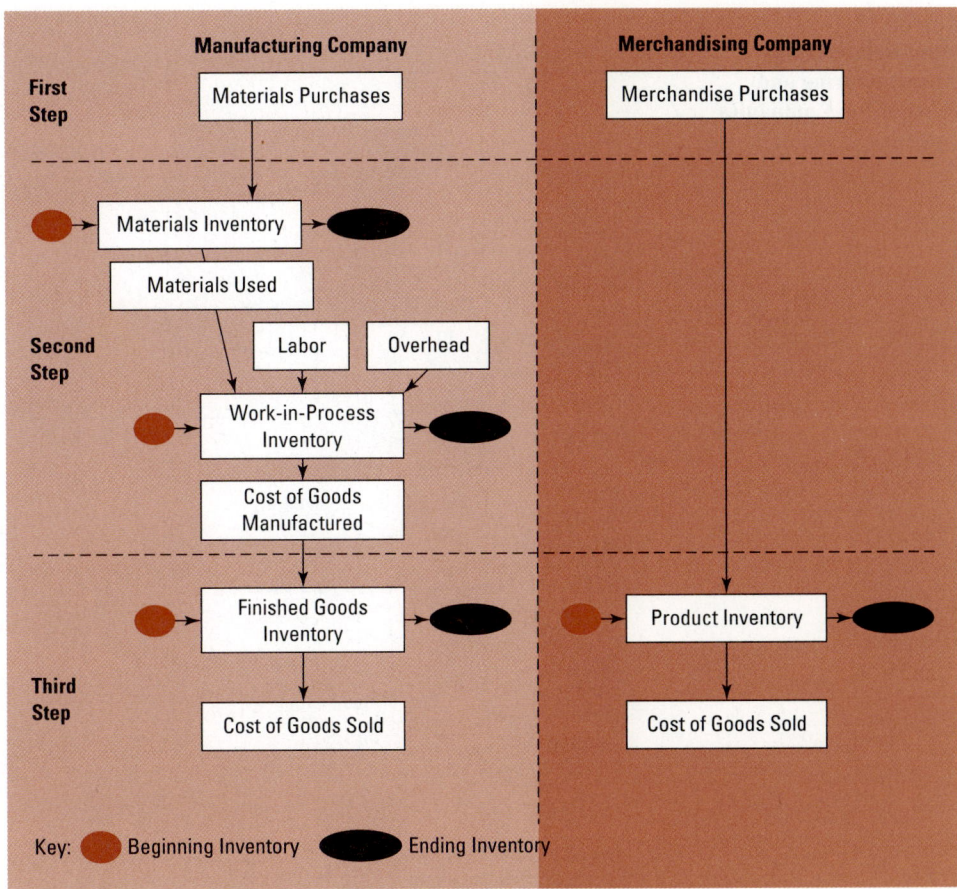

Key: ● Beginning Inventory ⬤ Ending Inventory

The inventory formula is a useful concept to show how materials, labor, and overhead costs flow into Work-in-Process Inventory, then into Finished Goods Inventory, and finally into Cost of Goods Sold. Exhibit 3.14 illustrates the effects of the cost flows on the accounts involved when the manufacturing firm converts materials into finished products and then sells them and when the merchandising firm sells merchandise inventory.

The illustration in Exhibit 3.14 shows the accounts for a manufacturing company that begins the period with $10 in Materials Inventory, $10 in Work-in-Process Inventory, and $20 in Finished Goods Inventory. During the period, it purchases $70 of materials, uses $75 of materials and $80 of direct labor, and spends $100 for factory overhead. The sum of materials used, labor, and overhead ($255 = $75 + $80 + $100) is called **total manufacturing cost** for the period. Also during the period, $215 of goods are completed and transferred from the Work-in-Process Inventory account to the Finished Goods Inventory account, and $210 of goods are sold. These events leave ending inventories of $5 in the materials account, $50 in the work-in-process account, and $25 in the finished goods account. The merchandising company purchased merchandise of $250 and had sales of $230, and its Merchandise Inventory account increases from $40 to $60.

Exhibit 3.15A shows how the accounting relationships are finally represented in the income statements for the two types of firms. Note that the manufacturing firm requires a two-part calculation for cost of goods sold: the first part combines the cost flows affecting the Work-in-Process Inventory account to determine the amount of **Cost of Goods Manufactured,** that is, the cost of the goods finished and transferred out of work in process during this period. The second part combines the cost flows for the Finished Goods Inventory account to determine the amount of the cost of the goods sold and operating income, assuming $50 of selling expense for the manufacturing firm and $40 of operating expense for the merchandising firm. Operating expenses for a merchandising company include all the nonproduct costs—facilities cost, advertising, staffing, and so on.

LEARNING OBJECTIVE 5

Prepare an income statement for both a manufacturing firm and a merchandising firm.

Total manufacturing cost
is the sum of materials used, labor, and overhead for the period.

Cost of Goods Manufactured
is the cost of goods finished and transferred out of the Work-in-Process Inventory account this period.

EXHIBIT 3.14
**Account Relationships
for Manufacturing and
Merchandising Companies**

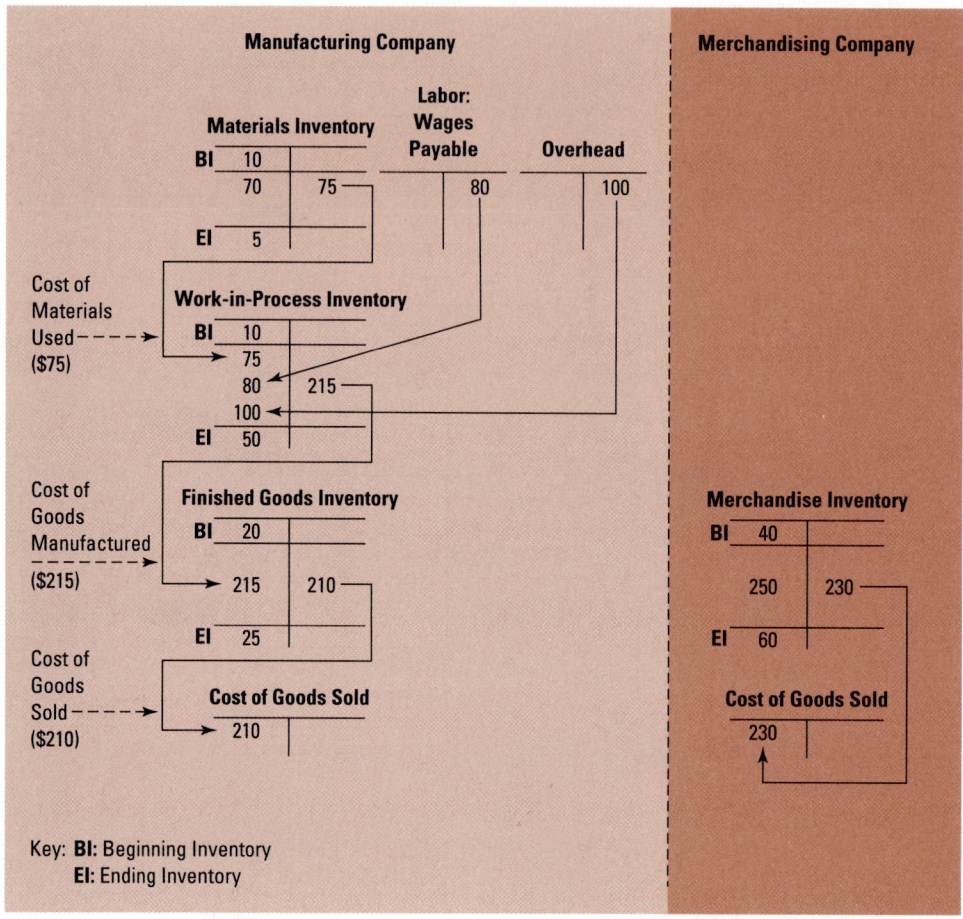

Exhibit 3.15B shows the relatively simple income statement for a service firm with $300 in sales, $10 in materials costs, $90 in labor costs, and $100 in other operating expenses for an operating income of $100. This provides an introduction to cost flows in the three types of firms. The process is shown in greater detail in Chapter 4.

Attributes of Cost Information

Accuracy

The experienced decision maker does not use accounting information without considering the potential for inaccuracy. Inaccurate data can mislead, resulting in potentially costly mistakes. A primary way to ensure accurate data for decision making is to design and monitor an effective system of internal accounting controls. The system of **internal accounting controls** is a set of policies and procedures that restrict and guide activities in the processing of financial data with the objective to prevent or detect errors and fraud. The emphasis on effective internal controls has increased significantly in recent years in response to Securities and Exchange Commission (SEC) requirements imposed by the Sarbanes-Oxley Act of 2002.

The system of **internal accounting controls** is a set of policies and procedures that restrict and guide activities in the processing of financial data with the objective of preventing or detecting errors and fraudulent acts.

Timeliness

Cost management information must be available to the decision maker in a timely manner to facilitate effective decision making. The cost of delay can be significant in many decisions, such as in filling rush orders that may be lost if the necessary information is not timely. The cost of identifying quality defects *early* in a manufacturing process can be far less than the cost of materials and labor wasted until the defect is detected later in the process.

EXHIBIT 3.15A   **Income Statements for Manufacturing and Merchandising Firms**

MANUFACTURING, INC.
Statement of Cost of Goods Manufactured
For the Year Ended December 31, 2010

(No need for a Cost of Goods Manufactured Statement for Merchandising Inc.)

Direct Materials		
Beginning Inventory	$ 10	
Purchases	70	
Direct Materials Available	80	
Less: Ending Direct Materials Inventory	5	
Direct Materials Used		$ 75
Direct Labor		80
Factory Overhead		100
Total Manufacturing Cost		255
Add: Beginning Work-in-Process Inventory		10
Total Manufacturing Cost to Account for		265
Less: Ending Work-in-Process Inventory		50
Cost of Goods Manufactured		$215

MANUFACTURING, INC.
Income Statement For the Year Ended December 31, 2010

Sales		$300
Cost of Goods Sold		
Beginning Finished Goods Inventory	$ 20	
Cost of Goods Manufactured	215	
Cost of Goods Available for Sale	235	
Less: Ending Finished Goods Inventory	25	210
Gross Margin		90
Selling and Administrative expenses		50
Operating Income		$ 40

MERCHANDISING, INC.
Income Statement For the Year Ended December 31, 2010

Sales		$300
Cost of Goods Sold		
Beginning Finished Goods Inventory	$ 40	
Purchases	250	
Cost of Goods Available for Sale	290	
Less: Ending Finished Goods Inventory	60	230
Gross Margin		$ 70
Operating expenses		40
Operating Income		$ 30

EXHIBIT 3.15B
Income Statement for a Service Firm

SERVICE, INC.
Income Statement
For the Year Ended December 31, 2010

Sales		$300
Operating Expenses		
Materials	$ 10	
Labor	90	
Other Operating Expenses	100	200
Operating Income		$100

Cost and Value of Cost Information

Thinking of cost management information as having a certain cost and value emphasizes that the management accountant is an information specialist, very much like other financial professionals, such as tax advisers, financial planners, and consultants. The management accountant provides an information service that has both a preparation cost and a value to the user. The preparation costs for cost management information should be controlled as should any other service provided within the firm. These preparation costs are likely influenced by the desired accuracy, timeliness, and level of aggregation; when increased accuracy, timeliness, and detail are desired, the preparation costs are higher.

Summary

There are several important concepts for the management accountant, which Chapter 3 presents in two groups: (1) cost objects, cost drivers, cost pools, and cost assignment and (2) product and service costing for the preparation of financial statements.

The first group of concepts includes the four types of cost drivers: activity-based, volume-based, structural, and executional. Activity-based cost drivers are at the detail level of operations: equipment setup, materials handling, and clerical or other tasks. In contrast, volume-based cost drivers are at the aggregate level: usually the number of units produced. Structural cost drivers involve plans and decisions having long-term effects; executional cost drivers have short-term decision frames. The most important volume-based concepts are variable costs, which change according to a change in the level of output, and fixed costs, which do not. Direct costs are defined as costs that can be traced directly to a cost object in contrast to indirect costs, which cannot.

The important concepts in product costing are product costs, which are the costs of direct materials, direct labor, and indirect manufacturing (called *overhead*) required for the product and production process. Nonproduct costs (also called *period costs*) are the selling, administrative, and other costs not involved in manufacturing. The inventory formula is used to determine the cost of materials used in production, the cost of goods manufactured, and the cost of goods sold for a given period.

Key Terms

allocation bases, 65	direct labor cost, 66	overhead, 67
average cost, 70	direct materials cost, 66	period costs, 73
conversion cost, 67	executional cost drivers, 73	prime costs, 67
cost, 64	factory overhead, 67	product costs, 73
cost allocation, 65	finished goods inventory, 74	relevant range, 68
cost assignment, 64	fixed cost, 69	step cost, 70
cost driver, 64	indirect cost, 64	structural cost drivers, 71
cost object, 64	indirect labor cost, 66	total manufacturing cost, 75
cost of goods manufactured, 75	indirect materials cost, 66	unit cost, 70
cost of goods sold, 73	internal accounting controls, 76	value stream, 64
cost pools, 64	materials inventory, 74	variable cost, 68
direct cost, 64	mixed cost, 69	work-in-process inventory, 74

Comments on Cost Management in Action

Cost per Bushel of Soybeans: United States and Brazil

The data is taken from an October 2001 Report of the Economic Research Service of the U.S. Department of Agriculture, based on 1998–1999 data. The report can be viewed at the following Web site: http://www.ers.usda.gov/Briefing/SoybeansOilcrops/pdf/SBProdExpCompOCS2001.pdf

1. What can you learn from this information about the cost competitiveness of the United States and Brazil in soybean production?

    Of particular value here is that the report distinguishes variable and fixed costs, which is not common in reports of this type. The distinction gives the reader an opportunity to better understand how cost production costs behave in the two countries. A wide number of observations are possible. In particular, we see the relatively high cost of land and equipment in the United States, partly balanced by relatively high labor and fertilizer and chemical costs in Brazil. Is the high labor cost a result of a substitution of labor for equipment or does it represent poorly trained or supervised workers? Similarly, does the high cost of chemicals and fertilizer in Brazil indicate that U.S. farmers have superior land use practices, or are the fertilizers and chemicals more expensive in Brazil for other reasons?

    While the figures clearly show that Brazil has a total cost advantage over the United States in the production of soybeans, other nonproduction, downstream costs are likely to be higher in Brazil— transportation (including fuel costs), marketing, and sales—because of its more remote location from world markets. Also, the United States has a cost advantage in variable costs, showing clearly the importance of the cost of land and farm equipment in the United States.

    Since the significance of the data is for understanding international competitiveness in global soybean production, it is also important to note that the above analysis does not include data on fluctuations in currency exchange rates, import restrictions, government subsidies, taxes, and other factors that are critical in global trade. Some of the strongest controversies among the World Trade Organization (WTO) countries at this time are the restrictions and subsidies involved in agricultural trade.

2. Critically evaluate the cost information.

A number of potential questions arise about the way the data is collected and presented. Here are some ideas to start with. First, what about the size of the farm: should this affect the fixed cost-per-acre calculations, since fixed costs are driven in part by the number of acres farmed but also by the fact that certain pieces of equipment are necessary for a farm of any size. Farm equipment might be more of a step cost than a fixed cost. If this is the case, the relatively low equipment cost per acre might simply be due to the fact that farm sizes are larger in Brazil. Are the fixed costs computed annually or monthly? And if land can be rented by the acre, is it not a variable cost?

Self-Study Problem
(For solution, please turn to the end of the chapter.)

The following data pertain to Spartan Products Company:

Sales revenue	$1,000,000
Direct materials inventory, Jan. 1, 2010	20,000
Direct labor—Wages	350,000
Depreciation expense—Plant and equipment	80,000
Indirect labor—Wages	5,000
Heat, light, and power—Plant	12,000
Supervisor's salary—Plant	40,000
Finished goods inventory, Jan. 1, 2010	35,000
Work-in-Process inventory, Dec. 31, 2010	25,000
Supplies—Administrative office	6,000
Property taxes—Plant	13,000
Finished goods inventory, Dec. 31, 2010	40,000
Direct materials inventory, Dec. 31, 2010	30,000
Sales representatives' salaries	190,000
Work-in-Process inventory, Jan. 1, 2010	35,000
Direct materials purchases	100,000
Supplies—Plant	4,000
Depreciation—Administrative office	30,000

Required   Prepare a statement of cost of goods manufactured and an income statement for Spartan Products Company for the year ended December 31, 2010, similar to the one in Exhibit 3.15A.

Questions

3-1   What is the difference between cost allocation and cost assignment?

3-2   Distinguish between direct and indirect costs and give several examples of each.

3-3   Are all direct costs variable? Explain.

3-4   Are all fixed costs indirect? Explain.

3-5   Define *cost driver.*

3-6   What is the difference between variable and fixed costs?

3-7   Explain step costs and give an example.

3-8   Define *relevant range* and explain its use.

3-9   What is a conversion cost? What are prime costs?

3-10   Why might the term *average cost* be misleading?

3-11   How do total variable costs, total fixed costs, average variable costs, and average fixed costs react to changes in the cost driver?

3-12   What does the term *unit cost* mean?

3-13   Distinguish between product costs and period costs.

3-14   Explain the difference between cost of goods sold and cost of goods manufactured.

3-15   What are the three types of inventory in a manufacturing firm?

3-16   Cost management information should be timely and accurate. Which of these attributes is most important? Why?

3-17   Provide an example of an executional cost driver.

3-18   Provide an example of a structural cost driver.

3-19   Provide an example of an indirect materials cost.

3-20   Provide an example of an indirect labor cost.

Brief Exercises

3-21 Identify what are likely to be variable costs for an airline such as Southwest Air. Also, what are the fixed costs likely to be?

3-22 Identify what are likely to be variable costs for a discount retailer such as Target. Also, what are the fixed costs likely to be?

3-23 Identify what are likely to be variable costs for a movie theater. Also, what are the fixed costs likely to be?

3-24 Identify what are likely to be variable costs for a brewery such as Molson or Budweiser. Also, what are the fixed costs likely to be?

3-25 Identify what variable costs are likely to be for a company that provides personal trainers. The personal trainers are paid a small salary plus a commission for each lesson. Also, what are the company's fixed costs?

3-26 Womble Inc has beginning inventory of $200 and an ending inventory of $400 for a given period in which it purchased $13,400 of materials. What is the dollar amount of materials used in this period?

3-27 Jordan Sports, Inc has labor costs and overhead totaling $2.6 million during a given period. The company purchased $10.5 million of materials during the period and used $10 million of this amount. What is the amount of total manufacturing cost for the period?

3-28 Lucas Diving Supplies Company, in its first year of business, had labor costs of $66,000, overhead costs of $98,000, materials purchases of $22,000, and ending materials and work-in-process inventories of $1,000 and $2,000 respectively. What is the amount of cost of goods manufactured in the first year of operations?

3-29 If a merchandising company has a beginning finished goods inventory of $400,000 and a finished goods ending inventory of $200,000, and the company purchased $1,600,000 of inventory during the month, what is the company's cost of goods sold?

3-30 The Walden Manufacturing Corp. has interest expense of $4,000, factory supplies of $1,000, indirect labor of $6,000, direct materials of $16,000, advertising expense of $2,500, office expense of $14,000, and direct labor of $20,000. What is the total period cost?

Exercises

3-31 **Classification of Costs** The following costs were taken from the accounting records of the Barnwell Manufacturing Company:
1. State income taxes
2. Insurance on the manufacturing facilities
3. Supplies used in manufacturing
4. Wages for employees in the assembly department
5. Wages for employees who deliver the product
6. Interest on notes payable
7. Materials used in the production process
8. Rent for the sales outlet in Sacramento
9. Electricity for manufacturing equipment
10. Depreciation expense on delivery trucks
11. Wages for the sales staff
12. Factory supervisors' salaries
13. Company president's salary
14. Advertising expense

Required Classify each item as either a product cost or a period cost. Also, classify all product costs as direct or indirect, assuming that the cost object is each unit of product manufactured.

3-32 **Classification of Costs** Following is a list of costs from Oakland Company, a furniture manufacturer:
1. Wood used in chairs
2. Salaries of inspectors
3. Lubricant used in machinery
4. Factory rent
5. Wages of assembly workers
6. Factory workers' compensation insurance
7. Sandpaper

8. Fabric used for upholstery
9. Property taxes on manufacturing plant
10. Depreciation on machinery

Required Classify each cost as direct or indirect assuming that the cost object is each item manufactured. Also indicate whether each cost is a variable or fixed cost.

3-33 Classification of Costs The following is a list of costs from the accounting records of Sunshine Pool Management, Inc. Each of Sunshine's 77 customers owns a pool. Sunshine maintains each customer's pool by providing supplies, cleaning, and repairs.

1. Lifesaving supplies
2. Salaries of Sunshine's managers
3. Pool chemicals
4. Sunshine's office rental expense
5. Wages of lifeguards
6. Workers' compensation insurance
7. Training for lifeguards
8. pH testing supplies
9. Office expense, including bookkeeping and clerical
10. Depreciation on cleaning and testing equipment

Required Classify each item as direct or indirect assuming that the cost objects are each of 77 pools.

3-34 Activity Levels and Cost Drivers Tartan Manufacturing Company produces four lines of high-quality lighting fixtures in a single manufacturing plant. Products are built to specific customer specifications. All products are made-to-order. Management of the plant lists the following as the key activities at the plant:

a. Product design
b. Production scheduling
c. Cost of purchasing department
d. Receipt and inspection of materials
e. Machine set-ups
f. Product inspection, done for each product
g. Plant security
h. Customer credit check
i. Machine operation
j. Machine maintenance

Required Identify a cost object and a cost driver for each activity.

3-35 Application of the Direct Cost Concept in the Fashion Industry Jane Wilson is the production manager for a company that produces high-fashion designer clothing for women. The product is made in small batches that are presold to high-end retailers, based on specific orders. The product is completed in batches, which consist of a single item of clothing being made for a single or small number of retail customers. In effect, Jane manages the flow of small batches of product through the company's design/production shop in New York. The materials and labor for each batch are purchased and scheduled well in advance of the time of production. The materials are unique to the job, and the employees assigned to the job will work on it till the job is done. The company has found that dedicating specific employees to each batch improves employee satisfaction, and most important, product quality.

Required Apply what you have just learned about the direct cost concept and explain its specific application with regard to this unique firm.

3-36 Manufacturing Direct Labor: Fixed or Variable?

To retain skilled employees instead of letting them go when demand falls, Lincoln Electric trains employees for other tasks in the company. The Cleveland-based manufacturer of welding and cutting parts has integrated the approach in all its operations, so that it can guarantee employment for all employees who have been with the company for three or more years. This policy has worked for 60 years.

Other companies such as Nestle and Apex Precision Technology accomplish the same goal of keeping their employees as demand fluctuates by using part-time arrangements with the employees.

Required   Discuss whether manufacturing labor should be considered a fixed or a variable cost at these companies.

3-37 Complexity of Operations and the Effect on Cost   In the mid-1990s, a large consumer goods manufacturer moved its customer-based department and specialty stores to mass merchandising in a a variety of retail stores, large and small. The strategic change required it to increase significantly the complexity of its operations—the number of products, prices, discounts, patterns, colors, and sizes. After noticing the firm's expense beginning to rise, the company hired a consultant to study the firm's cost structure. The findings:

- As many as 10 different vendors provided certain purchased items.
- Of the firm's customers after the strategic shift, 98% were responsible for only 7% of total sales volume.
- The wide variety of prices and discounts and promotional programs added complexity to the accounts receivable collection process because of increased disputes over pricing and customer balances.
- Seventy-five percent of the company sales involved products with five or more color combinations.
- Customer demands for fast delivery of new orders had caused a shift in manufacturing to smaller batch sizes and more frequent equipment setups. Thus, total setup-related costs increased.

Required   What would you advise the company to do?

3-38 Average and Total Costs   The Accounting Students Association wants to have a Christmas party for its members. The cost of renting space is $1,500, and the cost of refreshments will be $12 per person.

Required
1. What is the total cost if 100 people attend? What is the average cost?
2. What is the total cost if 200 people attend? What is the average cost?
3. Explain why average total cost differs with changes in total attendance.

3-39 Classification of Costs   Fran McPhair Dance Studios is a chain of 45 wholly owned dance studios that offer private lessons in ballroom dancing. The studios are located in various cities throughout the southern and southeastern states. McPhair offers a set of 12 private lessons; students may pay for the lessons one at a time, but each student is required to enroll for at least a 12-lesson plan. The 20-, 40-, and 100-lesson plans offer savings. Each dance instructor is paid a small salary plus a commission based on the number of dance lessons provided.

Required
1. McPhair's owner is interested in a strategic analysis of the business. The owner wants to understand why overall profitability has declined slightly in the most recent year while other studios in the area seem to be doing well. What is the proper cost object to begin this analysis? Explain your choice.
2. For each of the cost elements determine the cost classification from the following list for the cost object you chose in requirement 1. (In some cases, two or more classifications may apply.)

Cost Elements

1. Each dancing instructor's salary.
2. Manager's salary.
3. Music tapes used in instruction.
4. Utilities for the studio.
5. Part-time studio receptionist.
6. Planning and development materials sent from the home office.
7. Free lessons given by each studio as a promotion.
8. Regional TV and radio advertisements placed several times a year.

Cost Classifications

a. Direct
b. Indirect
c. Variable
d. Fixed

e. Controllable by studio manager

f. Uncontrollable by studio manager

3-40 **Activities and Cost Drivers in a Hospital**   Greenbelt Hospital has the following activities in its value chain of providing service to each inpatient admission:

1. Schedule patient.
2. Verify insurance.
3. Admit patient.
4. Prepare patient's room.
5. Review doctor's report.
6. Feed patient.
7. Order tests.
8. Move to/from laboratory.
9. Administer lab tests.
10. Order pharmaceuticals.
11. Complete patient report.
12. Check patient's vital signs.
13. Prepare patient for operation.
14. Move to/from operating room.
15. Operate.
16. Collect charges.
17. Discharge patient.
18. Bill insurance.

Required   Assume that the cost object is the individual patient. Determine the appropriate cost driver(s) for each activity.

3-41 **Fixed, Variable, and Mixed Costs**   Adams Manufacturing's five manufacturing departments had the following operating and cost information for the two most recent months of activity:

	May	June
Units produced	10,000	20,000
Costs in each department		
Department A	$10,000	$10,000
Department B	25,000	50,000
Department C	35,000	45,000
Department D	18,000	64,000
Department E	22,000	44,000

Required   Identify whether the cost in each department is fixed, variable, or mixed.

3-42 **Fixed, Variable, and Mixed Costs**   Habib Manufacturing has five manufacturing departments and operating and cost information for the most recent two months of activity.

	April	May
Units produced	4,000	6,000
Costs in each department:		
Department 1	$16,000	$18,000
Department 2	16,000	26,000
Department 3	20,000	20,000
Department 4	32,000	48,000
Department 5	16,000	24,000

Required   Identify whether the cost in each department is fixed, variable, or mixed.

3-43 **Strategy; Variable and Fixed Costs**

Zipcar (www.zipcar.com) is a car-sharing club founded in Cambridge, MA, in 1999. The club members pay an annual fee and then have the opportunity to rent a small car (usually a subcompact; the models include the Toyota Prius) for a fixed hourly rate. Zipcar is located largely in select metropolitan areas such as Boston, San Francisco, and Washington D.C. Members, called "Zipsters" make reservations for a car on the Zipcar Web site, and then use an access card to open the vehicle. The vehicle has a "home base" parking spot where the driver picks up and returns the vehicle. The club grew by 80 percent in 2007 and has great plans for the future, subject to potential competition from the existing car rental companies such as Hertz and Enterprise.

Required

1. What are the fixed and variable costs for Zipcar?
2. What are some of the competitive advantages and challenges of the Zipcar concept?

3-44 Interpreting Average Cost Concern for gas emissions and depletion of nonrenewable resources has caused environmentalists and others to push for higher fuel-efficiency standards for new cars. The current Corporate Automotive Fuel Efficiency (CAFE) standards require automakers to produce an overall fuel efficiency of 26.2 miles per gallon for all autos produced. Currently the U.S. government supports the development of hybrid autos that combine gas and electric power as the solution to the problem. Others propose simply raising the CAFE standards for auto manufacturers. To study the issue, the American Council for an Energy-Efficient Economy (ACEEE) conducted research to determine the cost for raising fuel efficiency for the different proposals. Their findings are as follows:

Option to reduce emissions and provide better fuel economy	Fuel Efficiency (mpg)	Cost for each Gallon of Gas Saved
Current mileage standards	26.2	—
Moderate increase in CAFE	40.8	$0.57
Significant increase in CAFE	45.8	$0.60
Partial hybrid (15% of power from electricity)	52.6	$1.38
Full hybrid (40% of power from electricity)	59.3	$1.80

The increase in fuel economy required by higher CAFE standards would require automakers to use conventional technology to improve engines and transmissions. The hybrid vehicles require newer technology and electric motors.

Required Give a brief critical review of the ACEEE's research results. What questions would you have for the researchers who presented these results?

3-45 Interpreting Average Cost Recently the American Institute of Certified Public Accountants (AICPA) and the Hackett Group, a consulting firm, partnered to study the trends in the nature and amount spent on the accounting function in corporations. A key finding was that the world's best accounting departments were able to function effectively at relatively low cost; these department's total costs were only about 1 percent of their firm's total revenues. In contrast, less efficient accounting departments required on the average 1.4 percent of total revenue, 40 percent higher. The world-class accounting departments were also faster in preparing regular financial reports (less than two days for the best departments, compared to five to eight days for the others). The study also found that larger firms spent less on accounting:

Manufacturing Firms	Finance Cost as a Percent of Total Revenue
Firms with less than $1 billion in revenues	1.6%
$1 billion to $5 billion	1.4%
More than $5 billion	1%
Service Firms	
Less than $1 billion in revenues	2.1%
More than $1 billion	1.6%

Required Give a brief critical review of these research results. What questions would you have for the researchers who presented these results?

3-46 Classification of Costs; Customer Profitability

Pet Partner is a small company that provides pet boarding, grooming, and minor medical services for dogs and cats. The company has been successful for its first three years because of its careful attention to customer expectations. The staff knows the names of each customer's pet, their food preferences, and their individual preferences. The company is now studying the profitability of the business, using each customer as a cost object. In the business, there are a number of costs:

1. Staff salaries.
2. Rent on office and work space used by the company.

3. Licenses and fees.

4. Supplies; grooming supplies and related items.

5. Medications.

6. Legal fees.

7. Accounting services provided part time by practicing accountant.

8. Pet food.

9. Utilities for office and work space.

10. Fire insurance for office and work space and its contents.

11. Liability insurance for the company business.

Required

1. For each cost category, indicate whether it is direct or indirect relative to the company's cost object.

2. Describe how Pet Partner could use the information in (1) to assess the profitability of each customer.

3-47 Classification of Costs

Papa's Pizza Heaven serves take-out pizza from three locations in Columbus, Maryland. Papa's considers each pizza delivered (even if the order is for two or more pizzas) as the cost object for the company. The company incurs the following costs:

1. Food costs including pizza dough, olive oil, tomato sauce, mozzarella cheese, mushrooms, bell peppers, Italian sausage, chopped fresh basil, pesto, pepperoni, onions, and ham.

2. Salaries for drivers.

3. Salaries for telephone operators.

4. Salaries for cooks.

5. Insurance for drivers.

6. Utilities.

7. Advertising.

8. Discount coupons offered in local newspapers to attract customers.

9. Food handling licenses, inspections, and fees.

10. Accounting and payroll services.

11. Cooking supplies.

12. Cleaning supplies.

13. Mortgage payments on the three locations owned by Papa's Pizza Heaven.

14. Insurance on facilities.

Required

1. For each cost item, indicate whether it is fixed or variable relative to the cost object.

2. For each cost item, indicate whether it is a product or a period cost.

3-48 Classification of Costs

Speedy Auto Service provides oil changes and minor repairs from 12 different locations in Wadesborough, Pennsylvania. The technicians who replace the oil and parts (mostly windshield wipers, air filters, and the like) are paid for an eight-hour day, irrespective of the number of customers in a give day. The cost object for Speedy is each customer visit. The cost elements for Speedy include:

1. Technicians who change the oil and replace parts.

2. Parts.

3. Oil.

4. Supplies, rags, cleanup equipment.

5. Tools.

6. Rental of each location.

7. Advertising.

8. Utilities.

9. Licenses and fees.

10. Employee training; 10 hours at time of hiring and 2 hours per month thereafter.

11. Security service to watch the locations during closing hours.

12. Online software system for managing sales, costs, and financial reports including tax returns and employee payroll.

Required

1. For each cost item, indicate whether it is fixed or variable relative to the cost object.

2. For each cost item, indicate whether it is a product or a period cost.

3-49 Cost of Goods Manufactured   The following information pertains to the Petrie Company:

Prime costs	$180,000
Conversion costs	215,000
Direct materials used	95,000
Beginning work in process	75,000
Ending work in process	65,000

Required   Determine the cost of goods manufactured.

Problems

3-50 Executional Cost Drivers, Internet Retailer   Assume that you are a consultant for a start-up Internet retailer, Bikes.com, which provides a variety of bicycle parts and accessories in a convenient and effective customer service approach. The firm operates from an office building and nearby warehouse located in Danville, Virginia. Currently, the firm has 10 permanent administrative staff, 6 customer service representatives who respond to customer inquiries, and 12 employees who pick, pack, and ship customer orders. All orders are placed over the firm's Web site. An 800 telephone number is available for customer service. The firm's sales increased at about 20 percent per year in the last two years, a decline from the 50 percent rate in its first three years of operation. Management is concerned that the decline will delay the firm's first expected profit, which had been projected to occur in the next two years. The firm is privately held and has been financed with a combination of bank loans, personal investments of top managers, and venture capital funding.

Required   What specific executional cost drivers are important in this business? How should the firm use them to improve its sales rate?

3-51 Structural Cost Drivers

    Case A.   Food Fare is a small chain of restaurants that has developed a loyal customer base by providing fast-food items with more choices (e.g., how the hamburger should be cooked; self-serve toppings) and a more comfortable atmosphere. The menu has a small number of popular items, including several different hamburgers, grilled chicken sandwiches, and salads. Recently, to broaden its appeal, Food Fare added barbecue, seafood, and steak to its menu.

    Case B.   Gilman Heating and Air Conditioning, Inc., provides a broad range of services to commercial and residential customers, including installation and repair of several different brands of heating and air conditioning systems. Gilman has a fleet of 28 trucks, each operated by one or more service technicians, depending on the size of a job. A recurrent problem for Gilman has been coordinating the service teams during the day to determine the status of a job and the need for parts not kept in the service vehicle as well as to identify which team to send on emergency calls. Gilman's service area is spread over an urban/rural area of approximately 20 square miles. The company has developed cost and price sheets so that the service technicians accurately and consistently price the service work they perform.

Required   For each case, identify the important structural cost drivers for the company and the related strategic issues that it should address to be competitive.

3-52 Cost of Goods Manufactured and Sold   Jordan Company produces women's clothing. During 2010, the company incurred the following costs:

Factory rent	$425,000
Direct labor	325,000
Utilities—Factory	35,000
Purchases of direct materials	625,000
Indirect materials	70,000
Indirect labor	80,000

Inventories for the year were as follows:

	January 1	December 31
Direct materials	$ 30,000	$50,000
Work in process	60,000	25,000
Finished goods	115,000	95,000

Required

1. Prepare a statement of cost of goods manufactured.
2. Calculate cost of goods sold.

3-53 **Cost of Goods Manufactured**   The following data pertain to Winstead Company for the year ended December 31, 2010:

	December 31, 2009	December 31, 2010
Purchases of direct materials		$120,000
Direct labor		85,000
Indirect labor		25,000
Factory insurance		12,000
Depreciation—Factory		65,000
Repairs and maintenance—Factory		15,000
Marketing expenses		110,000
General and administrative expenses		55,000
Direct materials inventory	$25,000	35,000
Work-in-process inventory	33,000	42,000
Finished goods inventory	18,000	20,000

Sales in 2010 were $650,000.

Required   Prepare a schedule of cost of goods manufactured and an income statement for 2010 for Winstead Company similar to those in Exhibit 3.15a.

3-54 **Cost of Goods Manufactured, Income Statement**   Consider the following information for Household Furnishings, Inc. for the year ended December 31, 2010:

Depreciation expense—Administrative office	$ 33,000
Depreciation expense—Plant and equipment	88,000
Direct labor—Wages	487,000
Direct materials inventory, Dec. 31, 2010	25,000
Direct materials inventory, Jan. 1, 2010	18,000
Direct materials purchases	155,000
Finished goods inventory, Dec. 31, 2010	38,000
Finished goods inventory, Jan. 1, 2010	15,000
Heat, light, & power—Plant	44,000
Indirect labor	25,000
Property taxes—Plant	34,000
Sales representatives' salaries	145,000
Sales revenue	1,500,000
Factory supervisor's salary	66,000
Supplies—Administrative office	16,000
Supplies—Plant	29,000
Work-in-Process inventory, Dec. 31, 2010	9,000
Work-in-Process inventory, Jan. 1, 2010	23,000

Required   Prepare a statement of cost of goods manufactured and an income statement for Household Furnishings for the year ended December 31, 2010, similar to the one in Exhibit 3.15A.

3-55 **Cost of Goods Manufactured; Income Statement**   Consider the following information for Blue Water Equipment, Inc., a manufacturer of sailboat rigging, blocks, and cordage.

Advertising expenses	$ 111,000
Depreciation expense—admin. office	88,000
Depreciation expense—plant and equip.	299,000
Depreciation expense—delivery trucks	55,000
Direct materials inventory, beginning	22,000
Direct materials inventory, ending	16,000
Direct materials purchases	348,000
Direct labor	455,000
Indirect labor	329,000
Finished goods inventory, beginning	66,000
Finished goods inventory, ending	42,000
Insurance on plant	44,000
Heat and light for plant	23,000
Repairs on plant building	34,000
Supervisor's salary—plant	85,000
Supplies—plant	118,000
Supplies—administrative office	42,000
Work-in-process inventory, beginning	14,000
Work-in-process inventory, ending	11,000
Sales representatives' salaries	216,000
Sales revenue	2,312,000

Required Prepare a statement of cost of goods manufactured and an income statement for Blue Water Equipment, Inc. for the year ended December 31, 2010.

3-56 **Cost of Goods Manufactured, Calculating Unknowns** The following information was taken from the accounting records of Tomek Manufacturing Company. Unfortunately, some of the data were destroyed by a computer malfunction.

	Case A	Case B
Sales	$150,000	$?
Finished goods inventory, Jan. 1, 2010	35,000	28,000
Finished goods inventory, Dec. 31, 2010	40,000	?
Cost of goods sold	?	61,000
Gross margin	25,000	23,000
Selling and administrative expenses	?	1,000
Operating income	10,000	22,000
Work in process, Jan. 1, 2010	?	14,000
Direct material used	18,000	8,000
Direct labor	35,000	9,000
Factory overhead	50,000	?
Total manufacturing costs	?	35,000
Work in process, Dec. 31, 2010	22,000	?
Cost of goods manufactured	?	45,000

Required Calculate the unknowns indicated by question marks.

3-57 **Cost of Goods Manufactured, Income Statement** Norton Industries, a manufacturer of cable for the heavy construction industry, closes its books and prepares financial statements at the end of each month. The statement of cost of goods sold for April 2010 follows:

NORTON INDUSTRIES
Statement of Cost of Goods Sold
For the Month Ended April 30, 2010
($000 omitted)

Inventory of finished goods, March 31	$ 50
Cost of goods manufactured	790
Cost of goods available for sale	$840
Less inventory of finished goods, April 30	247
Cost of goods sold	$593

Additional Information

- Of the utilities, 80 percent relates to manufacturing the cable; the remaining 20 percent relates to the sales and administrative functions.
- All rent is for the office building.
- Property taxes are assessed on the manufacturing plant.
- Of the insurance, 60 percent is related to manufacturing the cable; the remaining 40 percent is related to the sales and administrative functions.
- Depreciation expense includes the following:

Manufacturing plant	$20,000
Manufacturing equipment	30,000
Office equipment	4,000
	$54,000

- The company manufactured 7,825 tons of cable during May 2010.
- The inventory balances at May 31, 2010, follow:
  - Direct materials inventory $23,000
  - Work-in-process inventory $220,000
  - Finished goods inventory $175,000

NORTON INDUSTRIES
Preclosing Account Balances
May 31, 2010
($000 omitted)

Cash and marketable securities	$ 54
Accounts and notes receivable	210
Direct materials inventory (4/30/2010)	28
Work-in-process inventory (4/30/2010)	150
Finished goods inventory (4/30/2010)	247
Property, plant, and equipment (net)	1,140
Accounts, notes, and taxes payable	70
Bonds payable	600
Paid-in capital	100
Retained earnings	930
Sales	1,488
Sales discounts	20
Other revenue	2
Purchases of direct materials	510
Direct labor	260
Indirect factory labor	90
Office salaries	122
Sales salaries	42
Utilities	135
Rent	9
Property tax	60
Insurance	20
Depreciation	54
Interest expense	6
Freight-in for materials purchases	15

Required   Based on Exhibit 3.15A, prepare the following:

1. Statement of cost of goods manufactured for Norton Industries for May 2010.
2. Income statement for Norton Industries for May 2010.

(CMA Adapted)

Solution to Self-Study Problem

SPARTAN PRODUCTS COMPANY
Statement of Cost of Goods Manufactured
For the Year Ended December 31, 2010

Direct materials		
Direct materials inventory, Jan. 1, 2010	$ 20,000	
Purchases of direct materials	100,000	
Total direct materials available	$120,000	
Less: Direct materials inventory, Dec. 31, 2010	30,000	
Direct materials used		$ 90,000
Direct labor		350,000
Factory overhead		
Heat, light, and power—Plant	12,000	
Supplies—Plant	4,000	
Property taxes—Plant	13,000	
Depreciation expense—Plant and equipment	80,000	
Indirect labor	5,000	
Supervisor's salary—Plant	40,000	
Total factory overhead		154,000
Total manufacturing costs		$594,000
Add: Beginning work-in-process inventory, Jan. 1, 2010		35,000
Total manufacturing costs to account for		$629,000
Less: Ending work-in-process, Dec. 31, 2010		25,000
Cost of goods manufactured		$604,000

SPARTAN PRODUCTS COMPANY
Income Statement
For the Year Ended December 31, 2010

Sales revenue		$1,000,000
Cost of goods sold		
Finished goods inventory, Jan. 1, 2010	$ 35,000	
Cost of goods manufactured	604,000	
Total goods available for sale	$639,000	
Finished goods inventory, Dec. 31, 2010	40,000	
Cost of goods sold		599,000
Gross margin		$ 401,000
Selling and administrative expenses		
Sales representatives' salaries	190,000	
Supplies—Administrative office	6,000	
Depreciation expense—Administrative office	30,000	
Total selling and administrative expenses		226,000
Operating income		$ 175,000

CHAPTER FOUR

Job Costing

After studying this chapter, you should be able to . . .

1. Explain the types of costing systems
2. Explain the strategic role of costing
3. Explain the flow of costs in a job costing system
4. Explain the application of factory overhead costs in a job costing system
5. Calculate underapplied and overapplied overhead and show how it is accounted for
6. Apply job costing in service industries
7. Explain an operation costing system

Determining the accurate cost of a product or service plays a critical role in the success of firms in most industries. For example, Smith Fabrication Inc. of Kent, Washington (www.smithfabinc. com), uses a product costing system to estimate costs and to charge customers for the sheet metal products it provides to other manufacturers in the aviation, computer, telecom, and medical products industries. The product costing method it uses provides a competitive edge by providing accurate cost information in a form that customers can easily understand. Similarly, Hammert's Iron Works of St. Louis, Missouri (http://www.hammertsiron.com) uses job costing with a real-time labor and materials reporting system to provide the ability to account for materials and labor accurately at any point in the production process—important for managing the process of the job and for improving customer service. What these and many companies have found is that a simple yet accurate method for determining product cost is crucial to their competitive success. Another example is home construction and remodeling, where product costing plays a key role in cost estimating and pricing the work (www.housingzone.com).

Smith Fabrication, Hammert's Iron Works, and most home builders use a type of product costing called *job costing* which is explained in this chapter.

The following section explains all the different choices a management accountant must make in choosing a cost system, with job costing as one of the possibilities.

Costing Systems

Costing
is the process of accumulating, classifying, and assigning direct materials, direct labor, and factory overhead costs to products, services or projects.

LEARNING OBJECTIVE 1

Explain the types of costing systems.

Costing is the process of accumulating, classifying, and assigning direct materials, direct labor, and factory overhead costs to products, services, or projects.

In developing the particular costing system to fit a specific firm, the management accountant must make three choices, one for each of the three following characteristics of costing methods: (1) the cost accumulation method—job costing, process costing or joint costing; (2) the cost measurement method—actual, normal, or standard costing; and (3) the overhead assignment method—volume-based or activity-based. Each product costing system will reflect these three choices. For example, a company may choose to use job costing, normal costing, and activity-based costing, because that combination of choices best fits the firm's operations and strategic goals. Another firm might be better served by a product costing system based on process cost, standard cost, and volume-based costing.

The choice of a particular system depends on the nature of the industry and the product or service, the firm's strategy and management information needs, and the costs and benefits of acquiring, designing, modifying, and operating a particular system. Here are the three choices.

Cost Accumulation: Job or Process Costing?

Costs can be accumulated by tracing costs to a specific product or service, or by accumulating costs at the department level and then allocating these costs from the departments to the products or services. The first type is called *job costing* and the latter is *process costing*. In a job costing system the jobs consist of individual products or batches of products or services. A job costing system is appropriate when most costs incurred for the job can be readily identified with a specific product, batch of product, customer order, contract, or project. Types of companies that use job costing include those in construction, printing, special equipment manufacturing, shipbuilding, custom furniture manufacturing, professional services, medical services, advertising agencies, and others. Examples of companies using job costing systems include FedEx (fedex.com), Paramount Pictures (www.paramount.com), Jiffy Lube International (www.jiffylube.com), Accenture (www.accenture.com), Kaiser Permanente (www.kaiserpermanente.org), and Hyatt Corporation (www.hyatt.com). In job costing the job might consist of a single product or multiple products in a batch. For example, a batch might consist of 20 units of a product planned for distribution to a warehouse for future sale. Alternatively, a job could consist of the quantity of products ordered by a particular customer. The first approach is often called the *push* method because it fills the warehouse, while the latter is called the *pull* method because it is based on direct customer demand. The significance of the difference between these methods will be a recurring topic in later chapters.

In contrast, process costing is likely to be found in a firm that produces one or a few homogenous products or services. These firms often have continuous mass production. In this case, it is economically impractical to trace most costs to individual products. Industries where process costing is common include the chemical industry, bottling companies, plastics, food products, and paper products. Examples of companies using process costing systems include Shell Oil Co. (www.shell.com), Coca-Cola (www.coca-cola.com), International Paper (www.internationalpaper.com), and Kimberly-Clark (www.kimberly-clark.com). This chapter describes job costing systems and operation costing, a variation of job costing. Chapter 6 explains process costing systems, and Chapter 7 covers a variation of process costing in which there is joint processing of multiple products.

Cost Measurement: Actual, Normal, or Standard Costing?

Costs in either a job or process costing system can be measured in their actual, normal, or standard amount. An *actual costing system* uses actual costs incurred for all product costs including direct materials, direct labor, and factory overhead. Actual costing systems are rarely used because they can produce unit product costs that fluctuate significantly, causing potential errors in pricing, adding/dropping product lines, and in performance evaluations. Also, most actual factory overhead costs are known only at or after the end of the period rather than at the completion of the batch of products. Thus, actual costing systems cannot provide accurate unit product cost information on a timely basis.

A *normal costing system* uses actual costs for direct materials and direct labor and normal costs for factory overhead. Normal costing involves estimating a portion of overhead to be assigned to each product as it is produced. A normal costing system provides a timely estimate of the cost of producing each product or job.

A *standard costing system* uses standard costs and quantities for all three types of manufacturing costs: direct materials, direct labor, and factory overhead. Standard costs are expected costs the firm should attain. Standard costing systems provide a basis for cost control, performance evaluation, and process improvement. This chapter explains actual costing and normal costing systems; Chapters 14 and 15 explain standard costing systems. The different cost systems are summarized in Exhibit 4.1.

EXHIBIT 4.1
Cost Systems

Costing System	Types of Cost Used For		
	Direct Materials	Direct Labor	Factory Overhead
Actual costing	Actual cost	Actual cost	Actual cost
Normal costing	Actual cost	Actual cost	Estimated overhead cost (using predetermined rate(s))
Standard costing	Standard cost	Standard cost	Standard cost

Overhead Assignment under Normal Costing: Volume-Based or Activity-Based?

Volume-based product costing systems allocate overhead to products or jobs using a volume-based cost driver, such as units produced. This approach relies heavily on the assumption that each product uses the same amounts of overhead, since each product is charged the same amount. Many accountants argue that instead of an equal amount, the overhead in each product should be proportional to the direct labor hours needed to manufacture that unit, because more labor time also means increased overhead costs for equipment, supervision, and other facilities costs. Generally, neither of these assumptions turns out to be sufficiently accurate in many companies, so many firms use an activity-based approach.

Activity-based costing (ABC) systems allocate factory overhead costs to products using cause-and-effect criteria with multiple cost drivers. ABC systems use both volume-based and nonvolume-based cost drivers to more accurately allocate factory overhead costs to products based on resource consumption during various activities. Chapter 5 explains ABC systems.

The Strategic Role of Costing

LEARNING OBJECTIVE 2

Explain the strategic role of costing.

To compete successfully, firms need accurate cost information, regardless of their competitive strategies. And this is even more likely to be true for cost leadership firms that rely on a high level of manufacturing efficiency and quality to succeed. Effective management of manufacturing costs requires timely and accurate cost information. Getting this timely and accurate information requires that the firm choose a cost system that is a good match for its competitive strategy. For example, a cost leadership firm that produces a commodity product is also likely to be in a process industry, such as food or chemical processing, or assembly line manufacturing. Thus, process costing systems are likely to be a good fit. Because accurate costs are important, such firms are likely to use activity-based costing, which is more accurate than the volume-based method for overhead assignment. And finally, this type of firm is likely to choose a standard costing system to provide the cost targets and regular reports on meeting these targets. In sum, the commodity/cost leadership type of firm might very well use a cost system that combines elements of process costing (Chapter 6), activity-based costing (Chapter 5), and standard costing (Chapters 14 and 15).

Many firms' competitive environments are changing rapidly especially in the current economic recession. To provide useful information, a costing system must keep up with the constantly changing environment. To be competitive, the firm needs accurate cost information—for product pricing, profitability analysis of individual products, profitability analysis of individual customers, evaluation of management performance, and refinement of strategic goals.

Job Costing: The Cost Flows

LEARNING OBJECTIVE 3

Explain the flow of costs in a job costing system.

Job costing

is a product costing system that accumulates costs and assigns them to specific jobs, customers, projects, or contracts.

A **job cost sheet**

records and summarizes the costs of direct materials, direct labor, and factory overhead for a particular job.

Job costing is a costing system that accumulates costs and assigns them to specific jobs, customers, projects, or contracts. The basic supporting document (usually in electronic form) in a job costing system is the **job cost sheet**. It records and summarizes the costs of direct materials, direct labor, and factory overhead for a particular job.

An example of a job cost sheet for Thomasville Furniture Industries (TFI) of Thomasville, North Carolina, with disguised information, is shown in Exhibit 4.2. TFI (www.thomasville. com) is a large furniture manufacturer whose core values are quality and innovation, and whose products are sold through 150 TFI retail stores and more than 400 independent retailers. The job cost sheet in Exhibit 4.2 shows the materials, labor, and overhead required for the production of a batch of 20 end tables by TFI. The example is presented in the form of a Microsoft Access software application to emphasize that job costing is typically done by a database software system that collects all relevant job cost data and then prepares a variety of reports, such as the job cost sheet, reports of cost by department, listing of jobs by customer, and many others, including the firm's financial statements and tax return. Database software systems are used because of the large amounts of data that manufacturing firms such as TFI must maintain and use for a variety of purposes, such as the reports listed above. Often the software system is designed specifically for the industry (see softwarefinder.mbtmag.com for a comprehensive list of job costing software for the manufacturing industry). Microsoft Access is used here as a generic database system; the system used by a company like TFI could be any of a variety of the software systems available today.

A job cost sheet includes all three cost elements (materials, labor, overhead) as well as other detailed data management requires. The job cost sheet follows the product as it goes through the production process; all costs are recorded on the sheet as materials and labor are added. On completion of production, the overhead is added based usually on a certain dollar amount per labor hour, as shown in Exhibit 4.2. The total of all costs recorded on the job cost sheet is the total cost of the job.

Direct and Indirect Materials Costs

As part of the preparation for the job, TFI purchases materials that are needed for the job. The purchase, for $2,200, is illustrated with the following journal entry.

| (1) | Materials Inventory | 2,200 | |
| | Accounts Payable | | 2,200 |

EXHIBIT 4.2
Job Cost Sheet

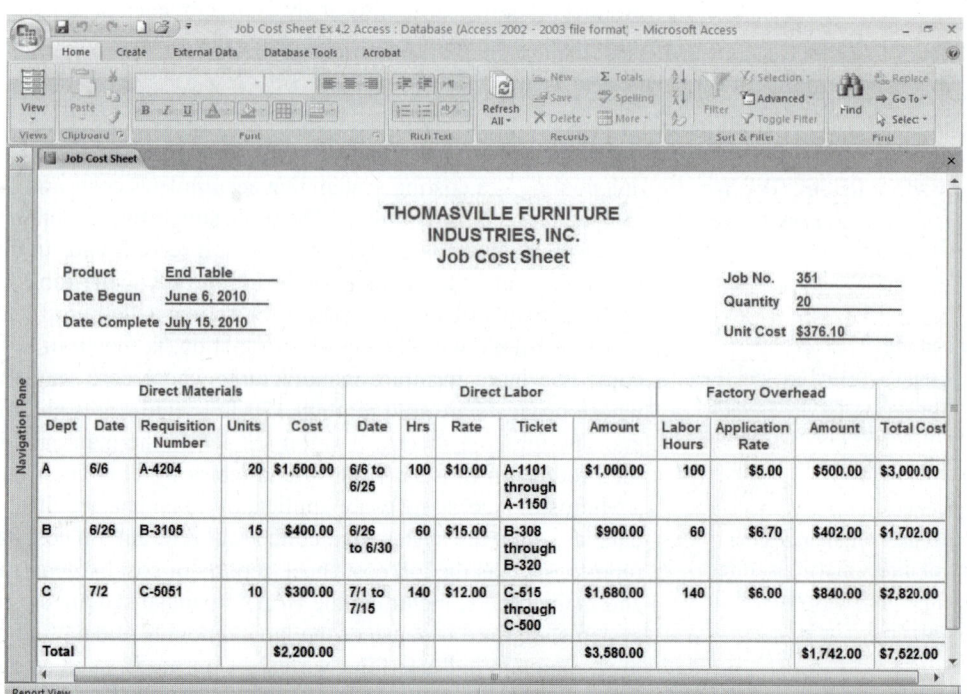

EXHIBIT 4.3
Materials Requisition

MATERIALS REQUISITION

No. A–4024

Job Number	351	Date	June 6, 2010
Department	A	Received by	Tom Chan
Authorized by	Juanita Perez	Issued by	Ted Mercer

Item Number	Description	Quantity	Unit Cost	Total Cost
MJI 428	Drawer Pull	20	$.75	$15

A **materials requisition** is a source document that the production department supervisor uses to request materials for production.

The purchased materials are used as TFI produces the job. A **materials requisition** is a source document or online data entry that the production department uses to request materials for production. The materials requisition indicates the specific job charged with the materials used. An example of a materials requisition for TFI is shown in Exhibit 4.3. The example shows that part of the Dept. A $1,500 materials requisition for the job shown in Exhibit 4.2 includes a drawer pull for each of the 20 end tables in the job, for a total cost of $15. A detailed listing of all the materials needed for a given job is often developed in what is called a bill of materials. For example, the bill of materials used by Thomasville Furniture Industries, Inc., in the manufacture of the end table is shown in Exhibit 4.4.

EXHIBIT 4.4 **Bill of Materials for End Table for Thomasville Furniture Industries, Inc.**

Thomasville Furniture Industries, Inc.
Bill of Materials

CHANGES FOR 14521–211

PLANT "T"

STYLE 14531–210 ARTICLE GEORGIAN END TABLE DATE 1–19–07 SHEET 1 OF 2

LINE		NO. PCS.	DESCRIPTION	FINISH SIZE L	FINISH SIZE W	FINISH SIZE T	FINISH SIZE BS	MULTI	ROUGH SIZE L	ROUGH SIZE W	ROUGH SIZE T	FOOTAGE	SKETCH
1	14531–210 ONLY	1	TOP	26	20	13/16		1	27	21	9/16		
2		1/2	TOP CORE					1	17	47 1/2	3/4		
3		1	TOP CORE SIDE BANDS	47 1/2	2	3/4		1	47 1/2	2	4/4		
4		2	TOP CORE FRT. & BK. BANDS	21	2	3/4		1	21	2	4/4		
5													
6		2	SIDE PANELS	22 3/8	4 15/16	3/4	21 3/8	4	23 7/8	21 3/4	5/8		4/4 POP CORE
7		2	SIDE APRON RAIL	22 3/8	1 7/8	1 7/16	21 3/8	1	23 3/8	2 1/8	8/4		
8		1	BACK PANEL	16 3/8	4 15/16	3/4	15 3/8	4	17 7/8	21 3/4	5/8		4/4 POP CORE
9		1	BACK APRON RAIL	16 3/8	1 7/8	1 7/16	15 3/8	1	17 3/8	2 1/8	8/4		
10		2	FRONT POST	22 3/4	2 1/2	2 1/2		1	23 3/4	2 3/4	3 pcs 5/4		
11		2	BACK POST	22 3/4	2 1/2	2 1/2		1	23 3/4	2 3/4	3 pcs 5/4		
12													
13	14531–210 ONLY	1	DRAWER FRONT	14 7/8	3 7/8	3/4		3	16 7/16	16 5/16	5/8		4/4 POP CORE
14		2	DWR. SIDES	20	3	7/16		1	21	3 1/4	5/8		
15		1	DWR. BACK	14 11/16	2 7/8	7/16							
16		1	DWR. BOTTOM	14 1/4	19 13/16	3/16		1	15 3/4	20 7/8	R.C.		
17		1	DWR. GUIDE—FEMALE	20 1/2	1 31/32	9/16	19 13/16	1	21 1/2	2 1/4	4/4		
18		1	DWR. GUIDE—MALE	22 1/2	1	1/2		1	23 1/2	1 1/4	4/4		
19		1	DWR. HOWE PULL										
20													

Thomasville Furniture Industries' Department A used a total of $1,500 in direct materials for Job 351. These costs are charged to work-in-process inventory until the job is completed, as shown in the following entry.

| (2) | Work-in-Process Inventory | 1,500 | |
| | Materials Inventory | | 1,500 |

Indirect materials are treated as part of the total factory overhead cost. Typical indirect materials are glue, nails, and factory supplies. The journal entry to record the use of indirect materials of $50 is

| (3) | Factory Overhead | 50 | |
| | Materials Inventory | | 50 |

Exhibit 4.5 describes cost flows for direct materials and indirect materials of transactions (1), (2), and (3).

Direct and Indirect Labor Costs

Direct labor costs are recorded on the job cost sheet by means of a time ticket prepared daily for each employee. A **time ticket,** usually part of a costing software system, shows the amount of time an employee worked on each job, the pay rate, and the total labor cost chargeable to each job. Analysis of the time tickets provides information for assigning direct labor costs to individual jobs. Note the typical time ticket in Exhibit 4.6. The total cost of the $1,000 direct labor incurred in TFI's Department A for Job 351 is recorded by the following journal entry:

A **time ticket**
shows the time an employee worked on each job, the pay rate, and the total labor cost chargeable to each job.

| (4) | Work-in-Process Inventory | 1,000 | |
| | Accrued Payroll | | 1,000 |

Indirect labor costs are treated as part of the total factory overhead cost. Indirect labor usually includes items such as salaries or wages for supervisors, inspectors, rework labor,

EXHIBIT 4.5
Materials Cost Flows

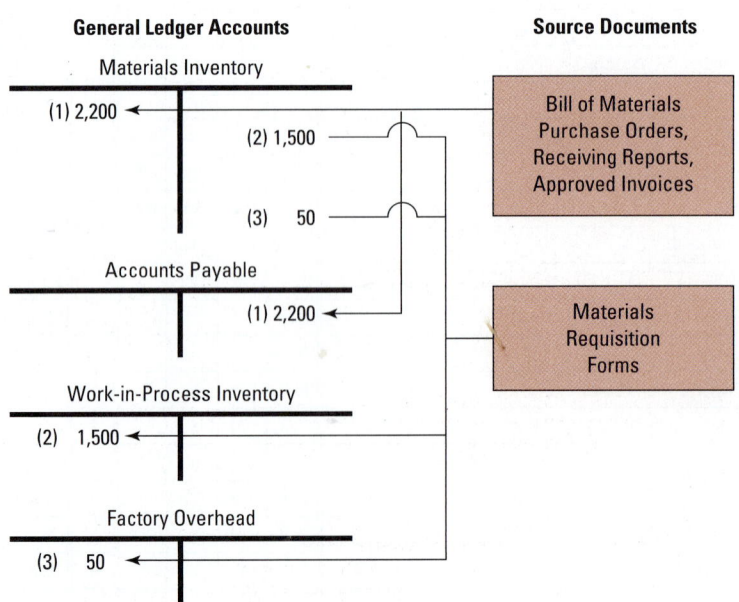

EXHIBIT 4.6
Time Ticket

TIME TICKET

Ticket Number _____ B-309 _____   Date _____ June 6, 2010 _____

Employee Name _____ Dale Johnson _____   Job Number _____ #351 _____

Operation _____ Assembly _____   Approved by _____ Juanita Perez _____

Time Started	Time Completed	Hours Worked	Rate	Cost
8:00 a.m.	11:00 a.m.	3.00	$10.00	$30.00
Total Cost				$30.00

and warehouse clerks. The following is a journal entry to record the $100 indirect labor cost incurred:

(5)	Factory Overhead	100	
	Accrued Payroll		100

Exhibit 4.7 shows direct labor and indirect labor cost flows through the accounts, and the related source documents.

Factory Overhead Costs

Overhead application is a process of allocating overhead costs to jobs. Allocation is necessary because overhead costs are not traceable to individual jobs. The two approaches to allocating overhead costs are actual costing and normal costing. A third approach, standard costing, is covered in Chapters 14 and 15.

Overhead application is a process of allocating overhead costs to jobs.

Actual Costing

An **actual costing system** uses actual costs incurred for direct materials and direct labor and applies actual factory overhead to the jobs.

Actual factory overhead costs are incurred each month for indirect materials, indirect labor, and other indirect factory costs, including factory rent, insurance, property tax, depreciation, repairs and maintenance, power, light, heat, and employer payroll taxes for factory personnel.

An **actual costing system** uses actual costs incurred for direct materials and direct labor and applies actual factory overhead to jobs.

EXHIBIT 4.7
Labor Cost Flows

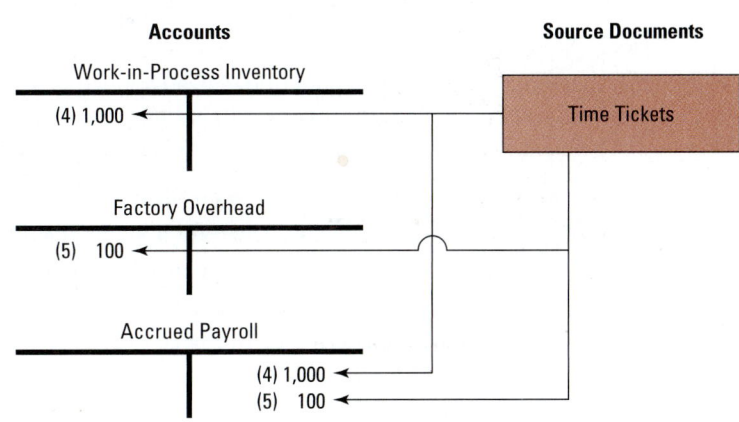

EXHIBIT 4.8
Monthly per-Unit Fixed Factory Overhead Cost Fluctuations under Actual Costing

Steece Machine Tools, Inc., has a monthly total fixed factory overhead of $60,000 and variable manufacturing costs per unit of $10 for its only product. The firm produced 50,000 units in January but only 10,000 units in February because it had a large inventory of unsold products at the end of January. The unit costs would be as follows if actual costing were used to determine the manufacturing cost per unit:

Month	Production Units	Variable Cost per Unit	Fixed Cost per Unit		Total Unit Cost
January	50,000	$10	$60,000/50,000 =	$1.20	$11.20
February	10,000	10	60,000/10,000 =	6.00	16.00

This fluctuation in unit cost arises because total fixed costs do not change, so unit costs change as volume changes, which is not desirable for cost estimation, budgeting, pricing, or product profitability analysis. Predetermined overhead rates, used for a year or longer, are easy to apply and reduce monthly fluctuations in job costs caused by changes in the production volume and/or overhead costs throughout the year.

Different firms use terms such as *manufacturing overhead, indirect manufacturing cost, overhead,* or *burden* in referring to factory overhead. Actual costing is illustrated in Exhibit 4.8

Generally, the total amount of actual overhead costs are not known until the end of the accounting period when total expenses are determined. Thus, the actual costing system is often applied to all of the company's jobs at the end of the accounting period. Revenues from all jobs and the actual expenses for materials, labor, and overhead are used to calculate overall profitability at that time. Using actual costing, the company could not know the cost or the profitability of each job when it is completed during the period, but only at the end of the period, and then the company would know the profitability of all the jobs combined. Most companies, like TFI, need to know for management planning and control purposes the cost and profitability of each job as it is completed, so they use normal costing rather than actual costing.

Normal Costing

Normal costing system
uses actual costs for direct materials and direct labor and applies factory overhead to jobs using a predetermined allocation rate.

In practice, most firms adopt a **normal costing system** that uses actual costs for direct materials and direct labor and applies factory overhead by adding to the job an amount of overhead for each unit of product in the job.

Normal costing avoids the fluctuations in cost per unit under actual costing resulting from changes in the month-to-month volume of units produced and changes in overhead costs. Using a predetermined *annual* factory overhead rate normalizes overhead cost fluctuations, hence, the term *normal costing*. The fluctuations in unit cost under actual costing are illustrated in Exhibit 4.8.

The Application of Factory Overhead in Normal Costing

The **predetermined factory overhead rate**
is an estimated rate used to apply factory overhead cost to a specific job.

Factory overhead applied
is the amount of overhead assigned to a job using a predetermined factory overhead rate.

The **predetermined factory overhead rate** is an estimated rate used to apply factory overhead cost to a specific job. The amount of overhead applied to a job using a predetermined factory overhead rate is called **factory overhead applied.**

To obtain the predetermined overhead rate, use these four steps:

1. Estimate total factory overhead costs for the operating period, usually a year.
2. Select the most appropriate cost driver for applying the factory overhead costs.
3. Estimate the total amount of the chosen cost driver for the operating period.
4. Divide the estimated factory overhead costs by the estimated amount of the chosen cost driver to obtain the predetermined overhead rate.

Cost Drivers for Factory Overhead Application

The cost driver selected for applying a predetermined overhead rate (step two above) can be either a volume- or activity-based cost driver. This chapter explains the use of volume-based cost drivers, and Chapter 5 explains activity-based cost drivers.

Direct labor-hours, direct labor costs, and machine-hours are among the most frequently used volume-based cost drivers for applying factory overhead. The proper bases or cost drivers for a labor-intensive firm are probably direct labor-hours, direct labor costs, or some labor-related measure. In contrast, if factory overhead costs are predominantly related to the equipment operation, the proper cost driver is probably machine-hours or a related measure. Surveys of practice show that direct labor (hours or dollars) and machine-hours are the most commonly used cost drivers for overhead application.

Applying Factory Overhead Costs

The predetermined overhead rate usually is calculated at the beginning of the year based on the four steps noted above:

$$\text{Predetermined factory overhead rate} = \frac{\text{Estimated total factory overhead amount for the year}}{\text{Estimated total amount of cost driver for the year}}$$

For example, suppose TFI has total estimated factory overhead cost of $200,070 for the coming year. TFI's cost system uses labor hours as the cost driver for overhead application. TFI has the following budgeted (i.e., estimated) and actual data.

Estimated annual overhead for all departments	$200,070
Estimated annual labor-hours for all departments	34,200
Actual labor-hours for Job 351 (Exhibit 4.2)	300

Thus, the predetermined overhead rate is

$$\frac{\text{Estimated factory overhead}}{\text{Estimated number of labor-hours}} = \frac{\$200,070}{34,200} = \$5.85 \text{ per labor-hour}$$

The overhead cost applied to Job 351 is $1,755 (=300 hours × $5.85 per labour hour). This amount would be recorded using the following journal entry

(6)	Work-in-Process Inventory	1,755	
	Factory Overhead		1,755

This approach is called the *plantwide method of normal costing,* since total overhead for all departments is used to determine the overhead rate. An alternative approach, and the one used by TFI, is to determine the overhead rate for each production department.

Departmental Overhead Rates

When the production departments in the plant are very similar as to the amount of overhead in each department and the usage of cost drivers in the departments, then the use of a plantwide rate (one rate for all production departments taken as a whole) is appropriate. In many cases, however, the various production departments differ significantly in the amount of cost and

Quality Printing Company (QPC) is profitable in a very competitive market within a large urban area. QPC attributes its success to customer service, especially quick turn-around on urgent print jobs. Jim Bernard, QPC's operating manager, is very effective at scheduling jobs so that customer order due dates are met, and urgent orders are handled expeditiously. As QPC has grown, it has developed a reputation for its ability to handle a wide range of print jobs, from simple tri-fold mailings to multiple page color brochures. For costing the jobs, QPC uses a job costing system that applies overhead based on operating hours, as follows, where BHR (budgeted hourly cost rate) is the overhead rate:

Job cost = Materials costs + Any outside purchases necessary for the order + BHR × Job hours

Pricing is based in part on job cost and Jim's knowledge of the printing competition in his area, so that some jobs are more profitable than others. Jim is interested in finding out more about job profitability. He wants to know which customers are really profitable and which are not. What would you suggest to Jim?

(Refer to Comments on Cost Management in Action at end of Chapter.)

cost drivers. Suppose, for example, that TFI has only three production departments (A, B, and C), and that the overhead costs and labor-hours in the three departments are shown below.

	Department A	Department B	Department C	Total
Overhead	$60,600	$65,670	$73,800	$200,070
Labor-hours	12,100	9,800	12,300	34,200

Note that the total overhead of $200,070 and total labor-hours of 34,200 hours are the same as in our above calculations for the plantwide rate.

Using the departmental approach, the rates are calculated as follows:

Overhead Rate for Department A

$60,600/12,100 labor hours = $5.00 per labor hour

Overhead Rate for Department B

$65,670/9,800 labor hours = $6.70 per labor hour

Overhead Rate for Department C

$73,800/12,300 labor hours = $6.00 per labor hour

Using the departmental approach, the overhead applied to Job 351 would be $1,742 as shown in Exhibit 4.2. The amount for the plantwide rate shown above, $1,755, differs by only $13 from the amount determined by the departmental approach, a very small difference. This means the usage of resources in the three departments by Job 351 is similar to that for the other TFI jobs, so that the plantwide rate and the departmental rate have a similar total cost. When the usage of resources in the three departments differs significantly for one job than others, then the departmental approach is considered the more appropriate and accurate since job cost is based on the actual usage of the different departments, not an overall average.

Disposition of Underapplied and Overapplied Overhead

Overapplied overhead is the amount of factory overhead applied that exceeds actual factory overhead cost.

Using a predetermined factory overhead rate to apply overhead cost to products can cause total overhead applied to the units produced to exceed the actual overhead incurred in periods when production is higher than expected. Alternatively, applied overhead might exceed incurred overhead if the amount incurred is less than estimated. **Overapplied overhead** is the amount of factory overhead applied that exceeds the actual factory overhead cost incurred.

Underapplied overhead is the amount by which actual factory overhead exceeds factory overhead applied.

On the other hand, it is possible that applied overhead will be less than the incurred amount of overhead, due either to the fact that the actual amount of incurred overhead was greater than expected and/or the actual production level was smaller than expected. **Underapplied overhead** is the amount by which actual factory overhead exceeds factory overhead applied. If the predetermined overhead rate has been determined carefully, and if actual production is similar to expected production, the overapplied or underapplied difference should be small.

What do we do with the difference between factory overhead applied and the actual amount of overhead incurred? Since actual production costs should be reported in the period they were incurred, total product costs at the end of the accounting period should be based on actual rather than applied overhead.

Underapplied or overapplied overhead can be disposed of in two ways:

1. Adjust the Cost of Goods Sold account.
2. Adjust the production costs of the period; that is, prorate the difference among the amounts of the current period's applied overhead remaining in the ending balances of the Work-in-Process Inventory, the Finished Goods Inventory, and the Cost of Goods Sold accounts.

When the amount of underapplied or overapplied overhead is not significant, it generally is adjusted to Cost of Goods Sold. On the other hand, if the amount is significant, it is often prorated. The proration method is explained in Chapter 15.

Adjustment to Cost of Goods Sold

Adjusting Cost of Goods Sold is the more expedient of the two methods for accounting for the overhead difference.

Suppose that TFI applied $200,000 overhead but found at the end of the year that the actual total amount of overhead incurred was $205,000. The $5,000 difference represents underapplied overhead. The appropriate adjusting entry to the Cost of Goods Sold account is:

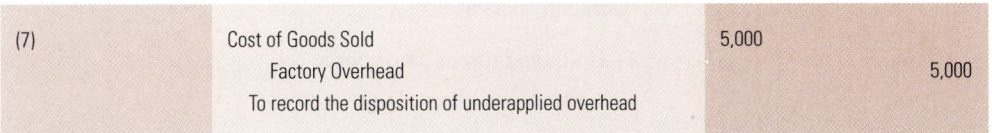

(7)	Cost of Goods Sold	5,000	
	Factory Overhead		5,000
	To record the disposition of underapplied overhead		

At the time of the adjusting entry, the Factory Overhead account had a debit balance of $5,000; the applied amount was credited to the account for $200,000 and the incurred amount was debited for $205,000, leaving a debit balance of $5,000. The entry removes this debit balance and transfers it to Cost of Goods Sold.

No matter which method is used (adjust cost of goods sold or prorate), underapplied or overapplied overhead is usually adjusted only at the end of a year. Nothing needs to be done during the year because the predetermined factory overhead rate is based on annual figures. A variance is expected between the actual overhead incurred and the amount applied in a particular month or quarter because of seasonal fluctuations in the firm's operating cycle. Furthermore, underapplied factory overhead in one month is likely to be offset by an overapplied amount in another month (and vice versa).

Job Costing in Service Industries; Project Costing

Job costing is used extensively in service industries such as advertising agencies, construction companies, hospitals, and repair shops, as well as consulting, architecture, accounting, and law firms. Instead of using the term *job,* accounting and consulting firms use the term *client* or *project;* hospitals and law firms use the term *case,* and advertising agencies and construction companies use the term *contract* or *project.* Many firms use the term *project costing* to indicate the use of job costing in service industries. Project costing is also used to track the costs and progress of nonrecurring tasks that take place within companies, for example, projects to develop a new marketing plan or to improve operating efficiency, projects to implement a new strategic direction for the company, or to introduce a new software system. These projects also have the characteristics that are suitable for job costing.

LEARNING OBJECTIVE 6

Apply job costing in service industries.

Job costing in service industries uses recording procedures and accounts similar to those illustrated earlier in this chapter except for direct materials involved (there could be none or an insignificant amount). The primary focus is on direct labor. The overhead costs are usually applied to jobs based on direct labor cost.

Suppose that Freed and Swenson, a Los Angeles law firm, has the following budget of estimated costs for the year.

Compensation of professional staff	$ 500,000
Other costs	500,000
Total budgeted costs for 2010	$1,000,000

Other costs include indirect materials and supplies, photocopying, computer-related expenses, insurance, office rent, utilities, training costs, accounting fees, indirect labor costs for office support personnel, and other office expenses.

Freed and Swenson charges overhead costs to clients or jobs at a predetermined percentage of the professional salaries charged to the client. The law firm's recent data show that chargeable hours average 80 percent of available hours for all categories of professional personnel. The nonchargeable hours are regarded as additional overhead. This nonchargeable time might involve training, idle time, and similar factors.

Using these data, the firm's budgeted (that is, estimated) direct labor costs and budgeted overhead costs are:

1. Budgeted direct labor costs:

$$\$500,000 \times 80\% = \$400,000$$

2. Budgeted overhead costs:

Other costs	$500,000
Salary costs for nonchargeable hours:	
$500,000 − $400,000 =	100,000
	$600,000

The predetermined overhead rate is:

$$\frac{\text{Budgeted overhead costs}}{\text{Budgeted direct labor costs}} = \frac{\$600,000}{\$400,000} = 150\% \text{ of direct labor cost}$$

Exhibit 4.9 presents relevant data and job costs for the law firm's recent client, George Christatos.

EXHIBIT 4.9
Job Costing for Freed and
Swenson Law Firm

Client: George Christatos

Employee Charges	Hours	Salary Rates	Billing Rates
Partners	10	$100	$250
Managers	20	80	200
Associates	100	30	100
	130		

Total Revenues and Costs for This Client's Job

Service revenues	($250 × 10) + ($200 × 20) + ($100 × 100) =	$16,500
Cost of services		
Direct labor ($100 × 10) + ($80 × 20) + ($30 × 100) = $5,600		
Overhead $5,600 × 150% =	8,400	
Total costs of services		14,000
Operating income for this client		$2,500

Operation Costing

Operation costing
is a hybrid costing system
that uses job costing to assign
direct materials costs to jobs
and process costing to assign
conversion costs to products or
services.

LEARNING OBJECTIVE 7

*Explain an operation costing
system.*

Operation costing is a hybrid costing system that uses job costing to assign direct materials costs to jobs, and a process costing approach to assign conversion costs to products or services.

Manufacturing operations whose conversion activities are very similar across several product lines, but whose direct materials used in the various products differ significantly use operation costing. After direct labor and factory overhead conversion costs have been accumulated by operations or departments, these costs are then assigned to products. On the other hand, direct materials costs are accumulated by jobs or batches, and job costing assigns these costs to products or services.

Industries suitable for applying operation costing include clothing, food processing, textiles, shoes, furniture, metalworking, jewelry, and electronic equipment. For example, sofa manufacturing has two standard operations: cutting and assembling. Different jobs, however, require different wood and fabric materials. Therefore, an operation costing system can be well-suited for this situation.

Suppose that Irvine Glass Company manufactures two types of glass for sheets, clear glass and colored glass. Department 1 produces clear glass sheets, some of which are sold as finished goods. Others are transferred to Department 2, which adds metallic oxides to clear glass sheets to form colored glass sheets, which are then sold as finished goods. The company uses operation costing.

Irvine Glass Company finished two jobs: Job A produced 10,000 sheets of clear glass and Job B produced 5,000 sheets of colored glass. Manufacturing operations and costs applied to these products follow.

Direct materials		
Job A (10,000 clear glass sheets)		$400,000
Job B (5,000 colored glass sheets)		
Materials for clear glass sheets in Department 1	$200,000	
Materials added to clear glass sheets in Department 2	100,000	300,000
Total direct materials		$700,000
Conversion costs		
Department 1		$180,000
Department 2		50,000
Total conversion costs		$230,000
Total costs		$930,000

Notice in this table that operation costing identifies direct materials by job but that it identifies conversion costs with the two production departments.

The product cost for each type of glass sheet is computed as follows:

	Clear Glass	Colored Glass
Direct materials		
Job A ($400,000/10,000)	$40	
Job B ($300,000/5,000)		$60
Conversion: Department 1 ($180,000/15,000)	12	12
Conversion: Department 2 ($50,000/5,000)		10
Total product cost per sheet	$52	$82

Notice in this table that each glass sheet receives the same conversion costs in Department 1 since this operation is identical for the two products. Total product costs are calculated as follows:

Clear glass sheets ($52 × 10,000)	$520,000
Colored glass sheets ($82 × 5,000)	410,000
Total	$930,000

The following journal entries record Irvine Glass Company's flow of costs. Department 1 makes the first entry by recording the requisition of direct materials when Job A entered production:

(1)	Work-in-Process Inventory: Department 1	400,000	
	Materials Inventory		400,000

Department 1 makes the following entry to record the requisition of direct materials when Job B enters production:

(2)	Work-in-Process Inventory: Department 1	200,000	
	Materials Inventory		200,000

Conversion costs are applied in Department 1 with the following journal entry:

(3)	Work-in-Process Inventory: Department 1	180,000	
	Conversion Costs Applied		180,000

The following entry records the transfer of completed clear glass sheets to finished goods:

(4)	Finished Goods Inventory	520,000	
	Work-in-Process Inventory: Department 1		520,000

Direct materials of $400,000 + Conversion ($12 × 10,000) = $520,000

The following entry for units of colored glass records the transfer of partially completed colored glass sheets to Department 2:

| (5) | Work-in-Process Inventory: Department 2 | 260,000 | |
| | Work-in-Process Inventory: Department 1 | | 260,000 |

Direct materials of $200,000 + \text{Conversion}(\$12 \times 5,000) = \$260,000$

The following entry records the requisition of the materials by Department 2 when job B enters production:

| (6) | Work-in-Process Inventory: Department 2 | 100,000 | |
| | Materials Inventory | | 100,000 |

Conversion costs are applied in Department 2 with the following journal entry.

| (7) | Work-in-Process Inventory: Department 2 | 50,000 | |
| | Conversion Costs Applied | | 50,000 |

The completed colored glass sheets are transferred to finished goods.

| (8) | Finished Goods Inventory | 410,000 | |
| | Work-in-Process Inventory: Department 2 | | 410,000 |

Department 2 work-in-process $260,000 + Materials for colored glass of $100,000 + $\text{Conversion}(\$10 \times 5,000) = \$410,000$

Summary

Product costing is the process of accumulating, classifying, and assigning direct materials, direct labor, and factory overhead costs to products or services. Product costing provides useful cost information for both manufacturing and nonmanufacturing firms for (1) product and service cost determination and inventory valuation, (2) management planning, cost control, and performance evaluation, and (3) managerial decisions.

Several different product costing systems are available and can be classified as the (1) cost accumulation method—job or processing costing systems, (2) cost measurement method—actual, normal, or standard costing systems, (3) overhead assignment method—volume- or activity-based costing systems. The choice of a particular system depends on the nature of the industry and the product or service; the firm's strategy and its management information needs; and the costs and benefits to acquire, design, modify, and operate a particular system.

Job costing uses several accounts to control the product cost flows. Direct materials costs are debited to the Materials Inventory account at time of purchase and debited to the Work-in-Process Inventory account when production requests materials. Direct labor costs are debited to the Work-in-Process Inventory account when they are incurred. Actual factory overhead costs are debited to the Factory Overhead account when they are incurred. Factory overhead applied using the predetermined factory overhead rate in normal costing is debited to the Work-in-Process Inventory account and credited to the Factory Overhead account. When a job is complete, the cost of goods manufactured is transferred from the Work-in-Process Inventory account to the Finished Goods Inventory account.

The predetermined factory overhead rate is an estimated factory overhead rate used to apply factory overhead cost to a specific job. The application of a predetermined overhead rate has four steps: (1) estimate factory overhead costs for an appropriate operating period, usually a year, (2) select the most appropriate cost driver for charging the factory overhead costs, (3) estimate the total amount of the chosen cost driver for the operating period, and (4) divide the estimated factory overhead costs by the estimated amount of the chosen cost driver to obtain the predetermined factory overhead rate.

The difference between the actual factory overhead cost and the amount of the factory overhead applied is the overhead variance; it is either underapplied or overapplied. It can be disposed of in two ways: (1) adjust the Cost of Goods Sold account or (2) prorate the difference among the Work-in-Process Inventory, the Finished Goods Inventory, and the Cost of Goods Sold accounts.

Job costing is used extensively in service industries such as advertising agencies, construction companies, hospitals, repair shops and consulting, architecture, accounting, and law firms.

Operation costing is used when most of the plant's products have a similar conversion cycle, but materials costs may differ significantly between jobs. In this case, materials costs are traced to jobs, while conversion costs are traced to departments and then to jobs.

Appendix

Spoilage, Rework, and Scrap in Job Costing

In today's manufacturing environment, firms adopt various quality-improvement programs to reduce spoilage, rework units, and scrap. **Spoilage** refers to unacceptable units that are discarded or sold for disposal value. **Rework** units are units produced that must be reworked into good units that can be sold in regular channels. **Scrap** is the material left over from the manufacture of the product; it has little or no value.

SPOILAGE

The two types of spoilage are normal and abnormal. **Normal spoilage** occurs under normal operating conditions; it is uncontrollable in the short term and is considered a normal part of production and product cost. That is, the cost of spoiled unit costs is absorbed by the cost of good units produced. **Abnormal spoilage** is in excess over the amount of normal spoilage expected under normal operating conditions; it is charged as a loss to operations in the period detected.

Normal spoilage is of two types: (1) specific normal spoilage, which is particular to a given job, and is not due to factors related to other jobs and (2) common normal spoilage, which is due to factors that affect two or more jobs, such as a machine malfunction that affected parts used in several jobs. Normal spoilage that is specific to a job is treated as a cost of that job, so that in effect the cost of spoilage is spread over the cost of the good units in the job. Normal spoilage that is common to two or more jobs is charged to factory overhead and, in this way, affects the costs of all jobs. Abnormal spoilage is charged to a special account, such as Loss from Abnormal Spoilage so that management attention can be given to spoilage of this type, and because product cost should not include abnormal elements such as abnormal spoilage.

Suppose a furniture manufacturer spoiled 1 sofa from an order of 100 sofas (job #1233) because of stains and tears in the fabric and that the spoilage was normal and particular to this job. At the time the spoilage was detected, a total of $500 had been incurred in the manufacture of the sofa. Suppose further that the spoiled sofa could be disposed of—sold as-is for $100, then the net cost of the spoilage is now $500 − $100 = $400. This means that $400 of work-in-process cost for the spoiled sofa will be spread over the remaining 99 sofas. The accounting treatment would be as follows:

Inventory of spoiled sofa for sale	100	
Work-in-process for job #1233		100

Margin definitions

Spoilage
refers to an unaccepted unit that is discarded or sold for disposal value.

Rework
is a produced unit that must be reworked into a good unit that can be sold in regular channels.

Scrap
is the material left over from the manufacture of the product; it has little or no value.

Normal spoilage
is waste that occurs under normal operating conditions.

Abnormal spoilage
is waste that should not arise under normal operating conditions.

Suppose the same information as above, except that the spoiled sofa described above was spoiled by a hard-to-detect malfunction in a fabric cutting machine that was also involved in other jobs in the plant, and had affected other jobs. The spoilage is now considered common normal spoilage, and the accounting treatment is:

Inventory of spoiled sofa for sale	100	
Factory overhead	400	
Work-in-process for job #1233		500

Finally, assume again the same information as above except that the malfunction in the fabric cutting machine is due to controllable operator error, and is now considered to be abnormal spoilage. The accounting treatment is now:

Inventory of spoiled sofa for sale	100	
Loss from abnormal spoilage	400	
Work-in-process for job #1233		500

REWORK

Like spoilage, there are three types of rework: (1) rework on normal defective units for a particular job, (2) rework on normal defective units common with all jobs, and (3) rework on abnormal defective units not falling within the normal range. The cost of rework units is charged to one of three accounts depending on its nature. Normal rework for a particular job is charged to that specific job's Work-in-Process Inventory account. Normal rework common to all jobs is charged to the Factory Overhead account and abnormal rework is charged to the Loss from Abnormal Rework account.

SCRAP

Scrap can be classified according to (1) a specific job and (2) common to all jobs. Suppose that the furniture manufacturer above incurred and sold the scrap from a specific job for $100 cash and sold the scrap common to all jobs for $200 cash. The proper journal entries follow:

Cash	100	
Work-in-Process Inventory		100
Cash	200	
Factory Overhead		200

Comments on Cost Management in Action

Job Costing in a Printing Company

Quality Printing Company has succeeded on the competitive knowledge of the manager, Jim Bernard, and on his ability to effectively manage operations. But the costing system stands in the way of Jim's further progress to profitability. The first problem with the costing system is that it uses a plantwide rate. The BHR system uses a rate derived from all the firms equipment and facilities. Since some print jobs are more complex (more colors, etc.) and must run on more expensive equipment while others are relatively simple, QPC needs overhead rates for each piece of equipment. The National Association for Printing Leadership (NAPL) publishes hourly cost rates (BHRs) for different types of machines, and these rates are updated twice a year. Using the NAPL rates would give Jim a more accurate basis for job costing; it is very much like the departmental approach mentioned in the chapter, except in this case the department is the printing machine.

Other issues Jim should consider in his analysis of customer profitability is that the customers who demand very quick turnaround are likely to increase operating costs by incurring overtime charges, delaying or interrupting other jobs, and in other ways. These additional costs should be considered in pricing these expedited jobs.

Jim can use job costing to measure the profitability of each job and, by extension, of each customer. This information can help him set prices and manage costs.

Source: Lisa Cross, "Benefiting from Costing and Pricing Tools," *Graphic Arts Monthly,* July 2004, pp. 32–34.

Self-Study Problem
(For solution, please turn to the end of the chapter.)

Journal Entries and Accounting for Overhead

Watkins Machinery Company uses a normal job costing system. The company has this partial trial balance information on March 1, 2010, the last month of its fiscal year:

Materials Inventory (X, $3,000; Y, $2,000; Indirect materials, $5,000)	$10,000
Work-in-Process Inventory—Job 101	6,000
Finished Goods Inventory—Job 100	10,000

These transactions relate to the month of March:

a. Purchased direct materials and indirect materials with the following summary of receiving reports:

Material X	$10,000
Material Y	10,000
Indirect materials	5,000
Total	$25,000

b. Issued direct materials and indirect materials with this summary of requisitions:

	Job 101	Job 102	Total
Material X	$5,000	$3,000	$ 8,000
Material Y	4,000	3,000	7,000
Subtotal	$9,000	$6,000	$15,000
Indirect materials			8,000
Total			$23,000

c. Factory labor incurred is summarized by these time tickets:

Job 101	$12,000
Job 102	8,000
Indirect labor	5,000
Total	$25,000

d. Factory utilities, factory depreciation, and factory insurance incurred is summarized by these factory vouchers, invoices, and cost memos:

Utilities	$ 500
Depreciation	15,000
Insurance	2,500
Total	$18,000

e. Factory overhead costs were applied to jobs at the predetermined rate of $15 per machine-hour. Job 101 incurred 1,200 machine-hours; Job 102 used 800 machine-hours.

f. Job 101 was completed; Job 102 was still in process at the end of March.

g. Job 100 and job 101 were shipped to customers during March. Both jobs had gross margins of 20 percent based on manufacturing cost.

The company closed the overapplied or underapplied overhead to the Cost of Goods Sold account at the end of March.

Required

1. Prepare journal entries to record the transactions and events. Letter your entries from a to g.
2. Compute the ending balance of the Work-in-Process Inventory account.
3. Compute the overhead variance and indicate whether it is overapplied or underapplied.
4. Close the overhead variance to the Cost of Goods Sold account.

Questions

4-1   What is the purpose of a costing system?

4-2   Give three ways that management uses product costs.

4-3   Distinguish between job costing and process costing.

4-4   Explain when companies are likely to use a job costing system or a process costing system. Provide examples.

4-5   Which costing system is extensively used in the service industry for hospitals, law firms, or accounting firms? Explain why.

4-6   What document is prepared to accumulate costs for each separate job in a job costing system? What type of costs are recorded in the document?

4-7   Explain how predetermined factory overhead rates are computed and why they are used to apply factory overhead to units of products instead of actual overhead costs.

4-8   What is the role of material requisitions in a job costing system? Time tickets? Bills of materials?

4-9   What does the statement that accounting for overhead involves an important cost-benefit issue mean? Why is that issue important?

4-10 Describe the flow of costs through a job costing system.

4-11 What do *underapplied overhead* and *overapplied overhead* mean? How are these amounts disposed of at the end of a period?

4-12 Why are some manufacturing firms switching from direct labor-hours to machine-hours as the cost driver for factory overhead application?

4-13 Explain why overhead might be overapplied in a given period.

4-14 Distinguish between an actual costing system and a normal costing system. What are the components of the actual manufacturing costs and the components of the normal manufacturing costs?

4-15 Factory overhead includes a variety of costs that vary greatly with respect to the production process. What is the best way to choose an appropriate cost driver when applying factory overhead?

4-16 What is the difference between cost of goods sold and adjusted cost of goods sold?

Brief Exercises

4-17 How is job costing in a service firm different from job costing in a manufacturer?

4-18 If the overhead rate is $10 per machine-hour, and there are 20 labor-hours, 16 machine-hours, and 2 personnel on the job, how much overhead should be applied to the job?

4-19 Nieto Machine Shop has 4,000 labor-hours and 8,000 machine-hours used in May. Total budgeted overhead for May is $80,000. What is the overhead rate using labor-hours and also using machine-hours? Which would you pick and why?

4-20 Assume that actual overhead is $613,000 in a given year and the overhead rate is $10 per unit, 60,000 units were sold, and 59,000 units were produced. For the end of the year, is overhead underapplied or overapplied, and by how much?

4-21 If the end-of-period balance for cost of goods sold is $90,000 and underapplied overhead is $10,000, what is the ending balance in cost of goods sold, after adjusting for the underapplied overhead?

4-22 A small consulting firm has an overhead rate of 200% of direct labor charged to each job. The materials cost (including travel and other direct costs) for a particular job is $10,000 and the direct labor is $20,000. What is the total job cost for this job?

4-23 Company A has a number of jobs that are processed through similar manufacturing processes. However, most jobs have labor-hour requirements ranging from 100 to 130 hours, while these jobs differ significantly in the number of machine-hours required for each job—some as low as 50, other as high as 5,000 hours. One reason for this is a well-trained labor pool that has the ability to work cross-functionally and perform a variety of duties. What do you think is the best overhead rate basis for this firm—labor-hours, machine-hours, or some other rate basis? Explain your answer.

4-24 When overhead is overapplied, is the balance of cost of good sold, before adjustment, too low or too high? Why?

4-25 Some firms pool overhead into a single plantwide overhead pool, while others collect overhead costs into manufacturing departments, each of which has an overhead cost pool and overhead cost application rate. Which approach is likely to provide more accurate cost numbers for cost estimating, pricing, and performance evaluation?

4-26 Assume the following for Black Top, Inc., for 2010. Black Top applies overhead on the basis of units produced.

Budgeted overhead	$210,000
Actual overhead	$222,000
Actual labor-hours	15,000
Actual number of units sold	43,000
Underapplied overhead	$ 20,400
Budgeted production (units)	50,000

Required How many units were produced in 2010?

4-27 Assume the following for Round Top, Inc., for 2010. Round Top applies overhead on the basis of units produced.

Budgeted overhead	$350,000
Actual overhead	$360,000
Actual labor-hours	22,000
Actual number of units sold	650,000
Overapplied overhead	$ 30,000
Budgeted production (units)	700,000

Required How many units were produced in 2010?

Exercises 4-28 **Job Costing** Johnson Inc. is a job-order manufacturing company that uses a predetermined overhead rate based on direct labor-hours to apply overhead to individual jobs. For 2010, estimated direct labor-hours are 95,000, and estimated factory overhead is $617,500. The following information is for September 2010. Job A was completed during September, and Job B was started but not finished.

September 1, 2010, inventories	
Materials inventory	$ 7,500
Work-in-process inventory (All Job A)	31,200
Finished goods inventory	67,000
Material purchases	104,000
Direct materials requisitioned	
Job A	65,000
Job B	33,500
Direct labor-hours	
Job A	4,200
Job B	3,500
Labor costs incurred	
Direct labor ($8.50/hour)	65,450
Indirect labor	13,500
Supervisory salaries	6,000
Rental costs	
Factory	7,000
Administrative offices	1,800
Total equipment depreciation costs	
Factory	7,500
Administrative offices	1,600
Indirect materials used	12,000

Required

1. What is the total cost of Job A?

2. What is the total factory overhead applied during September?

3. What is the overapplied or underapplied overhead for September?

4-29 Choice of Costing System

Required   The following is a list of Web sites for a number of companies. Briefly describe each company and indicate whether it is more likely to use job costing or process costing. Explain why in each case.

1. New Century Software Inc. at www.newcenturysoftware.com.

2. Kinko's at www.fedex.com/us/officeprint/main.

3. TXI Cement (TXI) at www.txi.com.

4. Paramount Pictures at www.paramount.com.

5. Evian at www.evian.com.

6. Ircon International Limited at www.irconinternational.com.

4-30 Choice of Costing System

Required   The following is a list of Web sites for a number of non–U.S. companies. Briefly describe each company and indicate whether it is more likely to use job costing or process costing. Explain why in each case.

1. Zurich Financial Services Group at www.zurich.com.

2. Reichhold Chemical Co. at www.reichhold.com

3. Nestle S.A. at www.nestle.com.

4. Coca-Cola at www.coca-cola.com

4-31 Job Costing in the Airline Industry
Manufacturers of large equipment such as aircraft and ships and companies involved in road construction have jobs that may require two or more years for completion. For example, Boeing Corporation might have an order for 50 aircraft for a particular airline, and the order will extend over a three- to five-year period. Aircraft are delivered as completed, but not in a batch of 50 at one time. In the typical fashion, the overhead application rate must be calculated and applied in such a way that each aircraft that is delivered has the proper amount of overhead for that aircraft.

Required   What unique difficulties do you see in the calculation and application of overhead in industries such as aircraft manufacturing or shipbuilding? How do you think these firms should respond to these difficulties in determining overhead rates and applying overhead costs?

4-32 **Journal Entries**   Erkens Company uses a job costing system with normal costing and applies factory overhead on the basis of machine-hours. At the beginning of the year, management estimated that the company would incur $1,980,000 of factory overhead costs and use 66,000 machine-hours.

Erkens Company recorded the following events during the month of April:

a.   Purchased 180,000 pounds of materials on account; the cost was $5.00 per pound.

b.   Issued 120,000 pounds of materials to production of which 15,000 pounds were used as indirect materials.

c.   Incurred direct labor costs of $240,000 and $40,000 of indirect labor costs.

d.   Recorded depreciation on equipment for the month, $75,700.

e.   Recorded insurance costs for the manufacturing property, $3,500.

f.   Paid $8,500 cash for utilities and other miscellaneous items for the manufacturing plant.

g.   Completed Job H11 costing $7,500 and Job G28 costing $77,000 during the month and transferred them to the Finished Goods Inventory account.

h.   Shipped Job G28 to the customer during the month. The job was invoiced at 35 percent above cost.

i.   Used 7,700 machine-hours during April.

Required

1.   Compute Erkens Company's predetermined overhead rate for the year.

2.   Prepare journal entries to record the events that occurred during April.

3.   Compute the amount of overapplied or underapplied overhead and prepare a journal entry to close overapplied or underapplied overhead into cost of goods sold on April 30.

4-33 **Working with Unknowns**   Gregson Company uses a job costing system that applies factory overhead on the basis of direct labor dollars. No job was in process on February 1. During the month of February, the company worked on these three jobs:

	Job Number		
	A23	**C76**	**G15**
Direct labor ($8/hour)	$24,000	?	$8,800
Direct materials	42,000	61,000	?
Overhead applied	?	24,750	6,050

During the month, the company completed and transferred Job A23 to the finished goods inventory. Jobs C76 and G15 were not completed and remain in work in process at the cost of $148,650 at the end of the month. Actual factory overhead costs during the month totaled $48,600.

Required

1.   What is the predetermined factory overhead rate?

2.   Compute the amount of underapplied or overapplied overhead for February.

3.   Compute the cost of direct materials issued to production during the month.

4-34 **Application of Factory Overhead**   Tomek Company uses a job costing system that applies factory overhead on the basis of direct labor-hours. The company's factory overhead budget for 2010 included the following estimates:

Budgeted total factory overhead	$568,000
Budgeted total direct labor-hours	71,000

At the end of the year, the company shows these results:

Actual factory overhead	$582,250
Actual direct labor-hours	71,500

The following amounts of the year's applied factory overhead remained in the various manufacturing accounts:

	Applied Factory Overhead
Work-in-process inventory	$139,000
Finished goods inventory	216,840
Cost of goods sold	200,160

Required

1. Compute the firm's predetermined factory overhead rate for 2010.
2. Calculate the amount of overapplied or underapplied overhead.
3. Prepare a journal entry to transfer the underapplied or overapplied overhead to the Cost of Goods Sold account (do not use proration).

4-35 **Overhead Rate, Pricing**   Norton Associates is an advertising agency in Austin, Texas. The company's controller estimated that it would incur $325,000 in overhead costs for 2010. Because the overhead costs of each project change in direct proportion to the amount of direct professional hours incurred, the controller decided that overhead should be applied on the basis of professional hours. The controller estimated 25,000 professional hours for the year. During October, Norton incurred the following costs to make a 20-second TV commercial for Central Texas Bank:

Direct materials	$32,000
Direct professional hours ($50/hour)	1,200

Actual overhead costs to make the commercial totaled $16,500. The industry customarily bills customers at 150 percent of total cost.

Required

1. Compute the predetermined overhead rate.
2. What is the total amount of the bill that Norton will send Central Texas Bank?

4-36 **Spoilage and Scrap (appendix)**   Lexan Textile Company's Job X12 had one of its 20 units spoiled. The cost incurred on the unit was $600. It was specific normal spoilage with an estimated disposal price of $300 for the spoiled unit. Job Y34 had common normal spoilage with the estimated cost of $400 from the general production process failure and abnormal spoilage of $200. The company also incurred scrap due to Job Y34 and sold it for $80. It also sold the scrap common to all jobs for $120 cash in May.

Required

1. Make the necessary journal entries to record normal and abnormal spoilage costs.
2. Make the necessary journal entries to record both types of scrap sold.

Problems   4-37 **Job Costing**   Work in process inventory for Bradley Inc. at the beginning of the year was a single job, Job 125 :

Job	Materials	Labor	Overhead	Total
125	$22,500	$22,000	$33,000	$77,500

The Company's actual cost incurred during the year are as follows:

	Incurred by Jobs			
Jobs	Materials	Labor	Other	Total
125	$1,000	$10,000	—	$11,000
128	26,000	18,000	—	44,000
129	12,000	34,000	—	46,000
130	4,000	16,000	—	20,000

	Materials	Labor	Other	Total
Indirect materials and supplies	$30,000	—	—	$30,000
Indirect labor	—	$23,000	—	23,000
Employee benefits	—	—	$46,000	46,000
Depreciation	—	—	12,000	12,000
Supervision	—	15,000	—	15,000

The Company's budgeted costs for the year are as follows:

Budgeted overhead	
Variable	
Indirect materials	$16,000
Indirect labor	56,000
Employee benefits	24,000
Fixed	
Supervision	20,000
Depreciation	12,000
Total	$128,000
Budgeted direct labor dollars	$ 80,000
Rate per direct labor dollar ($128,000/$80,000)	160%

Required

1. What was the actual factory overhead for Bradley, Inc for the year?
2. What was overapplied or underapplied overhead for the year?
3. Job 125 was the only job completed and sold in the year. What amount was included in the cost of the goods sold for this job?
4. What was the amount of Work-in-Process Inventory at the end of the year?

4-38 **Job Costing** Operations of Valport Company for the year ended November 30, 2010, have been completed, and all of the accounting entries have been made for the year except the transfer of costs from Work-in-Process to Finished Goods for the jobs completed in November, and the transfer of costs from Finished Goods to Cost of Goods Sold for the jobs that have been sold during November. Summarized data that have been accumulated from the accounting records as of October 31, 2010, and for November 2010, are shown below.

Jobs N11-007, N11-013, and N11-015 were completed during November 2010. All completed jobs except Job N11-013 had been turned over to customers by the close of business on November 30, 2010.

Required

1. Prepare a Statement of Cost of Goods Manufactured for Valport Company for the year ended November 30, 2010.
2. Determine the amount of Cost of Goods Sold for the year ended November 30, 2010.

		November 2010 Activity		
Work-in-Process	Balance 10/31/10	Direct Materials	Direct Labor	Machine-Hours
Job No.:				
N11-007	$ 87,000	$ 1,500	$ 4,500	300
N11-013	55,000	4,000	12,000	1,000
N11-015	-0-	25,600	26,700	1,400
D12-002	-0-	37,900	20,000	2,500
D12-003	-0-	26,000	16,800	800
Totals	$142,000	$95,000	$80,000	6,000

	Operating Activity	
	Through 10/31/10	November 2010
Manufacturing overhead applied		
Indirect materials	$ 125,000	$ 9,000
Indirect labor	345,000	30,000
Utilities	245,000	22,000
Depreciation	385,000	35,000
Total applied overhead	$1,100,000	$96,000
Other items		
Material purchases*	$ 965,000	$98,000
Direct labor costs	$ 845,000	$80,000
Machine-hours	73,000	6,000

	Account Balances at:	
	12/01/09	11/30/10
Materials inventory*	$105,000	$85,000
Work-in-process inventory	60,000	150,000
Finished goods inventory	125,000	225,000

*Material purchases and materials inventory consist of both direct and indirect materials.

4-39 **Job Costing**   The following information applies to the Colbert Company for March production. There are only two jobs (A and B) in production in March.

a. Purchased direct materials and indirect materials with the following summary of receiving reports:

Material A	$16,000
Material B	12,000
Indirect materials	3,000
Total	$31,000

b. Issued direct materials and indirect materials with this summary of requisitions:

	Job X	Job Y	Total
Material A	$6,000	$15,000	$21,000
Material B	2,000	7,000	9,000
Subtotal	$8,000	$22,000	$30,000
Indirect materials			42,000
Total			$72,000

c. Factory labor incurred is summarized by these time tickets:

Job X	$16,000
Job Y	12,000
Indirect labor	28,000
Total	$56,000

d.   Factory utilities, factory depreciation, and factory insurance incurred is summarized by these factory vouchers, invoices, and cost memos:

Utilities	$ 3,000
Depreciation	18,000
Insurance	2,500
Total	$23,500

e.   Factory overhead costs were applied to jobs at the predetermined rate of $46 per machine-hour. Job X incurred 1,300 machine-hours; Job Y used 900 machine-hours.

f.   Job X was completed; Job Y was still in process at the end of March.

g.   Job X was shipped to customers during March. Job X had a gross margin of 20 percent based on manufacturing cost.

The company closed the overapplied or underapplied overhead to the Cost of Goods Sold account at the end of March.

Required

1.   Calculate the amount of overapplied or underapplied overhead and state whether the cost of goods sold account will be increased or decreased by the adjustment.

2.   Calculate the total manufacturing cost for Job X and Job Y for March.

4-40   Job Costing

The following information is for Shiller Company for July 2010:

a.   Applied factory overhead costs to jobs at the predetermined rate of $39.50 per labor-hour. Job 1467 incurred 6,175 labor-hours; Job 1469 used 4,275 labor-hours.

b.   Shipped Job 1467 to customers during July. Job 1467 had a gross margin of 24 percent based on manufacturing cost.

c.   Job 1469 was still in process at the end of July.

d.   Closed the overapplied or underapplied overhead to the Cost of Goods Sold account at the end of July.

e.   Factory utilities, factory depreciation, and factory insurance incurred is summarized by these factory vouchers, invoices, and cost memos:

Utilities	$ 14,250
Depreciation	85,500
Insurance	11,875
Total	$111,625

f.   Purchased the following direct materials and indirect materials:

Material A	$ 25,000
Material B	43,000
Indirect materials	218,650
Total	$286,650

g.   Direct materials and indirect materials used are as follows:

	Job 1467	Job 1469	Total
Material A	$28,500	$71,250	$ 99,750
Material B	9,500	33,250	42,750
Subtotal	$38,000	$104,500	$142,500
Indirect materials			199,500
Total			$342,000

h.   Factory labor incurred for the two jobs and indirect labor is as follows:

Job 1467	$76,000
Job 1469	57,000
Indirect labor	133,000
Total	$266,000

Required

1. Calculate the amount of overapplied or underapplied overhead and state whether the cost of goods sold account will be increased or decreased by the adjustment.

2. Calculate the total manufacturing cost for Job 1467 and Job 1469 for July 2010.

4-41   **Journal Entries and Accounting for Overhead**   Humming Company manufactures high quality musical instruments for professional musicians. The company estimated that it would incur $120,000 in factory overhead costs and 8,000 direct labor-hours for the year. The April 1 balances in the inventory accounts follow:

Materials inventory	$27,000
Work-in-process inventory (S10)	10,500
Finished goods inventory (J21)	54,000

Job S10 is the only job in process on April 1. The following transactions were recorded for the month of April.

a.   Purchased materials on account, $90,000.

b.   Issued $91,000 of materials to production, $4,000 of which was for indirect materials. Cost of direct materials issued:

Job S10	$23,000
Job C20	42,000
Job M54	22,000

c.   Incurred and paid payroll cost of $20,460:

Direct labor cost ($13/hour; total 920 hours)	
Job S10	$ 6,110
Job C20	4,030
Job M54	1,820
Indirect labor	2,500
Selling and administrative salaries	6,000

d.   Recognized depreciation for the month:

Manufacturing assets	$2,200
Selling and administrative assets	1,700

e.   Paid advertising expenses $6,000

f.   Incurred factory utilities costs $1,300

g.   Incurred other factory overhead costs $1,600

h.   Applied factory overhead to production on the basis of direct labor-hours.

i. Completed Job S10 during the month and transferred it to the finished goods warehouse.

j. Sold Job J21 on account for $59,000.

k. Received $25,000 of collections on account from customers during the month.

Required

1. Calculate the company's predetermined overhead rate.
2. Prepare journal entries for the April transactions. Letter your entries from a to k.
3. What was the balance of the Materials Inventory account on April 30?
4. What was the balance of the Work-in-Process Inventory account on April 30?
5. What was the amount of underapplied or overapplied overhead?

4-42 **Journal Entries, Schedule of Cost of Goods Manufactured** Apex Corporation manufactures eighteenth-century, classical-style furniture. It uses a job costing system that applies factory overhead on the basis of direct labor-hours. Budgeted factory overhead for the year 2010 was $1,235,475, and management budgeted 86,700 direct labor-hours. Apex had no materials, work-in-process, or finished goods inventory at the beginning of August 2010. These transactions were recorded during August:

a. Purchased 5,000 square feet of oak on account at $25 per square foot.

b. Purchased 50 gallons of glue on account at $36 per gallon (indirect material).

c. Requisitioned 3,500 square feet of oak and 30.5 gallons of glue for production.

d. Incurred and paid payroll costs of $187,900. Of this amount, $46,000 were indirect labor costs; direct labor personnel earned $22 per hour on average.

e. Paid factory utility bill, $15,230 in cash.

f. August's insurance cost for the manufacturing property and equipment was $3,500. The premium had been paid in March.

g. Incurred $8,200 depreciation on manufacturing equipment for August.

h. Recorded $2,400 depreciation on an administrative asset.

i. Paid advertising expenses in cash, $5,500.

j. Incurred and paid other factory overhead costs, $13,500.

k. Incurred miscellaneous selling and administrative expenses, $13,250.

l. Applied factory overhead to production on the basis of direct labor-hours.

m. Completed goods costing $146,000 manufactured during the month.

n. Sales on account in August were $132,000. The cost of goods sold was $112,000.

Required

1. Compute the firm's predetermined factory overhead rate for the year.
2. Prepare journal entries to record the August events. Letter your entries from a to n.
3. Calculate the amount of overapplied or underapplied overhead to be closed to the Cost of Goods Sold account on August 31, 2010.
4. Prepare a schedule of cost of goods manufactured and sold.
5. Prepare the income statement for August.

4-43 **Journal Entries, Schedule of Cost of Goods Manufactured**

Accuzeit is a small New England company that manufactures custom clocks. It uses a job costing system that applies factory overhead on the basis of direct labor-hours. Budgeted factory overhead for the year 2010 was $527,805, and management budgeted 31,700 direct labor-hours. Accuzeit had no materials, work-in-process or finished goods inventory at the beginning of April. These transactions were recorded during April:

a. April insurance cost for the manufacturing property and equipment was $1,495. The premium had been paid in January.

b. Completed goods costing $62,390 manufactured during the month.

c. Recorded $1,025 depreciation on an administrative asset.

d. Purchased 21 pounds of high-grade wood fasteners on account at $15 per pound (indirect material).

e. Paid factory utility bill, $6,510 in cash.

f. Incurred and paid payroll costs of $80,300. Of this amount, $19,600 were indirect labor costs; direct labor personnel earned $20 per hour on average.

g. Incurred and paid other factory overhead costs, $5,770.

h. Purchased 2,100 unfinished mahogany blanks on account at $11 per blank.

i. Made sales on account in August, $56,410. The cost of goods sold was $47,860.

j. Requisitioned 1,495 mahogany blanks and 13 pounds of fasteners for production.

k. Incurred miscellaneous selling and administrative expenses, $5,660.

l. Incurred $3,505 depreciation on manufacturing equipment for April.

m. Paid advertising expenses in cash, $2,350.

n. Applied factory overhead to production on the basis of direct labor-hours.

Required

1. Compute the firm's predetermined factory overhead rate for the year.
2. Prepare journal entries to record the April events.
3. Calculate the amount of overapplied or underapplied overhead to be closed to the Cost of Goods Sold account on April 30.
4. Prepare a schedule of cost of goods manufactured and sold.
5. Prepare the income statement for April.

4-44 Job Costing; Service Industry   The Joshi CPA firm has the following budget for 2010:

Direct labor (for professional hours charged to clients)	$180,000
Overhead	
Indirect materials	$ 25,000
Indirect labor	125,000
Depreciation—Building	25,000
Depreciation—Furniture	2,500
Utilities	28,000
Insurance	2,400
Property taxes	2,600
Other expenses	14,500
Total	$225,000

The firm uses direct labor cost as the cost driver to apply overhead to clients.
During January, the firm worked for many clients; data for two of them follow:

Barry account	
Direct labor	$2,200
Miles account	
Direct labor	$8,400

Required

1. Compute Joshi's budgeted overhead rate. Explain how this is used.
2. Compute the amount of overhead to be charged to the Barry and Miles accounts using the predetermined overhead rate calculated in requirement 1.
3. Compute a separate job cost for the Barry and the Miles accounts.

E
x

4-45   **Job Cost Sheets; Departmental Rates, Pivot Tables in Excel (see also 4-50)**   Decker Screw Manufacturing Company produces special screws made to customer specifications. During June, the following data pertained to these costs:

		Summary of Direct Materials Requisitions		
Department Number	Job Number	Requisition Number	Quantity	Cost per Unit
1	2906	B9766	4,550	$ 1.34
2	2907	B9767	110	22.18
1	2908	B9768	1,000	9.00
1	2906	B9769	4,430	1.35
2	2908	B9770	23	48.00

		Summary of Direct Labor Time Tickets		
Department Number	Job Number	Ticket Number	Hours	Cost per Hour
1	2906	1056-1168	1,102	$6.50
2	2907	2121-2130	136	8.88
1	2908	1169-1189	151	6.50
2	2908	2131-1239	32	8.88
1	2906	1190-1239	810	6.50

	Summary of Factory Overhead Application Rates
Department Number	Basis of Application Rates
1	$3 per direct labor-hour
2	150% of direct labor cost

Decker had no beginning work-in-process inventory for June. Of the jobs begun in June, Job 2906 was completed and sold on account for $30,000, Job 2907 was completed but not sold, and Job 2908 was still in process.

Required

1. Calculate the direct materials, direct labor, factory overhead, and total costs for each job started in June, using EXCEL.

2. Perform the same calculations as in requirement (1), but assume that the direct labor-rate per hour increased by 10 percent in Department 1 and 25 percent in Department 2.

3. Perform the same calculations in part (1) except that you should use Pivot Tables in Excel to arrive at the answer.

4. Perform the same calculations in part (2) except that you should use Pivot Tables in Excel to arrive at the answer.

4-46   **Schedule of Cost of Goods Manufactured**

Cisneros Company uses a job costing system for its production costs and a predetermined factory overhead rate based on direct labor costs to apply factory overhead to all jobs. During the month of July, the firm processed three jobs: A12, C46, and M24, of which A12 was started in June.

Inventories	**July 1**	**July 31**
Direct materials	$42,500	?
Work in process	54,000	?
Finished goods	75,000	$196,080
Cost of Goods Sold, July	$?	
Direct materials purchased in July	45,000	
Issued to production:		
Job A12	21,340	
Job C46	26,000	
Job M24	16,000	
Factory labor hours used ($30/hour):		
Job A12	2,800	
Job C46	3,800	
Job M24	1,700	
Indirect labor	6,900	
Other factory overhead costs incurred:		
Rent	$129,500	
Utility	188,600	
Repairs and maintenance	194,600	
Depreciation	127,100	
Other	176,600	

As of July 31, Job A12 was sold and Jobs C46 and M24 were still in processing. Total factory overhead applied in July was $896,400.

IRequired

1. Compute the predetermined factory overhead rate.
2. Compute the amount of materials inventory at the end of July.
3. Compute the actual factory overhead cost incurred during the month of July.
4. Compute the ending balance of the work-in-process inventory account for July.
5. Prepare the statement cost of goods manufactured for July.
6. Compute the amount of over- or under-applied overhead.
7. What is the cost per unit of Job A12 if it has a total of 100 units?
8. Prepare the statement of cost of goods sold for July.

4-47 **Assigning Overhead to Jobs; Ethics**   Aero Systems is a manufacturer of airplane parts and engines for a variety of military and commercial aircraft. It has two production departments. Department A is machine-intensive; Department B is labor-intensive. Aero Systems has adopted a traditional plantwide rate using the direct labor-hour-based overhead allocation system. The company recently conducted a pilot study using a departmental overhead rate costing system. This system used two overhead allocation bases: machine-hours for Department A and direct labor-hours for Department B. The study showed that the system, which will be more accurate and timely, will assign lower costs to the government jobs and higher costs to the company's nongovernmental jobs. Apparently, the current (less accurate) direct labor-based costing system has overcosted government jobs and undercosted private business jobs. On hearing of this, top management has decided to scrap the plans for adopting the new departmental overhead rate costing system because government jobs constitute 40 percent of Aero Systems' business and the new system will reduce the price and thus the profit for this part of its business.

Required   As the management accountant participating in this pilot study project, what is your responsibility when you hear of top management's decision to cancel the plans to implement the new departmental overhead rate costing system? What would you do?

4-48 Operation Costing Brian Canning Co., which sells canned corn, uses an operation costing system. Cans of corn are classified as either sweet or regular, depending on the type of corn used. Both types of corn go through the separating and cleaning operations, but only regular corn goes through the creaming operation. During January, two batches of corn were canned from start to finish. Batch X consisted of 800 pounds of sweet corn and batch Y consisted of 700 pounds of regular corn. The company had no beginning or ending work-in-process inventory. The following cost information is for the month of January:

	Batch	Cost	Batch Size
Raw sweet corn	X	$5,200	800 LB
Raw regular corn	Y	2,450*	700 LB
Separating department costs		1,500	
Cleaning department costs		900	
Creaming department costs		210	

*Includes $300 for cream.

Required

1. Compute the unit cost for sweet corn and regular corn.
2. Record appropriate journal entries.

4-49 Spoilage, Rework, and Scrap (appendix) Richport Company manufactures products that often require specification changes or modifications to meet customer needs. Consequently, Richport employs a job costing system for its operations.

Although the specification changes and modifications are commonplace, Richport has been able to establish a normal spoilage rate of 2.5% of good units produced (before spoilage). The company recognizes normal spoilage during the budgeting process and classifies it as a component of factory overhead. Thus, the predetermined overhead rate used to apply factory overhead costs to jobs includes an allowance for net spoilage cost for normal spoilage. If spoilage on a job exceeds the normal rate, it is considered abnormal and then must be analyzed and the cause of the spoilage must be submitted to management.

Randa Duncan, one of Richport's inspection managers, has been reviewing the output of Job N1192-122 that was recently completed. A total of 122,000 units had been started for the job, and 5,000 units were rejected at final inspection, meaning that the job yielded 117,000 good units.

Randa noted that 900 of the first units produced were rejected due to a very unusual design defect that was corrected immediately; no more units were rejected for this reason.

Randa was unable to identify a pattern for the remaining 4,100 rejected units. They can be sold at a salvage value of $7 per unit.

The total costs accumulated for all 122,000 units of Job N1192-122 follow. Although the job is completed, all of these costs are still in the Work-in-Process Inventory account (i.e., the cost of the completed job has not been transferred to Finished Goods Inventory account).

Direct materials	$2,196,000
Direct labor	1,830,000
Applied factory overhead	2,928,000
Total cost of job	$6,954,000

Required

1. Explain the distinction between normal and abnormal spoilage.
2. Distinguish between spoiled units, rework units, and scrap.
3. Review the results and costs for Job N1192-122.

   a. Prepare an analysis separating the spoiled units into normal and abnormal spoilage by first determining the normal input required to yield 117,000 good units.

   b. Prepare the appropriate journal entries to account for Job N1192-122.

4-50 **Job Costing, Departmental Rates, Pivot Tables in Excel (see also 4-45)**   Boston Manufacturing Company had the following cost information for May.

| | **Summary of Direct Materials Requisitions** | | |
Department Number	Job Number	Quantity	Cost per Unit
1	88X	6,650	$8.31
1	88Y	2,130	2.52
1	88Z	1,818	9.16
1	88Y	921	4.18
1	88Z	63	3.23

| | **Summary of Direct Labor Time Tickets** | |
Department Number	Job Number	Hours
1	88X	554
2	88Y	321
2	88Z	618
1	88Y	25
1	88Z	613

The labor rate in Department 1 is $10.50 and in Department 2 is $9.50. The overhead rate in Department 1 is based on direct labor-hours, at $4.50 per hour; in Department 2 the rate is 125 percent of direct labor cost.

Boston had no beginning work-in-process inventory for May. Of the jobs begun in May, Job 88X was completed and sold on account for $86,000, Job 88Y was completed but not sold, and Job 88Z was still in process.

Required

1. Using Pivot Tables in Excel, calculate the direct materials, direct labor, factory overhead, and total costs for each job started in May.

2. Perform the same calculations as in requirement (1), but assume that labor rates in both departments have increased by 20 percent.

4-51 **Quarterly and Annual Overhead Application**   The Mansfield Machine Shop is a family-owned business with 25 employees. The founding brothers, Steve and George, started the business in 1974 with a single milling machine, a grinder, and a lathe. The brothers now own a business with 27 machines, and operating revenues of more than $5 million per year. The brothers have noticed that they are losing business to new competitors and they have heard from some of their customers that their competitors have better prices. So they have asked you to study their operations and summary financial reports for the prior year and to make recommendations.
The information available to you includes:

1. The business is very seasonal, as it reflects the seasonality of the businesses of its major customers in the manufacturing and construction industries. The first and third quarters of the year have relatively low demand, while their busiest periods are the second and fourth quarters. George and Steve measure the volume of their business in machine-hours, since they charge by the machine-hour and the materials costs are negligible. The machine-hours demand for last year was 5,000 hours in the first quarter, 12,500 in the second quarter, 7,500 in the third quarter, and 11,250 in the fourth quarter.

2. Mansfield has 27 machines in the plant, and while some are newer and more technologically advanced than others, the differences are not great. Because of this, the brothers charge the same price for machining on each of the machines. George and Steve realize that their business is very seasonal and that their machines and operators will be busier at times, but to keep the machines in good shape and operators rested, they try to limit the work to approximately 150 hours per month per machine.

3. Because of the seasonality of the business, George and Steve have always recalculated the overhead rate for each quarter. The overhead rate is determined at the end of each quarter based on actual total overhead costs for the quarter (which are $450,000 per quarter) and the actual machine-hours for that quarter. This machine-hours-based rate is then used in the following quarter, and is revised accordingly at the end of each quarter.

4. Mansfield's variable costs are $45 per machine-hour. The firm charges a 50 percent markup over full cost, the sum of variable costs and overhead charges per unit. Mansfield uses $85 full cost in pricing for the first quarter.

5. In addition to $450,000 fixed operating costs per quarter, Mansfield has $25,000 administrative fixed costs per quarter.

Required

1. Calculate the overhead rates and machine-hour pricing rates using the quarterly overhead system now used by the firm.

2. Recalculate the overhead rates and machine-hour pricing rates using an annual overhead rate.

3. Calculate total contribution and operating income for the year and for each quarter under both the quarterly and annual rates.

4. Interpret your findings in parts 1 through 3. How does the choice of a quarterly overhead rate affect pricing for Mansfield? Which overhead rate, quarterly or annual, do you think Mansfield should use and why? What are the strategic implications of the choice of overhead rates for the company?

4-52 **Overhead Rates Used for Each Machine in a Printing Plant**   Ennis Inc.'s Forms Solutions Group (http://www.ennis.com/) is a Texas-based machine-intensive printing company that produces business forms. The resources demanded by a specific job depend on the type and amount of paper used and the composition and the construction of the business form. All jobs are constrained by the time necessary on a press and on a collator capable of producing forms at the required size.

Ennis Inc.'s Forms Solutions (EFS) uses job costing for pricing and bidding decisions. EFS uses a separate factory overhead rate for each machine. Costs of machine operator, support personnel, and supplies are identified directly with presses and collators. Other factory overhead costs—including insurance, supervision, and office salaries—are allocated to machines based on their processing capacity (cost driver is the number of feet of business form per minute), weighted by the maximum paper width and complexity (the cost driver is the number of colors and other features) that they are capable of handling.

When EFS receives a request for a bid on a particular job, the company uses computer software to determine direct material costs based on the type and quantity of paper. Then it identifies the least expensive press and collator that are capable of handling the specifications for the business form ordered. The third step is to estimate the total press and collator processing costs by using specific cost-driver rates per machine time multiplied by the estimated processing time. The bid price is calculated by adding a standard markup to the total press, collator, and direct material costs. A higher markup is used for rush jobs and jobs requiring special features.

Required   Discuss the strengths and weaknesses of the EFS costing system and its strategic implications.

4-53 **Plantwide vs. Departmental Overhead Rate**   Rose Bach was recently hired as controller of Empco Inc., a sheet metal manufacturer. Empco has been in the sheet metal business for many years and is currently investigating ways to modernize its manufacturing process. At the first staff meeting Rose attended, Bob Kelley, chief engineer, presented a proposal for automating the drilling department. He recommended that Empco purchase two robots that could replace the eight direct labor workers in the department. The cost savings outlined in Bob's proposal included eliminating direct labor cost and reducing factory overhead cost to zero in the drilling department because Empco charges factory overhead on the basis of direct labor dollars using a plantwide rate.

Empco's president was puzzled by Kelley's explanation of cost savings, believing it made no sense. Rose agreed, explaining that as firms become more automated, they should rethink their factory overhead systems. The president then asked her to look into the matter and prepare a report for the next staff meeting.

Required

1. Describe the shortcomings of the Empco's current system for applying overhead.

2. Explain the misconceptions in Bob Kelley's statement that the factory overhead cost in the drilling department would be reduced to zero if the automation proposal were implemented.

3. How would you improve the allocation of overhead costs?

4-54 **Plantwide vs. Departmental Overhead Rate**   Adams Corporation manufactures auto steering systems. Cost estimates for one unit of the product for the year 2010 follow:

Direct materials	$200
Direct labor ($12/hour)	240
Machine-hours	20

This product requires 12 hours of direct labor in department A and 8 hours in department B. Also, it requires 5 machine-hours in department A and 15 machine-hours in department B. The factory overhead costs estimated in these two departments follow:

	A	B
Variable cost	$146,000	$77,000
Fixed cost	94,000	163,000

Management expects the firm to produce 1,000 units during 2010.

Required

1. Assume that factory overhead was applied on the basis of direct labor-hours. Compute the predetermined factory overhead rate.
2. If factory overhead were applied on the basis of machine-hours, what would be the plantwide overhead rate?
3. If the company produced 1,000 units during the year, what was the total amount of applied factory overhead in each department in requirements 1 and 2?
4. If you were asked to evaluate the performance of each department manager, which allocation basis (cost driver) would you use? Why?
5. Compute the departmental overhead rates for each department.

Solution to Self-Study Problem

Journal Entries and Accounting for Overhead

1. Journal entries:

(a)	Materials Inventory	25,000	
	Accounts Payable		25,000
	To record the purchase of direct materials and indirect materials		
(b)	Work-in-Process Inventory	15,000	
	Factory Overhead	8,000	
	Materials Inventory		23,000
	To record direct and indirect materials issued.		
(c)	Work-in-Process Inventory	20,000	
	Factory Overhead	5,000	
	Accrued Payroll		25,000
	To record factory labor incurred.		
(d)	Factory Overhead	18,000	
	Accounts Payable		500
	Accumulated Depreciation—Factory		15,000
	Prepaid Insurance		2,500
	To record actual overhead costs incurred, including factory utilities, depreciation, and insurance.		
(e)	Work-in-Process Inventory	30,000	
	Factory Overhead		30,000
	To record the application of factory overhead to jobs.		

Summary of factory overhead applied

Job 1($15 per machine hour × 1,200 hours.)	$18,000
Job 2 ($15 per machine hour × 800 hours)	12,000
Total	$30,000

(f)	Finished Goods Inventory	45,000	
	Work-in-Process Inventory		45,000
	To record the job finished		

Total manufacturing cost for Job 101

Beginning inventory	$6,000
Direct materials added	9,000
Direct labor incurred	12,000
Factory overhead applied	18,000
Total	$45,000

(g)	Accounts Receivable	66,000	
	Sales		66,000
	To record the total sales revenue of two jobs		
	Cost of Goods Sold	55,000	
	Finished Goods Inventory		55,000
	To record the total cost of goods sold		

Summary of the total cost in shipping orders

Job 100	$10,000
Job 101	45,000
Total	$55,000

Sales = $55,000 × 120% = $66,000

2. Ending balance of the Work-in-Process Inventory account for Job 102:

Direct materials	$ 6,000
Direct labor	8,000
Factory overhead applied	12,000
Total ending balance	$26,000

3. Factory overhead variance:

Actual factory overhead		
Indirect materials	$ 8,000	
Indirect labor	5,000	
Utilities	500	
Depreciation	15,000	
Insurance	2,500	$31,000
Less: Applied factory overhead (e)		30,000
Underapplied factory overhead		$ 1,000

4. To record the disposition of underapplied factory overhead by closing the Factory Overhead account to the Cost of Goods Sold account.

| (h) | Cost of Goods Sold | 1,000 | |
| | Factory Overhead | | 1,000 |

CHAPTER FIVE

Activity-Based Costing and Customer Profitability Analysis

After studying this chapter, you should be able to . . .

1. Explain the strategic role of activity-based costing
2. Describe activity-based costing (ABC), the steps in developing an ABC system, and the benefits of an ABC system
3. Determine product costs under both the volume-based method and the activity-based method and contrast the two
4. Explain activity-based management (ABM)
5. Describe how ABC/M is used in manufacturing companies, service companies, and governmental organizations
6. Use an activity-based approach to analyze customer profitability
7. Identify key factors for successful ABC/M implementation

Beware of little expenses. A small leak will sink a great ship.

Benjamin Franklin

This chapter has a lot to do with implementing the spirit of Benjamin Franklin's observation—in cost management terms—that it really does matter how accurately you calculate a cost. Why? Having accurate costs is important for a variety of reasons: a company might find that it has a difficult time determining which of its products is most profitable. Alternatively, it finds its sales increasing but profits declining and cannot understand why. Perhaps the company keeps losing competitive bids for products and services and does not understand why. In many cases, accurate cost information is the answer to these questions. Accurate cost information provides a competitive advantage. It helps a company or organization to develop and to execute its strategy by providing accurate information about the cost of its products and services, the cost of serving its customers, the cost of dealing with its suppliers, and the cost of supporting business processes within the company.

The Strategic Role of Activity-Based Costing

LEARNING OBJECTIVE 1

Explain the strategic role of activity-based costing.

Activity-based costing (ABC) is a method for determining accurate costs. While ABC is a relatively recent innovation in cost accounting, it is rapidly being adopted by companies across many industries and within government and not-for-profit organizations. Here is a quick example of how it works, and why it is important. Suppose you and two friends (Joe and Al) have gone out for dinner to have pizza. You each order an individual size pizza, and Al suggests that you all order a plate of appetizers for the table. You and Joe figure you will have a bite or two of the appetizers, so you say OK. Dinner is great, but at the end Al is still hungry, so he orders another plate of appetizers and as before, eats all of it. When it is time for the check, Al suggests the three of you split the cost of the meal equally. Is this fair? Perhaps Al should offer to pay for the two appetizer plates. The individual pizzas are direct costs for each of you so that an equal share is fair, but while the appetizer plates were intended to be shared equally, it turns out that Al consumed most of them.

There are similar examples in manufacturing. Suppose you and Joe and Al are also product managers at a plant that manufactures furniture. There are three product lines. Al is in charge of sofa manufacturing, Joe of dining room tables and chairs, and you are in charge of bedroom furniture. The direct materials and labor costs are traced directly to each product line. It is your responsibility to manage these direct costs. Also, there are indirect manufacturing costs (overhead) that cannot be traced to each product, including the following activities: materials acquisition, materials storage and handling, product inspection, manufacturing supervision, job scheduling, equipment maintenance, and fabric cutting. What if the company decides to charge each of the three product managers a "fair share" of the total indirect cost using the ratio of units produced in a manager's area to the total units produced for all managers? This approach is described in Chapter 4 and is commonly referred to as *volume-based costing.* Note that whether the proportions used are based on units of product, direct labor-hours, or machine-hours, each of these is volume-based.

But if, as is usually the case, the usage of these activities is not proportional to the number of units produced, then some managers will be overcharged and others undercharged under the volume-based approach. For example, suppose Al insists on more frequent inspections of his production; then he should be fairly charged a higher proportion of overhead (inspection) than that based on units alone. Moreover, why should you pay any portion of fabric cutting if your bedroom furniture does not require fabric?

Another consideration is that the volume-based method provides little incentive for the manager to control indirect costs. Unfortunately, the only way you could reduce your share of the indirect costs is to reduce your units produced (or hope that Joe and/or Al increase production)—not much of an incentive. On reflection, the approach that charges indirect costs to product based on units produced does not provide very accurate product cost for you or Joe or Al and certainly does not provide the appropriate incentives for managing the indirect costs. The solution is to use activity-based costing to charge these indirect costs to the products, using detailed information on the activities that make up the indirect costs—inspection, fabric cutting, and materials handling. This chapter shows how to do it.

A good example of one of many success stories for ABC is the application of ABC at the U.S. Postal Service (USPS). The ABC application at the USPS originated from the Postmaster General's directive to develop a costing system that would help the USPS to become more competitive and to serve as a basis for comparing performance among the various mail-processing facilities. The initial ABC system used 58 work activities and nine cost objects. The cost objects included handling of letters, flats, small parcels, large parcels, priority mail, express mail, registered mail, large mail containers, and small mail containers. In the initial application at a single mail-processing facility, there was a reduction of 13 percent in total cost as a result of the improved understanding of cost behavior in the facility. The USPS also used ABC to determine the cost differences in processing payments from customers who used cash, checks, or credit cards and from this analysis determined that the low-cost approach was to encourage the use of credit cards. The ABC-based analyses have helped the USPS to implement an effective, cost-competitive strategy.

Role of Volume-Based Costing

Volume-based costing can be a good strategic choice for some firms. It is appropriate generally when direct costs are the major cost of the product or service and activities supporting the production of the product or service are relatively simple, low-cost, and homogenous across different product lines. This may be the case, for example, for a commodity manufacturer that has one or a few very homogeneous product lines—for example, a firm that manufactures paper products or a firm that produces certain agricultural products. Similarly, a professional service firm (law firm, accounting firm) may not need ABC because labor costs for the professional staff are the largest cost of the firm, and labor is also easily traced to clients (the cost object). For firms other than these, the ABC approach is often preferred: the volume-based approach will cause significant inaccuracies in the product costs—some products will be overcosted and others undercosted because the usage of activities is not in proportion to the volume of output.

Activity-Based Costing

LEARNING OBJECTIVE 2

Describe activity-based costing (ABC), the steps in developing an ABC system, and the benefits of an ABC system.

To develop a costing system we need to understand relationships among resources, activities, and products or services. Resources are spent on activities, and products or services are a result of activities. Many of the resources used in an operation can be traced to individual products or services and identified as direct materials or direct labor costs. Most overhead costs relate only indirectly to final products or services. A costing system identifies costs with activities that consume resources and assign resource costs to cost objects such as products, services, or intermediate cost pools based on activities performed for the cost objects.

Resources, Activities, Resource Consumption Cost Drivers, and Activity Consumption Cost Drivers

Before discussing activity-based costing, we need to define several important terms: *activity, resource, cost driver, resource consumption cost driver,* and *activity consumption cost driver.*

An **activity**
is a specific task or action of work done.

An **activity** is a specific task or action of work done. An activity can be a single action or an aggregation of several actions. For example, moving inventory from workstation A to workstation B is an activity that may require only one action. Production set-up is an activity that may include several actions. Activities are often listed in what is called an *activity dictionary.* An illustration of key activities in a firm's internal supply chain is shown by the Supply Chain Council in what is called the SCOR® (Supply Chain Operations Reference) on the Council's Web site (www.supply-chain.org/).

A **resource**
is an economic element needed or consumed in performing activities.

A **resource** is an economic element needed or consumed in performing activities. Salaries and supplies, for example, are resources needed or used in performing manufacturing activities.

A *cost driver is* a factor that causes or relates to a change in the cost of an activity. Because cost drivers cause or relate to cost changes, measured or quantified amounts of cost drivers are excellent bases for assigning resource costs to activities and for assigning the cost of activities to cost objects.

A **resource consumption cost driver**
is a measure of the amount of resources consumed by an activity.

A cost driver is either a *resource consumption cost driver* or an *activity consumption cost driver.* A **resource consumption cost driver** is a measure of the amount of resources consumed by an activity. It is the cost driver for assigning a resource cost, consumed by or related to an activity, to a particular activity or cost pool. Examples of resource consumption cost drivers are the number of items in a purchase or sales order, changes in product design, and machine-hours.

An **activity consumption cost driver**
measures how much of an activity a cost object uses.

An **activity consumption cost driver** measures the amount of an activity performed for a cost object. It is used to assign activity cost pool costs to cost objects. Examples of activity consumption cost drivers are the number of machine-hours in the manufacturing of product X, or the number of batches used to manufacture Product Y.

What Is Activity-Based Costing?

Activity-based costing (ABC)
is a costing approach that assigns resource costs to cost objects based on activities performed for the cost objects.

Activity-based costing (ABC) is a costing approach that assigns resource costs to cost objects such as products, services, or customers based on activities performed for the cost objects. The premise of this costing approach is that a firm's products or services are the results of activities and activities use resources which incur costs. Costs of resources are assigned to activities based on the activities that use or consume resources (resource consumption drivers), and costs of activities are assigned to cost objects based on activities performed for the cost objects (activity consumption drivers). ABC recognizes the causal or direct relationships between resource costs, cost drivers, activities, and cost objects in assigning costs to activities and then to cost objects.

ABC assigns factory overhead costs to cost objects such as products or services by identifying the resources and activities as well as their costs and amounts needed to produce output.

Using resource consumption cost drivers, a firm determines the resource costs consumed by activities, calculates the cost of a unit of activity, and then assigns the cost of an activity to cost objects by multiplying the cost of each activity by the amount of the activity consumed by each of the cost objects.

The Two-Stage Cost Assignment Procedure

A **two-stage cost assignment** assigns resource costs to activity cost pools and then to cost objects.

A **two-stage cost assignment** procedure assigns resource costs such as factory overhead costs to activity cost pools and then to cost objects to determine the amount of resource costs for each of the cost objects. Volume-based costing systems assign factory overhead costs first to plant or departmental cost pools and second to products or services (see Exhibit 5.1). Volume-based systems, in the first stage, charge factory overhead costs to a single plant cost pool or to departmental cost pools. This approach is convenient and simple, because many accounting systems in use today accumulate cost information by department, which is easily aggregated to the plant level. In the second stage, a volume-based rate (based on units produced or hours used in production) is then used to apply overhead to each of the cost objects. The volume-based approach is used in Chapter 4 in job costing. A volume-based two-stage cost assignment procedure, however, is likely to distort product or service costs. This is true especially in the second stage where the volume-based costing system uses a cost driver such as direct labor-hours or output units to assign factory overhead costs. Because all products or services do not usually consume factory overhead resources in proportion to the volume-based measure the firm uses to assign factory overhead costs, a volume-based system often leads to inaccurate measures for the costs of support activities in its operations. This distortion becomes more serious when a substantial portion of factory overhead costs is not output-volume related and the firm manufactures a diverse mix of products with differences in volumes, sizes, or complexities.

Activity-based costing systems differ from volume-based costing systems by linking uses of resources to activities and linking activity costs to products, services, or customers (see Exhibit 5.2). The first stage assigns factory overhead costs to activities by using appropriate resource consumption cost drivers. The second stage assigns the costs of activities to cost objects using appropriate activity consumption cost drivers that measure the demands cost objects place on the activities. By using cost drivers in both the first and second stage cost assignments, activity-based costing systems provide more accurate measures of product or service costs for the cost of activities that are not proportional to the volume of outputs produced.

In summary, activity-based costing systems differ from volume-based costing systems in two ways. First, the ABC system defines cost pools as activities rather than production plant or department cost centers. Second, the cost drivers that the ABC system uses to assign activity

EXHIBIT 5.1 The Volume-Based Two-Stage Procedure

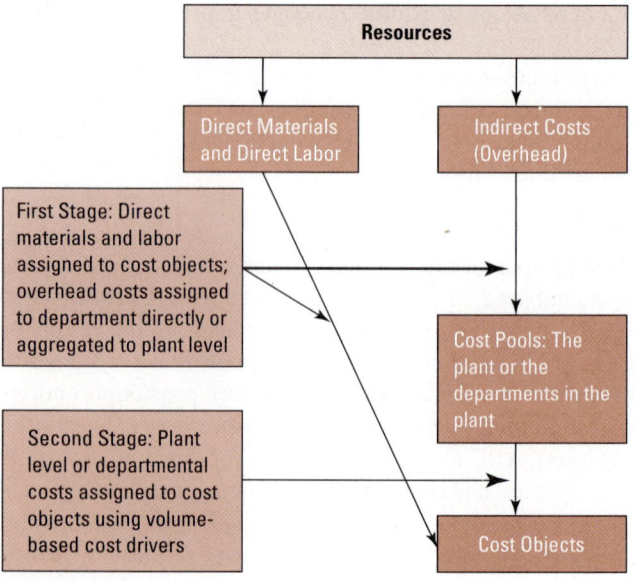

EXHIBIT 5.2 The Activity-Based Two-Stage Procedure

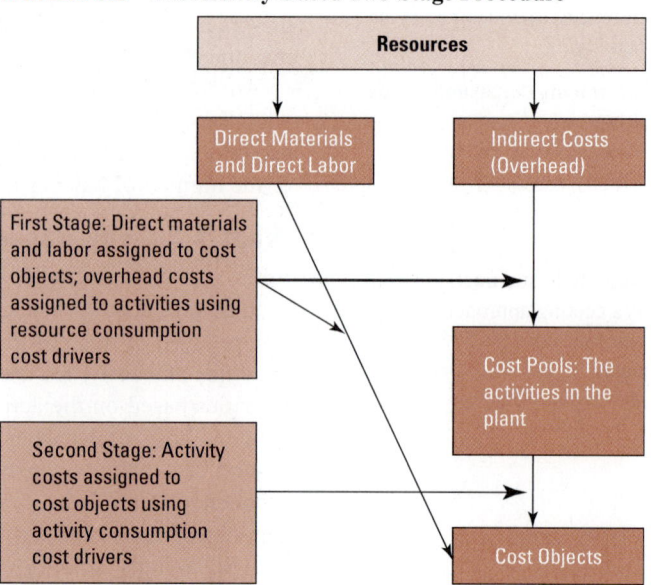

costs to cost objects are drivers based on an activity or activities performed for the cost object. The volume-based approach uses a volume-based cost driver that often bears little or no relationship to the consumption of resource costs by the cost objects.

Steps in Developing an Activity-Based Costing System

Developing an activity-based costing system entails three steps: (1) identifying resource costs and activities, (2) assigning resource costs to activities, and (3) assigning activity costs to cost objects. Steps 1 and 2 constitute stage 1 from Exhibit 5.2, and step 3 is equivalent to stage 2 from that exhibit.

Step 1: Identify Resource Costs and Activities

The first step in designing an ABC system is to conduct an activity analysis to identify the resource costs and activities of the firm. Most firms record resource costs in specific accounts in the accounting system. Examples of these accounts include supplies, purchasing, materials handling, warehousing, office expenses, furniture and fixtures, buildings, equipment, utilities, and salaries and benefits. However, special effort most likely will be needed to determine appropriate resource costs for activity-based costing because generally several different resource costs may be recorded in a single account or the costs for an activity may be recorded in several accounts. For example, a firm may use a single factory supplies account for all supplies in its operations that include several manufacturing operations. Costs to complete a purchasing order may be spread over several accounts including accounts for warehousing, purchasing, and receiving.

Through activity analyses a firm identifies the work it performs to carry out its operations. Activity analyses include gathering data from existing documents and records, as well as collecting additional data using questionnaires, observations, or interviews of key personnel. Questions that ABC project team members typically ask employees or managers in gathering activity data include:

- What work or activities do you do?
- How much time do you spend performing these activities?
- What resources are required to perform these activities?
- What value does the activity have for the product, service, customer, or organization?

With the help of industrial engineers and management accountants, the team also collects activity data by observing the work performed and making a list of all the activities involved.

Levels of Activities

To identify resource costs for various activities, a firm classifies all activities according to the way in which the activities consume resources.

A unit-level activity is performed for each unit of the cost object.

A batch-level activity is performed for each batch or group of products or services.

A product-level activity supports the production of a specific product or service.

A facility-level activity supports operations in general.

1. A **unit-level activity** is performed for each individual unit of product or service of the firm. Examples of unit-level activities include direct materials, direct labor-hours, inserting a component, and inspecting every unit. A unit-level activity is volume-based. The required activity varies in proportion with the quantity of the cost object. The resource consumption driver and the activity consumption driver are most likely to be the same for unit level activities.

2. A **batch-level activity** is performed for each batch or group of units of products or services. Examples of batch-level activities are setting up machines, placing purchase orders, scheduling production, conducting inspections by batch, handling materials, and expediting production.

3. A **product-level activity** supports the production of a specific product or service. Examples of product-level activities include designing products, purchasing parts required for products, and engaging in engineering changes to modify products.

4. A **facility-level activity** supports operations in general. These activities are not caused by products or customer service needs and cannot be traced to individual units, batches, or products. Examples of facility-level activities include providing security for the plant performing maintenance of general purpose machines, managing the plant, incurring factory property taxes and insurance, and closing the books each month. Some firms refer to these activities as business or infrastructure-sustaining activities.

Note that a unit-level activity can always be traced to a batch (one of the units in the batch), and a batch-level activity can always be traced to a product (one batch of this particular product), and a product-level activity can usually be traced to a manufacturing facility; but, the reverse is not possible. Exhibit 5.3 illustrates activity level classifications at Siemens Electric Motor Works.

Step 2: Assign Resource Costs to Activities

Activity-based costing uses resource consumption cost drivers to assign resource costs to activities. Because activities drive the cost of resources used in operations, a firm should choose resource consumption cost drivers based on cause-and-effect relationships. Typical resource consumption cost drivers include the number of (1) labor-hours for labor intensive activities; (2) employees for payroll-related activities; (3) setups for batch-related activities; (4) moves for materials-handling activities; (5) machine-hours for machine repair and maintenance; and (6) square feet for general maintenance and cleaning activities.

The cost of the resources can be assigned to activities by direct tracing or estimation. Direct tracing requires measuring the actual usage of resources by activities. For example, power used to operate a machine can be traced directly to that machine's operation by reading the meter attached to the machine. When direct tracing is not available, department managers and supervisors need to estimate the amount or percentage of time (or effort) employees spend on each identified activity. Exhibit 5.4 illustrates resources and resource consumption drivers for factory overhead costs at AT&T's New River Valley plant.

Step 3: Assign Activity Costs to Cost Objects

The final step is to assign costs of activities or activity cost pools to cost objects based on the appropriate activity consumption cost drivers. Outputs are the cost objects for which firms or organizations perform activities. Typical outputs for a cost system are products and services; however, outputs also can include customers, projects, or business units. For example, the outputs of an insurance company may be individual insurance policies sold to customers, claims processed, types of policies offered, insurance agents, or divisions or subunits of the company.

EXHIBIT 5.3

Activities and Activity Levels at Siemens Electric Motor Works

Activity	Activity Level
Using direct materials	Unit
Using direct labor-hours	Unit
Using machine-hours	Unit
Starting production orders	Batch
Adding special components	Batch

EXHIBIT 5.4
Resource and Resource Consumption Cost Drivers at AT&T's New River Valley Plant

Resource	Resource Consumption Cost Driver
Personnel	Number of workers
Storeroom	Number of items picked for an order
Engineers	Time worked
Materials management	Time worked
Accounting	Time worked
Research and development	Number of new codes developed
Quality	Time worked
Utilities	Square-footage

Benefits of Activity-Based Costing

Since the 1980s an increasing number of firms have adopted the activity-based costing system. These firms adopt ABC because of the benefits it offers.

Initially, many firms adopt activity-based costing to reduce distortions in product costs often found in their volume-based costing systems. Volume-based costing systems generate product or service costs bearing little or no relationship to activities and resources consumed in operations. ABC clearly shows the effect of differences in activities and changes in products or services on costs. Among the major benefits of activity-based costing that many firms have experienced are:

1. **Better profitability measures.** ABC provides more accurate and informative product costs, leading to more accurate product and customer profitability measurements and to better-informed strategic decisions about pricing, product lines, and market segments.
2. **Better decision making.** ABC provides more accurate measurements of activity-driving costs, helping managers to improve product and process value by making better product design decisions, better customer support decisions, and fostering value-enhancement projects.
3. **Process improvement.** The ABC system provides the information to identify areas where process improvement is needed.
4. **Cost estimation.** Improved product costs lead to better estimates of job costs for pricing decisions, budgeting, and planning.
5. **Cost of unused capacity.** Since many firms have seasonal and cyclical fluctuations in sales and production, there are times when plant capacity is unused. This can mean that costs are *incurred* at the batch-, product-, and facility-level activities but are *not used*. Capacity is supplied but not used in production. ABC systems provide better information to identify the cost of unused capacity and maintain a separate accounting for this cost. For example, if a particular customer's order requires the addition of a certain type of capacity in the plant, then the customer can be charged for that additional capacity. Alternatively, if a plant manager decides to add capacity in expectation of future increases in sales and production, then the cost of that additional capacity should not be charged to current production but charged as a lump-sum in the plant's costs. Overall, the goal is to manage capacity levels to reduce the cost of underutilization of capacity and to price products and services properly.

Each of these benefits can contribute significantly to a company's competitiveness by helping the company make better decisions and implement its strategy.

A Comparison of Volume-Based and Activity-Based Costing

LEARNING OBJECTIVE 3

Determine product costs under both the volume-based and the activity-based methods, and contrast the two.

The following example contrasts the volume-based costing system using direct labor-hours as the cost driver with an activity-based costing system that uses both volume-based and activity-based cost drivers. Since this illustration shows only step 3 of the ABC method, we also show an illustration (AIRCO Ltd) that includes all three steps of the ABC method in the section, "Real-World Activity-Based Costing/Management Applications," on page 141.

Haymarket BioTech Inc. (HBT) produces and sells two secure communications systems, AW(Anywhere) and SZ(SecureZone). AW uses satellite technology and allows customers to communicate anywhere on the earth. SZ uses similar technology except it allows communication between two parties that are within 10 miles of each other. HBT operates in a very small but competitive industry. The customers are governmental and corporate customers for which these products are critical; the customers rely on HBT's ability to quickly adapt its products to threats from devices that would compromise the security of the products. SZ has been successful for nearly 10 years and has undergone a number of improvements in this time; sales are expected to continue to grow at 8–10 percent per year. AW, a more recent product, has also been successful, but demand has not been as strong and sales growth is expected to be 3–5 percent per year. Because of the higher profitability of the AW system (Exhibit 5.5), HBT is considering an extensive advertising campaign to boost sales of AW, and to make plans for reallocating manufacturing facilities from SZ to AW to make this possible. HBT has the following operating data for the two products.

	AW	SZ
Production volume	5,000	20,000
Selling price	$400.00	$200.00
Unit direct materials and labor	$200.00	$ 80.00
Direct labor-hours	25,000	75,000
Direct labor-hours per unit	5	3.75

Volume-Based Costing

The volume-based costing system assigns factory overhead (OH) based on direct labor-hours (DLH). The firm has a total budgeted overhead of $2,000,000. Since the firm budgeted 100,000 direct labor-hours for the year, the overhead rate is $20 per direct labor-hour.

Total overhead		$2,000,000
Total DLH	25,000 + 75,000 =	100,000
Overhead rate per DLH		$ 20.00

EXHIBIT 5.5
Product Profitability Analysis under Volume-Based Costing

	AW	SZ
Unit selling price	$400	$200
Unit manufacturing cost:		
Direct materials and labor	$200	$80
Factory overhead	100	75
Cost per unit	300	155
Profit margin	$100	$ 45

Since the firm uses 25,000 direct labor-hours to manufacture 5,000 units of AW, the factory overhead assigned to AW is $500,000 in total and $100 per unit:

Total OH assigned to AW	$20 × 25,000 = $500,000
Number of units of AW	5,000
Factory overhead per unit of AW	$ 100.00

The factory overhead for SZ is $1,500,000 in total and $75 per unit since the firm spent 75,000 direct labor-hours to manufacture 20,000 units of SZ:

Total OH assigned to SZ	$20 × 75,000 = $1,500,000
Number of units of SZ	20,000
Factory overhead per unit of SZ	$ 75.00

Exhibit 5.5 shows a product profitability analysis using the firm's volume-based costing system.

Activity-Based Costing

In using activity-based costing, HBT identified the following activities, budgeted costs, and activity consumption cost drivers—the information necessary to complete Step 3: assign activity costs to cost objects.

Activity	Budgeted Cost	Activity Consumption Cost Driver
Engineering	$ 125,000	Engineering hours
Setups	300,000	Number of setups
Machine operation	1,500,000	Machine-hours
Packing	75,000	Number of packing orders
Total	$2,000,000	

HBT also gathered the following operating data pertaining to each of its products:

	AW	SZ	Total
Engineering hours	5,000	7,500	12,500
Number of setups	200	100	300
Machine hours	50,000	100,000	150,000
Number of packing orders	5,000	10,000	15,000

Using the above data, the cost driver rate for each activity consumption cost driver is calculated as follows:

(1) Activity Consumption Cost Driver	(2) Budgeted Cost	(3) Budgeted Activity Consumption	(4) = (2)/(3) Activity Consumption Rate
Engineering hours	$ 125,000	12,500	$ 10 per hour
Number of setups	300,000	300	1,000 per setup
Machine hours	1,500,000	150,000	10 per hour
Number of packing orders	75,000	15,000	5 per order

Factory overhead costs are assigned to both products by these calculations:

AW (5,000 units)				
(1) Activity Consumption Cost Driver	(2) Activity Consumption Rate	(3) Activity Consumption	(4) = (2) × (3) Total Overhead	(5) Overhead Per Unit
Engineering hours	$ 10	5,000	$ 50,000	$ 10
Number of setups	1,000	200	200,000	40
Machine hours	10	50,000	500,000	100
Number of packing orders	5	5,000	25,000	5
Overhead cost per unit			$775,000	$155

SZ (20,000 units)				
(1) Activity Consumption Cost Driver	(2) Activity Consumption Rate	(3) Activity Consumption	(4) = (2) × (3) Total Overhead	(5) Overhead Per Unit
Engineering hours	$ 10	7,500	$ 75,000	$ 3.75
Number of setups	1,000	100	100,000	5.00
Machine hours	10	100,000	1,000,000	50.00
Number of packing orders	5	10,000	50,000	2.50
Overhead cost per unit			$1,225,000	$61.25

Exhibit 5.6 presents a product profitability analysis under the activity-based costing system and Exhibit 5.7 compares product costs and profit margins under the two costing systems. The comparison shows that the volume-based product costing system significantly undercosts AW (a low-volume product) and overcosts SZ (a high-volume product) when considering the actual overhead consumption of the two products. This is sometimes called *cross-subsidization*, that

EXHIBIT 5.6
Product Profitability Analysis under the ABC Costing System

	AW		SZ	
Unit selling price		$400		$200.00
Unit manufacturing cost				
Direct materials and labor	$200		$80.00	
Factory overhead:				
Engineering	$ 10		$ 3.75	
Setups	40		5.00	
Machine running	100		50.00	
Packing	5	155	2.50	61.25
Cost per unit		355		141.25
Profit margin		$ 45		$ 58.75

EXHIBIT 5.7

Comparison of Alternative Costing Approaches

	AW	SZ
Unit overhead cost		
Volume-based	$100	$75.00
Activity-based	155	61.25
Difference	$ 55	$13.75
Profit margin		
Volume-based	$100	$45.00
Activity-based	45	58.75
Difference	$ 55	$13.75

is, the cost accounting subsidizes some products at the expense of others. Often the cross-subsidization is in the direction of undercosting the low-volume products (smaller batch size) and overcosting the high-volume products (large batch size) using the volume-based approach. The reason is that with ABC the batch-level costs are averaged over a larger number of units for high-volume products, thus bringing the costs of these products down, and vice-versa for the low-volume products.

For a short additional example, assume that product A is produced in a batch of 10 units, while product B is produced in a batch of 100 units, and that for both products the batch-level costs are $100 per batch. The ABC method would calculate the cost per unit of batch costs as $100/10 = $10 per unit for the low-volume batch and $100/100 = $1 per unit for the high-volume batch. In contrast, the volume-based method would calculate the cost of two batches and spread this equally to the 110 units produced; $200/110 = $1.82 per unit. Using the volume-based method, the high-volume product is overcosted ($1.82 vs. $1) and the low-volume product is undercosted ($1.82 vs. $10). Distorted or inaccurate product costing can lead to inappropriate inventory valuations, unrealistic pricing, ineffective resource allocations, misplaced strategic focus, misidentified critical success factors, and lost competitive advantage.

The Five Steps of Strategic Decision Making for Haymarket BioTech Inc

We can see how inaccurate costs under the volume-based method can affect HBT's success, by considering the five steps of strategic decision making.

1. **Determine the strategic issues surrounding the problem.** HBT, the maker of AW and SZ, competes on product leadership (differentiation) as its customers rely on the ability of these products to provide secure communications. Because innovation is a key customer buying criteria, HBT must take a long-term focus on developing innovations that meet expected future customer expectations and implement these innovations into successful, profitable products.

2. **Identify the alternative actions.** HBT is considering an advertising campaign and reallocation of manufacturing facilities to favor the AW product line over the SZ.

3. **Obtain information and conduct analyses of the alternatives.** The information available to HBT under the volume-based cost system shows a unit margin of $100 for AW and $45 for SZ, while the ABC-based cost system shows unit margins for AW and SZ of $45 and $58.75, respectively. As the ABC system provides more comprehensive and accurate cost information, HBT should rely on the latter figures which show that on a unit basis the SZ product is more profitable.

4. **Based on strategy and analysis, choose and implement the desired alternative.** Considering the ABC cost information and the higher margins for SZ relative to AW, the plans to promote AW and reallocate manufacturing facilities from SZ to AW are not consistent with HBT's long-term growth and profitability. The firm's best advantage for future growth and profitability would be to put resources behind SZ rather than AW.

5. **Provide an ongoing evaluation of the effectiveness of implementation in Step 4.** HBT should continue to review the ABC-based costs and profit margins of existing and new products, together with long-term projections of sales and customer expectations for these products, to choose the products with the best advantage for long-term growth and profitability.

Calculating the Cost of Capacity in ABC

The ABC application illustrated above uses activity-consumption rates based on budgeted activity costs and budgeted activity consumption. This is the same approach used in job costing (Chapter 4) to determine predetermined overhead rates. Since budgets are planned levels, we could say that budgeted activity costs are the planned level of spending, and the budgeted activity consumption is based on planned usage. The ABC costs assigned to cost objects are therefore based on planned levels of spending and usage of capacity. What if we want to know the cost of maintaining idle or excess capacity for planning capacity utilization? Perhaps the unused capacity can be used by other business units in the firm to expand their operations, or alternatively, the excess capacity can be sold or leased. Information on excess capacity allows the firm to manage and to reduce these costs when appropriate.

A straightforward adaptation of the ABC method provides the desired additional information—the cost of capacity. For example, suppose for simplicity that of the four activities for HBT we consider only the engineering activity. Engineering cost for HBT is budgeted at $125,000 as currently shown, but suppose that instead of a budgeted activity consumption of 12,500 hours, HBT were to use the practical capacity of the engineering staff, which is 15,625 hours. Practical capacity is the capacity available with the current resources of people, equipment, and facilities—the reasonable level of output if the resource is fully utilized. Using practical capacity, the activity consumption rate would be $8 per engineering hour (=$125,000/15,625). If only 12,500 hours were used, as shown in the example, then the overhead cost charged to AW and SZ would be reduced because of the lower rate ($8 instead of the original rate of $10). AW overhead would be reduced by $10,000 (5,000 hours × $2) and SZ overhead would be reduced by $15,000 (7,500 hours × $2). The total reduction for the two products, $25,000 (=$10,000 + $15,000) is the cost of unused capacity. The cost of unused capacity can also be calculated directly by taking the hours of unused capacity—3,125 hours (15,625 – 12,500)—and multiplying by the $8 activity consumption rate for engineering.

Determining the cost of capacity is a strategically important feature of ABC because it helps managers plan the short- and longer-term use of the operating resources. An example of an actual application of cost of capacity is shown in the Bellhaven Retirement Home Case below, in the section, "Real-World Activity-Based Costing/Management Applications." Also, the cost of capacity plays a central role in two methods that extend the basic ABC model; these are resource consumption accounting and time-driven activity-based costing. Both methods are explained at the end of the chapter.[1]

Activity-Based Management

LEARNING OBJECTIVE 4

Explain activity-based management (ABM).

Benefits of activity-based costing systems are not limited to improving product costing. After having an activity-based costing system in place, management often discovers that information from a well-designed ABC system helps to increase both the value customers received and the profits to the firm, especially for firms that embrace activity-based management.

What Is Activity-Based Management?

Activity-Based Management (ABM) manages resources and activities to improve the value of products or services to customers and increase the firm's competitiveness and profitability. ABM draws on ABC as its major source of information and focuses on the efficiency and effectiveness of key business processes and activities. Using ABM, management can pinpoint avenues for improving operations, reducing costs, or increasing values to customers. By identifying resources spent on customers, products, and activities, ABM improves management's focus on the firm's critical success factors and enhances its competitive advantage.

---

[1] *Statement of Financial Accounting Standards Number 151*, "Inventory Costs," requires abnormal amounts of idle capacity expense to be treated as a period cost, and not assigned to product. The *Standard* notes that some variation in production level from period to period is to be expected and that these variances should not affect the accounting for inventory, but when in the accountant's judgment the amount of idle capacity expense is abnormal, then the amount should be separated from inventory costs, as we have done in the above example, and charged against current income.

ABM applications can be classified into two categories: operational ABM and strategic ABM. Operational ABM enhances operational efficiency and asset utilization and lowers costs; its focuses are on doing things right and performing activities more efficiently. Operational ABM applications use management techniques such as activity analysis, business process improvement, total quality management, and performance measurement.

Strategic ABM attempts to alter the demand for activities and increase profitability through improved activity efficiency. Strategic ABM focuses on choosing appropriate activities for the operation, eliminating nonessential activities and selecting the most profitable customers. Strategic ABM applications use management techniques such as process design, customer profitability analysis, and value-chain analysis.

Exhibit 5.8 illustrates questions that strategic and operational ABC/ABM (ABC/M) can help to answer and the tools that are used. Some of the key tools of ABC/M are activity analysis, activity-based costing, performance measurement (covered in Chapters 18 and 19), and several contemporary management techniques explained in Chapter 1: benchmarking, total quality management, business process improvement, and others. Another technique, value-added analysis, is explained here.

Activity Analysis

To be competitive a firm must assess each of its activities based on its need by the product or customer, its efficiency, and its value content. A firm performs an activity for one of the following reasons:

- It is required to meet the specification of the product or service or satisfy customer demand.
- It is required to sustain the organization.
- It is deemed beneficial to the firm.

Examples of activities required to sustain the organization are providing plant security and compliance with government regulations. Although these activities have no direct effect on the product or service or customer satisfaction, they cannot be eliminated. Examples of discretionary activities deemed beneficial to the firm include a holiday party and free coffee. Exhibit 5.9 depicts an activity analysis.

Value-Added Analysis

Eliminating activities that add little or no value to customers reduces resource consumption and allows the firm to focus on activities that increase customer satisfaction. Knowing the values of activities allows employees to see how work really serves customers and which activities may have little value to the ultimate customers and should be eliminated or reduced.

A **high-value-added activity** increases significantly the value of the product or service to the customers. Removal of a high-value-added activity decreases perceptively the value of the product or service to the customer. Inserting a flange into a part, pouring molten metal into a mold, and preparing a field for planting are examples of high-value-added activities. Installing software to protect a computer from spam is a high-value-added activity to customers annoyed by unwanted e-mail. Designing, processing, and delivering products and services are high-value-added activities.

A **high-value-added activity** increases the value of the product or service to the customers.

EXHIBIT 5.8
The Role of ABC/M Tools

Critical Questions	ABC/M Tools
What do we do?	Activity analysis
How much does it cost?	Activity-based costing
How well do we do it?	Performance measurement, including the balanced scorecard
How can we do it better?	Benchmarking, total quality management, business process improvement, and business intelligence

EXHIBIT 5.9
Example of an Activity Analysis

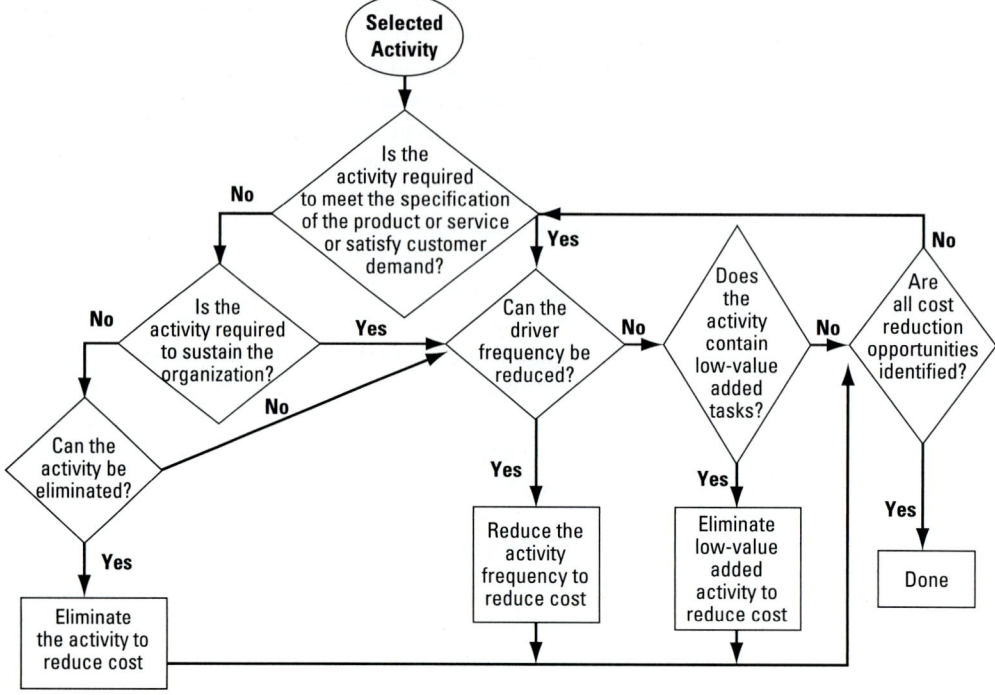

Exhibit 5.10 illustrates high-value-added and low-value-added activities of a television news broadcasting firm. For a television news broadcasting company a high-value-added activity is one that, if eliminated, would affect the accuracy and effectiveness of the newscast and decrease viewer satisfaction. An activity that shortens delivery from three to two days is a high-value-added activity. Activities that verify story sources to ensure the story's accuracy are high-value-added activities. Activities to plan newscasts so that viewers can follow transitions from one story to the next are high-value-added activities.

A low-value-added activity consumes time, resources, or space, but adds little to satisfying customer needs.

A **low-value-added activity** consumes time, resources, or space, but adds little in satisfying customer needs. If eliminated, customer value or satisfaction decreases inperceptively or

EXHIBIT 5.10
Television News Broadcasting Firm's High-Value-Added and Low-Value-Added Activities

A *high-value-added activity* is one that, if eliminated, would affect the accuracy and effectiveness of the newscast and decrease total viewers as well as ratings for that time slot.

1. Activities that augment accuracy
   • Verification of story sources and acquired information.
2. Activities that augment effectiveness
   • Efficient electronic journalism to ensure effective taped segments.
   • Newscast story order planned so that viewers can follow from one story to the next.
   • Field crew time used to access the best footage possible.
   • Meaningful news story writing.
   • Contents of the newscast planned so that viewers get the best possible package of stories.

A *low-value-added activity* is one that, if eliminated, would not affect the accuracy and effectiveness of the newscast. The activity contributes nothing to the quest for viewer retention and improved ratings.

   • Developing stories not used in a newscast.
   • Assigning more than one person to develop each facet of the same news story.
   • Newscast not completed on time because of one or more inefficient processes.
   • Too many employees on a particular shift or project.

EXHIBIT 5.11

A Classification of High-Value-Added and Low-Value-Added Activities

Activity	High-Value-Added	Low-Value-Added
Designing product	X	
Setting up		X
Waiting		X
Moving		X
Processing	X	
Reworking		X
Repairing		X
Storing		X
Inspecting		X
Delivering product	X	

remains unchanged. Moving parts between processes, waiting time, repairing, and rework are examples of low-value-added activities.

Reduction or elimination of low-value-added activities reduces cost. *Low-value-added activities* are those that:

- Can be eliminated without affecting the form, fit, or function of the product or service.
- Begin with prefix "re" (such as rework or returned goods).
- Result in waste and add little or no value to the product or service.
- Are duplicated in another department or add unnecessary steps to the business process.
- Produce an unnecessary or unwanted output.

Additional examples of high- and low-value adding activities are shown in Exhibit 5.11.

Real-World Activity-Based Costing/Management Applications

LEARNING OBJECTIVE 5

Describe how ABC/M is used in manufacturing companies, service companies, and governmental organizations.

Activity-based costing/management (ABC/M) applications are now common in most industries. This section illustrates some example applications in the manufacturing and service industries and within government.

ABC/M Application in Manufacturing: Industrial Air Conditioner Units

AIRCO Ltd (www.airco.co.za) of Johannesburg and Cape Town, South Africa, is a manufacturer of industrial air conditioning units. The units range in size and power from 5 to 20 tons.[2] Each unit has more than 200 parts, including holding tanks, electronic controllers, metal sheets, cooling coils, wires, and insulation material. Almost 90 percent of manufacturing workers are hourly workers, and the company operates two shifts. The organization of the manufacturing process is conventional, with separate departments for purchasing, engineering, job scheduling, materials handling, shipping, accounting, and human resources. AIRCO developed an ABC system to assist in the analysis of product profitability. Its first step was to identify the resource cost pools that make up total overhead of $4,458,610 at the plant (Exhibit 5.12). The resource costs (indirect labor, computer and software, etc.) are from the firm's accounting system, which collects resources costs in these 11 categories.

The next step is to identify production activities and to use resource consumption cost drivers to assign the resource costs to the activity cost pools. The activity cost pools are machines; data record maintenance; materials handling; production changeover (setup); scheduling and

---

[2] Heather Nachtmann and Mohammad Hani Al-Rifai, "An Application of Activity-Based Costing in the Air Conditioner Manufacturing Industry," *The Engineering Economist* 49 (2001), pp. 221–236. Used with permission. For simplicity, for the remainder of the chapter we will refer to resource consumption cost drivers as resource cost drivers and we will refer to activity consumption cost drivers as activity cost drivers.

EXHIBIT 5.12
AIRCO Overhead Cost Resources

Overhead Resource	Cost
Indirect labor	$2,786,900
Computer and software	731,405
Product transportation	319,800
Energy	170,600
Facility and vehicle rent	165,870
Business and training travel	66,000
Miscellaneous	65,480
Maintenance	60,000
Depreciation	48,200
Advertising	40,000
Office and utilities	4,355
	$4,458,610

production preparation; materials receiving and handling; product shipment; and customer service (Exhibit 5.13, column 1). The assignment of resources to activities typically uses resource cost drivers. Instead of using cost drivers, AIRCO determined the estimated contribution of each resource to each activity based on managers' and employees' experience. For example, the resource, maintenance costs of $60,000, was assigned entirely to the activity, machines. To illustrate, the cost of the machine activity was determined from the resources as follows (other activities were obtained in a similar way):

$$
\begin{aligned}
\text{Machine activity cost} \ =\ &20\% \text{ of the computer and software costs} \\
&+100\% \text{ of energy costs} + 15\% \text{ of miscellaneous expense} \\
&+100\% \text{ of maintenance expense} + 100\% \text{ of depreciation expense} \\
&+12\% \text{ of office and utilities expense} \\
=\ &(.2 \times \$731,405) + \$170,600 + (.15 \times \$65,480) + \$60,000 \\
&+ \$48,200 + (.12 \times \$4,355) \\
=\ &\$435,425
\end{aligned}
$$

The machine activity cost and the cost of other activities is shown in column 2 of Exhibit 5.13. The use of estimated percentages in place of other types of resource consumption cost drivers is a practical and convenient approach that is often used in implementing ABC costing.

EXHIBIT 5.13   **AIRCO Resource Consumption Cost Pools Assigned to Activities, Activity Cost Drivers, and Activity-Based Rates**

(1) Activity Cost Pool	(2) Budgeted Activity Cost	(3) Activity Cost Driver	(4) Budgeted Activity	(5) = (2)/(4) Activity-Based Application Rate
Machines	$ 435,425	Number of machine-hours	73,872	$ 5.89 per hour
Data record maintenance	132,596	Number of products lines	14	9,471 per line
Materials handling	1,560,027	Number of products	16,872	92.46 per product
Production changeover (setup)	723,337	Setup time (hours)	72	10,046 per hour
Scheduling and production preparation	24,876	Number of production runs	2,788	8.92 per run
Materials receiving and handling	877,106	Number of receipts	2,859	307 per receipt
Product shipment	561,013	Distance (miles)	13,784,015	.041 per mile
Customer service	144,230	Number of customer contacts	2,533	56.94 per contact
Total	$4,458,610			

EXHIBIT 5.14   **AIRCO: Overhead Allocation and Product Profitability under ABC Costing**

	5-ton	6-ton	7.5-ton	10-ton	12.5-ton	15-ton	20-ton
Direct labor	$ 342.20	$ 342.20	$ 342.20	$ 410.64	$ 410.64	$ 410.64	$ 410.64
Direct material	665.00	665.00	665.00	1,957.00	1,957.00	2,510.00	2,510.00
Overhead (ABC-based)	174.63	404.27	160.26	172.62	1,029.52	343.95	309.90
Total manufacturing cost	$ 1,181.83	$1,411.47	$1,167.46	$2,540.26	$3,397.16	$3,264.59	$3,230.54
Selling price	1,000.00	1,300.00	1,750.00	2,560.00	3,200.00	4,572.00	5,450.00
Product margin	$ (181.83)	$ (111.47)	$ 582.54	$ 19.74	$ (197.16)	$1,307.41	$2,219.46

The next step in ABC is to identify activity cost drivers, to identify the total amounts for these cost drivers, and then to determine the ABC-based application rate. This is shown in Exhibit 5.13, columns 3, 4, and 5, respectively. Thus, the cost of machine time is assigned to each of the products based on machine-hours used by that product times the rate of $5.89 per machine-hour ($5.89 = $435,425/73,872). This is done in the same manner for the other activities. The determination of ABC cost and profitability analysis for AIRCO's key product lines is the final step and is shown in Exhibit 5.14. Note that this analysis shows that the 5-ton, 6-ton, and 12.5-ton products are not profitable.

The ABC analysis can be compared to the volume-based approach that AIRCO used prior to ABC. The volume-based overhead costs were assigned to products based on a rate of $12.02 per direct labor-hour. The results are shown in Exhibit 5.15. Note that the ABC and volume-based methods show significantly different results for some of the products, particularly the 6-ton and 12.5-ton models. While the detailed calculations of the ABC costs for these products are not shown, the company reports that the 12.5-ton model required significantly more raw materials receipts (the cost driver for material receiving and handling) than other products, and it also required more setup time and customer service contacts. Thus, the ABC costs for the 12.5-ton model are significantly higher than for volume-based costs. Similarly, the 6-ton product has higher costs under ABC because of its relatively high use of setup time and customer service contact. The ABC information provides the company a useful basis for becoming more competitive, for example, by reconsidering the pricing of certain products and looking for ways to increase efficiency in the use of its activities.

ABC/M Application in the Service Industry: A Retirement and Assisted Living Community

The following is based on an actual 70-unit retirement and assisted living community, which we will call Bellhaven Homes, Inc.[3] Bellhaven has four levels of resident care: care-free living, semi-assisted living, assisted living, and short-term care. Each is offered in a studio or one-bedroom floor plan, except care-free living, which is also offered in a two-bedroom

EXHIBIT 5.15   **AIRCO: Overhead Allocation and Product Profitability under Volume-Based Costing**

	5-ton	6-ton	7.5-ton	10-ton	12.5-ton	15-ton	20-ton
Direct labor	$ 342.20	$ 342.20	$ 342.20	$ 410.64	$ 410.64	$ 410.64	$ 410.64
Direct material	665.00	665.00	665.00	1,957.00	1,957.00	2,510.00	2,510.00
Overhead (volume-based)	240.41	240.41	240.41	288.49	288.49	288.49	288.49
Total product cost	$1,247.61	$1,247.61	$1,247.61	$2,656.13	$2,656.13	$3,209.13	$3,209.13
Selling price	1,000.00	1,300.00	1,750.00	2,560.00	3,200.00	4,572.00	5,450.00
Product margin	$ (247.61)	$ 52.39	$ 502.39	$ (96.13)	$ 543.87	$1,362.87	$2,240.87

[3] Sidney J. Baxendale, Mahesh Gupta, and P. S. Raju, "Profit Enhancement Using an ABC Model," *Management Accounting Quarterly*, Winter 2005, pp. 11–21. Used with permission.

floor plan. These nine different care-level/floor-plan combinations are priced differently and are regarded as the cost objects at Bellhaven. There are currently 56 residents at Bellhaven, spread across the nine cost objects. The services at Bellhaven include resident care, housekeeping, maintenance of grounds and facility, food service, resident activities, and transportation. Each of these six services are the activities used by Bellhaven in developing an ABC model to determine the cost and profitability of each of its nine cost objects. The cost drivers for each activity are the number of hours worked by employees in each of these activities. The ABC application rates are then determined from the hours available in each of the service units, and the ABC costs for each cost object are calculated. Exhibit 5.16 illustrates the per resident costs within each of the nine cost objects. The ABC analysis provides Bellhaven useful information for pricing its services and for identifying activities where costs can be reduced and/or value added.

A special feature of the Bellhaven analysis is the calculation of the cost of unused capacity. Since Bellhaven maintains staff sufficient to cover all 70 units in the facility, it is important to track the costs of underutilization. Bellhaven has room for 14 more residents. This means that the application rates are based on 70-unit *capacity* and not budgeted usage, as is often the case in ABC. When rates are based on capacity, management is able to determine the additional information about the cost of unused capacity.

ABC/M Applications in Government

ABC/M is used widely in government. The U.S. Postal Service example that introduced this chapter is one good example. Another example is the U.S. Patent and Trademark Office (PTO) which uses ABC to better understand its cost structure. As the volume of patent requests has increased substantially, and since the PTO is not taxpayer supported but relies on user fees, the determination of accurate costs and the setting of appropriate user fees for its different services is critical. The ABC model at the PTO used 29 activities and the cost objects included utility patents, design patents, plant patents, reissues, reexaminations, trademarks, and appeals. One finding of the ABC implementation was that the cost of trademark processing was higher than expected.[4]

---

[4] For additional examples: Gary Cokins, *Activity-Based Cost Management in Government*, Management Concepts, Inc., 2001.

EXHIBIT 5.16 ABC Costing at Bellhaven Homes, Inc.

| | Care-Free Living | | | Semi-Assisted Living | | Assisted Living | | Short-Term Care | | Total Activity | Cost of Excess | Total Activity |
	Studio	One Bed	Two Bed	Studio	One Bed	Studio	One Bed	Studio	One Bed	Cost Assigned	Capacity	Cost Incurred
Resident care	$166	$166	$166	$332	$332	$554	$554	$332	$332	$14,114	$2,454	$16,568
Housekeeping	17	18	23	17	18	23	24	17	18	1,047	1,773	2,820
Maintenance	16	16	16	16	16	16	16	16	16	896	2,019	2,915
Food service	84	84	84	85	85	86	86	85	85	4,731	4,476	9,207
Resident activities	16	16	16	12	12	3	3	12	12	758	1,826	2,584
Transportation	8	8	8	8	8	8	8	8	8	448	631	1,079
	$307	$308	$313	$470	$471	$690	$691	$470	$471	$21,994	$13,179	$35,173

Other examples include the Internal Revenue Service (IRS), which uses ABC/M to calculate the costs of processing each of its different types of tax returns, and the U.S. Army, which uses ABC in the management of the delivery of medical care and the maintenance of military equipment, among other applications.

The U.S. federal government encourages the use of ABC within its various units. In 1990, three officials responsible for federal financial reporting established the Federal Accounting Standards Advisory Board (FASAB) as a federal advisory committee (www.fasab.gov). The officials were the Secretary of the Treasury, the Director of the Office of Management and Budget, and the Comptroller General of the United States. They created FASAB to develop accounting standards and principles for the U.S. government. *FASAB Standard Number 4,* "Managerial Cost Accounting Concepts and Standards for the Federal Government,*" explains the advantages of ABC for use in governmental units.

Customer Profitability Analysis

The customer is the most important part of the assembly line.

W. Edwards Deming

ABC/M is best known for its application in computing product costs, but many firms find that it is also very useful in determining the cost of serving customers and as a basis for evaluating the profitability of a specific customer or of a selected group of customers. Why is this important? Most managers agree that 80 percent of their profits come from the top 20 percent of their customers, and most important, the bottom 20 percent of their customers are unprofitable! For example, to better compete with Wal-Mart, Best Buy works hard to attract profitable customers (it calls them *angels*) and equally hard to discourage the unprofitable customers (the *devils*), those that are price shopping and looking for discounts and promotions, and comparing prices to Wal-Mart. This strategy involves improved service and fewer discount/promotion offers. Best Buy studies demographic and sales data for each store location to identify angels and devils. Similarly, the large food distributor, CONCO, studies its customer base (mostly restaurants) to identify profitable and unprofitable customers. CONCO found that certain food products and smaller customers tended to be unprofitable.[5]

Customer profitability analysis
identifies customer service activities, cost drivers, and the profitability of individual customers or groups of customers.

Customer profitability analysis identifies customer service activities and cost drivers and determines profitability of each customer or group of customers. Here, customer service includes all activities to complete the sale and satisfy the customer, including advertising, sales calls, delivery, billing, collections, service calls, inquiries, and other forms of customer service. Customer profitability analysis allows managers to:

- Identify most profitable customers.
- Manage each customer's costs-to-serve.
- Introduce profitable new products and services.
- Discontinue unprofitable products, services, or customers.
- Shift a customer's purchase mix toward higher-margin products and service lines.
- Offer discounts to gain more volume with low costs-to-serve customers.
- Choose types of after-sale services to provide.

A good understanding of the profitability of a firm's current and potential customers can help firms to improve overall profits and to become more competitive. This begins with an analysis of the cost to serve the customer.

---

[5] Stephen Schulist, "Using ABC to Manage and Improve at CONCO Foods," *The Journal of Corporate Accounting & Finance,* March/April 2004, pp. 29–34; Gary McWilliams, "Analyzing Customers, Best Buy Decides Not All Are Welcome," *The Wall Street Journal,* November 8, 2004, p. 1; Jaclyne Badal, "A Reality Check for the Sales Staff," *The Wall Street Journal,* October 16, 2006, p. B3.

LEARNING OBJECTIVE 6

Use an activity-based approach to analyze customer profitability.

Customer Cost Analysis

Not all customers require similar activities either before or after the sale. Examples of customer-specific activities include:

- Order processing costs.
- Billing, collection, and payment processing costs.
- Accounts receivable and carrying costs.
- Customer service costs.
- Selling and marketing costs.

Customer cost analysis
identifies activities and cost drivers to service customers.

Customer cost analysis identifies activities and cost drivers to service customers before and after sales, not including product costs. Traditionally these costs are hidden in the customer support, marketing, and sales function. ABC/M can help managers to understand their costs to serve customers.

Different activities often have different cost drivers. Based on the activities and cost drivers involved in services performed to acquire and complete a transaction, customer costs can be classified into the following categories:

- *Customer unit-level cost*—resources consumed for each unit sold to a customer. Examples include sales commissions based on the number of units sold or sales dollars, shipping cost when the freight charge is based on the number of units shipped, and cost of restocking each of the returned units.
- *Customer batch-level cost*—resources consumed for each sales transaction. Examples include order-processing costs, invoicing costs, and recording of sales returns or allowances every time a return or allowance is granted.
- *Customer-sustaining cost*—resources consumed to service a customer regardless of the number of units or batches sold. Examples are salespersons' travel costs to visit customers, monthly statement processing costs, and collection costs for late payments.
- *Distribution-channel cost*—resources consumed in each distribution channel the firm uses to service customers. Examples are operating costs of regional warehouses that serve major customers and centralized distribution centers that serve small retail outlets.
- *Sales-sustaining cost*—resources consumed to sustain sales and service activities that cannot be traced to an individual unit, batch, customer, or distribution channel. Examples are general corporate expenditures for sales activities, and salary, fringe benefits, and bonus of the general sales manager.

Exhibit 5.17 shows customer-related activities, cost drivers and their rates, and the cost category of each of the activities of Winsome Office Supply. These activities are based on the results of a careful study of the firm's selling, administrative, and general expenditures, as well as customer transactions for the last three years. Exhibit 5.18 shows the detailed

EXHIBIT 5.17
Customer-Related Activity, Cost Driver, Cost Rate, and Cost Category, Winsome Office Supply

Activity	Cost Driver and Rate	Cost Category
Order taking	$30 per order	Customer batch-level
Order processing	$20 per order,	Customer batch-level
	and $1 per item	Customer unit-level
Delivery	$100 per trip, and	Customer batch-level
	$1 per mile	Customer batch-level
Expedited order taking, processing, and delivery	$800 per order	Customer batch-level
Customer visit	$200 per visit	Customer-sustaining
Monthly billing:		
First statement	$5 per statement	Customer-sustaining
Subsequent reminder	$25 per notice	Customer-sustaining
Sales returns	$100 per occurrence	Customer batch-level
Restocking	$5 per item returned	Customer unit-level

EXHIBIT 5.18
Customer-Related Activity for Selected Customers, Winsome Office Supply

	GereCo.	HomeServ Inc.	Advance Tek
Net sales	$463,917	$477,600	$472,576
Number of orders and deliveries	2	20	80
Average number of items per order	400	38	8
Delivery miles	10	15	20
Number of expedited orders	0	0	5
Number of visits by salesperson	1	2	5
Sales returns			
Number of requests	2	1	10
Average units per return	3	4	2
Billing Reminder	0	0	2

EXHIBIT 5.19
Customer Cost Analysis, Winsome Office Supply

	GereCo.	HomeServ Inc.	Advance Tek
Customer unit-level cost			
Order processing	400 × 2 × $1 = $800	38 × 20 × $1 = $760	8 × 80 × $1 = $640
Restocking	2 × 3 × $5 = 30	1 × 4 × $5 = 20	10 × 2 × $5 = 100
Customer batch-level cost			
Order taking	2 × $30 = 60	20 × $30 = 600	80 × $30 = 2,400
Order processing	2 × $20 = 40	20 × $20 = 400	80 × $20 = 1,600
Delivery			
Trips	2 × $100 = 200	20 × $100 = 2,000	80 × $100 = 8,000
Miles	10 × 2 × $1 = 20	15 × 20 × $1 = 300	20 × 80 × $1 = 1,600
Expedited orders	—	—	$800 × 5 = 4,000
Sales returns	2 × $100 = 200	1 × $100 = 100	10 × $100 = 1,000
Customer-sustaining costs			
Sales visits	1 × $200 = 200	2 × $200 = 400	5 × $200 = 1,000
Monthly billings	1 × $5 = 5	1 × $5 = 5	1 × $5 = 5
Subsequent reminders	—	—	2 × $25 = 50
Sales-sustaining costs	—	—	—
Total	**$1,555**	**$4,585**	**$20,395**

customer-related activities that Winsome experienced for the sales to the firm's three major customers GereCo., HomeServ Inc., and Advance Tek.

Both customer activity costs, cost categories, and their cost drivers illustrated in Exhibit 5.17 and the detailed customer-related activities reported in Exhibit 5.18 provide the basis for analyzing customer costs. Exhibit 5.19 shows customer cost analyses for Winsome's three customers.

As illustrated in Exhibits 5.18 and 19, the costs to service customers often differ because they do not require the same amount of services. These three customers purchased approximately equal amounts from Winsome. The costs to serve these customers, however, ranged from $1,555 to $20,395.

Customer Profitability Analysis

Customer profitability analysis combines customer revenues and customer cost analyses to assess customer profitability and helps identify actions to improve customer profitability. Exhibit 5.20 illustrates customer profitability analysis for Winsome.

The reasons that GereCo. is not as profitable as HomeServ relate to sales activities. Winsome granted GereCo. much more favorable sales terms than the terms granted to HomeServ. GereCo. also had a high amount of sales returns and allowances; it returned twice as often as HomeServ did.

Sales returns are contributing factors for the low profitability of Advance Tek. Although Advance Tek had the highest total sales, it generated the lowest profit of the three customers. Winsome should be concerned about Advance Tek's high returns and its frequency of orders and number of expedited orders. The high returns could be a result of the customer's dissatisfaction with Winsome's products. Winsome needs to look into the reason for the high returns before losing the customer.

United Parcel Service, Harrah's Casinos, the Royal Bank of Canada, and Capital One have a special ability to understand customer profitability. In recent years, these companies have used their customer profitability strategy effectively to improve revenues and profits. Some would say their success has been due to hard work, or to good judgment, or just dumb luck. Perhaps you are a customer of one of these companies; how do you think they have been successful?

(Refer to Comments on Cost Management in Action at the end of chapter.)

EXHIBIT 5.20
Customer Profitability Analysis, Winsome Office Supply

	GereCo.	HomeServ Inc.	Advance Tek
Total sales	$500,000	$480,000	$540,000
Less: Sales discounts	25,000	—	27,000
Net invoice amount	$475,000	$480,000	$513,000
Less: Sales returns and allowances	4,750	2,400	30,780
Less: Cash discounts	6,333	—	9,644
Net sales	$463,917	$477,600	$472,576
Cost of goods sold	408,620	384,720	432,014
Gross margin	$ 55,297	$ 92,880	$ 40,562
Customer costs			
Order processing	$ 800	$ 760	$ 640
Restocking	30	20	100
Order taking	60	600	2,400
Order processing	40	400	1,600
Delivery			
Trips	200	2,000	8,000
Miles	20	300	1,600
Expedited orders	—	—	4,000
Sales returns	200	100	1,000
Sales visits	200	400	1,000
Monthly billings	5	5	5
Subsequent reminders	—	—	50
Total customer costs	$ 1,555	$ 4,585	$ 20,395
Net customer profit	$ 53,742	$ 88,295	$ 20,167

Late payments also add cost to serve Advance Tek; they might indicate Advance Tek's dissatisfaction with Winsome's sales and services or weakness of Advance Tek's financial condition.

Customer profitability analysis provides valuable information to the assessment of customer value. In addition, firms must weigh other relevant factors before determining the action appropriate for each customer. The following are among these relevant factors:

- Growth potential of the customer, the customer's industry, and its cross-selling potential.
- Possible reactions of the customer to changes in sales terms or services.
- Importance of having the firm as a customer for future sales references, especially when the customer could play a pivotal role in bringing in additional business.

Customer Lifetime Value and Customer Equity

Exhibit 5.20 shows how to determine the profitability of a customer at a given point in time. Many companies now see the importance of looking at the long-term value of the customer, the expected contribution to profit during the full period the company retains the customer. This concept is called **customer lifetime value (CLV),** and it is calculated as the net present value of all estimated future profits from the customer. Present value is used because the profits from the customer are expected to continue for a number of years. To provide a more comprehensive and strategically relevant measure of the value of the customer, CLV takes

Customer lifetime value (CLV)
is the net present value of all estimated future profits from the customer.

149

Sunil Gupta and Valerie Zeithaml have summarized the research that has examined the relationship between a variety of customer metrics and profitability. They integrated this large amount of knowledge into nine generalizations which they argue are supported by the research. These generalizations are important because they help us to understand the role of customer lifetime value (CLV) and customer equity (CE) in a firm's profitability.

1. Improvement in customer satisfaction has a significant and positive impact on firms' financial performance—shown by many studies

2. The link between customer satisfaction and profitability is asymmetric and nonlinear—an increase in satisfaction has less of a positive effect on profitability than the negative effect of declines in satisfaction; increases in satisfaction have a greater than linear effect on profits.

3. The strength of the satisfaction-profitability link varies across industries as well as across firms within an industry

4. There is a strong positive relationship between customer satisfaction and customer retention.

5. While customer satisfaction and service quality are strongly correlated with behavioral intentions, behavioral intentions imperfectly predict actual (buying) behavior.

6. The relationship between observable and unobservable metrics is nonlinear—as the relationship between satisfaction and profitability is nonlinear, so is the relationship between satisfaction and repurchase intention (an unobservable).

7. Marketing decisions based on observable customer metrics, such as CLV, improve a firm's financial performance.

8. Customer retention is one of the key drivers of CLV and firm profitability.

9. Customer metrics, especially CE, provide a good basis to assess the market value of the firm.

Source: Sunil Gupta and Valeria Zeithaml, "Customer Metrics and Their Impact on Financial Performance," *Marketing Science,* November–December 2006, pp. 718–739.

---

into account the company's expectations about the future potential growth in profits for a customer. The calculation of CLV can be quite complicated, but can be illustrated simply. For example, assume MidTown Medical Clinic purchases medical supplies from Johnson Medical Supply Company. Johnson calculates the CLV of the medical clinic by projecting profits from the clinic. Suppose the forecast is for $20,000 profit per year for the next three years. Further, suppose Johnson uses a discount rate of 6 percent (the relevant discount factor is 2.673 from the present value Table 2 at the end of Chapter 12 on page 521), then

$$CLV = \$53,460 = \$20,000 \times 2.673$$

CLV can be used to measure the value of a customer or group of customers and to determine how marketing and support services should be allocated to these customers to improve the firm's overall profitability. Since it is likely to be difficult to forecast future profits with a high level of accuracy, and because the choice of a discount rate involves judgment, it is important to compare different calculations of CLV made with different assumptions about profit forecasts and discount rates.

Customer equity (CE)
is the sum of the CLVs for all the firm's customers.

An extension of CLV is **customer equity (CE)** which is the sum of the CLVs for all the firm's customers.[6] The goal of using CE is to provide a roadmap for the firm to use in implementing its strategy. CE is viewed as a measure of total corporate value, much like the other measures of a firm's value explained in Chapter 20. The key is to understand the drivers of CE which can be described in three broad categories: value equity, brand equity, and retention equity. Value equity is the value the customers place on the firm's products or services because of the quality or features relative to the price. Value equity is higher when the customers think that the value (quality and features) are high relative to the price. One component of value equity, customer service, is extensively studied. For example, a Bain & Company survey of 362 firms in 2006 showed that 80 percent of these firms felt they delivered "superior service" while only 8 percent of the firms' customers agreed. Clearly, these firms have work to do on their value equity. The management of value equity is one way the firm can build individual customers' CLVs and by extension, customer equity.

Brand equity is the perception of the firm's products and services that are not explained by objective attributes. Brand equity is shaped by the firm's marketing strategy. The key subdrivers of brand equity are brand awareness, customer attitude toward the brand, and

---

[6] Much of the discussion in this section is based on the book by Roland T. Rust, Valerie Zeithaml, and Katherine N. Lemon, *Driving Customer Equity: How Customer Lifetime Value Is Reshaping Corporate Strategy* (New York: The Free Press, 2000).

customer perception of brand ethics. Brand equity in the context of a firm's strategy is covered in problem 1-41 at the end of Chapter 1.

Retention equity consists of programs and relationship-building activities that increase customer loyalty—loyalty programs that provide special benefits for customers that buy frequently, affinity programs that allow customers to benefit from lower prices on products from other companies, and consistent customer service, among others.

While all three drivers of customer equity are important, studies have shown that the relative importance of the drivers varies from industry to industry. For example, in contrast to the airline industry which is cutting frequent flyer benefits, the hotel industry focuses heavily on retention equity. It is much more common now to see hotels with loyalty programs, where membership in the program triggers room upgrades, free coffee, and other benefits. Hilton and Hyatt are among those that have these programs; they are called Hilton HHonors®, and Hyatt Gold Passport™, respectively.[7]

CLV and CE are most appropriate where the customers are the ultimate consumer of the product. This is called a B2C (a business to customer relationship), in contrast to a B2B relationship (business to business). In a B2B relationship, the customer relationship is maintained in a different way, and the issues of brand equity and retention do not apply.

Implementation Issues and Extensions

If you want to make enemies, try to change something.

Woodrow Wilson

LEARNING OBJECTIVE 7

Identify key factors for successful ABC/M implementation.

A successful ABC/M implementation requires close cooperation among management accountants, engineers, and manufacturing and operating managers. They need to act as a team in identifying activities, cost drivers, and requisite information, both financial and nonfinancial.

Understanding the production process and identifying cost drivers require careful effort. Efforts to redesign cost systems usually are rewarded when organizations have high product diversity, various cost drivers, multiple distribution channels, and heterogeneous batch sizes.

Following are processes found in many successful implementations of ABC/M:

Implementation Process	Why This Leads to Success
Involve management and employees in creating an ABC system	Allows them to become familiar with ABC/M. They could then be more willing to implement the system because they feel included and share in ownership of the new system.
Use ABC/M on a job that will succeed	Shows how and why the process works. Successfully completing one job enables individuals to see the benefits of ABC/M more clearly.
Keep the initial ABC/M design simple	Avoids overwhelming users and holds costs down; also reduces implementation time.

Extensions of the ABC model are becoming more common. We discuss three of these below: multistage ABC, resource consumption accounting (RCA), and time-driven activity-based costing (TDABC). All three respond directly to the inherent complexity of resource and activity cost assignments in actual applications, noted as one of the implementation issues above. The latter two take a resource-focused approach to ABC.

---

[7] Sarah Nassauer and Andrea Peterson, "Signing Bonus: Testing Hotel Loyalty Plans," *The Wall Street Journal,* September 25, 2008, p. D1. See also, Jack and Suzy Welch, "The Importance of Being Sticky," *BusinessWeek,* September 22, 2008, p. 112; here "sticky" refers to loyal customers.

EXHIBIT 5.21
Multistage Activity Cost Flows

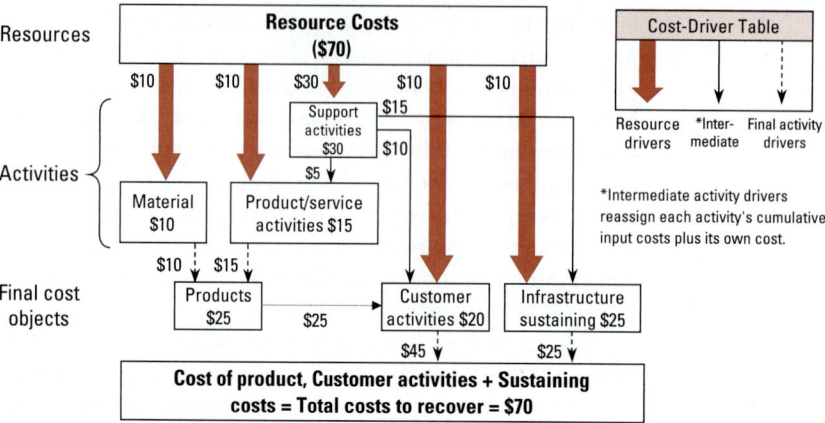

Multistage Activity-Based Costing

In practice, because of a firm's complexity due to the diversity of its products, services, and manufacturing or operating processes, some activities are intermediate cost objects for other activities while others are assigned directly to cost objects. To capture and calculate accurately the costs for this complexity, some firms use multistage activity-based costing rather than two-stage ABC described earlier in the chapter. In **multistage ABC,** resource costs are assigned to certain activities which in turn are assigned to other activities before being assigned to the final cost objects—the firm's products, services, or customers. Exhibit 5.21 illustrates such a case. The activity labeled "support activities" provides service to other activities later in the value chain—product/service activities, customer activities, and infrastructure-sustaining activities. The exhibit illustrates how a total of $70 of resource costs are assigned in multistage ABC costing. After multistage allocations, $25 is assigned to products, $20 is assigned to customer-related activities, and $25 is assigned to infrastructure-related costs (computer equipment and software, buildings, and other equipment, etc.).

Resource Consumption Accounting (RCA)

Resource consumption accounting (RCA) is an adaptation of ABC that emphasizes resource consumption by greatly increasing the number of resource cost pools, which allows more direct tracing of resource costs to cost objects than an ABC system with fewer cost centers.[8] RCA is particularly appropriate for large organizations with repetitive operations and high-level information systems such as those provided by SAP, Oracle, and SAS. These information systems, usually called enterprise resource planning systems (ERPs), allow the use of the large number of cost centers, which would be impractical or infeasible with simpler information systems. The RCA approach, with ERP support, allows much finer detail in the calculation of cost, by increasing the number of cost centers and thereby increasing the opportunity to trace costs directly to products and services; the objective is that cost assignment be based only on causality.

Important concepts in RCA include variable costing, resource interrelationships, detail level cost information at the resource level, the treatment of idle or excess capacity, and the use of replacement cost depreciation. We consider each of these. First, there is a focus on variable costing as the goal of RCA is to trace costs directly to cost objects by the use of many cost centers and by avoiding any cost allocations that do not reflect the use of the resource by the cost object. Second, as in multistage ABC, interrelationships among activities and resource pools are considered directly in RCA. Third, an important advantage of RCA, provided in part by ERP support, is that detailed cost information is available at the resource level so that cost information can be aggregated or tracked at many levels between resources and objects.

[8] In RCA, resource cost pools are called cost centers. Useful references for RCA include articles by Douglas Clinton and Sally Webber, "RCA at Clopay," *Strategic Finance* (October 2004) pp. 22–26 (this article describes an application of RCA in an actual plastics manufacturing company); Kip Krumwiede and Augustin Suessmair, "Getting Down to Specifics on RCA," *Strategic Finance* (June 2007), pp. 51–55; and Jeff Thomson and Jim Gurowka, "Sorting Out the Clutter," *Strategic Finance* (August 2005) pp. 27–33.

Fourth, because of the detailed information available, RCA is able to attribute the cost of idle or excess capacity to the appropriate cost center. Fifth, the RCA approach utilizes a measure of depreciation based on replacement cost; depreciation expense is based on an estimated replacement cost for the asset rather than purchase cost, as in conventional accounting.

Time-Driven Activity-Based Costing (TDABC)

Another resource-centric approach to the implementation of large ABC costing systems is based on the idea that the common element in the utilization of activities is the unit of time. ABC traces and reassigns resource expenses to the activities that consume them and then further reassigns them proportionately to the final cost objects based on the quantity of each activity's cost driver. When a substantial amount of the cost of a company's activities are in a highly repetitive process (much like in the RCA example above), the cost assignment can be based on the average time required for each activity. **Time-driven activity-based costing (TDABC)** assigns resource costs directly to cost objects using the cost per time unit of supplying the resource, rather than first assigning costs to activities and then from activities to cost objects.[9]

TDABC provides a direct way to measure unused capacity. To illustrate, we consider the activity, validate mailing address, in a credit card processing facility and we assume there are 10,000 validations per year. Traditional ABC calculates, we assume, $10.00 per validation and then applies this rate to assign the activity costs to the cost object where the activity is consumed. In contrast, TDABC considers the standard time for each validation, for example, 17 minutes for each validation. TDABC computes the cost per minute of the resources performing the work activity. In this example, we assume four clerical workers are paid $45,000 annually to work on validations, and we estimate that one-half the total productive time of each clerk is spent performing the validate-mailing-address activity. TDABC calculates the total cost as $45,000 × 4 employees × 50% of their time = $90,000; then TDABC calculates the total time available for the activity as 180,000 minutes (assuming 30 hours per week with two weeks vacation: 50% × 4 workers × 50 weeks × 30 hours × 60 minutes per hour = 180,000 minutes per year). The TDAC rate for the activity is $.50 per minute ($90,000 / 180,000). The cost of a given validation activity is $.50 × 17 minutes = $8.50; if the validation required 20 minutes, then the allocation would be $.5 × 20 = $10.

TDABC can then calculate the unused capacity cost by determining the activity cost and netting it from the total expense. In this example the TDABC activity cost is calculated as $85,000 (i.e., 17 minutes × 10,000 validations × $.50 per validation). This means that $5,000 (or 10,000 minutes at $.50 per minute) unused capacity is potentially available to be used for other work.

TDABC can be expanded to include complexities in the activity, in what is called a time equation. For example, we assume the time to validate an address is significantly increased for international address—an additional 22 minutes is required. Then the time equation can be determined as follows:

Time to validate address = 17 minutes + 22 minutes (if it is an international address)

The determination of the cost per minute is done in the same manner, but with the addition of the expected time for international addresses.

A difference between TDABC and ABC is that TDABC is capacity-sensitive and computes a standard activity cost using standard rates. That is, activity driver rates remain constant. In contrast, ABC might not include capacity, as in the HBT and AIRCO Ltd cases presented earlier (though capacity costs can be included, as in the Bellhaven case). ABC computes the activity cost each period as actual and therefore the final cost object's unit cost fluctuates each period. TDABC requires an upfront investment to measure activity times and to continuously maintain them.

Note that ABC can be adapted for the amount of time for an activity, to improve on the accuracy of the ABC cost rates. For example, an ABC system that uses number of setups to assign setup costs could be improved by instead using the amount of setup time used for each setup. The cost of the improvement is the necessity of determining budgeted time for the activity and the actual time for each setup. Note however, that this adaptation of ABC is different from TDABC; TDABC uses the time to drive costs directly from resources to assign costs to cost objects—there is no assignment of resource costs to activities and then from activities to cost objects.

Time-driven activity-based costing (TDABC)

assigns resource costs directly to cost objects using the cost per time unit of supplying the resource, rather than first assigning costs to activities and then from activities to cost objects.

[9] Robert S. Kaplan and Steven R. Anderson, *Time-Driven Activity-Based Costing* (Boston: Harvard Business School Press, 2007).

An example that illustrates the adaptation of ABC to include time is as follows. Consider that the three activities—machine setup, inspection, and packaging—require an average of 80 minutes, 15 minutes, and 20 minutes, respectively. Under ABC the activity consumption cost drivers for these activities are based on the total activity cost divided by the number of minutes available for that activity. For example, if the total cost of setup is $50,000, and there is a capacity of 1,250 minutes of setup time, then the activity rate is $50,000/1,250 = $40 per minute. This approach can improve the ABC application since actual time is used to assign costs. For example, if setup time for a special customer order requires an additional 15 minutes, the assigned setup cost would be based on $40 per minute times the total time of 80 + 15 = 95 minutes: 95 minutes × $40 = $3,800.

A disadvantage of TDABC is its reliance on the accuracy of the time estimates; also, the effort to determine these time-estimates could be very time-consuming and costly. Some activities are not time-driven and should not be included in a comprehensive TDABC; for example, in a chemical company, the cost of the setup and cleanup activities involves significant materials costs, apart from the cost of the time involved. However, these materials costs could be included in a modified TDABC where pounds of materials could be used rather than minutes of setup or cleanup; this is then a combination of time- and pounds-driven ABC. Finally, because of its distinction of resources and activities, traditional ABC can in some cases provide a better framework for identifying opportunities for cost savings, while TDABC can provide a better framework for identifying unused capacity.

Summary

Many companies have replaced their volume-based costing systems with activity-based costing systems for more accurate product costing and better decision making.

Volume-based costing systems use a volume-based overhead rate, either a single rate for the entire plant or departmental rates. These volume-based overhead rates typically use measures such as direct labor-hours, machine-hours, or direct labor costs for all products or services, even if the firm has diverse products, manufacturing processes, and volumes. For firms with more than one product or process, these overhead rates often generate inaccurate and significantly distorted product costs.

Activity-based costing systems recognize that products and services consume indirect costs in a manner that follows the usage of activities rather than the volume of output. ABC costing improves on costing accuracy because it identifies the detail-level activities which cause the consumption of resources; ABC costing assigns these activity-based costs to the products or services using activity-consumption cost drivers, rather than volume-based cost drivers.

Activity-based management manages resource costs and activities to improve the value of products or services to the customer by reducing product cost and/or increasing value-adding activities.

Customer profitability analysis, customer lifetime value, and customer equity are methods, enabled by activity-based costing, which provide important tools for determining the profitability of product lines, customer groups, or individual customers.

Multistage ABC, resource consumption accounting (RCA), and time-driven ABC (TDABC) are new tools which have been developed in recognition of the complexity of cost relationships in many organizations.

Key Terms

activity, *129*
activity-based costing (ABC), *129*
activity consumption cost driver, *129*
batch-level activity, *132*
customer cost analysis, *147*
customer equity (CE), *150*
customer lifetime value (CLV), *149*

customer profitability analysis, *146*
facility-level activity, *132*
high-value-added activity, *139*
low-value-added activity, *140*
multistage ABC, *152*
product-level activity, *132*
resource, *129*

resource consumption accounting (RCA), *152*
resource consumption cost driver, *129*
time-driven activity-based costing (TDABC), *153*
two-stage cost assignment, *130*
unit-level activity, *132*

Comments on Cost Management in Action

The answer to this one admittedly requires some guesswork. But here is the point. It has been proven time after time that data win over perceived expertise, experience, or unaided judgment. Each of these companies uses business analytics, a key form of business intelligence. Business analytics involves the use of computer-based models, statistical analysis, or simulations to test hypotheses about what drives customer loyalty and profitability.

UPS and Harrah's are examples of two companies that use models to predict when a customer is about to change to another company. At UPS, a phone message is sent to support customers whom the model predicts could switch from UPS. At Harrah's, the model predicts when customers are reaching their threshold of "too much" gambling losses; a "luck ambassador" is sent to encourage them to take a break and have a free meal, on Harrah's. Both models are based on extensive data obtained about their customers. Harrah's system is based on information from a loyalty program, a program in which customers use a swipeable card whenever they use the firm's services and receive "rewards," while the company receives vital data about the customers. Capital One uses the same approach to determine the best ways to recruit and retain credit card customers. And the Royal Bank of Canada uses customer data extensively, in combination with ABC costing, to assess customer profitability for each of its banking customers.

Ittner and Larcker, writing in the *Harvard Business Review,* observe that many companies still make these decisions based on expertise and judgment, but the most successful companies validate their assumptions about the factors that drive performance in these firms by seeking data and analyzing the data carefully. Ittner and Larcker present a six step process for validating performance drivers:

1. **Develop a causal model** that explains the hypothesized relationship between the performance drivers and desired performance.
2. **Pull together the data** that is relevant to test the hypothesized relationships. Loyalty programs such as the one used at Harrah's are a key source for data.
3. **Turn data into information** by using statistical models to test the causal model. Regression analysis is an example of a statistical model that is often used by these companies to test their causal models. It is used at Harrah's and Capital One, among others (other firms are described in the books by Ayres and Davenport & Harris cited below). Regression analysis is covered in Chapter 8.
4. **Continually refine the model**
5. **Base actions on findings,** that is, trust the statistical model over and above your own judgment and expertise. This is like trusting your GPS to tell you where you are rather than to go by your own guesswork.
6. **Assess outcomes** by an ongoing review of the outcomes of your actions, to determine if the model needs revision, the competitive environment has changed, and so on.

Source: Christopher D. Ittner and David F. Larcker, "Coming Up Short on Nonfinancial Performance Measures," *Harvard Business Review,* November 2003, pp. 88–95; Thomas H. Davenport and Jeanne G. Harris, *Competing on Analytics* (Boston: Harvard Business School Press, 2007) Ian Ayres, *Super Crunchers: Why Thinking-by-Numbers Is the New Way to Be Smart* (New York: Bantam, 2007).

Self-Study Problem

(For solution, please turn to the end of the chapter.)

Volume-Based Costing Versus ABC

Carter Company manufactures two products, Deluxe and Regular, and uses a traditional two-stage cost allocation system. The first stage assigns all factory overhead costs to two production departments A and B, based on machine-hours. The second stage uses direct labor-hours to allocate overhead to individual products.

For 2010, the firm budgeted $1,000,000 total factory overhead cost for these operations.

	Production Department A	Production Department B
Machine-hours	4,000	16,000
Direct labor-hours	20,000	10,000

The following information relates to the firm's operations for the month of January:

	Deluxe	Regular
Units produced and sold	200	800
Unit cost of direct materials	$100	$ 50
Hourly direct labor wage rate	$ 25	$ 20
Direct labor-hours in Department A per unit	2	2
Direct labor-hours in Department B per unit	1	1

Carter Company is considering implementing an activity-based costing system. Its management accountant has collected the following information for activity cost analysis for 2010:

Activity	Budgeted Overhead	Cost Driver	Budgeted Quantity	Driver Consumption Deluxe	Regular
Material movement	$ 7,000	Number of production runs	350	15	20
Machine setups	400,000	Number of setups	500	25	50
Inspections	588,000	Number of units	19,600	200	800
Shipment	5,000	Number of shipments	250	50	100
	$1,000,000				

Required

1. Calculate the unit cost for each of the two products under the existing volume-based costing system.
2. Calculate the overhead per unit of the cost driver under the proposed ABC system.
3. Calculate the unit cost for each of the two products if the proposed ABC system is adopted.

Questions

5-1   Explain why a costing system that uses a volume-based rate is likely to produce distorted product costs.

5-2   "Undercosting a product increases the profit from the product and benefits the firm." Do you agree? Why?

5-3   Firms sell products with high costs at high prices. High selling prices increase revenues and profits. Why then should managers worry about product overcosting?

5-4   What is activity-based costing, and how can it improve an organization's costing system?

5-5   Describe general levels of cost hierarchy in activity-based costing systems.

5-6   What is the second-stage procedure in assigning costs to products when using an activity-based costing system?

5-7   What type of company needs an activity-based costing system?

5-8   What are unit-level activities? Give two examples of unit-level activities.

5-9   What are batch-level activities? Give two examples of batch-level activities.

5-10   What are product-level activities? Give two examples of product-level activities.

5-11   What are facility-level activities? Give two examples of facility-level activities.

5-12   Why do product-costing systems using a single, volume-based cost driver tend to overcost high-volume products? Will there be any undesirable strategic effects from such product cost distortion?

5-13   What is activity-based management?

5-14   Give three examples of high-value-added activities in an organization that you choose.

5-15   Give three examples of low-value-added activities in an organization that you choose.

5-16   How can activity-based costing and management be used in service organizations?

5-17   Identify opportunities afforded by customer profitability analysis.

Brief Exercises

5-18   Tasty Beverage Co. produces soft drinks, specializing in fruit drinks. Tasty produces 5,000 cans of product per batch. Setup cost for each batch is $50 and each drink costs $0.10 to produce. What is the total cost per batch? How much would it cost to fill an order for 100,000 cans?

5-19   Montross Lumber processes wood to be shipped to construction companies. In order to keep their products uniform, Montross conducts inspections on 20 percent of the boards produced. Inspections cost the company $10 per hour and it takes one minute to inspect each board. How much would it cost to fill an order for 30,000 boards?

5-20   Orange Inc. grows cabbage. Each package shipped contains 20 vegetables. It costs Orange $5 to put together each package and $0.10 to clean and process each vegetable. How much more does it cost to produce an order for 60 heads of cabbage than an order of 50 heads?

5-21   Williams Performance Co. manufactures sports cars. After making a sale, the salesperson sends the car to be detailed before the customer takes it home. Detailing the car takes 30 minutes at a cost of $15 per hour for direct labor and $5 per car for materials. If the average salesperson sells five cars per day, what is the average cost per five-day week for detailing cars?

5-22 Stackhouse Computing produces high performance desktop computers. Labor cost data shows that the company spent $1,000,000 for 5,000 computers produced, and each computer requires two technician hours and five hours of direct labor. Direct labor is paid $10 per hour by the company. What is the cost of one technician hour?

5-23 Scott Cameras produces digital cameras and has decided to switch from a volume-based system to an activity-based system. Scott produced 100,000 digital cameras in the most recent quarter and has determined that total activity costs were: $3,000,000 materials cost, $500,000 labor costs, $50,000 inspection costs, and $500,000 packaging costs. It takes 30 minutes of labor to produce each camera, inspections are done for 20 percent of all cameras produced, and cameras are packaged individually. What are the rates for each of these activities?

5-24 Haywood Printing is processing a job with the following activity rates:

Activity	Cost Driver	Driver Rate
Direct labor	Number of hours	$ 8
Copying	Number of copies	$0.05

If this job requires five hours for the 1,000 copies, what is the activity-based cost of the job?

5-25 Locke Data Processing reported expenses of $5 million for indirect labor, of which $3 million was for data analysis and $2 million was for data entry. Locke recorded 30,000 hours of data analysis and 100,000 hours of data entry. What are the activity-based rates for each area of direct labor?

5-26 Mattresses-A-Million produces Pillow-Top mattresses. They have been using a volume-based costing system to allocate overhead based on direct labor-hours. The Pillow-Top requires two hours of direct labor. The company has been allocating overhead at the rate of $10 per direct labor-hour. The accounting manager thinks the company should switch to ABC and recognize two activities—materials handling and setup. If the Pillow-Top Mattress requires 30 pounds of materials (materials handling costs are $0.10 per pound) and two setups at $5 per setup, what is the ABC cost per unit? According to the activity-based costs, how much was the cost of making a mattress overstated/understated?

5-27 Plant overhead for ABC Corp is $150 million per year, a portion of which (20 percent) is attributable to inspection costs which are charged to products on the basis of the number of parts in the products. The plant produces 500,000 units per year, and on the average, each product has 20 parts. What is the average inspection cost in a product? What is the inspection cost for a product with 50 parts?

5-28 The materials handling charge for ABC Corp is $.50 per pound of finished product. What is the materials handling charge for a job that produced 10,000 units at a weight of 6 pounds per unit?

Exercises 5-29 **Activity Levels and Cost Drivers**   Al's Speedy Gourmet, a small hamburger shop, has identified the following resources used in its operations (assume each customer's order is a batch for this example):

a. Bread
b. Hourly help
c. Store rent
d. Ground beef
e. Catsup

f. Advertising for Triple-Burger special
g. Salary for the store managers
h. Utilities
i. $1-off-coupon for each order
j. Bags for each order

Required

1. Classify its costs as unit-level, batch-level, product-level, or facility-level costs.
2. Suggest a proper driver for each of the above items.

5-30 **Activity Levels and Cost Drivers**   Shroeder Machine Shop has the following activities:

a. Machine operation
b. Machine setup
c. Production scheduling
d. Materials receiving
e. Research and development

f. Machine maintenance
g. Product design
h. Parts administration
i. Final inspection
j. Materials handling

Required

1. Classify each of the activities as a unit-level, batch-level, product-level, or facility-level activity.
2. Identify a proper cost driver for each activity in requirement 1.

5-31 **Activity Levels and Cost Drivers** Richardson Industries manufactures industrial tools after creating a mold for each newly designed tool. Richardson personally inspects every unit during the trial run of a new mold and 10 percent of the units manufactured in the first three batches. Some of the activities of the firm follow:

a. Designing molds
b. Creating molds
c. Inspecting molds
d. Modifying molds
e. Setting up production

f. Requesting and moving materials
g. Machining
h. Insuring equipment
i. Paying suppliers
j. Heating the factory

Required

1. Classify each of the activities as a unit-level, batch-level, product-level, or facility-level activity.
2. Identify a proper cost driver for each activity in requirement 1.

5-32 **Activity-Based Costing** Hakara Company has identified the following overhead cost pools and cost drivers:

Cost Pools	Activity Costs	Cost Driver	Driver Consumption
Machine setup	$360,000	Setup hours	3,000
Materials handling	100,000	Pounds of materials	25,000
Electric power	40,000	Kilowatt-hours	40,000

The following cost information pertains to the production of two of its products, A and B:

	A	B
Number of units produced	4,000	20,000
Direct materials cost	$40,000	$50,000
Direct labor cost	$24,000	$40,000
Number of setup hours	200	240
Pounds of materials used	1,000	3,000
Kilowatt-hours	2,000	4,000

Required Use activity-based costing to calculate the unit cost for each product.

5-33 **Activity-Based Costing** CHAC Labs Inc. is a company that performs cutting-edge genetic tests and research. The management accountant has identified the following overhead cost pools and cost drivers:

Cost Pools	Activity Costs	Cost Driver	Driver Consumption
Specimen preparation/engineering	$120,000	Pounds of materials	2,500
Equipment calibration/setup	80,000	Setup hours	1,250
Electric power	30,000	Kilowatt-hours	30,000

The following cost information pertains to the production of two of CHAC's most popular genetic tests: T249 and T256:

	T249	T256
Number of units produced	2,000	900
Direct materials cost	$35,000	$40,000
Direct labor cost	$11,000	$20,000

(Continued)

Number of setup hours	140	300
Pounds of materials used	700	1,300
Kilowatt-hours	950	2,250

Required Use activity-based costing to calculate the unit cost for each test.

5-34 Role of Activity-Based Costing in Implementing Strategy Laurent Products is a manufacturer of plastic packaging products with plants located throughout Europe and customers worldwide. During the past 10 years Laurent Products has successfully developed a line of packaging materials and a unique bagging system that present an important opportunity to increase the productivity of checkout counters in grocery stores. The plastic bags manufactured by Laurent are produced in several sizes and different plastic film colors and may have attractive multicolor printed designs on one or both sides to meet the specification of a particular grocery store. The advantages provided by the Laurent bagging system include the lower cost of bags and labor at the checkout counter as well as improved customer service. The system has contributed to a significant growth in Laurent's sales in recent years.

Laurent's success in the grocery chain market has attracted an increasing number of competitors into the market. While the company had been very successful in bringing out a series of new product types with innovative labor-saving features for the grocery stores, the competitors have eventually been able to develop quite similar products. The result has been increased competition with a substantial reduction in Laurent's prices.

As a result of the increased competition in the grocery chain market, Laurent is planning to begin to focus on the small independent grocery stores that purchase bags from large wholesale distributors. The potential sales for this wholesaler segment is about the same size as the grocery chain market but includes a much larger number of independent store customers.

Investments in manufacturing equipment in recent years have been to support two principal objectives: to increase capacity and to reduce costs. The cost reduction initiatives principally concerned material costs and reduced processing times. Over the years Laurent has chosen to invest in machines that are similar to existing equipment in order to capitalize on the fact that the process is relatively simple and that products can, with relatively few exceptions, be processed on any machine in the plant. The only major restriction is the number of colors that a machine can accommodate on a single pass. Future investment proposals now being considered are based on this rationale.

Required What are the key strategic issues facing Laurent, and how can ABC costing assist in resolving these issues?

5-35 Tools for Successful ABC/M Implementation The Consortium for Advanced Manufacturing International (CAM-I) and the American Productivity and Quality Center (APQC) collaborated in the survey of 166 manufacturing and service firms to assess the implementation of ABC/M in these firms. Sixty-eight percent of the respondents were in manufacturing and 25 percent in service companies. The results showed that the majority of senior managers reported "very successful" implementations of the ABC/M system, while department managers were somewhat evenly split between "very successful" and "moderately successful." Line personnel tended to vote "moderately successful." So, the higher the level in the organization, the more perceived benefit of the ABC/M system.

Interviews with selected respondents and further data analysis showed that the three most common characteristics of successful systems were (1) a high level of top management support and commitment, (2) technical competence of the implementation team, and (3) effective change management, that is, companies driven by competitive pressures to strive to better understand their internal capabilities and external competition. Some of the responding companies made strategic changes, including changes in the supply chain and changes in target customers. These results are similar to those reported in prior studies of ABC/M implementation.

Required In addition to the three characteristics of successful ABC/M implementation noted above, list three or four other tools for ABC/M implementation.

5-36 Customer Loyalty and Profitability for Web Customers An important part of customer profitability is the cost to acquire a new customer. Bain and Company, a consulting firm, estimated that the cost of obtaining a new customer in the consumer electronics industry is so high that the firm needs an average of more than four years of business from each new customer to break even. However, industry statistics show that more than half the new customers will defect before the four-year breakeven point. The numbers are similar for the apparel industry. Many firms are now trying to acquire new customers at less cost, through the Web.

Required   Give an example of a firm you know that uses the Web to attract customers and explain why you think the strategy should (or should not) work for that company.

5-37 **Customer Profitability Analysis: Luxury Hotel Industry**   The luxury hotel chain Ritz-Carlton introduced a system called "Mystique" that collects information about its customers from employees and staff at the hotel. The information is used to personalize the services provided to each guest. For example, a bottle of the guest's favorite type of wine would be placed in the room without the guest having to request it. Similarly, the type of fruit a guest prefers will be waiting in the room on arrival. The information is available throughout the Ritz system so that when the guest checks into any Ritz-Carlton hotel, the special treatment is available. Other hotel chains such as Marriott, Hilton, and Hyatt have similar programs

Required

1. How do these information-gathering programs help the hotels become more competitive? What is the strategic role of these programs?

2. Do you see a role for activity-based accounting for these firms, as it relates to their information gathering and customer service?

3. What ethical issues, if any, do you see in the information-gathering systems?

5-38 **Applications of ABC in Government**   Activity-based costing is used widely within the U.S. government. One example is the Department of Agriculture's Animal and Plant Health Inspection Service (APHIS). APHIS helps to protect U.S. agriculture from exotic pests and diseases, to minimize wildlife/agriculture conflicts, and to protect the welfare of animals used for research or sold wholesale for pets. APHIS performs its services for a variety of users, some of whom pay a user fee. ABC was adopted to provide an accurate basis for determining these fees, and also for analysis of the effectiveness and efficiency of its programs in meeting the service's overall goals. The National Institute of Health and the U.S. Mint also use ABC/M to help these organizations achieve their missions effectively and efficiently.

Required

1. Identify an example or two of a governmental entity that you think could benefit from the application of activity-based costing, and explain why.

2. Identify some of the resources, activities, and cost drivers you would expect to see in this application.

5-39 **Activity-Based Costing in the Fashion Apparel Industry**   Fashion House, a manufacturer of high-fashion clothing for women, is located in South London. Its product line consists of trousers (45 percent), skirts (35 percent), dresses (15 percent), and other (5 percent). Fashion House has been using a volume-based rate to assign overhead to each product; the rate it uses is £2.25 per unit produced. The results for the trousers line, using the volume-based approach are as follows:

Number of units produced	10,000
Price (all figures in £)	20.525
Total revenue	205,250
Direct materials	33,750
Direct labor	112,500
Overhead (volume-based)	22,500
Total product cost	168,750
Nonmanufacturing expenses	31,500
Total cost	200,250
Profit margin for trousers	5,000

Recently, it has conducted a further analysis of the trousers line of product, using ABC. In the study, eight activities were identified, and direct labor was assigned to the activities. The total conversion cost (labor and overhead) for the eight activities, after allocation to the trousers line, is as follows:

Pattern cutting	£22,000
Grading	19,000
Lay planning	18,500
Sewing	21,000
Finishing	14,300
Inspection	6,500
Boxing up	3,500
Storage	7,000

Required Determine the profit margin for trousers using ABC and comment on the difference in comparison to the volume-based calculations. Is Fashion House more likely to use ABC as a U.K. company than a similar company in France or the U.S. (refer to real world focus boxes in the chapter)?

5-40 **Volume-Based Versus ABC Overhead Rate** Medical Arts Hospital (MAH) uses a hospital-wide overhead rate based on nurse-hours. The intensive care unit (ICU), which has 30 beds, applies overhead using patient-days. Its budgeted cost and operating data for the year follow:

Hospital Budget Information	
Hospital total overhead	$57,600,000
Hospital total nurse-hours	1,152,000

Budget Cost Driver Information for ICU for the Month of June			
Cost Pool	**Budget Cost**	**Cost Driver**	**Budget Cost Driver Activity**
Facilities and equipment	$2,400,000	Number of patient-days	7,500
Nursing care	3,000,000	Number of nurse-hours	80,000

In June, MAH's intensive care unit had the following operating data:

81,000 nurse-hours
7,250 patient-days

Required
1. Calculate the ICU's overhead costs for the month of June using
   a. The hospitalwide rate
   b. The ICU departmentwide rate
   c. The cost driver rates for the ICU department
2. Explain the differences and determine which overhead assignment method is more appropriate.

5-41 **Product Selection Strategy** Johans Computer Company has two product lines, Desktop and Tablet. The firm's costing system shows that each Desktop costs $550 to manufacture. Johans sells 9,000 Desktops at $660 per unit. A national low-price store has introduced a similar desktop computer with a market price of $380. Tablet computer is a new model that a handful of companies, including Johans, introduced recently. Each Tablet computer costs Johans $750 to produce and sells for $2,750. Johans sells approximately 150 Tablet computers. The marketing vice president suggests shifting the sales mix in favor of Tablet computer. Unfortunately, Tablet computer is more complicated to make and few are produced.

Required Should Johans focus its sales on the Desktop or Tablet computer? Explain your answer.

5-42 **High-Value-Added and Low-Value-Added Activities** The Lindex General Hospital has determined the activities of a nurse including the following:

a. Report for duty and review patient charts
b. Visit each patient and take her/his temperature
c. Update patients' records
d. Coordinate lab and radiology works
e. Wait for the attending physician to arrive
f. Accompany attending physician
g. Explain treatments to patients
h. Call kitchen to have the wrong meal tray replaced
i. Perform CPR

Required Classify each item as a high-value-added or a low-value-added activity.

5-43 **High-Value-Added and Low-Value-Added Activities**   Mazon.com sells merchandise through orders placed on its Web site. Some of the firm's activities are

a. Print order forms

b. Review orders to ensure the accuracy of prices and the totals

c. Secure approval of charges on credit cards

d. Deliver order forms to supervisor to secure her/his approval

e. Make a copy of each order to send to the warehouse

f. Pick and pack items ordered

g. E-mail customer for items not in stock

h. E-mail customer on the shipment of the order with a thank-you note

Required   Classify each item as a high-value-added or low-value-added activity.

5-44 **ABC and Job-Costing Working with Unknowns**   North Company designs and manufactures machines that facilitate DNA sequencing. Depending on the intended purpose of each machine and its functions, each machine is likely to be unique. The job-order costing system in its Norfolk plant has five activity cost pools, in addition to direct materials and direct labor. Job TPY–2306 requires 1,000 printed-circuit boards. The cost per board that passes the final inspection is $240. On average, only 50 percent of the completed units pass the final inspection. The prime costs per completed board are direct materials $25 and direct labor $5. Information pertaining to manufacturing overhead for printed-circuit boards follows:

Activity Cost Pool	Cost Driver	Activity Driver Rate	Unit of Cost Driver per Board	Factory Overhead per Board
Axial insertion	Number of axial insertions	$0.20	25	$A?
Hardware insertion	Number of hardware insertions	2.00	B?	37.00
Hand load	Boothroyd time	C?	5	35.50
Masking	Number of points masked	0.12	100	D?
Final test	Test time	E?	10	5.00

Required   Fill in the unknowns identified as A through E.

5-45 **Cost of Meal**   The following excerpt appeared in a syndicated advice column (March 20, 2003).

Dear Annie:

I attend out-of-town meetings and often am invited to join clients and associates for dinner. There is no way for me to politely refuse. The problem is, I can only afford so much for my meal. However, when the server comes to take our orders, one of the Big Shots invariably says to put the meal on one check. The others proceed to order expensive meals and wine, and we split the bill equally. I end up paying for a dinner that I can't afford, yet to ask for a separate check would be embarrassing.

How can I handle this situation?

Bottom of the Totem Pole in Wisconsin

Required   If you were Annie, how would you respond to this reader?

5-46 **Product-Line Profitability, ABC**   Supermart Food Stores (SFS) has experienced net operating losses in its frozen food products line in the last few periods. Management believes that the store can improve its profitability if SFS discontinues frozen foods. The operating results from the most recent period are:

	Frozen Food	Baked Goods	Fresh Produce
Sales	$120,000	$90,000	$158,125
Cost of goods sold	105,000	67,000	110,000

SFS estimates that store support expenses are approximately 20 percent of revenues.

The controller says that not every sales dollar requires or uses the same amount of store support activities. A preliminary analysis reveals store support activities for these three product lines are:

Activity (cost driver)	Frozen Food	Baked Goods	Fresh Produce
Order processing (number of purchase orders)	10	55	90
Receiving (number of deliveries)	10	70	120
Shelf-stocking (number of hours per delivery)	2	0.5	4
Customer support (items sold)	30,000	40,000	86,000

The controller estimates activity-cost rates for each activity as follows:

Order processing	$ 80 per purchase order
Receiving	110 per delivery
Shelf-stocking	15 per hour
Customer support	0.20 per item

Required

1. Prepare a product-line profitability report for SFS under the current costing system.

2. Prepare a product-line profitability report for SFS using the ABC information the controller provides.

3. What new insights does the ABC system in requirement 2 provide to SFS managers?

5-47 Customer Profitability Analysis   Doreen Company has gathered the following data pertaining to activities it performed for two of its major customers.

	Jerry Inc.	Donald Co.
Number of orders	5	30
Units per order	1,000	200
Sales returns:		
Number of returns	2	5
Total units returned	40	175
Number of sales calls	12	4

Doreen sells its products at $200 per unit. The firm's gross margin ratio is 25 percent. Both Jerry and Donald pay their accounts promptly and no accounts receivable is over 30 days. After a careful analysis using a business intelligence software on the operating data for the past 30 months the firm has determined the following activity costs:

Activity	Cost Driver and Rate
Sales calls	$ 1,000 per visit
Order processing	300 per order
Deliveries	500 per order
Sales returns	100 per return and $5 per unit returned
Sales salary	100,000 per month

Required

1. Classify activity costs into cost categories and compute the total cost for Doreen Company to service Jerry Inc. and Donald Co.

2. Compare the profitability of these two customers.

5-48 Product Line Profitability Analysis   Studemeir Paint & Floors (SPF) has experienced net operating losses in its Other Flooring Products line during the last few periods. SPF's management team thinks that the store will improve its profitability if they discontinue the Other Flooring Products line. The operating results from the most recent period are:

	Paint & Paint Supplies	Carpet	Other Flooring Products
Sales	$285,000	$235,000	$175,550
Cost of goods sold	165,000	150,000	135,250

SPF estimates that store support expenses are approximately 28.5 percent of revenues.

Harish Rana, SPF's controller, states that not every sales dollar requires or uses the same amount of store support activities. He conducts a preliminary investigation and his results and analysis are as follows:

Activity (cost driver)	Paint & Paint Supplies	Carpet	Other Flooring Products
Order processing (number of purchase orders)	110	200	25
Receiving (number of deliveries)	40	120	10
Inventory management (number of hours per delivery)	10	40	6
Customer support (hours required per sale)	0.50	8.50	0.25

Harish estimates activity-cost rates for each activity as follows:

Order processing	$135 per purchase order
Receiving	180 per delivery
Inventory management	30 per hour
Customer support	15 per hour

Required

1. Prepare a product-line profitability report for SPF under the current costing system.

2. Prepare a product-line profitability report for SPF using the ABC information the controller provides.

3. What new insights does the ABC system in requirement 2 provide to SPF managers?

5-49 **Customer Profitability Analysis**   Garner Industries manufactures precision tools. The firm uses an activity-based costing system. CEO Deb Garner is very proud of the accuracy of the system in determining product costs. She noticed that since the installment of the ABC system 10 years earlier the firm had become much more competitive in all aspects of the business and earned an increasing amount of profits every year.

In the last two years the firm sold 1 million units to 4,100 customers each year. The manufacturing cost is $600 per unit. In addition, Garner has determined that the order-filling cost is $100.50 per unit. The $784.56 selling price per unit includes 12 percent markup to cover administrative costs and profits.

The order-filling cost per unit is determined based on the firm's costs for order-filling activities. Order filling capacity can be added in blocks of 60 orders. Each block costs $60,000. In addition, the firm incurs $1,500 order-filling costs per order.

Garner serves two types of customers designated as PC (Preferred Customer) and SC (Small Customer). Each of the 100 PCs buys, on average, 5,000 units in two orders. The firm also sells 500,000 units to 4,000 SCs. On average each SC buys 125 units in 10 orders. Ed Cheap, a buyer for one PC, complains about the high price he is paying. Cheap claims that he has been offered a price of $700 per unit and threatens to take his business elsewhere. Garner does not give in because the $700 price Cheap demands is below cost. Besides, she has recently raised the price to SC to $800 per unit and experienced no decline in orders.

Required

1. Demonstrate how Garner arrives at the $100.50 order-filling cost per unit.

2. What would be the amount of loss (profit) per unit if Garner sells to Cheap at $700 per unit?

3. What is the amount of loss (profit) per unit at the $800 selling price per unit for units sold to SC?

5-50 **Activity-Based Costing**   Johnson Marine manufactures marine radios in three models—the 1600 model for the small boat enthusiast who will not venture far from shore, and the 2400 and 3600 models for the those with the need for more features, range, and sensitivity. Johnson manufactures only these three products. Johnson has the following manufacturing activities and the budgeted cost for each:

	Cost
Setup labor	$ 231,000
Equipment	135,660
Assembly	739,500
Materials handling	405,000
Purchasing	92,400
Inspection	325,000
	$1,928,560

Johnson uses a volume-based costing system that is based on labor-hours, since the assembly operation is the largest cost operation in the company. The direct labor rate is $22 per hour.

Johnson is considering an ABC approach to calculating product cost and has selected the following cost drivers for each activity:

Activity	Driver
Setup labor	Number of setups
Equipment	Machine-hours
Assembly	Direct labor-hours
Materials handling	Weight of materials
Purchasing	Materials cost
Inspection	Number of orders shipped

Johnson also has the following budgeted production data for the three products:

	1600	2400	3600
Units produced	10,000	4,000	1,000
Price	$ 200	$ 350	$ 600
Production orders	25	70	200
Production setups	10	50	50
Orders shipped	100	400	800
Direct materials cost per unit	$ 40	$ 70	$ 90
Weight of materials per unit	1	3	5
Direct labor-hours per unit	3	4	5
Machine-hours per unit	6	8	10

Required

1. Determine the unit cost for each of the three products using the current volume-based system.

2. Determine the unit cost for each of the three products using the ABC method.

3. Interpret the difference between your findings in requirements 1 and 2.

Problems   5-51   **Activity-Based Costing; Customer Group Cost Analysis**   Lenngton Furniture, Inc. (LFI) manufactures bedroom furniture in sets (a set includes a dresser, two queen-size beds, and one bedside table) for use in motels and hotels. LFI has three customer groups, which it calls the value, quality, and luxury groups. The value products are targeted to low-price motels that are looking for simple furniture, while the luxury furniture is targeted to the very best hotels. The value line is attractive to a variety of hotels and motels that appreciate the combination of quality and value. Currently there has been a small increase in the low-cost and value lines, and an appreciable increase in demand in the luxury line, reflecting cyclical changes in the marketplace. Luxury hotels are now in more demand for business travel, while a few years ago, the value segment was the most popular for business travelers. LFI wants to be able to respond to the increased demand with increased production but worries about the increased production cost and about price setting as its mix of customers and production change. LFI has used a volume-based rate based on direct labor-hours for some time. Direct labor cost is $12 per hour.

	Budgeted Cost	Cost Driver
Materials handling	$ 349,600	Number of parts
Product scheduling	160,000	Number of production orders
Setup labor	216,000	Number of setups
Automated machinery	1,750,000	Machine-hours
Finishing	619,500	Direct labor-hours
Pack and ship	290,400	Number of orders shipped
	$3,385,500	
General, selling, and adm. costs	$5,000,000	

The budgeted production data for the three product lines follows.

Product Lines	Value	Quality	Luxury
Units produced	15,000	5,000	500
Price	$ 650	$ 900	$1,200
Direct materials cost per unit	$ 80	$ 50	$ 110
Number of parts per unit	30	50	120
Direct labor-hours per unit	4	5	7
Machine-hours per unit	3	7	15
Production orders	50	70	200
Production setups	20	50	50
Orders shipped	1,000	2,000	300
Number of inspections	2	6	14

Required

1. Determine the cost per set and the total production cost of each of the three customer groups using activity-based costing.

2. Determine the production cost for each of the three customer groups using LFI's current volume-based approach.

3. The activity usage data given in the problem reflects current usage of the various cost drivers to manufacture the firm's product lines. Suppose you are given the following information regarding the firm's practical capacity for each of these activities, as follows:

Cost Driver	Practical Capacity
Number of parts	990,000
Number of production orders	800
Number of setups	200
Machine-hours	100,000
Direct labor-hours	123,900
Number of orders shipped	5,000

Comment on how you would use this additional information for costing the firm's products and assisting in strategic planning.

4. Compare the two approaches and discuss the strategic and competitive issues of using each of the two methods.

5-52 **Activity-Based Costing, Value-Chain Analysis** Hoover Company uses activity-based costing and provides this information:

Manufacturing Activity	Cost Driver	Overhead Rate
Materials handling	Number of parts	$ 0.45
Machinery	Number of machine-hours	51.00
Assembly	Number of parts	2.85
Inspection	Number of finished units	30.00

Hoover has just completed 80 units of a component for a customer. Each unit required 105 parts and 3 machine-hours. The prime cost is $1,200 per finished unit. All other manufacturing costs are classified as manufacturing overhead.

Required

1. Compute the total manufacturing costs and the unit costs of the 80 units just completed using ABC costing.

2. In addition to the manufacturing costs, the firm has determined that the total cost of upstream activities including research and development and product design is $180 per unit. The total cost of downstream activities, such as distribution, marketing, and customer service is $250 per unit. Compute the full product cost per unit, including upstream, manufacturing, and downstream activities. What are the strategic implications of this new cost result?

3. Explain to Hoover Company the usefulness of calculating the total value-chain cost and of knowing costs of different value-creating activities.

5-53 **Volume-Based Costing Versus ABC**   The California Cooking Oil Company (CCO) has been using machine-hours as the basis to determine overhead costs for all products. An ABC project team points out that the firm manufactures several products, each of which use significantly different factory supporting resources. As a start, the team suggests the following overhead cost pools, cost drivers, and estimated cost driver levels for manufacturing overheads:

Overhead Cost Pool	Cost Driver	Estimated Cost Driver Level	Budgeted Overhead
Machine setups	Number of setups	100	$100,000
Materials handling	Number of barrels	8,000	80,000
Quality control	Number of inspections	1,000	200,000
Other overhead cost	Machine-hours	10,000	100,000

CCO has recently completed production of 500 barrels each of P5 and G23. P5 is a corn-based oil distributed primarily through supermarkets. G23 is made from olive oil, flaxseed oil, and other exotic ingredients and sold to up scale restaurants as a gourmet food. P5 and G23 are two of the firm's many products. The production requires the following operations:

	Number of Cost Drivers	
Overhead Cost Pool	P5	G23
Machine setups	1 setup	50 setups
Materials handling	500 barrels	500 barrels
Quality inspections	2 times	20 times
Machine-hours	1,000 hours	1,000 hours

Required

1. Determine the overhead costs per barrel of P5 and G23 using the current single cost driver system based on machine-hours.

2. Determine the overhead costs per barrel of P5 and G23 using the multiple cost driver system suggested by the ABC project team.

3. Explain how the choice of costing system can be an important competitive factor for CCO. How can the costing system help the firm become more profitable and competitive?

5-54 **Volume-Based Costing Versus ABC**   West Chemical Company produces three products. The operating results of 2010 are:

Product	Sales Quantity	Target Price	Actual Price	Difference
A	1,000	$279.00	$280.00	$ 1.00
B	5,000	$294.00	$250.00	<$ 44.00>
C	500	$199.50	$300.00	$100.50

The firm sets the target price of each product at 150 percent of the product's total manufacturing cost. Recognizing that the firm was able to sell Product C at a much higher price than the target price of the product and lost money on Product B, Tom Watson, CEO, wants to promote Product C much more aggressively and phase out Product B. He believes that the information suggests that Product C has the greatest potential among the firm's three products since the actual selling price of Product C was almost 50 percent higher than the target price while the firm was forced to sell Product B at a price below the target price.

Both the budgeted and actual factory overheads for 2010 are $493,000. The actual units sold for each product also are the same as the budgeted units. The firm uses direct labor dollars to assign manufacturing overhead costs. The direct materials and direct labor costs per unit for each product are:

	Product A	Product B	Product C
Direct materials	$50.00	$114.40	$65.00
Direct labor	20.00	12.00	10.00
Total prime cost	$70.00	$126.40	$75.00

The controller noticed that not all products consumed factory overhead similarly. Upon further investigations, she identified the following usage of factory overhead during 2010:

	Product A	Product B	Product C	Total Overhead
Number of setups	2	5	3	$ 8,000
Weight of direct materials (pounds)	400	250	350	100,000
Waste and hazardous disposals	25	45	30	250,000
Quality inspections	30	35	35	75,000
Utilities (machine-hours)	2,000	7,000	1,000	60,000
Total				$493,000

Required

1. Determine the manufacturing cost per unit for each of the products using the volume-based method.
2. What is the least profitable and the most profitable product under both the current and the ABC costing systems?
3. What is the new target price for each product based on 150 percent of the new costs under the ABC system? Compare this price with the actual selling price.
4. Comment on the result from a competitive and strategic perspective. As a manager of West Chemical, describe what actions you would take based on the information provided by the activity-based unit costs.

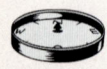

5-55 **Ethics, Cost System Selection** Aero Dynamics manufactures airplane parts and engines for a variety of military and civilian aircraft. The company is the sole provider of rocket engines for the U.S. military that it sells for full cost plus a 5 percent markup.

Aero Dynamics's current cost system is a direct labor-hour-based overhead allocation system. Recently, the company conducted a pilot study on the feasibility of using an activity-based costing system. The study shows that the new ABC system, while more accurate and timely, will result in the assignment of lower costs to the rocket engines and higher costs to the company's other products. Apparently, the current direct labor-based costing system overcosts the rocket engines and undercosts the other products. On hearing of this, top management has decided to scrap the plans to adopt the ABC system because its rocket engine business with the military is significant and the reduced cost would lower the price and, thus, the profit for this part of Aero Dynamics's business.

Required As the management accountant participating in this ABC pilot study project, what is your responsibility when you learn that top management has decided to cancel the plans for the ABC system? Can you ignore your professional ethics code in this case? What would you do?

5-56 **Resource and Activity-Based Cost Drivers** EyeGuard Equipment Inc. (EEI) manufactures protective eyewear for use in commercial and home applications. The product is also used by hunters, home woodworking hobbyists, and in other applications. The firm has two main product lines—the highest-quality product is called Safe-T, and a low-cost, value version is called Safe-V. Information on the factory conversion costs for EEI is as follows:

	Factory Costs
Salaries	$ 850,000
Supplies	150,000
Factory expense	550,000
	$1,550,000

EEI uses ABC costing to determine the unit costs of its products. The firm uses resource consumption cost drivers based on rough estimates of the amount that each activity consumes, as shown below. EEI has four activities: job setup, assembly, inspecting and finishing, and packaging.

	Setup	Assembly	Inspect & Finishing	Packaging	
Salaries	15%	55%	20%	10%	100%
Supplies	20%	60%	20%		100%
Factory expense		80%	20%		100%

The activity cost drivers for the two products are summarized below.

Activities	Activity Driver
Setup	Batch
Assembly	Units
Inspect and finishing	Hours
Packaging	Hours

	Safe-V	Safe-T
Batches	250	600
Units	60,000	72,000
Finishing hours, per unit	0.2	0.3
Packaging hours, per unit	0.1	0.15
Materials per unit	$ 3.50	$ 6.00

Required

1. Determine the amount of the cost pool for each of the four activities.
2. Determine the activity-based rates for assigning factory costs to the two products.
3. Determine the activity-based unit cost for each of the products.
4. What is the strategic role of the information obtained in part 3?

5-57 **Resource and Activity-Based Cost Drivers (Continuation of 5-56)** Assume the same information as in problem 5-56 above, except that, to improve the accuracy of the ABC-costs, EEI has determined resource consumption rates based on cost drivers instead of estimated-percentage-consumption rates. The resource consumption cost drivers and driver levels are given below:

Resource Driver	Resource Total	Setup	Assembly	Inspect & Finishing	Packaging
Number of employees	17	5	6	4	2
Number of machines	10	3	3	3	1
Square feet, floor space	22,000	4,000	8,000	6,000	4,000

Required

1. Determine the amount of the cost pool for each of the four activities.
2. Determine the activity-based rates for assigning factory costs to the two products.
3. Determine the activity-based total unit cost for each of the products.

5-58 **Volume-Based Costing Versus ABC** Superior Door Company (SDC) manufactures and sells two main product lines, interior doors and exterior doors. Its products are sold through industry and wholesale suppliers. SDC's products are known for their quality and value, and are often priced lower than competing brands. During a recent executive meeting, Jerry Rhodes, the vice president of marketing, made three observations: First, the price of the interior door (ID), a high-volume product for the firm, is often higher than that of competitors' products. Second, SDC has been struggling to maintain its market share of ID. Third, the firm has sold approximately the same number of units of its exterior door (ED), a high-margin product, despite a 7.5 percent increase in price. Noting that the profit margin per unit of ED is higher than that of ID, Rhodes has suggested that SDC should push for producing and selling ED. Regina Jones, the plant manager, objected to this strategy because the manufacturing processes of ED were much more complicated than those for ID. The total manufacturing costs would increase substantially if SDC shifted its product line to emphasize ED.

Joseph Higgins, the vice president of finance, observes that SDC uses a direct-labor cost-based system to determine the amount of manufacturing overhead for all of its products. Selected operating data for the year 2010 follow:

Product	Units Sold	Cost per Unit		Selling Price per Unit
		Direct Materials	Direct Labor	
ED	5,000	$40	$24	$150
ID	50,000	30	12	80

Joseph also has collected the following data on activity cost pools and their cost drivers:

Cost Pools/Activities	Cost Drivers
Machine operation	Machine-hours
Support labor overhead	Direct labor costs
Machine setup	Setup hours
Assembly	Number of operations
Inspection	Inspection hours

Estimated Overhead Costs and Activity Consumption Information for Cost Pools and Activities

Activity Cost Pool	Overhead	Activity Consumption Levels		
		Total Activity	ED	ID
Machine operation	$200,000	10,000	2,500	7,500
Support labor	150,800	$720,000	$120,000	$600,000
Machine setup	82,500	2,500	1,200	1,300
Assembly	140,875	402,500	192,500	210,000
Inspection	66,250	4,000	1,800	2,200
Total	$640,425			

Joseph explained why these cost drivers were appropriate:

- The overhead costs for machine operation had nothing to do with direct labor-hours. These costs were more likely to vary with the number of machine-hours.

- The support labor included allowances for benefits, break periods, and costs related to the supervising and engineering staff. This overhead was indirect to the products but was related to the direct labor costs.

- The setup overhead was generated by changing the job to be run and should be related to the setup hours rather than the direct labor-hours.

- The assembly overhead related to costs incurred for the cutting, trimming, and sanding operations. Therefore, the correct cost driver should be the number of operations.

- The inspection overhead arose from inspecting the finished goods. The higher the number of finished units, the higher the inspection overhead costs. The appropriate cost driver should be the number of hours spent on the inspection.

Required

1. Using the current costing system, which uses direct labor costs as the basis to determine overhead costs, calculate the unit manufacturing costs of the two products.

2. Using the activity-based costing system, calculate the unit manufacturing costs of the two products.

3. Under ABC, is the exterior door line as profitable as the vice president of marketing thinks it is under the existing costing system?

4. Evaluate the marketing vice president's suggestion to shift the sales mix in favor of exterior doors.

5. Give at least two reasons for the differences between the results for the two different costing systems.

5-59 **Volume-Based Costing Versus ABC**   ADA Pharmaceutical Company produces three drugs: Diomycin, Homycin, and Addolin belonging to the analgesic (pain-killer) family of medication. Since its inception four years ago, ADA has used a direct labor-hour-based system to assign manufacturing overhead costs to products.

Eme Weissman, the president of ADA Enterprises, has just read about activity-based costing in a trade journal. With some curiosity and interest, she asked her financial controller, Takedo Simon, to examine differences in product costs between the firm's current costing and activity-based costing systems.

ADA has the following budget information for the year:

	Diomycin	Homycin	Addolin
Cost of direct materials	$ 205,000	$265,000	$258,000
Cost of direct labor	250,000	234,000	263,000
Number of direct labor-hours	7,200	6,800	2,000
Number of capsules	1,000,000	500,000	300,000

ADA has identified the following activities as cost drivers and has allocated them to total overhead cost of $200,000 as follows:

Activity	Cost Driver	Budgeted Overhead Cost	Budgeted Cost Driver Volume
Machine setup	Setup hours	$ 16,000	1,600
Plant management	Workers	36,000	1,200
Supervision of direct labor	Direct labor-hours	46,000	1,150
Quality inspection	Inspection-hours	50,400	1,050
Expediting orders	Customers served	51,600	645
Total overhead		$200,000	

Takedo selected the cost drivers with the following justifications:

SETUP HOURS: The cost driver of setup hours is used because the same product takes about the same amount of setup time regardless of size of batch. For different products, however, the setup time varies.

NUMBER OF WORKERS: Plant management includes plant maintenance and corresponding managerial duties that make production possible. This activity depends on the number of workers. The more workers involved, the higher the cost.

SUPERVISION OF DIRECT LABOR: Supervisors spend their time supervising production. The amount of time they spend on each product is proportional to the direct labor-hours worked.

QUALITY INSPECTION: Inspection involves testing a number of units in a batch. The time varies for different products but is the same for all similar products.

NUMBER OF CUSTOMERS SERVED: The need to expedite production increases as the number of customers served by the company increases. Thus, the number of customers served by ADA is a good measure of expediting production orders.

Takedo gathered the following information about the cost driver volume for each product:

	Diomycin	Homycin	Addolin
Machine setups	200	600	800
Plant management	200	400	600
Supervision of direct labor	200	300	650
Quality inspection	150	200	700
Expediting production orders	45	100	500

Required

1. Use the firm's current costing system to calculate the unit cost of each product.

2. Use the activity-based cost system to calculate the unit cost of each product.

3. The two cost systems provide different results; give several reasons for this. Why might these differences be strategically important to ADA Enterprises? How does ABC add to ADA's competitive advantage?

4. How and why may firms in the pharmaceutical industry use ABC? What is the strategic advantage?

5-60　**Volume-Based Costing Versus ABC**　Alaire Corporation manufactures several different circuit boards, but two of the boards account for the majority of the company's sales. The first product, a television (TV) circuit board, has been a standard in the industry for several years. The market for this board is competitive and price sensitive. Alaire plans to sell 65,000 of the TV boards in 2010 at $150 per unit. The second product, a personal computer (PC) circuit board, is a recent addition to Alaire's product line. Because it incorporates the latest technology, it can be sold at a premium price. The 2010 plans include the sale of 40,000 PC boards at $300 per unit.

Alaire's management group is meeting to discuss strategies for 2010. The current topic of conversation is how to spend the sales and promotion dollars for 2010. The sales manager believes that the market share for the TV board could be expanded by concentrating Alaire's promotional efforts in this area. In response to this suggestion, the production manager said, "Why don't you go after a bigger market for the PC board? The cost sheets that I get show the contribution from the PC board is about double the contribution from the TV board. I know we get a premium price for the PC board; selling it should help overall profitability."

Alaire's current volume-based costing system shows these data for TV and PC boards:

	TV Board	PC Board
Direct materials	$80	$140
Direct labor	1.5 hours	4 hours
Machine time	.5 hour	1.5 hours

The current costing system uses three types of factory overhead: variable overhead, materials handling, and machine time. Variable factory overhead is applied on the basis of direct labor-hours. For 2010, Alaire budgeted $1,120,000 variable factory overhead and 280,000 direct labor-hours. The hourly rates for machine time and direct labor are $10 and $14, respectively. Alaire applies a materials-handling charge of 10 percent of direct materials cost, which is not included in variable factory overhead. Total 2010 expenditures for direct materials are budgeted at $10,800,000.

The company conducted an activity analysis and collected the following information for 10 activities:

Budgeted Overhead Costs		Cost Driver	Annual Activity for Cost Driver
Materials-related overhead			
Procurement	$ 400,000	Number of parts	4,000,000
Production scheduling	220,000	Number of boards	110,000
Packaging and shipping	440,000	Number of boards	110,000
	$1,060,000		
Variable overhead			
Machine setup	$ 446,000	Number of setups	278,750
Hazardous waste disposal	48,000	Pounds of waste	16,000
Quality control	560,000	Number of inspections	160,000
General supplies	66,000	Number of boards	110,000
	$1,120,000		
Manufacturing overhead			
Machine insertion	$1,200,000	Number of insertions	3,000,000
Manual insertion	4,000,000	Number of insertions	1,000,000
Wave soldering	132,000	Number of boards	110,000
	$5,332,000		

Required per Unit	TV Board	PC Board
Parts	25	55
Machine insertions	24	35
Manual insertions	1	20
Machine setups	2	3
Hazardous waste	0.02 lb.	0.35 lb.
Inspections	1	2

Ed Welch, Alaire's controller, believes that before the management group proceeds with the discussion about allocating sales and promotional dollars to individual products, it might be worthwhile to look at these products on the basis of the activities involved in their production. As Ed explained to the group, "Activity-based costing integrates the cost of all activities, known as cost drivers, into individual product costs rather than including these costs in overhead pools." He prepared the preceding information to help the management group understand this concept.

"Using this information," Ed explained, "we can calculate an activity-based cost for each TV board and each PC board and then compare it to the standard cost we have been using. The only cost that remains the same for both cost methods is the cost of direct materials. The cost drivers will replace the direct labor, machine time, and overhead costs in the old standard cost figures."

Required

1. On the basis of Alaire's current costing system and its cost data (direct materials, direct labor, materials-handling charge, variable overhead, and machine time overhead) given in the problem, calculate the total contribution margin expected in 2010 for Alaire Corporation's TV board and PC board.

2. On the basis of activity-based costs, calculate the total contribution margin expected in 2010 for Alaire Corporation's TV board and PC board.

3. Explain how the comparison of the results of the two costing methods might affect the sales, pricing, and promotion decisions made by Alaire Corporation's management group. How would it affect the strategic, competitive position of the firm?

5-61 **Volume-Based Costing Versus ABC**   Coffee Bean Inc. (CBI) processes and distributes a variety of coffee. CBI buys coffee beans from around the world and roasts, blends, and packages them for resale. Currently the firm offers 15 coffees to gourmet shops in one-pound bags. The major cost is direct materials; however, a substantial amount of factory overhead is incurred in the predominantly automated roasting and packing process. The company uses relatively little direct labor.

Some of the coffees are very popular and sell in large volumes; a few of the newer brands have very low volumes. CBI prices its coffee at full product cost, including allocated overhead, plus a markup of 30 percent. If its prices for certain coffees are significantly higher than the market, CBI lowers its prices. The company competes primarily on the quality of its products, but customers are price conscious as well.

Data for the 2010 budget include factory overhead of $3,000,000, which has been allocated by its current costing system on the basis of each product's direct labor cost. The budgeted direct labor cost for 2010 totals $600,000. The firm budgeted $6,000,000 for purchases and use of direct materials (mostly coffee beans).

The budgeted direct costs for one-pound bags of two of the company's products are as follows:

	Mona Loa	Malaysian
Direct materials	$4.20	$3.20
Direct labor	0.30	0.30

CBI's controller, Mona Clin, believes that its current product costing system could be providing misleading cost information. She has developed this analysis of the 2010 budgeted factory overhead costs:

Activity	Cost Driver	Budgeted Activity	Budgeted Cost
Purchasing	Purchase orders	1,158	$ 579,000
Materials handling	Setups	1,800	720,000
Quality control	Batches	720	144,000
Roasting	Roasting-hours	96,100	961,000
Blending	Blending-hours	33,600	336,000
Packaging	Packaging-hours	26,000	260,000
Total factory overhead cost			$3,000,000

Data regarding the 2010 production of two of its lines, Mona Loa and Malaysian, follow. There is no beginning or ending direct materials inventory for either of these coffees.

	Mona Loa	Malaysian
Budgeted sales	100,000 pounds	2,000 pounds
Batch size	10,000 pounds	500 pounds
Setups	3 per batch	3 per batch
Purchase order size	25,000 pounds	500 pounds
Roasting time	1 hour per 100 pounds	1 hour per 100 pounds
Blending time	0.5 hour per 100 pounds	0.5 hour per 100 pounds
Packaging time	0.1 hour per 100 pounds	0.1 hour per 100 pounds

Required

1. Using Coffee Bean Inc.'s current product costing system,

    a. Determine the company's predetermined overhead rate using direct labor cost as the single cost driver.

    b. Determine the full product costs and selling prices of one pound of Mona Loa coffee and one pound of Malaysian coffee.

2. Using an activity-based costing approach, develop a new product cost for one pound of Mona Loa coffee and one pound of Malaysian coffee. Allocate all overhead costs to the 100,000 pounds of Mona Loa and the 2,000 pounds of Malaysian. Compare the results with those in requirement 1.

3. What are the implications of the activity-based costing system with respect to CBI's pricing and product mix strategies? How does ABC add to CBI's competitive advantage?

(CMA Adapted)

5-62 **Cost of Capacity (Continuation of 5-61)**   Use the same information as above for Coffee Bean, Inc. (CBI) except assume now that Mona Loa and Malaysian are the only two products at CBI. Also, now include the following additional information about the practical capacity Coffee Bean has in each of its activities. For example, currently Coffee Bean has total practical capacity for processing 1,400 purchase orders, 2,400 setups, etc. These are the levels of activity work that are sustainable.

Activity	Practical Capacity
Purchasing	1,400
Materials handling	2,400
Quality control	1,200
Roasting	100,000
Blending	36,000
Packaging	30,000

Required

1. Determine the activity rates based on practical capacity and the cost of unused capacity for each activity.

2. Explain the strategic role of the information you have developed in part (1) above.

3. Assume the same information used in parts (1) and (2) above, but now assume also that the costs in the purchasing activity consists entirely of the cost of 8 employees; the cost in materials handling consists entirely of the cost of 20 employees; the cost of quality control consists entirely of the cost of 4 employees; the cost of roasting and blending consists entirely of the costs of machines—10 roasting machines and 10 blending machines; and the cost of packaging consists entirely of the cost of 3 employees. Based on this additional information, what can you now advise management about the utilization of capacity?

5-63 **Activity-Based Costing**   Miami Valley Architects Inc. provides a wide range of engineering and architectural consulting services through its three branch offices in Columbus, Cincinnati, and Dayton, Ohio. The company allocates resources and bonuses to the three branches based on the net income of the period. The results of the firm's performance for the year 2010 follows ($ in thousands):

	Columbus	Cincinnati	Dayton	Total
Sales	$1,500	$1,419	$1,067	$3,986
Less: Direct labor	382	317	317	1,016
Direct materials	281	421	185	887
Overhead	710	589	589	1,888
Net income	$ 127	$ 92	$ (24)	$ 195

Miami Valley accumulates overhead items in one overhead pool and allocates it to the branches based on direct labor dollars. For 2010, this predetermined overhead rate was $1.859 for every direct labor dollar incurred by an office. The overhead pool includes rent, depreciation, and taxes, regardless of which office incurred the expense. Some branch managers complain that the overhead allocation method forces them to absorb a portion of the overhead incurred by the other offices.

Management is concerned with the 2010 operating results. During a review of overhead expenses, management noticed that many overhead items were clearly not correlated to the movement in direct labor dollars as previously assumed. Management decided that applying overhead based on activity-based costing and direct tracing wherever possible should provide a more accurate picture of the profitability of each branch.

An analysis of the overhead revealed that the following dollars for rent, utilities, depreciation, and taxes could be traced directly to the office that incurred the overhead ($ in thousands):

	Columbus	Cincinnati	Dayton	Total
Direct overhead	$180	$270	$177	$627

Activity pools and their corresponding cost drivers were determined from the accounting records and staff surveys as follows:

General administration	$ 409,000
Project costing	48,000
Accounts payable/receiving	139,000
Accounts receivable	47,000
Payroll/Mail sort and delivery	30,000
Personnel recruiting	38,000
Employee insurance processing	14,000
Proposals	139,000
Sales meetings/Sales aids	202,000
Shipping	24,000
Ordering	48,000
Duplicating costs	46,000
Blueprinting	77,000
	$1,261,000

	Volume of Cost Drivers by Location		
Cost Driver	**Columbus**	**Cincinnati**	**Dayton**
Direct labor cost	$ 382,413	317,086	317,188
Timesheet entries	6,000	3,800	3,500
Vendor invoices	1,020	850	400
Client invoices	588	444	96
Employees	23	26	18
New hires	8	4	7
Insurance claims filed	230	260	180
Proposals	200	250	60
Contracted sales	1,824,439	1,399,617	571,208
Projects shipped	99	124	30
Purchase orders	135	110	80
Copies duplicated	162,500	146,250	65,000
Blueprints	39,000	31,200	16,000

Required (Round all answers to thousands)

1. What overhead costs should be assigned to each branch based on ABC concepts?
2. What is the contribution of each branch before subtracting the results obtained in requirement 1?
3. What is the profitability of each branch office using ABC?
4. Evaluate the concerns of management regarding the volume-based cost technique currently used.

5-64 **Time-Drive Activity-Based Costing (TDABC) in a Call Center** Marketing Specialists Inc. (MSI) provides a range of services to its retail clients—customer service for inquiries, ordering taking, credit checking for new customers, and a variety of related services. Auto Supermarket (AS) is a large auto dealer that provides financing for the autos and trucks that it sells. AS has approached MIS to manage the inquiries that come in regarding these loans. AS is not satisfied with the performance of the call center it currently uses for handling inquiries on these loans and is considering a change to MSI. MSI has been asked to estimate the cost of providing the service for the coming year.

There are two types of loans at AS, one for autos and SUVs and another for light trucks. The loans for auto and truck buyers typically have different types of customers and loan terms, so the nature and volume of the inquiries are expected to differ. MSI would use its own call center to handle the AS engagement. The MSI call center's annual costs are as follows:

Call Center Costs	
Salaries	$4,223,555
Utilities	2,387,446
Leasing of facilities	1,983,063
Other expenses	801,036
	$9,395,100

MSI's call center is staffed 12 hours per day with 60 call staff always available. Each staff has a paid 10-minute break for each hour worked, and an unpaid 1-hour break for a lunch/dinner during their 12-hour shift. Thus, the call center has 12,045,000 minutes (11 hrs. $\times$ 50 min. $\times$ 60 staff $\times$ 365 days) available for calls during the year.

AS and MSI work together to estimate the number of calls and time required for each call, based on AS's prior experience with its current call center.

Inquiries	Total Calls Answered	Average Number of Minutes/Call	Total Time (minutes)
Inquire re: rates and terms			
Autos	96,000	4	384,000
Trucks	32,000	7	224,000
Inquire re: loan application status			
Autos	37,500	6	225,000
Trucks	6,750	11	74,250
Inquire re: payment status			
Autos	39,000	3	117,000
Trucks	12,000	4	48,000
Inquire re: other matters			
Autos	29,000	11	319,000
Trucks	8,500	15	127,500
			1,518,750

Required

1. Determine the amount that MSI should propose to charge AS for the coming year using TDABC, assuming MSI desired a profit of 25 percent of incurred cost.

2. Suppose that AS wants the proposal broken down by type of loan (auto, truck). What would the proposal look like now?

5-65 **TDABC;** Continuation of Problem 5-64

Suppose that in addition to the call center engagement outlined above, AS also provides the following annual service to 10 other clients:

	Total Calls Answered	Average Number of Minutes/Call
Platinum Regional Bank	234,000	6.0
Healthwise Software Inc	66,788	5.0
Johnson Manufacturing	122,665	4.0
Lesco Online Shopping	233,756	6.0
Babcock Insurance Service	55,455	5.5
Garcia Electric Supply and Service	38,956	3.4
Gilbert's Online Garden Supplies	145,902	4.0
Financial Planning Services Inc	68,993	11.0
Porter's Camera and Optical	198,440	6.0

Required

1. What is the unused capacity at MSI, **not** assuming that AS becomes a customer? What are the implications for the operating and marketing strategies at AS?

2. Assume that AS comes back to MSI with a revised proposal. The revised proposal includes call center activity as described in problem 5-64, but in addition, AS wants MSI to provide error-checking services for those who apply for loans at AS. MSI would use some of the call center staff, after appropriate training, to complete the processing of the credit checks. AS expects the following service to be needed:

Processing Credit Checks	Requests	Min./request
Auto	45,600	10
Truck	12,500	18

What would be the unused capacity with the revised proposal? What would be the cost of the unused capacity?

Solution to Self-Study Problem

Volume-Based Costing Versus ABC

1. Volume-based costing system

Stage 1 Allocation: Machine Hours

Total overhead allocated to Department A

$$\$1,000,000 \times (4,000/20,000) = \$200,000$$

Total overhead allocated to Department B

$$\$1,000,000 \times (16,000/20,000) = \$800,000$$

Stage 2 Allocation: Labor Hours		
	Per Unit Cost	
	Deluxe	**Regular**
Overhead allocated to		
Department A		
($200,000/20,000) × 2 =	$ 20	
($200,000/20,000) × 2 =		$ 20
Department B		
($800,000/10,000) × 1 =	80	
($800,000/10,000) × 1 =		80
Total	$100	$100

Product cost per unit:

	Deluxe	**Regular**
Direct materials	$100	$ 50
Direct labor		
$25 × (2 + 1) =	75	
$20 × (2 + 1) =		60
Factory overhead	100	100
Unit cost	$275	$210

2. Budgeted overhead rates for cost drivers:

Cost Driver	Budgeted Overhead	Budgeted Cost Driver Quantity	Budgeted Overhead Rate
Number of production runs	$ 7,000	350	$ 20 per run
Number of setups	400,000	500	800 per setup
Number of units	588,000	19,600	30 per unit
Number of shipments	5,000	250	20 per shipment
	$1,000,000		

3. ABC system

	Deluxe	Regular
Overhead allocated to		
Material movement		
$20 × 15 =	$ 300	
$20 × 20 =		$ 400
Machine setups		
$800 × 25 =	20,000	
$800 × 50 =		40,000
Inspections		
$30 × 200 =	6,000	
$30 × 800 =		24,000
Shipment		
$20 × 50 =	1,000	
$20 × 100 =		2,000
Total	$27,300	$66,400
Unit overhead cost	$136.50	$ 83
Product cost per unit		
Direct materials	$100	$ 50
Direct labor	75	60
Factory overhead	136.50	83
Unit cost	$311.50	$ 193

Note that the volume-based costing system overcosts the high-volume regular product and undercosts the low-volume deluxe product.

CHAPTER SIX

Process Costing

After studying this chapter, you should be able to . . .

1. Identify the types of firms or operations for which a process costing system is most suitable
2. Explain and calculate equivalent units
3. Describe the five steps in process costing
4. Demonstrate the weighted-average method of process costing
5. Demonstrate the FIFO method of process costing
6. Analyze process costing with multiple departments
7. Prepare journal entries to record the flow of costs in a process costing system
8. Explain how process costing systems are implemented and enhanced in practice
9. (Appendix) Account for spoilage in process costing

The Coca-Cola Company (www.coca-cola.com) is the world's leading manufacturer, marketer, and distributor of soft drink concentrates, syrups, and soft drinks. Coca-Cola's strategy focuses on both price and differentiation.

Coca-Cola's differentiation strategy is apparent in its positioning. It positions itself as a unique and special product with a young, fresh image equal to none in the soft drink segment; it is a permanent reminder of classic values, of American culture inside and outside the country, and of all things American: entertainment, sports, and youth. Furthermore, its brand is recognized in practically every country in the world. Its exclusive formula makes it unique.

Coca-Cola uses process costing to track product and customer costs such as direct materials, direct labor, and factory overhead costs incurred in three major processes: (1) concentrate and syrup manufacturing, (2) blending, and (3) packaging. During the first process, mixing water with sugar, colorings, and other ingredients produces concentrates, and adding sweeteners and water to the concentrates produces syrups. In the second process, pure carbon dioxide is added to the blend of syrups and water to produce the beverage. In the third process, a filler injects a precise amount of the blended beverage into plastic bottles or cans, and a metal crown or plastic closure seals the package.

Process costing is a product costing system that accumulates costs according to processes or departments and assigns them to a large number of nearly identical products. The typical firm that uses process costing employs a standardized production process to manufacture homogeneous products. Process costing provides information for managers to analyze product and customer profitability and to make pricing, product-mix, and process improvement decisions.

In today's globally competitive environment, managers must know product costs to be able to make good decisions. Imagine a large corporation's top manager trying to decide whether to discontinue a product without knowing what it costs. Managers need cost information for setting goals; forming strategy; developing long- and short-term plans; and for control, performance measurement, and decision-making purposes.

Process costing also allows accountants to determine unit costs needed for valuing inventory and the cost of goods sold for external financial reports. For example, Milliken & Co. (www.milliken.com) uses an activity-based costing type of process costing to help managers focus on the actual costs in each process and to reduce non-value-added work in each process.

Characteristics of Process Costing Systems

LEARNING OBJECTIVE 1

Identify the types of firms or operations for which a process costing system is most suitable.

Firms having homogeneous products that pass through a series of similar processes or departments use process costing. These firms usually engage in continuous mass production of a few similar products. Manufacturing costs are accumulated in each process. The management accountant uses a production cost report to track production quantity and cost information for each department. Unit product cost is calculated by dividing process costs in each department by the number of equivalent units produced during the period.

The process cost system is used in many industries such as chemicals, oil refining, textiles, paints, flour, canneries, rubber, steel, glass, food processing, mining, automobile production lines, electronics, plastics, drugs, paper, lumber, leather goods, metal products, sporting goods, cement, and watches. Process costing can also be used by service organizations with homogeneous services and repetitive processes such as check processing in a bank or mail sorting by a courier. Companies using process costing include Coca-Cola (www.coca-cola.com), Royal Dutch Shell Group (www.shell.com), International Paper (www.internationalpaper.com), and Kimberly-Clark (www.kimberly-clark.com).

Equivalent Units

LEARNING OBJECTIVE 2

Explain and calculate equivalent units.

A manufacturing firm typically has partially completed units (work-in-process) at the end of an accounting period. Under the job costing system, these partially completed units are not difficult to handle because job costs are available on job cost sheets.

In a process costing system, however, product costs for partially completed units are not readily available. Because the focus in cost accounting has shifted from jobs to processes or departments, the interest is in the unit cost of performing a certain *process* for a given period. The goal is to find the combined unit cost of all product units processed in that period, including those that are partially complete at *either* the beginning or the end of the accounting period. Note that by *partially complete,* we mean partially complete for that department; a unit could be complete for a given department but still be in the Work-in-Process Inventory for a department that follows in the sequence of manufacturing processes.

With both complete and partially complete units, we need a way to measure the proper amount of production work performed during a period. An equivalent unit is the measure commonly used.

Equivalent units are the number of the same or similar complete units that could have been produced given the amount of work actually performed on both complete and partially complete units.

Equivalent units are the number of the same or similar complete units that could have been produced given the amount of work actually performed on both complete and partially complete units. Equivalent units are not the same as physical units. For example, suppose in a given month a chemical company had in process 30,000 gallons of a chemical, of which 20,000 gallons were complete at the end of the month but the remaining 10,000 gallons were only 50 percent complete. The equivalent units would be 25,000 gallons [20,000 + (10,000 × 50%)]. The percentage of completion is usually measured by percentage of total cost that has already been incurred in the production of the product.

The equivalent units should be calculated separately for direct materials, direct labor, and factory overhead because the proportion of the total work performed on the product units in the work-in-process inventories is not always the same for each cost element. Partially complete units are often complete for direct materials but incomplete for direct labor and factory overhead. Examples include chemical or brewing processes that add direct materials at the beginning but are not complete until the completion of processing, which can extend over hours or days. Because overhead is often applied on the basis of labor hours, some firms use the two categories—direct materials and conversion cost. *Conversion costs* are the sum of direct labor and factory overhead costs.

Conversion Costs

Because of the relatively small direct labor content in many process industries, such as the oil refining, aluminum, paper, chemical, and pharmaceutical industries, factory overhead and direct labor costs are sometimes combined and called conversion costs for the purpose of computing equivalent units of production. Linking these two cost elements is practical because direct labor cost is not a significant cost element in these process industries.

EXHIBIT 6.1   Equivalent Units for Direct Materials in Work-in-Process Ending Inventory

Type of Inventory	Physical Units Partially Complete	Percentage of Completion for Conversion	Equivalent Units in Ending Work-in-Process Inventory for Direct Materials			
			Materials Added Gradually	All Materials Added at the Beginning	All Materials Added at 40 Percent Point	All Materials Added at the End
Ending work-in-process inventory	1,500	60%	1,500 × 60% = 900	1,500 × 100% = 1,500	1,500 × 100% = 1,500	0

Many manufacturing operations incur conversion costs uniformly throughout production. The equivalent units of conversion costs are therefore the result of multiplying the percentage of work that is complete during the period by the number of units on which work is partially complete. For example, for 1,000 units estimated to be 30 percent complete in the work-in-process ending inventory, the equivalent units of conversion in the period are 300 (30 percent × 1,000 units).

Firms using nonlabor-based cost drivers (such as machine hours or the number of setups) for their factory overhead costs find that calculating separate equivalent units of production for factory overhead and direct labor costs is more appropriate.

Direct Materials

Direct materials can be added at discrete points or continuously during production. If the materials are added uniformly, the proportion used for computing equivalent units of direct materials is the same as the proportion for conversion costs. However, if the materials are added all at once, the proportion used in the computation depends on whether the point in the process where the materials are added has been reached.

Exhibit 6.1 illustrates the determination of equivalent units in direct materials for ending work-in-process (WIP) inventory. The example assumes that ending work-in-process (WIP) inventory has 1,500 product units that are 60 percent complete for conversion. Exhibit 6.1 has four materials-adding situations: (1) materials are added gradually throughout the process, (2) all materials are added at the beginning of the process, (3) all materials are added at the 40 percent point, and (4) all materials are added at the end of the process. Note that the equivalent units of materials in ending work-in-process inventory would be 900 (1,500 × .6) equivalent units under assumption (1).

Flow of Costs in Process Costing

In process costing, costs flow through different processes or departments. Exhibit 6.2 is a T-account model of direct materials, direct labor, and factory overhead cost flows in a two-department process costing system. Note four key points in this exhibit. First, a separate

EXHIBIT 6.2   T-Account Model of Flow of Costs for Two Departments in Process Costing

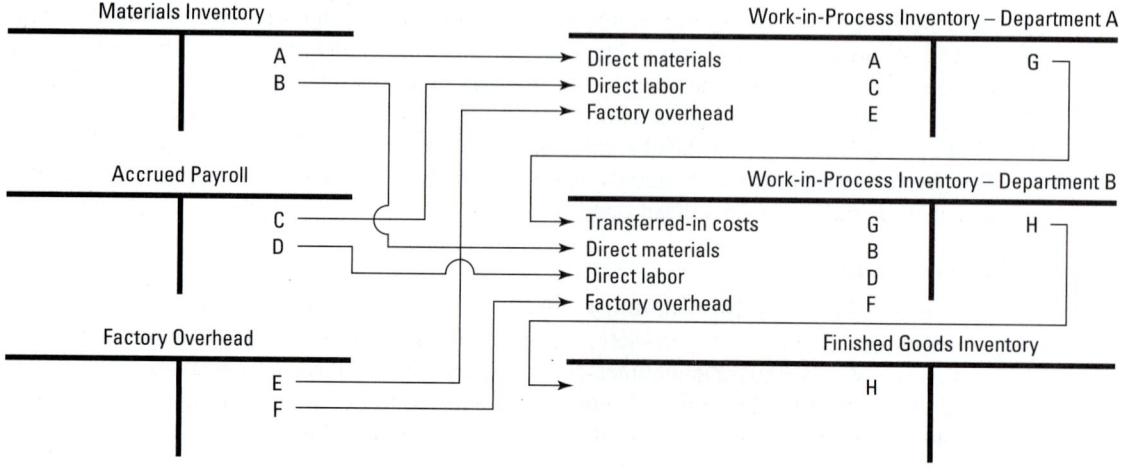

Work-in-Process Inventory account is used to record costs of each production department. Second, when Department A finishes its work, the costs of the goods completed are transferred to Department B's Work-in-Process Inventory account for further work. After this further work, the costs of goods completed are then transferred to the Finished Goods Inventory account. Third, direct materials, direct labor, and factory overhead costs can be entered directly into either production department's Work-in-Process Inventory account, not just that of the first department. Finally, starting with the second department (Department B), an additional cost element, *transferred-in-costs,* appears. These are costs of the goods completed in the prior department and transferred into this department during the period.

LEARNING OBJECTIVE 3

Describe the five steps in process costing.

Production cost reports
summarize the physical units and equivalent units of a department, the costs incurred during the period, and the costs assigned to both units completed and ending work-in-process inventories.

Steps in Process Costing

The key document in a typical process costing system is the production cost report, prepared at the end of each period for each production process or department. The **production cost report** summarizes the number of physical units and equivalent units of a department, the costs incurred during the period, and the costs assigned to both units completed and transferred out and ending work-in-process inventories. The preparation of a production cost report includes the five steps in Exhibit 6.3.

Step 1: Analyze the Physical Flow of Production Units

The first step determines the number of units on hand in beginning work-in-process, the number of units started into production (or received from a prior department), the number of units completed, and the number of units in ending work-in-process inventory.

The analysis of physical units includes accounting for both input and output units. *Input units* include beginning work-in-process inventory and all units that enter a production department during an accounting period. *Output units* include units that are complete and transferred out from a production department and units in the ending work-in-process inventory.

Step 2: Calculate Equivalent Units for Each Manufacturing Cost Element

The purpose of calculating equivalent units of production for direct materials, direct labor, and factory overhead is to measure the total work expended on production during an accounting period. The partially complete physical units are converted into the equivalent number of whole units.

Step 3: Determine Total Costs for Each Manufacturing Cost Element

The total manufacturing costs for each cost element (materials, labor, and overhead) include the current costs incurred and the costs of the units in work-in-process beginning inventory. The amount of these costs is obtained from material requisitions, labor time cards, and factory overhead allocation sheets. The total manufacturing cost for each cost element is also called *total cost to account for*. The total cost determined in step three must agree with the total cost assigned in step 5.

Step 4: Compute Cost per Equivalent Unit for Each Manufacturing Cost Element

The purpose of computing direct materials, direct labor, and factory overhead costs per equivalent unit of production is to have a proper product costing and income determination for an accounting period, which includes both complete and incomplete units.

Step 5: Assign Total Manufacturing Costs to Units Completed and Ending WIP

The objective of the production cost report is to assign total manufacturing costs incurred to the units completed during the period and the units that are still in process at the end of the

EXHIBIT 6.3
Five Steps in Process Costs

1. Analyze the physical flow of production units.
2. Calculate equivalent units for each manufacturing cost element (materials, labor, overhead).
3. Determine total costs for each manufacturing cost element.
4. Compute cost per equivalent unit for each manufacturing cost element.
5. Assign total manufacturing costs to units completed and ending WIP.

Many process industries such as paper manufacturing, chemical production, oil refining, and steel processing create environmentally sensitive waste products. Many of these firms use a sustainability scorecard as explained in Chapter 2 (refer to Exhibit 2.8). A critical cost management goal for these firms is to find cost-effective means to manage these waste products. For example, a steel plating facility in the United States recently faced the need to redesign its plant to meet U.S. environmental standards. The firm sought bids from environmental engineering firms for the redesign work. The average bid was $800,000, each requiring a significant rebuilding of the plant and extensive downtime at the plant. To avoid the cost and disruption of such a plant redesign, the company used cost management methods based in part on process cost information to develop a plan to reduce

cost within the plant's current facilities. The plan involved several changes in operations including new ways to handle raw materials, changes in product mix and scheduling, segregating wastewater flows, and treating some wastes within the plant rather than off-site. The cost of the plan was less than 25 percent of the cost of the plant redesign and it also was projected to have lower operating costs. Moreover, the plan offered a better integration of day-to-day decision making with environmental compliance, in comparison to the redesign plan of the consulting environmental engineers. Can you think of other examples of how a process industry could save money and also improve environmental sustainability?

(Refer to Comments on Cost Management in Action at end of Chapter.)

period. The total costs assigned in step 5 should equal the total costs to be accounted for in step 3.

Companies generally divide the five-step production cost report into three parts: (1) production quantity information, (2) unit cost determination, and (3) cost assignment. The first part includes step 1, analyze flow of physical units, and step 2, calculate equivalent units. The second part includes step 3, determine total costs to account for, and step 4, compute equivalent unit cost. The third part includes step 5, assign total manufacturing costs (total costs accounted for).

Process Costing Methods

The two methods used to prepare the departmental production cost report when the firm uses process costing are the weighted-average method and the first-in, first-out (FIFO) method. The **weighted-average method** includes all costs in calculating the unit cost, including both costs incurred during the current period and costs incurred in the prior period that are shown as the beginning work-in-process inventory of the current period. In this method, prior period costs and current period costs are averaged; hence, the name *weighted average.* The **FIFO method** includes in calculating the unit cost only costs incurred and work performed during the current period. FIFO considers the beginning inventory as a batch of goods separate from the goods started and completed within the period. FIFO assumes that the first work done is to complete the beginning work-in-process inventory. Thus, all beginning work-in- process inventories are assumed to be completed before the end of the current period.

Weighted-average method includes both current period and prior period costs in calculating unit cost.

FIFO method includes in calculating the unit cost only costs incurred and work performed during the current period.

Illustration of Process Costing

To illustrate these two process costing methods, assume that Naftel Toy Company has two production departments, molding and finishing. The molding department places a direct material (plastic vinyl) into production at the beginning of the process. Direct labor and factory overhead costs are incurred gradually throughout the process with different proportions.

Exhibit 6.4 summarizes the molding department's units and costs during June.

Weighted-Average Method

LEARNING OBJECTIVE 4

Demonstrate the weighted-average method of process costing.

The weighted-average method makes no distinction between the cost incurred prior to the current period and the cost incurred during the current period. As long as a cost is on the current period's cost sheet for a production department, it is treated as any other cost regardless of when it was incurred. Consequently, the average cost per equivalent unit includes costs incurred both during the current period and in the prior period that carry over into this period through beginning work-in-process inventory. We use the five-step procedure to assign direct materials, direct labor, and factory overhead costs to the cost object, the molding department for the month of June.

EXHIBIT 6.4
Basic Data for Naftel Toy Company—Molding Department

Work-in-process inventory, June 1	10,000 units
Direct materials: 100 percent complete	$10,000
Direct labor: 30 percent complete	1,060
Factory overhead: 40 percent complete	1,620
Beginning work-in-process inventory	$12,680
Units started during June	40,000 units
Units completed during June and transferred out of the molding department	44,000 units
Work-in-process inventory, June 30	6,000 units
Direct materials: 100 percent complete	
Direct labor: 50 percent complete	
Factory overhead: 60 percent complete	
Costs added during June	
Direct materials	$ 44,000
Direct labor	22,440
Factory overhead	43,600
Total costs added during June	$110,040

Step 1: Analyze the Physical Flow of Production Units

The first step is to analyze the flow of all units through production. Exhibit 6.5 presents the procedures for this step.

The two sections in Exhibit 6.5 show the two aspects of physical units flowing through production, *input units* and *output units.* This procedure ensures that all units in production are accounted for. Input units include all units that enter a production department during an accounting period or that entered during the prior period but were incomplete at the beginning of the period. These units come from two sources: (1) beginning work-in-process inventory started in a previous period that was partially complete at the end of the preceding period, which is 10,000 units in our example, and (2) work started or received in the current period, 40,000 units in our example. The sum of these two sources, 50,000 units here, is referred to as the number of **units to account for,** which is the sum of beginning inventory units and the number of units started during the period.

Units to account for are the sum of the beginning inventory units and the number of units started during the period.

Output units include those that have been completed and transferred out and those not yet complete at the end of a period. These units can be in one of two categories: the 44,000 units completed or the 6,000 units in the ending work-in-process inventory. The sum of these two categories, 50,000 units, is referred to as the *number of units accounted for*. This number should match the number of units to account for. **Units accounted for** includes the sum of units completed and transferred out plus ending inventory units.

Units accounted for are the sum of the units completed and transferred out plus ending inventory units.

The primary purpose of this first step is to ensure that all units in production are accounted for before we compute the number of equivalent units of production for each production element.

Step 2: Calculate Equivalent Units for Each Manufacturing Cost Element

The second step in the process costing procedure is to calculate the number of equivalent units of production activity for direct materials, direct labor, and factory overhead. A table of

EXHIBIT 6.5
Step 1: Analyze the Physical Flow of Units—Molding Department

Input	Physical Units
Work-in-process inventory, June 1	10,000
Units started during June	40,000
Total units to account for	50,000

Output	Physical Units
Units completed and transferred out during June	44,000
Work-in-process inventory, June 30	6,000
Total units accounted for	50,000

equivalent units, presented in Exhibit 6.6, is based on the table of physical units prepared in step 1 (Exhibit 6.5).

The weighted-average method computes the total equivalent units produced to date. The number of units in production in the current period for each manufacturing production element includes both (1) the units from previous periods that are still in production at the beginning of the current period and (2) the units placed into production in the current period.

In Exhibit 6.6, 44,000 physical units were complete and transferred out of the molding department. These units were 100 percent complete. Thus, they represent 44,000 equivalent units for direct materials, direct labor, and factory overhead. Note that the 44,000 units include 10,000 units placed into production prior to June and completed in June, and 34,000 units (44,000 units − 10,000 units) started and completed in June.

The 6,000 units in ending work-in-process inventory are complete with respect to direct materials because direct materials are added at the beginning of the process. Thus, they represent 6,000 equivalent units of direct materials. However, they are only 50 and 60 percent complete for direct labor and factory overhead, respectively. Therefore, the ending work-in-process inventories represent 3,000 equivalent units of direct labor (6,000 physical units × 50 percent complete) and 3,600 equivalent units of factory overhead (6,000 physical units × 60 percent complete).

From Exhibit 6.6, we calculate, for each cost element, the total number of equivalent units as follows:

Completed and transferred out units

+ Ending work-in-process equivalent units

= Total equivalent units of production

Combining completed units and ending work-in-process equivalent units, the equivalent units of production for the molding department under the weighted-average method are 50,000 units of direct materials, 47,000 units of direct labor, and 47,600 units of factory overhead.

Step 3: Determine Total Costs for Each Manufacturing Cost Element

The third step determines how much money was spent both in the beginning work-in-process inventory and current production for direct materials, direct labor, and factory overhead.

Exhibit 6.7 summarizes the total manufacturing costs to account for. As given in our example data, total manufacturing costs ($122,720) consist of the beginning work-in-process inventory balance, $12,680, plus the costs added during June, $110,040.

Step 4: Compute Cost per Equivalent Unit

For the fourth step in the process costing procedure, we compute the equivalent unit costs of production for direct materials, direct labor, and factory overhead; see Exhibit 6.8. The cost

EXHIBIT 6.6
Step 2: Calculate Equivalent Units—Molding Department: Weighted-Average Method

	Physical Units	Completion Percentage	EQUIVALENT UNITS Direct Materials	Direct Labor	Factory Overhead
Work-in-process, June 1	10,000				
Direct materials		100%			
Direct labor		30			
Factory overhead		40			
Units started	40,000				
Units to account for	50,000				
Units completed	44,000	100%	44,000	44,000	44,000
Work-in-process, June 30	6,000				
Direct materials		100	6,000		
Direct labor		50		3,000	
Factory overhead		60			3,600
Units accounted for	50,000				
Total equivalent units			50,000	47,000	47,600

EXHIBIT 6.7

Step 3: Determine Total
Costs—Molding Department

Beginning work-in-process inventory		
Direct materials	$10,000	
Direct labor	1,060	
Factory overhead	1,620	
Total		$ 12,680
Costs added during June		
Direct materials	$44,000	
Direct labor	22,440	
Factory overhead	43,600	
Total costs added		110,040
Total costs to account for		$122,720

EXHIBIT 6.8

Step 4: Compute Cost per
Equivalent Unit—Molding
Department: Weighted-
Average Method

	Direct Materials	Direct Labor	Factory Overhead	Total
Costs (from Exhibit 6.7)				
Work-in-process, June 1	$10,000	$ 1,060	$ 1,620	$ 12,680
Costs added during June	44,000	22,440	43,600	110,040
Total costs to account for	$54,000	$23,500	$45,220	$122,720
Divide by equivalent units (from Exhibit 6.6)	50,000	47,000	47,600	
Equivalent unit costs	$ 1.08 +	$ 0.50 +	$ 0.95 =	$ 2.53

per equivalent unit for direct materials ($1.08) is computed by dividing the total direct materials cost ($54,000), including the cost of the beginning work-in-process ($10,000) and the cost added during June ($44,000), by the total equivalent units (50,000). Similar procedures are used for direct labor and factory overhead costs. The total equivalent unit cost of $2.53 can be determined by adding the unit direct materials cost of $1.08, the unit direct labor cost of $0.50, and the unit factory overhead cost of $0.95.

Step 5: Assign Total Manufacturing Costs to Units Completed and Ending WIP

The final step of the process costing procedure is to assign total manufacturing costs to units completed and to units in the ending work-in-process inventory. Exhibit 6.9 summarizes the cost assignment schedule. Various unit information comes directly from Exhibit 6.6; various unit costs come from Exhibit 6.8. Note that the total costs accounted for in this step ($122,720) equals the total costs to account for in step 3 (Exhibit 6.7).

Cost Reconciliation

After finishing the five-step procedure, we need to determine whether the total manufacturing costs to account for in step 3 (i.e., total input costs) agree with the total costs accounted for

EXHIBIT 6.9

Step 5: Assign Total
Manufacturing Costs—
Molding Department:
Weighted-Average Method

	Completed and Transferred out	Ending Work-in-Process	Total
Goods completed and transferred out (44,000 × $2.53)	$111,320		$111,320
Ending work-in-process:			
Direct materials (6,000 × $1.08)		$ 6,480	6,480
Direct labor (3,000 × $0.50)		1,500	1,500
Factory overhead (3,600 × $0.95)		3,420	3,420
Total costs accounted for	$111,320	$11,400	$122,720

in step 5 (i.e., total output costs). This checking procedure is called the *cost reconciliation.* For example, for Naftel Toy Company's modeling department, $122,720 total manufacturing costs accounted for in step 3 equal the total costs accounted for in step 5.

Production Cost Report

Steps 1 through 5 provide all information needed to prepare a production cost report for the molding department for June. This report is in Exhibit 6.10.

EXHIBIT 6.10
Production Cost Report—
Molding Department:
Weighted-Average Method

Production Quantity Information					
	Step 1: Analyze Flow of Physical Units		Step 2: Calculate Equivalent Units		
	Physical Units	Completion Percentage	Direct Materials	Direct Labor	Factory Overhead
Input					
Work-in-process, June 1	10,000				
Direct materials		100%			
Direct labor		30			
Factory overhead		40			
Units started	40,000				
Units to account for	50,000				
Output					
Units completed	44,000	100%	44,000	44,000	44,000
Work-in-process, June 30	6,000				
Direct materials		100	6,000		
Direct labor		50		3,000	
Factory overhead		60			3,600
Units accounted for	50,000				
Total equivalent units			50,000	47,000	47,600

Unit Cost Determination				
Step 3: Determine Total Costs	Direct Materials	Direct Labor	Factory Overhead	Total
Work-in-process, June 1	$10,000	$ 1,060	$ 1,620	$ 12,680
Costs added during June	44,000	22,440	43,600	110,040
Total costs to account for	$54,000	$23,500	$45,220	$122,720
Step 4: Compute Cost per Equivalent Unit				
Divide by equivalent units	50,000	47,000	47,600	
Equivalent unit costs	$ 1.08	$ 0.50	$ 0.95	$ 2.53

Cost Assignment			
Step 5: Assign Total Manufacturing Costs	Completed and Transferred out	Ending Work-in-Process	Total
Goods completed and transferred out (44,000 × $2.53)	$111,320		$111,320
Ending work-in-process			
Direct materials (6,000 × $1.08)		$ 6,480	6,480
Direct labor (3,000 × $0.50)		1,500	1,500
Factory overhead (3,600 × $0.95)		3,420	3,420
Total costs accounted for	$111,320	$11,400	$122,720

First-In, First-Out (FIFO) Method

LEARNING OBJECTIVE 5

Demonstrate the FIFO method of process costing.

Another way to handle inventory in a process costing application is the first-in, first-out (FIFO) method, which assumes that the first units to enter a production process are the first units to be completed and transferred out.

Our illustration of the FIFO method of process costing again uses Naftel Toy Company's molding department data (see Exhibit 6.4). Unlike the weighted-average method, the FIFO method does not combine beginning inventory costs with current costs when computing equivalent unit costs. The costs from each period are treated separately. We follow the same five steps as in the weighted-average method, however, in determining product costs.

Step 1: Analyze the Physical Flow of Production Units

The physical flow of product units is unaffected by the process costing method used. Therefore, step 1 for the FIFO method is the same as the weighted-average method in Exhibit 6.5.

Step 2: Calculate Equivalent Units for Each Manufacturing Cost Element

The FIFO method considers the beginning inventory as a batch of goods separate from the goods started and completed within the same period. The equivalent units in the beginning work-in-process—work done in the prior period—are not counted as part of the FIFO method equivalent units. Only that part of the equivalent units of the beginning work in process to be completed this period is counted.

Two equivalent, alternative procedures are used to calculate equivalent units of production under the FIFO method.

Step 2, Alternative A

One way to calculate FIFO equivalent units is to subtract the equivalent units in beginning work-in-process from the weighted-average equivalent units to obtain the FIFO method equivalent units, as shown in the last three rows of Exhibit 6.11. The 10,000 physical units in June 1 work-in-process have 100 percent of direct materials, so these units have 10,000 equivalent units of direct materials prior to the current period. However, these units are only 30 percent and 40 percent complete for direct labor and factory overhead, respectively, so they contribute only 3,000 equivalent units of direct labor (10,000 × 30%) and 4,000 equivalent units of factory overhead (10,000 × 40%) prior to the current period.

To calculate the total number of FIFO equivalent units, the following equation is used for each cost element:

Completed and transferred out units

+ Ending work-in-process equivalent units

= Weighted-average equivalent units

− Beginning work-in-process equivalent units

= FIFO equivalent units of work done during this period

Exhibit 6.11 shows that Naftel Toy Company must account for a total of 50,000 units. Of these, 44,000 units are completed and 6,000 units are ending work-in-process inventory that is 100 percent complete for direct materials. The total equivalent units for the period for direct materials under the weighted-average method is 50,000. Of the 44,000 units completed during the period, 10,000 were in the beginning work-in-process inventory. These 10,000 units already had all direct materials added in the prior period. Subtracting 10,000 units from the 50,000 total equivalent units for the period, the FIFO equivalent units for work done only in June for direct materials is 40,000 units. Following the same procedure, equivalent units of production for the molding department using the FIFO method are 44,000 units of direct labor and 43,600 units of factory overhead.

The difference between the weighted-average method and the FIFO method is that under the weighted-average method, the equivalent units of production completed prior to the current

EXHIBIT 6.11
Step 2: Calculate Equivalent
Units—Molding Department:
FIFO Method—Alternative A

	Physical Units	Completion Percentage	Equivalent Units Direct Materials	Equivalent Units Direct Labor	Equivalent Units Factory Overhead
Input					
Work-in-process, June 1	10,000				
Direct materials		100%	10,000		
Direct labor		30		3,000	
Factory overhead		40			4,000
Units started	40,000				
Units to account for	50,000				
Output					
Units completed	44,000	100%	44,000	44,000	44,000
Work-in-process, June 30	6,000				
Direct materials		100	6,000		
Direct labor		50		3,000	
Factory overhead		60			3,600
Units accounted for	50,000				
Total equivalent units (weighted-average method)			50,000	47,000	47,600
Less: equivalent units in June 1 work-in-process			(10,000)	(3,000)	(4,000)
Equivalent units for work done in June only (FIFO method)			40,000	44,000	43,600

period are not subtracted from the total completed units, so equivalent units under the weighted-average method are always as large or larger than those under the FIFO method.

Step 2, Alternative B

An alternative way to determine the equivalent units using the FIFO method is to add equivalent units of work performed in the current period for each of the three components: (1) equivalent units added to complete the beginning work-in-process inventory, (2) units started and completed during the period, and (3) equivalent units of the ending work-in-process inventory. Exhibit 6.12 presents the FIFO equivalent units computation using the second procedure. Notice that under the FIFO method, the equivalent units in the beginning work-in-process inventory from last month's work effort are not added to equivalent units of work performed this month.

For example, the 10,000 units of beginning work-in-process inventory were 30 percent complete for direct labor. Naftel Toy Company completed the beginning work-in-process inventory by adding the remaining 70 percent of the direct labor during the current period to complete production. In addition, the firm started another 40,000 units in production during the period. Of these 40,000 units, the firm started and completed production of 34,000, and the remaining 6,000 were still in the manufacturing process at the end of the period. The firm has completed only 50 percent of the total direct labor in ending work-in-process inventory, or an equivalent of 3,000 units. To summarize the direct labor spent during the period, the firm spent an equivalent of 7,000 units of direct labor to complete the beginning work-in-process inventory on hand, started and completed 34,000 units, and spent an equivalent of 3,000 units to complete 50 percent of the 6,000 units of ending work-in-process inventory. The total direct labor of the period is equivalent to production of 44,000 FIFO units. Exhibit 6.13 graphically illustrates the difference between weighted-average and FIFO equivalent units.

Step 3: Determine Total Costs for Each Manufacturing Cost Element

The total costs incurred to manufacture product units are unaffected by the process costing method used. Therefore, step 3 is the same as the weighted-average method in Exhibit 6.7.

EXHIBIT 6.12   Step 2: Calculate Equivalent Units—Molding Department: FIFO Method—Alternative B

	Physical Units	Completion Percentage	Equivalent Units (FIFO)		
			Direct Materials	Direct Labor	Factory Overhead
Input					
Work-in-process, June 1	10,000				
Direct materials		100%	10,000		
Direct labor		30		3,000	
Factory overhead		40			4,000
Units started	40,000				
Units to account for	50,000				
Output					
Completed and transferred out from work-in-process, June 1	10,000				
Direct materials 10,000 × (1 - 100%)			0		
Direct labor 10,000 × (1 - 30%)				7,000	
Factory overhead 10,000 × (1 - 40%)					6,000
Started and completed (44,000 - 10,000)	34,000	100%	34,000	34,000	34,000
Work-in-process, June 30	6,000				
Direct materials		100	6,000		
Direct labor		50		3,000	
Factory overhead		60			3,600
Units accounted for	50,000				
Equivalent units of work for June (FIFO method)			40,000	44,000	43,600

It shows that Naftel Toy Company's modeling department has $122,720 total manufacturing costs to account for.

Step 4: Compute Cost per Equivalent Unit for Each Manufacturing Cost Element

Under the FIFO method, equivalent unit costs are calculated by dividing the costs added during the current period by the equivalent units for work completed only during the current period. No cost in the work-in-process beginning inventory is included in determining equivalent unit costs for cost elements. Exhibit 6.14 presents the calculations. The equivalent unit cost for direct materials ($1.10) is computed by dividing the direct materials cost added during June

EXHIBIT 6.13

Weighted-Average vs. FIFO Equivalent Units

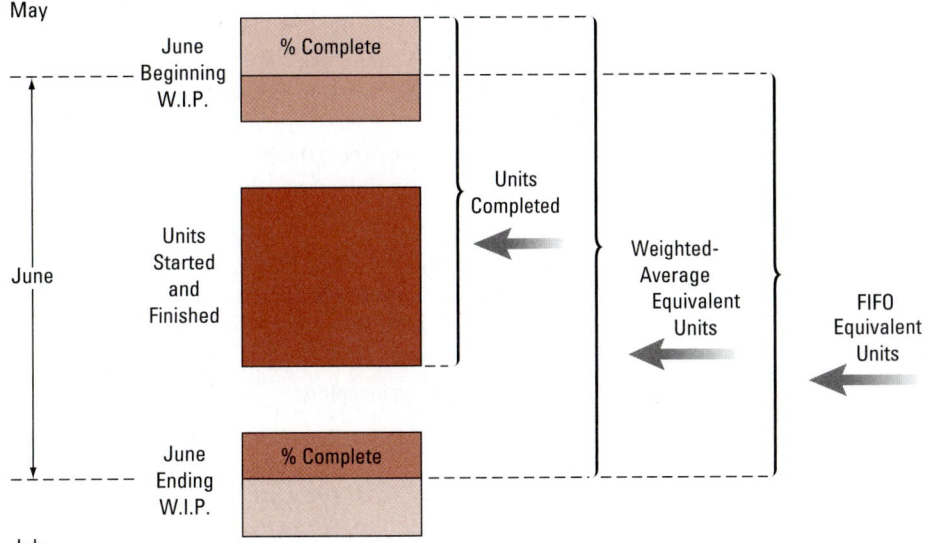

EXHIBIT 6.14

Step 4: Compute Cost per
Equivalent Unit—Molding
Department: FIFO Method

	Direct Materials	Direct Labor	Factory Overhead	Total
Costs (from Exhibit 6.7)				
Work-in-process, June 1				$ 12,680
Costs added during June	$44,000	$22,440	$43,600	110,040
Total costs to account for				$122,720
Divide by equivalent units (from Exhibit 6.11)	40,000	44,000	43,600	
Equivalent unit costs	$ 1.10 +	$ 0.51 +	$ 1.00 =	$ 2.61

($44,000) by the equivalent units for work done in June only (40,000). Similar procedures are used for direct labor and factory overhead costs. Notice that the total equivalent unit cost of $2.61 is determined by adding the unit direct materials cost of $1.10, the unit direct labor cost of $0.51, and the unit factory overhead cost of $1.00.

Step 5: Assign Total Manufacturing Costs to Units Completed and Ending WIP

The final step of the process costing procedure is to assign total manufacturing costs to units completed and to units in the ending work-in-process inventory. As for the weighted-average method, the FIFO method assigns the total costs of a period to the units completed, the units transferred out, and the units still in process at the end of the period. Unlike the weighted-average method, however, the FIFO method accounts separately for current and prior period costs.

The manufacturing process for units in the beginning work-in-process overlaps two periods. Thus, units completed from beginning work-in-process inventory incurred costs prior to the current period as well as during the current period. This fact makes the assignment of total manufacturing costs to units completed during a period a two-part process. In the first part, the total manufacturing cost for units completed from beginning work-in-process is determined. In the second part, the total manufacturing costs for units started and completed during the manufacturing process in the current period are calculated.

Step 5, Part A: Total Cost of Units Completed from Beginning Work-in-Process Inventory

To determine the total manufacturing costs for the units completed from beginning work-in-process, the firm adds the manufacturing costs assigned to the units during the current period to the costs of the beginning work-in-process inventory ($12,680).

The total additional cost incurred in the current period to complete these units is the sum of the equivalent units of each cost element added to complete the element. These are assigned to the units in beginning work-in-process and multiplied by the current period's unit cost for the cost element.

The costs assigned to the 10,000 units of the beginning work-in-process inventory that were completed and transferred out during the current period are calculated as follows:

Work-in-process inventory, June 1, 10,000 units	$12,680
Costs added during June to complete the beginning WIP inventory	
Direct labor 7,000 equivalent units × $0.51 per equivalent unit	3,570
Factory overhead 6,000 equivalent units × $1.00 per equivalent unit	6,000
Total for beginning inventory	$22,250

Step 5, Part B: Total Cost for Units Started and Completed

The production cost of units started and completed in the current period can be computed by multiplying the number of units in this category by the total cost per equivalent unit of the period.

The number of units started and completed in the period is the difference between the units completed and the number of units in beginning work-in-process. In the molding department example, we compute the number of units started and completed as follows:

$$\text{Units completed} - \text{Units in Beginning work-in-process} = \text{Units started and completed}$$
$$44{,}000 \text{ units} - 10{,}000 \text{ units} = 34{,}000 \text{ units}$$

Then the cost assigned to units started and completed is

$$34{,}000 \text{ units} \times \$2.61 = \$88{,}740$$

The total costs transferred out are the sum of the total cost from the beginning inventory and the total cost for units started and completed; that is

$$\$22{,}250 + \$88{,}740 = \$110{,}990$$

Ending Work-in-Process Inventory

The cost assigned under FIFO to ending work-in-process units is derived by multiplying the current period's cost per equivalent unit of each manufacturing cost element by the equivalent units of the ending work-in-process inventory.

The cost of 6,000 units in ending work-in-process inventory of the molding department is computed as follows:

Direct materials, 6,000 equivalent units × $1.10/equivalent unit	$ 6,600
Direct labor, 3,000 equivalent units × $0.51/equivalent unit	1,530
Factory overhead, 3,600 equivalent units × $1.00/equivalent unit	3,600
Total ending work-in-process inventory	$11,730

Exhibit 6.15 shows that the sum of the costs assigned to goods transferred out and in ending work-in-process inventory equals the total costs accounted for of $122,720.

Cost Reconciliation

Now we need to determine whether the total manufacturing costs to account for in step 3 agree with the total costs accounted for in step 5. Again, step 3 accounts for $122,720 total manufacturing costs; this equals the total costs of $122,720 accounted for in step 5.

Production Cost Report

Steps 1 through 5 provide all information needed to prepare a production cost report for the molding department for June (Exhibit 6.16).

EXHIBIT 6.15

Step 5: Assign Total Manufacturing Costs—Molding Department: FIFO Method

	Completed and Transferred out	Ending Work-in-Process	Total
Goods completed and transferred out			
Beginning work-in-process	$ 12,680		$ 12,680
Costs added during June			
Direct materials	0		0
Direct labor (7,000 × $0.51)	3,570		3,570
Factory overhead (6,000 × $1.00)	6,000		6,000
Total for beginning inventory	$ 22,250		$ 22,250
Started and completed (34,000 × $2.61)	88,740		88,740
Total costs completed and transferred out	$110,990		$110,990
Ending work-in-process			
Direct material (6,000 × $1.10)		$ 6,600	$ 6,600
Direct labor (3,000 × $0.51)		1,530	1,530
Factory overhead (3,600 × $1.00)		3,600	3,600
Total costs accounted for	$110,990	$11,730	$122,720

EXHIBIT 6.16
Production Cost Report—
Molding Department: FIFO
Method

Production Quantity Information

	Step 1: Analyze Flow of Physical Units		Step 2: Calculate Equivalent Units		
	Physical Units	Completion Percentage	Direct Materials	Direct Labor	Factory Overhead
Input					
Work-in-process, June 1	10,000				
Direct materials		100%	10,000		
Direct labor		30		3,000	
Factory overhead		40			4,000
Units started	40,000				
Units to account for	50,000				
Output					
Units completed	44,000	100%	44,000	44,000	44,000
Work-in-process, June 30	6,000				
Direct materials		100	6,000		
Direct labor		50		3,000	
Factory overhead		60			3,600
Units accounted for	50,000				
Total equivalent units (weighted-average method)			50,000	47,000	47,600
Less: equivalent units in June 1 work-in-process			(10,000)	(3,000)	(4,000)
Equivalent units for work performed in June only (FIFO method)			40,000	44,000	43,600

Unit Cost Determination

Step 3: Determine Total Costs	Direct Materials	Direct Labor	Factory Overhead	Total
Work-in-process, June 1				$ 12,680
Costs added during June	44,000	22,440	43,600	110,040
Total costs to account for	44,000	22,440	43,600	$122,720

Step 4: Compute Cost per Equivalent Unit				
Divide by equivalent units (from Step 2)	40,000	44,000	43,600	
Equivalent unit costs	$ 1.10	$ 0.51	$ 1.00	$ 2.61

Cost Assignment

Step 5: Assign Total Manufacturing Costs	Completed and Transferred out	Ending Work-in-Process	Total
Goods completed and transferred out			
Beginning work-in-process	$ 12,680		$ 12,680
Costs added during June			
Direct labor (7,000 × $0.51)	3,570		3,570
Factory overhead (6,000 × $1.00)	6,000		6,000
Total for beginning inventory	$ 22,250		$ 22,250
Started and completed (34,000 × $2.61)	88,740		88,740
Total costs completed and transferred out	$110,990		$110,990

(Continued; Ending work-in-process on next page)

EXHIBIT 6.16
(Continued)

Ending work-in-process			
Direct materials (6,000 × $1.10)		$ 6,600	$ 6,600
Direct labor (3,000 × $0.51)		1,530	1,530
Factory overhead (3,600 × $1.00)		3,600	3,600
Total costs accounted for	$110,990	$11,730	$122,720

Comparison of Weighted-Average and FIFO Methods

Both the weighted-average and the FIFO methods produce the same total costs accounted for (compare Exhibits 6.10 and 6.16). The key difference between the two methods is the handling of partially completed beginning work-in-process inventory units. The FIFO method separates the units in the beginning inventory from the units started and completed during the period. In contrast, the weighted-average method makes no separate treatment of the units in the beginning work-in-process inventory. Thus, there is a difference between the cost of goods completed under the weighted-average and FIFO methods. Similarly, there is a difference between ending work-in-process inventory under the two methods.

The weighted-average method generally is easier to use because the calculations are simpler. This method is most appropriate when work-in-process is relatively small, or direct materials prices, conversion costs, and inventory levels are stable. The FIFO method is most appropriate when direct materials prices, conversion costs, or inventory levels fluctuate significantly.

Some firms prefer the FIFO method over the weighted-average method for purposes of cost control and performance evaluation because the cost per equivalent unit under FIFO represents the cost for the current period's efforts only. Firms often evaluate department managers' performance on only current period costs without mixing in the effects of performance during different periods. Under the weighted-average method, the costs of the prior period and the current period are mixed, and deviations in performance in the current period could be concealed by interperiod variations in unit costs.

Process Costing with Multiple Departments

Most manufacturing firms have multiple departments or use several processes that require a number of steps. As the product passes from one department to another, the cost passes from department to department. The costs from the prior department are called *transferred-in costs* or *prior department costs*. This section discusses the concept of transferred-in costs and describes the weighted-average and FIFO methods of cost flow assumptions for firms with multiple departments.

Transferred-In Costs

Transferred-in costs
are costs of work performed in the earlier department that are transferred into the present department.

Transferred-in costs are costs of work performed in the earlier department that are transferred into the present department. Including these costs is a necessary part of process costing because we treat each department as a separate entity, and each department's production cost report includes all costs added to the product up to that point. If transferred-in costs were not included, each completed unit transferred out of a department would include only the value of the work performed by that department. It might help to think of transferred-in costs as similar to the direct materials introduced at the beginning of the production process. The equivalent units of production of transferred-in costs can be computed in the same manner as direct materials that are added at the beginning of a process. The difference between the direct materials cost and the transferred-in cost is that the former comes from the storeroom while the latter comes from another production department.

The equivalent units of the transferred-in cost for ending work-in-process inventory is always assumed to be the same as the number of units in ending work-in-process inventory. Because all units in process are complete for prior departments' costs, by definition the number of equivalent units transferred in is the same as the number of physical units transferred in.

Suppose that Naftel Toy Company's molding department transfers its production units to the finishing department. In the finishing department, direct materials are added at the end of the process. Conversion costs (direct labor and factory overhead) are applied evenly throughout the finishing department's process. The finishing department uses direct labor cost as the cost driver to apply factory overhead costs.

Data for the finishing department for June are shown in Exhibit 6.17.

Weighted-Average Method

LEARNING OBJECTIVE 6

Analyze process costing with multiple departments.

Follow the five-step procedure as we illustrate the weighted-average method for process costing with multiple departments.

Steps 1 and 2: Analyze Flow of Physical Units and Calculate Equivalent Units

The first step is to analyze the physical units of production. The second step is to calculate equivalent units. Exhibit 6.18 summarizes the computation of physical units and equivalent units. Note that because overhead is charged to the product based on direct labor cost in the finishing department, direct labor and overhead are combined into a single element, conversion, to simplify the production cost report.

The 8,000 units in ending work-in-process inventory are 100 percent complete with respect to transferred-in costs because they were 100 percent complete in the preceding department. There is no direct materials component because materials are added at the end of the finishing department. Because ending work-in-process inventory is only 50 percent complete with respect to conversion costs, ending work-in-process inventories represent 4,000 equivalent units of conversion costs (8,000 physical units $\times$ 50% complete).

As Exhibit 6.18 shows, the total number of equivalent units is calculated as follows:

$$\text{Completed units}$$
$$+ \text{ Ending work-in-process equivalent units}$$
$$= \text{ Total equivalent units of production}$$

That is, under the weighted-average method, the equivalent units of production for the finishing department include 58,000 units transferred in, 50,000 units of direct materials, and 54,000 units of conversion.

EXHIBIT 6.17

Basic Data for Naftel Toy Company—Finishing Department

Work-in-process, June 1:	14,000 units
Transferred-in: 100 percent complete	$ 34,250
Direct materials: 0 percent complete*	0
Conversion: 50 percent complete	7,000
Beginning work-in-process inventory	$ 41,250
Units transferred-in during June	44,000 units
Transferred-in costs during June	
Weighted-average method (From Exhibit 6.10)	$111,320
FIFO method (From Exhibit 6.15)	110,990
Units completed	50,000 units
Work-in-process, June 30	8,000 units
Transferred-in: 100 percent complete	
Direct materials: 0 percent complete	
Conversion: 50 percent complete	
Costs added by the finishing dept. during June	
Direct materials	$ 25,000
Conversion	47,000

* Materials are added at the *end* of the process.

The USDA's accounting standards manual urges the use of activity-based costing in conjunction with process costing. The USDA also suggests that process costing be used in situations involving a large volume of similar goods or services. An example is the use of process costing to cost the payment of entitlement benefits. The payment of entitlement benefits involves a series of processes: reviewing applications, computing the amount of benefits, and issuing checks. Process costing is well suited for this context.

Based on information in *U.S. Department of Agriculture Financial and Accounting Standards Manual,* Version 2.0, Chapter 5, Section 5.9 (U.S. Department of Agriculture, www.ocfo.usda.gov/acctpol/pdf/fasm.pdf.

EXHIBIT 6.18

Steps 1 and 2: Analyze Physical Flow of Units and Calculate Equivalent Units—Finishing Department: Weighted-Average Method

	Step 1		Step 2		
			Equivalent Units		
	Physical Units	**Completion Percentage**	**Transferred in Costs**	**Direct Materials**	**Conversion Costs**
Input					
Work-in-process, June 1	14,000				
Transferred-in		100%			
Direct materials		0			
Conversion		50			
Transferred-in	44,000				
Units to account for	58,000				
Output					
Units completed	50,000	100%	50,000	50,000	50,000
Work-in-process, June 30	8,000				
Transferred-in		100	8,000		
Direct materials		0			
Conversion		50			4,000
Units accounted for	58,000				
Total equivalent units			58,000	50,000	54,000

Steps 3 and 4: Determine Total Costs and Compute Unit Costs

The third step is to determine the total manufacturing costs to account for, and the fourth step is to compute equivalent unit costs for transferred-in, direct materials, and conversion costs.

Exhibit 6.19 summarizes the total manufacturing costs to account for and unit costs for all cost components. Total manufacturing costs to account for ($224,570) consist of the beginning work-in-process inventory balance, $41,250, plus the current costs added during June, $183,320 ($111,320 + $25,000 + $47,000).

The equivalent unit cost for units transferred in ($2.5098) is computed by dividing the total transferred-in cost ($145,570), including the cost of beginning work-in-process ($34,250) and the cost added during June ($111,320), by the total equivalent units transferred in (58,000). Similar procedures are used for direct materials and conversion costs.

Step 5: Assign Total Manufacturing Costs to Completed Units and Ending WIP

The final step of the process costing procedure is to assign total manufacturing costs to units completed and to units in ending work-in-process inventory. Exhibit 6.20 summarizes the cost assignment schedule with $224,568 total costs in step 5.

Cost Reconciliation

The small difference between the total cost accounted for in step 5 and the total cost in step 3 is due to a very small rounding error. To avoid unacceptable large rounding errors, at least

EXHIBIT 6.19

Steps 3 and 4: Determine Total Costs and Compute Cost per Equivalent Unit—Finishing Department: Weighted-Average Method

Step 3	Transferred-in Costs	Direct Materials	Conversion Costs	Total
Work-in-process, June 1	$ 34,250	$ 0	$ 7,000	$ 41,250
Costs added during June	111,320	25,000	47,000	183,320
Total costs to account for	$145,570	$25,000	$54,000	$224,570
Step 4				
Divide by equivalent units (from Exhibit 6.18)	58,000	50,000	54,000	
Equivalent unit costs	$ 2.5098 +	$ 0.50 +	$ 1.00 =	$ 4.0098

EXHIBIT 6.20

Step 5: Assign Total Manufacturing Costs—Finishing Department: Weighted-Average Method

Step 5	Completed and Transferred out	Ending Work-in-Process	Total
Goods completed and transferred out (50,000 × $4.0098)	$200,490		$200,490
Ending work-in-process			
Transferred-in (8,000 × $2.5098)		$20,078	20,078
Conversion (4,000 × $1.00)		4,000	4,000
Total costs accounted for	$200,490	$24,078	$224,568

three significant digits or more should be used in calculating the cost per equivalent unit in step 4.

The FIFO Method

Now we illustrate the FIFO method of process costing for multiple departments using data from the Naftel Toy Company's finishing department (see Exhibit 6.17).

Steps 1 and 2: Analyze Flow of Physical Units and Calculate Equivalent Units

Exhibit 6.21 summarizes the physical flow units and equivalent units of production for the finishing department.

The physical flow of product units is unaffected by the process costing method used. Therefore, step 1 is the same as with the weighted-average method.

The 14,000 physical units in the June 1 work-in-process inventory have 100 percent of transferred-in costs, so they represent 14,000 equivalent units of transferred-in work. Because the materials are added at the end of the process in the finishing department, zero equivalent units of direct materials for work-in-process inventory are on hand on June 1. The beginning work-in-process inventory is only 50 percent complete with respect to conversion activity, so this department has 7,000 equivalent units of conversion costs (14,000 × 50%).

As Exhibit 6.21 indicates, the total number of equivalent units is calculated as follows:

> Completed units
> + Ending work-in-process equivalent units
> − Beginning work-in-process equivalent units
> ───────────────────────────────────────
> = Equivalent units of work completed during this period (FIFO)

That is, equivalent units of production for the finishing department using the FIFO method are 44,000 transferred-in units, 50,000 direct material units, and 47,000 conversion activity units.

EXHIBIT 6.21
Steps 1 and 2: Analyze Flow of
Physical Units and Calculate
Equivalent Units—Finishing
Department: FIFO Method

	Step 1		Step 2		
			Equivalent Units		
	Physical Units	**Completion Percentage**	**Transferred-in Costs**	**Direct Materials**	**Conversion Costs**
Input					
Work-in-process, June 1	14,000				
Transferred-in		100%	14,000		
Direct materials		0		0	
Conversion		50			7,000
Transferred-in	44,000				
Units to account for	58,000				
Output					
Units completed	50,000	100%	50,000	50,000	50,000
Work-in-process, June 30	8,000				
Transferred-in		100	8,000		
Direct materials		0		0	
Conversion		50			4,000
Units accounted for	58,000				
Total equivalent units (weighted-average method)			58,000	50,000	54,000
Less: equivalent units in June 1 work-in-process			(14,000)	(0)	(7,000)
Equivalent units for work done in June only (FIFO method)			44,000	50,000	47,000

Steps 3 and 4: Determine Total Costs to Account for and Compute Unit Costs

Exhibit 6.22 shows the computation of total costs to account for and equivalent unit costs for the finishing department.

The beginning work-in-process inventory has a cost of $41,250. The $182,990 total costs added during June include $110,990 transferred-in costs from the modeling department, $25,000 direct materials costs and $47,000 conversion costs incurred in the finishing department as shown in Exhibit 6.22.

The equivalent unit cost for transferred-in units ($2.5225) is computed by dividing the transferred-in cost during June ($110,990) by the equivalent units for work completed only in June (44,000). Similar procedures are used for direct materials and conversion costs. Notice

EXHIBIT 6.22
Steps 3 and 4: Determine
Total Costs to Account For
and Compute Unit Costs—
Finishing Department: FIFO
Method

Step 3	Transferred-in Costs	Direct Materials	Conversion Costs	Total
Work-in-process, June 1	N/A	N/A	N/A	$ 41,250
Costs added during June*	$110,990	$25,000	$47,000	182,990
Total costs to account for				$224,240
Step 4				
Divide by equivalent units (from Exhibit 6.21):	44,000	50,000	47,000	
Equivalent unit costs	$ 2.5225 +	$ 0.50 +	$ 1.00 =	$ 4.0225

*Note: The transferred-in cost of $110,990 is taken from the FIFO report of the molding department, Exhibit 6.15.
N/A = Not applicable

that the costs of beginning inventory are excluded from this calculation. The calculations use only current costs added in June.

Step 5: Assign Total Manufacturing Costs

The final step of the process costing procedure is to assign total manufacturing costs to units completed and to units in the ending work-in-process inventory. Exhibit 6.23 summarizes the cost assignment schedule.

The total manufacturing cost associated with the 14,000 units of beginning work-in-process inventory is calculated as follows:

Work-in-process, June 1, 14,000 units	$41,250
Costs added during June to complete the beginning inventory:	
Direct material 14,000 equivalent units × $0.50	7,000
Conversion costs 7,000 equivalent units × $1.00	7,000
Total for beginning inventory	$55,250

The costs assigned to the 36,000 units started and completed during June are calculated:

$$50,000 \text{ units} - 14,000 \text{ units} = 36,000 \text{ units}$$

$$36,000 \text{ units} \times \$4.0225 = \$144,810$$

The total costs for units completed are the sum of the total costs from beginning inventory and the total costs for units started and completed, that is,

$$\$55,250 + \$144,810 = \$200,060$$

The cost of the finishing department's 8,000 units in ending work-in-process inventory is computed as follows:

Transferred-in: 8,000 equivalent units × $2.5225	$20,180
Conversion: 4,000 equivalent units × $1.00	4,000
Total ending work-in-process inventory	$24,180

In Exhibit 6.23, the sum of the costs assigned to goods completed and ending work-in-process inventory is $224,240. Note that the amount of total costs accounted for in step 5 should equal the total costs to account for in step 3 (as shown in Exhibit 6.22).

EXHIBIT 6.23
Step 5: Assign Total Costs—Finishing Department FIFO Method

	Completed and Transferred out	Ending Work-in-Process	Total
Goods completed and transferred out			
Beginning work-in-process	$ 41,250		$ 41,250
Costs added during June			
Direct materials (14,000 × $0.50)	7,000		7,000
Conversion (7,000 × $1.00)	7,000		7,000
Total from beginning WIP inventory	$ 55,250		$ 55,250
Started and completed (36,000 × $4.0225)	144,810		144,810
Total costs completed and transferred out	$200,060		$200,060
Ending work-in-process:			
Transferred-in (8,000 × $2.5225)		$20,180	20,180
Conversion costs (4,000 × $1.00)		4,000	4,000
Total costs accounted for	$200,060	$24,180	$224,240

Journal Entries for Process Costing

LEARNING OBJECTIVE 7

Prepare journal entries to record the flow of costs in a process costing system.

Process costing uses the same general ledger manufacturing accounts as job costing discussed in Chapter 4. However, instead of assigning product costs to specific jobs, we accumulate costs in production departments. Each department has a separate Work-in-Process Inventory account. These journal entries for Naftel Toy Company use the weighted-average method data from steps 3 and 5 of both Exhibit 6.10 (molding department) and Exhibits 6.19 and 6.20 (finishing department). Assume that 50 percent of the conversion costs in the finishing department are direct labor ($47,000 \times 50\% = \$23,500$).

The following direct materials were requisitioned and used:

(1)	Work-in-Process Inventory—Molding Department	44,000	
	Work-in-Process Inventory—Finishing Department	25,000	
	Materials Inventory		69,000
	To record direct materials costs added during June.		

The direct labor incurred follows:

(2)	Work-in-Process Inventory—Molding Department	22,440	
	Work-in-Process Inventory—Finishing Department	23,500	
	Accrued Payroll		45,940
	To record direct labor costs incurred during June.		

Factory overhead applied is as follows:

(3)	Work-in-Process Inventory—Molding Department	43,600	
	Work-in-Process Inventory—Finishing Department	23,500	
	Factory Overhead		67,100
	To record the application of factory overhead		
	to departments.		

Transferred-in costs from the molding department follows (using weighted-average):

(4)	Work-in-Process Inventory—Finishing Department	111,320	
	Work-in-Process Inventory—Molding Department		111,320
	To record the weighted-average method of the cost		
	of goods completed in the molding department and		
	transferred out to the finishing department.		

Product units finished are as follows (using weighted-average):

(5)	Finished Goods Inventory	200,490	
	Work-in-Process Inventory—Finishing Department		200,490
	To record the weighted-average method of the cost of		
	goods completed in the finishing department.		

Implementation and Enhancement of Process Costing

LEARNING OBJECTIVE 8

Explain how process costing systems are implemented and enhanced in practice.

Activity-Based Costing and the Theory of Constraints

Process costing systems are appropriate where there are one or a few homogeneous products, as in many process industries such as chemical or paper manufacturing. The goal of the costing system is to account for production costs in the cost of work-in-process units and finished products in the production cost report. There is little need for cost information to identify the cost of *different products* or *different customer jobs*, because there are only one or a few products and they all go through the same processing and thus have the same unit cost. But sometimes the process-based manufacturer has very different products going through different processes, making the process costing system by itself inadequate. For example, Reichhold Inc. (www.reichhold.com), a manufacturer of industrial chemicals, adhesives, and other products, is a process company that uses processing costing, but has adapted the system to include activity-based costing, because of its product variety. While most of its products go through similar processing steps (cleaning, reacting, filtration, and blending) some products require much more time in some steps than other products. For example, one Reichhold product requires careful cleanup of the vat where it is processed, because even very small quantities of the chemical can contaminate other products that are later processed in the vat. So, activity-based costing is used to properly charge the extra cleanup costs to this product.[1] Activity-based costing is an important enhancement to process costing when product and process variety arises.

Similarly, process costing information is not intended to help the firm determine the most profitable product mix or to identify the most profitable use of the plant. These questions require analyses that utilize the products' contribution margins and the location of production constraints in the plant. To determine the most profitable product mix, the process firm would use the contribution methods explained in Chapter 11 and the theory of constraints method explained in Chapter 13. For example, Reichhold could use the theory of constraints to identify the bottlenecks in the manufacture of its products. After determining which processing step (such as cleaning or reacting) constrains throughput for the plant, Reichhold could adjust production schedules to most profitably use this constraint.

Just-in-Time Systems and Backflush Costing

Firms use the just-in-time (JIT) method to minimize inventory and improve quality by carefully coordinating the receipt of raw materials and the delivery of product with the manufacturing processes in the plant. The goal is to have little or no raw material, work-in-process, or finished goods inventory in the plant. This saves costs that arise from holding inventory, including the risk of damage, theft, loss, or failure to find a customer for the finished product. Since inventory is minimal in an effective JIT system, there is no need for a system such as process costing to determine equivalent units and to account for production costs in work-in-process and finished goods. Simpler methods such as **backflush costing** can be used instead. These methods charge current production costs (using standard unit costs) directly to finished goods inventory, without accounting for the flows in and out of the Work-in-Process account. Any difference between these standard unit costs and actual costs is typically very small and is charged to cost of goods sold at the end of the year. While not in compliance with generally accepted accounting principles (because the small amount of work-in-process inventory is not valued and placed on the balance sheet), the backflush method is reasonable and convenient for a JIT production environment.

A brief illustration of backflush costing follows. Assume that a company has the following information for a given month of activity:

Purchase of direct materials	$100,000
Actual cost of materials used	$92,000
Conversion cost incurred	$145,000
Direct materials standard cost	$5 per unit
Conversion cost at standard	$8 per unit
Total standard cost	$13 per unit
Units produced	18,000 units
Units sold	17,000 units

The cost of production using the backflush method is $13 \times 18,000 = \$234,000$, of which $90,000 (= $5 \times 18,000$) is materials and $144,000 (= $8 \times 18,000$) is conversion.

Backflush costing
is a method that charges current production costs (using standard costs) directly to finished goods inventory without accounting for the flows in and out of work-in-process.

[1] "Edward Blocher, Betty Wong, and Christopher T. McKittrick, "Making Bottom-Up ABC Work at Reichhold, Inc," *Strategic Finance,* April 2002, pp. 51–55. Also, activity-based costing together with process costing has been used in health care applications: William N. Zelman, "Animated-Simulation Modeling Facilitates Clinical Process Costing, *Healthcare Financial Management,* September 2001.

The following journal entries show how the costs are applied and cost of goods sold is determined using the following five steps.

1. Materials inventory is increased for the amount of purchases, $100,000.
2. The conversion cost account is increased for the amount of conversion costs incurred, $145,000.
3. Finished goods are shown at the standard cost for 18,000 units completed, $234,000; this includes $90,000 of materials cost and $144,000 of applied conversion cost.
4. Cost of goods sold are shown for sales of 17,000 units, $221,000 = 17,000 × $13.
5. At the end of the accounting period, the difference ($1,000) between incurred ($145,000) and applied ($144,000) conversion costs is closed to the Cost of Goods Sold account. Also, the $2,000 difference between the actual usage of materials ($92,000) and the standard ($90,000) is closed to Cost of Goods Sold.

| (1) | Materials Inventory | 100,000 | |
| | Accounts Payable, Cash | | 100,000 |

| (2) | Conversion Cost Incurred | 145,000 | |
| | Wages payable, other accounts | | 145,000 |

(3)	Finished goods	234,000	
	Materials inventory (for actual usage)		90,000
	Conversion Cost applied		144,000

| (4) | Cost of Goods Sold | 221,000 | |
| | Finished Goods | | 221,000 |

(5a)	Conversion Cost Applied	144,000	
	Cost of Goods Sold	1,000	
	Conversion Cost Incurred		145,000

| (5b) | Cost of Goods Sold | 2,000 | |
| | Materials Inventory | | 2,000 |

The final amount for cost of goods sold is therefore $221,000 + $1,000 + $2,000 = $224,000. The above presents a simple approach that is used when work-in-process is negligible. The use of standard costs means that product costs can be quickly and conveniently calculated for both production and sales; the differences between actual and standard costs are usually small and are closed to Cost of Goods Sold at the end of the period. A full explanation of standard costs and standard cost variances is provided in Chapters 14 and 15.

Summary

Process costing is a product cost system that accumulates costs in processing departments and allocates them to all units processed during the period, including both completed and partially completed units. It is used by firms producing homogeneous products on a continuous basis to assign manufacturing costs to units in production during the period. Firms that use process costing include paint, chemical, oil-refining, and food-processing companies.

Process costing systems provide information so managers can make strategic decisions regarding products and customers, manufacturing methods, pricing options, overhead allocation methods, and other long-term issues.

Equivalent units are the number of the same or similar completed units that could have been produced given the amount of work actually performed on both complete and partially completed units.

The key document in a typical process costing system is the production cost report that summarizes the physical units and equivalent units of a production department, the costs incurred during the period, and the costs assigned to goods both completed and transferred out as well as to ending work-in-process inventories. The preparation of a production cost report includes five steps: (1) analyze physical units, (2) calculate equivalent units, (3) determine total costs to account for, (4) compute unit costs, and (5) assign total manufacturing costs.

The two methods of preparing the departmental production cost report in process costing are the weighted-average method and first-in, first-out (FIFO) method. The weighted-average method includes costs incurred in both current and prior periods that are shown as the beginning work-in-process inventory of this period. The FIFO method includes only costs incurred during the current period in calculating unit cost.

Most manufacturing firms have several departments or use processes that require several steps. As the product passes from one department to another, the costs from the prior department are transferred-in costs or prior department costs. Process costing with multiple departments should include the transferred-in cost as the fourth cost element in addition to direct materials, direct labor, and factory overhead costs.

Appendix

Spoilage in Process Costing

LEARNING OBJECTIVE 9

Account for spoilage in process costing.

In this appendix we explain the two types of spoilage—normal and abnormal. *Normal spoilage* occurs under normal operating conditions. It is uncontrollable in the short term and is considered a part of product cost. That is, the costs of lost units are absorbed by the good units produced. *Abnormal spoilage* exceeds expected losses under efficient operating conditions and is charged as a loss to operations in the period detected.

Two approaches are used to account for normal spoilage in process costing systems. The first approach is to count the number of spoiled units, prepare a separate equivalent unit computation with the cost per unit of the spoiled goods, and then allocate the cost to the good units produced. The second approach is to omit the spoiled units in computing the equivalent units of production; the spoilage cost is thus included as part of total manufacturing costs. The first approach provides more accurate product costs because it computes the costs associated with normal spoilage and spreads them over the good units produced. The second approach is less accurate because it spreads the costs of normal spoilage over all units—good completed units, units in ending work-in-process inventory, and abnormal spoiled units. This appendix discusses only the first approach.

Consider Diamond Company, which has the following data for the current period:

	Units	Cost
Beginning work-in-process inventory	2,000	
Direct materials (100 percent complete)		$100,000
Conversion costs (75 percent complete)		80,000
Units started in the period	8,000	
Costs incurred during the period		
Direct materials		300,000
Conversion costs		405,000
Ending work-in-process inventory	2,000	
Direct materials (100 percent complete)		
Conversion costs (80 percent complete)		
Completed and transferred out (good units produced)	7,000	
Normal spoilage is 10 percent of good units produced	700	

Diamond Company inspects all products at the completion point. Inspection at the completion point means that all costs incurred to the completion point are spoiled; the unit cost of spoilage is thus the total cost per equivalent unit. If the inspection point is earlier, then spoilage cost can be reduced; the cost of spoilage is then adjusted accordingly.

Using the five-step procedure described in the chapter, we need only add normal spoilage and abnormal spoilage components in calculations.

Step 1. Analyze Physical Flow of Production Units

With 7,000 good production units completed in May, the normal spoiled units total 700 (7,000 $\times$ 10%). Assume abnormal spoilage is 300 spoiled units.

Step 2. Calculate Equivalent Units

Equivalent units for spoilage are calculated in the same way as good units. Normal and abnormal spoiled units are included in the calculation of equivalent units. Since the company inspects all products at the completion point, the same amount of work is performed on each completed good unit and each spoiled unit.

Step 3. Determine Total Costs

These costs include all costs in the beginning work-in-process inventory and all costs added during the period. The detail of this step is similar to the process costing procedure without spoilage incurred.

Step 4. Compute Cost per Equivalent Unit

The detail of this step is similar to the process costing procedure without any spoilage.

Step 5. Assign Total Manufacturing Costs to Units Completed, Ending WIP, and Abnormal Spoilage

Exhibit 6A.1 summarizes the five-step procedure for the weighted-average process costing method, including both normal and abnormal spoilage. Exhibit 6A.2 is the production cost report under the FIFO process costing method.

EXHIBIT 6A.1
Diamond Company's Production Cost Report: Weighted-Average Method

	Production Quantity Information			
	Step 1: Analyze Flow of Physical Units		Step 2: Calculate Equivalent Units	
	Physical Units	**Completion Percentage**	**Direct Materials**	**Conversion Costs**
Input				
Work-in-process, May 1	2,000			
Direct materials		100%		
Conversion		75		
Number started	8,000			
Total to account for	10,000			
Output				
Units completed	7,000	100%	7,000	7,000
Normal spoilage (10%)	700		700	700
Abnormal spoilage	300		300	300
Work-in-process, May 31	2,000			
Direct materials		100	2,000	
Conversion		80		1,600
Total accounted for				
Total equivalent units	10,000		10,000	9,600

(Continued)

EXHIBIT 6A.1
(Continued)

Unit Cost Determination			
Step 3: Determine Total Costs	**Direct Materials**	**Conversion Costs**	**Total**
Work-in-process, May 1	$100,000	$ 80,000	$180,000
Costs added during period	300,000	405,000	705,000
Total costs to account for	$400,000	$485,000	$885,000
Step 4: Compute Cost per Equivalent Unit			
Divide by number of equivalent units	10,000	9,600	
Equivalent unit costs	$ 40.00	$ 50.521	$ 90.521

Cost Assignment			
Step 5: Assign Total Manufacturing Costs	**Completed and Transferred out**	**Ending Work-in-Process**	**Total**
Goods completed and transferred out [(Goods units 7,000 + Normal spoilage 700) × $90.521]	$697,011		$697,011
Abnormal spoilage (300 × $90.521)			27,156
Work-in-process, May 31 Direct materials (2,000 × $40.00)		$ 80,000	80,000
Conversion (1,600 × $50.521)		80,833	80,833
Total costs accounted for	$697,011	$160,833	$885,000

EXHIBIT 6A.2
Diamond Company's FIFO Production Cost Report

	Production Quantity Information		
	Step 1: Analyze Flow of Physical Units	**Step 2: Calculate Equivalent Units**	
	Physical Units	**Direct Materials**	**Conversion Costs**
Input			
Work-in-process beginning inventory	2,000	(100%)	(75%)
Started this period	8,000		
Total to account for	10,000		
Output			
Completed	7,000	7,000	7,000
Normal spoilage (10 percent)	700	700	700
Abnormal spoilage	300	300	300
Work-in-process ending inventory	2,000 (80%)	2,000	1,600
Total accounted for	10,000		
Total work done to date		10,000	9,600
Work-in-process beginning inventory		(2,000)	(1,500)
Total work done this period (Total equivalent units)		8,000	8,100

(Continued)

EXHIBIT 6A.2
(Continued)

		Unit Cost Determination		
Step 3: Determine Total Costs For		**Direct Materials**	**Conversion Costs**	**Total**
Work-in-process beginning inventory		$100,000	$ 80,000	$180,000
Current cost		300,000	405,000	705,000
Total costs to account for		$400,000	$485,000	$885,000
Step 4: Compute Cost per Equivalent Unit				
		($300,000/ 8,000) =	($405,000/ 8,100) =	
Cost per equivalent unit		$ 37.50	$ 50.00	$ 87.50

	Cost Assignment		
Step 5: Assign Total Manufacturing Costs	**Completed and Transferred out**	**Ending Work-in-Process**	**Total**
Units completed and transferred out (7,000)			
Beginning work-in-process	$180,000		$180,000
Current cost to complete			
conversion (500 × $50)	25,000		25,000
Total from beginning work-in-process	$205,000		$205,000
Units started & finished (5,000 × $87.50)	437,500		437,500
Normal spoilage (700 × $87.50)	61,250		61,250
Total cost completed and transferred out	$703,750		$703,750
Abnormal spoilage (300 × $87.50)			26,250
Ending work-in-process (2,000)			
Materials (2,000 × $37.50)		$ 75,000	75,000
Conversion (1,600 × $50)	—	80,000	80,000
Total costs accounted for	$703,750	$155,000	$885,000

Comments on Cost Management in Action

Achieving sustainability requires a carefully planned and executed policy for reducing the firm's environmental and social footprint. This could be measured in a number of ways, such as the amount of waste products, workplace injuries, carbon and sulfur emissions (as indicated in Exhibit 2.8), and other social and environmental indicators.

Marc Epstein notes that Royal Dutch Shell and Alcoa, two large process firms, employ review processes to assess human rights risks, health, safety, and other environmental issues before investing in a new location. Other initiatives include those by Wal-Mart in recent years to redesign its product distribution system to reduce fuel usage by over 30 percent. Other companies are using solar energy, some to the extent that they can sell energy back to the energy grid provided by the energy companies. In other initiatives in agriculture, genetic engineering and improved seed and planting methods have reduced the need for fertilizer and other soil treatments, saving the cost and also the environmental impact of these chemicals. There are many other stories that you may know of. The Epstein publications cited below provide additional examples.

Source: Marc J. Epstein, "Implementing Corporate Sustainability: Measuring and Managing Social and Environmental Impacts," *Strategic Finance,* January 2008, pp. 25–31; Marc J. Epstein, *Making Sustainability Work: Best Practices in Managing and Measuring Corporate Social, Environmental and Economic Impacts* (San Francisco: Berrett-Koehler, 2008).

Self-Study Problems
(For solutions, please turn to the end of the chapter.)

1. Weighted-Average Method versus FIFO Method

Smith Electronic Company's chip-mounting production department had 300 units of unfinished product, each 40 percent complete on September 30. During October of the same year, this department put another 900 units into production and completed 1,000 units and transferred them to the next production department. At the end of October, 200 units of unfinished product, 70 percent completed, were recorded in the ending work-in-process inventory. Smith Company introduces all direct materials when the production process is 50 percent complete. Direct labor and factory overhead (i.e., conversion) costs are added uniformly throughout the process.

Following is a summary of production costs incurred during October:

	Direct Materials	Conversion Costs
Beginning work-in-process		$2,202
Current costs	$9,600	6,120
Total costs	$9,600	$8,322

Required

1. Calculate each of the following amounts using weighted-average process costing:
   a. Equivalent units of direct materials and conversion.
   b. Unit costs of direct materials and conversion.
   c. Cost of goods completed and transferred out during the period.
   d. Cost of work-in-process inventory at the end of the period.
2. Prepare a production cost report for October using the weighted-average method.
3. Repeat requirement 1 using the FIFO method.
4. Repeat requirement 2 using the FIFO method.

2. Weighted-Average Method versus FIFO Method with Transferred-In Cost

Reed Company has two departments, a machining department and a finishing department. The following information relates to the finishing department: work-in-process, November 1, was 10 units, 40 percent completed, consisting of $100 transferred-in costs, $80 direct materials, and $52 conversion costs. Production completed for November totaled 82 units; work-in-process, November 30, is 8 units, 50 percent completed. All finishing department direct materials are introduced at the start of the process; conversion costs are incurred uniformly throughout the process. Transferred-in costs from the machining department during November were $800; direct materials added were $720; conversion costs incurred were $861. Following is the summary data of Reed Company's finishing department:

Work-in-process, November 1, 10 units:	
Transferred-in: 100 percent complete	$ 100
Direct materials: 100 percent complete	80
Conversion: 40 percent complete	52
Balance in work-in-process, November 1	$ 232
Units transferred in from machining department during November	80 units
Units completed during November and transferred out to finished goods inventory	82 units
Work-in-process, November 30	8 units
Transferred-in: 100 percent complete	
Direct materials: 100 percent complete	
Conversion: 50 percent complete	

(Continued)

Costs incurred during November	
Transferred-in	$ 800
Direct materials	720
Conversion	861
Total current costs	$2,381

Required

1. Prepare a production cost report for November using the weighted-average method.
2. Prepare a production cost report for November using the FIFO method.

Questions

6-1   What are the typical characteristics of a company that should use a process costing system?

6-2   List three types of industries that would likely use process costing.

6-3   Explain the primary differences between job costing and process costing.

6-4   What does the term *equivalent units* mean?

6-5   How is the equivalent unit calculation affected when direct materials are added at the beginning of the process rather than uniformly throughout the process?

6-6   What is a production cost report? What are the five key steps in preparing a production cost report?

6-7   What is the distinction between equivalent units under the FIFO method and equivalent units under the weighted-average method?

6-8   Identify the conditions under which the weighted-average method of process costing is inappropriate.

6-9   Specify the advantage of the weighted-average method of process costing in contrast to the FIFO method.

6-10 From the standpoint of cost control, why is the FIFO method superior to the weighted-average method? Is it possible to monitor cost trends using the weighted-average method?

6-11 What are transferred-in costs?

6-12 Suppose that manufacturing is performed in sequential production departments. Prepare a journal entry to show a transfer of partially completed units from the first department to the second department.

6-13 Under the weighted-average method, all units transferred out are treated the same way. How does this differ from the FIFO method of handling units transferred out?

6-14 Under the FIFO method, only current period costs and work are included in unit costs and equivalent units computation. Under the weighted-average method, what assumptions are made when unit costs and equivalent units are computed?

6-15 What is the main difference between journal entries in process costing and in job costing?

6-16 What is the difference between process costing and backflush costing?

6-17 Describe the effect of automation on the process costing system.

Brief Exercises

Required   For problems 6-18 to 6-21, fill in the missing amount.

6-18	Work-in-process inventory, February 1	80,000 units
	Work-in-process inventory, February 28	?
	Units started during February	60,000
	Units completed during February	75,000
6-19	Work-in-process inventory, June 1	?
	Work-in-process inventory, June 30	55,000 gallons
	Units started during June	75,000 gallons
	Units completed during June	83,000 gallons
6-20	Work-in-process inventory, September 1	5,500 tons
	Work-in-process inventory, September 30	3,400 tons
	Units started during September	?
	Units completed during September	7,300 tons

6-21   Work-in-process inventory, November 1   45,000 units

Work-in-process inventory, November 30   23,000 units

Units started during November   57,000 units

Units completed during November   ?

6-22   Beginning work-in-process is 2,000 units; units completed is 44,000 units, and ending work-in-process is 3,000 units, which are 100 percent complete for materials and 50 percent complete for conversion costs. The beginning work-in-process inventory is 100 percent complete for materials and 50 percent complete for conversion.

   a.   What are the equivalent units for materials and conversion using the weighted average method?

   b.   What are the equivalent units for materials and conversion using the FIFO method?

6-23   Cost per equivalent unit is $2 per EU for materials and $3 per EU for conversion. There are no transferred-in costs and no spoilage. What is the cost of goods completed if 10,000 units are completed and 1,000 are in ending inventory?

6-24   Abnormal spoilage is 100 units and normal spoilage is 400 units. Beginning work-in-process inventory consisted of 5,000 units; 20,000 units were started; and 22,000 units were completed this period. How many units are in ending work-in-process?

6-25   The number of abnormal spoiled units is 300 and the cost per equivalent unit is $2 for materials and $3 for conversion. The inspection point is at the end of processing. There are 600 units in ending work-in-process and 200 normal spoiled units. What is the cost of spoilage shown separately on the cost report?

6-26   There is no spoilage, the beginning work-in-process inventory is 6,000 units, and the ending work-in-process inventory is 4,000 units for the second department in a two department process. What is the number of units transferred in to the second department if good output of the second department is 35,000 units?

Exercises

6-27   **Equivalent Units; Weighted-Average Method**   Oregon Fisheries, Inc., processes salmon for various distributors. Two departments, processing and packaging, are involved. Data relating to tons of salmon sent to the processing department during May follow:

		Percent Completed	
	Tons of Salmon	Materials	Conversion
Work-in-process inventory, May 1	1,500	80%	70%
Work-in-process inventory, May 31	2,500	50	30
Started processing during May	8,000		

Required

1. Calculate the number of tons completed and transferred out during the month.

2. Calculate the number of equivalent units for both materials and conversion for the month of May, assuming that the company uses the weighted-average method.

6-28   **Process Costing in Sugar Manufacturing**   The food-processing industry, as for most process industries, is a common user of process costing. Consider for example the sugar manufacturing industry. The processes in sugar manufacturing can differ depending on the agricultural product used to produce sugar. When sugar cane is used, the sequence of processes looks something like this:

First: Cane shredding The sugar cane is shredded into small pieces to facilitate its movement through the milling machine.

Second: Milling The shredded cane is crushed between the rollers in the milling machine to produce the cane juice.

Third: Heating and adding lime In this step, the cane juice is heated to concentrate the juice, and lime is added to reduce acidity.

Fourth: Clarifying Impure elements are removed from the juice.

Fifth: Evaporating and Separating. Here the juice is heated, vacuum is applied, and the liquid is centrifuged to remove the molasses and to produce what is called raw sugar.

Sixth: Crystallizing The raw sugar is melted and carbon-filtered to produce the refined sugar.

Seventh: Drying. The refined sugar is dried and made ready for packaging.

Due to the nature of the seven processes, there is a relatively large amount of work-in-process inventory at any point in time. Also, sugar cane and raw sugar commodity prices can be stable for a period of time but there are periods of high volatility caused by, for example, India's mandate in 2007 to develop ethanol fuel; or the supply/demand imbalance in 1980 that sent prices up. Also, government price supports, import restrictions, and quotas affect the price of sugar cane. For example, as part of its development policy, the EU in recent years paid above market rates for sugar from a number of African, Caribbean, and Pacific countries, many of them former colonies of European countries.

Required

1. Are firms that produce sugar likely to incur transferred-in costs? Why or why not?

2. Should a sugar producer use the FIFO or the weighted-average method for the process cost report? Explain your answer.

3. Identify and explain any sustainability issues for the production of sugar.

4. Identify and interpret the significance of any global issues for the production of sugar.

6-29 Equivalent Units; Weighted-Average Method Eastern Oregon Lumber Company grows, harvests, and processes timber for use as building lumber. The following data pertain to the company's sawmill:

Work-in-process inventory, January 1 (materials: 60 percent; conversion: 40 percent)	30,000 units
Work-in-process inventory, December 31 (materials: 70 percent; conversion: 60 percent)	15,000 units

During the year the company started 150,000 units in production.

Required Prepare a physical flow schedule and compute the number of equivalent units of both direct materials and conversion for the year, using the weighted-average method.

6-30 Equivalent Units; Weighted-Average and FIFO Methods Industrial Chemical Company refines a variety of petrochemical products. These data are from the firm's Houston plant:

Work-in-process inventory, September 1	4,000,000 gallons
Direct materials	100 percent completed
Conversion	25 percent completed
Units started in process during September	4,850,000 gallons
Work-in-process inventory, September 30	2,400,000 gallons
Direct materials	100 percent completed
Conversion	60 percent completed

Required Compute the equivalent units of direct material and conversion for the month of September. Use both the weighted-average and the FIFO methods.

6-31 Equivalent Units; Weighted-Average and FIFO Methods Baker Company has the following information for December 1 to December 31. All direct materials are 100 percent complete; beginning materials cost $12,000.

Work-in-Process			
Beginning balance December 200 units, 9 percent complete for conversion	$14,000	Completed 800 units and transferred to finished goods inventory	$140,000
Direct materials	54,000		
Direct labor	34,000		
Factory overhead			
Property taxes	6,000		
Depreciation	32,000		
Utilities	18,000		
Indirect labor	4,000		
Ending balance December 31, 300 units, 12 percent complete	22,000		

Required Calculate equivalent units using the weighted-average and FIFO methods.

6-32 **Equivalent Units; Weighted-Average** Hawthorne Motor Company rebuilds automobile engines that have been damaged or are in need of extensive repair. The rebuilt engine has a 100,000-mile warranty and is purchased by auto shops, large motor pools in companies and governmental units, and some individual auto owners. The Dayton plant at Hawthorne specializes in the Ford V6 engine. Approximately 600 to 800 engines are rebuilt each month, and the costs of the plant are assigned to monthly production using weighted-average process costing. The current month began with a work-in-process inventory of 200 engines which were 50 percent complete for materials and 50 percent complete for conversion costs. The materials cost in beginning work-in-process was $50,000, while the conversion cost was $60,000. 600 engines were completed and shipped out during the month, and total materials cost of $550,000 and conversion cost of $640,000 were incurred during the month. The ending work-in-process of 200 units was 20 percent complete for materials and 40 percent complete for conversion costs.

Required Compute the cost per equivalent unit for materials and conversion for the month.

6-33 **Equivalent Units; Weighted-Average and FIFO Unit Cost** Solidad Company calculates the cost for an equivalent unit of production using process costing.

Data for June	
Work-in-process inventory, June 1: 30,000 units	
Direct materials: 100 percent complete	$ 60,000
Conversion: 20 percent complete	24,000
Balance in work-in-process, June 1	$ 84,000
Units started during June	50,000
Units completed and transferred	60,000
Work-in-process inventory, June 30	20,000
Direct materials: 100 percent complete	
Conversion: 70 percent complete	
Cost incurred during June	
Direct materials	$120,000
Conversion costs	
Direct labor	120,000
Applied overhead	180,000
Total conversion costs	$300,000

Required

1. Compute cost per equivalent unit for both the weighted-average and FIFO methods.
2. Explain the difference between the FIFO and weighted-average unit costs.

6-34 **Journal Entries** NYI Corporation manufactures decorative window glass in two sequential departments. These data pertain to the month of August:

	Department 1	Department 2
Direct materials used for production	$ 55,000	$ 32,000
Direct labor	160,000	320,000
Applied factory overhead	340,000	250,000
Costs of goods completed and transferred	850,000	740,000

Required Prepare journal entries to record these events:

1. Incurrence of direct materials and direct labor. Application of factory overhead in department 1.
2. Transfer of products from department 1 to department 2.

3. Incurrence of direct materials and direct labor. Application of factory overhead in department 2.

4. Transfer of complete products from department 2 to finished goods inventory.

6-35 FIFO Method   Taxes R Us (TRU), an income tax preparation firm, uses the FIFO method of process costing for the monthly reports. TRU has no materials cost in the preparation of the returns. The following shows its March information:

Returns in process, March 1 (30% complete)	100
Returns started in March	1,600
Returns in process, March 31 (90% complete)	200
Labor and overhead costs for returns in process, March 1	$ 2,500
Labor and overhead costs incurred in March	$173,250

Required   Calculate the following amounts for conversion costs using the FIFO method:

1. Equivalent units.
2. Cost per equivalent unit.
3. Cost of completed returns for the month of March.
4. Cost of returns in process as of March 31.

6-36 Backflush Costing   Chen Manufacturing uses backflush costing. Chen has the following information for the most recent month of activity:

Purchase of direct materials	$725,000
Direct materials used	$705,000
Conversion cost incurred	$1,450,000
Direct materials standard cost	$20 per unit
Conversion cost at standard	$40 per unit
Units produced	35,000 units
Units sold	33,000 units

Required

1. Prepare the journal entries for purchase of materials, conversion costs, the completion of product during the month, the sale of product, and the closing entry.
2. Under what conditions is backflush costing used in practice?

6-37 Backflush Costing   Grand Marine Inc. (GMI) manufactures sailcloth used by sailmakers that produce sails for sailboats. GMI's sailcloth is the conventional polyester-based sail material and is used widely in recreational boating. Sailmakers throughout the world use GMI's sailcloth. The manufacture of sailcloth has a small number of processes, and GMI integrates them carefully so that there is very little work-in-process inventory. The product is measured in yards of cloth, which is prepared in rolls 42 inches wide. Because it has little work-in-process inventory, GMI also uses backflush accounting to simplify the accounting for its operations. GMI has the following information for the most recent accounting period. The beginning inventory of polyester fiber was $142,000 and the ending inventory was $147,000.

Polyester fiber purchased	$690,000
Conversion cost incurred	$1,300,000
Direct materials standard cost	$4.35 per yard of cloth
Conversion standard cost	$8.50 per yard of cloth
Units produced	155,000 yards of cloth

Required   Show the entries for manufacturing costs, completion of 155,000 yards of product, and the closing entries.

Problems   6-38 **Weighted-Average Method**   Gifford, Inc. produces a single model of a popular cell phone in large quantities. A single cell phone moves through two departments, assembly and testing. The manufacturing costs in the assembly department during March follow:

Direct materials added	$187,500
Conversion costs	165,410
	$352,910

The assembly department has no beginning work-in-process inventory. During the month, it started 25,000 cell phones, but only 22,000 were fully completed and transferred to the testing department. All parts had been made and placed in the remaining 3,000 cell phones, but only 60 percent of the conversion had been completed. The company uses the weighted-average method of process costing to accumulate product costs.

Required

1. Compute the equivalent units and cost per equivalent unit for March in the assembly department.
2. Compute the costs of units completed and transferred to the testing department.
3. Compute the costs of the ending work-in-process.

6-39 **Weighted-Average Method**   South Atlantic Pulp Company processes wood pulp for manufacturing various paper products. The company employs a process costing system for its manufacturing operations. All direct materials are added at the beginning of the process, and conversion costs are incurred uniformly throughout the process. This is the company's production schedule for May:

		Percent Completed	
	Tons of Pulp	**Materials**	**Conversion**
Work-in-process inventory, May 1	6,000	100%	50%
Started during May	15,000		
Units to account for	21,000		
Units from beginning work-in-process, which were completed and transferred out during May	6000		
Started and completed during May	12,000		
Work-in-process inventory, May 31	3,000	100%	50%
Total units accounted for	21,000		

The following cost data are available:

Work-in-process inventory, May 1	
Direct materials	$ 88,000
Conversion	126,000
Costs incurred during May	
Direct materials	220,000
Conversion	356,000

Required

1. Calculate equivalent units of direct materials and conversion during May. Use the weighted-average method.
2. Calculate the cost per equivalent unit for both direct materials and conversion during May. Use the weighted-average method.

6-40 **FIFO Method**   Refer to the information in Problem 6-39.

Required   Complete Problem 6-39 using the FIFO method.

6-41 Weighted-Average Method   Cuevas Company manufactures a single product that goes through two processes, mixing and cooking. These data pertain to the mixing department for August:

Work-in-process inventory, August 1	
Conversion: 80 percent complete	33,000 units
Work-in-process inventory, August 31	
Conversion: 40 percent complete	27,000 units
Units started into production	54,000
Units completed and transferred out	?
Costs	
Work-in-process inventory, August 1	
Material X	$ 64,800
Material Y	89,100
Conversion	119,880
Costs added during August	
Material X	152,700
Material Y	135,900
Conversion	304,920

Material X is added at the beginning of work in the mixing department. Material Y is also added in the mixing department, but not until product units are 60 percent complete with regard to conversion. Conversion costs are incurred uniformly during the process. The company uses the weighted-average cost method.

Required

1. Calculate equivalent units of material X, material Y, and conversion for the mixing department.
2. Calculate costs per equivalent unit for material X, material Y, and conversion.
3. Calculate the cost of units transferred out.
4. Calculate the cost of ending work-in-process inventory.

6-42 FIFO Method   Jenice Company uses FIFO process costing to account for the costs of its single product. Production begins in the fabrication department, where units of direct materials are molded into various connecting parts. After fabrication is complete, the units are transferred to the assembly department, which adds no material. After assembly is complete, the units are transferred to the packaging department, which packages units for shipment. After the units have been packaged, the final products are transferred to the shipping department. A partially completed production cost report for the month of May in the fabrication department follows:

JENICE COMPANY
Fabrication Department—Production Cost Report
For the Month of May

Quantity Schedule	Units
Units to be accounted for	
Work-in-process inventory, May 1	
(materials: 100 percent; conversion: 40 percent)	3,000
Started into production	?
Total units to be accounted for	?
Units accounted for as follows	
Transferred to department Y	
Units from the beginning inventory	?
Units started and completed this month	?
Work-in-process inventory, May 31	4,000
(materials: 100 percent; conversion: 60 percent)	
Total units accounted for	?

(Continued)

Equivalent Units and Unit Costs	Materials	Conversion	Total
Cost added during May	$172,500	$224,900	?
Equivalent units	?	?	
Unit Cost	?	?	?
Cost Assignment			
Cost to be accounted for			
?			
Cost accounted for as follows:			
?			

The cost incurred in the fabrication department's work-in-process inventory at May 1 is $13,800. The assembly department's production cost report for the month of May shows that the number of transferred-in units is 68,000.

Required

1. Fill in the missing amounts in the quantity schedule and complete the equivalent units and costs.

2. Complete the cost assignment part of the production cost report.

6-43 **Weighted-Average Method**   China Pacific Company manufactures a variety of natural fabrics for the clothing industry in a suburb of Shanghai. The following data in Chinese currency called *yuan* pertain to the month of October.

Work-in-process inventory, October 1	25,000 units
Direct materials: 60 percent complete	57,000 yuan
Conversion: 30 percent complete	45,000 yuan
Cost incurred during October	
Direct materials	736,000 yuan
Conversion	1,094,950 yuan

During October, 175,000 units were completed and transferred out. At the end of the month, 30,000 units (direct materials 80 percent and conversion 40 percent complete) remain in work-in-process inventory.

Required   Calculate each of the following amounts using weighted-average process costing.

1. Equivalent units of direct materials and conversion.

2. Unit costs of direct materials and conversion.

3. Cost of goods completed and transferred out during October.

4. Cost of the work-in-process inventory at October 31.

5. Check the most recent issue of *The Wall Street Journal* or go to http://www.federalreserve.gov/releases/ H10/hist/ to learn the exchange rate between the U.S. dollar and the Chinese yuan.

6-44 **Weighted-Average Method; Transferred-in Costs**   Holton Tool Company has two departments, assembly and finishing. The assembly department takes purchased parts and assembles the final product. The finishing department performs testing and adds other materials and packages the product. Direct materials are added at the end of the process in the finishing department. The following summarizes the finishing department's operations for the month of July.

	Number of Units
Work-in-process, June 30, 50% complete for conversion costs	3,000
Transferred in during July	28,000
Completed during July	27,000
Work-in-process, July 31, 50% complete for conversion costs	4,000

	Costs
Work-in-process, June 30 (transferred-in costs: $40,000; conversion costs: $30,000)	$ 70,000
Transferred-in from assembly department during July	150,000
Direct materials added during July	60,000
Conversion added during July	80,000
Total to account for	$360,000

Required   Calculate each of the following amounts for the finishing department using the weighted-average process costing method:

1. Equivalent units of transferred-in direct materials and conversion.
2. Unit costs of transferred-in, direct materials, and conversion.
3. Cost of goods completed and transferred out during July.
4. Cost of work-in-process inventory at July 31.

6-45   Reconditioning Service; Weighted-Average Method   Golf World Inc. (GWI) sells products and services for the sport of golf. One of its key business units specializes in the repair and reconditioning of golf carts. GWI enters into contracts with a number of golf clubs throughout the U.S. in which the clubs send their carts to GWI for a complete recondition: motor, frame repair where necessary, and replacement of seat covers and canvas tops. The clubs usually will cycle 10–15 percent of their carts through this process each year. Because GWI's business has been growing steadily, it is very important to complete the reconditioning of the carts within a budgeted time and cost. The firm uses weighted-average process costing to keep track of the costs incurred in the reconditioning process.

GWI's golf cart operations has the following information for the month of November, in which 1,200 carts were started for reconditioning:

Beginning WIP: 150 units, 50 percent complete for materials ($15,000) and 30 percent complete for conversion ($20,000)

Current costs:
  Materials: $200,000
  Conversion: $385,000 (conversion costs for GWI usually average about $250 to $320 per unit, based on an average of 1,000–1,300 units completed each month)
Ending WIP: 300 units, 30 percent complete for materials and 20 percent complete for conversion

Required

1. Complete the cost report for the month of November.
2. GWI is scheduled to start another batch of 1,500 carts for reconditioning in December. Comment on the information the cost report contains regarding planning for December's work.

6-46   Weighted-Average Method   Sosna Company has a department that manufactures wood trusses (wood frames used in the construction industry). The following information is for the production of these trusses for the month of February:

Work-in-process inventory, February 1	5,000 trusses
Direct materials cost: 100 percent complete	$100,000
Conversion: 20 percent complete	$135,000
Units started during February	12,000 trusses
Units completed during February and transferred out	13,000 trusses
Work-in-process inventory, February 29	
Direct materials: 100 percent complete	
Conversion cost: 40 percent complete	
Costs incurred during February	
Direct materials	$ 50,000
Conversion	$ 95,000

Required Using the weighted-average method, calculate the following:

1. Costs per equivalent unit.
2. Cost of goods completed and transferred out.
3. Cost remaining in the ending work-in-process inventory.
4. Assume that you are the company's controller. The production department's February unit cost is higher than standard cost. If the manager of the first department asks you to do him a favor by increasing the ending inventory completion percentage from 40 to 60 percent to lower the unit costs, what should you do? How much would unit cost be affected by this request?

6-47 **FIFO Method** Refer to the information in problem 6-46.

Required Repeat Problem 6-46 using the FIFO method.

6-48 **FIFO Method; Journal Entries** You are engaged in the audit of the December 31, 2010, financial statements of Epworth Products Corporation. You are attempting to verify the costing of the work-in-process and finished goods ending inventories that were recorded on Epworth's books as follows:

	Units	Cost
Work-in-process (50 percent complete as to labor and overhead)	300,000	$660,960
Finished goods	100,000	504,900

Materials are added to production at the beginning of the manufacturing process, and overhead is applied to each product at the rate of 60 percent of direct labor costs. There was no finished goods inventory on January 1, 2010. Epworth uses the FIFO costing method. A review of Epworth's 2010 inventory cost records disclosed the following information:

		Costs	
	Units	Materials	Labor
Work-in-process inventory, January 1, 2010 (80 percent complete as to labor and overhead)	200,000	$ 200,000	$ 315,000
Started	1,000,000		
Completed	900,000		
Current period costs		1,300,000	1,995,000

Required Prepare a production cost report to verify the inventory balances and prepare necessary journal entries to correctly state the inventory of finished goods and work-in-process, assuming that the books have not been closed.

6-49 **Weighted-Average Method; Transferred-in Costs** Sanyo Corporation manufactures a popular model of business calculators in a suburb of Seoul, South Korea. The production process goes through two departments, assembly and testing. The following information (in thousands of South Korean currency, the *won*) pertains to the testing department for the month of July.

Work-in-process inventory, July 1		6,000 units
Transferred-in costs	57,800 won	(100 percent complete)
Costs added by the department		
Direct materials	23,400 won	(100 percent complete)
Conversion	23,360 won	(80 percent complete)

During the month of July, 15,000 units were transferred in from the assembly department at the cost of 141,700 won, and the testing department added costs of 201,820 won.

Direct materials	92,520 won
Conversion	109,300 won

During the month, 18,000 units were completed and transferred to the warehouse. At July 31, the completion percentage of work-in-process was as follows:

Direct materials	90 percent
Conversion	60 percent

Required

1. Prepare the production report of the testing department for the month of July using the weighted-average process costing.

2. Check the most recent issue of *The Wall Street Journal* or www.federalreserve.gov/releases/H10/hist/ to learn the exchange rate between the U.S. dollar and the South Korean won.

6-50 FIFO Method; Transferred-in Costs Wood Glow Manufacturing Company produces a single product, a wood refinishing kit that sells for $17.95. The final processing of the kits occurs in the packaging department. An internal quilted wrap is applied at the beginning of the packaging process. A compartmentalized outside box printed with instructions and the company's name and logo is added when the units have completed 60 percent of the process. Conversion costs consisting of direct labor and applied overhead occur evenly throughout the packaging process. Conversion activities after the addition of the box involve package sealing, testing for leakage, and final inspection. Rejections in the packaging department are rare and can be ignored. The following data pertain to the packaging department's activities during the month of October.

- Beginning work-in-process inventory was 10,000 units, 40 percent complete as to conversion costs.
- During the month, 30,000 units were started and completed.
- Ending work-in-process had 10,000 units, 80 percent complete as to conversion costs.

The packaging department's October costs follow:

Quilted wrap	$80,000
Outside boxes	50,000
Direct labor	22,000
Applied overhead ($3 per direct labor dollar)	66,000

The costs transferred in from prior processing were $3 per unit. The cost of goods sold for the month was $240,000, and the ending finished-goods inventory was $84,000. Wood Glow uses the first-in, first-out (FIFO) method of inventory valuation.

Wood Glow's controller, Mark Brandon, has been asked to analyze the packaging department's activities for the month of October. Mark knows that to properly determine the department's unit cost of production, he must first calculate the equivalent units of production.

Required

1. Prepare an equivalent units of production schedule for the packaging department's October activity.

2. Determine October production's cost per equivalent unit.

(CMA Adapted)

6-51 Weighted-Average Method; Two Departments Allgood, Inc., an automotive exhaust system manufacturer, has two departments in muffler production, the fabrication and the assembly departments.

All materials for the fabrication department were added at the beginning of the process. Data recorded for January follow:

	Units	Percent Completed	Direct Materials	Conversion
Fabrication department				
Work-in-process inventory, January 1	6,000	20%	$ 15,000	$ 20,000
Transferred to assembly				
department in January	50,000			
Work-in-process inventory, January 31	4,000	40%		
Assembly department				
Work-in-process inventory, January 1	10,000	40		$200,000
(transferred-in cost: $92,000)				
Completed and				
transferred out in January	55,000			
Work-in-process inventory, January 31	5,000	40		
Costs incurred in January				
Fabrication department			$117,500	$310,850
Assembly department				$723,400

Required   Calculate the following using the weighted-average method:

1. Equivalent units of direct materials and conversion in the fabrication department.
2. Unit costs of direct materials and conversion in the fabrication department.
3. Cost of goods transferred to the assembly department from the fabrication department in the month of January.
4. Cost of the work-in-process ending inventory in the fabrication department.
5. Equivalent units of transferred-in and conversion in the assembly department.
6. Unit costs of transferred-in and conversion in the assembly department.
7. Cost of goods transferred to finished goods from the assembly department in January.
8. Cost of the work-in-process ending inventory in the assembly department.

6-52   **FIFO Method; Two Departments**   Bhatti Company produces plastic photo frames. Two departments, molding and finishing, are involved in the manufacturing. The molding department fills the molds with hot liquid plastic that is left to cool and then opens them. The finishing department removes the plastic frame from the mold and strips the edges of the frames of extra plastic.

The following information is available for the month of January:

	January 1		January 31	
Work-in-Process Inventory	**Quantity (pounds)**	**Cost**	**Quantity (pounds)**	**Cost**
Molding department	None	—	None	—
Finishing department	5,000	$15,000	2,000	?

The work-in-process inventory in the finishing department is estimated to be 40 percent complete both at the beginning and end of January. Costs of production for January follow:

Costs of Production	Materials Used	Conversion
Molding department	$450,000	$90,000
Finishing department	—	80,000

The material used in the molding department weighed 50,000 pounds. The firm uses the FIFO method of process costing.

Required   Prepare a report for both the molding and finishing departments for the month of January. The report should include equivalent units of production (in pounds), total manufacturing costs, cost per equivalent unit (pounds), cost of ending work-in-process inventory, and cost of goods completed and transferred out.

6-53 **Weighted-Average Method; Two Departments**   Porter Company manufactures its one product by a process that requires two departments. The production starts in department A and is completed in department B. Materials are added at the beginning of the process in department A. Additional materials are added when the process is 50 percent complete in department B. Conversion costs are incurred proportionally throughout the production processes in both departments.

On April 1, department A had 500 units in work-in-process estimated to be 30 percent complete for conversion; department B had 300 units in work-in-process estimated to be 40 percent complete. During April, department A started 1,500 units and completed 1,600 units; department B completed 1,400 units. The work-in-process ending inventory on April 30 in department A is estimated to be 20 percent complete, and the work-in-process ending inventory in department B is estimated to be 70 percent complete.

The cost sheet for department A shows that the units in the work-in-process beginning inventory had $3,000 in direct materials costs and $1,530 in conversion costs. The production costs incurred in April were $12,000 for direct materials and $10,710 for conversion. Department B's work-in-process beginning inventory on April 1 was $6,100, of which $4,200 was transferred-in costs; it incurred $38,000 in direct materials costs and $24,350 in conversion costs in April.

Porter Company uses the weighted-average method for departments A and B.

Required

1. Prepare a production cost report for department A.
2. Prepare a production cost report for department B.

6-54 **Spoilage, Weighted-Average Method; Transferred-in Costs (Appendix)**   Romano Foods Inc. manufactures 12-inch Roman Surprise Fresh Frozen Pizzas that retail for $4.69 to $5.99, depending upon the topping. The company employs a process costing system in which the product flows through several processes. Joe Corolla, vice president of production, has had a long-running disagreement with the controller, Sue Marshall, over the way to handle spoilage cost. Joe resists every attempt to charge production with variance responsibilities unless they are favorable. Spoilage costs have not been significant in the past, but, in November, the mixing department had a substantial amount of spoilage. Romano Foods has traditionally treated 10 percent of good output as normal spoilage. The mixing department input 120,000 units of ingredients; inspection rejected 13,000 dough units. Sue is concerned about the abnormal spoilage and wants Joe to take corrective steps. He maintains, however, that the mixing department is operating properly and has prepared the following report to support his contention:

ROMANO FOODS—MIXING DEPARTMENT
Production Cost Report
Month Ended November 30, 2010

Input Units	Total Cost	Good Output Units	Normal Spoilage (10 percent)	Abnormal Spoilage	Good Unit Cost
120,000	$45,360	107,000	12,000	1,000	$ 0.42

Budgeted unit cost	$ 0.435
Actual cost per good unit	0.420
Favorable variance	$ 0.015

Cost Assignment

Cost of 107,000 good units @ $0.42 each	$44,940
Abnormal spoilage (charge to purchasing for buying inferior materials):	
1,000 units @ $0.42 each	420
Total cost	$45,360

Sue read the report and found out that Joe miscalculated both normal and abnormal spoilage units, and he ignored the normal spoilage in calculating the unit cost.

Required

1. Revise Joe Corolla's production cost report for November 2010 by calculating the correct numbers or amounts for the following:

   a. The number of units of normal spoilage.

   b. The number of units of abnormal spoilage.

   c. The total and per-unit costs of the mixing department's production of good units in November.

   d. The total and per-unit costs of abnormal spoilage.

2. Prepare the journal entry to transfer costs for the mixing department for November to the assembly department.

3. Describe how Joe Corolla's production cost report has shown the performance of the mixing department to be less favorable than that shown in the revised report in requirement 1.

(CMA Adapted)

6-55 **Weighted-Average Process Costing; Spoilage (Appendix)**   Wetherby Paint Company, which manufactures quality paint to sell at premium prices, uses a single production department. Production begins by blending the various chemicals that are added at the beginning of the process and ends by filling the paint cans. The gallon cans are then transferred to the shipping department for crating and shipment. Labor and overhead are added continuously throughout the process. Factory overhead is applied on the basis of direct labor hours at the rate of $3 per hour. The company combines labor and overhead in computing product cost.

Prior to May, when a change in the process was implemented, work-in-process inventories were insignificant. The change in the process allows increased production but results in considerable amounts of work-in-process inventory. Also, the company had 1,500 spoiled gallons in May—one-half of which was normal spoilage and the rest abnormal spoilage. The product is inspected at the end of the production process.

These data relate to actual production during the month of May:

	Costs
Work-in-process inventory, May 1	
Direct materials—chemicals	$ 45,500
Direct labor ($10 per hour)	8,500
May costs added:	
Direct materials—chemicals	228,400
Direct labor ($10 per hour)	38,500

	Units
Work-in-process inventory, May 1	
(25 percent complete)	4,000
Sent to shipping department	24,000
Started in May	26,000
Work-in-process inventory, May 31	
(80 percent complete)	4,500

Required   Prepare a production cost report for May using the weighted-average method.

(CMA Adapted)

6-56 **Spoilage; Weighted-Average Method; Transferred-in Costs (Appendix)**   APCO Company manufactures various lines of bicycles. Because of the high volume of each line, the company employs a process cost system using the weighted-average method to determine unit costs. Bicycle parts are manufactured in the molding department and then are consolidated into a single bike unit in the molding department and transferred to the assembly department where they are partially assembled. After assembly, the bicycle is sent to the packing department.

Annual cost and production figures for the assembly department are presented in the schedules that follow.

Defective bicycles are identified at the inspection point when the assembly labor process is 70 percent complete; all assembly materials have been added at this point. The normal rejection for defective bicycles is 5 percent of the bicycles reaching the inspection point. Any defective bicycles above the 5 percent quota are considered to be abnormal. All defective bikes are removed from the production process and destroyed.

Required

1. Compute the number of defective, or spoiled, bikes that are considered to be
   a. Normal.
   b. Abnormal.
2. Compute the equivalent units of production for the year for
   a. Bicycles transferred in from the molding department.
   b. Bicycles produced with regard to assembly material.
   c. Bicycles produced with regard to assembly conversion.
3. Compute the cost per equivalent unit for the fully assembled bike.
4. Compute the amount of the total production cost of $1,672,020 that will be associated with the following items:
   a. Normal spoiled units.
   b. Abnormal spoiled units.
   c. Good units completed in the assembly department.
   d. Ending work-in-process inventory in the assembly department.
5. Describe how to present the applicable dollar amounts for the following items in the financial statements:
   a. Normal spoiled units.
   b. Abnormal spoiled units.
   c. Completed units transferred in to the packing department.

Assembly Department Cost Data

	Transferred in from Molding Department	Assembly Materials	Assembly Conversion Cost	Total Cost of Bike through Assembly
Prior period costs	$ 82,200	$ 6,660	$ 11,930	$ 100,790
Current period costs	1,237,800	96,840	236,590	1,571,230
Total costs	$1,320,000	$103,500	$248,520	$1,672,020

Assembly Department Production Data

	Bicycles	Percentage Complete		
		Transferred in	Assembly Materials	Assembly Conversion
Beginning inventory	3,000	100%	100%	80%
Transferred in from molding during year	45,000	100	—	—
Transferred out to packing during year	40,000	100	100	100
Ending inventory	4,000	100	50	20

(CMA Adapted)

6-57 **Process Costing and Activity-Based Costing** Hampton Chemical Specialties, Inc. (HCS) is a manufacturer of specialty chemicals sold to manufacturers, hospitals, and other users. HCS produces 10 to 15 million gallons of its main product HCS-22 each month. The data for July 2010 follows (in thousands of gallons). The chemical raw materials are added at the beginning of processing.

Beginning work-in-process inventory (60% complete for conversion; materials $55,000, conversion $7,250)		200 gallons
Units started		1,000 gallons
Good units finished (no spoilage)		800 gallons
Ending work-in-process inventory (30% complete for conversion)		400 gallons
Current manufacturing costs		
Materials	$176,000	
Conversion	$ 66,900	

Each month HCS averages 100 batches of product with approximately 12,000 gallons per batch, though some batches are as large as 50,000 gallons or more, and some are as small as a few hundred gallons. Also, the pattern of customer orders is that large orders come in at all times of the month, while small orders tend to cluster around the last few days of the month. The small orders are due to salespersons trying to meet monthly sales quotas and to the buying patterns of smaller customers who want their shipments early in the following month. As a result, in the average month three-fourths of the total orders are started in the last few days of the month, and most are not completed until early in the following month. For example, in July 2010, 100 batches were produced, and 75 were still in the ending work-in-process inventory at the end of the month. Ted Brown, plant controller for HCS, thinks that the current costing method, using weighted-average process costing, underestimates the cost of the ending work-in-process inventory as well as the cost of smaller jobs.

Required

1. Prepare the production cost report using the weighted-average method.

2. Assume that $28,500 of the $66,900 current conversion costs could be traced to batch-related activities such as equipment setup. Further, assume that these batch-related costs are all incurred when the batch is started. Ted has asked you to recalculate the production cost report to separate the batch-related costs from total conversion costs. How do the results differ from the method in requirement 1? Is Ted right about underestimating the cost of ending work-in-process inventory?

6-58 **FIFO Method and Rising Prices**   Healthy Selections Cereals Inc. (HSC) is a large food-processing company specializing in whole-grain, high-energy, low-calorie and low-fat cereals that appeal to the health-conscious consumer. HSC has a premium image in the market and most of its customers are loyal and willing to pay a bit extra to get the healthy choice that HSC offers. HSC's cereals are made in a series of processes which begin with sorting, cleaning, preparing, and inspecting the raw materials (grains, nuts, and other ingredients). The materials are then mixed and processed for consistency, cooked, given a final inspection, and packaged. Raw materials are added only at the beginning of the first process. The inspections in the first and final processes are made at the end of those respective processes, so all materials and conversion costs are lost for waste detected at the inspection point. The company uses weighted-average process costing and accounts for all waste as normal spoilage.

Currently commodity prices are rising sharply, affecting the costs of many of the ingredients in HSC's products. The CFO, noting the sharp rise in the cost of the company's raw materials (the ingredients for its products), has considered using the FIFO method.

The following data is for the first process for the current month. All output is measured in pounds.

Beginning work-in-process:	14,000 pounds, 25% complete for conversion
Ending work-in-process:	12,000 pounds, 40% complete for conversion
Spoilage:	1,000 pounds
Pounds added this month	33,000 pounds

The cost information for the first process is as follows:

	Materials	Conversion	Total
Beginning WIP	$ 3,500	$ 3,400	$ 6,900
Current costs	66,000	104,000	170,000

Required

1. Calculate a process cost report for the first process using the weighted-average method.

2. Calculate a process cost report for the first process using the FIFO method.

3. Explain which of the two methods you would recommend to the CFO, considering the firm's competitive environment.

6-59   **Weighted-Average Method; Two Departments**   Precision Chemical Company (PCC) produces a variety of specialty chemicals used in the pharmaceutical industry and construction industry. PCC spends almost 20 percent of its net revenues on research, product development, and customer development to achieve its reputation as a high-quality producer of chemicals, a reliable supplier, and a great provider of customer service. PCC has a small number of large customers, each of which typically has one or more large orders being processed at PCC at any given point in time. These orders are typically completed over one to three months or longer. PCC uses job costing to keep track of total job costs over the duration of each order and process costing to keep track of monthly costs, department by department. The processing departments include mixing, reacting (in which chemicals are heated and sometimes vacuum is applied), cleaning, inspecting, packaging, and distribution. Much of the total product cost is accumulated in the first two processes, mixing and reacting. The following information is for activity and costs in the first two departments during the current month.

The mixing department started 84,000 gallons this month. No spoilage is measured in the mixing department, but a careful measure of the loss of material in reacting is taken after the completion of the reacting process. No materials are added in the reacting process. The number of gallons lost (spoilage) is considered normal spoilage and is considered to have lost the full cost of processing up to that point of inspection. PCC uses the weighted-average method for process costing.

Work-in-process for the two departments are as follows. Percentage completion for conversion costs are 60% and 80% in the mixing department for beginning and ending inventory, respectively. The percentage completion for conversion costs for the reacting department for beginning and ending inventory are 30% and 40%, respectively.

	Mixing Department (gallons)	Reacting Department (gallons)
Beginning work-in-process units	22,000	16,500
Ending work-in-process units	28,000	18,250
Normal spoilage (lost gallons)	0	2,250

Costs in the mixing department:

	Materials	Conversion
Beginning work-in-process	$ 63,420	$235,480
Current costs	288,500	989,400

Transferred-in beginning work-in-process costs are $234,050 and conversion costs in the reacting department are as follows:

	Conversion
Beginning work-in-process	$ 388,500
Current costs	1,245,320
	$1,633,820

Required

1. Prepare the production cost report for the mixing department
2. Prepare the production cost report for the reacting department
3. What comments and observations do you have about the two departments' cost reports?

Solutions to Self-Study Problems

1. Weighted-Average Method versus FIFO Method

1. Weighted-average method
   a. Equivalent units

Direct materials: 1,000 + (200 × 100%)	1,200
Conversion: 1,000 + (200 × 70%)	1,140

   b. Cost per equivalent unit

Direct materials: ($9,600/1,200)	$8.00
Conversion: ($2,202 + $6,120)/1,140	$7.30
Total unit costs: $8.00 + $7.30	$15.30

   c. Cost of goods completed and transferred out: $15.30 × 1,000 $15,300

d. Cost of work-in-process, 10/31

Direct materials: $8 × 200 × 100%	$1,600
Conversion: $7.30 × 200 × 70%	$1,022
Total: $1,600 + $1,022	$2,622

2. Weighted-average method production cost report

SMITH ELECTRONIC COMPANY
Chip-Mounting Production Department
Weighted-Average Production Cost Report

Production Quantity Information

	Step 1: Analyze Flow of Physical Units	Step 2: Calculate Equivalent Units	
	Physical Units	**Direct Materials**	**Conversion Costs**
Input			
Work-in-process			
beginning inventory	300		
Completion percentage			
Direct materials 0 percent			
Conversion 40 percent			
Started this period	900		
Total to account for	1,200		
Output			
Completed	1,000	1,000	1,000
Work-in-process			
ending inventory	200		
Completion percentage			
Direct materials 100 percent		200	
Conversion 70 percent			140
Total accounted for	1,200		
Total work done to date			
(Total equivalent units)		1,200	1,140

Unit Cost Determination

Step 3: Determine Costs to Account For	Total Direct Materials	Conversion Costs	Total
Work-in-process			
beginning inventory		$2,202	$ 2,202
Current cost	$9,600	$6,120	15,720
Total costs to account for	$9,600	$8,322	$17,922

Step 4: Compute Unit Costs			
Cost per equivalent unit	($9,600/1,200) = $ 8.00	($8,322/1,140) = $ 7.30	$ 15.30

Cost Assignment

Step 5: Assign Total Manufacturing Costs	Completed and Transferred out	Ending Work-in-Process	Total
Units completed			
and transferred out (1,000 × $15.30)	$15,300		$15,300
Ending work-in-process (200)			
Materials (200 × $8)		$1,600	1,600
Conversion (140 × $7.30)	–	1,022	1,022
Total costs accounted for	$15,300	$2,622	$17,922

3. FIFO method

   a. Equivalent units:

Direct materials: $(300 \times 100\%) + (1,000 - 300) + (200 \times 100\%)$	1,200
or $1,000 + (200 \times 100\%) - (300 \times 0\%)$	1,200
Conversion: $[300 \times (1 - 40\%)] + (1,000 - 300) + (200 \times 70\%)$	1,020
or $1,000 + (200 \times 70\%) - (300 \times 40\%)$	1,020

   b. Cost per equivalent unit

Direct materials: $9,600/1,200	$ 8
Conversion: $6,120/1,020	$ 6
Total unit costs = $8 + $6	$14

   c. Cost of goods completed and transferred out

      From beginning work-in-process inventory:

Direct materials: $0 + $8 \times 300 \times (1-0\%)$	$ 2,400
Conversion: $2,202 + $6 \times 300 \times (1-40\%)$	$ 3,282
Total: $2,400 + $3,282	$ 5,682
Started and completed: $14 \times (1,000 - 300)$	$ 9,800
Total cost of goods completed: $5,682 + $9,800	$15,482

   d. Cost of work in process, 10/31

Direct materials: $8 \times 200 \times 100\%$	$1,600
Conversion: $6 \times 200 \times 70\%$	$ 840
Total: $1,600 + $840	$2,440

4. FIFO method production cost report

SMITH ELECTRONIC COMPANY
Chip-Mounting Production Department
FIFO Production Cost Report

Production Quantity Information

	Step 1: Analyze Flow of Physical Units	Step 2: Calculate Equivalent Units	
	Physical Units	**Direct Materials**	**Conversion Costs**
Input			
Work-in-process beginning inventory	300		
Completion percentage			
Direct materials 0 percent		0	
Conversion 40 percent			120
Started this period	900		
Total units to account for	1,200		
Output			
Completed	1,000	1,000	1,000
Work-in-process ending inventory	200		
Completion percentage			
Direct materials 100 percent		200	
Conversion 70 percent			140
Total units accounted for	1,200	1,200	1,140
Total work performed to date			
Work-in-process beginning inventory	300	0	(120)
Total work performed this period		1,200	1,020
(FIFO equivalent units)			

(Continued)

Unit Cost Determination

Step 3: Determine Total Costs to Account For Flow	Direct Materials	Conversion Costs	Total
Work-in-process beginning inventory		$2,202	$ 2,202
Current cost	$9,600	6,120	15,720
Total costs to account for	$9,600	$8,322	$17,922

Step 4: Compute Unit Costs	($9,600/1,200) =	($6,120/1,020) =	
Cost per equivalent unit	$8	$6	$14

Cost Assignment

Step 5: Assign Total Manufacturing Costs	Completed and Transferred out	Ending Work-in-Process	Total
Units completed and transferred out (1,000)			
Beginning work-in-process	$2,202		$2,202
Current cost to complete			
Materials (300 × $8)	2,400		2,400
Conversion (180 × $6)	1,080		1,080
Total from beginning work-in-process	$5,682		$5,682
Units started and finished (700 × $14)	9,800		9,800
Total cost completed and transferred out	$15,482		$15,482
Ending work-in-process (2,000)			
Materials (200 × $8)		$1,600	1,600
Conversion (140 × $6)	–	840	840
Total costs accounted for	$15,482	$2,440	$17,922

2. Weighted-Average Method vs. FIFO Method with Transferred-In Cost

1. Weighted-average method

REED COMPANY
Finishing Department
Weighted-Average Production Cost Report

Production Quantity Information

	Step 1: Analyze Flow of Physical Units		Step 2: Calculate Equivalent Units	
	Physical Units	Transferred-in	Direct Materials	Conversion Costs
Input				
Work-in-process, November 1	10 (40%)			
Started this month	80			
Total units to account for	90			
Output				
Completed	82	82	82	82
Work-in-process, November 30	8 (50%)	8	8	4
Total accounted for	90			
Total work done to date				
(Total equivalent units)		90	90	86

(Continued)

Unit Cost Determination

Step 3: Determine Total Costs to Account For	Transferred-in	Direct Materials	Conversion Costs	Total
Work-in-process, November 1	$100	$ 80	$ 52	$ 232
Current costs	800	720	861	2,381
Total costs to account for	$900	$800	$913	$2,613
Step 4: Compute Unit Costs	($900/90) =	($800/90) =	($913/86) =	
Cost per unit	$10.00	$8.89	$10.62	$29.51

Cost Assignment

Step 5: Assign Total Manufacturing Costs	Completed and Transferred out	Ending Work-in-Process	Total
Units completed and transferred out (82 × $29.51)	$2,420		$2,420
Ending work-in-process (8)			
Transferred-in (8 × $10)		$80	80
Materials (8 × $8.89)		71	71
Conversion (4 × $10.62)		42	42
Total costs accounted for	$2,420	$193	$2,613

2. FIFO method

REED COMPANY
Finishing Department
FIFO Production Cost Report

Production Quantity Information

	Step 1: Analyze Flow of Physical Units		Step 2: Calculate Equivalent Units	
	Physical Units	Transferred-in	Direct Materials	Conversion Costs
Input				
Work-in-process, November 1	10 (40%)			
Started this month	80			
Total units to account for	90			
Output				
Completed	82	82	82	82
Work-in-process, November 30	8 (50%)	8	8	4
Total accounted for	90			
Total work done to date		90	90	86
Work-in-process, November 1		(10)	(10)	(4)
Total work done this month— FIFO equivalent units		80	80	82

Unit Cost Determination

Step 3: Determine Total Costs to Account For	Transferred-in	Direct Materials	Conversion Costs	Total
Work-in-process, November 1				$ 232
Current costs	$800	$720	$861	2,381
Total costs to account for				$2,613
Step 4: Compute Unit Costs	($800/80) =	($720/80) =	($861/82) =	
Cost per unit	$10.00	$9.00	$10.50	$29.50

(Continued)

Cost Assignment			
Step 5: Assign Total Manufacturing Costs	**Completed and Transferred out**	**Ending Work-in-Process**	**Total**
Units completed and transferred out (82)			
Beginning work-in-process	$232		$232
Current cost to complete			
conversion (6 × $10.50)	63		63
Total from beginning work-in-process	$295		$295
Units started & finished (72 × $ 29.50)	2,124		2,124
Total cost completed and transferred out	$2,419		$2,419
Ending work-in-process (8)			
Transferred-in (8 × $10)		$ 80	80
Materials (8 × $9)		72	72
Conversion (4 × 10.50)	–	42	42
Total costs accounted for	$2,419	$194	$2,613

CHAPTER SEVEN

Cost Allocation:
Departments, Joint Products, and By-Products

After studying the chapter, you should be able to . . .

1. Identify the strategic role of cost allocation

2. Explain the ethical issue of cost allocation

3. Use the three steps of departmental cost allocation

4. Explain the problems in implementing the different departmental cost allocation methods

5. Explain the use of cost allocation in service firms

6. Use the three joint product costing methods

7. Use the four by-product costing methods

In keeping with their firms' mission of continual improvement in their products and services, General Electric (GE) and many other firms such as Ford Motor Company, Johnson & Johnson, IBM, and Marriott have sought improved methods of providing administrative services within their firms. These administrative services are often called *shared services* because they are shared among the company's operating units. Shared services generally include such transaction-processing services as payroll processing, claims processing, human resources, and many accounting services, among others. The firms above have studied the cost to provide the services and have been alarmed at the relatively high costs, such as $10 or more to process a single vendor invoice. Some firms have chosen to outsource these services or to have the operating units provide the services locally, but, like GE, most firms are centralizing these services to reduce cost, provide a high and standardized level of service quality, and provide a single base of technology for easy use, communication, and future modification.

With the growth of these centralized services, the need for effective methods to allocate the shared costs to the operating units has increased. Generally, the allocation issue arises when cost is shared because of a shared facility, program, production process, or service. The methods used to allocate these common costs to products are explained in this chapter.

This chapter explains methods for allocating common costs to products for two broad types of common costs: (1) the costs of production and service departments shared by two or more individual products and (2) the joint manufacturing costs for products that are not separately identifiable until later in the manufacturing process. An example of the latter is the cost of refining crude oil (the joint cost) into the individual products: gasoline, heating oil, and other products.

We take a strategic perspective in developing these allocation methods and ask key strategic questions. How do the allocation methods we have chosen affect the motivations and behaviors of those in the operating units as well as the service units? Can we use ABC costing principles to develop more accurate methods of cost allocation? Does this service add value or should it be outsourced? The firm's answers to these questions can have a significant impact on its competitiveness and success.

The Strategic Role of Cost Allocation

The strategic role of cost allocation has four objectives:

1. Determine *accurate departmental and product costs* as a basis for the evaluation of the cost efficiency of departments and the profitability of different products, for financial reporting, and for tax compliance.
2. *Motivate* managers to exert a high level of effort to achieve the goals of top management.
3. Provide the right *incentive* for managers to make decisions that are consistent with the goals of top management.
4. *Fairly determine the rewards* earned by the managers for their effort and skill and for the effectiveness of their decision making.

LEARNING OBJECTIVE 1

Identify the strategic role of cost allocation.

The first and most important objective requires the cost allocation method to be sufficiently accurate to support effective management decision making about products and departments. The cost allocation methods must also comply with the financial reporting standards of FASB (and ultimately, the International Financial Reporting Standards of the International Accounting Standards Board, as the SEC moves to convergence of U.S. and international standards) and of the Internal Revenue Service. The management accountant recognizes that the desired cost allocation method might differ for the three objectives: cost management, financial reporting, and tax compliance.

The second objective, motivating managers, means that, to be effective, the cost allocation must reward department managers for reducing costs as desired. A key motivation issue is whether the manager *controls* the allocated cost. For example, when a department's cost allocation for equipment maintenance is based on the number of the department's machine breakdowns, the manager has an incentive to reduce them and therefore reduce the maintenance costs. On the other hand, when the cost of maintenance is allocated on the basis of a department's square feet of floor space, the manager—who cannot affect the amount of floor space—is not motivated.

The third objective, providing the incentive for decision making, is achieved when cost allocation effectively provides the incentives for the individual manager to act autonomously in a manner that is consistent with top management's goals. For example, a major advantage of cost allocation methods is that they draw managers' attention to shared facilities. The cost allocation provides an incentive for individual and joint efforts to manage these costs and to encourage the managers to use these facilities to improve the performance of their units.

The fourth objective, fairness, is met when the cost allocation is clear, objective, and consistently applied. The most objective basis for cost allocation exists when a *cause-and-effect relationship* can be determined. For example, the allocation of maintenance costs on the basis of the number of equipment breakdowns is more objective and fair than an allocation based on square feet, the number of products produced, or labor costs in the department. The reason is that a cause-and-effect relationship exists between maintenance costs and the number of breakdowns; square feet or labor costs, however, do not have a clear relationship to maintenance costs.

In some situations, cause-and-effect bases are not available and alternative concepts of fairness are used. One such concept is *ability-to-bear,* which is commonly employed with bases related to size, such as total sales, total assets, or the profitability of the user departments. Other concepts of fairness are based on equity perceived in the circumstance, such as *benefit received,* which often is measured in a nonquantitative way. For example, the cost of a firm's computer services might be allocated largely or entirely to the research and development department because the computer is more critical to this department's functioning and this department uses it more than other departments.

The Ethical Issues of Cost Allocation

LEARNING OBJECTIVE 2

Explain the ethical issues of cost allocation.

A number of ethical issues are important in cost allocation. First, ethical issues arise when costs are allocated to products or services that are produced for both a competitive market and a public agency or government department. Although government agencies very often purchase on a cost-plus basis, products sold competitively are subject to price competition. The incentive in these situations is for the manufacturer, using cost allocation methods, to shift manufacturing costs from the competitive products to the cost-plus products.

A second ethical issue in implementing cost allocation methods is the equity or fair share issue that arises when a governmental unit reimburses the costs of a private institution or when it provides a service for a fee to the public. In both cases, cost allocation methods are used to determine the proper price or reimbursement amount. Although no single measure of equity exists in these cases, the objectives of cost allocation identified at the beginning of the chapter are a useful guide.

A third important ethical issue is the effect of the chosen allocation method on the costs of products sold to or from foreign subsidiaries. The cost allocation method usually affects the cost of products traded internationally and therefore the amount of taxes paid in the domestic and the foreign countries. Firms can reduce their worldwide tax liability by increasing the costs of products purchased in high-tax countries or in countries where the firm does not have favorable tax treatment. For this reason, international tax authorities closely watch the cost allocation methods used by multinational firms. The methods most acceptable to these authorities are based on sales and/or labor costs.[1]

Cost Allocation to Service and Production Departments

LEARNING OBJECTIVE 3

Use the three steps of departmental cost allocation.

The preceding chapters on job costing (Chapter 4), activity-based costing (Chapter 5), and process costing (Chapter 6) provide a useful context for introducing cost allocation. Chapter 4 illustrated how overhead costs could be allocated to products in a single step, using a single overhead pool and single overhead rate in what we called the volume-based approach. Chapter 4 then showed an enhancement of the volume-based approach in which overhead was allocated to products in two steps, first to departments and then to products, in what we called the departmental approach. The departmental approach is an improvement over the single-step volume-based approach because it takes into account differences in costs incurred in the different departments and differences in consumption of the departments' resources by the products, thus leading to more accurate product costs.

The activity-based approach, explained in Chapter 5, follows a two-step approach like the departmental approach, with the difference that it assigns costs at a much more detailed level—that of the operating activity rather than the department. Because of the greater level of detail, the activity-based approach captures more accurately the usage of resources by the different

[1] For example, Glaxo SmithKline, a pharmaceutical company, settled a transfer-pricing dispute with the IRS for $5.2 billion. The dispute involved intercompany transactions and related transfer prices for the period 1989–2000. Also, Joanna Faith, "Transfer Pricing Helps Tax Avoidance, Says GAO Study," *International Tax Review,* September 2008; "Comparison of Tax Liabilities of Foreign- and U.S-Controlled Corporations, 1998–2005," United States Government Accountability Office (GAO), July 2008, at: www.gao.gov/products/GAO-08-957.

EXHIBIT 7.1

Three Types of Overhead Allocation

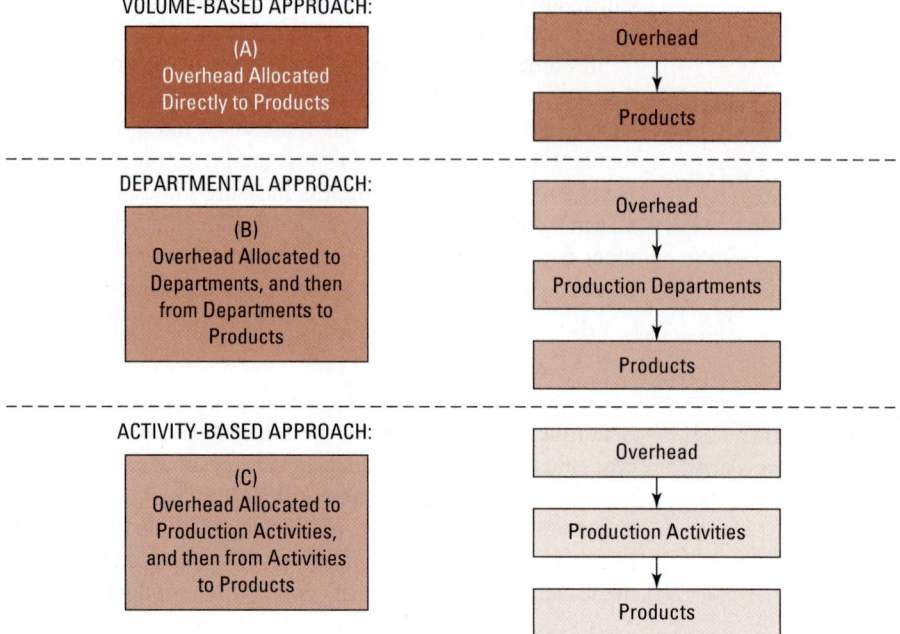

products, and therefore provides more accurate product costs. Because of the increased accuracy, the activity-based approach is generally preferred.[2] However, the activity-based approach is not preferred in all situations, such as those in which the company has homogeneous products and processes. Then the departmental approach is preferred because it is simpler, less costly, and produces results comparable to the activity-based approach. Also, there are some organizations that are required by law or regulation to use the departmental approach for cost reporting and cost reimbursement; a health care provider affected by the U.S. Medicare law is one such example.

The departmental approach recognizes that the typical manufacturing operation involves two types of manufacturing departments: production departments and service departments. Service departments provide human resources, maintenance, engineering, and other support to the production departments; production departments directly assemble and complete the product. The departmental approach has three phases: (1) trace all direct manufacturing costs and allocate manufacturing overhead costs to both the service departments and the production departments, (2) allocate the service department costs to the production departments, and finally (3) allocate the production department costs to the products.

Direct manufacturing costs are wages and materials that can be directly traced to a department; for example, direct materials and direct labor costs would be traced to the production departments where they are used. Direct labor and materials used in a service department would be traced to that service department. Indirect costs (manufacturing overhead) are the indirect materials and indirect labor costs that are allocated by means of a predetermined cost driver to the departments that use those resources. For example, the indirect labor cost of the plant supervisor who oversees all production and support departments would be allocated to all departments, while the indirect labor for inspection of the output of the two production departments would be allocated only to those two production departments.

The cost drivers commonly used include labor-hours, machine-hours, headcount (number of personnel in the department), and square feet of space in the department, among others. For example, the cost of the plant supervisor might be allocated to all departments based on the proportion of total labor-hours in the departments. The cost of the inspection in the production departments might be allocated based on the number of units of output in those two departments. In practice, a variety of cost drivers are used; the goal is to use a cost driver such that the cost allocation reflects the usage of the resource in the departments.

The three phases are illustrated in Exhibit 7.2.

[2] For a survey of the use of activity-based costing in the allocation of shared facility costs, see Ann Triplett and Jon Scheumann, "Managing Shared Services with ABM," *Strategic Finance*, February 2000, pp. 40–45.

EXHIBIT 7.2   **The Three Phases in Departmental Cost Allocation**

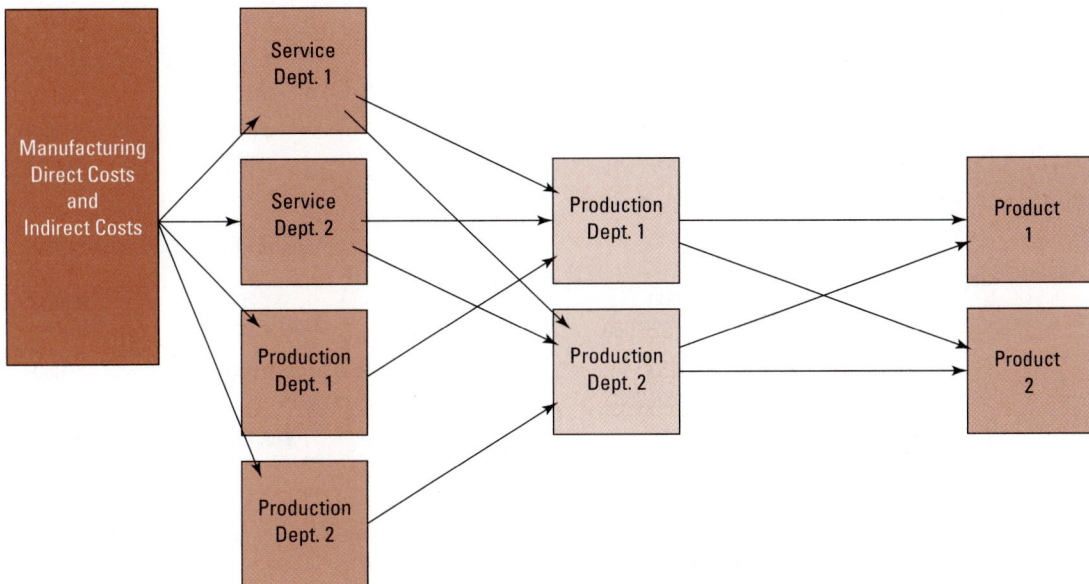

| FIRST PHASE: | SECOND PHASE: | THIRD PHASE: |
| Trace Direct Costs, and Allocate Indirect Costs to All Departments | Allocate Service Dept. Costs to Production Departments | Allocate Production Department Costs to Products |

First Phase: Trace Direct Costs and Allocate Indirect Costs to Departments

The first phase in the departmental allocation approach traces the direct costs and allocates the indirect manufacturing costs in the plant to each service and production department.

For the first-phase allocation, see the information for Beary Company in Exhibit 7.3. Beary manufactures two products and has two manufacturing departments and two service departments. $36,000 direct cost can be traced to each department, and an indirect cost of $30,000 ($25,000 labor and $5,000 materials) is common to all departments but cannot be traced directly to the departments. Beary uses labor-hours for allocating indirect labor cost and machine-hours for allocating indirect materials cost.

The first-phase allocation for Beary Company is shown in Exhibit 7.4. Total direct costs of $36,000 are traced to the four departments, and the overhead costs are allocated using labor-hours (for indirect labor) and machine-hours (for indirect materials). The exhibit presents the allocation base for labor-hour and machine-hour usage as a percent of total usage. The $25,000 of indirect labor is allocated to the four departments using the labor-hours allocation base. For example, the amount of indirect labor allocated to service department 1 is $3,750 (service department 1's share of total indirect labor, or 15% × $25,000). The allocations of indirect labor costs to the other departments are made in the same way. Similarly, the $5,000 of indirect materials cost is allocated to the four departments using machine-hours. The amount of indirect materials allocated to service

EXHIBIT 7.3

Data for Beary Company

	Service Department 1	Service Department 2	Production Department 1	Production Department 2	Total Hours	Total Amount
Labor-hours	1,800	1,200	3,600	5,400	12,000	
Machine-hours	320	160	1,120	1,600	3,200	
Direct costs	$1,600	$5,500	$15,500	$13,400		$36,000
Indirect labor		Not traceable				25,000
Indirect materials		Not traceable				5,000
						$66,000

EXHIBIT 7.4 **Departmental Allocation, First Phase: Beary Company**

Departmental Allocation Bases	All Departments				
	Service Department 1	Service Department 2	Production Department 1	Production Department 2	Total
Direct labor-hours	1,800	1,200	3,600	5,400	12,000
Percent	15%	10%	30%	45%	100%
Machine-hours	320	160	1,120	1,600	3,200
Percent	10%	5%	35%	50%	100%
First Phase: Trace Direct Costs and Allocate Indirect Costs to all Departments					
Direct costs	$1,600	$5,500	$15,500	$13,400	$36,000
Allocate indirect costs to departments:					
Indirect labor	3,750	2,500	7,500	11,250	25,000
	= 15% × $25,000	= 10% × $25,000	= 30% × $25,000	= 45% × $25,000	
Indirect materials	500	250	1,750	2,500	5,000
	= 10% × $5,000	= 5% × $5,000	= 35% × $5,000	= 50% × $5,000	
Totals for all departments	**$5,850**	**$8,250**	**$24,750**	**$27,150**	**$66,000**

department 1 is $500 (10% × $5,000). The totals for direct costs and allocated indirect costs are $66,000, the same as total cost from Exhibit 7.3.

Service department 1	$ 5,850
Service department 2	8,250
Production department 1	24,750
Production department 2	27,150
Total	$66,000

Allocation Phases Two and Three

The second phase allocates service department costs to the producing departments. This is the most complex of the allocation phases because services can flow back and forth between the service departments. These are often called **reciprocal flows.** For example, assume that 40 percent (720 hours) of service department 1's 1,800 labor-hours are spent serving service department 2. Also assume that 10 percent of service department 2's time is spent serving service department 1. You can see these two reciprocal flows for Beary Company in Exhibit 7.5.

The percentage of service relationships is commonly determined by reference to labor-hours, units processed, or some other allocation base that best reflects the service provided in the departments. At Beary Company, the service flow percentages for each service department are determined according to the labor-hours used for services provided to the other service department and to the production departments. Beary's first service department spends 40 percent of its labor time serving the service department 2 and 30 percent serving each of the two production departments. Service department 2 serves service department 1 10 percent of the time, the first production department 30 percent of the time, and the second production department 60 percent of the time.

Accountants use three common methods to allocate costs for the second phase: (1) the direct method, (2) the step method, and (3) the reciprocal method.

Reciprocal flows represent the flow of services back and forth between service departments.

EXHIBIT 7.5
Reciprocal Relationships in Beary Company

From:	To			
	Service Department 1	Service Department 2	Production Department 1	Production Department 2
Service Department 1	—	40%	30%	30%
Service Department 2	10%	—	30	60

The Direct Method

The **direct method**
of departmental cost allocation
is accomplished by using the
service flows *only to production
departments* and determining
each production department's
share of that service.

The **direct method** of departmental cost allocation is the simplest of the three methods because it ignores the reciprocal flows. The cost allocation is accomplished by using the service flows *only to production departments* and determining each production department's share of that service. For example, for service department 1, the share of time for each production department is 50 percent of the total production department service, determined as follows.

For service department 1:

> Net service to both production departments from service department 1:
>   =100% − Time of service to second service department
>   =100% − 40% = 60%
>   Production department 1's share: 30 percent/60 percent = <u>50 percent</u>
>   Production department 2's share: 30 percent/60 percent = <u>50 percent</u>

For service department 2:

> Net service to both production departments from service department 2:
>   100 percent − 10 percent = 90 percent
>   Production department 1's share: 30 percent/90 percent = <u>33.33%</u>
>   Production department 2's share: 60 percent/90 percent = <u>66.67%</u>

These percentage shares are used to allocate the costs from service departments to production departments, as shown in the second-phase section at the top of Exhibit 7.6. In that panel,

EXHIBIT 7.6   **Departmental Allocation Second and Third Phases, Using the Direct Method: Beary Company**

Second Phase: Allocate Service Department Costs to Production Departments

Direct Method		Production 1 Department	Production 2 Department	Total
Service Department 1	Service % to producing dept.	30%	30%	
	Allocation % per direct method	50% = 30/(30 + 30)	50% = 30/(30 + 30)	
	Allocation amount	**$2,925**	**$2,925**	**$5,850**
		= 50% × $5,850	= 50% × $5,850	
Service Department 2	Service % to producing dept.	30%	60%	
	Allocation % per direct method	33.33% = 30/(30 + 60)	66.67% = 60/(30 + 60)	
	Allocation amount	**2,750**	**5,500**	**8,250**
		= 33.33% × $8,250	= 66.67% × $8,250	
Plus: First-phase allocation		24,750	27,150	51,900
Totals for Production Departments		**$30,425**	**$35,575**	**$66,000**

Third Phase: Allocate Production Department Costs to Products

1. Allocation Base	Product 1	Product 2	
Base: labor-hours			
Hours	1,800	1,800	3,600
Percent	50%	50%	
Machine-hours			
Hours	400	1,200	1,600
Percent	25%	75%	

2. Cost Allocation to Products	Product 1	Product 2	
Production Department 1 (labor-hour basis)	**$15,212.50**	**$15,212.50**	
	= 50% × $30,425	= 50% × $30,425	
Production Department 2 (machine-hour basis)	**$8,893.75**	**$26,681.25**	
	= 25% × $35,575	= 75% × $35,575	
Totals for each product	**$24,106.25**	**$41,893.75**	**$66,000**

COST ALLOCATION AND MEDICARE REIMBURSEMENT IN HOSPITALS

A recent study of 105 hospitals found evidence of bias in their cost allocation practices. Since 1983, Medicare has reimbursed hospitals for inpatient services on the basis of specific, prospective rates and for outpatient services on the basis of cost. This reimbursement plan motivates hospitals to allocate as much common cost as possible to outpatient departments instead of inpatient services. The study examined the ratio of cost allocated to outpatient departments relative to total allocated cost for the period 1977 to 1991. Using regression analysis and data for each hospital, the study found a significant upward shift in costs allocated to outpatient departments after 1983.

DETERMINING THE COST OF HEALTH CARE PROCEDURES

A recent report by Cooper and Kramer shows that a common method used by providers of health care (hospitals, nursing homes, etc.) to calculate the cost of procedures (electrocardiogram, echocardiogram, cardiovascular stress test, etc.) based on revenue is equivalent to a method that produces equal profit margin for each procedure and each provider. The method is hailed as a useful way to determine cost information for making decisions, while it is simply a variation on the simple revenue-based methods once more commonly used, and thus does not actually provide the accurate cost information needed for decision making. ABC costing is one method that would provide more accurate cost information, but a recent study found that the rate of adoption of ABC in the health care industry has fallen from 16 percent in 1994 to 14 percent in 2004, and the rate of adoption in hospitals has fallen from 21 percent to 8 percent in the same period.

Based on information in: Leslie Eldenburg and Sanjay Kallapur, "Changes in Hospital Service Mix and Cost Allocations in Response to Changes in Medicare Reimbursement Schemes," *Journal of Accounting and Economics,* May 1997, pp. 31–51; Leslie Eldenburg and Sanjay Kallapur, "The Effect of Changes in Cost Allocation on the Assessment of Cost Containment Regulation in Hospitals," *Journal of Accounting & Public Policy,* Spring 2000, pp. 91–112; Robin Cooper and Theresa R. Kramer, "RBRVS Costing: The Inaccurate Wolf in Expensive Sheep's Clothing," *Journal of Health Care Finance,* Spring 2008, pp. 6–18; Robert M. Dowless, "What's the Procedure? Your Guide to Costing Methods and Terminology," *Nursing Management,* April 2007, pp. 52–56.

for example, $5,850 of service department 1's costs are allocated equally to the production departments; 50 percent each is $2,925. The $8,250 service department 2's costs are allocated 33.33 percent or $2,750 to production department 1 and 66.67 percent or $5,500 to production department 2. Total costs in production departments 1 and 2 at the end of the second phase allocations are $30,425 and $35,575, respectively.

The third and final phase is much like the first phase. The allocation from production departments to products typically is based on the number of labor-hours or machine-hours used in the production departments that produce the products. For Beary Company, using the direct method, costs are allocated to production department 1 on the basis of labor-hours and to production department 2 on the basis of machine-hours; see the third-phase panel of Exhibit 7.6. Assume that the production of product 1 required 1,800 hours of production department 1's total labor time of 3,600 hours, and thus is allocated 50 percent (1,800/3,600) of the total cost in production department 1. Similarly, assume that product 1 required 400 of the 1,600 machine-hours used in production department 2, and it is allocated 25 percent (400/1,600) of the costs of production department 2. Product 2's costs are determined in a similar manner, as shown in Exhibit 7.6. The total cost of $66,000 is allocated as $24,106.25 to product 1 and $41,893.75 to product 2.

The Step Method

The **step method**
uses a sequence of steps in the allocating service department costs to production departments.

The second method to allocate service department costs is the **step method,** so-called because it uses a sequence of steps in allocating service department costs to production departments. In the first step, one service department is selected to be allocated fully, that is, to the other service department as well as to each production department. The department to be allocated fully usually is chosen because it provides the most service to other service departments. At Beary Company, service department 1 provides more service (40%) and it goes first in the allocation. Service department 2 is allocated only to the production departments, in the same manner as the direct method. Overall, this means that the step method may provide more accurate allocations because one of the reciprocal flows between the two service departments (the one in the first step) is considered in the allocation, unlike the direct method that ignores all reciprocal flows.

The first phase of the step method (tracing direct costs and initial allocation of indirect costs) is the same as for the direct method as shown in Exhibit 7.4. However, in the second

EXHIBIT 7.7   Departmental Allocation, Second and Third Phases, Using the Step Method

Second Phase: Allocate Service Department Costs to Production Departments: Using the Step Method

	Service Department 2	Production Department 1	Production Department 2	Total
First Step				
Service Department 1				
Service percent	40%	30%	30%	
Amount	$2,340	$1,755	$1,755	$5,850
	= 40% × $5,850	= 30% × $5,850	= 30% × $5,850	
Second Step				
Service Department 2				
Service percent		30%	60%	
Allocation percent per direct method		33.33	66.67	
Amount	10,590	3,530	7,060	8250
	= $8,250 + $2,340	= 33.33% × $10,590	= 66.67% × $10,590	(= 3,530 + 7,060 − 2,340)
Plus: First-phase allocation		24,750	27,150	51,900
Totals for production departments		$30,035	$35,965	$66,000

Third Phase: Allocate Production Department Costs to Products

1. Allocation Base	Product 1	Product 2	
Labor-hours			
Hours	1,800	1,800	3,600
Percentage	50%	50%	
Machine-hours			
Hours	400	1,200	1,600
Percentage	25%	75%	
2. Cost Allocation to Products			
Production Department 1 (labor-hour basis)	$15,017.50	$15,017.50	
	= 50% × $30,035	= 50% × $30,035	
Production Department 2 (machine-hour basis)	$8,991.25	$26,973.75	
	= 25% × $35,965	= 75% × $35,965	
Totals for each product	$ 24,008.75	$41,991.25	$66,000

phase (Exhibit 7.7), service department 1, which is in the first step, is allocated to service department 2 and the two production departments. The allocation to service department 2 is $2,340 (40 percent × $5,850). The allocations for the two production departments are determined in a similar manner. Then, in the second step, service department 2 is allocated to the two production departments using the direct method in the same manner as in Exhibit 7.6. The only difference is that the total cost in service department 2 ($10,590) now includes the original cost in service department 2 ($8,250) plus the cost allocated from service department 1 in the first step ($2,340).

The third phase of the step method is completed in the same manner as in Exhibit 7.6. Using the step method, the total cost allocated to product 1 is $24,008.75 and the total cost allocated to product 2 is $41,991.25, for a total of $66,000.

The Reciprocal Method

The **reciprocal method**
considers *all* reciprocal flows
between service departments
through simultaneous equations.

The **reciprocal method** is the preferred of the three methods because, unlike the others, it considers *all* reciprocal flows between the service departments. This is accomplished by using simultaneous equations; the reciprocal flows are simultaneously determined in a system of equations.

An equation for each service department represents the cost to be allocated, consisting of the first-phase allocation costs plus the cost allocated from the other department. For Beary Company, the equation for service department 1 is as follows, using the symbol

Since the advent of Medicare in 1966 to cover medical expenses of aged, blind, and disabled individuals, health care providers have been required to use cost allocation methods to receive reimbursement from the federal government for services covered by Medicare. The costs of health care service activities are allocated to the patient revenue-generating services. Some examples of service activities and patient revenue-generating services in a hospital follow.

How do hospitals respond to Medicare requirements and allocate the costs of service activities to the patient revenue-generating services? What methods are likely to be preferred?

(Refer to Comments on Cost Management in Action at end of Chapter.)

Patient Revenue-Generating Services

Intensive care unit	Laboratory
Psychiatric care	Radiology
Coronary care	Emergency Room
Surgery	Pharmacy
Anesthesia	

Service Activities

Dietary	Operation of hospital
Laundry and linen	
Admissions	Administrative and general
Social services	Housekeeping
Nursing administration	

S1 to represent service department 1 costs and the symbol S2 to represent costs in service department 2.

Allocated S1 Costs = Initial allocation + Cost allocated from S2

$$S1 = \$5,850 + (10\% \times S2)$$

Similarly, the equation for the second service department is as follows:

Allocated S2 Costs = Initial allocation + Cost allocated from S1

$$S2 = \$8,250 + (40\% \times S1)$$

These two equations can be solved for S1 and S2 by substituting the second equation into the first as follows:

$$S1 = \$5,850 + [10\% \times (\$8,250 + 40\% \times S1)]$$
$$S1 = \$6,953.13$$

And substituting S1 back into the second equation:

$$S2 = \$11,031.25$$

These values for S1 and S2 are allocated to the producing departments using the percentage service amounts for each department. We illustrate the process for Beary Company in Exhibit 7.8. Note that since the reciprocal method has considered all reciprocal service department activities, the allocation in the second phase is based on the actual service percentages for each production department. For example, production department 1, which receives 30 percent of service department 1's work, is allocated 30 percent of service department 1's cost, $2,086 (30% × $6,953.13). The allocations are made in a similar manner to the allocation of service department 2's costs and to production department 2.

A simple and accurate way to calculate the reciprocal costs for S1 and S2 is to use the Solver function in Excel. Exhibit 7.9 illustrates how to use Solver for this purpose.

The third phase analysis in Exhibit 7.8 is done in the same manner as in Exhibits 7.6 and 7.7. The total cost allocated to product 1 is $24,036.25 and for product 2, $41,963.75.

Implementation Issues

LEARNING OBJECTIVE 4

Explain the problems in implementing the different departmental cost allocation methods.

The key implementation issue is the choice of the most accurate allocation method. Briefly review Exhibits 7.6, 7.7, and 7.8. Note that although total costs are the same ($66,000), the amounts allocated to the two products vary. Although these amounts do not vary greatly for Beary Company, wide variations can occur in practice. When significant differences exist, a management accountant should consider the value of the reciprocal method, which is more complete and accurate than the others because it fully considers the reciprocal flows between service departments.

EXHIBIT 7.8   **Departmental Allocation Second and Third Phases, Using the Reciprocal Method**

Second Phase: Allocate Service Department Costs to Production Departments Using the Reciprocal Method

First: Solve the simultaneous equations for Service 1 and Service 2 (see text):

Amount allocated from service 1	$ 6,953.13		
Amount allocated from service 2	$11,031.25		

	Production Department 1	Production Department 2	Total
Second: Allocate to producing departments			
Service Department 1			
Service %	30%	30%	
Allocated amount	$2,086	$2,086	**$4,172**
	= 30% × $6,953	= 30% × $6,953	
Service Department 2			
Service %	30%	60%	
Allocated amount	3,309	6,619	9,928
	= 30% × $11,031	= 60% × $11,031	
Plus: Costs allocated in first phase	24,750	27,150	51,900
Totals for Production Departments	**$30,145**	**$35,855**	**$66,000**

Third Phase: Allocate Production Department Costs to Products

1. Allocation Base	Product 1	Product 2	
Base: Direct labor-hours			
Hours	1,800	1,800	3,600
Percent	50%	50%	
Machine-hours			
Hours	400	1,200	1,600
Percent	25%	75%	

2. Cost Allocation to Products			
Production Department 1 (direct labor-hour basis)	$15,072.50	$15,072.50	
	= 50% × $30,145	= 50% × $30,145	
Production Department 2 (machine-hour basis)	$8,963.75	$26,891.25	
	= 25% × $35,855	= 75% × $35,855	
Totals for each product	$24,036.25	$41,963.75	$66,000

Three additional issues to consider when implementing the departmental allocation approach are (1) disincentive effects when the allocation base is unrelated to usage, (2) disincentive effects when the allocation base is actual usage, and (3) disincentive effects when allocated costs exceed external purchase cost.

Disincentive Effects When the Allocation Base Is Unrelated to Usage

Determining an appropriate allocation base and a percentage amount for service provided by the service departments is often difficult. For example, using labor-hours could be inappropriate in an automated plant where labor is a small part of total cost. Similarly, square feet of floor space could be inappropriate to allocate certain costs when a great deal of idle space exists. Furthermore, the use of square feet of floor space can have undesirable motivational consequences. For example, if we are allocating plantwide maintenance costs to production departments using floor space as a base, a department has inadequate incentive to limit its use of maintenance expense. Since the actual use of maintenance is unrelated to floor space, if a given department increases its use of maintenance, then the other departments pay for the increase as well, as illustrated in Exhibit 7.10. Here, department A increases its use of maintenance from 50 to 80 maintenance requests (panel 3 in Exhibit 7.10), while department B's usage stays the same. The effect of department A's increased usage (when allocation is based on square feet) is that department B pays one-half of the increased cost ($60,000), which is likely to be perceived as unfair and therefore a disincentive for department B. In contrast, using the number of requests as a base allocates to department A the full cost of its increased usage of maintenance ($60,000), while department B's allocated cost remains the same.

Disincentive Effects When the Allocation Base Is Actual Usage

When the cost allocation base is determined from actual usage, disincentives can arise because the usage of the resource by one department will affect the cost allocation to other departments, as illustrated in Exhibit 7.11. We continue with the same example as Exhibit 7.10 except we now assume that the cost to be allocated is made up of $100,000 fixed cost and $1,000 variable cost per maintenance request. Panel 2 shows that the amount of cost allocated will be the same for both departments if the usage is the same. Panels 3 and 4 illustrate how the cost allocation changes if the usage of one of the departments changes. If the usage in

EXHIBIT 7.9   **Solving for the Reciprocal Allocation Method Using the Solver Function in Microsoft Excel**

Solving reciprocal departmental allocation problems can become tedious if three or more departments are involved. In this case, we suggest the use of software programs such as the Solver tool in Excel. The following screen capture illustrates how the Solver tool can be used to solve the Beary Company example in the text. The column for "Allocated Cost" in the spreadsheet contains the cost in each service department, while the columns for "Service Rates" contain the reciprocal service rates. The column for "Initial Allocation to" contains the product of the "Allocated Cost" and "Service Rates" columns, using cell-based formulas. Cells E7 and F7 contain the formula-based sums of these columns. After selecting "Solver" from the Data menu, the Dialog Box in Exhibit 7.9 panel A appears and must be completed as shown. For example, the Target Cell (E7) must be set to a value of $5,850 (the cost of the first service department). When the dialog box is complete, select Solve, and the solution will appear in cells B5 and B6 (overwriting the amounts originally entered in the Allocated Cost column). The solution is $6,953.13 in cell B5 and $11,031.25 in cell B6. The solution is shown in panel B.

Note: The parameters of the Solver solution must be set to "Value" as indicated in the marked circle in Panel A.

Panel A: Solver Dialog Box

(Continued)

EXHIBIT 7.9   **Concluded**

Panel B: Solver Solution for Beary Example

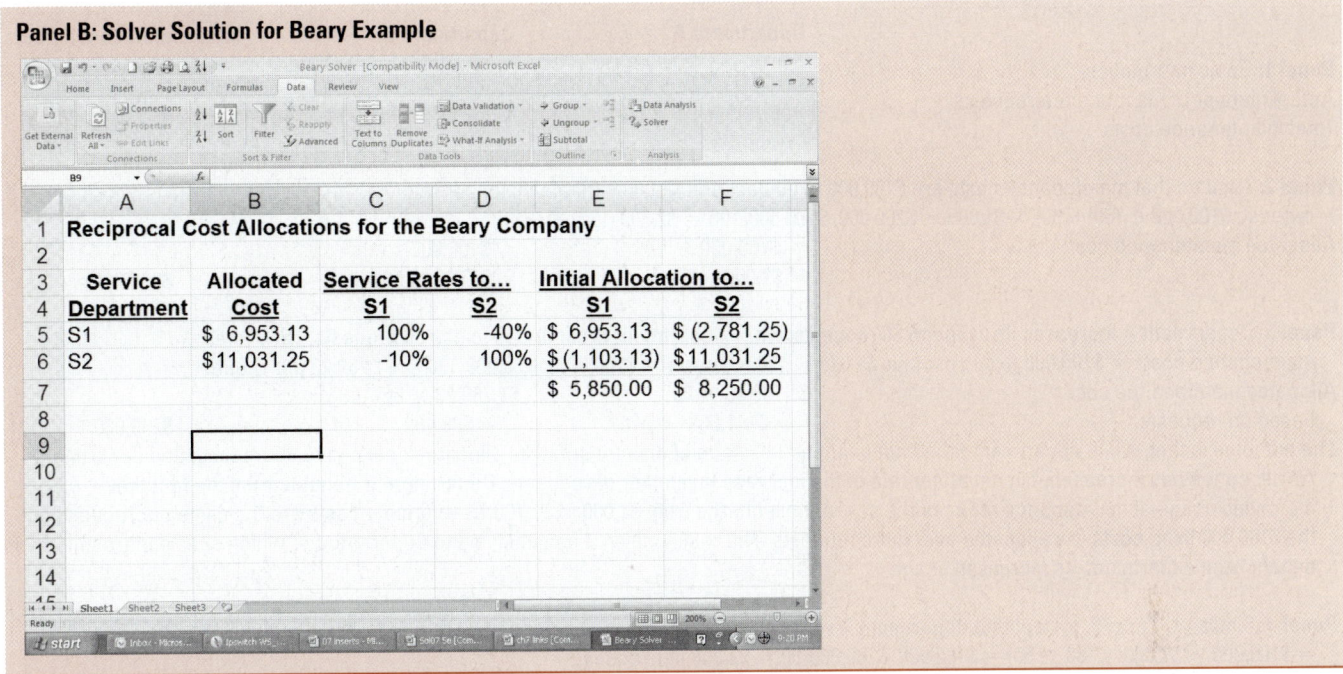

EXHIBIT 7.10   **Disincentive Effects When the Allocation Base is Unrelated to Usage**

	Department A	Department B	Total Maintenance Cost
Panel 1: Basic information			
Square feet of floor space	5,000	5,000	
Average number of maintenance requests	50	50	
Total maintenance costs			$200,000
Panel 2: Maintenance cost allocation in an average month using square feet of floor space or number of requests:			
Allocated maintenance cost	$100,000	$100,000	$200,000
Panel 3: Here we consider maintenance cost allocation based on square feet for a month when department A increases usage of maintenance from 50 to 80 maintenance requests, while department B's usage remains the same at 50 requests. For simplicity, assume that maintenance costs are variable with the number of maintenance requests, or $2,000 per request [$200,000/(50 + 50)], so that total maintenance costs increase to $260,000 [$2,000 × (50 + 80)]. The allocation based on square feet and number of requests is compared below:			
Number of maintenance requests	80	50	
Allocation of maintenance costs based on square feet	$130,000	$130,000	$260,000
Allocated maintenance cost based on number of maintenance requests	$2,000 × 80 = $160,000	$2,000 × 50 = $100,000	$260,000

department A increases (Panel 3) while department B's usage remains the same, then department B has an unexpected reduction in allocated cost from $100,000 to $88,462. The reason is that the fixed costs per maintenance request are now smaller due to the increase in total maintenance requests. Department A is unlikely to see this allocation as fair. In contrast, Panel 4 shows the outcome if department A reduces it usage of maintenance, while department B again maintains the same level of usage. Now department B's allocated cost increases from $100,000 to $112,500. The increase is due to the fact that fixed cost per maintenance request is now larger due to the overall reduction in maintenance requests. Now department B is unlikely to see that the allocation is fair.

EXHIBIT 7.11 **Disincentive Effects When the Allocation Base Is Actual Usage**

	Department A	Department B	Total Maintenance Cost
Panel 1: Basic information			
Actual number of maintenance requests	50	50	
Total maintenance costs			$200,000

Panel 2: Assume that maintenance costs are $100,000 fixed cost and $1,000 variable costs per request. The allocation base is $2,000 per request; $100,000 + (50 + 50) × $1,000 = $200,000; $200,000/100 = $2,000 per request

	Department A	Department B	Total Maintenance Cost
Allocated maintenance cost:	$100,000	$100,000	
	= $2,000 × 50	= $2,000 × 50	$200,000

Panel 3: Department A increases its usage to 80 requests, while department B continues to use 50 requests. New total maintenance costs = $100,000 fixed cost plus $1,000 × 130 requests = $230,000; $230,000/130 = $1,769.23 per request

	Department A	Department B	Total Maintenance Cost
Allocated maintenance cost	$1,769.23 × 80	$1,769.23 × 50	
based on requests:	= $141,538	= $88,462	$230,000

The outcome is that, while department B has not changed its usage of maintenance, its allocated costs have decreased; and department A's allocation has increased, but not at the rate of the increase in number of requests. Department B benefits from the fact that increased usage of maintenance reduces the per-request charge from $2,000 to $1,769.23—variable costs are the same per request, but the $100,000 fixed costs are allocated over more requests. The result may not be satisfying to department A, which sees department B benefit from department A's increased usage.

Panel 4: Similar to Panel 3, except that department A **reduces** its usage of maintenance to 30 requests. Now total maintenance costs = $100,000 + $1,000 × (30 + 50) = $180,000; $180,000/80 = $2,250 per request

	Department A	Department B	Total Maintenance Cost
Allocated maintenance costs	$2,250 × 30	$2,250 × 50	
based on requests:	= $67,500	= $112,500	$180,000

The outcome is that, while department B has not changed its usage of maintenance, its allocated costs have increased; and department A's allocation has decreased, but not at the rate of the decrease in number of requests. Department B suffers from the fact that decreased usage of maintenance increases the per-request charge from $2,000 to $2,250. While department B has not changed its usage, its cost increases because of department A's decreased usage.

Dual allocation
separates fixed and variable costs and traces variable costs to the departments based on actual usage; fixed costs are allocated based on either equal share among departments or a predetermined budgeted proportion.

Dual Allocation

The disincentives illustrated in Exhibit 7.11 can be resolved by using dual allocation. **Dual allocation** separates fixed and variable costs and traces variable costs to the departments based on actual usage; fixed costs are allocated based on either equal share among departments or a predetermined budgeted proportion. Exhibit 7.12 illustrates how dual allocation works. Again, Panels 1 and 2 follow the example from Exhibit 7.11. Panel 3 illustrates dual allocation in which fixed costs are equally shared among the departments. The reason for the equal-share approach is that each department pays in effect a fee for the right to receive future services from the maintenance department, irrespective of the amount of service to be used. This concept is similar to the minimum monthly charge on a checking account at the bank or a cell phone. Note that the effect of separating the fixed and variable costs is that department A pays for its increased usage, measured at variable cost, and department B's allocated cost does not change—a result that is likely to be satisfactory to both departments.

Panel 4 of Exhibit 7.12 illustrates the dual allocation method when fixed costs are allocated on the basis of a predetermined budget. This approach is used when usage differs significantly between departments; the rationale is that the allocation of fixed costs should reflect the long-term average usage by each department. In this example, we assume that the long-term rate of usage is 60 percent for department A and 40 percent for department B.

Disincentive Effects When Allocated Costs Exceed External Purchase Cost

Another limitation of the three departmental allocation methods is that in an uncommon circumstance they can allocate to a department a higher cost than the cost of the service that the department could purchase from an outside supplier. Should the department pay more for a service internally than an outside vendor would charge? To motivate managers to be efficient and to make the right decisions, the allocation should be based on the cost as if each department had to obtain the service outside the firm. Consider the data in Exhibit 7.13 for a firm with four departments that share a common data processing service costing $1,000.

EXHIBIT 7.12   Dual Allocation

	Department A	**Department B**	**Total Maintenance Cost**
Panel 1: Basic information			
Actual number of maintenance requests	50	50	
Total maintenance costs			$200,000

Panel 2: Assume that maintenance costs are mixed; $100,000 fixed and $1,000 variable per request. The allocation base is $2,000 per request; $100,000 + (50 + 50) × $1,000 = $200,000; $200,000/100 = $2,000

	Department A	**Department B**	**Total Maintenance Cost**
Allocated maintenance cost:	$100,000	$100,000	$200,000
	= $2,000 × 50	= $2,000 × 50	

Panel 3 (Dual Allocation; fixed costs shared equally): Department A increases its usage to 80 requests, while department B continues to use 50 requests. New total maintenance costs = $100,000 fixed cost plus $1,000 × 130 requests = $230,000.
This method allocates fixed costs equally between the departments and variable cost based on usage.

	Department A	**Department B**	**Total Maintenance Cost**
Allocated maintenance cost:	$50,000 + $1,000 × 80	$50,000 + $1,000 × 50	$230,000
	= $130,000	= $100,000	

The outcome is that department B's cost has not changed and department A's increase is in proportion to its increased usage. The result should be satisfying to both department A and department B.

Panel 4: (Dual Allocation; budget-based allocation of fixed costs) Assume, as in Panel 3 above, that department A increases its usage to 80 requests, while department B continues to use 50 requests. New total maintenance costs = $100,000 fixed cost plus $1,000 × 130 requests = $230,000. Budget-based allocation uses a predetermined budgeted amount of usage to allocate the fixed costs; in this example we use 60 requests for department A and 40 requests for department B. Thus, fixed costs are allocated $60,000 to department A and $40,000 to department B.

	Department A	**Department B**	**Total Maintenance Cost**
Budgeted number of maintenance requests	60	40	
Allocated maintenance cost:	$60,000 + $1,000 × 80	$40,000 + $1,000 × 50	$230,000
	= $140,000	= $90,000	

This outcome could be preferred to that of Panel 3 above, if the actual usage of the department fluctuates from period to period, but the long-term average usage by department A is 60% of the resources and for department B the long-term use is 40%.

Data processing costs are allocated using direct labor-hours in each department as shown in columns (B), (C), and (D) of Exhibit 7.13. The data processing service can also be obtained from an outside firm at the cost shown in column (E).

The direct labor-hours allocation base in this example penalizes department D, which can obtain the service outside the firm for $80 less than the inside cost ($200 − $120), perhaps because of the simplified nature of the requirements in department D. In contrast, department B can obtain the service outside only at a much higher price ($600 versus $400 inside), perhaps because of the specialized nature of the service. In this case, the allocation based on the *outside price* (column G in Exhibit 7.13) is fair to both departments B and D. It is a better reflection of the competitive cost of the service. The question of whether, and under what conditions, the department should be allowed to purchase outside the firm is a different issue, which is addressed in the coverage of management control in Chapters 18 and 19.

EXHIBIT 7.13   Cost Allocation Using External Prices

(A)	(B)	(C)	(D)	(E)	(F)	(G)
User Department	Direct Labor-Hours	Direct Labor-Hour Allocation Base	Cost Allocation Based on Labor-Hours	Outside Price	Allocation Base for Outside Price	Allocation Based on Outside Price
A	3,000	30% (3,000/10,000)	$ 300	$ 360	30% (360/1,200)	$ 300
B	4,000	40% (4,000/10,000)	400	600	50% (600/1,200)	500
C	1,000	10% (1,000/10,000)	100	120	10% (120/1,200)	100
D	2,000	20% (2,000/10,000)	200	120	10% (120/1,200)	100
Total	10,000		$1,000	$1,200		$1,000

Cost Allocation in Service Industries

LEARNING OBJECTIVE 5

Explain the use of cost allocation in service firms.

The concepts presented in this chapter apply equally well to manufacturing, service, or not-for-profit organizations that incur joint costs. For example, financial institutions such as commercial banks also use cost allocation. To illustrate, we use the Community General Bank (CGB), which provides a variety of banking services, including deposit accounts, mortgage loans, installment loans, investment services, and other services. Currently, CGB is analyzing the profitability of its mortgage loan unit, which has two main businesses, commercial construction loans and residential loans. An important part of the analysis of these loan businesses is determining how to trace or allocate costs to the two businesses.

The cost allocation begins by identifying which departments directly support the two loan businesses, the loan operations department and the marketing department. The *operations department* handles the processing of loan applications, safekeeping of appropriate documents, billing, and maintaining accounts for both commercial and residential loans. The *marketing department* provides direct advertising, promotions, and customer service for both types of loans. The operations and marketing departments in this illustration are comparable to the production departments in the Beary Company example used earlier in the chapter.

Other departments support the operations and marketing departments. Two important support departments are the administrative services department and the accounting department. The *administrative services department* provides legal and technical support. The *accounting department* provides financial services, including regular financial reports and the maintenance of customer records. The administrative services and accounting departments provide services to each other as well as to the operations and marketing departments, as illustrated in Exhibit 7.14. Each of the four departments has labor and certain supplies costs that can be traced directly to it. In addition, CGB's human resources department and computer services department provide services to all four departments. In this example, human resources and computer services are assumed to be part of the larger set of services that CGB provides to all of its business units; the mortgage loan unit being only one of these. Thus, human resources and computer services can be compared to the use of indirect labor and indirect materials in the Beary Company example earlier in the chapter; the accounting and administrative services departments provide service only to the loan unit and are comparable to the service departments used in the Beary Company example.

To summarize, the mortgage loan unit in CGB has two service departments (accounting and administrative services), two production departments (marketing and operations), and two products (commercial loans and residential loans). The indirect costs in the mortgage loan unit consist of $1,560,000 labor costs and $33,000 supplies cost which can be traced directly to the two service departments and the two production departments. In addition there are indirect costs of $80,000 human services cost and $66,000 computer service costs which must be allocated to the two service and two production departments.

CGB uses the step method to allocate costs from support departments to the loan businesses. See the step method in Exhibit 7.15, which follows the same approach as for Beary Company in Exhibit 7.7. The top of Exhibit 7.15 shows the allocation bases that CGB uses to allocate human resources costs and computer services costs to each department. The allocation base for human resources costs is the number of employees, or the head count, in each department, and the allocation of computer services costs is based on the number of computers in each department. The number of employees and the number of computers in each department are given.

EXHIBIT 7.14

Cost Flows in Community General Bank

	To			
From:	**Accounting Department**	**Administrative Service Department**	**Operations Department**	**Marketing Department**
Accounting Department (Service)	—	25%	35%	40%
Administrative Service Department (Service)	20%	—	40	40

The first phase of the allocation in Exhibit 7.15 shows tracing the totals of $1,560,000 of direct labor and $33,000 for supplies costs to each department as well as the allocation of the human resources costs ($80,000) and computer services costs ($66,000), using the allocation bases head count and number of computers, respectively. The result is that the total cost of $1,739,000 is allocated as follows:

Accounting department	$ 253,700
Administrative services department	381,500
Operations department	623,700
Marketing department	480,100
Total cost	$1,739,000

In the second phase, the accounting and administrative service department costs are allocated to the operations and marketing departments using the step method and the service percentages

EXHIBIT 7.15   **Cost Allocation at Community General Bank, Using the Step Method**

Departmental Allocation Bases	Accounting	Administrative Services	Operations	Marketing		Total
Human Resources						
Headcount	80	100	160	60		400
	20%	25%	40%	15%		100%
Computer Services						
Number of computers	60	60	150	30		300
	20%	20%	50%	10%		100%

First Phase: Trace Direct Costs and Allocate Overhead Costs to Departments

	Accounting	Administrative Services	Operations	Marketing	Total
Direct costs (given)					
Labor	$221,000	$339,500	$554,500	$445,000	$1,560,000
Supplies	3,500	8,800	4,200	16,500	33,000
Indirect costs					
Human Resources	16,000	20,000	32,000	12,000 (e.g., $12,000 = 15% × $80,000)	80,000
Computer Services	13,200	13,200	33,000	6,600 (e.g., $ 6,600 = 10% × $66,000)	66,000
Totals for all departments	$253,700	$381,500	$623,700	$480,100	$1,739,000

Second Phase: Allocate Service Department Costs to Operations and Marketing, Using the Step Method

		Accounting	Administrative Services	Operations	Marketing	Total
First step						
Accounting Department	Service percent		25%	35%	40%	
	Amount		$63,425	$88,795	$101,480 (e.g., $101,480 = 40% × $253,700)	
Second step						
Administrative services	Service percent			40%	40%	
	Allocation percent (per direct method)			50%	50%	
	Amount			$222,462.50	$222,462.50 [e.g., $222,462.50 = 50% × ($381,500 + $63,425)]	
Totals for production departments				$934,957.50	$804,042.50	$1,739,000

Third Phase: Allocate Operations and Marketing Costs to Commercial and Residential Loans

	Commercial Loans	Residential Loans	Total
Base: Number of banking transactions	15,000	10,000	25,000
Percent	60%	40%	
Number of loans	900	3,600	4,500
Percent	20%	80%	
Operations (Number of transactions)	$560,974.50	$ 373,983	
Marketing (Number of loans)	$160,808.50	$ 643,234	
Totals for commercial and residential loans	$ 721,783	$1,017,217	$1,739,000

EXHIBIT 7.16
Profitability Analysis of Commercial and Residential Loans for Community General Bank

	Commercial Loans	Residential Loans
Revenues	$2,755,455	$2,998,465
Less expenses		
Cost of funds	1,200,736	1,387,432
Allocated operating costs (Exhibit 7.15)	721,783	1,017,217
Contribution	$ 832,936	$ 593,816
Key ratios		
Contribution/revenue	30.23%	19.80%
Cost of funds/revenue	43.58%	46.27%

in Exhibit 7.14. The result is that the $1,739,000 of total cost is now allocated to the operations department ($934,957.50) and the marketing department ($804,042.50).

In the third and final phase, the costs from the operations and marketing departments are allocated to the two businesses, commercial and residential loans. The base that CGB uses to allocate operations department costs is the number of banking transactions handled within operations (15,000 for commercial loans and 10,000 for residential loans) and to allocate marketing costs is the number of loans of either type (900 commercial loans and 3,600 residential loans). The result of the final allocation is that the total cost of $1,739,000 is allocated to the commercial loans department ($721,783) and the residential loans department ($1,017,217), as illustrated for the third phase in Exhibit 7.15.

Cost allocation provides CGB a basis for evaluating the cost and profitability of its services. By taking the allocated operating costs just determined, the cost of funds provided, and the revenue produced by both commercial and residential loans, a profitability analysis of commercial and residential loans can be completed. Assume that the commercial and residential loan departments have revenues of $2,755,455 and $2,998,465, respectively, and direct cost of funds of $1,200,736 and $1,387,432, respectively.

The profitability analysis in Exhibit 7.16 shows that the relatively high allocated operating costs of the residential loan unit are an important factor in its overall poor performance (only 19.8 percent contribution per dollar of revenue in contrast to more than 30 percent for the commercial loan unit). In contrast, the cost of funds appears to be comparable for both types of loans (43.58 percent of revenues for commercial loans and 46.27 percent of revenues for residential loans). The analysis indicates that the bank should investigate the profitability of residential loans and, in particular, the cost of operations and marketing for these loans.

Joint Product Costing

LEARNING OBJECTIVE 6

Use the three joint product costing methods.

Joint products
are products from the same production process that have relatively substantial sales value.

By-products
are products whose total sales values are minor in comparison with the sales value of the joint products.

The split-off point
is the first point in a joint production process at which individual products can be identified.

Many manufacturing plants yield more than one product from a joint manufacturing process. For example, the petroleum industry processes crude oil into multiple products: gasoline, naphtha, kerosene, fuel oils, and residual heavy oils. Similarly, the semiconductor industry processes silicon wafers into a variety of computer memory chips with different speeds, temperature tolerances, and life expectancies. Beef and hides are products linked in the meatpacking process; neither of these items can be produced without producing the other. Other industries that yield joint products include lumber production, food processing, soap making, grain milling, dairy farming, and fishing.

Joint products and by-products are derived from processing a single input or a common set of inputs. **Joint products** are products from the same production process that have relatively substantial sales values. Products whose total sales values are minor in comparison to the sales value of the joint products are classified as **by-products.**

Joint products and by-products both start their manufacturing life as part of the same raw material. Until a certain point in the production process, no distinction can be made between the products. The point in a joint production process at which individual products can be identified for the first time is called the **split-off point.** Thereafter, separate production processes can be applied to the individual products. At the split-off point, joint products or by-products might be salable or require further processing to be salable, depending on their nature.

Joint costs include all manufacturing costs incurred prior to the split-off point (including direct materials, direct labor, and factory overhead). For financial reporting purposes, these costs are allocated among the joint products. Additional costs incurred after the split-off point that can be identified directly with individual products are called **additional processing costs** or **separable costs.**

Other outputs of joint production include scrap, waste, spoilage and defective units. Scrap is the residue from a production process that has little or no recovery value. Waste, such as chemical waste, is a residual material that has no recovery value and must be disposed of by the firm as required. In addition to waste and scrap, some products do not meet quality standards and can be reworked for resale. Spoiled units are not reworked for economic reasons. Defective units are reworked to become salable units.

Methods for Allocating Joint Costs to Joint Products

Joint costs are most frequently allocated to joint products using (1) the physical measure, (2) the sales value at split-off, and (3) the net realizable value methods.

The Physical Measure Method

The **physical measure method,** naturally enough, uses a physical measure such as pounds, gallons, yards, or units of volume produced at the split-off point to allocate the joint costs to joint products. The first step is to select the proper physical measure as the basis for allocation. We can use units of input or units of output. For example, if we are costing tuna products, the production of 100 pounds of tuna into quarter-pound cans would have an input measure of 100 pounds and an output measure of 400 cans. When units of output are used, this also is called the **average cost method.** Assume that Johnson Seafood produces tuna filets and canned tuna for distribution to restaurants and supermarkets in the southeastern United States. The cost of 14,000 pounds of raw, unprocessed tuna plus the direct labor and overhead for cutting and processing the tuna into filets and canned tuna is the joint cost of the process. The flow of production is illustrated in Exhibit 7.17.

The production process starts at point 1. A total $16,000 joint cost ($7,000 direct materials, $5,000 direct labor, and $4,000 overhead) is incurred. Point 2 is the split-off point where two joint products are separated: 2,000 pounds of tuna filets and 8,000 pounds of canned tuna. The remaining 4,000 pounds of by-products, scrap, and waste are not accounted for. (The appendix to the chapter explains how to account for by-products.) If we use a physical measure method, the joint cost of $16,000 is allocated as shown in Exhibit 7.18.

Based on the physical measure method (pounds in this example), when the joint products reach the split-off point, we can compute the relationship of each of the joint products to the

Additional processing costs or separable costs are those that occur after the split-off point and can be identified directly with individual products.

The **physical measure method** uses a physical measure such as pounds, gallons, yards, or units of volume produced at the split-off point to allocate the joint costs to joint products.

The **average cost method** uses units of output to allocate joint costs to joint products.

EXHIBIT 7.17
Diagram of Two Joint Product Cost Flows for Johnson Seafood

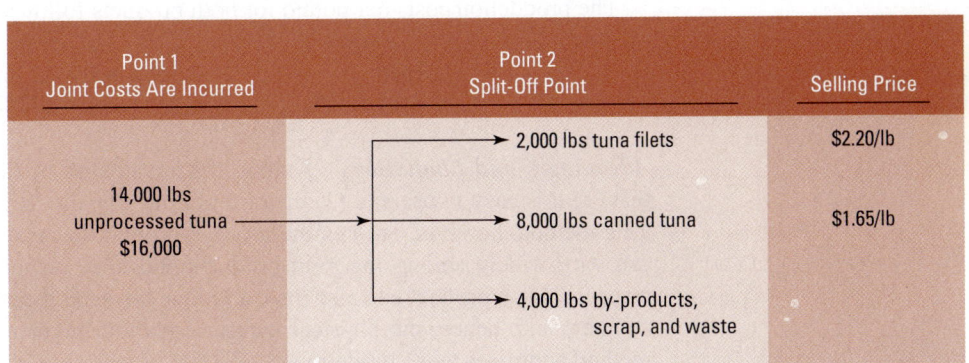

Point 1 Joint Costs Are Incurred	Point 2 Split-Off Point	Selling Price
14,000 lbs unprocessed tuna $16,000	2,000 lbs tuna filets	$2.20/lb
	8,000 lbs canned tuna	$1.65/lb
	4,000 lbs by-products, scrap, and waste	

EXHIBIT 7.18
Physical Measure Method

Product	Physical Measure	Proportion	Allocation of Joint Cost	Cost per Pound
Tuna filets	2,000 lbs	0.20	$16,000 × 20% = $ 3,200	$1.60
Canned tuna	8,000 lbs	0.80	16,000 × 80% = 12,800	1.60
Total	10,000 lbs	1.00	$16,000	

sum of the total units. The joint cost allocated to the products is the average cost per pound of the joint cost, which is $1.60 per pound.

The physical measure used to determine the relative weights for allocating the joint cost should be the measure of the products at the *split-off point,* not the measure when the production of the products is completed. Thus, the relevant measure in the example is the 2,000 pounds of filets and 8,000 pounds of canned tuna.

The production costs per pound for both products follow:

Filets	$1.60 per pound = $3,200/2,000 pounds
Canned tuna	$1.60 per pound = $12,800/8,000 pounds

Advantages and Limitations Among the advantages of the physical measure method are that (1) it is easy to use and (2) the criterion for the allocation of the joint costs is objective. This method, however, ignores the revenue-producing capability of individual products that can vary widely among the joint products and have no relationship at all to any physical measure. Each product can also have a unique physical measure (gallons for one, pounds for another) and, hence, the physical measure method might not be applicable. The following method addresses these limitations.

The Sales Value at Split-Off Method

The **sales value at split-off method**
allocates joint costs to joint products on the basis of their relative sales values at the split-off point.

The sales value at split-off method is an alternative and widely-used method. The **sales value at split-off method** (or more simply, *sales value method*) allocates joint costs to joint products on the basis of their relative sales values at the split-off point. This method can be used only when joint products can be sold at the split-off point. If we assume that Johnson can sell a pound of filets for $2.20 and a pound of canned tuna for $1.65 and that Johnson has produced

EXHIBIT 7.19
Sales Value at Split-Off
Method

Product	Units	Price per unit	Sales Value	Proportion	Joint Cost Allocated	Cost per Pound
Filets	2,000 lbs	$2.20	$ 4,400	0.25	$16,000 × 25% = $ 4,000	$2.00
Canned tuna	8,000 lbs	1.65	13,200	0.75	16,000 × 75% = 12,000	1.50
Total			$17,600	1.00	$16,000	

2,000 pounds of filets and 8,000 pounds of canned tuna, the $16,000 joint cost should be allocated between the products as shown in Exhibit 7.19.

The first step in the sales value method (Exhibit 7.19) is to compute the total sales value of the joint products at the split-off point. Note that the sales value is the sales price multiplied by the number of production units, *not the actual number of sales units*. Determining the proportion of the sales value of each joint product to the total sales value is the second step. The final operation allocates the total joint cost among the joint products based on those proportions.

In the Johnson Seafood example, the sales value of filets is $4,400 and of canned tuna is $13,200, a total of $17,600. The proportion of the individual sales values of the products to the total sales value are 0.25 ($4,400/$17,600) for filets and 0.75 ($13,200/$17,600) for canned tuna. The allocated costs are $4,000 to filets and $12,000 to canned tuna.

The production costs per pound for both products are calculated as follows:

Filets	$2.00 per pound = $4,000/2,000
Canned tuna	$1.50 per pound = $12,000/8,000

Note that filets have a higher unit cost under the sales value method than under the physical measure method. The reason is that filets have a higher sales value. If the sales prices are estimated accurately and no additional processing costs are involved, the sales value at split-off method generates the same gross margin percentage for both filets and canned tuna as shown in Exhibit 7.20.

Advantages and Limitations   The advantages of the sales value method are that it (1) is easy to calculate and (2) is allocated according to the individual product's revenues. This method is superior to the physical measure method because it allocates the joint costs in proportion to the products' ability to absorb these costs. This is an application of the ability-to-bear concept of fairness included in the objectives of cost allocation at the beginning of the chapter.

One limitation of the sales value method is that market prices for some industries change constantly. Also, the sales price at split-off might not be available because additional processing is necessary before the product can be sold.

The **net realizable value (NRV)** of a product is the estimated sales value of the product at the split-off point; it is determined by subtracting the additional processing and selling costs beyond the split-off point from the ultimate sales value of the product.

The Net Realizable Value Method

Not all joint products can be sold at the split-off point. Thus, there is no market price to attach to some products at the split-off point. In these cases, the concept of net realizable value is used. The **net realizable value (NRV)** of a product is the product's *estimated sales value* at the split-off point; it is determined by subtracting the additional processing and selling costs beyond the split-off point from the estimated ultimate sales value of the product.

$$\text{NRV} = \text{Ultimate sales value} - \text{Additional processing and selling cost}$$

EXHIBIT 7.20
**Product-Line Profitability
Analysis**

	Tuna Filets	Canned Tuna
Sales	$2.20 × 2,000 = $4,400	$1.65 × 8,000 = $13,200
Cost of goods sold	$2.00 × 2,000 = 4,000	$1.50 × 8,000 = 12,000
Gross margin	$ 400	$ 1,200
Gross margin percent	9.09%	9.09%

EXHIBIT 7.21   **Diagram of Three Joint Product Cost Flows for Johnson Seafood**

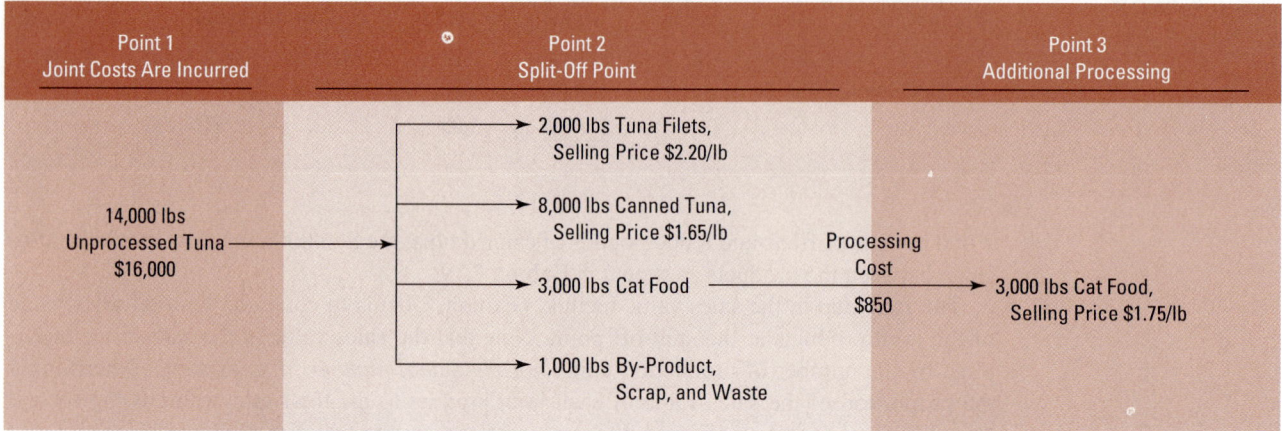

In the Johnson Seafood example, assume that in addition to filets and canned tuna, the firm processes cat food from raw, unprocessed tuna. Assume also that 14,000 pounds of tuna yield at the split-off point 2,000 pounds of filets and 8,000 pounds of canned tuna as before but now an additional 3,000 pounds of cat food. The remaining 1,000 pounds are scrap, waste, and by-products. For cat food the tuna must be processed further for sale to pet food distributors. The additional processing cost is $850 for minerals and other supplements that are important for cat nutrition but that add no weight to the product. The pet food distributors buy the prepared cat food from Johnson at $1.75 per pound and package it into 3-ounce cans for sale to pet stores and supermarkets. Exhibit 7.21 is a diagram of this situation.

Exhibit 7.22 shows the joint cost allocation calculation using the net realizable value method.

If Johnson Seafood sold all products it produced during the period, its gross margin amounts for the products would be as shown in Exhibit 7.23. Note that the gross margin percentage is lower for cat food than for filets because of the additional processing cost of $850.

Advantages and Limitations   The NRV method is superior to the physical measure method because, like the sales value at split-off method, it produces an allocation that yields a predictable, comparable level of profitability among the products. The physical measure method might provide misleading guidance to top management regarding product profitability.

EXHIBIT 7.22   **Joint Cost Allocation Using the Net Realizable Value Method**

Product	Pounds	Price	Sales Value	Additional Processing	Net Realizable Value	Percent of NRV	Allocated Cost	Total Cost	Cost per Pound
Filets	2,000	$2.20	$ 4,400	—	$ 4,400	20%	$ 3,200	$ 3,200	$1.60
Canned tuna	8,000	1.65	13,200	—	13,200	60	9,600	9,600	1.20
Cat food	3,000	1.75	5,250	$850	4,400	20	3,200	4,050	1.35
Total	13,000		$22,850	$850	$22,000	100%	$16,000	$16,850	

EXHIBIT 7.23
Johnson Seafood's Product-Line Profitability Analysis

	Tuna Filets	Canned Tuna	Cat Food
Sales	$2.20 × 2,000 = $4,400	$1.65 × 8,000 = $13,200	$1.75 × 3,000 = $5,250
Cost of goods sold	$1.60 × 2,000 = 3,200	$1.20 × 8,000 = 9,600	$1.35 × 3,000 = 4,050
Gross margin	$1,200	$ 3,600	$1,200
Gross margin percent	27.27%	27.27%	22.86%

Summary

This chapter introduces the objectives, concepts, and methods of cost allocation. There are two main cost allocation applications—departmental cost and joint product costing. Most important, the objectives and methods for cost allocation are determined based on the firm's strategy. Cost allocation is concerned with strategy in four key ways: (1) to determine accurate departmental and product costs as a basis for evaluating the departments' cost efficiency and profitability of different products, (2) to motivate managers to work hard, (3) to provide the proper incentive for managers to achieve the firm's goals, and (4) to provide a fair basis for rewarding managers for their effort.

Ethical issues often arise in cost allocation when managers must choose between alternative allocation methods. The manager must choose between methods that might decrease the cost of one product, customer, or business unit at the expense of increased costs for another product, customer, or unit.

Departmental cost allocation is performed in three phases: (1) trace all direct costs and allocate overhead to service and production departments, (2) allocate service department costs to production departments, and (3) allocate production department costs to products. The second phase is the most complex. Service department costs can be allocated to production departments using three methods—the direct method, the step method, and the reciprocal method. The three methods differ in the way they deal with service flows among service departments. The direct method ignores these flows, the step method includes some of them, and the reciprocal method includes all. For this reason, the reciprocal method is preferred.

A number of implementation issues arise when applying cost allocation methods including the strategic and ethical issues of the cost allocation. It is also important to allocate variable and fixed costs separately (in a process called *dual allocation*), to use budgeted rather than actual amounts in the allocation, and to consider alternative allocation methods when the result of an allocation to a department is a cost that is greater than the department could purchase the item from an outside entity.

The need for joint product costing arises when two or more products are made simultaneously in a given manufacturing process. The three methods for costing joint products are the (1) physical measure method, (2) sales value at split-off method, and (3) net realizable value method. The physical measure method is the simplest to use but also has a significant disadvantage. Because the allocation ignores sales value, the gross margins of joint products determined using the physical measure method can differ in significant and unreasonable ways. In contrast, the sales value and net realizable value methods tend to result in similar gross margins among the joint products. The sales value at split-off method is used when sales value at split-off is known; otherwise the net realizable value is used.

Appendix

By-Product Costing

LEARNING OBJECTIVE 7

Use the four by-product costing methods.

A by-product is a product of relatively small sales value that is produced simultaneously with one or more joint products. Two approaches are used for by-product costing: (1) the asset recognition approach and (2) the revenue approach. The main difference between these approaches lies in whether they assign an inventoriable value to by-products at the split-off point. The asset recognition approach records by-products as inventory at net realizable values; the by-product is therefore recognized as inventory when the by-product is produced. In contrast, the revenue approach does not assign values to the by-products in the period of production but recognizes by-product revenue in the period sold.

Each of the two approaches contain two alternative methods, depending on the way in which by-products are reported in the income statement. The two asset recognition methods follow:

Net Realizable Value Method. This method shows the net realizable value of by-products on the balance sheet as inventory and on the income statement as a deduction from the total manufacturing cost of the joint products. This is done in the *period in which the by-product is produced.*

EXHIBIT 7A.1
A Summary of By-Product Costing Methods

	Place in Income Statement	
Time to Recognize	**As Other Income**	**As a Deduction of Manufacturing Cost**
At time of production (asset recognition methods)	Other income at time of production	Net realizable value method; reduction in joint product cost at time of production
At time of sale (revenue methods)	Other income at time of sale	Reduction in cost of joint products at time of sale

Other Income at Production Point Method. This method shows the net realizable value of by-products on the income statement as other income or other sales revenue. This is done in the *period in which the by-product is produced.*

The two revenue methods follow:

Other Income at Selling Point Method. This method shows the net sales revenue from a by-product sold at time of sale on the income statement as other income or other sales revenue.

Manufacturing Cost Reduction at Selling Point Method. This method shows the net sales revenue from a by-product sold *at time of sale* on the income statement as a reduction of total manufacturing cost.

In Exhibit 7A.1 we summarize the four major by-product costing methods.

ASSET RECOGNITION METHODS

To illustrate the asset recognition methods, assume that Johnson Seafood believes that it can make additional profit by taking a portion of the 1,000 pounds of scrap and waste in each batch of unprocessed tuna and reprocessing them to produce a high-quality garden fertilizer. However, the selling price of the fertilizer is expected to be relatively low, 50 cents per pound. Moreover, additional processing and selling costs of 30 cents per pound would be necessary for preparing, packaging, and distributing the product. Since the sales value of fertilizer is relatively low, the firm decides to treat tuna filets, canned tuna, and cat food as joint products and fertilizer as a by-product. Suppose that Johnson sold all production of filets, canned tuna, and cat food, but sold only 400 of the 500 pounds of the fertilizer produced. Exhibit 7A.2 shows the cost flows of the three joint products and one by-product.

EXHIBIT 7A.2
Diagram of Three Joint Products and One By-Product Cost Flows for Johnson Seafood

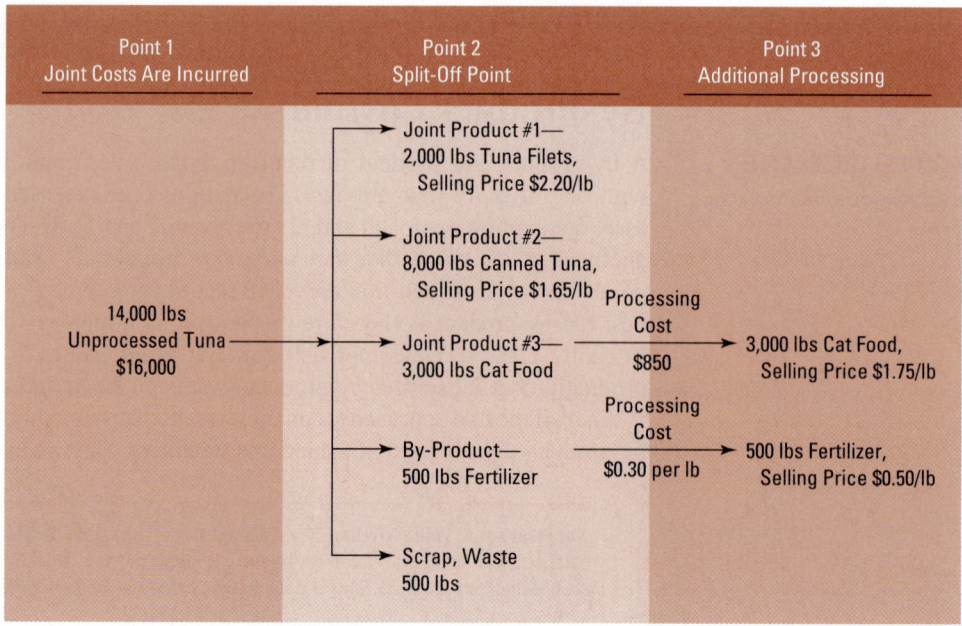

EXHIBIT 7A.3
By-Product Costing—Asset Recognition Methods

	Net Realizable Value Method	Other Income at Production Method
Sale of joint products (Exhibit 7.22)	$22,850	$22,850
Cost of joint products sold (Exhibit 7.22)	$16,850	$16,850
Less net realizable value of by-product	(100)	—
Cost of goods sold	$16,750	$16,850
Gross margin	$ 6,100	$ 6,000
Other income at production	—	100
Income before tax	$ 6,100	$ 6,100

From Exhibit 7.22, the total sales value of filets, canned tuna, and cat food is $22,850 ($4,400 + $13,200 + $5,250) and the total cost of the goods sold is $16,850 ($3,200 + $9,600 + $4,050). The net realizable value (NRV) of the 500 pounds of fertilizer produced is

$$\text{NRV} = \text{Sales value} - \text{Additional processing cost}$$
$$= (\$0.50 \times 500) - (\$0.30 \times 500)$$
$$= \$100$$

Johnson's accounting for the by-product using the asset recognition methods (the net realizable value method and the other income at production point method) appears in Exhibit 7A.3.

Asset recognition methods are based on the financial accounting concepts of asset recognition, matching, and materiality. By-products are *recognized* as assets with probable future economic benefits because a market exists for them. Asset recognition methods also have the preferred effect of *matching* the value of the by-product with its manufacturing cost; when the by-product is sold, its inventory cost is shown as the cost of sales. If the net realizable value of a by-product is *material* (that is, it will have a significant effect on inventory or profit), the asset recognition methods should be used because of the matching concept.

REVENUE METHODS

Revenue methods recognize by-products at the time of sale. Exhibit 7A.4 illustrates the two methods. Note that Exhibit 7A.4 shows the 400 pounds of by-product sold, not the 500 pounds of by-product produced.

Revenue methods are justified on the financial accounting concepts of revenue realization, materiality, and cost benefit. These methods are consistent with the argument that by-product net revenue should be recorded at the time of sale because this is the *point revenue is realized*. Revenue methods are also appropriate when the value of the by-product is *not material,* that is, very small in relation to net income. For *cost-benefit* considerations, many firms use a revenue method because of its simplicity.

EXHIBIT 7A.4
By-Product Costing—Revenue Recognition Methods

	Other Income at Selling Point Method	Manufacturing Cost Reduction Method
Sale of joint products	$22,850	$22,850
Cost of goods sold		
Cost of joint products sold	$16,850	$16,850
Less net sales revenue of by-product sold ($0.50 − $0.30) × 400	—	(80)
Cost of goods sold	$16,850	$16,770
Gross margin	$ 6,000	$ 6,080
By-product revenue	80	—
Income before tax	$ 6,080	$ 6,080

<table>
<tr><td>Key Terms</td><td>additional processing (separable) costs, 249
average cost method, 249
by-products, 248
direct method, 237</td><td>dual allocation, 244
joint products, 248
net realizable value (NRV), 251
physical measure method, 249
reciprocal flows, 236</td><td>reciprocal method, 239
sales value at split-off method, 250
split-off point, 248
step method, 238</td></tr>
</table>

Comments on Cost Management in Action

Health Care Providers Allocate Cost for Medicare Reimbursement

The direct method of the departmental approach to cost allocation explained in this chapter has never been permitted for Medicare cost reports. The only permissible method is the step method, which must be performed under Medicare guidelines and audited by a private intermediary (e.g., Blue Cross). A hospital chooses the order in which the step method occurs and the allocation bases (e.g., square feet, pounds of laundry, time spent, number of meals served). The order of the step method and the choice of allocation base are widely recognized to have a significant effect on allocated costs. Hospitals naturally choose methods that favor them in cost reimbursement. Many consultants, authors, and policy makers have called for improved guidance regarding the allocation of costs for Medicare reimbursement. Some have argued that since software tools are readily available to allocate costs using the reciprocal method, Medicare should require this more accurate method.

Marianne L Muise and Bonnie A Amoia, "Step Up to the Step-Down Method," *Healthcare Financial Management,* May 2006, pp. 72–77; William N. Zelman , Michael J. McCue, Alan R. Milikan, and Noah Glick, *Financial Management of Health Care Organizations,"* (Oxford: Blackwell Publishing, 2003). Also, the relevant guidance on Medicare costing is provided by the Centers for Medicare and Medicare Services, a U.S. federal agency to administer Medicare and Medicaid (www.cms.hhs.gov/). Medicare cost report information can be found at www.cms.hhs.gov/CostReports/.

Self-Study Problem
(For solution, please turn to the end of the chapter.)

Joint Product Costing

Northern Company processes 100 gallons of raw materials into 75 gallons of product GS-50 and 25 gallons of GS-80. GS-50 is further processed into 50 gallons of product GS-505 at a cost of $5,000, and GS-80 is processed into 50 gallons of product GS-805 at a cost of $2,000. Exhibit 1 depicts this manufacturing flow.

EXHIBIT 1
Joint Cost Flows for Northern Company

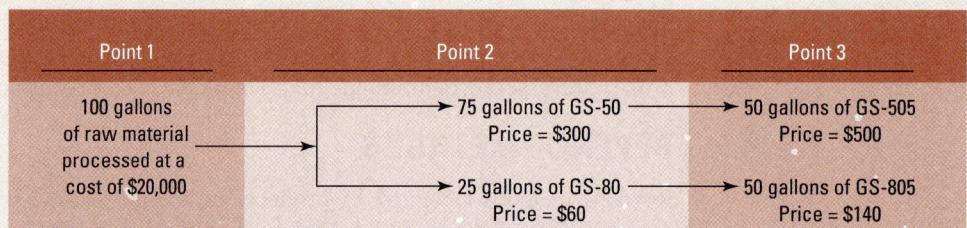

The production process starts at point 1. A total of $20,000 in joint manufacturing costs are incurred in reaching point 2. Point 2 is the split-off point of the process that manufactures GS-50 and GS-80. At this point, GS-50 can be sold for $300 a gallon, and GS-80 can be sold for $60 a gallon. The process is completed at point 3—products GS-505 and GS-805 have a sales price of $500 a gallon and $140 a gallon, respectively.

Required   Allocate the joint product costs using each of the three methods: (1) physical measure, (2) sales value at split-off, and (3) net realizable value.

Questions

7-1   What are the objectives of cost allocation? Which are most important in a retail firm? In a manufacturing firm? In a service firm?

7-2   Explain the difference between joint products and by-products.

7-3   What does the term *reciprocal* mean in the context of departmental cost allocation?

7-4   What are the three methods of departmental cost allocation? Explain how they differ, which is the most preferred, and why.

7-5   What are the three phases of the departmental allocation approach? What happens at each phase?

7-6   Give two or three examples of the use of cost allocation in service industries and not-for-profit organizations.

7-7   What are the four methods used in by-product costing, and how do they differ? Which is the preferred method and why?

7-8   What are the limitations of joint product cost allocation?

7-9   What are the implementation issues of departmental cost allocation?

7-10 What is the role of cost allocation from a strategic point of view?

Brief Exercises   Brief Exercises 7-11 through 7-14 involve departmental cost allocation with two service departments and two production departments. Use the following information for these four exercises:

		Percentage Service Provided to:			
Department	**Cost**	**S1**	**S2**	**P1**	**P2**
Service 1 (S1)	$ 30,000	0%	30%	35%	35%
Service 2 (S2)	20,000	20	0	20	60
Production 1 (P1)	100,000				
Production 2 (P2)	150,000				

7-11 What is the amount of service department cost allocated to P1 and P2 using the direct method?

7-12 What is the total cost in P1 and in P2 after allocation?

7-13 What is the amount of service department cost allocated to P1 and P2 using the step method with S1 going first?

7-14 How does your answer to 7-11 change if the cost in P1 is changed from $100,000 to $120,000?

Brief Exercises 7-15 and 7-16 require the following information:

		Percentage Service Provided to:			
Department	**Cost**	**S1**	**S2**	**P1**	**P2**
Service 1	$ 112,000	0%	40%	40%	20%
Service 2	44,000	20%	0%	40%	40%
Production 1	345,000				
Production 2	216,000				
	$ 717,000				

7-15 What percentage of service department 1's costs are allocated to P1 and to P2 under the direct method?

7-16 What percentage of service department 2's costs are allocated to P1 and to P2 under the direct method?

7-17 through 7-20 require the following information about a joint production process for three products, with a total joint production cost of $100,000. There are no separable processing costs for any of the three products.

Product	**Sales Value at Split-Off**	**Units at Split-Off**
1	$130,000	240
2	50,000	960
3	20,000	1,200
	$200,000	2,400

7-17 What amount of joint cost is allocated to each of the three products using the relative sales value method?

7-18 What amount of joint cost is allocated to each of the three products using the physical units method?

7-19 Assume that the total sales value at the split-off point for product 1 is $50,000 instead of $130,000 and the sales value of product 3 is $2,000 instead of $20,000. Assume also that, because of its relatively low sales value, the firm treats product 3 as a by-product and uses the net realizable value method for accounting for joint costs. There are no separable processing costs for product 3. What amount of joint cost would be allocated to the three products?

7-20 Assume the same as in 7-19 above except that product 3 is treated as a joint product. What amount of joint costs would be allocated to the three products using the relative sales value method?

Exercises

7-21 Cost Allocation, General An organization's service and administrative costs can be substantial, and some or all of these costs usually are allocated to cost objects. Thus, the allocations of service and administrative costs can have a significant impact on product cost and pricing, asset valuation, and segment profitability.

Required
1. What are service and administrative costs?
2. When service and administrative costs are allocated, they are grouped into homogeneous pools and then allocated to cost objects according to some allocation base.
   a. Compare and contrast the benefit and cost criteria for selecting an allocation base.
   b. Explain what the ability-to-bear criterion means in selecting an allocation base.

(CMA Adapted)

7-22 By-Products and Decision-Making Strategy Lowman Gourmet Products produces a wide variety of gourmet coffees (sold in pounds of roasted beans), jams, jellies, and condiments such as spicy mustard sauce. The firm has a reputation as a high-quality source of these products. Lowman sells the products through a mail-order catalog that is revised twice a year. Joe, the president, is interested in developing a new line of products to complement the coffees. The manufacture of the jams and jellies presently produces an excess of fruit liquid that is not used in these products. The firm is now selling excess liquid to other firms as flavoring for canned fruit products. Joe is planning to refine the liquid and add other ingredients to it to produce a coffee-flavoring product instead of selling the liquid. He figures that the cost of producing the jams and jellies, and therefore the fruit liquid, is irrelevant; the only relevant concern is the lost sales to the canneries and the cost of the additional ingredients, processing, and packaging.

Required Does this plan make financial and strategic sense?

7-23 Federal Reserve Banks; Cost Allocation The Monetary Control Act of 1980 (www.federalreserve .gov/paymentsystems/pricing/pricingpol.htm) requires the Federal Reserve (FED) to charge explicitly for certain services, in effect placing Federal Reserve banks in direct competition with large commercial banks for these services. The act also requires the FED to price these services based on full cost, including allocated indirect costs. Recent research indicates that the FED responded to the act by both improving the efficiency with which it provides these services and reallocating indirect costs to the less price-competitive services.

Required Describe briefly how the allocation of indirect costs could have made the FED's most price-sensitive services more competitive. Are there ethical or professional issues involved in this case?

7-24 Cost Allocation And Taxation At Nonprofit Organizations Nonprofit organizations are exempt from federal income tax except for income from any activities that are unrelated to the nonprofit's charitable purpose. An example is the use of a laboratory for both tax-exempt basic medical research and for testing a taxable product for commercial pharmaceutical firms. A concern in these cases is that the tax-exempt nonprofit organization will be able to compete unfairly with for-profit firms because of their tax-exempt status. The key argument is that common costs for the nonprofit's exempt and business activities will be used to "subsidize" the for-profit business (in this case, the taxable product testing).

Required How would cost allocation play a role in affecting the operating results of a nonprofit organization which has both business and charitable activities?

7-25 Fuel Surcharges: Allocating the Increased Cost of Fuel U.S. Railroads, including Burlington Northern Santa Fe Corp (BNSF) and CSX Corp., began using fuel surcharges in 2001 to recapture some of the additional costs due to the sharp rise in fuel costs in late 1999, continuing into 2000. Fuel costs have continued to increase and the fuel surcharges have continued to increase as well, accounting for approximately 12 percent of BNSF's revenues in the third quarter of 2008. Companies that use the railroads for shipping agricultural, chemical, and other commodities have been critical of the allocation methods the railroads use to apply the surcharges. The railroads have used surcharges based on a percentage of charges for the shipment. Shippers have argued that an allocation based on miles traveled in the shipment or other usage-based measure would be preferable. To resolve the conflict, the Surface Transportation Board (STB) in January 2007 prohibited the use of a surcharge based on shipping rates. Though it did not require the use of mileage, it required that railroads must use a method to allocate fuel surcharges that correlates with actual fuel costs. The STB is an economic regulatory agency that Congress charged with the fundamental missions of resolving railroad rate and service disputes and reviewing proposed railroad mergers. The STB is administratively affiliated with the Department of Transportation.

Required How would you propose that the increased cost of fuel be charged to shippers by the railroads? Do you think the STB ruling should solve the problem?

7-26 Joint Products Bravo Company produces joint products J, K, and B from a joint process. This information concerns a batch produced in April at a joint cost of $60,000:

| | | After Split-Off | |
Product	Units Produced and Sold	Total Additional Costs	Total Final Sales Value
J	1,000	$10,000	$90,000
K	2,000	10,000	50,000
B	4,000	5,000	10,000

Required How much of the joint cost should be allocated to each joint product using the net realizable value method?

7-27 Joint Products Nebraska Corporation manufactures liquid chemicals A and B from a joint process. It allocates joint costs on the basis of sales value at split-off. Processing 500 gallons of product A and 1,000 gallons of product B to the split-off point costs $4,560. The sales value at split-off is $10 per gallon for product A and $14 for product B. Product B requires an additional process beyond split-off at a cost of $2.50 per gallon before it can be sold.

Required What is Nebraska's cost to produce 1,000 gallons of product B?

7-28 Joint and By-Product Costing (Appendix) Silverman Company produces 20,000 units of A, 20,000 units of B, and 10,000 units of product C from the same manufacturing process at a cost of $340,000. A and B are joint products, and C is regarded as a by-product. The unit selling prices of the products are $50 for A, $25 for B, and $1 for C. None of the products require additional processing. Of the units produced, Silverman Company sells 18,000 units of A, 19,000 units of B, and 10,000 units of C. The firm uses the net realizable value method to allocate joint costs and by-product costs. Assume no beginning inventory.

Required
1. What is the value of the ending inventory of product A?
2. What is the value of the ending inventory of product B?

7-29 Departmental Cost Allocation HomeLife Life Insurance Company has two service departments (actuarial and premium rating) and two production departments (advertising and sales). The distribution of each service department's efforts (in percentages) to the other departments is

| | | To | | |
From	Actuarial	Premium Rating	Advertising	Sales
Actuarial	—	80%	10%	10%
Premium	20%	—	20%	60%

The direct operating costs of the departments (including both variable and fixed costs) are

Actuarial	$80,000
Premium rating	15,000
Advertising	60,000
Sales	40,000

Required
1. Determine the total cost allocated to the advertising and sales departments using the direct method.
2. Determine the total cost allocated to advertising and sales using the step method.
3. Determine the total cost allocated to advertising and sales using the reciprocal method.

7-30 Departmental Cost Allocation Robinson Products Company has two service departments (S1 and S2) and two production departments (P1 and P2). The distribution of each service department's efforts (in percentages) to the other departments is

		To		
From	**S1**	**S2**	**P1**	**P2**
S1	—	10%	20%	?%
S2	10%	—	?%	30%

The direct operating costs of the departments (including both variable and fixed costs) are

S1	$180,000
S2	60,000
P1	50,000
P2	120,000

Required
1. Determine the total cost of P1 and P2 using the direct method.
2. Determine the total cost of P1 and P2 using the step method.
3. Determine the total cost of P1 and P2 using the reciprocal method.

Problems

7-31 Departmental Cost Allocation; Outsourcing Tanner Company produces two software products (NetA and NetB) in two separate departments (A and B). These products are highly regarded network maintenance programs. NetA is used for small networks and NetB is used for large networks. Williams is known for the quality of its products and its ability to meet dates promised for software upgrades.

Department A produces NetA, and department B produces NetB. The production departments are supported by two support departments, systems design and programming services. The source and use of the support department time are summarized as follows:

		To			Total
From	**Design**	**Programming**	**Department A**	**Department B**	**Labor-Hours**
Design	—	4,000	2,000	10,000	16,000
Programming	400	—	400	800	1,600

The costs in the two service departments are as follows:

	Design	**Programming**
Labor and materials (all variable)	$30,000	$25,000
Depreciation and other fixed costs	38,000	29,000
Total	$68,000	$54,000

Required
1. What are the costs allocated to the two production departments from the two service departments using (a) the direct method, (b) the step method (design department goes first), and (c) the reciprocal method?
2. The company is considering outsourcing programming services to DDB Services, Inc., for $25 per hour. Should Tanner do this?

7-32 Departmental Cost Allocation Haywood Manufacturing has two production departments— assembly and finishing. These are supported by two service departments—sourcing (purchasing and handling of raw materials and human resources) and operations (work scheduling, supervision, and inspection). Haywood has the following labor-hours devoted by each of the service departments to the other departments.

	Total Labor-Hours Used by Departments			
	Sourcing	**Operations**	**Assembly**	**Finishing**
Sourcing		20,000	35,000	70,000
Operations	12,000	—	48,000	40,000

The costs incurred in the plant are as follows:

Departments	Departmental Costs
Sourcing	$ 155,000
Operations	222,000
Assembly	387,000
Finishing	466,000
Total	$1,230,000

Required

1. What are the costs allocated to the two production departments using (a) the direct method, (b) the step method with the sourcing department going first, and (c) the reciprocal method?

2. What are the total costs in the production departments after allocation?

7-33 **Departmental Cost Allocation; Outsourcing; Outside Price**   McKeoun Enterprises is a large machine tool company now experiencing alarming increases in maintenance expense in each of its four production departments. Maintenance costs are currently allocated to the production departments on the basis of labor-hours incurred in the production department. To provide pressure for the production departments to use less maintenance, and to provide an incentive for the maintenance department to become more efficient, McKeoun has decided to investigate new methods of allocating maintenance costs. One suggestion now being evaluated is a form of outsourcing: The producing departments could purchase maintenance service from an outside supplier. That is, they could choose either to use an outside supplier of maintenance or to be charged an amount based on their use of labor-hours. The following table shows the labor-hours in each department, the allocation of maintenance cost based on labor-hours, and the cost to purchase the equivalent level of maintenance service from an outside maintenance provider.

Production Department	Direct Labor-Hours Allocation Base (Percent)	Direct Labor-Hours Allocation Cost	Outside Price
A	20%	$ 90,000	$115,000
B	30	135,000	92,000
C	10	45,000	69,000
D	40	180,000	184,000
Total	100%	$450,000	$460,000

Required

1. As a first step in moving to the outsourcing approach, McKeoun is considering an allocation based on the price of the outside maintenance supplier for each department. Calculate the cost allocation on this basis and compare it to the current labor-hour basis.

2. If McKeoun follows the proposed plan, what is likely to happen to the overall use of maintenance? How will each department manager be motivated to increase or decrease the use of maintenance? What will be the overall effects of going to the new plan?

7-34 **Departmental Cost Allocation**   Swanick Corporation prepares business plans and marketing analyses for start-up companies in the Boston area. Swanick has been very successful in recent years in providing effective service to a growing number of clients. The company provides its service from a single office building in Boston, and is organized into two main client-service groups: one for market research and the other for financial analysis. The two groups are treated as cost centers with budgeted annual costs of $750,000 and $1,000,000, respectively. In addition, Swanick has a support staff that is organized into two main functions; one for clerical, facilities, and logistical support (called the CFL group) and another for computer-related support. The CFL group is also a cost center with budgeted annual costs of $500,000, while the annual cost of the computer group is $600,000.

Tom Miggs, CFO of Swanick, plans to prepare a departmental cost allocation for his four groups, and he assembles the following information:

Percentage of estimated dollars of work and time by CFL:

20%—service to the computer group
50%—service to market research
30%—service to financial analysis

Percentage of estimated dollars of work and time by the computer group:

12%—service to the CFL group
44%—service to market research
44%—service to financial analysis

Required   Using a spreadsheet, determine the total cost in the financial analysis and market research groups, after departmental allocation, using the direct method, the step method, and the reciprocal method.

7-35 **Departmental Cost Allocation**   Lempicke Corporation distributes its service department overhead costs to product departments. This information is for the month of June:

	Service Departments	
	Maintenance	**Utilities**
Overhead costs incurred	$60,000	$16,000
Service provided to departments		
Maintenance	—	10%
Utilities	30%	—
Producing—A	30	45
Producing—B	40	45
Totals	100%	100%

Required   What is the amount of maintenance and utility department costs distributed to producing departments A and B for June using (1) the direct method, (2) the step method, and (3) the reciprocal method?

7-36 **Joint Product Costing**   Choi Company manufactures two skin care lotions, Smooth Skin and Silken Skin, from a joint process. The joint costs incurred are $420,000 for a standard production run that generates 180,000 pints of Smooth Skin and 120,000 pints of Silken Skin. Smooth Skin sells for $2.40 per pint, while Silken Skin sells for $3.90 per pint.

Required
1. Assuming that both products are sold at the split-off point, how much of the joint cost of each production run is allocated to Smooth Skin on a net realizable value basis?
2. If no additional costs are incurred after the split-off point, how much of the joint cost of each production run is allocated to Silken Skin on the physical measure method basis?
3. If additional processing costs beyond the split-off point are $1.40 per pint for Smooth Skin and $0.90 per pint for Silken Skin, how much of the joint cost of each production run is allocated to Silken Skin on a net realizable value basis?
4. If additional processing costs beyond the split-off point are $1.40 per pint for Smooth Skin and $0.90 per pint for Silken Skin, how much of the joint cost of each production run is allocated to Smooth Skin on a physical measure method basis?

(CMA Adapted)

7-37 **Joint Product Costing**   Sonimad Sawmill manufactures two lumber products from a joint milling process: mine support braces (MSB) and unseasoned commercial building lumber (CBL). A standard production run incurs joint costs of $300,000 and results in 60,000 units of MSB and 90,000 units of CBL. Each MSB sells for $2 per unit, and each CBL sells for $4 per unit.

Required
1. Assuming that no further processing occurs after the split-off point, how much of the joint costs are allocated to commercial building lumber (CBL) on a physical measure method basis?
2. If no further processing occurs after the split-off point, how much of the joint cost is allocated to the mine support braces (MSB) on a sales value basis?
3. Assume that the CBL is not marketable at split-off but must be planed and sized at a cost of $200,000 per production run. During this process, 10,000 units are unavoidably lost and have no value. The remaining units of CBL are salable at $10 per unit. The MSB, although salable immediately at the split-off point, are coated with a tarlike preservative that costs $100,000 per production run. The braces are then sold

for $5 each. Using the net realizable value basis, how much of the completed cost should be assigned to each unit of CBL?

4. Should Sonimad Sawmill choose to process the MSB beyond split-off? What would be the contribution if it did so?

(CMA Adapted)

7-38 Joint Products   The Salinas Company produces three products, X, Y, and Z, from a joint process. Each product can be sold at the split-off point or processed further. Additional processing requires no special facilities, and the production costs of further processing are entirely variable and traceable to the products involved. Last year all three products were processed beyond split-off. Joint production costs for the year were $80,000. Sales values and costs needed to evaluate Salinas' production policy follow:

			If All Units Processed Further	
Product	Units Produced	Sales Value at Split-Off	Sales Value	Additional Costs
X	5,000	$25,000	$55,000	$9,000
Y	4,000	41,000	45,000	7,000
Z	1,000	24,000	30,000	8,000

Required
1. Determine the unit cost and gross profit for each product if Salinas allocates joint production costs in proportion to the relative physical volume of output.
2. Determine unit costs and gross profit for each product if Salinas allocates joint costs using the sales value method.
3. Should the firm sell any of its products after further processing?
4. Salinas has been selling all of its products at the split-off point. Selling any of the products after further processing will entail direct competition with some major customers. What strategic factors does the firm need to consider in deciding whether to process any of the products further?

7-39 Joint Products   Georgia Chemical makes three widely used industrial adhesives: G121, G143, and G189. See sales and production information for a gallon of each of the three adhesives in the following table. Most of Georgia's customers ask for a special blend of the three products which improves heat-resistance. The additional processing requires additional time and materials, and the price is increased accordingly, as shown in the table. Assume that Georgia produces only for specific customer orders, so there is no beginning or ending inventory. Assume also that all of Georgia's customers requested the heat-resistant version of the product, so that all production required additional processing.

	G121	G143	G189
Units sold	125,000	100,000	75,000
Price (after addt'l processing)	$ 30	$ 20	$ 25
Separable processing cost	$550,000	$125,000	$625,000
Total joint cost $3,000,000			
Sales price at split-off	$ 10	$ 8	$ 12

Required
1. Calculate the product cost of each of the three product lines using the following methods:
   (a) physical unit method, (b) sales value at split off method, and (c) the net realizable value method.
2. Which of the three methods do you think would be preferred in this case? Why?

7-40 Joint Products; By-Products (Appendix)   Multiproduct Corporation is a chemical manufacturer that produces two main products (Pepco–1 and Repke–3) and a by-product (SE–5) from a joint process. If Multiproduct had the proper facilities, it could process SE-5 further into a main product. The ratio of output quantities to input quantity of direct material used in the joint process remains consistent with the processing conditions and activity level.

Multiproduct currently uses the physical measure method of allocating joint costs to the main products. It uses the first-in, first-out (FIFO) inventory method to value the main products. The by-product is inventoried at its net realizable value, which is used to reduce the joint production costs before they are allocated to the main products.

Jim Simpson, Multiproduct's controller, wants to implement the sales value method of joint cost allocation. He believes that inventory costs should be based on each product's ability to contribute to the recovery of joint production costs. Multiproduct uses an asset recognition approach in accounting for by-products.

Data regarding Multiproduct's operations for November are presented in the following report. The joint cost of production totaled $2,640,000 for November.

	Main Products		By-Product
	Pepco–1	Repke–3	SE–5
Finished goods inventory in gallons on November 1	20,000	40,000	10,000
November sales in gallons	800,000	700,000	200,000
November production in gallons	900,000	720,000	240,000
Sales value per gallon at split-off point	$ 2.00	$ 1.50	$0.55*
Additional process costs after split-off	$1,800,000	$720,000	—
Final sales value per gallon	$ 5.00	$ 4.00	—

* Selling costs of 5 cents per gallon are incurred to sell the by-product.

Required

1. Describe the sales value method and explain how it would accomplish Jim's objective.

2. Assuming Multiproduct adopts the sales value method for internal reporting purposes, calculate the following:

   a. The allocation of the joint production cost for November.

   b. The dollar values of the finished goods inventories for Pepco–1, Repke–3, and SE–5 as of November 30.

3. Multiproduct plans to expand its production facilities to further process SE–5 into a main product. Discuss how the allocation of the joint production costs under the sales value method would change when SE–5 becomes a main product.

(CMA Adapted)

7-41 Joint Products   Alderon Industries manufactures chemicals for various purposes. One process that Alderon uses produces SPL–3, a chemical used in swimming pools; PST–4, a chemical used in pesticides; and RJ–5, a by-product sold to fertilizer manufacturers. Alderon uses the net realizable value of its main products to allocate joint production costs and the first-in, first-out inventory method to value the main products. The by-product is inventoried at its net realizable value, which is used to reduce the joint production costs before they are allocated to the main products. The ratio of output to input of direct material used in the joint process remains consistent from month to month.

Data regarding Alderon's operations for the month of November follow. During this month, Alderon incurred joint production costs of $1,702,000 in the manufacture of SPL–3, PST–4, and RJ–5.

	SPL–3	PST–4	RJ–5
Finished goods inventory in gallons (November 1)	18,000	52,000	3,000
November sales in gallons	650,000	325,000	150,000
November production in gallons	700,000	350,000	170,000
Sales value per gallon at split-off	—	$ 3.80	$0.70*
Additional processing costs	$874,000	$816,000	—
Final sales value per gallon	$ 4.00	$ 6.00	—

*Selling costs of 10 cents per gallon are incurred to sell the by-product.

Required

1. Determine Alderon Industries' allocation of joint production costs for the month of November. Be sure to present appropriate supporting calculations.

2. Determine the dollar values of the finished goods inventories for SPL–3, PST–4, and RJ–5 as of November 30.

3. Alderon has an opportunity to sell PST–4 at the split-off point for $3.80 per gallon. Prepare an analysis showing whether Alderon should sell PST–4 at the split-off point or process further.

4. As a production supervisor for Alderon, you have learned that small quantities of the critical chemical compound in PST–4 might be present in SPL–3. What should you do?

(CMA Adapted)

7-42 **Joint Products; By-Products (Appendix)** Lond Company produces joint products Jana and Reta, and by-product Bynd. Jana is sold at split-off; Reta and Bynd undergo additional processing. Production data pertaining to these products for the year ended December 31, 2010, were as follows:

	Jana	Reta	Bynd	Total
Joint costs				
Variable				$ 88,000
Fixed				148,000
Separate costs				
Variable		$120,000	$ 3,000	$123,000
Fixed		90,000	2,000	92,000
Production in pounds	50,000	40,000	10,000	100,000
Sales price per pound	$ 4.00	$ 7.50	$ 1.10	

Lond had no beginning or ending inventories and no materials were spoiled in production. Bynd's net realizable value is deducted from joint costs. Joint costs are allocated to joint products to achieve the same gross margin percentage for each joint product.

Required
Prepare the following information for Lond Company for the year ended December 31, 2010:

1. Total gross margin.
2. Allocation of joint costs to Jana and Reta.
3. Separate gross margins for Jana and Reta.

(CMA Adapted)

7-43 **Departmental Cost Allocation** Duvernoy Corporation is a manufacturing company with six support departments: finance, marketing, personnel, production engineering, research and development (R&D), and information systems, each administered by a vice president. The information systems department (ISD) was established in 2008 when Duvernoy decided to acquire a large computer and develop a new information system.

While systems development and implementation is an ongoing process at Duvernoy, many basic systems needed by each functional department were operational at the end of 2009. Thus, calendar year 2010 is considered the first year for which the ISD costs can be estimated with a high degree of accuracy. Duvernoy's president wants the other five functional departments to be aware of the magnitude of the ISD costs by allocating them in the reports and statements prepared at the end of the first quarter of 2010. The allocation to each department was based on its actual use of ISD services.

Jon Werner, vice president of ISD, suggested that the actual ISD costs be allocated on the basis of pages of actual computer output. He chose this basis because all departments use reports to evaluate their operations and make decisions. The use of this basis resulted in the following allocation of the $225,000 total ISD cost for the first quarter of 2010:

Department	Percentage	Allocated Cost
Finance	50%	$112,500
Marketing	30	67,500
Personnel	9	20,250
Production engineering	6	13,500
R&D	5	11,250

After the quarterly reports were distributed, the finance and marketing departments objected to this allocation method. Both departments recognized that they were responsible for most of the report output, but they believed that these output costs might be the smallest of ISD costs and requested that a more equitable allocation basis be developed.

After meeting with Jon, Elaine Jergens, Duvernoy's controller, concluded that ISD provides three distinct services: systems development, computer processing, and report generation. She recommended that a predetermined rate be developed for each service based on budgeted annual activity and costs. The ISD costs would then be assigned to the other functional departments using the predetermined rate times the actual activity used. ISD would absorb any difference between actual costs incurred and costs allocated to the other departments.

Elaine and Jon concluded that systems development could be charged on the basis of hours devoted to systems development and programming, computer processing based on time used for operations (exclusive of database development and maintenance), and report generation based on number of pages of output. The only cost they thought should not be included in any of the predetermined rates was for purchased software; these packages usually were acquired for a specific department's use. Thus, Elaine concluded that purchased software would be charged at cost to the department for which it was purchased. To revise the first-quarter allocation, she gathered this information on ISD costs and services:

| | Estimated Annual Costs | Actual First-Quarter Costs | Percentage Devoted to | | |
			Systems Development	Computer Processing	Report Generation
Wages/benefits					
Administration	$100,000	$ 25,000	60%	20%	20%
Computer operators	55,000	13,000		20	80
Analysts/programmers	165,000	43,500	100		
Maintenance					
Hardware	24,000	6,000		75	25
Software	20,000	5,000		100	
Output supplies	50,000	11,500			100
Purchased software	45,000	16,000*	—	—	—
Utilities	28,000	6,250		100	
Depreciation					
Mainframe computer	325,000	81,250		100	
Printing equipment	60,000	15,000			100
Building improvements	10,000	2,500		100	
Total department costs	$882,000	$225,000			

*All software purchased during the first quarter of 2010 was for the production engineering department.

Information Systems Department Services in First Quarter			
	Systems Development	Computer Operations (CPU)	Report Generation
Annual capacity	4,500 hours	360 CPU hours	5,000,000 pages
Actual usage during first quarter, 2010			
Finance	100 hours	8 CPU hours	600,000 pages
Marketing	250	12	360,000
Personnel	200	12	108,000
Production engineering	400	32	72,000
R&D	50	16	60,000
Total usage	1,000 hours	80 CPU hours	1,200,000 pages

Required

1. For ISD, determine the following:

   a. The predetermined rates for each service category: systems development, computer processing, and report generation.

   b. Using the predetermined rates developed in requirement 1a, calculate the amount each of the other five functional departments would be charged for ISD's services provided during the first quarter of 2010.

2. With the method proposed by Elaine Jergens for charging the ISD costs to the other five functional departments, ISD's actual costs incurred and the costs assigned to the five user department might differ.

   a. Explain the nature of this difference.

   b. Discuss whether this proposal will improve cost control in ISD.

3. Explain whether Elaine's proposed method of charging user departments for ISD costs will improve planning and control in the user departments.

4. Assume that a finance manager has suggested outsourcing ISD. What factors should Duvernoy consider in deciding whether to outsource ISD functions?

(CMA Adapted)

7-44 Departmental Cost Allocation   Computer Intelligence, a computer software consulting company, has three major functional areas: computer programming, information systems consulting, and software training. Carol Bingham, a pricing analyst in the accounting department, has been asked to develop total costs for the functional areas. These costs will be used as a guide in pricing a new contract. In computing these costs, Carol is considering three different methods of the departmental allocation approach to allocate overhead costs: the direct method, the step method, and the reciprocal method. She assembled the following data from the two service departments, information systems and facilities:

	Service Departments		Production Departments			
	Information Systems	**Facilities**	**Computer Programming**	**Information Systems Consulting**	**Software Training**	**Total**
Budgeted overhead	$80,000	$45,000	$150,000	$190,000	$135,000	$600,000
Information systems* (hours)		200	1,200	600	1,000	3,000
Facilities† (square feet)	200		400	600	800	2,000

*Allocated on the basis of hours of computer usage.
†Allocated on the basis of floor space.

Required

1. Using as the application base computer usage time for the information systems department and square feet of floor space for the facilities department, apply overhead from these service departments to the production departments, using these three methods. Use Excel and Solver to determine the allocations.

   a. Direct method.

   b. Step method.

   c. Reciprocal method.

2. Rather than allocate costs, how might Computer Intelligence better assign the information systems department's costs?

(CMA Adapted)

7-45 Joint Products   Yonica Petroleum is a global manufacturer of specialty chemicals that are made from the waste products of the petroleum industry. Yonica in effect recycles a good portion of the waste from the refineries used by the large oil companies. The specialty chemicals are used as cleaning solvents and lubricants in industrial applications. Yonica has three products—Y64, G22, and X17—and total joint production cost of $356,000. Yonica plans to process all three products beyond the split-off point in order to be able to sell the product at the higher price after additional processing.

	Y64	G22	X17
Gallons produced and sold	22,000	45,500	18,000
Sales price at split off point	$2.24	$2.88	$0.44
Separable processing cost	$65,500	$34,250	$55,400
Sales price after additional processing	$ 10.50	$ 6.75	$ 4.22
Number of customers	22	3	46

Required

1. Calculate the product cost of each of the three product lines using the following methods:
   (a) physical unit method, (b) sales value at split-off method, and (c) the net realizable value method.

2. Which of the three methods do you think would be preferred in this case? Why?

3. While Yonica chose to process all three products beyond the split-off point, do you think this is the correct decision? Which products, if any, do you think should have been processed beyond the split-off point, and why?

7-46 **Departmental Cost Allocation; Not-for-Profit**　The Fleming Foundation is a charitable organization founded by Gaylord Fleming and Sandy Fleming. The Flemings intended for the charity to provide programs in health care for the elderly, particularly those in poverty. The two main program divisions of the foundation are mental health for the elderly and housing for the elderly. In addition to these programs, the Foundation also provides health care educational programs and has a significant fund-raising effort to help the Foundation to grow and to accomplish the goals of the founders. The Foundation is organized into two main departments—education and program management. These departments are supported by two service departments—information technology (IT) and administration.

There are $418,000 of costs directly traceable to each of the four departments. An additional $65,000 of indirect costs are shared among the four departments—$50,000 of which is allocated to the departments based on direct labor-hours and $15,000 to the departments based on the number of personnel (headcount) in the departments.

The cost, labor-hours, and headcount in these departments in the most recent year are as follows:

	Direct Cost	Labor-Hours	No. of Personnel
Information technology	$ 6,000	2,000	2
Administration	122,000	6,000	3
Education	100,000	4,000	3
Program management	190,000	4,000	4
	$418,000		

IT serves Education, Administration, and Program Management 20 percent, 20 percent, and 60 percent of its time, respectively. Administration serves Education, IT, and Program Management 30 percent, 10 percent, and 60 percent, respectively.

The costs of the two main departments are allocated to the two programs as follows: the costs in education are allocated on the basis of labor-hours in the programs, while the costs in program management are allocated using the headcount used in the two programs. The following table shows the labor-hours and headcount consumption by the two programs.

	Labor-Hours	Headcount
Mental health	2,000	1
Housing	2,000	3
Labor-hours in education	4,000	
Headcount in program management		4

Required　Determine the costs allocated to the mental health and housing programs using the direct method, the step method (assuming that IT goes first), and the reciprocal method.

7-47 **Joint Products and By-Products**　Princess Corporation grows, processes, packages, and sells three apple products: slices that are used in frozen pies, applesauce, and apple juice. The outside skin of the apple, which is removed in the cutting department and processed as animal feed, is treated as a by-product. Princess uses the net realizable value method to assign costs of the joint process to its main products. The apple skin by-product net realizable value is used to reduce the joint production costs prior to allocation to the main products. Details of Princess' production process follow:

- The cutting department washes the apples and removes the outside skin. The department then cores and trims the apples for slicing. At this point, each of the three main products and the by-product are recognizable. Each product is then transferred to the next department for final processing.
- The slicing department receives the trimmed apples and slices and freezes them. Any juice generated during the slicing operation is frozen with the slices.
- The crushing department trims pieces of apple and processes them into applesauce. The juice generated during this operation is used in the applesauce.

- The juicing department pulverizes the core and any surplus apple from the cutting department into a liquid. This department experiences a loss equal to 8 percent of the weight of the good output produced.
- The feed department chops the outside skin into animal food and packages it. A total of 270,000 pounds of apples entered the cutting department during November. The following information shows the costs incurred in each department, the proportion by weight (based on pounds) transferred to the four final processing departments, and the selling price of each end product. Assume no beginning or ending inventory of apple slices, applesauce, or juice.

Department	Costs Incurred	Proportion of Product by Weight Transferred to Departments	Selling Price per Pound of Final Product
Cutting	$60,000	—	—
Slicing	11,280	33%	$.80
Crushing	8,550	30	.55
Juicing	3,000	27	.40
Feed	700	10	.10
Total	$83,530	100%	

Required

1. Princess Corporation uses the net realizable value method to determine inventory values for its main products and by-products. For the month of November, calculate each of the following:
   a. Output in pounds for apple slices, applesauce, apple juice, and animal feed.
   b. Net realizable value at the split-off point for each of the three main products.
   c. Cutting department cost assigned to each of the three main products and to the by-product in accordance with corporate policy.
   d. Gross margin in dollars for each of the three main products.
2. Comment on the significance to management of the gross margin dollar information by main product for planning and control purposes as opposed to inventory valuation.
3. List the important issues that Princess faces as a global company. What are its critical success factors? Which key issues arise because Princess operates in several countries? Should any of these issues affect the way Princess allocates costs, as determined in requirement 1?

(CMA Adapted)

7-48 **Joint Products and By-Products** Goodson Pharmaceutical Company manufactures three main products from a joint process: Altox, Lorex, and Hycol. Data regarding these products for the fiscal year ended May 31, 2010, follow:

	Altox	Lorex	Hycol
Units produced	170,000	500,000	330,000
Sales value per unit at split-off	$ 3.50	—	$ 2.00
Allocation of joint costs*	$450,000	$ 846,000	$504,000
Separable costs	—	$1,400,000	—
Final sales value per unit	—	$ 5.00	—

*Joint costs are allocated on the basis of net realizable value, and the net realizable value of any by-product is deducted from the joint costs before allocation.

Altox is currently sold at the split-off point to a vitamin manufacturer. Lorex is processed further after the split-off point and sold as a cold remedy. Hycol, an oil produced from the joint process, is sold at the split-off point to a cosmetics manufacturer.

Arlene Franklin, president of Goodson, is reviewing opportunities to change the processing and sale of these three products. Altox can be refined for use as a high blood pressure medication, but this would result in a loss of 20,000 units. The costs to further process Altox are estimated to be $250,000 annually. The medication would sell for $5.50 per unit. The company has an offer from another pharmaceutical company to purchase Lorex at the split-off point for $2.25 per unit. Goodson's research department has suggested that the company process Hycol further and sell it as an ointment to relieve muscle pain. The additional processing would cost $75,000 annually and would increase the units of product by 25 percent. The product would be sold for $1.80 per unit.

The joint process that Goodson currently uses also produces 50,000 units of Dorzine, a hazardous chemical waste product that costs the company $0.35 per unit for proper disposal. Dietriech Mills Inc. is interested in using the Dorzine as a solvent; however, Goodson must refine the Dorzine at an annual cost of $43,000. Dietriech would purchase all Dorzine Goodson can refine and is willing to pay $0.75 for each unit.

Required

1. Which of the three main products should Goodson Pharmaceutical Company sell at the split-off point? Which of the products should the company process further to maximize profits? Support your answers with appropriate calculations, using a spreadsheet system.

2. Assume that Goodson has decided to refine the waste product Dorzine as a by-product of the joint process in the future and to sell it to Dietriech Mill.

   a. Did Goodson make the correct decision regarding Dorzine? Support your answer with appropriate calculations.

   b. Explain whether the decision to treat Dorzine as a by-product will affect your answer to requirement 1.

(CMA Adapted)

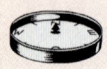

7-49 Joint Cost Allocation: Managerial Incentives   Cameron Manufacturing produces auto parts for auto manufacturers and parts wholesalers. The business is very competitive, and productivity measures are used throughout its eight manufacturing plants. Jill Owens, the manufacturing vice president, explains to her plant managers the importance of reducing cycle time, improving throughput, and reducing waste. One type of waste she keeps close track of is that due to accidents and injuries on the job. Jill believes that a safe work place also contributes to productivity. A reduction in accidents and injuries can also lead to a reduction in the insurance the firm pays to cover its liability in these incidents. The premium for this insurance coverage is a single policy and is a joint cost shared by all eight plants. One of the plant managers, Mike Griffin, notes that the current procedure for allocating the cost of insurance, which is based on total plant output, does not provide plant managers with the desired incentive to reduce accidents. It just means that the larger plants get charged more. Mike suggests that the insurance cost should be charged to the plants based on the number of manufacturing personnel in each plant.

Required   What do you think of Mike's suggestion? What alternative would you suggest, if any, for allocating the cost of insurance to the plants?

7-50 Cost Allocation; Equal Gross Margin Percentage; New Method   Ted Brown is the chief financial officer of Haywood Inc., a large manufacturer of cosmetics and other personal care products. Ted is conducting a financial analysis of the firm's line of hand lotions which consists of three products: SkinSalve, SkinCream, and SkinBalm. Total sales for the three products in the recent year were $400,000, $250,000 and $500,000, respectively. Because there is a small amount of additional processing cost for each of the three products, which differs between the products ($20,000, $50,000 and $30,000, respectively), Ted has been using the net realizable value method for allocating the joint production cost of $500,000. However, he is not satisfied with the result of somewhat different gross margin percentage ratios (gross margin/sales) for the three products when using this approach. He knows only of the physical units method, the sales value at split-off method, and the net realizable value method for allocating joint cost.

Required   Devise a new method of cost allocation for Ted so that after allocation of joint costs and separable costs, the gross margin percentage is the same for all three products.

7-51 Departmental Cost Allocation; Insurance Company   CareMark Insurance Company has two service lines, health insurance and auto insurance. The two product lines are served by three operating departments which are necessary for providing the two types of services: claims processing, administration, and sales. These three operating departments are supported by two departments: information technology and facilities. The support provided by information technology and facilities to the other departments is shown below.

| | Support Departments | | Operating Departments | | |
	Information Technology	Facilities	Claims Processing	Administration	Sales
Information technology	—	30%	30%	20%	20%
Facilities	10%	—	20	40	30

The total costs incurred in the five departments are:

Information technology	$ 600,000
Facilities	1,800,000
Claims processing	345,000
Administration	875,000
Sales	555,000
Total costs	$4,175,000

Required Allocate the $4,175,000 total departmental costs to the three operating departments using (a) the direct method, (b) the step method (for both information technology and facilities going first in the allocation), and (c) the reciprocal method.

7-52 **Cost Allocation and Legal Disputes** Cost allocation is often the centerpiece of conflict that is resolved in court cases. The litigation usually involves the dispute over how costs are allocated to a product or product line that is of interest to the plaintiff. This is particularly an issue when a company produces some products or services for a price-competitive market while other products or services are produced for a governmental unit on a cost-plus or reimbursement basis.

The following cost allocation disputes involve an organization (Nursing Care Inc, or NCI) that operates both a nursing home and an apartment building for retirees (retirement home). A single kitchen is used to provide meals to both the nursing home and retirement home. Also, certain labor costs and utilities costs of the kitchen are shared by the two homes. Many of those living in the nursing home are indigent and are on Medicaid. The state Department of Health and Family Services (DHFS) reimburses NCI at Medicaid approved cost reimbursement rates. The Medicaid reimbursement rates are based on cost information supplied by the organization, in this case NCI, and are assumed to be accurate; cost allocations are assumed to be reasonable. DHFS has examined the cost report of NCI and has raised the following issues which are now being litigated.

Required (The above is based upon an actual case, with names disguised.)

For each issue, consider whether you think the defendant (NCI) or the plaintiff (DHFS) has the valid position, based on your understanding of cost allocation.

1. DHFS alleges that NCI charged specific milk, condiments, and paper products to the nursing home, without following the usual 60 percent (nursing home) and 40 percent (retirement home) sharing for food costs. NCI asserts that these items are used in the nursing home to counteract the greater danger of spread of disease in the nursing home. DHFS claims that NCI's documentation to support charging these costs directly to the nursing home is inadequate

2. DHFS alleges that nourishments (liquid supplements, cookies, and some puree foods) that are consumed by nursing home residents at bedtime for their special health needs are akin to "seconds" at meals and should be allocated to both the nursing home and the retirement home

3. Three kitchen employees not involved in meal preparation are involved in service to both the nursing home and the retirement home; NCI asks the three employees to keep track of how much time they spend on the nursing home versus the retirement home. These time reports are then sent to management and are used as a basis for allocating the cost of the employees to the two homes. DHFS alleges that the practice is not sufficiently accurate, and relies largely on unsupported, self-reported information.

4. NCI allocates utility costs to the two homes using an industrial engineering study performed by the power company on five days in June four years ago. DHFS disputes that this allocation base is valid and says that NCI must use a square footage base rate.

Solution to Self-Study Problem

Joint Product Costing

The Physical Measure Method If we use a physical measure method, the joint cost of $20,000 is allocated as shown in Exhibit 1.

The production costs per gallon for both products are the same:

Product GS-50: $15,000/75 = $200

Product GS-80: $ 5,000/25 = $200

The Sales Value at Split-Off Method Assume that Northern Company sold 60 gallons of GS–50 and 20 gallons of GS–80. Then the $20,000 joint cost should be allocated among the products as shown in Exhibit 2.

Note that the gallons sold do not figure in the analysis, which is based on units produced only. The production costs per gallon for both products are calculated:

$$\text{Product GS-50 } \$18,750/75 = \$250$$
$$\text{Product GS-80 } \$ \ 1,250/25 = \$ \ 50$$

The Net Realizable Value Method   The net realizable values of GS–50 and GS–80 are $20,000 and $5,000, respectively, as shown in Exhibit 3. The allocated costs are $16,000 to GS–50 and $4,000 to GS–80. The costs per gallon for products GS–505 and GS–805 are calculated

$$\text{Product GS-505 } (\$16,000 + \$5,000)/50 = \$420$$
$$\text{Product GS-805 } (\$ \ 4,000 + \$2,000)/50 = \$120$$

EXHIBIT 1
Physical Measure Method

Product	Physical Measure	Proportion	Allocation of Joint Cost
GS–50	75 gallons	75%	$20,000 × 75% = $15,000
GS–80	25 gallons	25%	20,000 × 25% = 5,000

EXHIBIT 2
Sales Value at Split-Off Method

Product	Units	Price	Sales Value	Proportion	Joint Cost Allocated
GS–50	75	$300	$22,500	93.75%	$20,000 × 93.75% = $18,750
GS–80	25	60	1,500	6.25%	20,000 × 6.25% = 1,250
Total			$24,000	100%	$20,000

EXHIBIT 3   **Net Realizable Value Method**

Product	Production Units	Sales Price	Sales Value	Separable Cost	Net Realizable Value	Weight	Joint Cost Allocated
GS–50	50	$500	$25,000	$5,000	$20,000	80%	$20,000 × 80% = $16,000
GS–80	50	140	7,000	2,000	5,000	20%	20,000 × 20% = 4,000
Total	100		$32,000	$7,000	$25,000	100%	$20,000

Planning and Decision Making

The objective of these six chapters is to show how cost management information can be used strategically to support management planning and decision making. A key idea that ties these chapters together is that planning and decision making require a good understanding of cost drivers, that is, the activities or transactions that cause changes in costs, both from a short-term and a long-term perspective. There are both volume-based cost drivers (discussed in Chapter 4) and activity-based cost drivers (which we introduced in Chapter 5); both types of cost drivers are important in planning and decision making.

Because of this importance, the first chapter in this part, **Chapter 8,** is about cost estimation—how cost estimation equations can be developed to identify and measure the impact of cost drivers on cost objects. We cover both statistical and nonstatistical approaches to estimating cost equations. This foundational material is followed by a discussion of a short-run profit-planning tool, cost-volume-profit analysis, also called CVP, in **Chapter 9.**

Chapter 10 explains the master budget, which is one of the key planning tools that management accountants develop for their organizations. The master budget is often referred to as the most commonly used tool in management accounting for coordinating operations and for providing a set of financial targets to guide management. Linkages in Chapter 10 are made to some important topics covered earlier in the text, for example, budgeting for sustainability, preparation of activity-based budgets, and the impact of time-based activity-based costing on budgeting systems.

Chapter 11 shows how the management accountant uses cost calculations and a strategic understanding of the competitive context of an organization to address decisions such as whether to make or buy a component of a manufactured product or service, when to add features to a product, and when to accept one-time orders from customers. In each of these decisions, competitive context is crucial. For example, suppose that a company competes on the basis of *cost leadership* and is looking for ways to reduce manufacturing cost. The management accountant determines that it is cheaper to make rather than buy a part in the product; independently, the plant engineer figures out how to do away with the part while retaining the product's functionality. This accountant's analysis is flawed because it does not consider that the company can become more competitive by a redesign of the product.

Chapter 12, investment analysis, covers the topic of allocating capital (funds) to long-term projects, that is, those investments that require substantial amounts of capital and that provide financial returns over an extended period of time. As such, we extend the framework covered in Chapter 11 to include the analysis of decisions that have a long-term effect on the organization. The tools for decision making in this context incorporate the time-value of money and are called *discounted cash flow (DCF)* decision models.

Chapter 13 applies the concepts of the value chain and life-cycle analysis as cost-planning and cost-reduction tools. The value chain begins with the idea for a product or service; followed by market research, testing sample products, and manufacturing, and finally followed by sales and customer service. The chapter comprises four main parts: target costing at the front end of the value chain, the theory of constraints for the operational portion of the value chain, life cycle costing for the full value chain, and strategic pricing.

CHAPTER EIGHT

Cost Estimation

After studying this chapter, you should be able to . . .

1. Understand the strategic role of cost estimation
2. Understand the six steps of cost estimation
3. Use each of the cost estimation methods: the high-low method, and regression analysis
4. Explain the data requirements and implementation problems of the cost estimation methods
5. (Appendix A) Use learning curves in cost estimation when learning is present
6. (Appendix B) Use statistical measures to evaluate a regression analysis

LEARNING OBJECTIVE 1

Understand the strategic role of cost estimation.

Cost management information is critical in cost planning and decision making (planning for a new product or plant expansion and making other decisions). However, a basic requirement for cost effective planning is to use *accurate cost estimates* in the planning process. This chapter shows the methods to develop accurate estimates.

Cost estimation is particularly important for the construction industry. Large construction projects are often obtained on the basis of competitive bids. The contractors that bid on these projects must have accurate cost estimation methods to win their share of the bids and to be profitable. Cost estimation methods for contractors develop detailed analyses of the material and labor costs that are directly traceable to the project, as well as projections of the indirect costs, preferably using activity analysis as described in Chapter 5.

Cost estimation for construction contractors is such a critical aspect of these firms' success that a number of consultants and software developers have created tools and techniques to assist the contractors in cost estimation. The American Society of Professional Estimators (www.aspenational.com) and other professional organizations provide education and opportunities for professional development for cost managers involved in construction cost estimation. A number of consultants (e.g., Cost Concepts, Inc., www.costconcepts.com, and Davis Langdon Adamson Associates, www.davislangdon.com) and software providers such as Prosoft Inc. (www.prosoftinc.com) provide additional services.

An example of a large construction company that relies heavily on cost estimation is JE Dunn (www.jedunn.com), a builder of hospitals, resorts, office buildings, school buildings, and other projects across the United States.

Strategic Role of Cost Estimation

Carnegie's success can be attributed to another lesson he had learned on the way up: the value of meticulous cost accounting . . . As a result, when Union Iron or Keystone Bridge submitted a bid on a project, there was no guesswork involved. If Carnegie chose to undercut a rival's figure, he did so with absolute confidence that he could deliver what he promised and make a profit, for his was the only firm in the field with a near-fanatical devotion to cost accounting. As Charles Schwab would later put it, "Carnegie never wanted to know the profits. He always wanted to know the costs."[1]

As Carnegie understood, a critical starting point for strategic cost management is having accurate cost estimates. The strategic approach is forward looking, and thus cost estimation is

---

[1] Les Standiford, *Meet You in Hell* (New York: Crown Publishers, 2005), pp. 47–8, writing about Andrew Carnegie, business leader and philanthropist.

Cost estimation
is the development of a well-defined relationship between a cost object and its cost drivers for the purpose of predicting the cost.

an essential element of it. **Cost estimation** is the development of a well-defined relationship between a cost object and its cost drivers for the purpose of predicting the cost.

Cost estimation facilitates strategic management in two important ways. First, it helps predict future costs using previously identified activity-based, volume-based, structural, or executional cost drivers. Second, cost estimation helps identify the key cost drivers for a cost object and which of these cost drivers are most useful in predicting cost.

Using Cost Estimation to Predict Future Costs

Strategic management requires accurate cost estimates for many applications, including these:

1. **To facilitate strategy development and implementation.** Cost estimates are particularly important for firms competing on the basis of cost leadership. Cost estimates guide management in determining which management techniques, such as business intelligence, target costing, or total quality management, the firm should employ to succeed in its chosen strategy.

2. **To facilitate value-chain analysis.** Cost estimates help the firm identify potential opportunities for cost reduction by reconfiguring the value chain. For example, cost estimates are useful in determining whether overall costs and value to the product can be improved by manufacturing one of its components in-house or by purchasing it from a supplier.

3. **To facilitate target costing and pricing.** Cost estimates are an integral part of target costing and pricing. Management uses cost estimates of different product designs as part of the process of selecting the particular design that provides the best value to the customer while reducing manufacturing and other costs. Target costing and pricing are covered in Chapter 13.

4. **To facilitate effective performance measurement, evaluation, and compensation.** Cost estimates play a key role in determining costs in business units, which affect division managers' financial performance and opportunity for promotion and compensation and the ability to attract capital investment to their division. Accurate cost estimates play a crucial role in performance measurement which is covered in Chapters 18 through 20.

Cost Estimation for Different Types of Cost Drivers

The cost estimation methods explained in this chapter can be used for any of the four types of cost drivers: activity-based, volume-based, structural, or executional. The relationships between costs and activity-based or volume-based cost drivers often are best fit by the linear cost estimation methods explained in this chapter because these relationships are at least approximately linear within the relevant range of the firm's operations.

Structural cost drivers involve plans and decisions that have a long-term and therefore strategic impact on the firm. Such decisions include manufacturing experience, scale of product, product or production technology, and product or production complexity. Technology and complexity issues often lead management to use activity-based costing and linear estimation methods. In contrast, experience and scale often require nonlinear methods. As a cost driver, experience represents the reduction in unit cost due to learning. The effect on total cost of experience is nonlinear: that is, costs decrease with increased manufacturing experience. The learning effect is explained in Appendix A to the chapter. Similarly, the relationship between the structural cost driver, scale, and total cost is nonlinear. *Scale* is the term used to describe the manufacture of similar products that differ in size—for example, pipe valves of different capacity. A common effect of scale is that total manufacturing cost increases more rapidly than the increase in the size of the product. For example, the manufacture of a 22-inch industrial valve requires more than twice the cost of an 11-inch valve. The relationship between manufacturing cost and valve size can be predicted by a mathematical estimation model called the *power law* that is used in industrial engineering.[2]

Using Cost Estimation to Identify Cost Drivers

Often the most practical way to identify cost drivers is to rely on the judgment of product designers, engineers, and manufacturing personnel. Those who are most knowledgeable about

---

[2] Based on information in Phillip F. Ostwald and Timothy S. McLaren, *Cost Estimating for Engineering and Management* (Englewood Cliffs, NJ: Prentice Hall, 2004).

the product and production processes have the most useful information on cost drivers. Cost estimation sometimes plays a discovery role and at other times a collaborative role to validate and confirm the judgments of the designers and engineers. For example, Hewlett-Packard uses cost estimation to confirm the usefulness of cost drivers selected by teams of engineers and production personnel.

Six Steps of Cost Estimation

LEARNING OBJECTIVE 2

Understand the six steps of cost estimation.

The six steps of cost estimation are (1) define the cost object for which the related costs are to be estimated, (2) determine the cost drivers, (3) collect consistent and accurate data on the cost object and the cost drivers, (4) graph the data, (5) select and employ an appropriate estimation method, and (6) evaluate the accuracy of the cost estimate.

Step 1: Define the Cost Object to Be Estimated

Although it might seem elementary, defining the particular cost to be estimated requires care. For example, if the goal is to estimate product costs to improve product pricing, the relevant cost objects are the products manufactured in the plant. In contrast, if the goal is to reward managers for reducing cost, the most appropriate cost objects are the individual manufacturing departments in the plant since costs are most directly controllable by department managers.

Step 2: Determine the Cost Drivers

Cost drivers are the causal factors used in the estimation of the cost. Some examples of estimated costs and their related cost drivers follow:

Cost to Be Estimated	Cost Driver
Fuel expense for a delivery truck	Miles driven
Heating expense for a building	Temperature to be maintained in the building
Maintenance cost in a manufacturing plant	Machine-hours, labor-hours
Product design cost	Number of design elements, design changes

Identifying cost drivers is the most important step in developing the cost estimate. A number of relevant drivers might exist, yet some might not be immediately obvious. Fuel expense for a large delivery truck, for example, might be primarily a function of miles traveled, but it is also affected by the average weight delivered, the number of hours of operation, and the nature of the delivery area.

Step 3: Collect Consistent and Accurate Data

Once the cost drivers have been selected, the management accountant collects data on the cost object and cost drivers. The data must be consistent and accurate. *Consistent* means that each period of data is calculated using the same accounting basis and all transactions are properly recorded in the period in which they occurred. For example, using biweekly data for some variables and monthly data for other variables causes errors in estimates. Similarly, mismatch between periods occurs when data for one variable is based on the calendar month while data for another variable is based on four consecutive weekly periods that do not match the month. Difficulties also arise when supplies purchased during the month are used instead of supplies consumed.

The period used in cost estimating can vary from daily to weekly or annually. If the period is too short, the chance of mismatch between variables increases because of recording lags. On the other hand, if the period is too long, important short-term relationships in the data might be averaged out, and the estimate will not be as accurate. Moreover, a longer period reduces the number of data points available to improve the accuracy of the estimate. Management accountants must determine which time period best satisfies the competing objectives for accurate estimation.

Also the accuracy of the data depends on the source. Sometimes data developed within the firm are very reliable, as a result of management policies and procedures to ensure accuracy.

External sources of data, including governmental sources, trade and industry publications, universities, and other sources, have varying degrees of accuracy. The choice of cost drivers requires trade-offs between the relevance of the drivers and the consistency and accuracy of the data.

Step 4: Graph the Data

The objective of graphing data is to identify unusual patterns. Any shift or nonlinearity in the data must be given special attention in developing the estimate. For example, a week's down-time to install new equipment causes unusual production data for that week; such data should be excluded when developing a cost estimate. Any unusual occurrences can be detected easily by studying a graph.

Step 5: Select and Employ the Estimation Method

The two estimation methods presented in the next section of the chapter differ in their ability to provide superior accuracy in cost estimation relative to the cost of the expertise and resources required. The management accountant chooses the method with the best precision/cost trade-off for the estimation objectives.

Step 6: Assess the Accuracy of the Cost Estimate

A critical final step in cost estimation is to consider the potential for error when the estimate is prepared. This involves considering the completeness and appropriateness of cost drivers selected in step 2, the consistency and accuracy of data selected in step 3, the study of the graphs in step 4, and the precision of the method selected in step 5.

A common approach for assessing the accuracy of an estimation method is to compare the estimates to the actual results over time. For example, when a firm predicts overhead costs each year, over a 10-year period there are 10 estimation errors to evaluate. These errors can be evaluated using the **mean absolute percentage error (MAPE).** MAPE is calculated by taking the absolute value of each error, and then averaging these errors and converting the result to a percentage of the actual values of overhead.

> The **mean absolute percentage error (MAPE)** is calculated by taking the absolute value of each error, and averaging these errors and converting the result to a percentage of the actual values of overhead.

Cost Estimation Methods

> **LEARNING OBJECTIVE 3**
>
> *Use each of the cost estimation methods: the high-low method, and regression analysis.*

The two estimation methods are the high-low method and regression analysis. The high-low method is the least accurate but easiest to apply and regression analysis is the most accurate and most costly, requiring more time, data collection, and expertise. In choosing the best estimation method, management accountants must seek a balance between the level of accuracy desired and any limitations on cost, time, and effort.

An Illustration of Cost Estimation

To illustrate the two methods, we use the example of a management accountant, Ben Garcia, who is developing cost estimates of maintenance costs for a manufacturing plant. Garcia has the following data on maintenance costs:

	January	February	March	April	May	June	July
Maintenance cost ($)	22,843	22,510	22,706	23,030	22,413	22,935	23,175

As a first step, Garcia graphs the data (Exhibit 8.1) and observes that maintenance costs are increasing, although not steadily. Based only on a visual study of the graph, he also predicts that maintenance costs will be between $22,500 and $23,500 in the coming month, August. Since this prediction is rough and he wants to improve its accuracy, he turns to the cost estimation methods, beginning with the high-low method.

High-Low Method

The **high-low method** uses algebra to determine a *unique* estimation line between representative high and low points in the data. The high-low method accomplishes two important

> The **high-low method** uses algebra to determine a *unique* estimation line between representative high and low points in the data.

EXHIBIT 8.1
Graph of Maintenance Costs

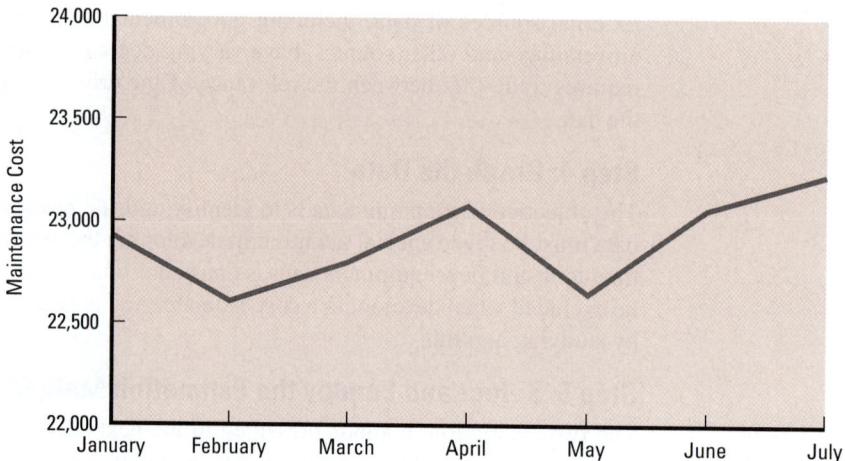

objectives for Garcia. First, it is based on a unique cost line rather than a rough estimate based on a view of the graph. Second, it permits him to add information that might be useful in predicting maintenance costs. For example, he knows that total maintenance costs are likely to include both variable and fixed costs. The fixed cost portion is the planned (preventive) maintenance that is performed regardless of the plant's volume of activity. Also, a part of maintenance cost varies with the number of operating hours; more operating hours mean more wear on the machines and thus more maintenance costs. Garcia collects the additional operating-hours information as follows:

	January	February	March	April	May	June	July
Total operating hours	3,451	3,325	3,383	3,614	3,423	3,410	3,500
Maintenance costs ($)	22,843	22,510	22,706	23,030	22,413	22,935	23,175

To use the high-low method, Garcia enters the data into a graph, as shown in Exhibit 8.2, and then selects two points from the data, one representative of the lower points and the other representative of the higher points. Often these can be simply the lowest and highest points

EXHIBIT 8.2
Ben Garcia's Data on Maintenance Cost and Hours

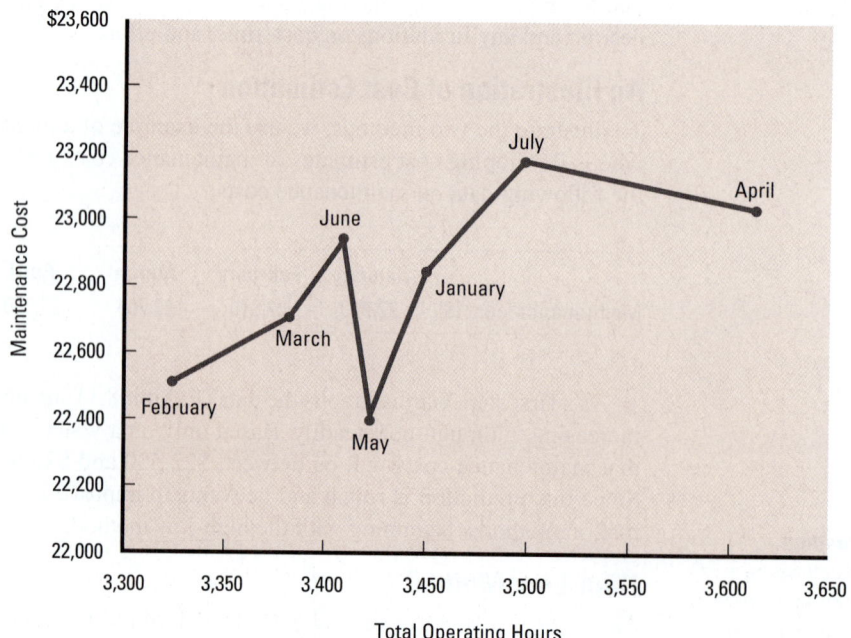

in the data. However, if either the highest or lowest point is a great distance from the other points around it, a biased estimation can result. Both points must be representative of the data around them.

The high-low estimate is represented as follows:

$$Y = a + (b \times X)$$

where: Y = the value of the estimated maintenance cost

X = the cost driver, the number of operating hours of operation for the plant

a = a fixed quantity that represents the value of Y when X = zero

b = the slope of the line. In the plant maintenance example, it is the unit variable cost for maintenance cost per operating hour.

To obtain the high and low points, Garcia draws a freehand line through the data to help select the high and low points (try this yourself on Exhibit 8.2). He then chooses a high and a low point reasonably close to the freehand line. Suppose that he has chosen the points for February and April. Then he calculates the value for b:

$$b = \text{Variable cost per hour}$$

$$= \frac{\text{Difference between } \textbf{costs} \text{ for high and low points}}{\text{Difference for the value of the } \textbf{cost driver} \text{ for the high and low points}}$$

$$b = \frac{\$23,030 - \$22,510}{3,614 - 3,325} = \$1.80 \text{ per hour}$$

Next, the value for a (the fixed quantity) can be calculated using either February or April data:

Using April Data

$$a = Y - (b \times X) = \$23,030 - (\$1.80 \times 3,614) = \$16,525$$

Using February data gives the same value for a because fixed cost is the same at both levels of operating hours; only total variable costs for the two levels differ:

Using February Data

$$a = Y - (b \times X) = \$22,510 - (\$1.80 \times 3,325) = \$16,52$$

So the estimation equation using the high-low method is:

$$Y = \$16,525 + (\$1.80 \times X)$$

This equation can be used to estimate maintenance cost for August. Suppose that 3,600 operating hours are expected in August. Then maintenance costs are estimated as follows:

$$\text{Maintenance cost in August} = \$16,525 + (\$1.80 \times 3,600)$$
$$= \$23,005$$

Management accountants find the high-low equation useful for estimating *total costs* but not the amount of fixed costs alone. The reason is that the estimate applies only to the *relevant range* of the cost driver used to develop the estimate, the range from 3,325 to 3,614 hours. The value of a, a measure that is relevant at zero hours only, is too far from the relevant range to be properly interpreted as a fixed cost. Its role is to serve only as the constant part of the estimation equation used to *predict total cost*.

The key advantage of the high-low method is that it provides a unique cost equation— once the high and low points are chosen, there is only one possible cost estimation equation. However, the high-low method is limited; it can represent only the best possible line for the two selected points, and the selection of the two points requires judgment. The next method, regression analysis, is generally more accurate because it uses statistical estimation, which provides greater mathematical precision.

Regression Analysis

Regression analysis
is a statistical method for
obtaining the unique cost-
estimating equation that best fits
a set of data points.

Regression analysis is a statistical method for obtaining the unique cost-estimating equation that best fits a set of data points. Regression analysis fits the data by *minimizing the sum of the squares* of the estimation errors. Each error is the distance measured from the regression line to one of the data points. Because regression analysis systematically minimizes the estimation errors in this way, it is called **least squares regression.**

Least squares regression,
which minimizes the sum of
the squares of the estimation
errors, is widely viewed as one
of the most effective methods for
estimating costs.

A regression analysis has two types of variables. The **dependent variable** is the cost to be estimated.[3] The **independent variable** is the cost driver used to estimate the value of the dependent variable. When one cost driver is used, the analysis is called a *simple regression.* When two or more cost drivers are used, it is called *multiple regression.*

The **dependent variable**
is the cost to be estimated.

The regression equation has both an intercept and a slope term, much like the high-low method. In addition, the amount of the estimation error is considered explicitly in the simple regression estimate, which is

The **independent variable**
is the cost driver used to estimate
the value of the dependent
variable.

$$Y = a + bX + e$$

where: Y = the amount of the *dependent variable,* the cost to be estimated

a = a *fixed quantity,* also called the *intercept* or *constant term,* which represents the amount of Y when $X = 0$

X = the value for the *independent variable,* the cost driver for the cost to be estimated; there may be one or more cost drivers

b = the *unit variable cost,* also called the *coefficient* of the independent variable, that is, the increase in Y (cost) for each unit increase in X (cost driver)

e = the *estimation error,* which is the amount by which the regression prediction $(y = a + bx)$ differs from the data point.

To illustrate the regression method, the following table and Exhibit 8.3A show three months of data on supplies expense and production levels. (To simplify the presentation, only three data points are used; applications of regression usually involve at least 12 data points.) The management accountant's task is to estimate supplies expense for month 4, in which the production level is expected to be 125 units.

Month	Supplies Expense (Y)	Production Level (X)
1	$250	50 units
2	310	100
3	325	150
4	?	125

The regression for the data is determined by a statistical procedure that finds the unique line through the three data points that minimizes the sum of the squared error distances. The regression line (see Exhibit 8.3B) is[4]

$$Y = \$220 + \$0.75X$$

Thus, the estimated value for supplies expense in month 4 is

$$Y = \$220 + (\$0.75 \times 125) = \$313.75$$

Regression analysis gives management accountants an objective, statistically precise method to estimate supplies expense. Its principal advantage is a unique estimate that produces the least estimation error for the data. On the other hand, since the errors are squared to find the best fitting line, the regression analysis can be influenced strongly by unusual data points called **outliers,** with the result that the estimation line is not representative of

Outliers
are unusual data points that
strongly influence a regression
analysis.

[3] Although the dependent variable is a cost in most of the cases we consider, the dependent variable also could be a revenue or some other type of financial or operating data.

[4] The derivation of the intercept ($220) and coefficient ($0.75) for this regression line is done in Excel or other software. Appendix B to this chapter also has an extended reference on regression analysis.

EXHIBIT 8.3A **Supplies Expense Data for Regression Application**

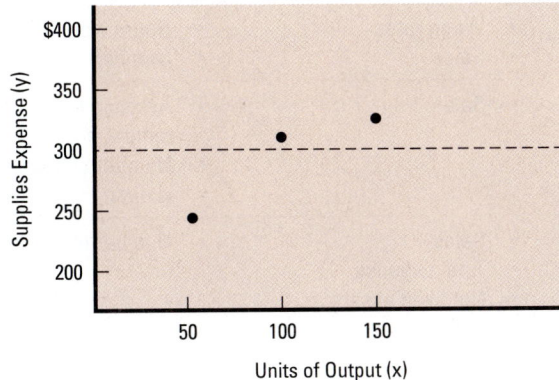

EXHIBIT 8.3B **The Regression Line for Supplies Expense with Units of Output as the Cost Driver (i.e., independent variable)**

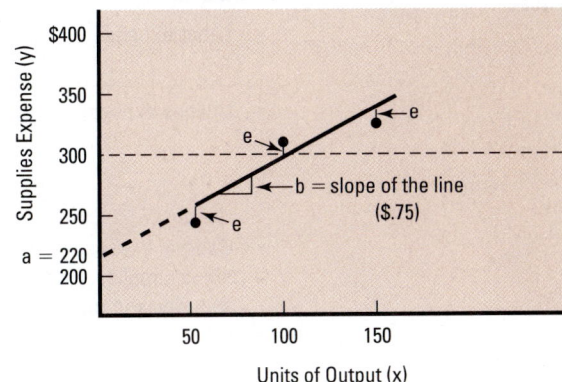

most of the data. Such a situation is illustrated in Exhibit 8.4. To prevent this type of distortion, management accountants often prepare a graph of the data prior to using regression and determine whether any outliers are present. Each outlier is reviewed to determine whether it is due to a data-recording error, normal operating condition, or unique and nonrecurring event. Guided by the objective of developing the regression that is most representative of the data, the accountant then decides whether to correct or remove the outlier.

Choosing the Dependent Variable

Development of a regression analysis begins with the choice of the cost object, the dependent variable. The dependent variable might be at a very aggregate level, such as total maintenance costs for the entire firm, or at a detail level, such as maintenance costs for each plant or department. The choice of aggregation level depends on the objectives for the cost estimation, data availability and reliability, and cost/benefit considerations. When a key objective is accuracy, a detailed level of analysis often is preferred.

Choosing the Independent Variable(s)

To identify the independent variables, management accountants consider all financial, operating, and other economic data that might be relevant for estimating the dependent variable. The goal is to choose variables that (1) are relevant; that is, they change when the dependent variable changes, and (2) do not duplicate other independent variables. As an example,

EXHIBIT 8.4

The Effect of Outliers on Regression

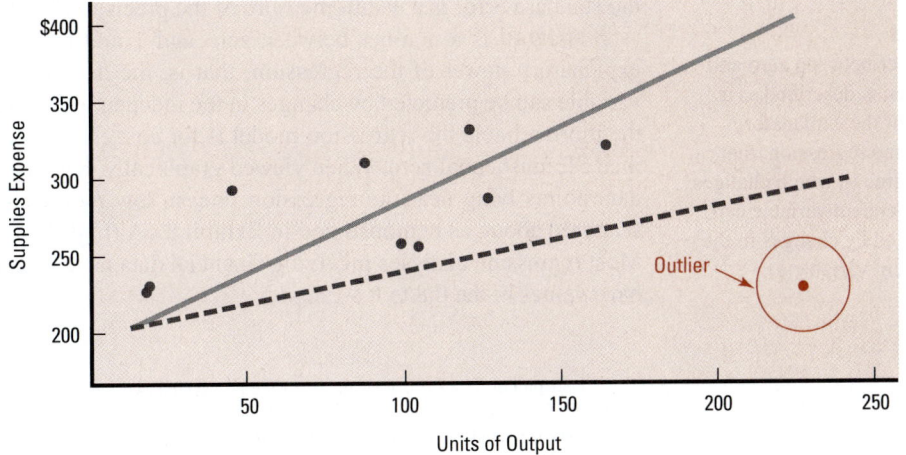

Key: ———————— proper regression line, excluding the outlier
- - - - - - - - improper regression line, influenced by the outlier

EXHIBIT 8.5

Selected Independent Variables and Dependent Variables for a Retail Store

Selected Dependent Variables	Independent Variables	
	Financial Data	**Operating Data**
• Labor expense	• Wage rates • Sales	• Hours worked • Number of employees
• Utilities expense	• Sales	• Average daily temperature • Number of hours store is open
• General expenses: office supplies, cleaning, security, and repairs	• Sales • Total expense • Net fixed assets	• Number of employees

A **dummy variable** is used to represent the presence or absence of a condition.

Exhibit 8.5 presents some dependent and independent variables that might be appropriate for the study of costs in a retail store.

Most often the data in a regression analysis are numerical amounts in dollars or units. Another type of variable, called a **dummy variable,** represents the presence or absence of a condition. For example, dummy variables can be used to indicate seasonality. If the management accountant is estimating costs of production, and if production is always high in March, a dummy variable with a value of 1 for March and 0 for the other months could be used.

Evaluating a Regression Analysis

In addition to a cost estimate, regression analysis also provides quantitative measures of its precision and reliability. *Precision* refers to the accuracy of the estimates from the regression, and *reliability* indicates whether the regression reflects actual relationships among the variables; that is, is the regression model likely to continue to predict accurately? These measures can aid management accountants in assessing the usefulness of the regression. Four key (and related) measures are explained here. These and other statistical measures are explained more fully in Appendix B.

1. R-squared, also called the *coefficient of determination.*
2. The *t*-value.
3. The standard error of the estimate (SE).
4. The *p*-value

R-squared, the *t*-value and the *p*-value are used to measure the reliability of the regression; the standard error is a useful measure of the precision, or accuracy, of the regression.

R-squared is a number between zero and 1 and often is described as a measure of the explanatory power of the regression; that is, the degree to which changes in the dependent variable can be predicted by changes in the independent variable(s). The higher the R-squared, the more reliable the regression model is for cost estimation; in fact if R-squared equals one, then SE must equal zero. When viewed graphically, regressions with high R-squared show the data points lying near the regression line; in low R-squared regressions, the data points are scattered about, as demonstrated in Exhibit 8.6A (high R-squared) and 8.6B (low R-squared). Most regression analyses involving financial data have R-squared values above 0.5, and many have values in the 0.8 to 0.9 range.[5]

R-squared

is a number between zero and 1 and often is described as a measure of the explanatory power of the regression, that is, the degree to which changes in the dependent variable can be predicted by changes in the independent variable(s).

---

[5] The square root of R-squared, or simply R, is called the *correlation coefficient* and is interpreted in the same manner as R-squared. The correlation coefficient is a number between −1 and +1; a value near zero is interpreted as a lack of relationship between the independent and dependent variables. When R is positive, the relationship is direct; that is, when one variable increases, so does the other. When R is negative, the relationship is inverse; that is, when one variable increases, the other decreases.

EXHIBIT 8.6A   **Regression with High R-Squared**

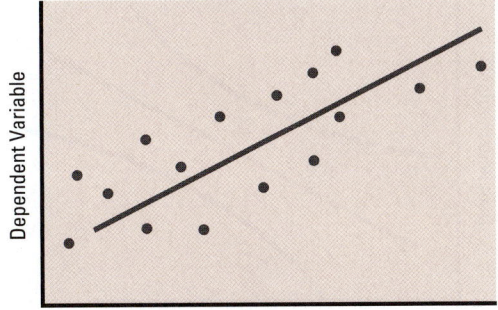

EXHIBIT 8.6B   **Regression with Low R-Squared**

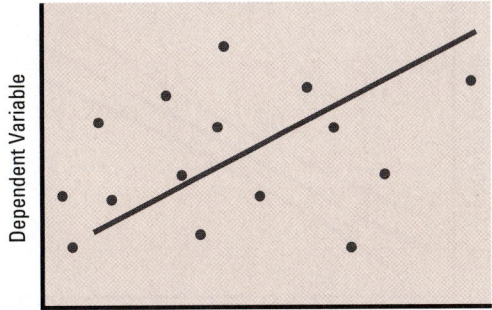

The *t*-value

is a measure of the reliability of each independent variable, that is, the degree to which an independent variable has a valid, stable, long-term relationship with the dependent variable.

Multicollinearity

means that two or more independent variables are highly correlated with each other.

Correlation

means that a given variable tends to change predictably in the same (or opposite) direction for a given change in the other, correlated variable.

The standard error of the estimate (SE)

is a measure of the accuracy of the regression's estimates.

A confidence interval

is a range around the regression line within which the management accountant can be confident the actual value of the predicted cost will fall.

The ***t*-value** is a measure of the statistical reliability of each independent variable. *Reliability* is the degree to which an independent variable has a valid, stable, long-term relationship with the dependent variable. A relatively small *t*-value (generally, the *t*-value should be more than 2) indicates little or no statistical relationship between the independent and dependent variables. A variable with a low *t*-value should be removed from the regression to simplify the model and to lead to more accurate cost estimates.[6]

When two or more independent variables exist, the presence of a low *t*-value for one or more of these variables is a possible signal of **multicollinearity,** which means that two or more independent variables are highly correlated with each other. As suggested by the name, independent variables are supposed to be independent of each other, not correlated. **Correlation** among variables means that a given variable tends to change predictably in the same (or opposite) direction of a given change in the other variable. For example, the number of machine-hours used in manufacturing is correlated with the number of labor-hours because both are affected by the same factor, the number of units produced. Moreover, because a common trend tends to affect many types of financial data, accounting and operating data are often highly correlated.

The effect of multicollinearity is that the regression estimates of the coefficients for the independent variables are unreliable. The cost estimates of the regression will be reliable, but the amount of the coefficient could not be reliably interpreted as the per-unit cost driver for the related independent variable. For example, if the independent variable is labor-hours, the coefficient for this variable does not give a reliable estimate of the labor cost per hour when multicollinearity is present. When practical, one or more of the correlated variables should be removed from the model.

The **standard error of the estimate (SE)** is a measure of the accuracy of the regression's estimate. It is a range around the regression estimate in which the unknown actual value can reasonably be expected to fall.

This range is called a **confidence interval** and is used to measure the accuracy of the prediction at any point for the independent variable, as illustrated in Exhibits 8.7A and 8.7B. A 67 percent confidence interval is determined by taking the regression line and identifying a range that is a 1 standard-error distance on either side of the regression line; a 95 percent confidence interval would be determined from 2 standard-error distances. Confidence intervals are useful and precise tools for management accountants to describe the degree of precision obtained from the regression prediction. To illustrate, if the regression prediction is $4,500 and the SE is $500, then the 67 percent confidence interval is $4,500 +/− $500; one can be 67 percent confident that the unknown true value of the dependent variable lies between $4,000 and $5,000. An equivalent interpretation is to say that there is a 67 percent probability that the unknown true value of the dependent

[6] As for the correlation coefficient (footnote 5), the *t*-value can be positive or negative, depending on the nature of the relationship between the dependent and independent variables.

EXHIBIT 8.7A **Regression with Narrow (Good) Standard Error**

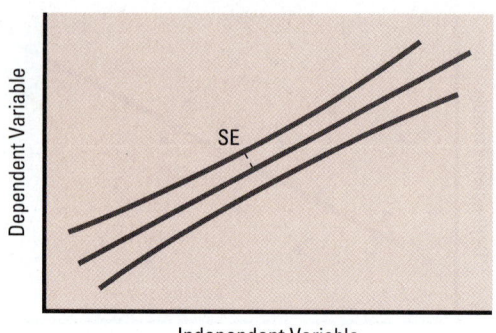

EXHIBIT 8.7B **Regression with Wide (Poor) Standard Error**

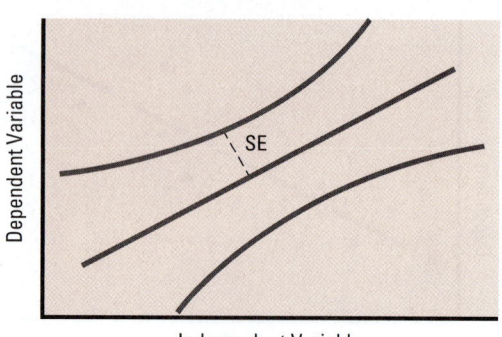

variable lies between $4,000 and $5,000. The confidence range for 95 percent would be $4,500 +/− 2 × $500, a range of $3,500 to $5,500.[7]

Because it is used to measure a confidence range, the SE must be interpreted by its relationship to the average size of the dependent variable. If the SE is small relative to the dependent variable, the precision of the regression can be assessed as relatively good. How small the SE value must be for a favorable precision evaluation is a matter of judgment, but a threshold of approximately 5 to 10 percent of the average of the dependent variable can be used. The confidence ranges for two regressions are illustrated in Exhibit 8.7A (good precision) and 8.7B (relatively poor precision).

The ***p*-value**
measures the risk that a particular independent variable has only a chance relationship to the dependent variable.

The ***p*-value** measures the risk that a particular independent variable has only a chance relationship to the dependent variable, and there is no significant statistical relationship. A small *p*-value (small risk) is desirable; a *p*-value of .05 to .1 or less is often used as a guide in practice. The *R*-squared, *t*-value, SE, and *p*-value are illustrated in the following example (Exhibit 8.8, p. 287) and are shown in the Excel spreadsheet for this example (Exhibit 8.9, p. 288). Note that the *t*-values greater than 2 have low *p*-values. Also, there is a *p*-value for the regression as a whole, which is labeled "Significance *F*" in Exhibit 8.9. As for the *p*-values for each independent variable, the significance of *F* should be less than approximately .05 for a statistically reliable regression. The explanation of the *F* statistic is found in Appendix B.

Using Regression to Estimate Maintenance Costs (Following the Six Steps)

We continue the case developed earlier, Ben Garcia's estimation of maintenance costs. Following the six steps outlined in the first section of the chapter, Garcia defined the cost object and the relevant cost driver as maintenance cost and operating hours, respectively. He also collected and graphed the data (Exhibit 8.2). The next step is to solve the regression using regression software such as the Excel spreadsheet program, with the following findings (*Y* represents maintenance cost and *X* represents operating hours):

$$Y = \$15{,}843 + (\$2.02 \times X)$$

Garcia expects approximately 3,600 operating hours in August, so the amount of maintenance cost for August is estimated to be

$$Y = \$15{,}843 + (\$2.02 \times 3{,}600) = \$23{,}115$$

---

[7] Note that the confidence intervals shown in Exhibits 8.7A and 8.7B are curved and move away from the regression line at low and high values for the independent variable. The reason is that *for a given value, or "point," of the independent variable (let's call the point "p"),* the standard error of that point, SE_p, can be calculated from two factors: the value of SE and the distance of the point *p* from the mean of the independent variable. SE_p is smallest at the mean of the independent variable and increases the further the point *p* is away from the mean. The calculation of SE_p is beyond the scope of this text but can be found in introductory statistics texts.

Regression analysis is used for cost estimation and a wide variety of financial management functions that the management accountant is likely to encounter. Four examples (and references for additional reading) are given here.

Business analytics is a type of business intelligence in which statistical models are used to develop information for decision making. The following examples show how business analytics are used in actual organizations.

IMPROVING PROFITABILITY USING REGRESSION ANALYSIS

How does a company improve its profitability? One approach is to study the high performers in the company's industry. Proprietary databases are available that provide detailed financial and operating information for comparable companies. After identifying low-performing and high-performing comparable companies, the management accountant can determine from the list of variables those that are under the control of management. Multiple-regression analysis can then be used to explain performance differences between the companies. This statistical information is then used to develop strategies for improving the company's own profitability. Cvar and Quelch (2007) used this data-driven approach to help improve a client's ROI from 33 percent to 57 percent—a gain of approximately 70 percent. As an example, outsourcing a component of the company's product, which was indicated by the regression analysis, accounted for a 10-point increase in the company's return on investment.

Source: Margeaux Cvar and John A. Quelch, "Which Levers Boost ROI?" *Harvard Business Review* 85, no. 6 (June 2007), pp. 21–22.

PREDICTING SUCCESS AT EHARMONY

The dating service, eHarmony, claims to produce 90 marriages per day, based on a recent Harris poll. The firm attributes its success to the use of regression. Neil Warren, the company's founder used data from 5,000 married couples to develop a model of marital compatibility using several variables based on cognitive style, relationship skills, and emotional temperament, among others. The regression was then used to match customers of eHarmony.

Source: Ian Ayres, *Super Crunchers* (New York: Bantam Books, 2007), pp. 23–26.

PREDICTING SUCCESS IN SCHOOL

The U.S. Department of Education undertook a project in the late 1990s called the Early Childhood Longitudinal Study (ECLS) with the goal of identifying the factors associated with academic progress of children from kindergarten through fifth grade. Twenty thousand children were selected for the study and extensive data analysis using regression analysis was employed to discover those factors. The eight leading factors in determining success were:

1. Parents' education.
2. Parents' socioeconomic status.
3. Age of the child's mother at the time of her first child's birth.
4. The child's birth weight.
5. Language spoken by parents at home.
6. Whether the child was adopted.
7. Parents' involvement in the PTA.
8. The number of books the child has at home.

Source: Steven D. Levitt and Stephen J. Dubner, *Freakonomics* (New York: HarperCollins, 2006).

CONSTRUCTION COSTS IN WASTE RECYCLING

The construction industry uses cost estimation extensively, and in many cases a project cost is estimated directly based on projected labor-hours, materials, and other elements of the project. Alternatively, the construction cost for a project can be estimated based upon the actual costs incurred for similar projects already completed. In this approach the management accountant identifies the key cost driver of construction cost, which might be square feet of space or similar measure of capacity. A regression is then used to develop a cost estimation equation to predict project cost based upon the cost driver. This approach has been used to estimate the cost of building waste recycling plants based on the capacity of each plant measured in tons per day (TPD). Regression analyses for TPD versus construction costs for a variety of completed waste recycling plants have shown a very good fit, with an R-squared of .88. The construction costs of a new plant can thus be estimated from the desired TPD of the new plant using this regression equation.

Source: Richard K. Ellsworth, "Cost-to-Capacity Analysis for Estimating Project Costs," *Construction Accounting and Taxation*, September/October 2005, pp. 5–10.

The statistical measures are:

R-squared $= .461$

t-value $= 2.07$ ($p = .09$)

Standard error of the estimate $= \$221.71$

Garcia notes that R-squared is less than 0.5, the t-value is greater than 2.0, and the SE is approximately 1 percent of the mean of the dependent variable. The SE and t-values are very good. However, since the R-squared is low, Garcia asks his accounting assistant, Jan, to review the regression.

Jan looks at the regression and the related graphs and notices immediately that in May maintenance cost dropped significantly, and operating hours experienced a modest drop. Garcia observes that the drop in May was probably due to the unusually poor economic conditions that

Regression analysis is commonly used as one means to estimate the value of commercial real estate properties. It is used for two key types of properties: income-producing properties, such as apartment buildings and office buildings, and nonincome-producing properties,

such as warehouses and manufacturing plants. Identify what you think are the two or three key independent variables for estimating the value for each type of property.

(Refer to Comments on Cost Management in Action at end of Chapter.)

month; thus, output was reduced and operating hours and maintenance fell accordingly. Recalling that dummy variables can be used to correct for isolated variations and seasonal or other patterns, Jan suggests that Garcia run the regression again with a dummy variable having a value of 1 in May and a value of zero otherwise (the symbol D represents the dummy variable). The new regression result is as follows:

$$Y = \$16,467 + (\$1.856 \times X) - (\$408.638 \times D)$$

The coefficients in the revised equation indicate that the poor performance in May reduced estimated costs by $408.64, and that each operating hour increases maintenance cost by $1.86. With the revised regression, the estimate of maintenance costs for August is as follows (assuming no unusual unfavorable event in August, and thus $D = 0$):

$$Y = \$16,467 + (\$1.856 \times 3,600) - (\$408.638 \times 0)$$
$$= \$23,149$$

The statistical measures are as follows:

R-squared = .772

t-values:

Hours: 2.60 ($p = .05$)

Dummy variable: -2.33($p = .07$)

Standard error of the estimate (SE) = $161.27

Garcia observes that the inclusion of the dummy variable improves *R*-squared, the *t*-values, the *p*-values, and the SE of the regression. For this reason, he relies on the estimate from the latter regression.

Using Spreadsheet Software for Regression Analysis

Taking a new example, suppose that WinDoor Inc. is developing a regression cost equation for the indirect costs in its plant. WinDoor manufactures windows and doors used in home construction; both products are made in standard and custom sizes. Occasionally, a very large order substantially increases the direct and indirect costs in a given month. The indirect costs primarily consist of supplies, quality control and testing, overtime, and other indirect labor. Regression is used to budget indirect costs for the coming year, primarily for cash management purposes. The management accountant, Charlotte Williams, knows from prior years that both direct labor-hours and machine-hours in the plant are good independent variables for estimating indirect costs. She gathers the data in Exhibit 8.8 for the most recent 12 months.

Williams develops the regression for these data using Excel. To use Excel, she selects the Regression option from the Data/Data Analysis tab, then selects the X and Y ranges for the independent and dependent variables, and obtains the regression results in Exhibit 8.9 on (where L represents labor-hours and M represents machine-hours):

$$Y = \$35,070 + (\$5.090 \times L) + (\$40.471 \times M)$$

The statistical measures follow:

R-squared = .935

t-values:

Labor-hours: 2.976 ($p = .015$)

Machine-hours: 2.505 ($p = .033$)

Standard error of the estimate (SE) = $17,480

EXHIBIT 8.8
Indirect Costs, Labor-Hours
and Machine-Hours for
WinDoor Inc.

Date	Total Indirect Costs	Direct Labor-Hours	Machine-Hours
June 2009	$274,500	26,940	2,009
July	320,000	35,690	3,057
August	323,200	32,580	3,523
September	219,900	24,580	1,856
October	232,100	19,950	2,168
November	342,300	34,330	3,056
December	427,800	43,180	3,848
January 2010	231,000	21,290	1,999
February	257,300	28,430	2,290
March	248,700	24,660	1,894
April	248,400	27,870	2,134
May	338,400	31,940	3,145

Multiple linear regression
is used to describe regression
applications having two or more
independent variables.

A simple linear regression
has a single independent
variable.

The regression satisfies our statistical criteria: R-squared is relatively high, and the t-values and SE are good. The p-value for the regression ("significance of F" in Excel on the right-hand side of Exhibit 8.9) is 4.44E-06, or .0000044, a very low and very good p-value. Thus, WinDoor can use the estimates with a reasonable degree of confidence.

The WinDoor example is an application of **multiple linear regression,** because it involves two or more independent variables. In contrast, the original Ben Garcia example, which used a single independent variable, operating hours, is an application of **simple linear regression.**

Illustration of the Use of Regression Analysis in the Gaming Industry

Harrah's owns many large casinos throughout the world, but particularly in Las Vegas, where it operates Flamingo Las Vegas, Caesars Palace, and Paris Las Vegas. Harrah's competes in a business that is very focused on customer satisfaction and customer loyalty. To be more competitive, Harrah's uses regression analysis to predict customer satisfaction. The approach is used by many other companies, including UPS and Google. The five-step model below explains how and why Harrah's uses regression analysis (the story is described in the book, *Super Crunchers,* by Ian Ayres, Bantam Books, 2007, pp. 30–32).

The Five Steps of Strategic Decision Making for Harrah's

1. **Determine the strategic issues surrounding the problem.** Since it operates in a very customer-focused business, Harrah's strategy is to develop and maintain customer loyalty (a differentiation strategy) and to improve customer profitability.

2. **Identify the alternative actions.** Harrah's knows that its customers have a "pain point," the amount of gaming losses at which the customer leaves the casino. The casinos have customer service representatives, called "luck ambassadors" who are responsible for maintaining customer satisfaction and, in particular, to make sure the customer does not reach the pain point.

3. **Obtain information and conduct analyses of the alternatives.** To obtain information about the pain points of individual customers, Harrah's began a "Total Rewards" program that involved a swipeable electronic card that provides certain rewards to customers but also provides data on the customers gaming in the casino. Harrah's uses this information together with other information provided by the Rewards customers to develop a regression analysis to predict the individual customer's pain point.

4. **Based on strategy and analysis, choose and implement the desired alternative.** Harrah's has implemented the regression-based system, so that when a given customer is gaming in the casino (Harrah's computer system lets it know real-time what the customer is gaming and the gains or losses for that day), the customer service representatives can be alerted when a given customer is approaching his or her predicted pain point and can be dispatched to urge that customer to take a break, and perhaps enjoy a free meal at Harrah's expense.

EXHIBIT 8.9 **Excel Regression Results for WinDoor Data, Showing Regression Dialog Box**

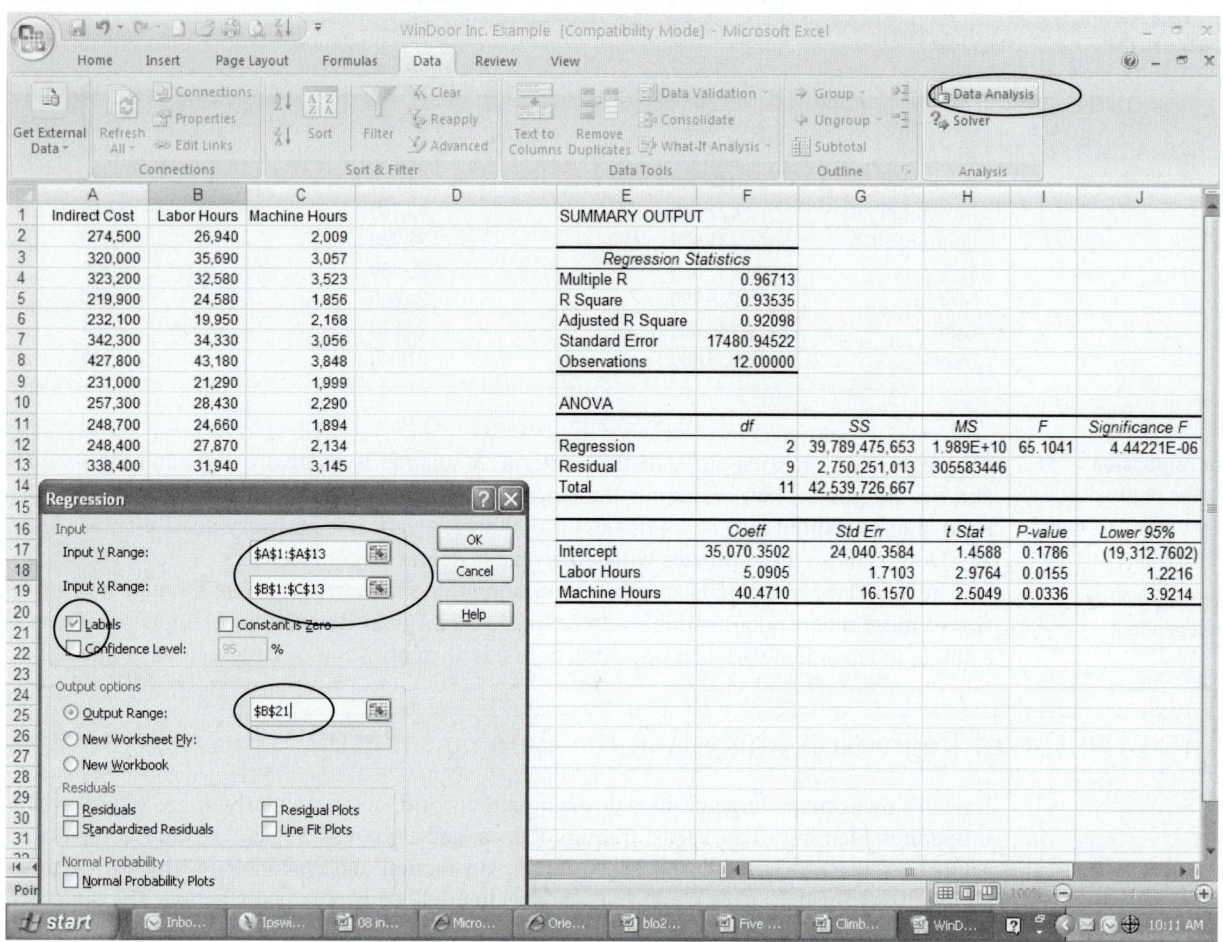

This exhibit shows both the regression results and the dialog box used to produce the regression results shown in the exhibit. Note that the independent variables (*X* Range) and dependent variable (*Y* Range) are entered into the dialog box. Labels are used in the top row of each column of data. The output is presented in the cells to the right and below the selected cell, F1. The dialog box is accessed by choosing **Data Analysis** at the right end of the ribbon under the DATA tab in Excel 2007. If Data Analysis is not on the ribbon, then it needs to be installed by clicking the Office button at the top left of the Excel spreadsheet and then clicking Excel Options. In the next screen click Add-ins on the left of the screen and then choose Analysis-ToolPak, which contains a number of statistical methods including regression. The location of Data Analysis and the key data entry in the regression dialog box are marked on the spreadsheet in Exhibit 8.9.

5. **Provide an ongoing evaluation of the effectiveness of implementation in step 4.** Harrah's system requires continuous updating for new customers and changes in customer behavior, so that the regression analyses can be kept current.

Implementation Problems: Nonlinearity

LEARNING OBJECTIVE 4

Explain the data requirements and implementation problems of the cost estimation methods.

Linear regression assumes a linear relationship between the variables, and the regression estimates are unreliable when the data relationships are nonlinear. Nonlinearity most often happens because of certain time-series patterns to the data such as trend and/or seasonality, an outlier in the data, and data shift, which are discussed below. Nonlinear regression analysis can be adapted for nonlinear relationships, so the following discussion applies to only the linear regressions that are illustrated in the chapter. (One example of a nonlinear regression is illustrated in Self-Study Problem 4).

1. **Trend and/or seasonality.** A common characteristic of accounting data is a significant trend that results from changing prices and/or seasonality. When trend or seasonality

EXHIBIT 8.10
Adjusting for Trend and
Seasonality Using First
Difference or a Price Index

		Price Index Adjustment	
Supplies Expense	First Difference	Hypothetical Price Index for Supplies Expense	Supplies Expense Adjusted for Price Index
$250	—	1.00	$250/1.00 = $250
310	$60	1.08	310/1.08 = 287
325	15	1.12	325/1.12 = 290

A **trend variable**
is a variable that takes on values
of 1, 2, 3, . . . for each period in
sequence.

is present, a linear regression is not a good fit to the data, and the management accountant should use a method to deseasonalize or to detrend a variable. The most common methods to do this follow:

- Use of a price change index to adjust the values of each variable to some common time period.
- Use of a trend variable. A **trend variable** takes on values of 1, 2, 3, . . . for each period in sequence.
- Replacement of the original values of each of the variables with the first differences. First difference for each variable is the difference between each value and the succeeding value in the time series.

The index approach and the first difference approach are shown in Exhibit 8.10 using the supplies expense data from Exhibit 8.3.

Trend is present in virtually all financial time series data used in management accounting because of inflation and growth in the economy. Thus, it is a pervasive issue in the proper development of a regression analysis.

2. **Outliers.** As mentioned earlier, when an error in the data or an unusual or nonrecurring business condition affects operations for a given period, the result might be a data point that is far from the others, an outlier. Because outliers can significantly decrease the precision and reliability of the estimate, they should be corrected or adjusted (using, for example, a dummy variable) if it is clear that they are unusual or nonrecurring.

3. **Data Shift.** In contrast to the outlier, if the unusual business condition is long lasting, such as the introduction of new production technology or other permanent change, the average direction of the data has a distinct shift that should be included in the estimate. One way to handle this is to use a dummy variable to indicate the periods before and after the shift.

Summary

Cost estimation is one of the most important activities the management accountant performs in supporting the firm's strategy. It has an important role in developing a strategic competitive position as well as in using value-chain analysis, target costing, and other planning and evaluation contexts within cost management.

To use cost estimation effectively, the management accountant develops and evaluates a cost-estimating model in six steps: (1) define the cost object, (2) determine the cost drivers, (3) collect consistent and accurate data, (4) graph the data, (5) select and apply a cost estimation method, and (6) evaluate the accuracy of the cost estimate.

This chapter presents two estimation methods. The high-low method develops a unique estimation equation using algebra and the representative low and high points in the data. Regression analysis, a statistical method, obtains a unique best-fitting line for the data. The chapter's focus is on the proper interpretation of the three key measures of the precision and reliability of the regression: R-squared, the t-value, and the standard error of the estimate.

The most reliable and accurate method available to the management accountant is regression analysis, which can be solved using spreadsheet software such as Microsoft Excel. An advantage of regression analysis is that its results include quantitative and objective measures of the reliability and accuracy of the regression estimate.

Appendix A

LEARNING OBJECTIVE 5

Use learning curves in cost estimation when learning is present.

Learning Curve Analysis

One prominent example of nonlinear cost behavior is a cost influenced by learning. When an activity has a certain labor component and repetition of the same activity or operation makes the labor more proficient, the task is completed more quickly with the same or a higher level of quality. Learning can occur in a wide variety of ways, from the individual level as new employees gain experience, to the aggregate level in which a group of employees experiences improvement in productivity. We consider the latter instance in this appendix.

Costs are affected by learning in a wide variety of contexts, especially in large-scale production settings, such as the manufacture of airplanes and ships. In each case, we can model the expected improvement in productivity and use this information in the estimation of future costs. A **learning curve analysis** is a systematic method for estimating costs when learning is present.

A **learning curve analysis** is a systematic method for estimating costs when learning is present.

One of the first well-documented applications of learning curves occurred in the World War II aircraft industry.[8] Studies showed that the total time to manufacture two airplanes declined by approximately 20 percent of the total time without learning. In other words, the average *per-unit* time to build the first two units was 80 percent of the time for the first unit. For example, if the time to build the first unit is 20 hours, the *average* time to build the first two units is 16 hours (20 × 0.8), or a total of 32 hours (16 × 2) for two units. Without learning, it would take 40 hours (20 × 2). The **learning rate** is the percentage by which average time (or total time) falls from previous levels *as output doubles*. In this example, the rate is 80 percent. The unit cost behavior of the learning curve is illustrated in Exhibit 8A.1.

The **learning rate** is the percentage by which average time (or total time) falls from previous levels as output doubles.

Additional evidence of the practical importance of learning curves is the common reference to start-up costs in corporate annual reports and the financial press. A commonly accepted business principle is that new products and production processes have a period of low productivity followed by increasing productivity. Thereafter, the rate of improvement in productivity tends to decline over time until it reaches some equilibrium level where it remains relatively stable until another change in the product line or production process occurs.[9]

LEARNING CURVES IN SOFTWARE DEVELOPMENT

SofTech, Inc., is a vendor of software for financial analysts. SofTech's development staff recently changed its development language, T-Base, to a new language, Z-Base, which permits faster development and provides certain object-oriented programming benefits. Now SofTech is calculating the learning time needed for its programmers to come up to speed in the new language. These estimates are important because programming costs have increased 10 percent to $65 per hour in the past year and are expected to rise as quickly in the coming years. For purposes of this analysis, SofTech estimates the learning rate for Z-Base to be 80 percent and the initial time for coding 500 lines of good code in Z-Base to be 100 hours. The time and related cost required for developing the first 4,000-line application in Z-Base can be determined by using the learning curve; see Exhibit 8A.2.

Learning rates are obtained by reviewing and analyzing historical data. The methods vary from the simple high-low method to regression analysis based on fitting a nonlinear relationship to the historical data.[10]

---

[8] Frank J. Andress, "The Learning Curve as a Production Tool," *Harvard Business Review,* January–February 1954; and Charles D. Bailey and Edward V. McIntyre, "Some Evidence on the Nature of Relearning Curves," *The Accounting Review,* April 1992, pp. 368–378.

[9] As in the World War II airplane production example, the common learning rate is approximately 80 percent. Two conventional models are used in learning curve analysis. One measures learning on the basis of average unit cost, the other on the basis of marginal cost. Both models are conceptually and mathematically similar, although the average cost model tends to lead to lower unit costs. The average cost model is the more common, and for clarity and simplicity, it is the only model we present here. For a full explanation and comparison of the two models, see J. Chen and R. Manes, "Distinguishing the Two Forms of the Constant Percentage Learning Curve Model," *Contemporary Accounting Research,* Spring 1985, pp. 242–52.

[10] For example, see methods described in Patrick B. McKenzie, "An Alternative Learning Curve Formula," *Issues in Accounting Education,* Fall 1987, pp. 383–88. Software can be used to facilitate the use of learning curves. Examples include an Excel add-in Foresee. See Charles D. Bailey, "Estimation of Production Costs and Labor Hours Using an Excel Add-in," *Management Accounting Quarterly,* Summer 2000, pp. 25–31.

Learning curve analysis is commonly used to improve cost estimates in situations when learning is likely to occur. Two example applications follow.

USING THE SALES LEARNING CURVE AS A STRATEGIC CONSTRUCT

Launching a new product involves a lot more than adding a large sales force. Just as there are learning effects in many manufacturing processes, there are learning effects in bringing products to market. A sales strategy that successfully brings a new product to market involves all functions that interact with customers and attempts to understand how customers will acquire and use the product. Leslie and Holloway (2006) suggest that to properly guide resource allocation, companies utilize the sales learning curve, which models sales per person as a function of time. The more a company learns about its product and the sales process, the more efficient it becomes in selling the product. The findings of analysis show that sales typically start out slow, increase for a period, and then finally become flat as the product matures. These changes over time can be estimated using a learning curve. The use of sales learning-curve models allows management to set more realistic expectations regarding sales, avoid excessive sales force costs, and reduce the time before a new product reaches the point of profitability by better deploying the sales force, marketing, and management resources. (Mark Leslie and Charles A. Holloway, "The Sales Learning Curve," *Harvard Business Review* 84, no. 7/8 (July–August, 2006), pp. 115–123.)

LEARNING RATES IN SURGICAL PROCEDURES

A hospital in Germany reports learning rates of over 90 percent for two types of common surgeries. Based on data from 1992 through 2002, researchers found a learning rate of 91 percent for 816 cases of knee replacement surgery, and a learning rate of 90.3 percent for 476 gall bladder surgeries. (Christian Ernst and Andrea Szczesny, "Cost Accounting Implications of Surgical Learning in the DRG Era—Data Evidence for a German Hospital," *Schmalenbach Business Review*, April 2005, pp. 127–166.)

EXHIBIT 8A.1
Average Cost with Learning

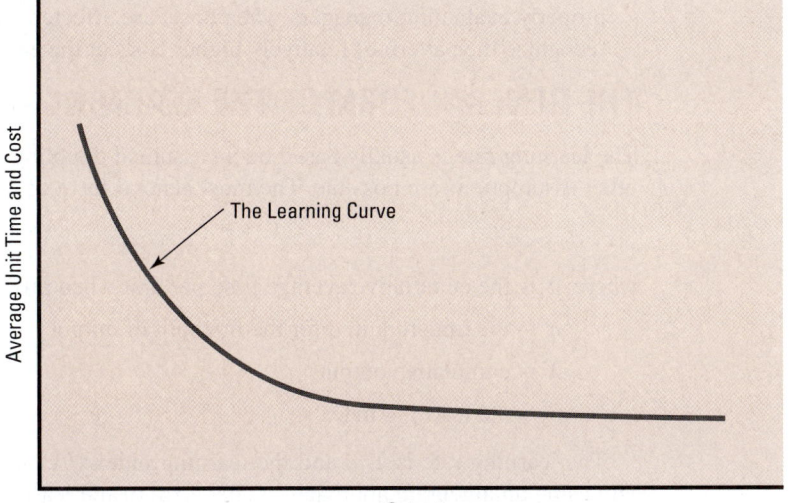

EXHIBIT 8A.2
SofTech, Inc.'s Learning Curve for Z-Base

Output (Multiples of 500 Lines)	Cumulative Average Time (Coding for 500 Lines)	Total Time
1 = 500 lines	100 hours	100 hours
2 = 1,000 lines	100 × .8 = 80 hours	80 × 2 = 160 hours
3 = 2,000 lines	80 × .8 = 64 hours	64 × 4 = 256 hours
4 = 4,000 lines	64 × .8 = 51.2 hours	51.2 × 8 = 409.6 hours

Note also that a learning rate of *1 is equivalent to no learning*. A *learning rate of .5 is best interpreted as the maximum learning rate* because the total time for actual production equals the time for a single unit. Thus, the learning rate is always a number greater than .5 and less than 1. Actual case studies reveal that the learning rate most often falls near .8.

WHAT DECISIONS ARE INFLUENCED BY LEARNING?

Because the productivity of labor is a vital aspect of any production process, learning curve analysis can be an important way to improve the quality of a wide range of decisions. For example, when product prices are based in part on costs, learning curves could be used to determine a life-cycle plan for pricing a new product. Moreover, learning curves would be helpful in these areas:

1. **Cost-volume-profit analysis (Chapter 9).** The determination of a breakeven point might be significantly influenced by the presence of learning.[11] Failing to consider learning causes overstatement of the actual number of units required for breakeven.

2. **Budgeting production levels and labor needs (Chapter 10).** Another useful application of learning curves is the development of the annual or quarterly production plan and related labor requirement budget. When the activity or operation is affected by learning, the production and labor budgets should be adjusted accordingly.

3. **The make-or-buy decision (Chapter 11).** When the cost to make a part is affected by learning, the analysis can be used to more accurately reflect the total cost over time of the make option.

4. **Capital budgeting (Chapter 12).** Learning curves capture cost behavior more accurately over the life of the capital investment by including the expected improvements in labor productivity due to learning.

5. **Preparation of bids for production contracts; target costing and life-cycle costing (Chapter 13).** Learning curves play an important role in ensuring that the contract cost estimates are accurate over the life of the contract.

6. **Development of standard product costs (Chapters 14 and 15).** When learning occurs, standard costs change over time, and the appropriate labor costs must be adjusted on a timely basis.[12]

7. **Management control (Chapters 18 and 19).** The use of learning curves is important in properly evaluating managers when costs are affected by learning. The evaluation should recognize the pattern of relatively higher costs at the early phase of the product life cycle.

THE GENERAL FORM OF THE LEARNING MODEL

The learning rate is usually based on an assumed doubling of output as illustrated above, but other assumptions are possible. The most general form of the learning model is as follows:

$$Y = aX^b$$

where: Y = the cumulative average time per unit when producing X units

   a = the time required for the first unit of output

   X = cumulative output

   b = the learning index

The learning rate is Y/a, and the learning index (b) can be determined from the learning rate using an algebraic approach.[13] This form of the learning model is very general and will

[11] Edward V. McIntyre, "Cost-Volume-Profit Analysis Adjusted for Learning," *Management Science,* October 1977, pp. 149–60.

[12] Jackson F. Gillespie, "An Application of Learning Curves to Standard Costing," *Management Accounting,* September 1981, pp. 63–65.

[13] To determine the learning index (b) for a given learning rate, first develop a linear expression for the general model by taking the natural log of both sides of the equation.

$$\ln(Y) = \ln(a) + b \times \ln(X)$$

so that:

$$b = \frac{\ln(Y) - \ln(a)}{\ln(X)} = \frac{\ln(Y/a)}{\ln(X)}$$

Thus, if we consider the changes in Y/a as X increases, the index b simplifies to the ratio of the learning rate to the rate of increase in output, or

$$b = \frac{\ln(\text{learning rate})}{\ln(\text{percent increase in output}/100)}$$

For example, to calculate the learning index for the doubling-output assumption (200 percent), we use:

$$b = \ln(\text{learning rate})/\ln(2)$$

And, for a learning rate of 80 percent, the learning index is therefore $\ln(.8)/\ln(2) = -.3219$. The index is negative because average unit labor time decreases with increasing output.

allow consideration of other learning assumptions, in addition to the doubling-of-output base commonly used.

LIMITATIONS OF LEARNING CURVE ANALYSIS

Although learning curve analysis can significantly enhance the ability to predict costs when learning occurs, three inherent limitations and problems are associated with the use of this method.

The first and key limitation of using learning curves is that the approach is most appropriate for labor-intensive contexts that involve repetitive tasks performed for long production runs for which repeated trials improve performance, or learning. When the production process is designed to maximize flexibility and very fast set-up times for manufacturing machinery using robotics and computer controls as many manufacturers now do, the manufacturing setting requires relatively little repetitive labor and consequently relatively little opportunity for learning.

A second limitation is that the learning rate is assumed to be constant (average labor time decreases at a fixed rate as output doubles). In actual applications, the decline in labor time might not be constant. For example, the learning rate could be 80 percent for the first 20,000 units, 90 percent for the next 35,000 units, and 95 percent thereafter. Such differences indicate the need to update projections based on the observed progression of learning.

Third, a carefully estimated learning curve might be unreliable because the observed change in productivity in the data used to fit the model was actually associated with factors other than learning. For example, the increase in productivity might have been due to a change in labor mix, a change in product mix, or some combination of other related factors. In such cases, the learning model is unreliable and produces inaccurate estimates of labor time and cost.

Appendix B

LEARNING OBJECTIVE 6

Use statistical measures to evaluate a regression analysis.

Regression Analysis

This appendix uses an example to explain the development of a regression estimate and the related statistical measures. Then we interpret the statistical measures to assess the precision and reliability of the regression.

THE REGRESSION ESTIMATE

To illustrate the manner in which a regression estimate is obtained, we use the data in Exhibit 8.3. Recall that regression analysis finds the unique line through the data that minimizes the sum of the squares of the errors, where the error is measured as the difference between the values predicted by the regression and the actual values for the dependent variable. In this example, the dependent variable, supplies expense (Y), is estimated with a single independent variable, production level (X). The regression for the three data points is

$$Y = a + b \times X = \$220 + \$0.75 \times X$$

The intercept term, labeled a, and the coefficient of the independent variable, labeled b, are obtained from a set of calculations performed by spreadsheet and other programs and are described in basic textbooks on probability and statistics. The calculations themselves are beyond the scope of this text. Our focus is on the derivation and interpretation of the statistical measures that tell management accountants something about the reliability and precision of the regression.

STATISTICAL MEASURES

The statistical measures of the reliability and precision of the regression are derived from an analysis of the variance of the dependent variable. *Variance* is a measure of the degree to

EXHIBIT 8B.1   Variance Components for Regression Analysis: Total Variance, Regression Variance, and Error Variance

				Variance Components		
1	2	3	4	5	6	7
Dependent Variable *Y*	Independent Variable *X*	Mean of *Y* (*YM*)	Regression Prediction for *Y* (*YE*)	Total Variance of *Y* (*T*) = (*Y* − *YM*)	Regression (Explained) Variance (*R*) = (*YE* − *YM*)	Error Variance (*E*) = (*Y* − *YE*)
250	50	295	257.5	(45)	(37.5)	(7.5)
310	100	295	295.0	15	0.0	15.0
325	150	295	332.5	30	37.5	(7.5)

which the values of the dependent variable vary about its mean. The term *analysis of variance* is used because the regression analysis is based on a separation of the total variance of the dependent variable into error and explained components. The underlying concept is that in predicting individual values for the dependent variable, the regression is *explaining changes (i.e., variance) in the dependent variable* associated with changes in the independent variable. The variance in the dependent variable that is not explained is called the residual, or *error variance.* Thus, the regression's ability to correctly predict changes in the dependent variable is a key measure of its reliability and is measured by the proportion of explained to error variances. Based on the data in Exhibits 8.3 and 8.4, Exhibit 8B.1 shows how the variance measures are obtained.

The first two columns of Exhibit 8B.1 show the data for the independent (*X*) and dependent (*Y*) variables. Column (3) shows the mean of the dependent variable (*YM*), and column (4) the regression prediction (*YE*) for each of the points. The last three columns indicate the three variance measures. Column (5) shows the total variance, or variance of the dependent variable, measured as the difference between each data point and the mean of the dependent variable (*Y* − *YM*). Column (6) shows the variance explained by the regression (*YE* − *YM*), and column (7) shows the error variance, (*Y* − *YE*). The measures in these last three columns are squared and summed to arrive at the desired values for *total* variance, explained variance, and error variance, respectively. The sum of the error and explained variance terms equals total variance. These terms are illustrated in Exhibit 8B.2 and the values calculated in Exhibit 8B.3.

The three variance terms are the basic elements of the statistical analysis of the regression. This is best illustrated in the analysis of variance table in Exhibit 8B.3. The **analysis of variance table** separates the total variance of the dependent variable into both error and explained components. The first two columns of the table show the type and amount of variance for each of the three variance terms. The third column shows the **degrees of freedom** for each

The **analysis of variance table** separates the total variance of the dependent variable into both error and explained variance components.

The **degrees of freedom** for each component of variance represent the number of independent choices that can be made for that component.

EXHIBIT 8B.2

Variance Components for Regression Analysis

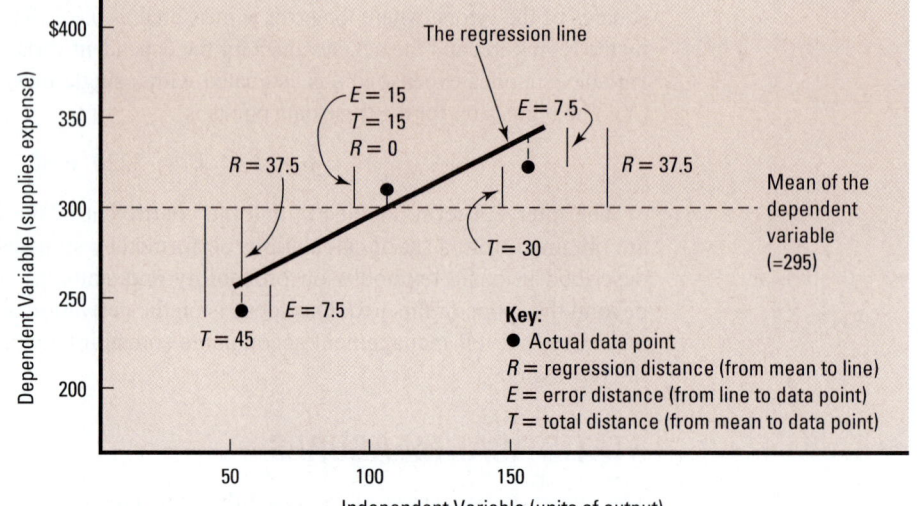

EXHIBIT 8B.3
Analysis of Variance Table
for Regression Analysis

Source of Variance	Variance of Each Component of the Regression (also called *sum of squares*)	Degrees of Freedom	Mean Squared Variance
Regression (explained)	$37.5^2 + 0^2 + 37.5^2 = $ **2,812.5**	1	2,812.5
Error	$7.5^2 + 15^2 + 7.5^2 = $ **337.5**	1	337.5
Total	$(45)^2 + (15)^2 + (30)^2 = $ **3,150.0**	2	1,575.0

component, which represents the number of independent choices that can be made for that component. Thus, the number of degrees of freedom for the explained variance component is always equal to the number of independent variables, and the total degrees of freedom is always equal to the number of data points less 1. The error degrees of freedom equal the total less the explained degrees of freedom.

Mean squared variance
is the ratio of the amount of
variance of a component to the
number of degrees of freedom
for that component.

The fourth column, **mean squared variance,** is the ratio of the amount of the variance of a component (in the second column) to the number of degrees of freedom (in the third column).

The analysis of variance table serves as a useful basis to discuss the key statistical measures of the regression. Of the six principal measures in Exhibit 8B.4, one measure refers to the precision of the regression and five measures refer to the reliability of the regression. *Precision* refers to the ability of the regression to provide accurate estimates—how close the regression's estimates are to the unknown true value. *Reliability* refers to the confidence the user can have that the regression is valid; that is, how likely the regression is to continue to provide accurate predictions over time and for different levels of the independent variables.

Precision of the Regression

The standard error of the estimate (SE) is a useful measure of the accuracy of the regression's estimates. The standard error is interpreted as a range of values around the regression estimate such that one can be approximately 67 percent confident the actual value lies in this range (see Exhibits 8.7A and 8.7B). An inverse relationship, and therefore a trade-off, exists between the confidence level and the width of the interval. The value of the SE for a given regression can be obtained directly from the analysis of variance table as follows:

$$SE = \sqrt{\text{Mean Square error}}$$
$$= \sqrt{337.5} = 18.37$$

The precision and accuracy of the regression improve as the variance for error is reduced and as the number of data points increases because the number of degrees of freedom increases, as illustrated in the preceding formula for SE.

Goodness of Fit (*R*-squared)

R-squared (also called the *coefficient of determination*) is a direct measure of the explanatory power of the regression. It measures the percent of variance in the dependent variable that can

EXHIBIT 8B.4
Six Key Statistical Measures

Precision

1. Precision of the regression (measured by the standard error of the estimate)

Reliability

2. Goodness of fit (*R*-squared)
3. Statistical reliability (*F*-statistic)
4. Statistical reliability for each independent variable (*t*-value)
5. Reliability of precision
6. Nonindependence of errors (Durbin-Watson statistic)

be explained by the independent variable. *R*-squared is calculated as follows, from the information in Exhibit 8B.3

$$R^2 = \frac{\Sigma \text{ of squares (explained)}}{\Sigma \text{ of squares (total)}}$$

$$= \frac{2,812.5}{3,150} = .892$$

The explanatory power of the regression improves as the explained sum of squares increases relative to the total sum of squares. A value close to 1 reflects a good-fitting regression with strong explanatory power. Note that *R*-squared and SE travel in opposite directions. A regression with a high *R*-squared will have a relatively small SE and vice versa.

Statistical Reliability (*F*-Statistic)

The **F-statistic** is a useful measure of the statistical reliability of the regression. Statistical reliability asks whether the relationship between the variables in the regression actually exists or whether the correlation between the variables is a chance relationship of the data at hand. If only a small number of data points are used, it is possible to have a relatively high *R*-squared (if the regression is a good fit to the data points), but this offers relatively little confidence that a statistical relationship exists because of the small number of data points.

> The **F-statistic**
> is a useful measure of the statistical reliability of the regression.

The larger the *F,* the lower the risk that the regression is statistically unreliable. The determination of an acceptable *F*-value depends on the number of data points, but the required *F*-value decreases as the number of data points increase. Most regression software programs show the *F*-value and the related *p*-value. The *p*-value should be less than approximately 5 percent. The *F*-statistic can be obtained from the analysis of variance table as follows:

$$F = \frac{\text{Mean square (explained)}}{\text{Mean square error}}$$

$$= \frac{2,812.5}{337.5} = 8.333$$

Statistical Reliability for Each of the Independent Variables (*t*-value)

The *t*-value is a measure of the reliability of each independent variable and as such, it has an interpretation very much like that of the *F*-statistic. The *t*-value equals the ratio of the coefficient of the independent variable to the standard error of the coefficient for that independent variable. The standard error of the coefficient is not the same as the standard error of the estimate, but it is interpreted in the same way. However, the standard error of the coefficient cannot be obtained directly from the analysis of variance table. For the data in Exhibit 8B.1, the value of the standard error for the coefficient is .2598.[14] The *t*-value is thus

$$t = .75/.2598 = 2.8868$$

A *t*-value larger than 2.0 indicates that the independent variable is reliable at a risk level less than approximately 5 percent and is therefore a reliable independent variable to include in the regression. Regression software such as Excel shows the 95 percent confidence range for the coefficient of each of the independent variables. The range of the standard error of the estimate should be relatively small. A small range provides confidence in the accuracy of the coefficient's value.

[14] The standard error of the coefficient of an independent variable is calculated as follows:

$$\text{Standard error} = \text{SE/(Std. deviation of the independent variable)}$$

$$= \frac{18.37}{\sqrt{(50-100)^2 + (100-100)^2 + (150-100)^2}} = .2598$$

EXHIBIT 8B.5
Nonconstant Variance

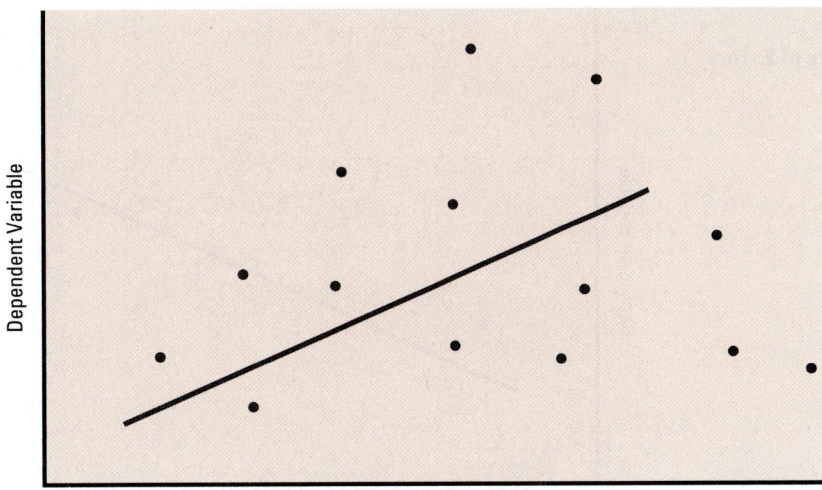

Nonconstant Variance
is the condition when the
variance of the errors is not
constant over the range of the
independent variable.

Reliability of Precision (Nonconstant Variance)

For certain sets of data, the standard error of the estimate varies over the range of the independent variable. The variance of the errors is not constant over the range of the independent variable. This is the case, for example, when the relationship between the independent and dependent variables becomes less stable over time. This type of behavior is illustrated in Exhibit 8B.5. If there is nonconstant variance, the SE value provided by the regression is not uniformly accurate over the range of the independent variable.[15]

To fix the problem of nonconstant variance, management accountants should transform the dependent variable with the log or square root. If it does not fix the condition, management accountants should be very cautious in interpreting the SE value.

Nonindependent Errors (Durbin-Watson Statistic)

Nonindependence of errors occurs when the amount and direction of each error term is related to those around it. For example, nonindependence of errors is illustrated in Exhibit 8B.6—the data points are all above the regression line for small values of the independent variable and then below the regression line for large values of the independent value. Nonindependent errors usually occur when there is nonlinearity in the data, as in the illustration for Exhibit 8B.6. When errors are not independent, the statistical measures are unreliable and the regressions predictions are biased.

The **Durbin-Watson statistic**
is a measure of the extent of
nonlinearity in the regression.

A common method that detects nonindependent errors is to use the **Durbin-Watson (DW) statistic.** It is calculated from the amount and change of the errors over the range of the independent variable. The DW value falls between zero and 4.0; with 20 or more data points, a value of DW between approximately 1.0 and 3.0 indicates little chance of a nonlinearity as described earlier; values less than 1.0 or greater than 3.0 should indicate the need to study the data and to choose appropriate fixes if necessary.

The problem of nonindependent errors usually can be fixed by deseasonalizing the data, using a dummy variable for seasonality, or using an index to remove the trend. Alternatively, what may be required is to convert a multiplicative relationship to an equivalent additive (that is, linear) relationship by taking the logarithm of the independent and dependent variables. The statistical measures, their indicators, and ways to fix the underlying conditions are summarized in Exhibit 8B.7.

[15] To detect nonconstant variance, calculate the rank-order correlation between the position of the data point and the size of the error at that point. The rank-order correlation is a statistic that measures the degree to which two sets of numbers tend to have the same order, or rank. A relatively high rank-order correlation is evidence of nonconstant variance. For the data in Exhibit 8B.1, the Spearman rank-order correlation coefficient is .125, a relatively small correlation that indicates little evidence of nonconstant variance. The calculation of rank-order correlation is beyond the scope of this introductory chapter but can be found in many statistics texts.

EXHIBIT 8B.6
Nonindependence of Errors

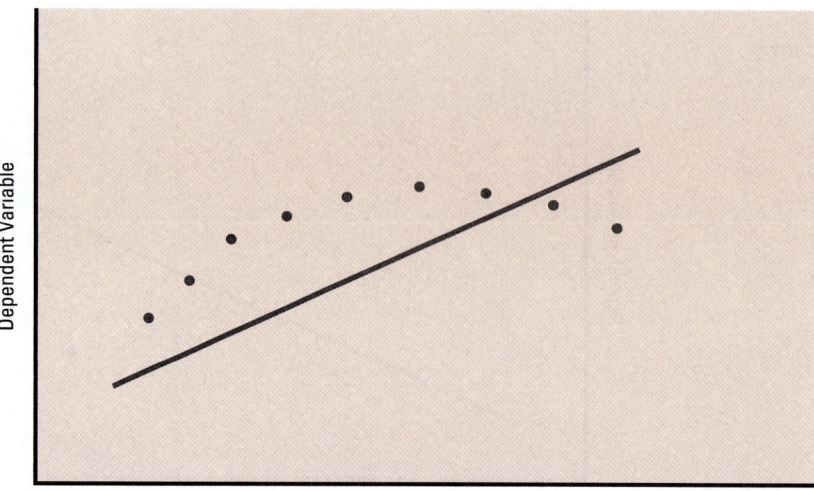

EXHIBIT 8B.7 **Summary of Statistical Measures**

Measure Concerns	Statistical Measure	What Is an OK Value?*	What Is the Right Fix If Not OK?	Consequence If Not Fixed
Reliability— Goodness of fit	R-squared	Should be approximately .75 or better	• Add or delete independent variables • If DW is poor, could need transforms (lag, log, first differences, . . .) • Correct measurement errors in the data, for example, cutoff errors, or reporting lags	• Inaccurate estimates
Statistical reliability for the regression	F-statistic	Depends on sample size	• Increase sample size • Other changes as suggested for reliability—goodness of fit (see above)	• Inaccurate estimates
Statistical reliability for the independent variables	t-value	Should be greater than 2.0	• Delete or transform the independent variable	• Inaccurate estimates
Precision of the regression	Standard error of the estimates (SE)	Should be small relative to the dependent variable	• Same considerations as for reliability—goodness of fit (see above)	• Inaccurate estimates
Reliability of precision (non-constant variance)	Rank-order correlation	Should be small	• Square root or log transform the dependent variable • Add a dummy variable	• SE is unreliable
Reliability— Potential nonlinearity (nonindependence of errors)	Durbin-Watson statistic (DW)	Between 2.0 and 3.0	*For certain series:* • Deseasonalize • Add trend variable • Use dummy variable for shift *For nonlinear relationship* • Log transform • Some other nonlinear transform	• Inaccurate estimates • SE is unreliable

* The values shown here are useful for a wide range of regressions. The exact values for a specific regression depend on a number of factors including the sample size and the number of independent variables. A recent study of regression analysis applied to 20 different overhead cost accounts showed that most of the R-squared values fall between .83 and .93. The values for the standard error of the estimates averaged 12 percent of the mean of the dependent variable, with most falling between 5 percent and 20 percent. See G. R. Cluskey Jr., Mitchell H. Raiborn, and Doan T. Modianos, "Multiple-Cost Flexible Budgets and PC-Based Regression Analysis," *Journal of Cost Management,* July–August 2000, pp. 35–47. Also, see the *Parametric Estimating Handbook,* 4th edition, the International Society of Parametric Analysis, April 2008, (Figure 3.6 on p. 84) for a list of thresholds for key statistical measures (www.ispa-cost.org/ISPA_PEH_4th_ed_Final.pdf).

TIME SERIES AND CROSS-SECTIONAL REGRESSION

Time-series regression
is the application of regression analysis to predict future amounts, using prior period's data.

Cross-sectional regression
estimates costs for a particular cost object based on information on other cost objects and other variables, where the information for all variables is taken from the same period of time.

The two examples used in this chapter, the Ben Garcia case and the WinDoor Inc. case, are both examples of what is called *time-series regression*. **Time-series regression** is the application of regression analysis to predict future amounts, using prior period's data. In contrast, **cross-sectional regression** estimates costs for a particular cost object based on information on other cost objects and variables, where the information for all variables is taken from the same period of time. For an example of cross-sectional regression, suppose a residential home builder uses regression to estimate the cost of constructing a new home, and the builder knows that the main cost driver for building cost is the size of the home, in square feet of floor space. The builder develops a regression model using the cost of homes built previously that year as the dependent variable and the size in square feet of these homes as the independent variable. The regression equation that the builder develops is then used to predict the cost of homes to be built, based on the expected size of the new home in square feet. All of the statistical measures of reliability and precision explained above apply equally to both types of regression, except for the issue, nonindependence of errors, which applies only in time-series regressions.

Key Terms

Comments on Cost Management in Action

Using Regression to Estimate the Value of Commercial Real Estate

Estimating Real Estate Values for Apartment Buildings and Office Buildings   As expected, real estate appraisers performing regression analysis to appraise the value of an apartment building or an office building use as the dominant independent variable the property's past, current, and expected future net operating income (NOI). That is, the chief determinant of the value of the property is its ability to produce cash flows and profits. Other variables regarding the property include its size (as measured by the number of units, number of square feet, number of two-bedroom and one-bedroom apartments, etc.), its age, and the relevant vacancy rate in the property and in the submarket area where it is located. Since the regression analysis is usually built from actual sales numbers over a period of time, these appraisers also use a trend variable to tie the sales price of the property to the year it was sold.

Estimating Real Estate Values for Warehouses and Manufacturing Plants   Similarly, real estate appraisers have developed regression analyses for warehouses and manufacturing plants using their size, age, and location. The NOI variable is usually not relevant. They also use a trend variable to distinguish sales of properties in different years. For example, an analysis of sales value (per square foot) of industrial properties in the Los Angeles area in the early 1990s showed a significant trend variable (-2.83 per square foot per year); the coefficient on the trend variable was negative because prices were falling during that period. A significant size variable (-2.43 per square foot, per 100,000 square feet of space) indicated that larger buildings had on average lower sales prices per square foot. Age was also a factor, the coefficient being -0.41 per square foot per year of age. The location variable was also significant, showing that properties in certain counties in the Los Angeles area (Orange County, San Bernardino, etc.) were predicted to have as much as a $2.32 difference in value per square foot.

Sources: Stephen T. Crosson, Charles G. Dannis, and Thomas G. Thibodeau, "Regression Analysis: A Cost-Effective Approach for the Valuation of Commercial Property," *Real Estate Finance,* Winter 1996; Maxwell O. Ramsland Jr. and Daniel E. Markham, "Market-Supported Adjustments Using Multiple Regression Analysis," *The Appraisal Journal,* April 1998, pp. 181–191; and Stephen C. Kincheloe, "Linear Regression Analysis of Economic Variables in the Sales Comparison and Income Approaches," *The Appraisal Journal,* October 1993.

Self–Study Problems

(For solutions, please turn to the end of the chapter.)

1. Using the High-Low Method

Hector's Delivery Service uses four small vans and six pickup trucks to deliver small packages in the Charlotte, North Carolina, metropolitan area. Hector spends a considerable amount of money on the gas, oil, and regular maintenance of his vehicles, which is done at a variety of service stations and repair shops. To budget his vehicle expenses for the coming year, he gathers data on his expenses and number of deliveries for each month of the current year.

	Total Vehicle Expenses	Total Deliveries
January	$145,329	5,882
February	133,245	5,567
March	123,245	5,166
April	164,295	6,621
May	163,937	6,433
June	176,229	6,681
July	180,553	7,182
August	177,293	6,577
September	155,389	5,942
October	150,832	5,622
November	152,993	5,599
December	201,783	7,433

Required   Use the high-low estimation method to determine the relationship between the number of deliveries and the cost of maintaining the vehicles.

2. Using Regression Analysis

George Harder is the Imperial Foods Company's plant manager of one of the processing plants. George is concerned about the increase in plant overhead costs in recent months. He has collected data on overhead costs for the past 24 months and has decided to use regression to study the factors influencing these costs. He has also collected data on materials cost, direct labor-hours, and machine-hours as potential independent variables to use in predicting overhead.

George runs two regression analyses on these data, with the following results:

	Regression 1 (labor-hours only)	Regression 2 (labor-hours and machine-hours)
R-squared	.65	.58
Standard error	$12,554	$13,793
Standard error as a percent of the dependent variable	12%	14%
t-values		
Materials cost	2.0	–1.6
Labor-hours	4.5	3.8
Machine-hours		1.4

Required   Which of the two regressions is better and why?

3. Using Both High-Low and Regression

John Meeks Company is a medium-size manufacturing company with plants in three small mid-Atlantic towns. The company makes plastic parts for automobiles and trucks, primarily door panels, exterior trim, and related items. The parts have an average cost of $5 to $20. The company has a steady demand for its products from both domestic and foreign automakers and has experienced growth in sales averaging between 10 and 20 percent over the last 8 to 10 years.

Currently, management is reviewing the incidence of scrap and waste in the manufacturing process at one of its plants. Meeks defines scrap and waste as any defective unit that is rejected for lack of functionality or another aspect of quality. The plants have a number of different inspection points, and failure or rejection can occur at any inspection point. The number of defective units is listed in the following table; management estimates the cost of this waste in labor and materials is approximately $10 per unit.

An unfavorable trend appears to exist with regard to defects, and management has asked you to investigate and estimate the defective units in the coming months. A first step in your investigation is to identify the cost drivers of defective parts, to understand what causes them, and to provide a basis on which to estimate future defects. For this purpose, you have obtained these recent data on the units produced, the units shipped, and the cost of sales since these numbers are easily available and relatively reliable on a monthly basis:

	Units Produced (000s)	Cost of Sales (000s)	Units Shipped (000s)	Defective Units
Jan 2009	55	$ 689	50	856
Feb	58	737	53	1,335
Mar	69	886	64	1,610
Apr	61	768	56	1,405
May	65	828	60	1,511
Jun	69	878	64	1,600
Jul	75	962	70	1,570
Aug	81	1,052	76	1,910
Sep	70	1,104	80	2,011
Oct	79	1,224	89	2,230
Nov	82	1,261	92	2,300
Dec	70	1,020	74	1,849
Jan 2010	67	850	62	1,549
Feb	72	916	67	1,669
Mar	85	1,107	80	2,012
Apr	75	968	70	1,756
May	81	1,037	76	1,889
Jun	85	1,103	80	1,650
Jul	92	1,208	87	2,187
Aug	100	1,310	95	2,387
Sep	91	1,380	101	2,514
Oct	101	1,536	111	2,787
Nov	105	1,580	115	2,310
Dec	88	1,270	92	2,311

Required   Use the high-low method and regression analysis to estimate the defective units in the coming months and to determine which method provides the best fit for this purpose.

4. Nonlinear Regression and Learning Curves

This self-study problem illustrates how nonlinear regression can be used to estimate the learning curve rate, given information on output levels and average processing times. To illustrate, we reproduce below the cumulative output (X) and the average time per unit (Y) for the SofTech Inc. illustration in Exhibit 8A.2 (page 291). Using regression analysis, we now show that this learning curve data is consistent with the general learning model. The general form of the learning model is $Y = aX^b$ where a = the time required for the first unit and b = the learning index. Using a log transform for Y, the general learning model can be shown in the equivalent log-linear form (see footnote 13 in Appendix A): $\log(Y) = \log(a) + b \times \log(X)$. The log transform is available in Excel in "Insert Function" under the Formulas tab.

The exhibit below shows that the X and Y values have been transformed (using log, base 10), and the results of a regression on log X and log Y are shown in the right two columns. Note that the regression R-squared is 1.0 because the data fit perfectly an 80 percent learning curve; the values for Y were calculated using the 80 percent rate. Also, note that the learning index $b = -.321928$ is the learning index for a model with an 80 percent learning rate, as shown in footnote 13 (page 292).

The value of Y can now be determined for any value of X using the general model. First we determine the value of the intercept, a. Since log (a) = 2.8688743, a is determined as follows: $a = 10^{2.8688743} = 739.39$. The value for $10^{2.8688743} = 739.39$ is determined using the Power function in Excel which is located in "Insert Function" under the Formulas tab. Thus, for example, the value of Y for $X = 1,500$ is determined as follows:

$$Y = 739.39 \times 1,500^{-.321928} = 70.2.$$

Log-Linear Regression of Learning Curve Data from Exhibit 8A.2

X	Y	LogX	LogY
500	100	2.69897	2
1000	80	3	1.90309
2000	64	3.30103	1.80618
4000	51.2	3.60206	1.70927

Regression Statistics	
Multiple R	1
R-square	1
Adj R-square	1
Standard error	1.677E-16
Observations	4

ANOVA	
	df
Regression	1
Residual	2
Total	3

	Coefficients
Intercept	2.8688743
Log$X$	−0.321928

Required Suppose that Virilli, Inc., a manufacturer of high-end furniture, has the following data for one of its products, where X is cumulative output, and Y is average unit time.

X	Y
10	45
18	40
25	38
43	32
55	30
70	25
93	22
110	20

1. Using log-linear regression, determine the general linear model for Virilli. Specifically, determine the values of a and b in the model $Y = aX^b$.
2. Using the model you developed in part 1, project the value of Y if output (X) is increased to 133.

Questions

8-1   Define *cost estimation* and explain its purpose.

8-2   Explain the assumptions used in cost estimation.

8-3   List the two methods of cost estimation. Explain the advantages and disadvantages of each.

8-4   Explain the implementation problems in cost estimation.

8-5   What are the six steps in cost estimation? Which one is the most important? Why?

8-6   Contrast the use of regression analysis and the high-low method to estimate costs.

8-7   How is cost estimation used in activity-based costing?

8-8   Explain how to choose the dependent and independent variables in regression analysis.

8-9   What are nonlinear cost relationships? Give two examples.

8-10   List four advantages of regression analysis.

8-11   Explain what a dummy variable is and how it is used in regression analysis.

8-12   How do we know when high correlation exists? Is high correlation the same as cause and effect?

8-13   What does the coefficient of determination (R-squared) measure?

Brief Exercises

8-14   Wallace Heating is attempting to estimate the production cost for heating ducts for the coming year using the high-low method. The cost driver is number of labor-hours. Wallace determines that the high and low costs are $25,830 and $18,414, respectively, and the values for the cost driver are 3,495 and 1,958 hours, respectively. What is the variable cost per hour?

8-15   Carter Dry Cleaning has developed two regression analyses for cost estimation. The accounting manager has presented statistical measures for both of these regressions. Regression A has an R-squared value of .53 and a t-value of 1.08 and Regression B has an R-squared of .89 and a t-value of 2.17. What do these statistical measures indicate about the regressions? Which regression should Carter Dry Cleaning use for cost estimation?

8-16   Williams Inc. produces fluorescent lightbulbs for commercial use. The accounting manager is attempting to estimate the total cost for the next quarter using the high-low method. He has compiled data and found the high and low costs are $10,000 and $6,000 and the associated cost drivers are 7,000 and 3,000 packs, respectively. He has also determined the variable cost to be $1.00 per pack. What is the value for a (the fixed quantity)?

8-17   Grant Healthcare provides plastic gloves for hospitals. Grant is forecasting costs for future production. The dependent variable is labor expense. List some possible independent variables for a regression analysis of financial data.

8-18   Smith Glass Co. produces industrial glass. Smith forecasts data using the high-low method and has compiled the following data from prior results:

	2006	2007	2008	2009	2010
Total operating hours	5,683	3,197	4,105	5,056	3,586
Inspection cost ($)	50,457	46,835	53,227	49,734	43,649

Which two years should Smith select for the high-low method analysis and why?

8-19   Johnson Plastics Inc. produces cases for CDs. The accounting manager has calculated a regression to determine future production costs. The regression estimate is $5,000 with an R-squared of .9, a t-value of 2.5, and a standard error of $400. Within what interval would she be reasonably (67 percent) confident that the actual values will fall?

8-20   Peppers Lockdown produces keys for homes and cars. As Peppers is planning for next year's production, he decided to implement a high-low system to forecast future costs. With total production of 2,500,000 keys at a total cost of $10,000, in 2009, and total production of 3,000,000 keys at a total cost of $20,000 in 2010 what is the variable cost per key?

8-21   Power Drink Inc. produces sports drinks. The accounting manager has decided to implement a high-low costing system to predict future materials handling costs. She has provided you with the following table of costs for the last five years. Which two years should be used for this method?

	2006	2007	2008	2009	2010
Production hours	100,000	138,679	98,843	203,517	188,352
Handling cost ($)	456,233	498,672	507,284	601,678	544,314

8-22 Jamison Construction has implemented a cost estimation system using a regression analysis. The variable cost per hour of labor is $35 and the fixed cost was determined to be $125,000. If Jamison projects it will be working 200,000 hours in 2010, what is the projected total cost?

8-23 Curry Rubber manufactures rubber bands for commercial retail companies. The accounting manager has created a regression analysis of past data. You notice that the formula has an R-squared of .6, a t-value of 2.3, and a standard error of the estimate of $200,000. The estimate for next quarter costs is $2,584,072. What do these statistics tell you about the reliability of his regression analysis?

8-24 Miller Landscaping is attempting to project costs for future quarters. Miller has compiled data and decided to use the high-low costing method. The low value is $250,000 for 5,000 hours and the high value is $400,000 for 8,000 hours. What is the variable cost per hour?

8-25 Sanders Bears produces stuffed animals. Sanders is in the process of implementing a cost forecasting system using the high-low method. The variable cost per animal is $2 and the high and low costs used were $80,000 for 120,000 animals and $40,000 for 100,000 animals. What is the value of the fixed cost for the cost estimating equation?

Exercises

8-26 Cost Classification: Match each cost to the appropriate cost behavior pattern shown in the graphs (a) through (l). Any graph can fit two or more patterns.

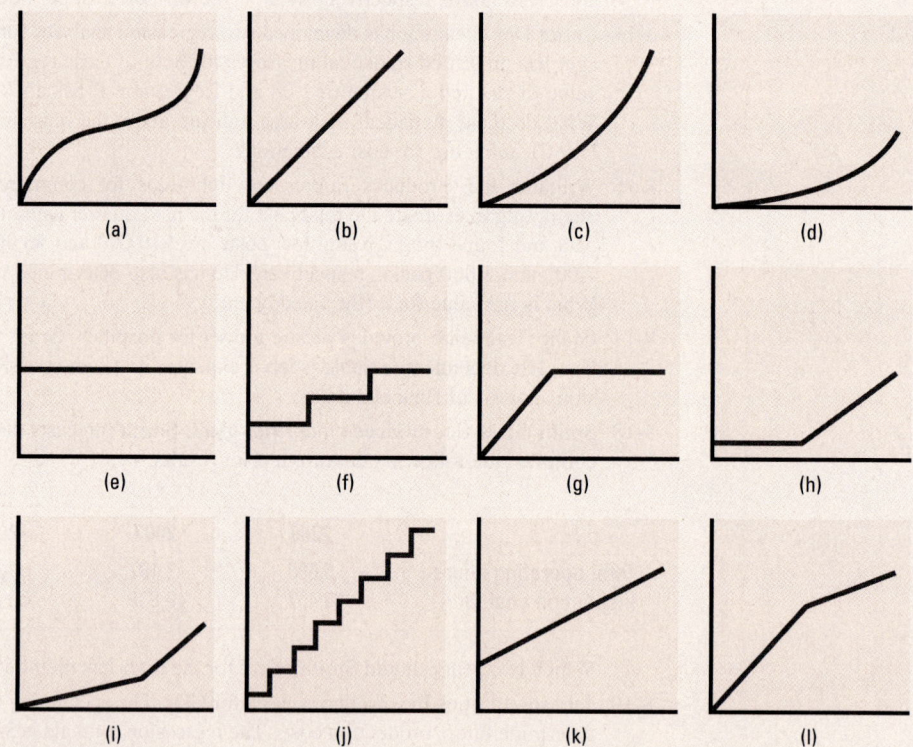

1. The cost of lumber used to manufacture wooden kitchen tables.

2. The cost of order fillers in a warehouse. When demand increases, the number of order fillers is increased, and when demand falls off, the number is decreased.

3. The salary of the plant's quality control inspector, who inspects each batch of products.

4. The cost of water and sewer service to the manufacturing plant. The local municipality charges a fixed rate per gallon for usage up to 10,000 gallons, and a higher charge per gallon for usage above that point.

5. The cost of an Internet connection of $23 per month.

6. The cost of an Internet connection of $10 per month plus $2 per hour of usage above 10 hours.

7. The cost to make copies of a given document at a printing shop, which reduces the per-copy charge for customers who make more than 100 copies of the document.

8. To discourage excess usage and to level the demand, especially in peak load times, the local electric utility increases the per-kilowatt-hour charge for each additional 5,000 kilowatt-hours' usage.

9. A clothing store in the SunnyVale Mall pays a fixed rental charge of $1,000 per month plus 2 percent of gross sales receipts.

10. A shoe store in the SunnyVale Mall pays 6 percent of gross sales receipts, up to a maximum of $3,000 per month as a rental charge.

8-27 **Cost Relationships**   Comptech hired Erwin & Associates to design a new computer-aided manufacturing facility that has the capacity to produce 250 computers per month. The variable costs for each computer are $150 and the fixed costs total $62,250 per month.

Required   What is the average cost per unit if the facility normally expects to operate at 80 percent of capacity?

8-28 **Cost Relationships**   The following costs are for Optical View Inc., a contact lens manufacturer:

Output in Units	Fixed Costs	Variable Costs	Total Costs
250	$4,750	$ 7,500	$12,250
300	4,750	9,000	13,750
350	4,750	10,500	15,250
400	4,750	12,000	16,750

Required

1. Graph total cost, total variable cost, and total fixed cost.
2. Graph the per-unit total cost, per-unit variable cost, and per-unit fixed cost.
3. Discuss the behavior of the fixed, variable, and total cost.

8-29 **Cost Estimation, Average Cost**   Maribeth's Cafe bakes croissants that it sells to local restaurants and grocery stores. The average costs to bake the croissants are $0.55 for 500 and $0.50 for 600.

Required   If the total cost function for croissants is linear, what will be the average cost to bake 560?

8-30 **Cost Estimation Using Graphs**   Lawson Advertising Agency is trying to persuade Kansas City Sailboards Company to spend more money on advertising. The agency's argument is that a positive linear relationship exists between advertising and sales in the sailboard industry. Sue Lawson presents these data taken from industry data for stores similar in size and market share to Kansas City Sailboards:

Advertising Expense	Annual Sales
$2,500	$ 95,000
3,000	110,000
3,500	124,000
4,000	138,000
4,500	143,000
5,000	147,000
5,500	150,000

Required

1. Graph annual sales and advertising expense.
2. Do the data prove Sue's point?

8-31 **Analysis of Regression Results**   Wang Manufacturing uses regression analysis to predict manufacturing overhead costs based on labor-hours and/or machine-hours and has developed the three following regression equations.

	Regression 1	Regression 2	Regression 3
SE	33,844	45,383	31,044
R-squared	0.55	0.35	0.58
t-values:			
Labor-hours	2.3		1.9
Machine-hours		1.1	0.8

Required Which regression would you choose and why?

8-32 **Cost Estimation: High-Low Method; MAPE** Horton Manufacturing Inc. produces blinds and other window treatments for residential homes and offices. The owner is concerned about the maintenance costs for the production machinery, as maintenance costs for the previous fiscal year were higher than he expected. The owner has asked you to assist in estimating future maintenance costs to better predict the firm's profitability. Together, you have determined that the best cost driver for maintenance costs is machine-hours. The data from the previous fiscal year for maintenance expense and machine-hours follows:

Month	Expense	Hours	Month	Expense	Hours
1	$2,625	1,499	7	$2,865	1,785
2	2,670	1,590	8	2,905	1,805
3	2,720	1,605	9	2,780	1,695
4	2,822	1,655	10	2,570	1,410
5	2,855	1,775	11	2,590	1,550
6	3,005	1,880	12	2,890	1,405

Required

1. What is the cost equation for maintenance cost using the high-low method? Graph the data points to check for outliers.
2. Calculate MAPE for the cost equation you developed in part 1.

8-33 **Cost Estimation, High-Low Method; MAPE** Ethan Manufacturing Inc. produces floor mats for automobiles. The owner, Joseph Ethan, has asked you to assist in estimating maintenance costs. Together, you and Joseph determine that the single best cost driver for maintenance costs is machine-hours. These data are from the previous fiscal year for maintenance expense and machine-hours:

Month	Maintenance Expense	Machine-Hours
1	$2,600	1,690
2	2,760	1,770
3	2,910	1,850
4	3,020	1,870
5	3,100	1,900
6	3,070	1,880
7	3,010	1,860
8	2,850	1,840
9	2,620	1,700
10	2,220	1,100
11	2,230	1,300
12	2,450	1,590

Required

1. What is the cost equation for maintenance cost using the high-low method?
2. Calculate MAPE for the cost equation you developed in part 1.

E_x

8-34 The Gompertz Equation; Learning Curves   The concept of learning curves has broad application in business, medicine, and many other fields. For example, the Gompertz equation is a mathematical model used to predict the number of deaths at a certain age. The Gompertz equation is very similar in form to that of the learning curve, except that e, the base of the natural logarithm, is used and there is a positive rather than a negative exponent in the equation. The Gompertz equation is as follows:

$$M(x) = Ae^{Gx}$$

Where:

$M(x)$ = the number of deaths in a population of 100,000 of those at age x; $M(x)$ is often called the *mortality rate.*

A = the initial mortality rate at age 0.

G = the exponential rate of increase in mortality for an increase in age, x.

e = a mathematical constant, the base of the natural logarithm, which equals approximately 2.718281828.

The Gompertz equation is used to estimate the number of deaths at a given age. The equation was estimated using nonlinear regression based on 2002 U.S. census data and the following estimated equation was derived (for ages 25–90). The regression had a very good fit, R-squared of 0.97.

$$M(x) = 8.84e^{.08x}$$

Required

1. Use the exponential function on your calculator or the EXP function in Excel to determine the mortality rate of any age you choose between 25 and 90.

2. Think of an application or two that an exponential equation like the Gompertz equation could be used in cost estimation.

8-35 Regression and Utility Rates; Sustainability   For several years many utilities have employed regression analysis to forecast monthly utility usage by residential customers using weather forecasts, the number of holidays, the number of days in the month, and other factors. For example, the Connecticut Department of Public Utility Control (CDPUC) has determined that regression, properly used, can accurately predict natural gas usage. Most gas public utilities serving Connecticut have reported levels of accuracy from 4 percent to 10 percent using regression. One company, Dominion Natural Gas Company of Ohio, uses this approach not to forecast but to explain to customers why their natural gas bills have gone up or down compared to the prior month, and also compared to the same month of the prior year. The bill shows total MCF (thousand cubic feet of natural gas) used by the customer for that month and why the total MCF usage has changed, based on three factors:

1. Change in temperature: each degree increase in temperature causes an increase in the number of MCFs consumed. The relationship between the change in temperature and the usage of MCF is not linear, but the monthly bill shows the average change in temperature for the month and the increase or decrease in MCF related to that change.

2. Number of billing days in the period.

3. The residual, the change in usage by the customer that is not attributable to temperature or the number of days in the billing period.

A customer of Dominion has used 13.7 MCF in December and is charged $12.50 per MCF for a total bill that month of $171.25. The following data are available to compare the current month's weather and billing period to the prior month and to the same month last year

Usage Factors	Current Month vs Last Month	Current Month to Last December
Weather	3 degrees cooler; +2.5MCF	8 degrees warmer; −3.5MCF
Number of billing days	5 more days; +.05 MCF	1 less day; −0.1 MCF
Customer-controlled usage	+.9 MCF	−1.8 MCF

Required

1. Determine the amount of difference in the customer's bill from the prior month and from the current month last year.

2. How does the Dominion Company's billing system affect environmental sustainability?

8-36 Interpreting Regression Results   Recent research into the cost of various medical procedures has shown the impact of certain complications encountered in surgery on the total cost of patient's stay in the hospital. The researchers used regression analysis and found the following results:

Total cost for patient = Constant, plus

$a \times$ length of stay (measured in days), plus

$b \times$ presence of one or more complications (= 1 if true, 0 if false), plus

$c \times$ use of a laparoscope (= 1 if true, 0 if false)

Where:

- a, b, c are coefficients of the regression model, and
- The laparoscope is an instrument somewhat like a miniature telescope with a fiber optic system which brings light into the abdomen. It is about as big around as a fountain pen and twice as long.

The research, based on 57 patients, showed the following regression results:

R-squared: 53%

constant term: $3,719

Coefficients and t-values for independent variables:

	Length of Stay	Complication	Laparoscope
coefficient	$ 861	$1,986	$ 908
t-value	10.76	4.89	2.54

Required

1. What is the estimated cost for a patient who has complications and stays in the hospital two days, and whose surgery requires a laparoscope?

2. Which, if any, dummy variables are used in this regression?

3. Comment on the statistical measures for the model.

8-37 Analysis of Regression Results; Appendix (Continuation of 8-36)   The following table shows additional regression results presented by the researchers in the study described in Exercise 8-36. There are two regressions. The right-hand column shows the results for all patients, including those treated with laparoscopic surgery. The left-hand column shows the results for the sample of patients who were treated without the laparoscopic surgery, and the related costs.

	Not Laparoscopic	All Patients
Coefficients for independent variables		
Regression intercept	$ 8,043	$ 3,719
Length of stay		
Coefficient*	Not significant	861
Standard error for the coefficient	Not applicable	80
Number of complications		
Coefficient	3,393	1,986
Standard error for the coefficient	1,239	406
Laparascopic		
Coefficient	Not applicable	908
Standard error for the coefficient	Not applicable	358
R-squared	0.11	0.53

* Note: All independent variables are significant at the level of $p = .05$ (and t-value >2) except for the length of stay variable in the nonlaparoscopic condition.

Required

1. Which of the two regressions has the better reliability and precision in estimating cost? Why?

2. Interpret the values of each coefficient and the standard error for each coefficient.

3. What are the *t*-values for each of the independent variables for each regression?

8-38 **Cost Estimation, High-Low Method** Albedo Inc. manufactures high-end replacement telescope lenses for amateur and professional astronomers that are seeking to upgrade the performance of their telescopes. You have just become employed as a staff accountant at Albedo and Jordan Coleman, the controller, has asked you to help with maintenance cost estimation for the lens manufacturing process. You review the manufacturing process and decide that the best cost driver for maintenance costs is machine-hours. These data are from the previous fiscal year for maintenance expense and machine-hours:

Month	Maintenance Cost	Machine-Hours
1	$3,210	2,750
2	4,650	3,900
3	5,175	4,050
4	3,350	2,690
5	3,100	2,500
6	2,950	2,580
7	2,900	2,300
8	2,900	2,500
9	4,120	3,160
10	4,350	3,325
11	3,500	2,780
12	3,775	3,000

Required What is the cost equation for maintenance cost using the high-low method?

Problems 8-39 **Cost Estimation, High-Low Method** Jay Bauer Company specializes in the purchase, renovation, and resale of older homes. Jay Bauer employs several carpenters and painters to do the work for him. It is essential for him to have accurate cost estimates so he can determine total renovation costs before he purchases a piece of property. If estimated renovation costs plus the purchase price of a house are higher than its estimated resale value, the house is not a worthwhile investment.

Jay has been using the home's interior square feet for his exterior paint cost estimations. Recently he decided to include the number of openings—the total number of doors and windows in a house—as a cost driver. Their cost is significant because they require time-consuming preparatory work and careful brushwork. The rest of the house usually is painted either by rollers or spray guns, which are relatively efficient ways to apply paint to a large area. Jay has kept careful records of these expenses on his last 12 jobs:

House	Square Feet	Openings	Cost
1	2,600	13	$3,300
2	3,010	15	3,750
3	2,800	12	3,100
4	2,850	12	3,150
5	4,050	19	4,700
6	2,700	13	3,250
7	2,375	11	2,800
8	2,450	11	2,800
9	2,600	10	2,875
10	3,700	16	4,100
11	2,650	13	3,200
12	3,550	16	3,950

Required

1. Using the high-low cost estimation technique, determine the cost of painting a 3,300-square-foot house with 14 openings. Also determine the cost for a 2,400-square-foot house with 8 openings.

2. Plot the cost data against square feet and against openings. Which variable is a better cost driver? Why?

8-40 **Cost Estimation, Machine Replacement, Ethics** SpectroGlass Company manufactures glass for office buildings in Arizona and Southern California. As a result of age and wear, a critical machine in the production process has begun to produce quality defects. SpectroGlass is considering replacing the old machine with a new machine, either brand A or brand B. The manufacturer of each machine has provided SpectroGlass these data on the cost of operation of its machine at various levels of output:

Output (square yards)	Machine A Estimated Total Costs	Machine B Estimated Total Costs
4,000	$ 54,600	$ 70,000
7,000	78,800	100,000
9,000	90,300	115,000
14,000	114,900	137,000
16,000	132,400	146,000
24,000	210,000	192,000

Required

1. Use the High-Low method to determine the cost equations for each machine, and then to determine if SpectroGlass's output is expected to be 22,000 square yards, which machine should it purchase? At 15,000 square yards? Is the High-Low method useful here? Why or why not?

2. As a cost analyst at SpectroGlass, you have been assigned to complete requirement 1. A production supervisor comes to you to say that the nature of the defect is really very difficult to detect and that most customers will not notice it, so he questions replacing it. He suggests that you modify your calculations to justify keeping the present machine to keep things the way they are and save the company some money. What do you say?

3. Assume that machine A is manufactured in Germany and machine B is manufactured in Canada. As a U.S.–based firm, what considerations are important to SpectroGlass, in addition to those already mentioned in your answer to requirement 1?

8-41 **Cost Estimation, High-Low Method** Antelope Park Amoco (APA) in Antelope Park, Alaska, has noticed that utility bills are substantially higher the colder the average monthly temperature is. The only thing in the shop that uses natural gas is the furnace. Because of prevailing low temperatures, the furnace is used every month of the year (though less in the summer months and very little in August). Everything else in the shop runs on electricity, and electricity use is fairly constant throughout the year.

For a year, APA has been recording the average daily temperature and the cost of its monthly utility bills for natural gas and electricity.

	Average Temperature	Utility Cost
January	31°F	$760
February	41	629
March	43	543
April	44	410
May	46	275
June	50	233
July	53	220
August	60	210
September	50	305
October	40	530
November	30	750
December	20	870

Required Use the high-low method to estimate utility cost for the upcoming months of January and February. The forecast for January is a near record average temperature of 10°F; temperatures in February are expected to average 40°F.

8-42 to 8-46   **Regression Analysis**   Problems 8-42 through 8-46 are based on Armer Company, which is accumulating data to use in preparing its annual profit plan for the coming year. The cost behavior pattern of the maintenance costs must be determined. The accounting staff has suggested the use of linear regression to derive an equation for maintenance hours and costs. Data regarding the maintenance hours and costs for the last year and the results of the regression analysis follow:

	Hours of Activity	Maintenance Costs
January	480	$ 4,200
February	320	3,000
March	400	3,600
April	300	2,820
May	500	4,350
June	310	2,960
July	320	3,030
August	520	4,470
September	490	4,260
October	470	4,050
November	350	3,300
December	340	3,160
Total	4,800	$43,200
Average	400	3,600

Average cost per hour ($43,200/4,800) = $9.00

a (intercept)	684.65
b coefficient	7.2884
Standard error of the estimate	34.469
R-squared	.99724
t-value for *b*	60.105

Required (8-42)   If Armer Company uses the high-low method of analysis, the equation for the relationship between hours of activity and maintenance cost follows:

a. $y = 400 + 9.0x$

b. $y = 570 + 7.5x$

c. $y = 3,600 + 400x$

d. $y = 570 + 9.0x$

e. None of the above

(CMA Adapted)

Required (8-43)   Based on the data derived from the regression analysis, 420 maintenance hours in a month mean that maintenance costs should be budgeted to the nearest dollar at

a. $3,780

b. $3,461

c. $3,797

d. $3,746

e. None of the above

(CMA Adapted)

Required (8-44)   The coefficient of determination for Armer's regression equation for the maintenance activities is

a. 34.469/49.515

b. .99724

c. square root of .99724

d. $(.99724)^2$

e. None of the above

(CMA Adapted)

Required (8-45)   The percent of the total variance that can be explained by the regression equation is

a. 99.724%

b. 69.613%

c. 80.982%

d. 99.862%

e. None of the above

(CMA Adapted)

Required (8-46)   At 400 hours of activity, Armer management can be approximately two-thirds confident that the maintenance costs will be in the range of

a. $3,550.50 to $3,649.53

b. $3,551.37 to $3,648.51

c. $3,586.18 to $3,613.93

d. $3,565.54 to $3,634.48

e. None of the above

(CMA Adapted)

8-47   **Regression Analysis**   Pilot Shop is a catalog business providing a wide variety of aviation products to pilots throughout the world. Maynard Shephard, the recently hired assistant controller, has been asked to develop a cost function to forecast shipping costs. The previous assistant controller had forecast shipping department costs each year by plotting cost data against direct labor-hours for the most recent 12 months and visually fitting a straight line through the points. The results were not satisfactory.

   After discussions with the shipping department personnel, Maynard decided that shipping costs could be more closely related to the number of orders filled. He based his conclusion on the fact that 10 months ago the shipping department added some automated equipment. Furthermore, he believes that using linear regression analysis will improve the forecasts of shipping costs. Cost data for the shipping department have been accumulated for the last 25 weeks. He ran two regression analyses of the data, one using direct labor-hours, and one using the number of cartons shipped. The information from the two linear regressions follows:

	Regression 1	Regression 2
Equation	$SC = 804.3 + 15.68DL$	$SC = 642.9 + 3.92NR$
R-squared	.365	.729
Standard error of the estimate	2.652	1.884
t-value	1.89	3.46

   where:

   SC = total shipping department costs

   DL = total direct labor-hours

   NR = number of cartons shipped

Required

1. Identify which cost function (regression 1 or regression 2) Pilot Shop should adopt for forecasting total shipping department costs and explain why.

2. If Pilot Shop projects that 600 orders will be filled the coming week, calculate the total shipping department costs using the regression you selected in requirement 1.

3. Explain two or three important limitations of the regression you selected in requirement 1, and identify one or two ways to address the limitations. Specifically include in your discussion the effect, if any, of the global nature of Pilot Shop's business.

(CMA Adapted)

8-48   **Analysis of Regression Results**   Rock n' Roll Heaven is an outdoor pavilion that presents musical performers throughout a six-month season, from late spring to early fall. Rock n' Roll presents a diverse venue of artists in a set of approximately 40 events each season. In order to better project its costs and expected attendance, Rock n' Roll uses regression analysis to project expected ticket sales for upcoming events for each performer. The regression results shown below are derived from the three most recent seasons. The dependent variable for Rock n' Roll is the number of paying tickets holders for each event, and the independent variables are

1. Whether or not this particular performer appeared at Rock n' Roll previously (a dummy variable, 0 if no and 1 if yes).
2. The spending on advertising targeted to the performer's appearance.
3. The performer's local sales of CDs in the most recent year prior to their appearance.
4. The number of television appearances for the performer in the most recent year.
5. The number of public performances in the United States by the performer in the recent year.

Independent Variables	Results
Regression intercept	1,224
Attendance at prior concert	
Coefficient	3,445
t-value	4.11
Spending on advertising	
Coefficient	0.113
t-value	1.88
Performer's CD sales	
Coefficient	0.00044
t-value	1.22
Television appearances	
Coefficient	898
t-value	2.4
Other public performances	
Coefficient	1,233
t-value	3.7
R-squared	0.88
Standard error of the estimate	2,447

Required

1. Using the above regression, what attendance would be predicted for a performer who had appeared at Rock n' Roll previously, had six other public performances but no TV appearances, had local CD sales of $10 million, and Rock n' Roll planned to spend $35,000 on advertising?

2. Evaluate the precision and reliability of the regression results shown above. What changes, if any, do you propose for the regression? Which variables should be deleted, and which do you think should be added, and why?

8-49 **Correlation Analysis** PolyChem is a large manufacturer of packaging materials for supermarkets and other retail applications; the packages are used by customers to carry away their purchases. PolyChem has succeeded for many years by providing a high-quality product and superior customer service. Recently, additional competitors have entered the market, both local and foreign, and PolyChem is finding that it must increasingly compete on price. PolyChem's strategy for dealing with the increased competition is to market its products to smaller retailers that would appreciate the firm's quality and service, as well as the firm's ability to customize the product—adding different designs and colors to the packaging material. Until recently, the firm determined product costs based on simple averages of materials purchases, plant labor, and overhead. The firm's management is now interested in improving, if possible, the accuracy of its cost information. As a start, Cheryl Greenberg, the management accountant, obtains the following sample of data (Table 1) from the plant manager, showing the machine number, the order size (quantity, in thousands), the machine setup time (in hours per unit; setup time also includes cleanup time after the order is run), run time (the operating time for the machine to produce the order), and a measure of the complexity of the order based on a subjective rating where 1 = less complex and 2 = more complex (complexity relates to the number and type of images and colors printed on the packaging material).

Cheryl wants to run some regression analyses to better understand this data and, as a first step, obtains a correlation analysis which shows the simple correlation between each of the variables in Table 1. The results are shown in Table 2. Cheryl understands that each of the correlation numbers in Table 2 is equivalent to the R-squared for a simple linear regression between the variable, as follows: (correlation between two variables)^2 = the R-squared for simple regression analysis between these two variables. To illustrate, note that the correlation between machine number and order quantity = $-.33919$. The R-squared for the regression between these two variables (with either as the dependent variable) is $(-.33919)^2 = .1151$. Cheryl also recalls that a negative correlation means that the two variables are inversely related—when one increases, the other decreases.

Table 1   Plant Data for PolyChem

Machine Number	Order Size	Order Complexity	Per Unit Setup Time	Per Unit Run Time
2	480	1	0.002	0.042
2	489	1	0.001	0.043
2	480	2	0.005	0.042
4	180	1	0.004	0.040
4	2160	1	0.002	0.035
4	1377	1	0.002	0.040
4	120	2	0.004	0.040
4	540	1	0.003	0.041
4	360	2	0.014	0.041
4	1080	2	0.011	0.038
4	300	1	0.004	0.043
4	2400	2	0.005	0.035
4	81	2	0.046	0.041
8	360	1	0.002	0.043
8	120	1	0.002	0.043
8	120	2	0.007	0.042
8	60	2	0.008	0.042
8	240	1	0.008	0.043
8	60	2	0.005	0.047

Table 2   Correlation Results for PolyChem's Plant Data

	Number	Order Size	Complexity	Setup Time	Run Time
Number	1				
Order size	−0.33919	1			
Complexity	0.071001	−0.07095	1		
Setup time	−0.03805	−0.20952	0.4521388	1	
Run time	0.346651	−0.80882	−0.140537	−0.06534	1

Note: Correlations with absolute value > .4 are statistically significant at $p < .10$; correlations with absolute value > .5 are statistically significant at $p < .05$.

Required

1. Analyze the findings in Table 2 and assess how, if at all, order size and complexity affect setup time and run time. What other findings in Table 2 are of particular interest?

2. How can your analysis in 1 above help PolyChem become more competitive?

8-50 **Regression Analysis**   United States Motors Inc. (USMI) manufactures automobiles and light trucks and distributes them for sale to consumers through franchised retail outlets. As part of the franchise agreement, dealerships must provide monthly financial statements following the USMI accounting procedures manual. USMI has developed the following financial profile of an average dealership that sells 1,500 new vehicles annually.

AVERAGE DEALERSHIP FINANCIAL PROFILE
Composite Income Statement

Sales	$30,000,000
Cost of goods sold	24,750,000
Gross profit	$ 5,250,000
Operating costs	
Variable expenses	862,500
Mixed expenses	2,300,000
Fixed expenses	1,854,000
Operating income	$ 233,500

USMI is considering a major expansion of its dealership network. The vice president of marketing has asked Jack Snyder, corporate controller, to develop some measure of the risk associated with the addition of these franchises. Jack estimates that 90 percent of the mixed expenses shown are variable for purposes of this analysis. He also suggested performing regression analyses on the various components of the mixed expenses to more definitively determine their variability.

Required

1. Calculate the composite dealership profit if 2,000 units are sold.

2. Assume that regression analyses were performed on the separate components of the mixed expenses and that a coefficient of determination value of .60 was determined as applicable to aggregate mixed expenses over the relevant range.

    a. Define the term *relevant range.*

    b. Explain the significance of an *R*-squared value of .60 to USMI's analysis.

    c. Describe the limitations that may exist in applying the composite-based relationships to specific new dealerships that have been proposed.

    d. Define the *standard error of the estimate.*

3. The regression equation that Jack Snyder developed to project annual sales of a dealership has an *R*-squared of 60 percent and a standard error of the estimate of $4,500,000. If the projected annual sales for a dealership total $28,500,000, determine the approximate 95 percent confidence range for Jack's prediction of sales.

4. What is the strategic role of regression analysis for USMI?

(CMA Adapted)

8-51   **Cost Estimation, High-Low Method, Regression Analysis**   DVD Express is a large manufacturer of affordable DVD players. Management recently became aware of rising costs resulting from returns of malfunctioning products. As a starting point for further analysis, Bridget Forrester, the controller, wants to test different forecasting methods and then use the best one to forecast quarterly expenses for 2010. The relevant data for the previous three years follows:

2007 Quarter	Return Expenses	2008 Quarter	Return Expenses	2009 Quarter	Return Expenses
1	$15,000	1	$16,200	1	$16,600
2	17,500	2	17,800	2	18,100
3	18,500	3	18,800	3	19,000
4	18,600	4	17,700	4	19,200

The result of a simple regression analysis using all 12 data points yielded an intercept of $16,559.09 and a coefficient for the independent variable of $183.22. (*R*-squared = .27, *t* = 1.94, *SE* = 1128).

Required

1. Calculate the quarterly forecast for 2010 using the high-low method and regression analyses. Recommend which method Bridget should use and explain why.

2. How does your analysis in requirement 1 change if DVD Express manufactures its products in multiple global production facilities to serve the global market?

8-52 **Regression Analysis; Use of the Internet** Economists and business planners often need to make projections of interest rates in order to effectively plan for the purchase of equipment and other assets. The timing of these investments is a critical part of the firm's financial management and can have a dramatic effect on the firm's profitability. This is particularly important during times of liquidity problems as we have had in the financial markets. As a CFO of a large retail firm that requires significant amounts of seasonal borrowing, you are interested in forecasting the prime rate for the next several months. You think you can get a good prediction for the consumer price index (CPI) and the unemployment rate months ahead, based on other studies and economic forecasts to which you have access. You have decided to use regression analysis to develop a model to predict the prime rate from the CPI and the unemployment rate. The data for monthly interest rate data (prime rate) from the Federal Reserve Board can be found at the FED Web site (www.stls.frb.org/fred/data/irates/mprime) and the employment and CPI information is provided by the U.S. Bureau of Labor Statistics (www.bls.gov/data/home.htm). The data for 24 months from October 2006 through September 2008 is provided below. The CPI data is for all U.S. items (indexed at year 1967); the unemployment rate is for all civilian unemployment.

Month/Year	Prime Rate	CPI	Unemployment Rate
10/2006	8.25	604.6	4.4
11/2006	8.25	603.6	4.5
12/2006	8.25	604.5	4.4
1/2007	8.25	606.3	4.6
2/2007	8.25	609.6	4.5
3/2007	8.25	615.4	4.4
4/2007	8.25	619.1	4.5
5/2007	8.25	622.9	4.5
6/2007	8.25	624.1	4.6
7/2007	8.25	624.0	4.7
8/2007	8.25	622.8	4.7
9/2007	8.03	624.5	4.7
10/2007	7.74	625.9	4.8
11/2007	7.50	629.6	4.7
12/2007	7.33	629.2	5.0
1/2008	6.98	632.3	4.9
2/2008	6.00	634.1	4.8
3/2008	5.66	639.6	5.1
4/2008	5.24	643.5	5.0
5/2008	5.00	648.9	5.5
6/2008	5.00	655.5	5.5
7/2008	5.00	658.9	5.7
8/2008	5.00	656.3	6.1
9/2008	5.00	655.4	6.1

Required

1. Develop a regression model to predict interest rates using the Bureau of Labor Statistics and Federal Reserve Board data above. Evaluate the results of the regression.

2. Use the model you developed to predict the prime rate for December 2008 if the CPI is expected to be 670 and the unemployment rate is expected to be 6.6 in December.

3. What other economic data can you find on the Web that would help in predicting the prime interest rate? Include the Web links in your answer, if appropriate.

4. To follow up on the regression analysis in part 1, go to the Web sites indicated above, include the most recent data, and rerun the regressions with the same objective of predicting the prime rate for December 2008. Compare your results to the finding for the regression in part 1 and to the actual prime rate in December 2008. Why the difference, if any?

8-53 **Regression; Applicants for MBA Programs** Business schools have commonly observed that when job opportunities are down, those interested in business seek to enter MBA programs. To test this hypothesis, we decided to look at the number of applicants for the Graduate Management Admissions Test (GMAT) which is required for application to most MBA programs and to compare that to the unemployment rate. The GMAT data is only available on an annual basis, so we also use annual unemployment data. The GMAT data is from the Graduate Management Admissions Council (www.gmac.com/gmac) while the unemployment data is taken from the Web site of the U.S. Bureau of Labor Statistics (www.bls.gov/data/home.htm). We have data for both the total unemployment rate and the rate for college graduates 25 years of age or older. The data for 2000 through September 2008 is shown below. The unemployment rate is the median value for the 12 months in the year (or the 9 months in 2008). The percentage change (from prior year) in GMAT exam takers is from the GMAC's publication "2008 Application Trends Survey."

	Unemployment Rate	Unemployment Rate for College Grads	Percentage Change in GMAT Takers
2000	4.0%	1.6%	4%
2001	4.6	2.2	3
2002	5.8	2.9	12
2003	6.0	3.1	(7)
2004	5.5	2.7	(9)
2005	5.1	2.3	(4)
2006	4.6	2	6
2007	4.7	2.1	5
2008	5.5	2.3	10

Required

1. Use regression on the above data to determine whether there is a relationship between the unemployment rate and the number of GMAT exam takers. Use both measures of unemployment and see if there is a difference in your results. State whether you expect the relationship to be positive or negative (inverse).

2. Assume that the relationship between the unemployment rate and the number of GMAT takers is a lagged relationship and a change in the unemployment rate in one year leads to a change in GMAT takers in the following year. Use regression again and compare your results to those in part 1.

8-54 **Learning Curves** The Air Force Museum Foundation has commissioned the purchase of 16 Four F Sixes, pre–World War II aircraft. They will be built completely from scratch to the exact specifications used for the originals. As further authentication, the aircraft will be made using the technology and manufacturing processes available when the originals were built. Each of the 16 will be flown to Air Force and aviation museums throughout the country for exhibition. Aviation enthusiasts can also visit the production facility to see exactly how such aircraft were built in 1938.

Soren Industries wants to bid on the aircraft contract and asked for and received certain cost information about the Four F Sixes from the Air Force. The information includes some of the old cost data from the builders of the original aircraft. The available information is for the total accumulated time as the first, eighth, and thirty-second aircraft, respectively, were completed. The data reflect a learning rate of 90%.

Output	Total Hours
1	250
8	1,458
32	4,724

Required

1. If Soren Industries expects that the manufacturing time will be the same as it was in 1938, how many hours will it take to build the 16 aircraft for the Air Force Museum Foundation?

2. What is the role of learning curves in Soren Industries' business for contracts such as this?

8-55 **Learning Curves** Ben Matthews and David Everhart work for a landscaping company in Twin Cities, Oklahoma. Their principal job is to lay railroad ties to line the sidewalks around apartment complexes and to install flower boxes. The first time Ben and David undertook one of these projects, they spent 17 hours. Their goal by the end of the summer was to be able to finish an apartment complex in 8 hours, one working day. They performed eight of these jobs and had an 80 percent learning curve. Assume that all apartment complexes are approximately the same size.

Required Did they reach their goal? If not, what would the learning rate have to have been for them to have accomplished their goal?

8-56 Learning Curves Emotional Headdress (EH) is a Des Moines, Iowa, manufacturer of avant garde hats and headwear. On March 11, 2010, the company purchased a new machine to aid in producing various established product lines. Production efficiency on the new machine increases with the workforce experience. It has been shown that as cumulative output on the new machine increases, average labor time per unit decreases up to the production of at least 3,200 units. As EH's cumulative output doubles from a base of 100 units produced, the average labor time per unit declines by 15 percent. EH's production varies little from month to month and averages 800 hats per month.

Emotional Headdress has developed a new style of men's hat, the Morrisey, to be produced on the new machine. One hundred Morrisey hats can be produced in a total of 25 labor-hours. All other direct costs to produce each Morrisey hat are $16.25, excluding direct labor cost. EH's direct labor cost per hour is $15. Fixed costs are $8,000 per month, and EH has the capacity to produce 3,200 hats per month.

Required Emotional Headdress wishes to set the selling price for a Morrisey hat at 125 percent of the hat production cost. At the production level of 100 units, what is the selling price?

8-57 Learning Curves Hauser Company, a family-owned business, engineers and manufactures a line of mopeds and dirt bikes under the trade-name Trailite. The company has been in business for almost 20 years and has maintained a profitable share of the recreational vehicle market due to its reputation for high-quality products. In addition, Hauser's engineering department has kept the company in the forefront by incorporating the latest technology in the Trailite bikes. Most sub-assembly work for the bikes is subcontracted to reliable vendors. However, the final assembly and inspection of all products is performed at Hauser's plant. Hauser recently developed a new braking system for the Trailite Model-500 dirt bike. Because of the company's current availability of production capacity, Jim Walsh, production manager, recommended that the first lot of the new braking system be manufactured in-house rather than by subcontractors. This 80-unit production run has now been completed. The cumulative average labor-hours per unit for the braking system was 60 hours. Hauser's experience with similar products indicates that a learning curve of 80 percent is applicable and that the learning factor can be expected to extend only through the fourth production run (80 per batch) for a total of 320 units. Hauser's direct labor cost is $14.50 per direct labor-hour. Its management must decide whether to continue producing the braking system in its own plant or to subcontract this work. Joyce Lane, Hauser's purchasing agent, has received a proposal from MACQ, a company specializing in component assembly. MACQ has done work in the past for Hauser and has proved to be of high quality and reliable. The terms of MACQ's proposal are negotiable, and before beginning discussions with them, Joyce has decided to conduct some relevant financial analysis.

Required

1. Hauser Company has an immediate requirement for a total of 1,000 units of the braking system. Determine Hauser's future direct labor costs to produce the required braking system units if it manufactures the units in-house.

2. A consultant has advised Joyce that the learning rate for this application might be closer to 75 percent. What is the effect on projected costs of using a 75 percent learning curve as opposed to an 80 percent learning curve?

3. What conditions in a manufacturing plant, if present, would offset the potential benefits of the learning curve? What is the strategic role of learning curve analysis for Hauser Company?

(CMA Adapted)

8-58 Cost Estimation, Regression Analysis Plantcity is a large nursery and retail store specializing in house and garden plants and supplies. Jean Raouth, the assistant manager, is in the process of budgeting monthly supplies expense for 2010. She assumes that in some way supplies expense is related to sales, either in units or in dollars. She has collected these data for sales and supplies expenses for June 2007 through December 2009, and has estimated sales for 2010:

Date	Supplies Expense	Sales Units	Sales Dollars
Jun 2007	$2,745	354	$2,009
Jul	3,200	436	2,190
Aug	3,232	525	2,878
Sep	2,199	145	1,856
Oct	2,321	199	2,168
Nov	3,432	543	2,152
Dec	4,278	1,189	2,463
Jan 2008	2,310	212	1,999
Feb	2,573	284	2,190
Mar	2,487	246	1,894
Apr	2,484	278	2,134
May	3,384	498	3,210
Jun	2,945	424	2,850
Jul	2,758	312	2,265
Aug	3,394	485	2,435
Sep	2,254	188	1,893
Oct	2,763	276	2,232
Nov	3,245	489	3,004
Dec	4,576	1,045	3,309
Jan 2009	2,103	104	2,195
Feb	2,056	167	2,045
Mar	3,874	298	2,301
Apr	2,784	398	2,345
May	2,345	187	1,815
Jun	2,912	334	2,094
Jul	2,093	264	1,934
Aug	2,873	333	2,054
Sep	2,563	143	1,977
Oct	2,384	245	1,857
Nov	2,476	232	2,189
Dec	3,364	1,122	3,433
Jan 2010 (estimated)		180	$1,600
Feb		230	2,000
Mar		190	1,900
Apr		450	2,400
May		350	2,300
Jun		350	2,300
Jul		450	2,500
Aug		550	3,000
Sep		300	2,500
Oct		300	2,500
Nov		450	3,200
Dec		950	3,900

Required

1. Develop the regression that Jean should use based on these data and use the regression procedure in Excel or an equivalent regression software program. Evaluate the reliability and precision of the regression you have chosen.

2. What are the predicted monthly figures for supplies expense for 2010?

8-59 **Cross-Sectional Regression Analysis**   WasteTec is a large construction company that specializes in the construction of large wastewater treatment plants and recycling plants. A major cost driver in either type of facility is the capacity of the plant. For example, the capacity of a recycling plant is measured by the number of tons of water per day (TPD) that the plant can process. These plants can vary in size from a few hundred TPD to as many as several thousand TPD. Regression analysis is a useful method to estimate the cost of a new plant by using a regression equation developed from prior plant construction projects. The dependent variable of the regression is the actual construction cost of each project, while the independent variable is the TPD for the plant. Below is a sample of some recent projects and the related construction costs (in thousands).

	TPD	Cost
Commerce, CA	360	$ 59,369
Hudson Falls, NY	400	77,013
Layton, UT	420	50,405
Oxford Township, NJ	450	75,779
Savannah, GA	500	87,439
Poughkeepsie, NY	506	57,463
Panama City, FL	510	60,730
Ronkonkoma, NY	518	84,457
Okahuma, FL	528	88,119
Spokane, WA	800	152,902
Arlington, VA	975	127,021
Camden, NJ	1,050	163,395
York, PA	1,344	139,302
Bridgeport, CT	2,250	344,852
Chester, PA	2,688	448,073

Required

1. Develop a regression model using Excel or an equivalent system to predict the cost of a proposed new plant in Babylon, New York, which will have a required capacity of 750 TPD. What is the predicted cost for the Babylon plant, using your regression?

2. Evaluate the precision and reliability of the regression you have developed. How could it be improved?

8-60 Regression Analysis: Cross-Sectional Analysis; Calculation of a Regression Equation   Jim Manzano is the general partner of an investment group that owns a number of commercial and industrial properties, including a chain of 15 convenience stores located in the greater metropolitan area of Cleveland, Ohio. Jim is concerned about the recent increase in inventory theft and waste (he calls it "spoilage") in his stores. Spoilage has increased by more than 20 percent in each of the past two years. In some stores, the main reason is theft; in others, it is damage and vandalism; and in still others, merchandise actually does spoil and must be thrown out. Jim has collected data on spoilage at each of his stores in the recent month and is looking for patterns of spoilage relative to store size (measured by square feet of floor space, number of employees, and total sales) and to the location of the store (location 1 is an area where few arrests for theft, disorderly conduct, or vandalism are made, and location 3 is for areas with high arrests). Jim is not sure, but he suspects, based on his experience managing convenience stores, that a relationship exists among these factors. A colleague told him that a type of regression called "cross-sectional" regression would suit his needs. The cross-sectional regression takes data from a single time period and determines predictions for the dependent variable at different cost objects (in this case, different stores). The objective of the cross-sectional regression is to compare the actual known value for the dependent variable to the predicted value as a basis for assessing the reasonableness of the actual value. This approach is often used in cases similar to Jim's in which the accuracy or reasonableness of the reported dependent variable is a concern. In effect, the cross-sectional regression develops a model that represents the overall patterns in all the data, and the unusual stores will be identified by the largest error terms in the regression. The following data are for the most recent month's operations:

Store Number	Inventory Spoilage	Square Footage	Number of Employees	Location	Sales
1	$ 1,512	2,400	8	1	$ 312,389
2	3,005	3,900	10	2	346,235
3	1,686	3,200	12	1	376,465
4	1,908	3,400	12	1	345,723
5	2,384	3,750	9	2	453,983

Store Number	Inventory Spoilage	Square Footage	Number of Employees	Location	Sales
6	4,806	4,800	10	3	502,984
7	2,253	3,500	8	1	325,436
8	1,443	3,000	10	1	253,647
9	3,755	5,550	15	2	562,534
10	1,023	2,250	15	1	287,364
11	1,552	2,500	9	1	198,374
12	2,119	3,500	16	2	333,984
13	5,506	7,500	15	3	673,345
14	3,034	5,700	16	2	588,947
15	772	2,200	8	1	225,364
Totals	$36,758	57,150	173		$5,786,774

Required

1. Using Excel or an equivalent software program, prepare a regression analysis that predicts inventory spoilage at each of the 15 stores. Use any of the four potential independent variables (or a combination) you think appropriate and explain your answer. Also evaluate the precision and reliability of the regression you select.

2. Using the regression equation you developed in requirement 1, determine which of the 15 stores might have inventory spoilage that is out of line relative to the entire chain of stores. Explain your choice.

8-61 **Cost Estimating for Defense Contracting; Using the Internet; Appendix B** Companies that do business with the U.S. Defense Department (e.g., The Boeing Company, Lockheed Martin Corporation, General Electric, Northrop Grumman, and General Dynamics) typically develop large multiyear proposals for large-scale defense-related projects. A key aspect of developing a successful proposal for the Department of Defense is to use proper cost estimation tools.

Required

1. Review the information at the site of the International Society of Parametric Analysis (ISPA), (www. ispa-cost.org/ISPA_PEH_4th_ed_Final.pdf), which sets out proper estimation methods for proposals to the Department of Defense. Look especially at Chapter 3 of the ISPA's handbook. In 100 words or less describe the cost estimation methods suggested in this document for use in developing proposals for the Department of Defense. What are some example of how cost estimation is used by defense contractors such as The Boeing Company.

2. Review Figure 3.6 in the handbook and compare it to Exhibit 8B.7 in this chapter.

Solutions to Self-Study Problems

1. Using the High-Low Method

Begin by graphing the data to determine whether there are any unusual (i.e., seasonal) patterns or outliers in Exhibit 1.

The graph shows no unusual patterns or outliers, so the high-low estimate can be determined directly from the low point (March) and the high point (December) as follows:

To determine the slope of the line (unit variable cost)

$$(\$201{,}783 - \$123{,}245)/(7{,}433 - 5{,}166) = \$34.644 \text{ per delivery}$$

To determine the intercept

$$\$201{,}783 - (7{,}433 \times \$34.644) = -\$55{,}726$$
$$\$123{,}245 - (5{,}166 \times \$34.644) = -\$55{,}726$$

The estimation equation is

$$\text{Vehicle costs} = -\$55{,}726 + (\$34.644 \times \text{Number of deliveries/Month})$$

Note that the intercept is a negative number, which simply means that the relevant range of 5,166 to 7,433 deliveries is so far from the zero point (where the intercept is) that the intercept cannot be properly interpreted as a fixed cost. The estimation equation therefore is useful only within the relevant range of approximately 5,000 to 7,500 deliveries and should not be used to estimate costs outside that range.

2. Using Regression Analysis

All relevant criteria favor the first regression based on higher R-squared and t-values and lower standard error. Moreover, the sign on the materials cost variable in regression 2 is negative, which is difficult to

EXHIBIT 1

Plot of Data for Hector's Delivery Service

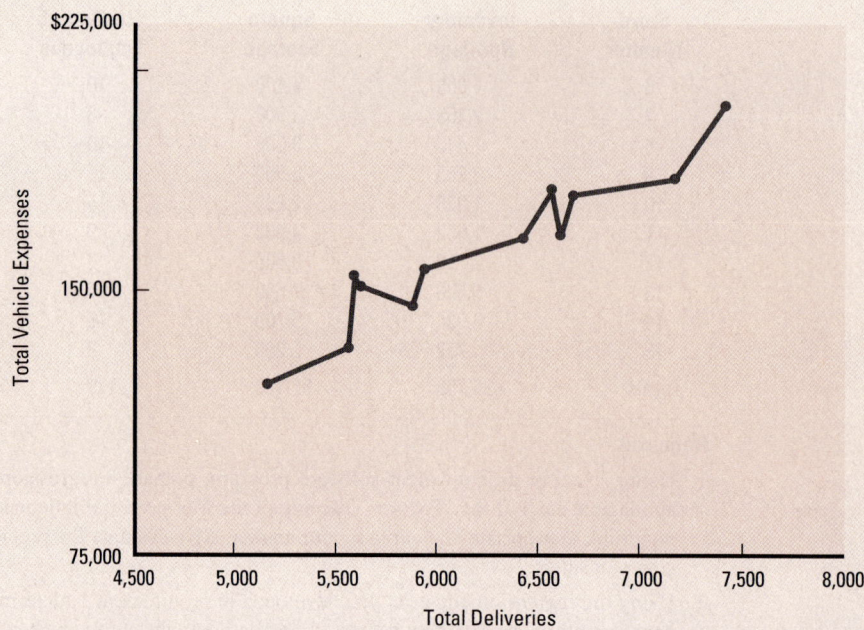

explain. This variable should have a direct relationship with overhead; thus, the sign of the variable should be positive. The reason for the improvement of regression 1 over regression 2 might be that machine-hours are highly correlated with either materials costs, labor-hours, or both, thus causing multicollinearity. By excluding machine-hours as an independent variable, George reduced or removed the multicollinearity, and the regression improved as a result. He should therefore use regression 1.

3. Using Both High-Low and Regression

Begin by graphing the data for the number of defective units, as shown in Exhibit 2. The objective is to identify any unusual patterns that must be considered in developing an estimate.

Exhibit 2 shows that the number of defective units varies considerably from month to month and that a steady increase has occurred over the past two years. Knowing that the production level also has been increasing (as measured either by cost of sales, units produced, or units shipped), we now want to determine whether the relationship between defects and production level (Exhibit 3) has changed.

We begin with units produced as the independent variable, since it should have the most direct relationship with defects; the other independent variables can be tried later. The second graph (Exhibit 3) makes clear that a relationship exists between units produced and the number of defects.

The next step is to quantify this relationship with the high-low method and regression analysis. We begin with the high-low analysis. For Exhibit 3, we identify February 2009 and December 2010 as representative low and high periods, respectively.

EXHIBIT 2

Defective Units from January 2009 to December 2010

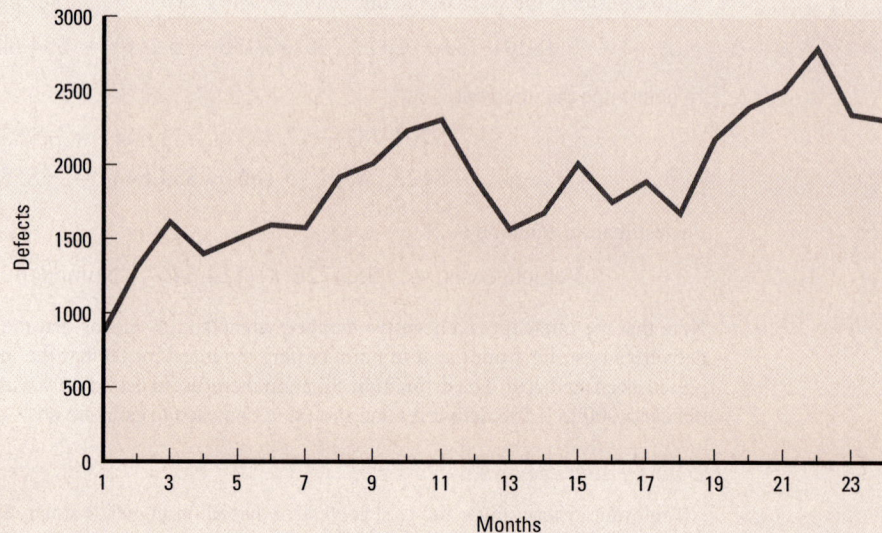

EXHIBIT 3
Defective Units vs.
Production Level from
January 2009 to December
2010

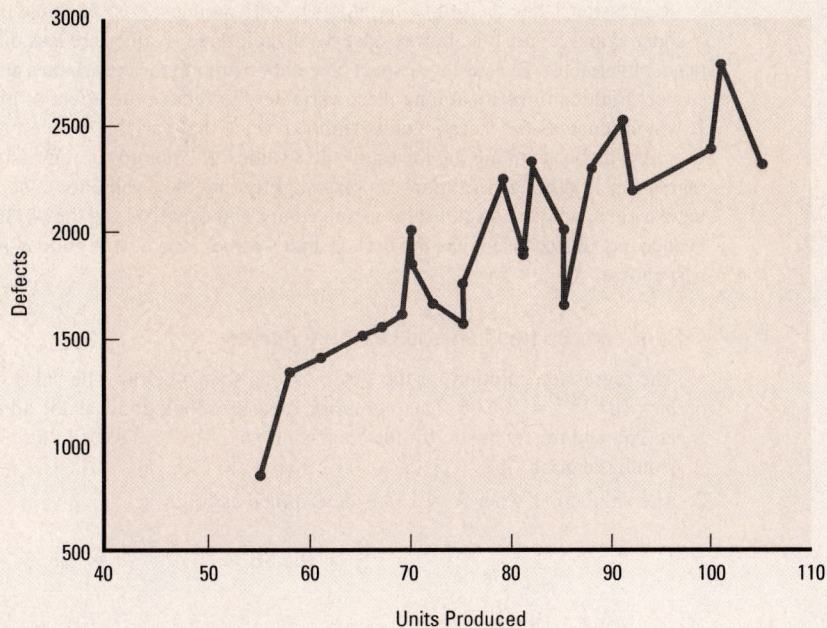

We calculate the high-low estimate as follows (these two points are not the absolute lowest and highest points, but they produce a line that is representative of the data):

$$\text{slope} = (2{,}311 - 1{,}335)/(88 - 58) = 32.533$$

And

$$\text{Intercept} = 2{,}311 - (32.533 \times 88) = 1{,}335 - (32.533 \times 58) = -552$$

Thus, the estimation equation is

$$\text{Number of defects} = -552 + (32.533 \times \text{Production level})$$

The high-low estimate is subject to the limitations of subjectivity in the choice of high and low points and because it uses only those two data points to develop the estimate. Regression is thus performed to provide a more precise estimate. Thus, the next step is to obtain a regression analysis from the previous data and to assess the precision and reliability of the regression estimate. The regression can be completed with a spreadsheet program or any of a number of available software systems. The results for three regression analyses are presented in Exhibit 4. The dependent variable in each case is the number of defective units.

EXHIBIT 4
Regressions for the Number
of Defects

Intercept	Coefficient of Independent Variable	t-value for Independent Variable	R-squared	Standard Error of the Estimate
Regression 1				
103.20			.883	161
	−38.974 (units shipped)	−.44		
	−2.849 (units produced)	−.38		
	4.702 (cost of sales)	.72		
Regression 2				
92.24			.881	158
	−2.230 (units produced)	−.309		
	1.837 (cost of sales)	4.54		
Regression 3				
43.95			.881	155
	1.720 (cost of sales)	12.77		

Regression 1 has the following independent variables: cost of sales, units shipped, and units produced. *R*-squared and *SE* are OK, but we observe that all three *t*-values are less than 2.0, indicating unreliable independent variables. Because we expect correlation among these variables and because of the low *t*- values, we suspect multicollinearity among these variables. To reduce the effect of multicollinearity, we try regression 2, which removes the variable units shipped, since that variable is likely to be least associated with defective units and has among the lowest of the *t*-values. *R*-squared for regression 2 is essentially the same as for regression 1, although *SE* improves very slightly, and the *t*-value for cost of sales is now OK. The results of regression 3, with the cost of sales variable only, show that *SE* and the *t*-value improve again while *R*-squared is unchanged. Because it has the best *SE* and *t*-values, and a very good *R*-squared, the third regression is the best choice.

4. Nonlinear Regression and Learning Curves

1. The regression solution for the Virilli case is shown below. The value of $b = -0.3394$, and the value of $a = 10^{2.02881} = 106.86$. The regression measures look good, as the adjusted *R*-squared is relatively high at .938 and the *t*-statistic for the coefficient, *b*, is 10.35. Overall these measures indicate that the regression has a good fit.

2. The value for *Y* when $X = 133$ is determined as follows.

$$Y = 106.86 \times 133^{-0.3394} = 20.33$$

X	Y	LogX	LogY
10	45	1	1.653213
18	40	1.255273	1.60206
25	38	1.39794	1.579784
43	32	1.633468	1.50515
55	30	1.740363	1.477121
70	25	1.845098	1.39794
93	22	1.968483	1.342423
110	20	2.041393	1.30103

Regression Statistics

Multiple *R*	0.97313
R-square	0.94698
Adjusted *R*-square	0.93815
Standard error	0.03162
Observations	8

ANOVA

	df	SS	MS
Regression	1	0.107148	0.107148
Residual	6	0.005999	0.001
Total	7	0.113147	

	Coefficient	Standard Error	t-Stat
Intercept	2.02881	0.053959	37.59928
Log*X*	−0.3394	0.032782	−10.3522

Profit Planning:
Cost-Volume-Profit Analysis

After studying this chapter, you should be able to . . .

1. Explain cost-volume-profit (CVP) analysis, the CVP model, and the strategic role of CVP analysis
2. Apply CVP analysis for breakeven planning
3. Apply CVP analysis for profit planning
4. Apply CVP analysis for activity-based costing
5. Employ sensitivity analysis to more effectively use CVP analysis when actual sales are uncertain
6. Adapt CVP analysis for multiple products
7. Apply CVP analysis in not-for-profit organizations
8. Identify the assumptions and limitations of CVP analysis and their effect on the proper interpretation of the results

For some companies, just about each product or service is new and different. This is true for Clear Channel Communications, Inc., (CCC; www.clearchannel.com), the world's largest owner of radio stations and provider of live entertainment events. CCC produces live entertainment, mostly musical entertainment, in more than 70 locations. Each show offers a new opportunity for CCC to be profitable, but careful planning is necessary to achieve success. A key part of this planning for CCC is to use cost-volume-profit analysis, the topic of this chapter. CCC uses cost-volume-profit (CVP) analysis to project estimated profits for each live event, given the company's projections about attendance; that is, CVP analysis shows the relationship between volume of attendance and the event's related costs and profits.

LEARNING OBJECTIVE 1

Explain cost-volume-profit (CVP) analysis, the CVP model, and the strategic role of CVP analysis.

Some of CCC's events are planned on a fixed-fee basis; that is, the entertainer is paid a fixed amount for the performance that is not tied to attendance. Other events are planned so that the entertainer receives a payment based on attendance. The fixed-fee arrangement is somewhat riskier for CCC because CCC bears the risk of low attendance and therefore low profits or losses; of course, the upside is that CCC does well if attendance is high. In contrast, the entertainer paid on the basis of attendance shares some of the risk.

For fixed-fee events, CCC uses attendance projections and cost-volume-profit analysis to carefully project costs and profits and to plan levels of advertising and other expenses. This type of short-term profit planning is critical for CCC's overall success and profitability.

Cost-Volume-Profit Analysis

Cost-volume-profit (CVP) analysis

is a method for analyzing how various operating decisions and marketing decisions will affect profit.

Cost-volume-profit (CVP) analysis is a method for analyzing how operating decisions and marketing decisions affect profit based on an understanding of the relationship between variable costs, fixed costs, unit selling price, and the output level. CVP analysis has many applications:

- Setting prices for products and services.
- Introducing a new product or service.
- Replacing a piece of equipment.
- Determining the breakeven point.

- Deciding whether to make or buy a given product or service.
- Determining the best product mix.
- Performing strategic what-if analyses.

CVP analysis is based on an explicit model of the relationships among the three factors—costs, sales, and profits—and how they change in a predictable way as the volume of activity changes. The CVP model is

$$\text{Operating profit} = \text{Sales} - \text{Total costs}$$

where operating profit is profit exclusive of unusual or nonrecurring items and is *before* tax. When there are no unusual or nonrecurring items, operating profit is simply before-tax income. Since we will be looking at how costs and sales vary with volume, it is important to distinguish variable and fixed costs, and to show the above equation in the equivalent form below:

$$\text{Sales} = \text{Fixed costs} + \text{Variable costs} + \text{Operating profit}$$

Now, replacing sales with the number of units sold times price, and replacing variable cost with unit variable cost times the number of units sold, the CVP model is

$$\text{Units sold} \times \text{Price} = \text{Fixed cost}$$
$$+ \text{Units sold} \times \text{Unit variable cost}$$
$$+ \text{Operating profit}$$

For convenient use, the model is commonly shown in a symbolic form:[1]

$Q = $ units sold

$p = $ unit selling price

$F = $ total fixed cost

$v = $ unit variable cost

$N = $ operating profit

$$p \times Q = F + (v \times Q) + N$$

Contribution Margin and Contribution Income Statement

Effective use of the CVP model requires an understanding of three additional concepts: the contribution margin, the contribution margin ratio, and the contribution income statement. The contribution margin is both a unit and a total concept. The **unit contribution margin** is the difference between unit sales price and unit variable cost:

$$p - v = \text{Unit contribution margin}$$

The unit contribution margin measures the increase in operating profit for a unit increase in sales. If sales are expected to increase by 100 units, profits should increase by 100 times the contribution margin. The **total contribution margin** is the unit contribution margin multiplied by the number of units sold.

For example, assume that Household Furnishings, Inc. (HFI), a manufacturer of home furnishings, is interested in developing a new product, a wooden TV table, that would be priced at $75 and would have variable costs of $35 per unit. Assume also that the new product will have no effect on sales of existing products. The investment would require new fixed costs of $5,000 per month ($60,000/yr). HFI expects sales of 2,400 units in the first year and 2,600 units in the second year. The data for HFI are summarized in Exhibit 9.1.

> The **unit contribution margin** is the difference between unit sales price and unit variable cost and is a measure of the increase in profit for a unit increase in sales.

> The **total contribution margin** is the unit contribution margin multiplied by the number of units sold.

---

[1] Note that in Chapter 8, Cost Estimation, we used the general form of the estimation equation: $Y = a + (b \times X)$. This is a general model that is used to estimate a variety of dependent variables including cost, the effect of learning on cost, sales, and different types of operating data. Since we are interested only in revenues, costs, and profits in CVP analysis, we use a specific notation in this chapter for price (p), unit variable cost (v), and fixed costs(F) in contrast to the more general notation.

EXHIBIT 9.1
Data for Household
Furnishings, Inc. (HFI):
TV Table

	Per Unit	2010	2011
Fixed cost		$60,000	$60,000
Revenue	$75		
Variable cost	35		
Planned production		2,400 units	2,600 units
Planned sales		2,400 units	2,600 units

EXHIBIT 9.2   **Contribution Income Statements for HFI's Proposed TV Table**

	2010		2011			
	Amount	Percent	Amount	Percent	Change	Notes
Sales	$180,000	100.00%	$195,000	100.00%	$15,000	
Variable costs	84,000	46.67	91,000	46.67	7,000	
Total contribution margin	$ 96,000	53.33%	$104,000	53.33%	$ 8,000	53.33% is the contribution margin ratio
Fixed costs	60,000		60,000		0	
Operating profit	$ 36,000		$ 44,000		$ 8,000	$8,000 = 0.5333 × $15,000

The unit contribution margin for each table would be $40 ($75 − $35). Using the unit contribution margin, we see that if HFI expects to sell 2,400 tables in 2010, it can expect to increase total contribution margin in 2010 by $96,000 ($40 × 2,400) and operating profit by $36,000 ($96,000 − $60,000 fixed cost). In 2011 profits increase as sales increase by 200 units, from 2,400 to 2,600 units. Since fixed costs are the same in both years, the increase in profits from 2010 to 2011 is equal to the change in total contribution margin from 2010 to 2011, that is, unit contribution of $40 times the increase in units sold, or $8,000 ($40 contribution per unit × 200 units). These results are shown in Exhibit 9.2.

The **contribution margin ratio**
is the ratio of the unit
contribution margin to unit sales
price $(p − v)/p$.

A measure of the profit contribution per sales dollar is the **contribution margin ratio,** which is the ratio of the unit contribution margin to unit sales price $(p − v)/p$. The contribution margin ratio for HFI's proposed TV table is 53.33% = ($75 − $35)/$75. The ratio identifies the amount of increase (or decrease) in profits caused by a given increase (or decrease) in sales dollars. What is the effect on operating profit of an increase of $15,000 in sales from 2010 to 2011? We can quickly calculate that profits will increase by $8,000 ($15,000 × 0.5333) from 2010 to 2011.

In the **contribution income statement**
variable costs are subtracted
from sales to get total
contribution margin.

A useful way to show the information developed in CVP analysis is to use the contribution income statement. The **contribution income statement** puts the focus on cost behavior—it separates fixed costs and variable costs. In contrast, the conventional income statement, as we used in prior chapters, puts the focus on cost type—product cost and nonproduct cost. In the contribution income statement, variable costs are subtracted from sales to get total contribution margin. In contrast, in the conventional income statement, product costs are subtracted from sales to get gross margin. Exhibit 9.2 shows the contribution income statement for HFI's TV tables. Note that the sales increase of 200 units and $15,000 caused an $8,000 increase in profits as predicted by the contribution margin and contribution margin ratio. It is not possible to predict the change in profit from a given change in sales with the conventional income statement, which does not separate variable and fixed costs.

Strategic Role of CVP Analysis

CVP analysis can help a firm execute its strategy by providing an understanding of how changes in its volume of sales affect costs and profits. Many firms, especially cost leadership firms, compete by increasing volume (often through lower prices) to achieve lower overall operating costs, particularly lower unit fixed costs. CVP analysis provides a means to predict the effect of sales growth on profits. It also shows the risks in increasing fixed costs if volumes fall.

EXHIBIT 9.3
Strategic Questions Answered by CVP Analysis

1. What is the expected level of profit at a given sales volume?
2. What additional amount of sales is needed to achieve a desired level of profit?
3. What will be the effect on profit of a given increase in sales?
4. What is the required funding level for a governmental agency, given desired service levels?
5. Is the forecast for sales consistent with forecasted profits?
6. What additional profit would be obtained from a given percentage reduction in unit variable costs?
7. What increase in sales is needed to make up a given decrease in price to maintain the present profit level?
8. What sales level is needed to cover all costs in a sales region or product line?
9. What is the required amount of increase in sales to meet the additional fixed charges from a proposed plant expansion?

Also, CVP analysis is important in using both life-cycle costing and target costing (Chapter 13). In life-cycle costing, CVP analysis is used in the early stages of the product's cost life cycle to determine whether the product is likely to achieve the desired profitability. Similarly, CVP analysis can assist in target costing at these early stages by showing the effect on profit of alternative product designs that have different target costs.

In addition, CVP analysis can be used at later phases of the life cycle, during manufacturing planning, to determine the most cost-effective manufacturing process. Such manufacturing decisions include when to replace a machine, what type of machine to buy, when to automate a process, and when to outsource a manufacturing operation. CVP analysis is also used in the final stages of the cost life cycle to help determine the best marketing and distribution systems. For example, CVP analysis can be used to determine whether to pay salespeople on a salary basis or a commission basis for lower cost. Similarly, it can help to assess the desirability of a discount program or a promotional plan. Some of the strategic questions answered by CVP analysis are outlined in Exhibit 9.3.

CVP analysis also has a role in strategic positioning. A firm that has chosen to compete on cost leadership needs CVP analysis primarily at the manufacturing stage of the cost life cycle. The role of CVP analysis here is to identify the most cost-effective manufacturing methods, including automation, outsourcing, and total quality management. In contrast, a firm following the differentiation strategy needs CVP analysis in the early phases of the cost life cycle to assess the profitability of new products and the desirability of new features for existing products. The same concepts apply for retail and service firms.

CVP Analysis for Breakeven Planning

LEARNING OBJECTIVE 2

Apply CVP analysis for breakeven planning.

We first survey the plot, then draw the model;
And when we see the figure of the house,
Then we must rate the cost of the erection;
Which, if we find outweighs ability,
What do we then but draw anew the model.

William Shakespeare, Henry IV, Part II, Act 1

The **breakeven point** is the point at which revenues equal total costs and profit is zero.

The starting point in many business plans is to determine the **breakeven point,** the point at which revenues equal total costs and profit is zero. This point can be determined by using CVP analysis. The CVP model is solved by inserting known values for unit variable cost (v), price (p), and total fixed cost (F), setting desired before tax profit (N) equal to zero, and then solving for Q. Here we assume that fixed costs cannot be changed over the planning period. We can solve for Q in two ways: the equation method and the contribution margin method. Each method can determine the breakeven point in units sold or sales dollars.

With gasoline prices increasing rapidly in recent years, consumers have moved to high miles-per-gallon (mpg) vehicles, in particular the hybrid autos that rely on a battery as well as a gasoline engine for even greater mpg. The new vehicles save money on gas but also reduce the motorist's "carbon footprint" in an environment of global warming. The increased cost of hybrids over regular vehicles is partially offset in the United States by a tax credit for purchasing a hybrid. The tax credit is diminished as the vehicle's sales increase, so for example, there is no tax credit for the Toyota Prius as it has sold over 60,000 vehicles. The question of cost/benefit arises for cost-conscious auto buyers, and the following data provide the information needed to conduct a breakeven analysis between a gasoline-powered car and the equivalent hybrid. Our analysis assumes the buyer will keep the car for four years and drive 15,000 miles per year (60,000 total miles). For example, the breakeven gas price per gallon for the Saturn VUE is $3.36, calculated as follows, where P is the breakeven gas price (data on the VUE is in the table below):

$$\$17,045 + [(60,000/23) \times P] = \$18,345 + [(60,000/27) \times P]$$
$$P = \$3.36$$

The breakeven price per gallon for the hybrids of the Ford Escape, the Toyota Corolla/Prius, and the Lexus are calculated in a similar manner.

A footnote on the issue of a carbon footprint: *Wired Magazine* points out that when one considers the very high energy consumption required to build a car (113,000 BTUs for the Toyota Prius), it is easy to show that the lesser carbon footprint would be achieved by buying an older, high-mileage gasoline vehicle and keeping it running. *Wired*'s calculations are that a Prius would have to be driven over 100,000 miles to achieve the carbon savings of driving a 1998 Toyota Tercel. Another issue: it is more costly to insure smaller cars than their larger cousins; insurance for the Honda Civic is on the average $412 per year higher than the Honda CR-C SUV.

Source: Mike Spector, "The Economics of the Hybrids," *The Wall Street Journal*, October 29, 2007, p. R5; Joseph B. White, "Why the Gas Engine Is Sticking Around," *The Wall Street Journal*, September 15, 2008, p. R1; "Used Cars, Not Hybrids" *Wired Magazine*, June 2008, p. 61; M.P. McQueen, "Higher Insurance Costs Erode Fuel Savings on Small Cars," *The Wall Street Journal*, October 23, 2008, p. D1. Jonathan Welsh, "The Hot New Car Is Your Old Car," *The Wall Street Journal*, January 14, 2009, p. D1; James R. White, "Under the Hood, Improvements Add Up," *The Wall Street Journal*, April 14, 2009, p. D5.

	Model	Price	Tax Credit	Price after Credit	MPG	Breakeven Gas Price
Saturn	VUE	$17,045		$17,045	23.0	
	VUE hybrid	18,995	$ 650	18,345	27.0	$ 3.36
Ford	Escape	22,021		22,021	22.6	
	Escape hybrid	25,985	2,600	23,385	29.7	2.15
Toyota	Corolla	14,926		14,926	31.9	
	Prius	22,110	—	22,210	46.0	12.63
Lexus	GS430	51,619		51,619	20.6	
	GS430h	52,065	—	52,065	24.0	1.08

Equation Method: For Breakeven in Units

The equation method uses the CVP model directly. For example, using information from Exhibit 9.2, the equation for the analysis of HFI's sale of TV tables is

$$\text{Sales} = \text{Fixed cost} + \text{Total variable cost} + \text{Operating profit}$$
$$p \times Q = F + (v \times Q) + N$$
$$\$75 \times Q = \$5,000 + (\$35 \times Q)$$

Solving for Q and assuming $N = 0$ the breakeven point is $Q = 125$ TV tables per month (1,500 units per year).

$$(\$75 - \$35) \times Q = \$5,000$$
$$Q = \$5,000/(\$75 - \$35)$$
$$Q = \$5,000/\$40 = 125 \text{ units per month}$$

The contribution to profit per TV table is measured directly by the unit contribution margin, $p - v$, which is $40 per table. So, since at sales of 125 units the profit is zero, at 126 units the profit is $40, at 127 units the profit is $2 \times \$40 = \$80$, and so on. Using the unit contribution

A global manufacturer of auto parts has manufacturing plants in three locations: Western Europe, Poland, and China. The firm is studying how to utilize or to increase manufacturing capacity in order to reduce total manufacturing costs worldwide. The findings of the study are shown in the chart below.

The background on the information above is that the plants in Poland and China are highly automated, and that a rapid decrease in costs in the Western Europe plant would require introducing automation and dramatically reducing labor costs. The firm also completed a competitive analysis and found that it had a key competitor in Western Europe whose plant was already automated and produced twice the volume at less the cost than the firm's plant there. Based on these findings, the company decided to retain two plants: in Poland and China. The plant in Poland would serve the European market and the one in China would serve the rest of the world. The study shows how a firm can use CVP to determine its manufacturing strategy.

Source: Booz Allen case study reported in: Kaj Grichnik and Conrad Winkler, *Make or Break* (New York: McGraw-Hill, 2008), p. 167.

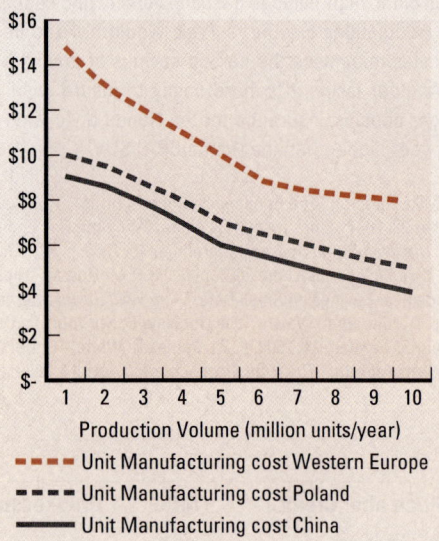

Production Volume (million units/year)
- - - - Unit Manufacturing cost Western Europe
- - - - Unit Manufacturing cost Poland
——— Unit Manufacturing cost China

margin gives us a quick way to determine the change in profit for a change in sales units. At the 128-unit level, profit is

Sales: 128 units at $75/unit	$9,600
Less:	
Variable costs: 128 at $35/unit	4,480
Contribution margin	$5,120
Fixed costs	5,000
Operating profit	$ 120

Equation Method: For Breakeven in Dollars

Sometimes units sold, unit variable cost, and sales price are not known, or it is impractical to determine them. For example, suppose that a firm has many products and is interested in finding the overall breakeven level for all products taken together. It is not practical to find the breakeven in units for each product, but it is possible to find the breakeven in sales dollars for all products. We use the equation method in a revised form, where Y is the breakeven point in *sales dollars*.

This model is equivalent to the model used for breakeven in units, except that Q is replaced by Y/p (i.e., sales in dollars divided by price = quantity; $Y/p = Q$), as follows:

$$\text{Sales} = \text{Fixed Cost} + \text{Total Variable Cost} + \text{Profit}$$
$$p \times Q = F + (v \times Q) + N$$
$$p \times (Y/p) = F + [v \times (Y/p)] + N$$
$$Y = F + [(v/p) \times Y] + N$$

Continuing with the HFI data in Exhibit 9.2, assume that because there are many different products, we know only total annual variable cost ($84,000), total annual sales ($180,000) and total monthly fixed costs ($5,000). We can obtain the ratio, $v/p = 0.4667$ ($84,000/$180,000), and solve for breakeven in dollars:

$$Y = (0.4667 \times Y) + \$5,000$$
$$Y = \$9,375 \text{ per month (125 units at \$75 each)}$$

Contribution Margin Method

A convenient method for calculating the breakeven point is to use the equation in its equivalent algebraic form (derived by solving the model for Q and assuming at breakeven $N = \text{profit} = 0$):

$$Q = \text{Fixed costs/Unit contribution margin}$$
$$= \frac{F}{p - v}$$

The contribution margin method (so-called because the contribution margin is the denominator of the ratio) produces the same result as the equation method:

$$Q = (\$5,000)/(\$75 - \$35) = 125 \text{ units per month}$$

The contribution margin method can also be used to obtain breakeven in dollars, using the contribution margin ratio (by solving $Y = F + [(v/p) \times Y]$)

$$Y = \frac{F}{(p - v)/p}$$

where:

$$(p - v)/p = \text{the contribution margin ratio}$$

For the HFI example, the contribution margin ratio is 0.5333 (the same as one minus the v/p ratio of .4667, as calculated above).

$$Y = \$5,000/0.5333 = \$9,375 \text{ per month}$$

Some find the equation method easier to use, and others prefer to use the contribution margin method. Both methods produce the same results.

CVP Graph and the Profit-Volume Graph

The **CVP graph** illustrates how the levels of revenues and total costs change over different levels of output.

Breakeven analysis is illustrated graphically in Exhibit 9.4. It shows the CVP graph at the top and the profit-volume graph beneath. The **CVP graph** illustrates how the levels of revenues and total costs change over different levels of sales volume in units. Note in the CVP graph that at sales levels lower than 125 units, the revenue line falls below the cost line, resulting in losses. In contrast, all points above the 125-unit level show profit.

The **profit-volume graph** illustrates how the level of profits changes over different levels of output.

The **profit-volume graph** in the lower portion of the exhibit illustrates how the level of profits changes over different levels of sales. At 125 units, profits are zero, and positive profits appear for sales levels greater than 125. The slope of the profit-volume line is the unit contribution margin; therefore, the profit-volume graph can be used to read directly how total contribution margin and profit changes as the sales level changes.

Summary of Breakeven Methods

The Equation Methods

1. Breakeven in sales units ($Q = $ sales in units)

$$p \times Q = (v \times Q) + F + N$$

2. Breakeven in sales dollars ($Y = $ sales in dollars)

$$Y = [(v/p) \times Y] + F + N$$

EXHIBIT 9.4
The CVP Graph and the
Profit-Volume Graph

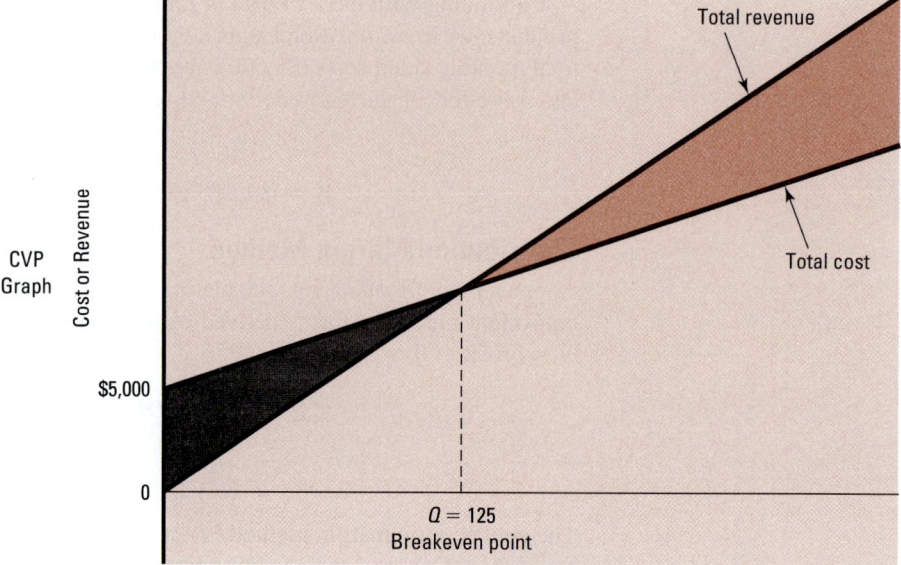

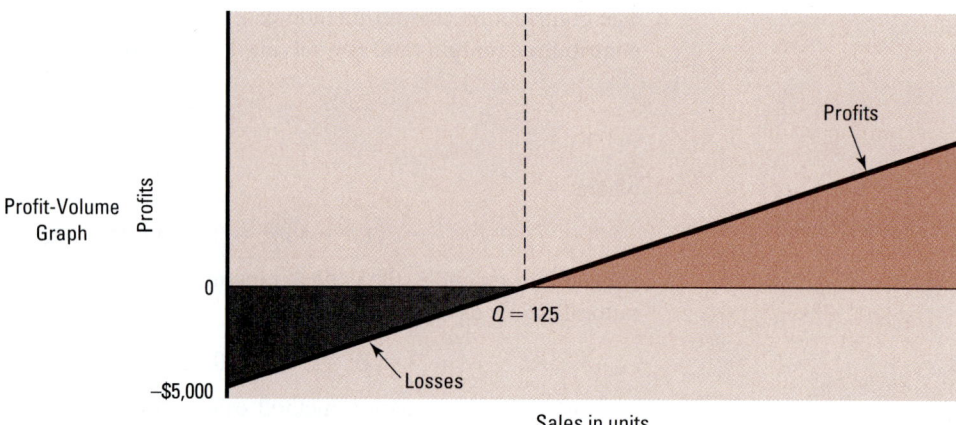

The Contribution Margin Methods

3. Breakeven in sales units =

$$Q = \frac{F + N}{p - v}$$

4. Breakeven in sales dollars =

$$Y = \frac{F + N}{(p - v)/p}$$

CVP Analysis for Profit Planning

LEARNING OBJECTIVE 3

Apply CVP analysis for profit planning.

CVP analysis can be used to determine the level of sales needed to achieve a desired level of profit. Finding the desired profit involves revenue planning, cost planning, and accounting for the effect of income taxes (when planning for the desired profit *after* tax).

Revenue Planning

CVP analysis assists managers in revenue planning to determine the revenue required to achieve a desired profit level. For example, if HFI's management wants to know the sales volume necessary to achieve $48,000 in annual profits, we substitute $60,000 for fixed costs and $48,000 for desired profit; the solution in units is

$$Q = \frac{F + N}{p - v} = \frac{\$60,000 + \$48,000}{\$75 - \$35} = 2,700 \text{ units per year}$$

The solution in sales dollars is

$$p \times Q = \$75 \times 2,700 = \$202,500 \text{ per year}$$

Cost Planning

For cost planning decisions, the manager assumes the sales quantity and the desired profit are known, but wants to find the value of the required variable cost or fixed cost to achieve the desired profit at the assumed sales quantity. Three examples follow.

Trade-Offs between Fixed and Variable Costs—Example One (One Machine)

To facilitate target costing, CVP analysis is used to determine the most cost-effective trade-off between different types of costs. To continue with the HFI example, assume sales of 2,700 units per year. Management is now considering the purchase of a new machine that will reduce variable costs but also increase fixed costs by $2,250 per month. How much must unit variable costs fall to maintain the current level of profit, assuming that sales volume and all other factors remain the same?

$Q = 2,700$ units $\qquad$ $F = \$5,000 + \$2,250 = \$7,250$ per month ($87,000 per year)

$p = \$75$ $\qquad\qquad\qquad$ $N = \$48,000$ per year

$v =$ an unknown (previously $35)

Now, instead of solving for Q (which is given as 2,700 units), we solve for v, as follows:

$$Q = \frac{F + N}{p - v}$$

$$p - v = \frac{F + N}{Q}$$

$$v = p - \frac{F + N}{Q}$$

$$v = \$75 - [(\$87,000 + \$48,000)/2,700] = \$25$$

In effect, for sales and profits to remain unchanged with the increase in fixed costs, unit variable costs must fall from $35 to $25.

The above calculations can be obtained directly using Goal Seek under the Data/DataTools/What-if Analysis tab in Excel (as circled in the exhibit). Exhibit 9.5 illustrates how this is done. Note that the information for the HFI case is entered in the spreadsheet, and profit is calculated for the current unit variable cost of $35 using the following formula in cell B8: "=B3 * (B4 − B5) − B6". The Goal Seek dialog box is shown in Exhibit 9.5. To achieve the desired profit of $48,000 by changing unit variable cost, we set Goal Seek to change cell B8, profit, to $48,000 by changing cell B5, unit variable cost. Selecting OK will enter the correct value for unit variable cost, $25, in cell B5.

Trade-Offs between Fixed and Variable Costs—Example Two (Two Machines)

A common management decision is choosing the right equipment for the work to be done. Assume as in example one that management is considering the purchase of a new machine and, in this case, has the choice between two machines. For example, a particular machine might

EXHIBIT 9.5   **Using Goal Seek in CVP Analysis**

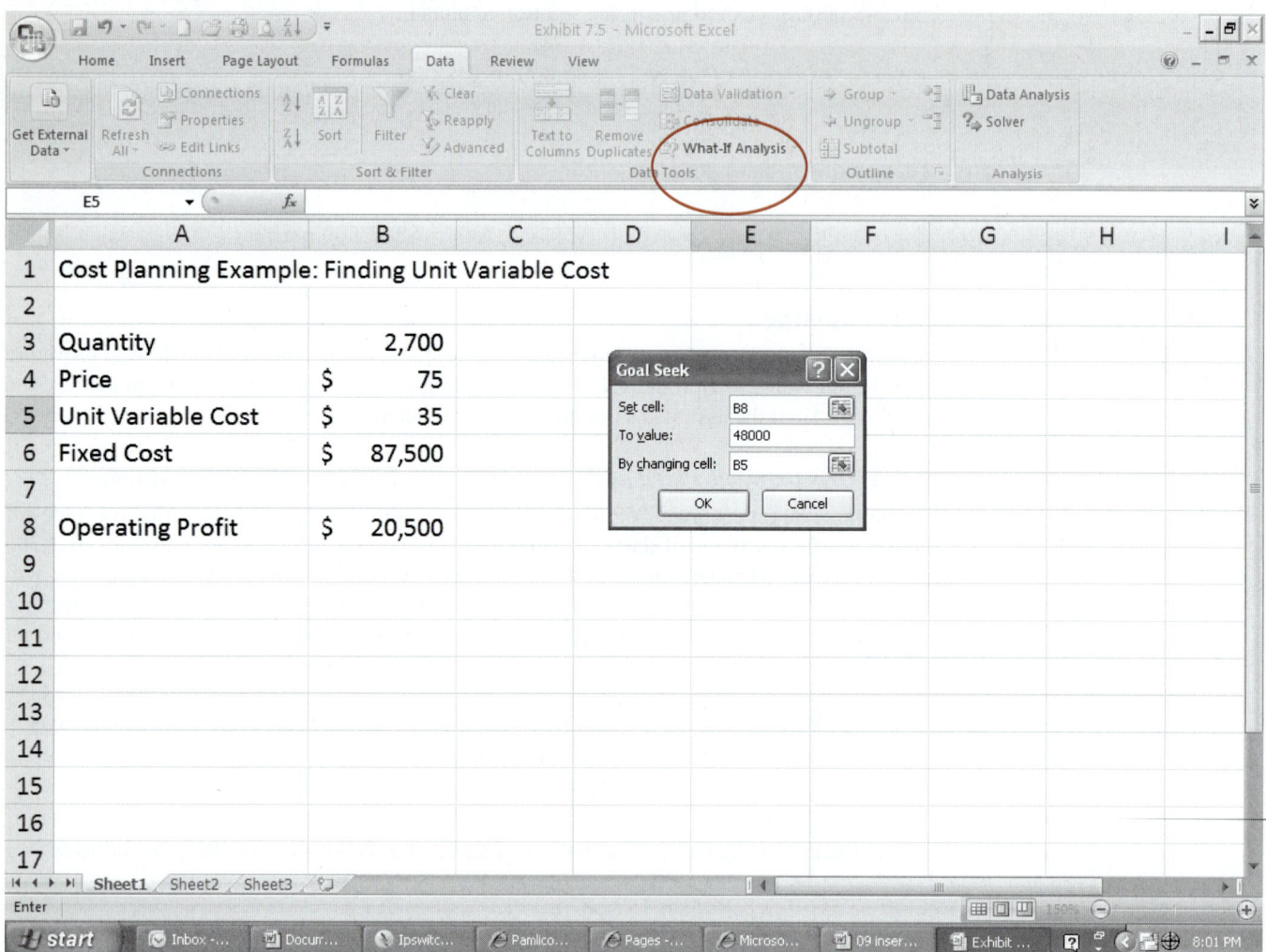

have a relatively high purchase cost but will provide lower operating costs in comparison to an alternative machine. So there is an option to trade off between high fixed costs and low unit variable costs (the high fixed-cost option) versus relatively low fixed costs and relatively higher unit variable costs (the low fixed-cost option). As volume increases, the high fixed-cost option will be more and more attractive, since it brings a reduction in total variable costs. Breakeven analysis can help to find the level of sales (called the *indifference point*), such that having sales greater than this level will favor the high fixed-cost option, and sales less than this level will favor the low fixed-cost option.

Example two assumes HFI can choose between two machines, either of which will complete the same operation with the same quality, but with different fixed and variable costs. Machine A has a fixed cost of $5,000 and a unit variable operating cost of $10, while machine B has a fixed cost of $15,000 and unit variable operating cost of $5. To find the indifference point, where the low fixed-cost (A) and high fixed-cost (B) options have the same total costs, we set the cost equations for each option equal and solve for sales quantity.

$$\text{Cost of machine A} = \text{Cost of machine B}$$
$$\$5,000 + (\$10 \times Q) = \$15,000 + (\$5 \times Q)$$
$$Q = \$10,000/\$5 = 2,000 \text{ units}$$

If HFI is operating at 2,000 units or more, then machine B should be chosen, and if it is operating at below 2,000 units, then machine A should be chosen. For example, at 3,000 units, the total cost of machine A is $5,000 + ($10 × 3,000) = $35,000, while the

ANALYSIS OF SOCIAL SECURITY RETIREMENT BENEFITS

By using data from the U.S. Social Security Administration (www.ssa.gov), a person thinking about retiring can develop a breakeven model to determine when to apply for benefits. The question is, if one delays applying for benefits until after age 62 (the earliest one can apply for benefits), how long will it take for the total of those larger (due to applying later) payments to add up to the total that would have been received by applying earlier? Two convenient Web sites provide the answer: (www.metlife.com/individual/retirement/retirement-planning-tools/social-security-decision-tool/index.html and www.ssa.gov/pubs/10147.html). For example, a person deciding whether to retire at the age of 65 or at 70 can use the analysis in the following graph. This analysis shows that retirees who survive beyond the breakeven age of 82 would receive greater lifetime benefits (not adjusted for the time value of money).

Total Cumulative Retirement Benefits at Different Ages

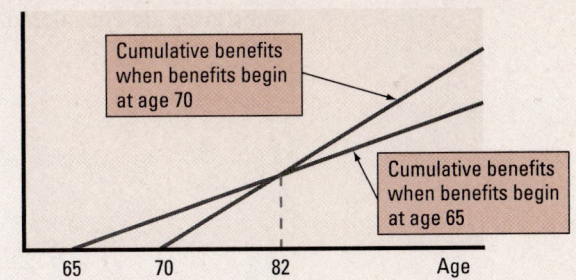

Cumulative benefits when benefits begin at age 70

Cumulative benefits when benefits begin at age 65

65 70 82 Age

Source: Jonathan Clements, "Delayed Gratification When Postponing Social Security Payments Is a Smart Move," *The Wall Street Journal*, May 10, 2006, p. D1.

---

cost of machine B is $15,000 + ($5 × 3,000) = $30,000, and thus the advantage goes to machine B at this sales level.

Sales Commissions and Salaries—Example Three

Another cost planning use of CVP analysis is to determine the most cost-effective means to manage selling costs. To illustrate, HFI management is reviewing sales salaries and commissions and finds that $1,000 of the monthly $5,000 fixed costs is for sales salaries, and that $7.50 of the $35.00 unit variable cost is a 10 percent sales commission. Suppose HFI management is considering a $450 increase in salary with an expected reduction in commission rate. How much must management reduce the commission rate to keep profits the same, assuming that sales volume and all other factors remain unchanged?

With the proposed changes in variable and fixed costs to accommodate the new salary and commission plan, fixed costs increase by $450 per month and variable costs decrease as a result of the decrease in the commission rate, r:

$$v = \text{Commision rate} \times \text{Sales price}$$
$$+ \text{ Other noncommission-based unit variable costs}$$
$$v = (r \times \$75) + \$27.50$$

And: F = Current monthly fixed costs + Increase in monthly salary
$$F = \$5,000 + \$450 = \$5,450 \text{ per month, or } \$65,400 \text{ per year}$$

Now we use the CVP model to solve for v:

$$Q = \frac{F + N}{p - v}$$

$$v = p - \frac{F + N}{Q}$$

and substituting for v and F with $N = \$48,000$ and $Q = 2,700$ as before:

$$(r \times \$75) + \$27.50 = \$75 - [(\$65,400 + \$48,000)/2,700]$$
$$r = 0.0733$$

In this situation, the manager must reduce the commission rate from 10 to 7.33 percent to keep annual profit the same and pay an additional monthly salary of $450 to the salespeople.

Including Income Taxes in CVP Analysis

The manager's decisions about costs and prices usually must include income taxes because taxes affect the amount of profit for a given level of sales. In the HFI example if we assume that the average income tax rate is 20 percent, to achieve the desired annual *after-tax* profit of $48,000, HFI must generate before-tax profits of at least $60,000 [$48,000/(1 − .2)]. Thus, when taxes are considered, the CVP model is as follows, where the average tax rate is *t:*

$$Q = \frac{F + \dfrac{\text{After-Tax Profit}}{(1 - t)}}{(p - v)}$$

or

$$Q = \frac{\$60,000 + [\$48,000/(1 - 0.2)]}{\$75 - \$35} = 3,000 \text{ units per yea}$$

This amount is an increase of 300 units over the 2,700 units required for the before-tax profit level.

CVP Analysis for Activity-Based Costing

LEARNING OBJECTIVE 4

Apply CVP analysis for activity-based costing.

The conventional approach to CVP analysis is to use a volume-based measure, that is, a measure based on units of product manufactured and sold. The preceding discussion has assumed a volume-based approach. An alternative approach is activity-based costing. Activity-based costing identifies cost drivers for detailed-level indirect cost activities, such as machine setup, materials handling, inspection, and engineering. In contrast, the volume-based approach combines the costs of these activities and treats them as fixed costs since they do not vary with volume.

Here's how activity-based CVP differs from the traditional volume-based approach. Recall from Chapter 5 the classification of activities into four levels: unit, batch, product, and facility. Unit-level costs are volume based, so they are treated in the same manner under volume-based and ABC-based CVP. Traditional volume-based CVP classifies the other three levels (batch, product, and facility) as indirect costs that do not vary with volume and thus are fixed costs. However, batch-level costs and product-level costs change with the number of batches or the number of product changes, and ABC-based CVP takes this into account. Facilities-level costs are not avoidable in a short-term planning horizon; these costs take many months or years to change, so facilities costs are treated as fixed costs under both volume-based and ABC-based CVP. So two activity cost levels, batch and product levels, are modeled as costs that can change in ABC-based CVP, but not in volume-based CVP.

Product-level costs such as a change in product design or features is a cost that has a shorter planning period because these changes can be incorporated into the manufacturing process in a shorter period of time, perhaps several months to a year before the change affects total costs. If the planning period is a year or less, as has been the common assumption in this chapter, then product-level costs will normally not be considered as a cost that can change in either ABC-based or volume-based CVP for that short planning period. If the planning period is extended to several months or years (the time it takes a change in product to affect costs), then product-level changes may be included in ABC-based CVP. In contrast, many batch-level costs (product setup, inspection, purchasing, etc.) can be changed in the short term, so batch-level costs can be considered in a short-term planning horizon. Our example below uses batch-level costs to illustrate ABC-based CVP.

Suppose that the cost accounting staff has been able to assign approximately $10,000 of last year's fixed costs to batch-level activities such as machine setup and inspection. This estimate was made when the firm was operating at 100 batches per year. These costs can be traced directly to each batch, although not to each unit of output. The staff has also learned that this year's production of 3,000 units is to be produced in batches of 30 units, so 100 batches will be produced again this year. We assume that batch-level costs increase in proportion to an increase in the number of batches produced during the year; that is, $100 per batch ($10,000/100). This assumption says in effect that the ABC rate of $100 per batch is a variable cost relative to the cost driver, number of batches. Alternative assumptions are possible. For example, if we assume that *total* batch-level costs do not change with the number of batches, then total batch-level costs are fixed relative to the number of batches. This would be true for example if the firm used the same number of batches each planning period, irrespective of volume. In this case volume-based and ABC-based CVP will always produce the same calculations, and the use of the ABC-based approach to CVP does not provide additional useful information. However, we expect that for most firms the number of batches is proportional to volume—batch sizes do not change significantly—so that at least a portion of batch-level costs change in a short-term planning period as volume changes.

One possible assumption is that total batch-level costs is a mixed cost, which has a fixed component that does not vary with the number of batches and a variable component that does vary with the number of batches. Note that assuming some portion of total batch-level costs vary with the number of batches is more consistent with the idea, introduced in Chapter 5, that it is important in using ABC to distinguish activity spending and activity usage. The objective is to reduce activity spending, which means that activity costs are at least in part variable and controllable.

For simplicity, we assume here that batch-level costs vary directly with the number of batches, not a mixed cost but a pure variable cost. An example where a batch cost would be variable relative to the number of batches is a chemical processing company that uses a vat for processing chemicals, and the batch activity is the cleaning of the vat after each use. The cleaning materials would be variable relative to the number of batches.

The activity-based CVP model can be developed in the following way.

First, we define new terms for fixed cost: $f = f^{UA} + f^{@A}$,

where:

f^{UA} = the volume-based fixed costs, the portion of fixed costs that *do not* vary with the activity cost driver, $50,000 ($60,000 − $10,000)

$f^{@A}$ = the portion of fixed costs that do vary with the activity cost driver, $10,000; we assume that $10,000 is necessary for 3,000 units of output, requiring 100 production batches of 30 units each

Second, we define the following terms:

$v^{@A}$ = the cost per batch for the activity-based cost driver, $10,000/100 = $100 per batch

b = the number of units in a batch, 30 units (3,000/100)

$v^{@A}/b$ = the cost per unit of product for batch-related costs when the batch is size b;
$v^{@A}/b = $3.333 ($100.00/30)

Third, the CVP model for activity-based costing is

$$Q = \frac{f^{VB} + N}{p - v - (v^{AB}/b)}$$

Fourth, substituting data from the HFI example,

$$Q = \frac{\$50,000 + \$48,000}{\$75 - \$35 - \$100/300} = 2,673 \text{ units}$$
$$= 89.1 \text{ batches } (2,673/30)$$

This method assumes that we hold batch size constant and vary the number of batches as the total volume changes. The number of batches must be a whole number, however. In this case, 90 batches are required for the 2,673 units: 89 batches of 30 units each (89 × 30 = 2,670 units) plus one additional batch. The analysis should be recalculated for exact break-even using 90 batches as follows, where the cost of 90 batches is 90 × $100/per batch = $9,000:

$$Q = \frac{\$50,000 + \$9,000 + \$48,000}{\$75 - \$35} = 2,675 \text{ units}$$

The solution for the activity-based model is slightly lower than for the volume-based model (2,675 units versus 2,700 units, p. 333) because the ABC method allows for lower total batch-level costs. Instead of a fixed batch-level cost of $10,000 under the volume-based approach, the ABC method allows the batch-level costs to decrease (or increase) as volume decreases (or increases); in this case it decreased from $10,000 to $9,000.

To illustrate the effect of batch size on the solution, suppose that production is scheduled in smaller batches of 20 units and that batch costs continue to be $100 each. How many units must be sold now to earn $48,000? The answer is 2,800 units and 140 batches, as shown below. Note that the cost of batch-level activities has now increased substantially, from $10,000 for 100 batches to $14,000 for 140 batches because of the smaller batch size.

$$Q = (\$50,000 + \$48,000)/(\$75 - \$35 - \$100/20)$$
$$= 2,800 \text{ units}$$

or

$$= 140 \text{ batches } (2,800/20) \text{ of } 20 \text{ units each}$$

We also could determine this from the following, using $14,000 for total batch level costs:

$$Q = \frac{\$50,000 + \$14,000 + \$48,000}{\$75 - \$35} = 2,800 \text{ units}$$

Notice that the number of units to achieve breakeven increases when the batch size is decreased. This is due directly to the increase in the total batch-level costs as batch size is decreased. CVP analysis based on activity-based costing can provide a more comprehensive analysis of the relationships among volume, costs, and profits by considering batch-level costs.[2]

Sensitivity Analysis of CVP Results

LEARNING OBJECTIVE 5

Employ sensitivity analysis to more effectively use CVP analysis when actual sales are uncertain.

CVP analysis becomes an important strategic tool when managers use it to determine the sensitivity of profits to possible changes in costs or sales volume. If costs, prices, or volumes can change significantly, the firm's strategy might also have to change. For example, if there is a risk that sales levels will fall below projected levels, management would be prudent to reduce planned investments in fixed costs (i.e., investments to increase production capacity). The additional capacity will not be needed if sales fall, but it would be difficult to reduce the fixed costs in the short term. **Sensitivity analysis** is the name for a variety of methods that examine how an amount changes if factors involved in predicting that amount change. Sensitivity analysis is particularly important when a great deal of uncertainty exists about the potential level of future sales volumes, prices, or costs. We present three of the most common methods for sensitivity analysis: (1) what-if analysis using the contribution margin and contribution margin ratio, (2) the margin of safety, and (3) operating leverage.

Sensitivity analysis
is the name for a variety of methods that examine how an amount changes if factors involved in predicting that amount change.

What-If Analysis of Sales: Contribution Margin and Contribution Margin Ratio

What-if analysis
is the calculation of an amount given different levels for a factor that influences that amount.

What-if analysis is the calculation of an amount given different levels for a factor that influences that amount. It is a common approach to sensitivity analysis when uncertainty is present. Many times it is based on the contribution margin and the contribution margin ratio. For example, the contribution margin ($40) and contribution margin ratio (0.5333) for HFI provide a direct measure of the sensitivity of HFI's profits to changes in volume. Each unit change in volume affects profits by $40; each dollar change in sales affects profits by $0.5333. Use of a spreadsheet such as Excel and tools such as Goal Seek can facilitate the analysis. An example of a data table for HFI is shown in Exhibit 9.6; units sold, fixed cost, and price are held constant, and we examine the effect of changes in unit variable cost on profits. Goal Seek is illustrated in Exhibit 9.5.

[2] See the discussion of CVP analysis for activity-based costing in Robert C. Kee, "Implementing Cost-Volume-Profit Analysis Using an Activity-Based Costing System," *Advances in Management Accounting* 10 (2001), pp. 77–94.

EXHIBIT 9.6
What-If Sensitivity Analysis for HFI, Inc. Using a Data Table

Units Sold	Unit Variable Cost	Fixed Cost	Price	Profit
1,500	$30	$60,000	$75	$7,500
1,500	35	60,000	75	—
1,500	40	60,000	75	−7,500
1,500	45	60,000	75	−15,000

Margin of Safety

The **margin of safety** is the amount of sales above the breakeven point.

The **margin of safety** is the amount of planned sales above the breakeven point:

$$\text{Margin of safety} = \text{Planned sales} - \text{Breakeven sales}$$

Returning to the HFI example, assume that the planned sales of TV tables is 3,000 units per year; since the breakeven quantity is 1,500 units, the margin of safety is

$$\text{Margin of safety in units} = 3,000 - 1,500 = 1,500 \text{ units}$$

or

$$\text{Margin of safety in sales dollars} = 1,500 \times \$75 = \$112,500$$

The margin of safety also can be used as a ratio, a percentage of sales:

$$\text{Margin of safety ratio} = \text{Margin of safety/Planned sales}$$
$$= 1,500/3,000 = .5$$

The **margin of safety ratio** is a useful measure for comparing the risk of two or more alternative products.

The **margin of safety ratio** is a useful measure for comparing the risk of two or more alternative products. The product with a relatively low margin of safety ratio is the riskier of the two products and therefore usually requires more of management's attention.

Operating Leverage

Changes in the contemporary manufacturing environment include improved production techniques through process improvement, lean manufacturing, and other techniques. As these changes take place, the nature of CVP analysis also changes. For example, in a fully automated production environment, labor costs are less important, and variable costs consist primarily of materials costs. In some cases, such as the manufacture of certain electrical parts and components, the materials cost is also relatively low so that fixed costs are very high relative to total cost. In this context, CVP analysis can play a crucial strategic role because profits are more sensitive to the number of units manufactured and sold. In other manufacturing operations, with low fixed costs and relatively high variable costs, profits are less sensitive to changes in sales, and CVP is relatively less important.

Consider two firms: one has relatively low fixed costs and relatively high unit variable costs (a labor-intensive firm), and the other has relatively high fixed costs and relatively low variable costs (a highly automated firm). Sample data for two such firms are shown in Exhibit 9.7.

These two situations are compared in Exhibit 9.8A (relatively high fixed costs) and Exhibit 9.8B (relatively low fixed costs). Note that the breakeven point is the same in each case, 50,000 units. However, if we examine the profit at 25,000 units above breakeven or the loss at 25,000 units below breakeven, a strong contrast emerges. For the firm with relatively high fixed costs (Exhibit 9.8A), the loss at 25,000 units is relatively large, $250,000, while the profit at 75,000 units is also relatively large, $250,000. In contrast, when fixed costs are

EXHIBIT 9.7
Contrasting Data for Automated and Labor-Intensive Firms

	Automated: High Fixed Cost	Labor-Intensive: Low Fixed Cost
Fixed cost/year	$500,000	$150,000
Variable cost/unit	2	9
Price	12	12
Contribution margin/unit	10	3

Cost Management in Action

Ford Motor Co. and GM: How Can They Become More Profitable?

In recent years, Detroit automakers have been struggling with declining sales and slowing profits—even losses in some recent quarterly periods. GM and Ford are particularly challenged by what investment analysts call *legacy costs*—the costs of retirement and other employee benefits. What do these retirement costs mean for operating leverage in these firms? How do you think these firms are, or should be, responding to become more competitive and profitable?

(Refer to Comments on Cost Management in Action at end of Chapter.)

EXHIBIT 9.8A

CVP Graph for a Firm with Relatively High Fixed Costs

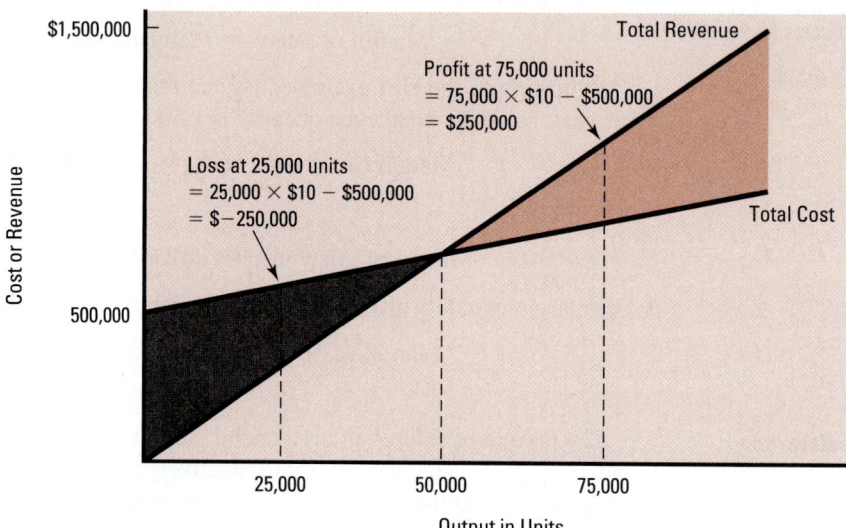

EXHIBIT 9.8B

CVP Graph for a Firm with Relatively Low Fixed Costs

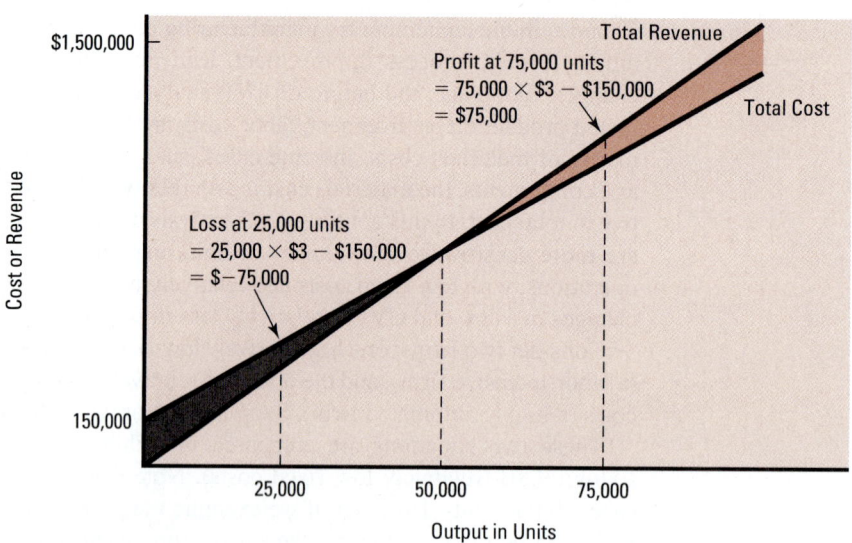

low (Exhibit 9.8B), the loss at 25,000 units is only $75,000 and the profit at 75,000 units is only $75,000.

A firm with high fixed costs is riskier because profits are very strongly affected by the level of sales. High profits are earned beyond breakeven, but high losses result from falling below breakeven. In this context, CVP analysis is particularly important in planning the use of new manufacturing technologies that have the potential to change the relationship between fixed and variable costs.

The potential effect of the risk that sales will fall short of planned levels, as influenced by the relative proportion of fixed to variable manufacturing costs, can be measured by the

Operating leverage
is the ratio of the contribution margin to profit.

degree of **operating leverage,** which is the ratio of the contribution margin to profit. For the HFI data (Exhibit 9.2), the operating leverage for 2010 is as follows:[3]

$$\text{Operating leverage} = \text{Contribution margin/Operating Profit}$$
$$= \$96,000/\$36,000 = 2.667$$

Operating leverage of 2.667 means that since HFI's sales increased 8.33 percent ($15,000/$180,000) from 2010 to 2011, profits should increase by 22.22 percent (2.667 × 8.33%). A quick calculation demonstrates that profit has grown by $8,000, a 22.22 percent ($8,000/$36,000) increase over the prior year.

Each firm chooses the level of operating leverage that is consistent with its competitive strategy. For example, a firm with a dominant position in its market might choose a high level of leverage to exploit its advantage. In contrast, a weaker firm might choose the less risky low-leverage strategy.

The Five Steps of Strategic Decision Making for CVP Analysis

Here is an example to illustrate strategic decision making in CVP analysis. Russ Talmadge operates a real estate service business that provides rental management services, real estate appraisal, and a variety of other services. Russ is successful because of his knowledge and experience and the reliability of his service which has gained him the trust of his customers, many of whom have been with him for several years. One of the key items in his office is a printer that prints copies of photos from his digital camera. The photos are used in appraisals and in other services. His printer was relatively inexpensive to buy ($99) but the ink cartridges are expensive—depending on the capacity of the cartridge, the cost is from $37.50 for a capacity of 500 copies to $80 for a capacity for 2,000 copies. Russ prints about 1,000 photos a month. He takes the following five steps to determine the best cartridge to buy for his printer.

1. **Determine the strategic issues surrounding the problem.** Russ's business is based on his knowledge and reliable service. The photos that are a part of his service must also be produced reliably (no printer jams or delays getting the photo to the customer) and be of high print quality.

2. **Identify the alternative actions.** Russ can purchase the high-capacity cartridge (2,000 copies) or the low-capacity cartridge (500 copies) for his printer. The high-capacity cartridge will cost 4 cents per copy ($80/2,000) while the low-capacity cartridge will cost 7.5 cents per copy ($37.50/500). Another option is to buy a new printer for $150 that has a cartridge costing $60 (capacity of 2,000 copies; 3 cents per copy).

3. **Obtain information and conduct analyses of the alternatives.**

Option One: Retain current copier   The high capacity cartridge will cost $40 per month (1,000 copies at 4 cents per copy) and the lower capacity cartridge which will cost $75 per month (1,000 copies at 7.5 cents per copy). The purchase cost of the copier can be ignored since it is a sunk cost, and therefore the high-capacity cartridge will always be the low cost option.

Option Two: New copier   The breakeven point for the new copier (assuming Russ is using the high capacity cartridge on his current copier) would be 15,000 copies—$150/(4 cents − 3 cents)—or, 15 months of usage.

4. **Based on Strategy and Analysis, Choose and Implement the Desired Alternative.**

Option One   The choice of cartridge has no effect on the quality or reliability of the printer, so the choice can be made on the basis of lower cost, and in this case the high-capacity cartridge is preferred. Also, the high-capacity cartridge would mean less frequent cartridge replacement and, therefore, less chance of a potential delay when a photo is needed quickly.

Option Two   Russ would achieve breakeven on the new copier in 15 months, not a particularly long period given the number of years he has been in business. And the addition of a new copier would give him a "backup" if one of them should fail. However, looking at a *Consumer*

---

[3] As defined here, the term *operating leverage* is also referred to as *degree of operating leverage (DOL).*

Reports study of copiers, Russ finds that the $150 copier does not have as high a reliability or quality rating as does his current copier. Considering the importance of quality and reliability in his business, Russ chooses option one with the high-capacity cartridge.

5. **Provide an ongoing evaluation of the effectiveness of implementation in step 4.** Russ continues to review the available printers. If he determines a way to reduce the need for photos or can print them on a color printer instead of photo paper, he may be able to reduce costs substantially. He may also be able to obtain the cartridges at lower cost from a new supplier.

CVP Analysis with Two or More Products

LEARNING OBJECTIVE 6

Adapt CVP analysis for multiple products.

Commonly, a company produces or retails two or more products. We have shown above how to calculate the CVP model for a single product. Suppose now that the company has several, perhaps hundreds or thousands, of products. It would be difficult to calculate and to interpret that many breakeven points. Moreover, it would be difficult to determine how the firm's fixed costs should be allocated among these products. For this reason, a common approach for firms with many products is to use the contribution margin ratio (CMR) approach explained earlier in the chapter. This approach allows the firm to estimate breakeven in dollar sales, based on an estimate of the weighted-average CMR for all of its products. For example, if the firm has a policy of setting price for all its products at twice variable cost, then CMR is estimated as follows, where $p = 2v$, or $v = \frac{1}{2}p$:

$$\text{CMR} = (p - v)/p = \left[p - \frac{1}{2}p\right]/p = 50\%$$

Using the CMR approach, a firm with $100 million in fixed costs and a CMR of 50 percent would have a breakeven of $200 million sales:

$$Y = \$100/.5 = \$200,000,000$$

Now suppose that the firm has only two or three (or a relatively small number of) products. In this case it is possible to calculate breakeven using the weighted-average contribution margin (CM) or weighted-average CMR determined directly for these products. The calculation of the weighted-average CM or CMR for the small number of products is based on the assumption that the sales mix, the proportion sold of each product, will remain constant. The sales mix in dollars is usually different than the sales mix in units. If we assume that the sales mix will remain constant in units, we use the CM approach to calculate breakeven. This is consistent because the sales mix is constant in units and the breakeven is calculated in units. Similarly, if we assume that the sales mix will remain constant in dollars, we use the CMR approach to calculate breakeven in dollars.

To illustrate, we use the example of Windbreakers, Inc., which sells light-weight sport/ recreational jackets. Windbreakers has three products, Calm, Windy, and Gale. Relevant information for these products is in Exhibit 9.9. The total fixed costs for the period are expected to be $168,000, and we assume that Windbreakers' sales will remain constant in sales dollars, at 50 percent, 40 percent, and 10 percent, respectively, for the three products.

From this information, we can calculate the weighted-average CMR as follows:

$$0.5(0.2) + 0.4(0.25) + 0.1(0.1) = 0.21$$

EXHIBIT 9.9

Sales and Cost Data for Windbreakers, Inc.

	Calm	Windy	Gale	Total
Last period's sales	$750,000	$600,000	$150,000	$1,500,000
Percent of sales	50%	40%	10%	100%
Price	$ 30	$ 32	$ 40	
Unit variable cost	24	24	36	
Contribution margin	$ 6	$ 8	$ 4	
Contribution margin ratio	0.20	0.25	0.10	

Sometimes showing the results of a sensitivity analysis in the form of a graph is useful. The U.S. Department of Energy has used this approach to study the decision to adopt fuel cell technology for generating electricity by such large users as the Pittsburgh International Airport, AT&T Research Laboratory in Morristown, New Jersey, and Kirtland Air Force Base in New Mexico. Fuel cell technology converts natural gas to electricity in a clean and efficient manner. Fuel cells are cost effective when the cost of natural gas is relatively low and the cost of other sources of electricity is relatively high. The study produced a breakeven analysis and related sensitivity analysis showing that a breakeven line can be determined (see the following) to clearly identify the preferred technology (fuel cell or conventional sources of electricity) based on variations in the cost of natural gas and conventional electricity.

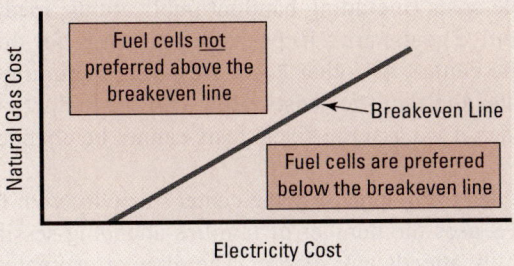

The breakeven line as shown is determined by solving the equation that sets total cost of one technology equal to that of the other. The two axes in the graph are the unit variable costs for each alternative.

To illustrate, using the data from Exhibit 9.7, we solve the equation that sets total cost of the automated factory equal to that of the labor-intensive factory. The fixed costs and volume level are assumed, and the equation is solved for the variable cost of each alternative as a function of the variable cost of the other alternative (where Y = unit variable cost for the automated factory and X = unit variable cost for the labor-intensive factory, volume = 50,000 units, and the remaining data are from Exhibit 9.7):

$$\text{Total cost of automated} = \text{Total cost of labor-intensive}$$
$$\text{factory} \qquad\qquad \text{factory}$$

$$(Y \times 50{,}000) + \$500{,}000 = (X \times 50{,}000) + \$150{,}000$$
$$Y = X - 7$$

The sensitivity graph for these data follows. The labor-intensive factory favors the area above the line and the automated factory favors the area below the line.

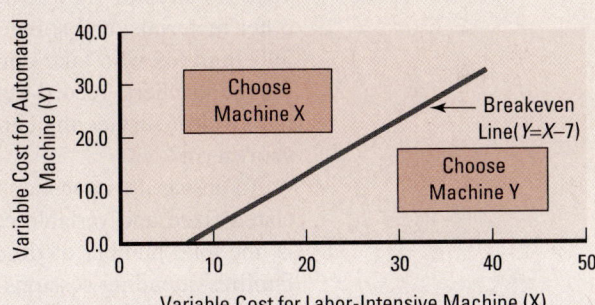

Variable Cost for Labor-Intensive Machine (X)

Source: Pacific Northwest National Laboratory, "Federal Technology Alerts: Natural Gas Fuel Cells," U.S. Department of Energy, www1.eere.energy .gov/femp/pdfs/FTA_natgas_fuelcell.pdf.

The breakeven point in dollars for all three products can be calculated as follows:

$$Y = \$168{,}000/0.21 = \$800{,}000$$

This means that for Windbreakers to break even, $800,000 of all three products must be sold in the same proportion as last year's sales mix. The sales for each product are as follows:

For Calm	0.5($800,000) = $400,000	(13,334 jackets at $30)
For Windy	0.4($800,000) = 320,000	(10,000 jackets at $32)
For Gale	0.1($800,000) = 80,000	(2,000 jackets at $40)
Total	$800,000	

The sale of jackets in the correct sales mix produces exactly the breakeven contribution margin of $168,000:

$$\$6(13{,}334) + \$8(10{,}000) + \$4(2{,}000) = \$168{,}000$$

Value Stream Accounting and CVP

When families of products are grouped into value streams in lean accounting, there is an opportunity to use CVP for the product group rather than for a single product or for multiple products. For example, families of products, or value streams, for a consumer electronics company might include one value stream for CD players (all the different types of CD players the company sells) and another for DVD players, and other value streams for other product groups. The use of value streams simplifies the calculation of CVP and can make it more meaningful and useful. Lean accounting is covered in Chapter 17.

CVP Analysis for Not-for-Profit Organizations

LEARNING OBJECTIVE 7

Apply CVP analysis in not-for-profit organizations.

Not-for-profit organizations and service firms can also use CVP analysis. To illustrate, consider a family support agency, Orange County Family Support Center, that provides training in a classroom setting for struggling young families. The training sessions cover health care for children, financial planning, and other issues; each session involves some handout materials (books, sample medications, etc.), and a paid instructor. Orange County Family Support Center (OCFS) receives financial support from the county, whose funding is falling because of a recession in the local economy. As a result, the county commissioners have set an across-the-board budget cut of 5 percent for the new fiscal year. The center's funding was $735,000 last year and is projected to be approximately $700,000 next year. Its director figures that variable costs (including handout publications, medications, other materials, and some administrative costs) are $10 per visit per family for the almost 300 families who take courses at the center. All other costs are fixed, including salaries for the teachers, record-keeping costs, and facilities costs. How will the budget cut affect the level of service the center provides if we assume fixed costs cannot be changed in the short term?

To answer this question, we must determine precisely the center's activity with the associated fixed and variable costs. OCFS uses the number of families-attending-sessions, that is, the total number of times any family attends any session. The director estimates 13,500 families-attending-sessions last year and that unit variable costs are constant at $10 per family-session in the range of 10,000 to 14,000 family-sessions per year; total variable costs were therefore $135,000 ($10 × 13,500) last year. We determine total fixed costs for last year as follows:

$$\text{Funding} = \text{Total cost}$$
$$= \text{Total fixed costs} + \text{Total variable costs}$$
$$\$735,000 = \text{Total fixed costs} + \$135,000$$
$$\text{Total fixed costs} = \$600,000$$

Now the director can analyze the effect of the budget change on the center's service levels. At the $700,000 budget level expected for next year, the activity level is approximately 10,000 family-sessions. Total cost of $700,000 less fixed cost of $600,000 leaves variable costs of $100,000; thus, $100,000/$10 = 10,000 family-sessions. The director can now see that the approximate 5 percent cut in the budget is expected to result in an approximate 26 percent drop in family-sessions [26% = (13,500 − 10,000)/13,500].

Assumptions and Limitations of CVP Analysis

LEARNING OBJECTIVE 8

Identify the assumptions and limitations of CVP analysis and their effect on the proper interpretation of the results.

Linearity, the Relevant Range, and Step Costs

The CVP model assumes that revenues and total costs are linear over the relevant range of activity. Although actual cost behavior is not linear, we use the concept of the relevant range introduced in Chapter 3 so that within a given limited range of output, total costs are expected to increase at an approximately linear rate. The caution for the manager is therefore to remember that the calculations performed within the context of a given CVP model should not be used outside the relevant range.

EXHIBIT 9.10
CVP Analysis with Step Cost
Behavior

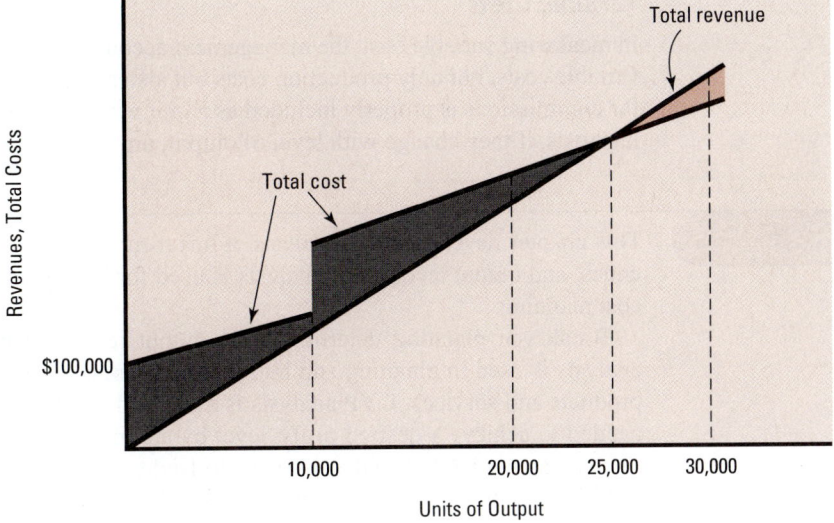

Step Costs

As illustrated in Exhibit 9.10, the cost behavior under examination may be so "lumpy" (step costs) that an approximation via a relevant range is unworkable. Although CVP analysis can be done, it becomes somewhat more cumbersome. Exhibit 9.10 illustrates a situation with a price of $18, a unit variable cost of $10, an initial fixed cost of $100,000, and an incremental fixed cost of another $100,000 when output exceeds 10,000 units. The expenditure of the additional fixed cost provides capacity for up to 30,000 units. A CVP analysis requires that the manager determine the breakeven point for each range (below and above the point at 10,000 units). For these data, we find no breakeven below the 10,000 unit level of output, but the breakeven point can be obtained for the upper range as follows:

$$Q = f/(p - v) = \$200{,}000/(\$18 - \$10) = 25{,}000 \text{ units}$$

Identifying Fixed and Variable Costs for CVP Analysis

Fixed Costs

Suppose that management wants to calculate the breakeven point for a new product for Household Furnishings, Inc. The new product is a computer table designed for easy assembly and intended for the low-price end of the market. Is the cost of the president's salary a relevant fixed cost for this calculation? It is not because the president's salary does not change whether HFI introduces the computer table; it is a fixed cost for the corporation, but it is irrelevant for the analysis of the short-term profitability of the new product.

In a short-term analysis, relevant fixed costs are those expected to change with the introduction of the new product. These include costs of any new production facilities, salaries of new production personnel, and similar costs.

If a new product does not require any new fixed costs because existing facilities and personnel can handle the added production, what is the breakeven point? For a *short-term analysis,* the breakeven point is zero since the new product must cover no new fixed costs. That is, each product sold, beginning with the first, contributes to profit in the excess of price over variable cost.

In contrast, for a *long-term analysis* of breakeven, all current and expected future fixed costs associated with the production, distribution, and sale of the product are relevant. The long-term view has been taken in this chapter. This is the view consistent with the idea that the company is a going-concern and will maintain at least approximately the current level of capacity.

Variable Costs

In measuring variable cost, the management accountant must be careful to include all relevant variable costs, not only production costs but also selling and distribution costs. Thus, expense for commissions is properly included as a unit variable cost. Any transportation or warehousing costs, if they change with level of output, are relevant.

Summary

This chapter develops CVP analysis, a linear model of the relationships between costs, revenues, and output levels. The analysis is used for breakeven planning, revenue planning, and cost planning.

Breakeven planning determines the output level at which profits are zero. Breakeven analysis is used in planning and budgeting to assess the desirability of current and potential products and services. CVP analysis is also used in revenue planning to determine the sales needed to achieve a desired profit level by adding desired profit to the breakeven equation. In cost planning, CVP analysis is used to find the required reduction in costs to meet desired profits or to find the required change in fixed cost for a given change in variable cost (or vice versa).

Two additional concepts—activity-based costing and sensitivity analysis—enhance revenue and cost planning. Activity-based costing breaks fixed costs into batch- and unit-related costs, so CVP analyses can be performed at either (or both) the batch or unit level.

Sensitivity analysis is useful because profits of firms with relatively high fixed costs are more sensitive to changes in the level of sales. The sensitivity, or risk, of changes in sales levels is measured by the margin of safety and operating leverage.

With two or more products, the use of CVP analysis requires the assumption of a constant sales mix between them, and the weighted-average contribution margin is used to calculate the breakeven point.

Not-for-profit and service firms also use breakeven analysis. We presented the example of a municipal family support agency's use of breakeven analysis to predict the effects of changing funding levels on its operations.

A number of limitations must be considered in using breakeven analysis. For example, we assume that total fixed costs and unit variable cost do not change.

Key Terms

breakeven point, *328*
contribution income
statement, *327*
contribution margin ratio, *327*
cost-volume-profit (CVP)
analysis, *325*

CVP graph, *331*
margin of safety, *339*
margin of safety ratio, *339*
operating leverage, *341*
profit-volume graph, *331*
sensitivity analysis, *338*

total contribution margin, *326*
unit contribution margin, *326*
what-if analysis, *338*

Comments on Cost Management in Action

Ford Motor Co. and GM: How Can They Become More Profitable?

Ford and GM are highly leveraged auto manufacturers. The high fixed costs include high labor-related costs—both current production labor and the costs of retirement benefits for retired workers. During the 1970s and 1980s the firms made decisions that locked in high labor capacity, based on a strategy that sales volume would grow and the labor capacity would be needed. But the desired sales increases have not happened, as foreign auto manufacturers continue to increase their market share.

High operating leverage leads to faster reductions in profits when sales fall, and this is the current experience for these automakers. A recent program by GM to boost sales by offering sales discounts to customers that were equivalent to the discounts given to employees of the auto manufacturers is an example of GM's strategy to increase sales to cover these fixed costs. The firms are also looking for ways to reduce the fixed costs, and recent plant closings employee buyouts, changes in benefit plans and renewed negotiations with the United Auto Workers' union are part of that strategy. High operating leverage also means high debt levels, and the Detroit automakers are significantly affected by changes in the credit markets; in particular, the liquidity crisis and recession of 2008–2009 have affected their ability to obtain needed financing. At this writing it is not clear to what extent the federal government will help these firms and whether the help will be effective.

Source: Jeffrey McCracken, "Detroit's Symbol of Dysfunction: Paying Employees Not to Work," *The Wall Street Journal,* March 1, 2006, p.1; Karen Lundegaard and Joseph B. White, "Detroit Finds a Bandwagon in 'Employee Discounts,' " *The Wall Street Journal,* July 6, 2005, p.1; Joann Muller, "Carmakers in the Credit Coalmine," *Forbes,* September 26, 2008; Matthew Dolan, "Michigan Sweats GM-Chrysler Talks," *The Wall Street Journal,* October 20, 2008, p. B1.

Self-Study Problem
(For solution, please turn to the end of the chapter.)

The following data refer to a single product, the TECHWHIZ, made by the Markdata Computer Company:

Sales price = $5,595
Materials cost (including purchased components) = $899
Direct labor cost = $233
Facilities cost (for a highly automated plant mainly includes rent, insurance, taxes, and depreciation) = $2,352,000 per year

Required

1. What is the unit contribution margin?
2. What is the breakeven point in units and dollars?
3. What is the desired level of sales if the company plans to increase fixed costs by 5 percent (to improve product quality and appearance) and achieve a desired before-tax profit of $200,000?
4. If the company's income tax rate is 22 percent, what unit sales are necessary to achieve an after-tax profit of $150,000?

Questions

9-1   What is the underlying relationship in CVP analysis?

9-2   When might it be better to find the breakeven point in sales dollars rather than in units?

9-3   What is the contribution margin ratio and how is it used?

9-4   What are the basic assumptions of CVP analysis?

9-5   Why might the percentage budget cut for a not-for-profit agency not equal the resultant change in the activity level?

9-6   If a new product does not require any new fixed costs because the company utilizes the existing capacity of facilities and personnel, what is the breakeven point?

9-7   Why do management accountants use sensitivity analysis?

9-8   Why does the issue of taxes not affect the calculation of the breakeven point?

9-9   Why is CVP analysis important in planning the use of new manufacturing technologies?

9-10 What type of risk does sensitivity analysis address?

9-11 Explain the four methods for calculating the breakeven point.

9-12 What is the margin of safety, and for what is it used?

9-13 What is operating leverage, and for what is it used?

9-14 How are step costs treated in CVP analysis?

9-15 Desired before-tax net income equals the desired after-tax net income multiplied by _____?

9-16 How is CVP analysis used to calculate the breakeven point for multiple products?

Brief Exercises

9-17 Doughton Bearings produces ball bearings for industrial equipment. In evaluating the financial data from the previous year, the accounting manager has determined that the company's unit sales price is $25 per bearing and the unit variable cost is $18 per bearing. What is the unit contribution margin?

9-18 Felton Paper produces paper for textbooks. Felton plans to produce 500,000 cases of paper next quarter to sell at a price of $100 per case. Each case costs the company $80 to produce. What is the total contribution margin for next quarter?

9-19 Montross Seating manufactures desk chairs for commercial distribution. Each chair is produced at a cost of $15 and sold for $25. What is the contribution margin ratio for desk chairs?

9-20 The Cobb Clinic treats walk-in patients for various illnesses. The accounting manager has estimated that the clinic has $5,000 in monthly fixed costs in addition to a $20 cost per patient visit. If the charge is $30 per visit, how many visits per month does the clinic need to break even?

9-21 Phelps Inc. manufactures several different types of candy for various retail stores. The accounting manager has requested that you determine the sales dollars required to break even for next quarter based on past financial data. Your research tells you that the total variable cost will be $500,000, total sales will be $750,000, and fixed costs will be $100,000. What is the breakeven point in sales dollars?

9-22 Williams & Williams Co. produces plastic spray bottles and wants to earn a before-tax profit of $100,000 next quarter. Variable costs are $0.50 per bottle, fixed costs are $500,000, and the selling price is $1 per bottle. How many bottles must the company sell to meet this goal?

9-23 Cunningham Audio sells headphones and would like to earn after-tax profits of $100 every week. Each set of headphones costs $5 and sells for $10. Rent and other fixed costs are $200 per week, and the tax rate is 20 percent. How many headphones must Cunningham sell per week to meet this goal?

9-24 Franklin Cards sells greeting cards for $2 each and plans to sell 100,000 cards every quarter. The accounting manager has determined the company must sell 80,000 cards every quarter to break even. What is the margin of safety in units and sales dollars?

9-25 May Clothing is a retail men's clothing store. May's cost is $10 per shirt and the sales price is $20 per shirt. May plans to sell 400,000 shirts each year and wants a before-tax profit of $500,000. What is the operating leverage?

9-26 Ford Tops manufactures hats for baseball teams. Ford has fixed costs of $100,000 per quarter and sells each hat for $20. If the hats cost $10 each to make, how many hats must Ford sell each quarter to break even?

9-27 Scott Power produces batteries. Scott has determined its contribution margin to be $2 per battery and its contribution margin ratio to be 0.5. What is the effect on profits of the sale of one additional battery? Of one additional dollar of sales?

Exercises

9-28 **Cost Planning; Machine Replacement** Calista Company manufactures electronic equipment. It currently purchases the special switches used in each of its products from an outside supplier. The supplier charges Calista $2 per switch. Calista's CEO is considering purchasing either machine X or machine Y so the company can manufacture its own switches. The projected data are as follows:

	Machine X	Machine Y
Annual fixed cost	$135,000	$204,000
Variable cost per switch	0.65	0.30

Required

1. For each machine, what is the minimum number of switches that Calista must make annually for total costs to equal outside purchase cost?

2. What volume level would produce the same total costs regardless of the machine purchased?

3. What is the most profitable alternative for producing 200,000 switches per year?

9-29 **Cost Planning; Gasoline Prices** In June 2008, when gasoline prices were at an all-time high, greater than $4 per gallon, Chrysler Motor Company promoted its Jeep vehicle with the offer of either $4,500 off the price of the vehicle or the guarantee that the buyer would not pay more than $2.99 per gallon of gas for the next three years (the details of the guarantee could vary by dealer).

Required

1. Assume that the Jeep vehicle you are interested in gets 15 mpg combined city/highway and that at the time of purchase you expected gasoline prices to average $5 per gallon over the next three years. How many miles would you have to drive the vehicle in the next three years to make the guarantee more attractive than the $4,500 discount?

2. Assume the same information as in part 1 above, except the average price of gas for the next three years is not known, but you are likely to drive 8,500 miles per year. What is the breakeven gasoline price in the coming three years so that you would be indifferent between the two options?

3. What are some important aspects of the decision that do not have to do with the price of gasoline and the $4,500 discount?

9-30 **Cost Planning: The Cost of an MBA; Time Value of Money** The motivation for getting the MBA degree has many aspects—the prestige, greater opportunity for promotion, change of occupation, and an increase in pay. To focus just on this last motivation, suppose that you are interested in getting an MBA and are studying the various programs in the United States. You want to balance the cost of getting the degree against the future benefits in increase of pay. You have information on the cost of two MBA programs, which includes the cost of tuition, living expenses, and forgone pre-MBA salary for the two years you are in the MBA program. School A has an average cost of $100,000 and School B, a far more prestigious school at which you think your grades would qualify you to be a successful applicant, has a cost of $250,000.

Required Assume that you have a five-year planning horizon, that the difference in pay for a job after both schools would remain the same for all five years, and the relevant cost of borrowing is 6 percent. Based on increase in pay only, how great would the increase for a job after leaving School B have to be relative to School A for you to be indifferent between the two schools? Hint: the present value factor for an annuity of five years at 6 percent is in Table 2 at the end of Chapter 12 and equals 4.212.

9-31 Cost Planning: Own Your Wheels, or Just Rent by the Hour You live in a large urban area that has a car-share program. For a small annual fee and small hourly fee, the program provides a rental car that can take you to town for shopping, to the airport to pick up someone, or wherever else you need to go. The savings over car ownership can be very significant. Two programs are currently available. One of the programs has a $140 annual fee and a $4 per hour usage fee. The other program has a smaller annual fee of only $50, but the hourly rate is $7.

Required
1. Which program would you choose and what type of analysis would you use to support your choice?
2. Rental car agencies such as Hertz and Avis are available for daily rentals which in some locations can be as low as $30 per day or less. When would you choose to use a rental agency instead of car-share, and why?

9-32 Cost Planning; High-End Copiers Companies that have a high demand for making copies, both color and black and white, often choose to lease a high-end copier that provides fast and reliable service at a reasonable cost. The lease is usually for three to five years and the cost to the user is $0.01 per page for black and white copies and typically $0.10 per page for color copies. These are the terms of your current three-year lease contract with Ricoh Company, which is up for renewal this month; the lease terms are expected to be the same for the next three years, if renewed.

Hewlett-Packard Company (H-P) has recently developed an innovative copier that can reduce the costs of color copies. The copier measures exactly how much color is used in a color copy, so that the price of the copy can be determined by the amount of color used rather than a fixed price per page, so the cost could be as low as $.070 per page for a color copy. H-P calls this a "flexible-pricing" approach. Assume for this example that the cost of the leased copier (three-year lease) is only the per page charge—the initial lease cost is negligible, and the service costs would not differ between the H-P copier and the copier you are using now.

Your company is an advertising agency, Tanner and Jones, LLC, and the quality of the color copies is critical to your business success. The ability to rely on the copier at any time is also very important, as some customer requests require urgent attention. You believe that the Ricoh and H-P printers are of the same reliability, but you have not had experience with the H-P copier to be sure of the copy quality. The demonstration of the H-P copier has shown as good or better copy quality, but you have not had three years' experience with it to know what it would be like day to day.

Required
1. Assume that your company is considering the lease of one of these H-P copiers, and you expect that the average price for a color copy for your company would be $0.075 because you would carefully prioritize color copy jobs and reduce the number of copies requiring a large amount of color. You expect that training your copy center staff to properly use the new copier would cost about $12,400 for materials and lost work time. What is the breakeven number of color copies per year that would make you indifferent between the new H-P copier and your current copier?
2. As in part 1 above, assume you expect that your per-copy cost for color copies with the H-P copier will be $0.075, the training costs are $12,400, and you expect to make 200,000 copies per year for the next three years. In your negotiations with Ricoh concerning the new lease and the cost of color copies, what price would you bargain for?
3. Consider your choice between the copiers within the context of the competitive and business environment of Tanner and Jones. What are the issues you should consider in addition to cost of copies?

9-33 Cost Structure of Retailers; The Internet Today's retailers are finding that online sales and service are a necessary ingredient of their overall marketing and selling strategy because of increased competition. In certain retail sectors, consumers are moving to the Internet in large numbers for the convenience and selection they find on the Internet. Unfortunately, the investment in resources, both equipment and labor, can be huge. Some studies show that less than a third of online retailers are profitable on Internet sales. As a result, some new consulting firms, software firms, and service providers have begun to provide e-commerce solutions for retailers.

Required

1. How does a consulting firm, service provider, or software firm help a retailer reduce cost and become more competitive for Internet sales? What is the role of operating leverage in the retailer's decision to outsource online sales and service?

2. What role if any does globalization play in a retailer's efforts to reduce costs on Internet sales?

9-34 Operating Leverage These sales and cost data (000s) are for two companies in the transportation industry:

	Company A		Company B	
	Amount	**Percent of sales**	**Amount**	**Percent of sales**
Sales	$100,000	100%	$100,000	100%
Variable costs	60,000	60	30,000	30
Contribution margin	$ 40,000	40%	$ 70,000	70%
Fixed costs	15,000		40,000	
Operating profit	$ 25,000		$ 30,000	

Required

1. Calculate the operating leverage for each company. If sales increase, which company benefits more? How do you know?

2. Assume that sales rise 10 percent in the next year. Calculate the percentage increase in profit for each company. Are the results what you expected?

9-35 CVP Analysis Connelly, Inc., a manufacturer of quality electric ice cream makers, has experienced a steady growth in sales over the past few years. Since her business has grown, Jan DeJaney, the president, believes she needs an aggressive advertising campaign next year to maintain the company's growth. To prepare for the growth, the accountant prepared the following data for the current year:

Variable costs per ice cream maker	
Direct labor	$ 13.50
Direct materials	14.50
Variable overhead	6.00
Total variable costs	$ 34.00
Fixed costs	
Manufacturing	$ 82,500
Selling	42,000
Administrative	356,000
Total fixed costs	$480,500
Selling price per unit	$ 65.00
Expected sales (units)	30,000

Required

1. If the costs and sales price remain the same, what is the projected operating profit for the coming year?

2. What is the breakeven point in units for the coming year?

3. Jan has set the sales target for 35,000 ice cream makers which she thinks she can achieve by an additional fixed selling expense of $200,000 for advertising. All other costs remain as in requirement 1. What will be the operating profit if the additional $200,000 is spent on advertising and sales rise to 35,000 units?

4. What will be the new breakeven point if the additional $200,000 is spent on advertising?

5. If the additional $200,000 is spent for advertising in the next year, what is the required sales level in units to equal the current year's income at 30,000 units?

9-36 The Role of Income Taxes In 2010, Triad Company had fixed costs of $200,000 and variable costs of 80 percent of total sales revenue, earned $70,000 of net income after taxes, and had an income tax rate of 30 percent.

Required Determine (1) before-tax income, (2) total contribution margin, (3) total sales, and (4) breakeven point in dollar sales.

9-37 CVP Analysis with Taxes   Jeffrey Company produces and sells socks. Variable costs are $3 per pair, and fixed costs for the year total $75,000. The selling price is $5 per pair.

Required   Calculate the following:
1. The breakeven point in units.
2. The breakeven point in sales dollars.
3. The units required to make a before-tax profit of $10,000.
4. The sales in dollars required to make a before-tax profit of $8,000.
5. The sales units and sales dollars required to make an after-tax profit of $12,000 given a tax rate of 40 percent.

9-38 Margin of Safety   Harold McWilliams owns and manages a general merchandise store in a rural area of Virginia. Harold sells appliances, clothing, auto parts, and farming equipment, among a wide variety of other types of merchandise. Because of normal seasonal and cyclical fluctuations in the local economy, he knows that his business will also have these fluctuations, and he is planning to use CVP analysis to help him understand how he can expect his profits to change with these fluctuations. Harold has the following information for his most recent year. Cost of goods sold represents the cost paid for the merchandise he sells, while operating costs represent rent, insurance, and salaries, that are entirely fixed.

Sales	$650,000
Cost of goods sold	422,500
Contribution margin	227,500
Operating costs	105,000
Operating profit	$122,500

Required
1. What is Harold's margin of safety in dollars? What is the margin of safety ratio?
2. What is Harold's margin of safety and operating profit if sales should fall to $500,000?

9-39 Budget Cuts   Pharmacy Health Services at Overland University provides certain medications to students free of charge. Currently, 40 percent of the pharmacy's costs are fixed; the other 60 percent are variable. The pharmacy's budget was $300,000 last year, but the university recently cut this year's budget by 10 percent.

Required   What is the percentage decrease in the amount of services the pharmacy can provide this year?

9-40 Multiple Products CVP   Julia Company can produce two types of carpet cleaners, the Brighter and Smarter. The data on the two machines is as follows:

	Brighter	Smarter
Sales volume in units	200	300
Unit sales price	$750	$1,000
Unit variable cost	225	450

The number of machine-hours to produce Brighter is 1 and to produce Smarter is 2. Total fixed costs for the manufacture of both products are $132,000.

Required   Using a spreadsheet, determine the breakeven point for Julia Company, assuming that the sales mix remains constant in sales dollars.

Problems   **9-41 CVP Analysis, Strategy**   Hank's Western Wear is a western hat retailer in Lubbock, Texas. Although Hank's carries numerous styles of western hats, each hat has approximately the same price and invoice (purchase) cost, as shown in the following table. Sales personnel receive large commissions to encourage them to be more aggressive in their sales efforts. Currently, the Lubbock economy is really humming, and sales growth at Hank's has been great. The business is very competitive, however, and Hank has relied on his knowledgeable and courteous staff to attract and retain customers who otherwise might go to other western wear stores. Because of the rapid growth in sales, Hank is also finding the management of certain aspects of the business, such as restocking of inventory and hiring and training new salespeople, more difficult.

Sales price	$ 45.00
Per unit variable expenses	
Purchase cost	25.50
Sales commissions	4.50
Total per unit variable costs	$ 30.00
Total annual fixed expenses	
Advertising	$ 22,000
Rent	18,000
Salaries	185,000
Total fixed expenses	$225,000

Required

1. Calculate the annual breakeven point in unit sales and dollar sales.
2. If Hank's sells 20,000 hats, what is its before-tax income or loss?
3. If Hank's sells 30,000 hats, what is its margin of safety and margin of safety ratio?
4. Hank is considering the elimination of sales commissions completely and increasing salaries by $106,500 annually. What would be the new breakeven point in units? What would be the before-tax income or loss if 20,000 hats are sold with the new salary plan?
5. Identify and discuss the strategic and ethical issues in the decision to eliminate sales commissions (see requirement 4). How do these strategic concerns affect Hank's decision?

9-42 **Cost Planning; Service Company**   Triangle Business Service Inc (TBS) is a delivery service specializing in small parcels, envelopes, and packages. TBS guarantees delivery of within 90 minutes for any business or residence in the Triangle (Greensboro–High Point–Winston-Salem) area. The owner of the business is currently evaluating the choice between two different cost structures for a planned increase in the business operations. One option is to buy 200 vehicles and hire delivery personnel to deliver the packages. Option two is to hire delivery personnel who would use their own vehicles for deliveries; the delivery personnel in this case would be compensated for their time and also for the use of their vehicles. For corporate purposes, the delivery personnel under option two would be required to attach a magnetic decal to their car or truck to identify it as a provider for TBS. Option one is the high fixed cost, high leverage option, and option two has the lower fixed cost but significantly higher variable costs. For simplicity, we assume that each package is delivered for the same price of $60.

Item	Drivers' Cars	TBS's Cars
Delivery price per package	$ 60	$ 60
Variable cost per package delivered	48	30
Contribution margin per unit	12	30
Fixed costs (per year)	$600,000	$3,000,000

Required

1. What is the breakeven point, in terms of number of deliveries per year, for the each alternative?
2. How many deliveries would have to be made under each alternative to generate a pretax profit of $25,000 per year?
3. How many deliveries would have to be made under option two (drivers use their cars) to generate a pretax profit equal to 15 percent of sales revenue?
4. Assume an effective income-tax rate of 40 percent. What number of deliveries would be needed to generate an after-tax profit of $36,000 for the TBS-Cars alternative?
5. Which decision alternative is the more profitable for TBS? Which alternative is more risky, and why?

9-43 Contribution Income Statements Using Excel; Sensitivity Analysis; Goal Seek

Required

1. Using the data in Exhibit 9.1, create an Excel spreadsheet to provide a sensitivity analysis of the effect on operating profit of potential changes in demand for HFI, Inc. Use Exhibits 9.2 and 9.6 as a guide.

2. Use the Goal Seek tool within Excel to determine which sales price would allow HFI to earn $100,000 operating profit, assuming that all the other cost information is the same as in Exhibit 9.1. Use Exhibit 9.5 as a guide.

9-44 Multiple Products
Most businesses sell several products at varying prices. The products often have different unit variable costs. Thus, the total profit and the breakeven point depend on the proportions in which the products are sold. Sales mix is the relative contribution of sales among various products sold by a firm. Assume that the sales of Jordan, Inc., are the following for a typical year:

Product	Units Sold	Sales Mix
A	18,000	80%
B	4,500	20
Total	22,500	100%

Assume the following unit selling prices and unit variable costs:

Product	Selling Price	Variable Cost per Unit	Unit Contribution Margin
A	$ 80	$ 65	$15 12
B	140	100	40 8

Fixed costs are $400,000 per year, of which $60,000 are batch-related and $340,000 are facilities-related. Assume sales mix is constant in units.

Required

1. Determine the breakeven point in units.

2. Determine the number of units required for a before-tax net profit of $40,000.

9-45 Multiple Products; ABC
Assume the same information as for Problem 9-44 above, with this additional information: product A is made in batches of 3,000 units and product B is made in batches of 750 units. The nature of the production process is such that each batch of product must be made in these quantities. We also assume that total batch-level costs of $60,000 vary directly with the number of batches used, so that a reduction in the number of batches produced will reduce total batch-level costs.

Required

1. Determine the breakeven point in units for each product using ABC.

2. Assume that expected sales of product A and B are 32,000 units and 8,000 units (instead of 18,000 and 4,500), and that the batch size for product A is 4,000 units per batch while the batch size for product B is 1,000 units per batch. All the remaining information from 9-44 is the same. Using ABC, determine the breakeven point in units for each product.

9-46 CVP Relationships
The following is taken from a recent media report about Gateway, Inc., which provides products and services in the PC industry.

"Gateway's loss in the quarter that ended June 30 nearly tripled to $61 million on revenues of $1 billion. . . . To break even, Gateway would need to boost unit sales a mind-numbing 43%, from 651,000 in the second quarter to 933,000 units."

Gateway has a mere 5.6 percent of the U.S. market. The media report is projecting a 5 percent rise in unit sales next quarter.

Required

1. Estimate Gateway's variable cost per unit and fixed cost per year.

   Hint: First determine price from the available information and then develop two breakeven models: one for the quarter ended June 30 in which there was a loss of $61 million and another for breakeven for the third quarter in which sales are expected to be 933,000 units. Using the two models, solve for v.

2. Determine the required market share Gateway needs to have in order to break even next quarter.

9-47   **CVP Relationships**   Recent news reports say that Expedia.com pays wholesale prices for hotel rooms and then adds an average of 26 percent markup over the price it pays, and then sells the rooms on its Web site. This approach is in contrast to other travel services that earn typically a 10 percent commission of the retail price on reservations they make for the hotel. Assume that the wholesale price that Expedia pays a hotel is 60 percent of the hotel's retail price, for the rooms that Expedia purchases.

Required

1. Compute the percentage return to Expedia from purchasing and reselling the rooms.

2. What must have been a hotel's expected vacancy rate if it sold rooms to Expedia at 60 percent of the wholesale price? Assume all the hotel's costs are fixed and that if the rooms are not sold to Expedia, the rooms will either remain empty, or for the rooms that are used, the room reservations will be made by a travel service that will require a 10 percent commission.

    Hint: Set up an equation for the amount received by the hotel without selling the room-days to Expedia equal to the amount received by the hotel by selling to Expedia, using three variables: the retail price of the room, the vacancy rate, and the number of rooms the hotel is considering selling to Expedia. Solve for the vacancy rate.

3. What is the minimum wholesale price discount that Expedia would accept from the hotel, such that Expedia would be indifferent between purchasing and reselling the rooms versus making reservations and receiving the 10 percent commission? Assume that Expedia can sell all the rooms it purchases.

9-48   **CVP Analysis**   Horton Manufacturing Inc. (HMI) is suffering from the effects of increased local and global competition for its main product, a lawn mower that is sold in discount stores throughout the United States. The following table shows the results of HMI's operations for 2010.

Sales (11,000 units @ $90)	$990,000
Less variable costs (11,000 @ $63)	693,000
Contribution margin	$297,000
Less fixed costs	324,000
Operating Loss	($ 27,000)

Required

1. Compute HMI's breakeven point in both units and dollars. Also, compute the contribution margin ratio.

2. The manager believes that a $60,000 increase in advertising would result in a $135,000 increase in annual sales. If the manager is right, what will be the effect on the company's operating profit or loss?

3. Refer to the original data. The vice president in charge of sales is certain that a 10 percent reduction in price in combination with a $50,000 increase in advertising will cause unit sales to increases by 20 percent. What effect would this strategy have on operating profit (loss)?

4. Refer to the original data. During 2010, HMI saved $5 of unit variable costs per lawn mower by buying from a different manufacturer. However, the cost of changing the plant machinery to accommodate the new part cost an additional $30,000 in fixed cost per year. Was this a wise change, and why or why not?

9-49   **CVP Analysis in a Professional Service Firm**   Lang and Thomas, a local CPA firm, has been asked to bid on a contract to perform audits for three counties in its home state. Should the firm be awarded the contract, it must hire one new staff member at a salary of $41,000 to handle the additional workload. (Existing staff are fully scheduled.) The managing partner is convinced that obtaining the contract will lead to additional new profit-oriented clients from the respective counties. Expected new work (excluding the three counties) is 800 hours at an average billing rate of $60.00 per hour. Other information follows about the firm's current annual revenues and costs:

Firm volume in hours (normal)	30,750
Fixed costs	$ 470,000
Variable costs	$ 20.00/hr

Should the firm win the contract, these audits will require 900 hours of expected work.

Required

1. If the managing partner's expectations are correct, what is the lowest bid the firm can submit and still expect to increase annual net income?

2. If the contract is obtained at a price of $30,000, what is the minimum number of hours of new business in addition to the county work that must be obtained for the firm to break even on total new business?

9-50 **CVP Analysis**   Lawn Master Company, a manufacturer of riding lawn mowers, has a projected income for 2010 as follows:

Sales		$46,000,000
Operating expenses		
Variable expenses	$32,200,000	
Fixed expenses	7,500,000	
Total expenses		39,700,000
Operating Profit		$ 6,300,000

Required

1. Determine the breakeven point in sales dollars.

2. Determine the required sales in dollars to earn a before-tax profit of $7,250,000.

3. What is the breakeven point in sales dollars if the variable cost increases by 10 percent?

9-51 **CVP Analysis, Activity-Based Costing, Taxes**   Sports Plus, Inc., produces software for personal computers. The company's main product is Swing!, a golf training program. The total variable cost of the product is $10. Fixed manufacturing expenses are $60,000 per month, and the price of the product is $300. In the coming year, the company plans to spend $100,000 for advertising and $50,000 for research and development. Because this proprietorship is managed from a personal residence, it incurs no other fixed costs. The federal and state tax rate for the proprietor is 40 percent. The company expects 6,000 units of sales for the next year.

Required

1. Determine the breakeven point for the coming year in number of units.

2. Suppose that 20 percent of the manufacturing fixed costs are batch-level costs from testing and packaging. Because of the nature of the testing process, all production has the same batch size of 20 units. Calculate the revised breakeven point.

3. Using a volume-based approach as in part 1 above, determine the number of units required for the coming year to cover a 100 percent increase in advertising expenses and a $12,000 after-tax profit per month.

9-52 **CVP Analysis**   The Brenham Hospital's Cardiac Diagnostic Screening Center (CDSC) is contemplating purchasing a blood gases analysis machine at a cost of $800,000. Useful life for this machine is 10 years. The screening center currently serves 5,000 patients per year, 30 percent of whom need blood gases analysis data as part of their diagnostic tests. The blood samples are presently sent to a private laboratory that charges $115 per sample. In-house variable expenses are estimated to be $65 per sample if CDSC purchases the analysis machine.

Required

1. Determine the indifference point between purchasing the machine or using the private laboratory.

2. Determine how many additional patients would be needed so that CDSC would be indifferent between purchasing the analysis machine and the $115 lab charge.

3. Determine the amount of the private laboratory charge so that CDSC would be indifferent as to purchasing the analysis machine or using the private laboratory, assuming the current service level of 5,000 patients per year.

9-53 **CVP Analysis; Sensitivity Analysis; Multiple Products; Strategy**   GoGo Juice is a combination gas station and convenience store located at a busy intersection. Recently a national chain opened a similar store only a block away; consequently sales have decreased for GoGo. In an effort to reclaim lost sales, GoGo has implemented a promotional effort; for every $10 purchase at GoGo, the customer receives a $1 coupon for the purchase of gasoline. The average gasoline customer purchases 15 gallons of gasoline at $2.50/gal. The results of an average month, prior to this coupon promotion are shown in the following chart.

Not included on the chart is the monthly cost of printing the coupons that is estimated to be $500. Coupons are issued on the basis of total purchases regardless of whether the purchases are paid in cash or paid by redeeming coupons. Assume that coupons are distributed to customers for 80 percent of the total sales. Also assume that all coupons distributed are used to purchase gasoline.

	Sales	Cost of Sales (per unit or % of retail)
Gasoline	$100,000	$1.875 per gallon
Food and beverages	60,000	60%
Other products	40,000	50%

	Other Costs
Labor—station attendants	$ 9,000
Labor—supervision	2,500
Rent, power, supplies, interest, and misc.	46,500
Depreciation (pumps, computers, counters, fixtures, and building)	2,500

Required

1. If GoGo Juice implements the promotional coupon effort, calculate the profit (loss) before tax if the sales volume remains constant and the coupons are used to purchase gasoline. Assume the sales mix remains constant.

2. Calculate the breakeven sales for GoGo Juice if the promotional effort is implemented. Assume that the product mix remains constant.

3. Disregarding your responses to Requirements 1 and 2, assume the weighted contribution margin ratio, after implementation of the coupon program, is 30 percent. Calculate the profit (loss) before tax for GoGo Juice, assuming sales increase 20 percent due to the new program. Assume that the sales mix remains constant.

4. GoGo Juice is considering using sensitivity analysis in combination with cost-volume-profit analysis. Discuss the use of sensitivity analysis with cost-volume-profit analysis. Include in your discussion at least three factors that make sensitivity analysis prevalent in decision making.

9-54 **CVP Analysis, Commissions, Ethics** Marston Corporation manufactures pharmaceutical products sold through a network of sales agents in the United States and Canada. The agents are currently paid an 18 percent commission on sales; that percentage was used when Marston prepared the following budgeted income statement for the fiscal year ending June 30, 2010.

MARSTON CORPORATION
Budgeted Income Statement
For the Year Ending June 30, 2010
($000 omitted)

Sales		$26,000
Cost of goods sold		
Variable	$11,700	
Fixed	2,870	14,570
Gross profit		$11,430
Selling and administrative costs		
Commissions	$ 4,680	
Fixed advertising cost	750	
Fixed administrative cost	1,850	7,280
Income before interest and taxes		$ 4,150
Fixed interest cost		650
Income before income taxes		$ 3,500
Income taxes (40 percent)		1,400
Net income		$ 2,100

Since the completion of the income statement, Marston has learned that its sales agents are requiring a 5 percent increase in their commission rate (to 23 percent) for the upcoming year. As a result, Marston's president has decided to investigate the possibility of hiring its own sales staff in place of the network of sales agents and has asked Tom Markowitz, Marston's controller, to gather information on the costs associated with this change.

Tom estimates that Marston must hire eight salespeople to cover the current market area, at an average annual payroll cost for each employee of $80,000, including fringe benefits expense. Travel and entertainment expense is expected to total $600,000 for the year, and the annual cost of hiring a sales manager and sales secretary will be $150,000. In addition to their salaries, the eight salespeople will each earn commissions at the rate of 10 percent. The president believes that Marston also should increase its advertising budget by $500,000 if the eight salespeople are hired..

Required

1. Determine Marston Corporation's breakeven point in sales dollars for the fiscal year ending June 30, 2010, if the company hires its own sales force and increases its advertising costs.

2. If Marston continues to sell through its network of sales agents and pays the higher commission rate, determine the estimated volume in sales dollars that would be required to generate the same operating profit as projected in the budgeted income statement.

3. Describe the general assumptions underlying breakeven analysis that limit its usefulness.

4. What is the indifference point in sales for the firm to either accept the agents' demand or adopt the proposed change? Which plan is better for the firm?

5. What are the ethical issues, if any, that Tom should consider?

(CMA Adapted)

9-55 **CVP Analysis, Different Production Plans**   The PTO Division of Galva Manufacturing Company produces power take-off units for the farm equipment business. The PTO Division, headquartered in Peoria, has a newly renovated, automated plant in Peoria and an older, less-automated plant in Moline. Both plants produce the same power take-off units for farm tractors that are sold to most domestic and foreign tractor manufacturers.

The PTO Division expects to produce and sell 192,000 power take-off units during the coming year. The division production manager has the following data available regarding the unit costs, unit prices, and production capacities for the two plants.

- All fixed costs are based on a normal year of 240 work days. When the number of work days exceeds 240, variable manufacturing costs increase by $3 per unit in Peoria and $8 per unit in Moline. Capacity for each plant is 300 working days.
- Galva Manufacturing charges each of its plants a per-unit fee for administrative services such as payroll, general accounting, and purchasing because management considers these services to be a function of the work performed at the plants. For each plant at Peoria and Moline, the fee is $6.50 and represents the variable portion of general and administrative expense.

Wishing to maximize the higher unit profit at Moline, PTO's production manager has decided to manufacture 96,000 units at each plant. This production plan results in Moline's operating at capacity and Peoria's operating at its normal volume. Galva's corporate controller is not happy with this plan because she does not believe it represents optimal usage of PTO's plants.

	Peoria	**Moline**
Selling price	$150.00	$150.00
Variable manufacturing cost	72.00	88.00
Fixed manufacturing cost	30.00	15.00
Commission (5 percent)	7.50	7.50
General and administrative expense	25.50	21.00
Total unit cost	$135.00	$131.50
Unit profit	$ 15.00	$ 18.50
Production rate per day	400 units	320 units

Required

1. Determine the annual breakeven units for each PTO plant.

2. Determine the operating income that would result from the division production manager's plan to produce 96,000 units at each plant.

3. Determine the optimal production plan to produce the 192,000 units at PTO's plants in Peoria and Moline and the resulting operating income for the PTO Division. Be sure to support the plan with appropriate calculations.

(CMA Adapted)

9-56   CVP Analysis, Probability Analysis   Don Carson and two colleagues are considering opening a law office in a large metropolitan area to make inexpensive legal services available to people who cannot otherwise afford these services. They intend to provide easy access for their clients by having the office open 360 days per year, 16 hours each day from 7:00 @-L - to 11:00 O-L - A lawyer, paralegal, legal secretary, and clerk-receptionist would staff the office for each of the two 8-hour shifts.

To determine the feasibility of the project, Don hired a marketing consultant to assist with market projections. The consultant's results show that if the firm spends $500,000 on advertising the first year, the number of new clients expected each day would have the following probability distribution:

Number of New Clients per Day	Probability
10	.10
20	.30
40	.40
60	.20

Don and his associates believe these numbers to be reasonable and are prepared to spend the $500,000 on advertising. Other pertinent information about the operation of the office follows.

The only charge to each new client would be $30 for an initial consultation. The firm will accept all cases that warrant further legal work on a contingency basis with the firm earning 30 percent of any favorable settlements or judgments. Don estimates that 20 percent of new client consultations will result in favorable settlements or judgments averaging $15,000 each. He does not expect repeat clients during the first year of operations.

The hourly wages for the staff are projected to be $185 for the lawyer, $50 for the paralegal, $30 for the legal secretary, and $20 for the clerk-receptionist. Fringe benefit expense will be 40 percent of the wages paid. A total of 400 hours of overtime is expected for the year; this will be divided equally between the legal secretary and the clerk-receptionist positions. Overtime will be paid at one and one-half times the regular wage, and the fringe benefit expense will apply to the full wage.

Don has located 6,000 square feet of suitable office space that rents for $48 per square foot annually. Associated expenses will be $22,000 for property insurance and $32,000 for utilities. The group must purchase malpractice insurance expected to cost $180,000 annually.

The initial investment in office equipment will be $60,000; this equipment has an estimated useful life of four years. The cost of office supplies has been estimated to be $10 per expected new client consultation.

Required

1. Determine how many new clients must visit the law office that Don and his colleagues are considering for the venture to break even in first year of operations.

2. Using the probability information provided by the marketing consultant, determine whether it is feasible for the law office to achieve breakeven operations.

3. Explain how Don and his associates could use sensitivity analysis to assist in this analysis.

(CMA Adapted)

9-57   CVP Analysis, Strategy, Critical Success Factors   Garner Strategy Institute (GSI) presents executive-level training seminars nationally. Eastern University (EU) has approached GSI to present 40 one-week seminars during 2010. This activity level represents the maximum number of seminars that GSI is capable of presenting annually. GSI staff would present the week-long seminars in various cities throughout the United States and Canada.

Terry Garner, GSI's president, is evaluating three financial options for the revenues from Eastern: accept a flat fee for each seminar, receive a percentage of Eastern's profit before tax from the seminars, and form a joint venture to share costs and profits.

Estimated costs for the 2010 seminar schedule follow.

	Garner Strategy Institute	Eastern University
Fixed costs		
Salaries and benefits	$200,000	N/A*
Facilities	48,000	N/A*
Travel and hotel	0	$210,000
Other	70,000	N/A*
Total fixed costs	$318,000	$210,000

(Continued)

Variable costs		Per Participant
Supplies and materials	0	$47
Marketing	0	18
Other site costs	0	35

*Eastern's fixed costs are excluded because the amounts are not considered relevant for this decision (i.e., they will be incurred whether or not the seminars are presented). Eastern does not include these costs when calculating the profit before tax for the seminars.

EU plans to charge $1,200 per participant for each one-week seminar. It will pay all variable marketing, site costs, and materials costs.

Required

1. Assume that the seminars are handled as a joint venture by GSI and EU to pool costs and revenues.

   a. Determine the total number of seminar participants needed to break even on the total costs for this joint venture. Show supporting computations.

   b. Assume that the joint venture has an effective income tax rate of 30 percent. How many seminar participants must the joint venture enroll to earn a net income of $169,400? Show supporting computations.

2. Assume that GSI and EU do not form a joint venture, but that GSI is an independent contractor for EU. EU offers two payment options to GSI: a flat fee of $9,500 for each seminar, or a fee of 40 percent of EU's profit before tax from the seminars. Compute the minimum number of participants needed for GSI to prefer the 40 percent fee option over the flat fee. Show supporting computations.

3. What are the strategic and implementation issues for GSI to consider in deciding whether to enter into the joint venture? For Eastern?

(CMA Adapted)

9-58 **CVP Analysis, Strategy, Uncertainty** Computer Graphics (CG) is a small manufacturer of electronic products for computers with graphics capabilities. The company has succeeded by being very innovative in product design. As a spin-off of a large electronics manufacturer (ElecTech), CG management has extensive experience in both marketing and manufacturing in the electronics industry. A long list of equity investors is betting that the firm will really take off because of the growth of specialized graphic software and the increased demand for computers with enhanced graphics capability. A number of market analysts say, however, that the market for the firm's products is somewhat risky, as it is for many high-tech start-ups because of the number of new competitors entering the market, and CG's unproven technology.

CG's main product is a circuit board (CB3668) used in computers with enhanced graphics capabilities. Prices vary depending on the terms of sale and the size of the purchase; the average price for the CB3668 is $100. If the firm is able to take off, it might be able to raise prices, but it also might have to reduce the price because of increased competition. The firm expects to sell 150,000 units in the coming year, and sales are expected to increase in the following years. The future for CG looks very bright indeed, but it is new and has not developed a strong financial base. Cash flow management is a critical feature of the firm's financial management, and top management must watch cash flow numbers closely.

At present, CG is manufacturing the CB3668 in a plant leased from ElecTech using some equipment purchased from ElecTech. CG manufactures about 70 percent of the parts in this circuit board.

CG management is considering a significant reengineering project to significantly change the plant and manufacturing process. The project's objective is to increase the number of purchased parts (to about 55 percent) and to reduce the complexity of the manufacturing process. This would also permit CG to remove some leased equipment and to sell some of the most expensive equipment in the plant.

The per-unit manufacturing costs for 150,000 units of CB3668 follow:

	Current Manufacturing Cost	**Proposed Manufacturing Costs**
Materials and purchased parts	$ 6.00	$ 15.00
Direct labor	12.50	13.75
Variable overhead	25.00	30.00
Fixed overhead	40.00	20.00
Manufacturing information for CB3668		
Number of setups	3,000	2,300
Batch size	50	50
Cost per setup	$ 300	$ 300
Machine-hours	88,000	55,000

General, selling, and administrative costs are $10 variable cost per unit and $1,250,000 fixed; these costs are not expected to differ for either the current or the proposed manufacturing plan.

Required

1. Compute the contribution margin and breakeven in units for CB3668, both before and after the proposed reengineering project. Assume all setup costs are included in fixed overhead.

2. Determine the number of sales units at which CG would be indifferent as to the current manufacturing plan or the proposed plan.

3. Explain briefly (a) what CG's strategy is (b) what you think it should be and (c) why.

4. Should CG undertake the proposed reengineering plan? Using a spreadsheet, support your answer with sensitivity analysis and a discussion of short-term and long-term considerations.

9-59 CVP Analysis; ABC Costing Using the information in Problem 9-58, complete the following:

Required

1. Compute the breakeven in units for both the current and proposed manufacturing plans, assuming that setup costs vary with the number of batches. Assume that setup costs are the only costs that vary with the number of batches.

2. Compare your solution above to that for Problem 9-58 and interpret the difference.

9-60 New Manufacturing Facility, Strategy Julius Brooks, plant manager for ICL, Inc., a manufacturer of auto parts, has been successful in recent years because of the very high quality of his products and the speed of delivery. A growing market for ICL is automakers who want it to participate in the design of the car and to design certain parts. The ICL design team supervised by Julius has developed an excellent reputation among the automakers for quality designs, which have reduced warranty and service costs for the automakers. The result has been that a substantial part of the plant's revenues are now from design work, and sometimes ICL subcontracts the actual manufacturing to other manufacturers. Nevertheless, competitors continue to cut prices, and Julius is finding it more difficult to cut costs to meet the competition. Working with top management, he has helped design a new, automated factory in Georgia to take advantage of the tax breaks allowed by the State of Georgia and the local community.

Required Discuss the strategic aspects of the plan for the new factory.

9-61 CVP Analysis Babbott Bicycle Company (BBC) is a high-end manufacturer of bicycles. Its products are sold in specialty retail bike stores throughout the United States and Canada. This year's expected production is 10,000 units, but demand in the bicycle market has fluctuated in recent years so that BBC is also predicting that the actual production/sales figure could be anywhere between 7,000 and 15,000 bikes. To control quality, BBC currently makes most of the parts for its bikes, including the rear brake. BBC's accountant reports the following costs for making the 10,000 rear brake assemblies:

	Per-Unit Costs	Costs for 10,000 Units
Direct materials	$10.00	$100,000
Direct manufacturing labor	6.00	60,000
Variable manufacturing overhead (power and utilities)	3.00	30,000
Inspection, setup, materials handling	2.00	20,000
Machine lease	3.40	34,000
Allocated fixed plant administration, taxes, and insurance	6.00	60,000
Total costs		$304,000

An outside vendor has offered to supply up to 20,000 brake assemblies to BBC for $25 each. The following additional information is available:

• BBC's machine lease costs are for the equipment used to make the brakes. If BBC buys all brakes from the outside vendor, it will be able to cancel the lease and avoid this cost. All other fixed costs will not be affected.

Required Assume that if BBC purchases the brake assemblies from the outside supplier, the facility where it currently makes them will remain idle for at least the next year. At that point, BBC might consider leasing the space or using it for an alternative use. Should BBC accept the outside supplier's offer? Support your answer using CVP analysis. Include an assessment of the strategic issues facing BBC that might affect your answer.

9-62 CVP Analysis; ABC Costing Using the information in Problem 9-61 above, complete the following.

Required Assume that inspection, setup, and materials-handling costs vary directly with the number of batches in which the bikes are produced, and that BBC produces brakes in batches of 1,000 units. Compute the indifference quantity between making the brakes or purchasing the brakes. Compare your solution to that in Problem 9-61 and interpret the difference.

9-63 CVP Analysis, Strategy SolarFlex is a small but very innovative manufacturer of cutting-edge solar panels. A significant portion of the company's success is due to technologically superior product design. SolarFlex has invented a flexible photovoltaic panel that utilizes solar energy much more efficiently than traditional panels. Due to its flexible properties, SolarFlex's panels are also very resistant to weathering and the normal wear and tear associated with traditional panels. This has made Solar-Flex panels especially popular among certain green-minded companies and individual consumers. SolarFlex's management team is made up of a number of high-profile executives that have extensive experience in the energy industry. Many equity investors and analysts believe the firm is poised to experience exponential growth in the coming years because of the growing popularity of environmentally friendly products and green engineering. However, a number of key industry experts warn that the market for SolarFlex's new technology is much riskier than what many believe. They point out that the market is always risky for high-tech start-ups, especially those with new and unproven technology.

The regular price for SolarFlex's main product, the Flex 1000 panel, is $600. The firm expects to sell 380,000 units in the coming year, and sales are expected to increase during the following years.

Right now SolarFlex produces its Flex 1000 panel at a small factory it recently purchased and uses some equipment it purchased from a leading industry manufacturer, the rest of the equipment is on lease. Currently, SolarFlex manufactures about 62 percent of the parts in their photovoltaic panels.

SolarFlex's management team has decided that it must reconfigure its manufacturing process in order to remain competitive. They decide to implement a plan to increase the number of purchased parts (to about 82 percent) and to reduce the complexity of the manufacturing process. This would allow SolarFlex to remove the leased equipment and to raise some cash by selling some of the purchased equipment currently used in the plant.

The per unit manufacturing costs for 380,000 units of Flex 1000 follow:

	Current Manufacturing Cost	Proposed Manufacturing Costs
Materials and purchased parts	180	195
Direct labor	55	62.5
Variable overhead	70	80
Fixed overhead	90	55

General, selling, and administrative variable costs are $25 per unit and total fixed costs are $2,050,000; these costs are not expected to differ for either the current or the proposed manufacturing plan.

Required

1. Compute the contribution margin and breakeven in units for the Flex 1000 panel, both before and after the proposed reengineering project. Assume all setup costs are included in fixed overhead.

2. Determine the number of sales units at which SolarFlex would be indifferent between the current manufacturing plan and the proposed plan.

3. Explain briefly (a) SolarFlex's strategy and (b) if SolarFlex should undertake the proposed reengineering plan? Using a spreadsheet, support your answer with sensitivity analysis and a discussion of short-term and long-term considerations.

9-64 CVP Analysis Hemp, an agricultural product, is a natural fiber that has many industrial and commercial uses, including handbags, backpacks, hats, paper, rope, industrial fabrics, and clothing. In some areas of the world, particularly Australia, Canada, and the United States, hemp is viewed as a potentially significant new opportunity for agricultural production, and business and agricultural leaders are studying the strategic issues involved in making further investments in the crop. For example, an agricultural analysis by the Manitoba, Canada, Department of Agriculture has developed the following estimated costs for producing hemp. This analysis is based on an average farm in which 180 acres would be planted. Assume machinery operating costs, crop insurance, land taxes, licensing fees, sampling and analytical fees, and other costs are fixed relative to the production of hemp, while the other costs are variable per pound produced. Also, assume seed prices of $4.00 per pound, a 20-pound per acre seeding rate, and crop yield of 400 pounds per acre. The costs associated with investment in land and machinery are ignored in the analysis, on the assumption that these costs would remain the same whether or not the farmer grows hemp.

Required Calculate the price per pound that a farmer on an average-sized farm would have to receive to break even on the production of hemp.

Estimated Operating Costs per Acre for the Production of Hemp	
Seed	$80.00
Fertilizer	38.15
Chemicals	10.00
Fuel	11.00
Machinery operating costs	15.00
Crop insurance	6.00
Other costs	7.50
Land taxes	5.50
Licensing fee	15.00
Sampling and analytical fees	15.00
Drying costs	3.57
Cleaning costs	5.00
Interest on operating costs	7.44

9-65 **Multiple Product CVP Analysis** Headlines Publishing Company (HPC) specializes in international business news publications. Its principal product is *HPC-Monthly,* which is mailed to subscribers the first week of each month. A weekly version, called *HPC-Weekly,* is also available to subscribers over the Web at a higher cost. Sixty percent of HPC's subscribers are nondomestic customers. The company experienced a fast growth in subscribers in its first few years of operation, but sales have begun to slow in recent years as new competitors have entered the market. HPC has the following cost structure and sales revenue for its subscription operations on a yearly basis. All costs and all subscription fees are in U.S. dollars.

Fixed Cost

$306,000 per year

Variable Costs

Mailing	$0.60 per issue
Commission	3.00 per subscription
Administrative	1.50 per subscription

Sales Mix Information (constant in sales units)

HPC-Weekly	20%
HPC-Monthly	80%

Selling Price

HPC-Weekly	$47 per subscription
HPC-Monthly	19 per subscription

Required Use these data to determine the following:
1. Contribution margin for weekly and monthly subscriptions.
2. Contribution margin ratio for weekly and monthly subscriptions.
3. HPC's breakeven point in sales units and sales dollars.
4. HPC's breakeven point to reach a target before-tax profit of $75,000.
5. What are the critical success factors for HPC? For its domestic subscribers? For its international subscribers? How can CVP analysis be used to make HPC more competitive?

Solution to Self-Study Problem

Breakeven Analysis

1. Unit contribution margin = $5,595 − $899 − $233 = $4,463
2. Breakeven

   In units:

   $$Q = (F + N)/(p - v)$$
   $$Q = \$2,352,000/\$4,463 = 527 \text{ units}$$

   In dollars:

   $$p \times Q = \$5,595 \times 527 = \$2,948,565$$

   Or

   $$p \times Q = \frac{F + N}{(p - v)/p} = \frac{\$2,352,000}{0.797676} = \$2,948,565$$

3. New level of fixed costs = $2,352,000 (1 + .05) = $2,469,600

   Breakeven:

   $$Q = (F + N)/(p - v)$$
   $$Q = (\$2,469,600 + \$200,000)/\$4,463$$
   $$= 598 \text{ units}$$

4. Incorporate a tax rate of 22 percent and desired profit of $150,000:

   $$Q = \{\$2,352,000 + [\$150,000/(1 - 0.22)]\}/\$4,463$$
   $$= 570 \text{ units}$$

CHAPTER TEN

Strategy and the Master Budget

After studying this chapter, you should be able to . . .

1. Describe the role of budgets in the overall management process
2. Discuss the importance of strategy and its role in the master budgeting process
3. Outline the budgeting process
4. Prepare a master budget and explain the interrelationships among its supporting schedules
5. Deal with uncertainty in the budgeting process
6. Identify unique characteristics of budgeting for service companies
7. Understand alternative approaches to budgeting (zero-base budgeting, activity-based budgeting, time-driven activity-based budgeting, and kaizen budgeting)
8. Discuss various behavioral considerations in budgeting

If you don't know where you're going, you'll end up somewhere else.

Yogi Berra

Johnson & Johnson (J&J), one of the largest manufacturers of health-care products in the world, started (in 1887) as a small manufacturer of health and well-being-related products. Today, it has more than 99,000 employees and more than 190 operating companies in 51 countries. J&J sells its products in more than 175 countries. Surveys conducted over the years by *BusinessWeek, Forbes, Fortune,* and other business journals repeatedly have ranked J&J as one of the most innovative, well-managed, and admired firms in the world.

How does Johnson & Johnson do it? It relies on a comprehensive formal planning, budgeting, and control system in formulating and implementing strategy, coordinating and monitoring operations, and reviewing and evaluating performance. Every January, each operating unit reviews and revises its 5- and 10-year plans from the previous year and prepares the budget for the coming year as well as a two-year plan. The budgeting process is not completed until the approval of the profit plan in December.[1]

Johnson & Johnson is not unique. Growth and long-term profitability are results of a well-formulated strategy with good planning and implementation of the strategy. Firms need to plan for success. Budgeting is a common tool that organizations use for planning and controlling what they must do to serve their customers and succeed in the marketplace. This chapter discusses the budgeting processes and techniques that many successful companies such as J&J use as part of its overall management processes.

---

[1] A description of the budgeting process at Johnson & Johnson can be found in Robert Simon, "Planning, Control, and Uncertainty: A Process View," in William J. Bruns, Jr., and Robert S. Kaplan, eds., *Accounting and Management: Field Study Perspectives* (Boston: Harvard University Press, 1987), pp. 339–62. A case study, *Codman & Shurtleff, Inc.* (Harvard Business School: 187–081), describes the budgeting process of a subsidiary of Johnson & Johnson.

Role of Budgets

LEARNING OBJECTIVE 1

Describe the role of budgets in the overall management process.

A **budget**
is a detailed plan for the acquisition and use of financial and other resources over a specified period of time—typically a fiscal year.

Budgeting
is the process of projecting continuing operations and projects and then reflecting their financial impact.

A **budget** is a detailed plan for the acquisition and use of financial and other resources over a specified period of time—typically a fiscal year. A budget includes both financial and nonfinancial aspects of planned operations and projects. The budget for a period is both a guideline for operations and a projection of the operating results for the budgeted period. The process of preparing a budget is called **budgeting.**

Budget preparations allow management time to work out any problems the organization might face in the coming periods. This extra time enables the organization to minimize the adverse effects that anticipated problems could have on operations. Completion of a budget for all units of an organization facilitates the coordination of activities across departments and other organizational units. The budget also can help managers identify current and potential bottlenecks in operations. Critical resources can then be acquired to ease any bottlenecks and prevent such bottlenecks from becoming obstacles to attaining budgetary goals.

A budget also serves as a communication device through which top management defines its plans and goals for the period so that other managers and employees have access to this information. The operating plan of a budget allows each division to know what it needs to do to satisfy the needs of other divisions. The manufacturing division knows, for example, that it needs to complete the production of so many units of a given product before a certain date if the marketing division schedules the delivery of that product to customers for various dates. Budgets prescribe what performance the organization expects of all divisions and all employees for the period.

A budget can also be a motivating device. With the expected activities and operating results clearly delineated in the budget, employees know what is expected of them; this in turn motivates employees to work to attain the budgeted goals. To enhance the role of the budget as a motivating device, many organizations have employees participate in the budgeting process, thus helping employees embrace the budget as their own.

Budgets also provide authority to acquire and to use resources. The authorization function of budgets is especially important for government and not-for-profit organizations because budgeted amounts, sometimes referred to as *appropriations,* often serve both as approval of activities and as a ceiling for expenditures.

At the end of an operating period, the budget for the period can serve as a basis for assessing performance by reporting variances between actual and budgeted spending and operating results. The budget represents the specific results expected of the firm's divisions and employees for the period against which actual performance can be compared.[2]

Strategy, the Long-Term Plan, and the Master Budget

LEARNING OBJECTIVE 2

Discuss the importance of strategy and its role in the master budgeting process.

Importance of Strategy in Budgeting

A firm's strategy is the path it chooses for attaining its long-term goals and mission. The importance of strategy in planning and budgeting cannot be overemphasized. Too often organizations view the budget for the coming period as a continuation of the budget for the current period with at best a scant attempt to link the budget to their strategy. A budget should start with a careful review and study of the organization's strategic plan. The objective is to build a budget to achieve the organization's strategic goals and objectives. By not relying on its strategic plan, an organization very likely would not be able to fully utilize its strengths and take full advantage of opportunities. Ignoring the strategic plan can result in not adequately funding the projects and initiatives that are critical to achieving results aside from the daily operations of taking and fulfilling sales orders.

Formulation of Strategy

The success stories of many organizations are stories of good strategy formulation and execution. Formulation of strategy starts with analyzing external factors and assessing internal capabilities. Examining external factors surrounding an organization, such as the economy, politics, regulations, society, environment, and competition, helps the organization to identify opportunities, limitations, and threats. Opportunities available during a booming economy can be substantially different from those available in other times. Political situations and regulations often define the best course of action for firms and organizations. Assessing internal capabilities of the organization (e.g., strength and capability

---

[2] Analysis of actual versus budgeted results is the essence of the traditional model of financial control and is covered in Chapters 14, 15, and 16.

of management; structure, morale, and organizational culture) can help the organization recognize its strengths, weaknesses, and competitive advantages. Exhibit 10.1 shows the development of a company's product strategy.

Having analyzed external factors surrounding the organization and having assessed the internal situations it possesses, management can then match opportunities with the strengths and competitive advantages of the organization and determine the organization's strategic goals and long-term objectives.

Strategic Goals and Long-Term Objectives

Long-range plan
identifies required actions over a 5- to 10-year period to attain the firm's strategic goal(s).

Capital budgeting
is a process for evaluating, selecting, and financing long-term projects.

An organization expresses its strategic goals and long-term objectives in its capital and master budgets. Strategy provides the framework within which a long-range plan is developed. The organization's **long-range plan** identifies required actions over a 5- to 10-year period to attain the firm's strategic goal(s).

Long-range planning often entails **capital budgeting,** which is a process for evaluating, selecting, and financing major projects such as purchases of new equipment, construction of a new factory, and addition of new products. Capital budgets are prepared to bring an organization's capabilities into line with the needs of its long-range plan and long-term sales forecast. An organization's capacity is a result of capital investments made in prior budgeting periods.[3]

Strategic budget expenditures
are planned spending on projects and initiatives that lead to long-term value and competitive advantage.

The strategic goals and objectives of the organization are, ultimately, accomplished through a focused set of initiatives and projects. Put another way, it is this set of initiatives and projects that creates value for the organization. As such, it is important that the organization's annual budgeting process give prominence to a particular class of capital-budgeting expenditures: **strategic budget expenditures,** including those related to *sustainability.* Because such expenditures lead to long-term value creation and competitive advantage, it is important that they be clearly indentified and, to the extent possible, protected. Too often, such budgetary amounts are buried in ledger accounts and therefore subject to reduced support if not outright cutting. This is true particularly when short-term financial performance is falling short of expectations, with the consequent "need" to cut spending.

Short-Term Objectives and the Master Budget

Short-term objectives are goals for the coming period, which can be a month, a quarter, a year, or any length of time desired by the organization for planning purposes. An organization determines short-term objectives for the budget period based on strategic goals, long-term objectives and plans, operating results of past periods, and expected future operating and environmental factors including economic, industry, and marketing conditions. These objectives serve as the basis for preparing the **master budget** for a period.

A master budget
is an organization's operating and financing plan for the upcoming period; it translates short-term objectives into action steps.

Recognizing that the objective of an organization is multidimensional, more and more organizations are employing strategy maps and their companion, the balanced scorecard, to translate their strategy into objectives.[4] Exhibit 10.2 depicts a translation of strategy into short-term objectives with the balanced scorecard.[5] The arrows suggest that the process is both top-down and bottom-up.

A master budget translates the organization's short-term objectives into action steps. A master budget reflects an organization's operating and financing plans for the upcoming budget period. Exhibit 10.3 illustrates the relationships among strategic goals, long-term objectives and plans, short-term goals, budgets, operations, and controls.

Operating budgets
are plans for all phases of operations and include production, purchasing, personnel, and marketing budgets.

The master budget is also a comprehensive financial summary of the organization's budgets. As such, it comprises both operating budgets and financial budgets. **Operating budgets** are plans that identify resources needed to implement strategic projects and to carry out budgeted activities such as sales and customer services, production, purchasing,

---

[3] Capital budgeting is the subject of Chapter 12.

[4] Strategy maps and the balanced scorecard (BSC) are covered in Chapters 2 and 18.

[5] Adapted from Paul R. Niven, *Balanced Scorecard* (New York: John Wiley & Sons, Inc., 2002), p. 107.

EXHIBIT 10.1

Formulation of Strategy

Adapted from Robert N. Anthony and Vijay Govindarajan, *Management Control Systems,* 11th ed. (Burr Ridge, IL: Richard D. Irwin, 2003).

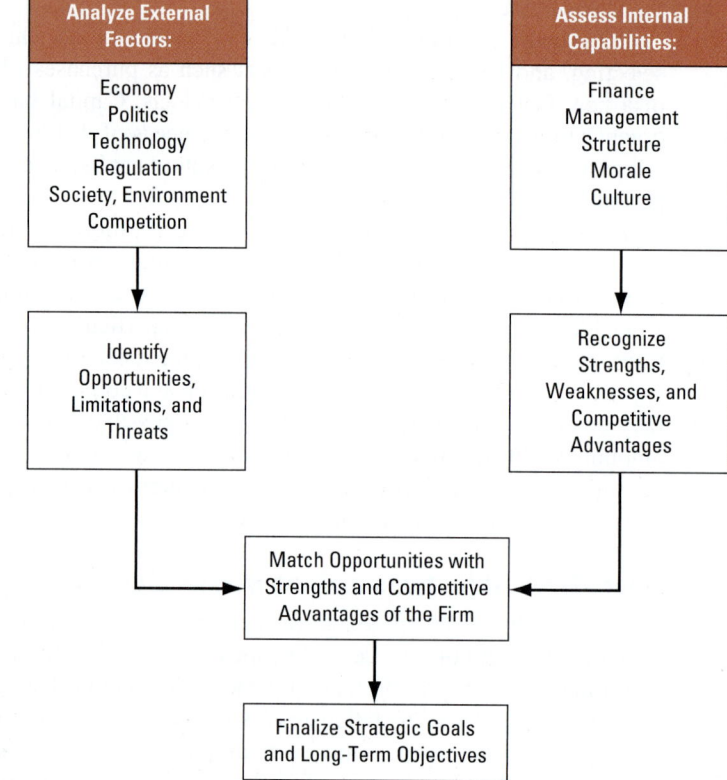

EXHIBIT 10.2 Translating Strategy with Strategy Maps and the Balanced Scorecard (BSC)

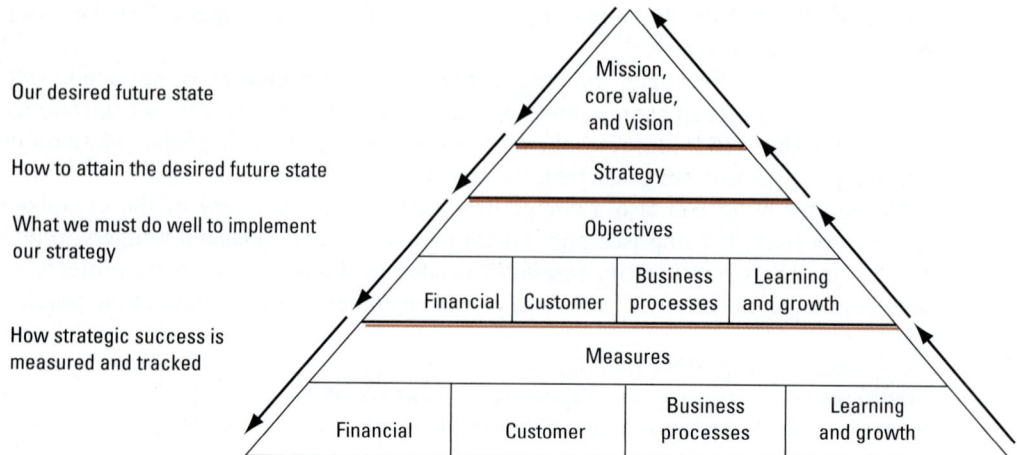

EXHIBIT 10.3
The Relationships Among Strategic Goals, Long-Term Objectives, Master Budgets, and Operations

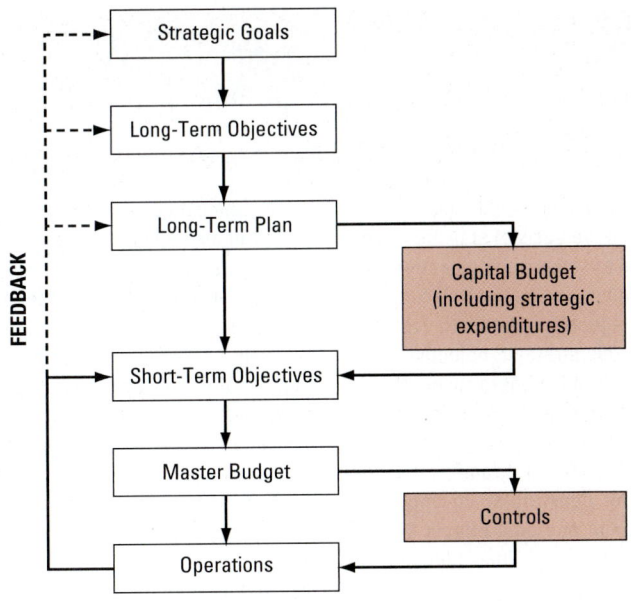

marketing, and research and development, and the acquisition of these resources. For a manufacturer, operating budgets include production, purchasing, personnel, and marketing budgets. The set of operating budgets culminates in a budgeted income statement. **Financial budgets** identify sources and uses of funds for the budgeted operations, including strategic projects and initiatives. Financial budgets include the cash budget, budgeted statement of cash flows, the budgeted balance sheet, and the capital expenditures (including strategic expenditures) budget.

Financial budgets
identify sources and uses of funds for budgeted operations and capital expenditures.

The Budgeting Process

LEARNING OBJECTIVE 3

Outline the budgeting process.

The traditional budgeting process can range from the informal simple processes small firms use that take only days or weeks to complete to elaborate, lengthy procedures large firms or governments employ that span months from start to final approval. The process usually includes the formation of a budget committee; determination of the budget period; specification of budget guidelines; preparation of the initial budget proposal; budget negotiation, review, and approval; and budget revision.

Budget Committee

The budget committee oversees all budget matters and often is the highest authority in an organization for all matters related to the budget. The committee sets and approves the overall budget goals for all major business units, coordinates budget preparation, resolves conflicts and differences that may arise during budget preparation, approves the final budget, monitors operations as the year unfolds, and reviews the operating results at the end of the period. The budget committee also approves major revisions of the budget during the period. A typical budget committee includes the chief executive officer (CEO) or one or more vice presidents, heads of strategic business units, and the chief financial officer (CFO).[6]

Budget Period

A budget usually is prepared for a set time, most commonly for the fiscal year with subperiod budgets for each of the constituent quarters or months. Synchronizing the budget period with

---

[6] In some organizations, the CEO makes all budget decisions and there is no committee.

Adding Value to the Overall Performance-Assessment Process: The Role of Technology

Budgets can be used strategically in the overall planning and control process *if* they are constructed on the basis of activities, processes, and strategic projects needed to support the objectives and strategies the organization is pursuing. For example, an organization might embrace a strategic objective related to "revenue growth." Two strategies to achieve this strategic objective might be "maintain existing distributor base" and "generate new sales." In turn, a number of tactics might be designed to accomplish each strategy. For example, tactics associated with the "generate new sales" strategy might be a "communications program" and a "loyalty program." Budgets can then be constructed to implement the programs and to cover the revenue and cost effects of each tactic. It is through a mechanism such as this that budgets can be used within the organization to ensure that resource planning and consumption are linked to the strategies the organization has formulated.

A common complaint among managers charged with the responsibility of managing and reporting on the execution of organizational strategy is the lack of an effective means to view and analyze all of the cause-and-effect relationships (objectives, strategies, tactics, and activities) embodied in the strategic plan. Technology, for example SAS's Performance Management Software, can be used to improve the visibility of the cause-and-effect relationships of corporate strategies, day-to-day activities, and the resources that support them. This software allows managers to view the entire strategic plan of the organization, to understand whether planned activities have been implemented, and to identify areas where results are falling short of budgeted goals.

Source: Geac, *6 Steps for Linking Corporate Budgeting to Strategy* (White Paper), August 2005 (available for download at: www.performance.geac.com).

---

the organization's fiscal period for external financial reporting eases budget preparation and facilitates comparisons and reconciliation of actual results with the budgeted amounts.

In practice, firms seldom have budgets for only one year. The budgets for the years beyond the coming year, however, usually contain only essential operating data. For example, Johnson & Johnson has only skeleton budgets for its 5- and 10-year budgets. Having a long-term budget in parallel with the master budget allows alignment of strategic goals and short-term operations.

Budget Guidelines

In a traditional budgeting process the budget committee is responsible for providing initial budget guidelines that set the tone for the budget and govern its preparation. The committee issues budget guidelines after careful considerations on the general outlook of the economy and the market; the organization's strategic goals, long-term plan, strategic projects, and expected operating result of the current period; specific corporate decisions or policies such as mandates for downsizing, reengineering, pollution control, and special promotions; and short-term objectives. All responsibility centers (or budget units) follow the budget guidelines in preparing their budgets.

Initial Budget Proposal

Each responsibility center prepares its initial budget proposal based on the budget guidelines. In addition, budget units need to consider a number of internal factors in preparing their budget proposals, including:

- Changes in availability of equipment or facilities.
- Adoption of new or improved operating processes and planned efficiency gains.
- Changes in product and/or service design and mix of offerings.
- Introduction of new products and services.
- Consumption rates of activities and their resources for the recurring volume and mix of products and services.

- Changes in expectations or operating processes of other budget units that the budget unit relies on for its input materials or other operating factors.
- Changes in other operating factors or in the expectations or operating processes in those other budget units that rely on the budget unit to supply them components.

Inevitably, external factors have effects on operations and a budget cannot be completed without careful examination of important external factors such as:

- The industry's outlook for the near term.
- Competitors' actions.
- Threat to entry.
- Substitute products.
- Bargaining power of customers.
- Bargaining power (availability and price) of input suppliers (raw materials, components, and labor).[7]

Negotiation, Review, and Approval

The executives of budget units examine initial budget proposals. The examination includes determining adherence to the budget guidelines, verifying that the budget goals can be reasonably attained and are in line with the goals of the immediately higher organizational unit, and assuring that the budgeted operations are consistent with those of other budget units.

As budget units complete their budgets within the units, the budgets go through successively higher levels of the organization until they reach the top level and the combined unit budgets become the organization's budget. The budget committee reviews the budget for consistency with the budget guidelines, attainment of the desired short-term goals and strategic objectives of the organization. The budget committee gives final approval, and the CEO then approves the entire budget and submits it to the board of directors.

Revision

No budget is ever cast in stone. As operations unveil, newly learned internal factors or external situations may make it necessary to revise the budget. Procedures for budget revisions vary among organizations. For organizations that allow budget revisions only under special circumstances, obtaining approval to modify a budget can be difficult. Not all events, however, unfold as predicted in a budget. Strictly implementing a budget as prescribed, even when the actual events differ significantly from those expected, certainly is not a desirable behavior. In such cases, managers should be encouraged not to rely on the budget as the absolute guideline in operations.

The finest plans are often spoiled through the pettiness of those who are supposed to carry them out, since even emperors can do nothing without the support of their soldiers and hangers-on.

Bertolt Brecht

The strategic role of budgeting for a hypothetical company, Kerry Window Systems, Inc., is given on the next page. This is followed by a detailed example of preparing a master budget for this company.

---

[7] Michael Porter considers the last five factors as five competing forces that firms need to scrutinize in determining strategy and planning for action. For details, see Cynthia A. Montgomery and Michael E. Porter, *Strategy* (Boston: Harvard Business Review Press, 1991).

Comprehensive Budgeting Example: Kerry Window Systems, Inc. (KWS)

KWS is a manufacturer of aluminum window frames and storm window frames. Kerry's product is sold to a glass manufacturer that inserts the glass panes and then sells the completed windows to retailers. KWS sells an upscale window, made in strong aluminum, which is priced somewhat higher than the vinyl windows sold by competitors. In fact, Kerry's prices are similar to high-end wooden windows. To compete in this portion of the market, KWS stresses manufacturing quality and offers the final customer a comprehensive warranty against defects. Many view KWS as having among the best windows available.

With winter heating costs going up, there has been strong demand for storm windows, especially for older homes. Also, many families who are finding it more difficult to move up to a larger home as they had planned are remodeling or adding rooms to their existing homes, thus increasing demand for Kerry's windows. The result of these economic forces is that KWS is growing very fast. Another factor affecting KWS is that the business is very seasonal, as the building and remodeling season is limited to those months with good weather. KWS's manufacturing process is year-round, but its sales are seasonal. As the company grows, this means negative cash flows at certain times of the year. KWS management is particularly concerned about maintaining its product lines, and this must be done in a business environment in which available credit is hard to find, a consequence of the mortgage loan losses at many financial institutions in recent years. The owners of this business will use a comprehensive budgeting system to facilitate planning and decision making for KWS. A discussion of the five steps the company will take follows.

The Five Steps of Strategic Decision Making for Kerry Window Systems, Inc.

1. **Determine the strategic issues surrounding the problem.** KWS operates in an industry that is very competitive and seasonal. Cash-flow management is a common issue in the industry, particularly for fast-growing companies. Cost-cutting measures would damage the KWS brand at this stage of the company's growth, so the company depends on financing from a variety of sources.

2. **Identify the alternative actions.** The company can raise financing through additional short- or long-term debt, or the sale of stock.

3. **Obtain information and conduct analyses of the alternatives.** The company's stock price has remained steady in the prior several months, reflecting in part the market's overall concern for the industry and uncertainty about the degree of success that will be achieved by KWS's recent growth. The availability for debt is limited by the current poor conditions in the banking industry.

4. **Based on strategy and analysis, choose and implement the desired alternative.** KWS is in a difficult situation regarding cash-flow management. The use of the master budget, paying *particular attention* to the cash budget, is crucial for the company's continued success. Forecasting sales and costs, using the tools explained in Chapter 8, is also particularly important for KWS. With accurate budgets, the company thinks it will be able to more effectively project cash needs and have a plan in place for providing the needed financing when necessary. Comprehensive and carefully prepared financial plans and cash budgets are great tools to have in approaching a bank for financing; these tools can help the company make its case for the needed financing.

5. **Provide an ongoing evaluation of the effectiveness of implementation in step 4.** As the company matures and its growth rate slows, and as conditions in the banking industry improve, the focus on financing can shift to other issues, such as advancing and protecting the company's competitive position in the market, improving profitability, and developing effective management and control systems.

In the next section of this chapter we provide an overview of the master budgeting process for a one-year period for KWS.

Master Budget

LEARNING OBJECTIVE 4

Prepare a master budget and explain the interrelationships among its supporting schedules.

A master budget is a comprehensive budget for a specific period. It consists of a capital budget and a set of interrelated operating and financial budgets. As noted earlier, the capital budget includes budgets to support strategic initiatives, programs, and projects. Exhibit 10.4 delineates the relationships among components of a master budget for a hypothetical manufacturing firm.

Sales Budget

A **sales budget**

shows expected sales in units at their expected selling prices.

Manufacturing and service firms attain their desired goals through sales. Almost all activities of the firm emanate from efforts to attain sales goals and sales growth. For this reason, a sales budget often is regarded as the cornerstone of the entire master budget. The **sales budget** has three components: forecasted sales volume, forecasted sales mix, and budgeted selling prices.

The starting point in preparing a sales budget is the sales forecast. An inaccurate sales forecast can render the entire budget a futile exercise and, when inaccurate, can impose costly expenses to the firm as well as to its suppliers.[8]

Sales forecasting by its nature is, in part, subjective. To reduce subjectivity in forecasts, many firms generate more than one independent sales forecast before preparing the sales budget for the period. The following factors should be considered in sales forecasting:[9]

- Current sales levels and sales trends of the past few years.
- General economic and industry conditions.
- Competitors' actions and operating plans.
- Pricing policies.

[8] At the end of its fiscal year on July 29, 2000, Cisco reported $1.2 billion in inventory. The firm reported in early February 2001 that it had inventories of $2.5 billion—an increase of more than 100 percent in six months, despite the fact that Cisco's sales grew only 25 percent during that same period. The increase in inventory led Cisco's suppliers to suffer a similar fate. The inventory of Solectron, one of Cisco's major suppliers, went up from $1.8 billion in February 2000 to $4.5 billion at year-end. Flextronics, another supplier to Cisco, reported increases in inventories from $470 million at the end of 1999 to $1.73 billion at the end of 2000. Much of Solectron's and Flextronics' inventory was intended for Cisco. "Cisco's (sales) forecasts were wrong . . . and these guys are feeling its pain." At a cost of 1 percent per month, the increases in inventory added tremendous financial burdens to these firms and increased Cisco's costs. Fred Vogelstein, "Valley Talk Missed Earnings: The Contagion is Spreading and Oracle may be Next," *Fortune*, March 5, 2001, p. 42.

[9] *Time* magazine attributes the use of an advanced data mining system to perform sales forecasting as one reason for Wal-Mart's success. "By analyzing years' worth of sales data—and then cranking in variables such as the weather and school schedules—the [advanced data mining] system could predict the optimal number of cases of Gatorade, in which flavors and sizes, a store in Laredo, Texas, should have on hand on Friday before Labor Day. Then, if the weather forecast suddenly called for temperatures 5° hotter than last year, the delivery truck would automatically show up with more." Bill Saporito, "Can Wal-Mart Get Any Bigger?" *Time*, January 13, 2003, p. 43.

EXHIBIT 10.4
The Master Budget for a Manufacturer

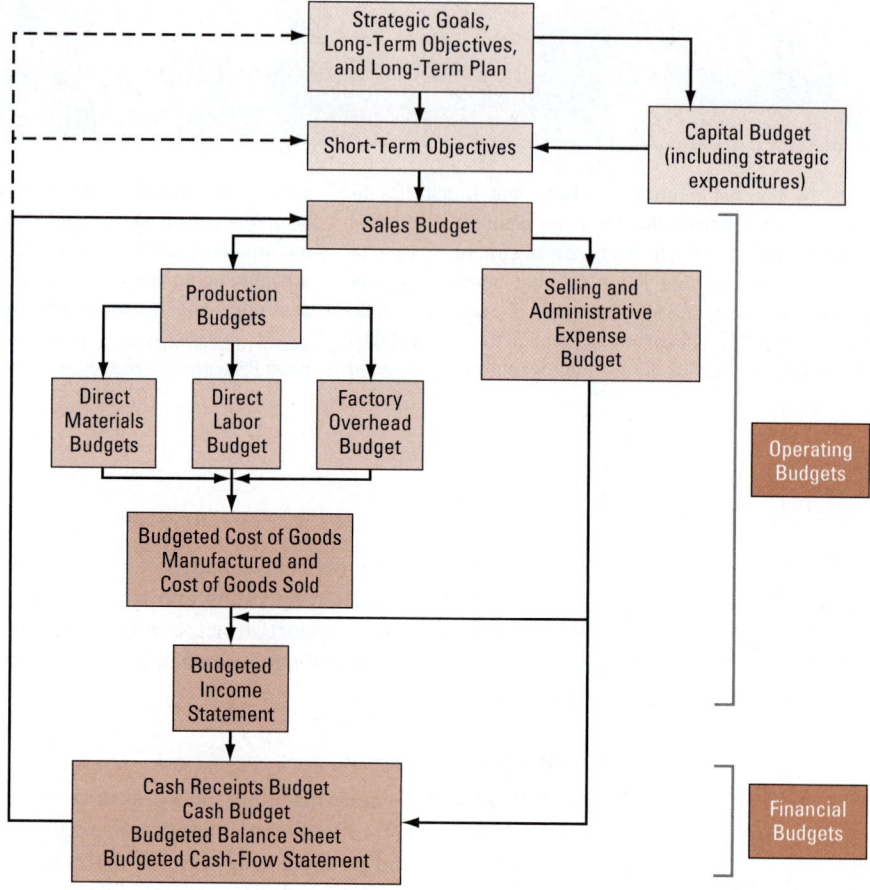

EXHIBIT 10.5
Sales Budget

KERRY WINDOW SYSTEMS, INC. Sales Budget For the Quarter Ended June 30, 2010				
	April	**May**	**June**	**Quarter**
Sales in units	20,000	25,000	35,000	80,000
Selling price per unit	× $30	× $30	× $30	× $30
Gross sales revenue	**$600,000**	**$750,000**	**$1,050,000**	**$2,400,000**

- Credit policies.
- Advertising and promotional activities.
- Unfilled back orders.

Exhibit 10.5 illustrates the sales budget for Kerry Window System, Inc. for the first quarter of the 2010 fiscal year. After examining its sales forecast for the coming year, operating results of the year to date, strategic goals, long-range plans for the firm and the product, and the budget guidelines, Kerry forecasts the sales levels shown and a selling price of $30 per unit. It then prepares its manufacturing budgets for the quarter.

Manufacturing Budgets

Production Budget

A **production budget**
shows planned production for a
given period.

A **production budget** shows planned production for a given period. For manufacturers, planned production in a given period depends on budgeted sales, the desired units of finished goods ending inventory, and the units of finished goods beginning inventory, as described in the following equation:

$$
\begin{array}{ccccc}
\text{Budgeted} & \text{Budgeted} & & \text{Desired ending} & \text{Beginning} \\
\text{production} = & \text{sales} & + & \text{inventory} & - & \text{inventory} \\
\text{(in units)} & \text{(in units)} & & \text{(in units)} & \text{(in units)}
\end{array}
$$

To illustrate, Kerry expects to have 5,000 units on hand at the beginning of the quarter, April 1. The firm's policy is to have on hand at the end of each month inventory equal to 30 percent of the following month's predicted sales. Kerry expects its total sales in May 2010 to be 25,000 units. The desired ending inventory on April 30, therefore, is 7,500 units, as shown in step 1. Step 2 shows that 22,500 units are to be manufactured in April.

Step 1. Determine the desired ending inventory (April 30):

Expected sales in May	25,000 units
× Desired percentage of next month's sales to be on hand on April 30	× 30%
Desired ending inventory (April 30)	7,500 units

Step 2. Calculate budgeted production for April:

Budgeted sales for April	20,000 units
+ Desired ending inventory (April 30)	+ 7,500 units
Total number of units needed in April	27,500 units
− Beginning inventory (April 1)	− 5,000 units
Budgeted production for April	22,500 units

Exhibit 10.6 shows Kerry's production budget for the first quarter of 2010. This budget is based on the sales budget (Exhibit 10.5) and the expected sales in July (40,000, assumed).

Most of the quarterly amounts are simply the sums of the appropriate monthly figures. For example, in Exhibit 10.5 the budgeted sales for the quarter, 80,000 units, is the sum of the budgeted sales in April (20,000 units), May (25,000 units), and June (35,000 units). The desired ending inventory of the quarter, however, is the desired ending inventory of June, the end of the quarter, not the sum of the desired ending amount in each of the three months. The amount of beginning inventory for the quarter is the beginning inventory of the first month of the quarter. These two amounts refer to specific times in the quarter, not the amount for the entire period.

Before finalizing a production budget, the production manager reviews the feasibility of the budgeted production in view of the available facilities and other activities scheduled for the same period. In the event that budgeted production exceeds the maximum capacity available, management needs to either revise the budgeted sales level or find alternatives to satisfy the demand. If the available capacity exceeds the budgeted production level, the budget allows management ample time to find alternative uses of the idle capacity or to schedule other activities such as preventive maintenance and trial runs of new production processes. This ability to coordinate sales needs and production activities is another benefit of having a budget that allows firms to identify mismatches between capacity and output.

The sales budget for the quarter shows that Kerry expects increasing sales. When sales vary over periods, management can either change the production level as needed, as Kerry did, or choose to maintain a stable production level and schedule the entire quarter's production evenly at 29,000 units per month.

Maintaining a constant production level enables the firm to keep a constant employment level. However, manufacturing excess units during slow periods builds up inventory that is costly to hold. The new manufacturing environment and increasing use of just-in-time (JIT) production-scheduling methods have led many companies to adjust production activity to changes in anticipated sales volume (and mix). JIT requires a more flexible workforce with broader skills to move the employee to the work center needed for immediate production. As well, JIT involves deploying relatively more temporary and contract laborers to match labor supply with the short-term demand for products and services.

Direct Materials Usage Budget and Direct Materials Purchases Budget

A **direct materials usage budget** shows the amount and budgeted cost of direct materials required for production.

The information in the production budget becomes the basis for preparing several manufacturing-related budgets. One is the **direct materials usage budget** (Exhibit 10.7), which shows the amount and budgeted cost of direct materials required for production. The last line of the production budget (Exhibit 10.6) shows the number of units of the product that Kerry plans to manufacture in April: 22,500 units. This amount is reflected in line 1 of Exhibit 10.7, Kerry's direct materials usage budget. Assume that the product specification requires 3 pounds of aluminum alloy for each unit of the product, which is entered into line 2 of Exhibit 10.7. Therefore, Kerry needs a total of 67,500 pounds of aluminum (line 3) to produce the 22,500 units budgeted in April. The remainder of the direct materials usage budget (Exhibit 10.7, part B) identifies the cost of direct materials for the budget period, which can be completed only after Kerry prepares the direct materials purchases budget for the month (Exhibit 10.7). Finally, assume that Kerry uses a FIFO cost-flow assumption.

A **direct materials purchases budget**
shows the physical amount and cost of planned purchases of direct materials.

A **direct materials purchases budget** shows the amount of direct materials, such as raw materials or component parts, to be purchased during the period (in both units and cost) to meet the production and ending materials inventory requirements. A direct materials purchases budget starts with the amount of direct materials needed in production for the current period, which was determined in Line 3 of Exhibit 10.7. Kerry needs 67,500, 84,000, and 109,500 pounds of aluminum alloy to meet the production needs for April, May, and June, respectively.

The firm's policy is to have in ending materials inventory each period an amount equal to 10 percent of the next period's production needs (line 2). Line 3 of Exhibit 10.7 shows that the firm needs 84,000 pounds of aluminum alloy for the budgeted production in May. Thus, the firm needs to maintain 8,400 pounds of aluminum alloy on hand at the end of April (10% of 84,000), as shown in line 2 of Exhibit 10.8. (Assume that direct materials needed for production in July = 108,000 lbs.) The sum of lines 1 and 2 (Exhibit 10.8) is the total amount of direct materials needed for April, 75,900 pounds.

Kerry expects to have 7,000 pounds of aluminum alloy on hand at the beginning of April (March's ending inventory). Subtracting the quantity expected to be on hand on April 1 from the total amount needed for April, we see that Kerry must purchase 68,900 pounds in April

EXHIBIT 10.6
Production Budget

KERRY WINDOW SYSTEMS, INC. Production Budget For the Quarter Ended June 30, 2010				
	April	**May**	**June**	**Quarter**
Budgeted sales (units)	20,000	25,000	35,000	80,000
Add: Desired ending inventory of finished units	7,500	10,500	12,000*	12,000
Total units needed	27,500	35,500	47,000	92,000
Less: Beginning inventory of finished units	5,000†	7,500	10,500	5,000
Budgeted production (units)	**22,500**	**28,000**	**36,500**	**87,000**

* Assumed, based on anticipated sales in July.
† Assumed.

EXHIBIT 10.7 Direct Materials Usage Budget

KERRY WINDOW SYSTEMS, INC.
Direct Materials Usage Budget
For the Quarter Ended June 30, 2010

Line	Item	April	May	June	Quarter	Calculation
A.	**Production Requirements**					
1.	Budgeted production	22,500	28,000	36,500	87,000	*
2.	Pounds of aluminum alloy for one unit of product	× 3	× 3	× 3	× 3	
3.	**Total pounds of aluminum alloy needed in production**	67,500	84,000	109,500	261,000	
B.	**Cost of Direct Materials**					
4.	Pounds of aluminum alloy from beginning inventory	7,000	8,400	10,950	7,000	
5.	Cost per pound (FIFO basis)	× $ 2.40	× $ 2.45	× $ 2.50	× $ 2.40	
6.	Total cost of aluminum alloy beginning inventory	$ 16,800	$ 20,580	$ 27,375	$ 16,800	(4) × (5)
7.	Total cost of aluminum alloy purchases	+ 168,805	+ 216,375	+ 284,310	+ 669,490	†
8.	Total cost of aluminum alloy available	$185,605	$236,955	$311,685	$686,290	(6) + (7)
9.	Desired ending inventory of aluminum alloy in units	8,400	10,950	10,800‡	10,800	†
10.	Cost per unit (FIFO basis)	× $ 2.45	× $ 2.50	× $ 2.60	× $ 2.60	†
11.	Aluminum alloy ending inventory	− $ 20,580	− $ 27,375	− $ 28,080	− $ 28,080	(9) × (10)
12.	**Total cost of aluminum alloy used in production**	$165,025	$209,580	$283,605	$658,210	(8) − (11)

* = Exhibit 10.6
† = Exhibit 10.8
‡ = Assumed

(line 5 of Exhibit 10.8) to meet the expected needs in April. These steps summarize the calculations in Exhibit 10.8:

Total amount of direct materials needed in production during the month	Line 1
+ Required direct materials inventory at the end of the month	+ Line 2
= Total direct materials needed for the month	= Line 3
− Direct materials on hand at the beginning of the month	− Line 4
= Direct materials to be purchased during the month	= Line 5

Kerry's purchasing department estimates the cost of aluminum alloy to be $2.45 per pound in April. Thus, the total cost for the 68,900 pounds to be purchased in April is $168,805, as shown in line 7 of Exhibit 10.8.

At the beginning of April, assume that Kerry has on hand 7,000 pounds of aluminum alloy. At a cost of $2.40 per pound, the total cost of the beginning inventory is $16,800 (Exhibit 10.7, line 6). Adding the purchase cost of $168,805 in April (line 7 of Exhibit 10.8), the total cost of the direct materials available in April is $185,605 (line 8 of Exhibit 10.7). Under FIFO, Kerry's cost of ending inventory in April is priced at the most recent purchase price paid, which is $2.45 per pound, or $20,580 (line 11). Subtracting the cost of ending inventory, $20,580, from the total cost of direct materials available, $185,605, the total cost of direct materials to be used in April is $165,025 (line 12).

Following the same procedure, Kerry completes the purchase budgets for May and June. June's direct materials ending inventory of 10,800 pounds is based on the 36,000 units to be

EXHIBIT 10.8
Direct Materials Purchases
Budget

	KERRY WINDOW SYSTEMS, INC.				
	Direct Materials Purchases Budget				
	For the Quarter Ended June 30, 2010				
Line	Item	April	May	June	Quarter
1.	Total direct materials needed in production (from part A of Exhibit 10.7), in lbs.	67,500	84,000	109,500	261,000
2.	Add: Desired direct materials ending inventory +	8,400 +	10,950 +	10,800* +	10,800
3.	Total direct materials needed	75,900	94,950	120,300	271,800
4.	Less: Direct materials beginning inventory −	7,000 −	8,400 −	10,950 −	7,000
5.	**Total direct materials purchases**	68,900	86,550	109,350	264,800
6.	Purchase price per pound	× $ 2.45	× $ 2.50	× $ 2.60	
7.	**Total cost of direct materials purchases**	**$168,805**	**$216,375**	**$284,310**	**$669,490†**

* Assumed, based on estimated production in July.
† $669,490 = $168,805 + $216,375 + $284,310

manufactured in July (3 pounds per unit × 36,000 (assumed units) = 108,000 pounds and 10% × 108,000 = 10,800 pounds).

Direct Labor Budget

To prepare the direct labor budget, Kerry would take information from its production budget. Each firm needs a requisite number of employees with the required skills to carry out production activity, as budgeted. The direct labor budget enables the personnel department to plan for hiring and repositioning of employees. A good labor budget helps the firm avoid emergency hiring, prevent labor shortages, and reduce or eliminate the need to lay off workers.

Some firms have stable employment policies or labor contracts that prevent them from hiring and laying off employees in direct proportion to their production needs. A direct labor budget enables the firm to identify circumstances when it can either reschedule production or plan temporary employee reassignments to perform other tasks. Manufacturing cells common to many firms that adopt new manufacturing technologies often use the direct labor budget to plan for maintenance, minor repairs, installation, testing, learning and growth, or other activities.

A company usually prepares a direct labor budget for each type (or class) of labor; for instance, Kerry has skilled and semiskilled factory workers. The production process uses 0.5 hour of semiskilled labor and 0.2 hour of skilled labor for each unit. The hourly wages are $8 and $12 for semiskilled and skilled laborers, respectively. Exhibit 10.9 illustrates the direct labor budget for the first quarter of 2010.

Factory Overhead Budget

A factory overhead budget includes all production costs other than direct materials and direct labor. Some firms, such as Kerry, separate factory overhead into variable and fixed costs. Exhibit 10.10 shows Kerry's factory overhead cost budget for the first quarter of 2010. Note that variable overhead cost is assumed related to the number of direct labor-hours (DLH) worked. (For a more accurate budget of factory overhead costs, activity-based budgeting [ABB] procedures can be used. ABB is discussed later in this chapter.)

Cost of Goods Manufactured and Sold Budget

The cost of goods manufactured and the cost of goods sold budgets are then prepared. Exhibits 10.6 through 10.10 provide the data needed to complete these budgets for each of the months and for the quarter. Exhibit 10.11 shows a combined cost of goods manufactured and sold budget for the first quarter of 2010 for Kerry. The company's finished goods inventory on April 1 shows a unit cost of $18.

EXHIBIT 10.9
Direct Labor Budget

KERRY WINDOW SYSTEMS, INC.
Direct Labor Budget
For the Quarter Ended June 30, 2010

Line		April	May	June	Quarter
	Semiskilled Labor				
1.	Budgeted production (Exhibit 10.6)	22,500	28,000	36,500	87,000
2.	Semiskilled direct labor-hours per unit	× 0.5 ×	0.5 ×	0.5 ×	0.5
3.	Total semiskilled direct labor-hours needed	11,250	14,000	18,250	43,500
4.	Hourly wage rate of semiskilled labor	× $8 ×	$8 ×	$8 ×	$8
5.	Total wages for semiskilled labor	$ 90,000	$112,000	$146,000	$348,000
	Skilled Labor				
6.	Budgeted production (Exhibit 10.6)	22,500	28,000	36,500	87,000
7.	Skilled direct labor-hours per unit	× 0.2 ×	0.2 ×	0.2 ×	0.2
8.	Total skilled direct labor-hours needed	4,500	5,600	7,300	17,400
9.	Hourly wage for skilled labor	× $12 ×	$12 ×	$12 ×	$12
10.	Total wages for skilled labor	$ 54,000	$ 67,200	$ 87,600	$208,800
11.	**Total cost for direct manufacturing labor (5 + 10)**	**$144,000**	**$179,200**	**$233,600**	**$556,800**
12.	Total direct manufacturing labor-hours (3 + 8)	15,750	19,600	25,550	60,900

Information from the cost of goods manufactured and cost of goods sold budgets for a period appear in two other budgets for the same period. The budgeted income statement uses the cost of goods sold figure to determine the gross margin for the period, and the balance sheet includes the finished goods ending inventory in total assets. These two pro forma financial statements are discussed later.

EXHIBIT 10.10
Factory Overhead Budget

KERRY WINDOW SYSTEMS, INC.
Factory Overhead Budget
For the Quarter Ended June 30, 2010

	Rate Per DLH*	April	May	June	Quarter
Total direct labor-hours (Exhibit 10.9)		15,750	19,600	25,550	60,900
Variable factory overhead:					
Supplies	$0.12	$ 1,890	$ 2,352	$ 3,066	$ 7,308
Indirect labor	1.00	15,750	19,600	25,550	60,900
Fringe benefits	3.00	47,250	58,800	76,650	182,700
Power	0.20	3,150	3,920	5,110	12,180
Maintenance	0.08	1,260	1,568	2,044	4,872
Total variable factory overhead	$4.40	$ 69,300	$ 86,240	$ 112,420	$ 267,960
Fixed factory overhead:					
Depreciation		$ 30,000	$ 30,000	$ 40,000†	$ 100,000
Factory insurance		2,500	2,500	2,500	7,500
Property taxes		900	900	900	2,700
Supervision		8,900	8,900	8,900	26,700
Power		1,250	1,250	1,250	3,750
Maintenance		750	750	750	2,250
Total fixed factory overhead		$ 44,300	$ 44,300	$ 54,300	$ 142,900
Total factory overhead		$113,600	$ 130,540	$ 166,720	$ 410,860
Less: Depreciation		30,000	30,000	40,000	100,000
Cash disbursements for factory overhead		$ 83,600	$ 100,540	$ 126,720	$ 310,860

* Direct labor-hour.
† Kerry purchased equipment in January for $200,000, to be delivered and installed in May (see item 5 on page 384). Exhibit 10.10 includes one month of depreciation expense for this asset (June).

EXHIBIT 10.11
Cost of Goods Manufactured
and Cost of Goods Sold Budget

KERRY WINDOW SYSTEMS, INC.
Cost of Goods Manufactured and Cost of Goods Sold Budget
For the Quarter Ended June 30, 2010

	April	May	June	Quarter
Direct materials (Line 12, Exhibit 10.7)	$165,025	$209,580	$283,605	$ 658,210
Direct labor (Line 11, Exhibit 10.9)	144,000	179,200	233,600	556,800
Total factory overhead (Exhibit 10.10)	113,600	130,540	166,720	410,860
Total cost of goods manufactured	$422,625	$519,320	$683,925	$1,625,870
Finished goods beginning inventory	90,000*	140,875	194,745	90,000
Total cost of goods available for sale	$512,625	$660,195	$878,670	$1,715,870
Finished goods ending inventory†	140,875	194,745	224,852	224,852
Cost of goods sold	**$371,750**	**$465,450**	**$653,818**	**$1,491,018**

* Finished goods beginning inventory, April 1, 5,000 units (Exhibit 10.6, p. 376) at $18 per unit.
† Computations for cost per unit and finished goods ending inventory (FIFO basis):

Cost of goods manufactured		$422,625	$519,320	$683,925
Budgeted production (Exhibit 10.6, last line)	÷	22,500	÷ 28,000	÷ 36,500
Manufacturing cost per unit		$18.7833	$18.5471	$18.7377
Desired ending inventory (Exhibit 10.6, line 2)	×	7,500	× 10,500	× 12,000
Finished goods ending inventory, FIFO basis		$140,875	$194,745	$224,852

Merchandise Purchases Budget

A merchandising firm does not have a production budget; instead, it prepares a merchandise purchases budget. A firm's **merchandise purchases budget** shows the amount of merchandise it needs to purchase during the period. The basic format of a merchandise purchases budget is the same as the production budget. Instead of budgeted production as shown in Exhibit 10.6, however, the last items in a merchandise purchases budget are budgeted purchases.

Selling and General Administrative Expense Budget

The selling and general administrative expense budget is then prepared. As shown in Exhibit 10.12, Kerry's selling and general administrative expense budget for the first quarter of 2010 includes all the planned expenditures for selling and general administrative expenses. This budget serves as a guideline for selling and administrative activities during the budget period.

Many selling and general administrative expenditures are the result of sales and marketing activities and programs. Firms are known to reduce or eliminate selling and administrative expenses to increase operating income for the period. For example, in an attempt to increase operating income and to show good control of operating expenses, the manager of a retail business proposes to decrease customer service expenditures by $15 million from $20 million to $5 million. Although reduced customer services are likely to lead to decreases in sales, the budgeted total saving in expenditures exceeds the budgeted decrease in earnings for the year and the firm expects its budgeted operating income for the year to increase by $11 million as a result. Decreases in customer services, however, will likely have negative effects on the firm's reputation as well as its future sales.

Note that we have subdivided the total selling and administrative expense budget into *total expenses* (for income statement purposes) and *total cash expenses* (for preparing the cash budget for the period). Noncash expenses for Kerry include estimated bad-debts expense (assumed equal to 5 percent of sales made on open account) plus depreciation expense. Thus, in April total budgeted noncash expenses amount to $36,000, as follows: estimated bad-debts expense, $9,000; depreciation expense—selling, $20,000; and, depreciation expense—administrative, $7,000.

EXHIBIT 10.12   Selling and General Administrative Expense Budget

KERRY WINDOW SYSTEMS, INC.
Selling and General Administrative Expense Budget
For the Quarter Ended June 30, 2010

	April	May	June	Quarter
Selling expenses				
Variable selling expenses:				
Sales commissions (given)	$ 30,000	$ 37,500	$ 52,500	$120,000
Delivery expenses (given)	2,000	2,500	3,500	8,000
Bad debts expense (allowance method)*	9,000	11,250	15,750	36,000
Total variable selling expenses	$ 41,000	$ 51,250	$ 71,750	$164,000
Fixed selling expenses:				
Sales salaries (given)	$ 8,000	$ 8,000	$ 8,000	$ 24,000
Advertising (given)	50,000	50,000	50,000	150,000
Delivery expenses (given)	6,000	6,000	6,000	18,000
Depreciation (given)	20,000	20,000	20,000	60,000
Total fixed selling expenses	$ 84,000	$ 84,000	$ 84,000	$252,000
Total selling expenses	$125,000	$135,250	$155,750	$416,000
Administrative expenses (all fixed)				
Administrative salaries	$ 25,000	$ 25,000	$ 25,000	$ 75,000
Accounting and data processing	12,000	12,000	12,000	36,000
Depreciation	7,000	7,000	7,000	21,000
Other administrative expenses	6,000	6,000	6,000	18,000
Total administrative expenses	$ 50,000	$ 50,000	$ 50,000	$150,000
Total selling and administrative expenses	**$175,000**	**$185,250**	**$205,750**	**$566,000**
Less: noncash expenses (bad debts expense + depreciation)	$ 36,000	$ 38,250	$ 42,750	$117,000
Cash disbursements for selling and administrative expenses	**$139,000**	**$147,000**	**$163,000**	**$449,000**

* Estimated bad debts = gross sales in a month × 30% × 5%:

Gross sales (Exhibit 10.5)	$600,000	$750,000	$1,050,000	$2,400,000
% credit sales in a month	30%	30%	30%	30%
estimated % of credit sales that are uncollectible	5%	5%	5%	5%
estimated B/D expense	$9,000	$11,250	$15,750	$36,000

Cash Receipts (Collections) Budget

The cash receipts budget provides details regarding anticipated collections of cash from operations for an upcoming period. Cash receipts from investing and financing activities are shown elsewhere on the cash budget. Kerry has three different sources of cash receipts from operations: (1) cash sales, (2) bank credit-card sales, and (3) collection of credit sales (i.e., sales made by the company on "open account").

Past history indicates that, on average, cash plus bank credit-card sales for Kerry represent 70 percent of gross sales revenue; the balance each month is credit sales to customers on open account. Kerry estimates that the breakdown between cash and bank credit-card sales is 60%/40% (60% cash). The bank charges a 3 percent service fee to process credit-card sales. In the cash receipts budget, estimated collections of bank credit-card sales are reflected *net* of this service fee.

In terms of credit sales, Kerry e-mails invoices to its customers on the first of each month. Credit terms are 2/10, n/eom. This means that customers who pay within 10 days receive a 2 percent discount; otherwise, the account is due on or before the end of the month (eom). *(Discounts for early payment of credit sales are recorded on the income statement as deductions from gross sales to arrive at net sales.)* These customers can access their accounts anytime on Kerry's Web site to find out the status of their accounts. Eighty percent of these customers pay within the month; of these, 60 percent pay within the discount period. Seventy-five percent of the remaining balances at the end of the month pay within the following month. The remaining accounts are likely bad debts. (As indicated previously, the company uses the allowance method to account for bad-debts expense. *Bad-debts expense is included on the income statement as a noncash component of variable selling expenses.*) Most payments are made via electronic transfer of funds.

Gross sales revenue was $400,000 in February and $450,000 in March of 2010.

Given the preceding information, and the gross sales revenues reported in Exhibit 10.5, the accountant for Kerry can now prepare the cash receipts budget for the quarter ended June 30, 2010 (see Exhibit 10.13). Information from the last line of this budget is then incorporated into the cash budget for the quarter.

Cash Budget

A cash budget depicts effects on cash of all budgeted activities.

Having adequate cash on hand at all times is crucial for a business's survival and growth. A **cash budget** brings together the cash effects of all budgeted activities. A cash budget depicts the firm's cash position during the budget period. By preparing a cash budget, management can take steps to ensure having sufficient cash on hand to carry out the planned activities, allow sufficient time to arrange for additional financing that may be needed during the budget period (and thus avoid high costs of emergency borrowing), and plan for investments of excess cash on hand to earn the highest possible return. For smaller firms and those with seasonal business, the cash budget is especially critical to ensuring smooth operations and avoiding crises.

A cash budget includes all items that affect cash flows and pulls data from almost all parts of the master budget. Preparing a cash budget requires a careful review of all budgets to identify all revenues, expenses, and other transactions that affect cash. A cash budget generally includes three major sections: (1) net cash flows from *operating activities*; (2) net cash flows from *investing activities*; and (3) net cash flows from *financing activities*.

The cash budget can thus be prepared to parallel the statement of cash flows that is prepared for financial-reporting purposes. This statement (and related budget) provides information about how the company generated cash (so the reader can judge whether those sources

EXHIBIT 10.13 **Cash Receipts Budget—Operating Activities**

KERRY WINDOW SYSTEMS, INC. Cash Receipts Budget—Operating Activities For the Quarter Ended June 30, 2010					
Sales Data	**March**	**April**	**May**	**June**	**Quarter**
Cash and bank credit card sales (70% of total sales)	$315,000	$420,000	$525,000	$ 735,000	$1,680,000
Credit sales (30% of total sales)	135,000	180,000	225,000	315,000	720,000
Gross sales revenue (Exhibit 10.5)	$450,000	$600,000	$750,000	$1,050,000	$2,400,000
Cash received from cash sales (60% of cash plus bank credit card sales)		$252,000	$315,000	$441,000	$1,008,000
Cash received from bank credit card sales (40% of cash and bank credit card sales × 97%)		162,960	203,700	285,180	651,840
Collections of accounts receivable: From credit sales the month before this month: Within cash discount period (Prior month's credit sales × 80% × 60% × 98%)		63,504	84,672	105,840	254,016
After the cash discount period (Prior month's credit sales × 80% × 40%)		43,200	57,600	72,000	172,800
From credit sales two months before this month (75% of 20% of credit sales two months prior)		18,000	20,250	27,000	65,250
Total cash receipts, net of bank service charge (3%)		**$539,664**	**$681,222**	**$931,020**	**$2,151,906**

are predictable or transitory), and what the company did with the cash it had at its disposal. In short, the cash budget (and related statement of cash flows) provides the user with information regarding the cash-management ability of the company.

Cash flows from operating activities reflect cash flows from the company's transactions and events related to its main operating activity. Cash flows from investing activities provide information regarding the net cash effect of acquisitions and divestitures of investments and long-term assets. Cash flows from financing activities provide information regarding the net effect of issuances of, payments toward, and retirements of borrowings (debt) and equity.

Exhibit 10.14 shows the cash budget of Kerry for the quarter ended June 30, 2010. In addition to reviewing the information illustrated in Exhibits 10.5 through 10.13 to identify items that involve either cash inflow or cash outflow, management must gather additional information about the firm's operating characteristics and policies to complete the cash budget.

EXHIBIT 10.14   Cash Budget

	April	May	June	Quarter
KERRY WINDOW SYSTEMS, INC. Cash Budget For the Quarter Ended June 30, 2010				
Cash balance, beginning of period	$ 75,000	$ 84,781	$ 91,916	$ 75,000
Cash flow from operations:				
Operating cash inflows (cash receipts from cash sales, credit-card sales, and collections of accounts receivable, Exhibit 10.13)	$539,664	$681,222	$ 931,020	$2,151,906
Operating cash outflows:				
Purchases of direct materials:				
From current month purchases (60% of current month's purchases, Exhibit 10.8)	$101,283	$129,825	$ 170,586	$ 401,694
From purchases made last month (40% of last month's purchases, Exhibit 10.8)	62,000*	67,522	86,550	216,072
Total cash payments for direct material purchases	$163,283	$197,347	$ 257,136	$ 617,766
Direct labor (Exhibit 10.9, line 11)	144,000	179,200	233,600	556,800
Factory overhead (Exhibit 10.10, last line)	83,600	100,540	126,720	310,860
Selling and administrative expenses (Exhibit 10.12, last line)	139,000	147,000	163,000	449,000
Net cash flow from operations	$ 9,781	$ 57,135	$ 150,564	$ 217,480
Investing activities:				
Equipment purchase	$ -0-	$200,000	$ -0-	$ 200,000
Cash balance before financing activities	$ 84,781	$ (58,084)	$ 242,480	$ 92,480
Financing activities:				
Bank borrowing beginning of month		$150,000		$ 150,000
Payments (i.e. cash outflows):				
Repayment of principal (end of month)			(150,000)	(150,000)
Interest (end of month; 1% per month)			(1,500)	(1,500)
Net effect of financing activities	$ 0	$150,000	$ (151,500)	$ (1,500)
Ending cash balance	$ 84,781	$ 91,916	$ 90,980	$ 90,980

* March purchases = $155,000 (assumed)

The following are relevant operating characteristics and policies of Kerry that affect the availability of cash or the requirement to expend cash during the budget period:

1. The firm expects to have $75,000 cash on hand on April 1 and has a requirement of maintaining a minimum cash balance of $50,000 each month.
2. Kerry purchases direct materials with a term of n/30. The firm pays 60 percent of its purchases in the month of purchase and the remainder in the following month.
3. All expenses and wages are paid as incurred.
4. The firm purchased $155,000 of direct materials in March.
5. Equipment purchased in January for $200,000 will be delivered in May, terms COD. Depreciation deductions will commence in June.
6. The firm has a revolving 30-day account at 1 percent per month with the First National Bank for all temporary financing needs. The account must be drawn in increments of $50,000 with repayment occurring no sooner than 30 days. All borrowings take place at the beginning of the month while repayments (and interest payments) occur at the end of the month.

Budgeted Income Statement

The budgeted (pro forma) income statement describes the expected net income for an upcoming period. In the event that the budgeted income for the period falls short of the prespecified goal, management can investigate, during the budget-negotiation process, actions to improve operating results.

Once the budgeted income statement has been approved, it can be used as the benchmark against which the performance of the period is evaluated. Exhibits 10.5, 10.11, and 10.12 provide information needed to prepare the budgeted income statement for the period (Exhibit 10.15).

Budgeted Balance Sheet

The last step in a budget-preparation cycle usually is to prepare the budgeted (pro forma) balance sheet. The starting point in preparing a budgeted balance sheet is the expected financial position at the beginning of the budget period. Exhibit 10.16 presents the expected balance sheet as of March 31, 2010, the beginning of the current budget period.

The budgeted balance sheet incorporates the effects of all operations and cash flows during the budget period and shows projected balances at the end of the budget period. Exhibit 10.17

EXHIBIT 10.15
Budgeted Income Statement

KERRY WINDOW SYSTEMS, INC.
Budgeted Income Statement
For the Quarter Ended June 30, 2010

	April	May	June	Quarter
Gross sales revenue (Exhibit 10.5)	$600,000	$750,000	$1,050,000	$2,400,000
Less: Cash discounts for early payment of credit sales (last month's credit sales × 80% × 60% × 2%)	$ 1,296	$ 1,728	$ 2,160	$ 5,184
Bank service charge (3% of bank credit-card sales)	$ 5,040	$ 6,300	$ 8,820	$ 20,160
Net sales	$593,664	$741,972	$1,039,020	$2,374,656
Less: Cost of goods sold (Exhibit 10.11)	371,750	465,450	653,818	1,491,018
Gross profit	$221,914	$276,522	$ 385,202	$ 883,638
Selling and general administrative expenses (Exhibit 10.12)	175,000	185,250	205,750	566,000
Net operating income	$ 46,914	$ 91,272	$ 179,452	$ 317,638
Less: Interest expense (Exhibit 10.14)	0	0	1,500	1,500
Income before income taxes	$ 46,914	$ 91,272	$ 177,952	$ 316,138
Less: Income taxes (@30%)	14,074	27,382	53,386	94,841
Income after tax	**$ 32,840**	**$ 63,890**	**$ 124,566**	**$ 221,297**

EXHIBIT 10.16
Beginning-of-Budget-Period
Balance Sheet

KERRY WINDOW SYSTEMS, INC.
Balance Sheet
March 31, 2010

Assets

Current assets:

Cash (Exhibit 10.14)	$ 75,000	
Net accounts receivable*	146,250	
Direct materials inventory (Exhibit 10.7)	16,800	
Finished goods inventory (Exhibit 10.11)	90,000	
Total current assets		$328,050

Plant, property, and equipment:

Land (given)		$ 40,000	
Buildings and equipment, gross	$769,750		
Less: Accumulated depreciation	168,000	601,750	
Total plant, property, and equipment			641,750
Total assets			**$969,800**

Liabilities and Stockholders' Equity

Current liabilities:

Accounts payable (Exhibit 10.14)	$ 62,000	
Income taxes payable	0	
Total liabilities		$ 62,000

Stockholders' equity:

Common stock (given)	$303,300	
Retained earnings (given)	604,500	
Total stockholders' equity		907,800
Total liabilities and stockholders' equity		**$969,800**

* **Net accounts receivable, March 31, 2010:**

Gross accounts receivable:		
From credit sales made in February (20% [a])	$ 24,000	
From credit sales made in March (100% of March's credit sales)	135,000	
Gross accounts receivable, end of March		$159,000
Less: Allowance for doubtful accounts:		
For February's credit sales (5%)	$6,000	
For March's credit sales (5%)	6,750	12,750
Net accounts receivable, March 31, 2010		$146,250

[a] That is, a total of 20% of each month's credit sales will be collected or written off in the second month following the month of sale.

EXHIBIT 10.17
Budgeted Balance Sheet,
June 30, 2010

KERRY WINDOW SYSTEMS, INC.
Budgeted Balance Sheet
June 30, 2010

Assets

Current assets:

Cash (Exhibit 10.14)	$ 90,980	
Net accounts receivable[a]	333,000	
Direct materials inventory (Exhibit 10.7, line 11)	28,080	
Finished goods inventory (Exhibit 10.11)	224,852	
Total current assets		$ 676,912

Plant, property, and equipment:

Land (Exhibit 10.16)		$ 40,000	
Buildings and equipment, gross	$969,750		
Less: Accumulated depreciation[b]	349,000	620,750	
Total plant, property, and equipment			660,750
Total assets			**$1,337,662**

(Continued)

Liabilities and Stockholders' Equity		
Current liabilities:		
Accounts payable[c]	$113,724	
Income-tax payable (Exhibit 10.15)	94,841	
Total liabilities		$ 208,565
Stockholders' equity:		
Common stock (Exhibit 10.16)	$303,300	
Retained earnings[d]	825,797	
Total stockholders' equity		1,129,097
Total liabilities and stockholders' equity		**$1,337,662**

[a] Ending balance of accounts receivable, net of allowance for bad debts:

Gross A/R:		
From sales made in May (20%)	$ 45,000	
From sales made in June (100%)	315,000	$360,000
Less: Allowance for doubtful accounts:		
From May's sales (5%)	$ 11,250	
From June's sales (5%)	15,750	27,000
Net accounts receivable, June 30, 2010		$333,000

[b] Accumulated depreciation, beginning of quarter (Exhibit 10.16) $168,000

Plus: Depreciation expense for the quarter ending June 30, 2010:		
Factory (Exhibit 10.10)	$ 100,000	
Selling (Exhibit 10.12)	60,000	
Administrative (Exhibit 10.12)	21,000	181,000
Accumulated depreciation, June 30, 2010		$349,000

[c] End-of-quarter balance in accounts payable:

Direct material purchases in June (Exhibit 10.8)	$284,310
Payments made in month of purchase (June), 60%	170,586
Accounts payable balance, June 30, 2010	$113,724

[d] End-of-quarter balance in retained earnings:

Beginning-of-quarter balance (Exhibit 10.16)	$604,500
Plus: net income for quarter (Exhibit 10.15)	221,297
Retained earnings balance, June 30, 2010	$825,797

shows the budgeted balance sheet at the end of the budget period. For example, the amount of cash in Exhibit 10.17, $90,980, is taken from the ending cash balance of the cash budget for the period (Exhibit 10.14). The ending balance of direct materials, $28,080, is from Exhibit 10.7. The gross amount for Buildings and Equipment, $969,750, is the sum of the beginning balance in the Building and Equipment account reported in Exhibit 10.16, $769,750, and the purchase of new equipment during the budget period, $200,000, as shown in the cash budget for May and, again, for the quarter (Exhibit 10.14).

Uncertainty and the Budgeting Process

LEARNING OBJECTIVE 5

Deal with uncertainty in the budgeting process.

The preceding section provides an overview of the master budgeting process, which culminates in a set of pro forma (i.e., budgeted) financial statements. As you can imagine, the validity of these statements is directly affected by the accuracy of the forecasted data going into the component budgets. Such data, because they are forecasts, are subject to various levels of uncertainty. Spreadsheet software (such as Excel) can be used to deal with uncertainty associated with the budget-preparation process. This software can be used to perform *what-if analysis* and *sensitivity analysis*. Most integrated budgeting and planning software programs include a module on sensitivity analysis and therefore allow managers to evaluate alternative budgetary plans and scenarios.

What-If Analysis

The intent of what-if analysis is to examine how a change in one or more budgetary items affects another variable or budget of interest. For example, management of Kerry might use Excel to address the following questions:

- What would be the resulting impact on cash flow, or operating income, if management were able to increase product selling price by 8 percent while holding other factors constant?
- What would be the net effect on operating profit if Kerry were to engage in a one-year product-promotion campaign that would increase sales by 20 percent?

- Assume Kerry can invest in a new manufacturing technology. If direct labor costs, as a result of this investment, were to decrease by 8 percent, what would be the net impact on the company's short-term operating income?

- What would be the impact on operating income of a 7 percent increase in raw material costs accompanied by a commensurate percentage increase in selling price per unit?

- What would be the cash-flow impact of investing in a program to better assess the financial wherewithal of potential customers if this investment reduced estimated bad-debt expense by 50 percent?

An example of conducting a what-if analysis for Kerry is presented in Exhibit 10.18.[10] In this simple example the analysis responds to the following question: What would be the impact on the production schedule for each month of the quarter if the targeted ending inventory level were decreased from 30 percent to 20 percent of the following month's projected sales. As can be seen, budgeted production levels for Kerry are relatively insensitive to changes in the targeted level of ending inventory. A similar analysis could be performed in terms of other budgeted items of interest, for example, the effect of the proposed change of targeted ending finished goods inventory on budgeted operating income or on budgeted cash flow from operations.

EXHIBIT 10.18
Results of What-If Analysis

Decision Variable: Targeted Ending Inventory, Finished Goods				
		Budgeted Production (units) (Exhibit 10.6)		
		April	**May**	**June**
Original assumption	30%	22,500	28,000	36,500
Revised assumption	20%	20,000	27,000	36,000
Percentage change	(33)	(11.1%)	(3.6%)	(1.4%)

Sensitivity Analysis

As you might imagine, the pro forma financial statements that are produced as part of the master budgeting process assume a given operating strategy and scenario (state of the economy, level of product demand, achieved selling prices, etc.). Software, such as Excel, can be used to provide information about the sensitivity of the pro forma financial statements to various assumptions made in preparing the component budgets. In fact, one can think of sensitivity analysis as a tool (or method) that budget planners use to determine the extent to which a change in the forecasted value of one or more budgetary inputs affects

EXHIBIT 10.19
Results of Sensitivity Analysis: April 2010

Selling Price per Unit	Sales Volume (units)	Budgeted Net Operating Income	% Change from Master Budget Amount
$25.00	17,500	$(67,877)	(244.6)%
25.00	20,000	(50,746)	(208.2)
25.00	22,500	(33,249)	(170.9)
30.00	17,500	17,575	37.5
30.00	**20,000**	**46,914**	**N/A**
30.00	22,500	76,619	163.3
35.00	17,500	103,028	219.6
35.00	20,000	144,574	308.2
35.00	22,500	186,487	397.5

[10] The Excel spreadsheet containing all of the budgets and the pro forma financial statements from this chapter is available from your instructor. The following tutorials provide guidance for conducting what-if analysis using Excel 2007: *Introduction to What-If Analysis* (office.microsoft.com/en-us/excel/HA102431641033.aspx); *Using Excel to Perform Scenario Analysis* (office.microsoft.com/en-us/excel/HP100726691033.aspx); and *Using Solver to Perform What-If Analysis* (office.microsoft.com/en-us/excel/HA102190021033.aspx).

individual budgets and the set of pro forma financial statements produced as part of the master budgeting process.

An example of sensitivity analysis for Kerry is provided in Exhibit 10.19. Management of the company is unsure about both the level of sales demand and product selling price. In addition to a best-guess estimate (Exhibit 10.5) used to prepare the master budget, management elicits from the marketing manager both high-end (optimistic) and low-end (pessimistic) estimates for both sales volume (in units) and selling price per unit. High-end and low-end estimated selling prices per unit were $35 and $25, respectively, while high-end and low-end estimates of sales volume were 17,500 and 22,500. Exhibit 10.19 provides estimated net operating income for a single month, April 2010, for Kerry under nine different scenarios (that is, combinations of selling price and sales volume). Note that in this analysis all other budgetary inputs (e.g., total fixed costs and variable cost per unit) are held constant.

One of the primary advantages of conducting sensitivity analysis is the ability to isolate risks associated with particular components of operations and to develop contingency plans for dealing with these risks. To the extent that the output variable of interest (operating income, for example) is sensitive to changes in input factors (e.g., sales volume), management needs to know this. The ability to isolate these important factors is the primary planning benefit of performing sensitivity analysis as part of the master budgeting process.

In the present case (Exhibit 10.19), we see significant sensitivity of budgeted net operating income as a function of both sales volume and selling price. In fact, if the realized selling price can be set no higher than $25 per unit, our analysis shows that it is virtually impossible with the current cost structure for Kerry to earn a profit. This situation would prompt managers to develop contingency plans to deal with this less-than-favorable situation. Kerry could complement the analysis reported in Exhibit 10.19 by developing alternative scenarios for any of the budgets presented earlier in the chapter.

Integrated Budgeting and Planning Software

Spreadsheet software, such as Excel, can facilitate the preparation of the master budget. However, the usefulness of spreadsheets in budgeting varies greatly with the abilities of those who develop the component budgets. Furthermore, spreadsheets lack the ability to easily coordinate the budgets of various divisions and therefore render a fragmented budgeting process.

Integrated budgeting and planning software programs now include strategic planning, budgeting, rolling financial forecasts, management reporting, and financial consolidations into one package. The online architecture of most of these programs makes it easy to involve more people in the budgeting process, provide instant feedback to users, and allow constant updates of budgets in response to changing circumstances. The online budgeting-planning capability facilitates communication and enables firms to use both top-down and bottom-up budgeting approaches.

A computer-based budgeting and planning system also facilitates sensitivity analysis. Executives can pose what-if questions, which are easily handled by the software program. For example, a manager can use integrated planning software to test changes in strategic assumptions and different budget scenarios, such as a new hiring plan, a new pricing schedule, a change in the cost of materials, a 10 percent decrease in sales because of a higher-than-expected unemployment in an area, a 5 percent cut in travel expenses across the board, or a supplemental incentive program for high performers. The manager can then see the impact of such changes on operating profit, cash flows, financial position, and so on.

Budgeting in Service Companies

LEARNING OBJECTIVE 6

Identify unique budgeting characteristics of service companies.

Service companies have different operating characteristics, operating environments, and considerations than those of manufacturing and merchandising firms. This section examines special concerns in budgeting for service companies.

Budgeting in Service Industries

Similar to budgeting for manufacturing or merchandising firms, budgeting for service firms consists of an integrated set of plans for an upcoming period. The difference is in the absence of production or merchandise purchase budgets and their ancillary budgets. A service organization achieves its budgeted goals and fulfills its mission through providing services. Therefore, an important focal point in its budgeting is personnel planning. A service firm must ensure that it has personnel with the appropriate skills to perform the services required for the budgeted service revenue.

As an example, AccuTax, Inc., provides tax services to small firms and individuals. It expects to have the following revenues from preparing tax returns for the year ended August 31, 2010:

Tax returns for business firms		$1,000,000
Individual tax returns:		
Simple returns	$1,640,000	
Complex returns	1,200,000	2,840,000
Total revenues		$3,840,000

The firm has 2 partners, 8 senior consultants, and 20 consultants. On average, a partner works 50 hours a week and is paid $250,000 a year. Both senior consultants and consultants are expected to work 40 hours a week and are paid, respectively, $90,000 and $60,000 a year. The annual compensation for supporting staff is $40,000 per full-time equivalent. The number of supporting staff varies with the size of the firm. In general, one staff is needed for every 2 partners, one for every 4 senior consultants, and one for every 10 consultants. After allowing for vacation, sickness, and continuing education days, the weeks per year available to work with clients are 40 weeks for each partner, 45 weeks for each senior consultant, and 48 weeks for each consultant. All partners and senior consultants are full-time employees. The firm estimates the following required staff times for each hour spent to complete a tax return:

	Business Return	Complex Individual	Simple Individual
Partner	0.4 hour	0.1 hour	—
Senior consultant	0.6 hour	0.4 hour	0.1 hour
Consultant	—	0.5 hour	0.9 hour

General and administrative expenses are estimated as $150,000 per year, plus 10 percent of the total payroll. The firm charges $250 per hour for business returns, $100 per hour for individual returns with complicated tax matters, and $50 per hour for simple individual tax returns. The budgeted revenues and the total hours for each of the returns for the coming year are as follows:

	Budgeted Revenue		Hourly Charge Rate		Required Hours
Business returns	$1,000,000	÷	$250	=	4,000
Individual returns:					
Simple returns	$1,640,000	÷	$ 50	=	32,800
Complex returns	$1,200,000	÷	$100	=	12,000
Total					48,800

The following table shows the staff requirements for the budgeted revenue:

	Total Hours	Partner	Senior Consultant	Consultant
Business returns	4,000	1,600	2,400	—
Complex individual returns	12,000	1,200	4,800	6,000
Simple individual returns	32,800	—	3,280	29,520
Total hours	48,800	2,800	10,480	35,520
Hours per week (given)		÷ 50	÷ 40	÷ 40
Number of weeks worth of work		56	262	888
Weeks per year/employee		÷ 40	÷ 45	÷ 48
Number of employees needed		2	6	18.5

The budget shows that AccuTax has sufficient staff to support the expected activity. Assuming AccuTax plans no change in personnel and maintains the same staff level, its budgeted operating income will be $808,000, as shown in Exhibit 10.20.

EXHIBIT 10.20
Budgeted Operating Income with No Change in Staffing

ACCUTAX INC.				
Budgeted Income Statement				
For the year ended August 31, 2010				
Revenue				$3,840,000
Payroll expenses:				
Partners	2 × $ 250,000 =	$ 500,000		
Senior consultants	8 × $ 90,000 =	720,000		
Consultants	20 × $ 60,000 =	1,200,000		
Supporting staff	5 × $ 40,000 =	200,000	2,620,000	
General and administrative expenses	$150,000 + (10% × $2,620,000) =		412,000	
Operating income				$ 808,000

Alternative Budgeting Approaches

LEARNING OBJECTIVE 7

Understand alternative approaches to budgeting (viz., zero-base, activity-based, time-driven activity-based, and kaizen budgeting).

Over the years alternative approaches have been proposed to facilitate budget preparation and improve operations. When used properly these approaches—zero base, activity-based, time-driven activity-based, and kaizen budgeting—improve budget effectiveness.

What complications exist regarding the budgeting process of U.S. multinational companies that have foreign affiliates? According to Milani and Rivera, the following complications exist:

- Foreign exchange rates: These rates affect a multinational business through:
  - Translation exposure—operational performance reviews should be assessed only after the effects of shifting exchange rates are factored out.
  - Transaction exposure—because of transaction exposure, multinationals typically hedge their international cash flows. The additional expenses and transactions associated with the hedging process need to be recognized in the budgeting process.
- Interest rates: Because such changes affect the flow of goods and capital across borders, there is a need to accurately estimate forward exchange rates (at a minimum, such estimations will affect both budgeted sales prices and budgeted purchase costs for raw materials).
- Inflation: Anticipated inflation rates help companies determine real versus nominal rates of return for capital-budgeting purposes.

This information is critical when comparing investment opportunities between different countries.

- Inflation: For financial performance assessment, the effect of inflation (in some cases, hyperinflation) should be recognized by applying the actual inflation rates in the flexible budgeting process before determining revenue and expense variances.
- Capital budgeting: The U.S. company needs to adjust cash flows for fees, royalties, and tax considerations associated with foreign investments.
- Cash budgeting: The finalized budget should incorporate the effects of currency exchange controls (if any).
- Inventory policy: Because of increased risk, inventory investments in foreign affiliates might be larger than for domestic-based operations.

The bottom line is that preparation of budgets for foreign affiliates of U.S. multinationals is more time-consuming, costly, and complicated as compared to budgeting for domestic firms.

Source: K. Milani and J. Rivera, "The Rigorous Business of Budgeting for International Operations," *Management Accounting Quarterly,* Winter 2004, pp. 38–50.

Zero-Base Budgeting (ZBB)

Zero-base budgeting (ZBB)
is a budgeting process that requires managers to prepare budgets from a zero base.

Zero-base budgeting (ZBB) requires managers to prepare budgets each period from a zero base. A typical budgeting process incremental in nature in the sense that it starts with the current budget. The process assumes that most, if not all, current activities and functions will continue into the budget period. The primary focus in a typical budgeting process is on changes to the current operating budget.

In contrast, ZBB allows no activities or functions to be included in the budget unless managers can justify their needs. ZBB requires budgeting teams to perform in-depth reviews of all budget items. Such a budgeting process encourages managers to be aware of activities or functions that have outlived their usefulness or have been a waste of resources.

The amount of work and time needed to perform a true ZBB to all aspects of operations of an organization can be monumental. An organization may find it practically impossible to review and examine all of its activities from the zero-budget level every year. As an alternative, the organization can schedule ZBB periodically or perform ZBB for different divisions each year. For example, the highway department of a state government could adopt a rotating five-year ZBB process. All divisions of the department would be subject to in-depth review of their activities every fifth year, not every year as true ZBB requires, with the process applied to different divisions each year.

Activity-Based Budgeting (ABB)

Activity-based budgeting (ABB)
is a budgeting process based on activities and cost drivers of operations.

Activity-based budgeting (ABB) is an extension of activity-based costing (ABC).[11] ABB starts with the budgeted output and segregates costs required for the budgeted output into homogeneous activity cost pools such as unit, batch, product-sustaining, customer-sustaining, and facility-sustaining activity pools. Traditional budgeting and ABB are conceptually very different. For the majority of organizations, budgeting revolves around the chart-of-accounts structure. As a consequence, costs are budgeted on a departmental basis using descriptive accounts (salaries, depreciation, marketing, etc.). Budgets expressed in these terms tell us little about

---

[11] Chapter 5 discusses activity-based costing (ABC) in detail.

the drivers of success for the organization. ABB attempts to fill this information void by focusing on the activities and associated resources needed to satisfy the projected level of customer demand.

ABB begins by budgeting activity requirements for the upcoming budget period. It then budgets the cost of resources needed to perform the set of budgeted activities. In so doing, a better match of the supply of and the demand for resources is effected. For example, management can budget intelligently for additional resources in specific areas or can plan to redeploy resources from one area of the organization to another. These insights would be difficult, if not impossible, to achieve in a traditional budgeting environment.

Of particular interest to most organizations today is the budgeting for labor (headcount). How does the organization cut costs or manage its human capital when everyone appears fully employed? Which employees are involved in value-added activities, and which employees are performing non-value-added activities? What opportunities are there for re-deploying people to activities within the organization that are value-added and strategically aligned? The application of ABB allows the organization to address these critical issues.

One important by-product of using an ABB planning approach is that managers, who are typically not accountants, can budget for their areas of responsibility in terms that these managers understand. This empowerment can, in turn, lead to more accurate forecasts and, ultimately, to stricter cost control and to tighter strategic alignment.

ABB can be a simple extension of a firm's ABC system that has grouped its costs into activity cost pools. Note, however, that the firm needs to periodically review the appropriateness of its activity cost pools and accuracy of its activity costs. Either internal or external relevant operating factors may have changed and rendered the data from the current ABC system less accurate or irrelevant. For example, management may have decided to increase batch size so that fewer batches and fewer batch-related costs such as setup and materials requisition costs are needed for the budgeted output.

Exhibit 10.21 illustrates an ABB for the factory overhead budget of the quarter ended June 30, 2010, for Kerry Window Systems, Inc. In addition to data used in Exhibit 10.10, the ABB used data given in Part A of Exhibit 10.21.

EXHIBIT 10.21
Factory Overhead Budget Using Activity-Based Budgeting (ABB)

KERRY WINDOW SYSTEMS, INC.
Factory Overhead Budget (Activity-Based Budgeting)
For the Quarter Ended June 30, 2010

	Activity Cost Rate	April	May	June	Quarter
A: Data					
Units of output (Exhibit 10.6)		22,500	28,000	36,500	87,000
Direct labor-hours:					
Semiskilled (Exhibit 10.9, Line 3)		11,250	14,000	18,250	43,500
Skilled (Exhibit 10.9, Line 8)		4,500	5,600	7,300	17,400
Machine-hours (given)		6,650	8,220	10,510	25,380
Number of batches (2,500/batch)		9	11.2	14.6	34.8
Number of products		5	6	7	
B: Activity-Based Budget					
Overhead cost pools:					
Semiskilled-hour-related	$ 0.60	$ 6,750	$ 8,400	$ 10,950	$ 26,100
Skilled-hour-related	$ 0.20	900	1,120	1,460	3,480
Machine-hour-related	$ 3.20	21,280	26,304	33,632	81,216
Batch-related	$ 1,700	15,300	19,040	24,820	59,160
Product-related	$ 5,000	25,000	30,000	35,000	90,000
Facility/per month	$50,000	50,000	50,000	50,000	150,000
Total budgeted factory overhead		$119,230	$134,864	$155,862	$409,956

EXHIBIT 10.22

Traditional versus Activity-Based Budgeting (ABB)

	Traditional Budgeting	Activity-Based Budgeting (ABB)
Budgeting unit	Expressed as the cost of functional areas or spending categories	Expressed as the cost of activities and cost drivers
Focus on	Input resources	High-value-added activities
Orientation	Historical	Continuous improvement and capacity management
Roles of suppliers and customers	Does not formally consider suppliers and customers in budgeting	Coordinates with suppliers and considers the needs of customers
Control objective	Maximize managers' performance	Synchronize activities with level of demand
Budget base	Description accounts in departmental budgets	Value-added versus non-value-added activities

The result of an activity-based costing by Kerry suggests that factory overhead cost varies with hours of semiskilled labor ($0.60 per hour), hours of skilled labor ($0.20 per hour), machine-hours ($3.20 per hour), number of batches ($1,700 per batch), and number of products ($5,000 each). In addition, there is a $50,000 facility-level cost per month. The firm has a standard batch size of 2,500 units and expects to operate 6,650, 8,220, and 10,510 machine-hours, respectively, in April, May, and June. Starting with five products in April, Kerry plans to introduce one additional product each month.

Exhibit 10.22 contrasts traditional budgeting and ABB. As noted above, firms with traditional costing systems usually prepare budgets for departmental units such as cutting, assembling, and finishing using volume-based drivers, as Kerry did for the budget shown in Exhibit 10.10. Note that for Kerry the traditional budget for April was $113,600 compared with $119,320 under ABB. Aggregations of resource costs into functional units obscures relationships between resource consumption and output and complicates decisions regarding resource planning. As a result, traditional cost systems emphasize allocations of indirect costs to products via a broadly averaged and simplified volume-based measure, such as labor-hours, machine-hours, units of materials used, or output units. Such allocations generally do not represent resource demands (or resource consumption) of the organization's outputs and customers. Of course, some resources come in discontinuous amounts. For example, it may not be possible to hire one-third of a person. Thus, the last step in ABB is for managers to decide whether to round up (and incur some idle-capacity costs) or to round down (which may adversely affect customer-service levels).

ABB facilitates continuous improvement. The process of preparing a budget under ABB highlights opportunities for cost reduction and elimination of wasteful activities. ABB facilitates identification of high-value-added activities and reduction or elimination of low-value-added activities. In contrast, history often is the underlying guidance in a traditional budget.

Time-Driven Activity-Based Budgeting

As discussed in Chapter 5, time-driven activity-based costing (TDABC) has been proposed as an alternative to traditional ABC.[12] As we pointed out in Chapter 5, to build a TDABC system management needs to provide only two estimates for each department or business process: (1) the total cost and amount of resources supplied for a period, and (2) the amount of resource capacity, measured in time, that is consumed by the organization's cost objects (products, services, and customers).

In stage one of the two-stage TDABC process, cost rates are calculated. For example, for an activity defined as *packaging activity*, we would divide the cost of resources supplied for this activity (labor, systems, etc.) by the amount of resources supplied, measured in *time* (e.g.,

---

[12] R. S. Kaplan and S. R. Anderson, *Time-Driven Activity-Based Costing: A Simpler and More Powerful Path to Higher Profits* (Boston: Harvard Business School Press, 2007).

minutes). In stage two, costs are then allocated to cost objects by multiplying estimated cost rates (e.g., $2 per minute) by the time requirements of the cost object (for example, 4.0 minutes to package a standard, nonhazardous product that is shipped by air). Resource demands, and therefore allocated costs, of more complicated packaging activities can be captured through the use of time equations.

Time-driven activity-based budgeting (TDABB)
represents budgets prepared in conjunction with a TDABC system.

Time-driven activity-based budgeting (TDABB) is a method of budget preparation used in conjunction with TDABC. As with activity-based budgeting (ABB), time-driven activity-based budgeting works backwards from forecasted sales volume (and mix) to calculate in a straightforward way resource spending needed to support production and sales plans. That is, the organization will have to estimate resource requirements in each process and department if the production and sales forecasts for the coming period are to be realized. To generate these estimates, time equations (discussed in Chapter 5) for each major activity or process can be used to extend the basic approach described above. All of this detail can be supplied by the organization's enterprise resource planning (ERP) system. In sum, TDABC models can be used to streamline, and therefore significantly reduce the cost of, activity-based budgeting (ABB) processes. The resulting system allows managers to more accurately plan for the level of capacity needed to accomplish short-term profit goals.

Resource Capacity Planning

Practical capacity
is the measure of capacity used to estimate cost-driver rates under ABC and TDABC systems.

In both ABC and TDABC systems, we calculate cost-driver rates (e.g., the cost to ship an item, and the cost to process a customer order). As we argued in Chapter 5, these rates are best defined by dividing budgeted resource costs by the practical capacity of resources supplied for each activity or process. The use of this level of capacity allows us to estimate the cost of unused capacity at the end of each period for each activity or process. This estimate is defined as the difference between the total cost of resources *supplied* and the cost of resources *used* (or planning to be used) during the period, where the latter is defined as the product of the activity-cost rate (based on practical capacity) and the actual activity units used (or planned to be used) during the period.

A question arises as to what the appropriate treatment of unused capacity costs should be. Such costs should not be assigned to customers served or products produced during the period. To do so would overestimate the resource demands of these cost objects. Rather, these costs should be assigned to the level (product line, department, or a given manager) within the organization where the decision to acquire the capacity was made. For example, if the excess capacity was acquired to meet the anticipated demands of a given customer or market segment, then the cost of unused capacity, as a lump-sum amount, should be assigned to these segments.

The primary benefit of reporting the cost of unused capacity for each activity or resource is that this information can be used to manage the demand for and supply of capacity within the organization. For example, if excess capacity is identified during the budgeting process, then management can take steps to reduce spending in these areas or to find alternative uses for this available capacity. This insight in large part distinguishes both ABB and TDABC budgeting from traditional budgeting practices. These issues are explored further in Exercise 10-55.

Kaizen (Continuous Improvement) Budgeting

Kaizen budgeting
is a budgeting approach that incorporates continuous improvement expectations in the budget.

Kaizen budgeting is a budgeting approach that incorporates continuous improvement expectations in the budget. A kaizen budgeting approach adjusts required resource demands based on targeted efficiency and productivity gains. As such, it is an excellent complement to both traditional and activity-based budgeting systems.

A kaizen budget decrease is not the same as the budget cuts we often see firms or governments make when facing a budget crunch because of diminishing profits, decreasing sales, or declining tax revenues. A budget cut often is a reluctant passive response to a mandate that is accomplished by reducing productive activities or services. In contrast, kaizen budgeting promotes active engagement in reforming or altering practices. A decrease in cost in a kaizen budget is a result of performing the same activity more efficiently and with higher quality; it is not a result of arbitrary elimination of activities or components.

Kaizen budgeting is not limited to internal improvements. Some firms expect and demand continuous improvements from their suppliers and explicitly incorporate consequent effects in budgeted production cost and manufacturing schedules. For example, Citizen Watch demands that its suppliers decrease costs a minimum of 3 percent per year and includes this decrease in its own budget. Suppliers keep any cost savings in excess of 3 percent.[13]

Behavioral Issues in Budgeting

LEARNING OBJECTIVE 8
Discuss various behavioral considerations in budgeting.

A budget can be successful only if those responsible for its implementation make it happen. To encourage a successful budgeting process management must consider a number of behavioral issues, as discussed below.

Budgetary Slack

Budgetary slack
is the "cushion" managers intentionally build into budgets to help ensure success in meeting the budget.

Budgetary slack, or padding the budget, is the practice of managers knowingly including a higher amount of expenditures (or lower amount of revenue) in the budget than they actually believe will occur. When the actual cost (or revenue) amounts are realized and compared to "budgeted" figures, an appearance of successful effort is indicated.

Managers often justify such practices as insurance against uncertain future events. After all, no one knows exactly how the future will unfold. Budgetary slack, however, wastes resources and could lead employees to make half-hearted efforts to meet or exceed the budget.

Goal Congruence

Goal congruence
is consistency between the goals of the firm, its subunits, and its employees.

Goal congruence is a term that refers to the degree of consistency between the goals of the firm, its subunits, and its employees. In general, a firm's goals should be as consistent as possible with the goals of its employees. A budget devoid of considerations for goal congruence is not likely to achieve the most desirable results. A budget that aligns the firm's goals with those of its employees has a much better chance to realize successful operations and attain desirable results. As discussed below, there are at least three major factors that affect the level of goal congruence achieved: (1) the extent to which employees participate in the budgeting process; (2) the level of difficulty embedded in the budget; and (3) whether and how compensation is linked to budgeted performance.

Authoritative or Participative Budgeting?

Budgeting processes can be either top down or bottom up. In a top-down budgeting process, top management prepares budgets for the entire organization, including those for lower-level operations. This process often is referred to as *authoritative budgeting*. A *participative budgeting* process, on the other hand, is a bottom-up approach that involves the people affected by the budget, including lower-level employees, in the budget-preparation process.

Authoritative budgeting provides better decision-making control than does participative budgeting. Top management sets the overall goals for the budget period and prepares a budget for operating personnel to attain the goals. An authoritative budget, however, often lacks the commitment ("buy-in") of lower-level managers and employees responsible for implementing it.

A participative budget is a good communication device. The process of preparing a budget often gives top management a better grasp of the problems their employees face and provides the employees a better understanding of the dilemmas that top management deals with. A participative budget also is more likely to gain employee commitment to fulfill budgetary

[13] Robin Cooper, *Citizen Watch Company, Ltd.*, Harvard Business School case 9–194033. © 1993 by the President and Fellows of Harvard College.

EXHIBIT 10.23
Budget Difficulty and Effort

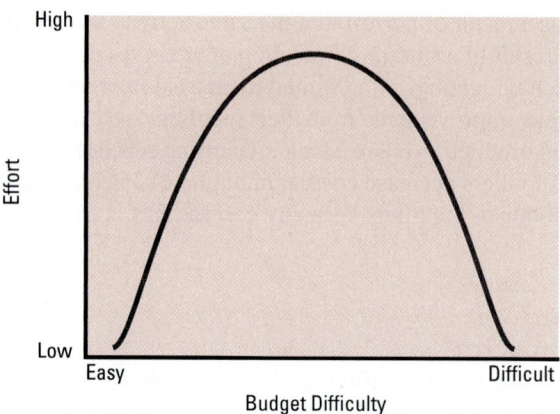

goals. Unless properly controlled, however, a participative budget can lead to easy budget targets or targets not in compliance with the organization's overall strategy.

An effective budgeting process often combines both top-down and bottom-up budgeting approaches. Divisions prepare their initial budgets based on the budget guidelines issued by the firm's budget committee. Senior managers review and make suggestions to the proposed budget before sending it back to the divisions for revisions. The final budget usually is reached after several rounds of negotiations. For this reason, this is generally referred to as a *negotiated budgeting* process.

Difficulty Level of the Budget Target

An easy budget target may fail to encourage employees to give their best efforts. A budget target that is very difficult to achieve can, however, discourage managers from even trying to attain it. Exhibit 10.23 depicts research findings on the relationship between the level of employee effort and level of difficulty of budget targets. Ideally, budget targets should be challenging yet attainable. But what is a challenging and attainable budget target?

Research by Merchant and Manzoni suggests that a "highly achievable target," that is, one achievable by most managers 80 to 90 percent of the time, serves quite well in the vast majority of organizations, especially when accompanied by extra rewards for performances exceeding the target.[14] According to Merchant (1990), the advantages of using such a target include:

1. Increasing managers' commitment to achieving the budget target.
2. Maintaining managers' confidence in the budget.
3. Decreasing the cost of organizational control.
4. Reducing the risk that managers will engage in harmful "earnings management" practices or violate corporate ethical standards.
5. Allowing effective and efficient managers greater operating flexibility.
6. Improving predictability of earnings or operating results.
7. Enhancing the usefulness of a budget as a planning and coordinating tool.

Linkage of Compensation and Budgeted Performance

Traditionally, budgets have played a role in determining employee and executive compensation. The traditional model is that such compensation would be at least partially a function of the difference between actual performance (sales, operating profit, net income, etc.) and budgeted performance for a given budget period, usually a year. This type of compensation

---

[14] K. A. Merchant, "How Challenging Should Profit Budget Targets Be?" *Management Accounting,* November 1990, pp. 46–48; K. A. Merchant, *Rewarding Results: Motivating Profit Center Managers* (Cambridge, MA: Harvard Business School Press, 1989); and K. A. Merchant and J. Manzoni, "The Achievability of Budget Targets in Profit Centers: A Field Study," *The Accounting Review,* July 1989, pp. 539–58.

Fixed performance contract is an incentive compensation plan whereby compensation is a function of actual performance compared to a fixed (budgeted) target.

Gaming the performance measure is a result of non-value-adding actions taken by managers to improve indicated performance.

plan is sometimes referred to as a **fixed performance contract** because actual performance is compared to a fixed (budgeted) target.

While this traditional model may work well in some situations, we know that its usage can have dysfunctional consequences. That is, significant incentive (and ethical) issues arise when compensation is linked to a fixed-performance target. For example, such a reward system provides incentives for managers to submit biased information in their budgets. Budgetary slack, discussed earlier, is one example. In addition, the use of fixed targets reinforced by incentives motivates some managers to **game the performance measure,** that is, to take actions that make the performance indicator look better but do not increase the value of the firm. Finally, some would argue that the use of fixed budget targets unfairly rewards managers when actual performance is affected by factors, such as macroeconomic conditions, that are beyond the control or influence of the manager. In short, critics of the conventional fixed-performance model linked to compensation contend that this process is fundamentally flawed. At least two alternatives have been proposed as a way to deal with this problem: the use of linear compensation plans and the use of rolling forecasts combined with relative performance indicators.

Use of Linear Compensation Plans [15]

Essentially, this option would sever the relationship between budgets and managerial compensation. In its place, incentive compensation would be based on a linear compensation plan. This strategy has two characteristics: (1) managerial reward is independent of budgeted targets, and (2) managerial reward is a linear function of actual performance: the greater the performance, the greater the managerial reward (both monetary and nonmonetary). In other words, this incentive system rewards people for what they actually do, not for what they do relative to what they say they can do. However, from a practical standpoint this strategy may be difficult to implement because of the use of budgeted targets in determining managerial rewards.

Use of Rolling Forecasts and Relative Performance Results [16]

The displeasure with respect to current budgeting practices is perhaps best epitomized by a group referred to as the Beyond Budgeting Roundtable (BBRT—see: www.bbrt.org and www.project.bbrt.org). Instead of fixed performance contracts, the BBRT recommends the use of *relative performance (improvement) contracts* and *rolling financial forecasts.*

[15] This section draws on the following source: Michael C. Jensen, "Corporate Budgeting Is Broken—Let's Fix It," *Harvard Business Review* (November 2001), pp. 94–101.

[16] This discussion draws on the following source: Jeremy Hope and Robin Fraser, *Beyond Budgeting: How Managers Can Break Free from the Annual Performance Trap* (Boston: Harvard Business School Press, 2003).

Cost Management in Action

What's Wrong with the Budget Process?

A recent survey of chief financial officers (CFOs) by Pricewaterhouse Coopers shows that 74 percent of these executives believe that the master budget has one of the highest priorities in the coming years. On a 5-point scale to rank importance, the executives scored the master budget as 4.1. Unfortunately, the executives also reported that the master budget was poorly implemented at their firms (an average score of 2.1 out of 5). Those writing up the study also noted that Jack Welch, former CEO of General Electric, has called the master budget the "bane of corporate America." What are some of the implementation problems these CFOs are concerned about, and how do you think they might address these problems?

(Refer to Comments on Cost Management in Action at end of Chapter.)

REAL-WORLD FOCUS

Increasing Motivational Effects of Budgeting: The Use of "Rolling Financial Forecasts"

In its survey of 200 senior-level finance professionals, PwC (2007) found that while a slight majority of organizations (52%) use a static budget for planning purposes, a significant minority of respondents (42%) are using rolling forecasts, that is, budgets that extend beyond the end of the fiscal year. Survey respondents indicated that such forecasts enable companies to react quickly to market conditions and to alter long-range plans accordingly without worrying about artificial end points, such as the end of a fiscal year. Some organizations indicate that they have moved away entirely from the annual budget-planning process to a continuous planning model. *CFO* magazine (June 1, 2008) reports that CaseCentral, a San Francisco-based litigation-support firm, was being challenged by its customers trying to renegotiate their contracts with the firm. Partners in the firm wanted a system that would enable the firm to quickly estimate how changes in client contracts would affect the projected financial performance of the firm. To generate the information it needed, CaseCentral invested in an integrated budgeting and planning software system. Managers of CaseCentral are now able, on a monthly basis, to both review actual results and to reforecast 90 days out. Once every quarter, senior managers of the firm make new forecasts for the following three quarters and all of the following year, looking for trends in pricing and revenue. In short, the software allows the firm to quickly estimate the financial impact of all major decisions, such as renegotiated client contracts (e.g., a price cut for a large customer) or the hiring of a senior employee. Continuous planning is accomplished through the use of rolling financial forecasts.

Sources: Karen M. Kroll, "Staying on Course: It's Hard to Weather an Economic Slowdown without a Sound Budget to Steer By," *CFO* magazine (June 1, 2008); and, 2007 *PwC Budgeting and Forecasting Study,* available online at: www.pwc.com/us/performance improvement.

Relative performance contracts reward managers for performance based on comparison of actual results with specified benchmarks, not budgeted targets.

Relative performance (or relative improvement) contracts essentially reward managers for how their business units perform relative to some appropriate benchmark performance, not a fixed budget target. For example, an operating unit or division might be evaluated on the basis of its return on investment (ROI) for a period relative to the market or to best-in-class performance. Some organizations benchmark actual performance to the top quartile of their peer group. This change in incentive, at least conceptually, avoids much of the dysfunctional consequences associated with traditional budgeting systems. Units and managers are motivated to achieve to their highest level because their compensation/reward is tied to how they performed relative to a prespecified (external or internal) benchmark. In essence, this represents radical decentralization and significant reliance on self-regulation. Employees and operating managers in this model are vested with significant decision authority and are asked to use their own best judgment to achieve superior results, without being constrained by the plan embodied in a budget.

Rolling financial forecast provides a constant planning horizon with the use of regularly updated forecasts.

In addition to the use of relative performance contracts, the BBRT model calls for the use of **rolling financial forecasts** rather than the annual master budget (described earlier in this chapter). These forecasts are updated regularly, for example every quarter, to provide a constant planning horizon (e.g., five quarters into the future). Of particular note is the fact that these forecasts are separated from performance evaluation and control. They are prepared for a small set of key performance indicators (e.g., cash flow, sales, and number of customer orders) and serve as a high-level view of future performance. Their use is designed to allow employees to adapt to changing environments (including competitive threats) and to achieve the level of radical decentralization envisioned by the BBRT.

Summary

An organization's budget is a quantitative plan that identifies the resources required and commitments to fulfill the organization's goals for the budget period. Budgeting allows management to plan ahead, communicate the plan and performance expectations to all divisions and employees, and, when properly implemented, motivate employees. A budget can also serve as a basis for performance evaluation.

Strategy helps a firm to be more focused in its operations and to take advantage of its strengths and opportunities. A firm executes its strategy through long-range plans and master budgets. An annual master budget is an extension of the organization's long-range plan to fulfill organizational goals and objectives.

The master budget for a manufacturer includes sales, production, direct materials, direct labor, factory overhead, selling, and administration expense budgets, as well as a cash budget, and budgeted financial statements.

A service firm prepares a budget following set procedures just as a manufacturing or merchandising firm does. A major difference between budgets for service firms and those for manufacturing or merchandising firms is the absence of a production budget or merchandise purchases budget for service firms. The budgeting procedures and all other budget items are essentially the same for both service and manufacturing or merchandising firms.

Budgets, by definition, are forward-looking and include estimates for key inputs such as sales volume, sales mix, total fixed (capacity-related) costs, variable cost per unit, and selling price per unit. What-if analysis can be performed to determine the effects of alternative scenarios (states of nature) and alternative plans. Sensitivity analysis allows us to determine the extent to which resulting budgets are affected by changes in the input factors. Together, these analyses allow the budget analyst to deal with uncertainty that is inherent in the budgeting process.

Refinements or alternatives to traditional budgeting practices include zero-base budgeting (ZBB), activity-based budgeting (ABB), time-driven activity-based budgeting (TDABB), and kaizen budgeting. By requiring budgets that start from a zero base each period, ZBB attempts to achieve a more realistic allocation of resources within the organization. ABB and TDABB are both extensions to modern cost-allocation systems, as discussed in Chapter 5. Kaizen budgeting incorporates continuous improvements into budgets that are produced.

In some quarters (e.g., BBRT) there is growing dissatisfaction, indeed frustration, with traditional budgeting practices, such as those described in this chapter. Critics contend that incentive compensation/employee reward should not be a function of the difference between budgeted and actual performance, a widespread approach in practice. In place of the annual fixed-performance contract these critics suggest either that a linear compensation plan based on actual results be used or that budgets be replaced altogether with rolling forecasts and relative-performance contracts.

Key Terms

activity-based budgeting (ABB), *391*
budget, *365*
budgetary slack, *395*
budgeting, *365*
capital budgeting, *367*
cash budget, *382*
direct materials purchases budget, *376*
direct materials usage budget, *376*
financial budgets, *369*

fixed-performance contract, *397*
gaming the performance measure, *397*
goal congruence, *395*
kaizen budgeting, *394*
long-range plan, *367*
master budget, *367*
merchandise purchases budget, *380*
operating budgets, *367*
practical capacity, *394*

production budget, *374*
relative performance contracts, *398*
rolling financial forecast, *398*
sales budget, *373*
strategic budget expenditures, *367*
time-driven activity-based budgeting (TDABB), *394*
zero-base budgeting (ZBB), *391*

Comments on Cost Management in Action

What's Wrong with the Budget Process?

While most chief financial officers (CFOs) are convinced of the importance of the master budget, many are not satisfied with the budget process in their firms. Among the issues the CFOs identify for improvement are:

1. Many firms use a bottom-up budget process—department managers initiate the process and prepare detailed budgets for top management's review and approval. However, firms that use a top-down budgeting process find the top-down approach is preferable because it places a greater focus on the strategic plans developed by top management and because it is faster and more flexible to execute. Most important, it can be more difficult to integrate strategy into the budget when it has a bottom-up process. General Electric, in particular, insists that strategic thinking must be integrated throughout the budget process.

2. Many firms that use the annual budget process fail to update for changes during the year. As a result, these firms are not prepared for changes in market conditions and operating factors—changes that require fast response and perhaps a change in strategy. Johnson & Johnson, General Electric, Roche, and other firms use *continuous budgets* that require frequent updates of forecasts and reassessment of competitive factors throughout the year.

3. At some firms, a problem is that financial managers are not effective in communicating the importance and the benefits of the master budget to department heads. This means that the budget is not fully and properly utilized. Firms such as Warner Lambert and General Electric work hard to make sure that financial managers working on the budget are effective at supporting the department heads, and that the budget process is understood and valued throughout the firm.

Source: Richard Harborne, "Power Planning: An Integrated Business Planning Process," *Strategic Finance,* October 1999, pp. 47–53.

Self-Study Problems
(For solutions, please turn to the end of the chapter)

1. Master Budget

Hansell Company's management wants to prepare budgets for one of its products, duraflex, for July 2010. The firm sells the product for $80 per unit and has the following expected sales (in units) for these months in 2010:

April	May	June	July	August	September
5,000	5,400	5,500	6,000	7,000	8,000

The production process requires 4 pounds of dura-1000 and 2 pounds of flexplas. The firm's policy is to maintain an ending inventory each month equal to 10 percent of the following month's budgeted sales, but in no case less than 500 units. All materials inventories are to be maintained at 5 percent of the production needs for the next month, but not to exceed 1,000 pounds. The firm expects all inventories at the end of June to be within the guidelines. The purchase department expects the materials to cost $1.25 per pound and $5.00 per pound for dura-1000 and flexplas, respectively.

The production process requires direct labor at two skill levels. The rate for labor at the K102 level is $50 per hour and for the K175 level is $20 per hour. The K102 level can process one batch of duraflex per hour; each batch consists of 100 units. The manufacturing of duraflex also requires one-tenth of an hour of K175 workers' time for each unit manufactured.

Variable manufacturing overhead is $1,200 per batch plus $80 per direct labor-hour. The company uses an actual cost system with a LIFO cost-flow assumption.

Required On the basis of the preceding data and projections, prepare the following budgets:
a. Sales budget for July (in dollars).
b. Production budget for July (in units).
c. Production budget for August (in units).
d. Direct materials purchases budget for July (in pounds).
e. Direct materials purchases budget for July (in dollars).
f. Direct manufacturing labor budget for July (in dollars).

2. Cash Budget and Budgeted Income Statement

Hansell Company expects its trial balance on June 30 to be as follows:

HANSELL COMPANY
Budgeted Trial Balance
June 30, 2010

	Debit	Credit
Cash	$ 40,000	
Accounts receivable	80,000	
Allowance for bad debts		$ 3,500
Inventory	25,000	
Plant, property, and equipment	650,000	
Accumulated depreciation		320,000
Accounts payable		95,000
Wages and salaries payable		24,000
Note payable		200,000
Stockholders' equity		152,500
Total	$795,000	$795,000

Typically, cash sales represent 20 percent of sales while credit sales represent 80 percent. Credit sales terms are 2/10, n/30. Hansell bills customers on the first day of the month following the month of sale. Experience has shown that 60 percent of the billings will be collected within the discount period, 25 percent by the end of the month after sales, 10 percent by the end of the second month after the sale, and 5 percent will ultimately be uncollectible. The firm writes off uncollectible accounts after 12 months.

The purchase terms for materials are 2/15, n/60. The firm makes all payments within the discount period. Experience has shown that 80 percent of the purchases are paid in the month of the purchase and the remainder are paid in the month immediately following. In June 2010, the firm budgeted purchases of $25,000 for dura-1000 and $22,000 for flexplas.

In addition to variable overhead, the firm has a monthly fixed factory overhead of $50,000, of which $20,000 is depreciation expense. The firm pays all manufacturing labor and factory overhead when incurred.

Total budgeted marketing, distribution, customer service, and administrative costs for 2010 are $2,400,000. Of this amount, $1,200,000 is considered fixed and includes depreciation expense of $120,000. The remainder varies with sales. The budgeted total sales for 2010 are $4 million. All marketing and administrative costs are paid in the month incurred.

Management desires to maintain an end-of-month minimum cash balance of $40,000. The firm has an agreement with a local bank to borrow its short-term needs in multiples of $1,000 up to $100,000 at an annual interest rate of 12 percent. Borrowings are assumed to occur at the end of the month. Bank borrowing at July 1 = $0.

Required

1. Prepare the cash budget for July 2010.
2. Prepare the budgeted income statement for July 2010.

Questions

10-1   Describe at least three benefits that an organization can expect to realize from budgeting. (CMA adapted)

10-2   Explain the difference between a strategic plan and a master budget.

10-3   Is a capital budget part of a master budget?

10-4   Differentiate master, operating, and financial budgets.

10-5   Some critics of budgeting believe that budgets are effective tools for planning but not for control purposes. What is the essence of this argument?

10-6   Many accountants believe that the most important benefit of the master budgeting process is the end result: a set of pro forma financial statements. What is the rationale for this view?

10-7   Why is the sales budget considered the cornerstone of the organization's master budget?

10-8 In addition to the sales budget, what information does a firm need to complete its materials purchases budget?

10-9 List the major components of a cash budget.

10-10 Contrast the budget characteristics of service organizations and manufacturing companies.

10-11 Distinguish between the terms *sensitivity analysis* and *what-if analysis.*

10-12 What is zero-base budgeting (ZBB)?

10-13 Is kaizen budgeting the Japanese term for activity-based budgeting (ABB)?

10-14 Define the term *budgetary slack.* Why is it common to find slack in budgets?

10-15 How does the use of a time-driven activity-based costing (TDABC) system facilitate the preparation of budgets for an organization?

10-16 What is a highly achievable budget? Why might organizations prefer such a budget?

10-17 List the role of top management in participative budgeting.

10-18 What is the essence of a fixed-performance contract and what dysfunctional consequences can occur through the use of this type of incentive system?

10-19 Distinguish between a linear-preformance contract and a fixed performance contract in terms of motivational/incentive effects.

10-20 Define the terms *relative performance contract* and *rolling financial forecast.* What role for these is envisioned by critics of the traditional budgeting process?

Brief Exercises

10-21 Kraft Bakeries introduced in 2010 a new line of frozen apple pie. For 2010, sales by quarter were as follows: 11,000 units; 16,000 units; 15,000 units; and 20,000 units. Because of aggressive marketing and promotion, the company expects that sales for each quarter of 2011 will be 25 percent higher than the respective quarter in 2010. The selling price per unit in 2011 is expected to be $4. What are the expected sales, in units and dollars, for the second quarter of 2011? For the third quarter of 2011?

10-22 Resco, a local retail establishment, expects to make inventory purchases as follows for the first quarter of 2010: January, $5,500; February, $6,500; and March, $8,000. Prior experience shows that 25 percent of a given month's purchases are paid in the month of purchase with the balance paid in the following month. No purchase discounts apply. What is the total expected cash disbursement for February? For March?

10-23 Ajax Manufacturing produces a single product, which takes 8.0 pounds of direct materials per unit produced. We are currently at the end of the first quarter of the year and there are 50,000 pounds of material on hand. The company's policy is to maintain an end-of-quarter inventory of materials equal to 25 percent of the following quarter's material requirements for production. How many units of product were produced in the first quarter of the year? Under the assumption that production will increase by 10 percent in the second quarter, what are the direct materials requirements (in pounds) for planned production in the second quarter?

10-24 Grey Manufacturing Company expects sales to total 13,000 in the first quarter, 12,000 units in the second quarter, and 15,000 units in the third quarter of the current fiscal year. Company policy is to have on hand at the end of each quarter an amount of inventory equal to 10 percent of the following quarter's sales. Given this information, how many units should be scheduled for production in the second quarter?

10-25 Easy Clean operates a chain of dry cleaners. It is experimenting with a continuous improvement (i.e., kaizen) budget for operating expenses. Currently, a typical location has operating expenses of $10,000 per month. Plans are in place to achieve labor and utility savings. The associated operational changes are estimated to reduce monthly operating costs by a factor of 0.99 beginning in January. What is the estimated operating cost for January? For June? For December?

10-26 Campbell's Wholesale Company is preparing monthly cash budgets for the fourth quarter of 2010. Monthly sales revenue in this quarter is estimated as follows: October, $30,000; November, $24,000; and December, $20,000. All sales are made on open credit with 70 percent collected in the month of sale and 30 percent collected in the following month. What is the estimated total cash collected in November? December?

10-27 Royal Cigar Company is preparing a budget for cash collections. Its sales for November and December are estimated as $90,000 and $100,000 respectively. Past practice indicates that sales in any given month are collected as follows: month of sale, 75 percent; month following the month of sale, 20 percent; uncollectible accounts, 5 percent. The company allows a 2 percent discount for cash collections in the month of sale. What is the net cash estimated to be collected in December?

10-28 The George Company has a policy of maintaining an end-of-month cash balance of at least $30,000. In months where a shortfall is expected, the company can draw in $1,000 increments on a line of credit it has with a local bank, at an interest rate of 12 percent per annum. All borrowings are assumed for budgeting purposes to occur at the beginning of the month, while all loan repayments (in $1,000 increments of principal) are assumed to occur at the end of the month. Interest is paid at the end of each month. For April, an end-of-month cash balance (prior to any financing and interest expense) of $18,000 is budgeted; for May, an excess of cash collected over cash payments (prior to any interest payments and loan repayments) of $22,000 is anticipated. What is the interest payment estimated for April (there is no bank loan outstanding at the end of March)? What is the total financing effect (cash interest plus loan transaction) for May?

10-29 If the December 1 balance in the Direct Materials (DM) Inventory account was $37,000, the December 31 balance was $39,500, and $150,000 of DM were issued to production during December, what was the amount of DM purchased during the month?

10-30 A company is formulating its marketing expense budget for the last quarter of the year. Sales in units for the third quarter amounted to 4,000; sales volume for the fourth quarter are expected to increase by 10 percent. Variable marketing expenses per unit sold amount to approximately $0.05, paid in cash in month of sale. Fixed marketing expenses per month amount to $10,000 of salaries, $5,000 of depreciation (delivery trucks), and $2,000 of insurance (paid monthly). What is the total budgeted marketing *expense* for the fourth quarter of the year? What is the estimated *cash payment* for marketing expenses for the fourth quarter?

Exercises

10-31 **What-If Analysis**   As the management accountant for the Tyson Company you have been asked to construct a *financial planning model* for collection of accounts receivable and then to perform a what-if analysis in terms of the assumption regarding estimated uncollectible accounts. You are provided with the following information:

Collection Pattern for Credit Sales: 75 percent of the company's credit sales are collected in the month of sale, 20 percent in the month following month of sale, and 5 percent are uncollectible.

Credit Sales: January 2010, $100,000; February 2010, $120,000; March 2010, $110,000.

Required

1. What is meant by the term *what-if analysis?*

2. Generate a spreadsheet model regarding estimated bad debts expense under the following assumptions regarding the rate of uncollectible accounts: 1 percent, 3 percent, 5 percent (base case), and 8 percent. Prepare an estimate of bad debts expense for each of three months, January through March, and for the quarter as a whole.

3. What is the value to Tyson Company of creating a model and then performing the what-if analysis described above?

10-32 **Purchases Budget and Payments**   Janet DeVolris, purchasing manager of Corkin Manufacturing, a small Midwest manufacturer of specialty tools, was frustrated because her efforts to reduce the use of expensive overnight shipping appeared to be futile. Rush orders, last-minute changes, and other operating emergencies seemed to be the firm's way of life. Although she vowed to keep last-minute actions to a minimum, overnight shipping shows no sign of abatement after six months.

At a recent convention, several suppliers mentioned that Corkin Manufacturing rarely takes advantage of the discount terms she worked so hard for them to grant. She was very surprised because sales terms of 2/10, n/30 or better yielded an annual return of at least 36 percent.

Tony Blair, the firm's CEO, recently praised Janet lavishly for her performance for the last six months and gave her a generous raise. Still, she feels frustrated and unfulfilled.

Required   What could Janet do to overcome her frustration?

10-33 **Budgetary Slack and Zero-Base Budgeting (ZBB)**   Bob Bingham is the controller of Atlantis Laboratories, a manufacturer and distributor of generic prescription pharmaceuticals. He is currently preparing the annual budget and reviewing the current business plan. The firm's business unit managers prepare and assemble the detailed operating budgets with technical assistance from the corporate accounting staff. The business unit managers then present the final budgets to the corporate executive committee for approval. The corporate accounting staff reviews the budgets for adherence to corporate accounting policies but not for reasonableness of the line items within the budgets.

Bob is aware that the upcoming year for Atlantis could be a difficult one because of a major patent expiration and the loss of a licensing agreement for another product line. He also knows that during the budgeting process slack is created in varying degrees throughout the organization.

Bob believes that this slack has a negative effect on the firm's overall business objectives and should be eliminated where possible.

Required

1. Define the term *budgetary slack.*

2. Explain the advantages and disadvantages of budgetary slack from the point of view of (a) the business unit manager who must achieve the budget, and (b) corporate management.

3. Bob Bingham is considering implementing zero-base budgeting (ZBB) in Atlantis Laboratories.

   a. Define *zero-base budgeting.*

   b. Describe how *zero-base budgeting* could be advantageous to Atlantis Laboratories in controlling budgetary slack.

   c. Discuss the disadvantages Atlantis Laboratories might encounter in using ZBB.

(CMA Adapted)

10-34 **Cash Disbursements Budget** The Ajax Company budgets the following purchases of direct materials for the first quarter of the year:

	January	February	March
Budgeted purchases	$100,000	$120,000	$110,000

All purchases of direct materials are made on credit. On average, the company pays 75 percent of its purchases in the month of sales, and the remainder in the following month.

Required

1. For the months of February and March, what are the estimated cash payments for purchases of direct materials under the assumption that there is no (cash) discount for early payment?

2. For the months of February and March, what are the estimated cash payments for purchases of direct material under the assumption that the purchase terms are 2/10, net 30? The company's policy is to take advantage of all cash discounts for early payment.

3. Provide an economic argument as to why it is good (economic) policy to take advantage of early payment discounts, as in (2) above.

10-35 **Budgeted Cash Receipts and Cash Payments** The Dyson Company, a retailer, makes both cash and credit sales (i.e., sales on open account). Information regarding budgeted sales for the last quarter of the year is as follows:

	October	November	December
Cash sales	$100,000	$120,000	$ 80,000
Credit sales	100,000	150,000	90,000
Total	$200,000	$270,000	$170,000

Past experience shows that 5 percent of credit sales are uncollectible. Of the credit sales that are collectible, 65 percent are collected in the month of sale; the remaining 35 percent are collected in the month following the month of sale. Customers are granted a 2 percent discount for payment within 10 days of billing. Approximately 80 percent of collectible credit sales take advantage of the cash discount.

Inventory purchases each month are 100 percent of the *cost* of the following month's projected sales. (The gross profit rate for Dyson is approximately 30 percent.) All merchandise purchases are made on credit, with 25 percent paid in the month of purchase and the remainder paid in the following month. No cash discounts for early payment are in effect.

Required

1. Calculate the budgeted total cash receipts for November and December.

2. Calculate budgeted cash payments for November and December (budgeted total sales for January of the coming year = $200,000).

10-36 Production and Materials Purchases Budgets DeVaris Corporation's budget calls for the following sales for next year:

Quarter 1	45,000 units	Quarter 3	34,000 units
Quarter 2	38,000 units	Quarter 4	48,000 units

Each unit of the product requires 3 pounds of direct material. The company's policy is to begin each quarter with an inventory of the product equal to 10 percent of that quarter's sales requirements and an inventory of direct materials equal to 20 percent of that quarter's direct materials requirements for production.

Required Determine the production and materials purchases budgets for the second quarter.

10-37 Purchase Discounts It is typically beneficial for companies to take advantage of early-payment discounts allowed on purchases made on credit. To see why this is the case, determine the effective rate of interest associated with *not* taking advantage of the early-payment discount for each of the following situations. Assume in each case that payment is made on the 30th day of the billing cycle.

Required

1. What is the opportunity cost of not taking advantage of the discount associated with purchases made under the following terms: 2/10, n/30?

2. What is the opportunity cost of not taking advantage of the discount associated with purchases made under the following terms: 1/10, n/30?

3. What is the appropriate accounting treatment for purchase discounts?

10-38 Production and Materials Budgets—Process Costing Uecker Company budgets on an annual basis. The planned beginning and ending inventory levels (in units) for the fiscal year of July 1, 2010, through June 30, 2011, for one of its products, XPL30, are as follows:

	July 1, 2010	June 30, 2011
Raw materials	40,000	50,000
Work in process	10,000	20,000
Finished goods	80,000	50,000

Two units of raw materials are needed to complete one unit of finished product. All materials are added at the beginning of production. The firm completes all work-in-process before starting a new batch and plans to sell 480,000 units during the 2010–2011 fiscal year.

Required

1. How many units of XPL30 must Uecker Company complete in fiscal 2010?

2. How many units of XPL30 must Uecker Company start into production during the 2010–2011 fiscal year?

3. How many units of raw materials must Uecker Company purchase during the 2010–2011 fiscal year?

4. In general, how would your answer change if the company adds all require materials immediately before completion of the manufacturing process for XPL30?

10-39 Cash Budget—Financing Effects You are a relatively recent hire to Hartz & Co., a local manufacturer of plumbing supply products. You have been asked to prepare, for a presentation to the company's management, a condensed cash-flow statement for the months of November and December 2010.

Assume the cash balance at November 1 will be $75,000. It is the company's policy to maintain a minimum cash balance of $50,000 at the end of each month. Cash receipts (from cash sales and collection of accounts receivable) are projected to be $525,000 for November and $450,000 for December. Cash disbursements (sales commissions, advertising, delivery expense, wages, utilities, etc.) prior to financing activity are scheduled to be $450,500 in November and $550,000 in December.

Borrowing, when needed, is done at the beginning of the month in increments of $1,000. The annual interest rate on any such loans is estimated to be 12 percent. Interest on any outstanding loans is paid in cash at the end of the month. Repayments of principal (if any) are assumed to occur at the end of the month. As of November 1, the company has a $50,000 short-term loan from the local bank. This loan is payable at the end of November.

Required   Use the preceding information to prepare the cash budget for November and December. (*Hint:* the December 31 cash balance should be $50,480.)

10-40 Cash Budget   Carla Inc. has the following budgeted data for 2010:

Cash balance, beginning	$ 10,000
Collections from customers	150,000
Expenses:	
Direct materials purchases	25,000
Operating expenses	50,000
Payroll	75,000
Income taxes	6,000
Machinery purchases	30,000

Operating expenses include $20,000 depreciation for buildings and equipment. The company requires a minimum cash balance of $20,000.

Required   Compute the amount the company needs to finance or the excess cash available for Carla to invest.

10-41 Cash Budget   Bill Joyce, CEO of Joyce and Associates, expects the firm to have $6,000 cash on hand at the end of 2009. He estimates the total revenues in 2010 to be $250,000, of which $175,000 will be collected during the year. Payroll and fringe benefits constitute the bulk of the firm's expenditures and will amount to $160,000 in 2010. Other operating expenses, including $5,000 for depreciation and $3,000 for property taxes, are $18,000. The property tax expense is an increase of $500 from the current year. In addition, Bill Joyce plans to update the office equipment for $24,000 in 2010. He expects the payment in 2010 for the office equipment will be $6,000. The county in which the firm is located requires payment of at least one-half of property taxes before the end of the year and the remainder before June 30 of the following year. The desired ending cash balance is $6,000.

Required   Can Bill meet the minimum cash balance? Show calculations.

10-42 Cash Budgeting: Not-for-Profit Context   *(contributed by Helen M. Savage)* Tri-county Social Service Agency is a not-for-profit organization in the Midwest. Use the following information to complete the *cash budget* for the year ending December 31, 2010.

- The Board of Trustees requires that Tri-county maintain a minimum cash balance of $8,000.
- If cash is short, the agency may borrow from an endowment fund enough to maintain the $8,000 minimum. Repayment must be made as soon as possible. No interest is charged.
- It is anticipated that the year 2010 will begin with an $11,000 cash balance.
- Contract revenue is received evenly during the year.
- Mental health income is expected to grow by $5,000 in the second and third quarters, but not change in the fourth quarter.

Required

1. Within the context of a not-for-profit organization, what is an *endowment fund?*
2. Complete the cash budget for 2010, for each quarter and the year as a whole, using the template that follows.
3. Determine the amount that the agency will owe the *endowment fund* at year end.
4. Does the borrowing indicate a problem? What options would the agency have to increase revenues?
5. Do you think that a requirement to pay interest on the borrowings would have a positive impact on the agency's activities? Why or why not?

Cash Budget for Tri-county Social Service Agency
2010 (in thousands)

	Quarters				
	I	II	III	IV	Year
Cash balance, beginning	$ 11	?	?	?	$ 11
Receipts:					
Grants	$ 80	$ 70	?	?	$ 300
Contracts	?	?	?	?	$ 80
Mental health income	$ 20	?	?	?	$ 105
Charitable donations	$250	?	$200	$400	?
Total cash available	?	$473	$333	?	?
Less disbursements:					
Salaries and benefits	?	$342	?	?	$1,365
Office expenses	$ 70	?	$ 71	$ 50	$ 256
Equipment purchases & maintenance	$ 2	$ 4	$ 6	?	$ 17
Specific assistance	$ 20	$ 15	$ 18	?	$ 73
Total disbursements	?	?	?	?	?
Excess (defic.) of cash available over disbursements	$ (46)	?	?	$112	?
Financing:					
Borrowings from endowment fund	?	?	$112	?	?
Repayments	?	$ (39)	?	?	?
Total financing effects	?	?	?	?	?
Cash balance, ending	?	?	?	?	?

10-43 **Accounts Receivable Collections** Esplanade Company's credit sales have the following historical pattern:

> 70 percent collected in the month of sale
> 15 percent collected in the first month after month of sale
> 10 percent collected in the second month after month of sale
> 4 percent collected in the third month after month of sale
> 1 percent uncollectible

The following sales on open account (credit sales) have been budgeted for the last six months in 2010:

July	$60,000	October	90,000
August	70,000	November	100,000
September	80,000	December	85,000

Required

1. Determine the estimated total cash collections from accounts receivable during October 2010.
2. Compute the estimated total cash collections during the fourth quarter *from credit sales of the fourth quarter.*

(CMA Adapted)

10-44 **Accounts Receivable Collections and Sensitivity Analysis** Doreen Company is preparing its cash budget for the month of May. The following information is available concerning its accounts receivable:

Actual credit sales for March	$120,000
Actual credit sales for April	$150,000
Estimated credit sales for May	$200,000
Estimated collections in the month of sale	25%
Estimated collections in the first month after the month of sale	60%
Estimated collections in the second month after the month of sale	10%
Estimated provision for bad debts made in the month of sale	5%

The firm writes off all uncollectible accounts at the end of the second month after the month of sale.

Required Create an Excel spreadsheet and determine for Doreen Company for the month of May:

1. The estimated cash receipts from accounts receivable collections.
2. The gross amount of accounts receivable at the end of the month.
3. The net amount of accounts receivable at the end of the month.
4. Recalculate requirements (1) and (2) under the assumption that estimated collections in month of sale = 60 percent and in first month following month of sale = 25 percent.
5. What are the benefits and likely costs of moving to the situation described above in (4)?

10-45 Budgeting: Not-for-Profit Context (*contributed by Helen M. Savage*) Catholic Charities Regional Agency serves several contiguous counties in Ohio. The finance committee of its board of directors monitors financial activity for the agency. This oversight includes decisions regarding the investment of excess funds and the management of endowment funds. These decisions are relevant to the annual budget preparation since the investment accounts serve as a source of needed funds and/or a use of excess funds.

As a Catholic Charities agency, the regional organization must adhere to guidelines adopted by the U.S. Council of Catholic Bishops. Visit the council's Web site at http://www.usccb.org/finance/srig.htm and review its *Socially Responsible Investment Guidelines,* which discuss basic principles for investments and the stated Investment policy of the organization.

Required

1. What is the meaning of the word *stewardship?* Should the religious or philosophical position of an organization affect decisions that are made as part of the budgeting process?
2. How should a board of directors for this organization apply these principles in making investment decisions tied to the annual budget?
3. Would you, as a board member, ignore such principles to increase investment gains? Why or why not?
4. If the agency's monies are managed by an investment firm, should the board request information about the stocks included in individual investment funds to verify compliance with the stated investment policy of the organization?

10-46 Budgeting Cash Receipts: Cash Discounts Allowed on Receivables Yeopay Plumbing Supply accepts bank charge cards and offers established plumbers charge accounts with terms of 1/eom, n/45. Yeopay's experience is that 25 percent of its sales are for cash and bank credit cards. The remaining 75 percent are on credit. Of the cash sales, 40 percent pay cash and the remaining 60 percent pay with bank credit cards. Yeopay receives payments from the bank on credit card sales at the end of the day. However, Yeopay has to pay 3 percent for these services. An aging schedule for accounts receivable shows the following pattern on credit sales:

20 percent pay in the month of sale.
50 percent pay in the first month following the sale.
15 percent pay in the second month following the sale.
12 percent pay in the third month following the sale.
 3 percent are never collected.

All accounts not paid by the end of the second month following the month of sale are considered overdue and are subject to 2 percent monthly late charge. Yeopay has prepared the following sales forecasts:

June	$60,000
July	80,000
August	90,000
September	96,000
October	88,000

Required

1. Prepare a schedule of cash receipts for September.
2. What is the appropriate accounting treatment for the bank service fees and the cash discounts allowed on collection of receivables?

10-47 Cash Discount with Spreadsheet Application   Use the data for Yeopay Plumbing Supply in Exercise 10-46.

Required

1. At the top of a new spreadsheet, create an "Original Data" section with four subheads: Sales Data, Sales Breakdown and Terms, Breakdown of Cash/Bank Credit Card Sales, and collection of Credit Sales.

2. Enter all pertinent data from Exercise 10-46 for determination of cash receipts.

3. Create a new section to calculate cash receipts for September with rows for Cash Sales, Bank Credit Card Sales, Collections of Accounts Receivable (4 rows), Total Cash Inflow, and columns for: Total Sales; Percentage of Sales for cash, bank credit card sales, and credit sales; Payment Percentage for the proportions collected (i.e., percentage collected to allow for cash discounts or late charges); and Cash Receipts.

4. Program your spreadsheet to perform all necessary calculations for determinations of cash receipts for September. Do not type in any amounts. All the amounts you enter into this new section should derive from data from the Original Data section using a formula.

5. Verify the accuracy of your spreadsheet by calculating the total cash receipts in September: $86,082.

6. Create a new section entitled October. Program your spreadsheet to perform all necessary calculations for determinations of cash receipts for October and verify the accuracy of your spreadsheet by showing that the total cash receipts for October is $88,141.

10-48 Activity-Based Budgeting (ABB)   OFC Company of Kansas City prints business forms and other specialty paper products, such as writing paper, envelopes, note cards, and greeting cards. Its Business Services division offers inventory-management services and desktop delivery on request. The division uses an activity-based costing system. The budgeted usage of each activity cost driver and cost-driver rates for January 2010 for the Business Services division are:

Activity	Cost Driver	Budgeted Activity	Cost-Driver Rate
Storage	Cartons in inventory	400,000	$0.4925/carton/month
Requisition handling	Requisitions	30,000	$ 12.50
Pick packing	Lines	800,000	$ 1.50
Data entry	Lines	800,000	$ 0.80
	Requisitions	30,000	$ 1.20
Desktop delivery	Per delivery	12,000	$ 30.00

The division made 11,700 deliveries to deliver 1,170,000 cartons to customers. The division expects the average delivery size in January 2010 to remain unchanged.

Required

1. What is the total budgeted cost for each activity and for the Business Services Division in January 2010?

2. What is the budgeted cost per delivered carton and the total budgeted cost for the Business Services Division if the firm uses a single cost rate (based on the number of cartons delivered) to estimate cost?

3. Dories Supply Chain Management Company offers to install an electronic order processing system that transmits customer requisitions via the Internet to the Business Services Division for immediate pick, packing, and delivery. No requisition handling and data entry will be needed once the system is fully functional. How much savings can the Business Services Division expect from switching to the new system before considering the payment to Dories? Can you estimate the amount if the firm uses a single cost rate (based on the number of cartons delivered) to determine the budgeted cost for the division?

10-49 Activity-Based Budgeting (ABB) with Continuous Improvements   OFC Company (Exercise 10-48) has decided to implement a continuous improvements program to improve operational efficiency. After a careful study, management and employees agree that the firm will be able to reduce cost rates for batch-level activities by 2 percent and unit-level activities by 1 percent per month during the first year of the program starting February 2010. The firm has decided to delay the implementation of the program for customer-sustaining and facility-level activities until 2011. The firm expects the amount of cost-driver usage in each of the next two months to be the same as those in January. (Use 4 decimal points for all cost rates.)

Required

1. Identify unit-level and batch-level activities.

2. What are the total budgeted costs for each activity and for the division as a whole in February and March?

3. Identify three factors that are likely to be critical for a successful kaizen program.

4. What are primary criticisms regarding Kaizen budgeting?

10-50 Cash Receipts and Payments   Information pertaining to Noskey Corporation's sales revenue follows:

	November 2009 (Actual)	December 2009 (Budgeted)	January 2010 (Budgeted)
Cash sales	$ 80,000	$100,000	$ 60,000
Credit sales	240,000	360,000	180,000
Total sales	$320,000	$460,000	$240,000

Management estimates 5 percent of credit sales to be uncollectible. Of collectible credit sales, 60 percent is collected in the month of sale and the remainder in the month following the month of sale. Purchases of inventory each month include 70 percent of the next month's projected total sales (stated at cost) plus 30% of projected sales for the current month (stated at cost). All inventory purchases are on account; 25 percent are paid in the month of purchase, and the remainder is paid in the month following the month of purchase. Purchase costs are approximately 60 percent of the selling price.

Required   Determine for Noskey:

1. Budgeted cash collections in December 2009 from November 2009 credit sales.

2. Budgeted total cash receipts in January 2010.

3. Budgeted total cash payments in December 2009 for inventory purchases.

(CPA Adapted)

10-51 Budgeting for a Service Firm   Refer to the AccuTax, Inc., example in the chapter. One of the partners is planning to retire at the end of the year. May Higgins, the sole remaining partner, plans to add a manager at an annual salary of $90,000. She expects the manager to work, on average, 45 hours a week for 45 weeks per year. She plans to change the required staff time for each hour spent to complete a tax return to the following:

	Business Return	Complex Individual Return	Simple Individual Return
Partner	0.3 hour	0.05 hour	—
Manager	0.2 hour	0.15 hour	—
Senior consultant	0.5 hour	0.40 hour	0.2 hour
Consultant	—	0.40 hour	0.8 hour

The manager is salaried and earns no overtime pay. Senior consultants are salaried but receive time and a half for any overtime worked. The firm plans to keep all the senior consultants and adjust the number of consultants as needed including employing part-time consultants, who also are paid on an hourly basis. The partner has also decided to have five supporting staff at $40,000 each. All other operating data remain unchanged. The manager will share 10 percent of any profit over $500,000 before bonus.

Required   Set up an Excel spreadsheet to answer the following questions:

1. What is the budgeted total cost for overtime hours worked by senior consultants?

2. How many full-time consultants should be budgeted?

3. Determine the manager's total compensation and total pretax operating income for the firm, assuming that the revenues from preparing tax returns remain unchanged.

10-52 **Budgetary Pressure and Ethics** Midwest Industries produces and distributes industrial chemicals in its Belco Division, which is located in Michigan's upper peninsula. Belco's earnings increased sharply in 2010, and bonuses were paid to the management staff for the first time in three years. Bonuses are based in part on the amount by which reported income exceeds budgeted income.

Maria Gonzales, vice president of finance, was pleased with reported earnings for 2010 and therefore thought that pressure to "show" financial results would subside. However, Tom Lin, Belco's division manager, told Gonzales that he "saw no reason why bonuses for 2011 should not be double those of 2010." As a result, Gonzales felt pressure to increase reported income to exceed budgeted income by an even greater amount, a situation that would ensure increased bonuses.

Gonzales met with Bill Wilson of P&R, Inc., a primary vendor of Belco's manufacturing supplies and equipment. Gonzales and Wilson have been close business contacts for many years. Gonzales asked Wilson to identify all of Belco's purchases of perishable supplies as "equipment" on sales invoices issued by P&R. The reason Gonzales gave for her request was that Belco's division manager had imposed stringent budget constraints on operating expenses, but not on capital expenditures. Gonzales planned to capitalize (rather than expense) the cost of perishable supplies and then include them in the equipment account on the balance sheet. In this way, Gonzales could defer the recognition of expenses to a later year. This procedure would increase reported earnings, which in turn would lead to higher bonuses (in the short run). Wilson agreed to do as Gonzales had asked.

While analyzing the second quarter financial statements, Gary Wood, Belco's director of cost accounting, noticed a large decrease in supplies expense from a year ago. Wood reviewed the Supplies Expense account and noticed that only equipment, not supplies, had been purchased from P&R, a major source for such supplies. Wood, who reports to Gonzales, immediately brought this to the attention of Gonzales.

Gonzales told Wood of Lin's high expectations and of the arrangement made with Wilson (from P&R). Wood told Gonzales that her action was an improper accounting treatment for the supplies purchased from P&R. Wood requested that he be allowed to correct the accounts and urged that the arrangement with P&R be discontinued. Gonzales refused the request and told Wood not to become involved in the arrangement with P&R.

After clarifying the situation in a confidential discussion with an objective and qualified peer within Belco, Wood arranged to meet with Lin, Belco's division manager. At that meeting, Wood disclosed the arrangement Gonzales had made with P&R.

Required

1. Explain why the use of alternative accounting methods to manipulate reported earnings is unethical, if not illegal.
2. Is Gary Wood, Belco's director of cost accounting, correct in saying that the supplies purchased from P&R, Inc. were accounted for improperly? Explain.
3. Assuming that the agreement of Gonzales with P&R was in violation of the IMA's *Statement of Ethical Professional Practice* (www.imanet.org), discuss whether Wood's actions were appropriate or inappropriate.

(CMA Adapted)

10-53 **Scenario Analysis** As part of the process of preparing the master budget for the coming year, you've been asked to perform what-if analyses, in the form of scenarios, on the original planning assumptions regarding Product A produced by your company. The following is the baseline planning data for the coming year for this product:

Sales volume (annual, in units)	1,000
Selling price per unit	$ 750
Variable cost per unit	$ 500
Fixed costs (per year)	$100,000

Required

1. Define what is meant by the terms *what-if analysis* and *scenario analysis.*
2. Based on the baseline planning data, what is the budgeted operating income for Product A for the coming year?

3. Determine the estimated operating income under each of the following scenarios (for each scenario you should report both the new budgeted operating income and the percentage change in operating income from the baseline budgeted result):

a. Selling price per unit is 10 percent higher than planned, while fixed costs per year are also 10 percent higher than planned.

b. Variable cost per unit is 5 percent higher than planned, while fixed costs are lower by this same percentage.

c. Selling price per unit is 10 percent higher than planned, while volume is decreased by 8 percent.

10-54 **Profit Planning and Sensitivity Analysis** You are currently trying to decide between two cost structures for your business, one that has a greater proportion of short-term fixed costs, the other that is more heavily weighted to variable costs. Estimated revenue and cost data for each alternative is as follows:

	Cost Structure	
	Alternative #1	Alternative #2
Selling price per unit	$ 100	$ 100
Variable cost per unit	$ 85	$ 80
Short-term fixed costs/year	$ 40,000	$ 45,000

Required

1. What sales volume, in units, is needed for the total costs in each cost-structure alternative to be the same?

2. Suppose your profit goal for the coming year is 5 percent on sales (i.e., operating profit/sales = 5%). What sales level in units is needed under each alternative to achieve this goal?

3. Suppose again that your profit goal for the coming year is 5 percent on sales. What sales volume in dollars is needed under each alternative to achieve this goal?

10-55 **Time-Driven Activity-Based Budgeting (TDABB)** The company for which you work recently implemented time-driven activity-based costing (TDABC) in conjunction with its ERP system. Management is pleased with the revised product and customer cost information that the TDABC system produces. It is now wondering how this system can be used for budgeting purposes. You have been asked to provide an example of using time-driven activity-based budgeting, given the following information:

1. There are two resources (departments): indirect labor and computer support.

2. There are two primary activities that these resources support: handling production runs and product-level support.

3. Indirect labor support is consumed as follows:

a. To handle production runs: 10 hours/run

b. To support products: 500 hours/product

4. Computer support is consumed as follows:

a. To handle production runs: 0.4 hr./run

b. To support products: 50 hours/product

5. Resource practical capacity levels:

a. Indirect labor: 20,000 hours per quarter

b. Computer support: 500 hours per quarter

6. Cost of supplying resources:

a. Indirect labor: $1,000,000 per quarter

b. Computer support: $500,000 per quarter

Required

1. Calculate the budgeted resource cost per hour (at practical capacity) for each of the two resources, *indirect labor support* and *computer support.*

2. Determine the budgeted cost-driver rates for each of two activities, *handle production runs,* and *support products.*

3. Suppose that the total cost of resources supplied for the quarter just ended was exactly as budgeted (i.e., $1,500,000), but that only 18,000 indirect labor hours were used along with 450 computer hours. Calculate, for each resource, the cost of unused capacity. How should this cost be handled for internal reporting purposes?

4. After implementing a TQM program, the company was able to implement process-efficiency changes, the end result of which was a 10 percent reduction in the indirect labor time associated with the activity handling production runs. Re-estimate the indirect labor cost component of the cost to handle a production run. Also, recalculate the cost of unused capacity for indirect labor assuming the original facts but with the 10 percent efficiency gain. Assume that in the original case facts, 16,000 of the 18,000 hours related to the activity handling production runs (while the remaining 2,000 hours related to the activity support product).

10-56 **Rolling Financial Forecasts**   You are given the following budgeted and actual data for the Grey Company for each of the months January through June of the current year.

In December of the prior year, sales were forecasted as follows: January, 100 units; February, 95 units; March, 100 units; April, 110 units; May, 120 units; June, 125 units. In January of the current year, sales for the months February through June were reforecasted as follows: February, 90 units; March, 100 units; April, 105 units; May, 110 units; June, 120 units. In February of the current year, sales for the months March through June were reforecasted as follows: March, 95 units; April, 105 units; May, 105 units; June, 120 units. In March of the current year, sales for the months April through June were reforecasted as follows: April, 105 units; May, 100 units; June, 110 units. In April of the current year, sales for the months May and June were reforecasted as follows: May, 90 units; June, 105 units. In May of the current year, sales for June were reforecasted as 105 units.

Actual sales for the six-month period were as follows: January, 98 units; February, 95 units; March, 92 units; April, 108 units; May, 98 units; June, 100 units.

Required

1. For each of the months January through June, inclusive, prepare a rolling forecast of sales volume. (*Hint:* there will be only one forecasted number for January—this is the forecast done in December. For February, there will be two forecasts: one done in December and a second done in January. For June, there will be six forecasts, one for each of the preceding six months.)

2. For each of the months March through June, determine the three-month forecast error rate, defined as 1 minus the absolute percentage error. For example, the forecast error rate for March's sales is found by dividing the *absolute value* of the forecast error for this month by the actual sales volume for the month. The *forecast error* for any month (e.g., March) is defined as the difference between the actual sales volume for the month and the sales volume for that month forecasted three months earlier (e.g., December).

Problems   10-57 **Profit Planning and What-If Analysis**   As a newly hired management accountant, you have been asked to prepare a profit plan for the company for which you work. As part of this task, you've been asked to do some what-if analyses. Following is the budgeted information regarding the coming year:

Selling price per unit	$ 40.00
Variable cost per unit	$ 32.00
Fixed costs (per year)	$450,000

Required

1. What is the breakeven volume, in units and dollars, for the coming year?

2. Assume that the goal of the company is to earn a pretax (operating) profit of $180,000 for the coming year. How many units would the company have to sell to achieve this goal?

3. Assume that, of the $32 variable cost per unit, the labor-cost component is $10. Current negotiations with the employees of the company indicate some uncertainty regarding the labor-cost component of the variable cost figure presented above. What is the effect on the breakeven point in units if selling price and fixed costs are as planned, but the labor cost for the coming year is 4 percent higher than anticipated? What if labor costs are 6 percent higher than anticipated? What if labor costs turn out to be 8 percent higher than anticipated? (Show calculations.)

4. Assume now that management is convinced that labor costs will be 5 percent higher than originally planned when the budget for the year was put together. What selling price per unit must the company

charge to maintain the budgeted ratio of contribution margin to sales? (*Hint:* Use the Goal-Seek function in Excel to answer this question.)

5. Explain the role of what-if analysis in the budgeting process.

10-58 Profit Planning and Strategic Considerations Because of competitive pressures and potential increases in product quality, your company is evaluating whether it should replace an existing piece of machinery that is used in the manufacture of a key product produced by the company. Because of anticipated decreases in manufacturing cycle time and increases in product quality, you anticipate that, if the company purchases the new machine, it would be able to increase the selling price for the product. Baseline budgeted data are as follows:

Product-Related Information	Existing Machine	New Machine
Sales price per unit	$ 15.00	$ 17.50
Variable cost per unit	$ 12.00	$ 12.00
Fixed costs per month	$100,000	$200,000

Required

1. What is the monthly breakeven volume for each of the two decision alternatives?

2. Assume that in the past the company's targeted ratio of operating profit to sales was 12 percent. What sales level, in units per month, would the company have to generate for each alternative in order to meet this stated profitability target?

3. In evaluating this investment proposal, management is interested in knowing the monthly sales volume (in units) at which the two decision alternatives yield the same operating profit (in dollars). Determine what this monthly volume is. Construct a graph to depict the operating profit equation for each decision alternative. Be sure to fully label the graph, to include the profit equation for each alternative, the breakeven point for each alternative, and the volume level at which the company would be indifferent between the two alternatives.

4. What strategic factors or considerations might affect the decision as to whether the company should keep or replace the existing equipment?

10-59 Ethics in Budgeting/Budgetary Slack Norton Company, a manufacturer of infant furniture and carriages, is in the initial stages of preparing the annual budget for 2010. Scott Ford recently joined Norton's accounting staff and is interested in learning as much as possible about the company's budgeting process. During a recent lunch with Marge Atkins, sales manager, and Pete Granger, production manager, Scott initiated the following conversation:

Scott: Since I'm new around here and am going to be involved with the preparation of the annual budget, I'd be interested to learn how the two of you estimate sales and production numbers.

Marge: We start out very methodically by looking at recent history, discussing what we know about current accounts, potential customers, and the general state of consumer spending. Then, we add that usual dose of intuition to come up with the best forecast we can.

Pete: I usually take the sales projections as the basis for my projections. Of course, we have to make an estimate of what this year's closing inventories will be, and that sometimes is difficult.

Scott: Why does that present a problem? There must have been an estimate of closing inventories in the budget for the current year.

Pete: Those numbers aren't always reliable since Marge makes some adjustments to the sales numbers before passing them on to me.

Scott: What kind of adjustments?

Marge: Well, we don't want to fall short of the sales projections so we generally give ourselves a little breathing room by lowering the initial sales projection anywhere from 5 to 10 percent.

Pete: So you can see why this year's budget is not a very reliable starting point. We always have to adjust the projected production rates as the year progresses and, of course, this changes the ending inventory estimates. By the way, we make similar adjustments to expenses by adding at least 10 percent to the estimates; I think everyone around here does the same thing.

Required

1. Marge Atkins and Pete Granger have described the use of *budgetary slack.*

   a. Explain why Marge and Pete might behave in this manner, and describe the benefits they expect to realize from the use of budgetary slack.

   b. Explain how the use of budgetary slack can adversely affect Marge and Pete personally, and the organization as a whole.

2. As a management accountant, Scott Ford believes that the behavior described by Marge and Pete may be unethical and that he may have an obligation not to support this behavior. By citing the specific standards from the IMA's "Statement of Ethical Professional Practice" (www.imanet.org), explain why the use of budgetary slack may be unethical.

(CMA Adapted)

10-60 **Comprehensive Profit Plan**   Spring Manufacturing Company makes two components identified as C12 and D57. Selected budgetary data for 2010 follow:

	Finished Components	
	C12	**D57**
Requirements for each finished component:		
RM 1	10 pounds	8 pounds
RM 2	0	4 pounds
RM 3	2 pounds	1 pound
Direct labor	2 hours	3 hours
Product information:		
Sales price	$150	$220
Sales (units)	12,000	9,000
Estimated beginning inventory (units)	400	150
Desired ending inventory (units)	300	200

	Direct Materials Information		
	RM1	**RM2**	**RM3**
Cost per pound	$ 2.00	$ 2.50	$ 0.50
Estimated beginning inventory in pounds	3,000	1,500	1,000
Desired ending inventory in pounds	4,000	1,000	1,500

The firm expects the average wage rate to be $25 per hour in 2010. Spring Manufacturing uses direct labor-hours to apply overhead. Each year the firm determines the overhead application rate for the year based on the budgeted output for the year. The firm maintains negligible work-in-process inventory and expects the cost per unit for both beginning and ending finished products inventories to be identical.

	Factory Overhead Information
Indirect materials—variable	$ 10,000
Miscellaneous supplies and tools—variable	5,000
Indirect labor—variable	40,000
Supervision—fixed	120,000
Payroll taxes and fringe benefits—variable	250,000
Maintenance costs—fixed	20,000
Maintenance costs—variable	10,080
Depreciation—fixed	71,330
Heat, light, and power—fixed	43,420
Heat, light, and power—variable	11,000
Total	$580,830

(Continued)

	Selling and Administrative Expense Information
Advertising	$ 60,000
Sales salaries	200,000
Travel and entertainment	60,000
Depreciation—warehouse	5,000
Office salaries	60,000
Executive salaries	250,000
Supplies	4,000
Depreciation—office	6,000
Total	$645,000

The effective income tax rate for the company is 40 percent.

Required Prepare an Excel spreadsheet that contains the following schedules or statements for 2010:

1. Sales budget
2. Production budget
3. Direct materials purchases budget (units and dollars)
4. Direct labor budget
5. Factory overhead budget
6. Cost of goods sold and ending finished goods inventory budgets
7. Selling and general administrative expense budget
8. Budgeted income statement

10-61 Comprehensive Profit Plan   (Use information in Problem 10-60 for Spring Manufacturing Company.) C12 is a mature product. The sales manager believes that the price of C12 can be raised to $160 per unit with no effect on sales quantity. D57 is a new product introduced last year. Management believes D57 has a great potential and is considering lowering the price to $180 to expand market size and gain market share. The lowering of D57's price is likely to double the total units of D57 sold.

Required

1. Amend the spreadsheet you constructed in Problem 10-60 to incorporate the changes outlined above. What effect do the changes have on the firm's after-tax operating income?
2. Would you recommend that the firm execute this strategy?

10-62 Comprehensive Profit Plan (Kaizen Budgeting)   (Use information in Problem 10-60 for Spring Manufacturing Company.) Spring Manufacturing Company has had a continuous improvement (kaizen) program for the last two years. According to the kaizen program, the firm is expected to manufacture C12 and D57 with the following specifications:

Cost Element	C12	D57
Raw material 1	9 pounds	7 pounds
Raw material 2	- 0 -	3.6 pounds
Raw material 3	1.8 pounds	0.8 pounds
Direct labor	1.5 hours	2 hours

The firm specifies that the variable factory overhead is to decrease by 10 percent while the fixed factory overhead is to decrease by 5 percent, except for depreciation expenses. The firm does not expect the price of the raw materials to change. However, the hourly wage rate is likely to be $30.

Required

1. What is the budgeted after-tax operating income if the firm can attain the expected operation level as prescribed by its kaizen program?
2. What are the benefits of Spring Manufacturing Company adopting a continuous improvement program? What are the limitations?

10-63 **Retailer Budget**   D. Tomlinson Retail seeks your assistance in developing cash and other budget information for May, June, and July. The store expects to have the following balances at the end of April:

Cash	$ 5,500
Accounts receivable	437,000
Inventories	309,400
Accounts payable	133,055

The firm follows these guidelines in preparing its budgets:

- **Sales.** All sales are on credit with terms of 3/10, n/30. Tomlinson bills customers on the last day of each month. The firm books receivables at gross amounts and collects 60 percent of the billings within the discount period, 25 percent by the end of the month, and 9 percent by the end of the second month. The firm's experience suggests that 6 percent is likely to be uncollectible and is written off at the end of the third month.
- **Purchases and expenses.** All purchases and expenses are on open account. The firm pays its payables over a two-month period with 54 percent paid in the month of purchase. Each month's units of ending inventory should equal 130 percent of the next month's cost of sales. The cost of each unit of inventory is $20. Selling and general and administrative expenses, of which $2,000 is depreciation, equal 15 percent of the current month's sales.

  Actual and projected sales follow:

Month	Dollars	Units	Month	Dollars	Units
March	$354,000	11,800	June	342,000	11,400
April	363,000	12,100	July	360,000	12,000
May	357,000	11,900	August	366,000	12,200

Required

1. Prepare schedules showing budgeted purchases for May and June.
2. Prepare a schedule showing budgeted cash disbursements during June.
3. Prepare a schedule showing budgeted cash collections during May.
4. Determine gross and net balances of accounts receivable on May 31.

(CMA Adapted)

10-64 **Sales Budget and Pro Forma Financial Statements**   Mark Dalid founded Molid Company three years ago. The company produces PDAs that are compatible with the most operating systems including Palm, MS Windows, and Linux with USB connection and WiFi capability. Since the company's inception its business has expanded rapidly.

Maria Sanchez, the company's general accountant, prepared a budget for the fiscal year ending August 31, 2011, based on the prior year's sales and production activity. In view of the general business slowdown, Mark believes that the sales growth experienced during the prior year will not continue at the same pace. The pro forma statements of income and cost of goods sold prepared as part of the budget processes follow:

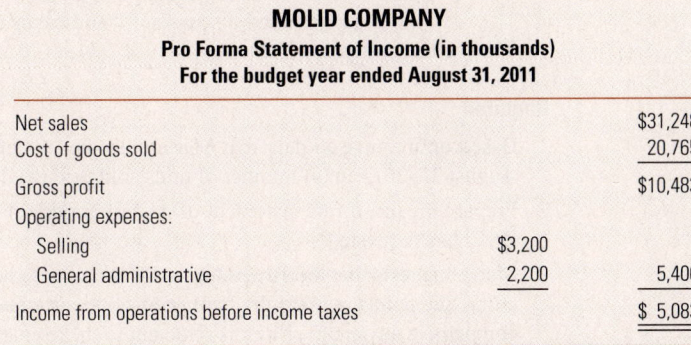

MOLID COMPANY
Pro Forma Statement of Income (in thousands)
For the budget year ended August 31, 2011

Net sales		$31,248
Cost of goods sold		20,765
Gross profit		$10,483
Operating expenses:		
Selling	$3,200	
General administrative	2,200	5,400
Income from operations before income taxes		$ 5,083

MOLID COMPANY
Pro Forma Statement of Cost of Goods Sold (in thousands)
For the budget year ended August 31, 2011

Direct materials:		
Materials inventory, 9/1/2010	$ 1,360	
Materials purchases	14,476	
Materials available for use	$15,836	
Materials inventory, 8/31/2011	1,628	
Cost of direct materials used		$14,208
Direct labor		1,134
Factory overhead:		
Indirect materials	$ 1,421	
General factory overhead	3,240	4,661
Cost of goods manufactured		$20,003
Finished goods inventory, 9/1/2010		1,169
Cost of goods available for sale		$21,172
Finished goods inventory, 8/31/2011		407
Cost of goods sold		$20,765

On December 10, 2010, Mark and Maria met to discuss the first quarter operating results (September 1 through November 30, 2010). Maria believed that several changes should be made to the original budget assumptions that had been used to prepare the pro forma statements. She prepared the following notes summarizing the changes that had not become known until the first quarter results had been compiled. She submitted the following data to Mark:

a. The estimated production in units for the fiscal year should be revised upward from 162,000 units to 170,000 units with the balance of production being scheduled in equal segments over the last nine months of the fiscal year. Actual first quarter production was 35,000 units.

b. The planned ending inventory for finished goods of 3,300 units at the end of the fiscal year remains unchanged. The finished goods inventory of 9,300 units as of September 1, 2010, had dropped to 9,000 units by November 30, 2010. The finished goods inventory at the end of the fiscal year will be valued at the average manufacturing cost for the year.

c. The direct labor rate will increase 8 percent as of June 1, 2011, as a consequence of a new labor agreement signed during the first quarter. When the original pro forma statements were prepared, the expected effective date for this new labor agreement had been September 1, 2011.

d. Direct materials sufficient to produce 16,000 units were on hand at the beginning of the fiscal year. The plan to have sufficient direct materials inventory at the end of the fiscal year for 18,500 units of production remains unchanged. Direct materials inventory is valued on a first-in, first-out (FIFO) basis. Direct materials equivalent to 37,500 units of output were purchased for $3,300,000 during the first quarter of the fiscal year.

   Molid's suppliers have informed the company that direct materials prices will increase 5 percent on March 1, 2011. Direct materials needed for the rest of the fiscal year will be purchased evenly through the last nine months.

e. On the basis of historical data, indirect materials cost is projected at 10 percent of the cost of direct materials consumed.

f. One-half of general factory overhead and all of selling and general administrative expenses are considered fixed in the short run.

   After an extended discussion, Dalid asked for new pro forma statements for the fiscal year ending August 31, 2011.

Required

1. Based on the revised data that Maria presented, calculate Molid Company's sales for the year ending August 31, 2011 in (a) number of units sold, and (b) dollar volume of net sales.

2. Prepare the pro forma statement of cost of goods sold for the year ending August 31, 2011, that Mark Dalid had requested.

3. Maria suggests that the firm adopt a JIT strategy to better serve customers and to reduce obsolescence costs. She points out that the firm needs to incorporate new manufacturing technologies to maintain its competitive advantage. Mark is reluctant to make changes because he does not want to upset the proven successful business. He knows that any changes cost money, and he does not want to commit fresh

capital just to change the business procedures. Maria argues that no additional capital will be needed to fund the changes. She points out that a JIT system maintains no finished goods inventory and no more materials than those needed to produce 100 units of the finished products.

   a. How much will the firm save by changing to a JIT system? (*Hint:* Estimate the cost savings per year as the product of the firm's cost of capital, say 10 percent and the estimated reduction in net working capital under JIT.)

   b. Should the firm follow Maria's suggestion?

   c. What other factors should be considered in making the decision?

(CMA Adapted)

10-65 **Budget for a Merchandising Firm**   Kelly Company is a retail sporting goods store that uses an accrual accounting system. Facts regarding its operations follow:

- Sales are budgeted at $220,000 for December and $200,000 for January, terms 1/eom, n/60.
- Collections are expected to be 60 percent in the month of sale and 38 percent in the month following the sale. Two percent of sales are expected to be uncollectible and recorded in an allowance account at the end of the month of sales. Bad debts expense is included as part of operating expenses.
- Gross margin is 25 percent of sales.
- All accounts receivable are from credit sales. Bad debts are written off against the allowance account at the end of the month following the month of sale.
- Kelly desires to have 80 percent of the merchandise for the following month's sales on hand at the end of each month. Payment for merchandise is made in the month following the month of purchase.
- Other monthly operating expenses to be paid in cash total $22,600.
- Annual depreciation is $216,000, one-twelfth of which is reflected as part of monthly operating expenses.

Kelly Company's statement of financial position at the close of business on November 30 follows:

KELLY COMPANY
Statement of Financial Position
November 30, 2010

Assets	
Cash	$ 22,000
Accounts receivable (net of $4,000 allowance for doubtful accounts)	76,000
Inventory	132,000
Property, plant, and equipment (net of $680,000 accumulated depreciation)	870,000
Total assets	$1,100,000

Liabilities and Stockholders' Equity	
Accounts payable	$ 162,000
Common stock	800,000
Retained earnings	138,000
Total liabilities and equity	$1,100,000

Required

1. What is the total of budgeted cash collections for December?
2. How much is the book value of accounts receivable at the end of December?
3. How much is the income (loss) before income taxes for December?
4. What is the projected balance in inventory on December 31, 2010?
5. What are budgeted purchases for December?
6. What is the projected balance in accounts payable on December 31, 2010?

(CMA Adapted)

10-66 **Budgets for a Service Firm** Triple-F Health Club (Family, Fitness, and Fun) is a not-for-profit family-oriented health club. The club's board of directors is developing plans to acquire more equipment and expand club facilities. The board plans to purchase about $25,000 of new equipment each year and wants to establish a fund to purchase the adjoining property in four or five years. The adjoining property has a market value of about $300,000.

The club manager, Jane Crowe, is concerned that the board has unrealistic goals in light of the club's recent financial performance. She has sought the help of a club member with an accounting background to assist her in preparing a report to the board supporting her concerns.

The member reviewed the club's records, including this cash-basis income statement:

TRIPLE-F HEALTH CLUB
Income Statement (Cash Basis)
For Years Ended October 31 (in thousands)

	2011	2010
Cash revenues:		
Annual membership fees	$355.0	$300.0
Lesson and class fees	234.0	180.0
Miscellaneous	2.0	1.5
Total cash revenues	$591.0	$481.5
Cash expenses:		
Manager's salary and benefits	$ 36.0	$ 36.0
Regular employees' wages and benefits	190.0	190.0
Lesson and class employees' wages and benefits	195.0	150.0
Towels and supplies	16.0	15.5
Utilities (heat and light)	22.0	15.0
Mortgage interest	35.1	37.8
Miscellaneous	2.0	1.5
Total cash expenditures	$496.1	$445.8
Increase in cash	$ 94.9	$ 35.7

- Other financial information as of October 31, 2011:

  Cash in checking account, $7,000.

  Petty cash, $300.

  Outstanding mortgage balance, $360,000.

  Accounts payable arising from invoices for supplies and utilities that are unpaid as of October 31, 2011, and due in November 2011, $2,500.

- No other unpaid bills existed on October 31, 2011.

- The club purchased $25,000 worth of exercise equipment during the current fiscal year. Cash of $10,000 was paid on delivery, with the balance due on October 1, but which had not been paid as of October 31, 2011. An additional $25,000 (cash) of equipment purchases is planned for the coming year.

- The club began operations in 2007 in rental quarters. In October 2007, it purchased its current property (land and building) for $600,000, paying $120,000 down and agreeing to pay $30,000 plus 9 percent interest annually on the unpaid loan balance each November 1, starting November 1, 2008.

- Membership rose 3 percent in 2011. The club has experienced approximately this same annual growth rate since it opened and this rate is expected to continue in the future.

- Membership fees increased by 15 percent in 2011. The board has tentative plans to increase these fees by 10 percent in 2012.

- Lesson and class fees have not been increased for three years. The board policy is to encourage classes and lessons by keeping the fees low. The members have taken advantage of this policy, and the number of classes and lessons has increased significantly each year. The club expects the percentage growth experienced in 2011 to be repeated in 2012.

- Miscellaneous revenues are expected to grow at the same rate as in 2011.

• Operating expenses expected to increase:

   Hourly wage rates and the manager's salary: 15 percent.

   Towels and supplies, utilities, and miscellaneous expenses: 25 percent.

Required

1. Prepare a cash budget for 2012 for the Triple-F Health Club.

2. Identify any operating problems that this budget discloses for the Triple-F Health Club. Explain your answer.

3. Is Jane Crowe's concern that the board's goals are unrealistic justified? Explain your answer.

(CMA Adapted)

10-67 **Budgeting for Marketing Expenses; Strategy** You have been recruited by a former classmate, Susanna Wu, to join the finance team of a company that she founded recently. The company produces a unique product line of hypoallergenic cosmetics and relies for its success on an aggressive marketing program. The company is in a start-up phase and therefore has no significant history of expenses and revenues upon which to rely for budgeting and planning purposes. Given the restriction on available funds (most of the available capital has been used for new-product development and to recruit a management team), the control of costs, including marketing costs, is thought by the management team to be essential for the short-term viability of the company.

   You have held a number of intensive discussions with Susanna and John Thompson, director of marketing for the firm. They have asked you to prepare an estimated budget for marketing expenses for a month of operations.

   You are provided with the following data, which represent average actual monthly costs over the past three months:

Cost	Amount
Sales commissions	$120,000
Sales staff salaries	40,000
Telephone and mailing	38,000
Rental—office building	25,000
Gas (utilities)	12,000
Delivery charges	70,000
Depreciation—office furniture	8,000
Marketing consultants	25,000

   Your discussions with John and Susanna indicate the following assumptions and anticipated changes regarding monthly marketing expenses for the coming year.

• Sales volume, because of aggressive marketing, should increase on a monthly basis by 10 percent.

• Sales prices are expected to decrease, to meet competitive pressures, by 5 percent.

• Sales commissions are based on a percentage of sales revenue.

• Sales staff salaries, because of a new hire, will increase by 10 percent per month, regardless of sales volume.

• Because of recent industrywide factors, rates for telephone and mailing costs, as well as delivery charges, are expected to increase by 6 percent. However, both of these categories of costs are variable with sales volume.

• Rent on the office building is based on a two-year lease, with 18 months remaining on the original lease.

• Gas utility costs are largely independent of changes in sales volume. However, because of industrywide disruptions in supply, these costs are expected to increase by 15 percent per month, regardless of changes in sales volume.

• Depreciation on the office furniture used by members of the sales staff should increase because of new equipment that will be acquired. The planned cost for this equipment is $30,000, which will be depreciated using the straight-line (SL) method, with no salvage value, over a five-year useful life.

• Because of competitive pressure, the company plans to increase the cost of marketing consultants by $5,000 per month.

Required

1. Use the preceding information to develop an Excel spreadsheet that can be used to generate a monthly budget for marketing expenses. (Use the built-in function "SLN" to calculate monthly depreciation charges for the new equipment to be purchased.) What is the percentage change, by line item and in total, for items in your budget?

2. The management team is worried about the short-term financial position of the new company. Given the strain on available cash, the president has expressed a desire to keep marketing expenses over the next few months to a maximum of $350,000. Discussions with the marketing department indicate that telephone and mailing costs are the only category, in the short run, that can reasonably bear the planned-for reduction in marketing costs. The budget you have prepared includes an assumed 6 percent increase in telephone and mailing costs. What must this percentage change (positive or negative) be in order to achieve targeted monthly marketing costs? (*Hint:* Use the Goal-Seek function in Excel, which is found under Data Tools, then What-If Analysis.)

3. Comment on the use of the budget in this situation for cost-control purposes.

10-68 Strategy, Product Life-Cycle, and Cash Flow   Burke Company manufactures various electronic assemblies that it sells primarily to computer manufacturers. Burke has built its reputation on quality, timely delivery, and products that are consistently on the cutting edge of technology. Burke's business is fast paced: a typical product has a short life; the product is in development for about a year and in the growth stage, with spectacular growth sometimes, for about a year. Each product then experiences a rapid decline in sales as new products become available.

Burke has just hired a new vice-president of finance, Devin Ward. Shortly after reporting for work at Burke, he had a conversation with Andrew Newhouse, Burke's president. A portion of the conversation follows.

Andrew: The thing that fascinates me about this business is that change is its central ingredient. We knew when we started out that a reliable stream of new products was one of our key variables, in fact, the only way to cope with the threat of product obsolescence. You see, our products go through only the first half of the traditional product life-cycle—the development stage and then the growth stage. Our products never reach the traditional mature product stage or the declining product stage. Toward the end of the growth stage, products die as new ones are introduced.

Devin: I suppose your other key variables are cost controls and efficient production scheduling?

Andrew: Getting the product to market on schedule, whether efficiently or not, is important. Some firms in this business announce a new product in March to be delivered in June, and they make the first shipment in October, or a year from March, or sometimes, never. Our reputation for delivering on schedule could account for our success as much as anything.

Devin: Where I previously worked, we also recognized the importance of on-time deliveries. Our goal was a 93 percent on-time rate.

Andrew: The key variable that is your responsibility is cash management. It took us a while to recognize that. At first, we thought that profit was the key and that cash would naturally follow. But now we know that cash is the key and the profits naturally follow. Still, we don't manage cash well. Improving our cash management is the main thing we expect from you.

Required

1. Discuss the cash-generating and cash-usage characteristics of products in general in each of the four stages of the product life cycle—development, growth, maturity, and decline.

2. Describe the cash-management problems confronting Burke Company.

3. Suggest techniques that Devin might implement to cope with Burke Company's cash-management problems.

(CMA Adapted)

10-69 Budgeting Customer Retention and Insurance-Policy Renewal; Sensitivity Analysis   National Insurance company underwrites property insurance for homeowners. You have been charged with the responsibility of developing a portion of the monthly budget for the coming 12-month period for the company.

You have collected the following driver volumes, consumption rates, unit resource costs, and other data needed to prepare your 12-month budget for those active policyholders whose policy runs from January to December:

Number of active policyholders beginning of month #1	100,000
Average monthly premium per policy	$100.00
Monthly mid-term cancellation rate	0.50%
Policy renewal rate	85.00%

Required

1. Prepare, in good form, a monthly budget for customer retention and insurance premium revenue for the period January through December. Columns in your budget should represent months, while the rows in your budget should consist of the following: number of policyholders at beginning of the month; midterm cancellation rate (%); number of active policyholders at end of the month; average number of active policyholders during the month; average monthly premium per policy; and total premiums earned per month from active policyholders. How many policies are projected to be renewed at the end of the year?

2. Within the context of budgeting, what do we mean by the term *what-if analysis?*

3. Recreate the original 12-month budget you prepared in (1) above to reflect what would happen if the policy-renewal rate falls to 80 percent and the monthly midterm cancellation rate increases to 0.75 percent. Of what potential significance is the analysis you just performed?

4. What other information or data would be included in the full budget prepared each month for the company?

10-70 **Budgeting Insurance Policy Volume and Monthly Revenues**   National Auto Insurance company underwrites automobile coverage for the consumer market. As part of the annual planning process, National requires monthly estimates for number of policies in force and the amount of premium revenue associated with this volume of business. You have been asked to prepare these estimates for the coming six-month period. Past experience indicates that number of policies outstanding during a given month is influenced both by macro factors [e.g., market size (total number of households) and market growth rate] and company-specific factors (e.g., market share, cancellation rate experience).

At the beginning of January for the new budget year, the number of households is estimated as 100 million; further, past experience indicates that this will increase by approximately 0.05 percent per month. Your own research indicates that approximately 80 percent of households have one or more cars. On average, each household owns 2.2 cars. Because of legal requirements, the average percentage of cars insured is high—your best estimate is that this number is 85 percent and growing by 0.1 percent per month. Current market share of National Auto in the consumer market is approximately 10 percent. Over the past 24 months, the rate of increase in market share for National has been 0.005 percent per month. Because of aggressive levels of customer service, National has been able to keep its monthly cancellation rate below average, to approximately 0.125 percent. Average monthly premium paid per auto insured for the coming year is assumed to be $100.

Required

1. For each of the months January–June in the coming year prepare, a budget broken down in three parts:

   a. Market size and volume.

   b. Volume for National Auto Insurance (number of policies outstanding).

   c. Premium revenues generated.

   For (a) above, you should have six rows of data, as follows: total number of households (i.e., market size), percentage of households owning one or more cars; number of cars owned per household; percentage of car owners with insurance; total number of insured cars (marketwide); market share of National Auto; and number of autos insured by National Auto, end of the month. For (b) above, your budget should have four rows, as follows: number of cars insured, beginning of the month; cancellations during the month; number of insured autos, end of the month; and average number of insured autos during the month. For (c) above, your budget should have the following three rows: average number of cars insured during the month; average insurance premium per car per month; total monthly premium revenue.

2. What additional real-life refinements do you envision for the budgets you prepared above in (1)? What additional budgets would you anticipate preparing for the company if you were in charge of the budget-preparation process?

3. The budgets you prepared above in (1) can be referred to as *driver-based budgets.* List some of the pros and the cons of such budgets, relative to traditional budgeting practices.

10-71 Comprehensive Budget; Strategy   Gold Sporting Equipment (GSE) is in the process of preparing its budget for the third quarter of 2010. The budgeting staff has gathered the following data:

1. Account balances as of June 30:

Cash	$ 25,000
Accounts receivable	15,000
Short-term payable (equipment purch.)	0
Merchandise inventory	47,520
Building and equipment (net)	200,000
Bank loans pay	0
Income tax payable	0

2. Recent and forecasted sales:

June (actual)	$ 75,000
July	80,000
August	82,000
September	90,000
October	100,000

3. Sales are 80 percent cash and 20 percent on credit. Credit accounts are all collected 30 days after sale.

4. At gross purchase prices of inventories, GSE's gross margin averages 40 percent of revenues. GSE records all inventory purchases net of available purchase discounts.

5. Operating expenses: Salaries and wages, $8,000 per month plus 5 percent of revenue; rent and property tax, $1,000 per month; other operating expenses, excluding depreciation, 2 percent of revenues; depreciation $800 per month. All cash operating expenses in a month are paid before the end of the month.

6. GSE has no minimum inventory requirement. The policy is to purchase each month on the 15th the expected sales (@ cost) for the following month. Terms of purchases are 1/10, n/30. Purchases usually arrive on or before the 20th. GSE's policy is to take all cash discounts offered.

7. GSE is negotiating the purchase of new equipment for $127,000 to be installed in September. Terms are 50 percent in the month before and 50 percent after the month of installation.

8. Minimum cash balance is $30,000. All borrowings are effective at the beginning of the month and all repayments are made at the end of the month of repayment. Loans are repaid when sufficient cash is available. The interest rate is 15 percent per year, payable at the end of each month. Both borrowings and repayments are in multiples of $10,000. Management does not want to borrow any more cash than is necessary and wants to repay whenever the cash on hand exceeds the minimum requirement.

9. GSE plans to pay no dividend to stockholders.

Required

1. Complete schedules A through E.

Schedule A: Budgeted Monthly Cash Receipts

Item	June	July	August	September
Cash sales				
Credit sales				
Total sales				
Receipts:				
Cash sales	N/A			
Collections on accounts	N/A			
Total cash collections				

(Continued)

Schedule B: Budgeted Monthly Cash Disbursements for Purchases

Item	July	August	September	3rd Quarter
Purchases (gross)				
Cash discount				
Total				

Schedule C: Budgeted Monthly Cash Disbursements for Operating Costs

Item	July	August	September	3rd Quarter
Salaries and wages				
Rent and property taxes				
Other cash operating costs				
Total				

Schedule D: Budgeted Total Cash Disbursements Prior to Financing

Item	July	August	September	3rd Quarter
Cash operating costs				
Purchases				
Equipment				
Total				

Schedule E: Cash Budget

Item	July	August	September	3rd Quarter
Cash balance, beginning				
Total cash receipts				
Total cash disbursements prior to financing				
Cash balance before financing				
Financing:				
Borrowing required				
Interest expense				
Borrowing repaid				
Cash balance, ending				

2. Prepare a budgeted income statement for the third quarter and beginning and end-of-quarter balance sheets. GSE estimates its income tax rate at 25 percent, payable in the second quarter of the following year. (*Hint:* Cost of goods sold % is 59.4%.)

3. Gold Sporting Equipment has been using the loan described in Item 8 to meet its needs for funds. Alternatively, Gold can issue long-term bonds at no more than 12 percent annual interest rate to increase funds available for operations. What is the most sensible type of loan GSE should use to meet its needs? Explain your reasoning.

4. The underlying business situation has been greatly simplified. List at least three complicating factors that may exist in a real business setting.

10-72 **Cash-Flow Analysis; Sensitivity Analysis** CompCity, Inc., sells computer hardware. It also markets related software and software-support services. The company prepares annual forecasts for sales, of which the first six months of 2010 are given below.

In a typical month, total sales are broken down as follows: cash sales, 25 percent; VISA® credit card sales, 55 percent; and 20 percent open account (the company's own charge accounts). For budgeting purposes, assume that cash sales plus bank credit card sales are received in the month of sale; bank credit card sales are subject to a 3 percent processing fee, which is deducted daily at the time of deposit into CompCity's cash account with the bank. Cash receipts from collection of accounts receivable typically occur as follows: 25 percent in the month of sale, 45 percent in the month following the month of sale, and 27 percent in the second month following the month of sale. The remaining receivables generally turn out to be uncollectible.

CompCity's month-end inventory requirements for computer hardware units are 30 percent of the following month's estimated sales. A one-month lead time is required for delivery from the hardware distributor. Thus, orders for computer hardware units are generally placed by CompCity on the 25th of each month to ensure availability in the store on the first day of the month needed. These units are purchased on credit, under the following terms: n/45, *measured from the time the units are delivered to CompCity.* Assume that CompCity takes the maximum amount of time to pay its invoices. On average, the purchase price for hardware units runs 65 percent of selling price.

COMPCITY, INC.
Forecasted Sales (units and dollars)
January–June, 2010

	No. of Units	Hardware Sales	Software/Support Sales	Total Revenue
January	120	$ 360,000	$140,000	$ 500,000
February	130	390,000	160,000	550,000
March	90	270,000	130,000	400,000
April	100	300,000	125,000	425,000
May	110	330,000	150,000	480,000
June	120	360,000	140,000	500,000
Totals	670	$2,010,000	$845,000	$2,855,000

Required

1. Calculate estimated cash receipts for April 2010 (show details).
2. The company wants to estimate the number of hardware units to order on January 25th.
   a. Determine the estimated number of units to be ordered.
   b. Calculate the dollar cost (per unit and total) for these units.
3. Cash planning in this line of business is critical to success. Management feels that the assumption of selling price per unit ($3,000) is firm—at least for the foreseeable future. Also, it is comfortable with the 30 percent rate for end-of-month inventories. It is not so sure, however, about (a) the CGS rate (because of the state of flux in the supplier market), and (b) the level of predicted sales in March 2010. Discussions with marketing and purchasing suggest that three outcomes are possible for each of these two variables, as follows:

Outcome	March Sales	CGS%
Optimistic	100 units	60%
Expected	90 units	65%
Pessimistic	80 units	70%

The preceding outcomes are assumed to be independent, which means that there are nine possible combinations (3 × 3). You are asked to conduct a sensitivity analysis to determine the range of possible cash outflows for April 10th, under different combinations of the above. Assume, for simplicity, that sales volume for April is fixed. Complete the following table:

Scenario	March Sales (units)	CGS %	Cash Payment April 10
1	100	60%	$_____
2	100	65%	$_____
3	100	70%	$_____
4	90	60%	$_____
5	90	65%	$_____
6	90	70%	$_____
7	80	60%	$_____
8	80	65%	$_____
9	80	70%	$_____

Maximum = ?
Minimum = ?
Range   = ?

4. As part of the annual budget process, CompCity, Inc., prepares a cash budget by month for the entire year. Explain why a company such as CompCity would prepare monthly cash-flow budgets for the entire year. Explain the role of *sensitivity analysis* in the monthly planning process.

(CMA adapted)

10-73 **Criticisms of Traditional Budgeting/Incentive Issues**   As noted in the chapter, some individuals allege that the practice of tying managerial rewards to budgeted performance has dysfunctional consequences, including (but not limited to) gaming behavior. Search the Internet and pertinent literature (e.g., Michael C. Jensen, "Corporate Budgeting Is Broken—Let's Fix It," *Harvard Business Review,* November 2001, pp. 94–101) to further explore the issue of negative incentive effects associated with traditional budgeting practices. What alternatives are suggested to correct these negative consequences?

Solutions to Self-Study Problems

1. Master Budget

a.

HANSELL COMPANY
Sales Budget
For July 2010

Budgeted sales in units	6,000
Budgeted selling price per unit	× $ 80
Budgeted sales	$480,000

b.

HANSELL COMPANY
Production Budget (in units)
For July 2010

Desired ending inventory (July 31) (The higher of 500 and 7,000 × 0.1)	700
Budgeted sales for July 2010	+ 6,000
Total units needed for July 2010	6,700
Beginning inventory (July 1) (The higher of 500 and 6,000 × 0.1)	− 600
Units to manufacture in July	6,100

c.

HANSELL COMPANY
Production Budget (in units)
For August 2010

Desired ending inventory (The higher of 500 and 8,000 × 0.1)	800
Budgeted sales	+ 7,000
Total units needed	7,800
Beginning inventory (Aug 1)	− 700
Units to manufacture in August	7,100

d.

HANSELL COMPANY
Direct Materials Purchases Budget (in pounds)
For July 2010

	Direct Materials	
	Dura-1000 **(4 lb. each)**	**Flexplas** **(2 lb. each)**
Materials required for budgeted production (6,100 units of duraflex)	24,400	12,200
Add: Target inventories (lower of 1,000 or 5 percent of August production needs)	+ 1,000	+ 710
Total materials requirements	25,400	12,910
Less: Expected beginning inventories (lower of 1,000 or 5 percent of July needs)	− 1,000	− 610
Direct materials to be purchased	24,400	12,300

e.

HANSELL COMPANY
Direct Materials Purchases Budget (in dollars)
For July 2010

	Budgeted Purchases Pounds	Expected Purchase Price per Unit	Total
Dura-1000	24,400	$1.25	$30,500
Flexplas	12,300	$5.00	61,500
Budgeted purchases			$92,000

f.

HANSELL COMPANY
Direct Manufacturing Labor Budget
For July 2010

Direct Labor Class	Direct Labor-Hours per Batch	Number of Batches	Total Hours	Rate per Hour	Total
K102	1	61*	61	$50	$ 3,050
K175	10	61*	610	$20	12,200
Total			671		$15,250

* No. of units ÷ 100 units/batch = 6,100/100 = 61 batches

2. Cash Budget and Budgeted Income Statement

HANSELL COMPANY
Cash Budget
For July 2010

Cash balance, beginning (given)			$ 40,000
Cash flow from operations:			
July cash sales	$480,000 × 20% =	$ 96,000	
Collections of receivables from credit sales in June:			
Within the discount period	(5,500 × $80) × 80% × 60% × 98% =	$206,976	
After the discount period	(5,500 × $80) × 80% × 25% =	88,000	
Collections of receivables from credit sales in May	(5,400 × $80) × 80% × 10% =	34,560	$425,536

(Continued)

Cash Disbursements:

Materials purchases:

June purchases	($25,000 + $22,000) × 20% × 98% =	$ 9,212	
July purchases	$92,000 × 80% × 98% =	72,128	$ 81,340
Direct manufacturing labor			15,250
Variable factory overhead	($1,200 × 61) + ($80 × 671) =		126,880
Fixed factory overhead	$50,000 − $20,000 =		30,000
Variable marketing, customer services, and administrative expenses	[($2,400,000 − $1,200,000) ÷ $4,000,000] × $480,000 =		144,000
Fixed marketing, customer services, and administrative expenses	($1,200,000 − $120,000) ÷ 12 =		90,000
Total cash flow from operations			($61,934)

Investment activities:

Purchases of investments and other long-term assets		$ 0	
Sales of investments and other long-term assets		$ 0	$ 0

Financing activities:

Repayment of existing debt, end of month		$ 0	
Interest payments, end of month		$ 0	
New borrowing, end of the month		$ 62,000	$ 62,000
Cash balance, July 31, 2010			$ 40,066

HANSELL COMPANY
Budgeted Income Statement
For July 2010

Sales			$480,000
Cost of goods sold, LIFO basis*	$46.50 × 6,000 =		279,000
Gross margin			$201,000
Selling and administrative expenses:			
Variable (see cash budget, above)		$144,000	
Fixed	$1,200,000 ÷ 12 =	100,000	244,000
Operating income (Loss) before tax			($ 43,000)

* Actual manufacturing cost per unit; July:

Direct materials:			
Dura-1000	4 lb. × $1.25 =	$ 5.00	
Flexplas	2 lb. × $5.00 =	10.00	$ 15.00
Direct labor:			
K102 labor	0.01 hour × $50 =	$ 0.50	
K175 labor	0.1 hour × $20 =	2.00	2.50
Factory overhead:			
Batch-related	(61 × $1,200)/6,100 =	$ 12.00	
DLH-related	($80 × 671)/6,100 =	8.80	
Fixed	($50,000/6,100) =	8.20	$ 29.00
Cost per unit, units produced in July			$ 46.50

CHAPTER ELEVEN

Decision Making with a Strategic Emphasis

After studying this chapter, you should be able to . . .

1. Define the decision-making process and identify the types of cost information relevant for decision making
2. Use relevant cost analysis and strategic analysis to make special order decisions
3. Use relevant cost analysis and strategic analysis in the make, lease, or buy decision
4. Use relevant cost analysis and strategic analysis in the decision to sell before or after additional processing
5. Use relevant cost analysis and strategic analysis in the decision to keep or drop products or services
6. Use relevant cost analysis and strategic analysis to evaluate service and not-for-profit organizations
7. Analyze decisions with multiple products and limited resources
8. Discuss the behavioral, implementation, and legal issues in decision making

The family sedan segment of the U.S. auto market—especially the Honda Accord and Toyota Camry—experiences an intense level of competition. The competition between these two cars illustrates an important cost management issue—striking a balance between product features and price. The two cars do not differ greatly in price, but most analysts argue that the cost and price reductions in the 1997 remake of the Camry brought it to the top of U.S. car sales.

Toyota and Honda know that a number of strategic issues are involved in developing a competitive car, including fuel economy, safety features, low-cost manufacturing methods, and a competitive price. In this chapter we will discuss how to conduct relevant cost analysis and strategic analysis of decisions about product pricing, selecting cost-effective manufacturing methods, and deciding when to keep or drop a product, among others.

The decision maker has both short-term and long-term objectives for each type of decision. A decision with a short-term objective is one whose effects are expected to occur within about a year from the time of the decision. A decision with a long-term objective is expected to affect costs and revenues for a period longer than a year. Both types of decisions should reflect the firm's overall strategy, but it is often said that the decision maker has a long-term strategy if the focus is primarily on the decision's long-term objectives and a short-term strategy if the focus is on the short term.

Decision makers should consider both short-term and long-term effects in making the best decision. Although the art and science of decision making has many elements, including leadership, vision, execution, and other characteristics, cost management provides two important resources to improve decisions: relevant cost analysis and strategic analysis. Relevant cost analysis has a short-term focus; strategic analysis has a long-term focus. Relevant cost analysis and strategic analysis are important parts of the manager's decision process.

The Five Steps of the Decision-Making Process

In deciding among alternatives for a given situation, managers employ the five-step process outlined in Exhibit 11.1. The first step, and the most important, is to consider the organization's business environment and competitive strategy. This helps focus the decision maker on

EXHIBIT 11.1 **The Decision-Making Process**

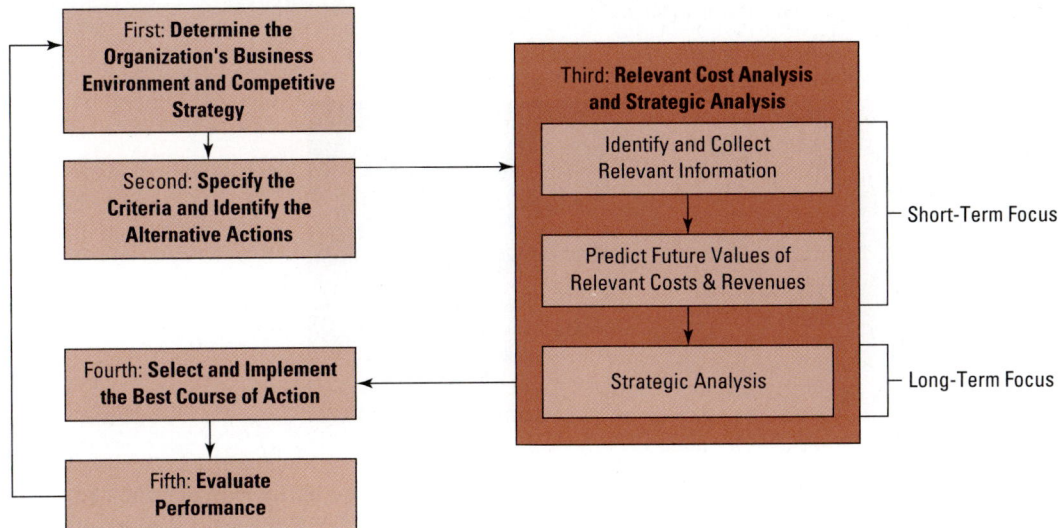

answering the right question. Strategic thinking is important to avoid decisions that might be best only in the short term. For example, a plant manager might incorrectly view the choice as whether to make or to buy a part for a manufactured product when the correct decision might be to determine whether the product should be redesigned so the part is not needed.

The manager's second step is to specify the criteria by which the decision is to be made and to identify the alternative actions. Most often the manager's principal objective is an easily quantified, short-term, achievable goal, such as to reduce cost, improve profit, or maximize return on investment. Other interested parties (e.g., owners or shareholders) have their own criteria for these decisions. Therefore, a manager most often is forced to think of multiple objectives, both the quantifiable short-term goals, and the more strategic, difficult-to-quantify goals.

In the third step, a manager performs an analysis in which the relevant information is developed and analyzed, using relevant cost analysis and strategic analysis. This step involves three sequential activities. The manager (1) identifies and collects relevant information about the decision, (2) makes predictions about the relevant information, and (3) considers the strategic issues involved in the decision.

Fourth, based on the relevant cost analysis and strategic analysis, the manager selects the best alternative and implements it. In the fifth and final step, the manager evaluates the performance of the implemented decision as a basis for feedback to a possible reconsideration of this decision as it relates to future decisions. The decision process is thus a feedback-based system in which the manager continually evaluates the results of prior analyses and decisions to discover any opportunities for improvement in decision making.

Relevant Cost Analysis

Relevant Cost Information

Relevant costs
are costs that will be incurred at some future time; they differ for each option available to the decision maker.

Sunk costs
are costs that have been incurred in the past or are committed for the future and are therefore irrelevant to decision making.

Relevant costs for a decision are costs that should make a difference in choosing among the options available for that decision. A cost that has been incurred in the past or is committed for the future is not relevant; it is a **sunk cost** as it will be the same whichever option is chosen. Similarly, costs that have not been incurred but that would be the same whichever option is chosen are not relevant. In effect, for a cost to be relevant it must be a *cost that will be incurred in the future and will differ between the decision maker's options.* For example, consider the decision to purchase a new automobile. The purchase cost of the new auto is relevant, while the price paid previously for the current auto is irrelevant—you can't change that. Similarly, the cost of your auto club membership, which will not change whichever car you choose, is irrelevant. This would be true also for licenses and fees that would be the same

EXHIBIT 11.2
Relevant and Not Relevant Costs: The Car Purchase Decision

Cost Classification and Cost Relevance
(With examples for the car purchase decision)

	Committed, or Sunk (Generally, in the Past)	Not Committed, Discretionary (Generally, in the Future)
Costs That Differ among Options	**Not Relevant** Example: Cost of shopping for each new car being considered—differences in the cost of travel to the different auto dealerships	**Relevant** Example: Purchase price of the new car
Costs That Do Not Differ among Options	**Not Relevant** Example: Price of old car; also, the cost of the Buyers' Guide used to shop for the new car	**Not Relevant** Example: Cost of membership in an auto club such as the AAA

LEARNING OBJECTIVE 1

Define the decision-making process and identify the types of cost information relevant for decision making.

regardless of the car you select. Suppose further that you have narrowed your choice to two vehicles, and the dealer for one is located some distance away, while the other dealer is nearby. The costs of travel to the different dealers are irrelevant; they are "sunk" at the time the decision is made to travel to both dealers (see Exhibit 11.2).

A relevant cost can be either variable or fixed. Generally, variable costs are relevant for decision making because they differ for each option and have not been committed. In contrast, fixed costs often are irrelevant, since typically they do not differ for the options. Overall, variable costs often are relevant but fixed costs are not. So the use of the concept of relevant cost follows naturally from the development of the methods we used in cost estimation, cost-volume-profit analysis, and master budgeting in prior chapters.

Occasionally, some variable costs are not relevant. For example, assume that a manager is considering whether to replace or repair an old machine. If the electrical power requirements of the new and old machines are the same, the variable cost of power is not relevant. Some fixed costs can be relevant. For example, if the new machine requires significant modifications to the plant building, the cost of the modifications (which are fixed costs) are relevant because they are not yet committed.

To illustrate, assume a machine was purchased for $4,200 a year ago, it is depreciated over two years at $2,100 per year, and it has no trade-in or disposal value. At the end of the first year, the machine has a net book value of $2,100 ($4,200 − $2,100) but the machine needs to be repaired or replaced. Assume that the purchase price of a new machine is $7,000 and it is expected to last for one year with little or no expected trade-in or disposal value. The repair of the old machine would cost $3,500 and would be sufficient for another year of productive use. The power for either machine is expected to cost $2.50 per hour. The new machine is semiautomated, requiring a less-skilled operator and resulting in a reduction of average labor costs from $10.00 to $9.50 per hour for the new machine. If the firm is expected to operate at a 2,000-hour level of output for the next year, the total variable costs for power will be $2,000 × $2.50 = $5,000 for either machine, and labor costs will be $19,000 ($9.50 × 2,000) and $20,000 ($10 × 2,000) for the new and old machines respectively.

Data for Machine Replacement Example

Old machine	
Level of output	2,000 hours/year
Current net book value	$2,100
Useful life (if repaired)	1 year
Operating cost (labor)	$10 per hour
Repair cost	$3,500
New machine	
Level of output	2,000 hours/year
Purchase price	$7,000
Useful life	1 year
Operating cost (labor)	$9.50 per hour

EXHIBIT 11.3
Relevant Cost Analysis in
Equipment Replacement

	Relevant Costs		Difference
	Repair	**Replace**	**Replace Minus Repair**
Variable costs			
Labor (2,000 × $10, $9.50)	$20,000	$19,000	$(1,000)
Fixed costs (relevant costs)			
Old machine repair cost	3,500		(3,500)
New machine		7,000	7,000
Total costs	$23,500	$26,000	$ 2,500
Repair cost lower by: $2,500			

The summary of relevant costs for this decision is in Exhibit 11.3, showing a $2,500 advantage for repairing the old machine. The $1,000 decrease in labor costs for the new machine is less than the $3,500 difference of replacement cost over repair cost ($7,000 − $3,500). Note that the power costs and the depreciation on the old machine are omitted because they are not relevant; they do not differ between the options.

To show that the analysis based on total costs provides the same answer, Exhibit 11.4 shows the analysis for total costs that includes the power costs and the depreciation of the old machine; neither cost is relevant. The left portion of Exhibit 11.4 is the same as Exhibit 11.3. Note that both analyses lead to the same conclusion. The relevant cost approach in Exhibit 11.3 is always preferred, however, because it is simpler and, therefore less prone to error; it also provides better focus for the decision maker.

Batch-Level Cost Drivers

The above analysis has included the fixed cost associated with the purchase or repair of the machine, but has not included the fixed cost of labor for machine setup. Setup cost is a batch-level cost that varies with the number of batches and not the units or hours of output on the machine. Suppose that there will be 120 setups done during the year, irrespective of whether the machine is replaced or repaired. This sounds irrelevant, because the number of setups remains the same. But suppose further, that because the automated machine is easier to set up, it takes only one hour to set up the new machine, while the old machine takes four hours to set up. Also, assume that the automated machine requires less-skilled setup labor, so that the $9.50 per hour labor rate applies and the firm uses only the needed setup labor; there is no unused capacity in setup labor. The machine replacement analysis should also include the differential setup time and cost as follows:

Setup Costs for New Machine	Setup Costs for Old Machine
$9.50 per hour for labor	$10 per hour for labor
× 120 setups per year	× 120 setups per year
× 1 hour per setup	× 4 hours per setup
= $1,140	= $4,800

EXHIBIT 11.4
Relevant Cost and Total
Cost Analysis in Equipment
Replacement

	Relevant Costs		Total Costs		Difference
	Repair	**Replace**	**Repair**	**Replace**	**Replace – Repair**
Variable costs					
Labor	$20,000	$19,000	$20,000	$19,000	$(1,000)
Power			5,000	5,000	0
Fixed costs					
Old machine					
Depreciation			2,100	2,100	0
Repair cost	3,500		3,500		(3,500)
New machine		7,000		7,000	7,000
Total costs	$23,500	$26,000	$30,600	$33,100	$ 2,500

EXHIBIT 11.5
Relevant Costs in Equipment
Replacement (including
consideration of setup costs)

	Relevant Costs		Total Costs		Difference
	Repair	Replace	Repair	Replace	Replace–Repair
Variable costs					
Labor	$20,000	$19,000	$20,000	$19,000	$ (1,000)
Batch-level costs					
Setup costs	4,800	1,140	4,800	1,140	(3,660)
Fixed costs					
Old machine					
Repair cost	3,500		3,500		(3,500)
New machine		7,000		7,000	7,000
Total costs	$28,300	$27,140	$35,400	$34,240	$ (1,160)

The new machine saves $3,660 ($4,800 − $1,140) in setup labor as well as $1,000 in direct labor. The labor savings total is $4,660 ($3,660 + $1,000). This more than offsets the excess of the cost of the new machine over the cost of repair, $3,500 ($7,000 − $3,500), for a $1,160 = ($4,660 − $3,500) net benefit of replacing the machine. See the revised analysis in Exhibit 11.5.

Fixed Costs and Depreciation

A common misperception is that depreciation of facilities and equipment is a relevant cost. In fact, depreciation is a portion of a committed cost (the allocation of a purchase cost over the life of an asset); therefore, it is sunk and irrelevant. There is an exception to this rule: when tax effects are considered in decision making. In this context, depreciation has a positive value in that, as an expense, it reduces taxable income and tax expense. If taxes are considered, depreciation has a role to the extent that it reduces tax liability. The decision maker often must consider the impact of local, federal, and sometimes international tax differences on the decision situation.

Other Relevant Information: Opportunity Costs

Opportunity cost
is the benefit lost when the chosen option precludes the benefits from an alternative option.

Managers should include in their decision process information such as the capacity usage of the plant. Capacity usage information is a critical signal of the potential relevance of **opportunity costs,** the benefit lost when one chosen option precludes the benefits from an alternative option. When the plant is operating at full capacity, opportunity costs are an important consideration because the decision to produce a special order or add a new product line can cause the reduction, delay, or loss of sales of products and services currently offered. In contrast, a firm with excess capacity might be able to produce for current demand as well as handle a special order or new product; thus, no opportunity cost is present. When opportunity costs are relevant, the manager must consider the value of lost sales as well as the contribution from the new order or new product.

Another important factor is the *time value of money* that is relevant when deciding among alternatives with cash flows over two or more years. These decisions are best handled by the methods described in Chapter 12. Also, differences in quality, functionality, timeliness of delivery, reliability in shipping, and service after the sale could strongly influence a manager's final decision and should be considered in addition to the analysis of relevant costs. Although these factors often are considered in a qualitative manner, when any factor is strategically important, management can choose to quantify it and include it directly in the analysis.

Strategic Analysis

The task of management is not to apply a formula but to decide issues on a case-by-case basis. No fixed, inflexible rule can ever be substituted for the exercise of sound business judgment in the decision-making process.

Alfred P. Sloan, early president and CEO of General Motors

EXHIBIT 11.6
Relevant Cost Analysis versus
Strategic Cost Analysis

Relevant Cost Analysis	Strategic Cost Analysis
Short-term focus	Long-term focus
Not linked to strategy	Linked to the firm's strategy
Product cost focus	Customer focus
Focused on individual product or decision situation	Integrative; considers all customer-related factors

Alfred Sloan had an important role in developing many of the financial management tools we use today, including relevant cost analysis and strategic analysis. Sloan knew that an inflexible "run the numbers" approach would not lead to good decision making. Instead, he used a consideration of the business and competitive context of the decision, together with the use of relevant costs, which we call *strategic cost analysis*. A consideration of the business and competitive context of the decision, together with an understanding of the firm's strategy and the relevant costs ensures that each decision will advance the firm's strategy, performance, and success.

To illustrate, a strategic decision to design the manufacturing process for high efficiency to produce large batches of product reduces overall production costs. At the same time, it might reduce the firm's flexibility to manufacture a variety of products and thus could increase the cost to produce small, specialized orders. The decision regarding cost efficiency cannot be separated from the determination of marketing strategy, that is, deciding what types and sizes of orders can be accepted.

For another example, the decision to buy rather than to make a part for the firm's product might make sense on the basis of relevant cost but might be a poor strategic move if the firm's competitive position depends on product reliability that can be maintained only by manufacturing the part in-house. A good indication of a manager's failing to take a strategic approach is that the analysis will have a product cost focus, while a strategic cost analysis also addresses broad and difficult-to-measure strategic issues. The strategic analysis directly focuses on adding value to the customer, going beyond only cost issues. (See Exhibit 11.6.)

We now consider the application of the relevant cost analysis and strategic cost analysis to four types of decisions that management accountants often face. For each decision, we develop the cost information that should be used. In the decision to make the best use of capacity, this cost information includes both relevant cost analysis and strategic cost analysis as discussed earlier. The four decisions are as follows: (1) the special order decision; (2) the make, lease, or buy decision; (3) the decision to sell before or after additional processing; and (4) profitability analysis.

Special Order Decision

Relevant Cost Analysis

LEARNING OBJECTIVE 2

Use relevant cost analysis and strategic analysis to make special order decisions.

A special order decision occurs when a firm has a one-time opportunity to sell a specified quantity of its product or service. It is called a *special order* because it is typically unexpected. The order frequently comes directly from the customer rather than through normal sales or distribution channels. Special orders are infrequent and commonly represent a small part of a firm's overall business. To make the special order decision, managers begin with a cost analysis of the relevant costs for the special order. To illustrate, consider the special order situation facing Tommy T-Shirt, Inc. (TTS). TTS is a small manufacturer of specialty clothing, primarily T-shirts and sweatshirts with imprinted slogans and brand names. TTS has been offered a contract by the business honor society, Alpha Beta Gamma (ABG) for 1,000 T-shirts printed with artwork publicizing a fund-raising event. ABG offers to pay $6.50 for each shirt. TTS normally charges $9.00 for shirts of this type for this size order.

Cost Element	Costs Per Unit	Batch-Level Costs Per Batch	Batch-Level Costs Fixed Costs	Plant-Level Costs (all fixed)
Shirt	$3.25			
Ink	0.95			
Operating labor	0.85			
Subtotal	$5.05			
Setup		$130	$29,000	
Inspection		30	9,000	
Materials handling		40	7,000	
Subtotal		$200	$45,000	
Machine related				$315,000
Other				90,000
Total	$5.05	$200	$45,000	$405,000

TTS's master budget of manufacturing costs for the current year is given in Exhibit 11.7. The budget is based on expected production of 200,000 T-shirts from an available capacity of 250,000. The 200,000 units are expected to be produced in 200 different batches of 1,000 units each. The three groups of cost elements are as follows:

1. **Unit-level costs** vary with each shirt printed and include the cost of the shirt ($3.25 each), ink ($0.95 each), and labor ($0.85), for a total of $5.05.

2. **Batch-level costs** vary, in part, with the number of batches produced. The batch-level costs include machine setup, inspection, and materials handling. These costs are partly variable (change with the number of batches) and partly fixed. For example, setup costs are $130 per setup ($26,000 for 200 setups) plus $29,000 fixed costs that do not change with the number of setups (e.g., setup tools or software). Setup costs for 200 batches total $55,000 ($26,000 + $29,000). Similarly, inspection costs are $30 per batch plus $9,000 fixed costs—$15,000 total [($30 × 200) + $9,000]. Materials-handling costs are $40 per batch plus $7,000 fixed costs—$15,000 total [($40 × 200) + $7,000]

3. **Plant-level costs** are fixed and do not vary with the number of either units produced or batches. These costs include depreciation and insurance on machinery ($315,000) and other fixed costs ($90,000), for a total of $405,000. Total fixed cost is the sum of fixed batch-level costs ($45,000) and fixed facilities-level costs ($405,000), or $450,000. And the total cost estimation equation for TTS is

$$\text{Total Cost} = \$5.05 \text{ per unit} + \$200 \text{ per batch} + \$450,000.$$

Exhibit 11.8 presents TTS's analysis of the relevant costs. The ABG order requires the same unprinted T-shirt, ink, and labor time as other shirts, for a total of $5.05 per unit. In addition, TTS uses $200 of batch-level costs for each order.

Analysis of Contribution from the Alpha Beta Gamma Order		
Sales	1,000 units @ $6.50	$6,500
Relevant costs (Exhibit 11.8)	1,000 units @ $5.25	5,250
Net contribution	1,000 units @ $1.25	$1,250

The correct analysis for this decision is to determine the relevant costs of $5.25, and then to compare the relevant costs to the special order price of $6.50. The irrelevant costs are not considered because they remain the same whether or not TTS accepts the ABG order. There is a $1.25 ($6.50 − 5.25) contribution to income for each shirt sold to Alpha Beta Gamma, or a total contribution of $1,250.

EXHIBIT 11.8
Special Order Decision
Analysis for TTS

Cost Type	Unit Costs	Total Cost for One Batch of 1,000 Units
Relevant Costs		
Unit-level costs		
Unprinted shirt	$3.25	$3,250
Ink and other supplies	0.95	950
Machine time (operator labor)	0.85	850
Total unit-level costs	$5.05	$5,050
Batch-level costs (that vary with the number of batches)		
Setup		130
Inspection		30
Materials handling		40
Total ($200/batch; $0.20/unit)	$0.20	$ 200
Total relevant costs	$5.25	$5,250

Strategic Analysis

The relevant cost analysis developed for TTS provides useful information regarding the order's profitability. However, for a full decision analysis, TTS also should consider the strategic factors of capacity utilization and short-term versus long-term pricing.

Is TTS Now Operating at Full Capacity?

TTS currently has 50,000 units of excess capacity, more than enough for the ABG order. But what if TTS is operating at or near full capacity; would accepting the order cause the loss of other possibly more profitable sales? If so, TTS should consider the opportunity cost arising from the lost sales. Assume that TTS is operating at 250,000 units and 250 batches of activity, and that accepting the ABG order would cause the loss of sales of other T-shirts that have a higher contribution of $3.75 ($9.00 − $5.25). The opportunity cost is $3.75 per shirt and the proper decision analysis is as follows:

Contribution from Alpha Beta Gamma order	$ 1,250
Less: Opportunity cost of lost sales (1,000 units × $3.75)	(3,750)
Net contribution (loss) for the order	$(2,500)

Exhibit 11.9 shows the effect of accepting the Alpha Beta Gamma order at full capacity; under full capacity, the Alpha Beta Gamma order would reduce total profits by $2,500 due to lost sales.

Excessive Relevant Cost Pricing

The relevant cost decision rule for special orders is intended only for those infrequent situations when a special order can increase income. Done on a regular basis, relevant cost pricing can erode normal pricing policies and lead to a loss in profitability for firms such as TTS. The failure of large companies in the airline, auto, and steel industries has been attributed to

EXHIBIT 11.9
Special Order Decision for
TTS under Full Capacity

	With ABG Order	Without ABG Order
Sales		
250,000 units at $9.00		$2,250,000
249,000 at $9.00; 1,000 at $6.50	$2,247,500	
Variable cost at $5.25	1,312,500	1,312,500
Contribution margin	$ 935,000	$ 937,500
Fixed cost	450,000	450,000
Operating income	$ 485,000	$ 487,500
Advantage in favor of rejecting the ABG order		$ 2,500

their excessive relevant cost pricing because a strategy of continually focusing on the short-term can deny a company a successful long-term. Special order pricing decisions should not become the centerpiece of a firm's strategy.

Other Important Strategic Factors

In addition to capacity utilization and long-term pricing issues, TTS should consider Alpha Beta Gamma's credit history, any potential complexities in the design that might cause production problems, and other strategic issues such as whether the sale might lead to additional sales of other TTS products.

Value Stream Accounting and the Special Order Decision

A **value stream** consists of all the activities required to create customer value for a family of products or services.

When using lean accounting (see Chapter 17 for more information on this topic) the management accountant puts families of products together in what is called a **value stream,** which consists of all the activities required to create customer value for that family of products or services. An example of a product family for a consumer electronics firm would be its group of DVD players, while another family of products would be its digital televisions. An example for a service firm, a bank, would be value streams for installment loans, mortgage loans, and commercial loans. When using lean accounting, special orders are evaluated within the context of the value stream in which they are located, so the analysis of costs includes relevant costs throughout the value stream and the strategic analysis is for the entire family of products in the value stream.

Make, Lease, or Buy Decision

Relevant Cost Analysis

LEARNING OBJECTIVE 3

Use relevant cost analysis and strategic analysis in the make, lease, or buy decision.

Generally, a firm's products are manufactured according to specifications set forth in what is called the bill of materials, which is a detailed list of the components of the manufactured product. A bill of materials for the manufacture of furniture is illustrated in Chapter 4. An increasingly common decision for manufacturers is to choose which of these components to manufacture in the firm's plant and which to purchase from outside suppliers.

The relevant cost information for the make-or-buy decision is developed in a manner similar to that of the special order decision. The relevant cost information for making the component consists of the short-term costs to manufacture it, ordinarily the variable manufacturing costs, which would be saved if the part is purchased. These costs are compared to the purchase price for the part or component to determine the appropriate decision. Costs that will not change whether the firm makes the part or not are ignored. For example, consider Blue Tone Manufacturing, maker of clarinets and other reed-based musical instruments. Suppose that Blue Tone is currently manufacturing the mouthpiece for its clarinet but has the option to buy it from a supplier. The mouthpiece is plastic, while the remainder of the clarinet is made from wood. The following cost information assumes that fixed overhead costs will not change whether Blue Tone chooses to make or buy the mouthpiece:

Cost to buy the mouthpiece, per unit		$24.00
Cost to manufacture, per unit		
Materials	$16.00	
Labor	4.50	
Variable overhead	1.00	
Total variable costs	$21.50	
Fixed overhead	6.00	
Total costs	$27.50	
Total relevant costs		$21.50
Savings from continuing to make		$ 2.50

In this example, the relevant cost to make is $21.50. Since the decision will not affect fixed overhead, the total $27.50 cost is irrelevant. The relevant cost to make is $2.50 less than the purchase cost. The next step is for Blue Tone to complete a strategic analysis that considers, for example, the quality of the part, the reliability of the supplier, and the potential alternative uses of Blue Tone's plant capacity. With the combined cost and strategic analysis, Blue Tone is prepared to make the decision.

A similar situation arises when a firm must choose between leasing or purchasing a piece of equipment. Such decisions are becoming ever more frequent as the cost and terms of leasing arrangements continue to become more favorable.

To illustrate the lease or buy decision, we use the example of Quick Copy, Inc., a firm that provides printing and duplicating services and other related business services. Quick Copy uses one large copy machine to complete most big jobs. It leases the machine from the manufacturer on an annual basis that includes general servicing. The annual lease includes both a fixed fee of $40,000 and a per copy charge of $0.02.

The copier manufacturer has suggested that Quick Copy upgrade to the latest model copier that is not available for lease but must be purchased for $160,000. Quick Copy would use the purchased copier for one year, after which it could sell it back to the manufacturer for one-fourth the purchase price ($40,000). In addition, the new machine has a required annual service contract of $20,000 which includes all repair, service, and replacement of ink cartridges. Quick Copy's options for the coming year are to renew the lease for the current copier or to purchase the new copier. The relevant information is outlined in Exhibit 11.10.

EXHIBIT 11.10
Quick Copy Lease or Buy Information

	Lease Option	Purchase Option
Annual lease	$40,000	N/A
Charge per copy	0.02	N/A
Purchase cost	N/A	$160,000
Annual service contract	N/A	$ 20,000
Value at end of period	N/A	$ 40,000
Expected number of copies a year	6,000,000	6,000,000

The lease-or-buy decision will not affect the cost of paper, electrical power, and employee wages, so these costs are irrelevant and are excluded from the analysis. For simplicity, we also ignore potential tax effects of the decision and the time value of money.

The initial step in the analysis is to determine which machine produces lowest total cost. The answer depends on the expected annual number of copies. Using cost-volume-profit analysis (Chapter 9 and Exhibit 11.11), Quick Copy's manager determines the indifference point, the number of copies at which both machines cost the same. The calculations are as follows, where Q is the number of copies:

$$\text{Lease cost} = \text{Purchase cost}$$
$$\text{Annual fee} + \text{Per copy charge} = \text{Net purchase cost} + \text{Service contract}$$
$$\$40,000 + (\$0.02 \times Q) = (\$160,000 - \$40,000) + \$20,000$$
$$Q = \$100,000/\$0.02$$
$$= 5,000,000 \text{ copies per year}$$

EXHIBIT 11.11
The Lease or Buy Example

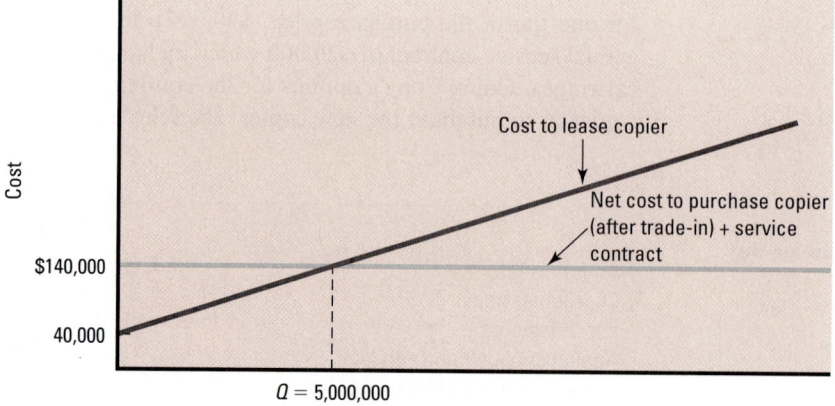

The indifference point, 5,000,000 copies, is lower than the expected annual machine usage of 6,000,000 copies. This indicates that Quick Copy will have lower costs by purchasing the new machine. Costs will be lower by $20,000:

$$\text{Cost of lease} - \text{Cost of purchase}$$
$$= [\$40,000 + (\$0.02 \times 6,000,000)] - (\$160,000 - \$40,000 + \$20,000)$$
$$= \$160,000 - \$140,000$$
$$= \$20,000 \text{ in favor of purchase}$$

In addition to the relevant cost analysis, Quick Copy should consider strategic factors such as the quality of the copy, the reliability of the machine, the benefits and features of the service contracts, and any other factors associated with the use of the machine that might properly influence the decision.

Strategic Analysis

The make, lease, or buy decision often raises strategic issues. For example, a firm using value-chain analysis could find that certain of its activities in the value chain can be more profitably performed by other firms. The practice of choosing to have an outside firm provide a basic service function is called *outsourcing*. Make, lease, or buy analysis has a key role in the decision to outsource by providing an analysis of the relevant costs. Many firms recently have considered outsourcing manufacturing and data processing, janitorial, or security services to improve profitability. Thomas Friedman, in his recent book, *The World Is Flat: A Brief History of the Twenty-First Century,* explains the breadth of outsourcing practices in the world today.[1] Even such simple activities as taking hamburger orders at the drive-thru of a fast food restaurant are being outsourced around the world.

Because of the important strategic implications of a choice to make, lease, or buy, these decisions are often made on a two- to five-year basis, using projections of expected relevant costs and taking into account the time value of money (Chapter 12) where appropriate.

Sell Before or After Additional Processing

Relevant Cost Analysis

LEARNING OBJECTIVE 4

Use relevant cost analysis and strategic analysis in the decision to sell before or after additional processing.

Another common decision concerns the option to sell a product or service before an intermediate processing step or to add further processing and then sell the product or service for a higher price. The additional processing might add features or functionality to a product or add flexibility or quality to a service. For example, a travel agent preparing a group tour faces many decisions related to optional features to be offered on the tour, such as side-trips, sleeping quarters, and entertainment. A manufacturer of consumer electronics faces a number of decisions regarding the nature and extent of features to offer in its products.

The analysis of features also is important for manufacturers in determining what to do with defective products. Generally, they can either be sold in the defective state to outlet stores and discount chains or be repaired for sale in the usual manner. The decision is whether the product should be sold with or without additional processing. Relevant cost analysis is again the appropriate model to follow in analyzing these situations.

To continue with the TTS example, assume that a piece of equipment used to print its T-shirts has malfunctioned, and 400 shirts are not of acceptable quality because some colors are missing or faded. TTS can sell the defective shirts to outlet stores at a greatly reduced price ($4.50) or can run them through the printing machine again. A second run will produce a salable shirt in most cases. The costs to run them through the printer a second time are for

---

[1] Thomas L. Friedman, *The World Is Flat: A Brief History of the Twenty-First Century* (New York: Farrar, Straus, and Giroux, 2005). See also, Thomas L. Friedman, *Hot, Flat, and Crowded,* Farrar, Straus, and Giroux, New York, 2008.

Cost Management in Action

Trends in Make-or-Buy Strategies

A recent study of 328 U.S. manufacturing firms revealed that the purchasing managers at most of these firms prefer to purchase parts from outside suppliers rather than to assign the work to an internal manufacturing unit. Factors given as favoring outsourcing include the quality and speed of delivery for the external suppliers, while factors favoring insourcing include concerns for capacity utilization, overhead absorption, employee loyalty, and union contracts. The purchasing managers also tend to prefer to use a number of suppliers in order to develop multiple sourcing relationships. For example, in recent years General Motors (in its U.S. operations) had approximately 3,500 suppliers, while Toyota in Japan had only about 200. How does Toyota keep such a relatively small number of suppliers?

(Refer to Comments on Cost Management in Action at end of Chapter.)

EXHIBIT 11.12

Analysis of Reprinting 400 Defective T-Shirts

	Reprint	Sell to Discount Store
Revenue (400 @ $9.00, $4.50)	$3,600	$1,800
Relevant costs		
Supplies and ink ($.95)	380	
Labor ($.85)	340	
Setup	130	
Inspection	30	
Materials handling	40	
Total relevant costs	$ 920	
Contribution margin	$2,680	$1,800
Net advantage to reprint	$2,680 − $1,800 = $880	

the ink, supplies, and labor, totaling $1.80 per shirt, plus the setup, inspection, and materials-handling costs for a batch of product. See the relevant cost analysis in Exhibit 11.12. Note that the cost of the unprinted T-shirt is the same for both options and is therefore irrelevant.

The analysis shows there is an $880 advantage to reprinting the shirts rather than selling the defective shirts to discount stores.

Strategic Analysis

Strategic concerns arise when considering selling to discount stores. Will this affect the sale of T-shirts in retail stores? Will the cost of packing, delivery, and sales commissions differ for these two types of sales? TTS management must carefully consider these strategic issues in addition to the information provided in the relevant cost analysis in Exhibit 11.12.

Profitability Analysis

Profitability Analysis: Keep or Drop a Product Line

LEARNING OBJECTIVE 5

Use relevant cost analysis and strategic analysis in the decision to keep or drop products or services.

An important aspect of management is the regular review of product profitability. This review should address issues such as these:

- Which products are most profitable?
- Are the products priced properly?
- Which products should be promoted and advertised most aggressively?
- Which product managers should be rewarded?

This review has both a short-term and a long-term strategic focus. The short-term focus is addressed through relevant cost analysis. To illustrate, we use Windbreakers, Inc., a manufacturer of sport clothing. Windbreakers manufactures three jackets: Calm, Windy, and Gale. Management has requested an analysis of Gale due to its low sales and low profitability (see Exhibit 11.13).

EXHIBIT 11.13
Sales and Cost Data for Windbreakers, Inc.

	Calm	Windy	Gale	Total
Units sold last year	25,000	18,750	3,750	47,500
Revenue	$750,000	$600,000	$150,000	
Price	$ 30.00	$ 32.00	$ 40.00	
Relevant costs				
Unit variable cost	24.00	24.00	36.00	
Unit contribution margin	$ 6.00	$ 8.00	$ 4.00	
Nonrelevant fixed costs	3.54	3.54	3.54	$168,000
Operating profit per unit	$ 2.46	$ 4.46	$ 0.46	

EXHIBIT 11.14
Contribution Income Statement Profitability Analysis: Gale Dropped

	Calm	Windy	Total
Sales	$750,000	$600,000	$1,350,000
Relevant costs			
Variable cost ($24 ea)	600,000	450,000	1,050,000
Contribution margin	$150,000	$150,000	$ 300,000
Nonrelevant costs			
Fixed cost			168,000
Operating profit without Gale			$ 132,000

The analysis of Gale should begin with the important observation that the $3.54 fixed cost per unit is irrelevant for the analysis of the current profitability of the three products. Because the $168,000 total fixed costs are unchangeable in the short run, they are irrelevant for this analysis. That is, no changes in product mix, including the deletion of Gale, will affect total fixed costs in the coming year. The fact that the fixed costs are irrelevant is illustrated by comparing the contribution income statements in Exhibit 11.14, which assumes that Gale is dropped, and Exhibit 11.15, which assumes that Gale is kept. The only changes caused by dropping Gale are the loss of its revenues and the elimination of variable costs. We assume there is no effect on the sales or costs of the other two products. Thus, dropping Gale causes a reduction in total contribution margin of $4 per unit times 3,750 units of Gale sold, or $15,000, and a corresponding loss in operating profit ($15,000 = $147,000 − $132,000).

Benefit: Saved variable costs of Gale	$ 135,000	$(36 × 3,750)
Cost: Opportunity cost of lost sales of Gale	(150,000)	$(40 × 3,750)
Decrease in profit from decision to drop Gale	$ (15,000)	$ (4 × 3,750)

Assume that further analysis shows that $60,000 of the $168,000 fixed costs are advertising costs to be spent directly on each of the three products: $25,000 for Calm, $15,000 for Windy, and $20,000 for Gale. The remainder of the fixed costs, $108,000 ($168,000 − $60,000), are not traceable to any of the three products and are therefore allocated to each product as before.

EXHIBIT 11.15
Contribution Income Statement Profitability Analysis: Gale Retained

	Calm	Windy	Gale	Total
Sales	$750,000	$600,000	$150,000	$1,500,000
Relevant costs				
Variable cost ($24, 24, 36)	600,000	450,000	135,000	1,185,000
Contribution margin	$150,000	$150,000	$ 15,000	$ 315,000
Nonrelevant costs				
Fixed cost				168,000
Operating profit with Gale				$ 147,000

EXHIBIT 11.16
Profitability Analysis: Including Traceable Advertising Costs

	Calm	Windy	Gale	Total
Sales	$750,000	$600,000	$150,000	$1,500,000
Relevant costs				
Variable cost	600,000	450,000	135,000	1,185,000
Contribution margin	$150,000	$150,000	$ 15,000	$ 315,000
Other relevant costs (traceable)				
Advertising	25,000	15,000	20,000	60,000
Contribution after all relevant costs	$125,000	$135,000	$ (5,000)	$ 255,000
Nonrelevant costs (not traceable)				
Fixed cost				$ 108,000
Operating profit				$ 147,000

Because advertising costs are directly traceable to the individual products, and assuming that the advertising plans for Gale can be canceled without additional cost, the $20,000 of advertising costs for Gale should be considered a relevant cost in the decision to delete Gale. This cost will differ in the future.

Exhibit 11.16 shows that the total contribution margin for Gale is now a net loss of $5,000, providing a potential $5,000 gain by dropping Gale because of the expected $20,000 savings in avoidable advertising costs. Alternatively, management may choose to forgo the advertising for Gale and assess whether sales will fall with the loss of advertising; Gale could be profitable without advertising. We can interpret the contribution figures for Calm and Windy in the same way. The loss in deleting Calm or Windy would be $125,000 and $135,000, respectively.

Strategic Analysis

In addition to the relevant cost analysis, the decision to keep or drop a product line should include relevant long-term strategic factors, such as the potential effect of the loss of one product line on the sales of another. For example, some florists price cards, vases, and other related items at or below cost to better serve and attract customers to the most profitable product, the flower arrangements.

Other important strategic factors include the potential effect on overall employee morale and organizational effectiveness if a product line is dropped. Moreover, managers should consider the sales growth potential of each product. Will a product considered to be dropped place the firm in a strong competitive position sometime in the future? A particularly important consideration is the extent of available production capacity. If production capacity and production resources (such as labor and machine time) are limited, consider the relative profitability of the products and the extent to which they require different amounts of these production resources.

An example of a user of the contribution income statement is STIHL, Incorporated, a manufacturer of leaf blowers, chain saws, trimmers, edgers, and many other landscaping products. STIHL uses the contribution income statement to assess the profitability of both product lines and customer groups.[2]

Profitability Analysis: Service and Not-for-Profit Organizations

LEARNING OBJECTIVE 6

Use relevant cost analysis and strategic analysis to evaluate service and not-for-profit organizations.

Triangle Women's Center (TWC) uses relevant cost analysis to determine the desirability of new services. TWC provides several services to the communities in and around a large southeastern city. It has not offered child-care services but has received a large number of requests to do so in recent years. Now TWC is planning to add this service. The relevant cost analysis follows. TWC expects to hire a director ($65,000) and two part-time assistants ($30,000 each) for the child-care service. TWC estimates variable costs per child at $60 per month. No other costs are relevant because none of the other operating costs of TWC are expected to change. TWC expects to receive funding of $100,000 from the United Way plus

[2] Carl S. Smith, "Going for GPK," *Strategic Finance*, April 2005, pp. 36–39.

EXHIBIT 11.17
Triangle Women's Center Analysis of Child-Care Services

Relevant annual costs	
Salary of director	$ 65,000
Salary for two part-time assistants	60,000
Variable costs for 20 children at $60 per month each	14,400
Total relevant costs	$139,400
Total funding	
United Way	$100,000
City Council	30,000
	$130,000
Expected deficit in the first year	$ 9,400

$30,000 from the city council. The analysis for the child-care service's first year of operation is shown in Exhibit 11.17, which assumes that 20 children, the maximum number, will use the service.

The TWC analysis shows that the child-care service will have a deficit of approximately $9,400 in the first year. Now TWC can decide whether it can make up the deficit from current funds or by raising additional funds. Relevant cost analysis provides TWC a useful method to determine the resource needs for the new program.

Multiple Products and Limited Resources

LEARNING OBJECTIVE 7

Analyze decisions with multiple products and limited resources.

The preceding relevant cost analyses were simplified by using a single product and assuming sufficient resources to meet all demands. The analysis changes significantly with two or more products and limited resources. The revised analysis is considered in this section. We continue the example of Windbreakers, Inc., except that we assume that the Calm product is manufactured in a separate plant under contract with a major customer. Thus, the following analysis focuses only on the Windy and Gale products, which are manufactured in a single facility.

A key element of the relevant cost analysis is to determine the most profitable sales mix for Windy and Gale. If there are no production constraints, the answer is clear; we manufacture what is needed to meet demand for both Windy and Gale. However, when demand exceeds production capacity, management must make some trade-offs about the quantity of each product to manufacture, and therefore, what demand is unmet. The answer requires considering the production possibilities given by the production constraints. Consider two important cases: (1) one production constraint and (2) two or more production constraints.

Case 1: One Production Constraint

Assume that the production of Windy and Gale requires an automated sewing machine to stitch the jackets and that this production activity is a limited resource: sales demand for the two products exceeds the capacity on the plant's three automated sewing machines. Each machine can be run up to 20 hours per day five days per week, or 400 hours per month, which is its maximum capacity allowing for maintenance. This gives 1,200 (3 × 400) available hours for sewing each month. Assume further that the machine requires three minutes to assemble a Windy and two minutes to assemble a Gale.

Because only 1,200 hours of machine time are available per month and the Gale jacket requires less machine time, more Gale jackets can be made in a month than Windy jackets. The maximum number of Windy jackets is 24,000 jackets per month (1,200 hours times 20 jackets per hour, at 3 minutes per jacket). Similarly, if the sewing machine were devoted entirely to Gale jackets, then 36,000 jackets per month could be produced (1,200 times 30 jackets per hour). This information is summarized in Exhibit 11.18.

A continuous trade-off possibility exists for the extreme situations: zero output of Windy and 36,000 of Gale or 24,000 of Windy and zero of Gale. These production and sales mix

EXHIBIT 11.18
Windbreakers Data for the Windy and Gale Plant
One Constraint: The Sewing Machine

Find the most profitable product this way:	Windy	Gale
Since		
Contribution margin/unit	$8	$4
Sewing time per jacket	3 min	2 min
Then, because sewing time is limited to 1,200 hours per month, we determine the contribution margin per machine-hour		
Number of jackets per hour (60min/3min = 20; 60/2 = 30)	20	30
Contribution margin per hour (20 × $8; 30 × $4)	$160	$120
Also, the maximum production for each product, given the 1,200-hour constraint		
For Windy: 1,200 × 20 jackets per hour	24,000	
For Gale: 1,200 × 30 jackets per hour		36,000

possibilities can be shown graphically; all sales mix possibilities are represented by all possible points on the line in Exhibit 11.19. The line in Exhibit 11.19 can be determined as follows:

$$\text{Slope} = -36,000/24,000 = -3/2$$

$$\text{Intercept} = 36,000$$

The line in Exhibit 11.19 is thus given by

$$\text{Units of Gale} = 36,000 - (3/2 \times \text{Units of Windy})$$

To illustrate, assume that Windbreakers is producing 12,000 units of Windy so that

$$\text{Units of Gale} = 36,000 - (3/2 \times 12,000) = 18,000$$

Now that we know the production possibilities, we can determine the best product mix. Note from Exhibit 11.18 that Windy has the higher overall contribution margin, $160 per hour (20 jackets per hour × $8 per jacket). Because 1,200 machine-hours are available per month, the maximum total contribution from the production possibilities is to produce only Windy and achieve the total contribution of 1,200 × $160 = $192,000 (or $8 per unit × 24,000 units = $192,000) per month. If Windbreakers were to produce and sell only Gale, the maximum total contribution margin would be $144,000 per month (1,200 hours × $120 per hour), a $48,000 reduction over the contribution from selling only Windy. *Thus, when there is only one production constraint and excess demand, it is generally best to focus production and sales on the product with the highest contribution per unit of scarce resource.* Of course, it is unlikely in a practical situation that a firm would be able to adopt the extreme position of deleting one

EXHIBIT 11.19
Windbreakers Production and Sales Possibilities
One Production Constraint—The Sewing Machine

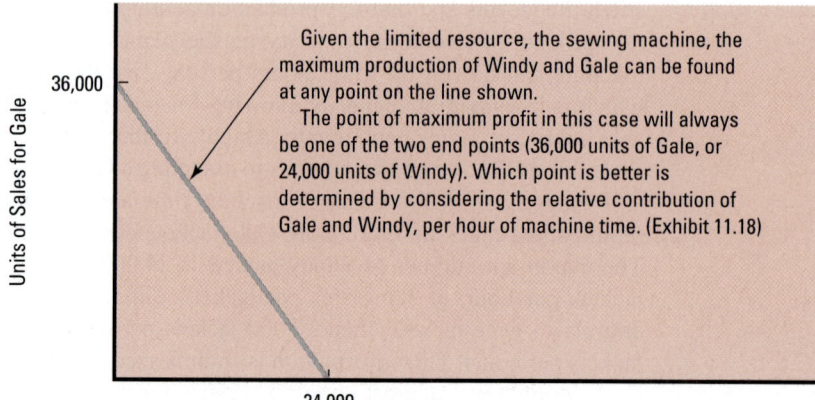

Given the limited resource, the sewing machine, the maximum production of Windy and Gale can be found at any point on the line shown.
The point of maximum profit in this case will always be one of the two end points (36,000 units of Gale, or 24,000 units of Windy). Which point is better is determined by considering the relative contribution of Gale and Windy, per hour of machine time. (Exhibit 11.18)

Units of Sales for Gale

36,000

24,000

Units of Sales for Windy

product and focusing entirely on the other. However, the previous results show the value of considering a strong focus on the more profitable product based on the contribution per unit of a scarce resource.

Case 2: Two or More Production Constraints

When the production process requires two or more production constraints, the choice of sales mix involves a more complex analysis, and in contrast to the case of one production constraint which solves for a single product, the solution can include both products when two constraints are involved. To continue with the Windbreakers case, assume that in addition to the automated sewing machine, a second production activity is required. The second activity inspects the completed jackets, adds labels, and packages the completed product. This operation is done by 40 workers, each of whom can complete the operation for the Windy jacket in 15 minutes and for the Gale jacket in 5 minutes (because of differences in material quality, less inspection time is required for the Gale jacket). This means that 4 (60 min./15 min.) Windy jackets can be completed in an hour, or 12 Gale (60 min./5 min.). Because of the limited size of the facility, no more than 40 workers can be employed effectively in the inspection and packaging process. These employees work a 40-hour week, which means 35 hours of actually performing the operation, given times for breaks, training, and other tasks. Thus, 5,600 hours (40 workers × 35 hours × 4 weeks) are available per month for inspecting and packing.

The maximum output per month for the Windy jacket is 22,400 (5,600 hours × 4 jackets per hour). Similarly, the maximum output for the Gale jacket is 67,200. All of this information is summarized in Exhibit 11.20.

The production possibilities for two constraints are illustrated in Exhibit 11.21. In addition to the production possibilities for machine time, we show the production possibilities for inspection and packing. The darker shaded area indicates the range of possible outputs for

EXHIBIT 11.20

Windbreakers Data for the Windy and Gale Plant
The Second Constraint: Inspecting and Packing

	Windy	Gale
Since		
Contribution margin/unit	$8	$4
Inspection and packaging time per jacket	15 min	5 min
Then		
Number of jackets per hour	4	12
Contribution margin per labor-hour (4 × $8; 12 × $4)	$32	$48
Also		
The maximum production for each product, given the 5,600-hour constraint		
For Windy: 5,600 × 4 jackets per hour	22,400	
For Gale: 5,600 × 12 jackets per hour		67,200

EXHIBIT 11.21

Windbreakers Production and Sales Possibilities
Two Production Constraints— Sewing Machine and Inspection

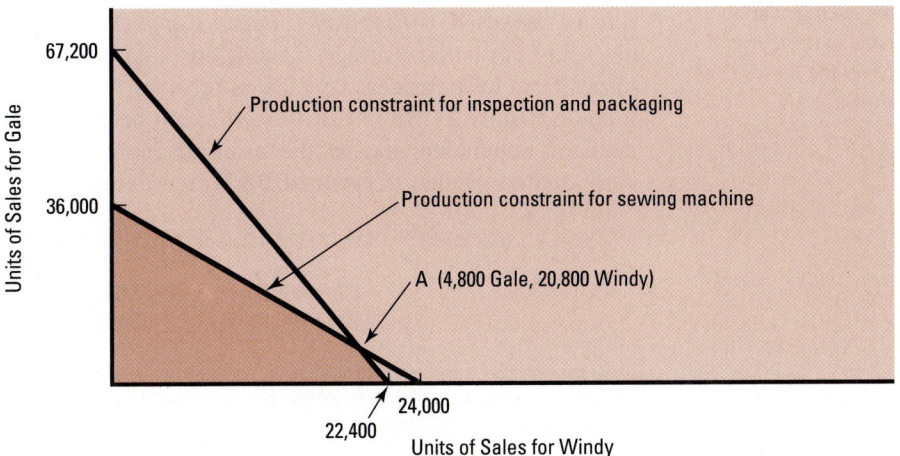

both Gale and Windy. Note that it is not possible to produce more than the 22,400 units of Windy because all 40 workers inspecting and packing full time would not be able to handle more than that number, even though the sewing machine is capable of producing 24,000 units. Similarly, although Windbreakers could pack and ship 67,200 units of Gale by having all 40 packers work full-time on that jacket, the firm could manufacture only 36,000 units of Gale because of limited capacity on the sewing machines.

The production planner can determine the best production mix by examining all of the possible production possibilities in the darker shaded area, from 36,000 on the Gale axis to point A where the constraints intersect, and then to the point 22,400 on the Windy axis. The sales mix with the highest contribution must be one of these three points: 36,000 of Gale, point A, or 22,400 units of Windy. The solution, called the *corner point analysis,* is obtained by finding the total contribution at each point and then choosing the point with the highest contribution. The solution achieved in this manner is for production at point A, 20,800 units of Windy and 4,800 units of Gale.[3]

The analysis of sales mix and production constraints is a useful way for managers to understand both how a difference in sales mix affects income and how production limitations and capacities can significantly affect the proper determination of the most profitable sales mix.

Behavioral and Implementation Issues

Consideration of Strategic Objectives

LEARNING OBJECTIVE 8

Discuss the behavioral, implementation, and legal issues in decision making.

A well-known problem in business today is the tendency of managers to focus on short-term goals and neglect the long-term strategic goals because their compensation is based on short-term accounting measures such as net income. Many critics of relevant cost analysis have raised this issue. As noted throughout the chapter, it is critical that the relevant cost analysis be supplemented by a careful consideration of the firm's long-term, strategic goals. Without strategic considerations, management could improperly use relevant cost analysis to achieve a short-term benefit and potentially suffer a significant long-term loss. For example, a firm might choose to accept a special order because of a positive relevant cost analysis without properly considering that the nature of the special order could have a significant negative impact on the firm's image in the marketplace and perhaps a negative effect on sales of the firm's other products. The important message for managers is to keep the strategic objectives in the forefront in any decision situation.

Predatory Pricing Practices

Predatory pricing

exists when a company has set prices below average variable cost and plans to raise prices later to recover the losses from the lower prices.

The Robinson Patman Act, administered by the U.S. Federal Trade Commission, addresses pricing that could substantially damage competition in an industry. This is called **predatory pricing,** which the U.S. Supreme Court defined in a 1993 decision, *Brooke Group Ltd. vs. Brown & Williamson Tobacco Corp.* (B&W), as a situation in which a company has set prices below average variable cost and planned to raise prices later to recover the losses from lower prices. This law is relevant for short-term *and* long-term pricing since it could require a firm to justify significant price cuts. However, the Court in the *Brooke* decision concluded that on the basis of economic theory, predatory pricing does not work and concluded in favor of B&W, the defendant in the case. The Court's reasoning

---

[3] The point A, 20,800 for Windy (W) and 4,800 for Gale (G), is obtained by solving the two equations:

$$15W + 5G = 35 \times 40 \times 4 \times 60 = 336,000 \text{ minutes of inspection time}$$
$$3W + 2G = 400 \times 3 \times 60 = 72,000 \text{ minutes of sewing time}$$

Linear programming, a mathematical method, permits the solution of much larger problems involving many products and production activities. A linear program technique to solve the Windy and Gale case is shown in appendix A. This technique uses the Solver function of Microsoft Excel.

has stood the test of time, because all 37 predatory pricing cases since its 1993 decision have been found in favor of the defendant. In spite of this, some economists and lawyers in 1999–2000 believed that economic theories of competition had changed since 1993. On the basis of these new theories, they took issue with the aggressive pricing practices of American Airlines, especially at the Dallas–Fort Worth airport, where a number of competing carriers had been driven to financial distress. In 2001 their suit against American was thrown out by a federal judge, causing some to argue this is the end of suits regarding predatory pricing. Another example of the failure of a predatory pricing suit is the case of a small chain of convenience stores, in which activity-based costing assisted the defendant to support its position that it was not selling gasoline below cost.[4]

A variation on the issue of predatory pricing is the recent increase in the number of countries levying fines against global firms for "dumping" their products at anticompetitive prices. A recent World Trade Organization report shows the number of cases per year increased by 100 percent from 1995 to 2000 and then decreased by 30% from 2000 to 2005. The U.S. antidumping laws were enacted more than 90 years ago to protect against predatory pricing by global firms exporting to the United States. The laws state that the import price cannot be lower than the cost of production or the price in the home market. Unfortunately the laws often have been used to protect uncompetitive industries in the home country. Facing increasing global pressure on the issue, U.S. congressional leaders are debating the need to reform the U.S. law.[5]

Replacement of Variable Costs with Fixed Costs

Another potential problem associated with relevant cost analysis is that managers who are evaluated on their ability to reduce controllable variable costs will have the incentive to replace variable costs with fixed costs. This happens if mid-level and lower-level managers realize that because top managers rely on relevant cost analysis, upper management might overlook fixed costs. Lower-level managers might choose to upgrade or increase fixed assets in order to reduce variable costs, although this might increase fixed costs significantly. For example, a new machine might replace direct labor. The overall costs increase because of the cost of the new machine, although variable costs under the manager's control decrease and the contribution

---

[4] Dan Carney, "Predatory Pricing: Cleared for Takeoff," *BusinessWeek*, May 14, 2001, p. 50; Thomas L. Barton and John B. MacArthur, "Activity-Based Costing and Predatory Pricing," "The Case of the Petroleum Retail Industry," *Management Accounting Quarterly*, Spring 2003, pp. 1–5. Note that price fixing, in which firms collude to set higher prices, differs from predatory pricing as described above.

[5] Paul Magnusson, "A U.S. Trade Ploy That Is Starting to Boomerang," *BusinessWeek*, July 29, 2002, pp 64–65; "The WTO Rules Against a Globally Unpopular U.S. Legislation," *Business Standard*, February 13, 2003; "Steel Wire Imports May Have Violated Antidumping Laws," *The Wall Street Journal*, March 18, 2003, p. A12; Murray Hiebert, "When It Comes to Law, China Buys American," *The Wall Street Journal*, February 17, 2006, p. B1.

margin increases. Management's proper goal is to maximize contribution margin and to minimize fixed operating costs at the same time. Managers should use relevant cost analysis as a tool to maximize contribution and must also develop methods to manage fixed costs.

Proper Identification of Relevant Factors

Also, managers can fail to properly identify relevant costs. In particular, untrained managers commonly include irrelevant, sunk costs in decision making.[6] Similarly, many managers fail to see that allocated fixed costs are irrelevant. When fixed costs are shown as fixed cost per unit many managers tend to improperly find them relevant. It is easier for these managers to see the fixed cost as irrelevant when it is given in a single sum; it is more difficult to see unit fixed costs as irrelevant.

These are illustrations of the pervasive biases present in many managers' decision making. Effective use of relevant cost analysis requires careful identification of relevant costs, those future costs that differ among decision alternatives, and correctly recognizing sunk costs and unit fixed costs as irrelevant in the short term.

Summary

Relevant cost analysis uses future costs that differ for the decision maker's options. The principle of relevant cost analysis can be applied in a number of specific decisions involving manufacturing, service, and not-for-profit organizations. The decisions considered in the chapter include

- The special order decision for which the relevant costs are the direct manufacturing costs and any incremental fixed costs.
- The make, lease, or buy decision for which the relevant costs are the direct manufacturing costs and any avoidable fixed costs.
- The decision to sell a product before or after additional processing for which the relevant costs are the additional processing costs.
- The decision to keep or drop a product line or service for which the relevant costs are the direct costs and any fixed costs that change if the product or service is dropped.
- The decision of a not-for-profit organization to offer a service.

Strategic analysis complements relevant cost analysis by having the decision maker consider the strategic issues involved in the situation.

When two or more products or services are involved, another type of decision must be made: to determine the correct product mix. The solution depends on the number of production activities that are at full capacity. With one production constraint, the answer is to produce and sell as much as possible of the product that has the highest contribution margin per unit of time on the constrained activity. With two or more constrained activities, the analysis uses graphical and quantitative methods to determine the correct product mix.

A number of key behavioral, implementation, and legal issues must be considered in using relevant cost analysis. Many who use the approach fail to give sufficient attention to the firm's long-term, strategic objectives. Too strong a focus on relevant costs can cause the manager to overlook important opportunity costs and strategic considerations. Other issues include the tendency to replace variable costs with fixed costs when relevant cost analysis is used in performance evaluation and the pervasive tendency of people not to correctly view fixed costs as sunk but to view them as somehow controllable and relevant.

[6] For a comprehensive coverage of decision-making biases, see John S. Hammond, Ralph L. Keeney, and Howard Raiffa, "The Hidden Traps in Decision Making," *Harvard Business Review,* September–October 1998, pp. 47–58; also D. L. Heerema and R. L. Rogers, "Is Your Cost Accounting System Benching Your Team Players?" *Management Accounting,* September 1991, pp. 35–40, gives useful illustrations of the improper use of relevant cost analysis in the automobile industry, the military, and elsewhere. Prospect theory suggests that people underweigh alternatives that are uncertain in comparison to alternatives known to be certain. The theory has been offered as a potential explanation of the tendency people have to include sunk costs in decision making. See D. Kahneman and A. Tversky, "Prospect Theory: An Analysis of Decision under Risk," *Econometrica,* March 1979, pp. 263–92; and Glen Whyte, "Escalating Commitment to a Course of Action: A Reinterpretation," *Academy of Management Review,* 1986, pp. 311–21.

Appendix

Linear Programming and the Product Mix Decision

Linear programming
is a mathematical technique that can be used to solve for the best product mix.

Solver
is a an analytical tool available on the Data tab in Excel that can be used to solve linear programming problems.

This appendix explains how **linear programming** can be used to solve product mix decisions such as the Windbreakers case illustrated in the chapter. Linear programming is particularly useful when the product mix decision involves three or more constraints since these larger problems are difficult to solve graphically or with the simple corner point analysis explained in the chapter. A number of linear programming tools are available; we use the **Solver** function of Microsoft Excel because of its wide availability. To access this tool, you simply install it when installing Excel; Solver will appear as an option on Excel's Data tab. If Solver is not installed for your Excel, go to the Office button at the top left of the Excel spreadsheet and then choose Excel Options. In the next screen choose Add-ins on the left of the screen and then choose Solver Add-in.

The first step in using Solver is to enter the data for the problem into an Excel spreadsheet, in the form shown in Exhibit 11A.1.

Column A: Shows the product names.

Column B: Solver requires an initial guess at what might be an appropriate solution; for this purpose, we chose the point 10,000 units of Windy and 2,000 units of Gale; the point should be any of the possible points within the feasible region shown as the darker shaded area in Exhibit 11.21 on page 447.

Columns C, D, and E: These contain data entered from the problem information.

Columns F, G, and H: These contain formulas based on the data in columns, C, D, and E; for example, cell F5 contains B5 × C5; cell G5 contains B5 × D5, and so on.

EXHIBIT 11A.1   **Enter Data and Solver Parameters: Solution for the Windy and Gale Problem**

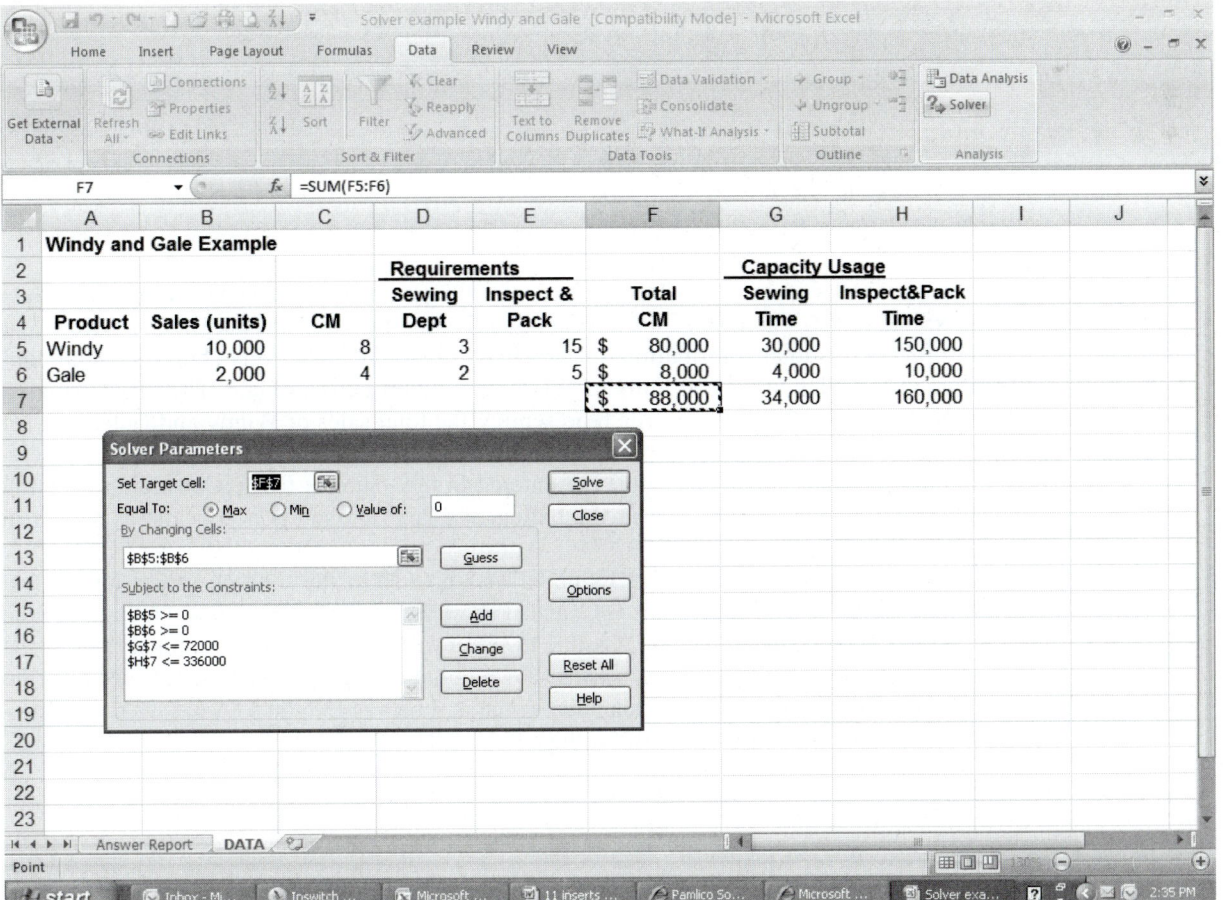

EXHIBIT 11A.2 **Solver Solution for the Windy and Gale Problem**

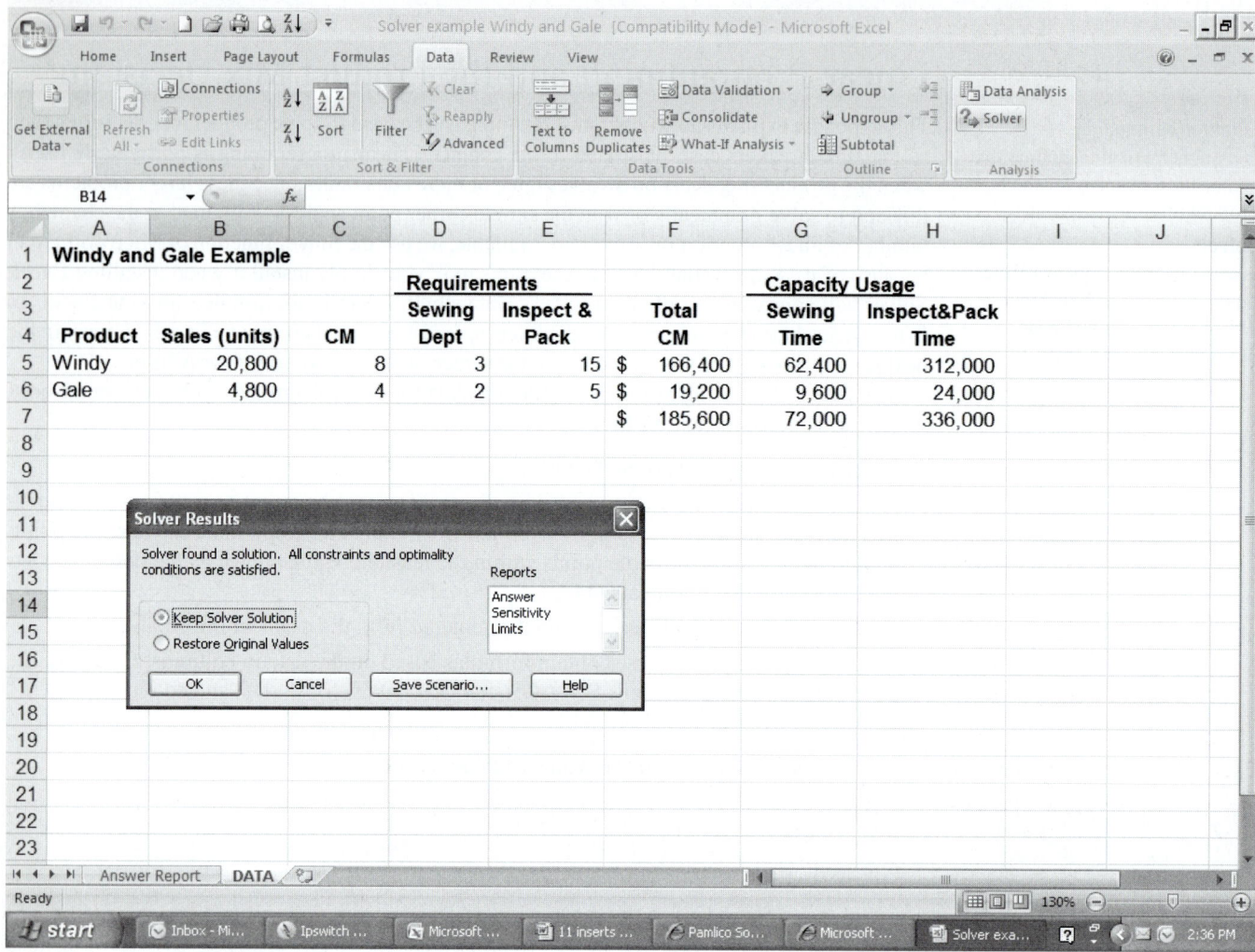

The second step in using Solver is to enter the parameters as shown in the dialog box in Exhibit 11A.1. The dialog box appears by selecting Solver from the Data tab. Note that the target cell is total contribution, located in cell F7, which currently shows the total contribution for sales of 10,000 units of Windy and 2,000 units of Gale. The "By Changing Cells" section includes those cells representing the total sales of Windy and Gale, now set at an initial value of 10,000 and 2,000 units, respectively. Then the constraints for sewing time and inspect and pack time are entered in the "Subject to the Constraints" section as shown. Finally, select Solve in the dialog box, and the solution appears, as shown in Exhibit 11A.2.

Notice that cells B5 and B6 in Exhibit 11A.2 now show the solution values for the two products, and the cells in columns F, G, and H show the total contribution and total use of the two constraints. At this time, it is possible to see any of three possible additional reports, the Answer, Sensitivity, and Limit reports as shown in the dialog box. We have selected only the Answer report for illustration at this time, which is shown in Exhibit 11A.3. This report summarizes the initial and final values for the problem data.

EXHIBIT 11A.3   Solver Solution for the Windy and Gale Problem: Answer Report

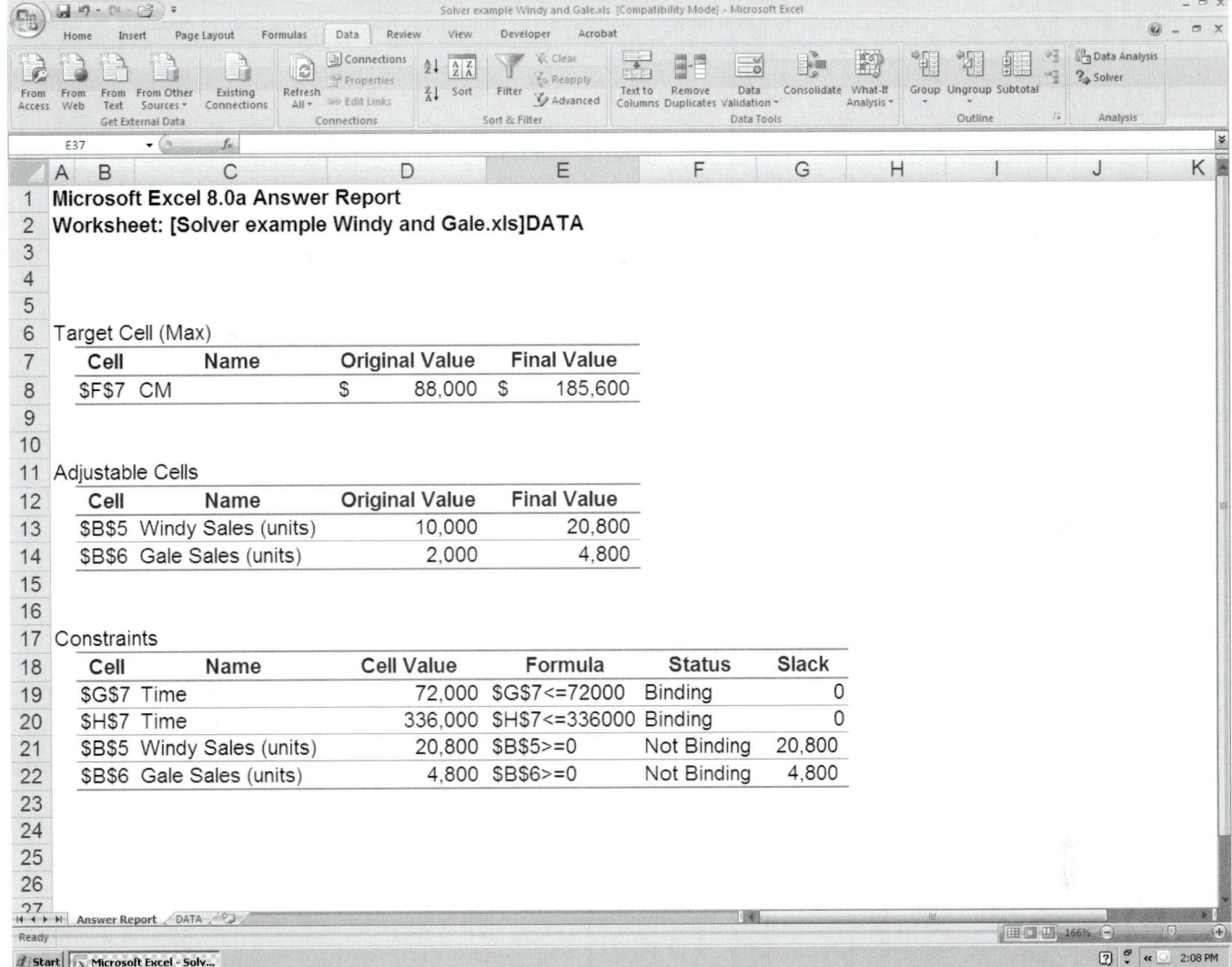

Comments on Cost Management in Action

Trends in Make-or-Buy Strategies

Toyota Motor Company is able to maintain a small number of suppliers by using two key strategies. First, it develops a hierarchy of suppliers; Toyota deals directly with approximately 200, which are called the *top-tier suppliers*. These 200 suppliers in turn deal with second-tier suppliers who provide products and services to those at the top tier. These second-tier suppliers in turn deal with third-tier suppliers. In this way, Toyota delegates the responsibility for managing the supply function in a way that motivates suppliers at each tier to work effectively with those above and below it in the supply chain. Second, Toyota distinguishes two types of suppliers, general and specialty. Toyota has relatively simple relationships with those in the general category of suppliers but develops close financial and technological ties with the specialty suppliers. The objective is to recognize the strategic importance of the specialty suppliers and to develop strong relationships with them to ensure success.

In a recent change the airline carriers are beginning to manufacture replacement parts for their fleets, rather than purchase the replacement parts from the manufacturers. For example, Continental Airlines can manufacture a flight deck door for a Boeing 767 for $150 in contrast to the purchase price from

Boeing of $960. Similarly, American Airlines manufactures air filters for its Boeing 777 fleet for $33, in contrast to the Boeing price of $132. For the air carriers, it is definitely cheaper to make than to buy.

Other trends include a move by some firms to return some manufacturing back to domestic factories, as the cost of shipping product from China and other countries has increased dramatically with the increase in fuel prices; the cost of shipping a 40-foot, 5,000-pound container from China to the west coast has increased from $2,000 in 2000 to $5,000 in 2008.

In another reversal of outsourcing, the financial services industry, suffering through historic losses in 2008, has cut back in 2008 by one-half the amount of 2007 outsourcing in which computer services, customer services, and other banking activities are "off-shored."

Source: "Machete Time," *BusinessWeek,* April 9, 2001, pp. 42–43; Melanie Trottman, "To Cut Costs: Airlines Make More of Their Own Parts; Jettisoning a $719 Toilet Seat," *The Wall Street Journal,* Tuesday May 3, 2005, p. B1; Timothy Aeppel, "Stung by Soaring Transport Costs, Factories Bring Jobs Home Again," *The Wall Street Journal,* June 13, 2008, p. 1. "In a Pinch," *The Economist,* October 11, 2008, p. 86.

Self-Study Problems

(For solutions, please turn to the end of the chapter.)

1. Special Order Pricing

HighValu Inc. manufactures a moderate-price set of lawn furniture (a table and four chairs) that it sells for $225. It currently manufactures and sells 6,000 sets per year. The manufacturing costs include $85 for materials and $45 for labor per set. The overhead charge per set is $35, which consists entirely of fixed costs.

HighValu is considering a special purchase offer from a large retail firm, which has offered to buy 600 sets per year for three years at a price of $150 per set. HighValu has the available plant capacity to produce the order and expects no other orders or profitable alternative uses of the plant capacity.

Required Should HighValu accept the offer?

2. The Make-or-Buy Decision

Assume that HighValu Inc., as described, currently purchases the chair cushions for its lawn set from an outside vendor for $15 per set. HighValu's chief operations officer wants an analysis of the comparative costs of manufacturing these cushions to determine whether bringing the manufacturing in-house would save the firm money. Additional information shows that if HighValu were to manufacture the cushions, the materials cost would be $6 and the labor cost would be $4 per set and that it would have to purchase cutting and sewing equipment, which would add $10,000 to annual fixed costs.

Required Should HighValu make the cushions or continue to purchase them from the vendor?

3. Profitability Analysis

Consider again the Windbreakers firm described in the text. Suppose that Windbreakers determines that dropping the Gale product line will release production capacity so that it can manufacture additional units of Windy. Assume that, as described in the text, the two production constraints are the automated sewing machine and the inspection and packing operation. The automated sewing machine can make 20 Windys or 30 Gales per hour. As before, the inspection operation requires 15 minutes for a Windy (4 per hour) and 5 minutes for a Gale (12 per hour). Currently, 3,750 Gales and 18,750 Windys are being manufactured and sold. Sales projections show that sales of Windy could be increased to 30,000 units if additional capacity were available.

Required
1. If Windbreakers deletes Gale entirely, how many units of Windy can it manufacture with the released capacity?
2. What is the dollar effect on net income if Windbreakers drops the production and sale of Gale and uses the released capacity for Windy?
3. What other factors should Windbreakers consider in its decision to drop Gale and use the released capacity to produce additional units of Windy?

Questions

11-1 What are relevant costs? Provide several examples for the decision to repair or replace a piece of equipment.

11-2 Define *outsourcing* and explain how the relevant cost analysis model is used in the outsourcing decision.

11-3 List at least four different decisions for which the relevant cost analysis model can be used effectively.

11-4 How does the relevant cost analysis model differ for manufacturing and service firms?

11-5 What is the relevant cost when determining whether or not to process a product further?

11-6 List four to six strategic factors that are often important in the make-or-buy decision.

11-7 Explain what *not relevant* cost means and provide two examples of it.

11-8 Why are variable costs usually more relevant than fixed costs in short-term decision making?

11-9 Give an example of how a firm can decrease variable costs by increasing fixed costs.

11-10 Give an example of how a firm can decrease fixed costs by increasing variable costs.

11-11 How do short-term evaluations affect a manager's incentives and performance?

11-12 List four or five important limitations of relevant cost analysis.

11-13 How do strategic factors affect the proper use of relevant cost analysis?

11-14 List some of the behavioral, implementation, and legal problems to be anticipated in the use of relevant cost analysis.

11-15 How does the presence of one production constraint affect the relevant cost analysis model? Two or more production constraints?

11-16 What is the relationship, if any, between the relevant cost analysis method and cost-volume-profit analysis?

11-17 Explain why depreciation is a nonrelevant cost.

Brief Exercises

11-18 Purchase price is $35 for a part that can be manufactured for $33; the $33 manufacturing costs include $5 per unit fixed cost. What is the savings to make rather than to buy?

11-19 Products X and Y are produced in a joint process that costs a total of $300,000. At the end of this process, X can be sold for $20 per unit and Y for $40 per unit. X can be processed further for an additional $2 per unit and sold for $25. Also, product Y can be processed further for $4 per unit and sold for $50 per unit. Which product should be processed further, and why?

11-20 Adams Furniture receives a special order for 10 sofas for a special price of $3,000. The materials and direct labor for each sofa are $100. In addition, the setup, supervision, and other overhead costs are $150 per sofa. Should Adams accept the special order? Why or why not? Would it make a difference to your answer if Adams is at full capacity and its current line of sofas sell for $500 each?

11-21 Wings Diner has a box lunch that it sells on football game days at the local university. Each box lunch sells for $6, which includes $2.50 variable costs and $2.50 fixed cost plus a $1 markup. What is the lowest price Wings can sell its box lunch so that Wings will still make a profit?

11-22 Williams Auto has a machine that installs tires. The machine now is in need of repair. The machine originally cost $10,000 and the repair will cost $1,000, but the machine will then last two years. The variable (labor) cost of operating the machine is $0.50 per tire. Instead of repairing the old machine, Williams could buy a new machine at a cost of $5,000 that would also last two years; the labor cost per tire would be reduced to $0.25 per tire. Should Williams repair or replace the machine if it is installing 10,000 tires in the next two years?

11-23 Ford Manufacturing has received an order from Roy Inc. for 500 sport shirts. Ford could produce the shirts or Ford could buy the shirts from another supplier to fill the Roy order, at $20 per shirt. The production at Ford is $10 per shirt plus $1,000 cost per batch. Which option will be preferable to Ford?

11-24 Jamison Health Care is trying to decide if it should eliminate its orthopedic care division. In the last year, the orthopedic division had a contribution margin of $100,000 and allocated overhead costs of $200,000, of which $90,000 could be eliminated if the division is dropped. Should Jamison keep the division?

11-25 Guthridge Soap Corporation is evaluating a new soap cutting machine that could eliminate some direct labor costs. The machine would cost $900,000 per year and would cost $0.10 per bar to cut the soap. Currently, Guthridge uses direct labor to cut the soap into bars, which costs $1 per bar. The company currently produces 500,000 bars of soap per year. Should it buy the machine?

11-26 ElecPlus Batteries has two different products, AAA and AA batteries. The AA batteries have a contribution margin of $1 per package, and the AAA batteries have a contribution margin of $2 per package. ElecPlus has a capacity for 1 million batteries per month, and both batteries require the same amount of processing time. If a special order for 10,000 AAA exceeds the monthly capacity, should ElecPlus accept the special order?

11-27 Jackson Inc. disposes of other companies' toxic waste. Currently Jackson loads the waste by hand into the truck, which requires labor of $20 per load. Jackson is considering a machine that would reduce the amount of time needed to load the waste. The machine would cost $200,000, but would reduce labor cost to $5 per load. Should Jackson buy the machine if it averages 10,000 loads per year?

11-28 Durant Co. manufactures glass bottles for dairy products. The contribution margin is $0.10 per bottle. Durant just received notification that one of their orders for 100,000 bottles contained misprinted labels, and thus had to recall and reprint the bottle labels. If it will cost $0.05 per bottle to reprint the labels and $1,000 to reship the bottles, what will the net contribution margin be after the recall?

11-29 Wings Airlines targets budget travelers with its low-cost fares. Assume Wings provides no in-flight service except for meals and beverages that the passengers must pay for. The baggage handling and gate services are fixed costs. What is the lowest price Wings should charge for a ticket?

11-30 Lance's Diner has a hot lunch special each weekday and Sunday afternoon. Food and other variable costs for the lunch are $3.50, and the daily fixed costs are $1,000. Lance has an average of 500 customers per day. What is the lowest price Lance should charge for a special group of 200 that wants to come on Saturday for a family reunion? What should be the lowest price Lance charges on a normal weekly basis?

11-31 Sweet Dream Hotel has labor costs that are mostly fixed, including registration desk, maintenance, and general repairs and cleaning. The housekeeping staff is hired in sufficient numbers to clean the rooms that need cleaning, so that housekeeping is a variable cost for the number of occupied rooms. Which of these costs is relevant for determining the price of a room?

Exercises

11-32 **Special Order** Marshall Company recently approached Johnson Corporation regarding manufacturing a special order of 4,000 units of product CRB2B. Marshall would reimburse Johnson for all variable manufacturing costs plus 35 percent. The *per-unit* data follow:

Unit sales price	$28
Variable manufacturing costs	13
Variable marketing costs	5
Fixed manufacturing costs	4
Fixed marketing costs	2

Johnson would have a retooling cost of $12,000 for the special order. Johnson has no alternative use of capacity.

Required Should the special order be accepted?

11-33 **Special Order** Alton Inc. is working at full production capacity producing 20,000 units of a unique product. Manufacturing costs per unit for the product are

Direct materials	$ 9
Direct labor	8
Manufacturing overhead	10
Total manufacturing cost	$27

The unit manufacturing overhead cost is based on a $4 variable cost per unit and $120,000 fixed costs. The nonmanufacturing costs, all variable, are $8 per unit, and the sales price is $45 per unit.

Sports Headquarters Company (SHC) has asked Alton to produce 5,000 units of a modification of the new product. This modification would require the same manufacturing processes. SHC has offered to share the nonmanufacturing costs equally with Alton. Alton would sell the modified product to SHC for $35 per unit.

Required

1. Should Alton produce the special order for SHC? Why or why not?

2. Suppose that Alton Inc. had been working at less than full capacity to produce 16,000 units of the product when SHC made the offer. What is the minimum price that Alton should accept for the modified product under these conditions?

11-34 **Make or Buy; Continuation of Problem 9-28 (Chapter 9)** Calista Company manufactures electronic equipment In 2009, it purchased the special switches used in each of its products from an outside supplier. The supplier charged Calista $2 per switch. Calista's CEO considered purchasing either machine X or machine Y so the company could manufacture its own switches. The CEO decided at the beginning of 2010 to purchase Machine X, based on the following data:

	Machine X	Machine Y
Annual fixed cost	$135,000	$204,000
Variable cost per switch	0.65	0.30

Required

1. For machine X, what is the indifference point between purchasing the machine and purchasing from the outside vendor?

2. At what volume level should Calista consider purchasing Machine Y?

11-35 **Special Order**   Grant Industries, a manufacturer of electronic parts, has recently received an invitation to bid on a special order for 20,000 units of one of its most popular products. Grant currently manufactures 40,000 units of this product in its Loveland, Ohio, plant. The plant is operating at 50 percent capacity. There will be no marketing costs on the special order. The sales manager of Grant wants to set the bid at $9 because she is sure that Grant will get the business at that price. Others on the executive committee of the firm object, saying that Grant would lose money on the special order at that price.

Units	40,000	60,000
Manufacturing costs		
Direct materials	$ 80,000	$120,000
Direct labor	120,000	180,000
Factory overhead	240,000	300,000
Total manufacturing costs	$440,000	$600,000
Unit cost	$ 11	$ 10

Required

1. Why does the unit cost decline from $11 to $10 when production level rises from 40,000 to 60,000 units?

2. Is the sales manager correct? What do you think the bid price should be?

3. List some additional factors Grant should consider in deciding how much to bid on this special order.

11-36 **Profitability Analysis**   Barbour Corporation, located in Buffalo, New York, is a retailer of high-tech products known for its excellent quality and innovation. Recently the firm conducted a relevant cost analysis of one of its product lines that has only two products, T-1 and T-2. The sales for T-2 are decreasing and the purchase costs are increasing. The firm might drop T-2 and sell only T-1.

Barbour allocates fixed costs to products on the basis of sales revenue. When the president of Barbour saw the income statement, he agreed that T-2 should be dropped. If this is done, sales of T-1 are expected to increase by 10 percent next year; the firm's cost structure will remain the same.

	T-1	T-2
Sales	$200,000	$260,000
Variable cost of goods sold	70,000	130,000
Contribution margin	$130,000	$130,000
Expenses		
Fixed corporate costs	60,000	75,000
Variable selling and administration	20,000	50,000
Fixed selling and administration	12,000	21,000
Total expenses	$ 92,000	$146,000
Operating income	$ 38,000	$(16,000)

Required

1. Find the expected change in annual operating income by dropping T-2 and selling only T-1.

2. What strategic factors should be considered?

11-37 **Relevant Cost Exercises**   Each of the following situations is independent

a. **Make or Buy**   Terry Inc. manufactures machine parts for aircraft engines. CEO Bucky Walters is considering an offer from a subcontractor to provide 2,000 units of product OP89 for $120,000. If Terry does not purchase these parts from the subcontractor, it must continue to produce them in-house with these costs:

	Costs per Unit
Direct materials	$28
Direct labor	18
Variable overhead	16
Fixed overhead	4

Required   Should Terry Inc. accept the offer from the subcontractor? Why or why not?

b.   **Disposal of Assets**   A company has an inventory of 2,000 different parts for a line of cars that has been discontinued. The net book value of inventory in the accounting records is $50,000. The parts can be either remachined at a total additional cost of $25,000 and then sold for $30,000 or sold as is for $2,500. What should it do?

c.   **Replacement of Asset**   An uninsured boat costing $90,000 was wrecked the first day it was used. It can be either sold as is for $9,000 cash and replaced with a similar boat costing $92,000 or rebuilt for $75,000 and be brand new as far as operating characteristics and looks are concerned. What should be done?

d.   **Profit from Processing Further**   Deaton Corporation manufactures products A, B, and C from a joint process. Joint costs are allocated on the basis of relative sales value at the end of the joint process. Additional information for Deaton Corporation follows:

	A	B	C	Total
Units produced	12,000	8,000	4,000	24,000
Joint costs	$144,000	$ 60,000	$36,000	$240,000
Sales value before additional processing	240,000	100,000	60,000	400,000
Additional costs for further processing	28,000	20,000	12,000	60,000
Sales value if processed further	280,000	120,000	70,000	470,000

Required   Which, if any, of products A, B, and C should be processed further and then sold?

e.   **Make or Buy**   Eggers Company needs 20,000 units of a part to use in producing one of its products. If Eggers buys the part from McMillan Company for $90 instead of making it, Eggers could not use the released facilities in another manufacturing activity. Fifty percent of the fixed overhead will continue irrespective of CEO Donald Mickey's decision. The cost data are

Cost to make the part	
Direct materials	$35
Direct labor	16
Variable overhead	24
Fixed overhead	20
	$95

Required   Determine which alternative is more attractive to Eggers and by what amount.

f.   **Selection of the Most Profitable Product**   DVD Production Company produces two basic types of video games, Flash and Clash. Pertinent data for DVD Production Company follows:

	Flash	Clash
Sales price	$250	$140
Costs		
Direct materials	50	25
Direct labor ($25/Hr)	100	50
Variable factory overhead*	50	25
Fixed factory overhead*	20	10
Marketing costs (all fixed)	10	10
Total costs	$230	$120
Operating profit	$ 20	$ 20

* Based on labor-hours.

The DVD game craze is at its height so that either Flash or Clash alone can be sold to keep the plant operating at full capacity. However, labor capacity in the plant is insufficient to meet the combined demand for both games. Flash and Clash are processed through the same production departments.

Required   Which product should be produced? Briefly explain your answer.

g.   **Special Order Pricing**   Barry's Bar-B-Que is a popular lunch-time spot. Barry is conscientious about the quality of his meals, and he has a regular crowd of 600 patrons for his $5 lunch. His variable cost for each meal is about $2, and he figures his fixed costs, on a daily basis, at about $1,200. From time to time, bus tour groups with 50 patrons stop by. He has welcomed them since he has capacity to seat 700 diners in the average lunch period, and his cooking and wait staff can easily handle the additional load. The tour operator generally pays for the entire group on a single check to save the wait staff and cashier the additional time. Due to competitive conditions in the tour business, the operator is now asking Barry to lower the price to $3.50 per meal for each of the 50 bus tour members.

Required Should Barry accept the $3.50 price? Why or why not? What if the tour company were willing to guarantee 200 patrons (or four bus loads) at least once a month for $3.00 per meal?

11-38 **Special Order** Earth Baby Inc. (EBI) recently celebrated its tenth anniversary. The company produces organic baby products for health-conscious parents. These products include food, clothing, and toys. Earth Baby has recently introduced a new line of premium organic baby foods. Extensive research and scientific testing indicate that babies raised on the new line of foods will have substantial health benefits. EBI is able to sell its products at prices higher than competitors' because of its excellent reputation for superior products. EBI distributes its products through high-end grocery stores, pharmacies, and specialty retail baby stores.

Joan Alvarez, the founder and CEO of EBI recently received a proposal from an old business school classmate, Robert Bradley, the vice president of Great Deal Inc (GDI), a large discount retailer. Mr. Bradley proposes a joint venture between his company and EBI, citing the growing demand for organic products and the superior distribution channels of his organization. Under this venture EBI would make some minor modifications to the manufacturing process of some of its best-selling baby foods and the foods would then be packaged and sold by GDI. Under the agreement EBI would receive $3.10 per jar of baby food and would provide GDI a limited right to advertise the product as manufactured for Great Deal by EBI. Joan Alvarez set up a meeting with Fred Stanley, Earth Baby's CFO, to discuss the profitability of the venture. Mr. Stanley made some initial calculations and determined that the direct materials, direct labor, and other variable costs needed for the GDI order would be about $2 per unit as compared to the full cost of $3 (materials, labor, and overhead) for the equivalent EBI product.

Required Should Earth Baby Inc. accept the proposed venture from GDI? Why or why not?

11-39 **Special Order; Strategy, International** Williams Company, located in southern Wisconsin, manufactures a variety of industrial valves and pipe fittings that are sold to customers in nearby states. Currently, the company is operating at about 70 percent capacity and is earning a satisfactory return on investment.

Glasgow Industries Ltd. of Scotland has approached management with an offer to buy 120,000 units of a pressure valve. Glasgow Industries manufactures a valve that is almost identical to Williams' pressure valve; however, a fire in Glasgow Industries' valve plant has shut down its manufacturing operations. Glasgow needs the 120,000 valves over the next four months to meet commitments to its regular customers; the company is prepared to pay $21 each for the valves.

Williams' product cost for the pressure valve, based on current attainable standards, is

Direct materials	$ 6
Direct labor (0.5 hr per valve)	8
Manufacturing overhead (1/3 variable)	9
Total manufacturing cost	$23

Additional costs incurred in connection with sales of the pressure valve are sales commissions of 5 percent and freight expense of $1 per unit. However, the company does not pay sales commissions on special orders that come directly to management. Freight expense will be paid by Glasgow.

In determining selling prices, Williams adds a 40 percent markup to product cost. This provides a $32 suggested selling price for the pressure valve. The marketing department, however, has set the current selling price at $30 to maintain market share.

Production management believes that it can handle the Glasgow Industries order without disrupting its scheduled production. The order would, however, require additional fixed factory overhead of $12,000 per month in the form of supervision and clerical costs.

If management accepts the order, Williams will manufacture and ship 30,000 pressure valves to Glasgow Industries each month for the next four months. Shipments will be made in weekly consignments, FOB shipping point.

Required

1. Determine how many additional direct labor-hours will be required each month to fill the Glasgow order.

2. Prepare an analysis showing the impact on profit before tax of accepting the Glasgow order.

3. Calculate the minimum unit price that Williams' management could accept for the Glasgow order without reducing net income.

4. Identify the strategic factors that Williams should consider before accepting the Glasgow order.

5. Identify the factors related to international business that Williams should consider before accepting the Glasgow order.

(CMA Adapted)

11-40 **Opening a New Restaurant; Use of Relevant Cost Analysis**   Brad and Judy Bailey both enjoy preparing food and creating new recipes. So they are taking their passion to the workplace and plan to open a new restaurant called Baileys'. They have a two-year, renewable lease on a property that was previously used as a fast food restaurant. You are a good friend of the couple. They know of your expertise in cost management, so they have asked for your advice.

Required   Give an example (no numbers necessary) of how the Baileys could use the following cost management methods in planning and operating their new restaurant.

1. Special order analysis.

2. The make-or-buy decision.

3. Sell now or process further.

4. Profitability analysis for current and/or new products.

11-41 **Special Order; Use of Opportunity Cost Information**   Sharman Athletic Gear Inc (SAG) is considering a special order for 15,000 baseball caps with the logo of East Texas University (ETU) to be purchased by the ETU alumni association. The ETU alumni association is planning to use the caps as gifts and to sell some of the caps at alumni events in celebration of the university's recent national championship by its baseball team. Sharman's cost per hat is $3.50 which includes $1.50 fixed cost related to plant capacity and equipment. ETU has made a firm offer of $35,000 for the hats, and Sharman, considering the price to be far below production costs, decides to decline the offer.

Required

1. Did Sharman make the wrong decision? Why or why not?

2. Consider the management decision-making approach at Sharman that resulted in this decision. How was opportunity cost included or not included in the decision? What decision biases are apparent in this decision?

11-42 **When Does Buying a Gas Guzzler Make Sense?**   Gasoline prices increased and also fluctuated widely during 2007 and 2008, and car purchases fell, even for fuel-efficient cars. Many new cars were selling for a discount and/or special promotions including reduced interest rates on car loans. These discounts and promotions were especially prominent for SUVs and larger cars, those with the lowest gas mileage. The discounts and promotions were also prominent for used cars; in the used car market it was hard to find a fuel efficient vehicle, but SUVs and larger cars were in abundance.

Required   You are shopping for a car for your youngest son who has just received his driver's license. By clear agreement with your son, and because of local legal restrictions on new drivers such as those limiting the time of day they can drive, you do not expect the car to be driven many miles in the average month. Your son will be the only one allowed to use the car and he by agreement must purchase the gasoline for it. You will pay for insurance and for any mechanical repairs. Your criteria for the purchase of the car are first safety and then reliability and the cost of insurance. What type of car would you consider—a small fuel-efficient car or a large car?

Problems   11-43 **Special Order**   Award Plus Co. manufactures medals for winners of athletic events and other contests. Its manufacturing plant has the capacity to produce 10,000 medals each month; current monthly production is 7,500 medals. The company normally charges $175 per medal. Variable costs and fixed costs for the current activity level of 75 percent follow:

	Current Product Costs
Variable costs	
Manufacturing	
Labor	$ 375,000
Material	262,500
Marketing	187,500
Total variable costs	$ 825,000
Fixed costs	
Manufacturing	$ 275,000
Marketing	175,000
Total fixed costs	$ 450,000
Total costs	$1,275,000

Award Plus has just received a special one-time order for 2,500 medals at $100 per medal. For this particular order, no variable marketing costs will be incurred. Cathy Senna, a management accountant with Award Plus, has been assigned the task of analyzing this order and recommending whether the company should accept or reject it. After examining the costs, Senna suggested to her supervisor, Gerard LePenn who is the controller, that they request competitive bids from vendors for the raw materials since the current quote seems high. LePenn insisted that the prices are in line with other vendors and told her that she was not to discuss her observations with anyone else. Senna later discovered that LePenn is a brother-in-law of the owner of the current raw materials supply vendor.

Required

1. Determine if Award Plus Co. should accept the special order and why.

2. Discuss at least three other considerations that Cathy Senna should include in her analysis of the special order.

3. Explain how Cathy Senna should try to resolve the ethical conflict arising out of the controller's insistence that the company avoid competitive bidding.

(CMA Adapted)

11-44   **Special Order**   Duvernoy Industries produces high-quality automobile seat covers. Its success in the industry is due to its quality, although all of its customers, the automakers, are very cost conscious and negotiate for price cuts on all large orders. Noting that the auto supply business is becoming increasingly competitive, Duvernoy is looking for a way to meet the challenge. It is negotiating with Chen, Inc., a large mail-order auto parts and accessories retailer, to purchase a large order of seat covers. Much of Duvernoy's business is seasonal and cyclical, fluctuating with the varying demands of the large automakers. Duvernoy would like to keep its plants busy throughout the year by reducing these seasonal and cyclical fluctuations. Keeping the flow of product moving through the plants at a steady level is helpful in keeping costs down; extra overtime and machine setup and repair costs are incurred when production levels fluctuate. Chen has agreed to a large order but only at a price of $30 per set. The special order can be produced in one batch with available capacity. Duvernoy prepared these data:

Next month's operating information without the special order (per unit, for 10,000 units, made in 10 batches of 1,000 each)	
Sales price	$80
Per unit costs	
Variable manufacturing costs	20
Variable marketing costs	8
Fixed manufacturing costs	40
Fixed marketing costs	3
Special order information	
Sales	2,000 units
Sales price per unit	$30

No variable marketing costs are associated with this order, but Marc Jones, the firm's president, has spent $6,000 during the past three months trying to get Chen to purchase the special order.

Required

1. How much will the special order change Duvernoy Industries' total operating income?

2. How might the special order fit into Duvernoy's competitive situation?

11-45   **Special Order: ABC Costing (Continuation of Problem 11-44)**   Assume the same information as for Problem 11-44, except that the $40 fixed manufacturing overhead consists of $15 per unit batch related costs and $25 per unit facilities level fixed costs. Also, assume that each new batch causes increased costs of $15,000 per batch; the remainder of the fixed costs do not vary with the number of units produced or the number of batches.

Required

1. Calculate the relevant unit and total cost of the special order, including the new information about batch related costs.

2. If accepted, how would the special order affect Duvernoy's operating income?

3. Suppose that Chen notifies Duvernoy it must reduce its order to 1,000 units because of changes in orders it has received. How would this change affect your answer in Parts 1 and 2?

Required

11-46   **Make or Buy**   Martens, Inc., manufactures a variety of electronic products. It specializes in commercial and residential products with moderate to large electric motors such as pumps and fans. Martens is now looking closely at its production of attic fans, which included 10,000 units in the prior year and had the following costs. These costs included $100,000 of allocated fixed manufacturing overhead. Martens has capacity to manufacture 15,000 attic fans per year.

Martens believes demand in the coming year will be 20,000 attic fans. The company has looked into the possibility of purchasing the attic fans from another manufacturer to help it meet this demand. Harris Products, a steady supplier of quality products, would be able to provide up to 9,000 attic fans per year at a price of $46 per fan delivered to Martens's facility.

For each unit of product that Martens sells, regardless of whether the product has been purchased from Harris or is manufactured by Martens, there is an additional selling and administrative cost of $20, which includes an allocated $6 fixed overhead cost per unit. The following is based on the production of 10,000 units in the prior year.

Selling price per unit		$72.00
Costs per unit		
Electric motor	$ 6.00	
Other parts	8.00	
Direct labor ($15/hr.)	15.00	
Manufacturing overhead	15.00	
Selling and administrative cost	20.00	64.00
Profit per unit		$ 8.00

Required

1. Assuming Martens plans to meet the expected demand for 20,000 attic fans, how many should it manufacture and how many should it purchase from Harris Products? Explain your reasoning with calculations.

2. Independent of Part 1 above, assume that Beth Johnson, Martens's product manager, has suggested that the company could make better use of its fan department capacity by manufacturing marine pumps instead of fans. Johnson believes that Martens could expect to use the production capacity to produce and sell 25,000 pumps annually at a price of $60 per pump. Johnson's estimate of the costs to manufacture the pumps is presented below. If Johnson's suggestion is not accepted, Martens would sell 20,000 attic fans instead. Should Martens manufacture pumps or attic fans? Information on the sales price and costs for the marine pumps follows.

Selling price per pump		$60.00
Costs per unit		
Electric motor	$ 5.50	
Other parts	7.00	
Direct labor ($15/hr.)	7.50	
Manufacturing overhead	9.00	
Selling and administrative cost	20.00	49.00
Profit per pump		$11.00

3. What are some of the long-term considerations in Martens's decisions in Parts 1 and 2 above?

11-47 **Special Order** BallCards Inc. sells baseball cards in packs of 15 in drugstores throughout the country. It is the third leading firm in the industry. BallCards has been approached by Pennock Cereal Inc., which would like to order a special edition of cards to use as a promotion with its cereal. BallCards would be solely responsible for designing and producing the cards. Pennock wants to order 25,000 sets and has offered $23,750 for the total order. Each set will consist of 33 cards. BallCards currently produces cards in sheets of 132.

Production, marketing, and other costs (per sheet)	
Direct materials	$ 1.20
Direct labor	0.20
Variable overhead	0.40
Fixed overhead	0.15
Variable marketing	0.10
Fixed marketing	0.35
Insurance, taxes, and administrative salaries	0.10
Costs for special order	
Design	2,000
Other setup costs	5,500

BallCards would incur no marketing costs for the special order. It has the capacity to accept this order without interrupting regular production.

Required

1. Should Ballcards accept the special order? Support your answer with appropriate computations.

2. What are the important strategic issues in the decision?

11-48 **Special Order**   Green Grow Inc. (GGI) manufactures lawn fertilizer and because of its very high quality often receives special orders from agricultural research groups. For each type of fertilizer sold, each bag is carefully filled to have the precise mix of components advertised for that type of fertilizer. GGI's operating capacity is 22,000 one-hundred-pound bags per month, and it currently is selling 20,000 bags manufactured in 20 batches of 1,000 bags each. The firm just received a request for a special order of 5,000 one-hundred-pound bags of fertilizer for $125,000 from APAC, a research organization. The production costs would be the same, although delivery and other packaging and distribution services would cause a one-time $2,000 cost for GGI. The special order would be processed in two batches of 2,500 bags each. The following information is provided about GGI's current operations:

Sales and production cost data for 20,000 bags, per bag	
Sales price	$38
Variable manufacturing costs	15
Variable marketing costs	2
Fixed manufacturing costs	12
Fixed marketing costs	2

No marketing costs would be associated with the special order. Since the order would be used in research and consistency is critical, APAC requires that GGI fill the entire order of 5,000 bags.

Required

1. Should GGI accept the special order? Explain why or why not.

2. What would be the change in operating income if the special order is accepted?

3. Suppose that after GGI accepts the special order, it finds that unexpected production delays will not allow it to supply all 5,000 units from its own plants and meet the promised delivery date. It can provide the same materials by purchasing them in bulk from a competing firm. The materials would then be packaged in GGI bags to complete the order. GGI knows the competitor's materials are very good quality, but it cannot be sure that the quality meets its own exacting standards. There is not enough time to carefully test the competitor's product to determine its quality. What should GGI do?

11-49 **Special Order; ABC Costing (Continuation of Problem 11-48)**   Assume the same information as for Problem 11-48, except that the $12 fixed manufacturing overhead consists of $8 per unit batch related costs and $4 per unit facilities level fixed costs. Also, assume that each new batch causes increased costs of $5,000 per batch; the remainder of the batch level costs consists of tools and supervision labor that do not vary with the number of batches. The remainder of fixed costs do not vary with the number of units produced or the number of batches.

Required

1. Calculate the relevant unit and total cost of the special order, including the new information about batch related costs.

2. If accepted, how would the special order affect GGI's operating income?

11-50 **Profitability Analysis, Scarce Resources**   Santana Company has met all production requirements for the current month and has an opportunity to produce additional units of product with its excess capacity. Unit selling prices and costs for three models of one of its product lines are as follows:

	No Frills	Standard Options	Super
Selling price	$30	$35	$50
Direct materials	9	11	11
Direct labor ($10/hour)	5	10	15
Variable overhead	3	6	9
Fixed overhead	3	6	6

Variable overhead is charged to products on the basis of direct labor dollars; fixed overhead is charged to products on the basis of machine-hours.

Required

1. If Santana Company has excess machine capacity and can add more labor as needed (neither machine capacity nor labor is a constraint), the excess production capacity should be devoted to producing which product or products?

2. If Santana Company has excess machine capacity but a limited amount of labor time, the production capacity should be devoted to producing which product or products?

11-51 **Profitability Analysis** "I'm not looking forward to breaking the news," groaned Charlie Wettle, the controller of Meyer Paint Company. He and Don Smith, state liaison for the firm, were returning from a meeting with representatives of the Virginia General Services Administration (GSA), the agency that administers bidding on state contracts. Charlie and Don had expected to get the specifications to bid on the traffic paint contract, soon to be renewed. Instead of picking up the bid sheets and renewing old friendships at the GSA, however, they were stunned to learn that Meyer's paint samples had performed poorly on the road test and the firm was not eligible to bid on the contract.

Meyer's two main product lines are traffic paint, used for painting yellow and white lines on highways, and commercial paints, sold through local retail outlets. The paint production process is fairly simple. Raw materials are kept in the storage area that occupies approximately half of the plant space. Large tanks that resemble silos are used to store the latex that is the main ingredient in their paint. These tanks are located on the loading dock just outside the plant so that when a shipment of latex arrives, it can be pumped directly from the tank truck into these storage tanks. Latex is extremely sensitive to cold. It cannot be stored outside or even shipped in the winter without heated trucks, which are very expensive for a small firm such as Meyer.

Currently, Meyer has the traffic paint contracts for the states of Pennsylvania, North Carolina, Delaware, and Virginia. Of last year's total production of 380,000 gallons, 90 percent was traffic paint. Of this amount, 88,000 gallons were for the Virginia contract. Each state has unique specifications for color, thickness, texture, drying time, and other characteristics of the paint. For example, paint sold to Pennsylvania must withstand heavy use of salt on roads during the winter. Paint for North Carolina highways must tolerate extended periods of intense heat during summer months.

Due to the high cost of shipping paint, most paint producers can be competitive on price only in locations fairly close to their production facilities. Accordingly, Meyer has enjoyed an advantage in bidding on contracts in the eastern states close to Virginia. However, one of their biggest competitors, Heron Paint Company of Houston, Texas, is building a new plant in North Carolina. With lower costs due to their efficient new facility and their proximity, Heron will become a major competitive threat.

Meyer's commercial paint line includes interior and exterior house paints in a wide range of colors formulated to approximate authentic colonial colors. Because of the historical association, the line has been well received in Virginia. Most of these paints are sold through paint and hardware stores as the stores' second or third line of paint. The large national firms such as Benjamin Moore or Sherwin Williams provide extensive services to paint retailers such as computerized color matching equipment. Partly because they lack the resources to provide such amenities and partly because they have always considered the commercial paint a sideline, Meyer has never tried to market the commercial line aggressively. Meyer sells 38,000 gallons of commercial paint per year.

Charlie is worried about the future of the company. The firm's strategic goal is to provide a quality product at the lowest possible cost and in a timely fashion. After absorbing the shock of losing the Virginia contract, Charlie wondered whether the firm should consider increasing production of commercial paints to lessen the company's dependence on traffic paint contracts. Carl Bunch, who manages the day-to-day operation of the firm, believes the company can double its sales of commercial paint if it undertakes a promotional campaign estimated to cost $60,000. The average price of traffic paint sold last year was $10 per gallon. For commercial paint, the average price was $12.

Charlie Wettle has assembled the following data to evaluate the financial performance of the two lines of paint. The primary raw material used in paint production is latex. The list price for latex is $16 per pound; 450 pounds of latex are needed to produce 1,000 gallons of traffic paint. Commercial paint requires 325 pounds of latex per 1,000 gallons of paint. In addition to the cost of the latex, other variable costs are as shown below.

	Traffic	Commercial
Raw materials cost per gallon of paint:		
Camelcarb (limestone)	0.38	0.54
Silica	0.37	0.52
Pigment	0.12	0.38
Other ingredients	0.06	0.03
Direct labor cost per gallon	0.46	0.85
Freight cost per gallon	0.78	0.43

Last year, fixed overhead costs attributable to the traffic paint totaled $85,000, including an estimated $25,000 of costs directly associated with the Virginia contract; the $25,000 can be eliminated in approximately two years. Fixed overhead costs attributable to the commercial paint are $13,000. Other manufacturing overhead costs total $110,000. Charlie estimates that $40,000 of this amount is inventory handling costs that will be avoided due to the loss of the Virginia contract. Both the remaining manufacturing overhead and the general and administrative costs of $140,000 are allocated equally to all gallons of paint produced.

Required

1. Calculate the contribution margin for each type of paint and total firmwide contribution under each of the following scenarios:

   Scenario A Current production, including the Virginia contract

   Scenario B Without either the Virginia contract or the promotion to expand sales of commercial paint

   Scenario C Without the Virginia contract but with the promotion to expand sales of the commercial paint

2. Determine whether scenario B or C (per Part 1 above) should be chosen by Meyer and explain why, including a consideration of the strategic context.

11-52 **Special Order**   New Life, Inc., manufactures skin creams, soaps, and other products primarily for people with dry and sensitive skin. It has just introduced a new line of product that removes the spotting and wrinkling in skin associated with aging. It sells these products in pharmacies and department stores at prices somewhat higher than those of other brands because of New Life's excellent reputation for quality and effectiveness.

New Life currently has very low utilization of plant capacity. Two years ago, in anticipation of rapid growth, the company opened a large new manufacturing plant, which has yet to be utilized more than 50 percent. Partly for this reason, New Life has sought new partners and was able, with the help of financial analysts, to locate suitable business partners. The first potential partner identified in this search was a large supermarket chain, SuperValue, which is interested in the partnership because it wants New Life to manufacture an age cream to sell in its stores. The product would be essentially the same as the New Life product but packaged with the SuperValue brand name. The agreement would pay New Life $2.00 per unit and would allow SuperValue a limited right to advertise the product as manufactured for SuperValue by New Life. New Life's CFO has made some calculations and has determined that the direct materials, direct labor, and other variable costs needed for the SuperValue order would be about $1.00 per unit as compared to the full cost of $2.50 (materials, labor, and overhead) for the equivalent New Life product.

Required   Should New Life accept the proposal from SuperValue? Why or why not?

11-53 **Project-Analysis, Sales Promotions**   Hillside Furniture Company makes outdoor furniture from recycled products, including plastics and wood by-products. Its three furniture products are gliders, chairs with footstools, and tables. The products appeal primarily to cost-conscious consumers and those who value the recycling of materials. The company wholesales its products to retailers and various mass merchandisers. Because of the seasonal nature of the products, most orders are manufactured during the winter months for delivery in the early spring. Michael Cain, founder and owner, is dismayed that sales for two of the products are tracking below budget. The following chart shows pertinent year-to-date data regarding the company's products.

Certain that the shortfall was caused by a lack of effort by the sales force, Michael has suggested to Lisa Boyle, the sales manager, that the company announce two contests to correct this situation before it deteriorates. The first contest is a trip to Hawaii awarded to the top salesperson if incremental glider sales are attained to close the budget shortfall. The second contest is a golf weekend, complete with a new set of golf clubs, awarded to the top salesperson if incremental sales of chairs with footstools are attained to close the budget shortfall. The Hawaiian vacation would cost $16,500 and the golf trip would cost $12,500.

	Glider		Chair with Footstool		Table	
	Actual	**Budget**	**Actual**	**Budget**	**Actual**	**Budget**
Number of units	2,600	4,000	6,900	8,000	3,500	3,300
Average sales price	$80.00	$85.00	$61.00	$65.00	$24.00	$25.00
Variable costs						
Direct labor						
Hours of labor	2.50	2.25	3.25	3.00	0.60	0.50
Cost per hour	$11.00	$10.00	$ 9.50	$ 9.25	$ 9.00	$ 9.00
Direct material	$16.00	$15.00	$11.00	$10.00	$ 6.00	$ 5.00
Sales commission	$15.00	$15.00	$10.00	$10.00	$ 5.00	$ 5.50

Required

1. Explain whether either contest is desirable or not.

2. Explain the strategic issues guiding your choice about these contests.

(CMA Adapted)

11-54 **Make or Buy**   GianAuto Corporation manufactures parts and components for manufacturers and suppliers of parts for automobiles, vans, and trucks. Sales have increased each year based in part on the company's excellent record of customer service and reliability. The industry as a whole has also grown as auto manufacturers continue to outsource more of their production, especially to cost-efficient manufacturers such as GianAuto. To take advantage of lower wage rates and favorable business environments around the world, Gian has located its plants in six different countries.

Among the various GianAuto plants is the Denver Cover Plant, one of Gian Auto's earliest plants. The Denver Cover Plant prepares and sews coverings made primarily of leather and upholstery fabric and ships them to other GianAuto plants where they are used to cover seats, headboards, door panels, and other GianAuto products.

Ted Vosilo is the plant manager for the Denver Cover Plant, which was the first GianAuto plant in the region. As other area plants were opened, Ted was given the responsibility for managing them in recognition of his management ability. He functions as a regional manager although the budget for him and his staff is charged to the Denver Cover Plant.

Ted has just received a report indicating that GianAuto could purchase the entire annual output of Denver Cover from suppliers in other countries for $60 million. He was astonished at the low outside price because the budget for Denver Cover Plant's operating costs for the coming year was set at $82 million. He believes that GianAuto will have to close operations at Denver Cover to realize the $22 million in annual cost savings.

Denver Cover's budget for operating costs for the coming year follows:

DENVER COVER PLANT
Budget for Operating Costs
For the Year Ending December 31, 2010
(000s omitted)

Materials		$ 32,000
Labor		
Direct	$ 23,000	
Supervision	3,000	
Indirect plant	4,000	30,000
Overhead		
Depreciation—equipment	$ 5,000	
Depreciation—building	3,000	
Pension expense	4,000	
Plant manager and staff	2,000	
Corporate allocation	6,000	20,000
Total budgeted costs		$ 82,000

Additional facts regarding the plant's operations are as follows:

- Due to Denver Cover's commitment to use high-quality fabrics in all its products, the purchasing department placed blanket purchase orders with major suppliers to ensure the receipt of sufficient materials for the coming year. If these orders are canceled as a result of the plant closing, termination charges would amount to 15 percent of the cost of direct materials.

- Approximately 400 plant employees will lose their jobs if the plant is closed. This includes all direct laborers and supervisors as well as the plumbers, electricians, and other skilled workers classified as indirect plant workers. Some would be able to find new jobs, but many would have difficulty doing so. All employees would have difficulty matching Denver Cover's base pay of $14.40 per hour, the highest in the area. A clause in Denver Cover's contract with the union could help some employees; the company must provide employment assistance to its former employees for 12 months after a plant closing. The estimated cost to administer this service is $1 million for the year.

- Some employees would probably elect early retirement because GianAuto has an excellent plan. In fact, $3 million of the 2010 pension expense would continue whether Denver Cover is open or not.

- Ted and his staff would not be affected by closing Denver Cover. They would still be responsible for managing three other area plants.

- Denver Cover considers equipment depreciation to be a variable cost and uses the units-of-production method to depreciate its equipment and the customary straight-line method to depreciate its building.

Required

1. Explain GianAuto's competitive strategy and how this strategy should be considered with regard to the Denver Plant decision. Identify the key strategic factors that should be considered in the decision.

2. GianAuto Corporation plans to prepare a strategic analysis to use in deciding whether to close the Denver Cover Plant. In your analysis, use the above information, and include consideration of global competition and GianAuto's competitive strategy.

(CMA Adapted)

11-55 **Make or Buy** Bernard's Specialty Manufacturing (BSM) produces custom vehicles—limousines, buses, conversion vans, and small trucks—for special order customers. It customizes each vehicle to the customer's specifications. BSM has been growing at a steady rate in recent years in part because of the increased demand for specialty luxury vehicles. The increased demand has also caused new competitors to enter the market for these types of vehicles. BSM management considers its competitive advantage to be the high quality of its manufacturing. Much of the work is handmade, and the company uses only the best parts and materials. Many parts are made in-house to control for highest quality. Because of the increased competition, price competition is beginning to become a factor for the industry, and BSM is becoming more concerned about cost controls and cost reduction. It has controlled them by purchasing materials and parts in bulk, paying careful attention to efficiency in scheduling and working different jobs, and improving employee productivity.

The increased competition has also caused BSM to reconsider its strategy. Upon review with the help of a consultant, BSM management has decided that it competes most effectively as a differentiator based on quality of product and service. To reinforce the differentiation strategy, BSM has implemented a variety of quality inspection and reporting systems. Quality reports are viewed at all levels of management, including top management.

To decrease costs and improve quality, BSM has begun to look for new outside suppliers for certain parts. For example, BSM can purchase a critical suspension part, now manufactured in-house, from Performance Equipment Inc. for a price of $105. Buying the part would save BSM 10 percent of the labor and variable overhead costs and $68 of materials costs. The current manufacturing costs for the suspension assembly are as follows:

Materials	$192
Labor	75
Variable overhead	150
Fixed overhead	150
Total cost for suspension assembly	$567

Required

1. How would total costs be affected if BSM chose to purchase the part rather than to continue to manufacture it?

2. Should BSM purchase or manufacture the part? Include strategic considerations in your answer.

11-56 **Make or Buy, Review of Learning Curves** Henderson Equipment Company has produced a pilot run of 50 units of a recently developed cylinder used in its finished products. The cylinder has a one-year life, and the company expects to produce and sell 1,650 units annually. The pilot run required 14.25 direct labor-hours for the 50 cylinders, averaging 0.285 direct labor-hours per cylinder. Henderson has experienced an 80 percent learning curve on the direct labor-hours needed to produce new cylinders. Past experience indicates that learning tends to cease by the time 800 parts are produced.

Henderson's manufacturing costs for cylinders follows:

Direct labor	$12.00 per hour
Variable overhead	10.00 per hour
Fixed overhead	16.60 per hour
Materials	4.05 per unit

Henderson has received a quote of $7.50 per unit from Lytel Machine Company for the additional 1,600 cylinders needed. Henderson frequently subcontracts this type of work and has always been satisfied with the quality of the units produced by Lytel.

Required

1. If Henderson manufactures the cylinders, determine

   a. The average direct labor-hours per unit for the first 800 cylinders (including the pilot run) produced. Round calculations to three decimal places.

   b. The total direct labor-hours for the first 800 cylinders (including the pilot run) produced.

2. After completing the pilot run, Henderson must manufacture an additional 1,600 units to fulfill the annual requirement of 1,650 units. Without regard to your answer in requirement 1, assume that

   • The first 800 cylinders produced (including the pilot run) required 100 direct labor-hours.
   • The 800th unit produced (including the pilot run) required 0.079 hour.

   Calculate the total manufacturing costs for Henderson to produce the additional 1,600 cylinders required.

3. Determine whether Henderson should manufacture the additional 1,600 cylinders or purchase them from Lytel. Support your answer with appropriate calculations.

(CMA Adapted)

11-57 **Profitability Analysis; Review of Master Budget** RayLok Incorporated has invented a secret process to improve light intensity and manufactures a variety of products related to this process. Each product is independent of the others and is treated as a separate profit/loss division. Product (division) managers have a great deal of freedom to manage their divisions as they think best. Failure to produce target division income is dealt with severely; however, rewards for exceeding one's profit objective are, as one division manager described them, lavish.

The DimLok Division sells an add-on automotive accessory that automatically dims a vehicle's headlights by sensing a certain intensity of light coming from a specific direction. DimLok has had a new manager in each of the three previous years because each manager failed to reach RayLok's target profit. Donna Barnes has just been promoted to manager and is studying ways to meet the current target profit for DimLok.

DimLok's two profit targets for the coming year are $800,000 (20 percent return on the investment in the annual fixed costs of the division) plus an additional profit of $20 for each DimLok unit sold. Other constraints on division operations are

• Production cannot exceed sales because RayLok's corporate advertising program stresses completely new product models each year, although the models might have only cosmetic changes.
• DimLok's selling price cannot vary above the current selling price of $200 per unit but may vary as much as 10 percent below $200.
• A division manager can elect to expand fixed production or selling facilities; however, the target objective related to fixed costs is increased by 20 percent of the cost of such expansion. Furthermore, a manager cannot expand fixed facilities by more than 30 percent of existing fixed cost levels without approval from the board of directors.

Donna is now examining data gathered by her staff to determine whether DimLok can achieve its target profits of $800,000 and $20 per unit. A summary of these reports shows the following:

• Last year's sales were 30,000 units at $200 per unit.
• DimLok's current manufacturing facility capacity is 40,000 units per year but can be increased to 80,000 units per year with an increase of $1,000,000 in annual fixed costs.
• Present variable costs amount to $80 per unit, but DimLok's vendors are willing to offer raw materials discounts amounting to $20 per unit, beginning with unit number 60,001.

- Sales can be increased up to 100,000 units per year by committing large blocks of product to institutional buyers at a discounted unit price of $180. However, this discount applies only to sales in excess of 40,000 units per year.

Donna believes that these projections are reliable and is now trying to determine what DimLok must do to meet the profit objectives that RayLok's board of directors assigned to it.

Required

1. Determine the dollar amount of DimLok's present annual fixed costs.

2. Determine the number of units that DimLok must sell to achieve both profit objectives. Be sure to consider all constraints in determining your answer.

3. Without regard to your answer in Part 2, assume that Donna decides to sell 40,000 units at $200 per unit and 24,000 units at $180 per unit. Prepare a master budget income statement for DimLok showing whether her decision will achieve DimLok's profit objectives.

4. Assess DimLok's competitive strategy.

5. Identify the strategic factors that DimLok should consider.

(CMA Adapted)

11-58 **Profitability Analysis; Pricing**   HomeSuites Inn is a national chain of high-quality hotels, which is popular with business travelers. Many of HomeSuites' best customers will stay for a week or longer during their business trip. Top management of the hotel chain made a strategic move in the prior year to raise profitability by raising room rates an average of 10 percent, from an average of $80 to $88. HomeSuites' main competitors (the total market for hotels that compete with Home-Suites is about 50,000,000 daily room occupancy per year) responded by keeping their rates low, and as a result, HomeSuites' sales fell from 5,000,000 annual room occupancy to 4,000,000 rooms, a 20 percent fall in room sales, and a new low in occupancy rate for the firm. The fall in room sales was greater than expected, so HomeSuites consulted a marketing expert who explained that customers in this market are very sensitive to price changes, and furthermore, that while a reduction in price increases volume and an increase in price reduces volume, the effect is not proportional; price decreases improve sales at a faster rate than price increases reduce sales. HomeSuites is now considering a reduction in price to $76, with the expectation of increasing sales by as much as 50 percent over the current level of 4,000,000 rooms. The consultant assures HomeSuites that if it returned to the $80 price, sales would return to the 5,000,000 level. The table below shows the room costs per occupied rooms at various annual occupancy levels.

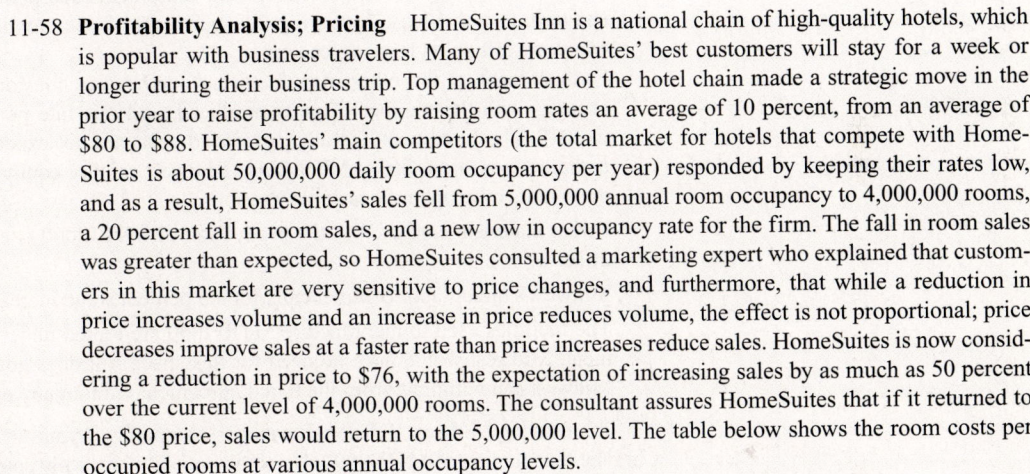

	Room Occupancy (thousands)					
	4,000	**4,500**	**5,000**	**5,500**	**6,000**	**6,500**
Per Room Costs						
Supplies	$ 3.30	$ 3.32	$ 3.28	$ 3.31	$ 3.31	$ 3.30
Direct labor	15.41	15.37	15.41	15.40	15.38	15.31
Overhead (see note)						
Room level	10.55	10.48	10.46	10.44	10.59	10.48
Hotel level	23.35	21.01	19.12	18.01	16.33	15.11
Total operating cost	$52.61	$50.18	$48.27	$47.16	$45.64	$44.20
Selling and administrative	30.11	27.66	25.12	22.88	21.01	19.43
Total cost	$82.72	$77.84	$73.39	$70.04	$66.65	$63.63

Note: Room-level overhead costs are laundry, housekeeping, and supplies, which vary with the number of rooms occupied; hotel-level overhead includes general maintenance, registration staff, pool expense, and other expenses, which do not vary with the number of rooms occupied. Selling and administrative expense is the cost of hotel management, the reservation network, and other fixed costs.

Required   What do you think is the best strategy for HomeSuites regarding room pricing? Develop a spreadsheet analysis that shows what would be the effect on contribution of the different pricing policies HomeSuites has used or is considering.

11-59 **Make or Buy**   The Midwest Division of the Paibec Corporation manufactures subassemblies used in Paibec's final products. Lynn Hardt of Midwest's profit planning department has been assigned the task of determining whether Midwest should continue to manufacture a subassembly component, MTR-2000, or purchase it from Marley Company, an outside supplier. Marley has submitted a bid to manufacture and supply the 32,000 units of MTR-2000 that Paibec will need for 2010 at a unit price of $17.30. Marley has assured Paibec that the units will be delivered according to Paibec's production specifications and needs. The contract price of $17.30 is applicable only in 2010, but Marley is interested in entering into a long-term arrangement beyond 2010.

Lynn has submitted the following information regarding Midwest's cost to manufacture 30,000 units of MTR-2000 in 2009.

Direct material	$195,000
Direct labor	120,000
Factory space rental	84,000
Equipment leasing costs	36,000
Other manufacturing costs	225,000
Total manufacturing costs	$660,000

Lynn has collected the following information related to manufacturing MTR-2000:

- Equipment leasing costs represent special equipment used to manufacture MTR-2000. Midwest can terminate this lease by paying the equivalent of one month's lease payment for each of the two years left on its lease agreement.
- Forty percent of the other manufacturing overhead is considered variable. Variable overhead changes with the number of units produced, and this rate per unit is not expected to change in 2010. The fixed manufacturing overhead costs are not expected to change whether Midwest manufactures or purchases MTR-2000. Midwest can use equipment other than the leased equipment in its other manufacturing operations.
- Direct materials cost used in the production of MTR-2000 is expected to increase 8 percent in 2010.
- Midwest's direct labor contract calls for a 5 percent wage increase in 2010.
- The facilities used to manufacture MTR-2000 are rented under a month-to-month rental agreement. Midwest would have no need for this space if it does not manufacture MTR-2000. Thus, Midwest can withdraw from the rental agreement without any penalty.

John Porter, Midwest divisional manager, stopped by Lynn's office to voice his opinion regarding the outsourcing of MTR-2000. He commented, "I am really concerned about outsourcing MTR-2000. I have a son-in-law and a nephew, not to mention a member of our bowling team, who work on MTR-2000. They could lose their jobs if we buy that component from Marley. I really would appreciate anything you can do to make sure the cost analysis shows that we should continue making MTR-2000. Corporate is not aware of materials cost increases and maybe you can leave out some of those fixed costs. I just think we should continue making MTR-2000."

Required

1. Prepare a relevant cost analysis that shows whether the Midwest Division should make MTR-2000 or purchase it from Marley Company for 2010.

2. Identify and briefly discuss the strategic factors that Midwest should consider in this decision.

3. By referring to the specific ethical standards for management accountants outlined in Chapter 1, assess the ethical issues in John Porter's request of Lynn Hardt.

(CMA Adapted)

11-60 **Profitability Analysis** High Point Furniture Company (HPF) manufactures very high-quality furniture for sale directly to exclusive hotels, interior designers, and select retail outlets throughout the world. HPF's products include upholstered furniture, dining tables, bedroom furniture, and a variety of other products, including end tables. Through attention to quality and design innovation, and by careful attention to changing consumer tastes, HPF has become one of the most successful furniture manufacturers worldwide. Hal Blin, the chief operating officer of HPF, is reviewing the most recent sales and profits report for the three best-selling end tables in HPFs product line—the Parker, Virginian, and Weldon end tables. Hal is concerned about the relatively poor performance of the Weldon line. He discusses the prospects for the line with HPF's marketing and sales vice-president, Joan Hunt. Joan notes that there has been no significant trend up or down in any of the end table lines, though the direction of consumer tastes would probably favor the Virginian and Parker lines. Hal and Joan agree that this may be the time for further analysis to determine whether the Weldon line should be discontinued.

HPF Sales and Profits Report: End Tables

	Parker		Virginian		Weldon		
	Per Unit	**Total**	**Per Unit**	**Total**	**Per Unit**	**Total**	**Total**
Sales units		150,000		335,000		165,000	
Sales dollars	$459.00	$68,850,000	$365.00	$122,275,000	$248.00	$40,920,000	$232,045,000
Factory Costs							
Labor	125.00	18,750,000	118.00	39,530,000	62.00	10,230,000	68,510,000
Raw materials	88.50	13,275,000	66.00	22,110,000	78.00	12,870,000	48,255,000
Power	23.50	3,525,000	15.60	5,226,000	13.80	2,277,000	11,028,000
Repairs	12.25	1,837,500	12.25	4,103,750	12.25	2,021,250	7,962,500
Factory equipment	33.50	5,025,000	33.50	11,222,500	33.50	5,527,500	21,775,000
Other costs	14.00	2,100,000	12.50	4,187,500	13.25	2,186,250	8,473,750
Total factory cost	296.75	44,512,500	257.85	86,379,750	212.80	35,112,000	166,004,250
Selling and Administrative Expenses							
Selling expense	45.00	6,750,000	36.00	12,060,000	25.00	4,125,000	22,935,000
Office expense	16.80	2,520,000	16.80	5,628,000	16.80	2,772,000	10,920,000
Administrative expense	27.50	4,125,000	27.50	9,212,500	27.50	4,537,500	17,875,000
Other admin. expense	6.50	975,000	6.50	2,177,500	6.50	1,072,500	4,225,000
Total cost	392.55	58,882,500	344.65	115,457,750	288.60	47,619,000	221,959,250
Operating profit (loss)	$ 66.45	$ 9,967,500	$ 20.35	$ 6,817,250	$ (40.60)	$ (6,699,000)	$ 10,085,750

Note: Selling expense consists of fixed salaries for the sales staff, advertising, and the cost of marketing/sales management. Power is for equipment used in manufacturing and varies with the number of units produced. Other factory costs, including repairs and equipment, are considered to be fixed costs.

Required

1. Using Excel or an equivalent spreadsheet, develop an analysis that can help Hal decide about the future of the Weldon line. Should the Weldon line be dropped? Why or why not?

2. Using the spreadsheet you developed in Part 1, determine whether your answer would change if sales of Weldon are expected to fall by 80 percent.

3. Again using the spreadsheet in Part 1, determine whether the Weldon line should be discontinued if the resources devoted to Weldon could be used to increase sales by 10 percent in each of the other two lines.

4. Again using the spreadsheet in Part 1 and using Goal Seek in Excel or an equivalent, determine the sales increase (or decrease) in the sales of the Parker line that would be necessary if the Weldon line were discontinued to maintain the firm's overall profit in Part 1. For an illustration of Goal Seek, seek Exhibit 9.5 in Chapter 9.

5. Given your answers to Parts 1 through 4 above, consider the overall competitive environment facing HPF and make your recommendations regarding the firm's strategic position and direction at this time.

11-61   Profitability Analysis; Linear Programming (Appendix)   Home Service Company offers monthly service plans to provide prepared meals that are delivered to customers' homes and need only be heated in a microwave or conventional oven. Home Service offers two monthly plans, premier cuisine and haute cuisine. The premier cuisine plan provides frozen meals that are delivered twice each month; the premier generates a contribution of $150 for each monthly service plan sold. The haute cuisine plan provides freshly prepared meals delivered on a daily basis and generates a contribution of $100 for each monthly plan sold. Home Service's strong reputation enables it to sell all meals that it can prepare.

Each meal goes through food preparation and cooking steps in the company's kitchens. After these steps, the premier cuisine meals are flash frozen. The time requirements per monthly meal plan and hours available per month follow:

	Preparation	**Cooking**	**Freezing**
Hours required			
Premier cuisine	3	2	1
Haute cuisine	1	3	0
Hours available	80	120	45

For planning purposes, Home Service uses linear programming to determine the most profitable number of premier and haute cuisine meals to produce.

Required

1. Using the Solver function of Microsoft Excel, determine the most profitable product mix for Home Service given the existing constraints and contribution margins.

2. Using the Solver function of Microsoft Excel, determine the most profitable product mix for Home Service given the existing contribution margins and all constraints except the preparation time constraint.

(CMA Adapted)

11-62 **Bid Pricing; Review of CVP Analysis** Deaton Fibers Inc. specializes in the manufacture of synthetic fibers that the company uses in many products such as blankets, coats, and uniforms for police and firefighters. Deaton has been in business since 1975 and has been profitable each year since 1983.

Deaton recently received a request to bid on the manufacture of 800,000 blankets scheduled for delivery to several military bases. The bid must be stated at full cost per unit plus a return on full cost of no more than 12 percent after income taxes. *Full cost* has been defined as all variable costs of manufacturing the product, a reasonable amount of fixed overhead, and a reasonable incremental administrative cost associated with the manufacture and sale of the product. The contractor has indicated that bids in excess of $30 per blanket are not likely to be considered.

To prepare the bid for the 800,000 blankets, John Taylor, cost management analyst, has gathered the following information concerning the costs associated with the production of the blankets. The fixed overhead costs represent an allocation of the cost of currently used facilities. No new fixed costs are needed for the order.

Raw material per pound of fibers	$ 1.50
Direct labor per hour	7.00
Direct machine costs per blanket*	10.00
Variable overhead per direct labor-hour	3.00
Fixed overhead per direct labor-hour	10.00
Added administrative costs per 1,000 blankets	2,500.00
Special fee per blanket[†]	0.50
Material usage	6 pounds per blanket
Production rate	4 blankets per labor-hour
Effective tax rate	40%

* Direct machine costs consist of variable costs such as special lubricants, replacement needles used in stitching, and maintenance costs that are not included in the normal overhead rates.
[†] Deaton recently developed a new blanket fiber at a cost of $750,000. To recover this cost, it adds a $0.50 fee to the cost of each blanket using the new fiber. To date, the company has recovered $125,000. John knows that this fee does not fit within the definition of full cost because it is not a cost to manufacture the product.

Required

1. What is the breakeven price per blanket using Deaton's full cost system?

2. Calculate the minimum price per blanket that Deaton could bid without reducing the company's net income.

3. Using the *full cost* criteria and the maximum allowable return specified, calculate the bid price per blanket for Deaton Fibers.

4. Without prejudice to your answer to requirement 3, assume that the price per blanket that Deaton calculated using the cost-plus criteria specified is higher than the maximum allowed bid of $30 per blanket. Discuss the strategic factors that the company should consider before deciding whether to submit a bid at the maximum acceptable price of $30 per blanket.

(CMA Adapted)

11-63 **Outsourcing Call Centers** Merchants' Bank (MB) is a large regional bank operating in 634 locations in the Southeast U.S. MB has grown steadily over the last 20 years, because of the region's growth and the bank's prudent and conservative business practices. The bank has been able to acquire less successful competitors in recent years, further enhancing its growth. Until 2005, the bank operated a call center for customer inquiries out of a single location in Atlanta, GA. MB understood the importance of the call center for overall customer satisfaction and made sure that the center was managed effectively. However, in early 2004, it became clear that the cost of running the center was

increasing very rapidly, along with the firm's growth, and that some issues were arising about the quality of the service. To improve the quality and dramatically reduce the cost of the service, MB moved its call center to Bangalore, India, where it is now run by an experienced outsourcing firm, Naftel, which offers similar services to other banks like MB.

The Naftel contract was for five years, and now in late 2008 it is time to consider whether to renew the contract, change to another call center service provider (in India or elsewhere), or bring the call center back to Atlanta.

Some important factors to consider in the decision:

- The value of the dollar has been increasing relative to most other currencies at the time of the decision in late 2008.
- The financial crisis of 2008 continues to affect the banking business, and the outlook for growth for MB is not as rosy as it has been for the last few years. Top management and economic advisors for the bank have basically no idea what is the right forecast for the coming five years.
- The employment rate in Atlanta has fallen in the last several months and there is a good supply of talented employees who might be recruited into the call center if it were relocated back to Atlanta.
- The bank has just completed a new headquarters building in Atlanta and has a good bit of space in the building that MB has yet to lease. The outlook for the Atlanta economy is such that MB does not expect to lease much of this space for at least the next three years. If the call center were returned to Atlanta, it would occupy a space that would be rented for $100,000 per month, if there were a company that wanted to lease the space.
- If renewed, the Naftel contract would cost $4,200,000 per year for the next five years.
- The cost of salaries to staff the call center in Atlanta are expected to be $2,300,000 per year, the equipment would be leased for $850,000 per year, telecommunication services are expected to cost $500,000 per year, administrative costs for the call center are expected to be $600,000 per year, and the call center's share of corporate overhead is expected to be $400,000 per year.

Required

1. Should MB return the call center to Atlanta or renew the contract with Naftel? Develop your answer for both a one-year and a five-year time horizon. Consider the strategic context of the decision as an integral part of your answer. (Hint: using discounted cash flow is not required but would improve your answer; MB uses a discount rate of 6%.)
2. What are the global issues that should be considered in the decision?
3. What ethical issues, if any, should be considered in the decision?

11-64 **Opportunity Cost; Lost Sales** Wood Flooring Inc. (WFI) is an industry leader in wood flooring installed in new homes and sold in home improvement stores such as Wal-Mart and Lowes. The company has recently suffered a significant loss in sales because one of its suppliers, Lucas Products Inc, due to its own production problems was unable (though contractually required) to provide in a timely manner the coating that WFI uses in the manufacture of its product. WFI makes its product to order so that each customer chooses the particular stain, coating, and other features of the product before it is manufactured by WFI. There is no production for inventory. All orders require a deposit from the customer and the remainder is paid upon delivery; sometimes the deposit is held by the vendor, and in other cases it is forwarded to WFI. Thus, the failure to receive the coating from Lucas meant that WFI lost a number of sales orders and had to return some deposits.

In retrospect, WFI understands the mistake of relying on a single source of supply for a critical element of their manufacturing process and has now developed a set of suppliers, each of which can be relied upon to provide the needed coating. WFI has estimated lost sales of $ 3.5 million as a result of the failure of Lucas Products, a portion of which ($2.9 million) is due to orders canceled by customers because of the delay in receiving their orders. The remaining orders were canceled by WFI in order to give these customers an opportunity to buy the product from another company, and thereby to maintain some degree of goodwill with these customers. In all, WFI lost about one-third of a month's sales.

WFI is now pursuing legal action against Lucas to recover at least a portion of the lost profits on these sales. Jeff Jones, the management accountant, has been asked to determine the amount of the lost profit which the court would consider recoverable.

The relevant facts, that Jeff has obtained are:

- The company spent $18,000 for additional, temporary administrative support personnel to handle the cancellation of the orders and return of deposits.

- WFI approximates its distribution costs at 12 percent of sales price; these costs include the cost of delivery to the customer, an allowance for returned items, and fees paid to vendors, such as Wal-Mart. The estimate of 12 percent is based on average results for the prior three years for WFI.

- WFI approximates its total variable manufacturing costs at 45 percent of sales; fixed manufacturing costs are allocated to the product based on labor hours and are approximately 25 percent of sales, based on averages of application rates used over the prior three years.

- WFI did receive and paid for $30,000 of coating that was used to complete some customers orders, but the orders were not ready for shipment when the customer canceled the order. The company sold these completed orders to building contractors at a salvage price that Jones says is approximately equal to manufacturing cost. There was also $45,000 of coating from Lucas that was received and paid for by WFI but has not been used.

Required Develop the estimate of recoverable opportunity cost and other costs that Jeff Jones should present to top management and WFI's attorneys. In providing the estimate, be sure to include a discussion of which portions of the estimate are more subjective and therefore more easily denied by the defendant were the matter to go to trial.

Solutions to Self–Study Problems

1. Special Order Pricing

The key to this exercise is to recognize that the variable manufacturing costs of $130 ($85 material and $45 labor) are the relevant ones and that the fixed overhead costs, since they will not change, are not relevant.

Thus, the correct decision is to accept the offer, since the price of $150 exceeds the variable manufacturing cost of $130. HighValu also should consider strategic factors. For example, will the three-year contract be desirable? Perhaps the market conditions will change so that HighValu will have more profitable uses of the capacity in the coming years. Will the special order enhance or diminish the firm's competitive position?

2. The Make-or-Buy Decision

The relevant costs for this analysis are the outside purchase cost of $15 per set versus the make costs of $10 per set ($6 material plus $4 labor), and $10,000 annual fixed costs.

First, determine the amount of annual savings from the reduction in variable costs for the make option:

$$6,000 \text{ annual sales} \times (\$15 - \$10) = \$30,000 \text{ annual savings}$$

Second, compare the savings in variable costs to the additional fixed costs of $10,000 per year. The net savings, an advantage to make rather than buy, is $20,000 ($30,000 − $10,000).

HighValu also should consider relevant strategic factors, such as the quality and reliability of the supply for the cushion. How will HighValu use the released capacity at its plant? Are any employees' jobs affected?

3. Profitability Analysis

1. To determine the number of Windys that can be manufactured if the 3,750 units of Gale are no longer produced, we consider the capacity released for each of the two constraints.

   For the automated sewing machine: The machine produces 20 Windys per hour or 30 Gales per hour, so that the number of Windys that could be produced from the released capacity of Gale is

   $$3,750 \times 20/30 = 2,500 \text{ Windys}$$

   For the inspection and packing operation: The operation requires 15 minutes for Windy (4 per hour) and 5 minutes for Gale (12 per hour), so the number of Windys that could be inspected and packed in the released time is

   $$3,750 \times 4/12 = 1,250 \text{ Windys}$$

   In this case, the inspection and packing is the effective limitation, so that if Gale is deleted, the firm can produce 1,250 Windys with the released capacity.

2. If 3,750 units of Gale are replaced with 1,250 units of Windy, the proper relevant cost analysis should consider the contribution margin of each product:

	Windy	Gale
Unit contribution margin	$ 8	$ 4
Units sold (giving up 3,750 units Gale gives 1,250 of Windy, per part 1)	1,250	3,750
Total contribution margin	$10,000	$15,000

Thus, the deletion of Gale and replacement with Windy would reduce the total contribution margin by $5,000 ($15,000 − $10,000).

3. Since the effect on total contribution is significant (as shown in Part 2), Windbreakers should continue to make Gale. Other factors to consider follow:

   a. At existing sales levels of 18,750 of Windy and 3,750 of Gale, Windbreakers is operating at full capacity; if there are additional sales opportunities for Windy, the firm should consider adding to available capacity so that the current sales of Gale can be made plus the additional sales of Windy. The analysis of the cost benefit of additional capacity is best addressed through the techniques of capital budgeting as described in Chapter 12.

   b. The effect of the loss of Gale on the firm's image and therefore the potential long-term effects on the sales of Windy.

   c. The long-term sales potential for Gale. Will its sales likely exceed the current 3,750 level in future years?

CHAPTER TWELVE

Strategy and the Analysis of Capital Investments

After studying this chapter, you should be able to

1. Explain the strategic role of capital-investment analysis
2. Describe how accountants can add value to the capital-budgeting process
3. Provide a general model for determining relevant cash flows associated with capital-investment projects
4. Apply discounted cash flow (DCF) decision models for capital-budgeting purposes
5. Deal with uncertainty in the capital-budgeting process
6. Discuss and apply other capital-budgeting decision models
7. Identify behavioral issues associated with the capital-budgeting process
8. (Appendix A): Understand alternative templates for setting up a DCF analysis
9. (Appendix B): Identify selected advanced considerations in making capital-investment decisions

LEARNING OBJECTIVE 1

Explain the strategic role of capital-investment analysis.

Consider the following examples of strategic investments made recently by a variety of companies and industries:

- In August 2008 General Motors (GM) Corporation announced a planned investment of $350 million at its Lordstown, Ohio, assembly plant. This investment is designed to support the production of GM's next generation of small cars, including the Cruze, which is scheduled to replace the Chevy Cobalt. (Source: *The Wall Street Journal,* August 22, 2008, p. B-5)

- In July 2008 Ford Motor Company announced an aggressive plan to spend as much as $3 billion to retool three of the company's North American truck plants to enable these plants to build at least six small vehicles, including the Ford Fiesta, which the company currently makes and sells in Europe. (Source: *The Wall Street Journal,* September 8, 2008, p. B3)

- Walt Disney Company's California Adventure theme park celebrated its grand opening in 2001, but has since not lived up to expectations in terms of attendance and profitability. Thus, in 2007 the company announced that it planned to spend $1.1 billion (over a five-year period) for a massive overhaul of the park. (Source: *The Wall Street Journal,* October 17, 2007, p. B1)

- Consumer demand for online video and other bandwidth-hungry Internet services (file sharing, Internet phone service, etc.) has forced telecommunications carriers to significantly improve available capacity. Projected spending in 2007 by North American telecom companies alone was estimated at $70 billion. Worldwide spending on new telecom infrastructure in 2008 was expected to rise to around $240 billion. (Source: *The Wall Street Journal,* February 14, 2007, p. A1)

- Gillette Company spent more than $750 million in new manufacturing equipment and research and development (R&D) to bring its MACH3™ razor to market. In support of its new product, the company committed an additional $300 million of advertising costs designed principally to build a brand image suggestive of high-performance, aerodynamic flight. (Source: www.gillette.com/men/product_news/intro.html)

- Anheuser-Busch, Inc. in 2005 completed a major modernization/redesign of its Williamsburg, Virginia, brewery. The $200 million project provides enhancements to control systems, cleaning systems, beer-delivery systems, production lines, utility systems, and improvements to logistics systems. According to company management, this investment was designed to accomplish multiple objectives: improve product quality, reduce production costs, and improve efficiencies in plant operations—all of which should allow the company to better compete in the marketplace. (Source: www.anheuser-busch.com/news/WilliamsburgModern.htm)
- To meet the data-security and processing-reliability demands of its core customer group, and in an attempt to expand its mainframe customer base to emerging markets such as Russia, China, and Brazil, IBM spent more than $1 billion (over a three-year period) to develop a new supercomputer (the "x9"), which can process up to 1 billion transactions per day. (Source: www.forbes.com/technology/)

Strategy and the Analysis of Capital Expenditures

Underlying Nature of Capital Expenditures

A **capital investment** is a project that involves a large expenditure of funds and expected future benefits over a number of years.

What do each of the preceding examples have in common? In each case, the organization is committing a significant amount of capital for an investment project that provide expected future benefits over an extended number of years. Through such well-planned **capital investments,** business entities are able to restore profitability, regain or expand market share, respond to changing business climates, reduce costs, improve quality, and strengthen strategic business processes throughout their value chain. Examples of capital investments include: the purchase of new manufacturing equipment, implementation of a new manufacturing technology, installation of a computer-based recordkeeping system, the offering of new services by a governmental entity, and the expansion of a business into new territories.

Fundamentally, capital-investment decisions should support the underlying strategy of the organization. As noted in Chapter 1, firms can secure competitive advantage by pursuing either a low-cost (i.e., cost-leadership) strategy or a product-differentiation strategy. In the case of the former, we would expect the use of large, highly automated manufacturing facilities, designed to capture economies of scale, and production efficiencies associated with the use of advanced manufacturing technologies (e.g., computer-integrated manufacturing, or CIM). In the case of the latter, the organization would likely devote a greater share of its capital-investment budget to research, development, and product-promotion activities.

Organizational Strategy and Capital-Investment Analysis

Capital budgeting is the process of identifying, evaluating, selecting, and controlling capital investments.

As stated in Chapter 2, an alternative framework for describing an organization's strategy is in terms of whether it chooses to "build," "hold," or "harvest." Given the strategic nature of capital-investment decisions, organizations generally use a formal process to plan and control such expenditures. The process of identifying, evaluating, selecting, and controlling capital investments is called **capital budgeting.** Exhibit 12.1 provides an overview of the relationship between elements of the capital-budgeting process and an organization's chosen strategy.

An organization that chooses to *build* often faces many uncertainties, uses evolving technologies, and operates in environments that change rapidly. The control of capital expenditures in this environment is often less formal, uses more nonfinancial data, and is more subjective in nature. Uncertainties faced by an organization that chooses to *build* generally require the adoption of a long-term perspective, the allowance for long payback periods (i.e., recovery of the cost of a capital investment), and the use of relatively low discount rates (for converting projected future cash inflows to a present-value basis). Long payback periods or low discount rates are justified in this situation because the firm is choosing to "build" and enjoy a long payoff period if it is successful. However, because of the risks involved, such investments are likely to require approval at a relatively high level of management.

In contrast, a firm that chooses to "harvest" is likely a mature organization or one that competes in a mature market (i.e., one that is ripe for change). The capital-budgeting practices for a firm pursuing this strategy are more likely to be formal, and most of the data for making

EXHIBIT 12.1

Strategic Missions and Capital Budgeting

Factor in Capital Budgeting	Strategic Mission		
	Build	**Hold**	**Harvest**
Formalization of capital expenditure decisions	Less formal DCF analysis	→	More formalized DCF analysis
Capital expenditure evaluation criteria	More emphasis on nonfinancial data (market share, efficient use of R&D dollars, etc.)	→	More emphasis on financial data (cost efficiency; straight cash-on-cash incremental return)
	Longer payback	→	Shorter payback
Hurdle rate	Relatively low	→	Relatively high
Capital investment analysis	More subjective and qualitative	→	More quantitative and financial
Project approval limit at business-unit level	Relatively high	→	Relatively low
Frequency of postaudit	Frequent	→	Less frequent

Based on: Vijay Govindarajan and John K. Shank, "Strategic Cost Management: Tailoring Controls to Strategies," *Journal of Cost Management,* Fall 1992, pp. 14–25.

investment decisions in this environment are likely to be quantifiable and financial in nature. By necessity, a capital investment's payback period in this context needs to be short, and the "discount rate" must be relatively high (e.g., at least as high as the firm's cost of capital). A firm that chooses to *harvest* most likely would not undertake major capital investments, which suggests that many investment projects (given lower investment costs) could be approved by managers at relatively low levels of the organization.

Effect of Capital Expenditures on Strategic Cost Drivers

In Chapter 5 we introduced the notion of cost drivers as part of our discussion of activity-based costing (ABC). Capital expenditures are important to organizations because they can affect both structural and executional cost drivers.

Structural cost drivers are factors that relate to the firm's strategic decisions on the fundamental structure of the organization, such as its technology, scale, product-line complexity, scope of vertical integration, or experience. Capital expenditures can change the organization's structural cost drivers. Thus, a complete capital-investment analysis should include the effects of the investment on the organization's *structural cost drivers.*

Executional cost drivers affect an organization's cost position and its ability to work successfully within the economic structure it chooses. Executional cost drivers include:

- Workforce involvement (participative management).
- Workforce commitment to continuous improvement.
- Adherence to total quality management (TQM) concepts (see Chapter 17).
- Utilization of effective capacity.
- Efficiency of production flow/layout.
- Effectiveness of product design.
- Exploitation of linkages with suppliers and customers throughout the value chain.

In the early 1990s, Motorola derived one of its cost advantages from its ability to reduce defect rates in manufacturing integrated circuits to no more than three units per million. This feat was achieved through years of continual capital investments in quality training and process improvements. This example shows the impact of an executional cost driver. The cost advantage led Motorola to enter the business of making billets for fluorescent lamps. Motorola management believes that its quality skills provided a strategic advantage for successful entry into this new line of business.

Chapter Overview—Where Are We Headed?

This chapter presents a discussion of the following issues related to the capital-budgeting process: the role of accounting in the capital-budgeting process; the identification of relevant financial information for the analysis of capital-expenditure projects; the use of discounted cash flow (DCF) models for making capital-budgeting decisions; handling uncertainties in the decision-making process; the use of non-DCF decision models; and, selected behavioral issues. Some advanced issues related to the use of DCF decision models are covered in Appendix B.

The Role of Accounting in the Capital-Budgeting Process

LEARNING OBJECTIVE 2

Describe how accountants can add value to the capital-budgeting process.

You might wonder why the topic of capital budgeting is covered in an accounting textbook. You might say, "Isn't capital budgeting a finance topic?" These are legitimate questions, particularly since the theory behind modern capital-budgeting decision models comes from the field of finance. Thus, if accounting adds value to the capital-budgeting process, it must come from somewhere other than model development. We consider the following four contributions that accounting makes to the capital-budgeting process: linkage to an organization's *master budget* (planning); linkage to strategy (planning) and to the organization's *balanced scorecard* (control); generation of *relevant data for investment analysis* purposes (decision making); and, conducting *post-audits* (control) of capital-investment projects.

Linkage to the Master Budget

A **capital budget** is a listing of approved investment projects for a given accounting period.

For any given accounting period, a listing of approved investment projects is reflected in the organization's **capital budget.** As indicated in Chapter 10, the capital budget is part of the overall planning system of the organization—called the "master budget." The master budget is part of a larger system of planning and control, which we refer to as an organization's comprehensive management accounting and control system (MACS). Such a system has strategic, operational, and management control dimensions. Accounting plays both a coordinating and a leadership role in the design of an organization's MACS. That is, accounting adds value by guiding the development and use of comprehensive planning and control systems, including an effective capital-budgeting process. As a component of the master budget, the organization's capital budget is used for both strategic and management control purposes.

Linkage to Strategy and to the Balanced Scorecard (BSC)

A **strategic control system** refers to the processes and procedures organizations use to monitor progress toward strategic goals of the organization.

In Chapter 2 we introduced you to the notion of the balanced scorecard (BSC) as a critical element of an organization's **strategic control system.** The BSC can be an effective tool to communicate to employees and managers the mission and strategy of the organization. Fundamentally, a BSC represents a series of linked (i.e., cause-and-effect) relationships across four broad performance perspectives: learning and growth, customer, business processes, and, financial. Included in these four dimensions is a mixture of financial and nonfinancial, internal and external, and lead versus lagged performance indicators.

It is management's responsibility, working with individuals throughout the organization (including accountants), to develop the list of relevant performance metrics. Presumably, the BSC will include some of the performance indicators—both financial and nonfinancial—used to evaluate capital-investment proposals. Accounting's special role in this process is to collect and periodically summarize the performance metrics—both financial and nonfinancial—included within the organization's BSC.

Kaplan and Norton (2008)[1] describe a five-stage "closed-loop" management system that can be used to develop strategy, translate the strategy into operational actions, and monitor and improve the effectiveness of both. Stage 2 of this process includes the development of a strategy

[1] Robert S. Kaplan and David P. Norton, "Mastering the Management System," *Harvard Business Review*, January 2008, pp. 63–77.

Overcapacity of the global shipping industry and decreased demand forecasts made cost-cutting a priority at American President Lines (APL), a global shipping company founded in 1848. At the same time, the shipping industry was becoming more IT-intensive. Cost cutting and the emerging business model required increasing reliance on conducting transactions online. Investment in information technology has been a recurring issue throughout the firm.

Projects with a strong ROI get priority while those characterized by soft-dollar benefits get a harder look through a balanced-scorecard approach. APL's scorecard is heavily weighted toward ROI, payback, and net present value, while also considering a range of soft benefits. The scorecard requires weighted averages of scores on a long list of items, including strategic alignment, costs, benefits to the company and its customers, and risks, among others. All hard-dollar returns require identification of the cost center and account to which benefits will accrue. For example, to justify a project that claims a savings of $1 million in labor or 10 full-time

employees, the scorecard has to specify which cost center will eliminate those jobs and which of the company's accounts will turn red ink into black.

Once approved, the project's progress is reviewed every month. The review committee assigns a red, yellow, or green light to the project. According to Chuck Lenatti, "A yellow light indicates that the project has a problem but can get back on track with some modifications. A red light means that there are significant issues. The biggest challenge is saying, Stop the project. Once a project has gotten wheels and is moving along, it is very difficult to stop."

After a project is completed, the committee conducts two post-mortem reviews. Upon completion, the committee examines whether the project was completed on time and on budget, and whether it delivered the benefits promised. The second review is conducted six months after completion.

Source: Chuck Lenatti, "Grinding Away on ROI," *CFO*, Summer 2003, pp. 23–29.

---

map and associated balanced scorecard (BSC) and the identification of a set of strategic initiatives (investments) needed to achieve the organization's strategic objectives. The authors define (p. 68) strategic initiatives as "discretionary projects or programs, of finite duration, designed to close a performance gap." Such programs would complement capital expenditures designed to support current operations and would include, for example, a customer-loyalty program or the implementation of a training program for Six-Sigma. Strategic expenditures can also be made to support the organization's environmental-performance and/or sustainability goals. As explained in Chapter 10, this approach gives prominence to strategy-related capital expenditures by separating total investment spending into two categories: strategic capital expenditures (StratEx), and capital expenditures needed to support current operations (CapEx).

The evaluation of capital-investment projects in terms of their relationship to strategy in general, and to the BSC in particular, is an interesting problem. That is, how do organizations evaluate proposed projects in a comprehensive manner—to include both financial and non-financial/qualitative considerations and to ensure that such investments support the underlying strategy of the organization? The answer to this question may lie in the use of what are called **multicriteria decision models,** which include more than a single decision criterion (such as after-tax rate of return, or projected future cash flows). One of the more popular multicriteria decision models is the analytic hierarchy process (AHP).

The **analytic hierarchy process (AHP)** is a multicriteria decision technique that can combine qualitative and quantitative factors in the overall evaluation of decision alternatives; as such, the AHP can be used for capital-budgeting purposes.[2] The AHP organizes a problem into smaller and smaller parts and then calls for the use of simple pair-wise comparisons to develop a hierarchy of decision-maker preferences. This hierarchy is then manipulated analytically to produce a final matrix representing the overall priorities of the decision alternatives relative to one another. One can then make a logical decision based on the pair-wise comparisons made between the decision alternatives (for example, choice of competing capital-budgeting projects) and the various criteria used for decision-making purposes (such as quality, cash flows, impact on brand image, and payback period). The AHP allows managers to consider both tangible and intangible factors when constructing the decision hierarchy,

A **multicriteria decision model** is one that includes more than one decision criterion.

The **Analytic Hierarchy Process (AHP)** is a multicriteria decision technique that can combine qualitative and quantitative factors in the overall evaluation of decision alternatives.

---

[2] A five-step procedure for implementing the AHP in a capital-budgeting context is given in T. F. Monahan, M. J. Liberatore, and D. E. Stout, "Decision Support for Capital Budgeting: A Model for Classroom Presentation," *Journal of Accounting Education* 8 (1990), pp. 225–239, and in D. E. Stout, M. J. Liberatore, and T. F. Monahan, "Decision Support Software for Capital Budgeting," *Management Accounting*, July 1991, pp. 50–53.

thereby allowing managers to link capital-budgeting decisions to strategy.[3] This ensures that the decision will be based on more than just financial or other quantitative characteristics of proposed capital investments. Accountants can add value to the decision-making process by providing accurate information and by participating in the pair-wise comparison process.

In addition to the AHP, other multicriteria decision approaches include scoring models and multi-attribute utility theory (MAUT). The advantages of AHP over these alternatives include the following:

- Unlike scoring models, the AHP uses a ratio-scale measurement process that produces ratio-scale results.
- Pair-wise comparisons represent a natural way for eliciting preferences of decision makers (unlike the use of lotteries in MAUT).
- Unlike scoring models and MAUT, the AHP allows some inconsistency in judgments.
- Unlike MAUT, the AHP does not require the determination of a measurement function.
- The AHP is easy to use—in fact, there are many published accounts of its successful application to a variety of decision contexts.

Generation of Relevant Financial Data for Decision-Making Purposes

In Chapter 11 we defined relevant financial information for decision making as future costs or revenues that differ between decision alternatives. At that time we made the point that accounting assumes a primary responsibility for providing managers with such information. These points apply as well to capital budgeting: managerial accountants supply decision makers with relevant *after-tax* cash-flow data for analyzing the desirability of proposed capital-investment projects.

Part of the relevant financial data pertaining to capital-budgeting decisions are the income-tax consequences of proposed capital expenditures. As we point out later in this chapter, tax savings due to depreciation deductions are of paramount importance in capital-expenditure analysis.[4] Income tax laws pertaining to the acquisition, use, and disposal of investment assets are exceedingly complex. Thus, accounting can add value by ensuring that all relevant tax-related items, especially depreciation deductions, are included as part of the information set provided to managers for capital-budgeting purposes.

---

[3] A discussion of using the AHP to link capital-budgeting decisions to strategy, within a Mission-Objectives-Strategy planning framework, is provided in M. J. Liberatore, T. F. Monahan, and D. E. Stout, "A Framework for Integrating Capital Budgeting Analysis with Strategy," *The Engineering Economist* 38, no. 1 (Fall 1992), pp. 31–43, and in M. J. Liberatore, T. F. Monahan, and D. E. Stout, "Strategic Capital Budgeting Analysis for Investments in Advanced Manufacturing Technology," *Journal of Financial and Strategic Decisions* 6, no. 2 (Summer 1993), pp. 55–72.

[4] Current rules for determining depreciation deductions are contained in IRS Publication 946, available on the Web at: www.irs.gov/publications/p946/.

A **post-audit**
is an in-depth review of a
completed capital-investment
project.

Conducting Post-Audits

Accountants can also add value in the final stage of the capital-budgeting process. Various terms have been used to describe this stage, including post-audit, post-completion audit, project reappraisal, post-appraisal, and project review. We prefer the term **post-audit** and define this as an in-depth review of a completed capital-investment project for the purpose of comparing its realized benefits and costs with the preinvestment estimates of these items.

The use of post-audits of capital-budgeting decisions is particularly important for larger, longer-term investments, and investments in new manufacturing technologies. The audit for such investments should include an analysis of both cash-flow results and of operating benefits, such as forecasted improvements in manufacturing flexibility or improved manufacturing cycle times.

In general, the value of the post-audit is in its capacity as a *feedback* and *control* mechanism for the organization. The following specific benefits are associated with capital expenditure post-audits:

- Such audits help keep projects on target by, for example, limiting the ability of managers to divert project funds (without authorization) to other uses.

- The post-audit provides a formal mechanism (feedback) for determining whether existing projects should be continued, expanded, or terminated. That is, the post-audit provides valuable information that can be used to correct problems before the success of an investment is undermined.

- The process of conducting post-audits helps improve the quality of future investment proposals; since managers know that project results will be evaluated, there is an incentive for managers to make accurate estimates rather than presenting overly optimistic estimates in an effort to get projects approved.

- The feedback from post-audits allows top management to identify the biases of individual managers; such information can be used to improve the future capital-budgeting process.

Difficulties (or problems) associated with conducting capital-investment post-audits generally fall into one of the following three categories:

1. *Organizational problems*—for example, lack of qualified personnel to perform the audit and the resentment of personnel being audited.
2. *Economic problems*—for example, the cost of conducting the audit itself.
3. *Technical problems*—for example, the inability of the accounting system to produce the needed information to perform the audit, or the inability to identify the profit stemming from a particular investment.

By anticipating the preceding problems, the management accounting team can help develop a successful capital-investment post-audit process.

The following real-life example is offered as an overview of the strategic dimensions of the capital-budgeting process. The rest of this chapter covers the technical and then behavioral factors associated with this process.

The Five Steps of Strategic Decision Making: Cost-Benefit Analysis of a Hospital Bar-Code Technology Investment[5]

1. **Determine the strategic issues surrounding the problem.** Errors in dispensing medications represent a significant and strategically important problem for hospital pharmacies. Costs, both out-of-pocket and opportunity (reputation effects, for example), for such errors can be considerable. Thus, most hospitals attempt to control these quality-related costs. Recent

---

[5] This example is drawn from the following: S. M. Maviglia, J. Y. Yoo, C. Franz, E. Featherstone, W. Churchill, D. W. Bates, T. K. Gandhi, and E. G. Poon, "Cost-Benefit Analysis of a Hospital Pharmacy Bar Code Solution," *Archives of Internal Medicine* 167, no. 8 (April 23, 2007), pp. 788–794. The five steps discussed in this section constitute a higher-level aggregation of the eight key principles of project appraisal presented in *Project Appraisal Using Discounted Cash Flow* (New York: IFAC, June 2008).

When it comes to post-audits of information technology (IT) projects, survey evidence from chief information officers (CIOs) indicates that there is much to be done. A recent example from Partners HealthCare System (which runs 10 hospitals in eastern Massachusetts, including two large academic medical centers) shows why. Diabetics need regular cardiovascular checkups and cholesterol tests. Annual eye exams are a must, as eye disease is a sign that the diabetes may be progressing. All these factors lend themselves to *systems tracking*. These hospitals observed, however, that their diabetic patients were not routinely getting their eye exams. This prompted the CIO of the organization to authorize an update to the electronic medical records system that added an automatic reminder system that would pop up and tell physicians and nurses to make sure their diabetes patients go to their eye exams.

In theory, this investment in IT would both increase the quality of patient care and, over the long run, reduce patient-care costs. Such was not the case, however: the percentage of diabetes patients getting an annual exam increased only slightly, from 10 percent to 17 percent. The irony is that management felt the system update had such a clear-cut perceived value that IT had not followed up on the project. The CIO felt this was an outstanding opportunity to make sure the company was getting value out of existing IT implementations as well as new ones. Among changes the CIO instituted was the conduct of post-implementation audits for selected (i.e., key) projects.

Failure to implement post-implementation audits for IT projects is not unique to Partners HealthCare System. A recent survey indicated that fewer than 2 in 10 firms conduct such audits. Perhaps ironically, data suggest that fewer than 20 percent of IT projects are successfully completed. What is the moral of this story? There are plenty of processes and tools to measure post-implementation value of IT projects. If CIOs don't use these tools they are basically guaranteeing that they are not going to get what they should from their IT investments.

Source: M. Fitzgerald, "Don't Stop Thinking about the Value," *CIO Magazine*, July 15, 2004, accessed at www.cio.com/archive/071504/value.html.

advances in technology, including the use of a bar-code system, can be used by hospitals to manage the risk and costs of such errors.

2. **Identify the alternative actions.** Hospital administrators can invest either in employee training and updating of existing monitoring systems associated with the control of pharmacy dispensing errors, or they can invest in and implement a new bar-code system that is designed to virtually eliminate human errors. Because this technology is relatively new, it is very expensive. Thus, one alternative is to delay the investment for a year, at which time the price of the technology will likely be significantly lower.

3. **Obtain information and conduct analyses of the alternatives.** The hospital would have to estimate the required investment outlay for the new dispensing system, both today and approximately one year from now. It would also have to estimate ongoing operating costs associated with the new monitoring system. These costs would be compared to anticipated benefits of the system, both financial and nonfinancial in nature. Financial benefits are costs avoided by eliminating adverse effects from dispensing errors. Thus, both number of event reductions and the dollar savings per event would have to be estimated. Other, more difficult, benefits are qualitative or strategic in nature and would complement the cost-benefit analysis described above.

4. **Based on strategy and analysis, choose and implement the desired alternative.** The proposed investment would be evaluated using a discounted analysis of anticipated future cash outflows and inflows (cost savings). This analysis of financial results would be supplemented by a strategic analysis of this investment, done either informally or by using a multicriteria decision model such as the analytic hierarchy process (AHP). Finally, the cash-flow analysis could be supplemented by including the effect of the option to delay the investment, which is one example of a *real option*. Given the uncertainties associated with the projected costs and benefits of this proposed investment, management would likely conduct a sensitivity analysis using, for example, a Monte Carlo simulation procedure.

5. **Provide an ongoing evaluation of the effectiveness of implementation in Step 4.** Assuming the investment in the new technology is made, the hospital administrators could institute a *post-audit review* of the decision, to see how close the actual results were to the projected costs and benefits.

Identification of Relevant Cash-Flow Data for Capital-Expenditure Analysis

Data for evaluating the financial consequences associated with capital-investment proposals differ from data used to prepare an organization's financial statements. The former relies on forecasted *cash-flow* data, while the latter relies on the use of *accrual-accounting* amounts.

Why Focus on Cash Flows?

Accrual-based accounting income is determined under the matching principle. As such, there is no attempt to track cash flows into and out of an organization. However, in capital budgeting the focus is on cash flows and the timing of these cash flows. This is true for two reasons. One, conceptually, the financial markets value companies according to their abilities to generate "free cash flow." Alternatively, companies are valued differently depending on their dividend-paying ability, which in turn is a function of their ability to generate free cash flow. Two, from a market perspective, the timing of cash flows generated by a company matters: a cash return to shareholders in the future does not have the same value (economic worth or buying power) as a dollar received today. In short, money has a time value.

Thus, managers strive to use capital-budgeting decision models that (a) focus on cash-flow amounts, and (b) take into consideration the time value of money. The use of such decision models has the potential for increasing the value or economic worth of the firm.

Cash Flows—A Framework for Analysis

A capital investment, such as the replacement of a machine, usually starts with a large cash outflow, followed by future benefits in the form of reductions in cash expenditures, increases in cash inflows, or both. Additional funds could also be needed to support the investment over its useful life. The following structure can be used to accumulate relevant financial information associated with a proposed capital-investment project:

1. **Project initiation**—Cash flows at this point include:

   a. Cash outflows, including installation costs, to acquire the investment and to begin operations (e.g., employee training costs, machine-testing costs).

   b. Cash commitments for increases in *net* working capital (i.e., current assets − current liabilities).

   c. Cash inflow or outflow, net of tax, associated with the disposal of the asset being replaced. (For simplicity, we assume throughout this chapter that any such cash-flow effects are realized in the year of asset disposal.)

2. **Project operation**—Cash flows during the operating stage of a capital investment include:

   a. Outflows for operating expenditures and, in some cases, additional capital investment(s) after the initial outlay.

   b. Commitments for additional *net* working capital needed to support operations.

   c. Inflows of cash (or reductions in cash operating expenses) generated by the investment, and cash released from reductions in *net* working capital.

3. **Project disposal**—Cash flows at project disposal include:

   a. Cash inflows or outflows, net of tax, related to the investment's disposal. (As noted above, assume that any such cash-flow effects are realized fully in the year of asset disposal.)

   b. Cash inflows from the reduction/release of *net* working capital.

Sample Data Set: Mendoza Company—Equipment-Replacement Decision

To illustrate the calculation of relevant cash flows, we use the following example. The Mendoza Company manufactures high-pressure pipes for deep-sea oil drilling. The company is considering purchasing a new drilling machine at a base cost of $465,000, which will improve the efficiency of its drilling operations and therefore provide increased cash operating income. The controller expects the company to be in the 34 percent federal income tax bracket and the state and local governments to levy a combined 6 percent income tax.

Installation costs associated with the new machine are expected to be $5,000, while associated testing and adjusting expenses incurred before the machine is put into production will be $10,000. After its expected useful life of four years, the company expects to sell the machine for $100,000. In conjunction with this sale, the company expects to incur machine-removal and site-clearing expenses that total $95,000, all of which are assumed to be deductible for tax purposes. The firm elects to use straight-line (SL) depreciation for tax purposes; a zero salvage value is used for determining depreciation charges for tax purposes. After disposing of the investment, the company feels it can reassign all but 10 employees to other divisions without incurring significant expenses. However, at the end of year 4, the company expects to spend $150,000 for relocation, retraining, and work adjustment for these 10 employees. This expense is expected to be fully deductible for income-tax purposes.

The company expects the new investment to bring in $1 million of cash revenue from increases in production volume in each of the next four years. This increase in sales activity is expected to increase cash operating expenses, such as labor, materials, energy, selling and administrative expenses, by $733,333 per year. Mendoza expects additional cash costs of $50,000 (pretax) in the first year of operating the new machine, including expenditures for employee training, work adjustments, and learning effects.

Mendoza Company estimates that once the proposed machine is in operation, its inventory and accounts receivable will increase $200,000 beyond the expected increase in current liabilities. That is, the amount of *net* working capital—current assets other than cash, minus current liabilities—is expected to increase because of the increased sales volume associated with the purchase of the machine. The company expects to fully recover (i.e., convert to cash) the $200,000 amount at the end of the four-year life of the machine.

The purchase of the new machine is not expected to increase any corporate-level support costs. However, the new investment will increase the cost-allocation base of the division that is acquiring the machine. As such, the new investment will serve to increase the corporate-level support costs that are allocated to the division. The cost-allocation rate used for performance-assessment purposes is $0.025 per dollar of sales. As noted above, the new machine is expected to generate increased sales of $1 million annually. Thus, total divisional expenses will increase by $25,000 per year in each of the four years of the new machine's life. Note, however, that the total corporate headquarters' expenses are not expected to increase because of the new investment undertaken by the division.

If Mendoza purchases the new machine, it will make redundant the machine the company is currently using. Mendoza purchased the existing machine seven years ago for $320,000. The accumulated depreciation on this machine, on the replacement date, will be $200,000. A used equipment broker, who charges a commission of 10 percent of the selling price, has secured a buyer for the existing machine. The buyer is willing to pay $80,000 for the old machine; however, Mendoza would have to pay all asset removal expenses, estimated to be $2,000. Assume a WACC of 10% for purposes of discounting all future cash flows.

The preceding set of facts is summarized in Exhibit 12.2. It is through the proper assemblage of such data that the accounting function can add value to the organization.

Determining After-Tax Cash Flows for Capital-Investment Analysis

As noted above, cash flows for capital-investment analysis must be stated on an *after-tax* basis. In the space below we offer an analysis of the data for the Mendoza Company regarding the capital-investment project the company is considering; a summary analysis is presented in Exhibit 12.3. For the cash-flow calculations presented below, assume that the combined income tax rate is 40 percent.

Project Initiation

Asset Acquisition As shown in Exhibit 12.3, the net cost of the machine is $480,000 ($465,000 + $5,000 + $10,000). This is the depreciable basis of the asset.

Incremental Investment in Net Working Capital In addition to the cost of the new asset, Mendoza Company feels that it must commit additional *net* working capital (current assets other than cash, less current liabilities) to support the investment. Mendoza estimates that,

EXHIBIT 12.2
Data for Mendoza Company
Capital-Investment Decision

MENDOZA COMPANY Capital-Budgeting Data Machine-Replacement Decision	
New Machine	
Purchase price of replacement (i.e., new) machine, year 0	$465,000
Machine installation cost	$5,000
Testing and adjustments of new machine prior to new machine's use	$10,000
Expected life of new machine	4 years
Depreciation method (ignore salvage value for tax purposes)	SL
Estimated sales (disposal) value of equipment at end of four years	$100,000
Salvage value assumed for tax-depreciation purposes	$0
Estimated costs related to sale of asset at end of four years	$95,000
Old (i.e., Existing) Machine	
Purchase price of machine (7 years ago)	$320,000
Accumulated depreciation to date	$200,000
Machine removal expenses upon sale	$2,000
Commission on sale of old machine	10% of selling price
Current disposal value (selling price) of machine, year 0	$80,000
Other Data	
Expected increase in *net* working capital, year 0	$200,000
Expected reduction in *net* working capital, end of year 4	$200,000
Increase in annual cash sales because of new machine	$1,000,000
Increase in annual cash expenses	$733,333
Pretax operating cash-flow *increase* because of new machine	$266,667
Marginal income tax rate (34% + 6%)	40%
Corporate headquarters allocation percentage	$0.025 per dollar of sales*
Additional pretax cash outlays, year 1 (employee training, etc.)	$50,000
Employee pretax relocation expenses, end of year 4	$150,000
Weighted-average cost of capital (WACC)	10.00%

* Note: The total corporate headquarters' expense is unaffected by whether or not the new machine is purchased. That is, the purchase of the new machine will not entail an increase in operating expenses at the corporate level.

beyond a projected increase in current liabilities, its inventories and accounts receivable will increase by $200,000 per year during the life of the project. Thus, the excess of *additional* current assets (other than cash) over *additional* current liabilities is treated as an *additional* investment outlay in year 0. (Essentially, cash will be tied up until other working capital items are recovered.) Note in this example that the firm is making a simplifying assumption that the dollar investment in additional net working capital is constant. Also, note that at the end of year 4 the company expects to fully recover (i.e., convert back into cash) the $200,000 incremental investment in net working capital.

Not all investments require additional net working capital, however. Some investments may actually decrease net working capital. Any decreased need for net working capital should be shown as a cash inflow in the period in which the decrease takes place. Companies that adopt supply-chain management, just-in-time (JIT), and computer-integrated manufacturing (CIM) systems often experience a decreased need for net working capital.

In sum, a decrease in net working capital represents a recovery of net working capital (i.e., conversion back to cash); as such, it is treated as a non-tax-deductible cash inflow. An increase in net working capital during the year is an investment; as such, it is treated as a non-tax-deductible cash outflow.

After-Tax Proceeds from Sale of Existing Asset Cash flow at time 0 is also affected by the after-tax proceeds associated with the sale of the asset that is being replaced. As indicated in Exhibit 12.4, a taxable gain or loss may be realized on such disposals. Thus, the net cash proceeds (selling price minus sales-related costs, such as sales commissions) from the sale are adjusted by the income-tax effect of the transaction: taxes paid on a gain are treated as a cash *outflow;* taxes saved by the deductibility of a loss are shown as a cash *inflow* at the time of the asset's sale.

EXHIBIT 12.3
After-Tax Cash-Flow Data

MENDOZA COMPANY
After-Tax Cash-Flow Data
Machine-Replacement Decision (000s)

		Years			
	0	**1**	**2**	**3**	**4**
Project Initiation					
Net cost of new machine (a)	$ (480.00)				
Incremental net working capital	$ (200.00)				
Sale of old (existing) machine:					
Pretax proceeds from sale of old asset (b)	70.00				
Tax effect of sale of old machine (c)	20.00				
Net initial cash outflow, after tax	$ (590.00)				
Project Operation					
Cash revenues		$1,000.00	$1,000.00	$1,000.00	$1,000.00
Operating expenses:					
Cash items (d)		783.33	733.33	733.33	733.33
Depreciation (e)		120.00	120.00	120.00	120.00
Total operating expenses		903.33	853.33	853.33	853.33
Pretax operating income		96.67	146.67	146.67	146.67
Income taxes on operating income		38.67	58.67	58.67	58.67
After-tax operating income		58.00	88.00	88.00	88.00
Plus: Noncash expenses		120.00	120.00	120.00	120.00
After-tax cash operating income		$ 178.00	$ 208.00	$ 208.00	$ 208.00
Project Disposal					
Net working capital released					$ 200.00
After-tax proceeds from sale of machine (f)					3.00
After-tax employee relocation expenses (g)					(90.00)
Net cash flow, after tax, at project disposal					$ 113.00
Net (after-tax) cash flows	**($590)**	**$178**	**$208**	**$208**	**$321**

Notes:
(a) Net cost of new machine = Gross purchase price + Installation cost + Testing costs
        = $465,000 + $5,000 + $10,000 = **$480,000**
(b) Net selling price of old machine = Gross selling price − Sales commission − Machine removal expenses
        = $80,000 − (10% × $80,000) − $2,000 = **$70,000** *pretax*
(c) Tax effect of sale of old machine: Gain (loss) × Tax rate = (Net selling price − NBV) * *t*
        = [$70,000 − ($320,000 − $200,000)] × 0.40 = **$20,000** *tax savings*
(d) For year 1, amount = $733,333 + $50,000 (one-time employee training costs) = **$783,333**; for all other years, amount = **$733,333**
(e) Annual depreciation (SL basis) = Depreciable cost/Useful life in years = $480,000/4years = **$120,000** (note that we are assuming that for tax purposes a salvage value of $0 is assumed)
(f) After-tax proceeds = Net selling price + Tax effect; Net selling price = $100,000 − $95,000 = $5,000;
        Tax effect = (Net selling price − NBV) × *t* = ($5,000 − $0) × 0.40 = $2,000 taxes due because the asset will be sold at a gain;
        thus, after-tax proceeds = $5,000 − $2,000 = **$3,000**
(g) After-tax employee relocation expense = Pretax amount × (1 − *t*) = $150,000 × 0.60 = **$90,000**

EXHIBIT 12.4
After-Tax Proceeds from Asset Disposal

Net Effect of Asset Disposal on After-Tax Cash Flow, Year 0

Terminology
Net book value (NBV) = Original cost − Accumulated depreciation
Net proceeds = Selling (disposal) price of asset − Disposal costs (selling commissions, etc.)
Gain on disposal: If Net proceeds > NBV
Loss on disposal: If Net proceeds < NBV
Net cash effect (inflow):
    For *gain* situation: Net cash effect = Net proceeds − (Gain on disposal × tax rate)
    For *loss* situation: Net cash effect = Net proceeds + (Loss on disposal × tax rate)

Note: Assume, for simplicity, that any tax effects are realized in full in the year of asset disposal.

As indicated in Exhibit 12.3, the pretax proceeds from the sale of the existing asset for Mendoza Company would be $70,000 ($80,000 selling price − $8,000 sales commission − $2,000 asset-removal costs). Because this asset is sold at a $50,000 loss, the income tax savings, at 40 percent, are $20,000. Thus, the net-of-tax cash inflow at time zero is $90,000 (i.e., $70,000 + $20,000).

Project Operation

After-Tax Cash Operating Receipts The new machine expects to generate an additional $1 million of cash revenue per year. Such an amount, everything else held constant, will increase the annual income tax liability of the company. That is, the after-tax amount for this taxable cash receipt is found by subtracting from the gross cash inflow of $1,000,000 the associated $400,000 increase in income tax liability ($1,000,000 × 0.40). Thus, the after-tax cash receipt each year is only $600,000. In summary, this transaction has two cash effects: a cash *inflow,* and a cash *outflow* represented by the increased income tax liability. This leads to the following formula that can be used to determine the after-tax effect of taxable cash receipts:

$$\text{After-tax cash receipt} = \text{Taxable cash receipt} \times (1 - \text{Tax rate})$$

After-Tax Cash Operating Expenses As shown in Exhibit 12.2, the increased revenue is expected to require $733,333 of cash operating expenses per year. Assuming that these expenses are fully deductible for income-tax purposes, this annual transaction has two cash effects: a cash *outlay* of $733,333, and a reduction of income taxes in the amount of $293,333 ($733,333 × 0.40). Thus, the net effect of the expense is $440,000. In effect, the net cost to the company is only $440,000 after taking into consideration the tax savings realized because of the deductibility of the expense. This leads to the following formula that can be used to determine the after-tax effect of cash operating expenses:

$$\text{After-tax cash expense} = \text{Pretax cash expense} \times (1 - \text{Tax rate})$$

After-Tax Cash Operating Income Of course, the analyst can combine incremental cash operating revenues (or cost savings) and incremental operating expenses to produce *incremental cash operating income* associated with an investment. In the case of the Mendoza Company, the expected increase in pretax cash operating income in year 1 would be $216,667 ($1,000,000 − $783,333). On an after-tax basis, this pretax cash operating income would yield $130,000. The following formula can be used to estimate each year's after-tax cash operating income:

$$\text{After-tax cash operating income} = \text{Pretax cash operating income} \times (1 - \text{Tax rate})$$

Noncash Revenues A word of caution is needed here. Noncash revenues that have tax effects also affect cash flows because of their effect on the tax liability of the company for the year. Because the income-tax liability is determined on an accrual-accounting basis, a noncash revenue, such as a credit sale planned to be collected in the following year, does not increase cash available to the firm this year, but does increase the company's taxable income for the current year. In turn, this transaction increases the cash outflows (taxes) for the current year. Thus, a noncash revenue for the current year *decreases,* not increases, cash available to the firm. The amount of the decrease is the increase in taxes resulting from the noncash revenue.

For example, assume that a company at the end of the year makes a $10,000 credit sale, the amount of which will be collected in the following year. Although the company receives no cash this year from the sale, it nevertheless increases its tax liability for the current year. Therefore, for a tax-paying organization, a noncash revenue is effectively a cash *outflow,* not a cash *inflow,* in the year the revenue is recognized for tax purposes.

Note, however, that for the Mendoza Company the only information we have is for *cash* revenues and *cash* operating expenses associated with the proposed investment. As such, noncash revenues are not an issue in this example.

Noncash Expenses   An increase in noncash expenses (e.g., depreciation, amortization costs), on the other hand, decreases taxable income, which reduces income taxes for the current period. Thus, a noncash expense increases, not decreases, cash flow. The deductibility of the noncash expense for income tax purposes reduces the tax liability that otherwise would exist.

Depreciation Calculations for Income-Tax Purposes (MACRS)   Depreciation for income-tax purposes is determined using the procedures specified in the Modified Accelerated Cost Recovery System (MACRS). MACRS assigns all depreciable assets to one of eight classes, referred to as *recovery periods*. Exhibit 12.5 describes these classes and their depreciation methods, and provides examples of assets in each class.

Exhibit 12.6 shows the depreciation rates each year for depreciable assets other than residential or nonresidential real estate. These percentages reflect the use of an accelerated depreciation method—150 percent or 200 percent of the straight-line (SL) depreciation rate, depending on the property class. Note that under MACRS disposal (salvage) value is ignored for calculating depreciation expense. With the exception of residential and nonresidential real estate properties (see last two classes of assets in Exhibit 12.5), a half-year convention is used to determine the depreciation expense for the first and last year of the asset's recovery period.

To illustrate, the first-year depreciation for a five-year property is 20 percent of the asset's cost—regardless of when the asset was placed into service during the year. The depreciation deduction for the second year for this asset would be 32 percent of the asset's cost. This amount is determined using the double-declining-balance (DDB) approach. That is, the SL rate for an asset with a five-year recovery period would be 20 percent per year. In year 1 (under the half-year convention) 20 percent of the asset's cost would be written off, leaving 80 percent to be deducted over the remaining four years. For year 2, the depreciation deduction (32 percent) is equal to 40 percent of this 80 percent. To ensure that 100 percent of an

EXHIBIT 12.5   **Asset Classes (Recovery Periods) under MACRS**

Class	Depreciation Method	Example
3-year property	200% declining balance	Light tools and handling equipment
5-year property	200% declining balance	Computers and peripheral equipment, office machinery, automobiles, light trucks
7-year property	200% declining balance	Office furniture, appliances, carpet, and furniture in residential rental property and any asset that does not have an assigned class
10-year property	200% declining balance	Manufacturing assets for food products, petroleum refining, tobacco
15-year property	150% declining balance	Road and shrubbery, telephone distribution plant
20-year property	150% declining balance	Multipurpose farm structures
27.5 year property	Straight line	Residential rental property
31.5 year property	Straight line	Nonresidential real property, office building, warehouse

EXHIBIT 12.6
MACRS Depreciation Rates

Year	3-year	5-year	7-year	10-year	15-year	20-year
1	33.33	20.00	14.29	10.00	5.00	3.75
2	44.45	32.00	24.49	18.00	9.50	7.22
3	14.81	19.20	17.49	14.40	8.55	6.68
4	7.41	11.52*	12.49	11.52	7.70	6.18
5		11.52	8.93*	9.22	6.93	5.71
6		5.76	8.92	7.37	6.23	5.28
7			8.92	6.55*	5.90*	4.89
8			4.47	6.55	5.90	4.52
9				6.56	5.91	4.46*
10				6.55	5.90	4.46
11				3.28	etc.	etc.

* First year of switching to the straight-line method.
Source: http://www.irs.gov/publications/p946/

asset's cost is written off over the specified recovery period, the depreciation method under MACRS ultimately reverts to the SL method. For example, the switch-over for five-year property occurs in year 4.

Taxpayers can choose to use the optional SL method in lieu of the percentages specified in the MACRS tables. Except for the midyear, or in some cases midquarter, convention that affects the amount of depreciation charges for the first and last year of an asset's life, the optional SL method provides for a constant depreciation deduction per year. For example, for a three-year property subject to the midyear convention, the relevant depreciation rates would be: 16 2/3 percent for year 1; 33.33 percent for years 2 and 3; and 16 2/3 percent for year 4. Note that under MACRS the salvage value is ignored for depreciation calculations, including situations where the optional SL method is chosen. The use of the optional SL method may be attractive to start-up firms (because they generally are unprofitable during the early stages of the business) and to firms experiencing financial difficulties. For such situations, the firm in question may want to defer rather than accelerate its depreciation deductions.

In Exhibits 12.2 and 12.3 we made a simplifying assumption that Mendoza chose the optional SL method under MACRS but is not subject to the midyear convention; the latter is not currently in accordance with current tax law. However, this assumption simplifies the capital-budgeting analysis that follows. Remember, however, that in most situations a company would not choose the SL optional approach and regardless of this decision *would* be subject to the midyear (or midquarter) convention. Knowledge of detailed income tax requirements regarding the determination of depreciation deductions is yet another way that accountants can add value to the capital-budgeting process.[6] As shown in Exhibit 12.3, the depreciation deduction for Mendoza Company, under the simplifying assumption noted above, is $120,000 per year. Given a 40 percent tax rate, this deduction provides annual income-tax savings of $48,000.

Project Disposal

Investment Disposal At the project-disposal stage, there are potential cash-flow effects that should be included in any capital-investment analysis.

In some situations there are end-of-project cash expenses that should be included on an after-tax basis. These costs include asset-removal costs, restoration costs (that is, costs needed to bring the asset, such as land, back to an original state), and any employee-related costs (e.g., severance pay, relocation costs, retraining costs).

In addition, at the end of the project's life the investment asset could, perhaps, be sold—an event that could trigger a taxable gain or loss. Any cash received from the disposal of the asset at the end of its life must be adjusted by the tax effect of the transaction. Refer back to Exhibit 12.4 for a summary of the procedures used for determining the after-tax cash flow effect of an asset disposal.

In the case of the Mendoza Company (Exhibit 12.3), the after-tax cash inflow from the sale of the four-year-old asset is projected to be $3,000; that is, $5,000 net sales proceeds minus $2,000 income tax paid on the gain.

Recovery of Investment in Net Working Capital Recall that Mendoza Company committed $200,000 in additional net working capital at the onset of the investment, which at the end of year 4 is no longer needed. Thus, at the end of year 4 we include a $200,000 cash inflow for the conversion of this net working capital back into cash.

---

[6] For example, the provides certain incentives to businesses, including: (a) a special 50 percent depreciation allowance for purchases made in 2009, and (b) an increase in the small-business expensing limitation for tax year 2009. The former provision is similar to the "bonus depreciation" provisions previously allowed certain taxpayers. Under the new law a qualifying business can expense up to $250,000 of Section 179 property purchased by the taxpayer in a tax year beginning in 2009. (Absent this legislation, the expense limit for Section 179 property would have been $133,000. Note that the $250,000 is reduced if the amount of Section 179 property placed in service by the taxpayer during the tax year exceeds $800,000.) This illustrates the somewhat complicated and changing nature of tax laws. As participants in the decision-making team, it is incumbent on accounting professionals to keep abreast of income-tax provisions that affect the after-tax cash flows associated with capital-investment projects.

Additional Measurement Issues

Following are four additional measurement issues that need to be considered by accountants as they gather relevant information for the analysis of capital-expenditure proposals.

Inflation   For simplicity, we have assumed that the annual cash revenues and cash expenses associated with the proposed project, including the recovery of net working capital at the end of the project's life, are constant in amount; that is, they are not affected by inflation. In an actual capital-budgeting analysis, however, the accountant would incorporate inflation adjustments for future cash flows. Typically, the discount rate that is used in capital-budgeting models is an inflation-adjusted rate. Thus, to achieve consistency in the discounting process, the cash flows that are being discounted should incorporate the anticipated effects of inflation.

Opportunity Costs—Include Them in Your Cash-Flow Analysis   As noted in Chapter 11, opportunity costs are always relevant for decision making, including the analysis of proposed capital expenditures. Consider, for example, the decision to expand manufacturing facilities to meet projected demand for a firm's product(s). Suppose that the land on which the facilities would be built could otherwise be sold for $250,000. While an out-of-pocket cost would not be involved, there is nonetheless an economic cost of using the land for the new manufacturing facilities. In this example, the opportunity cost is equal to the after-tax amount that the firm could get by selling the land; as such, this amount should be included as a relevant cash flow for capital-budgeting purposes.

Sunk Costs—Ignore These   In Chapter 11 it was noted that these costs, because they are historical or "down-the-drain," are irrelevant for decision-making purposes. Consider the example above. The original purchase price of the land is irrelevant to the facilities-expansion decision—it is a sunk cost. Because such costs will be the same regardless of whether or not the firm invests in the new facilities, these costs should be ignored for capital-budgeting purposes.

Allocated Overhead Costs—Be Careful of These!   As discussed elsewhere in the text, there are various circumstances in which accountants must allocate common, or shared, costs of the organization. The requirement of generating full product cost information for financial statement purposes is one such use. However, there are certain circumstances in which the allocation of these kinds of costs should be avoided.

The basic rule here is to ask whether overhead costs (administrative and/or manufacturing) will increase if a given project is accepted, or whether these costs will be largely unaffected in total. In the former case, the *incremental* overhead should be included (as an after-tax cash outflow) for capital-budgeting purposes. In the latter case, regardless of the amount allocated to the project for accounting purposes, these costs should not be charged against the project for decision-making purposes.

In the Mendoza Company example (Exhibit 12.2) corporate headquarters' expenses are not likely to change in total if the company invests in the new machine. Thus, even though an allocation of such expenses may be appropriate for some other reason (such as full product costing), no portion of these expenses should be charged against the project for capital-budgeting purposes.

Recap—After-Tax Cash Flow Information for the Mendoza Company Investment Proposal

After-tax cash flow information for the Mendoza Company investment proposal is summarized in Exhibit 12.3. Data in this exhibit have been divided according to the three primary stages of the proposed project: (1) project initiation, (2) project operation, and (3) project disposal.

How can managers use this information to assess the financial consequences of the proposed investment? We turn now to a discussion of various capital-budgeting decision models that can be used to answer this question.

The University of Texas M.D. Anderson Cancer Center in Houston, Texas has a staff of about 8,000 located in several buildings that include a 518-bed hospital, a 10-story outpatient clinic, and several remote patient-care sites. Although it kept some patient information on computer, many records were paper-based. Files for repeat patients became unwieldy, requiring regular compiling and thinning. A computer-based patient record (CPR) that integrates financial and clinical information can be an important tool for improving the quality of care and lowering its cost. However, purchasing, implementing, and maintaining a CPR requires a significant investment that management must justify.

The CPR project at the Anderson Cancer Center was the responsibility of an executive team consisting of the vice president for patient care, the vice president for hospital and clinic operations, and the executive vice president for administration and finance. A project steering committee directed the cost-benefit analysis and other aspects of evaluation. A stakeholders' group consisting of managers from departments that would be affected by CPR implementation

provided much of the data for the cost-benefit analysis. The chief information officer (CIO) and the associate vice president of medical information served on all teams and were involved at all levels.

The cost-benefit analysis followed these steps:

- Identified goals for a CPR.
- Determined quantifiable and nonquantifiable benefits.
- Estimated costs.
- Projected costs and benefits over 10 years and calculated the net present value (NPV) of the project.
- Monitored the results.

The cost-benefit analysis enabled executives at the Anderson Cancer Center to make informed strategic and tactical decisions regarding acquisition and implementation of a CPR.

Based on Leslie A. Kian and Michael W. Stewart, "Justifying the Cost of a Computer-Based Patient Record," *Healthcare Financial Management* 49, no. 7, pp. 58–63.

Discounted Cash Flow (DCF) Capital-Budgeting Decision Models

LEARNING OBJECTIVE 4

Apply discounted cash flow (DCF) decision models for capital-budgeting purposes.

Discounted cash flow (DCF) models

represent capital-budgeting decision models that incorporate the present value of future cash flows.

Non-DCF models

for capital budgeting are those that are not based on the present value of future cash flows.

Types of Capital-Budgeting Decision Models

Models for evaluating capital-investment proposals fall into one of two categories: **discounted cash flow (DCF) models** and **non-DCF models.** The former category includes the net present value (NPV) model, the internal rate of return (IRR) model, and the profitability index (PI) model. The latter category includes the payback model and the accounting (book) rate of return (ARR) model. As indicated by the survey results from large firms reported in Exhibit 12.7, two of the DCF models (NPV and IRR) enjoy widespread use in practice: approximately three-quarters of such firms "always" or "almost always" use both NPV and IRR for capital-budgeting purposes.

As indicated in Exhibit 12.8, recent survey evidence from owners of small businesses (that is, those with 20 or fewer employees) suggests that such businesses do not routinely use modern (DCF) models when analyzing capital-investment proposals. Rather, these owners tend to rely on informal decision models (gut feeling) or on payback information for decision-making purposes.

Given the prominence of DCF models in practice today, particularly for large companies, we discuss these models next, using data from the Mendoza Company. We discuss the non-DCF models (payback and accounting rate of return) in a separate section of the chapter.

DCF Models: Specifying the Discount Rate

The discounted cash flow (DCF) models evaluate capital-investment projects by converting anticipated future cash flows to a present-value basis. That is, in evaluating capital investments, DCF models explicitly take into consideration the time value of money. This process is conceptually appealing because it is consistent with the process that investors use in assigning value to securities issued by individual firms.

The discount rate

is a generic term that refers to the rate used in capital budgeting for converting future cash flows to a present-value basis.

Unfortunately, the terminology regarding the discounting process can be confusing. In this text, when we speak in general of the rate used to convert future cash flows to a present value basis we use the term **discount rate.** For capital-budgeting purposes, the discount rate can be approximated as the firm's weighted-average cost of capital (WACC). The use of a

PricewaterhouseCoopers, the largest accounting firm in the world, publishes an annual set of examples as to how some forward-looking companies are responding to the increasing need for transparency of reporting beyond the requirements of the existing financial reporting model. One recent example is a disclosure of the Ascott Group Limited, a Singapore company in what is called the *serviced residence industry* (essentially, the company operates hotels that are relatively smaller and that have few non-room areas, such as multiple restaurants, ballrooms, etc.). The 2004 Annual Report provides the following estimates of the company's weighted-average cost of capital: 6.5 percent (2004), 5.8 percent (2003).

Note 4 to the annual report provides the following details regarding the calculation of the estimated WACC for the Ascott Group Limited:

1. The Cost of Equity Capital is estimated using the Capital Asset Pricing Model (CAPM) with a market risk premium of 6 percent for both 2003 and 2004

2. Risk-free interest rate was 3.78 percent for 2004 and 2.78 percent for 2003 (based on yield-to-maturity of 10-year government bonds)

3. Unlevered beta coefficient of 0.6, both for 2004 and 2003

4. Cost of debt was 3.7 percent (2004) and 2.68 percent (2003), based on a five-year Singapore Dollar Swap Offered rate plus 75 basis points

The company indicates that it provides information about its estimated WACC so that investors can better assess the risk position of the company.

Source: PricewaterhouseCoopers, *Trends 2006: Good Practices in Corporate Reporting.* 2005. This document is presented in an on-line format at www.corporatereporting.com.

EXHIBIT 12.7

Relative Use of Various Capital-Budgeting Models by Large Firms

Source: J. Graham and C. Harvey, "How Do CFOs Make Capital Budgeting and Capital Structure Decisions?" *Journal of Applied Corporate Finance* 15, no. 1 (Spring, 2002), pp. 8–23; and P. A. Ryan and G. P. Ryan, "Capital Budgeting Practices of the Fortune 1000: How Have Things Changed?" *Journal of Business and Management* 8, no. 4 (Fall 2002), pp. 355–364.

Method/Model	Percentage of Firms That "Always" or "Almost Always/Often" Use the Indicated Method	
	Graham & Harvey (2002) (N = 392 CFOs)	Ryan & Ryan (2002) (N = 205 CFOs)
Payback	57	53
Discounted payback	30	38
Accounting (book) rate of return	20	15
NPV	75	85
IRR	76	77
Profitability index (PI)*	12	12

* PI = NPV per dollar invested.

EXHIBIT 12.8

Relative Use of Various Capital-Budgeting Models by Small Firms

Source: M. Daniels and J. A. Scott, "The Capital Budgeting Decisions of Small Businesses," Working paper, Erivan K. Haub School of Business, Saint Joseph's University, Philadelphia, PA, 2005.

Decision Model	Percentage of Respondents Indicating That This Is the Primary Tool Used to Assess a Project's Viability
"Gut feeling"	29%
Payback period	22
Accounting (book) rate of return	16
DCF methods (NPV/IRR)	14
Combination of methods	12
Other	8

Average-risk projects

are those that approximate the risk of the firm's existing assets and operations; the WACC is used to evaluate average-risk investment projects.

firm's WACC as the discount rate for capital-budgeting purposes is, however, appropriate (as explained below) only for **average-risk projects.** In the situation where a project under consideration exhibits higher or lower risk than average, an adjustment to the firm's WACC is needed (upwards for higher-risk projects, downwards for lower-risk projects).[7] For this reason, some

[7] In the study by J. Graham and C. Harvey, "How Do CFOs Make Capital Budgeting and Capital Structure Decisions," *Journal of Applied Corporate Finance* 15, no. 1 (Spring 2002), 60 percent of respondents said they used a single companywide rate for investment analysis purposes; 51 percent said they used a "risk-matched" rate for a given project (thereby suggesting that some companies use *both* approaches).

493

EXHIBIT 12.9

Survey Evidence Regarding the Definition of "Discount Rate" for Capital-Budgeting Purposes (N = 205)

Discount Rate Definition	Percentage That Consider This to Be the Best Definition of the Discount Rate
WACC	83.2
After-tax cost of debt	7.4
Retained earnings	1.5
Cost of new equity	1.0
Other	6.9
Total	100.0

Source: P. A. Ryan and G. P. Ryan, "Capital Budgeting Practices of the Fortune 1000: How Have Things Changed?" *Journal of Business and Management* 8, no. 4 (Winter 2002), pp. 355–364.

For capital-budgeting purposes, the **hurdle rate** represents the minimum acceptable rate of return on an investment; also referred to as the required rate of return.

The **weighted-average cost of capital (WACC)** is an average of the (after-tax) cost of debt and equity capital for a firm; in general, the WACC is the appropriate discount rate to use for future cash flows associated with "average risk" projects.

Capital structure refers to the means by which a company is financed; the mix between debt and equity capital.

The **yield-to-maturity** is a long-term bond yield (rate of return) expressed as an annual rate; the calculation takes into account the current market price of the bond, its par value, the coupon interest rate, and the time-to-maturity; the total performance of a bond, coupon payments as well as capital gain or loss, from the time of purchase until maturity.

The **capital asset pricing model (CAPM)** depicts the risk-return relationship for equity securities and can be used to estimate the required rate of return on equity for a given company; equal to the risk-free rate of return plus a risk premium measured as the product of β and the market-risk premium.

individuals refer to a project-specific discount rate as the **hurdle rate** for a project. They consider this the minimum acceptable rate of return. In order to accept a given capital-investment project, the projected economic return on the project must exceed the "hurdle rate."

Unless otherwise noted, for purposes of discussion assume that the appropriate discount rate used for capital-budgeting purposes is the firm's WACC. Exhibit 12.9 indicates that, in fact, the majority of companies today define the discount rate for capital-budgeting purposes as the WACC.

Estimating the WACC

A company obtains funds (capital) from both equity and debt sources. The cost to the firm for each source of funds is the return demanded by lenders and investors who buy the firm's securities. A firm's **weighted-average cost of capital (WACC),** therefore, is defined as "a composite of the cost of various sources of funds comprising a firm's capital structure." [8] You could think of the WACC as the expected rate of return that investors would demand on a portfolio consisting of all of the firm's securities.[9] The weights in determining the WACC are based on the firm's **capital structure,** that is, its mix of debt and equity capital, expressed in market-value terms.[10]

After-Tax Cost of Debt

Because interest payments are tax deductible, we must calculate the after-tax cost of debt. Because market values are used to determine the weight attached to each type of security (including debt instruments), we need to estimate the current yield (**yield-to-maturity**) of the debt instruments in a company's capital structure. That is, we need to use the effective, not nominal, interest rate of the debt.[11] Thus, we define the after-tax cost of debt, K_d, as follows:

$$K_d = \text{Effective interest rate} \times (1 - t)$$

where

$$t = \text{marginal income tax rate}$$

Cost of Common Equity

The cost of common stock (and retained earnings) is defined as the rate of return demanded by investors; that is, it is the risk-adjusted return needed to attract investors to purchase the common stock of a company. For companies whose shares of stock are listed on an exchange, the **capital asset pricing model (CAPM)** can be used to estimate this rate of return, K_e, as follows:

$$K_e = r_f + \beta(r_m - r_f)$$

[8] Institute of Management Accountants (IMA), *Statement Number 4A:* "Cost of Capital" (Montvale, NJ: 1984), p. 1.

[9] R. A. Brealey, S. C. Myers, and A. J. Marcus, *Fundamentals of Corporate Finance,* 6th Edition (New York: McGraw-Hill/Irwin, 2009).

[10] The rest of this section draws on the material contained in M. S. Pagano and D. E. Stout, "Estimating a Firm's Cost of Capital," *Management Accounting Quarterly* 5, no. 3 (Spring 2004), pp. 13–20.

[11] For example, the *effective interest rate* on a 10-year, 8 percent, $100,000 bond with semiannual interest payments that was sold for $88,448 is 10 percent, not 8 percent, since the *effective interest rate* on the bond is 10 percent. If the issuing firm faces a marginal income tax rate of 40 percent, the after-tax cost of this security is 6 percent.

where

r_f = Risk-free rate

r_m = The percentage return (dividends + capital gains) on a market portfolio of securities

The **beta coefficient (β)** is a measure of the sensitivity of a given stock's return to fluctuations in the overall market; the average beta of all stocks is 1.0; betas > 1 imply greater sensitivity to market fluctuations.

β = The firm's **beta coefficient** (an index of how the price of a particular security moves as the price of the market moves)

An intuitive explanation of the CAPM is that the expected rate of return on a given stock is a function of two factors: the current risk-free rate of return (e.g., the yield on U.S. Treasury bills), and a market risk premium equal in amount to the second component on the right-hand side of the preceding equation. Alternatively, you can view the former term as compensation for the time value of money and the second term as a premium that investors demand. This second term is a function of the sensitivity of a given stock's return to the fluctuations in the overall market (i.e., its β coefficient) and the **market risk premium** (defined as the spread between the expected rate of return on a market portfolio of securities, r_m, and the risk-free rate of return, r_f). In sum, under the CAPM the expected rate of return on a stock is equal to the risk-free rate plus the specific stock's beta coefficient times the market risk premium.

The **market risk premium** is the spread between the expected rate of return on a market portfolio of securities and the risk-free rate of return; represented as $(r_m - r_f)$, where r_m = return on the market and r_f = risk-free rate of return.

If the CAPM model is used to estimate the cost of equity capital for a company, you might want to use an alternative estimate as a check on your calculation. One such estimate is based on what is called the *constant growth, dividend discount model.* Using this model, we would estimate the cost of equity capital, K_e, for a company as follows:

$$K_e = (D_1/P_0) + g$$

where

D_1 = Expected dividend per share one period (year) forward

P_0 = Current price per share of common stock

g = Dividend growth rate (assumed constant to perpetuity)

Cost of Preferred Stock

The cost of preferred stock, K_p, is conceptually equal to the current yield that holders (i.e., investors) of the stock demand. This is also referred to as the *dividend yield* on the share of preferred stock. That is,

$$K_p = \text{Current dividend on preferred stock/current market price per share}$$

Determining Weights

Market, not book (accounting), values are needed conceptually to determine the weights associated with each source of funds in determining the WACC. As an example, consider a company in the 40 percent marginal income-tax bracket. This company has outstanding: a $100,000 long-term bank loan with a 12 percent interest rate; $500,000 face value of 8.396 percent, 20-year bonds, currently selling at 90 percent of face value (interest on the bonds is paid semi-annually; the bonds mature in 10 years); $200,000 of 15 percent, $20 preferred stock with a current market value of $300,000; and, 10,000 shares of $1 par value common stock that the firm sold originally for $5 per share. The common stock has a current market price of $75 per share. Assume that application of the CAPM (as described above) yields an estimated rate of return (yield) of approximately 20 percent. Given this information, the company's WACC is approximately 13.4 percent, as shown in Exhibit 12.10.

Software that calculates a company's WACC and that generates estimates of underlying common stock value for the company is available (e.g., www.valuepro.net). Also, you can obtain from www.ibbotson.com cost of capital (both cost of equity and WACC) information from a sample of U.S. industries, income-tax rate and beta information for individual U.S. stocks, and international industry data that would be of interest to U.S. investors.

Following are estimates of the WACC for a sample of New Zealand companies as of the first quarter of 2005. Note that since the cost of capital for Sky Network Television Ltd. (14.6%) is greater than the cost of capital for the New Zealand Refining Co. Ltd. (8.2%), Sky Network must earn a higher return (on average) on the projects in which it invests.

Company Name	NZSE Code	Industry	WACC Estimate
Sanford Ltd	SAN	Agriculture	7.8%
New Zealand Refining Co. Ltd.	NZR	Energy	8.2
Carter Holt Harvey Ltd.	CAH	Forestry/forest products	11.0
Sky Network Television Ltd.	SKY	Media/telecommunications	14.6
Mainfreight Ltd.	MFT	Transportation	10.9

Source: PricewaterhouseCoopers, *The Cost of Capital Report*, March 31, 2005.

EXHIBIT 12.10   Estimation of Weighted-Average Cost of Capital (WACC) (Hypothetical Example)

	(1)	(2)	(3)	(4)	(5)	(6) = (3) × (5)
Source of Funds	Book Value	Pretax Effective Rate of Return	After-tax Rate or Expected Return	Total Current Market Value	Weight (Based on Market Values)	Components for WACC Calculation
Bank loan	$100,000	12%	7.20%	$ 100,000	0.06250	0.4500%
Bonds	500,000	10[a]	6.00	450,000	0.28125	1.6875
Preferred stock	200,000	15	10.00[b]	300,000	0.18750	1.8750
Common stock	50,000		20.00	750,000	0.46875	9.3750
Total	**$850,000**			**$1,600,000**	**1.00**	**13.3875%**

Notes:

[a] The estimated effective interest rate (yield to maturity) on the bonds, 10%, was found using the YIELD function in Excel.

[b] Number of preferred shares outstanding = $200,000/$20 par value per share = 10,000 shares. Current market price per share = $300,000/10,000 shares outstanding = $30.00. Preferred stock dividend per share = 15% × $20 par value per share = $3.00. Therefore, the current dividend yield on preferred stock = $3.00/$30.00 = 10%.

Net Present Value (NPV) Decision Model

Determining a Project's NPV

The **net present value (NPV)** equals the difference between the present value of future cash inflows and the present value of future cash outflows of an investment project.

The **present value (PV)** of a future cash flow is its current equivalent value; also referred to as time-adjusted value.

The **net present value (NPV)** of an investment is equal to the difference between the present value of the project's cash inflows and the present value of the project's cash outflows. The **present value (PV)** of a future cash flow is its current equivalent dollar value, using an appropriate discount rate; for example, using the firm's WACC. The decision rule is to accept a proposed investment if the projected NPV of the project is positive; that is, accept a project if the PV of cash inflows is greater than the PV of cash outflows. If a project has a positive NPV, then the project adds to shareholder value.

Determining NPV with Uniform Net Cash Inflows

Some capital-expenditure projects are characterized by an investment outlay in year 0 followed by an annuity, that is, a uniform stream of future cash inflows. Such a project's NPV can be determined in either of two ways. Let's assume a four-year project that requires an outlay at time 0 of $555,000 and after-tax inflows of $200,000 per year. The WACC is assumed to be 10 percent.

Method 1: Annuity Table

To convert the future stream of cash inflows back to its present value, you could obtain from Appendix C, Table 2, the appropriate annuity factor for 10 percent, four years: 3.170. Note that this factor is simply the sum of the four present-value factors presented in Appendix C, Table 1 under the 10% column. Thus, the PV of the future annuity is $634,000 ($200,000 × 3.170), and the NPV of this project is: $634,000 − $555,000 = $79,000. This implies that the investment is expected to provide an economic return greater than 10 percent. Alternatively, you can say that this investment is expected to earn a 10 percent return on the funds invested *plus* an additional $79,000 (in current dollars).

Method 2: Excel Formula

You can use a built-in function in Excel to estimate a project's NPV, as indicated in the screenshot presented below. Note that the difference of $26.91 in indicated NPVs that you observe is due to rounding (to three decimal points) that took place when Table 2 was constructed.

	A	B	C	D	E
1	Investment Outlay		$555,000		
2	After-tax Cash Inflows:				
3	Year 1	$200,000			
4	Year 2	$200,000			
5	Year 3	$200,000			
6	Year 4	$200,000			
7	Discount Rate		10.00%		
8				Formula in Cell B9	
9	NPV =	$78,973.09	=NPV(C7,B3,B4,B5,B6)-C1		

Determining NPV with Uneven Cash Inflows

Refer now to the cash-flow data for the Mendoza Company presented in Exhibit 12.3. The net investment outlay at time zero is $590,000. The after-tax cash inflows from the proposed investment are: $178,000 (year 1), $208,000 (year 2), $208,000 (year 3), and $321,000 (year 4). Given a 10 percent discount rate (WACC), we calculate the NPV of this proposed investment as $119,240, as follows:[12]

	A	B	C	D
1	WACC	0.1		
2	After-tax Cash Inflows:			
3	Year 0	($590,000)		
4	Year 1	$178,000		
5	Year 2	$208,000		
6	Year 3	$208,000		
7	Year 4	$321,000		
8			Formula in Cell B9	
9	NPV=	$119,240	=B3+NPV(B1,B4:B7)	

Internal Rate of Return (IRR) Decision Model

The **internal rate of return (IRR)** represents an estimate of the true (i.e., economic) rate of return on an investment. Mathematically, the IRR is defined as the rate of return that produces an NPV of zero. The decision rule using the IRR model is simple: accept an investment if its projected IRR exceeds the firm's discount rate (WACC). If a project's IRR is greater than the company's WACC, it means that the project has a positive NPV.

The **internal rate of return (IRR)** is an estimate of the true (i.e., economic) rate of return on an investment.

Determining a Project's IRR: Uniform Cash Inflows

If the project consists of an initial investment outlay followed by a stream of constant cash inflows, the project's IRR is defined as the discount rate that satisfies the following equation:

Initial investment outlay = PV of future cash inflows at a specified discount rate

= Annual after-tax cash inflow × Annuity discount factor associated with the life of the project

---

[12] Alternatively, we could use the PV factors in Appendix C, Table 1, to determine the PV of the stream of after-tax cash inflows. From this, we would subtract the required investment outlay, $590,000, to arrive at the project's estimated NPV.

Using $A_{r,n}$ to denote the last term in the above equation, the equation can be restated as follows:

$$A_{r,n} = \text{Initial investment outlay/Annual after-tax cash inflow from the investment}$$

where

$A_{r,n}$ = Annuity factor that makes the PV of the stream of future after-tax cash inflows equal to the initial investment outlay

n = Life of the project (e.g., in years)

r = Discount rate.

For a four-year project that has an initial investment outlay of $555,000 and annual after-tax cash inflows of $200,000, the estimated IRR for this project is determined as follows:

$$\$555,000 = \$200,000 \times A_{r,4}$$

$$A_{r,4} = \$555,000/\$200,000 = 2.775$$

An annuity factor of 2.775 in Appendix C, Table 2 for a project with a four-year useful life corresponds to a discount rate, r, of between 15 percent and 20 percent. Because this rate exceeds the firm's WACC(10.0%), the project should be accepted.[13]

Determining a Project's IRR: Uneven Cash Inflows (Mendoza Company example)

When the projected future cash inflows are not even, the project's IRR can be estimated using a trial-and-error approach. That is, a discount rate, say 10%, is chosen to begin the process. Using this discount rate, you would compute the project's NPV. If the resulting NPV at this discount rate is positive, the discount rate you chose is too low (and vice versa). Thus, a higher discount rate is chosen and the project's NPV at this new rate is determined. The process stops when the resulting NPV is close to zero: the discount rate at this point represents the project's estimated IRR. The interpolation process explained in footnote 13 can be used to generate a more accurate estimate of a project's IRR.

Alternatively, you can use the IRR function in Excel to estimate a project's IRR. Using the cash-flow data for Mendoza Company (Exhibit 12.3) we generate an IRR of 18.2 percent, as follows:

	A	B	C	D
1	After-tax Cash Inflows:			
2	Year 0	($590,000)		
3	Year 1	$178,000		
4	Year 2	$208,000		
5	Year 3	$208,000		
6	Year 4	$321,000		
7			Cell Formulas	
8	IRR =	18.2%	=IRR(B2:B6,0.10)	
9	NPV =	($0)	=NPV(B8,B2:B6)	

[13] To generate a more accurate estimate of this project's IRR, we can use the following interpolation procedure:

	Interest rate, r		Annuity factor, $A_{r,4}$	
At lower rate	15.00%	15.00%	2.855	2.855
Target rate	?	?		2.775
At higher rate	20.00%		2.589	—
Difference	5.00%	—	0.266	0.080

The difference in annuity factors between the interest rates on either side of the target annuity factor (2.775) is 0.266. This suggests that an increase of 5% in interest rates, from 15% to 20%, increases the annuity factor by 0.266. Thus, to get to 2.775 we need to increase the interest rate proportionately to the decrease in the annuity factor. That is, the annuity factor must be reduced by 30.08% (0.080/0.266). Thus, the needed increase in interest rate to decrease the annuity factor by 0.266 is 30.08% of 5%, or 1.50%. The project's estimated IRR is therefore 16.50% [i.e., 15% + (30.08% × 5.00%)]. Note that this linear interpolation process produces an *estimate* of the true IRR. The true IRR, found using the built-in Excel function, is 16.42%. See if you can reproduce this result and verify that at this discount rate the NPV of the project is zero.

Note that we confirm that the project's IRR is 18.2 percent: at this discount rate, the NPV of the project is zero. Given a WACC of 10 percent for the Mendoza Company, this project should therefore be accepted. Managers generally find the IRR decision rule intuitively appealing: *accept projects that provide a rate of return* (e.g., 18.2%) *that exceeds the company's WACC* (e.g., 10%).

Of course, you can also use the built-in function in Excel to estimate a project's IRR when the future cash inflows are equal (rather than using the trial-and-error procedure described above).

The Modified Internal Rate of Return (MIRR)

Survey evidence suggests that IRR is widely used in practice, in large part because of its intuitive appeal to managers. Students in accounting should be aware of a particular controversy regarding the use of IRR for evaluating capital-budgeting projects: the reinvestment rate assumption.

Critics[14] maintain that the IRR metric ignores the reinvestment potential of intermediate positive cash flows from a project. These same critics maintain that IRR inherently assumes that such cash flows are reinvested at the IRR rate and that in most cases this rate is unrealistically high. Thus, they maintain, conventional IRR calculations build in reinvestment assumptions that make bad projects look better and good ones look great. Such practice can result in major capital-budgeting distortions.

These critics suggest that a more conservative assumption regarding the reinvestment rate rate of return on interim cash flows be used. In most cases, this rate is better approximated by the organization's discount rate (WACC). In response to this controversy, the **modified internal rate of return (MIRR)** can be used to assess capital-budgeting projects. As the name implies, MIRR is a modification of the conventional IRR measure. The MIRR assumes all positive cash flows are reinvested at a particular rate of return (usually at the WACC) for the remaining duration of the project.

A built-in function in Excel, MIRR, provides an estimate of a project's modified internal rate of return, as follows:[15]

$$\text{MIRR(values, finance\_rate, reinvest\_rate)}$$

Values is an array or a reference to cells that contain a series of payments (negative values) and income (positive values) occurring at regular periods; **finance_rate** is the discount rate (i.e., WACC) used for DCF analysis of capital-budgeting projects; and **reinvest_rate** is the estimated reinvestment rate (i.e., the rate of return on the periodic cash flows provided by the project—generally, this will also be the WACC).

Based on the after-tax cash-flow data for the Mendoza Company presented in Exhibit 12.3, we find an estimated MIRR of 15.18 percent, as follows:

	A	B	C	D
1	After-tax cash flows:			
2	Year 0	($590,000)		
3	Year 1	$178,000		
4	Year 2	$208,000		
5	Year 3	$208,000		
6	Year 4	$321,000		
7			Cell formula	
8	MIRR =	15.18%	=MIRR(B2:B6,0.1,0.1)	

Three points are worth making regarding the reinvestment rate controversy. One, the MIRR suffers from some of the same drawbacks as the more conventional IRR metric: relying on either can lead to an incorrect choice between mutually exclusive investments; as noted below, we deal with this issue in Appendix B. Two, a search of the Internet under "MIRR" suggests heated debate as to whether or not the conventional IRR metric has an inherent reinvestment rate assumption. Some of these arguments are arcane and embedded in mathematical theory. Students of accounting should therefore simply be aware that there are different points of view regarding this issue. Third, as noted below, in most cases (e.g., other than when capital

The **modified internal rate of return (MIRR)** is IRR adjusted to account for an assumed rate of return associated with interim project cash inflows.

---

[14] See, for example, J. C. Kelleher and J. J. MacCormack, "Internal Rate of Return: A Cautionary Tale," *The McKinsey Quarterly,* October 20, 2004 (available at www.cfo.com/article.cfm/3304945).

[15] See office.microsoft.com/en-us/excel/HP100623681033.aspx.

needs to be rationed), a safe bet would be to use NPV as the financial-performance metric associated with proposed investments.

Comparison of NPV and IRR Methods: Which to Use?

If the decision is limited to accepting or rejecting a given investment project, the NPV model and the IRR model will lead to the same conclusion. There are, however, several situations that complicate capital-budgeting decisions in the real world. Appendix B to this chapter deals with three of these issues: (1) the problem of multiple IRRs, (2) choosing between mutually exclusive projects, and (3) capital budgeting under the situation of capital rationing. Given such real-world complications, modern financial theory generally argues for the use of the NPV decision model, except in the case of capital rationing. In this case, a company's capital budget should be allocated to projects on the basis of *relative profitability,* that is, on the basis of NPV per dollar invested.[16]

Templates for Structuring a DCF Capital-Budgeting Analysis

Before discussing several non-DCF capital-budgeting decision models, we direct your attention to Appendix A in which we present alternative templates that can be used to structure a DCF analysis of a capital-budgeting problem. All data used in Appendix A relate to the Mendoza Company example discussed thus far in the chapter. Panels A and B in Appendix A contain two versions of the differential approach, to which you were introduced in Chapter 11. Panel C contains an example of the total approach to analyzing an asset-replacement decision. Note that in Panel C depreciation expense in the total column includes both the existing asset and the new asset that is being proposed. Which of these templates you use is a matter of personal choice/preference. Note, too, that the basic templates included in Appendix A can be customized by including additional lines. For example, in equipment-replacement decisions, the decision to keep an existing asset may require periodic repairs and upgrades at future intervals. The actual templates contained in Appendix A can be obtained from your instructor.

Uncertainty and the Capital-Budgeting Process

LEARNING OBJECTIVE 5

Understand approaches to dealing with uncertainty in the capital-budgeting process.

Capital-budgeting decision models rely on estimates of key input variables, such as the discount rate, life of a proposed project, after-tax cash flows associated with a project, and alternative future states of nature (e.g., good economy vs. bad economy, high price of oil/energy vs. low price of oil/energy). By definition, these estimates and states of nature are subject to uncertainty; and the longer the time horizon for the investment, the greater is the uncertainty regarding these estimates. Management accountants, as part of the decision-making team, need to understand approaches that can be used to address this uncertainty. Here we consider two broad approaches to the problem: one, conducting sensitivity analysis as part of the capital-budgeting process; and two, incorporating real options into the analysis of proposed investments.

Decision makers want to know how sensitive their capital-budgeting decisions (e.g., whether to accept or reject a proposed investment) are to estimates of the decision inputs (e.g., discount rate). In more formal terms, this assessment process is referred to as **sensitivity analysis.** There are several ways that managers can conduct a sensitivity analysis in conjunction with the capital-budgeting process.

In the space below we provide an overview of three types of sensitivity analysis: what-if analysis, scenario analysis, and Monte Carlo simulation. This material is followed by a discussion of the use of "real options" as a way to more formally model uncertainty in the analysis of capital-expenditure proposals.

Sensitivity analysis

is the process of selectively varying a key input variable, for example, the discount rate, to identify the range over which a capital-budgeting decision is valid.

What-If Analyses

What-if questions attempt to determine the impact on project profitability of changes in the value of a single input variable. For example, we might be interested in knowing the impact on NPV if the after-tax cash flows for a project are only 90 percent of their projected amount? Separately, what if a given project has a three-year rather than four-year life? The more general question to be asked is: Which variables in the decision model have the greatest potential to

---

[16] See, for example, Brealey et al. (2009).

alter the indicated profitability (and hence desirability) of an investment? Once this is known, management may want to refine its estimate of the variables that have, or variable that has, the greatest impact on project profitability.

Following is an Excel screen shot of a basic what-if analysis for a project with an investment outlay of $18 and a three-year life. The table in the shot shows the independent impact of changes in the discount rate and changes in the amount of annual after-tax cash flows on the estimated NPV of the investment.

	A	B	C	D
1	NPVs as a Function of Changes in After-tax Cash			
2	Flows and Discount Rate (Initial Cash Outflow =			
3	$18; project life = 3 years)			
4				
5		**Annual After-tax Cash Flows**		
6	**Discount Rate**	$7.00	$8.00	$9.00
7	0.10	($0.59)	$1.89	$4.38
8	0.11	($0.89)	$1.55	$3.99
9	0.12	($1.19)	$1.21	$3.62

Instead of choosing the values in the preceding table somewhat arbitrarily, the decision maker can specify *optimistic* and *pessimistic* values for a variable of interest, say, the after-tax cash flows. Thus, $8 per year might be the expected amount of cash flow, $7 might be defined as a *pessimistic* estimate, and $9 per year might be defined as an *optimistic* estimate.

In addition, the decision maker might be interested, as part of the what-if analysis, of determining the breakeven point associated with a given variable. In the preceding example, managers might feel fairly certain that the appropriate discount rate (WACC) is 11 percent. A reasonable question to ask is: What is the **breakeven after-tax cash flow,** that is, the minimum annual after-tax cash inflows needed for an investment project to be acceptable. In other words, what is the annual cash inflow amount that would result in a zero NPV? The **Goal Seek** function in Excel can be used to answer this question.

Assume a model that calculates the NPV of a three-year project with an initial investment cost of $18, annual after-tax cash inflows of $7 per year, and a discount rate of 11 percent. The NPV function of Excel for this example shows a projected NPV of ($0.89), as indicated below:

Breakeven after-tax cash flow equals the minimum annual after-tax cash inflows needed for an investment project to be acceptable.

	A	B	C	D	E	F
1	Original Investment Outlay		$18.00			
2	Annual after-tax cash flow		$7.00			
3	Discount rate		0.11			
4	NPV		($0.89)	(=NPV(C3,C2,C2,C2)-C1)		

To find the breakeven after-tax cash flow, use the following method:

Goal Seek ☒

Set cell: $C$4

To value: 0

By changing cell: $C$2

OK   Cancel

After clicking OK in the dialogue box above, the following solution should appear:

	A	B	C	D	E	F
1	Original Investment Outlay		$18.00			
2	Annual after-tax cash flow		$7.37			
3	Discount rate		0.11			
4	NPV		$0.00	(=NPV(C3,C2,C2,C2)-C1)		

Thus, a project that costs $18 and that has an after-tax cash flow of $7.37 for each of three years will, at a discount rate of 11 percent, result in an NPV of $0. (See the end-of-chapter Self-Study Problem for another application of the **Goal Seek** option in Excel.)

A word of caution regarding what-if analyses is in order: the basic approach looks at the *independent effects* of individual variables. In reality, variables included in the NPV model may be related to one another. That is, a change in one variable (e.g., variable costs) might be related to a change in another variable (e.g., fixed costs). The effect of such inter-relationships cannot be captured by the use of what-if analyses, which look only at the effects of changing one variable at a time. In short, there are technical limits as to how far you can take this type of sensitivity analysis.

Scenario analysis represents an attempt to look at how a proposed investment project would fare under different combinations of variables, called *scenarios;* a special form of sensitivity analysis that is appropriate when the variables in a decision model are interrelated.

Scenario Analysis

Decision makers may be interested in how their proposed investment would look under different combinations of variables, called *scenarios.* **Scenario analysis** is a form of sensitivity analysis that does just this: it looks at the profitability of a project (e.g., its indicated NPV) according to one or more plausible scenarios.

Typically, decision makers specify the expected outcomes of an investment project as the base case. The associated NPV of this project assumes a specific scenario, e.g., the market price of oil, whether the U.S. economy is in recession or expansion, the state of labor relations with a key supplier, and so forth.

One could construct a separate NPV analysis for each of several additional scenarios beyond the base case. It is common to label such scenarios with descriptive terms such as *disaster scenario* (i.e., worst-case scenario for related variables such as sales price, sales demand, and variable costs), *disappointing* (reflecting less-than-favorable values for related variables), and *optimistic* (reflecting greater-than-favorable values for a set of related variables). In generating these scenarios it is not uncommon for accountants to work with marketing managers and/or the V.P. of strategic planning of the company. These individuals should be most knowledgeable about possible macro-economic and uncontrollable factors that determine various scenarios. In short, scenario analysis allows managers to examine the effects of different scenarios represented as the joint effect of a set of related variables captured in the NPV model. These scenarios are developed through the use of a cross-functional team of individuals within the organization.

Monte Carlo Simulation[17]

As noted above, risk analysis of capital-budgeting projects using traditional spreadsheets is inherently limited. For example, scenario analysis yields only a single output value (e.g., expected NPV) for a set of inputs. Scenario analysis does not have the ability to measure an outcome's probability of occurrence, which is a key measure of risk within a modeled relationship.

Thus, risk analysis can be enhanced if managers are able to generate probabilities associated with alternative values of the outcome variable (e.g., NPV, IRR) in a capital-budgeting decision model. Spreadsheet add-ons, such as @RISK,[18] are able to generate such probability distributions, provided we are able to specify a probability distribution for each input variable in the decision model. The @RISK Excel add-on product specifies over 30 possible probability distributions (normal, uniform, binomial, triangular, etc.) that can be used to describe each input variable (such as project life or discount rate). The end result is that this process transforms what was previously a deterministic model (e.g., NPV or IRR) into a probabilistic model that can be analyzed through **Monte Carlo simulation.** Monte Carlo simulation is an extension to scenario analysis in which a computer provides a distribution of possible outcomes (for example, project NPVs) based on repeated sampling from a distribution associated with each input variable in a decision model.

Monte Carlo simulation
is an extension to scenario analysis in which a computer provides a distribution of possible outcomes, for example, project NPVs, based on repeated sampling from a distribution associated with each input variable in a decision model.

A capital-budgeting simulation computes the value of an outcome variable of interest (e.g., a project's NPV) many times over. Each time it simulates the project's NPV it draws a combination of input values (sales price per unit, variable cost per unit, sales volume, etc.) based on a prespecified probability distribution associated with each of these variables. Based on these inputs, an associated NPV is generated. In essence, the simulation allows the decision maker to substitute a probability distribution for the mean value of each input variable in a decision model. When the simulation is complete, for example after 10,000 iterations, a probability distribution of NPVs for a given investment proposal is generated. Associated output from the simulation includes the mean, maximum result, minimum result, standard deviation, skewness, and percentile probabilities. The latter are particularly important as they allow statements such as "Given the probability distributions of the variables in our capital-budgeting model, this investment proposal has a 48 percent probability of having a negative NPV and a 35 percent probability of having an NPV of at least $25,000."

Real Options[19]

The use of DCF models, such as NPV, is recommended as the preferred method of evaluating capital-budgeting proposals, as noted in the "International Good Practice" document cited in the Real-World Focus box presented on page 507. However, these models have an inherent assumption that may not comport with reality. That is, these models assume passive behavior

[17] This discussion draws on the following source: D. F. Togo, "Risk Analysis for Accounting Models: A Spreadsheet Simulation Approach," *Journal of Accounting Education* 22, no. 2 (2004), pp. 153–163.

[18] See www.palisade.com. A student version of the @RISK add-on for Excel is available at a reduced cost. Similar software, Crystal Ball, is available from Decisioneering (www.crystalball.com). An academic version of this software is available for student/faculty use.

[19] The material in this section is drawn from the following two sources: D. E. Stout, Y. A. Xie, and H. Qi, "Improving Capital Budgeting Decisions with Real Options," *Management Accounting Quarterly* 9, no. 4 (Summer 2008), pp. 1–10; and, D. E. Stout, H. Qi, Y. A. Xie, and S. Liu, "Incorporating Real Options into the Capital Budgeting Process: A Primer for Accounting Educators," *Journal of Accounting Education* 26 (2008), pp. 213–230.

As noted in the text, adjusting conventional DCF analysis of capital-budgeting proposals can be advantageous to the firm in terms of maximizing shareholder value. A related question is whether incorporating real options into net present value (NPV) analysis helps reduce the problem of "escalation of commitment." Escalation of commitment refers to the tendency of decision makers to continue to commit resources to a failing course of action—that is, negative feedback regarding an investment project that has been made. One type of real option that decision makers can consider is the "abandonment option" associated with a given investment proposal. In a laboratory (i.e., behavioral) study, Denison (2009) finds evidence that users of real options exhibit less escalation of commitment to a failing course of action than do users of NPV analysis alone. The author's study contributes to accounting practice by offering managers a way to improve firm performance by reducing escalation of commitment. Escalation of commitment is discussed later in the chapter as one of the primary behavioral issues associated with the capital-budgeting process.

Source: Christine A. Denison, "Real Options and Escalation of Commitment: A Behavioral Analysis of Capital Investment Decisions," *The Accounting Review* 84, no. 1 (January 2009), pp. 133–135.

Real options

represent flexibilities and/or growth opportunities embedded in capital-investment projects.

Real assets

represent investments in both tangible property (e.g., a manufacturing facility) and intangible property (e.g., a new information system).

on the part of management once an investment decision has been made. Alternatively, we can describe the traditional analysis as "take it or leave it." But in reality, some investment projects are dynamic in nature. They may contain one or more options for dealing with risk and uncertainty as new information (e.g., market conditions) is revealed over time. Management might expand a project in the future if things go well or it might scale back or abandon a project altogether if things are not going well. These opportunities are collectively referred to as **real options** (or options on **real assets**). In this context, real assets represent investments in both tangible property (e.g., a new manufacturing facility) and intangible property (e.g., a new information system). Traditional capital-budgeting decision models, such as DCF models, do not explicitly incorporate options on real assets that may be embedded in a proposed investment.

Real options are analogous to financial options—puts and calls. The latter gives the holder of the option the right, but not obligation, to purchase stock at a fixed price, called the *strike price* or *exercise price,* up to the expiration date of the option; the former gives the holder of the option the right, but not obligation, to sell stock for a fixed price on or before the exercise date of the option. These financial options have value and in fact are traded between investors on an organized exchange. Financial options have value precisely because they allow investors to capitalize on new information about a company that unfolds over time. In an analogous fashion, options on real assets have value because they allow decision makers to react to favorable or unfavorable new situations by dynamically adjusting the capital-budgeting decision. Unfortunately, conventional capital-budgeting decision models, such as DCF, do not incorporate into the valuation process the value of real options. Not explicitly including the value of embedded options effectively assigns any such options a value of zero.

There are four common types of real options: (1) the option to *expand* an investment (i.e., to make follow-on investments if the immediate investment project succeeds); (2) the option to *abandon* a project on the basis of new information revealed, over time, regarding states of nature that affect projected returns to the project; (3) the option to wait and learn before investing (i.e., the option to *delay* an investment–some refer to this as an investment-timing option), or (4) the option to *scale back* the magnitude of a project (e.g., by varying output or its production methods). Items (1) and (3) are analogous to call options, while items (2) and (4) are similar in nature to put options. We discuss the topic of real options in this section of the chapter because their inclusion in the capital-budgeting process provides an additional opportunity for dealing formally with risk and uncertainty. As we demonstrate with the following example, real options may change a project's expected cash flows and risk, and for this reason should be formally considered in the analysis of capital-investment projects.

Incorporating Real Options into the Capital-Budgeting Process

There are, in general, two approaches to incorporating real options into the analysis of long-term investment projects: the use of *scenario analysis combined with decision trees,* and the use of an *options-pricing model* (such as the Black-Scholes model). The following discussion illustrates the former approach. The latter approach is illustrated in selected finance texts, such as intermediate financial management.

For purposes of illustration, assume that XYZ Company is considering investing in the production of a new technology (e.g., hand-held communications device), the target market for which is young college graduates. The estimated investment cost for this project is $100 million. Demand for the product, and therefore the project's risk, is a function of the demand for wireless Internet connections "on-the-go." The CFO of XYZ, working with marketing, estimates a 25 percent chance that such demand will be high, 50 percent probability that demand will be medium, and 25 percent probability that demand will be low. Associated after-tax cash flows under each of these market scenarios are as follows: $70 million, $50 million, and $5 million. For projects of this nature, a 15 percent discount rate is assumed.

XYZ can make the investment today (time period 0), or it can delay the decision for one year. The advantage of the delay option is that over the coming year additional information regarding consumer demand for this project will be revealed. For simplicity, assume the same investment outlay cost ($100 million) and the same projected after-tax cash flows. The difference, however, is that if XYZ delays its investment by a year, the cash inflows will also be delayed (and therefore worth less in a present-value sense). Finally, assume (and this is a strong assumption) that if the project is delayed one year, the true level of consumer demand will be revealed with certainty (or near certainty). You can see that this investment-timing option is similar to a call option on a stock. In essence, management of XYZ needs to decide whether to defer the investment one year. If the company does delay the investment, then one year from now XYZ can exercise its option to invest in the project. Note, however, that it will choose to do this only if the expected NPV at $t = 0$ is positive. In this sense, the inclusion of real options complements a traditional DCF analysis of a proposed investment, as discussed earlier in this chapter.

Traditional (DCF) Analysis

Details regarding the proposed investment are provided in the decision tree depicted in Panel A of Exhibit 12.11. Each state of nature (level of demand in our example) in the tree is shown as a separate branch of the decision tree. The expected NPV of the project is defined as the weighted average of the three possible states of nature (outcomes), with the weights represented by the demand probabilities. Given an after-tax discount rate of 15 percent, the expected NPV of this investment is *negative* $0.109 million. Based on this conventional analysis, the project should not be undertaken: the project's expected rate of return is less than the weighted-average cost of capital (15 percent); as such, this project would not add to shareholder value.

Investment Analysis with Investment-Timing Option

As shown above, the expected NPV of the proposed investment is slightly negative. However, that analysis of the project failed to incorporate the value of the timing (or delay) option associated with the project. In reality, XYZ company has the option to delay, by one year, an investment in the project. This situation is analogous to having a call option on a stock. In this case, the company has the ability to "purchase" the investment next year, for the indicated price, based on the revealed level of consumer demand for the proposed product.

EXHIBIT 12.11
Decision Trees: Real Options Analysis (Investment-Timing Option)

Panel A: Expected NPV--Invest in Project Today ($t = 0$), amounts in $ millions

discount rate = 15.00%

Cash Outflow	Market Demand (Scenario)	probability	1	Cash Inflows 2	3	NPV of Scenario	Weighted NPV
$t = 0$	high	0.25	$70	$70	$70	$59.83	$14.956
$100	medium	0.50	$50	$50	$50	$14.16	$7.081
	low	0.25	$5	$5	$5	($88.58)	($22.146)
		1.00				Expected NPV =	($0.109)

Panel B: Expected NPV--Delay Investment by One Year, Only if NPV is increased, amounts in $ millions

discount rate = 15.00%
risk-free rate = 5.00%
cash outflow one year from the present (?) = $100

	Market Demand (Scenario)	probability	1	Cash Flows 2	3	4	PV of Cash Outflows*	PV of Cash Inflows**	Weighted NPV @ $t = 0$
	high	0.25	($100.00)	$70	$70	$70	($95.24)	$138.98	$10.935
	medium	0.50	($100.00)	$50	$50	$50	($95.24)	$99.27	$2.016
	low	0.25	$0.00	$0	$0	$0	$0.00	$0.00	$0.000
		1.00						Expected NPV =	$12.951

*discounted at risk-free rate of interest
**discounted at weighted-average cost of capital

The essence of the approach is to estimate, as before, the NPV (at $t = 0$) of the proposed investment. What is different, however, is that the planning horizon must now be extended to four periods. Also, **in the determination of the weighted-average NPV of the project, we include only those individual scenarios that have a positive NPV.** For example, if the NPV of any scenario at $t = 1$ is negative, then this scenario is not included in the computation of the weighted-average return on the project. This is precisely because at $t = 1$ the company is assumed to possess revealed information regarding the level of consumer demand. If, for example, it is revealed at $t = 1$ that demand is going to be low, then XYZ would not be forced to exercise its option to purchase the investment. On the other hand, if at $t = 1$ the revealed level of consumer demand is high, then most likely the NPV of this scenario, at $t = 1$, would be positive. As such this scenario is included in the computation of the expected value of the proposed investment. Note, however, that in order to be able to compare our NPV analysis with the conventional approach (Panel A of Exhibit 12.11) we must bring all future cash flows (both inflows and outflows) back to time period 0. Because we assume that the investment outlay cost of $1 million is known with certainty (or near certainty), it would be appropriate to use the risk-free rate of return to discount this amount to present value at $t = 0$. For the current example, we assume that the risk-free rate of return is 5 percent. All of the information pertaining to the investment-timing option analysis is presented in Panel B of Exhibit 12.11.

We see from Panel B that at $t = 1$, XYZ Company would invest in the project *only if* the revealed level of demand was either high or medium. If the company invests (at $t = 1$) in the project, then it will spend $100 million and will expect to receive either $70 million or $50 million in cash inflows for each of three years. If consumer demand turns out to be low, then no investment is made at $t = 1$. Thus, given the probabilities for the three specified levels of demand, we can proceed to calculate the weighted present value of each scenario (see cells J20:J22 in Exhibit 12.11) and finally the weighted-average NPV of the project. As shown in cell J23, this value is $12.95 million, an amount considerably higher than indicated in the conventional NPV analysis presented in Panel A of Exhibit 12.11. In short, the project's expected NPV is considerably higher after considering the existence of the investment-timing option. As indicated earlier in the chapter, the decision maker normally would, as part of the evaluation of a proposed investment, conduct a sensitivity analysis on the inputs to the decision model. This issue is pursued in Exercise 12-51.

Finally, we note that the same approach as discussed above, and revealed in Exhibit 12.11, can be used to deal with other types of real options. Exercise 12-52 provides an alternative example of a real option embedded in a proposed investment. The approach, however, is basically the same as that illustrated above. A decision tree can be used to represent various scenarios or states of nature (e.g., levels of consumer demand). The NPV of the proposed project can first be determined using the conventional approach and then again after incorporating the effect of the real option. The decision, from a purely financial standpoint, is a function of the NPVs of the decision alternatives. Just remember that these NPVs, for comparability purposes, are calculated at $t = 0$.

Determinants of the Value of Real Options

As members of the decision-making team that evaluates capital-budgeting proposals, accountants should have some knowledge of the drivers or determinants of value for real options. In effect, the same factors that affect the value of financial options also affect the inherent value of real options. In this regard, we offer the following three comments:

1. *Ceteris paribus,* the value of a real option is higher if the value of the underlying asset is high relative to the exercise price of the option (for XYZ, an estimate of the value of the asset is $99.89 million, while the exercise price of the project is $100 million).
2. The farther away the expiration date is, the higher the value of an option is. (The one-year expiration period in the case of XYZ is probably considered long.)
3. Perhaps most important, the value of an option increases as the risk of the project increases. (In the case of XYZ, the value of the delay option increases as the volatility of project returns increases. In essence, when project returns are considered risky, there is greater value in delaying the decision until consumer demand levels are revealed, or at least better revealed. The delay option available to XYZ therefore provides value to the company in terms of dealing with project risk.)

REAL-WORLD FOCUS — Motivating the Study of "Real Options"

Accountants worldwide interested in obtaining certification in management accounting from the Institute of Management Accountants (IMA) must pass the Certified Management Accounting (CMA) exam. Part three of this exam ("Strategic Management") contains the following learning objectives related to the topic of real options: (1) demonstrate an understanding of the concept of real options in the capital-budgeting process; (2) identify four common types of real options; (3) classify each of these real options as either a "put" or a "call" option; and, (4) demonstrate an understanding of the variables and factors that affect the value of options. Recently, the Professional Accountants in Business Committee of the International Federation of Accountants (IFAC, 2008) had this to say (p. 15) about the topic of real options: "Real options analysis is an emerging and evolving area of practice in valuation and investment appraisal; it can be seen as an extension of DCF analysis. . .to accommodate real-life scenarios in which cash flows often depend on decisions that will only be made after resolving uncertainties. . ." Further, this document indicates (p. 24) that "real options. . . should be considered as part of an evolutionary process to improve the valuation of investments and the allocation of capital." In short, the study of real options is important for the training of future accounting professionals worldwide.

Sources: Professional Accountants in Business committee, International Federation of Accountants (IFAC), *International Good Practice guidance: Project Appraisal Using Discounted Cash Flow* (New York: IFAC, June 2008; Institute of Management Accountants (IMA), *Certified Management Accountant* (CMA) *Learning Outcome Statements,* effective July 1, 2004, updated July 2008, and available at www.imanet.org.

Other Capital-Budgeting Decision Models

LEARNING OBJECTIVE 6

Discuss and apply other capital-budgeting decision models.

The **payback period** of an investment is the length of time required for the cumulative after-tax cash inflows from an investment to recover the initial investment outlay.

Payback Period

The **payback period** of an investment is the length of time required for the cumulative after-tax cash inflows from an investment to recover the initial investment outlay. At that point the investor has recovered the amount of money invested in the project, hence the term *payback period.*

Determining the Payback Period with Uniform Annual Cash Inflows

For an investment that provides uniform future after-tax cash inflows, the payback period (in years) can be determined as follows:

Payback period = Total initial capital investment/Annual after-tax cash inflows

For example, assume an initial capital-investment outlay (year 0) of $1,110,000. This project is projected to have a four-year life. Each year, the investment is expected to provide an after-tax cash inflow of $387,000. Based on this information, the project has a payback period of 2.87 years (i.e., $1,110,000/$387,000).

Determining the Payback Period with Uneven Cash Inflows (Mendoza Company example)

Refer back to Exhibit 12.3, which contains cash-flow information regarding the equipment-replacement decision facing the Mendoza Company. With uneven cash inflows, as is the case here, the payback period is defined as the number of years it takes for the *cumulative* after-tax cash inflows to equal the initial investment outlay ($590,000). The necessary analysis is presented in Exhibit 12.12.

EXHIBIT 12.12

Payback Period Calculation for the Mendoza Company example

(1) Year	(2) After-Tax Cash Flows (Exhibit 12.3)	(3) Cumulative After-Tax Net Cash Flows
0	($590,000)	($590,000)
1	$178,000	($412,000)
2	208,000	($204,000)
3	208,000	$4000
4	321,000	

The amount needed in year 3 to reach the payback period is $204,000; under the assumption that the after-tax cash inflows in year 3 occur evenly throughout the year, the payback period is 2 + ($204,000/$208,000) years = 2.98 years. If we assume, as is the case when we calculate a project's NPV or IRR, that the cash inflows occur at year-end, then the payback period for this project would be 3 years.

Evaluation of the Payback Period Model

Advantages The principal advantage of the payback period model is that, once cash-flow data have been collected, the payback period is easy to compute and comprehend. Business-people, particularly owners of small businesses, seem to have an intuitive understanding of payback periods.

The length of payback period can serve as a rough measure of the risk associated with a proposed investment. The longer the payback period, the more risky the project is. The underlying logic is that the farther out into the future the payback period is, the more uncertainty associated with the future cash flows. For example, the longer it takes to recover the original investment, the more likely it is that the underlying product or service will become obsolete or attract competition, making it more difficult to earn cash flows as projected.

Limitations The use of payback period information for investment decision making is subject to four primary limitations:

1. *The model fails to consider returns over the entire life of the investment.* That is, the payback model considers cash inflows from the initiation of the project until its payback period but ignores cash flows after the payback period.

2. *The payback period, in its unadjusted state, ignores the time value of money.* It considers only the length of time required to recover the investment regardless of differences in the timing or pattern of cash flows. For example, as long as the payback period for each of two projects is the same, the model considers them equally desirable. This is the case even if one project generates most of its cash inflows in the early years of its payback period while the other project generates most of its cash inflows in the latter years of its payback period.

3. *The decision criterion for accepting/rejecting a project is not well defined; that is, it is subjective.* This situation can be compared to the two DCF decision models we discussed earlier in this chapter. For the NPV model, the decision rule was: accept a project if its NPV is greater than 0; for the IRR model, the decision rule was: accept a project if its IRR is greater than WACC (or otherwise specified hurdle rate).

4. *Use of the model may encourage excessive investment in short-term projects, at the expense of investments critical to long-term success.* Some investments needed to secure competitive advantage—such as an investment in computer-integrated manufacturing (CIM)—can take many years to recover the original investment. A company that fails to make such strategic investments may not be competitive in the long run.

Present Value (or, Discounted) Payback Period

The **present value payback period** of an investment is the length of time required for the cumulative *present value* of after-tax cash inflows to recover the initial investment outlay.

To avoid the second criticism listed above, some companies use the present value of future cash inflows to determine the investment's payback period. Because discounted cash flows are used, the resulting payback period is referred to as the **present value payback period.** As with the NPV model, the present value of future after-tax cash inflows from an investment is estimated using the firm's WACC (or otherwise specified "hurdle rate").

As shown in Exhibit 12.13, the present value payback period for the equipment-replacement investment by the Mendoza Company is approximately 3.5 years. As noted above, the unadjusted (i.e., non-discounted) payback period is approximately 3 years.

Because it considers the time value of money, the present value payback model is considered superior to the unadjusted payback period model. Because it relies on the use of discounted cash inflows, this version of the payback model has an important implication: *if the discounted payback period is less than the life of the project, then the project must have a positive NPV.* This result holds because the cash inflows that accrue up to the discounted payback period are,

EXHIBIT 12.13
Present Value Payback Period
for the Mendoza Company
Investment Proposal

Year	After-Tax Cash Flow	Discount Factor @ 10%	PV of After-Tax Cash Flow	Cumulative PV of After-Tax Cash Flows
0	$(590,000)	1.000	$(590,000)	$(590,000)
1	178,000	0.909	161,802	(428,198)
2	208,000	0.826	171,808	(256,390)
3	208,000	0.751	156,208	(100,182)
4	321,000	0.683	219,243	

Note: Amount needed in year 4 to reach the payback period = $100,182; under the assumption that the after-tax inflows in year 4 occur evenly throughout the year, the discounted payback period = 3 + ($100,182/$219,243) years = 3.46 years. If we assume, as is the case when we calculate a project's NPV or IRR, that the cash flows occur at year-end, then the discounted payback period for this example would be 4 years.

by definition, just sufficient (in a present-value sense) to cover the initial investment outlay; any cash inflows that come after the cut-off period will ensure a positive NPV for the project.

However, the discounted payback model suffers the same weaknesses of the unadjusted payback model in other respects: use of the model for capital-budgeting decision making can motivate excessive investments in short-term projects; the model ignores investment returns beyond the (discounted) payback period; and the decision criterion under this model is not set objectively, that is, the cut-off period for determining project acceptance is set by trial and error. The second limitation is particularly important since it may lead managers to incorrectly reject some positive NPV investment opportunities.

Accounting (Book) Rate of Return

The **accounting (book) rate of return (ARR)** on a project is equal to some measure of accounting profit to some measure of investment in the project. One specification of the ARR is:

The **accounting (book) rate of
return (ARR)**
of a project is equal to some
measure of accounting profit to
some measure of investment in
the project.

ARR = Average annual net operating income/Average investment

Be aware that there are differences in practice regarding how both the numerator and the denominator for the ARR are defined. That is, there is more than a single way to calculate the ARR of an investment.

One way to define the denominator of the ARR is to take a simple average of the book value of the investment at the beginning and at the end of the project's life and to add to this amount the average incremental investment in working capital net of the after-tax cash flow received in year 0 from the sale of the existing asset.

Refer back to Exhibit 12.3 for financial information regarding the equipment-replacement decision for the Mendoza Company. In this case, the average book value of the proposed investment can be calculated as follows:

Book value of asset at beginning of project's life = Net cost of new asset = $480,000

Book value of asset at end of project's life = $0

Average book value over life of project = ($480,000 + $0)/2 = $240,000

Average incremental investment in working capital, net of the after-tax proceeds from the sale of the existing asset in year 0, equals $110,000 (i.e., $200,000 − $90,000). What this means is that for each year of the life of this project, there is a required incremental investment in net working capital of $110,000. Thus, one estimate of the average book value of the investment for the Mendoza project is $350,000 ($240,000 + $110,000).

The proposed investment for the Mendoza Company is expected to earn an average annual net-of-tax operating income of $80,500, as follows:

Year	Operating Income After-Tax
1	$58,000
2	88,000
3	88,000
4	88,000
Average	80,500

Thus, when the denominator of the calculation is defined as *average investment,* the proposed project's ARR is 23.0 percent ($80,500/$350,000). This result means that, on average, the proposed project returns approximately 23 cents of after-tax operating profit per year for each dollar associated with the investment.

Note, however, that some companies define the denominator of the ARR as the original (i.e., gross) book value of the investment. Again, there are different ways to define this number. One approach is to use the net initial cash outflow (year 0) associated with the investment project. If the ARR is calculated based on this measure ($590,000), the calculated ARR for the proposed project would be 13.6 percent.

Evaluation of the Accounting (Book) Rate of Return Model

Advantages To a large extent, the ARR model uses the same kind of data routinely generated for financial reporting purposes. For this reason, the ratio is called the *accounting rate of return.* As indicated in Chapter 19, accounting rate of return measures are used by many companies to evaluate the financial performance of operating divisions and managers. Thus, the use of ARR for capital-budgeting purposes would be consistent with the way subsequent financial performance is typically measured.

The ARR has an additional advantage over the payback period model in that it looks at financial returns (e.g., increases in after-tax operating income) over the entire life of a project.

Limitations As with the payback period model, the ARR decision model ignores the time value of money. Another limitation pertains to the use of accounting numbers in the numerator and denominator. While such numbers are useful for financial reporting purposes, financial theory tells us that cash-flow information is preferable for making capital-budgeting decisions. In essence, the use of DCF decision models aligns internal decision making with the process that, in theory, investors use in valuing stocks in the financial marketplace.

As indicated above, there are multiple ways to define both the numerator and the denominator in the ARR calculation. For example, one possibility is to define the denominator simply as the net cost of the asset acquired ($480,000 in the case of the Mendoza Company). While simplifying the calculation (i.e., average investment would now be defined as ($480,000 + $0)/2 = $240,000), this approach ignores the fact that the proposed project required a commitment of net working capital during the life of the project. It also would ignore the fact that the initial investment outlay was reduced by the after-tax proceeds ($90,000) from the sale of the existing asset. In short, there is no universally accepted practice as to how the components of ARR are measured. At a minimum, this leads to comparability problems across companies and potentially within divisions of the same company.

Finally, as with the case of the payback model (and, for that matter, the discounted payback model as well), there is no objectively defined decision criterion for making project acceptance decisions. What is an acceptable ARR? Any such response is determined heuristically (i.e., subjectively, using rules of thumb).

Behavioral Issues in Capital Budgeting

LEARNING OBJECTIVE 7

Identify behavioral issues associated with the capital-budgeting process.

To this point, we have dealt mainly with technical issues associated with the capital-budgeting process. It is worth noting that the success of this process is affected by a number of behavioral considerations, as discussed below.

Common Behavioral Problems: Cost Escalation, Incrementalism, and Uncertainty Intolerance

Studies have found that escalating commitment is common in the capital-budgeting process. In an attempt to recoup past losses, a decision maker may consider past costs or losses as relevant in making capital-budgeting decisions. For example, elimination or reduction of losses from past investments may, erroneously, be included as savings associated with a proposed investment. As indicated in Chapter 11, such amounts do not meet the test of information relevancy and as such should not be included in formal decision models, such as those used for analyzing

A manufacturer of telecommunications devices is about to review proposals for investment to increase its manufacturing capacity for manufacturing one of its key components. In the past, the proposals vary in the level of technology and the degree of computer integration required for manufacturing process. So far, the firm has minimal experience with advanced manufacturing technology and is using semiautomated machines in key parts of its manufacturing process of the components. Over the last several years, company executives have been conscious of the growing competitive pressures that may eventually require investment in advanced manufacturing technology. As a result the firm has been actively seeking out such investment proposals. Many proposals had been reviewed in the last few years. However, no proposals have ever passed the review stage. "The numbers just don't support it," according to one member of the review committee, who has been a staunch advocate of advanced manufacturing technologies.

The firm evaluates all major investment proposals using the net present value method with the estimated long-term (five years) cost of capital as the discount rate. In addition, the firm also uses the payback method in its analysis of investment proposals. However, a short payback period is not necessary to justify investment in a project if the project is considered to be among the best in terms of investment proposals. A review of the proposals submitted over the last few years revealed that these proposals ranked consistently higher based upon the net present value method.

You believe that it is critically important for the long-term profitability of the firm to acquire new advanced manufacturing technology. You are of the opinion that the firm will lose its competitive edge, or may not even survive, if it fails to respond to this demand. As the manager of the manufacturing process, who has submitted several unsuccessful proposals for investment in advanced manufacturing technologies, how would you modify your proposal?

(Refer to Comments on Cost Management in Action at end of Chapter.)

capital-investment projects. Research suggests that escalating commitments are more likely to occur when current managers are the ones responsible for the negative results of past actions.[20]

Needed capital investments may not be pursued because of the amount of time and work required to secure their approval. Projects that cost less than those that must be approved as a capital investment are undertaken instead. As a result, managers may choose to invest in multiple small additions that require no approval from above, rather than investing in a major capital project such as computer-integrated manufacturing (CIM) or a flexible manufacturing system (FMS) that would vastly improve the firm's competitive position. Failure to make necessary capital investments can reduce the firm's competitiveness, erode its market share, and jeopardize its long-term profitability and survival.

Intolerance of uncertainty may lead managers to require short payback periods for capital investments. Once a project pays for itself, the amount of risk is substantially reduced. This makes projects with short payback periods the preferred choice to some decision makers. However, many capital investments of strategic import do not have short payback periods. These projects may require a lengthy time to install, test, adjust, train personnel, and gain market acceptance; examples include investments in new manufacturing technologies, new product development, and expansion into new territories. Requiring too short a payback period makes the acceptance of such projects unlikely, even if the firm would enjoy long-term benefits from these projects.

Goal-Congruency Issues

Perhaps the greatest behavioral challenge in capital budgeting relates to the need to align DCF decision models (such as NPV) with models used to evaluate subsequent financial performance. Typically, accrual-based measures of profitability, such as return on investment (ROI), are used to evaluate financial performance of managers and organizational subunits. As the following example shows, managers may not be motivated to make decisions that are in the best interest of the organization when NPV is used for decision making but accrual accounting income numbers are used subsequently for performance-evaluation purposes.

Assume an investment outlay of $12,000 today that will generate, for each of three years, an increase in cash contribution margin (CM) of $5,000. Further, assume no income taxes, a three-year depreciation period for the investment, zero salvage value, and the use of straight-line depreciation. Finally, assume that the financial performance of the manager and subunit is evaluated each year using accounting rate of return (ROI), defined as operating income

[20] G. Whyte, "Escalating Commitment to a Course of Action: A Reinterpretation," *Academy of Management Review,* 1986, pp. 311–321.

divided by beginning-of-year (B-O-Y) book value of the asset. Given these assumptions, the following rates of return would be anticipated:

Item	Year 1	Year 2	Year 3
Cash CM	$ 5,000	$5,000	$5,000
Less: Depreciation	$ 4,000	$4,000	$4,000
Operating income	$ 1,000	$1,000	$1,000
NBV of asset (B-O-Y)	$12,000	$8,000	$4,000
ROI (accounting rate of return)	8.33%	12.50%	25.00%

Assuming a discount rate of 11.0 percent, this project has a projected NPV of $218.57 (details omitted) and therefore should be accepted.

The issue, however, is whether a rational decision-maker/manager would be motivated to accept the investment given the projected accounting rates of return over the coming three years. If compensation is tied to reported ROI, there may be a disincentive to invest, in spite of the fact that accepting the project would be consistent with adding shareholder value. This disincentive would be stronger:

- If the individual were likely to be transferred out of the division (job advancement, retirement, etc.).
- If the project life is long (wherein the cash flow benefits are not realized until later in the project's life).
- If the discount rate is high.
- If the disposal of any existing assets would result in a reported loss (which would, in turn, reduce reported ROI in year 1).
- If accelerated depreciation methods are used for accounting purposes.

Addressing the Goal-Congruency Problem

The preceding example illustrates a pervasive problem in control system design: conflicts can arise when DCF-based models are used for decision-making purposes and accrual-based accounting income numbers are used subsequently for evaluating the financial performance of managers and organizational subunits. Top management cannot expect goal congruence under these conditions. Unfortunately, such conditions tend to characterize existing business practice.

What can organizations do, then, to better align the goals of decision makers with the goals of the overall organization? To a large extent, this issue is one of the unsolved problems in control system design. An extended discussion of these issues is presented in Chapter 19. Within the context of capital budgeting, however, three possible solutions are offered.

Economic Value Added (EVA®)

Economic Value Added (EVA®)
is a measure of financial performance designed to approximate an entity's economic profit; calculated most often as net operating profit after taxes (adjusted for accounting "distortions") less an imputed charge based on the level of invested capital.

As will be discussed more fully in Chapter 19, **Economic Value Added (EVA®)** is a financial-performance indicator that includes a charge for use of invested capital. That is, *economic profitability* is not indicated until the organization generates sufficient cash flow to cover *all* expenses, including an imputed charge for capital invested in the business. As such, both NPV and EVA® assume that shareholder value is created only when projects recover their capital costs. Thus, the use of EVA® for evaluation of financial performance is one way to avoid the behavioral conflict noted above.

Separating Incentive Compensation from Budgeted Performance

In Chapter 10 we discussed some of the negative incentive effects of traditional budgeting systems, including those where an annual fixed-performance contract is used to determine compensation.[21] Budgeted performance, against which actual performance (income earned, ROI, etc.), is

[21] See Michael C. Jensen, "Corporate Budgeting Is Broken—Let's Fix It," *Harvard Business Review* (November 2001), pp. 94–101.

reflected in the master budgeting process and set of pro forma financial statements produced as a result of that process. Among other things, linking managerial reward to a comparison between budgeted and actual performance penalizes managers for factors that emerge during the year that are beyond their control (general price-level changes, changes in worldwide demand for and pricing of oil, etc.). It simultaneously rewards such managers for market (or industrywide) positive results. Further, linking compensation to budgeted performance encourages dysfunctional, perhaps even unethical, behaviors as managers game the performance indicator in order to make budget. As we discussed in Chapter 10, some commentators feel that relative performance indicators are superior to the fixed-performance model described above. In such a case, actual financial performance for a subunit or manager is compared to some internal or external benchmark for the purpose of determining incentive rewards and executive compensation. As such, greater degrees of goal congruence are expected to be realized.

Post-Audit

Another way to achieve goal congruence in terms of the capital-budgeting process is to forgo in the evaluation process the use of accrual-based accounting income numbers altogether. Rather, top management might focus on, or at least give considerable weight to, a post-decision comparison between forecasted and realized amounts for a given investment project. As indicated earlier in this chapter, such a comparison is referred to as a *post-audit*. The principal benefit of post-audits is the collection, for performance-evaluation purposes, of the same cash inflow and outflow information used for investment decision-making purposes (e.g., NPV). In turn, this should eliminate disincentives associated with the use of different models for decision making and assessment of subsequent financial performance.

Summary

Capital-budgeting decisions represent long-term commitments of substantial amounts of resources. As such, these decisions are of strategic concern to organizations; in a very real sense these decisions affect financial results (returns) of organizations for many years into the future.

As indicated in Chapter 10, the capital budget (i.e., the allocation of capital to long-term investment projects) is a key component of an organization's overall planning system, referred to as its *master budget*. Recent advances in the field of cost management, including the balanced scorecard (BSC) and the analytic hierarchy process (AHP), can be used to help align capital investments with an organization's strategy.

Accountants can add value to the capital-budgeting process of an organization in at least three ways: (1) development of relevant financial (i.e., cash flow) and nonfinancial information for decision making; (2) the design of an effective post-audit mechanism; and (3) educating small-business owners on the value and conceptual superiority of discounted cash flow (DCF) decision models. Alternative templates for structuring a DCF analysis are presented in Appendix A.

In general, managers can optimize an organization's capital budget by using the net present value (NPV) decision model, which compares the present value of cash inflows to the present value of cash outflows. Typically, the discount rate used in DCF models is the organization's weighted-average cost of capital (WACC).

Cash outflows from investments can occur at three points: (1) *project initiation*—to acquire the investment and begin operations, to provide needed net working capital for the project, and to dispose of any replaced or discarded assets; (2) *project operation*—to cover operating expenditures, any additional investments, and additional net working capital; and (3) *project disposal*—to dispose of the investment, to restore facilities, and to provide training or relocation benefits for personnel whose positions have been terminated. An investment generates net cash inflows during its existence through increases in revenues or decreases in expenses, through recovery of its investment in net working capital, and from the disposal of assets. For a profit-seeking organization, all such cash flows should be stated on an after-tax basis.

Exhibit 12.14 summarizes the definitions, computation procedures, advantages, and weaknesses of the various capital-budgeting decision models covered in the chapter. Some advanced considerations in using DCF models for the analysis of capital investments are presented in Appendix B to this chapter.

EXHIBIT 12.14 Capital Investment Decision Models

Model	Definition	Computation Procedure	Advantages	Disadvantages
Payback period	Number of years to recover the initial investment	*Uniform flow:* Investment *divided by* net cash flow *Uneven flow:* Number of years for the cumulative cash inflow to equal the initial investment	1. Simple to use and understand 2. Focuses on liquidity 3. Rough measure of risk	1. Ignores timing and time value of money 2. Ignores cash flows beyond payback period 3. Decision rule = "rule of thumb"
Accounting (book) rate of return (ARR)	Ratio of average annual net income to the initial (or average) investment (book value)	Average net income *divided by* investment book value	1. Data are readily available 2. Consistent with other financial measures	1. Ignores timing and time value of money 2. Uses accounting numbers, not after-tax cash flows
Net present value (NPV)	Difference between present value (PV) of cash inflows and PV of cash outflows	PV of after-tax cash inflows − PV of cash outflows	1. Considers the time value of money 2. Focuses on after-tax cash flows 3. Consistent with goal of maximizing shareholder value	1. Can possibly lead to suboptimal capital budgeting under condition of capital rationing
Internal rate of return (IRR)	Discount rate that makes PV of cash inflows equal PV of cash outflows	For uniform cash inflows—solving for i in the following equation: PV annuity factor for $i \times$ Annual after-tax cash inflow = Initial investment	1. Considers time value of money 2. Focuses on after-tax cash flows 3. Ratios are intuitively appealing to managers	1. Inherent assumption regarding reinvestment rate could be unrealistic 2. Complex to compute if done manually 3. May not lead to optimum capital budget
Modified internal rate of return (MIRR)	Discount rate that makes the PV of cash inflows equal to the PV of cash outflows, under the assumption that interim cash inflows are reinvested at a specified rate	Rate at which: PV costs = PV terminal value, where the left-hand term is the PV of outlays, discounted at the WACC, and the numerator of the right-hand term is the compounded future vale of the interim cash inflows, reinvested at the WACC, and the denominator is $(1 + MIRR)^n$, where n = number of periods.	1. Considers the time value of money 2. Focuses on after-tax cash flows 3. Ratios are intuitively appealing to managers 4. Avoids overly optimistic rates of return associated with the use of IRR	1. Complex to compute, if done manually 2. May not lead to optimum capital budget 3. Discrepancy as to whether there is a reinvestment rate assumption inherent in the IRR calculation
Profitability index (PI) (see Appendix B)	Ratio of PV of cash inflows (or, NPV) to initial investment	PV of after-tax cash inflows (or NPV) *divided by* initial investment	1. Considers time value of money 2. Focuses on after-tax cash flows 3. Useful under conditions of capital rationing	1. When capital budget is not limited, use could lead to suboptimal capital budget

The determination of a project's NPV requires the use of forecasts and assumptions. Sensitivity analysis can be used to determine how sensitive the capital-budgeting decision is with respect to these assumptions. The chapter presents three examples of sensitivity analysis: what-if analysis, scenario analysis, and Monte Carlo simulation analysis. An alternative approach to dealing with the problem of risk and uncertainty is to incorporate the existence of real options that may be embedded in a capital-investment project.

Finally, managers need to understand that the capital-budgeting process is affected by a number of important behavioral considerations. Foremost among these considerations is the conflict that arises from using DCF models for investment decision making but accrual accounting numbers (such as ROI) for subsequent appraisal of financial performance, and also from incentive conflicts associated with the use of fixed-performance contracts. The use of EVA® for performance appraisal, the use of relative performance for compensation and reward, and the use of post-audits may help reduce this conflict and achieve greater congruency between the goals of decision makers and the goals of the organization as a whole.

Appendix A

LEARNING OBJECTIVE 8
Understand alternative templates for setting up a DCF analysis

Spreadsheet Templates for Conducting a DCF Analysis

The following data, related to the equipment-replacement decision facing the Mendoza Company, are used in the three templates included in this appendix.

	A	B	C	D	E	F	G
1	**Input Data (from Exhibit 12-3)**						
2	Discount rate (WACC) =				10.00%		
3	Combined income tax rate =				40.00%		
4	Net cost of new equipment, year 0 =				$480,000		
5	Useful life of asset (in years) =				4		
6	Estimated salvage value, Yr. 4 =				$0		
7	After-tax proceeds, sale of old machine (Yr. 0) =				$90,000		
8	One-time employee training costs, Yr. 1 =				$50,000		
9	Incremental working capital required, Yr. 1 =				$200,000		
10	Return of working capital, Yr. 4 =				$200,000		
11	After-tax proceeds, sale of machine (Yr. 4) =				$3,000		
12	After-tax employee relocation costs (Yr. 4) =				$90,000		
13	Incremental cash revenues, per year =				$1,000,000		
14	Incremental cash operating costs, per year =				$733,333		
15	Recurring after-tax operating cash flows, years 1 - 4:						
16				Year	Cash Revenues	Recurring Cash Expenses	Pre-tax Operating Cash Flows	Operating Cash Flows, After Tax
17				1	$1,000,000	$733,333	$266,667	$160,000
18				2	$1,000,000	$733,333	$266,667	$160,000
19				3	$1,000,000	$733,333	$266,667	$160,000
20				4	$1,000,000	$733,333	$266,667	$160,000
21	Annual depreciation charges (SL basis):						
22				Year	Depreciation Expense	Income Tax Rate, t	Depreciation tax shield	
23				1	$120,000	40.00%	$48,000	
24				2	$120,000	40.00%	$48,000	
25				3	$120,000	40.00%	$48,000	
26				4	$120,000	40.00%	$48,000	

Panel A (below) contains the first of two alternative templates that can be used in conjunction with what we call the *differential approach* to a decision analysis. The 10 percent discount factors shown in cells L30:L33 were calculated using the following formula: factor $= 1/(1 + 0.10)^i$, where i represents year (1, 2, 3, 4). (Note: all numbers in cells I31 through I37 were determined using actual discount factors from cells L30 through L34, not the rounded values shown in column H.)

	A	B	C	D	E	F	G	H	I	J	K	L
27	Panel A: DCF Analysis--Differential Approach #1											
28						Amount	Year(s)	PV Factor (@ WACC)	PV of Cash Flows			
29	After-tax Cash Inflows:										Discount Factors, 10%	
30		PV of annual after-tax operating cash flow:									Year 1 =	0.909091
31			Recurring operating cash flows after taxes			$160,000	1-4	3.16987	$507,179		Year 2 =	0.826446
32			One-time emplyee training costs, after taxes			$30,000	1	0.9091	($27,273)		Year 3 =	0.751315
33			Depreciation tax shield =			$48,000	1-4	3.16987	$152,154		Year 4 =	0.683013
34		PV of terminal value:									Annuity =	3.169865
35			Working capital returned =			$200,000	4	0.6830	$136,603			
36			After-tax proceeds, sale of machine =			$3,000	4	0.6830	$2,049			
37			After-tax employee relocation expenses =			$90,000	4	0.6830	($61,471)			
38	Net Investment:											
39		Net cost of new equipment, Yr. 0 =				$480,000	0	1.0000	($480,000)			
40		After-tax salvage value, old equipment (Yr. 0) =				$90,000	0	1.0000	$90,000			
41		Increase in working capital, Yr. 0 =				$200,000	0	1.0000	($200,000)			
42						$590,000		NPV =	$119,240			

Panel B (below) contains an alternative format for the "differential approach" to structuring a decision analysis. Note that the PV factors in line 64 are copied from cells L30:L33. Note also that the estimated NPV of the project (cell F68) is exactly the same as the amount contained in Panel A (cell I42).

	A	B	C	D	E	F	G	H	I
43	Panel B: DCF Analysis--Differential Approach #2								
44		Discount Rate (WACC) =			10.00%				
45							Year		
46					0	1	2	3	4
47	I. Net Cash Flow at Time Investment is Made								
48		Net cost of new equipment			$480,000				
49		Increase in working capital required			$200,000				
50		After-tax salvage value of existing asset			$90,000				
51				Total	$590,000				
52	II. Operating Cash Flows Over Life of the Asset:								
53		One-time cash outlay, after tax				$30,000			
54		Annual net operating cash flows, after tax				$160,000	$160,000	$160,000	$160,000
55		Annual depreciation tax shield				$48,000	$48,000	$48,000	$48,000
56				Totals		$178,000	$208,000	$208,000	$208,000
57	III. Terminal (end of investment) After-tax Cash Flows:								
58		Working capital returned							$200,000
59		After-tax salvage value of asset							$3,000
60		Additional end-of-investment costs, after tax							$90,000
61				Total					$113,000
62	IV. Net Cash Flow per Year				($590,000)	$178,000	$208,000	$208,000	$321,000
63	V. NPV Determination:								
64			PV factors		1.000000	0.909091	0.826446	0.751315	0.683013
65									
66			PV of After-tax Cash Flows =			$709,240			
67			Net Investment Outlay =			$590,000			
68			NPV =			$119,240			
69	VI. IRR Estimation:								
70			IRR =			18.2%			

Finally, in Panel C (below) we present an alternative approach to structuring a decision analysis, viz., the total approach. (As you can see, to implement this approach we had to add the assumed data contained in cells A73:G87.) As explained in Chapter 11, in this approach we include total revenues and costs (or, cash inflows and cash outflows) under each of the decision alternatives, regardless of whether a given item is relevant to the decision. It is for this reason that we refer to this as the *total approach*. Note that, if properly constructed, the estimated NPV of the proposed investment should be exactly the same as the NPV contained in Panels A and B. This demonstrates the point made in the chapter that which of these templates you use (if any) is a matter of personal choice: they should all lead to the same decision (in this case, the company should purchase the new equipment because to do so increases shareholder value).

72	Panel C: Analysis of Equipment-Replacement Decision--Total Approach						
73	Additional *Assumptions* --Existing Machine:						
74		Annual cash revenues		$3,000,000				
75		Annual cash operating costs, pre-tax		$2,750,000				
76		Current NBV of existing machine		$120,000				
77		Remaining depreciable life of exisiting machine		4				
78		Salvage value estimate for deprec. Calculation		$0				
79				Existing Machine	New Machine			
80		Annual cash revenues		$3,000,000	$4,000,000			
81		Less: Annual cash operating costs, pre-tax		$2,750,000	$3,483,333			
82		Less: Depreciation expense, SL basis		$30,000	$150,000	(note that total depreciation,		
83		Annual pre-tax cash operating income		$220,000	$366,667	is listed here, not just		
84		Less: Income taxes		$88,000	$146,667	the incremental amount)		
85		After-tax income		$132,000	$220,000			
86		Plus: Depreciation expense		$30,000	$150,000			
87		After-tax cash operating income per year		$162,000	$370,000			
88								
89	Decision Alternatives			Amount	Year(s)	PV Factor (@ WACC)	PV of Cash Flows	
90	Purchase New Machine:							
91		Net incremental investment, after tax		$480,000	0	1.000000	($480,000)	
92		Increased investment in working capital, Yr. 0		$200,000	0	1.000000	($200,000)	
93		Net-of-tax salvage value, sale of old (Yr. 0)		$90,000	0	1.000000	$90,000	
94		Annual after-tax cash income (total)		$370,000	1-4	3.169865	$1,172,851	
95		One-time operating cash outflow, after-tax, Yr. 1		$30,000	1	0.909091	($27,273)	
96		Ater-tax proceeds from sale of the asset, Yr. 4		$3,000	4	0.683013	$2,049	
97		After-tax employee relocation expenses, Yr. 4		$90,000	4	0.683013	($61,471)	
98		End-of-investment recovery of working capital, Yr. 4		$200,000	4	0.683013	$136,603	
99		Net present value of this decision alternative					$632,759	
100	Keep Exisiting Machine:							
101		After tax cash operating income, per year		$162,000	1-4	3.169865	$513,518	
102		After tax salvage value of existing equipment, 4 years hence		$0	4	0.683013	$0	
103		Net present value of this decision alternative					$513,518	
104	Difference in NPV, Purchase New Machine vs. Keep Exisiting Machine						$119,240	

Appendix B

LEARNING OBJECTIVE 9

Identify selected advanced considerations in making capital-investment decisions.

DCF Models: Some Advanced Considerations

Thus far we have considered the rather simple situation where the firm is evaluating independent projects, each on a "go/no-go" basis. In such situations, the NPV method and the IRR method normally lead to the same decision as to whether the project should be accepted or rejected. However, there are some pitfalls associated with the use of IRR for capital-budgeting purposes. We deal briefly with these pitfalls below. In addition, we look briefly at the capital-budgeting decision when the firm faces a capital (funds) constraint. Except for the capital-rationing situation, the primary conclusion of this appendix is that managers should be guided by project NPVs in making capital-budgeting decisions.

THE POTENTIAL FOR MULTIPLE IRRs

In a normal investment project, there will be a large cash outflow in year 0 of the project, followed by a series of positive after-tax cash inflows during the life of the project. In this case there is only one "sign change" in the pattern of cash flows, and as such there will be only a single IRR.

Some projects, however, have a nonnormal pattern of cash flows. For example, new machinery might require a major overhaul (cash outflow) sometime during the life of the asset. A strip-mining company might incur end-of-project reclamation costs, for example, to restore to its original state the land that was mined. In both cases, there are two sign changes in the pattern of cash flows. In each of these two cases, there can be *up to* two IRRs associated with the project—one IRR for each sign change. If there are five sign changes, then there can be *up to* five IRRs. Thus, the basic rule to "accept a project if its IRR is greater than the firm's weighted-average cost of capital" breaks down. The solution to this problem is to base the decision on the NPV of the proposed investment: *if the NPV is greater than 0, accept the project.*

MUTUALLY EXCLUSIVE PROJECTS

Mutually exclusive projects represent an extreme form of project interdependence: the acceptance of one investment alternative precludes the acceptance of one or more other alternatives.

All of the examples in the body of the chapter involve "take-it or leave-it" decisions. That is, each investment project is considered independently of other investments. The basic decision therefore is whether to accept or reject the individual project being considered. However, in the real world, almost all capital-budgeting decisions involve a choice in which the selection of one alternative precludes the selection of one or more other alternatives. For example, your university may be considering whether to build a three-story or a four-story parking garage on campus—the university can invest in one but not both alternatives. The new lot could involve the use of electronic surveillance equipment or the use of security guards. These alternatives are said to be **mutually exclusive projects** in the sense that acceptance of one investment alternative precludes the acceptance of one or more other alternatives.

In analyzing mutually exclusive projects on a DCF basis, should the analyst use NPV or IRR? Although there are situations where NPV and IRR both give the same result regarding which of two (or more) competing investments should be chosen, there are also situations where the two methods provide different signals to managers. For discussion purposes, consider the following two examples of mutually exclusive projects:

1. Each of two projects has roughly the same initial investment outlay but different useful lives; the project with the longer life also has more distant returns and a higher NPV but a lower IRR compared to the project with the shorter life
2. Each of two projects has the same useful life but a different initial outlay.

Given the project choices listed above, modern financial theory specifies that the decision maker should choose the project with the higher NPV.[22] In the case of the first example, it

---

[22] In general, the existence of two mutually exclusive projects with different useful lives requires a so-called secondary analysis. That is, one cannot rely on raw, or unadjusted, NPV estimates alone. Rather, the decision maker uses either a replacement chain (or, "common life") approach or an equivalent annual annuity (EAA) to determine which of the two alternatives is preferable in a present-value sense. In the former case, we replicate the two investments out to a common ending point, defined mathematically as the least (or smallest) common multiple. For any two integers, *a* and *b*, the least common multiple is the smallest positive integer that is a multiple of both *a* and *b*. Since it is a multiple, it can be divided by *a* and *b* without a remainder. For example, the least common multiple of 3 and 4 is 12. In the latter case, we calculate the annual payments each project would provide if it were an annuity. That is, we determine the stream of constant annuity cash flow (the *equivalent annual annuity*) that has the same present value as each project's calculated NPV. The project with the higher EAA will always have the higher NPV when extended out to any common life. Therefore, when comparing projects of unequal lives, we choose the one with the higher EAA.

can be shown that the IRR method mistakenly favors the project with the quicker payback and higher IRR in spite of the fact that the alternative project has a higher NPV. In the case of the second example, it can be shown that the IRR decision rule can mistakenly favor smaller projects with high rates of return but lower NPVs. The arguments are developed more fully in a finance textbook, such as Brealey et al. (2009).

In general, the point here is that high economic rates of return (project IRRs) are not an end in and of themselves. The shareholders of a company benefit to the extent that managers choose projects that increase share value, and this increase is accomplished by choosing among investment alternatives on the basis of projected NPVs.

CAPITAL RATIONING (CAPITAL CONSTRAINT)

Capital rationing
refers to the case where investment capital for a given accounting period is limited—hence the need for these funds to be "rationed."

The **profitability index (PI)**
of a project is a rate-of-return measure, defined as the ratio of the NPV of a project to the original investment outlay for the project.

We stated above that, in general, decision makers should use the NPV criterion for capital-budgeting purposes. This rule states that all projects with a positive NPV should be accepted. This rule, however, assumes that the organization has access to capital markets to raise, if need be, additional capital (presumably at its WACC). For many large companies, this assumption would seem to be reasonable. But many small companies, and some larger companies as well, have either self-imposed or externally imposed constraints on their ability to raise capital. This situation is referred to as **capital rationing;** in the context of a capital constraint, the overall goal of management is to allocate in an optimal manner the investment funds (capital) it has available.

In fact, the situation here is similar to the constrained optimization problem we considered in Chapter 11 when we addressed the issue of determining the optimal short-run product mix. Under capital rationing, the appropriate decision rule is: allocate capital to investment projects on the basis of the NPV per dollar of the investment capital associated with each project. This relative measure of profitability is referred to as the **profitability index (PI)** and is calculated as follows:

$$PI = NPV/Initial\ investment$$

Under the situation of capital rationing, managers should allocate available capital (investment funds) to projects that provide the greatest NPV per dollar of investment. Consider the following two independent projects and an after-tax discount rate of 10 percent for the firm attempting to set an optimum capital budget for the period:

Project	After-Tax Cash Flows (Undiscounted)				NPV	PI = NPV/I
	Period 0	Period 1	Period 2	Period 3		
1	$(36.00)	$20.00	$20.00	$15.00	$9.98	0.28
2	(50.00)	25.00	25.00	25.00	12.17	0.24

If there is no capital rationing, the firm would accept both projects since the NPV of each project, at 10 percent, is positive. Under capital rationing, Project 1 would be preferred over project 2, since it has the higher ratio of NPV to investment (0.28) than Project 2 (0.24). In a sense, the underlying logic is one of getting the most bang for the buck. Remember, though, that the use of PI for ranking investment projects is appropriate only under conditions of capital rationing.

Present Value Tables

TABLE 1 Present Value of $1

Periods	4%	5%	6%	7%	8%	9%	10%	11%	12%	13%	14%	15%	20%	25%	30%
1	0.962	0.952	0.943	0.935	0.926	0.917	0.909	0.901	0.893	0.885	0.877	0.870	0.833	0.800	0.769
2	0.925	0.907	0.890	0.873	0.857	0.842	0.826	0.812	0.797	0.783	0.769	0.756	0.694	0.640	0.592
3	0.889	0.864	0.840	0.816	0.794	0.772	0.751	0.731	0.712	0.693	0.675	0.658	0.579	0.512	0.455
4	0.855	0.823	0.792	0.763	0.735	0.708	0.683	0.659	0.636	0.613	0.592	0.572	0.482	0.410	0.350
5	0.822	0.784	0.747	0.713	0.681	0.650	0.621	0.593	0.567	0.543	0.519	0.497	0.402	0.328	0.269
6	0.790	0.746	0.705	0.666	0.630	0.596	0.564	0.535	0.507	0.480	0.456	0.432	0.335	0.262	0.207
7	0.760	0.711	0.665	0.623	0.583	0.547	0.513	0.482	0.452	0.425	0.400	0.376	0.279	0.210	0.159
8	0.731	0.677	0.627	0.582	0.540	0.502	0.467	0.434	0.404	0.376	0.351	0.327	0.233	0.168	0.123
9	0.703	0.645	0.592	0.544	0.500	0.460	0.424	0.391	0.361	0.333	0.308	0.284	0.194	0.134	0.094
10	0.676	0.614	0.558	0.508	0.463	0.422	0.386	0.352	0.322	0.295	0.270	0.247	0.162	0.107	0.073
11	0.650	0.585	0.527	0.475	0.429	0.388	0.350	0.317	0.287	0.261	0.237	0.215	0.135	0.086	0.056
12	0.625	0.557	0.497	0.444	0.397	0.356	0.319	0.286	0.257	0.231	0.208	0.187	0.112	0.069	0.043
13	0.601	0.530	0.469	0.415	0.368	0.326	0.290	0.258	0.229	0.204	0.182	0.163	0.093	0.055	0.033
14	0.577	0.505	0.442	0.388	0.340	0.299	0.263	0.232	0.205	0.181	0.160	0.141	0.078	0.044	0.025
15	0.555	0.481	0.417	0.362	0.315	0.275	0.239	0.209	0.183	0.160	0.140	0.123	0.065	0.035	0.020
16	0.534	0.458	0.394	0.339	0.292	0.252	0.218	0.188	0.163	0.141	0.123	0.107	0.054	0.028	0.015
17	0.513	0.436	0.371	0.317	0.270	0.231	0.198	0.170	0.146	0.125	0.108	0.093	0.045	0.023	0.012
18	0.494	0.416	0.350	0.296	0.250	0.212	0.180	0.153	0.130	0.111	0.095	0.081	0.038	0.018	0.009
19	0.475	0.396	0.331	0.277	0.232	0.194	0.164	0.138	0.116	0.098	0.083	0.070	0.031	0.014	0.007
20	0.456	0.377	0.312	0.258	0.215	0.178	0.149	0.124	0.104	0.087	0.073	0.061	0.026	0.012	0.005
22	0.422	0.342	0.278	0.226	0.184	0.150	0.123	0.101	0.083	0.068	0.056	0.046	0.018	0.007	0.003
24	0.390	0.310	0.247	0.197	0.158	0.126	0.102	0.082	0.066	0.053	0.043	0.035	0.013	0.005	0.002
25	0.375	0.295	0.233	0.184	0.146	0.116	0.092	0.074	0.059	0.047	0.038	0.030	0.010	0.004	0.001
30	0.308	0.231	0.174	0.131	0.099	0.075	0.057	0.044	0.033	0.026	0.020	0.015	0.004	0.001	0.000
35	0.253	0.181	0.130	0.094	0.068	0.049	0.036	0.026	0.019	0.014	0.010	0.008	0.002	0.000	0.000
40	0.208	0.142	0.097	0.067	0.046	0.032	0.022	0.015	0.011	0.008	0.005	0.004	0.001	0.000	0.000

TABLE 2 Present Value of Annuity of $1

Periods	4%	5%	6%	7%	8%	9%	10%	11%	12%	13%	14%	15%	20%	25%	30%
1	0.962	0.952	0.943	0.935	0.926	0.917	0.909	0.901	0.893	0.885	0.877	0.870	0.833	0.800	0.769
2	1.886	1.859	1.833	1.808	1.783	1.759	1.736	1.713	1.690	1.668	1.647	1.626	1.528	1.440	1.361
3	2.775	2.723	2.673	2.624	2.577	2.531	2.487	2.444	2.402	2.361	2.322	2.283	2.106	1.952	1.816
4	3.630	3.546	3.465	3.387	3.312	3.240	3.170	3.102	3.037	2.974	2.914	2.855	2.589	2.362	2.166
5	4.452	4.329	4.212	4.100	3.993	3.890	3.791	3.696	3.605	3.517	3.433	3.352	2.991	2.689	2.436
6	5.242	5.076	4.917	4.767	4.623	4.486	4.355	4.231	4.111	3.998	3.889	3.784	3.326	2.951	2.643
7	6.002	5.786	5.582	5.389	5.206	5.033	4.868	4.712	4.564	4.423	4.288	4.160	3.605	3.161	2.80
8	6.733	6.463	6.210	5.971	5.747	5.535	5.335	5.146	4.968	4.799	4.639	4.487	3.837	3.329	2.925
9	7.435	7.108	6.802	6.515	6.247	5.995	5.759	5.537	5.328	5.132	4.946	4.772	4.031	3.463	3.019
10	8.111	7.722	7.360	7.024	6.710	6.418	6.145	5.889	5.650	5.426	5.216	5.019	4.192	3.571	3.092
11	8.760	8.306	7.887	7.499	7.139	6.805	6.495	6.207	5.938	5.687	5.453	5.234	4.327	3.656	3.147
12	9.385	8.863	8.384	7.943	7.536	7.161	6.814	6.492	6.194	5.918	5.660	5.421	4.439	3.725	3.190
13	9.986	9.394	8.853	8.358	7.904	7.487	7.103	6.750	6.424	6.122	5.842	5.583	4.533	3.780	3.223
14	10.563	9.899	9.295	8.745	8.244	7.786	7.367	6.982	6.628	6.302	6.002	5.724	4.611	3.824	3.249
15	11.118	10.380	9.712	9.108	8.559	8.061	7.606	7.191	6.811	6.462	6.142	5.847	4.675	3.859	3.268
16	11.652	10.838	10.106	9.447	8.851	8.313	7.824	7.379	6.974	6.604	6.265	5.954	4.730	3.887	3.283
17	12.166	11.274	10.477	9.763	9.122	8.544	8.022	7.549	7.120	6.729	6.373	6.047	4.775	3.910	3.295
18	12.659	11.690	10.828	10.059	9.372	8.756	8.201	7.702	7.250	6.840	6.467	6.128	4.812	3.928	3.304
19	13.134	12.085	11.158	10.336	9.604	8.950	8.365	7.839	7.366	6.938	6.550	6.198	4.843	3.942	3.311
20	13.590	12.462	11.470	10.594	9.818	9.129	8.514	7.963	7.469	7.025	6.623	6.259	4.870	3.954	3.316
22	14.451	13.163	12.042	11.061	10.201	9.442	8.772	8.176	7.645	7.170	6.743	6.359	4.909	3.970	3.323
24	15.247	13.799	12.550	11.469	10.529	9.707	8.985	8.348	7.784	7.283	6.835	6.434	4.937	3.981	3.327
25	15.622	14.094	12.783	11.654	10.675	9.823	9.077	8.422	7.843	7.330	6.873	6.464	4.948	3.985	3.329
30	17.292	15.372	13.765	12.409	11.258	10.274	9.427	8.694	8.055	7.496	7.003	6.566	4.979	3.995	3.332
35	18.665	16.374	14.498	12.948	11.655	10.567	9.644	8.855	8.176	7.586	7.070	6.617	4.992	3.998	3.333
40	19.793	17.159	15.046	13.332	11.925	10.757	9.779	8.951	8.244	7.634	7.105	6.642	4.997	3.999	3.333

Key Terms

accounting (book) rate of return (ARR), *509*

analytic hierarchy process (AHP), *480*

average-risk projects, *493*

beta coefficient, *495*

breakeven after-tax cash flow, *501*

capital asset pricing model (CAPM), *494*

capital budget, *479*

capital budgeting, *477*

capital investment, *477*

capital rationing, *519*

capital structure, *494*

discounted cash-flow (DCF) models, *492*

discount rate, *492*

economic value added (EVA®), *512*

hurdle rate, *494*

internal rate of return (IRR), *497*

market risk premium, *495*

modified internal rate of return (MIRR) *499*

Monte Carlo simulation, *503*

multicriteria decision model, *480*

mutually exclusive projects, *518*

net present value (NPV), *496*

non-DCF models, *492*

payback period, *507*

post-audit, *482*

present value (PV), *496*

present value payback period, *508*

profitability index (PI), *519*

real assets, *504*

real options, *504*

scenario analysis, *502*

sensitivity analysis, *500*

strategic control system, *479*

weighted-average cost of capital (WACC), *478*

yield-to-maturity, *494*

Comments on Cost Management in Action

Many benefits of advanced manufacturing technology are difficult to quantify in dollar amounts or even in numbers. To make matters worse, these benefits, more often than not, are long-term in nature, and the firm will see no immediate tangible results. A large confectionery firm rejected an automated storage and distribution facility because it did not include the benefits that better customer services would bring. Better customer services often lead to higher sales volume and market share and, eventually, higher profits. Realizing these difficulties, middle managers of a kitchen unit manufacturer, with an established reputation for innovative design, forced an investment in computer-assisted design equipment by exaggerating financial benefits—a practice that should be discouraged and disallowed!

Appraisals of investments in advanced manufacturing technology need to be evaluated in terms of quantitative analysis and strategic consideration. Advanced manufacturing technology can expand the firm's product portfolio, enhance corporate image, and increase manufacturing flexibility, in addition to potentially decreasing production time and costs. Firms need to assess both the quantifiable short-term incremental cash inflows and the long-run strategic benefits in judging an investment's merits. In addition to cash-flow analysis, an investment proposal can go a long way if it also includes the investment's strategic benefits. A firm manufacturing high-pressure casings decided to convert its manufacturing operations to cell manufacturing. The firm enjoyed such unplanned benefits as a 50 percent reduction in inventory, a 75 percent improvement in quality, substantial reduction in lead times, and flexible machining with overall labor reduction. An electrical switch gear products manufacturer with sales of $32 million and a total staff of 550 invested in CAD to increase its design capacity in anticipation of a 25 percent growth. The firm's original expectations included reduced lead time in the drawing office and reduced number of employees and WIP inventory. The additional benefits offered more accurate and timely transfer of data that greatly improved the firm's competitive edge and propelled the firm into a new marketing position.

Based on Michael Bromwich and Al Bhimani, "Strategic Investment Appraisal," *Management Accounting,* March 1991, pp. 45–48. See also M. J. Liberatore, T. F. Monahan, and D. E. Stout, "Strategic Capital Budgeting Analysis for Investments in Advanced Manufacturing Technology," *Journal of Financial and Strategic Decisions,* Summer 1993, pp. 55–72; and M. J. Liberatore, T. F. Monahan, and D. E. Stout, "A Framework for Integrating Capital Budgeting Analysis with Strategy," *The Engineering Economist,* Fall 1992, pp. 31–43.

Self-Study Problem

(For solution, please turn to the end of the chapter.)

Capital Budgeting for Expanding Productive Capacity

Ray Summers Company operates at full capacity of 10,000 units per year. The company, however, is still unable to fully meet the demand for its product, estimated at 15,000 units annually. This level of demand is expected to continue for at least another four years.

To meet the demand, the firm is considering the purchase of new equipment for $580,000. This equipment has an estimated useful life of four years and can be sold for $50,000 at the end of the fourth year. The engineering division estimates that installing, testing, and adjusting the machine will cost $12,000 before it can be put in operation.

An adjacent vacant warehouse can be leased for the duration of the project for $10,000 per year. The warehouse needs $58,000 of renovations to make it suitable for manufacturing. The lease terms call for restoring the warehouse to its original condition at the end of the lease. The restoration is estimated to cost $20,000. Current pre-tax operating profit per unit is as follows:

			Per Unit
Sales price			$200
Variable costs			
Manufacturing	$60		
Marketing	20	$80	
Fixed costs			
Manufacturing	$25		
Marketing and administrative	15	40	120
Operating profit before tax			$ 80

The new equipment would have no effect on the variable costs per unit. All current fixed costs are expected to continue with the same total amount. The per-unit fixed cost includes depreciation expenses of $5 for manufacturing and $4 for marketing and administration.

Additional fixed manufacturing costs of $140,000 (excluding depreciation) will be incurred each year if the equipment is purchased. The firm must hire an additional marketing manager to serve new customers. The annual cost for the new marketing manager, support staff, and office expense is estimated at approximately $100,000. The company expects to be in the 40 percent tax bracket for each of the next four years. The company requires a minimum after-tax rate of return of 12 percent on investments and uses straight-line depreciation.

Required

1. What is the required net initial investment outlay (year 0)?
2. What effect will the acquisition of the new equipment have on total operating profit after-tax in each of the four years?
3. What effect will the acquisition of the new equipment have on after-tax cash inflows in each of the four years?
4. Compute the payback period of the proposed investment under the assumption that cash inflows occur evenly throughout the year.
5. Compute the book (accounting) rate of return (ARR) of the proposed investment, based on the average book value of the investment.
6. Compute the net present value (NPV) of the proposed investment under the assumption that all cash inflows occur at year-end.
7. Compute the discounted payback period of the proposed investment under the assumption that cash inflows occur evenly throughout the year.
8. Compute the internal rate of return (IRR) of the proposed investment under the assumption that all cash inflows occur at year-end.
9. Use the MIRR function in Excel to estimate the modified internal rate of return for the proposed investment.
10. The company expects the variable manufacturing cost per unit to increase once the new equipment is in place. What is the most that the unit variable manufacturing cost can increase and still allow the company to earn the minimum rate of return on this investment? (*Hint:* Use the **Goal Seek** option in Excel.)

Questions

12-1   What are the distinguishing characteristics of capital-budgeting decisions?

12-2   In what ways can accountants add value to the capital-budgeting process?

12-3   What is the analytic hierarchy process (AHP) and how can it be used in making capital-budgeting decisions?

12-4   List cash flows that a hospital is likely to incur in conjunction with the installation of a new CAT scanner.

12-5   Identify costs that a chemical plant may incur after 20 years of operation (in connection with a planned closing of the plant).

12-6   In capital-budgeting analysis, what is meant by the *income tax effect?* Give three examples of the tax effect pertaining to the acquisition of new factory (manufacturing) equipment.

12-7   "Book value of an existing asset that we are contemplating replacing is nothing but a bookkeeper's figure and, as such, is irrelevant in capital-expenditure analysis." Do you agree? Why or why not?

12-8   What are the limitations of the payback period method for making capital-budgeting decisions (e.g., whether to accept or reject a proposed investment)? Does the present value payback period overcome these limitations?

12-9 Does the book (accounting) rate of return (ARR) method provide a true measure of the return on investment? How about the investment's internal rate of return (IRR)?

12-10 What should be the decision criterion when using the NPV method to evaluate capital investments? Does the IRR method use the same criterion?

12-11 "Let's be more practical. DCF is not the only gospel. Many managers have become too absorbed with DCF." Can such a statement be justified? Why?

12-12 Within the context of capital-budgeting decisions, what is meant by the term *sensitivity analysis?* What kinds of sensitivity analysis can be used to support the capital-budgeting process?

12-13 List at least three important behavioral issues related to the capital-budgeting process.

12-14 "The net present value (NPV) method weighs early receipts of cash much more heavily than more distant receipts of cash." Do you agree? Why?

12-15 "Depreciation expenses have no effect on cash flows and, therefore, are not relevant in capital-expenditure analysis." Do you agree? Why or why not?

12-16 A company alters its minimum rate of return from year-to-year or from project-to-project. What underlying factors may prompt a company to change its minimum rate of return for capital-budgeting purposes?

12-17 Should the firm accept the independent projects described below? Why or why not?

 a. The firm's cost of capital is 10 percent and the estimated internal rate of return (IRR) of the project is 11 percent.

 b. A capital investment requires a $150,000 initial investment. The firm's cost of capital is 10 percent, and the present value of the expected cash inflows from the project is $148,000.

12-18 How would the capital-budgeting procedures of a firm that chooses to "build" differ from those used by a firm that chooses to "harvest"? Why might they differ?

12-19 C.W. Yale, president of Hotchikiss, Inc., a client of yours, recently attended a seminar at which a speaker discussed the planning and control of capital expenditures, which he described as *capital budgeting*. Yale tells you he is not quite sure he understands the concept.

Required

1. Explain the nature of capital budgeting and provide several examples of capital-budgeting decisions.

2. What are the basic differences between the payback period decision model and the net present value (NPV) model? Explain.

3. Define the term *weighted-average cost of capital (WACC)*. Of what importance is the concept of WACC to the capital-budgeting process?

4. Financial accounting data are not entirely suitable for use in making capital-budgeting decisions. Explain.

5. Explain the role of the post-audit in the capital-budgeting process.

12-20 Provide an intuitive explanation of the modified internal rate of return (MIRR) financial performance metric. How does MIRR differ from IRR?

12-21 (Appendix B): What decision criterion should be used to choose investment projects for a firm with unlimited funds available at a weighted-average cost of 10 percent (after tax)? Can the firm use the same decision criterion if it has only a limited amount of available funds, say $100 million? Explain.

12-22 (Appendix B): When analyzing a proposed capital investment, what conditions or factors may lead the results to differ between the net present value (NPV) and internal rate of return (IRR) decision models?

12-23 (Appendix B): How does the size of the initial investment affect the indicated internal rate of return (IRR) and net present value (NPV) of a proposed investment?

Brief Exercises

12-24 For a firm facing a marginal income tax rate of 34 percent, what is the after-tax cash-flow effect of: (a) a $1,000 increase in contribution margin during the year, and (b) a $500 increase in cash operating expenses?

12-25 What is the present value of $1,000 to be received two years from now, if the discount rate is: (a) 10 percent, (b) 14 percent, and (c) 20 percent? Use both the appropriate table in the text (Appendix C, Table 1) and the appropriate function in Excel to answer these questions.

12-26 What is the present value of a stream of 5 end-of-year annual cash receipts of $500 given a discount rate of 14 percent? Use both the appropriate table in the text (Appendix C, Table 2) and the appropriate function in Excel to answer this question.

12-27 Use the appropriate function in Excel to calculate the annual straight-line (SL) depreciation charge for an asset that has a $10,000 acquisition cost, a salvage value of $500, and a useful life of four years.

12-28 Given the following information, calculate the amount of after-tax profit for the period: sales, $260; expenses other than depreciation, $140; depreciation, $50; marginal income tax rate, 35 percent. Calculate the net after-tax cash flow effect of the preceding information. (*Hint:* You can use either a direct or an indirect approach to arrive at the appropriate answer.)

12-29 Refer to Exhibit 12.6 in the text. What is the depreciation expense deduction in each of four years for a $10,000 asset classified under MACRS as three-year property?

12-30 A company purchases an asset that costs $10,000. This asset qualifies as three-year property under MACRS. The company uses an after-tax discount rate of 12 percent and faces a 40 percent income-tax rate. Use the appropriate present value factors found in Appendix C, Table 1 to determine the present value of the depreciation deductions for this firm over the specified four-year period.

12-31 Create an Excel spreadsheet for exercise 12-30 and demonstrate that the PV of the depreciation deductions, when the income tax rate is 40 percent, is $3,218. Given an after-tax discount rate of 12 percent, what tax rate would be needed in order for the PV of the depreciation deductions to equal $4,000? Use the **Goal Seek** function of Excel.

12-32 Given an asset with a net book value (NBV) of $25,000, what are the after-tax proceeds for a firm in the 34 percent tax bracket if this asset is sold for $35,000 cash? What are the after-tax proceeds for this same firm if the asset is sold for $15,000 cash? (Show calculations.)

12-33 Given the following attributes of an investment project with a five-year life, and an after-tax discount rate of 12 percent, calculate the net present value (NPV) and the payback period of the project: investment outlay, year 0, $5,000; after-tax cash inflows, year 1, $800; year 2, $900; year 3, $1,500; year 4, $1,800; and year 5, $3,200. (Use the built-in function of Excel to estimate the NPV of this project.)

12-34 Use the data in exercise 12-33 and the appropriate function in Excel to estimate both the IRR and the MIRR of the proposed investment. What accounts for the difference in these two measures?

12-35 MicroTech Corporation is subject to a 35 percent income tax rate. Given the following information about the firm's capital structure, calculate the corporation's weighted-average cost of capital (WACC):

Source of Funds	Market Value	Required Rate of Return
Long-term debt	$40 million	7.0%
Preferred stock	$20 million	9.0%
Common stock	$60 million	12.0%

Exercises

12-36 Basic Capital-Budgeting Techniques

a. Project A costs $5,000 and will generate annual after-tax net cash inflows of $1,800 for five years. What is the payback period for this investment under the assumption that the cash inflows occur evenly throughout the year?

b. Project B costs $5,000 and will generate after-tax cash inflows of $500 in year one, $1,200 in year two, $2,000 in year three, $2,500 in year four, and $2,000 in year five. What is the payback period (in years) for this investment assuming that the cash inflows occur evenly throughout the year?

c. Project C costs $5,000 and will generate net cash inflows of $2,500 before taxes for five years. The firm uses straight-line depreciation with no salvage value and is subject to a 25 percent tax rate. What is the payback period?

d. Project D costs $5,000 and will generate sales of $4,000 each year for five years. The cash expenditures will be $1,500 per year. The firm uses straight-line depreciation with an estimated salvage value of $500 and has a tax rate of 25 percent.

   (1) What is the book rate of return based on the original investment?

   (2) What is the book rate of return based on the average book value?

e. What is the NPV for each of the projects a through d above? Assume that the firm requires a minimum after-tax return of 8 percent on all investments.

12-37 Weighted-Average Cost of Capital (WACC)

a. Micro Advantage, Inc., issued a $5,000,000, 20-year bond a year ago at 98 with a stated rate of 9 percent. Today, the bond is selling at 110. If the firm's tax bracket is 30 percent, what is the current after-tax cost of this debt?

b. Micro Advantage, Inc., has $5,000,000 preferred stock outstanding that it sold for $24 per share. The preferred stock has a per share par value of $25 and pays a $3 dividend per year. The current market price is $30 per share. The firm's tax bracket is 30 percent. What is the after-tax cost of the preferred stock?

c. In addition to the bonds and preferred stocks described in (a) and (b) above, Micro Advantage has outstanding 50,000 shares of common stock that has a par value of $10 per share and a current market price of $170 per share. The expected after-tax market return on the firm's common equity is 20 percent. What is Micro Advantage's weighted-average cost of capital (WACC)?

12-38 Future and Present Values, Spreadsheet Application

a. It is said (S. Branch Walker) that the Indian who sold Manhattan for $24 was a sharp salesman. If he had put his $24 away at 6 percent compounded semiannually, it would now be worth over $9 billion, and he could buy most of the now-improved land back! Assume that this seller invested on January 1, 1701, the $24 he received.

Required

1. Use Excel to determine the balance (in billions) of the investment as of December 31, 2009, assuming a 6 percent interest rate compounded semiannually. (*Hint:* Use the FV function in Excel.)

2. Carry out the same calculation using an 8 percent annual interest rate, compounded semiannually.

3. What would be the balances for requirements 1 and 2 if interest is compounded quarterly?

4. Assume that the account consisting of this investment had a balance of $9.5 billion as of December 31, 2009. How much would the total amount be on December 31, 2015, if the annual interest rate is 8 percent, compounded semiannually?

b. In 2000, Alex Rodriguez signed a 10-year, $252 million dollar contract with the Texas Rangers. Assume that equal payments would have been made each year to Alex and that the owner's cost of capital (discount rate) was 12 percent at the time the contract was signed. What is the present value cost of the contract to the owners as of January 1, 2000, the date the contract was signed, in each of the following independent situations?

Required

1. Alex received the first payment on December 31, 2000.

2. Alex received the first payment on January 1, 2000, the date the contract was signed.

3. Assuming the owner is in the 45 percent income tax bracket, calculate your answer for requirement 1.

12-39 Cash Receipts Frequency and Present-Value Consequences   Assume that you are about to sell property (a vacant parcel of real estate) you own but otherwise have no use for. The net-of-sales-commission selling price for the property is $500,000. You are willing to finance this transaction over a 20-year period and have told the buyer that you expect a 12 percent pretax return on the transaction. The buyer has asked you for a payment schedule under several alternatives.

Required

1. What will be your periodic cash receipt, to earn a 12 percent return, if payments are received from the purchaser:
   a. at the end of each week.
   b. at the end of each month.
   c. at the end of each quarter.
   d. at the end of each year.

2. What general conclusion can you draw based on the calculations above in (1)?

12-40 After-Tax Net Present Value and IRR (non-MACRS rules)

a. eEgg is considering the purchase of a new distributed network computer system to help handle its warehouse inventories. The system costs $60,000 to purchase and install and $30,000 to operate each year. The system is estimated to be useful for four years. Management expects the new system to reduce by $62,000 a year the cost of managing inventories. The firm's cost of capital is 10 percent.

Required   What is the net present value (NPV) of the proposed investment under each of the following independent situations?

1. The firm is not yet profitable and pays no taxes.

2. The firm is in the 30 percent income tax bracket and uses straight-line depreciation with no salvage value. Assume MACRS rules do not apply.

3. The firm is in the 30 percent income tax bracket and uses double-declining-balance depreciation with no salvage value. Assume MACRS rules do *not* apply.

  b. Use the data for eEgg and answer the first two questions. This time, however, compute the internal rate of return (IRR) in each case.

12-41 Basic Capital-Budgeting Techniques, No Taxes, Uniform Net Cash Inflows Irv Nelson, Inc., purchased a $500,000 machine to manufacture specialty taps for electrical equipment. Nelson expects to sell all it can manufacture in the next 10 years. To encourage capital investments, the government has exempted taxes on profits from new investments. This legislation is to be in effect in the foreseeable future. The machine is expected to have a 10-year useful life with no salvage value. Nelson uses straight-line depreciation. The net cash inflow is expected to be $120,000 each year for 10 years. Nelson uses a 12 percent discount rate in evaluating capital investments. Assume, for simplicity, that MACRS depreciation rules do not apply.

Required Using Excel, compute for the proposed capital investment the:

1. Payback period under the assumption that cash inflows occur evenly throughout the year.
2. Book rate of return based on (a) initial investment and (b) average investment.
3. Net present value (NPV) of the proposed investment under the assumption that cash inflows occur at year-end.
4. Present value payback period of the proposed investment under the assumption that cash inflows occur evenly throughout the year.
5. Internal rate of return (IRR).
6. Modified internal rate of return (MIRR).

12-42 Basic Capital-Budgeting Techniques, Uneven Net Cash Inflows With Taxes, Spreadsheet Application Use the same information for this problem as you did for Exercise 12-41, except that the investment is subject to taxes and that the pre-tax operating cash inflows are as follows:

Year	Pre-tax Cash Inflow	Year	Pre-tax Cash Inflow
1	$50,000	6	$300,000
2	80,000	7	270,000
3	120,000	8	240,000
4	200,000	9	120,000
5	240,000	10	40,000

Irv Nelson has been paying 30 percent for combined federal, state, and local income taxes, a rate that is not expected to change during the period of this investment. The firm uses straight-line depreciation. Assume, for simplicity, that MACRS depreciation rules do not apply.

Required Using Excel, compute for the proposed investment the:

1. Payback period for the proposed investment under the assumption that the cash inflows occur evenly throughout the year.
2. Book rate of return based on (a) initial investment and (b) average investment.
3. Net present value (NPV).
4. Present value payback period of the proposed investment under the assumption that the cash inflows occur evenly throughout the year.
5. Internal rate of return (IRR).
6. Modified internal rate of return (MIRR).

12-43 Basic Capital-Budgeting Techniques, Uneven Net Cash Inflows and MACRS Use the data in Exercise 12-42 for Irv Nelson, Inc., and MACRS. The asset qualifies as a 5-year property.

Required Compute for the investment its:

1. Payback period under the assumption that the cash inflows occur evenly throughout the year.
2. Book rate of return based on: (a) the initial investment, and (b) an average investment (calculated as a simple average of the 10 average annual book values).
3. Net present value (NPV).
4. Internal rate of return (IRR).
5. Modified internal rate of return (MIRR).

12-44 **Straightforward Capital Budgeting with Taxes; Sensitivity Analysis**   Dorothy & George Company is planning to acquire a new machine at a total cost of $30,600. The machine's estimated life is six years and its estimated salvage value is $600. The company estimates that annual cash savings from using this machine will be $8,000. The company's after-tax cost of capital is 8 percent and its income tax rate is 40 percent. The company uses straight-line depreciation (non-MACRS-based).

Required

1. What is this investment's net after-tax annual cash inflow?

2. Assume that the net after-tax annual cash inflow of this investment is $5,000; what is the payback period?

3. Assume that the net after-tax annual cash inflow of this investment is $5,000; what is the net present value (NPV) of this investment?

4. What are the minimum net after-tax annual cost savings that make the proposed investment acceptable (i.e., the dollar cost savings that would yield a NPV of $0)?

(CPA Adapted)

12-45 **Capital Budgeting with Tax (non-MACRS Depreciation) and Sensitivity Analysis**   Gravina Company is planning to spend $6,000 for a machine that it will depreciate on a straight-line basis over 10 years with no salvage value. The machine will generate additional cash revenues of $1,200 a year. Gravina will incur no additional costs except for depreciation. Its income tax rate is 35 percent.

Required

1. What is the payback period of the proposed investment under the assumption that the cash inflows occur evenly throughout the year?

2. What is the book rate of return (ARR) based on the initial investment outlay?

3. What is the maximum amount that Gravina Company should invest if it desires to earn an internal rate of return (IRR) of 15 percent?

4. What is the minimum annual (pretax) cash revenue required for the project to earn a 15 percent internal rate of return?

5. Prepare a single schedule to show the NPVs associated with a 10-year life under annual after-tax cash flows of $500, $1,000, and $2,000 *and* discount rates of 10 percent, 15 percent, and 20 percent.

(CPA Adapted)

12-46 **Basic Capital Budgeting**   Rockyford Company must replace some machinery that has zero book value and a current market value of $1,800. One possibility is to invest in new machinery costing $40,000. This new machinery would produce estimated annual pretax cash operating savings of $12,500. Assume the new machine will have a useful life of four years and depreciation of $10,000 each year for book and tax purposes. It will have no salvage value at the end of four years. The investment in this new machinery would require an additional $3,000 investment of net working capital.

If Rockyford accepts this investment proposal, the disposal of the old machinery and the investment in the new one will occur on December 31 of this year. The cash flows from the investment will occur during the next four calendar years.

Rockyford is subject to a 40 percent income tax rate for all ordinary income and capital gains and has a 10 percent weighted-average after-tax cost of capital. All operating and tax cash flows are assumed to occur at year-end.

Required   Determine:

1. The after-tax cash flow arising from disposing of the old machinery.

2. The present value of the after-tax cash flows for the next four years attributable to the cash operating savings.

3. The present value of the tax shield effect of depreciation for year 1.

4. Which one of the following is the proper treatment for the additional $3,000 of net working capital required in the current year?

   a. It should be ignored in capital budgeting because it is not a capital investment.

   b. It is a sunk cost that needs no consideration in capital budgeting.

   c. It should be treated as part of the initial investment when determining the net present value.

   d. It should be spread over the machinery's four-year life as a cash outflow in each of the years.

   e. It should be included as part of the cost of the new machine and depreciated.

(CMA Adapted)

12-47 Working Backward: Determine Initial Investment Based on Book Rate of Return Bread Company is planning to purchase a new machine that it will depreciate on a straight-line basis over 10 years. Estimated salvage value = $0. A full year's depreciation will be taken in the year of acquisition. The machine is expected to produce a net before-tax cash inflow of $6,750 from operations in each of the 10 years. The book rate of return (ARR) is expected to be 10 percent on the initial investment. The firm's tax rate is 20 percent.

Required What is the cost of the new machine?

(CPA Adapted)

12-48 Working Backward: Determine Initial Investment Based on Internal Rate of Return (IRR) Gene, Inc., invested in a machine with a useful life of six years and no salvage value. It depreciated the machine using the straight-line method; the machine was expected to produce a $20,000 annual cash inflow from operations, after cash expenses but before taxes. Gene has determined that the time-adjusted rate of return (IRR) on the investment is 10 percent. The firm is in the 20 percent tax bracket. The appropriate annuity factor for this situation is 4.355.

Required What was the cost of the machine?

(CPA Adapted)

12-49 Working Backward: Determine Periodic Cash Flow Based on Book (Accounting) Rate of Return Dillon, Inc., purchased a new machine for $60,000 on January 1, 2010. The machine is being depreciated on a straight-line basis over five years with no salvage value. The book rate of return is expected to be 15 percent on the initial investment. The machine will generate a uniform cash flow. The firm's tax rate is 25 percent.

Required What is the expected annual pre-tax cash flow from operations from this investment?

(CPA Adapted)

12-50 Real Options—Basic Concepts This exercise pertains to the XYZ Company example in the body of the chapter and the associated discussion of real options.

Required

1. Define the term *real option.* Provide an example of each of the four common types of real options.
2. Define the terms *put option* and *call option.* Which of the four common types of *real options* are similar to put options? Which are similar to call options?
3. Based on the stated probabilities for the individual states of nature (i.e., level of consumer demand):
   a. What is the expected value each year of the after-tax cash inflows from the proposed investment, without considering the investment delay option?
   b. What is the estimated NPV of the proposed investment, without considering the investment delay option?
4. We see from Panel B of Exhibit 12.11 that XYZ would invest in the project only if the revealed level of consumer demand was high or medium. Show calculations as to why no investment would be made if the revealed level of demand were low.
5. In Panel B of Exhibit 12.11, show for each of the three scenarios the calculation for present value (at $t = 0$) of cash inflows (cells H20:H22), present value of cash outflows (cells I20:I22), and weighted net present value (cells J20:J22). What is the interpretation of the expected NPV of the project (i.e., a *positive* $12.95 million)?

12-51 Real Options and Sensitivity Analysis Refer to the XYZ Company example in the chapter. Based on the results in Panels A and B of Exhibit 12.11, management of the company decided to delay the implementation of the project for one year. Those managers are now interested in knowing how sensitive this decision is with respect to the assumptions they've made regarding the basic analysis. Therefore, they've asked you to prepare some supplementary analyses regarding Panel B of Exhibit 12.11.

Required

1. Holding everything else constant, what is the impact on expected NPV of the decision if the probabilities for the three scenarios change as follows: high (20%), medium (50%), low (30%). Does your decision change based on these revised assumptions? Why or why not? (Show calculations.)
2. Holding everything else constant, what is the impact on expected NPV of the decision if the probabilities for the three scenarios change as follows: high (30%), medium (40%), low (30%). Does your decision change based on these revised assumptions? Why or why not? (Show calculations.)

3. Prepare a 5 × 3 table containing the estimated NPV of the decision to delay for each combination of the following: risk-free rate of interest (4%, 5%, 6%) and weighted-average cost of capital (13%, 14%, 15%, 16%, and 17%). For example, one cell in your table would be the estimated NPV of the project if the risk-free rate of interest is 4 percent and the weighted-average cost of capital is 13 percent. What does your analysis suggest?

12-52 **Real Options—the Option to Abandon a Project**   You and several of your classmates have just graduated from college and are evaluating various investment opportunities, including a start-up company that would produce high-quality jackets embroidered with a college logo. If demand for this customized product is high, you expect to sell approximately 100,000 units per year, at a price per unit of $80. On the other hand, because of stiff competition in the field, a pessimistic estimate is that demand for your new product would be only 40,000 units per year at a selling price of $70. Anticipated variable costs per jacket amount to $40. Capacity-related (i.e., short-term fixed) costs other than the cost of manufacturing equipment are thought to be negligible. Manufacturing equipment (with a 10-year life, a cost of $12 million, and a zero salvage value) would have to be purchased as part of this project. Assume that for income-tax purposes your company will use straight-line depreciation over the life of the proposed investment. Your anticipated income-tax bracket for this endeavor is 33 1/3 percent. You are unsure of what discount rate to use for capital-budgeting purposes, but you believe the appropriate rate is somewhere between 10 percent and 14 percent on an after-tax basis.

Required

1. What is the anticipated after-tax cash flow for this investment for each of the two possible states of nature/scenarios?

2. Under the assumption that the two scenarios (level of product demand) are equally likely, what is the expected NPV of the proposed investment? Assume a discount rate of 12 percent. Based on the amount you estimated, should you invest in the project?

3. How sensitive is your decision to the assumption regarding the discount rate? To answer this question, prepare an estimated NPV for the proposed project using discount rates, in 1 percent increments, from 10 percent to 14 percent. Is the decision to accept or reject the investment sensitive to the discount rate used in the calculation of NPV?

4. Suppose your company could abandon the project and dispose of the manufacturing equipment for $10.4 million if demand for your product turns out to be weak. You and your colleagues would make this decision at the end of the first year of operations. Does the abandonment option change your decision as to whether to invest in the project? (Use a discount rate of 12%.)

Problems   12-53 **Equipment Replacement and Strategic Considerations**   The management of Devine Instrument Company is considering the purchase of a new drilling machine, model RoboDril 1010K. According to the specifications and testing results, RoboDril will substantially increase productivity over AccuDril X10, the machine Devine is currently using.

The AccuDril was acquired 8 years ago for $120,000 and is being depreciated over 10 years expected useful life with an estimated salvage value of $20,000. The engineering department expects the AccuDril to keep going for another three years after a major overhaul at the end of its expected useful life. The estimated cost for the overhaul is $100,000. The overhauled machine will be depreciated using straight-line depreciation with no salvage value. The overhaul will improve the machine's operating efficiency approximately 20 percent. No other operating conditions will be affected by the overhaul.

RoboDril 1010K is selling for $250,000. Installing, testing, rearranging, and training will cost another $30,000. The manufacturer is willing to take the AccuDril as a trade-in for $40,000. The RoboDril will be depreciated using the straight-line method with no salvage value. New technology most likely will make RoboDril obsolete to the firm in five years.

Variable operating cost for either machine is the same: $10 per hour. Other pertinent data follow:

	AccuDril X10	RoboDril 1010K
Units of output (per year)	10,000	10,000
Machine-hours	8,000	4,000
Selling price per unit	$100	$100
Variable manufacturing cost (not including machine-hours)	$40	$40
Other annual expenses (tooling and supervising)	$95,000	$55,000
Disposal value—today	$25,000	
Disposal value—in five years	0	$50,000

Devine Instrument Company's weighted-average cost of capital (WACC) is 12 percent, and it is in the 40 percent tax bracket.

Required

1. Determine the effect on cash flow for items that differ for the two alternatives.

2. Compute the payback period for purchasing RoboDril 1010K rather than having AccuDril X10 overhauled in two years.

3. What is the present value of each decision alternative?

4. What other factors, including strategic issues, should the firm consider before making the final decision?

12-54 Sensitivity Analysis Use the information in problem 12-53 to answer the following questions:

Required

1. What is the maximum machine operating cost of the overhauled AccuDril for the replacement decision to be an incorrect financial decision?

2. Use the **Goal Seek** function in Excel to determine the maximum amount that the annual after-tax operating costs for the new machine can be before changing the decision.

3. New technologies make it possible to overhaul this machine now for $80,000. Both the overhaul cost and the undepreciated cost (book value) of the existing asset are to be depreciated over two years. The overhaul will improve its productivity by 20 percent and reduce the cost of a major overhaul two years from now to $30,000. All overhaul costs will be depreciated using the straight-line method. With either overhaul, the machine will have no salvage value. Either overhaul can be scheduled during regular maintenance and will not affect production. Despite the old saying, "If it ain't broke, don't fix it," should you overhaul it now or wait for two years to do the overhaul as planned originally, assuming that no funds are currently available to purchase RoboDril 1010K?

4. Performing the overhaul now also improves product quality. Management believes that the quality improvement is rather subtle and very difficult to quantify. Should the firm overhaul now?

12-55 Comparison of Capital-Budgeting Techniques, Sensitivity Analysis Nil Hill Corporation has been using its present facilities at its annual full capacity of 10,000 units for the last three years. Still, the company is unable to keep pace with continuing demand for the product that is estimated to be 25,000 units annually. This demand level is expected to continue for at least another four years. To expand manufacturing capacity and take advantage of the demand, Nil Hill must acquire equipment costing $995,000. The equipment will double the current production quantity. This equipment has a useful life of 10 years and can be sold for $195,000 at the end of year 4 or $35,000 at the end of year 10. Analysis of current operating data provides the following information:

			Per Unit
Sales price			$195
Variable costs			
Manufacturing	$90		
Marketing	10	$100	
Fixed costs			
Manufacturing	$45		
Other	25	70	170
Pretax operating income			$ 25

The fixed costs include depreciation expense of the current equipment. The new equipment will not change variable costs, but the firm will incur additional fixed manufacturing costs (excluding depreciation) of $250,000 annually. The firm needs to spend an additional $200,000 in fixed marketing costs per year for additional sales. Nil Hill is in the 30 percent tax bracket. Management has set a minimum rate of return of 14 percent after-tax for all capital investments. Assume, for simplicity, that MACRS depreciation rules do *not* apply.

Required

1. Assume that the equipment will be depreciated over a four-year period. What effects will the new equipment have on after-tax operating income in each of the four years?

2. What effect will the new equipment have on cash flows in each of the four years?

3. Compute the proposed investment's payback period (in years), under the assumption that cash inflows occur evenly throughout the year.

4. Compute the book rate of return (ARR) based on the average investment.

5. Compute the net present value (NPV) of the proposed investment.

6. Compute the internal rate of return (IRR) of the proposed investment.

7. Compute the modified internal rate of return (MIRR) for the proposed investment.

8. Management has decided to invest in the new equipment, but is unsure of the reliability of some of the estimates and as such has asked some what-if questions. Treat each of the following two cases independently.

   a. By how much can the unit variable cost for units produced by the new equipment increase and still justify the purchase of the equipment (i.e., have the investment generate an after-tax IRR of exactly 14 percent, its cost of capital)?

   b. The company is anticipating an increase in competition. Management believes that, in response, it will have to reduce the selling price of the product. By how much can the firm decrease the selling price (of all units sold) and still be able to justify the purchase of the new equipment?

9. What strategic considerations might bear on this investment decision? How can such considerations be dealt with formally in the planning and decision-making process?

12-56 **Replacing a Small Machine: Capital-Budgeting Techniques and Sensitivity Analysis** Hightec Corporation has a seven-year contract with Magichip Company to supply 10,000 units of XT-12 at $5 per unit. Increases in materials and other costs since signing the contract two years ago make this product a cash drain to Hightec. As the manager of the subsidiary that manufactures and sells XT-12, you have discovered that a new machine, SP1000, has a higher productivity. The following is a summary of pertinent information:

	Machine in Use	**SP1000**
Capacity	10,000 units/year	18,000 units/year
Materials	$4.00 per unit	$3.00 per unit
Labor and other variable costs	$1.00 per unit	$0.20 per unit
Maintenance costs	$1.00 per unit	$0.10 per unit

(For simplicity, assume that all revenues and expenses are received and paid at year-end.)

The current machine can be sold for $3,000 today. Its salvage value will be $1,000 if the firm continues to use the machine for another five years. The new machine costs $100,000, will be depreciated over a five-year life, and will have a net disposal value of $5,000 in five years. The company's after-tax cost of capital is 10 percent. If the company decides to keep the old machine, which is fully depreciated, production can continue with it for at least another five years. All machines are depreciated on a straight-line basis with no salvage value. (Assume, for simplicity, that MACRS depreciation rules do *not* apply.) The firm expects to continue to pay approximately 20 percent for both federal and state income taxes in the foreseeable future. **At present the Magichip Company is the only user of XT-12.**

Required Compute:

1. The effects on the cash flow each year, including year 0, if the new machine is purchased.

2. The net present value (NPV) of the new machine.

3. The payback period of the new machine, under the assumption that cash inflows occur evenly throughout the year.

4. The internal rate of return (IRR) on the new machine, assuming that the new machine's annual cash inflows are $25,000 and that neither the new machine nor the existing machine will have salvage value at the end of the five-year period.

5. The internal rate of return (IRR) assuming that the after-tax cash inflows are as follows and that the estimated salvage value for both machines at the end of five years is $0.

Year 1	$20,000
Year 2	22,000
Year 3	25,000
Year 4	30,000
Year 5	40,000

6. By how much can the variable costs of the new machine increase (or decrease) and the company be indifferent on the replacement, assuming all the other costs will be as estimated?

12-57 **Capital Budgeting with Sum-of-Years'-Digits Depreciation** Bernie Company purchased a new machine, with an estimated useful life of five years and no salvage value, for $45,000. The machine is expected to produce net cash inflows from operations, before income taxes, as follows:

1st year	$ 9,000
2nd year	12,000
3rd year	15,000
4th year	9,000
5th year	8,000

Bernie will use the sum-of-the-years'-digits method to depreciate the new machine. Bernie uses 10 percent for evaluating capital investments and is currently in a 24 percent income tax bracket.

Required Set up an Excel spreadsheet to determine:

1. The payback period of the proposed investment (assume that cash inflows occur evenly throughout the year).
2. The net present value (NPV) of the proposed investment.
3. The internal rate of return (IRR) of the proposed investment.
4. The discounted payback period of the proposed project.
5. The modified internal rate of return (MIRR) of the proposed investment. Explain the difference between IRR and MIRR.

(CPA Adapted)

12-58 **Machine Replacement and Sensitivity Analysis Without Considering Taxes** Ann & Andy Machine Company bought a cutting machine, Model KC12, on March 5, 2010, for $5,000 cash. The estimated salvage value and estimated life were $600 and 11 years, respectively. On March 5, 2011, Ann, the company CEO, learned that she could purchase a different cutting machine, Model AC1, for $8,000 cash. The new machine would save the company an estimated $750 per year in cash operating costs compared to KC12. AC1 has an estimated salvage value of $400 and an estimated life of 10 years. The company could get $3,000 for KC12 on March 5, 2011. The company uses the straight-line method for depreciation (non-MACRS-based) and a 12 percent discount rate.

Required

1. Compute, for AC1, the:
   a. Payback period of the proposed investment, under the assumption that the cash inflows occur evenly throughout the year.
   b. Book rate of return (ARR) using the average investment; assume that any loss on the disposal of the existing machine is spread out evenly over the 10-year life of the new machine.
   c. Net present value (NPV).
   d. Internal rate of return (IRR).
   e. Modified internal rate of return (MIRR) also, explain the difference between a project's IRR and its MIRR.
2. Should the firm purchase AC1? Why?
3. What is the minimum (or maximum) savings that AC1 must have without altering your decision in requirement 2?

12-59 **Value of Accelerated Depreciation** Freedom Corporation acquired a fixed asset for $100,000. Its estimated life at time of purchase was four years, with no estimated salvage value. Assume a discount rate of 8 percent and an income tax rate of 40 percent.

Required

1. What is the present value of the tax benefits resulting from calculating depreciation using the sum-of-the-years'-digits method as opposed to the straight-line method on this asset?
2. What is the present value of the tax benefits resulting from calculating depreciation using the double-declining-balance method as opposed to straight-line method on this asset?
3. What is the present value of the tax benefits resulting from using MACRS as opposed to straight-line depreciation? The asset qualifies as a three-year asset. Use the half-year convention.

(CPA Adapted)

12-60 Solving for Unknown Costs The Mendoza Company discussed in the chapter is now considering replacing a piece of equipment that the company uses to monitor the integrity of metal pipes used for deep-sea drilling purposes. The company's pretax WACC is estimated as 12 percent. The following data are pertinent to the question you've been asked to analyze:

	Existing Asset	Replacement
Annual (pretax) variable operating expenses	$200,000	(?)
Current purchase price	N/A	$500,000
Current salvage value	$ 40,000	N/A
Expected useful life (years)	6	6
Expected salvage value, end of year 6	$ 10,000	$100,000

Required

1. What is the maximum amount of annual variable operating expenses, pretax, that would make this an attractive investment from a present-value standpoint?

2. Assume now that the company expects, over the coming six years, to be subject to a combined income-tax rate of 40 percent, including any gain/loss realized on the sale of the existing equipment. Assume that the current book value of the existing asset is $50,000 and that the after-tax WACC for Mendoza is 10 percent. Finally, assume that the company will use SL depreciation, with no salvage value, for income-tax purposes. In this situation, what is the maximum amount of variable operating costs that can be incurred in order to make the proposed purchase attractive in a present-value sense?

3. What strategic considerations might affect the decision whether to invest in this new equipment?

12-61 Solving for Unknowns; Strategy Because of increased consumer demand for fuel-efficient, alternative energy automobiles, Global Auto Company is considering investing in a new hybrid crossover vehicle. Development costs each year for a two-year period for this new vehicle are estimated as $750 million. Tooling and other set-up costs in year 2 are estimated at $1 billion. Actual production and sales are estimated to begin in year 3. It is anticipated that the plant being envisioned could produce vehicles for six years. Each vehicle sold is estimated to provide $3,500 of net cash flow (pre-tax). The estimated salvage value of the manufacturing plant after six years of operation is thought to be $250 million. Assume that all cash flows take place at year-end, and that the pre-tax WACC for Global Auto is 15 percent. Income-tax effects can be ignored in this problem.

Required

1. What is the minimum volume of car sales, per year, in the six-year life of the plant that is needed to make this proposed investment acceptable using NPV as decision criterion?

2. How does your answer in (1) change if the company's pretax WACC is 14 percent? 16 percent? Do you think the estimated NPV of this project is sensitive to the estimate of the company's discount rate?

3. What strategic considerations, including those related to risk management, would likely bear on this decision?

12-62 MACRS Depreciation and Capital-Budgeting Analysis You and your spouse have recently inherited money from a distant relative and are considering a number of investment opportunities, one of which would involve residential real estate. Specifically, you have an opportunity to purchase an apartment complex with 25 rental units. The total price for these units, including sales commission expense, is estimated as $500,000. You estimate that to make each unit suitable for renting, average remodeling costs of $20,000 per unit would be needed. Fifteen of the units have a single bedroom, and rent for $500 per month; the remaining units contain two bedrooms and rent for $650 per month. A friend of yours who is in the business suggests that ordinary maintenance and repair costs be budgeted, annually, at 16 percent of rental revenue. Both the purchase price of the units and the remodeling costs qualify as 27.5-year MACRS property.

In terms of calculating depreciation expense for tax purposes, you can assume that MACRS-based deductions for the first 27 years will be the same; in year 28 one-half year of depreciation will be deducted. (The present value, at 10 percent, of each dollar of cost-recovery spread this way is $0.3372.) If the remodeling is undertaken and annual maintenance is done as scheduled, the investment should last at least 30 years. The estimated salvage value of the investment 30 years from now is $0. You can assume that any gain/loss on this sale will be taxed at your ordinary income-tax rate.

Assume an opportunity cost of capital of 10 percent for purposes of evaluating this investment proposal. You and your spouse feel that your combined income tax rate for the foreseeable future would be approximately 40 percent (Note: The required PV factors are not in Appendix C. Thus, you will need to use Excel functions to generate a PV annuity factor for 27 periods and a PV factor for period 28, at various discount rates, in order to solve this problem.)

Required

1. What is the estimated after-tax NPV of this proposed investment? On the basis of your analysis of cash flows, is this investment desirable? Why or why not?

2. How is the estimated NPV affected if the discount rate were 8 percent rather than 10 percent? How would your estimate change if the discount rate were 12 percent rather than 10 percent? (*Hint:* Unlike (1) above, in which you were provided a MACRS present value conversion factor, you will have to develop a 28-year depreciation schedule and associated income-tax savings based on the stated tax rate. You must then discount this 28-year stream of cash savings back to present value using both the 8 percent and 12 percent discount rates. The PV annuity factor for 27 periods and the PV factor for period 28, at various discount rates, are *not* included in Appendix C. Thus, you will have to generate these yourself, using Excel.)

3. What additional factors might you have to consider before investing in this apartment complex?

12-63 New Venture Analysis After completing your MBA degree recently, you and your friends decided to evaluate alternative business opportunities. As a result of marketing research the four of you did for a course, you are convinced that an investment in a new home-to-airport transit service in your locale would be a profitable venture. (The region in which the four of you live is surrounded by three airports, the closest of which is 55 miles away.) One strategy would be to provide multiple pick-up and drop-off points, some in suburban locations, and others located downtown and at two area shopping malls. Your research team has gathered the following pertinent information:

- Given the anticipated volume, you anticipate the need for five part-time drivers, at a total payroll cost per year of approximately $100,000 ($20,000 per person).
- You anticipate purchasing six used vans, at a cost of $54,000 each, to support your operation. For tax purposes, these vans will be depreciated using the SL method (3-year life) with no anticipated salvage value assumed for the depreciation calculation.
- The opportunity cost of capital for an investment of this magnitude and risk is estimated at 12 percent, after tax.
- Additional cash operating expenses per year are estimated as follows: maintenance and repair costs, $6,000 (total); insurance, $2,000 (per van); gasoline, $20,000; and advertising, $5,000.
- Estimates regarding fare receipts are as follows: assume an operating year of 30 weeks; the cost per one-way ticket is $25, while the cost per round-trip ticket is $40; the total number of trips to the airport and back per van per week is estimated as 10; each trip, on average, carries four individuals. Three quarters of all passengers pay the round-trip fare, while the rest of them pay the one-way fare.

Required

1. What is the average annual pretax profit anticipated for this new venture? What is the average annual profit after tax, under the assumed 40 percent income tax?

2. What is the annual amount of both pretax and after-tax cash flows generated from this proposed investment?

3. What is the anticipated NPV of this project? If the current anticipated ticket prices per trip are insufficient to make the project desirable in a present-value sense, what selling price is needed (keeping the same $10 differential for two one-way trips versus one round-trip ticket)?

4. What is the accounting rate of return (ARR) on this investment, using average after-tax earnings as the numerator and average book value of the investment as the denominator of the ARR calculation? What is the anticipated IRR for this investment? What accounts for the difference between these two rates of return?

12-64 Capital Budgeting with Sensitivity Analysis Meidi Johnson has owned a medical professional building for the last 20 years. She leased the land from an adjacent medical school 22 years ago for 30 years and had the building constructed. At the end of the lease period, the medical school becomes the sole owner of the land, its improvements, and any structures on the land. The construction took two years. The building is in excellent condition and fully occupied at favorable rental rates. The value of the property has appreciated considerably. Because depreciation is based on the original construction cost, Meidi's taxable income is unusually large.

George Kardell, a commercial real estate broker, has approached Meidi with a proposal from a group of investors. He believes that Meidi can sell the building and the balance of the leasehold at a price that will be profitable to all parties. The sale, if made, would be a cash sale that will provide her with the cash she needs for another project. She is currently negotiating with a bank for financing of this other project she is considering. The bank is asking for 12 percent interest.

Meidi, however, would use 10 percent as her cost of capital if she can sell the building for cash. The potential investor group's cost of capital is 12 percent.

The buyer is in the 30 percent tax bracket. Meidi believes that she has been paying a marginal income tax rate of 40 percent in the last five years, and she expects no change in the next eight years. Unfortunately for her, the tax law in effect since last year eliminates any special tax rate for capital gains earned. This condensed income statement is taken from Meidi's latest tax return.

Income Statement for 2010		
Rental revenue		$2,000,000
Expenses		
Operations	$950,000	
Administration	70,000	
Property taxes	280,000	
Depreciation (straight line)	100,000	1,400,000
Net income before taxes		$ 600,000
Income taxes at 40 percent		240,000
Net income after taxes		$ 360,000

The buyer will use the straight-line depreciation method. No change in either rental revenue or expenses is expected.

Required

1. What is the maximum the buyer should pay? (Show details.)

2. What is the minimum selling price Meidi can accept if she has to pay George a 5 percent commission? Assume that Meidi would want to be compensated for the lost rental incomes, plus any capital gains tax she'd have to pay in conjunction with the sale, plus the sales commission paid to the broker.

3. What is the maximum the buyer would be willing to pay if the purchase is for a MACRS five-year property? Use the half-year convention.

12-65 **Cash-Flow Analysis and NPV**   Lou Lewis, the president of the Lewisville Company, has asked you to give him an analysis of the best use of a warehouse the company owns.

a. Lewisville Company is currently leasing the warehouse to another company for $5,000 per month on a year-to-year basis.

b. The warehouse's estimated sales value is $200,000. A commercial realtor believes that the price is likely to remain unchanged in the near future. The building originally cost $60,000 and is being depreciated at $1,500 annually. Its current net book value (NBV) is $7,500.

c. Lewisville Company is seriously considering converting the warehouse into a factory outlet for furniture. The remodeling will cost $100,000 and will be modest because the major attraction will be rock-bottom prices. The remodeling cost will be depreciated over the next five years using the double-declining-balance method. (Note: Use the VDB function in Excel to calculate depreciation charges.)

d. The inventory and receivables (net of current liabilities) needed to open and sustain the factory outlet would be $600,000. This total is fully recoverable whenever operations terminate.

e. Lou is fairly certain that the warehouse will be condemned in 10 years to make room for a new highway. The firm most likely would receive $200,000 from the condemnation.

f. Estimated annual operating data, exclusive of depreciation, are

Sales	$900,000
Operating expenses	$500,000

g. Nonrecurring sales promotion costs at the beginning of year 1 are expected to be $100,000.

h. Nonrecurring termination costs at the end of year 5 are $50,000.

i. The minimum annual rate of return desired is 14 percent. The company is in the 40 percent tax bracket.

Required

1. Show how you would handle the individual items in determining whether the company should continue to lease the space or convert it to a factory outlet. Use the company's analysis form, which is set up as follows:

			Cash Flows in Year					
Item	Description	Net Present Value	0	1	2	3	4	5
a.								
b.								
.								
.								
.								
i.								

Identify any item that is irrelevant.

2. After analyzing all relevant data, compute the net present value (NPV). Indicate which course of action, based only on these data, should be taken.

12-66 Machine Replacement with Tax Considerations   A computer chip manufacturer spent $2,500,000 to develop a special-purpose molding machine. The machine has been used for one year, and will be obsolete after an additional three years. The company uses straight-line (SL) depreciation for this machine.

At the beginning of the second year, a machine salesperson offers a new, vastly more efficient machine. It will cost $2,000,000, will reduce annual cash manufacturing costs from $1,800,000 to $1,000,000, and will have zero disposal value at the end of three years. Management has decided to use the double-declining-balance depreciation method for tax purposes for this machine if purchased. (Note: make sure to switch to SL depreciation in year 3 to ensure that the entire cost is written off. You may find it useful to use the VDB function in Excel to calculate depreciation charges.)

The old machine's salvage value is $300,000 now, and will be $50,000 three years from now; however, no salvage value is provided in calculating straight-line depreciation for tax purposes. The firm's income tax rate is 45 percent. The firm desires to earn a minimum after-tax rate of return of 8 percent.

Required   Using the net present value (NPV) technique, show whether the firm should purchase the new machine.

12-67 Equipment Replacement   Oilers Company makes a computer desk that it sells for $30 under a contract to a large computer retailer. The company operates one shift in its Ohio plant. The annual normal capacity is 100,000 units.

Oilers pays direct labor at $8.00 per hour. An employee can produce a desk in 2 hours. Each desk requires 8 board feet of hardboard costing $0.25 per board foot. Indirect manufacturing costs (manufacturing overhead) at normal capacity of 100,000 units are described by the following formula:

Total costs = Fixed costs + (Variable cost per unit × units manufactured)

Total costs = $25,000 + ($0.30/unit × units manufactured)

Some years ago, Oilers installed a saw that now has a carrying (book) value of $20,000, which is being depreciated at $2,000 a year. At the time of installation, the saw was expected to have no salvage value at the end of its useful life because that value would equal its dismantling costs.

A sales agent from Whalers Company is encouraging Oilers Company to replace the saw with a numerical saw. In addition to being able to perform precision cutting, the new saw also will reduce by half the time to make a desk. Because the new saw is more powerful than the present one, utility costs are expected to increase by $0.10 per unit.

The new saw will cost $100,000, including installation, testing, and transportation charges. Its estimated useful life is 10 years and will be depreciated using the straight-line (SL) method with $10,000 estimated salvage value.

Whalers Company agrees that, if Oilers buys the saw, Whalers will buy the old one for $4,000 and charge Oilers no dismantling costs. The income tax rate is 40 percent. Oilers management expects a 15 percent after-tax return on investment. The loss on the trade-in of the current saw is allowable as an income-tax deduction.

Required

1. As a financial analyst for Oilers, you are charged with analyzing the purchase of the new saw. In preparing a report for the president, you must determine the following for management's consideration:

   a. The contribution margin per unit under current operating conditions.

   b. The standard overhead rate (application rate) per unit under current operating conditions.

   c. The formula for indirect manufacturing costs (manufacturing overhead), assuming the purchase and installation of the new saw.

   d. The new saw's manufacturing overhead standard rate (application rate) per unit, based on a normal capacity of 100,000 units.

   e. The contribution margin per unit, assuming the sales price remains unchanged, if the new saw is purchased and installed.

   f. The net additional investment for the new saw, assuming that Oilers decides to purchase and install it.

   g. The expected net additional cash flow per year if the new saw is purchased and installed. Assume that the company sells all that it produces.

2. The firm will be able to reduce approximately half of the hourly production workers currently on its payroll if the new saw is purchased. The plant has been in its current location for more than 50 years. Over 40 percent of the households in this small southeast Ohio town have at least one member who works for the firm. Should the firm purchase the state-of-the-art equipment? Why or why not?

(IMA Adapted)

12-68 **Equipment Replacement, MACRS** VacuTech is a high-technology company that manufactures sophisticated instruments for testing microcircuits. Each instrument sells for $3,500 and costs $2,450 to manufacture. An essential component of the company's manufacturing process is a sealed vacuum chamber where the interior approaches a pure vacuum. The technology of the vacuum pumps that the firm uses to prepare its chamber for sealing has been changing rapidly. On June 1, 2009, VacuTech bought the latest in electronic high-speed vacuum pumps that can evacuate in only six hours a chamber for sealing. The company paid $400,000 for the pump. Recently, the pump's manufacturer approached VacuTech with a new pump that would reduce the evacuation time to two hours.

VacuTech's management is considering the purchase of this new pump and has asked Doreen Harris, the company controller, to evaluate the financial impact of replacing it with the new model. Doreen has gathered the following information prior to preparing her analysis:

- The new pump could be installed and placed in service on January 1, 2013. The pump's cost is $608,000; installing, testing, and debugging it will cost $12,000. The pump would be assigned to the three-year class for depreciation under the Modified Accelerated Cost Recovery System (MACRS) and is expected to have an $80,000 salvage value when it is sold at the end of four years. Depreciation on the equipment would be recognized starting in 2013, and MACRS rates (rounded) would be as follows:

Year 1	33%
Year 2	45
Year 3	15
Year 4	7

- The current pump is being depreciated under MACRS and will be fully depreciated by the time the new pump is placed in service. If the firm purchases the new pump, it will sell the current pump for $50,000.

- At the current rate of production, the new pump's greater efficiency will result in annual pretax cash savings of $125,000.

- VacuTech is able to sell all testing instruments that it can produce. Because of the new pump's increased speed, output is expected to increase by 30 units in 2013, 50 units in both 2014 and 2015, and 70 units in 2016. Manufacturing costs for all additional units would be reduced by $150 per unit (in addition to the $125,000 savings noted above).

- VacuTech is subject to a 40 percent income tax rate. For evaluating capital-investment proposals, *management assumes that annual cash flows occur at the end of the year* and uses a 15 percent after-tax discount rate.

Required

1. Determine whether VacuTech should purchase the new pump by calculating the net present value (NPV) at January 1, 2013, of the estimated after-tax cash flows that would result from its acquisition.

2. Describe the factors, other than the net present value, that VacuTech should consider before making the pump replacement decision.

(CMAAdapted)

12-69 Joint Venture Perez Group has the opportunity to enter into a joint venture giving it a 49 percent ownership with local investors in an emerging country. The firm would be required to invest the entire $3,000,000 initial outlay needed for the venture and would receive 80 percent of the expected $900,000 yearly net cash flows for 10 years. At the end of 10 years, ownership will be turned over to the local investors. Cost of capital is 10 percent. Because of the inherent risk of overseas investments, Perez will accept such projects only if the projected IRR is more than 20 percent.

Required Should Perez invest in the project?

12-70 Risk and NPV J. Morgan of SparkPlug Inc. has been approached to take over a production facility from B.R. Machine Company. The acquisition will cost $1,500,000, and the after-tax net cash inflow will be $275,000 per year for 12 years.

SparkPlug currently uses 12 percent for its after-tax cost of capital. Tom Morgan, production manager, is very much in favor of the investment. He argues that the total after-tax net cash inflow is more than the cost of the investment, even if the demand for the product is somewhat uncertain. "The project will pay for itself even if the demand is only half the projected level." Cindy Morgan (corporate controller) believes that the cost of capital should be 15 percent because of the declining demand for SparkPlug products.

Required

1. Should Morgan accept the project if its after-tax cost of capital is 12 percent?

2. If Cindy Morgan is correct and uses 15 percent, does that change the investment decision?

3. Use the built-in function in Excel to estimate the project's IRR. Use the **Goal Seek** function in Excel to calculate the maximum amount that can be invested up front in order to generate an economic rate of return equal to the 15 percent rate of return specified by management as appropriate for the proposed investment.

4. Is adjusting the discount rate or the desired rate of return an effective way to deal with risk or uncertainty?

12-71 Sensitivity Analysis Griffey & Son operate a plant in Cincinnati and are considering opening a new facility in Seattle. The initial outlay will be $3,500,000 and should produce after-tax net cash inflows of $600,000 per year for 15 years. Due to the effects of the ocean air in Seattle, however, the plant's useful life may be only 12 years. Cost of capital is 14 percent.

Required

1. Will the project be accepted if 15 years' useful life is assumed? What if 12 years of useful life is used?

2. How many years will be needed for the Seattle facility to earn at least a 14 percent return?

12-72 Uneven Cash Flows, NPV MaxiCare Corporation, a not-for-profit organization, specializes in health care for senior citizens. Management is considering whether to expand operations by opening a new chain of care centers in the inner city of large metropolises. For a new facility, initial cash outlays for lease, renovations, net working capital, training, and other costs are expected to be about $15 million in year 0. The corporation expects the cash inflows of each new facility in its first year of operation to equal the total cash outlays for the year. Net cash inflows are expected to increase to $1 million in each of years 2 and 3, $2.5 million in year 4, and $3 million in each of years 5 through 10. The lease agreement for the facility will expire at the end of year 10, and MaxiCare expects the cost to close a facility will pretty much exhaust all cash proceeds from the disposal. Cost of capital for MaxiCare is 12 percent.

Required Compute the net present value (NPV) and the IRR for this venture. What is the break-even selling price for this investment, that is, the price that would yield an NPV of $0?

12-73 Environmental Cost Management Myers Manufacturing, Inc., wants to build a booth for painting the boxes it makes for small transformers to be used to power neon signs. The company can choose either a solvent-based or a powder paint process. The following table summarizes the costs and investment required by each approach:

	Solvent Paint System	Powder Paint System
Initial investment	$400,000	$1,200,000
Unit paint cost	$0.19	$0.20
Estimated life in years	10	10
Annual units	2,000,000	2,000,000

The firm will incur additional environmental costs with the solvent paint system but not with the powder paint system. The firm estimates annual environmental costs for the solvent paint system as follows:

	Units	Unit Cost
Monthly pit cleaning	12	$1,000
Hazardous waste disposal	183	3,000
Superfund fee	18,690	0.17
Worker training	2	1,500
Insurance	1	10,000
Amortization of air-emission permit	0.2	1,000
Air-emission fee	44.6	25
Recordkeeping	0.25	45,000
Wastewater treatment	1	50,000

The firm estimates its after-tax cost of capital to be 12 percent. Either system is a 10-year property under MACRS. The firm pays a total of 40 percent in income taxes.

Required

1. What is the difference in cost in today's dollar for the two systems?

2. What is the most the firm is willing to pay for the powder-based system?

(Adapted from German Boer, Margaret Curtin, and Louis Hoyt, "Environmental Cost Management," *Management Accounting* [September 1998], pp. 28–38.)

12-74 **Research Assignment, Strategy**   Obtain from your library a copy of following article: Clayton M. Christensen, Stephen P. Kaufman, and Willy C. Shih, "Innovation Killers: How Financial Tools Destroy Your Capacity to Do New Things," *Harvard Business Review,* January 2008, pp. 98–105. The article focuses on bias against innovation that is attributable to the misuse of certain financial tools. In fact, they conclude (p. 104) that "managers in established corporations use analytical methods that make innovation investments extremely difficult to justify."

Required   After reading the above-referenced article, answer the following questions:

1. According to the authors of the article, how does the use of DCF tools by managers in practice bias against innovation? What solution do the authors propose to counter this problem?

2. Define the terms *fixed costs* and *sunk costs.* According to the authors of this article, what is the bias against innovation that is created by how some decision makers view such costs? What remedies do the authors recommend for dealing with this problem?

3. The authors suggest that bias in the evaluation of innovation projects is caused, as well, by an overemphasis on (short-term) earnings per share statistics. What is the essence of this argument? What do the authors propose as a recommendation for addressing this problem?

12-75 **Assessing Customer Lifetime Value**   How important to profitability are customer referrals? What customers feel about your company (and you) and what they are prepared to tell others about you can be just as important as what your customers do themselves. The authors of the following article hypothesize that overall customer value, what they call *customer lifetime value,* as consisting of two components: the amount a customer brings in from purchases and the value of referrals. See V. Kumar, J. A. Petersen, and R. P. Leone, "How Valuable Is Word of Mouth?" *Harvard Business Review,* October 2007, pp. 139–146, prior to answering the following questions.

Required

1. What is the primary managerial question or issue that the authors of this article are addressing?

2. Define the terms *customer lifetime value (CLV)*, and *customer referral value (CRV)*. Which of these values do the authors believe is more important for financial success? Why"

3. Which of the two components of value, CLV or CRV, is the more difficult to estimate? Why?

4. Explain the *customer value matrix* developed by the authors and presented on page 144 of their article. Of what strategic importance is this matrix?

5. In what way can the management accountant aid in the estimation of CLV and CRV (and, by extension, the creation of the customer value matrix)?

Solution to Self–Study Problem

Capital Budgeting for Expanding Productive Capacity

1. Net initial investment outlay, year 0:

Cost of the new equipment	$580,000
Installation, testing, and training	12,000
Capitalized renovation costs for the leased warehouse	58,000
Total cash outflow, year 0	$650,000

2. Effect of the acquisition on total after-tax operating profit, years 1 through 4:

Incremental sales	$200 × 5,000		$1,000,000
Cost of goods sold:			
Variable manufacturing costs	$ 60 × 5,000	$300,000	
Additional fixed manufacturing overhead			
($140,000 + $10,000)		150,000	
Depreciation on new equipment (SL basis)			
($650,000 – $50,000)/4 years*		150,000	600,000
Gross margin			$ 400,000
Marketing and administrative expenses:			
Variable marketing expenses	$ 20 × 5,000	$100,000	
Additional fixed marketing expenses		100,000	200,000
Incremental operating profit before tax			$ 200,000
Less: Income taxes (@40%)			80,000
Incremental after-tax operating profit, years 1 through 3			$ 120,000
The company can expect its after-tax operating profit in year 4			
to increase by $108,000, as follows:			
Net operating income before restoration expenses (see above)			$ 120,000
Less: After-tax restoration expenses:			
Restoration expenses		$ 20,000	
Less: Income-tax savings on restoration expenses (@40%)		8,000	12,000
Incremental after-tax operating profit, year 4			$ 108,000

*Unlike the example in the body of the chapter, we are assuming here that for tax purposes, the depreciable cost of the asset is cost less estimated salvage value, an assumption that may or may comport with current tax law.

3. The incremental after-tax cash inflow is anticipated to be $270,000 for each of the first three years and $308,000 in year 4, as follows:

	Years 1 to 3	Year 4
After-tax operating profit (see part 2 above)	$120,000	$108,000
Add: Noncash expenses included in determination		
of after-tax operating profit: depreciation expense	150,000	150,000
Add: After-tax cash inflow from disposal of equipment	-0-	50,000
Incremental after-tax cash inflows	$270,000	$308,000

4. The (unadjusted) payback period for this investment (under the assumption that cash inflows occur evenly throughout the year) is approximately 2.4 years, as follows:

$$\text{Payback period} = \text{Initial investment/Annual cash inflow after-tax}$$
$$= \$650,000/\$270,000 = 2.407 \text{ years, or 2 years and 5 months}$$

5. The accounting (book) rate of return, based on average investment, is approximately 33.4 percent, as follows:

$$\text{Average net operating income} = [(\$120,000 \times 3) + \$108,000]/4 \text{ years} = \$117,000 \text{ per year}$$
$$\text{Average investment} = (\text{Book value beginning of year 1} + \text{Book value at end of year 4})/2$$
$$= (\$650,000 + \$50,000)/2 = \$350,000$$
$$\text{Accounting rate of return (ARR)} = \$117,000/\$350,000 = 33.43\%$$

6. The net present value (NPV) of the proposed investment, at a 12% discount rate, is $194,428, as follows (under the assumption that cash inflows occur at year-end):

PV of after-tax cash inflows, years 1 through 3, at 12%:	
$270,000 × 2.402 =	$648,540
PV of after-tax cash inflow, year 4: $308,000 × 0.636 =	195,888
Total PV of after-tax cash inflows	$844,428
Initial investment outlay (i.e., year 0)	650,000
NPV	$194,428

Alternative Solution: Using an Excel Spreadsheet

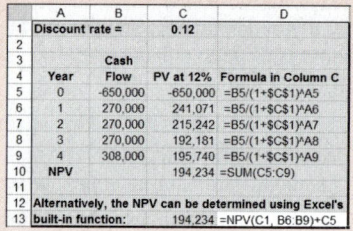

	A	B	C	D
1	Discount rate =		0.12	
2				
3		Cash		
4	Year	Flow	PV at 12%	Formula in Column C
5	0	-650,000	-650,000	=B5/(1+$C$1)^A5
6	1	270,000	241,071	=B5/(1+$C$1)^A6
7	2	270,000	215,242	=B5/(1+$C$1)^A7
8	3	270,000	192,181	=B5/(1+$C$1)^A8
9	4	308,000	195,740	=B5/(1+$C$1)^A9
10	NPV		194,234	=SUM(C5:C9)
11				
12	Alternatively, the NPV can be determined using Excel's			
13	built-in function:		194,234	=NPV(C1, B6:B9)+C5

Note that the Excel-generated solutions are exact while the method based on the Present Value tables is an approximation because the present value factors in the tables are rounded to three decimal places.

7. Under the assumption that cash inflows occur evenly throughout the year, the discounted payback period for the proposed project is slightly more than three years, as follows:

	A	B	C	D	E
1					Cumulative
2		After-tax	Discount	PV of After-	PV of After-
3		Cash	Factor	tax Cash	tax Cash
4	Year	Inflow	@ 12.0%	Flow	Flows
5	0	($650,000)	1.000	($650,000)	($650,000)
6	1	$270,000	0.893	$241,110	($408,890)
7	2	$270,000	0.797	$215,190	($193,700)
8	3	$270,000	0.712	$192,240	($1,460)
9	4	$308,000	0.636	$195,888	$194,428

8. Under the assumption that cash inflows occur at year-end, the estimated internal rate of return (IRR) for this investment is 25.3 percent, which can be determined using either a trial-and-error approach or using a built-in function for Excel, as follows:

Trial-and-Error: We can surmise from 6 above that the IRR must be significantly greater than the discount rate, 12 percent. Thus, we might choose IRR candidates of 25 percent and 30 percent in our attempt to find a rate that produces an NPV of 0.

	@25%	@30%
PV of after-tax cash inflows (details omitted)	$653,320	$598,120
Less: Initial investment outlay	650,000	650,000
NPV at indicated discount rate	$ 3,320	$(51,880)

Thus, the IRR of this project lies between 25 percent and 30 percent. By interpolation we have

$$IRR = 25\% + [\$3,320/(\$3,320 + \$51,880)] \times 5\%$$
$$= 25\% + [\$3,320/\$55,200] \times 5\% = 25\% + [0.06 \times 5\%] = \mathbf{25.3\%}$$

Excel-based formula approach:

	A	B	C	D
1		**After-tax**		
2	**Year**	**Cash Inflow**		
3	0	($650,000)		
4	1	$270,000		
5	2	$270,000		
6	3	$270,000		
7	4	$308,000		
8			Formula	
9	**IRR =**	**25.27%**	=IRR(B3:B7,0.12)	

(**Note:** In the IRR function, the "0.12" represents an initial guess; if omitted, Excel uses 10 percent as the starting point in its algorithm to estimate the IRR of an investment project.)

9. The MIRR of the proposed investment is approximately 20 percent, as follows:

	A	B	C	D
1		**After-Tax**		
2	**Year**	**Cash Flow**		
3	0	($650,000)		
4	1	$270,000		
5	2	$270,000		
6	3	$270,000		
7	4	$308,000		
8	**WACC =**	12.00%		
9			Formula	
10	**MIRR =**	**19.57%**	=MIRR(B3:B7,B8,B8)	

10. The most that variable costs can increase and still have the project return the minimum rate of return (12%), *holding everything else constant,* is $21.34 per unit, as follows:

The current projected NPV of the project is $194,428; thus, the PV of future after-tax cash inflows can drop by a maximum of $194,428 (if they fell by this amount, then the IRR on the project would be exactly 12%). The amount by which the annual pretax cash flows could decrease is $106,700, as follows:

Maximum annual decrease in annual *after-tax* cash inflows
(through increased variable costs, using annuity factor @ 12%) = $194,428/3.037 = $ 64,020

Given a 40% marginal income tax rate, the above amount
represents 60% (i.e., 1 − 40%) of the pretax amount;
thus, the maximum amount that pretax income can fall = $64,020/(1 − 0.40) = $106,700

Therefore, the variable cost per unit can increase by $106,700/5,000 units = $21.34 per unit. If everything else remained constant and the variable cost per unit increased by $21.34, the proposed project will yield a 12.0 percent return.

Alternatively, we can use the **Goal Seek** function in Excel to determine the maximum change in variable costs that could be realized such that the investment would yield an IRR of 12 percent. Use the following two-step process:

Step 1: Set Up the Current Situation

	A	B	C	D	E
1	Incremental sales per year (in units) =		5,000		
2	Selling price per unit =		$200.00		
3	Variable costs per unit =		$80.00		
4	Cash fixed costs per year =		$250,000		
5	Marginal income tax rate =		0.4		
6	Annual depreciation deduction (SL) =		$150,000		
7	Current level of after-tax operating cash flows per year =		$270,000		
8					
9	Current NPV of investment proposal =		$194,428	(given, Part 6)	
10	PV annuity factor, 12%, 4 years =		3.037	(Appendix C, Table 2)	
11					
12	Thus, decrease in annual *after-tax* cash inflows can be		$64,020	=C9/C10	
13	New level of annual *after-tax* cash inflows can decrease to		$205,980	=C7-C12	
14					
15	Incremental annual *pre-tax* cash income =		$350,000	=C1*(C2 C3) C4	
16	Minus: Income taxes on above (@40%) =		$140,000	=C5*C15	
17	Plus: Depreciation tax savings =		$60,000	=C5*C6	
18	After-tax, annual increase in operating cash flows =		$270,000	=C15-C16+C17	

This initial spreadsheet reflects the current investment proposal and the allowable decrease in after-tax annual cash inflows (cell C12) that can occur, given the goal of generating an IRR of 12.0 percent on the project.

Step 2: Use the Goal Seek Function of Excel

Next, go to the **Goal Seek** option under Data, then Data Tools. Given the preceding spreadsheet, complete the box as follows:

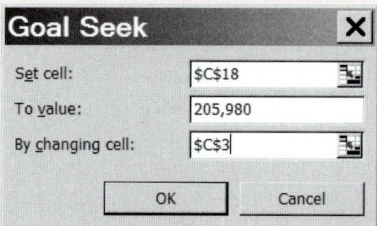

The preceding entries tell Excel to vary cell C3 (variable costs per unit) until the amount of annual cash operating profit after-tax (cell C18) has been reduced to $205,980 ($270,000 − $64,020). After clicking "OK," your spreadsheet should change to:

	A	B	C	D	E
1	Incremental sales per year (in units) =		5,000		
2	Selling price per unit =		$200.00		
3	Variable costs per unit =		$101.34		
4	Cash fixed costs per year =		$250,000		
5	Marginal income tax rate =		0.4		
6	Annual depreciation deduction (SL) =		$150,000		
7	Current level of after-tax operating cash flows per year =		$270,000		
8					
9	Current NPV of investment proposal =		$194,428	(given, Part 6)	
10	PV annuity factor, 12%, 4 years =		3.037	(Appendix C, Table 2)	
11					
12	Thus, decrease in annual *after-tax* cash inflows can be		$64,020	=C9/C10	
13	New level of annual *after-tax* cash inflows can decrease to		$205,980	=C7-C12	
14					
15	Incremental annual *pre-tax* cash income =		$243,300	=C1*(C2-C3)-C4	
16	Minus: Income taxes on above (@40%) =		$97,320	=C5*C15	
17	Plus: Depreciation tax savings =		$60,000	=C5*C6	
18	After-tax, annual increase in operating cash flows =		$205,980	=C15-C16+C17	

Thus, variable costs per unit can increase to $101.34 (or, $21.34 over the initial assumption of $80.00 per unit); if everything else other than variable cost per unit is held constant, the IRR of the project would be 12 percent.

Cost Planning for the Product Life Cycle: Target Costing, Theory of Constraints, and Strategic Pricing

After studying this chapter, you should be able to . . .

1. Explain how to use target costing to facilitate strategic management
2. Apply the theory of constraints to strategic management
3. Describe how life-cycle costing facilitates strategic management
4. Outline the objectives and techniques of strategic pricing

Having two of the world's best selling cars, the Camry and the Corolla, as well as a number of other popular models, Toyota is among the world's most successful automakers. The reason for Toyota's success is that it is able to consistently produce high-quality cars with attractive features at competitive prices. Target costing, a method Toyota pioneered in the 1960s, is one method it uses to achieve high quality and desirable features at a competitive price. Target costing is a design approach in which cost management plays a large part, as we will see in this chapter. Using target costing, a company designs a product to achieve a desired profit while satisfying the customer's expectations for quality and product features. The balancing of costs, features, and quality takes place throughout the design, manufacturing, sale, and service of the car but has the strongest influence in the first phase, design. When design alternatives are being examined and selected, Toyota has the maximum flexibility for choosing options that affect manufacturing and all other product costs such as customer service and warranty work.

Once the design is complete and manufacturing has begun, the cost consequences of the choice of features and manufacturing methods are set until the next model change. As a result, the development of a good, cost-effective design is critical. Target costing places a strong focus on using the design process to improve the product and reduce its cost. For example, in the redesign of the Camry, Toyota made the running lamps part of the headlamp assembly and made the grill part of the bumper, which saves time and materials in manufacturing and produces a more crash-resistant bumper—a win/win for Toyota and the car buyer.

Target costing is the first of four costing methods we study in the chapter. Each of the four methods is used for cost planning during the product (or service) life cycle. For example, target costing is used at an early phase in the product's life cycle to help an organization design the product to achieve a desired profit. The other methods, which are used at different phases in the life cycle, are the theory of constraints, life-cycle costing, and strategic pricing. While once managers focused only on manufacturing costs, they now look at costs upstream (before manufacturing) and downstream (after manufacturing) in the product life cycle to get

EXHIBIT 13.1
The Cost Life Cycle of a Product or Service

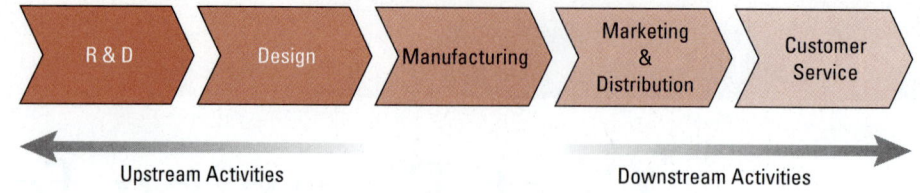

R & D → Design → Manufacturing → Marketing & Distribution → Customer Service

← Upstream Activities   Downstream Activities →

The **cost life cycle**
is the sequence of activities within the firm that begins with research and development followed by design, manufacturing, marketing/distribution, and customer service.

The **sales life cycle**
is the sequence of phases in the product's or service's life in the market from the introduction of the product or service to the market, growth in sales, and finally maturity, decline, and withdrawal from the market.

a comprehensive analysis of product cost and profitability (Exhibit 13.1). For example, in target costing we consider the role of product design (an upstream activity) in reducing costs in the manufacturing and downstream phases of the life cycle. Then, we see how the theory of constraints is used in the manufacturing phase to reduce manufacturing costs and to speed up delivery downstream. Then we look at life-cycle costing, which provides a comprehensive evaluation of the profitability of the different products, including costs throughout the product life cycle. Finally, strategic pricing uses life-cycle concepts in pricing decisions.

Of the four methods for cost planning, target costing, theory of constraints, and life-cycle costing are based on the product or service's cost life cycle, while the last method, strategic pricing, considers both the cost life cycle and the sales life cycle. The **cost life cycle** is the sequence of activities within the organization that begins with research and development followed by design, manufacturing (or providing the service), marketing/distribution, and customer service. It is the life cycle of the product or service from the viewpoint of costs incurred. The cost life cycle is illustrated in Exhibit 13.1.[1] The **sales life cycle** is the sequence of phases in the product's or service's life in the market from the introduction of the product or service to the market, the growth in sales, and finally maturity, decline, and withdrawal from the market. Sales are at first small, peak in the maturity phase, and decline thereafter, as illustrated in Exhibit 13.2.

These four methods are commonly used by manufacturing firms, where new product development, manufacturing speed, and efficiency are important. Because a product with physical characteristics is involved, applications in manufacturing firms are more intuitive and easily understood. However, each method can also be used in service firms. For example, a local government could use the theory of constraints to speed the process of billing residents for water services (and to reduce the processing cost) or to speed the operations for processing and depositing the collections from these residents.

EXHIBIT 13.2
The Sales Life Cycle of a Product or Service

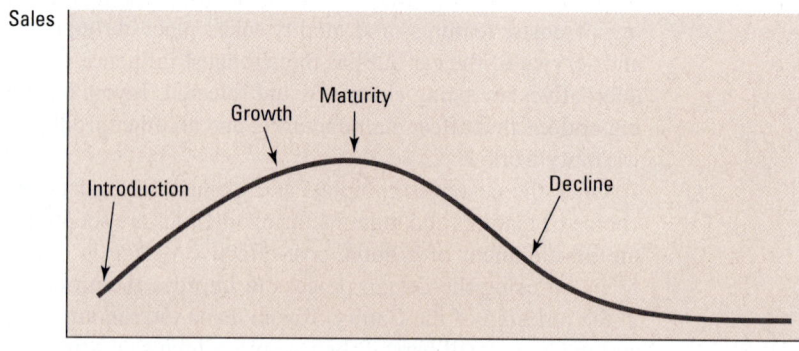

Sales

Introduction / Growth / Maturity / Decline

Time

---

[1] The *cost life cycle* also is called a *value chain* by many writers to emphasize that each activity must add value for the ultimate consumer [Michael Porter, *Competitive Advantage* (New York: Free Press, 1985)]. Note that this concept of the value chain differs from that introduced in Chapter 2. Chapter 2 describes the industry-level value chain; the cost life-cycle concept in this chapter describes the firm-level value chain. We use the broader concept of the industry-level value chain in Chapter 2 to facilitate the strategic focus in that chapter. For a discussion of the two types of value chains, see "Value Chain Analysis for Assessing Competitive Advantage," *Statement on Management Accounting*, Institute of Management Accountants, www.imanet.org/publications_statements.asp.

Target Costing

Henry Ford's thinking would fit well in today's corporate boardrooms, where global competition, increased customer expectations, and competitive pricing in many industries have forced companies to look for ways to reduce costs year after year at the same time producing products with increased levels of quality and functionality.

> Our policy is to reduce the price, extend the operations, and improve the article. You will notice that the reduction of price comes first. We have never considered costs as fixed. Therefore we first reduce the price to the point where we believe more sales result. Then we go ahead and try to make the prices. We do not bother about the costs. The new price forces the costs down. The more usual way is to take the costs and then determine the price, and although that method may be scientific in the narrow sense; it is not scientific in the broad sense, because what earthly use is it to know the cost if it tells you that you cannot manufacture at a price at which the article can be sold? But more to the point is the fact that although one may calculate what a cost is, and of course all of our costs are carefully calculated, no one knows what a cost ought to be. One of the ways of discovering is to name a price so low as to force everybody in the place to the highest point of efficiency. The low price makes everybody dig for profits. We make more discoveries concerning manufacturing and selling under this forced method than by any method of leisurely investigation.
>
> *Henry Ford,* My Life and My Work, *1923*

LEARNING OBJECTIVE 1

Explain how to use target costing to facilitate strategic management.

Ford is describing a technique called *target costing,* in which the firm determines the allowable (i.e., target) cost for the product or service, given a competitive market price, so the firm can earn a desired profit:

$$\text{Target cost} = \text{Competitive price} - \text{Desired profit}$$

Target costing is especially important during particularly competitive times, as during an economic recession, when many firms struggle for survival. The firm has two options for reducing costs to a target cost level:

1. By integrating new manufacturing technology, using advanced cost management techniques such as activity-based costing, and seeking higher productivity.
2. By redesigning the product or service. This method is beneficial for many firms because it recognizes that design decisions account for much of total product life cycle costs. By careful attention to design, significant reductions in total cost are possible.

Many firms employ both options: efforts to achieve increased productivity gains and target costing to determine low-cost design.

Auto manufacturers, software developers, and other consumer product manufacturers must also determine in the design process the number and types of features to include in periodic updates of a product using cost and market considerations. Target costing, based on analysis of functionality/cost trade-offs, is an appropriate management tool for these firms. With its positioning in the early, upstream phases of the cost life cycle, target costing can clearly help a firm reduce total costs (see Exhibit 13.3).

Japanese industry and a growing number of firms worldwide are using target costing. Toyota; Honda Motor Company; Boeing; Intel, Inc.; and many others use target costing. Many firms find it difficult to compete successfully on cost leadership or differentiation alone; they

EXHIBIT 13.3

Target Costing in the Cost Life Cycle

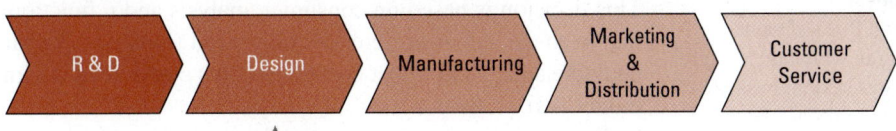

R & D   Design   Manufacturing   Marketing & Distribution   Customer Service

Target Costing

must compete on both price and functionality. Target costing is a very useful way to manage the needed trade-off between functionality and cost.

Implementing a target costing approach involves five steps:

1. Determine the market price.
2. Determine the desired profit.
3. Calculate the target cost at market price less desired profit.
4. Use value engineering to identify ways to reduce product cost.
5. Use kaizen costing and operational control to further reduce costs.

The first three steps require little additional explanation. However, the determination of desired profit can be done in a variety of ways. A common way is to set a desired per unit profit. This approach means that, if the product's price falls and target costs fall proportionally, then profits will remain the same after the price change, assuming the firm meets the new price and sales in units do not change. Another approach is to set the desired profit as a percentage of sales dollars. The section on pricing at the end of this chapter gives some additional examples of pricing methods. The following sections explain the fourth and fifth steps: the use of value engineering, kaizen costing, and operational control.

Value Engineering

Value engineering is used in target costing to reduce product cost by analyzing the trade-offs between different types of product functionality (different types of product features) and total product cost. An important first step in value engineering is to perform a consumer analysis during the design stage of the new or revised product. The consumer analysis identifies critical consumer preferences that define the desired functionality for the new product.

The type of value engineering used depends on the product's functionality. For one group of products—including automobiles, computer software, and many consumer electronic products such as cameras and audio and video equipment—functionality can be added or deleted relatively easily. These products have frequent new models or updates, and customer preferences change frequently. The manufacturer in effect chooses the particular bundle of features to include with each new model of the product. For automobiles, this can mean new performance and new safety features; for computer software, it might mean the ability to perform certain new tasks or analyses.

In contrast, for another group of products, the functionality must be designed into the product rather than added on. These are best represented by specialized equipment and industrial products such as construction equipment, heavy trucks, and specialized medical equipment. In contrast to the first group, customer preferences here are rather stable.

Target costing is more useful for products in the first group because the firm has some discretion about a larger number of features. A common type of value engineering employed in these firms is **functional analysis,** a process of examining the performance and cost of each major function or feature of the product. The objective of the analysis is to determine a desired balance of functionality and cost. An overall desired level of performance achievement for each function is obtained while keeping the cost of all functions below the target cost.

Benchmarking is often used at this step to determine which features give the firm a competitive advantage. In a release of new software, for example, each desired feature of the updated version is reviewed against the cost and time required for its development. The objective is an overall bundle of features for the software that achieves the desired balance of meeting customer preferences while keeping costs below targeted levels. In another example, auto manufacturers must decide which performance and safety features to add to the new model. This decision is based on consumer analysis and a functional analysis of the feature's contribution to consumer preferences compared to its cost. For instance, improved safety air bags could be added, but target cost constraints could delay an improved sound system until a later model year.

Design analysis is the common form of value engineering for products in the second group, industrial and specialized products. The design team prepares several possible designs of the product, each having similar features with different levels of performance and different costs.

Value engineering
is used in target costing to reduce product cost by analyzing the trade-offs between different types of product functionality and total product cost.

Functional analysis
is a common type of value engineering in which the performance and cost of each major function or feature of the product is examined.

Design analysis
is a common form of value engineering in which the design team prepares several possible designs of the product, each having similar features with different levels of performance and different costs.

Cost Management in Action

Why Go Abroad? Ralph Lauren, Apple, Kodak, and IBM

In competitive industries such as computers, consumer electronics, and autos, manufacturers continuously look for ways to reduce cost and increase value throughout the value chain. Because of intense pricing pressures and increased customer expectations, target costing methods can help identify and analyze the options for competitive advantage. Going abroad is the solution for many firms but for different reasons. We look at the practices in two industries: apparel companies, and consumer electronics and computer products.

APPAREL COMPANIES

Apparel manufacturers such as Ralph Lauren and Liz Claiborne have moved much of their product development as well as manufacturing to China. Fashion designers, fabric suppliers, button makers, and other parts of the product development process work together in the single location in China. What is the advantage to these companies?

CONSUMER ELECTRONICS AND COMPUTER PRODUCTS

Computer and electronics companies including Apple, Kodak, and IBM have outsourced manufacturing to plants operated by contract manufacturers in China and Mexico, such as Flextronics International, Ltd. and SCI Systems. IBM, for example, owns relatively few manufacturing plants, opting instead to contract out its manufacturing needs. Why is this an advantage to these three companies?

(Refer to Comments on Cost Management in Action at end of Chapter.)

Benchmarking and value-chain analysis help guide the design team in preparing designs that are both low cost and competitive. The design team works with cost management personnel to select the one design that best meets customer preferences while not exceeding the target cost.

A useful comparison of different target costing and cost-reduction strategies in three Japanese firms, based on the field research of Robin Cooper, is illustrated in Exhibit 13.4. Note that the different market demands for functionality result in different cost-reduction approaches. Where customers' expectations for functionality are increasing, as for Nissan and Olympus, there is more significant use of target costing. In contrast, at Komatsu, the emphasis is on value engineering and productivity improvement. Note also that firms such as Nissan, which use both internal and external sourcing for parts and components, use target costing at both the product level and the component level. The overall product-level target cost is achieved when targeted costs for all components are achieved.[2]

Other cost-reduction approaches include cost tables and group technology. **Cost tables** are computer-based databases that include comprehensive information about the firm's cost drivers. Cost drivers include, for example, the size of the product, the materials used in its manufacture, and the number of features. Firms that manufacture parts of different size from the

Cost tables
are computer-based databases that include comprehensive information about the firm's cost drivers.

EXHIBIT 13.4 Target Costing in Three Japanese Firms

Firm/Industry	Functionality	Cost Reduction Approach	Strategy
Olympus/Cameras	Increasing rapidly; is designed in	Target costing using value engineering; the concept of distinctive functionality for the **price point**, plus supportive functionality	Heavy focus on managing functionality
Nissan/Auto	Rapidly increasing; easy to add or delete functionality	**Value engineering** by product and by each component of each product; then increase price or reduce functionality	Prices are set by desired customers' expectations about functionality; after functionality is set, target cost is used to find savings, especially from suppliers
Komatsu/Construction equipment	Static; must be designed in	**Design analysis** to determine alternative designs. **Functional analysis** to develop cost/functionality trade-offs. **Productivity programs** to reduce the remaining costs	Primary focus is on cost control rather than redesign or functionality analysis

[2] Robin Cooper and Regine Slagmulder, "Develop Profitable New Products with Target Costing," *Sloan Management Review,* Summer 1999, pp. 23–33; and Robin Cooper and Regine Slagmulder, "Target Costing for New Product Development; Component-Level Target Costing," *Journal of Cost Management,* September–October, 2001, pp. 36–43.

Group technology
is a method of identifying similarities in the parts of products manufactured so the same part can be used in two or more products, thereby reducing costs.

Concurrent engineering,
or *simultaneous engineering,* is an important new method that integrates product design with manufacturing and marketing throughout the product's life cycle.

same design (pipe fittings, tools, and so on) use cost tables to show the difference in cost for parts of different sizes and different types of materials.

Group technology is a method of identifying similarities in the parts of products manufactured so the same parts can be used in two or more products, thereby reducing costs. Large manufacturers of diverse product lines, such as in the automobile industry, use group technology in this way. A point of concern in the use of group technology is that it reduces manufacturing costs but might increase service and warranty costs if a failed part is used in many different models. The combination of group technology and total quality management can, however, result in lower costs in both manufacturing and service/warranty.

Concurrent engineering, or *simultaneous engineering,* is an important new development in the design of products that is replacing the basic engineering approach in which product designers work in isolation on specialized components of the overall design project. In contrast, concurrent engineering relies on an integrated approach, in which the engineering/design process takes place throughout the cost life cycle using cross-functional teams. Information is solicited from and used at each phase of the value chain to improve the product design. For example, customer feedback in the service phase is used directly in product design. Manufacturers such as Toyota Motor Corp. and Moen, Inc. are increasingly using product design in a very flexible manner; they incorporate improvements in the product continuously. Some experts argue that this approach has saved firms as much as 20 percent of total product cost.

An important part of value engineering is the use of advanced costing methods, such as ABC costing, to accurately determine the product cost for each feature of the product, each function of the product, or each design option that is being considered. ABC costing is particularly useful for helping product designers, purchasing managers, manufacturing managers, and marketing managers work together with a common understanding of the costs of different features and options.[3]

Be a yardstick of quality. Some people aren't used to an environment where excellence is expected.

Steve Jobs, CEO of Apple, Inc

Target Costing and Kaizen

The fifth step in target costing is to use continuous improvement (kaizen) and operational control to further reduce costs. Kaizen occurs at the manufacturing stage where the effects of value engineering and improved design are already in place; the role for cost reduction at this phase is to develop new manufacturing methods (such as flexible manufacturing systems) and to use new management techniques such as operational control (Chapters 14, 15, and 16), total quality management (Chapter 17), and the theory of constraints (next section) to further reduce costs. *Kaizen* means *continuous* improvement, that is, the ongoing search for new ways to reduce costs in the manufacturing process of a product with a given design and functionality. Toyota and a small number of other firms are leaders in the implementation of continuous improvement. Toyota is using kaizen to reduce manufacturing costs on its hybrid vehicles, so that it can bring down the premium it must now charge for these vehicles.

Exhibit 13.5 shows the relationship between target costing and kaizen. Price is assumed to be stable or decreasing over time for firms for which target costing is appropriate because of intense competition on price, product quality and product functionality. These firms respond to the competitive pressure by periodically redesigning their products using target costing to simultaneously reduce the product price and improve their value. Consider the two points in Exhibit 13.5 labeled first and second target cost. The time period between product redesigns is approximately the product's sales life cycle. In the time between product redesigns, the firm uses kaizen to reduce product cost in the manufacturing process by streamlining the supply chain and improving both manufacturing methods and productivity programs. Thus, target costing and kaizen are complementary methods used to continually reduce cost and improve value.

---

[3] Gary Cokins, "Integrating Target Costing and ABC," *Journal of Cost Management*, July/August 2002, pp. 13–22.

EXHIBIT 13.5
Price, Cost, Kaizen,
and Target Costing

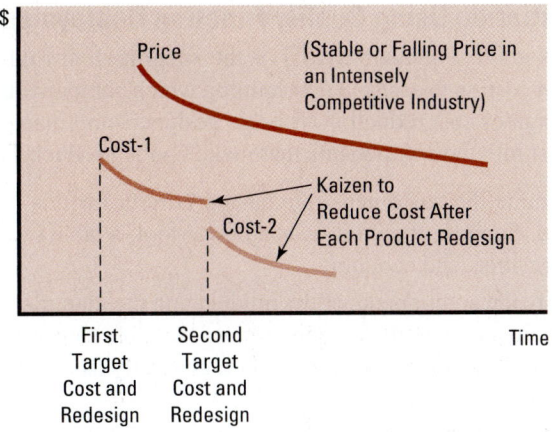

An Illustration: Target Costing in Health Product Manufacturing

Health Products International, Inc. (HPI), is conducting a value engineering project by making a target costing analysis of a major product, a hearing aid. HPI sells a reliable second-generation hearing aid (HPI-2) for $750 (cost of $650) and has obtained 30 percent of this market worldwide at a profit of $100 per aid. However, a competitor recently introduced a new third-generation hearing aid that incorporates a computer chip that improves performance considerably and increases the price to $1,200. Through consumer analysis, HPI has determined that cost-conscious consumers will stay with HPI, which will maintain its market share as long as its price does not exceed $600. HPI must meet the new lower price and maintain its current rate of profit ($100 per unit) by redesigning the hearing aid and/or the manufacturing process.

The target cost for the hearing aid is $600 − $100 = $500, a reduction in cost of $150 ($650 − $500). Because the product has no add-on features, HPI decides to use design analysis with the following alternatives for changes and related savings per unit:

> **Alternative A.** Reduce research and development expenditures ($50), replace the microphone unit with one of nearly equivalent sensitivity ($30), replace toggle power switch with a cheaper and almost as reliable slide switch ($30), replace the current inspection procedure with an integrated quality review process at each assembly station ($40). Total savings: $150.

> **Alternative B.** Replace the amplifier unit with one having slightly less power, not expected to be a noticeable difference for most users ($50), replace the microphone unit with one of nearly equivalent sensitivity ($30), replace toggle power switch with a cheaper and almost as reliable slide switch ($30), replace the current inspection procedure with an integrated quality review process at each assembly station ($40). Total savings: $150.

> **Alternative C.** Increase research and development activity to develop the new third-generation computer chip type of hearing aid (the total R&D commitment would require a price *increase* of $40). Replace the amplifier unit with one of slightly less power, not expected to be a noticeable difference for most users ($50), replace the microphone unit with one of nearly equivalent sensitivity ($30), replace toggle power switch with a cheaper and almost as reliable slide switch ($30), replace the current inspection procedure with an integrated quality review process at each assembly station ($40), renegotiate contract with supplier of plastic casing ($20), replace plastic earpiece material with material of slightly lower quality but well within the user's expectations for 6 to 10 years of use ($20). Net savings: $150.

After a review of its alternatives, HPI chose alternative C, primarily because it included an increase in research and development expenditures that would enable the firm at some future time to compete in the market for the new type of hearing aid. Manufacturing and marketing managers agreed that the design changes proposed in all the options would not significantly alter the market appeal of the current product. Key managers also determined that this alternative was strategically important because the new technology, while only a fraction of the market now, could be dominant in the next 10 to 15 years as prices come down on the new units and users become more aware of the benefits of the computer chip.

An Illustration Using Quality Function Deployment (QFD)

Quality function deployment (QFD)

is the integration of value engineering, marketing analysis, and target costing to assist in determining which components of the product should be targeted for redesign.

Quality function deployment (QFD) is the integration of value engineering, marketing analysis, and target costing to assist in determining which components of the product should be targeted for redesign or cost reduction. It helps designers and managers break down the total product target cost into the components that make up the product. There are four steps in QFD:

1. Determine the customer's purchasing criteria for this product and how these criteria are ranked. Suppose the product is a power tool, a table saw. The customer criteria are safety, performance, and economy.

2. Identify the components of the product and the manufacturing cost of each component. For simplicity, assume the components of the table saw are the motor, the saw and the frame. (QFD in an actual application would generally use many more components and more customer criteria).

3. Determine how components contribute to customer satisfaction. How much does the motor contribute to the customer's desired safety, performance, and economy? This is done for all the components.

4. The final step is to determine the importance index of each component, by combining the information in steps one and three and then comparing this to the cost information in step 2.

To illustrate, suppose the information in step one shows the customer criteria as follows. The importance rating might be obtained from a survey or from interviews. We assume in this example that the customers rated safety a value of 95, performance a value of 60, and economy a value of 50. The key here is the relative importance rating, which is 46.3 percent, 29.3 percent, and 24.4 percent, respectively.

First: Customer Criteria and Ranking

	Importance	Relative Importance
Safety	95	46.3%
Performance	60	29.3
Economy	50	24.4
Total	205	100.0%

Second, we identify the components and cost of each:

Second: Product Components and Cost

	Cost	Percent of Total
Motor	$40	53.3%
Saw	20	26.7
Frame	15	20.0
Total	$75	100.0%

Third, we determine the contribution of each component to satisfying customer criteria. This step usually requires a team of marketing, operations, and cost management analysts. In this example, the desired criteria of safety is achieved primarily by the frame (60%) and then by the saw (30%) and motor (10%).

Third: Determine How Components Contribute to Customer Satisfaction

Components	Customer Criteria		
	Safety	Performance	Economy
Motor	10%	10%	60%
Saw	30	50	10
Frame	60	40	30
	100%	100%	100%

Fourth, we determine the importance index for each component, which reflects the value of the component to the customer. It is shown in the right column below.

Fourth: Determine Importance Index for Each Component

	Customer Criteria			Importance Index
	Safety	Performance	Economy	
Relative importance of this criteria (step one)	46.3%	29.3%	24.4%	
The % contribution of each component to each customer criteria (from step 3):				
Motor	10%	10%	60%	22.2%
Saw	30	50	10	31.0
Frame	60	40	30	46.8
	100%	100%	100%	100.0%

The importance index values are 22.2 percent for the motor, 31.0 percent for the saw, and 46.8 percent for the frame. For example, the 22.2 percent index for the motor is determined as follows (the index for the other two components is computed in a similar way):

$$(46.3\% \times 10\%) + (29.3\% \times 10\%) + (24.4\% \times 60\%) = 22.2\%$$

The importance index can now be compared to the cost information in step two to identify components where cost reductions are needed, and components where additional design features might be appropriate.

Components	Importance Index	Relative Cost
Motor	22.2%	53.3%
Saw	31.0	26.7
Frame	46.8	20.0
	100.0%	100.0%

The comparison above shows that far too much is being spent on the motor relative to its value to the customer. In contrast, not enough is being spent on the frame, relative to customer criteria.

This information is a guide to the redesign of the product and to the determination of the target cost for each component.

Benefits of Target Costing

Target costing can be beneficial because it

- Increases customer satisfaction, as design is focused on customer values.
- Reduces costs, through more effective and efficient design.
- Helps the firm achieve desired profitability on new or redesigned products.
- Can decrease the total time required for product development, through improved coordination of design, manufacturing, and marketing managers.
- Can help provide a competitive edge in times of economic recession.
- Can improve overall product quality, as the design is carefully developed and manufacturing issues are considered explicitly in the target design phase.

The Theory of Constraints

Remember that time is money.

Benjamin Franklin

LEARNING OBJECTIVE 2

Apply the theory of constraints to facilitate strategic management.

Benjamin Franklin must be right. Most strategic initiatives undertaken by firms today focus on improving the speed of their operations throughout the cost life cycle. Why is speed so important? For many companies, it is a competitive edge. Customers expect quick response to inquiries and fast delivery of the product. Shorter sales life cycles in many industries mean that manufacturers are working to reduce product development time. Some of the most successful business models of recent years, such as those of Dell Inc. and Amazon.com, are built on speed. Amazon's Web site states when the product will be shipped; many times this is within 24 hours.

In this part of the chapter, we present one of the key methods used to improve speed, the theory of constraints (TOC). Before looking closely at TOC, we consider the issue of how speed is measured and improved throughout the cost life cycle, as illustrated in Exhibit 13.6. The measures are defined in different ways by different firms, depending on the nature of the firm's operations. For example, manufacturing **cycle time** (or manufacturing *lead time or throughput time*) is commonly defined as follows:

Cycle time

is the amount of time between the receipt of a customer order and the shipment of the order.

$$\text{Cycle time} = \text{Amount of time between the receipt of a customer order and the shipment of the order}$$

Depending on the firm's operations and objectives, the start of the cycle time can also be defined as the time a production batch is scheduled, the time the raw materials are ordered, or the time that production on the order is started. The finish time of the cycle can also be defined as the time that production is completed or the time the order is ready for shipping.

Manufacturing cycle efficiency (MCE)

is the ratio of processing time to total cycle time.

Another useful measure is **manufacturing cycle efficiency (MCE)**:

$$\text{MCE} = \frac{\text{Processing time}}{\text{Total cycle time}}$$

For example, if the processing time is 2 days and the cycle time is 10 days, then the MCE ratio is 2/10, or 20 percent.

EXHIBIT 13.6 **Measures of Speed and How to Improve Speed at Each Step of the Cost Life Cycle**

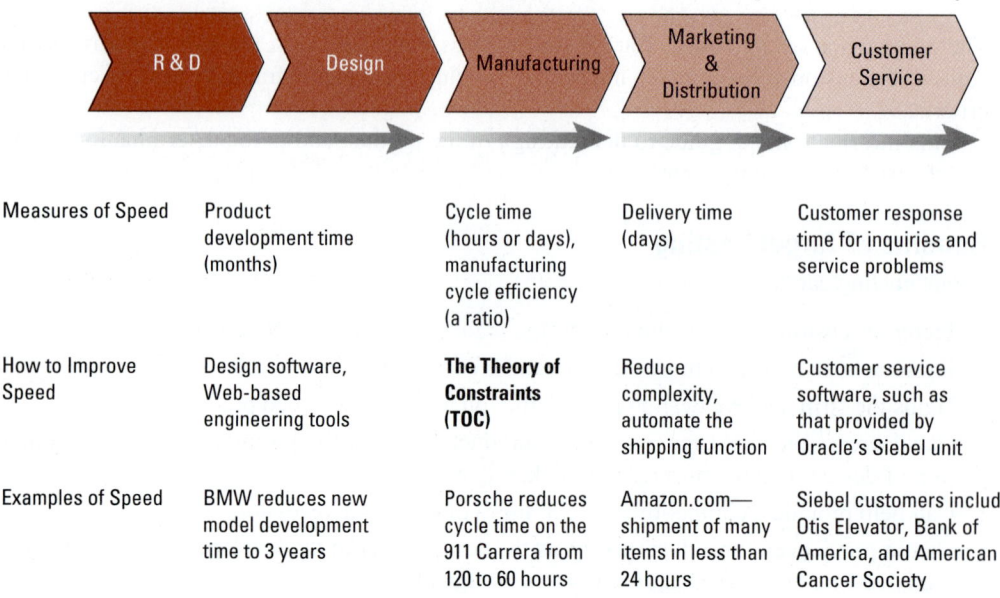

	R & D	Design	Manufacturing	Marketing & Distribution	Customer Service
Measures of Speed	Product development time (months)		Cycle time (hours or days), manufacturing cycle efficiency (a ratio)	Delivery time (days)	Customer response time for inquiries and service problems
How to Improve Speed	Design software, Web-based engineering tools		**The Theory of Constraints (TOC)**	Reduce complexity, automate the shipping function	Customer service software, such as that provided by Oracle's Siebel unit
Examples of Speed	BMW reduces new model development time to 3 years		Porsche reduces cycle time on the 911 Carrera from 120 to 60 hours	Amazon.com—shipment of many items in less than 24 hours	Siebel customers include Otis Elevator, Bank of America, and American Cancer Society

MCE separates total cycle time into the time required for each of the various activities: processing (value-adding work on the product), inspection, materials handling, waiting, and so on. Most firms would like to see their MCE close to 1, which reflects less time wasted on moving, waiting, inspecting, and other non-value-adding activities.[4]

Constraints
are those activities that slow the product's cycle time.

The theory of constraints (TOC) was developed to help managers reduce cycle times and operating costs.[5] Prior to TOC, managers often devoted efforts to improve efficiency and speed *throughout* the manufacturing process instead of focusing attention on just those activities that were constraints (i.e., bottlenecks) in the process. **Constraints** are activities that slow a product's total cycle time. Goldratt and Cox use as an example a troop of boy scouts on a hike; the slowest hiker is the constraint and sets the overall pace for the troop. Manufacturers have learned that increased efficiency and speed with activities that are not constraints could be dysfunctional. Unnecessary efficiency is likely to result in the buildup of work-in-process inventory for activities prior to the constraint (just as the scouts would be "bunched up" behind the slowest scout) and to divert attention and resources from the actual slowdown in cycle time. TOC has turned the attention to improving speed at the constraints, which causes a favorable decrease in the overall cycle time and inventory. TOC can be compared to just-in-time manufacturing (JIT) in that both are aimed at reducing cycle time and reducing inventory levels. JIT accomplishes this by methods that coordinate manufacturing processes so that materials are available just in time for the process, thereby increasing processing speed and reducing or eliminating inventory.[6]

The Use of the Theory of Constraints Analysis in Health Product Manufacturing

To illustrate the use of TOC and its five steps, we again consider Healthcare Products International, Inc. (HPI). Suppose that HPI is currently manufacturing both the second generation (HPI-2) and third generation (HPI-3) hearing aids. The prices for the HPI-2 and HPI-3 are competitive at $600 and $1,200, respectively, and are not expected to change. Because of manufacturing delays and increasing cycle times, HPI has a backlog of orders for both the HPI-2 and the HPI-3. Its monthly number of orders for the HPI-2 is 3,000 units and for the HPI-3 is 1,800 units. New customers are told that they may have to wait three weeks or more for their orders. Management is concerned about the need to improve speed in the manufacturing process and is planning to use TOC. Here are the steps HPI would take to use TOC.

Steps in the Theory of Constraints Analysis

TOC analysis has five steps:

1. Identify the constraint.
2. Determine the most profitable product mix given the constraint.
3. Maximize the flow through the constraint.
4. Add capacity to the constraint.
5. Redesign the manufacturing process for flexibility and fast cycle time.

---

[4] While 100 percent is a theoretical maximum for MCE, many firms find their MCE ratios somewhat smaller because of delays and wasted time in the manufacturing process. For example, statistics from the auto industry show that some firms have cycle times of over 30 days and product assembly times of 1 to 2 days—an MCE of approximately 5 percent. Also, note that the terms used here are *manufacturing* measurements, and that similar measures are used by firms to examine the firm's progress in *filling customer orders*. For example, customer lead time (or customer cycle time) is usually defined as the time from the receipt of an order to the delivery of the product.

[5] E. Goldratt and J. Cox, *The Goal* (New York: Free Press, 1986); and E. Goldratt, *The Theory of Constraints* (New York: North River Press, 1990). See also Thomas Corbett, *Throughput Accounting* (New York: North River Press, 1998); and Thomas Corbett, "Three Questions Accounting," *Strategic Finance*, April 2006, pp. 48–55.

[6] A comprehensive comparison of TOC and JIT is provided by Bih-Ru Lea and Hokey Min, "Selection of Management Accounting Systems in Just-In-Time and Theory of Constraints-Based Manufacturing," *International Journal of Production Research*, 2003, pp. 2879–2910.

EXHIBIT 13.7
Flow Diagram for HPI, Inc.

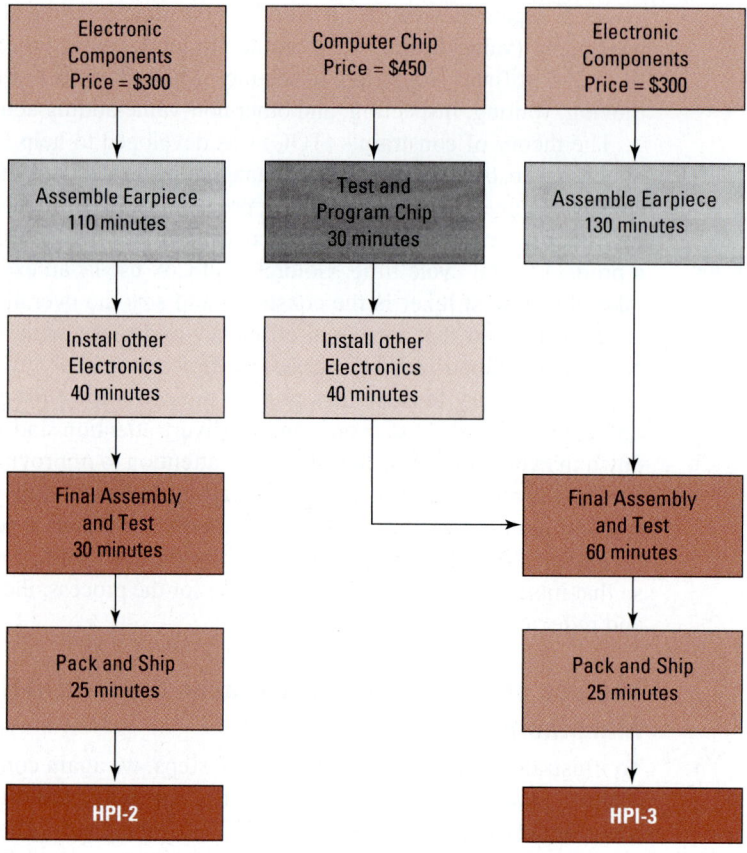

Step 1: Identify the Constraint

A **flow diagram**
is a flowchart of the work done
that shows the sequence of
processes and the amount of
time required for each.

The management accountant works with manufacturing managers and engineers to identify any constraint in the manufacturing process by developing a **flow diagram** of the work done. The flow diagram shows the sequence of processes and the amount of time each requires. The five processes for HPI follow, and their flow diagram is shown in Exhibit 13.7.

Process 1. Assemble earpiece.
Process 2. Test and program computer chip (product HPI-3 only).
Process 3. Install other electronics.
Process 4. Perform final assembly and test.
Process 5. Pack and ship.

The raw materials cost for each unit is $300 for the HPI-2 and $750 for the HPI-3 ($450 for the computer chip and $300 for other electronics).

The constraint is identified by using the flow diagram to analyze the total time required for each process given the current level of demand. Exhibit 13.8 shows a summary of the data for this analysis, including the number of employees available for each process and the total time available per month for all employees (assuming a 40-hour work week in which 30 hours are available for work and 10 hours are used for breaks, training, etc.). HPI processes are very specialized, and employees are able to work only within their assigned process. Moreover, because of the specialized skills required, HPI has difficulty maintaining adequate staffing in all processes except process 5, pack and ship.

Step 1 in Exhibit 13.8 shows the total time required in each process given the current level of demand. Each of the five processes except process 4 has slack time. Therefore, the constraint occurs with process 4, perform final assembly and test. Because of inadequate time (900 hours too few) available in this process, HPI will not be able to meet the total demand for HPI-2 and HPI-3 and will delay some orders or perhaps not fill them at all. HPI

EXHIBIT 13.8   **Summary of Data for HPI, Inc., TOC Analysis**

	HPI-2	HPI-3
Demand (per month)	3,000	1,800
Price	$600	$1,200
Materials cost	$300	$ 750

	Minutes Required for Each Product Per Unit		Number of Employees	Total Hours Available Per Month
Process	HPI-2	HPI-3		
1: Assemble earpiece	110	130	80	9,600
2: Test and program computer chip	0	30	8	960
3: Install other electronics	40	40	30	3,600
4: Perform final assembly and test	30	60	20	2,400
5: Pack and ship	25	25	18	2,160

Step 1: Identify the Constraint (the process for which total hours required for the given demand exceeds available hours-Process 4)

	Hours Required				
	HPI-2	HPI-3	Total Hours	Hours Available	Slack Hours
Process 1: Assemble earpiece	5,500	3,900	9,400	9,600	200
(5,500 hrs = 3,000 × 110/60, etc)					
Process 2: Test and program chip	0	900	900	960	60
Process 3: Install other electronics	2,000	1,200	3,200	3,600	400
Process 4: Perform final assembly and test	1,500	1,800	3,300	2,400	(900)
Process 5: Pack and ship	1,250	750	2,000	2,160	160

Step 2, Part 1: Identify Most Profitable Product = HPI-2

	HPI-2	HPI-3
Price	$600.00	$1,200.00
Materials cost	300.00	750.00
Throughput margin	$300.00	$ 450.00
Constraint time (for Process 4)	30	60
Throughput margin per minute	$ 10.00	$ 7.50

Step 2, Part 2: Identify the Most Profitable Product Mix

	HPI-2	HPI-3	
Total demand in units	3,000	1,800	
Units of product in optimal mix	3,000	900	(Total HPI-2 demand is met first; then remaining capacity is used for HPI-3)
Unmet demand	—	900	

must now determine which orders to fill and which not to fill. This takes us to the second step of TOC.

Step 2: Determine the Most Profitable Product Mix Given the Constraint

The most profitable product mix is the combination of products that maximizes total profits for both products. Should we produce all 3,000 units of HPI-2 and whatever we can of HPI-3, or should we produce all 1,800 units of HPI-3 and whatever we can of HPI-2? Or some other mix? The step 2 analysis in Exhibit 13.8 provides the answer.[7]

To determine the most profitable product mix, we first determine the most profitable product, given the constraint. TOC measures product profitability using the **throughput margin,** which is the product price less materials cost (includes the costs of all materials used,

Throughput margin
is a TOC measure of product profitability; it equals price less materials cost, including all purchased components and materials handling costs.

[7] Note that the analysis in step 2 part 1 and step 2, part 2 of Exhibit 13.8 is identical to that explained in Chapter 11 under the heading of "Multiple Products and Limited Resources," for one production constraint. The determination of the optimal product mix is arrived at in the same manner. Step 2, part 2 can be solved using the Solver tool in Excel, as illustrated in Chapter 11.

purchased components, and materials-handling costs). All other manufacturing costs are excluded in determining profitability because they are assumed to be fixed and will not change regardless of which product mix is chosen.[8] Step 2, part 1 in Exhibit 13.8 shows that throughput margins for the HPI-2 and HPI-3 are $300 and $450, respectively. Although HPI-3 has the higher margin, the profitability analysis is not complete without considering the time required by the constraint, final assembly and test for each product. Since HPI-3 takes twice as much time in final assembly and test as HPI-2 (60 versus 30 minutes), HPI can produce twice as many HPI-2 models for each HPI-3 produced. In effect, the relevant measure of profitability is throughput margin *per minute of time in final assembly and test,* that is, a throughput per minute of $10 for HPI-2 and $7.50 for HPI-3. This means that each minute that final assembly and test is used to produce HPI-2 earns $10 while each minute used to produce HPI-3 earns only $7.50. HPI-2 is the most profitable product when final assembly and test is the constraint.

The best product mix is determined in step 2, part 2 of Exhibit 13.8. HPI produces all 3,000 units or demand for HPI-2 since it is the most profitable product. Next, HPI determines the remaining capacity in final assembly. Then HPI determines the number of units of HPI-3 it can produce with the remaining capacity on the constraint, process 4. Despite the demand for 1,800 units of HPI-3, only 900 can be produced with the available capacity, determined as follows: First, the process 4 capacity used in production of HPI-2 is calculated, 3,000 units $\times$ 30 minutes/unit equals 90,000 minutes or 1,500 hours. This leaves 900 hours (2,400 total process 4 hours $-$ 1,500) for HPI-3. Second, in 900 hours, HPI can produce 900 units of HPI-3, which requires one hour per unit processing time. Thus, the optimal product mix is 3,000 units of HPI-2 and 900 units of HPI-3, given the constraint on process 4.

The assumption in our illustration of the TOC approach is that minimal or no inventory of HPI-3 is maintained, so that it is not possible to fill the unmet demand for HPI-3 out of inventory. This assumption is in keeping with the TOC approach which emphasizes the reduction of cost and speed of product flow by removing constraints and reducing inventory levels.

Step 3: Maximize the Flow through the Constraint

In this step, the management accountant looks for ways to speed the flow through the constraint by simplifying the process, improving the product design, reducing setup time, and reducing other delays due to unscheduled and non-value-added activities such as inspections or machine breakdowns, among others.

A commonly used method for identifying constraints and smoothing production flow is the use of **Takt time.** Takt is a German word meaning the conductor's baton, or rhythm. It is the ratio of the total time available to the expected customer demand. For example, suppose a manufacturing plant operates for eight hours per day, and that after allowing for break time, 400 minutes of manufacturing time are available per day. Also, since the average customer demand per day is 800 units, the Takt time is 30 seconds per unit:

Takt time

is the speed at which units must be manufactured to meet customer demand.

$$\text{Takt time} = \frac{\text{Available manufacturing time}}{\text{Customer demand}}$$

$$\text{Takt time} = \frac{400 \text{ minutes}}{800 \text{ units}} = \frac{1}{2} \text{ minute or 30 seconds per unit}$$

This means that each unit must be manufactured in an average of 30 seconds to meet customer demand. To illustrate how Takt time can be used to identify constraints, consider a product that has demand of 18,000 units per week, with total operating time available per week at 75 hours. The Takt time is:

$$\frac{\text{Available time}}{\text{Demand}} = \frac{75 \text{ hr.} \times 60 \text{ min.} \times 60 \text{ seconds}}{18,000 \text{ units}}$$

$$= \frac{270,000 \text{ seconds}}{18,000 \text{ units}}$$

$$= 15 \text{ seconds per unit}$$

---

[8] Note that TOC analysis assumes that factory labor is not a direct and variable cost but is a fixed cost. This assumption applies when labor is a small or an unchanging part of total cost.

REDUCING CYCLE TIMES IN CUSTOMER PAYMENT

Starbucks has decided to deal with the long lines that scare off some customers by decreasing the time needed to pay from 20 seconds to 4 seconds. The swipeable card that allows customers to pay instantly also provides Starbucks with important marketing information. McDonald's is doing the same thing for fast food by using credit cards to reduce customer paying time to 5 seconds instead of the 10 seconds needed with cash.

BMW, HONDA, AND NISSAN: SPEED THROUGH FLEXIBILITY

Improvements in the design of auto manufacturing plants to use labor and machines more flexibly allow BMW, Honda, and Nissan to improve throughput and reduce costs. Flexible manufacturing improvements come through automation, flexible labor agreements, strategic outsourcing, and fast change-over times.

Sources: "Starbucks' Card Smarts," *BusinessWeek,* March 18, 2002, p. 14; "BMW Keeps the Home Fires Burning," *BusinessWeek,* May 30, 2005, p. 52; Kate Linebaugh, "Honda's Flexible Plants Provide Edge," *The Wall Street Journal,* September 23, 2008, p. B1.

The plant must produce a unit each 15 seconds to keep up with demand. Assume the manufacturing process has three operations in sequence, each of which requires 15 seconds processing time. Then, on the average, a product will be completed every 15 seconds. Now, assume that the first operation requires 10 seconds, the second operation requires 20 seconds, and the third requires 15 seconds. Now, the processing line is unbalanced; the first operation moves quickly and work in process will build up at the second operation, which is relatively slow. Furthermore, the total demand of 18,000 units cannot be met because the second process requires more than the 15 seconds of Takt time. The second operation is a constraint. In fact, the plant will only be able to meet a demand of 13,500 units (13,500 = 270,000 seconds/20 seconds) because of the slow second operation. Only when the three operations are balanced at or near the Takt time of 15 seconds will the demand be met. The goal of implementing Takt time is to balance the processing of the operations, so that the processing time of each operation is preferably a little below the overall Takt time. An operation that has a very low processing time relative to Takt time has too much capacity, and it would be more efficient to reduce capacity (and thus increase processing time) on that operation, as long as processing time remains below Takt time.

Step 4: Add Capacity to the Constraint

As a longer-term measure to relieve the constraint and improve cycle time, management should consider adding capacity to the constraints by adding new or improved machines and/or additional labor.

Step 5: Redesign the Manufacturing Process for Flexibility and Fast Cycle Time

The most complete strategic response to the constraint is to redesign the manufacturing process, including the introduction of new manufacturing technology, deletion of some hard-to-manufacture products, and redesign of some products for greater ease of manufacturing. Simply removing one or more minor features on a given product might speed up the production process significantly. The use of value engineering as described earlier might help at this point.

The Five Steps of Strategic Decision Making for Speed and Efficiency in the Fashion Industry

Burberry Group PLC is a London-based fashion retailer with several hundred retail stores worldwide providing its famous trench coats and a variety of women's and men's fashion clothing. Burberry CEO, Angela Ahrendts, upon taking the position in July 2006, noticed that the company was making "way too much stuff." There were too many product lines—for example, 20 different versions of men's and women's polo shirts. The complexity of the large number of products resulted in delay throughout the value chain—design, manufacturing, and distribution.[9]

The Five Steps of Strategic Decision-Making for Burberry, the Fashion Retailer

1 **Determine the strategic issues surrounding the problem.** Burberry, as a fashion retailer, competes on the basis of design and fashion innovation, a differentiation strategy.

2 **Identify the alternative actions.** The company can continue to focus on product development, design, and innovation, with the expectation that the delays will not affect customer satisfaction or profitability. Alternatively, the company could review its product lines and look for efficiency throughout the value chain and expect to maintain the unique designs that have satisfied Burberry customers in the past.

3 **Obtain information and conduct analyses of the alternatives.** Ahrendts directed the CFO to prepare a report showing what amount each product contributed to overall sales. The findings were that 20 percent of the products produced 80 percent of total sales. In order to determine product profitability, Ahrendts directed the CFO to develop appropriate computer-based accounting and operating systems. The enterprise system, SAP, was introduced in 2007.

4 **Based on strategy and analysis, choose and implement the desired alternative.** Based on the CFO's information and her understanding that the firm's strategy required comprehensive, coherent product development, Ahrendts decided to reduce the number of Burberry's products by one-third and to switch from two large collections of fashion per year to five smaller collections. At the same time, she coordinated product development from London, so that all Burberry lines provided ". . .one brand and one message." The changes allowed the company to design and produce its fashions much more quickly, to adjust much more rapidly to changes in customer expectations, and to reduce costs through more efficient processes—design through retail sales.

5 **Provide an ongoing evaluation of the effectiveness of implementation in step 4.** The changes made by the new CEO have made the company more profitable and better able to meet its customer expectations—a more competitive company. However, since design and innovation are the hallmarks of the fashion industry and for Burberry, the company must maintain a priority on these facets of the business as well.

Theory of Constraints Reports

When a firm focuses on improving cycle time, eliminating constraints, and improving speed of delivery, the performance evaluation measures also focus on these critical success factors. A common approach is to report throughput margin as well as selected operating data in a *theory of constraints report*. An example of this report used by a manufacturer of automotive glass is shown in Exhibit 13.9. Note in the exhibit that window styles H and B are the most profitable because they have far higher throughput margin based on the binding constraint, hours of furnace time. The throughput margin per hour is $3,667 and $2,371 for styles H and B, respectively; in contrast, the throughput margin per hour for styles C and A is less than $1,000. TOC reports are useful for identifying the most profitable product and for monitoring success in achieving the critical success factors.

Activity-Based Costing and the Theory of Constraints

Firms using such cost management methods as target costing and the theory of constraints commonly employ activity-based costing (ABC). ABC is used to assess the profitability of products, just as TOC was used in the previous illustration. The difference is that TOC takes a short-term approach to profitability analysis while ABC costing develops a long-term

[9] The information is from Burberry's 2007 annual report and from Cecilie Rohwedder, "Burberry CEO Retrenches: Fewer Items, Faster Delivery," *The Wall Street Journal*, May 24, 2007, p. B1. Other high fashion designers including Valentino , Gucci, and Zara are also changing design and manufacturing processes for greater speed and flexibility: Christina Passariello, "Logistics Are in Vogue with Designers," *The Wall Street Journal*, Friday June 27, 2008, p. B1; Kerry Capell, "Zara Thrives by Breaking All the Rules," *BusinessWeek*, October 20, 2008, p. 66; Christina Binkley," Tracking the Trousers Cycle," *The Wall Street Journal*, August 16, 2007, p. D1.

EXHIBIT 13.9
The TOC Report for an Auto Glass Manufacturer

Source: R. J. Campbell, "Pricing Strategy in the Automotive Glass Industry," *Management Accounting*, July 1989, pp. 26–34.

	March 2010			
	Style C	**Style A**	**Style H**	**Style B**
Window size	0.77	.073	7.05	4.95
Sales volume	High	Moderate	High	Moderate
Units in unfilled orders	1,113	234	882	23
Average lead time (days)	16	23	8	11
Market price	$2.82	$6.68	$38.12	$24.46
Direct production costs				
Materials	0.68	0.64	5.75	4.02
Scrap allowance	0.06	0.05	0.42	0.34
Material handling	0.12	0.12	1.88	1.61
Subtotal	.86	.81	8.05	5.97
Throughput margin	$1.96	$5.87	$30.07	$18.49
Furnace hours per unit	.0062	.0061	.0082	.0078
Throughput margin per hour	$316	$962	$3,667	$2,371

EXHIBIT 13.10
Comparison of the TOC and ABC Costing Methods

	TOC	**ABC**
Main objective	**Short-term focus;** throughput margin analysis based on materials and materials-related costs	**Long-term focus;** analysis of all product costs, including materials, labor, and overhead
Resource constraints and capacities	Included explicitly; a principal focus of TOC	Not included explicitly except as shown in Time-Driven ABC (Chapter 5)
Cost drivers	No direct utilization of cost drivers	Develop an understanding of cost drivers at the unit, batch, product, and facility levels
Major use	Optimization of production flow and short-term product mix	Strategic pricing and profit planning

analysis. The TOC analysis has a short-term focus because of its emphasis on only materials-related costs, but ABC includes all product costs.

On the other hand, unlike TOC, ABC does not explicitly include the resource constraints and capacities of production activities. Thus, ABC cannot be used to determine the short-term best product mix, as for example in Exhibit 13.9. ABC and TOC are thus *complementary* methods; ABC provides a comprehensive analysis of cost drivers and accurate unit costs as a basis for strategic decisions about long-term pricing and product mix. In contrast, TOC provides a useful method for improving the short-term profitability of the manufacturing plant through short-term product mix adjustments and through attention to production constraints. The differences between ABC and TOC are outlined in Exhibit 13.10.[10]

Life-Cycle Costing

LEARNING OBJECTIVE 3
Describe how life-cycle costing facilitates strategic management.

Typically, product or service costs are measured and reported for relatively short periods, such as a month or a year. Life-cycle costing provides a long-term perspective because it considers the entire cost life cycle of the product or service (see Exhibit 13.11). It therefore provides a more complete perspective of product costs and product or service profitability. For example, a product that is designed quickly and carelessly, with little investment in design costs, could

[10] For a comparison of TOC and ABC, see Robert Kee, "Integrating Activity-Based Costing with the Theory of Constraints to Enhance Production-Related Decision Making," *Accounting Horizons*, December 1995, pp. 48–61; Robin Cooper and Regine Slagmulder, "Integrating Activity-Based Costing and the Theory of Constraints," *Management Accounting*, February 1999, p. 2; and Robert Kee and Charles Schmidt, "A Comparative Analysis of Utilizing Activity-Based Costing and the Theory of Constraints for Making Product-Mix Decisions," *International Journal of Production Economics* 63 (2000), pp. 1–17.

EXHIBIT 13.11
Life-Cycle Costing in the Cost Life Cycle

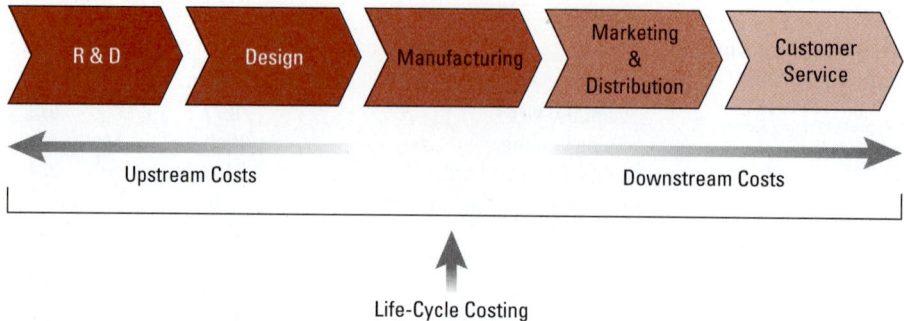

have significantly higher marketing and service costs later in the life cycle. Managers are interested in the total cost, over the entire life cycle, not manufacturing costs only.

While cost management methods have tended to focus only on manufacturing costs, upstream and downstream costs can account for a significant portion of total life-cycle costs, especially in certain industries:

Industries with High Upstream Costs

Computer software

Specialized industrial and medical equipment

Pharmaceuticals

Industries with High Downstream Costs

Fashion apparel

Perfumes, cosmetics, and toiletries

Upstream and downstream costs are managed in a number of ways including improved relationships with suppliers and distributors; the most crucial way is the design of the product and the manufacturing process. Value chain analysis, as explained in Chapter 2, can also provide a useful way to identify upstream and downstream linkages (see Exhibit 13.12 for an example showing the effects of poor design and quality on life cycle costs).

The Importance of Design

As managers consider upstream and downstream costs, decision making at the design stage is critical. Although the costs incurred at the design stage could account for only a very small percentage of the total costs over the entire product life cycle, design-stage decisions commit a firm to a given production, marketing, and service plan. Therefore, they lock in most of the remaining life cycle costs.

The critical success factors at the design stage include the following:

Reduced time to market. In a competitive environment where the speed of product development and the speed of delivery are critical, efforts to reduce time to market have high priority.

EXHIBIT 13.12
Value Chain Showing Upstream and Downstream Linkages for a Manufacturer

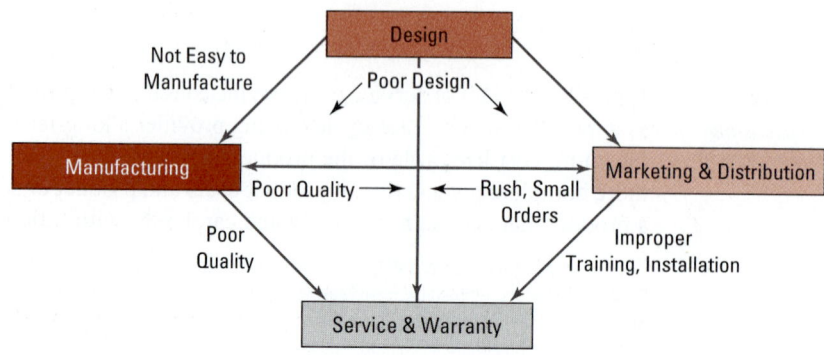

Reduced expected service costs. By careful, simple design and the use of modular, interchangeable components, the expected service costs can be greatly reduced.

Reduced product environmental impact. The product is designed with a focus on sustainability—low carbon footprint (use of greenhouse gasses) in manufacturing and in the later use of the product, use of recycled materials, and other means to lower the environmental impact of the product and the manufacturing of the product.[11]

Improved ease of manufacture. To reduce production costs and speed production, the design must be easy to manufacture.

Process planning and design. The plan for the manufacturing process should be flexible, allowing for fast setups and product changeovers, using flexible manufacturing concepts, computer-integrated manufacturing, computer-assisted design, and concurrent engineering.

The Use of Life-Cycle Costing in a Software Firm

As an example of applying life-cycle costing, consider software developer Analytical Decisions, Inc. (ADI), that provides specialized software for banks and other financial institutions to use to analyze loan loss reserves and to plan loan portfolios. ADI has two products, ADI–1 for large banks and ADI–2 for small banks and savings and loans. Each product is updated annually, with an occasional special update during the year. Each update improves the product's functionality in some significant way.

Initially, ADI analyzed profitability by using the accounting software widely used in the industry, which provided the report shown in Exhibit 13.13. This analysis shows both products to be quite profitable, even in the presence of heavy R&D and selling costs; ADI–1 shows a somewhat higher gross margin (72%; $3,260,000/$4,500,000) than ADI–2 (60%; $1,495,000/$2,500,000). However, the analysis is incomplete since most of ADI's costs (R&D and selling) are not included in the product comparison. Because ADI's systems designers and programmers work in project teams, determining how the R&D costs should be assigned to the two products is relatively simple. Similarly, because ADI's sales and customer-service efforts are logged by product, these costs also can be traced, as shown in Exhibit 13.14.

The life-cycle cost analysis clearly identifies ADI–2 as the more profitable of the two products because ADI–1 incurs the bulk of the R&D and selling costs. Moreover, the revised analysis provides a basis for ADI management to seek possible cost reductions. For example, the ratio of research and development, selling and service costs to sales dollars, is much higher for ADI–1 (67%; $3,000,000/$4,500,000) than for ADI–2 (40%; $1,000,000/$2,500,000). Management should investigate whether these higher costs are due to the nature of the different customers or quality problems in ADI–1. Management can use this breakdown of costs throughout the product's life cycle to identify opportunities for cost savings.

EXHIBIT 13.13
Product-Line Income Statement for Analytical Decisions, Inc.

	ADI–1	ADI–2	Total
Sales	$4,500,000	$2,500,000	$7,000,000
Cost of sales	1,240,000	1,005,000	2,245,000
Gross margin	$3,260,000	$1,495,000	$4,755,000
Research and development			2,150,000
Selling and service			1,850,000
Operating profit			$ 755,000

[11] Brian Hindo, "Everything Old Is New Again," *BusinessWeek,* September 25, 2006, pp. 65–70. See also, Marc J. Epstein, *Making Sustainability Work: Best Practices in Managing and Measuring Corporate Social, Environmental, and Economic Impacts* (San Francisco: Berrett-Koehler, 2008).

EXHIBIT 13.14
Life-Cycle Costing for
Analytical Decisions, Inc.

	ADI–1	ADI–2	Total
Sales	$4,500,000	$2,500,000	$7,000,000
Cost of sales	1,240,000	1,005,000	2,245,000
Gross margin	$3,260,000	$1,495,000	$4,755,000
Research and development	1,550,000	600,000	2,150,000
Selling and service	1,450,000	400,000	1,850,000
Operating profit	$ 260,000	$ 495,000	$ 755,000

Strategic Pricing Using the Product Life Cycle

LEARNING OBJECTIVE 4

Outline the objectives and techniques of strategic pricing.

Management accountants are involved in three pricing situations: The first is the special order decision explained in Chapter 11 in which a nonrecurring sales opportunity arises; the proper price in this case is based on relevant cost analysis and strategic analysis. The second context is target costing explained earlier in this chapter in which a firm faces a market price and determines how to achieve the level of costs necessary to make a profit, using product design and kaizen. The third type of pricing decision—not involving special orders or market-determined prices—is the focus in this section. These are the long-term, strategic pricing decisions facing many managers. They are complex decisions involving strategic issues and careful use of cost information. To assist in these pricing decisions, the management accountant prepares cost information from the perspective of the cost life cycle, the sales life cycle, and the use of analytical pricing methods.

Pricing Using the Cost Life Cycle

Pricing based on cost is a common approach for manufacturing and service firms. Those that compete on cost leadership use cost information to improve operating efficiency to reduce costs and price. Prices are set by the most efficient producers; the ones that are best able to reduce costs. In contrast, firms that compete on differentiation have more discretion in setting prices. The differentiated firm's goal might be to increase profits by setting an initial high price for those willing to pay, followed by lower prices for the cost-conscious customers (called skimming). Alternatively, the firm's goal might be to increase market share by lowering the price (called penetration). A third approach would be to build longer-term customer relationships by utilizing "value pricing" in which pricing is based on meeting specific customer needs. A firm's pricing policy is also influenced by patterns in the industry. For example, firms with seasonal demand (clothing, appliances, furniture, among others) usually offer discounts and promotions during the slow periods of the year. Other industries are sensitive to interest rates, stock market returns, other factors in the economy (automobiles and construction, among others), and new products or pricing policies of competitors. To deal with the complexity of the pricing decision, firms like GE Lighting, DHL, and Hewlett-Packard use Web-based software systems to determine prices more quickly and accurately for different customers. The systems speed up the process of quoting prices and assist in determining the timing and location of discount programs. Thus, a number of seasonal, cyclical, economic, and other strategic factors influence the pricing policies of the firm, and cost information is only the starting point of the pricing decision. The cost information for pricing is commonly based on one of the four methods: (1) full manufacturing cost plus markup, (2) life cycle cost plus markup, (3) full cost and desired gross margin percent, and (4) full cost plus desired return on assets.

Full Manufacturing Cost Plus Markup

In this method, a firm determines full manufacturing cost (the total of variable and fixed manufacturing costs) and applies a markup percentage to cover other operating costs plus profit. The markup percentage could be determined by industry practice, judgment, or a desired level of profit (equivalent to method 4). Suppose a firm has the following unit costs (using ABC costing), and a markup rate of 40 percent. Then, the price would be calculated as $210.

Manufacturing cost	
Materials	$ 40
Labor	50
Batch level costs	20
Other plant overhead	40
Total manufacturing cost	$150
Price based on full manufacturing cost: $150 × 140% = $210	

Life-Cycle Cost Plus Markup

The life-cycle approach to pricing uses the full life-cycle cost instead of manufacturing cost only. Suppose that in addition to manufacturing costs of $150 per unit, the example firm has selling and administrative costs of $25 per unit, for a total of $175 life-cycle cost. The firm uses a markup rate of 25 percent based on life-cycle costs. The calculated price is now $218.75:

$$\text{Total life-cycle costs} \times \text{markup} = \text{price}$$
$$\$175 \times 125\% = \$218.75$$

The life-cycle approach has the advantage that all costs are included, so that the markup percentage can be directly tied to a desired level of profit. Both the full manufacturing cost and life-cycle cost approaches are commonly used.

Full Cost and Desired Gross Margin Percent

In this variation, the price is determined so that a desired gross margin percent is achieved. To continue with the previous example, suppose that the desired gross margin is 30 percent of sales. Then, the price would be $214.29:

$$\text{Price} = \frac{\text{Full manufacturing cost}}{(1 - \text{Desired gross margin percentage})}$$
$$= \frac{\$150}{(1 - .3)} = \$214.29$$

This price would produce a gross margin of $214.29 − $150 = $64.29, which is 30 percent of sales. Alternatively, a variation of this method could be used to achieve a desired percentage return on life-cycle costs. For example, if the desired percentage return on life-cycle costs is 15 percent, then the price would be $205.88:

$$\text{Price} = \frac{\text{Full life-cycle cost}}{(1 - \text{Desired life-cycle margin percentage})}$$
$$= \frac{\$175}{(1 - .15)} = \$205.88$$

Full Cost and Desired Return on Assets

Another common pricing approach is to set the price to achieve a desired return on assets. Assume again that the same information applies, that the firm has $3.5 million assets committed to the production of the product, and desires a 10 percent before-tax return on assets. Sales are expected to be 10,000 units. Using a life-cycle cost approach (a full manufacturing-cost approach could be used in a similar manner), the markup percentage would be 20 percent.

$$\text{Markup rate} = \frac{\text{Desired before-tax profit}}{\text{Life-cycle cost of expected sales}}$$
$$= \frac{\$3,500,000 \times 10\%}{10,000 \times \$175} = 20\%$$

And the price would then be $210:

$$\text{Price} = \text{Life-cycle cost} \times 120\% = \$175 \times 120\% = \$210$$

Each of these illustrations assumes that all sales are for the price determined. The desired price could be adjusted to reflect expected discounts or losses due to spoilage or theft.

Strategic Pricing for Phases of the Sales Life Cycle

Strategic pricing depends on the position of the product or service in the sales life cycle. As the sales life cycle becomes shorter (only months in some industries such as consumer electronics), the analysis of the sales life cycle becomes increasingly important. In contrast to the cost life cycle just described, the sales life cycle refers to the phase of the product's or service's sales in the market, from introduction of the product or service to decline and withdrawal from the market. (Exhibit 13.2 illustrates the phases of the sales life cycle.)

Phase 1: Introduction. The first phase involves little competition, and sales rise slowly as customers become aware of the new product or service. Costs are relatively high because of high R&D expenditures and capital costs for setting up production facilities and marketing efforts. Prices are relatively high because of product differentiation and the high costs at this phase. Product variety is limited.

Phase 2: Growth. Sales begin to increase rapidly as does product variety. The product continues to enjoy the benefits of differentiation. Competition increases, and prices begin to fall.

Phase 3: Maturity. Sales continue to increase but at a decreasing rate. The number of competitors and of product variety decline. Prices fall further, and differentiation is no longer important. Competition is based on cost given competitive quality and functionality.

Phase 4: Decline. Sales and prices decline, as do the number of competitors. Control of costs and an effective distribution network are key to continued survival.

In the first phase, the focus of management is on design, differentiation, and marketing. The focus shifts to new product development and pricing strategy as competition develops in the second phase. In the third and fourth phases, management's attention turns to cost control, quality, and service as the market continues to become more competitive. Thus, the firm's strategy for the product or service changes over the sales life cycle from differentiation in the early phases to cost leadership in the final phases.

Similarly, the strategic pricing approach changes over the product or service life cycle. In the first phase, pricing is set relatively high to recover development costs and to take advantage of product differentiation and the new demand for the product. In the second phase, pricing is likely to stay relatively high as the firm attempts to build profitability in the growing market. In the latter phases, pricing becomes more competitive, and target costing and life-cycle costing methods are used as the firm becomes more a price taker than a price setter and makes efforts to reduce upstream and downstream costs.

Strategic Pricing: Analytical Pricing Methods

Increasingly, retailers and some manufacturers use a strategic approach to pricing in which they determine prices by what the customer is willing to bear, often using analytical methods based upon extensive data analysis of customer buying behavior. Industries in which this is common include the airlines, hotels, and department stores. A common example is the use of data analysis of customer behavior to determine the optimum amount of markdowns during seasonal downturns in the business. Another example is the use of a "fighter brand," a low-priced version of the well-known product. The fighter brand is especially common in a recessionary environment, as consumers of high-end products look for less expensive substitutes.[12]

[12] Thomas H. Davenport and Jeanne G. Harris, *Competing on Analytics*, (Boston: Harvard Business School Press, 2007); Timothy Aeppel, "Seeking Perfect Prices, CEO Tears Up the Rules," *The Wall Street Journal*, March 27, 2007, p. 1; Josh Hyatt, "And in This Corner, the Fighter Brand," CFO.com, December 1, 2008; Yukari Kane "To Sustain iPhone, Apple Halves Price," *The Wall Street Journal*, June 9, 2009, p B1; John Jannarone, "Procter's Gamble: Down-Market Move," *The Wall Street Journal*, June 9, 2009, p C10.

Summary

The strategic cost management concepts introduced in the preceding chapters are extended here. First, we discuss four cost management methods used to analyze the product or service's life cycle: target costing, the theory of constraints, life-cycle costing, and strategic pricing. Target costing is a tool for analyzing the cost structure to help management identify the proper design features and manufacturing methods to allow the firm to meet a competitive price. The five steps in target costing are (1) determine the market price, (2) determine the desired profit, (3) calculate the target cost (market price less desired profit), (4) use value engineering to identify ways to reduce product cost, and (5) use kaizen costing and operational control to further reduce costs.

The theory of constraints (TOC) is a tool that assists managers in identifying bottlenecks (constraints) and scheduling production to maximize throughput and profits. TOC analysis has five steps: (1) identify the constraint, (2) determine the most efficient product mix given the constraint, (3) maximize the flow through the constraint, (4) add capacity to the constraint, and (5) redesign the manufacturing process for flexibility and fast throughput.

Life-cycle costing assists managers in minimizing total cost over the product's or service's entire life cycle. Life-cycle costing brings a focus to the upstream activities (research and development, engineering) and downstream activities (marketing, distribution, service), as well as the manufacturing and operations that cost systems focus on. Especially important is a careful consideration of the effects of design choices on downstream costs.

Strategic pricing helps management determine the price of the product or service based on life-cycle costs or in its position in the different phases of its sales life cycle.

Appendix

Using the Flow Diagram to Identify Constraints

This chapter has illustrated the use of the flow diagram to identify the constraint when there are two or more products being produced through a common set of processes, with no specific completion time. The flow diagram can also be used when there is a single product or project and a specific completion time. In the latter case, which is illustrated in this appendix, the flow diagram is used to identify the processes that must be finished on time for the product or project to be completed on time.

To illustrate, suppose that a small pharmaceutical firm, Skincare Products, Inc. (SPI), manufactures an insect repellent with sun screen. To produce a batch of product, the firm mixes the active and inert ingredients in a large vat. Because of Food and Drug Administration requirements, SPI provides three inspections: (1) the raw materials it receives, (2) the mix of raw materials during the mixing process, and (3) the final product. The first and second inspections check the materials for correct chemical content and potency; the third inspection focuses on correct weight or item count. The manufacturing process has six processes, which are illustrated in Exhibit 13A.1.

Process 1: Receive and inspect raw materials.
Process 2: Mix raw materials.
Process 3: Perform second inspection.
Process 4: Fill and package.
Process 5: Perform third inspection.
Process 6: Attach labels.

Exhibit 13A.1 is a flow diagram of the work done that shows the sequence of processes and the amount of time required for each. The flow diagram is used to identify the constraints. Computer techniques do this for large networks, but the constraints for a smaller one such as Exhibit 13A.1 can be identified by visual inspection. As defined earlier, a *constraint* is any process that delays the entire manufacturing process. The amount of the delay is often called *slack time*. Processes that can be delayed without delaying the finish time for the entire

EXHIBIT 13A.1
Flow Diagram for Skincare Products, Inc.

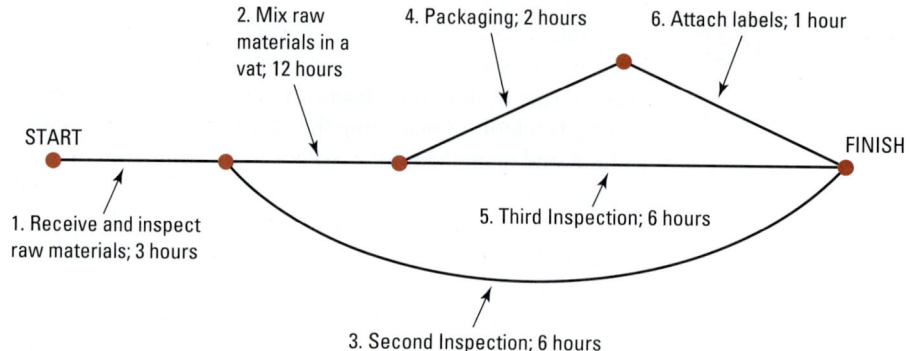

process are called *nonconstraints* or simply *slack* processes since the processes have some slack time in which to be completed. The constraints for SPI are as follows:

Process 1: Receive and inspect raw materials; required time, 3 hours.
Process 2: Mix raw materials in vat; required time, 12 hours.
Process 5: Perform third inspection; required time, 6 hours.

The total time for the entire manufacturing process cannot be less than the total time of these three processes added together (3 + 12 + 6 = 21 hours) since these processes must follow in sequence and cannot overlap. The remaining processes—3, 4, and 6—are not constraints and can be delayed one or more hours without delaying the entire production process. The amount of the delay can be determined as follows. Process 3 requires 6 hours and must be finished while processes 2 and 5 are being completed, but because processes 2 and 5 require 18 hours (12 + 6) and process 3 requires only 6 hours, process 3 has 12 hours (18 − 6) of slack time. Similarly, since processes 4 and 6 together require only 3 hours (2 hours plus 1 hour, respectively) and must be completed during process 5 (which requires 6 hours), in effect 3 hours of slack exist for processes 4 and 6 combined. Often the constraint processes (1, 2, and 5 in this case) are called critical processes since they cannot be delayed without delaying the entire batch of product. Also, the sequence of critical processes is often called the *critical path*.

Key Terms

Comments on Cost Management in Action

Why Go Abroad? Ralph Lauren, Apple, Kodak, and IBM

In competitive industries such as apparel, consumer electronics, and computers, manufacturers continuously look for ways to reduce cost and increase value throughout the value chain. These industries have chosen to locate extensive manufacturing operations and/or partners in Latin America to reduce cost and to benefit from innovative manufacturing methods and facilities. Wage costs are lower and, using target costing and value engineering, manufacturing processes are built around modular manufacturing methods that reduce the number of parts in the product, speeding the manufacturing process and reducing costs.

Consumer Electronics   Why is outsourcing manufacturing to plants an advantage to IBM, Apple, and Kodak? The contract manufacturers' manufacturing experience and technology give them a cost advantage. Flextronics and the other contract manufacturers also can focus on the manufacturing process rather than the entire product value chain. Moreover, they gain economies of scale by manufacturing similar products for different clients. The use of contract manufacturing is an important part of the strategy to achieve target costs while maintaining product leadership in design and customer service.

Apparel Manufacturing   Liz Claiborne and Ralph Lauren are saving lots of time and money by outsourcing many phases of the product development, from design to manufacturing, to plants in China. Having the product development and manufacturing in one place has helped the firms introduce new products more quickly and has also allowed them to deliver their product more quickly around the world.

Sources: Gary McWilliams, "In Electronics, U.S. Companies Seize Momentum from Japan," *The Wall Street Journal,* March 10, 2005, p. P1; Gabriel Kahn, "Making Labels for Less," *The Wall Street Journal,* August 13, 2004, p. B1; Mark Heinzl, "Nortel and Flextronics Discuss $500 Million Outsourcing Pact," *The Wall Street Journal,* January 23, 2004, p. A12; Justin Scheck, "Dell Plans to Sell Factories in Effort to Cut Costs," *The Wall Street Journal,* September 5, 2008, p1.

Self-Study Problem

(For solution, please turn to the end of the chapter.)

Best Brand Lighting, Inc.

Best Brand Lighting Inc. (BBL) manufactures lighting fixtures. The two major markets for BBL products are major retailers, including Home Depot, Wal-Mart, and Kmart, and specialty lighting stores. The former sell primarily to homeowners, and the latter primarily to electrical contractors.

Although its standard sizes and models typically are sold to the large retailers, BBL sells its products with more specialized features and sizes only to the specialty stores. Thus, the design and manufacturing costs of the products going to the specialty stores are slightly higher. The products in both markets have similar sales life cycles of about two years.

Because of the difference in consumers, BBL has a larger marketing cost for the products sold to the large retailers—advertising in major media to attract homeowners. In contrast, the marketing for the specialty shops consists mainly of catalogs and advertisements in trade publications resulting in a lower overall marketing cost. The sales policies also differ somewhat for the two markets. Sales to specialty stores are priced higher but include significant discounts and attractive return policies. In contrast, sales to the major retailers have restrictive return policies and offer little, if any, discount.

BBL management is interested in an in-depth analysis of the profitability of its two markets. As a first step, it has asked for the average costs and other data for all BBL products:

	Major Retailers	**Specialty Stores**
Design costs	$ 0.80	$ 1.10
Manufacturing costs	5.20	5.90
Marketing costs	0.95	0.10
Returns	0.05	0.95
Discounts	0.10	0.95
Average price	10.55	12.50
Total market ($000) in BBL's sales region	188,000	32,000
Current unit sales ($000)	9,200	8,000

Required   Using the methods discussed in this chapter, analyze BBL's two market segments. What questions would you want to ask management and which fact-finding studies would be appropriate to support this analysis?

Questions

13-1   Explain the two methods for reducing total product costs to achieve a desired target cost. Which is more common in the consumer electronics industries? In the specialized equipment manufacturing industries?

13-2   What does the term *sales life cycle* mean? What are the phases of the sales life cycle? How does it differ from the cost life cycle?

13-3   Do pricing strategies change over the different phases of the sales life cycle? Explain how.

13-4   Do cost management practices change over the product's sales life cycle? Explain how.

13-5   What is target costing? What types of firms use it?

13-6   What is life-cycle costing? Why is it used?

13-7   Name the five steps of the theory of constraints and explain the purpose of each. Which is the most important step and why?

13-8   What does the term *constraint* mean in the theory of constraint analysis?

13-9   What is the role of the flow diagram in the theory of constraints analysis?

13-10 How important is product design in life cycle costing? Why?

13-11 What does the concept of *value engineering* mean? How is it used in target costing?

13-12 What is the main difference between activity-based costing and the theory of constraints? When is it appropriate to use each one?

13-13 For what types of firms is the theory of constraints analysis most appropriate and why?

13-14 For what types of firms is target costing most appropriate and why?

13-15 For what types of firms is life-cycle costing most appropriate and why?

13-16 Explain the difference in intended application between strategic pricing and life-cycle costing.

13-17 How is Takt time calculated and what is it used for?

13-18 Distinguish pricing based on the cost life cycle and pricing based on the sales life cycle and give an example method for each.

Brief Exercises

13-19 The market price for a product has been $50 per unit, but competitive pressures have reduced the market price to $45. The firm manufactures 10,000 of these products per year at a manufacturing cost of $38 per unit (including $22 fixed cost and $16 variable cost per unit). Other selling and administrative costs for the product are $8 per unit. What is the firm's target cost for this product?

13-20 The firm in 13-19 above ignores competitive prices because it has a differentiated product. It uses full-cost-based pricing with a 40 percent markup. What is the firm's price?

13-21 The firm in 13-19 above ignores competitive prices because it has a differentiated product. It uses cost life-cycle-based pricing with a 10 percent markup. What is the firm's price?

13-22 At what phase in the product sales life cycle will prices likely be the highest: introduction, growth, maturity, or decline?

13-23 If customer demand is 200,000 units per month, and available manufacturing capacity is 6,000 hours per week, what is the Takt time for this firm?

13-24 If a customer order is placed on May 1 and the company expects to begin processing it on May 10, and the order is shipped on May 20, the cycle time is then how many days long?

13-25 If Toyota Motor Company receives an order on May 1, begins production on May 19, and ships the order on May 20 immediately following production, then what is the manufacturing cycle efficiency (MCE) ratio?

13-26 Hanes Sport Wear is facing increased price competition, and its market price has fallen by $3. What approach besides target costing can Hanes use to reduce manufacturing cost?

13-27 Comdex Inc. manufactures parts for the telecom industry. One of its products that currently sells for $160 is now facing a new competitor that offers the same product at $140. The parts currently cost Comdex $130. Comdex believes it must reduce its price to $140 to remain competitive. What is the target cost of the product if Comdex desires a 25 percent profit on sales dollars?

13-28 England, Inc., a furniture manufacturer in Tazewell, Tennessee, has found a competitive advantage and increasing sales through speed in delivering customer orders. England, Inc. uses precision scheduling throughout the cost life cycle to achieve delivery times in as few as three weeks, much better than the industry average. This means tightly coordinated order taking, production scheduling, labor scheduling, purchasing, and the use of company-owned delivery trucks. What management technique is England using?

13-29 Why do prices at Orlando's theme parks remain high despite seasonal and economic cyclical ups and downs? What type of strategic pricing is used by these theme parks?

Exercises

13-30 **Target Costing** MaxiDrive manufactures a wide variety of parts for recreational boating, including a gear and driveshaft part for high-powered outboard boat engines. Original equipment manufacturers such as Mercury and Honda purchase the components for use in large, powerful outboards. The part sells for $610, and sales volume averages 25,000 units per year. Recently, MaxiDrive's major competitor reduced the price of its equivalent unit to $550. The market is very competitive, and Maxi-Drive realizes it must meet the new price or lose significant market share. The controller has assembled these cost and usage data for the most recent year for MaxiDrive's production of 25,000 units:

	Budgeted Quantity	Budgeted Cost	Actual Quantity	Actual Cost
Materials		$ 6,500,000		$ 7,000,000
Direct labor		2,500,000		2,625,000
Indirect labor		2,500,000		2,400,000
Inspection (hours and cost)	920	300,000	1,000	350,000
Materials handling (number of purchases and cost)	3,500	500,000	3,450	485,000
Machine setups (number and cost)	1,400	750,000	1,500	725,000
Returns and rework (number of times and cost)	300	80,000	500	130,000
		$13,130,000		$13,715,000

Required

1. Calculate the target cost for maintaining current market share and profitability.

2. Can the target cost be achieved? How?

13-31 **Strategic Pricing with Rising Commodity Prices**   In the recession of 2008 one of the important factors was the rise in certain commodity costs, particularly food commodities. In June 2008 the price of the average four-person family food budget had risen by almost 9 percent from January 2008, a period of less than six months. Families reacted by buying less and buying more selectively. Further aggravating the situation, U.S. inventories of key commodities such as soybeans, corn, and wheat had fallen to historically low levels in the spring of 2008.

Required   How do you think the producers of packaged foods, cereals, meat products, and other supermarket items change their pricing to react to the increased commodity prices and the change in consumer behavior?

13-32 **Manufacturing Cycle Efficiency**   Waymouth Manufacturing operates a contract manufacturing plant located in Dublin, Ireland. The plant provides a variety of electronics products and components to consumer goods manufacturers around the world. Cycle time is a critical success factor for Waymouth, which has developed a number of measures of manufacturing speed. Waymouth has studied the matter and found that competitive contract manufacturers have manufacturing cycle times (MCE) of about 40 percent. When last calculated, Waymouth's MCE was 35 percent.

Some key measures from the recent month's production, averaged over all the jobs during that period, are as follows:

Activity	Average Time
New product development	30 hours
Materials handling	3
Order setup	6
Machine maintenance	3
Order scheduling	1
Inspection of completed order	5
Pack and move to storage or ship	2
Manufacturing assembly	23
Order taking and checking	3
Receiving and stocking raw materials	6
Inspection of raw materials	2

Required   Determine the manufacturing cycle efficiency (MCE) for the recent month. What can you infer from the MCE you calculated?

13-33 **Takt Time**   Johnson Electronics manufactures a power supply used in a variety of electronic products including printers, modems, and routers. The demand for the part is 8,400 units per week. The production of the power supply requires six different manufacturing operations, each in sequence and each having the following processing times. The net available time to work is 70 hours per week, using two shifts.

Operation	Processing Time
Operation 1	25 sec
Operation 2	34 sec
Operation 3	22 sec
Operation 4	24 sec
Operation 5	30 sec
Operation 6	28 sec

Required

1. What is the Takt time for this product?

2. Is the processing line properly balanced for this product? Why or why not?

3. What is the strategic role of Takt time, and how is it implemented by the cost management analyst?

13-34 **Life Cycle Costing; Service Department**   In the chapter we illustrated the use of the life cycle concept for both the cost and sales life cycle of a company's product lines. It can also be useful to extend the cost life cycle to the service department. In Chapter 7 we were interested in the allocation of service department costs to product lines. Here we are interested in managing the costs of a service department over its life cycle. The information technology department (IT) is a good example. The costs incurred in IT have the following phases:

1. Acquisition of IT assets including computers, hubs, cables, and other assets.
2. Acquisition of software and deployment of IT for the desired application and functionality.
3. Maintain management and operations of the IT assets.
4. Provide user support.
5. Retire the assets on a planned schedule and replace as needed.

Required   How can life cycle costing help in the management of the IT department?

13-35 **Target Costing**   Bowman Specialists Inc. (BSI) manufactures specialized equipment for polishing optical lenses. There are two models—one (A–25) principally used for fine eyewear and the other (A–10) for lenses used in binoculars, cameras, and similar equipment.

   The manufacturing cost of each unit is calculated, using activity-based costing, for these manufacturing cost pools:

Cost Pools	Allocation Base	Costing Rate
Materials handling	Number of parts	$2.25 per part
Manufacturing supervision	Hours of machine time	$23.50 per hour
Assembly	Number of parts	$2.55 per part
Machine setup	Each setup	$44.60 per setup
Inspection and testing	Logged hours	$35.00 per hour
Packaging	Logged hours	$15.00 per hour

BSI currently sells the A–10 model for $1,050 and the A–25 model for $725. Manufacturing costs and activity usage for the two products follow:

	A–10	A–25
Direct materials	$143.76	$66.44
Number of parts	121	92
Machine-hours	6	4
Inspection time	1	0.6
Packing time	0.7	0.4
Setups	2	1

Required

1. Calculate the product cost and product margin for each product.

2. A new competitor has entered the market for lens-polishing equipment with a superior product at significantly lower prices, $825 for the A–10 model and $595 for the A–25 model. To try to compete, BSI has made some radical improvements in the design and manufacturing of its two products. The materials costs and activity usage rates have been decreased significantly:

	A–10	A–25
Direct materials	$78.65	$42.45
Number of parts	110	81
Machine-hours	5	2
Inspection time	1	0.5
Packing time	0.7	0.2
Setups	1	1

Calculate the total product costs with the new activity usage data. Can BSI make a positive gross margin with the new costs, assuming that it must meet the price set by the new competitor?

3. Assume the information in requirement 2, but that BSI management is not satisfied with the gross margin on the A–10 after the cost improvements. BSI wants a $50 gross margin on A–10. Suppose you are able to change the number of parts to reduce costs further to achieve the desired $50 margin. How much would the number of parts have to change to provide the desired gross margin? [Hint: Use the Excel **Goal Seek** function.]

4. What cost management method might be useful to BSI at this time, and why?

13-36 **Target Costing in a Service Firm**   Take-a-Break Travel Company offers spring break travel packages to college students. Two of its packages, a seven-day, six-night trip to Cancun and a five-day, four-night trip to Jamaica, have the following characteristics:

Package Specifications	Cancun	Jamaica	Cost Data
Oceanfront room; number of nights	6	4	$ 30/night
Meals:			
Breakfasts	7	5	$ 5/ea
Lunches	7	5	$ 7/ea
Dinners	6	0	$ 10/ea
Scuba diving trips	4	2	$ 15/ea
Water skiing trips	5	2	$ 10/ea
Airfare (round trip from Miami)	1	1	$200 (Cancun), $355 (Jamaica)
Transportation to and from airport	1	1	$ 15 (Cancun), $ 10 (Jamaica)

The Cancun trip sells for $750, and the Jamaica trip sells for $690.

Required

1. What are the current profit margins on both trips?

2. Take-a-Break's management believes that it must drop the price on the Cancun trip to $710 and on the Jamaica trip to $650 in order to remain competitive in the market. Recalculate profit margins for both packages at these price levels.

3. Describe two ways that Take-a-Break Travel could cut its costs to get the profit margin back to their original levels.

13-37 **Target Costing**   Jared Monsma, Weekend Golfer's vice president for marketing, has concluded from his market analysis that sales have been dwindling for the standard golf cart because of aggressive pricing by competitors. Weekend Golfer sells these golf carts online for $3,000, whereas the competition sells a comparable cart online in the $2,800 range. Jared has determined that dropping the price to $2,850 would regain the firm's annual market share of 8,000 golf carts. Cost data based on sales of 8,000 gas golf carts follow:

	Budgeted Amount	Actual Amount	Actual Cost
Direct materials	$4,200,000		$4,500,000
Direct labor	100,000 hrs.	125,000 hrs.	1,750,000
Machine setups	75,000 hrs.	75,000 hrs.	750,000
Mechanical assembly	375,000 hrs.	400,000 hrs.	5,000,000

Required

1. Calculate the current cost and profit per unit.

2. How much of the current cost per unit is attributable to non-value-added activities?

3. Calculate the new target cost per unit for a sales price of $2,850 if the profit per unit is maintained.

4. What strategy do you suggest for Weekend Golfer to attain the target cost calculated in requirement 3?

13-38 **Pricing**   Williams Inc. produces a single product, a part used in the manufacture of automobile transmissions. Known for its quality and performance, the part is sold to luxury auto manufacturers around the world. Because this is a quality product, Williams has some flexibility in pricing the part. The firm calculates the price using a variety of pricing methods and then chooses the final price based on that information and other strategic information. A summary of the key cost information follows. Williams expects to manufacture and sell 48,500 parts in the coming year. While the demand for Williams' part has been growing in the past two years, management is not only aware of the cyclical nature of the automobile industry but also concerned about market share and profits during the industry's current downturn.

	Total Costs
Variable manufacturing	$ 4,680,000
Variable selling and administrative	855,650
Plant-level fixed overhead	2,345,875
Fixed selling and administrative	675,495
Batch-level fixed overhead	360,000
Total investment in product line	22,350,000
Expected sales (units)	48,500

Required

1. Determine the price for the part using a markup of 45 percent of full manufacturing cost.
2. Determine the price for the part using a markup of 25 percent of full life-cycle cost.
3. Determine the price for the part using a desired gross margin percentage to sales of 40 percent.
4. Determine the price for the part using a desired life-cycle cost percentage to sales of 25 percent.
5. Determine the price for the part using a desired before-tax return on investment of 15 percent.
6. Determine the contribution margin and operating profit for each of the methods in requirements 1 through 5. Which price would you choose, and why?

13-39 **Life-Cycle Pricing**   Matt Simpson owns and operates Quality Craft Rentals, which offers canoe rentals and shuttle service on the Nantahala River. Customers can rent canoes at one station, enter the river there, and exit at one of two designated locations to catch a shuttle that returns them to their vehicles at the station they entered. Following are the costs involved in providing this service each year:

	Fixed Costs	Variable Costs
Canoe maintenance	$ 2,300	$2.50
Licenses and permits	3,000	0
Vehicle leases	5,400	0
Station lease	6,920	0
Advertising	6,000	0.50
Operating costs	21,000	0.50

Quality Craft Rentals began business three years ago with a $21,000 expenditure for a fleet of 30 canoes. These are expected to last seven more years, at which time a new fleet must be purchased.

Required   Matt is happy with the steady rental average of 6,400 per year. For this number of rentals, what price should he charge per rental for the business to make a 20 percent life-cycle return on investment?

13-40 **Matching Market Characteristics with Sales Life-Cycle Stages**

Activities and Market Characteristics

Decline in sales
Advertising
Boost in production
Stabilized profits
Competitors' entrance into market
Market research
Market saturation
Start production
Product testing
Termination of product
Large increase in sales

Required   Determine the appropriate life-cycle stage for each activity.

13-41 Pricing Military Contracts   The Pentagon is constantly seeking ways to procure the most effective combat equipment and systems at the lowest possible cost. A key element in most procurement contracts is fixed fee based on percentage of full cost for the contract, plus a percentage fixed fee that is incentive based. The latter is based on meeting contract deadlines and meeting or exceeding other contract performance measures. A recent Pentagon contract with Boeing involves a 10 percent fixed fee on cost incurred and another 5-percent-of-incentive award.

Required   Evaluate the compensation plan for this contract, with the fixed fee of 10 percent and the incentive fee of 5 percent. What do you think is the role of the incentive fee, and do you think it is too large or too small?

13-42 Target Costing Using Quality Function Deployment (QFD)   Rick's is a popular restaurant for fine dining. The owner and chef, Rick Goetz, is pleased with his success and is now considering expanding his existing restaurant or perhaps opening a second restaurant. Before making his decision, Rick wants to find out more about his competitive position. There are three other restaurants that compete directly with him on food quality and price. Rick knows that his profitability depends on his ability to provide a satisfying meal at the market price. His first step is to gather some information about his customers, using an independent market research firm, which informed him that his customers were looking for taste, comfort (the ambiance, service, and overall presentation of the food), and enjoyment (the distinctiveness of the dining experience, a degree of excitement). He was surprised to find that comfort and enjoyment ranked highest.

First: Customer Criteria and Ranking

	Importance	Relative Importance
Taste	50	16.7%
Comfort	100	33.3
Enjoyment	150	50.0
Total	300	100.0%

Next, he worked with his key wait staff and chefs to try to identify the three main components, and related cost, of the service Rick's provided:

Second: Components and Cost

Components	Cost	Percent of Total
Menu and Food Preparation	$ 8	30.77%
Wait Staff	12	46.15
Food Ingredients	6	23.08
Total	$ 26	100.00%

Having the customer criteria and components, Rick now again worked with his staff to assess how each component contributed to the desired customer criteria.

Third: Determine How Components Contribute to Customer Satisfaction

	Customer Criteria		
Components	Taste	Comfort	Enjoyment
Menu and Food Preparation	30%	20%	50%
Wait Staff	40	60	30
Food Ingredients	30	20	20
	100%	100%	100%

Required

1. Using the information Rick has developed, determine the importance index for each component (menu and food preparation, wait staff, and food ingredients).

2. Compare your findings in Part 1 to the cost of the components. What conclusions can you draw from this comparison?

Problems

13-43 **Target Costing in a Service Firm** Alert Alarm Systems installs home security systems. Two of its systems, the ICU 100 and the ICU 900, have these characteristics:

Design Specifications	ICU 100	ICU 900	Cost Data
Video cameras	1	3	$150/ea.
Video monitors	1	1	$ 75/ea.
Motion detectors	5	8	$ 15/ea.
Floodlights	3	7	$ 8/ea.
Alarms	1	2	$ 15/ea.
Wiring	700 ft.	1,100 ft.	$ 0.10/ft.
Installation	16 hrs.	26 hrs.	$ 20/hr.

The ICU 100 sells for $810 installed, and the ICU 900 sells for $1,520 installed.

Required

1. What are the current profit margins on both systems?

2. Alert's management believes that it must drop the price on the ICU 100 to $750 and on the ICU 900 to $1,390 to remain competitive in the market. Recalculate profit margins for both products at these price levels.

3. Describe two ways that Alert could cut its costs to get the profit margins back to their original levels.

13-44 **Target Costing, Strategy** Benchmark Industries manufactures large workbenches for industrial use. Wayne Garrett, Benchmark's vice president for marketing, has concluded from his market analysis that sales are dwindling for the standard table because of aggressive pricing by competitors. This table sells for $875 whereas the competition sells a comparable table in the $800 range. Wayne has determined that dropping the price to $800 is necessary to maintain the firm's annual market share of 10,000 tables. Cost data based on sales of 10,000 tables follow:

	Budgeted Amount	Actual Amount	Actual Cost
Direct materials	400,000 sq. ft.	425,000 sq. ft.	$2,700,000
Direct labor	85,000 hrs.	100,000 hrs.	1,000,000
Machine setups	30,000 hrs.	30,000 hrs.	300,000
Mechanical assembly	320,000 hrs.	320,000 hrs.	4,000,000

Required

1. Calculate the current cost and profit per unit.

2. What amount of the current cost per unit is attributable to non-value-added activities?

3. Calculate the new target cost per unit for a sales price of $800 if the profit per unit is maintained.

4. What strategy do you suggest for Benchmark to attain the target cost calculated in requirement 3?

13-45 **Target Costing; Review of Chapter 11** Morrow Company is a large manufacturer of auto parts for automakers and parts distributors. Although Morrow has plants throughout the world, most are in North America. Morrow is known for the quality of its parts and for the reliability of its operations. Customers receive their orders in a timely manner and there are no errors in the shipment or billing of these orders. For these reasons, Morrow has prospered in a business that is very competitive, with competitors such as Delphi, Visteon, and others.

Morrow just received an order for 100 auto parts from National Motors Corp., a major auto manufacturer. National proposed a $1,500 selling price per part. Morrow usually earned 20 per cent operating margin as a percent of sales. Morrow recently decided to use target costing in pricing its products. An examination of the production costs by the engineers and accountants showed that this part was assigned a standard full cost of $1,425 per part (this includes $1,000 production, $200 marketing, and $225 general and administration costs per part). Morrow's Value Assessment Group (VAG) undertook a cost reduction program for this part. Two production areas that were investigated were the defective unit rate and the tooling costs. The $1,000 production costs included a normal defective cost of $85 per part. Group leaders suggested that production changes could reduce defective cost to $25 per part.

Forty-five tools were used to make the auto part. The group discovered that the number of tools could be reduced to 30 and less expensive tools could be used on this part to meet National's product specifications. These changes saved an additional $105 of production cost per part. By studying other problem areas, the group found that general and administration costs could be reduced by $50 per unit through use of electronic data interchange with suppliers and just-in-time inventory management.

In addition, Morrow's sales manager told the group that National might be willing to pay a higher selling price because of Morrow's quality reputation and reliability. He believed National's proposed price was a starting point for negotiations. Of course, National had made the same offer to some of Morrow's competitors.

Required

1. What should be Morrow's target cost per auto part? Explain.

2. As a result of the Value Engineering Group's efforts, determine Morrow's estimated cost for the auto part. Will Morrow meet the target cost for the part? Do you recommend that Morrow take the National offer? Explain your reasons.

(Adapted from a problem by Joseph San Miguel)

13-46 **Target Costing; Health Care**   VIP-MD is a health maintenance organization (HMO) located in North Carolina. Unlike the traditional fee-for-service model that determines the payment according to the actual services used or costs incurred, VIP-MD receives a fixed, prepaid amount from subscribers. The per member per month (PMPM) rate is determined by estimating the health care cost per enrollee within a geographic location. The average health care coverage in North Carolina costs $368 per month which is the same amount irrespective of the subscriber's age. Because individuals are demanding quality care at reasonable rates, VIP-MD must contain its costs to remain competitive. A major competitor, Doctors Nationwide, is entering the North Carolina market in early 2010 with a monthly premium of $325. VIP-MD wants to maintain its current market penetration and hopes to increase its enrollees in 2010. The latest data on the number of enrollees and the associated costs follow:

Age	Enrollment in 2010	Projected Enrollment in 2011	Average Monthly Cost in 2010
1–4	45,688	48,977	$ 11,147,872
5–14	82,456	84,663	10,059,632
15–19	95,873	95,887	8,436,824
20–24	66,246	67,882	9,539,424
25–34	133,496	132,554	26,432,208
35–44	166,876	175,446	38,882,108
45–54	85,496	90,889	22,741,936
55–64	99,624	101,923	28,691,712
65–74	156,288	161,559	48,918,144
75–84	67,895	72,465	33,132,760
85 years and older	23,499	26,849	24,086,475
	1,023,437	1,059,094	$262,069,095

Required

1. Calculate the target cost required for VIP-MD to maintain its current market share and profit per enrollee in 2010.

2. Costs in the health care industry applicable to VIP-MD and Doctors Nationwide are expected to increase by 6 percent in the coming year, 2011. VIP-MD is planning for the year ahead and is expecting all providers, including VIP-MD and Doctors Nationwide, to increase their rates by $15 to $340. Calculate the new target cost assuming again that VIP-MD wants to maintain the same profit per enrollee as in 2010.

13-47 **Target Cost; Warehousing**   McFee Supply, a wholesaler, has determined that its operations have three primary activities: purchasing, warehousing, and distributing. The firm reports the following operating data for the year just completed:

Activity	Cost Driver	Quantity of Cost Driver	Cost per Unit of Cost Driver
Purchasing	Number of purchasing orders	1,000	$150 per order
Warehousing	Number of moves	8,000	30 per move
Distributing	Number of shipments	500	80 per shipment

McFee buys 100,000 units at an average unit cost of $10 and sells them at an average unit price of $20. The firm also has a fixed operating cost of $250,000 for the year.

McFee's customers are demanding a 10 percent discount for the coming year. The company expects to sell the same amount if the demand for price reduction can be met. McFee's suppliers, however, are willing to give only a 2 percent discount.

Required McFee has estimated that it can reduce the number of purchasing orders to 700 and can decrease the cost of each shipment $5 with minor changes in its operations. Any further cost saving must come from reengineering the warehousing processes. What is the maximum cost (i.e., target cost) for warehousing if the firm desires to earn the same amount of profit next year?

13-48 **Target Costing; International** Harpers, Ltd., is a U.K. manufacturer of casual shoes for men and women. It has sustained strong growth in the U.K. market in recent years due to its close attention to fashion trends. Harpers' shoes also have a good reputation for quality and comfort. To expand the business, Harpers is considering introducing its shoes to the U.S. market, where comparable shoes sell for an average of $90 wholesale, more than $16 above what Harpers charges in the United Kingdom (average price, £ 45). Management has engaged a marketing consultant to obtain information about what features U.S. consumers seek in shoes if they desire different features. Harpers also has obtained information on the approximate cost of adding these features:

Features Desired in the United States	Cost to Add (in U.S. $)	Importance Rating (5 is most important)
Colorfast material	$4.50	3
Lighter weight	6.75	5
Extra-soft insole	3.00	4
Longer-wearing sole	3.00	2

The current average manufacturing cost of Harpers' shoes is £34 (approximately $56 U.S.), which provides an average profit of £11 ($18 U.S.) per pair sold. Harpers would like to maintain this profit margin; however, the firm recognizes that the U.S. market requires different features and that shipping and advertising costs would increase approximately $10 U.S. per pair of shoes.

Required

1. What is the target manufacturing cost for shoes to be sold in the United States?
2. Which features, if any, should Harpers add for shoes to be sold in the United States?
3. Strategically evaluate Harpers' decision to begin selling shoes in the United States.

13-49 **Target Costing Quality Function Deployment** Ranger Yacht manufactures a line of family cruiser/racing sailboats. The boats are well-known for their quality, safety, and performance. Ranger hired Matthew Perry, a well-known sailboat designer and racer, to design a new sailboat, the M33. The M33 will have advanced materials in the hull and rigging to enhance the safety and performance of the boat, and also to improve its overnight comfort. Safety and comfort are the two most important boat-buying criteria of Ranger's customers, rated at 33 percent and 32 percent respectively, on a 100 point scale. The other two criteria are performance (20 percent) and styling (15 percent). The overall length of the boat is about 33 feet; its two sleeping areas have room for five or six people. Ranger projects a sale price of approximately $200,000 and estimates the costs of manufacturing the M33 as shown in Table 1.

Table 1

Component	Target Cost	Percentage of Total
Hull and keel	$36,000	30%
Standing rig	18,000	15
Sails	20,000	17
Electrical	16,000	13
Other	30,000	25
		100%

A team of engineers and sales managers studied the projected cost and was able to identify how each component of the planned boat contributed to satisfying the customers' criteria. The results of this study, based on careful estimates, is shown in Table 2. For example, the estimates show that 30 percent of the customers' desire for safety is satisfied by the construction of the hull and keel, another 30 percent by the standing rigging.

Table 2

	Criteria			
Component	**Safety**	**Styling**	**Performance**	**Comfort**
Hull and keel	30%	40%	50%	30%
Standing rig	30	20	20	10
Sails	10	10	30	10
Electrical	20	10	—	—
Other	10	20	—	50
	100%	100%	100%	100%

Required

1. Using the information in Table 2 developed by the team of engineers and sales managers, together with the customer criteria, determine which components of the boat are most important to customers, and why.

2. Take your findings in requirement 1 and compare them against the target cost figures in Table 1. What conclusions can you draw from this comparison?

13-50 **Target Costing: Quality Function Deployment** Bridal Photography Inc. (BPI) specializes in preparing wedding pictures, including a large book of photos for the wedding couple. Each BPI couple works directly and individually with a single BPI photographer who helps the couple plan the photos to be made on the wedding day and make the selection of photos to go into the wedding photo book and the choice of a wedding-photo book. The standard fee for each wedding is $6,000 which includes all of the firm's services including the book of wedding photos. BPI has several experienced photographers and has been managed well but is experiencing increased competition, especially based on price. BPI wants to protect its reputation and to continue to expand its business, and for this purpose has decided to use Quality Function Deployment (QFD) to better understand the cost and value trade-offs in its business. As a first step, BPI defined the four key "buying criteria" that couples use in choosing and evaluating photographers — (1) fast service, (2) great photos at the wedding, (3) quality of the photo finishing (color, clarity . . .), and (4) the quality of the photo book. A select sample of prior customers was asked to rate these criteria and, on a 300 point scale, provided scores of 30, 120, 60, and 90 respectively.

The BPI accounting records showed that the cost of the average wedding was $5,000, and the cost could be traced to four activities: (1) the planning meeting in which the couple and the photographer determined what types of photos were desired, set dates for the photography and proofs, etc., (2) the photography on the wedding day, (3) the preparation of proofs from which the couple would select the photos to be used in the book, and (4) the preparation of the final photos and the wedding photo book. The average costs of the four activities were $800, $2,400, $600, and $1,200, respectively.

As a final step, BPI managers, photographers, and staff worked together to determine an estimate of the contribution of each of the four activities to achieving the four buying criteria. The result is as follows (for example, the criteria of fast service was equally served by the planning meeting, the preparation of proofs and the preparation of the photo book, and only 10 percent from taking photos the day of the wedding):

Activity/ Criteria	Fast Service	Good Photos	Finishing	Book Quality
Planning meeting	30%	40%	-	30%
Take photos	10	60	-	10
Prepare proofs	30	-	50%	-
Prepare photo book	30	-	50	60
	100%	100%	100%	100%

Required

1. Determine which activities are most valuable to the wedding couple and compare this finding to the cost of the activities. Which activities should be given greater attention in time and cost, and which should be given less time and cost?

2. Indicate some business and competitive issues that should be taken in account in considering your answer to part 1 above.

13-51 **Theory of Constraints** Research Equipment Inc. (REC) is a small manufacturer of precision tools used to construct research equipment for engineering departments at colleges and universities. It sells its two main products, REC-1 and REC-2, for $450 and $600, respectively. Due to increasing demand and shortage of specialized labor, REC has found it increasingly difficult to meet the current weekly demand of 100 units of REC-1 and 60 units of REC-2. The following flow diagram shows the manufacturing requirements for the two products and the three types of materials required. Material A is used in REC-1 only, Material C is used in REC-2 only, and Material B is used in both REC-1 and REC-2.

The amount of weekly labor available for the four manufacturing operations follows:

Receiving and testing materials: 6,000 minutes
Machining (for Material A only): 10,000 minutes
Assembly: 5,000 minutes
Finishing: 10,000 minutes

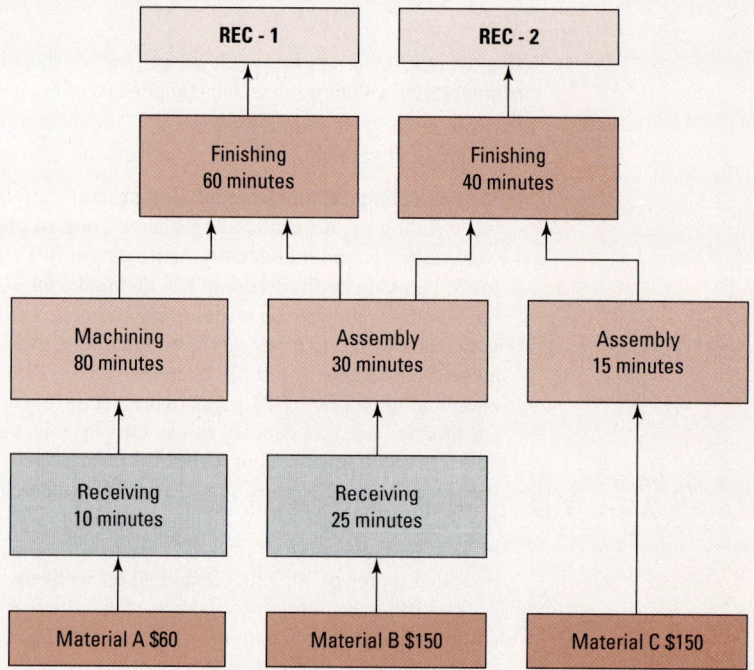

Assume that the labor for each operation is specialized and cannot be moved from one activity to another, that all operations except receiving and testing require a high level of skill, and that REC cannot increase the capacity on these operations in the short run.

Required What is the best production plan for REC? Why?

13-52 **Theory of Constraints; Strategy** Colton Furniture Co. is a small but fast-growing manufacturer of living room furniture. Its two principal products are end tables and sofas. The flow diagram for the manufacturing at Colton follows. Colton's manufacturing involves five processes: cutting the lumber, cutting the fabric, sanding, staining, and assembly. One employee cuts fabric and two do the staining. These are relatively skilled workers who could be replaced only with some difficulty. Two workers cut the lumber, and two others perform the sanding operation. There is some skill to these operations, but it is less critical than for staining and fabric cutting. Assembly requires the lowest skill level and is currently done by one full-time employee and a group of part timers who provide a total of 175 hours of working time per week. The other employees work a 40-hour week, with 5 hours off for breaks, training, and personal time. Assume a four-week month and that by prior agreement, none of the employees can be switched from one task to another. The current demand for Colton's products and sales prices are as follows, although Colton expects demand to increase significantly in the coming months if it is able to successfully negotiate an order from a motel chain.

	End Tables	Sofas
Price	$250	$450
Current demand (units per month)	400	150

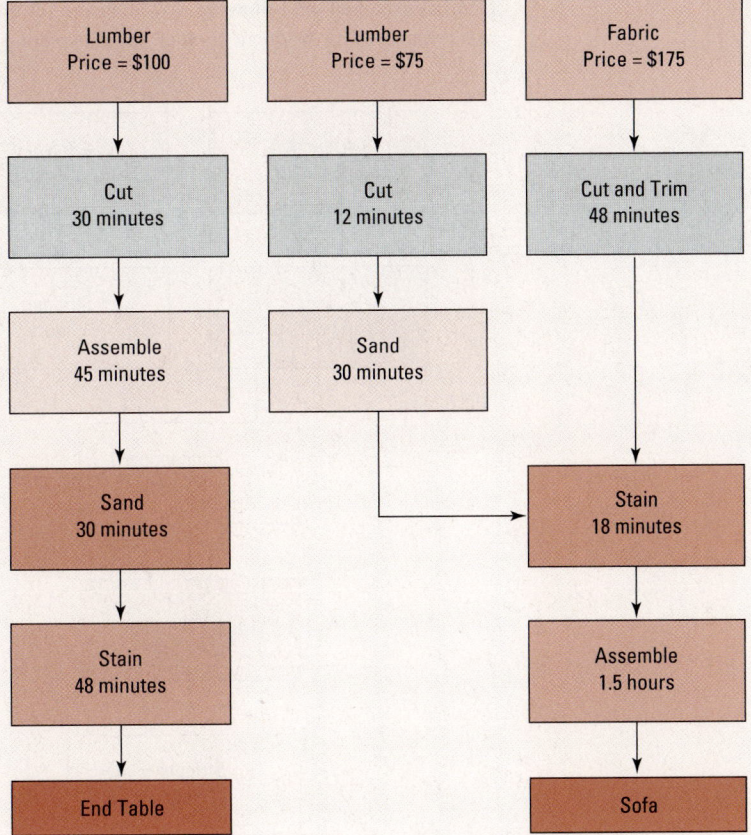

Required

1. What is the most profitable production plan for Colton? Explain your answer with supporting calculations.

2. How would you apply the five steps of the theory of constraints to Colton's manufacturing operations? What would you recommend for each step?

13-53   **Theory of Constraints**   Chemical Products Company (CPC) produces a variety of chemicals, primarily adhesives, lubricants, and polymers for industrial use by manufacturers to produce plastics and other compounds. Don Leo, the production vice president, has been informed of a disturbing trend of increasing customer complaints regarding late deliveries from the Canton, Kentucky, plant. The Canton plant is one of the firm's newest and most modern plants and is dedicated to the manufacture of two products, Polymer 1 and Polymer 2. Don has downloaded some incomplete recent information about the Canton plant onto his laptop; he plans to analyze the information in the hour or so he has before his next meeting of the CPC executive committee. He is concerned that some comments will be made about the problems at Canton, and he wants to have an idea of how to respond. Because CPC views Polymer 1 and Polymer 2 as very promising in terms of both sales and profit potential, the news of these problems is likely to spark some comment. The data downloaded by Don is as follows:

Activity	Number of Hours Required for Each Product		Number of Hours Available per Week
	Polymer 1	Polymer 2	
Filtering	2	4	320
Stripping	2	3	320
Reacting	3	5	320
Final filtering	2	1	160
Mixing	3	3	320
Other information			
Current sales demand (per week)	60	40	
Price	$145	$185	

Don has sketched the following flow diagram for the Canton plant. He believes it is relatively accurate because of his frequent contact with the plant.

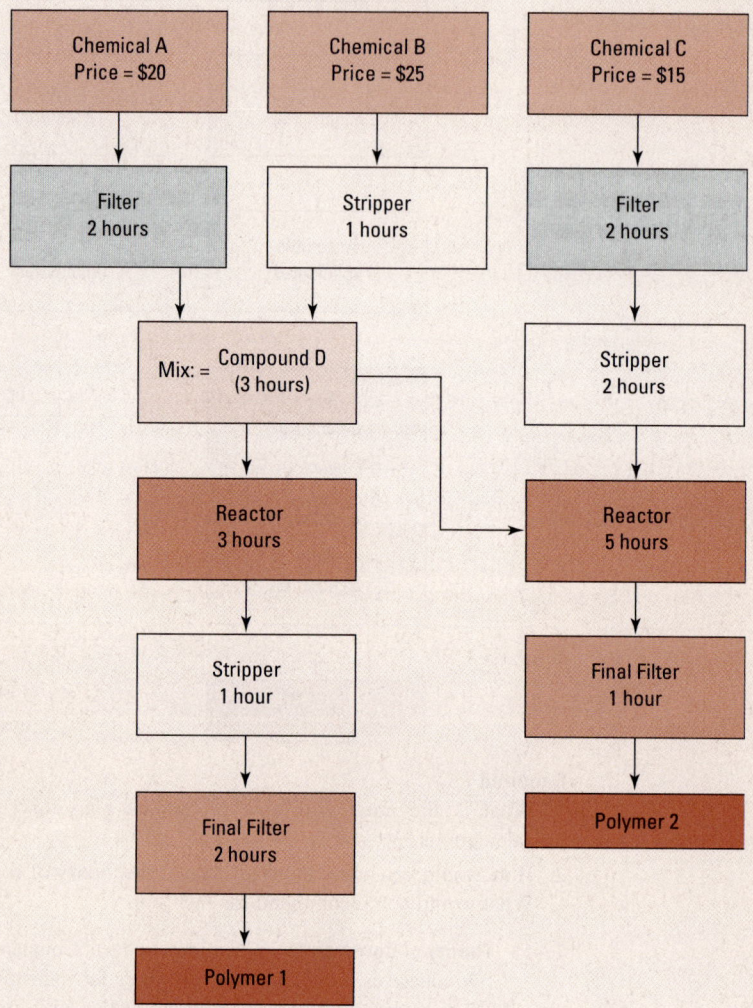

Required   Prepare a set of notes that Don can use in the executive meeting if questions come up about the problems at the Canton plant.

13-54   **Theory of Constraints**   Bakker Industries sells three products (611, 613, and 615) that it manufactures in four departments. Both labor and machine time are applied to products in each of the four departments. The machine-processing and labor skills required in each department prohibit switching either machines or labor from one department to another. However, Bakker has a good supply of both full-time and part-time labor and does not expect hiring or retention of employees to be a problem. Because of the availability of part-time labor, Bakker considers labor a variable cost and includes it in the calculation of throughput margin.

Bakker's management is planning its production schedule for the next several months. Some machines will be out of service for extensive overhauling. Available machine times by department for each of the next six months are as follows:

	Department			
	1	**2**	**3**	**4**
Normal machine capacity in machine-hours	3,500	3,500	3,000	3,500
Capacity of machines being repaired, in machine-hours	500	400	300	200
Available capacity in machine-hours	3,000	3,100	2,700	3,300

Labor and machine specifications per unit of product follow:

Product	Labor and Machine Time	Department 1	2	3	4
611	Direct labor-hours	2	3	3	1
	Machine-hours	2	1	2	2
613	Direct labor-hours	1	2	0	2
	Machine-hours	1	1	0	2
615	Direct labor-hours	2	2	1	1
	Machine-hours	2	2	1	1

The Sales Department's forecast of product demand over the next six months is as follows:

Product	Monthly Sales
611	500 units
613	400 units
615	1,000 units

Bakker's inventory levels will not increase or decrease during the next six months. The unit price and cost data valid for the next six months follow:

	Product 611	613	615
Price	$196	$123	$167
Direct materials	7	13	17
Direct labor			
Department 1	12	6	12
Department 2	21	14	14
Department 3	24	—	16
Department 4	9	18	9
Variable overhead	27	20	25
Fixed overhead	15	10	32
Variable selling	3	2	4

Required

1. Determine whether Bakker can meet the monthly sales demand for the three products. What department is a constraint, if any?

2. What monthly production schedule would be best for Bakker Industries? Assume that Bakker includes all variable manufacturing costs in calculating throughput.

(CMA Adapted)

13-55 **Life-Cycle Costing**   Tim Waters, the COO of BioDerm, has asked his cost management team for a product-line profitability analysis for his firm's two products, Xderm and Yderm. The two skin care products require a large amount of research and development and advertising. After receiving the following statement from BioDerm's auditor, Tim concludes that Xderm is the more profitable product and that perhaps cost-cutting measures should be applied to Yderm.

	Xderm	Yderm	Total
Sales	$3,000,000	$2,000,000	$5,000,000
Cost of goods sold	(1,900,000)	(1,600,000)	(3,500,000)
Gross profit	$1,100,000	$ 400,000	$1,500,000
Research and development			(900,000)
Selling expenses			(100,000)
Profit before taxes			$ 500,000

Required

1. Explain why Tim may be wrong in his assessment of the relative performances of the two products.

2. Suppose that 80 percent of the R&D and selling expenses are traceable to Xderm. Prepare life-cycle income statements for each product. What does this tell you about the importance of accurate life-cycle costing?

3. Consider again your answers in requirements 1 and 2 with the following additional information. R&D and selling expenses are substantially higher for Xderm because it is a new product. Tim has strongly supported development of the new product, including the high selling and R&D expenses. He has assured senior managers that the Xderm investment will pay off in improved profits for the firm. What are the ethical issues, if any, facing Tim as he reports to top management on the profitability of the firm's two products?

13-56 **Theory of Constraints for a Restaurant**   Taylor's is a popular restaurant that offers customers a large dining room and comfortable bar area. Taylor Henry, the owner and manager of the restaurant, has seen the number of patrons increase steadily over the last two years and is considering whether and when she will have to expand its available capacity. The restaurant occupies a large home, and all the space in the building is now used for dining, the bar, and kitchen, but space is available to expand the restaurant. The restaurant is open from 6 p.m. to 10 p.m. each night (except Monday) and has an average of 24 customers enter the bar and 50 enter the dining room during each of those hours. Taylor has noticed the trends over the last two years and expects that within about four years the number of bar customers will increase by 50 percent and the dining customers will increase by 20 percent. Taylor is worried that the restaurant will be not be able to handle the increase and has asked you to study its capacity. In your study you consider four areas of capacity: the parking lot (which has 80 spaces), the bar (54 seats), the dining room (100 seats), and the kitchen. The kitchen is well staffed and can prepare any meal on the menu in an average of 12 minutes per meal. The kitchen when fully staffed is able to have up to 20 meals in preparation at a time, or 100 meals per hour (60 min./12 min. × 20 meals). To assess the capacity of the restaurant, you obtain the additional information:

- Diners typically come to the restaurant by car with an average of three persons per car, while bar patrons arrive with an average of 1.5 persons per car.
- Diners on the average occupy a table for an hour while bar customers usually stay for an average of two hours.
- Due to fire regulations, all bar customers must be seated.
- The bar customer typically orders two drinks at an average of $7 per drink; the dining room customer orders a meal with an average price of $22; the restaurant's cost per drink is $1, and the direct costs for meal preparation is $5.

Required   (Note: When calculating capacity usage, you may round numbers up to the nearest whole digit)

1. a. Given the current number of customers per hour, what is the amount of excess capacity in the bar, dining room, parking lot, and kitchen?

   b. Calculate the expected total throughput margin for the restaurant per hour, day, and month (assuming a 26-day month).

2. a. Given the expected increase in the number of customers, determine if there is a constraint for any of the four areas of capacity. What is the amount of needed capacity for each constraint?

   b. If there is a constraint, reduce the demand on the constraint so that the restaurant is at full capacity (assume some customers would have to be turned away). Calculate the expected total throughput margin for the restaurant per hour, day, and month (assuming a 26-day month).

3. Taylor has obtained construction estimates. To increase the capacity of her bar to 80 seats and dining room to 120 seats and kitchen to 25 meals at the same time would cost $250,000 which she could finance for $5,000 per month for the next four years. There would be no change to the parking lot. Given your analysis above, prepare a brief recommendation to Taylor regarding expanding the restaurant.

13-57 **Life-Cycle Costing, Health Care, Present Values**   Cure-all, Inc., has developed a drug that will diminish the effects of aging. Cure-all has spent $1,000,000 on research and development and $2,108,000 for clinical trials. Once the drug is approved by the FDA, which is imminent, it will have a five-year sales life cycle. Laura Russell, Cure-all's chief financial officer, must determine the best alternative for the company among three options. The company can choose to manufacture, package, and distribute the drug; outsource only the manufacturing; or sell the drug's patent. Laura has compiled the following annual cost information for this drug if the company were to manufacture it:

Cost Category	Fixed Costs	Variable Cost per Unit
Manufacturing	$5,000,000	$68.00
Packaging	380,000	20.00
Distribution	1,125,000	6.50
Advertising	2,280,000	12.00

Management anticipates a high demand for the drug and has benchmarked $235 per unit as a reasonable price based on other drugs that promise similar results. Management expects sales volume of 3,000,000 units over five years and uses a discount rate of 10 percent.

If Cure-all chooses to outsource the manufacturing of the drug while continuing to package, distribute, and advertise it, the manufacturing costs would result in fixed costs of $1,500,000 and variable cost per unit of $80. For the sale of the patent, Cure-all would receive $300,000,000 now and $25,000,000 at the end of every year for the next five years.

Required   Determine the best option for Cure-all. Support your answer.

13-58   **Constraint Analysis, Flow Diagrams (Appendix)**   Silver Aviation assembles small aircraft for commercial use. The majority of its business is with small freight airlines serving areas whose airports do not accommodate larger planes. The remainder of Silver's customers are commuter airlines and individuals who use planes in their businesses, such as the owners of larger ranches. Silver recently expanded its market into Central and South America, and the company expects to double its sales over the next three years.

To schedule work and track all projects, Silver uses a flow diagram. The diagram for the assembly of a single cargo plane is shown in Exhibit 1. The diagram shows four alternative paths with the critical path being *ABGEFJK*. Bob Peterson, president of Coastal Airlines, recently placed an order with Silver Aviation for five cargo planes. During contract negotiations, Bob agreed to a delivery time of 13 weeks (five work days per week) for the first plane with the balance of the planes being delivered at the rate of one every four weeks. Because of problems with some of the aircraft that Coastal is currently using, Bob contacted Grace Vander, sales manager for Silver Aviation, to ask about improving the delivery date of the first cargo plane. Grace replied that she believed the schedule could be shortened by as much as 10 work days or two weeks, but the cost of assembly would increase as a result. Bob said he would be willing to consider the increased costs, and they agreed to meet the following day to review a revised schedule that Grace would prepare.

Because Silver Aviation previously assembled aircraft on an accelerated basis, the company has a list of costs for this purpose. Grace used the data shown in Exhibit 2 to develop a plan to cut 10 working days from the schedule at a minimum increase in cost to Coastal Airlines. Upon completing her plan, she reported to Bob that Silver would be able to cut 10 working days from the schedule for an associated increase in cost of $6,600. Grace's Exhibit 3 shows accelerated assembly schedule for the cargo plane starting from the regularly scheduled days and cost.

EXHIBIT 1   **Flow Diagram for Plane Assembly**

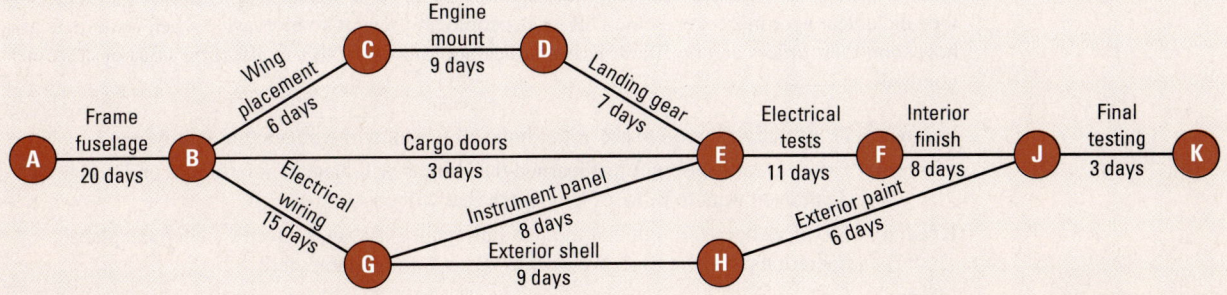

EXHIBIT 2
Crash Cost Listing

Activity		Expected Activity Times		Direct Cost		Added Crash Cost
		Regular	Accel.	Regular	Accel.	Per Reduced Day
AB	Frame fuselage	20 days	16 days	$12,000	$16,800	$1,200
BC	Wing placement	6	5	3,600	5,000	1,400
CD	Engine mount	9	7	6,600	8,000	700
DE	Landing gear	7	5	5,100	6,700	800
BE	Cargo doors	3	3	1,400	1,400	—
BG	Electrical wiring	15	13	9,000	11,000	1,000
GE	Instrument panel	8	6	5,700	8,300	1,300
EF	Electrical tests	11	10	6,800	7,600	800
GH	Exterior shell	9	7	4,200	5,200	500
FJ	Interior finish	8	7	3,600	4,000	400
HJ	Exterior paint	6	5	3,600	4,000	400
JK	Final testing	3	2	3,500	4,400	900
				$65,100	$82,400	

EXHIBIT 3
Accelerated Plane Assembly Schedule

Activity Accelerated	Additional Cost per Day	Total Direct Cost
		$65,100
HJ by one day	$400	65,500
FJ by one day	400	65,900
GH by two days	500	66,900
CD by two days	700	68,300
EF by one day	800	69,100
DE by two days	800	70,700
BG by one day	1,000	71,700

Required

1. Is Grace's plan satisfactory? Why or why not?

2. Revise the accelerated assembly schedule so that Coastal Airlines will take delivery of the first plane ahead of schedule at the least incremental cost to Coastal.

3. Calculate the incremental costs that Bob will have to pay for this revised accelerated delivery.

(CMA Adapted)

13-59 **Production Planning and Control Strategy**   This is a story about manufacturing performance at one plant of a large company. It begins with Kristen Reynolds, a relatively new plant manager, coming to visit Bryan Simpkins, the plant's head of manufacturing. Kristen and Bryan work for ITR Incorporated, a manufacturer of lighting fixtures with plants located in six countries and worldwide sales. The plant that Kristen and Bryan manage is located in Canada near Hamilton, Ontario. It is the one plant in ITR's system that focuses on custom orders that require special materials, setup, and assembly. The other five plants supply ITR's high-volume, standardized products. Because of changes in the residential and commercial construction industries, the demand for custom orders at the Ontario plant has been increasing steadily. Unfortunately, it has not been filling these orders as quickly as Kristen would like. Many solid customers are waiting days or weeks longer for their orders than they did a year ago; moreover, some ITR sales people have begun to be evasive when customers ask how soon their orders can be filled. Kristen does not know how this is affecting sales or customer goodwill.

Kristen: Hi, Bryan. It's good to see you. I hope all is well with you and the family.

Bryan: Going great—though I just learned that Jimmy will have to have braces on his teeth. I don't even want to think of how much that will cost.

Kristen: Hey, I've been through that too. No fun. (pause) Bryan, I haven't visited the plant operations in some time. Would you take me for a quick tour?

Bryan: Let's go.

Bryan and Kristen first visit an operation where a skilled worker is operating a machine that molds a metal frame on which multiple light fixtures will later be installed. They watch as the worker (name badge says Ed) completes the last of a batch of 15 frames. Kristen asks how long this batch took him, and he says 82 minutes. "I know this exactly because I have productivity standards to meet, and I must record my time on all jobs. My standard is 6 minutes per item, so I beat my goal." Ed then examines each frame and finds that one has a bad twist and must be rejected; this takes about 10 minutes. He then pushes a button near the machine that calls another worker to remove the defective frame. Meanwhile, Ed loads the 14 good ones on a cart and moves them to the next manufacturing station. Bryan and Kristen note that many frames are already waiting at the next station.

The worker who was called to remove the defective frame tags it, writes up the potential cause(s) for the defect, and then moves the frame to the area of the plant designated for scrap and rework. Kristen and Bryan look at the defect report and note that it indicates two possibilities which will be studied further by another worker assigned to the scrap and rework area. The two possibilities are poor-quality materials, as determined by apparent weaknesses in portions of the framing material and poor work quality (Ed could have damaged the frame accidentally by banging it against one of the roof support beams located next to his work area). Kristen and Bryan note that Ed's workstation area is indeed pretty cramped.

They move to another workstation, which has no operator. By asking a worker at the adjacent station, they determine that the station is down because the machine needs repair. "Joe usually works that station, but he is helping out in the shipping department until his machine is repaired."

They move to another workstation that looks very busy. An order marked "urgent" is waiting at this station, while Dan, the operator, quickly finishes another order. Bryan asks Dan why he has not started the urgent order, and Dan explains that he cannot afford to stop the machine and set it up for another order. This would cost him some time that would lower his productivity on the current job. Dan explains that it is important that he get the items done in the current order quickly, within a standard level of productivity, or production supervisors will be coming to call. Dan says he sees the urgent sign and is working quickly to get to it. He says he might even delay lunch to start it.

To investigate some of the things they observed, Kristen and Bryan next visit the purchasing department. Here they find that the frame material Ed used was purchased from a relatively new vendor at an unbelievably low price. The purchasing department manager approved the purchase because other purchases in the month had gone over budget and this was a way to help meet the budget. The budget is a predetermined amount that the purchasing department is expected to spend each month. Plant policy requires an investigation of any large variances from the budget.

Next Kristen and Bryan inquire about Joe's machine. A check at the job scheduler's desk shows that the workstation had been in use constantly for the last few weeks. Joe said that he noticed a funny noise but had not reported it because he had some jobs to finish and his productivity is measured by how quickly he finished them. His time between jobs is not measured, but doing jobs quickly is important. Bryan asks the job scheduler why Ed's work area is so crowded since there appears to be plenty of room elsewhere in the plant. The job scheduler says that he is not sure, but that it probably has to do with the fact that each production department is charged a certain amount of plant overhead based on the amount of square feet of space that department occupies. Thus, the department manager for whom Ed works is likely to have reduced the space as much as possible to reduce these overhead charges.

As the story ends, Bryan and Kristen are looking for an answer to how urgent orders are scheduled and moved through the plant.

Required   Consider the manufacturing processes observed in ITR's Ontario plant. What recommendations do you think Bryan and Kristen should make?

Solution to Self-Study Problem

Best Brand Lighting, Inc.

A thorough analysis will require a good deal more inquiry of management and fact finding than is available from the limited information provided earlier, but a few useful observations can be made.

1. Encourage BBL to consider increasing the effort put into design to reduce manufacturing costs and to reduce the relatively high rate of product returns in the specialty segment. The cost of design appears low relative to manufacturing and downstream costs, especially in the specialty segment. Inquire about which types of design approaches are being used. Urge BBL to adopt concurrent engineering-based methods, especially because of the relatively short market life cycles in the industry.

2. Consider additional analysis of pricing. Because of BBL's strong acceptance in the specialty segment and because the differentiation strategy is likely to be important in that segment, a price increase might yield higher profits with little or no loss in market share.

   Cost leadership appears to be the appropriate strategy in the major retail segment; inquire what methods the company is using to reduce overall product costs in this segment.

   Also, investigate further the rate of customer returns for each product. Is this due to design problems or problems in sales management?

3. Consider a further analysis of marketing expenses. Would an increase in marketing effort in the major retailer segment improve sales in this segment?

4. Consider the need to perform a detailed analysis by product category within each market segment. A detailed analysis might uncover important information about opportunities to reduce cost and add value within the products' value chain.

5. Because of the relatively short sales life cycles, consider whether target costing could be used effectively at BBL. How intense is the level of competition in the industry, and to what extent are trade-offs made between functionality and price in the development and introduction of each new product? If the level of competition is very intense, and trade-offs between functionality and price are key strategic decisions, target costing should be a useful management tool.

6. Investigate the costing system. Is it activity based? How accurate are the cost figures that it develops?

Operational-Level Control

The objective of the four chapters in Part Three is to present some key tools used to evaluate the performance of mid-level managers and operating personnel, what we refer to as *operational control*. By its nature, operational control focuses on short-term financial and relevant nonfinancial performance. The performance of high-level managers (i.e., *management control*) is examined in Part Four. The essence of control is a comparison of actual performance to budgeted or expected performance.

In **Chapters 14** through **16** we cover traditional *financial-control* models, that is, models based on the use of standard costs and flexible budgets. The flexible budget allows a comparison of expected financial performance to the actual performance for a given period. The use of flexible budgets and standard costs provides a number of ways to break down and explain what we call the total operating income variance for the period—that is, the difference between actual operating profit and budgeted operating profit. Since profit is a function of five factors (sales volume, selling price, variable cost per unit, sales mix, and total fixed costs), the total operating income variance can be broken down into components associated with each of these five factors.

In **Chapter 14** we begin by defining the total operating income variance and then breaking this total variance down into a sales volume variance and a total flexible-budget variance. We show how the latter variance can be broken down into a selling-price variance and component variances related to two direct manufacturing costs (labor and materials). Chapter 14 also looks at relevant nonfinancial performance indicators that are useful supplements to the variances calculated earlier in the chapter.

Chapter 15 focuses on the variances that arise from differences between budgeted and actual indirect manufacturing costs (i.e., manufacturing overhead). As with Chapter 14, we use flexible budgets and standard costs to further break down the total flexible-budget variance for the period.

Chapter 16 completes the operating-income variance analysis by looking in more detail at the sales volume variance. Specifically, we show how the total sales volume variance can be broken down into components based on market size and market share, among others. Chapter 16 also looks at various measures of operating productivity.

Part Three closes with a study, in **Chapter 17,** of the management and control of quality, including topics of cost of quality (COQ), six sigma, lean manufacturing, and lean accounting. These topics are presented from the standpoint of how cost-management systems can be refined to support strategic initiatives on the part of management.

Operational Performance Measurement: Sales, Direct-Cost Variances, and the Role of Nonfinancial Performance Measures

After studying this chapter, you should be able to . . .

1. Explain the essence of control systems in general and operational control systems in particular
2. Explain the total operating-income variance for a given period
3. Develop a general framework for subdividing the total operating-income variance into component variances
4. Develop standard costs for product costing, performance evaluation, and control
5. Record manufacturing cost flows and associated variances in a standard cost system
6. Discuss major operating functions and the need for nonfinancial performance indicators

Schmidt Machinery, the example company for this chapter and the next, is a well-established (hypothetical) firm that produces a high-quality line of all-weather furniture for use on patios and decks and in sunrooms. Product XV-1 is a lightweight but durable lounge chair. Because of its very high quality and reputation for design innovation, Schmidt's products are sold largely by catalog, and over the firm's Web site; a few high-end retailers also carry the brand. The company currently has few direct competitors in this country, but there is a growing number of competitors from Europe and Asia. At present, the falling dollar has helped Schmidt maintain its domestic sales and to have some opportunities for foreign sales, but management is concerned that the foreign competitors will soon be able to reduce price and compete effectively. For this reason, the company is looking for ways to better manage its costs and to improve manufacturing efficiency.

The underlying business of Schmidt can conceptually be broken down into four major processes: operating processes, customer-management processes, innovation processes, and regulatory/social processes. Schmidt desires to design and implement a comprehensive management accounting and control system that enables it to successfully meet competitive threats in a sustainable manner. As a start, the company has decided to focus on a control system associated with its operating processes—*operational control,* for short.

The topic of operational control systems, as part of a more comprehensive management accounting and control system, is the subject of Part Three of the text. In this chapter we introduce you to the notion of *financial control,* which begins at the end of a period (e.g., month or quarter) by comparing actual operating income to budgeted income. This difference, which we call a variance, can then be broken down into component variances related to costs, sales volume, sales price, and sales mix.

In this chapter we focus on the determination of the sales volume variance and what is called the *total flexible-budget variance.* The latter variance can be further broken down into a sales price variance, and component variances associated with two direct manufacturing costs: labor and materials. In Chapter 15 we extend the analysis to include a breakdown and analysis of variances associated with indirect manufacturing costs (i.e., manufacturing support costs). In Chapter 16 we provide a further discussion of sales-related and productivity variances. Finally, in Chapter 17 we look at the issue of operational control from the standpoint of quality initiatives and how management accounting systems can be refined to support such initiatives. In all four chapters we make the point that in order to develop a comprehensive management accounting and control system, we need to supplement financial-performance indicators with relevant nonfinancial measures of performance. Thus, operational control systems can be thought of as including both financial and nonfinancial performance metrics.

> You can't get caught up in things that you can't control. . . . We cannot control our selling price. We can control our cost of manufacturing. We can control our efficiencies.
>
> *Steven Appleton, CEO of Micron Technology*

Management Accounting and Control Systems

LEARNING OBJECTIVE 1

Explain the essence of control systems in general and operational control systems in particular.

Control
refers to the set of procedures, tools, and systems organizations use to reach their goals.

A **management accounting and control system**
is an organization's core performance-measurement system.

Operational control
focuses on short-term operating performance.

Financial control
consists of a comparison between actual and budgeted financial results.

Variances
are the differences between budgeted and actual financial amounts.

In business we use the term **control** in a general sense to refer to the set of procedures, tools, and systems organizations use to ensure that progress is being made toward accomplishing the goals and objectives of the organization. In accounting, we refer to an organization's **management accounting and control system** as its core performance-measurement system, one that includes both planning and evaluation (feedback) components.

Comprehensive management accounting and control systems can be subdivided for discussion purposes into management control systems and operational control systems. In this text we use the term **operational control** to refer to the subset of an organization's overall management accounting and control system that focuses on *short-term operational performance.* That is, operational control focuses on the control of basic business processes (or activities) that are performed to produce and deliver to customers the organization's outputs (goods or services).

There are fundamentally two performance dimensions covered by operational control systems: financial and nonfinancial. Thus, an effective operational control system will include performance indicators of both types.

By convention, **financial control** is accomplished by comparing actual to budgeted financial amounts. Thus, budgets are useful in the financial-control process because they provide the standard against which actual financial results can be compared. Differences between budgeted amounts and actual financial results are referred to as **variances.** In this text, we use the labels F and U to refer, respectively, to favorable and unfavorable variances. Favorable variances are those that increase short-term operating income, while unfavorable variances have the opposite effect.

The following example provides a broad overview of the tasks involved in developing an effective operational control system for Schmidt Machinery Company.

Developing an Operational Control System: The Five Steps of Strategic Decision Making for Schmidt Machinery

1. **Determine the strategic issues surrounding the problem.** Schmidt is a differentiated manufacturer, selling a high-priced product to those who value its quality, design, and

functionality. With the growth of foreign competition and the possibility of price competition in the coming years, Schmidt is now looking for ways to maintain its profitability and quality by improving operational efficiency.

2. **Identify the alternative actions.** One approach, as explained in Chapter 13, would be to use target costing in the context of product redesign aimed at reducing the cost while maintaining the quality of the product that Schmidt produces. Another approach would be to implement an operational control system. Thus, the company is currently considering whether to implement such a system, either in conjunction with or in lieu of the target-costing procedures discussed in Chapter 13.

3. **Obtain information and conduct analyses of the alternatives.** An operational control system, if fully implemented, will capture both financial and nonfinancial performance data. Financial data include budgeted results (sales volume, sales mix, selling prices, variable cost per unit, and total fixed costs). Budgeted costs on a per-unit basis are referred to as *standard costs*. To experiment with a new financial control system, Schmidt develops standard costs for the production of one of its products, XV-1 (see Exhibit 14.5 on page 599). Product design engineers have been asked to consider the possibility of redesigning XV-1 and to estimate the potential savings from the redesign.

4. **Based on strategy and analysis, choose and implement the desired alternative.** Management decides that a product redesign would be too risky at this point, jeopardizing the quality image of the company. So the firm chooses to proceed with the development and implementation of an operational control system associated with product XV-1.

5. **Provide an ongoing evaluation of the effectiveness of implementation in step 4.** As the competitive environment becomes clearer, including changes in the value of the dollar, management should continue to review its approach on how to continue to deliver its differentiated product profitably. In the future, therefore, the company will evaluate each of the following options: the management and control of quality (Chapter 17), productivity analysis (Chapter 16), and theory of constraints, TOC (Chapter 13).

Short-Term Financial Control

LEARNING OBJECTIVE 2
Explain the total operating-income variance for a given period.

The total **operating-income variance** of a period is the difference between the actual operating income of the period and the budgeted operating income for the period; also referred to as the **master (static) budget variance** for the period.

An important short-term financial goal for a company is to achieve the budgeted operating income for the period. At the end of a period, management wants to know whether the planned operating income was attained. The difference between the actual operating income and the master budget operating income is called the total **operating-income variance.** This variance is also referred to as the **master (static) budget variance** for the period.

Consider the analysis of operations for Schmidt Machinery Company presented in Exhibit 14.1. The bottom line of column (2) shows that the budgeted operating income for the period is $200,000, while column (1) reports that the firm actually earned an operating income of $128,000 for the period. This difference is the total operating-income variance for the period, $72,000 unfavorable [column (3)].

In addition to the operating-income variance, Exhibit 14.1 reports the difference between the master (static) budget and the actual result for units sold, sales dollars, variable cost per unit, and total fixed costs. For example, we see from Exhibit 14.1 that actual units sold, 780 units, is 220 units less than the sales units in the master budget, a 22 percent shortfall.

Exhibit 14.1 also reports that total variable costs in October were $99,050 less than budget; we refer to this difference as a favorable variance. This result may lead us to conclude that the primary reason for Schmidt's failure to be effective in earning its budgeted operating income is the shortfall in sales, not its failure to control variable costs. The shortfall is so large that even with a good control of expenses, as evidenced by the substantial favorable variance in total variable costs, the firm still failed to achieve its budgeted operating income.

That conclusion is misleading. Direct comparisons between the actual operating results and the master (static) budget amounts for total variable costs can be meaningless. In this

EXHIBIT 14.1
Comparison of Actual and
Budgeted Operating Income

	SCHMIDT MACHINERY COMPANY					
	Analysis of Operating Income					
	For October 2010					
	(1)		**(2)**		**(3)**	
	Actual Operating Income		**Master (Static) Budget**		**Variances**	
Units	780		1,000		220U*	
Sales	$639,600	100%	$800,000	100%	$160,400U	
Variable costs	350,950	55	450,000	56	99,050F†	
Contribution margin	$288,650	45%	$350,000	44%	$ 61,350U	
Fixed costs	160,650	25	150,000	19	10,650U	
Operating income	$128,000	20%	$200,000	25%	$ 72,000U	

* U denotes an *unfavorable* effect on operating income.
† F denotes a *favorable* effect.

instance, the variable expenses in the master budget are for operations at a higher level than that actually attained. Variable expenses for 780 units should be less than the variable expenses for 1,000 units. Schmidt should not credit its management for having good control of variable expenses based only on the fact that the variable costs incurred are below the master budgeted amount for the period.

The operating-income variance ($72,000 unfavorable for Schmidt in October) reveals only whether the firm achieved the budgeted operating income for the period; it does not identify causes for the deviation or help the firm identify courses of action to reduce or eliminate similar deviations in the future. The firm needs to conduct additional analyses to learn the reason for missing the target. Flexible budgets and standard costs can be used to break down and explain the total operating-income variance for a period. It is to this process of variance decomposition that we now turn.

Flexible-Budgets and Profit-Variance Analysis

LEARNING OBJECTIVE 3

Develop a general framework for subdividing the total operating-income variance into component variances.

The Flexible Budget

The budget prepared prior to the beginning of a period, as discussed in Chapter 10, is a *master budget* for the period; it lays out expectations and provides blueprints of operations for the coming period. This budget is referred to as a *static budget* because it is developed for only a single output level.

The master budget is useful for initial planning and coordination of activities for a given period. It also serves as a guideline or benchmark in monitoring and controlling operations and for performance evaluation. Operating conditions, however, seldom turn out exactly the way they were expected or forecasted when the budget was prepared. Whenever the output (e.g., sales volume) attained differs from the budgeted output, the organization needs to revise the master budget before assessing short-run financial performance. This revised budget is referred to as a *flexible budget*.

The **flexible budget** is a budget that adjusts revenues and costs to the actual output level achieved.

A **flexible budget** is a budget that adjusts revenues and expenses to the actual output level achieved. Changes in output (for example, units manufactured or sold for a manufacturing firm, number of patient-days for a hospital, or number of students for a school district) change the firm's expected revenues and expenses. For financial control purposes, a firm prepares a flexible budget at the end of a period when the total work done or the actual output level for the period is known.

Flexible budgets are useful for assessing short-term financial performance. The data for Schmidt Machinery Company in Exhibit 14.1 show that the period's operating income is

$72,000 less than the budgeted amount. On receiving the report, management would likely raise the following questions:

1. Why was operating income less than expected?
2. Why have expenses gone from 75 to 80 percent of sales? Can management do something to prevent the same thing from happening next year?
3. Why were short-term fixed costs $10,650 more than expected?
4. Were the disappointing financial results attributable to changes in:
   a. Units sold?
   b. Sales price?
   c. Sales mix?
   d. Production costs?
   e. Selling and general expenses?

Preparing a flexible budget allows management to adjust the budget to the output level achieved and to answer these questions. That is, the use of flexible budgets and standard costs (discussed later in this chapter) allows us to subdivide the total operating-income variance for the period into component variances related to each of the five factors that combine to determine short-run operating profit, viz., selling price, sales volume, sales mix, variable cost per unit, and total fixed costs. A framework for subdividing the total operating-income variance into component variances is presented in Exhibit 14.2. This exhibit gives you an overall picture of the variance-decomposition process. All of the component variances that can be calculated, when summed, equal the total operating-income variance for the period. The ability to explain this overall variance is the essence of the traditional financial control model.

Flexible budgets differ from the master budget only in terms of the number of units embodied in the budget. Exhibit 14.3 illustrates the flexible budget for Schmidt for October 2010. Schmidt developed this flexible budget in three steps:

Step 1. **Determine the output of the period.** Schmidt manufactured and sold 780 units. The flexible budget, therefore, would be based on an output level of 780 units.

Step 2. **Use the selling price and the variable cost per unit data from the master budget to calculate the budgeted sales revenues and budgeted variable expenses, respectively, for the output of the period and to compute the flexible budget contribution margin.** The selling price per unit and variable cost per unit in the master budget are $800 and $450, respectively. Thus, at 780 units:

Flexible budget total sales = 780 units × $800 per unit	$624,000
Flexible budget total variable expenses = 780 units × $450 per unit	351,000
Flexible budget contribution margin = 780 units × $350 per unit*	$273,000

* $800 − $450 (total variable cost per unit consists of manufacturing costs of $400 plus $50 of selling and administrative expenses)

Alternatively, the flexible budget contribution margin can be computed by multiplying actual sales volume by the budgeted contribution margin per unit:

$$780 \text{ units} \times \$350 \text{ per unit} = \$273,000$$

Step 3. **Determine the budgeted amount of fixed cost and then compute the flexible-budget operating income.** Schmidt Company has determined that the manufacturing and selling of 780 units is within the same operating range as the master budget operating level. Thus, the total fixed cost for the flexible budget is $150,000, and the flexible-budget operating income is:

$$\$273,000 - \$150,000 = \$123,000.$$

EXHIBIT 14.2   Operating-Income Variances (Single-Product Example)

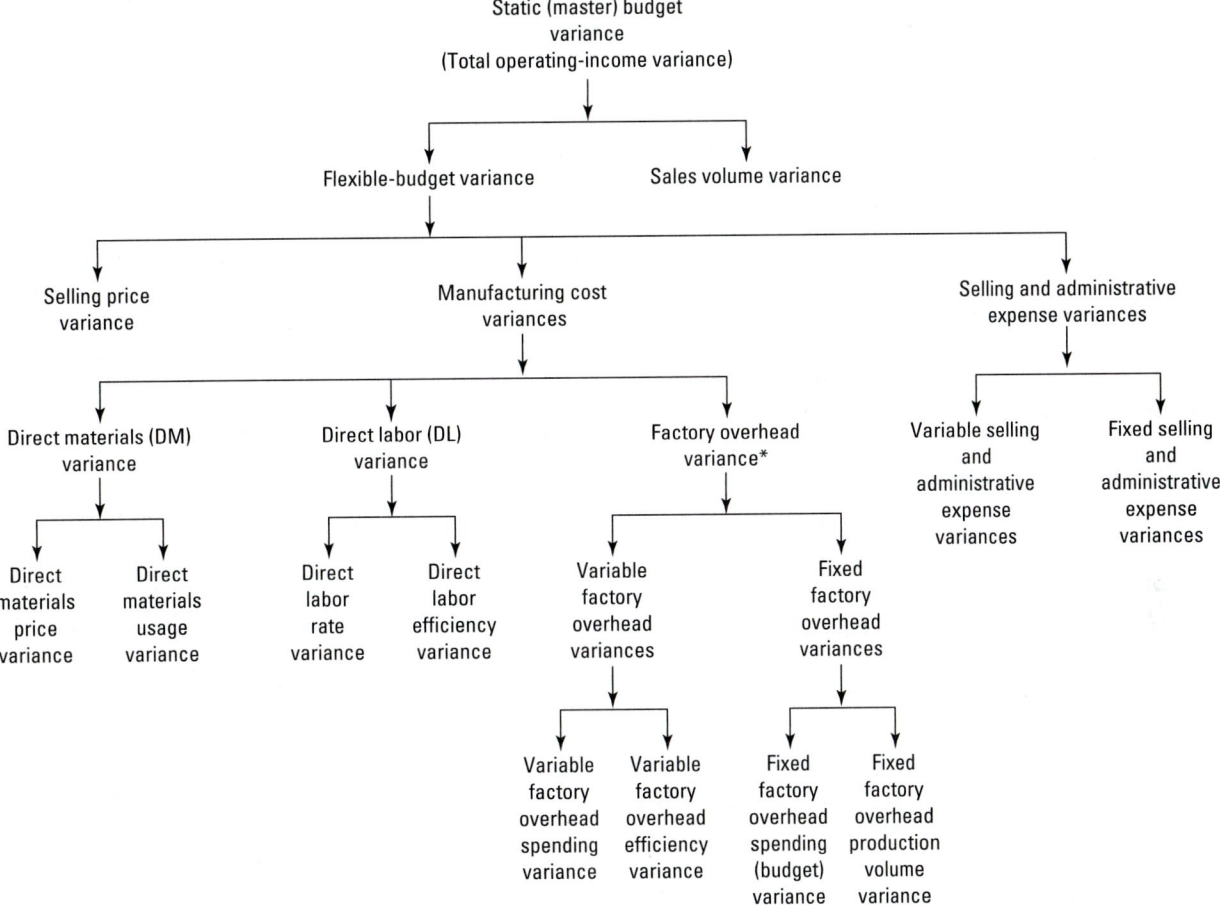

* The decomposition of this variance is covered in Chapter 15.

EXHIBIT 14.3

Flexible and Master Budgets for Schmidt Machinery Company

	(1) Flexible Budget		(2) Master (Static) Budget	
Units	780		1,000	
Sales ($800/unit)	$624,000	100.00%	$800,000	100.00%
Variable expenses ($450/unit)	351,000	56.25	450,000	56.25
Contribution margin ($350/unit)	$273,000	43.75%	$350,000	43.75%
Fixed expenses	150,000	24.04	150,000	18.75
Operating income	$123,000	19.71%	$200,000	25.00%

Note that the amount of fixed costs in a flexible budget may differ from the amount in the master budget if the actual operating level is substantially different from the operating level anticipated by the firm at the time it prepared the master budget.

In summary, total sales and total expenses for a flexible budget are calculated using these formulas:

Total sales = Actual number of units sold × Budgeted selling price per unit

Total variable expenses = Actual number of units sold × Budgeted variable cost per unit

Total fixed expenses = Amount of fixed expenses in the master budget

A firm can prepare a budget for different levels of output or activity. In this text we use the term *pro forma* when referring to budgets prepared for multiple output levels. We use the term *flexible budget* in a more limited sense, that is, the budget based on the actual activity level achieved during a period.

Sales Volume Variance and the Total Flexible-Budget Variance

With the help of a flexible budget, we can now separate the $72,000U total operating-income variance (Exhibit 14.1) into two components: a *flexible-budget variance* and a *sales-volume variance*. The details for this decomposition are shown in Exhibit 14.4. Note that the total operating-income variance is also referred to as the total master (static) budget variance.

Sales Volume Variance

Sales volume variance
for each income statement item is the difference between the flexible budget amount for that item and the amount for that item reflected in the master budget for the period.

The **sales volume variance** of a period is the difference between the flexible-budget amount and the amount in the master (static) budget of the period for the corresponding income statement item. A sales volume variance measures the effect of changes in sales volume on revenue, expenses, contribution margin, or operating income of the period. Column (4) of Exhibit 14.4 shows the sales volume variances for October 2010.

The master budget [column (5)] shows that Schmidt planned to sell 1,000 units in October 2010. However, actual sales in October were only 780 units. Column (3) shows the budget for this sales volume. The difference between the flexible and the master budgets is the sales volume variance. Thus, the sales volume variance is 220 unfavorable in units and $77,000 unfavorable in operating income [column (4)].

Note that the sales volume variance in terms of operating income is normally the same as the contribution margin sales volume variance. This is because, as noted above, fixed expenses in the master budget and in the flexible budget usually are the same. Thus, an alternative way to compute the sales volume variance is to multiply the master budget contribution margin per unit (here $350) by the difference between the actual units sold and the units in the master (static) budget.

$$\text{Sales volume variance in terms of operating income} = \left(\begin{array}{c}\text{Actual units} \\ \text{sold}\end{array} - \begin{array}{c}\text{Units budgeted} \\ \text{to be sold}\end{array}\right) \times \begin{array}{c}\text{Master budget contribution} \\ \text{margin per unit}\end{array}$$

$$= (780 - 1{,}000) \text{ units} \times \$350/\text{unit}$$

$$= \$77{,}000U$$

The sales volume variance expressed in terms of operating income shows that, holding everything else constant, a sales volume decrease of 220 units would decrease operating income by $77,000. The sales volume variance may be a result of one or more of the following:[1]

1. The market for the product has changed. The total demand for the product grew (declined) at a rate higher than expected.
2. The firm lost market share to competitors.
3. The firm failed to set a proper goal for the period.
4. The firm set an inappropriate selling price for the product.
5. The marketing and promotion programs were not effective.

Each of these causes may be a result of one or more contributing factors. For example, a firm might have lost market share because of quality problems that led to customers' dissatisfaction, shifts in customer preferences and tastes, ineffective advertising, reduction in the number of sales calls or salespeople, or products not available due to production problems, among others. The proper response to a sales volume variance depends on the cause of the variance.

[1] For a multiproduct firm (not considered in this chapter), the sales volume variance can be decomposed into a pure volume variance and a sales-mix variance. This topic is covered in Chapter 16. Also, in Chapter 16 we discuss how to separate the pure sales-volume variance into market-size and market-share components.

EXHIBIT 14.4
Breakdown of Total Operating-
Income Variance

SCHMIDT MACHINERY COMPANY
Analysis of Financial Results
For October 2010

	(1) Actual	(2) Flexible-Budget Variances	(3) Flexible Budget	(4) Sales Volume Variances	(5) Master (Static) Budget
Units	780	0	780	220U	1,000
Sales	$639,600	$15,600F	$624,000	$176,000U	$800,000
Variable costs	350,950	50F	351,000	99,000F	450,000
Contribution margin	$288,650	$15,650F	$273,000	$ 77,000U	$350,000
Fixed costs	160,650	10,650U	150,000	0	150,000
Operating Income	$128,000	$ 5,000F	$123,000	$ 77,000U	$200,000

Analysis of Operating-Income Variance

Total operating-income variance*
$= \$128,000 - \$200,000 = \$72,000U$

Flexible-budget variance
$= \$128,000 - \$123,000$
$= \$5,000F$

Sales volume variance
$= \$123,000 - \$200,000$
$= \$77,000U$

* Also called the *total master (static) budget variance*

Flexible-Budget (FB) Variances

Flexible-budget (FB) variances refer to differences between actual and flexible-budget amounts. As indicated in column (2) of Exhibit 14.4, for any income statement item a

$$\text{Flexible-budget variance} = \text{Actual results} - \text{Flexible-budget results}$$

Thus, there are flexible-budget variances for sales, variable costs, fixed costs, and operating income.

The **total flexible-budget variance** of a period is the difference between the flexible-budget operating income and the operating income actually earned during the period. In Exhibit 14.4, we see that the total flexible-budget variance for October is $5,000 favorable, as follows:

$$\begin{array}{rl} \text{Total flexible-} & = \text{(Actual) operating} - \text{Flexible-budget} \\ \text{budget variance} & \quad \text{income earned} \quad \text{operating income} \\ & = \$128,000 - \$123,000 \\ & = \$5,000F \end{array}$$

This total flexible-budget variance is the result of a $15,600 favorable sales price variance, a $50 favorable variable cost variance, and a $10,650 unfavorable variance in fixed costs.

Breakdown of the Total Flexible-Budget Variance

Factors that contribute to the total flexible-budget variance include deviations in selling prices, variable costs, and fixed costs from their standard or budgeted amounts.

Selling Price Variance

As the name implies, the selling price variance reflects the effect on operating income of a difference between actual and budgeted selling prices. Thus, the **selling price variance** can be determined by taking the difference between actual sales revenues for a period and the sales revenue

Flexible-budget (FB) variances
refer to differences between actual and flexible-budget amounts on the income statement.

The **total flexible-budget variance**
for a period is the difference between the flexible budget-operating income and the actual operating income for the period.

Selling price variance
is the difference between the actual sales revenue for a period and the sales revenue in the flexible budget for the period.

in the flexible budget for the period. The difference between these two amounts, if any, results from deviations of the actual selling price per unit from the budgeted selling price per unit:

$$\text{Actual sales revenue} = \text{Units sold} \times \textit{Actual} \text{ selling price per unit}$$

$$\text{Flexible budget sales revenue} = \text{Units sold} \times \textit{Budgeted} \text{ selling price per unit}$$

In the above, both sales revenue figures are for the actual number of units sold during the period. The difference between these two sales revenue amounts is due solely to the difference between actual and budgeted selling price per unit. For this reason we refer to this difference as the selling price variance for the period.

$$\begin{aligned}\text{Selling price} \atop \text{variance} &= {\text{Actual sales} \atop \text{revenue}} - {\text{Flexible budget} \atop \text{sales revenue}} \\[2mm]
&= \left({\text{Units} \atop \text{sold}} \times {\text{Actual selling} \atop \text{price per unit}}\right) - \left({\text{Units} \atop \text{sold}} \times {\text{Budgeted selling} \atop \text{price per unit}}\right) \\[2mm]
&= \left({\text{Actual selling} \atop \text{price per unit}} - {\text{Budgeted selling} \atop \text{price per unit}}\right) \times {\text{Units} \atop \text{sold}} \\[2mm]
&= \text{Selling price variance}\end{aligned}$$

Exhibit 14.4 shows that in October 2010 Schmidt sold 780 units of XV–1 for $639,600, or $820 per unit. The budgeted selling price, however, was $800 per unit. Using the budgeted selling price of $800 per unit, the total sales revenue in the flexible budget for 780 units is $624,000. The difference, $15,600, is a result of the actual selling price per unit being $20 higher than the budgeted selling price per unit for each of the 780 units sold, as shown here:

$$\begin{aligned}\text{Selling price} \atop \text{variance} &= {\text{Actual} \atop \text{sales revenue}} - {\text{Flexible budget} \atop \text{sales revenue}} \\[2mm]
&= \$639,600 - \$624,000 = \$15,600 \text{ F} \\[2mm]
\text{Selling price} \atop \text{variance} &= \left({\text{Actual selling} \atop \text{price per unit}} - {\text{Budgeted} \atop \text{selling price per unit}}\right) \times {\text{Units} \atop \text{sold}} \\[2mm]
&= (\$820 - \$800) \times 780 \text{ units} \\[2mm]
&= \$15,600\text{F}\end{aligned}$$

Variable Cost Flexible-Budget Variances

The **total variable cost flexible-budget variance** is the difference between the total variable cost incurred during a period and the total variable cost in the flexible budget for the period. Thus, this variance reflects the deviation of the actual variable cost incurred during the period from the standard variable cost for the output of the period.

Note in Exhibit 14.4 that Schmidt incurred $350,950 total variable costs in October 2010 to produce and sell 780 units of XV–1. Budgeted variable costs per unit for Schmidt are referred to as *standard costs* and are reflected on the standard cost sheet illustrated as Exhibit 14.5. The standard variable manufacturing cost is $400 per unit (including $140 for direct materials, $200 for direct labor, and $60 for variable manufacturing overhead). For 780 units, the total standard variable manufacturing cost is therefore $312,000 ($400 per unit × 780 units). In addition, the standard variable selling and administrative expense is $50 per unit, or $39,000 in total ($50 per unit × 780 units). This brings the total budgeted variable cost for manufacturing and selling 780 units to $351,000 ($312,000 + $39,000). The difference between the actual variable cost incurred during the period and the total variable cost in the flexible budget for the units manufactured and sold during the period is the *total variable cost flexible-budget variance,* which in the present case is $50 favorable:

$$\begin{aligned}{\text{Total variable cost flexible-} \atop \text{budget variance}} &= {\text{Total variable} \atop \text{cost incurred}} - {\text{Total flexible budget} \atop \text{variable cost}} \\[2mm]
&= \$350,950 - [(\$140 + \$200 + \$60 + \$50) \times 780 \text{ units}] \\[2mm]
&= \$350,950 - (\$450 \times 780) \\[2mm]
&= \$350,950 - \$351,000 \\[2mm]
&= \$50\text{F}\end{aligned}$$

EXHIBIT 14.5
Standard Cost Sheet

SCHMIDT MACHINERY COMPANY				
Standard Cost Sheet				
Product: XV–1				
Descriptions	Quantity	Unit Cost	Subtotal	Total
Direct materials:				
Aluminum	4 pounds	$25	$100	
PVC	1 pound	40	40	
Direct labor	5 hours	40	200	
Variable factory overhead	5 hours	12	60	
Total variable manufacturing cost				$400
Fixed factory overhead	5 hours	24	120	180
Standard manufacturing cost per unit				$520
Standard variable selling and administrative expense per unit				$ 50

Further Analysis of the Total Variable Cost Flexible-Budget Variance

The total variable cost flexible-budget variance is the sum of flexible-budget variances of all variable costs and expenses, including flexible-budget variances for direct materials, direct labor, variable overhead, and variable selling and administrative expenses.

$$
\begin{array}{c}
\text{Total variable} \\
\text{cost flexible-} \\
\text{budget} \\
\text{variance}
\end{array}
=
\begin{array}{c}
\text{Total direct} \\
\text{materials} \\
\text{flexible-budget} \\
\text{variance}
\end{array}
+
\begin{array}{c}
\text{Total direct} \\
\text{labor flexible-} \\
\text{budget} \\
\text{variance}
\end{array}
+
\begin{array}{c}
\text{Total variable} \\
\text{overhead} \\
\text{flexible-budget} \\
\text{variance}
\end{array}
+
\begin{array}{c}
\text{Total variable selling} \\
\text{and administrative} \\
\text{expenses flexible-} \\
\text{budget variance}
\end{array}
$$

More detailed information regarding the total variable cost flexible-budget variance is provided in Exhibit 14.6. The $50 favorable total variable cost flexible-budget variance may not in and of itself be of concern to the management of Schmidt Machinery Company. However, this seemingly insignificant net variance could be the result of large but offsetting component variances. For this reason, we can decompose this net variance using a two-step process. Step one is to calculate a flexible-budget variance for each variable cost, as shown in Exhibit 14.8. For example, the total direct labor cost variance for October was $8,580F. Step two is to use the following model to break down (decompose) this variable cost variance into its price and quantity components.

General Model for the Analysis of Variable Cost Variances

Any purely variable cost is a function of two factors, price (P) and quantity (Q). Thus, any flexible-budget variance for a given variable cost, such as direct materials or direct labor, should be able to be decomposed into a *price* (rate) *variance* and a *quantity* (efficiency) *variance*. A general model for the analysis of variable cost flexible-budget variances is provided in Exhibit 14.7.

We note that the price variance for direct materials can be calculated either at the time of purchase or at the time of production. If the former is the case, then AQ in Exhibit 14.7 means "actual quantity of materials *purchased*" and the resulting variance is referred to as a *materials purchase-price variance*. Regardless of when the price variance for materials is calculated, the quantity variance is calculated at the end of the period, once production is known. The term AQ in the materials quantity variance *always* refers to the actual quantity of materials consumed for a given period's output.

We now apply the general model to the analysis of variable cost flexible-budget variances for the Schmidt Machinery Company, October 2010.

The traditional variance-decomposition model for variable costs, such as the framework presented in Exhibit 14.7, produces two component variances: price (rate) and quantity (efficiency). In reality, there is a third variance that can be calculated: the portion of the total standard cost variance that is jointly attributable to price *and* quantity, i.e., the portion of the total variance that cannot be explained in terms of a change in price or in terms of a change in quantity. In practice, this *joint variance* is typically included as part of the price variance component of the overall standard cost variance. (Using the terminology in the chapter, the joint price-quantity variance is calculated as: (AP–SP) × (AQ–SQ).) Historically, the joint variance has been given little attention because of the assumption that the amounts involved are likely to be small. Also as discussed in the chapter, standard cost variance models have been applied to date primarily in the manufacturing sector.

Can such models be used in nonmanufacturing settings? Is the assumption of a small joint variance in such settings justified? Mitchell

and Thomas address these two questions by looking at the application of a variance-decomposition model within the context of an advertising campaign, the output of which was defined as "gross rating points (GRP)," which is the product of two advertising activities, "frequency" and "reach." In this context, marketing managers would like to know which of the two deviations from plan (frequency vs. reach) had the greater impact on advertising performance (GRP). The example they include shows three items: (1) impact on GRP due solely to the change of frequency, (2) impact on GRP due solely to the change of reach, and (3) residual impact on GRP due to simultaneous changes in reach and frequency. (Note: The formula for this joint variance is slightly different from the conventional joint price-quantity formula presented above.)

The authors suggest that this type of report would be useful to media planners in terms of developing effective strategies for increasing advertising effectiveness.

Source: T. Mitchell and M. Thomas, "Can Variance Analysis Make Media Marketing Managers More Accountable?" *Management Accounting Quarterly* 7, no. 1 (Fall 2005), pp. 51–61.

EXHIBIT 14.6
Comparison of Actual Variable Costs and Flexible-Budget Variable Costs

SCHMIDT MACHINERY COMPANY			
October 2010			
Product XV–1			
Units Manufactured: 780			
Actual Results			
Direct materials:			
Aluminum	3,630 pounds at $26 per pound	$94,380	
PVC	720 pounds at $41 per pound	29,520	$123,900
Direct labor	3,510 hours at $42 per hour		147,420
Variable factory overhead			40,630
Total variable cost of goods manufactured			$311,950
Variable selling and administrative expenses			39,000
Total variable costs for the period			$350,950
Flexible Budget			
Budgeted variable cost of goods manufactured:			
Standard variable manufacturing cost per unit (from Exhibit 14.5)		$400	
Number of units manufactured		× 780	$312,000
Budgeted variable selling and administrative expenses (780 × $50)			39,000
Total budgeted variable costs for the period			$351,000
Total variable cost flexible-budget variance for the period			$ 50F*

* F denotes a *favorable* variance.

Direct Materials Variances

As indicated in Exhibit 14.7, the direct materials flexible-budget variance *for each material* is the difference between the actual direct materials cost and the total standard direct materials cost for this period's output. This variance reflects efficiency (or inefficiency) in buying and in using direct materials. Attaining efficiency in buying and using materials

EXHIBIT 14.7
General Model for Analyzing Variable Cost Variances

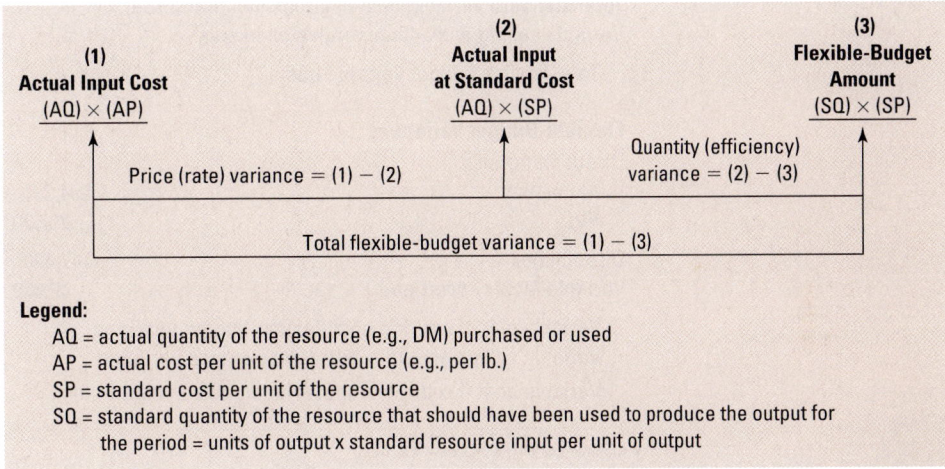

requires good controls over both the price paid for the materials and the quantity of the materials used in production. Since price and usage can move in opposite directions, we must analyze a total variance for each raw material by breaking the variance down into its price and quantity components.

Exhibits 14.8 and 14.9 illustrate an analysis of direct materials costs using the October 2010 operating data of the Schmidt Company. In this example, there are two direct materials: aluminum, and PVC. We illustrate here the analysis of the flexible-budget variance for aluminum. Exhibit 14.8 shows that Schmidt used 3,630 pounds of aluminum at a total cost of $94,380 to manufacture 780 units of XV–1. The standard cost sheet reported in Exhibit 14.5 indicates that the standard cost for one unit of XV–1 is 4 pounds of aluminum at $25 per pound. For October, the total flexible-budget cost for aluminum, given an output of 780 units, is $78,000. (See the middle section of Exhibit 14.8.)

Direct Materials Flexible-Budget Variance

The **direct materials flexible-budget variance** for each material is the difference between the total direct material cost incurred and the flexible-budget amount for this period's output. Schmidt spent $94,380 for aluminum (Exhibit 14.8). Thus, the total flexible-budget

The **direct materials flexible-budget variance** for each material is the difference between total direct materials cost incurred and the flexible-budget amount for this period's output.

EXHIBIT 14.8

A Detailed Comparison of
Actual Variable Costs and
Flexible-Budget Variable Costs

SCHMIDT MACHINERY COMPANY			
October 2010			
Product XV–1			
Units Manufactured: 780			
Actual Variable Costs Incurred			
Direct materials:			
Aluminum	3,630 pounds* at $26 per pound	$94,380	
PVC	720 pounds at $41 per pound	29,520	$123,900
Direct labor	3,510 hours at $42 per hour		147,420
Variable factory overhead			40,630
Total variable cost of goods manufactured			$311,950
Variable selling and administrative expenses			39,000
Total variable costs incurred			$350,950
Flexible Budget for Variable Costs			
Direct materials:			
Aluminum	780 units × 4 pounds × $25 = $78,000		
PVC	780 units × 1 pound × $40 =	31,200	$109,200
Direct labor	780 units × 5 hours × $40 =		156,000
Variable factory overhead	780 units × 5 hours × $12 =		46,800
Total standard variable cost of goods manufactured			$312,000
Variable selling and administrative expenses			39,000
Total flexible budget variable costs			$351,000
Flexible-Budget Variances			
Direct materials:			
Aluminum	$94,380 − $78,000 = $16,380U[†]		
PVC	29,520 − 31,200 =	1,680F[‡]	$14,700U
Direct labor	147,420 − 156,000 =		8,580F
Variable factory overhead	40,630 − 46,800 =		6,170F
Variable manufacturing cost flexible-budget variance			$ 50F
Variable selling and administrative expense variance			0
Variable cost flexible-budget variance (see Exhibit 14.6)			$ 50F

* Assume that lbs. purchased = lbs. used.
[†] U denotes an *unfavorable* variance.
[‡] F denotes a *favorable* variance.

variance for aluminum for October is $16,380 unfavorable ($94,380 − $78,000). This same approach can be used to calculate the total flexible-budget variance for PVC, $1,680F (Exhibit 14.8).

The **direct materials price variance** for each material is the difference between the actual and standard cost per unit multiplied by the quantity of direct materials used during the period.

Further Analysis of the Direct Materials Flexible-Budget Variance

Price Variance   The **direct materials price variance** for each material is the difference between the actual and the standard cost per unit of direct material multiplied by the quantity of the direct materials used during the period.[2] Exhibit 14.8 shows that in October Schmidt Machinery Company paid $26 per pound for the 3,630 pounds of aluminum used in production. The standard cost sheet (Exhibit 14.5) specifies the standard price to be $25 per pound. Thus,

---

[2] As we discuss later in this chapter, for control purposes it is preferable to calculate the materials price variance at the time materials are purchased. In this case, we use the more specific term *materials purchase-price variance.* See Exhibit 14.11 and the related discussion.

EXHIBIT 14.9
Direct Materials Flexible-Budget Variance—Aluminum

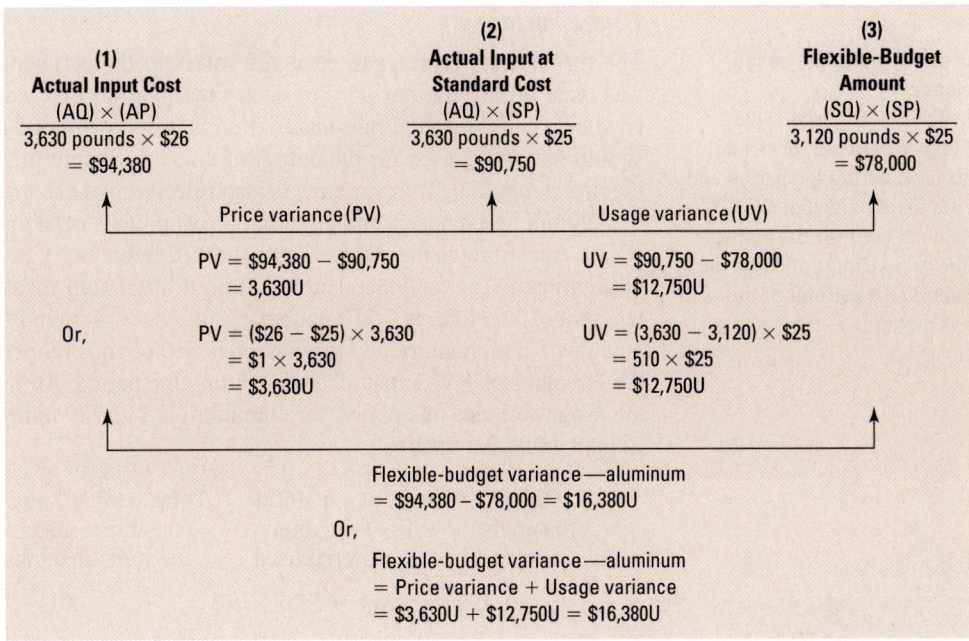

actual price paid is $1 per pound more than standard. For the 3,630 pounds used, the price variance is $3,630 unfavorable (column (1) − column (2), Exhibit 14.9). Alternatively,

$$\begin{matrix} \text{Direct} \\ \text{materials price} \\ \text{variance} \end{matrix} = \left(\begin{matrix} \text{Actual price paid} \\ \text{for one unit of} \\ \text{direct material} \end{matrix} - \begin{matrix} \text{Standard price} \\ \text{for one unit of} \\ \text{direct material} \end{matrix} \right) \times \begin{matrix} \text{Total number of units} \\ \text{of the direct material} \\ \text{used in production} \end{matrix}$$

$$
\begin{aligned}
PV &= (AP - SP) \times AQ \\
&= (\$26 - \$25) \times 3{,}630 \\
&= \$1 \times 3{,}630 \\
&= \$3{,}630 \text{ Unfavorable}
\end{aligned}
$$

Interpreting the Direct Materials Price Variance (PV)   A direct materials price variance (PV) can result from failure to take purchase discounts, unexpected price change of materials, changes in freight costs, variation in grades of materials, or other causes. The purchasing department is often the office most likely to provide an explanation or have the responsibility for materials price variances.

Care must be taken in interpreting direct materials price variances. A favorable direct materials price variance could lead to high manufacturing costs if the low-cost materials are of poor quality. Downstream costs such as scrap, rework, schedule disruptions, or field-service costs could exceed the price savings from lower materials prices. A firm with a differentiation strategy is likely to fail when it pursues favorable price variances through purchases of low-quality materials. A firm that competes on low cost also is likely to be adversely affected if the quality of its products is below customer expectations or it increases downstream costs.

Carrying costs and additional materials-handling costs can exceed the savings from low purchase prices. A firm with a cost-effective purchasing department that has several warehouses full of materials and supplies purchased in bulk at low prices could have a higher total overall cost than a firm that buys in small quantities as needed, and maintains only a minimum amount of direct materials on hand, even though the firm paid higher purchase prices for these materials.

In addition to price variances, many firms also use usage ratios in evaluating the performance of purchasing departments. A **materials usage ratio** is the ratio of quantity used over quantity purchased. A low materials usage ratio suggests that the purchasing department purchased for materials inventory rather than the operational needs of the period. Such a move can be costly if the firm considers all costs. In this case, the benefit of any favorable price variance should be evaluated along with the cost of inventory storage of the surplus purchases.

Materials usage ratio
is the ratio of quantity used over quantity purchased.

The **direct materials usage variance**

for each raw material is the difference between the actual units used during the period and the standard units that should have been used for the output of the period, multiplied by the standard cost per unit of the direct material.

Usage Variance

The **direct materials usage variance** refers to the efficiency with which each raw material was used during the period. For each raw material this variance is calculated as the difference between the actual raw-material units used during the period and the standard units that should have been used for the output of the period, multiplied by the standard cost per unit of the direct material. This variance is also referred to as an *efficiency* or *quantity variance.*

Schmidt Machinery Company used 3,630 pounds of aluminum to manufacture 780 units of XV–1. According to the standard cost sheet (Exhibit 14.5), each unit of XV–1 requires 4 pounds of aluminum. The total standard quantity of aluminum for the 780 units manufactured during the period, therefore, is 3,120 pounds (780 units × 4 pounds per unit). This says that the 3,630 pounds of aluminum used in production is 510 pounds more than the total standard quantity for the 780 units of XV–1 manufactured during the period. At the standard price of $25 per pound, the usage variance this period for aluminum is $12,750 unfavorable (column (2) – column (3), Exhibit 14.9). Alternatively,

$$\begin{matrix} \text{Direct} \\ \text{materials} \\ \text{usage variance} \end{matrix} = \left(\begin{matrix} \text{Total quantity} \\ \text{of the direct} \\ \text{material used} \end{matrix} - \begin{matrix} \text{Total standard quantity of} \\ \text{the direct material for} \\ \text{the units manufactured} \end{matrix} \right) \times \begin{matrix} \text{Standard cost per} \\ \text{unit of the direct} \\ \text{material} \end{matrix}$$

$$\begin{aligned} \text{UV} &= (\text{AQ} - \text{SQ}) \times \text{SP} \\ &= (3,630 - 3,120) \times \$25 \\ &= 510 \times \$25 \\ &= \$12,750 \text{ Unfavorable} \end{aligned}$$

Interpreting the Direct Materials Usage Variance

A significant direct materials usage variance suggests that operations consumed a significantly different amount of direct materials than the amount specified for the output of the period. This variance measures efficiency in using direct materials. A direct materials usage variance can result from the efforts of production personnel, substitutions of materials or production factors, variation in the quality of direct materials, inadequate training or inexperienced employees, poor supervision, or other factors.

Direct Labor Variances

As indicated in Exhibit 14.7, a direct labor flexible-budget variance is a result of the total direct labor cost of a period being different from the total standard direct labor cost for the output of the period. As with the direct materials flexible-budget variance, a direct labor flexible-budget variance also can be divided into two components: a rate (price) and an efficiency (quantity) variance. As shown in Exhibit 14.8 the total direct labor flexible-budget variance for October 2010 is $8,580F. The procedure for further analysis of this variance is similar to the procedure discussed above for direct materials. Exhibit 14.10 shows calculations of the direct labor rate variance and the direct labor efficiency variance for Schmidt Machinery Company for October 2010.

Direct Labor Rate Variance

Direct labor rate variance

is the difference between the actual and the standard wage rate multiplied by the actual direct labor hours worked during the period.

The **direct labor rate variance** is the difference between the actual and the standard wage rate multiplied by the actual direct labor hours worked during the period. Schmidt Machinery Company paid an average wage rate of $42 per hour for 3,510 direct labor hours in October. The standard cost sheet, however, calls for a wage rate of $40 per hour. The firm paid $2 per hour more than the standard hourly rate. With 3,510 total hours actually worked, the total direct labor rate variance is $7,020 unfavorable (Exhibit 14.10, column (1) – column (2)). Alternatively,

$$\begin{matrix} \text{Direct labor} \\ \text{rate variance} \end{matrix} = \left(\begin{matrix} \text{Actual hourly} \\ \text{wage rate paid} \end{matrix} - \begin{matrix} \text{Standard hourly} \\ \text{wage rate} \end{matrix} \right) \times \begin{matrix} \text{Total direct labor} \\ \text{hours worked} \end{matrix}$$

$$\begin{aligned} \text{RV} &= (\text{AP} - \text{SP}) \times \text{AQ} \\ &= (\$42.00 - \$40.00) \times 3,510 \text{ direct labor hours} \\ &= \$7,020\text{U} \end{aligned}$$

EXHIBIT 14.10
Direct Labor Flexible-Budget
Variance—Schmidt Machinery
Company October 2010

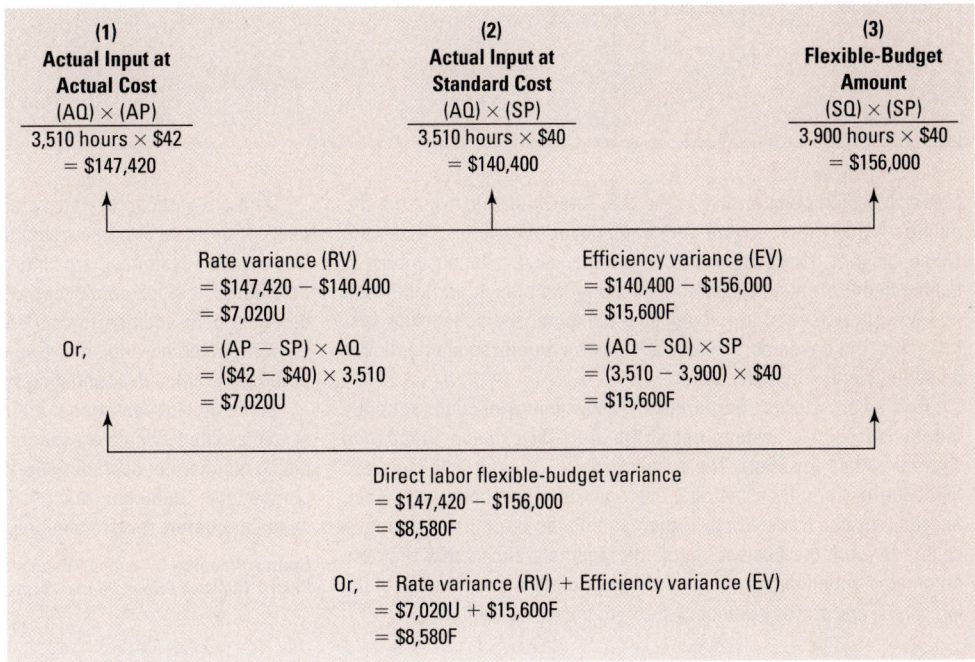

A direct labor rate variance reflects the effect on operating income when the actual hourly wage rate deviates from the standard hourly wage rate. This could result from not using workers with the skill level specified in the standard cost sheet for the work performed or from using an out-of-date standard.

The personnel department usually is responsible for direct labor rate variances. Production, however, could be responsible for the variance if it chooses to use employees with a different skill level than that specified in the standard cost sheet.

Direct Labor Efficiency Variance

The **direct labor efficiency variance** is the difference between the actual hours worked and the standard hours allowed for the units manufactured, multiplied by the standard wage rate.

A **direct labor efficiency variance** occurs when the total direct labor hours worked deviates from the total standard direct labor hours for the output of the period. It is calculated by multiplying the difference between the actual and the standard allowed hours by the standard hourly wage rate, as follows:

$$\begin{array}{l}\text{Direct labor} \\ \text{efficiency} \\ \text{variance}\end{array} = \left(\begin{array}{cc}\text{Total direct} & \text{Total standard direct} \\ \text{labor hours} - & \text{labor hours for the} \\ \text{worked} & \text{output of the period}\end{array}\right) \times \begin{array}{l}\text{Standard} \\ \text{direct labor} \\ \text{hourly rate}\end{array}$$

As indicated in Exhibit 14.8, Schmidt Machinery Company spent 3,510 direct labor hours to manufacture 780 units of XV–1 in October 2010. The standard cost sheet (Exhibit 14.5) allows five direct labor hours for one unit of XV–1. The total standard hours allowed for 780 units of XV–1, therefore, is 3,900 hours (780 × 5). Thus, Schmidt used 390 fewer direct labor hours than standard this period. At a standard wage rate of $40 per hour, the total direct labor efficiency (quantity) variance is $15,600 favorable (Exhibit 14.10, column (2) – Column (3)). Alternatively,

$$\begin{array}{l}\text{Direct labor} \\ \text{efficiency variance}\end{array} = \left(\begin{array}{cc}3,510\ \text{actual} & 3,900\ \text{total} \\ \text{hours} - & \text{standard hours}\end{array}\right) \times \$40\ \text{per hour}$$

$$\text{EV} = (\text{AQ} - \text{SQ}) \times \text{SP}$$

$$= \$15,600\text{F}$$

A direct labor efficiency variance reflects the effect on operating income of using a nonstandard amount of direct labor hours during the period. This variance usually is the responsibility of the production department. Besides the employees' efficiency or inefficiency in carrying out their tasks, however, several other factors—including these—can lead to a direct-labor efficiency variance:

1. Employees or supervisors are new on the job or are inadequately trained.
2. Employees' skill levels are different from those specified in the standard cost sheet.
3. Batch sizes are different from the standard size.
4. Materials are different from those specified.
5. Machines or equipment are not in proper working condition.
6. Supervision is inadequate.
7. Scheduling is poor.

Timing of Variance Recognition

Identification of variances helps managers to be aware of deviations from expected performance. For maximum control, managers should recognize variances at the earliest feasible time.

As noted earlier, a direct materials price variance can be identified either at the *time of purchase* or at the *time the materials are issued to production*. The discussion in the chapter to this point has assumed that the price variance for materials is calculated at the time of production. By contrast, recognition of the price variance at point of purchase allows the firm to take proper actions preventing the continuation of an unfavorable price variance or attaining the most benefit from favorable price variances. As indicated in the top half of Exhibit 14.11, when the materials price variance is calculated at point of purchase, *actual quantity* (AQ) refers to the quantity of materials *purchased*. In this case, the materials price variance is referred to by the more descriptive term, *materials purchase-price variance*.

As well, recognizing materials price variances at the time of purchase lets the firm carry all units of the same material at one price—the standard cost of the material. Using one price for the same materials greatly simplifies accounting work. For example, such a firm needs to maintain subsidiary ledgers for materials only in terms of quantity.

If a price variance is not recorded until the materials are issued to production, then AQ in the price-variance formula refers to the quantity of materials *used* in production and the direct materials are carried on the books at their actual purchase prices.

Regardless of when a direct materials price variance is recognized, the number of units actually consumed in production is used to compute the direct materials usage variance, as shown in the lower portion of Exhibit 14.11.

EXHIBIT 14.11
Analyzing Direct Materials Variances When the Quantity Purchased and Quantity Used Are Different

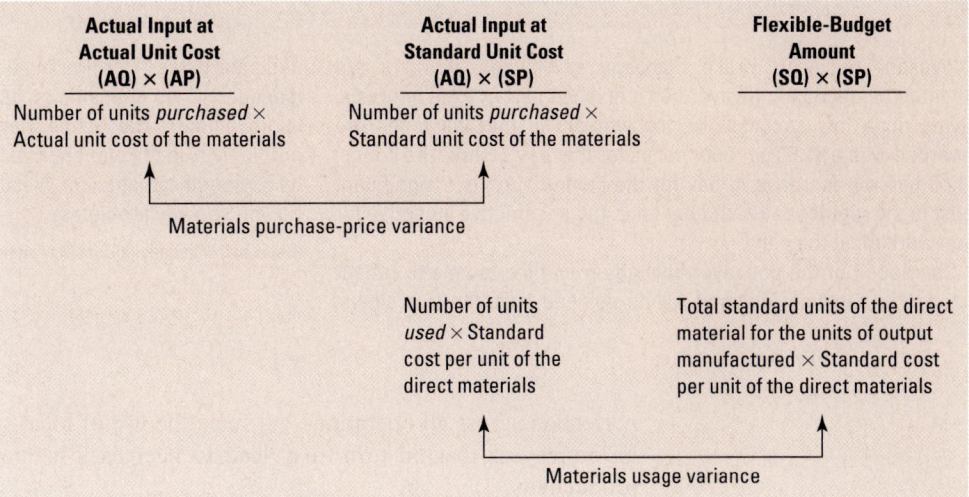

Standard Costs

LEARNING OBJECTIVE 4

Develop standard costs for product costing, performance evaluation, and control.

A **standard cost**
is the cost a firm should incur for an operation.

A **standard cost system**
is one in which standard, not actual, costs flow through the formal accounting records.

An **ideal standard**
reflects maximum efficiency in every aspect of the operation.

A **standard cost** is a carefully determined cost a firm or organization sets for an operation—the cost the firm or organization should incur for the operation. A standard cost usually is expressed on a per-unit basis. Standard costs are incorporated into budgets and as such can be used to monitor and control operations, and to evaluate performance.

Standard Costs versus a Standard Cost System

A standard cost prescribes expected performance. A complete standard cost for a product or service includes carefully established standards for each cost element, including manufacturing, selling, and administrative expenses. Although the discussions in this and the next chapter focus on standard cost systems for manufacturing operations, these concepts and procedures can be applied to service contexts as well.

It is useful to distinguish between standard costs and a **standard cost system.** The latter refers to an accounting system in which standard costs, and associated standard cost variances, are recorded in the formal accounting system. The flow of direct manufacturing costs in the accounting records is illustrated in the next section of this chapter.[3] Note, however, that standard costs can be used for control purposes outside of the formal accounting system. That is, at the end of the accounting period accountants can compare actual and standard costs and analyze variances using the procedures discussed in the previous section of this chapter, regardless of whether standard costs are incorporated formally in the accounting system.

A standard cost system can be applied in either a job-order or a process cost context. Because of the repetitive nature of operations, it is generally simpler to establish standards in conjunction with a process cost system. Also, the use of standard costs in a process cost system greatly simplifies the determination of equivalent-unit costs: the standard (predetermined) costs serve as the cost per equivalent unit for direct materials, direct labor, and manufacturing overhead.

Types of Standards

Firms have different expectations for the proper level at which to set their standards. Differences in expectations lead to two types of standards: ideal, and currently attainable standards.

Ideal Standards

An **ideal standard** reflects maximum efficiency in every aspect of an operation. By definition, ideal standards are difficult, but not impossible, to achieve. They assume peak operating efficiency and the absence of any production disruptions. That is, ideal standards assume

---

[3] Journal entries for recording standard indirect manufacturing costs (i.e., manufacturing overhead), as well as associated standard cost variances, are presented in Chapter 15.

Cost Management in Action

Is Two Minutes and Twenty Seconds Enough for a Brake Part?

At Westinghouse Air Brake Company in Chicago, workers are expected to "feed" a conveyor belt a finished part at fixed intervals. Having done this successfully, the workers in that work cell are rewarded with a $1.50 per hour bonus for that day's work. The bonus, a 12.5 percent increase in pay for the same hours, is a significant boost to the regular pay of $12 per hour and an effective incentive for most workers at the plant.

The speed of the conveyor changes from time to time to reflect changes in customer demand. When demand falls, the rate slows, and vice versa. The firm installed the bonus plan upon the recommendations of consultants and specialists in *kaizen* (continuous improvement). The bonus plan allowed Westinghouse to improve productivity in the plant by over 10 times the 1991 level. This seems to be a win-win situation for Westinghouse and Westinghouse workers. Do you see any problems?

(Refer to Comments on Cost Management in Action at end of Chapter.)

---

perfection across all operations. As such, the use of ideal standards can lead to undue stress on employees that, in turn, may lead to decreases in morale and ultimately decreases in productivity.

As an alternative to the use of ideal standards, some organizations employ what are referred to as **continuous-improvement standards.** Such standards, as a function of time (e.g., months), become progressively tighter (i.e., more difficult to achieve). The use of this approach is somewhat analogous to the Japanese use of kaizen costing.

Organizations that use ideal standards often modify performance evaluation and reward structures so that employees are not frustrated by frequent failures to attain the standards. Organizations can, for example, use progress toward an ideal standard rather than deviations from it as the primary benchmark in its performance-evaluation and reward system.

> **A continuous-improvement standard** is one that gets progressively tighter over time.

Currently Attainable Standards

A **currently attainable standard** sets the performance criterion at a level that a person with proper training and experience can attain most of the time without having to exert extraordinary effort. A currently attainable standard emphasizes normality and allows for some imperfections and inefficiencies.

Suppose that a firm sets the standard for the amount of plywood needed to produce 1,000 tabletops at 525 sheets of plywood, although two tabletops can be cut from one sheet. The additional 25 sheets allow for such things as less-than-ideal input quality, occasional maladjustment of the equipment used in production, worker fatigue, and varying experience and skill levels of the personnel involved in production. By using a standard that allows for normal fluctuations in relevant manufacturing factors, employees usually can meet the standard with reasonable effort.

> **A currently attainable standard** sets the performance criterion at a level that a person with proper training and experience can attain most of the time without having to exert extraordinary effort.

Selection of Standards

Which standards—ideal or currently attainable—should a firm use? There is no single answer for all situations.

Firms struggling for survival in intensely competitive industries may choose to use ideal (or continuous-improvement) standards to motivate employees to put forth their best efforts. Ideal standards are not effective, however, if frequent failures in meeting the standards discourage employees or lead them to ignore the standards.

Currently attainable standards, however, may have built into them some degree of inefficiency. Allowing some inefficiencies is strategically unwise if the firm operates in an intensely competitive environment. For example, a standard that allows 25 additional sheets of plywood conveys to production that it has attained acceptable performance as long as it does not make more than 25 mistakes for every 500 sheets of plywood it cuts.

> **An authoritative standard** is determined solely or primarily by management.

> **A participative standard** calls for active participation throughout the standard-setting process by employees affected by the standard.

Standard-Setting Procedures

A firm can use either an authoritative or a participative procedure in setting standards. An **authoritative standard** is determined solely or primarily by management. In contrast, a **participative standard** calls, throughout the standard-setting process, for active participation of employees affected by the standard. A firm uses an authoritative process to ensure proper consideration of all operating factors, to incorporate management's desires or expectations, or to expedite the standard-setting process. Firms using an authoritative process in standard setting, however, should keep in mind that a standard is useless if ignored by employees.

By contrast, participative standards are thought to produce important behavioral effects. For example, employees are more likely to accept standards they helped to determine. Participation also reduces the chance that employees will view the standard as unreasonable and increases the likelihood that they will buy into or adopt it as their own.

Establishing Standard Costs

Establishing a standard cost often is a joint effort of management, product-design engineers, industrial engineers, management accountants, production supervisors, the purchasing department, the personnel department, and employees affected by the standard.

Establishing the Standard Cost for Direct Materials

A standard cost for direct materials of a product has three facets: quality, quantity, and price. The first step in establishing a standard cost is to specify the quality of the direct materials. The quality of direct materials determines the quality of the product and affects many phases of the manufacturing process including quantity of direct materials needed or used in manufacturing, prices of direct materials, processing time, and the extent and frequency of supervision needed to complete manufacturing. Once a firm determines the quality of the direct materials, management accountants work with the industrial engineering and production departments to set the standard for the quantity of direct materials needed to manufacture the product.

Quality, quantity, and at times the timing of purchases can all affect price standards of materials. In a competitive environment, many companies emphasize long-term relationships with selected suppliers that are reliable in delivering quality materials on time. For a firm that emphasizes long-term benefits and reliability of its supply chain, the price standard needs to be revised only when a change occurs in the underlying long-term factors that affect material prices.

Establishing the Standard Cost for Direct Labor

Direct labor costs vary with types of work, product complexity, employee skill level, nature of the manufacturing process, and the type and condition of the equipment to be used. After considering these factors, industrial engineering, production, personnel, labor union representatives, and management accountants jointly determine the quantity standard for direct labor.

The personnel department determines the standard wage rate for the type and skill level of employees needed for the manufacturing process. The standard labor rate for either direct or indirect labor includes not only the wage paid but also the fringe benefits provided to employees and the required payroll taxes associated with wages and salaries. Fringe benefits include health and life insurance, pension plan contributions, and paid vacations. Payroll taxes include unemployment taxes and the employer's share of an employee's Social Security assessment.

Overtime premium
refers to the *excess* wage rate over the standard hourly wage rate.

A question normally arises as to how overtime premiums are treated, both for product costing and subsequent variance-analysis purposes. In many cases, **overtime premiums** are treated as part of factory overhead. This is true when production (or service) scheduling is random or when the overtime is caused by taking on more jobs than can be handled during a standard workweek. In this case, the overtime premium should be spread over production in general— that is, over all output for the period. In other cases, however, the overtime premium might be attributed to a specific job, client, or customer—for example, a rush order. In this case, the premium can be traced and, therefore, should be treated as part of direct labor cost. Such excess payments would typically appear as part of the direct labor rate variance for the period.

Standard Cost Sheet

A **standard cost sheet**
specifies the standard cost of manufacturing and selling one unit of a product.

A **standard cost sheet** specifies the standard costs (including both price and quantity) for all manufacturing cost elements (i.e., direct materials, direct labor, and factory overhead) required in the production of one unit of a product. Exhibit 14.5, discussed earlier, shows a standard cost sheet for Schmidt Machinery Company for manufacturing one unit of XV–1. The standard cost for one unit of XV–1 includes 4 pounds of aluminum at $25 per pound, 1 pound of PVC at $40 per pound, 5 hours of direct labor at $40 per hour, and factory overhead of $36 ($12 + $24) per direct labor hour. Also included on the standard cost sheet for product XV-1 is the budgeted variable selling and administrative expense of $50 per unit.

Recording Cost Flows and Variances in a Standard Cost System

LEARNING OBJECTIVE 5
Record manufacturing cost flows and associated variances in a standard cost system.

Standard cost systems use the same accounts for inventory and for recording manufacturing costs that actual or normal costing systems use. Thus, they have accounts such as Materials Inventory, Accrued Payroll, Factory (manufacturing) Overhead, Work-in-Process Inventory, Finished Goods Inventory, and Cost of Goods Sold. Manufacturing costs flow through inventory and manufacturing cost accounts in ways that are similar to cost flows in an actual or normal cost system. Of course, standard cost systems have standard costs instead of actual or normalized costs flowing through the accounts.

Another difference is the use of variance accounts in standard cost systems. Firms that use a standard cost system have a separate ledger account for each variance. Favorable variances will have *credit* balances while unfavorable variances will have *debit* balances. The end-of-period

EXHIBIT 14.12   **Standard Manufacturing Cost Flows (Direct Labor and Direct Materials)***

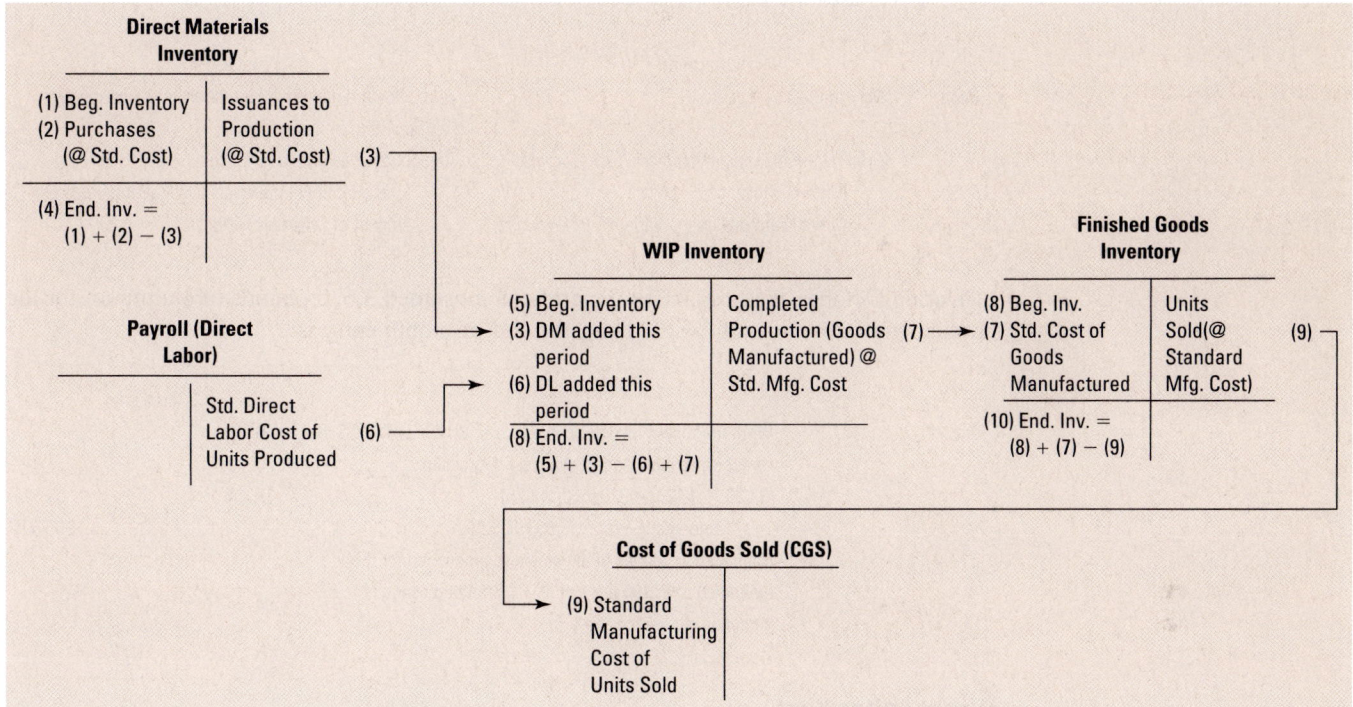

* **Note:** The accounting for standard *manufacturing overhead costs* is covered in Chapter 15.

disposition (closing) of these variance accounts is covered in Chapter 15. A diagramatic representation of the cost-recording process for a standard cost system is given in Exhibit 14.12.

Direct Materials Cost

A firm that uses a standard cost system *and that recognizes material price variances at point of purchase* records purchases of direct materials as follows:

	Account	Amount
Debit:	Materials Inventory	Total standard cost of the purchased materials
	Direct Materials Purchase-Price Variance *(if unfavorable)*	Amount of *unfavorable* variance
Credit:	Cash or Accounts Payable	Purchase cost of materials
	Direct Materials Purchase-Price Variance *(if favorable)*	Amount of *favorable* variance

To illustrate, on October 7, Schmidt Machinery Company purchased 3,630 pounds of aluminum at $26 per pound. The term of the purchase is 1/EOM, n/180. The standard cost sheet (Exhibit 14.5) lists the cost at $25 per pound. The firm records all cash discounts when earned. The journal entry for the purchase is as follows:

Date	Account	Amount	
Oct. 7	Materials Inventory (3,630 × $25)	90,750	
	Materials Purchase-Price Variance—Aluminum (3,630 × $1)	3,630	
	Accounts Payable (3,630 × $26)		94,380
	Purchase of 3,630 pounds of aluminum at $26 per pound.		
	Terms 1/EOM, n/180; standard price is $25 per pound.		

The purchase price Schmidt agreed to pay is $3,630 higher than the total standard cost for 3,630 pounds of aluminum—an unfavorable direct materials purchased-price variance. Schmidt records the unfavorable variance by *debiting* the variance account.

The journal entry at the end of the month to record the issuance of direct materials, after the output for the month could be determined, takes the following form:

	Account	Amount
Debit:	Work-in-Process Inventory	Total standard quantity of materials, at standard cost, for the output of the period
	Direct Materials Usage Variance *(if unfavorable)*	Amount of *unfavorable* variance
Credit:	Materials Inventory	Total quantity of materials used, at standard cost
	Direct Materials Usage Variance *(if favorable)*	Amount of *favorable* variance

During October, the production department consumed 3,630 pounds of aluminum for the production of 780 units of XV–1. Thus, the end-of-month entry is:

Date	Account	Amount	
Oct. 31	Work-in-Process Inventory (780 × 4 = 3,120; 3,120 × $25)	78,000	
	Direct Materials Usage Variance—Aluminum		
	(3,630 − 3,120 = 510; 510 × $25)	12,750	
	Materials Inventory (3,630 × $25)		90,750
	Issued 3,630 pounds of aluminum to production for the		
	manufacture of 780 units of XV–1. Standard usage is		
	4 pounds per unit of XV–1.		

Direct Labor Cost

The cost of the units manufactured is increased by direct labor costs. To accomplish this, the Work-in-Process Inventory account is debited for the total standard direct labor cost for the units manufactured. An associated credit entry is made to the Accrued Payroll account for the total direct labor wages incurred for the period.

	Account	Amount
Debit:	Work-in-Process Inventory	Total number of standard hours, at the standard hourly wage rate, for the units manufactured
	Direct Labor Rate or Efficiency Variance *(if unfavorable)*	Amount of variance
Credit:	Accrued Payroll	Actual wage expense
	Direct Labor Rate or Efficiency Variance *(if favorable)*	Amount of variance

The difference between the amount debited (the amount that *should have been incurred* for the units manufactured) and the amount credited (the total amount of direct labor wages incurred) can result from a difference in either the wage rate or labor-hour efficiency during the period. Differences between the actual wage rate and the standard wage rate are recorded in the Direct Labor Rate Variance account. Differences in the number of total hours spent in production and the number of total standard hours that should have been spent for the output of the period are recorded in the Direct Labor Efficiency Variance account.

During October, Schmidt spent 3,510 direct labor-hours for $147,420 to complete the production of 780 units of XV–1, or $42 per hour. The standard (Exhibit 14.5) calls for 5 direct labor-hours per unit of XV–1 at $40 per hour. Thus, the end-of-month entry is:

Date	Account	Amount	
Oct. 31	Work-in-Process Inventory (780 × 5 = 3,900; 3,900 × $40)	156,000	
	Direct Labor Rate Variance (3,510 × [$42 − $40 = 2])	7,020	
	Direct Labor Efficiency Variance (390 × $40)		15,600
	Accrued Payroll (3,510 × $42)		147,420
	Used 3,510 direct labor hours to manufacture 780 units of XV–1.		
	Standard cost allows 5 hours per unit of XV–1 at $40 per hour		

Completion of Production

Upon completion of production, the total standard cost of the units manufactured is transferred out of the Work-in-Process Inventory account and into the Finished Goods Inventory account. The standard cost sheet (Exhibit 14.5) specifies that the total standard manufacturing cost per unit of XV–1 is $520. The following journal entry, on October 31, records the completion of 780 units of XV–1:

Date	Account	Amount
Oct. 31	Finished Goods Inventory (780 × $520)	405,600
	Work-in-Process Inventory	405,600
	Completed 780 units of XV–1 at standard manufacturing cost per unit of $520.	

Exhibit 14.13 summarizes cost flows through ledger accounts in a standard cost system. (The recording of manufacturing overhead costs, including overhead cost variances, is covered in Chapter 15.)

EXHIBIT 14.13

Partial Cost Flows and General Ledger Entries in a Standard Cost System

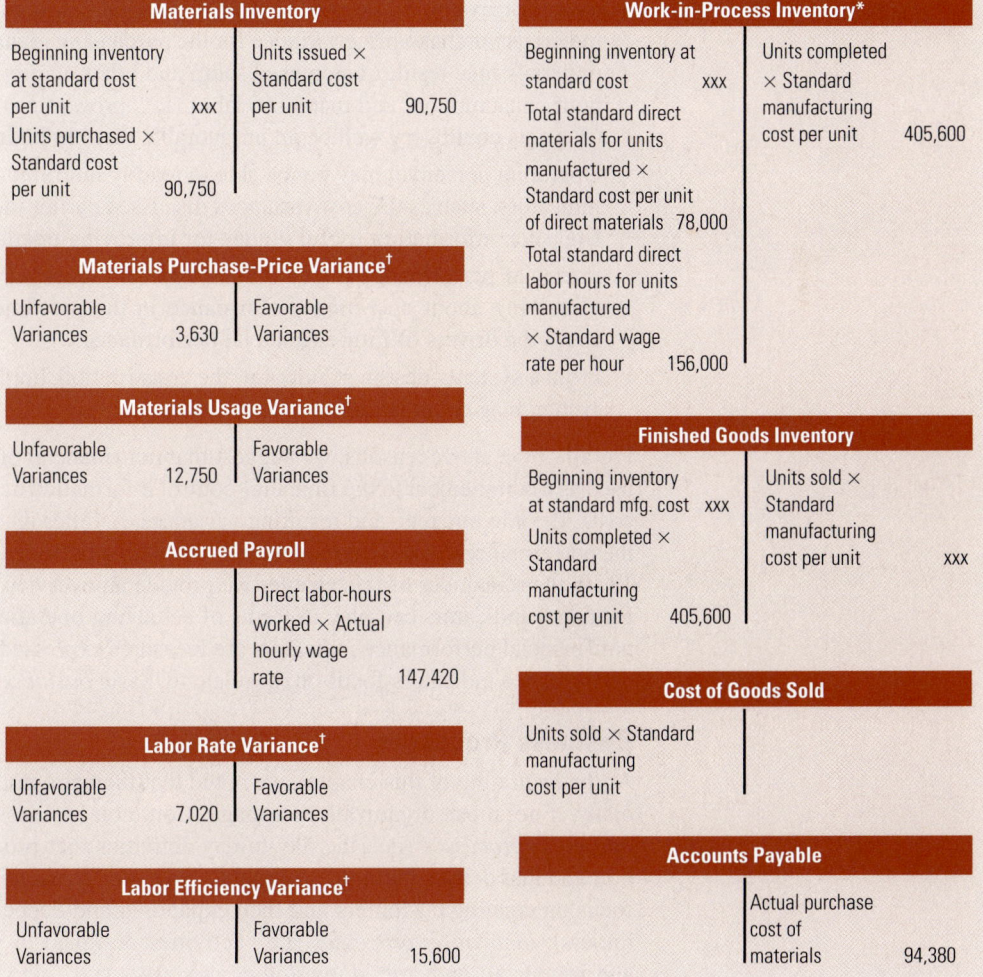

Materials Inventory

Beginning inventory at standard cost per unit xxx	Units issued × Standard cost per unit 90,750
Units purchased × Standard cost per unit 90,750	

Materials Purchase-Price Variance†

Unfavorable Variances 3,630	Favorable Variances

Materials Usage Variance†

Unfavorable Variances 12,750	Favorable Variances

Accrued Payroll

	Direct labor-hours worked × Actual hourly wage rate 147,420

Labor Rate Variance†

Unfavorable Variances 7,020	Favorable Variances

Labor Efficiency Variance†

Unfavorable Variances	Favorable Variances 15,600

Work-in-Process Inventory*

Beginning inventory at standard cost xxx	Units completed × Standard manufacturing cost per unit 405,600
Total standard direct materials for units manufactured × Standard cost per unit of direct materials 78,000	
Total standard direct labor hours for units manufactured × Standard wage rate per hour 156,000	

Finished Goods Inventory

Beginning inventory at standard mfg. cost xxx	Units sold × Standard manufacturing cost per unit xxx
Units completed × Standard manufacturing cost per unit 405,600	

Cost of Goods Sold

Units sold × Standard manufacturing cost per unit	

Accounts Payable

	Actual purchase cost of materials 94,380

Notes:
* A full accounting would include debits for manufacturing overhead costs as well—a topic covered in Chapter 15.
† The end-of-period disposition (closing) of those accounts is covered in Chapter 15.

The Strategic Role of Nonfinancial Performance Indicators

LEARNING OBJECTIVE 6

Discuss major operating functions and the need for nonfinancial performance indicators.

Thus far, this chapter has focused on the use of flexible budgets, standards, and various operating-income variances to assess short-run operating performance. However, long-term organizational success will not likely be achieved if the focus of the accounting and control system is solely on short-run financial performance indicators. This section explains some of the limitations of short-term financial performance indicators and introduces you to the use of nonfinancial performance indicators as part of a comprehensive management accounting and control system.

Limitations of Short-Term Financial-Performance Indicators

When put into perspective, and interpreted carefully, the financial-control model discussed thus far in the chapter can be useful for organizations as they strive for competitive advantage. However, management accountants need to recognize the following major limitations of the use of standard costs and variance-analysis for operational control purposes:

- Because of the short-term nature of the performance indicators, employees and decision makers may take actions that improve short-term financial performance at the expense of long-term performance; that is, they may induce behavior that is not goal-congruent. For example, favorable labor rate variances may be realized by employing substandard labor. The use of such labor may, however, result in a deterioration of product or service quality, which could result in eroding market shares and profitability.

- Focusing on individual variances may result in optimizing local, but not global, performance. For example, the purchase of nonstandard raw materials may result in a favorable materials purchase-price variance for the purchasing manager. However, those lower-quality materials may result in increased scrap and other quality-related costs, increased machine-hour consumption, and increased labor (i.e., processing) costs. The net effect of this chain of events could very well be an unfavorable flexible-budget variance for the period.

- Operating personnel may not be able to readily interpret or act upon financial-performance indicators, such as the cost variances discussed earlier in this chapter. That is, they may not find such information useful guides for improving operating performance.

- Financial performance indicators are basically backward-looking measures. They tell us something about operating performance in the past but do not necessarily tell us much about the drivers of future financial performance.

- From a systems-design standpoint, the construction, application, and use of a standard cost system may entail significant costs.

For all of the above reasons, we suggest that nonfinancial operating performance measures be used as a complement to the financial-control information achieved through the use of standard costs, flexible budgets, and resulting variances. A fuller discussion of expanding the scope of the performance-evaluation model, in the form of a balanced scorecard, is presented in Chapter 18. In the remainder of this chapter we provide an overview of the role that nonfinancial performance indicators can play in terms of achieving operational control. As the name implies, nonfinancial performance indicators are measures expressed in terms other than dollars. These performance indicators focus on, or relate to, basic *business processes,* as described below.

Business Processes

At the beginning of this chapter, we noted that there are multiple business processes in which many, if not most, organizations engage. Common business processes include the following: *operating processes* (i.e., the day-to-day activities that produce the outputs of the organization and that deliver them to customers); *customer-management processes* (i.e., activities that focus on creating customers and then expanding and deepening relationships with these customers); *innovation processes* (i.e., activities designed to produce new processes, services, and products); and, *social/regulatory processes* (i.e., activities related to the organization's environmental and community responsibilities, as well as its legal responsibilities, at both local and national levels).

Organizations succeed by managing the set of activities associated with each of these four classes of business processes. Thus, an effective operational control system would establish specific objectives for each of the four business processes and then monitor performance by developing one or more key performance measures for each specified objective. For example, in the innovation-process category, management might specify the following two critical objectives: (1) manage the development-cycle cost, and (2) reduce new-product development time. To monitor performance of the former, the organization might compare actual spending versus budgeted spending on each project at each development stage. To monitor performance in terms of the latter objective, management might collect information as to the development-cycle time (elapsed time from initial concept to the time the product in question comes to market) and/or the number of projects delivered on time (i.e., according to plan). In the space below, we provide a more detailed discussion of the use of both financial and nonfinancial performance indicators for improving operating processes. The monitoring of customer-management processes, the innovation process, and social/regulatory processes is covered in greater detail in Chapter 18.

Operating Processes

As noted above, operating processes include all activities such as acquiring raw materials from suppliers, producing outputs (i.e., services or products), and delivering products or services to customers. Depending on the strategy the organization is pursuing, it would likely give differential weight to each of the following operating-process objectives: time, cost, and quality. For each of these critical dimensions on which the organization could compete, the management accountant would help to identify a series of specific objectives and associated measures, similar to the example given above. In the remainder of this section, we provide an extended discussion of a particular operating strategy: the switch from a conventional manufacturing process to a just-in-time (JIT) process.

The goal of the discussion is to illustrate the expansion of a management accounting system for control of an operating process.

Just-in-Time (JIT) Manufacturing

A JIT process is one in which production at any stage of a process does not take place until an order, from an internal or external customer, is received. In this sense, the underlying system is sometimes referred to as demand-pull. One implication of JIT manufacturing is the reduction, if not elimination, of inventory buffer stocks (which, many would argue, serve as a cushion for poor-quality outputs). When inventory stocks are kept to a minimum, quality at each stage of the production process is expected. Obviously, the adoption of a JIT philosophy, with a focus on the elimination of waste and inefficiency, is a strategic choice made by management. What are the costs and benefits associated with a move to JIT? The management accountant can help answer this question.

Costs of Implementing JIT

Organizations make investments in four general categories: people, tangible assets (e.g., equipment and machinery), information systems, and organizational processes/culture. In concept, a JIT system is straightforward: reduce inventories, eliminate waste, and produce only to order.

In reality, however, the successful implementation of a JIT system, as an operating process, can require significant resources—to educate and train employees, to reconfigure the production layout (e.g., to a cellular approach), and to monitor operating performance in the new environment (i.e., to revise the organization's management accounting and control system). The organization's management accounting system can help by identifying and reporting to management the sources of delay, error, and waste in the system. While conventional systems monitor labor and materials usage, with large-batch production, the focus on a JIT system would be on measures such as defect rates, cycle times, percent of on-time deliveries, and machine up-times.

Benefits of Implementing JIT

A switch from a conventional to a JIT manufacturing system provides the following key benefits, all of which could be estimated by the organization's management accounting system:

- Reduction in out-of-pocket inventory-carrying costs. Under JIT, the clerical process of recording and monitoring inventory levels (raw materials, work-in-process inventory, and finished goods) is significantly reduced. This results in both labor savings as well as reduced information-processing costs.
- Reduction in inventory-related opportunity (holding) costs. All assets that are held require that capital be tied up (i.e., not available for an alternative use). Reductions in inventory result in reductions in imputed costs associated with holding inventory.
- Possible increases in sales, market share, and profitability.
  - Increases in product/service *quality* can result in increased sales and market share for the organization, particularly if it is pursuing a differentiation strategy.
  - Reductions in cycle/processing time (i.e., faster customer response times) may also lead to increased sales and market share for the organization.
- Decreased production costs. Improvements in product/service quality are reflected in reduced manufacturing costs. For example, under JIT, we would anticipate reductions in defect-related quality costs (e.g., the cost of reworking defective outputs).

The preceding discussion focuses on financial performance indicators associated with a strategic move to a JIT operating process. Such indicators, in a mature management accounting system, should be supplemented with relevant nonfinancial operating performance indicators, as discussed below.

Exhibit 14.14 provides an example of a model **(customer-response time)** that the management accountant can use to monitor and report to management time-based performance in conjunction with the adoption of a JIT production system. This model would be particularly useful for an organization that competes on the basis of time. You notice that the total customer response time (CRT) can be broken down into three major elements: receipt time, manufacturing lead (cycle) time, and delivery time. Cycle time (or, manufacturing lead time) represents the total time from the start of production to the time the product is finished. As you see from Exhibit 14.14, cycle time can be further broken down into manufacturing wait time and actual processing (manufacturing) time. Behind each of these times we would envision one or more activities that are being performed.

Customer response time (CRT) is a measure of operating performance defined as the elapsed time between the time a customer places an order and the time the customer receives the order.

EXHIBIT 14.14
Model of Customer Response Time (CRT)

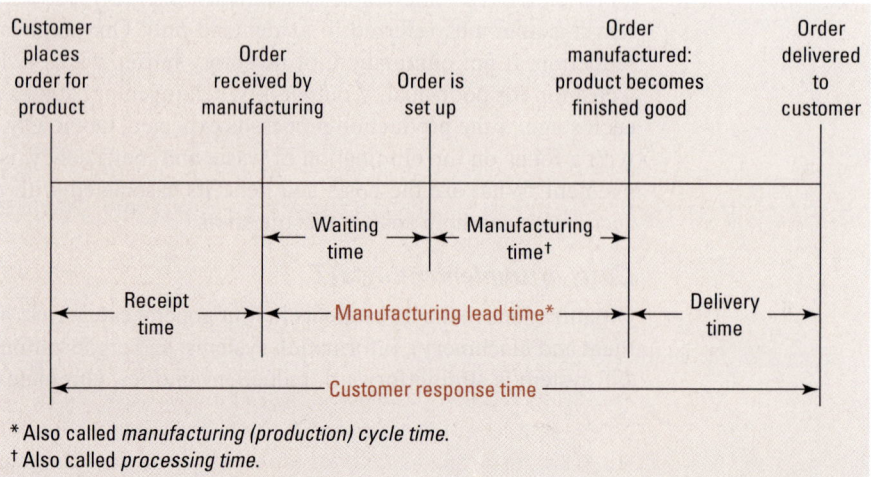

* Also called *manufacturing (production) cycle time.*
† Also called *processing time.*

An activity analysis, similar to the analysis required in conjunction with the implementation of an ABC system (Chapter 5) can be performed to motivate improvements in these time-based measures. The main point, however, is that the CRT model is but one example of a nonfinancial performance indicator that could be used as part of an operational control system.

Processing Cycle Efficiency (PCE)

Processing cycle efficiency (PCE) is a measure of operating performance defined as the ratio of processing time to total manufacturing time.

An alternative (and complementary) measure of operating process efficiency is called **processing cycle efficiency (PCE)**. PCE is a method of assessing process efficiency, based on the relationship between *actual processing time* and *total production time*. In formula form, we can define PCE as:

PCE = Processing time/Total manufacturing time

PCE = Processing time/(Processing time + Moving time + Storage time + Inspection time)

Alternatively, we can view PCE as the ratio of value-added time to the sum of value-added time + non-value-added time. The notion of value-added and non-value-added is precisely the same as we saw in Chapter 5: the classifications are viewed from the standpoint of the customer. That is, an external, not internal, perspective is taken when classifying activities as value-added or non-value-added. Notice that increases in performance are reflected by increases in PCE. The optimum situation is when PCE equals 1.

Advantages of Nonfinancial Measures of Business-Process Performance

Nonfinancial performance measures complement the financial measures discussed earlier in the chapter and in conjunction with the JIT example presented above. Both types of measures are useful in terms of building a comprehensive management accounting and control system. As well, both types of measures can be incorporated into an organization's strategic management system, such as its balanced scorecard (BSC). That is to say, the two groups of measures complement one another.

Relative to financial measures, nonfinancial performance measures have the following advantages:

- Such measures are often easy to quantify and understand. That is, they are readily understandable by operating personnel. This is a significant benefit when building an effective operational control system.
- They direct attention to basic business *processes* and hence focus attention on the precise problem areas that need attention.
- Nonfinancial performance measures can be useful indicators of *future* financial performance. That is, these measures can be viewed as the drivers of future financial performance.

Summary

This chapter is the first of four that together address the topic of operational control. We define operational control systems as a subset of an organization's overall (i.e., comprehensive) management accounting and control system. A modern operational control system consists of *both* financial and nonfinancial performance indicators. Financial control is achieved through the use of flexible budgets, standard costs, and associated variances for reporting and interpreting the short-term financial results of operations. A comprehensive operational control system will also include performance indicators associated with basic business processes (operating, customer, innovation, and regulatory/social).

For any given period (e.g., a month or a quarter), an organization will typically realize an actual amount of operating income that differs from the operating income reflected in its master (static) budget. Any such difference is referred to as the *total operating-income variance* for the period. Other terms used to describe this amount are the *static budget variance* or the *master budget variance* for the period. This total variance is a function of five factors: sales volume, selling price per unit, variable cost per unit, total fixed costs, and sales mix. Through the use of flexible budgets and standard costs, we are able at the end of the period to subdivide the total operating-income variance into amounts associated with each of these five factors. This variance-decomposition process is the essence of the short-term financial control model that is used today by many organizations. Exhibit 14.15 provides a summary of the variance-decomposition

EXHIBIT 14.15   **Variance Summary: Schmidt Machinery Company Example, October 2010**

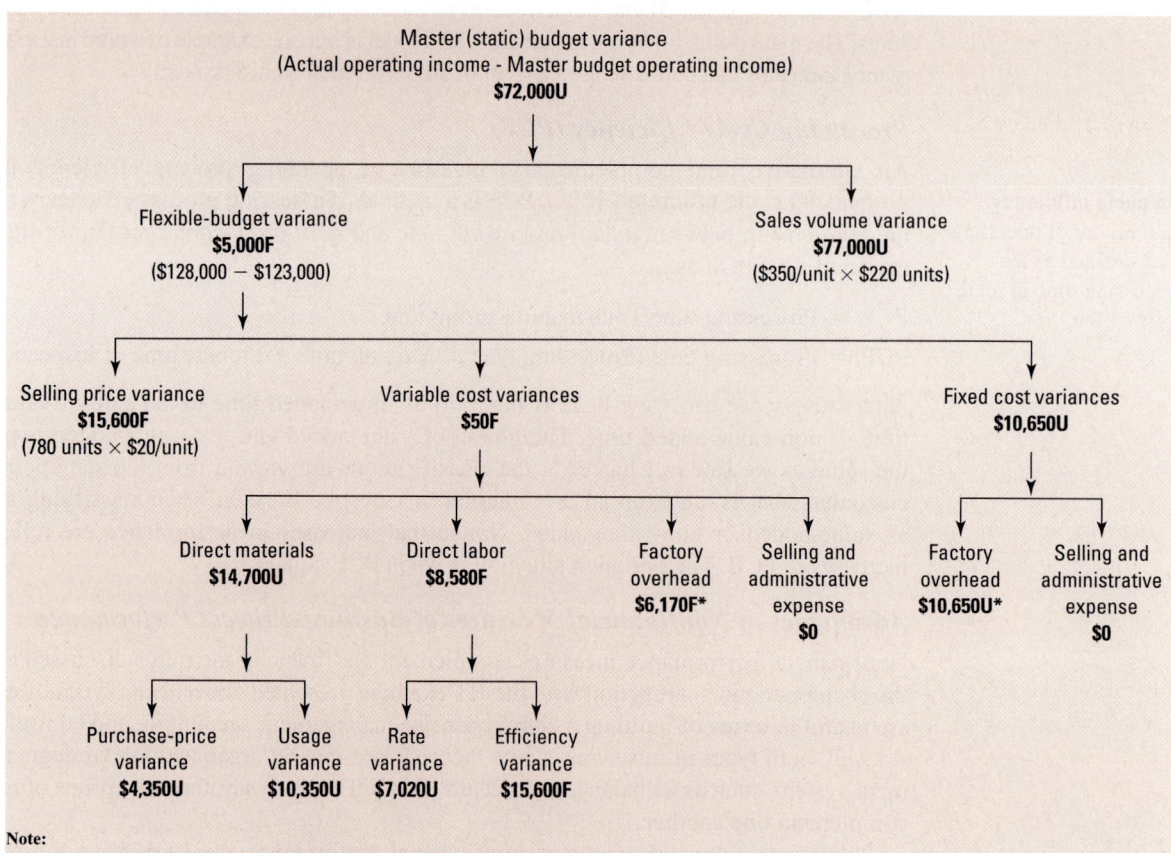

Note:
* Decomposition (breakdown) of these variances is covered in Chapter 15.

process we conducted for the Schmidt Machinery Company for October 2010. Our goal in this regard was to explain the $72,000U operating-income variance for the month.

In this chapter, we assume a single product/output and show you how to calculate the selling price variance and the total flexible-budget variance for any given operating period. As can be see in Exhibit 14.15, the total flexible-budget variance can be subdivided into a series of fixed cost variances and variable cost variances. All variable cost variances can then be subdivided into a price (rate) component and a quantity (efficiency) component. In Chapter 15 we continue the variance-decomposition process by calculating and interpreting variances for indirect manufacturing costs. In Chapter 16 we take a further look at sales variances (e.g., by introducing sales mix into the analysis) and to complement the analysis we look at various productivity indices.

When standard costs are incorporated into the formal accounting system, the organization is said to be using a standard cost system. The standard cost for each product is reflected on what is called a standard cost sheet. Except for the inclusion of standard cost variances (e.g., materials purchase-price variance), the recording of manufacturing costs under a standard cost system parallels the process we discussed earlier in the text for job-cost and process-cost systems. (We leave until Chapter 15 the accounting issue of how standard cost variances are disposed of at the end of an accounting period.)

In this chapter we discuss major classes of business processes, including operating processes. Each business process consists of a number of activities. Thus, the control of operating processes focuses on managing these activities, a point we made earlier in the text (Chapter 5) in our discussion of ABC. This implies the use of nonfinancial operating performance indicators as a complement to the financial indicators discussed earlier in the chapter. We argue that an effective operational control system includes both financial and nonfinancial performance indicators. One example of an operating process is the production/manufacturing process. The chapter concludes with an extended discussion of one manufacturing strategy: just-in-time (JIT) production. As an example of how nonfinancial performance indicators of operating performance can be constructed to support the organization's strategy, we discuss the following two time-related metrics: customer response time (CRT) and process cycle efficiency (PCE).

Key Terms

authoritative standard, *608*
continuous-improvement standard, *608*
control, *591*
currently attainable standard, *608*
customer-response time (CRT), *616*
direct labor efficiency variance, *605*
direct labor rate variance, *604*
direct materials flexible-budget variance, *601*
direct materials purchase-price variance, *602*

direct materials usage variance, *604*
financial control, *591*
flexible budget, *593*
flexible-budget (FB) variance, *597*
ideal standard, *607*
management accounting and control system, *591*
master (static) budget variance, *592*
materials usage ratio, *603*
operational control, *591*
overtime premium, *610*
participative standard, *608*

processing cycle efficiency (PCE), *617*
sales volume variance, *596*
selling price variance, *597*
standard cost, *607*
standard cost sheet, *610*
standard cost system, *607*
total flexible-budget variance, *597*
total operating-income variance, *592*
total variable cost flexible-budget variance, *598*
variances, *591*

Comments on Cost Management in Action

Is Two Minutes and Twenty Seconds Enough for a Brake Part?

The improvement in plant productivity brought about by the bonus system and conveyor belt system at Westinghouse Air Brake Company was just what was needed to save the old Chicago plant. Without these improvements, the business would likely have gone overseas. However, the increased demand on workers' attention and effort caused stress. Workers found themselves operating two or more machines, each of which could operate at a different speed. Workers were usually in constant motion. To decrease stress, the machines were located close together in U-shaped cells when the plant was renovated. This allowed the workers to operate the machines more efficiently, and reduced the time required to move parts around the plant.

An unfortunate side effect of the system is that workers often would set aside a half-dozen or more finished parts to have some to feed the conveyor belt if there was a distraction or disruption of any kind. The few extra finished parts each worker set aside added up to a substantial amount for the plant. Plant managers frowned upon this hidden inventory practice and were constantly on the lookout for it.

Source: Timothy Aeppel, "Factory Lifts Productivity, But Staff Finds It's No Picnic," *The Wall Street Journal,* May 18, 1999, p. A10.

Self-Study Problems
(For solutions, please turn to the end of the chapter.)

1. Sales Volume and Flexible-Budget (FB) Variances/JIT Manufacturing

Solid Box Fabrications manufactures boxes for workstations. The firm's standard cost sheet prior to October and actual results for October 2010 are as follows:

	Budget Information		Actual
	Standard Price and Variable Costs per Unit	Fixed Costs	Results October 2010
Units			9,500
Sales	$50.00		$551,000
Variable costs:			
Direct materials			
5 pounds at $2.40 per pound =	$12.00		48,000 lbs.* × $3 = $144,000
Direct labor			
0.5 hour at $14 per hour =	7.00		4,800 hours × $16 = 76,800
Manufacturing overhead	2.00		19,000
Selling and administrative	5.00		55,100
Total variable cost	$26.00		$294,900
Contribution margin	$24.00		$256,100
Fixed costs:			
Manufacturing (factory) overhead		$50,000	$ 55,000
Selling and administrative		20,000	24,000
Total fixed costs		$70,000	$ 79,000
Operating income			$177,100

* Assume that #lbs. purchased = #lbs. issued to production (i.e., a JIT inventory policy).

In preparing the master budget for October 2010, the firm recognized that several items on the standard cost sheet would change. For example, the selling price of the product would increase by 8 percent. Suppliers have notified the firm that starting October 1, materials prices would be 5 percent higher. The labor contract prescribes a 10 percent increase, starting October 1, on wages and benefits. Fixed manufacturing costs will increase $5,000 for insurance, property taxes, and salaries. Fixed selling and administrative expenses will increase as follows: $2,000 in managers' salaries, and $2,000 for advertising during October 2010. The unit sales for October 2010 are expected to be 10,000 units. Solid Box Fabrications uses JIT systems in all of its operations including materials acquisitions and product manufacturing.

Required

1. Prepare the master (static) budget and pro forma budgets for 9,500 units and 11,000 units for October 2010.

2. Calculate and label as favorable or unfavorable the static (master) budget variance (total operating-income variance) for October 2010. Break this variance down into the sales volume variance and the total flexible-budget variance for the period.

3. Compute and label as favorable or unfavorable each of the following variances for October 2010: selling price variance; total variable cost flexible-budget (FB) variance; and total fixed cost variance.

4. Break down the total direct materials flexible-budget variance and the total direct labor flexible-budget variance into their price (rate) and quantity (efficiency) components. Label each component variance as favorable or unfavorable.

5. Define what is meant by a just-in-time (JIT) manufacturing process. What are the primary benefits, both financial and nonfinancial, of a JIT system compared to a conventional manufacturing process?

2. Direct Materials Price and Usage Variances, Direct Labor Rate and Efficiency Variances, and Journal Entries

Chemical, Inc., has set the following standards for direct materials and direct labor for each 20-pound bag of Weed-Be-Doom:

	Per Bag
Direct materials: 25 pounds XF–2000 @ $0.08/lb.	$2.00
Direct labor: 0.05 hour @ $32/hr.	1.60

The firm manufactured 100,000 bags of Weed-Be-Doom in December and used 2,700,000 pounds of XF–2000 and 5,200 direct labor hours. During the month the firm purchased 3,000,000 lbs. of XF–2000 at $0.075 per pound and incurred a total payroll of $182,000 for direct labor. The firm records purchases at standard cost and therefore recognizes material price variances at point of purchase.

Required

1. Compute the price and usage variances for direct materials, and the rate and efficiency variances for direct labor.

2. Prepare journal entries to record the preceding events.

Questions

14-1 Explain how standard costs and flexible budgets can be used for short-term profit analysis, i.e., for financial control purposes.

14-2 Can standard costs be used in job-order costing? In process costing? Explain.

14-3 Distinguish between the terms "standard costs" and "standard cost system."

14-4 What is the difference between standard costs and budgeted costs?

14-5 What is the difference between a master budget, pro forma budgets, and a flexible budget?

14-6 Explain primary reasons why actual direct materials cost for a given period would be different from direct materials cost contained in the master (static) budget that was prepared before the start of the period.

14-7 Verbatim Company's budget for last year included $80,000 for variable costs. The total actual variable costs for the period were $72,000. Can we say that the plant manager has done a good job in controlling these costs if actual production was 80 percent of budgeted production?

14-8 Which of the following should a firm use as the standard in assessing production efficiencies: standards based on ideal performance, standards based on attainable performance, or standards based on the average of recent historical performance? Explain.

14-9 Why does management need to separate direct labor variances into rate and efficiency components?

14-10 The manager of a firm is happy to receive a report that shows a favorable total materials variance of $75. The manager decides that no more action is needed since the total variance is such an insignificant amount for an operation that has a total direct materials cost of over $100,000. Do you agree?

14-11 Which variances discussed in this chapter would be directly affected by a learning curve phenomenon?

14-12 Will overtime premiums affect direct labor variances? If so, which ones?

14-13 Should the performance of a division be deemed less than satisfactory if all of its variances are "unfavorable"? Explain.

14-14 Explain what is meant by the term "management by exception." What is the relationship between the process of standard cost variance analysis and management by exception?

14-15 Todco planned to produce 3,000 units of its single product, Teragram, during November. The standard specifications for one unit of Teragram include 6 pounds of material at $0.30 per pound. The firm uses JIT in all operations. Actual production in November was 3,100 units of Teragram. The accountant computed a $380 favorable materials purchase-price variance and a $120 unfavorable materials usage variance.

Required Which of the following conclusions do these variances best support?

1. More materials were purchased than were used.
2. More materials were used than were purchased.
3. The actual cost of materials was less than the standard cost.
4. The actual usage of materials was less than the standard allowed.
5. The actual cost and usage of materials were both less than standard.

(CMA Adapted)

14-16 Why do firms using JIT systems often have little interest in materials price variances?

14-17 Identify the effects that new technologies such as JIT, flexible manufacturing systems, and TQM have on standard cost systems.

14-18 Discuss behavioral concerns in establishing and implementing a standard cost system.

14-19 Explain the possible causes for direct materials *price* and direct materials *usage* variances. Who in the organization normally has influence over or responsibility for these variances?

14-20 Explain some of the possible causes of direct labor *rate* (price) and direct labor *efficiency* (quantity) variances. Who normally has responsibility for or influence over these variances?

14-21 This chapter deals with control systems associated with business processes, such as operating processes. Provide a definition and some examples of operating processes. In what other processes would an organization engage in the normal course of business?

14-22 Describe how a just-in-time (JIT) manufacturing system is fundamentally different from a conventional manufacturing system. List two primary financial benefits associated with a shift to JIT manufacturing. What effect does the adoption of JIT have on the design of management accounting and control systems?

14-23 One of the purported benefits of moving to a JIT system is improvements in customer response time (CRT). Define the following terms: *total customer response time; manufacturing (production) cycle time; cycle-time efficiency; value-added time;* and *non-value-added time.*

Brief Exercises

14-24 The Ace Company sells a single product, at a budgeted selling price per unit of $20. Budgeted fixed manufacturing costs for the coming period are $10,000, while budgeted fixed marketing expenses for the period are $24,000. Budgeted variable costs per unit include $2 of selling expenses (commission) and $4 of manufacturing costs. What is the budgeted operating income if the anticipated sales volume for the period is (a) 10,000 units, and (b) 15,000 units?

14-25 The Baldwin Company, in its master budget for 2010, predicted total sales of $160,000, variable costs of $48,000, and fixed costs of $52,000 ($24,000 manufacturing and $28,000 nonmanufacturing). Actual sales revenue for 2010 turned out to be $180,000. Actual costs were as follows: variable, $54,000, and fixed, $50,000. What was the total static budget (operating-income) variance for 2010? Was this total variance favorable (F) or unfavorable (U)?

14-26 Chapman, Inc., sells a single product, Zud, which has a budgeted selling price of $24 per unit and a budgeted variable cost of $12 per unit. Budgeted fixed costs for the year amount to $45,000. Actual sales volume for the year (47,000) fell 3,000 units short of budgeted sales volume. Actual fixed costs were $46,000. With everything else held constant, what impact did the shortfall in volume have on profitability for the year?

14-27 Davidson Corp. produces a single product: fireproof safety deposit boxes for home use. The budget going into the current year anticipated a selling price of $55 per unit. Because of competitive pressures, the company had to cut selling prices by 10 percent during the year. Budgeted variable costs per unit are $32, and budgeted total fixed costs are $156,000 for the year. Anticipated sales volume for the year was 10,000 units. Actual sales volume was 5 percent less than budget. What was the sales price variance for the year? Label this variance F (favorable) or U (unfavorable), as appropriate.

14-28 Edwards and Bell market a single line of home computer, dubbed the XL-98. The master budget for the coming year contained the following items: sales revenue, $400,000; variable costs, $250,000; fixed costs, $100,000. Actual results for the year were as follows: sales revenue, $350,000; variable costs, $225,000; fixed costs, $95,000. The flexible-budget operating income for the year was $35,000. What is the total static (master) budget variance in operating profit for the period? What portion of the total static (master) budget variance is attributable to actual sales volume being different from planned sales volume? What portion is due to a combination of selling price and costs (variable cost per unit and total fixed costs) being different from budgeted amounts?

14-29 Refer to Exhibit 14.8 and the accompanying discussion in the text. Demonstrate that the materials usage variance for PVC during 2010 was $2,400F.

14-30 Refer to Exhibit 14.8 and the accompanying discussion in the text. Demonstrate that the purchase-price variance for PVC during 2010 was $720U.

14-31 Refer to Exhibit 14.8 and the accompanying discussion in the text. Demonstrate that the flexible-budget variance for PVC during 2010 was $1,680F.

14-32 Mom's Apple Pie Company uses a standard cost system. The standard direct labor time for each pie is 10 minutes. During the most recent month, the company produced and sold 6,000 pies. The standard direct labor rate is $8 per hour; the actual labor rate per hour for the month was $8.40. The company used a total of 980 labor-hours. What was the direct labor efficiency (usage) variance for the month? (Show calculations.)

14-33 Refer to the data in 14-32 above. What was the direct labor rate (price) variance for the month? (Show calculations.)

Exercises 14-34 **Applicability of Standard Cost Systems** Portfolio management is a powerful concept in finance and marketing. The marketing application of the concept is to develop and manage a balanced portfolio of products. Market share and market growth can be used to classify products for portfolio purposes, and the product classifications often are extended to the organizational units that make the product. The market share/growth classifications can be depicted as follows:

	Market Share	
Market Growth Rate	**High**	**Low**
High	Rising star	?
Low	Cash cow	Dog

The question mark is the classification for products that show high-growth rates but have small market shares, such as new products that are similar to their competitors. A rising star is a high-growth, high-market-share product that tends to mature into a cash cow. A cash cow is a slow-growing established product that can be milked for cash to help the question mark and introduce new products. The dog is a low-growth, low-market-share item that is a candidate for elimination or segmentation. Understanding where a product falls within this market share/growth structure is important when applying a standard cost system.

Required

1. Discuss the major advantages of using a standard cost accounting system.

2. Describe the types of information that are useful in setting standards and the conditions that must be present to support the use of standard costing.

3. Discuss the applicability or nonapplicability of using standard costing for a product classified as (a) a cash cow, and (b) a question mark.

4. What are some primary criticisms of using standard cost systems in today's manufacturing environment?

(CMA Adapted)

14-35 **Flexible Budget and Operating-Income Variances** Assume that Schmidt Machinery Company (Exhibit 14.1) manufactured and sold 900 units for $840 each in June. The company incurred $414,000 total variable expenses and $180,000 total fixed expenses.

Required for the Month of June:

1. Prepare a flexible budget for the production and sale of 900 units.
2. Compute for June:
    a. The sales volume variance, in terms of operating income.
    b. The sales volume variance, in terms of contribution margin.
3. Calculate for June:
    a. The total flexible-budget (FB) variance.
    b. The total variable cost flexible-budget variance.
    c. The total fixed cost flexible-budget (FB) variance.
    d. The selling price variance.

14-36 Flexible Budget and Operating-Income Variances   Kermit Company's master budget calls for production and sale of 12,000 units for $48,000; variable costs of $18,000; and fixed costs of $16,000. During the most recent period, the company incurred $24,000 of variable costs to produce and sell 15,000 units for $64,000. During this same period, the company earned $25,000 of operating income.

Required

1. Determine the following for Kermit Company:
    a. Flexible-budget operating income.
    b. Flexible-budget variance, in terms of contribution margin.
    c. Flexible-budget variance, in terms of operating income.
    d. Sales volume variance, in terms of contribution margin.
    e. Sales volume variance, in terms of operating income.
2. Explain why the contribution margin sales volume variance and the operating income sales volume variance for the same period are likely to be identical.
3. Explain why the contribution margin flexible-budget variance is likely to differ from the operating income flexible-budget variance for the same period.

14-37 Flexible Budgets and Operating-Income Variance Analysis   The following information is available for Mitchelville Products Company for the month of July:

	Actual	Master Budget
Units	3,800	4,000
Sales revenue	$53,200	$60,000
Variable manufacturing costs	19,000	16,000
Fixed manufacturing costs	16,000	15,000
Variable selling and administrative expenses	7,700	8,000
Fixed selling and administrative expenses	10,000	9,000

Required

1. Set up a spreadsheet to compute the July sales volume variance and the flexible-budget variance for the month in terms of both contribution margin and operating income.
2. Discuss implications of these variances on strategic cost management for Mitchelville.
3. Create an electronic spreadsheet that will allow the firm to prepare pro forma budgets for activities within its relevant range of operations and prepare flexible budgets when sales are:
    a. 3,800 units.
    b. 4,100 units.

(CMA Adapted)

14-38 Direct Materials and Direct Labor Variances   Schmidt Machinery Company (Exhibit 14.5) used 3,375 pounds of aluminum in June to manufacture 900 units. The firm paid $30 per pound during the month to purchase aluminum. On June 1, the company had 50 pounds of aluminum on hand. At the end of June, the firm only had 25 pounds of aluminum in its warehouse. Schmidt spent 4,200 direct labor-hours in June, at an average cost of $42 per hour.

Required   Compute for June, Schmidt Machinery Company's

1. Purchase-price and usage variances for aluminum.
2. Direct labor rate and efficiency variances.

14-39 **Journal Entries**   Use the data in Exhibit 14.5. On October 7, Schmidt Machinery Company purchased 720 pounds of PVC at $41 per pound. On October 9, Schmidt's production department used
720 pounds of PVC for the 780 units of XV–1 it manufactured.

Required   Make the necessary journal entries to record the purchase and usage of PVC during October.

14-40 **Materials Variances—Working Backwards**   SMP Company has the following operating data for
the month just completed:

Direct materials purchased	40,000 pounds
Direct materials used	38,000 pounds
Total cost of direct materials purchased	$120,000
Standard price of direct materials	$3.50 per pound
Direct materials usage variance—unfavorable	$6,500

Required   Compute for SMP the following:

1. Purchase price per pound for direct materials.
2. Direct materials purchase-price variance.
3. Total standard quantity of direct materials allowed for units produced during the period.

14-41 **Behavioral and Strategic Considerations**   Chen, Inc., produces a line of soy-based products, including a premium soy-milk that comes in different flavors. This company, founded by Alan Chen, has been
doing business in the United States for the past 15 years. In the face of competition associated with
recent entrants into this line of business, the controller of the company, Rosita Chang, implemented a
standard cost system to better control costs of the soy-milk product line. Financial reports for tracking
performance are issued monthly, and any unfavorable cost variances are investigated by management.

Recently, the production manager of the soy-milk line complained to Chang that the standards
were unrealistic, that they have a negative impact on motivation (because the system focuses only on
unfavorable variances), and that, because of global forces of supply and demand, they quickly become
out of date. The production manager noted that his recent switch to a newly available homogenizing
agent resulted in higher material-acquisition costs but decreased labor hours to produce the soy-milk.
These two changes, when combined, had a negligible effect on manufacturing cost per unit. However,
the monthly performance reports continued to show a favorable labor variance (despite evidence that
the workers were slowing down or slacking off a bit) and an unfavorable material variance.

Required

1. Describe several ways that a standard cost system could improve (i.e., strengthen) an overall management control system.
2. Give at least two reasons how a standard cost system could have a negative impact on employee
motivation.
3. Explain strategic issues regarding the decision to adopt a standard costing system, particularly in light of
competitive forces confronting this company. (*Hint:* think in terms of the costs and benefits associated
with the use of standard costs as part of a comprehensive management accounting and control system.)

(**CMA Adapted**)

14-42 **Direct Materials Variances—Journal Entries**   Steinberg Company had the following direct materials costs for the manufacturing of product T in March:

Actual purchase price per pound	$7.50
Standard direct materials allowed for units of Product T produced	2,100 pounds
Decrease in direct materials inventory	100 pounds
Direct materials used in production	2,300 pounds
Standard price per pound of material	$7.25

Required

1. What was Steinberg's direct materials purchase-price variance and its direct materials usage variance
for March?
2. Give the appropriate journal entries for March.

14-43 **Determining Standard Direct Materials Cost**   Agrichem manufactures Insect-Be-Gone. Each bag of the product contains 60 pounds of direct materials. Twenty-five percent of the materials evaporate during manufacturing. The budget allows the direct materials to be purchased at $2.50 a pound under terms of 2/10, n/30. The company's stated policy is to take all available cash discounts. Determine the standard direct materials cost for one bag of Insect-Be-Gone.

14-44 **Determining Standard Direct Materials Cost**   Rusty Industries manufactures a sugar-substitute, SS–2, from a natural ingredient, natura. Each 10-pound package of SS–2 is manufactured using twelve pounds of natura. The company has determined the purchase price per pound of natura to be $5.00 with a purchase term of 3/15, n/45 and FOB, destination. Rusty has a policy of taking all discounts offered. Determine the standard direct materials cost for one package of SS–2.

14-45 **Master (Static) Budget Variance and Components**   As the new accountant for B&B, Inc., you've been asked to provide a succinct analysis of financial performance for the year just ended. You obtain the following information that pertains to the company's sole product.

	Actual	Master (Static) Budget
Units sold	40,000	45,000
Sales	$390,000	$450,000
Variable costs	$220,000	$270,000
Fixed costs	$140,000	$138,000

Required

1. What was the actual operating income for the period?
2. What was the company's master budget operating income for the period?
3. What was the total master (static) budget variance, in terms of operating income, for the period? Is this variance favorable (F) or unfavorable (U)? Why?
4. From the information given above, are you able to decompose the total master (static) budget variance into a total flexible-budget variance and a sales volume variance? Why or why not?
5. Define the meaning of the total flexible-budget variance and the sales volume variance.

14-46 **Financial versus Operational Control; Behavioral Considerations in the Standard-Setting Process**   You have been assigned to a strategic leadership committee that has been charged by the CEO with developing and implementing a comprehensive management accounting and control system. At the first planning session that you attended the subject of financial control systems arose, but there was some uncertainty regarding the nature of such systems and some of the behavioral considerations that might have to be made in the design process. You have been asked by the chair of the committee to prepare a short written document that could be used as the basis of discussion at the next meeting. Specifically, you have been asked to: define and distinguish between operational control and financial control and how such systems relate to an organization's management accounting and control system; explain the theory behind the use of flexible budgets, standard costs, and variance analysis as elements of a financial control system; and how standards/budgets for performance evaluation should be set (i.e., whether authoritative standards, or participative standards, or a consultative approach should be used in the standard-setting process). Compose your response as requested.

14-47 **Standard Costing/Journal Entries**   Create an Excel spreadsheet to record, in proper form, the journal entries for each of the following events and transactions.

a. Purchased, on open account, 4,000 pounds of direct materials at a total cost of $20,200. The standard cost of these materials, at $5.00 per pound, was $20,000. The company records any price variance for direct materials at point of purchase.

b. During the current month 1,000 units of output were produced. Each unit of output, at standard, requires 2 pounds of direct materials, at $5.00 per pound. A total of 1,950 pounds of material was consumed in production during the month.

c. The direct labor payroll for the period was $25,000 and has yet to be paid. The standard direct labor hours to produce each unit is 2 and the standard wage rate per hour is $11. The actual wage rate per hour was $10.

    d. The standard direct manufacturing cost for each unit is $32. During the month, 1,000 units were produced.

    e. During the month, 900 units were sold, at a cost of $50 per unit. Give the summary journal entry to record each of the following:

        1. The cost of the units sold (direct manufacturing costs only)

        2. The sales revenue for the period

14-48 Standard Labor Rate and Labor Efficiency Variance Elof's direct labor costs for the month of January follow:

Direct labor hourly rate paid	$30.00
Total standard direct labor hours for units produced this period	12,000
Direct labor hours worked	11,000
Direct labor rate variance	$33,000 favorable

Required Compute these:

1. Standard direct labor wage rate per hour in January.
2. Direct labor efficiency variance.

14-49 Basic Analysis of Direct Labor Variances Day-Mold was founded several years ago by two designers who developed several popular lines of living room, dining room, and bedroom furniture for other companies. The designers believed that their design for dinette sets could be standardized and would sell well. They formed their own company and soon had all the orders they could handle in their small plant in Dayton, Ohio.

    The owners bought a microcomputer and software to produce financial statements. They thought all the information they needed was included in these statements.

    Recently the employees have been requesting raises. The owners wonder how to evaluate these requests. At the suggestion of Day-Mold's CPA, who prepares the tax return, the owners have hired a CMA as a consultant to implement a standard cost system. The consultant believes that the calculation of variances will aid management in setting responsibility for labor performance.

    The supervisors believe that under normal conditions, a dinette set can be assembled with 5 hours of direct labor at a cost of $25 per hour. The consultant has assembled labor cost information for the most recent month and would like your advice in calculating direct labor variances.

    During the month, the company paid $159,500 direct labor wages for 5,800 hours. The factory produced 1,200 dinette sets during the month.

Required

1. Compute direct labor variances for management's consideration.
2. Provide management with possible reasons for the variances.

(CMA Adapted)

14-50 Control of Operating Processes/Nonfinancial Performance Indicators This chapter deals with the design of effective control systems associated with business, including operating, processes. As indicated in the text, a comprehensive management accounting and control system will have both financial indicators and nonfinancial performance indicators. Financial indicators can include the operating-income variances that can be calculated each period by using standard costs and flexible budgets. This question deals with the use of nonfinancial performance indicators as a complement to the financial-performance indicators that are useful for controlling operating processes.

Required

1. List and define the primary business processes in which organizations engage in their attempt to meet customer expectations.
2. Fundamentally, control systems (including management accounting and control systems) collect information regarding the extent to which specified objectives are being accomplished. For each of the operating processes identified in (1), provide a listing of possible objectives that the organization might

pursue. For each listed objective, provide one or more relevant *nonfinancial performance indicators* (performance metrics) that the organization's management accounting and control system might collect and report to management.

14-51 **Process Cycle Efficiency (PCE) and JIT** The manufacturing company for which you currently serve as plant controller is contemplating moving from a conventional manufacturing layout to a just-in-time (JIT) system. The overall strategy is to improve manufacturing operations, thereby enabling the company to compete more effectively in an increasingly competitive environment. As a member of the decision-making team, you have been asked to provide input regarding the decision at hand.

Required Prepare a memo for management in which you address the following issues:

1. Comment on the relative costs and benefits of adopting a JIT manufacturing strategy.
2. For which type of companies, from a competitive standpoint, would the adoption of JIT be most useful? Why?
3. Define the term *processing cycle efficiency (PCE)*. Given the estimated data below, calculate the PCE for your plant under the existing manufacturing layout and after the proposed implementation of JIT:

Activity	Current System	After JIT Implementation
Storage	3 hours	1 hour
Inspection	40 minutes	8 minutes
Moving	75 minutes	20 minutes
Processing	2 hours	75 minutes

4. Distinguish between *value-added time* and *non-value-added time* within the present decision context.

14-52 **JIT and Process Cycle Time Efficiency (PCE)** Zodiac Sound Co. manufactures audio systems, both made-to-order and more mass-produced systems that are typically sold to large-scale manufacturers of electronics equipment. For competition reasons, the company is trying to increase its processing cycle efficiency (PCE) measure. As a strategy for improving its PCE performance, the company is considering a switch to JIT manufacturing. While the company managers have a fairly good feel for the cost of implementing JIT, they are unsure about the benefits of such a move, both in financial and nonfinancial terms. To help inform the ultimate decision regarding a move to a JIT system, you've been asked to provide some input. Fortunately, you've recently attended a continuing professional education (CPE) workshop on the costs and benefits of moving to JIT and therefore feel comfortable responding to management's request.

Required

1. Define the terms *value-added time, non-value-added time,* and *process cycle efficiency (PCE)*. Conceptually, how are activities included in the first two categories determined? (That is, how does one know what activities are considered "value-added"?)
2. Define the terms *cycle time* and *processing (manufacturing) time*. How can processing time be broken down further?
3. Given the estimated data below, calculate and interpret the PCE for both the current manufacturing process and the proposed process after implementing JIT:

Activity	Current System	After JIT Implementation
Storage	60 minutes	20 minutes
Inspection	30 minutes	15 minutes
Moving	45 minutes	15 minutes
Processing	60 minutes	30 minutes

4. What is the percentage change in average PCE anticipated under JIT?
5. What additional nonfinancial performance indicators might management monitor in conjunction with the move to JIT?

E_x

14-53 **Generating a Flexible Budget**   Balmer Corporation's master (static) budget for the year is shown below:

Sales (50,000 units)		$1,600,000
Cost of goods sold:		
Direct materials	$150,000	
Direct labor	450,000	
Overhead (Variable overhead		
applied at 40% of direct labor cost)	240,000	840,000
Gross profit		$ 760,000
Selling expenses:		
Sales commissions (all variable)	$160,000	
Rent (all fixed)	40,000	
Insurance (all fixed)	30,000	
General expenses:		
Salaries (all fixed)	92,000	
Rent (all fixed)	77,000	
Depreciation (all fixed)	51,000	450,000
Operating income		$ 310,000

Required

1. During the year the company actually manufactured and sold 42,000 units of product. Prepare an Excel spreadsheet that contains a flexible budget for this level of output.

2. Suppose, however, that the actual level of output had been 52,000 units of output. Rerun your spreadsheet to generate a flexible budget for this level of output.

3. Of what relevance is the notion of "relevant range" when preparing pro forma budgets or a flexible budget for control purposes?

14-54 **Labor Rate and Efficiency Variances**   Keck Company's direct labor costs to manufacture its only product in October follow:

Standard direct labor hours per unit of product	1.5
Number of finished units produced	10,000
Standard wage rate per direct labor hour	$16
Total payroll for direct labor	$207,000
Wage paid per direct labor hour	$18

Differences in hourly wage rates reflect skill levels of workers.

Required   Determine the following for October:

1. Direct labor rate variance.

2. Direct labor efficiency variance.

3. Production manager's performance in managing direct labor costs.

14-55 **Ethical Considerations**   A number of ethical issues arise in the design of management control systems. For example, such issues might arise when an individual's performance relative to budget or standard cost affects the individual's compensation or reward. Assume you are the cost accountant for a manufacturing firm. The reward system at your firm is such that the purchasing manager earns a financial reward when a significant favorable materials purchase-price variance is realized. Suppose, too, that this manager has an opportunity to get an extremely low price on raw materials that the manager knows are of substandard quality. Finally, assume that the purchasing manager believes that any problems attributable to the low-grade materials are not likely to surface until the product from which these materials is made has been in use for a while by consumers.

Required

1. Access the IMA's *Statement of Ethical Professional Practice* (www.imanet.org). Which, if any, of the IMA standards contained in the statement are at issue in this case, either from the standpoint of the purchasing manager or of the cost accountant?

2. Assume you are the cost accountant at the manufacturing plant where the preceding scenario takes place. According to the IMA's *Statement of Ethical Professional Practice,* what are your obligations in this situation?

14-56 **Journal Entries in a Standard Cost System** Boron Chemical Company produces a synthetic resin that is used in the automotive industry. The company uses a standard cost system. For each gallon of output, the following direct manufacturing costs are anticipated:

Direct labor: 2 hours at $25.00 per hour	$50.00
Direct materials: 2 gallons at $10.00 per gallon	$20.00

During December of 2010, Boron produced a total of 2,500 gallons of output and incurred the following direct manufacturing costs:

Direct labor: 4,900 hours worked @ an average wage rate of $19.50 per hour
Direct materials:
    Purchased: 6,000 gallons @ $10.45 per gallon
    Used in production: 5,100 gallons

Boron records price variances for materials at the time of purchase.

Required Give journal entries for the following events and transactions:

1. Purchase, on credit, of direct materials.
2. Direct materials issued to production.
3. Direct labor cost of units completed this period.
4. Direct manufacturing cost (direct labor plus direct materials) of units completed and transferred to Finished Goods Inventory.
5. Sale, for $150 per gallon, of 2,000 gallons of output. (*Hint:* You will need two journal entries here.)

14-57 **Behavioral Considerations and Continuous-Improvement Standards** At a recent seminar you attended, the invited speaker was discussing some of the advantages and disadvantages of standard costs in terms of evaluating performance and motivating goal-congruent behavior on the part of employees. One criticism of standard costs in particular caught your attention: the use of conventional standard costs may not provide appropriate incentives for improvements needed to compete effectively with world-class organizations. The speaker then discussed so-called "continuous-improvement standard costs." Such standards embody systematically lower costs over time. For example, on a monthly basis, it might be appropriate to budget a 1 percent reduction in per-unit direct labor cost.

Assume that the standard wage rate into the foreseeable future is $40 per hour. Assume, too, that the budgeted labor-hour standard for October 2010 is 1.0 hour and that this standard is reduced each month by 1 percent. During December of 2010 the company produced 10,000 units of XL-10, using 9,980 direct labor hours. The actual wage rate per hour in December was $42.50.

Required

1. Prepare a table that contains the standard labor-hour requirement per unit and standard direct labor cost per unit for the four months, October 2010 through January 2011.
2. Compute the direct labor efficiency variance for December 2010.
3. What behavioral considerations apply to the decision to use continuous-improvement standards?

14-58 **Financial versus Nonfinancial Performance Indicators for Operational Control** As indicated in the text, both financial and nonfinancial performance indicators play important roles in an organization's overall operational control system. Explain, concisely, the relative advantage of each type of performance indicator. That is, what role would each type of performance indicator play in helping to ensure that operations are in control? (*Hint:* Think about this issue both from the standpoint of managers and from the standpoint of operating personnel.)

14-59 **Standard Costs and Ethics** Ohio Apple Orchards (OAO), Inc., produces an organic, super-premium apple juice that it markets to specialty food outlets. OAO purchases its apples from a select group of farmers located in the Midwest. Recently, a graduate of the local university, Susanna Wu, joined the staff of OAO. Among Susanna's first responsibilities was the change to develop and implement a standard costing system for OAO, this in response to competition arising from new and aggressive entrants to the organic foods market. Susanna discussed her task with the controller of the company, Mary Whitman, who indicated that unrefined apple juice would cost $1.50 per liter, the price she intended to pay her college pal, Bill O'Neal, who had since graduation been operating his own apple orchard at a loss. Because of favorable weather conditions during the most recent growing season, the price for comparable apple juice in the region has dropped to $1.10 per liter. Mary felt that the $1.50 price, if maintained throughout the current year, would be sufficient to make Bill's operation profitable—at last.

Required Is Mary's behavior regarding the cost information she provided to Susanna ethical? Support your answer by reference to the Institute of Management Accountant's *Statement* of *Ethical Professional Practice* (www.imanet.org).

(CMA Adapted)

14-60 Flexible Budgets and Direct Labor Variances Duo Co. has the following processing standards for its clerical employees:

Number of hours per 1,000 papers processed	150
Normal number of papers processed per year	1,500,000
Wage rate per 1,000 papers	$1,200
Total standard variable cost (including labor) of processing 1,500,000 papers	$2,700,000
Fixed costs per year	$ 150,000

The following information pertains to the 1,200,000 papers processed during the year:

Total cost	$1,995,000
Labor cost	$1,710,000
Labor hours	190,000

Required Prepare an Excel spreadsheet that can be used to compute for Duo Co. the following:

1. Expected total cost for the year to process 1,200,000 papers, assuming standard performance.
2. Labor rate variance for the year.
3. Labor efficiency variance for the year.

(CPA Adapted)

Problems

14-61 Standard Cost System—Behavioral Considerations Mark-Wright Inc. (MWI) is a specialty frozen food processor located in the midwestern states. Since its founding in 1982, MWI has enjoyed a loyal local clientele willing to pay premium prices for the high-quality frozen foods prepared from special recipes. In the last two years, MWI has experienced rapid sales growth in its operating region and has had many inquiries about supplying its products on a national basis. To meet this growth, MWI expanded its processing capabilities, which resulted in increased production and distribution costs. Furthermore, MWI has been encountering pricing pressure from competitors outside its normal marketing region.

Because MWI desires to continue its expansion, Jim Condon, CEO, has engaged a consulting firm to assist the company in determining its best course of action. The consulting firm concluded that, although premium pricing is sustainable in some areas, MWI must make some price concessions if sales growth is to be achieved. Also, to maintain profit margins, the company must reduce and control its costs. The consulting firm recommended using a standard cost system that would facilitate a flexible budgeting system to better accommodate the changes in demand that can be expected when serving an expanding market area.

Jim met with his management team and explained the consulting firm's recommendations. He then assigned the team the task of establishing standard costs. After discussing the situation with their respective staffs, the management team met to review the matter.

Jane Morgan, purchasing manager, noted that meeting expanded production would necessitate obtaining basic food supplies from sources other than MWI's traditional ones. This would entail increased raw materials and shipping costs and could result in supplies of lower quality. Consequently, the processing department would have to make up these increased costs if current cost levels are to be maintained or reduced.

Alan Chen, processing manager, countered that the need to accelerate processing cycles to increase production, coupled with the possibility of receiving lower-grade supplies, could result in a slip in quality and a higher product rejection rate. Under these circumstances, per-unit labor utilization cannot be maintained or reduced, and forecasting future unit labor content becomes very difficult.

Tina Lopez, production engineer, advised that failure to properly maintain and thoroughly clean the equipment at prescribed daily intervals could affect the quality and unique taste of the frozen food products. Jack Reid, vice president of sales, stated that if quality could not be maintained, MWI could not expect to increase sales to the levels projected.

When the management team reported these problems to Jim, he said that if agreement could not be reached on appropriate standards, he would arrange to have the consulting firm set the standards, and everyone would have to live with the results.

Required

1. With respect to a standard cost system, list:
   a. Its major advantages.
   b. Its disadvantages.
2. Identify those who should participate in setting standards and describe the benefits of their participation.
3. Explain the general features and characteristics associated with the introduction and operation of a standard cost system that make it an effective tool for cost control.
4. What could the consequences be if Jim Condon, CEO, has the outside consulting firm set MWI's standards?

(CMA Adapted)

14-62 **Standard Cost Sheet** Singh Company is a small manufacturer of wooden household items. Al Rivkin, corporate controller, plans to implement a standard cost system. He has information from several co-workers that will help him develop standards for Singh's products.

One product is a wooden cutting board. Each cutting board requires 1.25 board feet of lumber and 12 minutes of direct labor time to prepare and cut the lumber. The cutting boards are inspected after they are cut. Because they are made of a natural material that has imperfections, one board is normally rejected for each five boards accepted. Four rubber pads are attached to the corners of each good cutting board. A total of 15 minutes of direct labor time is required to attach all four pads and finish each cutting board. The lumber for the cutting boards costs $10 per board foot, and each pad costs 50 cents. Direct labor is paid at the rate of $18 per hour.

Required

1. Develop the standard cost sheet for the direct manufacturing cost components of the cutting board. For each direct cost component, the standard cost should identify the following:
   a. Standard quantity.
   b. Standard rate.
   c. Standard cost per unit of output.
2. Identify the advantages of implementing a standard costing system.
3. Explain the role of each of the following persons in developing standards:
   a. Purchasing manager.
   b. Industrial engineer.
   c. Cost accountant.

(CMA Adapted)

14-63 **Standard Cost Sheet and Use of Variance Data** ColdKing Company is a small producer of fruit-flavored frozen desserts. For many years, its products have had strong regional sales because of brand recognition; however, other companies have begun marketing similar products in the area, and price competition has become increasingly important. Janice Wakefield, the company's controller, is planning to implement a standard cost system for ColdKing and has gathered considerable information from her co-workers about production and materials requirements for ColdKing's products. Janice believes that the use of standard costs will allow the company to improve cost control, make better pricing decisions, and enhance strategic management.

ColdKing's most popular product is raspberry sherbet. The sherbet is produced in 10-gallon batches, each of which requires 6 quarts of good raspberries and 10 gallons of other ingredients.

The fresh raspberries are sorted by hand before they enter the production process. Because of imperfections in the raspberries and normal spoilage, one quart of berries is discarded for every four accepted. The standard direct labor time for sorting to obtain one quart of acceptable raspberries is 3 minutes. The acceptable raspberries are then blended with the other ingredients; blending requires 12 minutes of direct labor time per batch. After blending, the sherbet is packaged in quart containers. Janice has gathered the following price information:

- ColdKing purchases raspberries for $4.00 per quart. All other ingredients cost $2.25 per gallon.
- Direct labor is paid at the rate of $15 per hour.
- The total packaging cost (labor and materials) for the sherbet is $0.50 per quart.

Required

1. Develop the standard cost for the direct cost components of a 10-gallon batch of raspberry sherbet. For each direct cost component, the standard cost should identify the following:
   a. Standard quantity.
   b. Standard rate.
   c. Standard cost per batch.

2. As part of the implementation of a standard cost system at ColdKing, Janice plans to train those responsible for maintaining the standards to use variance analysis. She is particularly concerned with the causes of unfavorable variances.

   a. Discuss the possible causes of unfavorable materials price variances, identify the individuals who should be held responsible for them, and comment on the implications of these variances on strategic cost management.

   b. Discuss the possible causes of unfavorable labor efficiency variances, identify the individuals who should be held responsible for them, and comment on the implications of these variances on strategic cost management.

(CMA Adapted)

14-64 **Master Budgets, Flexible Budgets, and Profit-Variance Analysis**   As part of its comprehensive planning and control system, Menendez Company uses a master budget and subsequent variance analysis. You are given the following information that pertains to the company's only product, XL-10, for the month of December.

Required

1. Using text Exhibit 14.4 as a guide, complete the missing parts of the following profit report for December.

	Actual Results	Flexible-Budget Variance	Flexible Budget	Sales Volume Variances	Master (Static) Budget
Unit sales	50,000				40,000
Sales	$450,000				$400,000
Variable costs	375,000				280,000
Contribution margin	$ 75,000				$120,000
Fixed costs	65,000				75,000
Operating income	$ 10,000				$ 45,000

2. Based on your completed profit report, determine the dollar amount and label (F or U) each of the following variances for December:
   a. Total master (static) budget variance.
   b. Total flexible-budget variance.
   c. Sales volume variance, in terms of operating income.
   d. Sales volume variance, in terms of contribution margin.
   e. Selling price variance.

3. Explain what is meant by the labels "favorable" and "unfavorable" in terms of a profit-variance report of the type you just prepared for the Menendez Company.

4. What information is contained in the total flexible-budget variance for the period? Include in your answer a short discussion of the component variances that can be calculated to explain the causes of the total flexible-budget variance.

5. Some individuals have recently criticized the use of standard costs and flexible budgets to perform the kinds of variance analyses covered in this chapter. Provide an overview of the arguments for and against the use of standard costs and flexible budgets for operational control purposes.

14-65 **Master Budgets, Flexible Budgets, and Profit-Variance Analysis** The Ono Tuna Company uses flexible budgets at the end of each period to evaluate the financial performance of each operating unit. As the accountant in charge, you have been asked to explain to management why actual results during the past year differed from the results contained in the master budget that was prepared before the start of the year.

Required

1. Using text Exhibit 14.4 as a guide, fill in the missing amounts and labels. (Note: A and B are labels.)

	Actual Results	A?	Flexible Budget	B?	Master Budget
Units	205,000	C?	D?	E?	200,000
Sales revenues	$2,255,000	F?	$2,203,750	G?	H?
Variable costs	J?	$6,000U	I?	K?	$660,000
Fixed costs	$170,000	L?	$180,000	M?	N?
Operating income	O?	P?	Q?	R?	S?

2. What was the total master (static) budget variance for the period? How much of this variance was attributable to sales volume for the period being different from planned? How much is attributable to a combination of selling price, variable cost per unit, and spending on fixed costs being different from plans?

3. A production manager who is attending your presentation asks about the total flexible-budget variable cost variance of $6,000 (U) that was incurred during the past year. Explain how this variance might be further analyzed to provide managerial insight. Assume, for this problem, that there are only three variable costs for the company: direct materials, direct labor, and variable selling/administrative expenses.

4. What nonfinancial performance indicators might be appropriate in this context as part of a comprehensive performance-evaluation system?

14-66 **Summary Problem: All Variances** Funtime, Inc., manufactures video game machines. Market saturation and technological innovations caused pricing pressures that resulted in declining profits. To stem the slide in profits until new products can be introduced, top management turned its attention to both manufacturing economics and increased production. To realize these objectives, management developed an incentive program to reward production managers who contribute to an increase in the number of units produced and a decrease in costs.

The production managers responded to the pressure of improving manufacturing in several ways that increased the number of completed units beyond normal production levels. The assembly group puts together video game machines that require parts from both the printed circuit boards (PCB) and the reading heads (RH) groups. To attain increased production levels, the PCB and RH groups began rejecting parts that previously would have been tested and modified to meet manufacturing standards. Preventive maintenance on machines used to produce these parts has been postponed; only emergency repair work is being performed to keep production lines moving. The maintenance department is concerned about serious breakdowns and unsafe operating conditions.

The more aggressive assembly group production supervisors pressured maintenance personnel to attend to their machines rather than those of other groups. This resulted in machine downtime in the PCB and RH groups that, when coupled with demands for accelerated parts delivery by the assembly group, led to more frequent rejection of parts and increased friction among departments.

Funtime operates under a standard cost system. The standard costs per video game machine are as follows:

| | Standard Cost per Unit | | |
Cost Item	Quantity	Cost	Total
Direct materials:			
Housing unit	1.0	$20	$ 20
Printed circuit boards	2.0	15	30
Reading heads	4.0	10	40
Direct labor:			
Assembly group	2.0 hours	10	20
PCB group	1.0 hour	11	11
RH group	1.5 hours	12	18
Total standard cost per unit			$139

Funtime prepares monthly performance reports based on standard costs. The following is the contribution report for May 2010 when production and sales both reached 2,200 units.

FUNTIME INC.
Contribution Report
For the Month of May 2010

	Budget	Actual	Variance
Units	2,000	2,200	200F
Revenue	$400,000	$396,000	$ 4,000U
Variable costs:			
Direct materials	$180,000	$220,400	$40,400U
Direct labor	98,000	112,260	14,260U
Total variable costs	278,000	332,660	54,660U
Contribution margin	$122,000	$ 63,340	$58,660U

Funtime's top management was surprised by the unfavorable contribution margin variance in spite of the increased sales in May. Constance Brown, the firm's cost accountant, was asked to identify and report on the reasons for the unfavorable contribution margin as well as the individuals or groups responsible for them. After her review, Constance prepared the following usage report:

FUNTIME INC.
Usage Report
For the Month of May 2010

Cost Item	Quantity	Actual Cost
Direct materials:		
Housing units	2,200 units	$ 44,000
Printed circuit boards	4,700 units	75,200
Reading heads	9,200 units	101,200
Direct labor:		
Assembly	3,900 hours	31,200
Printed circuit boards	2,400 hours	31,060
Reading heads	3,500 hours	50,000
Total variable cost		$332,660

Constance reported that the PCB and RH groups supported the increased production levels but experienced abnormal machine downtime, causing idle time that required the use of overtime to keep up with the accelerated demand for parts. This overtime was charged to direct labor. She also reported that the production managers of these two groups resorted to parts rejections, rather than testing and modifying them, as was done routinely in the past. Constance determined that the assembly group met management's objectives by increasing production while utilizing fewer-than-standard hours.

Required

1. Set up an Excel spreadsheet to calculate the following variances:
   a. Direct material price variance, calculated at point of production.
   b. Direct material usage variance.
   c. Direct labor efficiency variance.
   d. Direct labor rate variance.
   e. Selling price variance.
   f. Sales volume variance, in terms of contribution margin.
2. Determine the components of the $58,660 unfavorable variance between budgeted and actual contribution margin during May 2010.
3. Identify and briefly explain the behavioral factors that could promote friction among the production managers and between them and the maintenance manager.
4. Evaluate Constance Brown's analysis of the unfavorable contribution results in terms of the report's completeness and its effect on the behavior of the production groups.

(CMA Adapted)

14-67 **Revision of Standards** NuLathe Co. produces a turbo engine component for jet aircraft manufacturers. It has used a standard costing system for years with good results.

Unfortunately, NuLathe recently experienced production problems. The source for its direct materials went out of business. The new source produces similar but higher quality materials. The price per pound from the old source averaged $7.00; the price from the new source is $7.77. The use of the new materials results in a reduction in scrap that lowers the actual consumption of direct materials from 1.25 to 1.00 pounds per unit. In addition, the direct labor decreased from 24 to 22 minutes per unit because of less scrap labor and machine setup time.

The direct materials problem occurred when labor negotiations resulted in an increase of more than 14 percent in hourly direct labor costs. The average rate rose from $12.60 per hour to $14.40 per hour. Production of the main product requires a high level of skilled labor. Because of a continuing shortage in that skill area, NuLathe had to sign an interim wage agreement.

NuLathe began using the new direct materials on April 1 of this year, the same day the new labor agreement went into effect. The company had been using standards set at the beginning of the calendar year. The direct materials and direct labor standards for the turbo engine component are as follows:

Direct materials 1.2 lbs. @ $6.80/lb.	$ 8.16
Direct labor 20 min. @ $12.30 DLH	4.10
Standard direct manufacturing cost per unit	$12.26

Howard Foster, cost accounting supervisor, had been examining the following performance report that he had prepared at the close of business on April 30. Jane Keene, assistant controller, came into Howard's office. He said, "Jane, look at this performance report. Direct materials price increased 11 percent and the labor rate increased over 14 percent during April. I expected larger variances, but direct manufacturing costs decreased over 5 percent from the $13.79 we experienced during the first quarter of this year. The proper message just isn't coming through."

"This has been an unusual period," Jane said. "With the unforeseen changes, perhaps we should revise our standards based on current conditions and start over."

Howard replied, "I think we can retain the current standards but expand the variance analysis. We could calculate variances for the specific changes that have occurred to direct materials and direct labor before we calculate the normal price and quantity variances. What I really think would be useful to management right now is to determine the impact the changes in direct labor had in reducing our direct manufacturing costs per unit from $13.79 in the first quarter to $13.05 in April—a reduction of $0.74."

NULATHE CO.
Direct Manufacturing Costs:
Standard Cost Variance Analysis for April

	Standard	Price Variance	Quantity Variance	Actual
Direct materials	$6.8 × 1.2 = $8.16	($7.77 − $6.80) × 1.0 = $0.97U	(1.0 − 1.2) × $6.8 = $1.36F	$7.77 × 1.0 = $7.77
Direct labor	$12.3 × 0.33 = $4.10	($14.4 − $12.3) × 22/60 = $0.77U	(22/60 − 20/60) × $12.30 = $0.41U	$14.4 × 22/60 = $5.28
Total	$12.26			$13.05

Comparison of Actual Per-Unit Costs

	First Quarter	April	Percentage
Direct materials	$ 8.75	$ 7.77	(11.2)%
Direct labor	5.04	5.28	4.8
Total	$13.79	$13.05	(6.4)%

Required

1. Discuss the advantages of immediately revising the standards and of retaining the current standards and expanding the analysis of variances.

2. Prepare an analysis that reflects the impact of the new direct materials supplier and the new labor contract on reducing NuLathe Co.'s costs per unit from $13.79 in the first quarter to $13.05 in April. This analysis should be in sufficient detail to identify the changes due to the direct materials price, the direct labor rate, the effect of direct materials quality on direct materials usage, and the effect of direct materials quality on direct labor usage. The analysis should show the changes in cost per unit due to the following.

   a. Use of the direct materials from new suppliers. (*Hint:* There should be three components: change due to price; change due to the effect of materials quality on materials usage; and, change in labor usage based on materials quality. The net effect of these three factors is $1.40 per unit.)

   b. The new labor contract. (Note the sum of (a) and (b) should equal $0.74 per unit.)

(CMA Adapted)

14-68 **Standard Cost in Process Costing; All Variances and Journal Entries**   Dash Company adopted a standard costing system several years ago. The standard costs for the prime costs (i.e., direct materials + direct labor) of its single product are

Material	(8 kilograms × $5.00/kg)	$ 40.00
Labor	(6 hours × $18.20/hr.)	$109.20

All materials are added at the beginning of processing. The following data were taken from the company's records for November:

In-process beginning inventory	none
In-process ending inventory	800 Units, 75 percent complete as to labor
Units completed	5,600 Units
Budgeted output	6,000 Units
Purchases of materials	50,000 Kilograms
Total actual labor costs	$600,000
Actual hours of labor	36,500 Hours
Materials usage variance	$1,500 Unfavorable
Total materials variance	$750 Unfavorable

Required

1. Compute for November:
   a. The labor efficiency variance.
   b. The labor rate variance.
   c. The actual number of kilograms of material used in the production process during the month.
   d. The actual price paid per kilogram of material during the month.
   e. The total amounts of material and labor cost transferred to the finished goods account.
   f. The total amount of material and labor cost in the work-in-process inventory account at the end of November.
2. Prepare journal entries to record all transactions including the variances in requirement 1.

(CMA Adapted)

14-69 **Joint Direct Materials Variance**   Benderboard produces corrugated board containers that the nearby wine industry uses to package wine in bulk. Benderboard buys kraft paper by the ton, converts it to heavy-duty paperboard on its corrugator, and then cuts and glues it into folding boxes. The boxes are opened and filled with a plastic liner and then with the wine.

Many other corrugated board converters are in the area and competition is strong. Benderboard is eager to keep its costs under control. The company has used a standard cost system for several years. Responsibility for variances has been established. For example, the purchasing agent was responsible for the direct materials price variance, and the general supervisor answered for the direct materials usage variance.

Recently, the industrial engineer and the company's management accountant participated in a workshop sponsored by the Institute of Management Accountants at which there was some discussion of variance analysis. They noted that the workshop proposed that the responsibility for some variances was properly dual. The accountant and engineer reviewed their system and were not sure how to adapt the new information to it.

Benderboard has the following standards for its direct materials:

Standard direct materials cost per gross of finished boxes = 4½ tons of kraft paper at $10 per ton = $45.00

During May, the accountant assembled the following data about direct materials:

Finished product: 5,000 gross of boxes
Actual cost of direct materials used during month: $300,000 for 25,000 tons
Direct materials put into production (used): 25,000 tons
Benderboard began and finished the month of May with no inventory

Required   Determine the following for Benderboard:

1. Direct materials price variance, calculated at point of production.
2. Direct materials efficiency (usage) variance.
3. Direct materials joint price-quantity variance (defined as: $(AP-SP) \times (AQ-SQ)$).

(CMA Adapted)

14-70 **Flexible Budget and Operating-Profit Variances**   Phoenix Management helps rental property owners find renters and charges the owners one-half of the first month's rent for this service. For August 2010, Phoenix expects to find renters for 100 apartments with an average first month's rent of $700. Budgeted cost data per tenant application for 2010 follow:

- Professional labor: 1.5 hours at $20 per hour.
- Credit checks: $50.

Phoenix expects other costs, including lease payment for the building, secretarial help, and utilities, to be $3,000 per month. On average, Phoenix is successful in placing one tenant for every three applicants.

Actual rental applications in August 2010 were 270. Phoenix paid $9,500 for 400 hours of professional labor. Credit checks went up to $55 per application. Other support costs in August 2010 were $3,600. The average first monthly rentals for August 2010 were $800 per apartment unit for 90 units.

Required

1. Prepare a profit-variance report similar to text Exhibit 14.4. Compute the total flexible-budget variance and the sales volume variance for Phoenix's operations in August 2010.

2. Determine the professional labor rate and efficiency variances for August 2010.

3. What nonfinancial factors should Phoenix consider in evaluating the effectiveness and efficiency of professional labor?

14-71 **Master Budget, Flexible Budget, and Profit-Variance Analysis**   Going into the period just ended, Ortiz & Co., manufacturer of a moderately priced espresso maker for retail sale, had planned to produce and sell 3,900 units at $100 per unit. Budgeted variable manufacturing costs per unit are $50. Ortiz pays its salespeople a 10 percent sales commission, which is the only variable nonmanufacturing cost for the company. Fixed costs are budgeted as follows: manufacturing, $50,000; marketing, $36,000.

Actual financial results for the period were disappointing. While sales volume was up (4,000 units sold), actual operating profit was only $20,000 for the period. Fixed manufacturing costs were as budgeted, but fixed marketing expenses exceeded budget by $4,000. Actual sales revenue for the period was $390,000, and actual variable costs were $70 per unit (the actual sales commission was 10 percent of sales revenue generated).

Required

1. Develop an Excel spreadsheet that is able to produce a profit-variance report similar to the one presented in text Exhibit 14.4.

2. Use the spreadsheet you developed in (1) and the data presented above to complete the profit-variance report for the period. Below the table you create, show separately the following variances:

   a. Total master (static) budget variance (i.e., the total operating-income variance for the period).

   b. Total flexible-budget variance.

   c. Flexible-budget variance for total variable costs, plus the flexible-budget variance for:

      (1) variable manufacturing costs.

      (2) variable nonmanufacturing costs.

   d. Flexible-budget variance for total fixed costs, plus the flexible-budget variance for:

      (1) fixed manufacturing costs.

      (2) fixed nonmanufacturing costs.

3. Provide a concise interpretation for each of the variances calculated above in (2).

4. Using the variances you calculated above in (2), prepare in as much detail as the data allow, a separate summary report similar to text Exhibit 14.2.

14-72 **Purchase-Price Variance and Foreign Exchange Rates**   Applied Materials Science (AMS) purchases its materials from several countries. As part of its cost-control program, AMS uses a standard cost system for all aspects of its operations including materials purchases. The company establishes standard costs for materials at the beginning of each fiscal year.

Pat Butch, the purchasing manager, is happy with the result of the year just ended. He believes that the purchase-price variance for the year will be favorable and is very confident that his department has at least met the standard prices. The preliminary report from the controller's office confirms his jubilation. This is a portion of the preliminary report:

Total quantity purchased	36,000 kilograms
Average price per kilogram	$50
Standard price per kilogram	$60
Budgeted quantity per quarter	4,000 kilograms

In the fourth quarter, the purchasing department increased purchases from the budgeted normal volume of 4,000 to 24,000 kilograms to meet the increased demands, which was a result of the firm's unexpected success in a fiercely competitive bidding. The substantial increase in the volume to be purchased forced the purchasing department to search for alternative suppliers. After frantic searches, it found suppliers in several foreign countries that could meet the firm's needs and could provide materials with higher quality than that of AMS's regular supplier. The purchasing department, however, was very reluctant to make the purchase because the negotiated price was $76 per kilogram, including shipping and import duty.

The actual cost of the purchases, however, was much lower because of currency devaluations before deliveries began, which was a result of the financial turmoil of several countries in the region.

Patricia Rice, the controller, does not share the purchasing department's euphoria. She is fully aware of the following quarterly purchases:

	First Quarter	Second Quarter	Third Quarter	Fourth Quarter
Quantity	4,000	4,000	4,000	24,000
Purchase price (per kilogram)	$68	$69	$73	?

Required

1. Calculate purchase-price variances for the fourth quarter and for the year. How much of the price variance is attributable to changes in foreign currency exchange rates?

2. Evaluate the purchasing department's performance.

14-73 **Variance Analysis and Accountability** In late November, the sales department of Sanchez Manufacturing accepted a rush order for 8,000 units of one of its products. The sales department did not consult with any of the operating departments before committing to a firm December 20 delivery date. The standard direct material and direct labor costs for this product are as follows:

Direct materials: 1.5 pounds @ $10.00 per pound	$15.00
Direct labor: Class III, 1.2 hours @ $18.00 per hour	$21.60
Total direct manufacturing cost per unit	$36.60

Unfortunately, all of the labor normally used to manufacture this product was already scheduled to manufacture 12,000 units for delivery by the end of December. In addition, the regular raw material supplier could only furnish the quantity needed for the 12,000 units originally scheduled. To meet its regular commitments as well as the rush order, Sanchez did the following:

1. In addition to 18,200 pounds of raw material from Sanchez's regular supplier (cost was $180,862.50), the purchasing department was able to obtain raw material from a new supplier at a favorable price—provided that 18,000 pounds were purchased. These alternative raw materials were supposed to be of the same quality and had a total cost of $177,750.

2. The production department was able to shift Class II labor from another product to assist in producing the 20,000 units (12,000 regular units, plus 8,000 rush-order units) of product. The standard labor rate for Class II labor is $20 per hour.

At the end of December, the production department received the following summary report regarding the production costs related to the manufacture of this product. Raw material price variances are not included in this report because they are isolated at the time of purchase and charged directly to the purchasing department. When raw materials are requisitioned, they are charged to the production department at standard cost.

Cost charged to the production department:	
Material—regular (18,200 pounds purchased and used)	$182,000
Material—alternate (18,000 pounds purchased/15,800 pounds used)	158,000
Class III labor: 15,200 hours worked	281,200
Class II labor: 10,300 hours worked	204,970
Total cost charged to the production department	$826,170
Standard direct manufacturing cost of completed production	
= 20,000 units × $36.60/unit	732,000
Unfavorable cost variance	$ 94,170

The following discussion took place between Sarah Young, cost accountant, and Carlos Sanchez, production department, regarding this report.

Young: Carlos, what happened this month with this product? Your costs for this product are usually in line with standard. If I calculated a labor variance, it would be huge! The boss wants me to do an analysis of the cost overrun. Can you help me?

Sanchez: I am not at all surprised by the cost overrun. We had all kinds of problems this month—none of which were under my control!

Young: What do you mean?

Sanchez: We scheduled production for 12,000 units, based on contract orders received. Then, without warning, Sales accepted an order for 8,000 more units to be delivered mid-month! Well, I had to transfer Class II labor from another production run to cover that order—and these individuals earn about $2 an hour more per hour. If I could have left them on the other project for which they are better suited, I would probably have had a favorable labor rate variance.

Young: By transferring the Class II labor, you are probably behind on the other project, too, right? In addition, I bet the Class II workers were slow and inefficient because this was a new product for them.

Sanchez: Well, we are OK on the project the Class II workers were supposed to work on because we arranged with the buyer to delay delivery for 30 days. The Class II workers were really not that inefficient once they learned the routine. What was really bad was the material the purchasing department bought for us.

Young: What do you mean about "bad" material?

Sanchez: Well, our regular supplier for this project could only provide enough material for 12,000 units. Purchasing had to find another source. They did and seemed to get a good deal, but the material we received was not of the same quality. Our spoilage really increased. The problem was that sometimes we could not tell whether or not it was bad until we put the labor into it. Interestingly, both the Class II and Class III laborers had the same problems and, I would guess, the same error rate. You could really tell when we started using that substitute material!

Young: Do you have any breakdown to help me? Maybe I can show my boss what happened here.

Sanchez: Sure, I have some data. I watched it closely. You ought to charge all of the variance to the sales department; after all, they caused all of the problems with that rush order!

Sanchez was able to determine when the switch to the substitute material took place, and Young was able to determine how many direct labor-hours were worked before and after the switch to the substitute materials. Following is a summary of their findings.

	Regular Materials	Alternative Materials
Direct materials used (in pounds)	18,200	15,800
Production output:		
Class III	7,200	4,800
Class II	4,800	3,200
Total output	12,000	8,000
Actual direct labor hours:		
Class III labor	8,600	6,600
Class II labor	5,900	4,400
Total direct labor hours	14,500	11,000

Required

1. Determine, by calculating a direct material efficiency (usage) variance for both the regular and the alternative materials, whether or not Carlos Sanchez was correct in his analysis of direct material usage.

2. Sarah Young has decided to prepare a detailed analysis of the total direct labor cost variance. Calculate the following components of the total direct labor variance:

   a. Labor rate variance, by labor class.

   b. Labor substitution variance, Class II labor (calculate this as the difference in standard wage rate per hour for Class II vs. Class III labor, times the actual number of Class II labor hours worked).

   c. Labor variance from use of substandard material, by labor class.

   d. Labor efficiency variance associated with use of regular materials, by labor class.

3. Sanchez stated that the variances arising from the rush order should be charged to the sales department.

   a. Identify which of the variances calculated in Requirements 1 and 2 above, if any, could be associated with the rush order. For each variance identified, provide a brief explanation of why it is related to the rush order.

   b. Discuss whether or not Sanchez is justified in stating that the variances related to the rush order should be charged to the sales department.

(CMA Adapted)

14-74   Standard Costing, Variance Analysis, and Strategic Considerations   In a recent *Wall Street Journal* article, the author notes that various retailers in the U.S. (e.g., Meijer, Inc., Gap, Inc., Office Depot, Inc., and Toys "R" Us, Inc.) are turning to consulting firms, such as Accenture, to develop engineered labor standards for cashiers and other retail workers. Monitoring labor-hour consumption (i.e., labor efficiency) under such standards involves timing from the first scan of an item in a customer's purchase to the production of a sales receipt for the customer. A commentator for Meijer, Inc. states that the system now in use had enabled the company to more efficiently staff stores while concomitantly increasing customer-service ratings. A representative from another client of Accenture states that the new system allows the retailer to determine how many workers to schedule at a given time, resulting in a labor-cost reduction of approximately 8 percent. Engineered standards were developed many years ago in a manufacturing environment, at places such as Westinghouse, by time-and-motion study experts. Unlike factor workers, however, most retail clerks deal directly with customers. This raises interesting questions as to whether and how the use of such monitoring (i.e., control) systems affects customer relations, including customer satisfaction. Uncertainties associated with nonstandard transactions or events are also thought to have negative motivational effects on employees whose performance is assessed using such engineered standards. (**Source:** Vanessa O'Connell, "Stores Count Seconds to Cut Labor Costs," *The Wall Street Journal,* November 13, 2008, pp. A1, A15. For additional information regarding "workforce-management systems," go to the Web site of Accenture, Ltd. (www.accenture.com/home.asp) and search under "Operations Workforce Optimization.")

Required

1. The article refers to the terms *engineered labor standards* and *time-and-motion studies.* Define each of these two terms.

2. Define the terms *labor rate variance* and *labor efficiency variance.* Which of these two variances is the basis for monitoring a cashier's performance, as described in the above-referenced article?

3. What cashier activities might invalidate cashier time measures? What recommendation(s) do you have for addressing this problem?

4. As described in the chapter, any control/monitoring system is likely to have behavioral consequences. In the present context, what employee morale and customer-service problems might arise from the system that was implemented? What steps do you think a retailer, such as those described in the article, can take to monitor this situation?

5. How can information about cashier time-management be used strategically by a retailer? For example, how can such information be used to lower labor costs for retail stores? For which types of firms would such detailed information likely be of greater value?

Solutions to Self-Study Problems

1. Sales Volume and Flexible-Budget (FB) Variances/JIT manufacturing

1. Master and pro forma budgets:

	Master (Static) Budget	Pro forma Budgets	
Units	10,000	9,500	11,000
Sales ($54/unit)	$540,000	$513,000	$594,000
Variable costs:			
Direct materials ($12.60/unit)	$126,000	$119,700	$138,600
Direct labor ($7.70/unit)	77,000	73,150	84,700
Manufacturing overhead	20,000	19,000	22,000
Selling and administrative	50,000	47,500	55,000
Total variable cost ($27.30/unit)	$273,000	$259,350	$300,300
Contribution margin ($26.70/unit)	$267,000	$253,650	$293,700
Fixed costs:			
Manufacturing	$ 55,000	$ 55,000	$ 55,000
Selling and administrative	24,000	24,000	24,000
Total fixed costs	$ 79,000	$ 79,000	$ 79,000
Operating income	$188,000	$174,650	$214,700

2. Total master (static) budget variance = Actual operating income − Master budget operating income
   = $177,100 − $188,000 = **$10,900U**

   Sales volume variance, in terms of operating income = Flexible-budget operating income − Master (static) budget operating income
   = $174,650 − $188,000 = **$13,350U**

   or = Standard cm/unit × (Actual sales volume − Master budgeted sales volume)
   = ($54.00 − $27.30)/unit × (9,500 − 10,000) units = **$13,350**

   Total flexible-budget variance = Actual operating income − Flexible-budget operating income
   = $177,100 − $174,650 = **$2,450F**

3. Selling price variance = Actual sales revenue − Flexible-budget sales revenue
   = $551,000 − $513,000 = **$38,000F**

   or = AQ × (AP − SP) = 9,500 units × ($58.00 − $54.00)/unit = **$38,000F**

   Total variable cost flexible-budget variance = Actual total variable costs − Flexible-budget total variable costs
   = $294,900 − $259,350 = **$35,550U**

   or AQ × (AP − SP) = 9,500 units × ($31.0421 − $27.30)/unit = **$35,550U**

   Total fixed cost flexible-budget variance = actual fixed costs − flexible-budget fixed costs
   = $79,000 − $79,000 = **$0**

   Check: Total flexible-budget variance = selling price variance + total variable cost flexible-budget variance + total fixed cost flexible-budget variance
   $2,450F = $38,000F + $35,550U + $0

4. Direct materials purchase-price variance, direct materials usage variance, direct labor rate variance, and direct labor efficiency variance

Direct Materials

$3 × 48,000 lbs. = $144,000 $2.52 × 48,000 lbs. = $120,960 $2.52 × 47,500 lbs. = $119,700

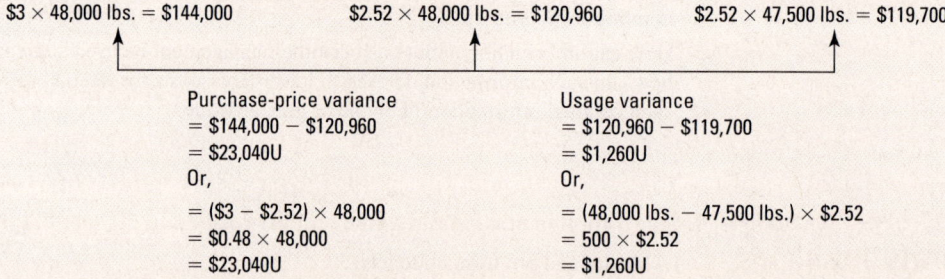

Purchase-price variance
= $144,000 − $120,960
= $23,040U
Or,
= ($3 − $2.52) × 48,000
= $0.48 × 48,000
= $23,040U

Usage variance
= $120,960 − $119,700
= $1,260U
Or,
= (48,000 lbs. − 47,500 lbs.) × $2.52
= 500 × $2.52
= $1,260U

Direct Labor

$16 × 4,800 hrs. = $76,800 $15.40 × 4,800 hrs. = $73,920 $15.40 × 4,750 hrs. = $73,150

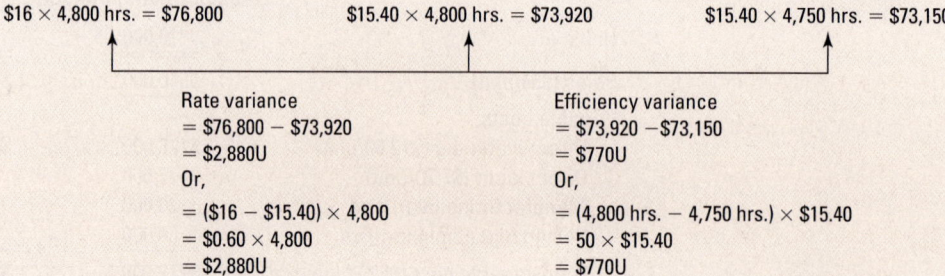

Rate variance
= $76,800 − $73,920
= $2,880U
Or,
= ($16 − $15.40) × 4,800
= $0.60 × 4,800
= $2,880U

Efficiency variance
= $73,920 − $73,150
= $770U
Or,
= (4,800 hrs. − 4,750 hrs.) × $15.40
= 50 × $15.40
= $770U

5. A just-in-time (JIT) process is one in which products, components, and subassemblies are produced only when needed—that is, on a so-called demand-pull basis. Based originally on the Toyota production system, this philosophy requires a commitment to total quality (to ensure smooth flowing of the production

line), elimination of waste and inefficiency, and a minimization of inventory holdings. In effect, the JIT philosophy reflects a new business model for the organization, as follows:

> Make only what you've sold, rather than stockpiling large quantities of goods that may remain in inventory for an extended period of time. Make use of raw materials as soon as they are delivered. Deliver to customers finished goods shortly after rolling off the assembly line.

Financial benefits from implementing a JIT manufacturing strategy include: increased sales/market share (especially for companies embracing a differentiation strategy), reduction in inventory-holding costs (both out-of-pocket costs and opportunity costs), and decreased quality-related costs (e.g., internal failure costs and external failure costs). Nonfinancial benefits associated with JIT manufacturing systems include: faster cycle times, reductions in inventory turnover ratios, improvements in defect rates, increased up-time for machinery and equipment, and improvements in on-time deliveries to customers. Of course, to obtain these benefits, the organization generally must make sizable investments in employee training, information systems, and a reconfigured plant layout (e.g., a move to *cellular manufacturing*).

2. Direct Materials Purchase-Price and Usage Variances, Direct Labor Rate and Efficiency Variances, and Journal Entries

1. Variance Calculations

Direct Materials—XF-2000
Total standard quantity of direct materials for the product manufactured (SQ)
= 100,000 bags × 25 pounds of XF-2000 per bag = 2,500,000 pounds

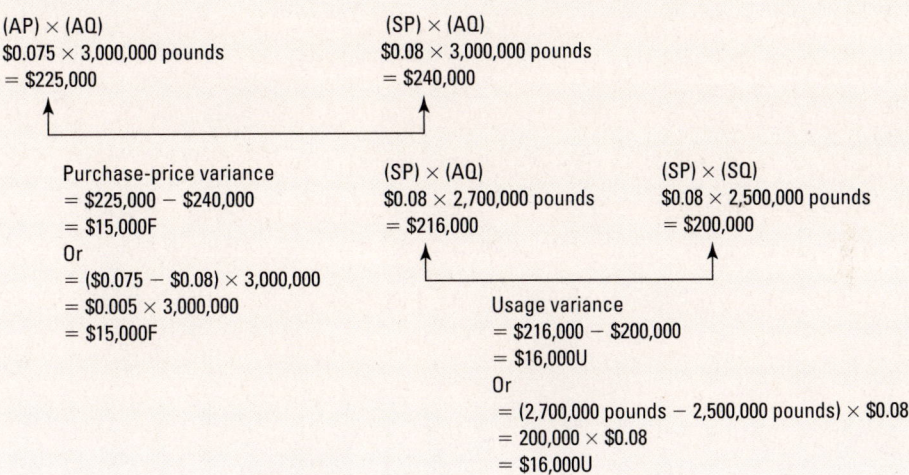

Direct Labor
Actual wage rate per direct labor-hour (AP)
= $182,000 ÷ 5,200 hours = $35 per hour
Total standard direct labor-hours for the product manufactured (SQ)
= 100,000 bags × 0.05 hours per bag = 5,000 hours

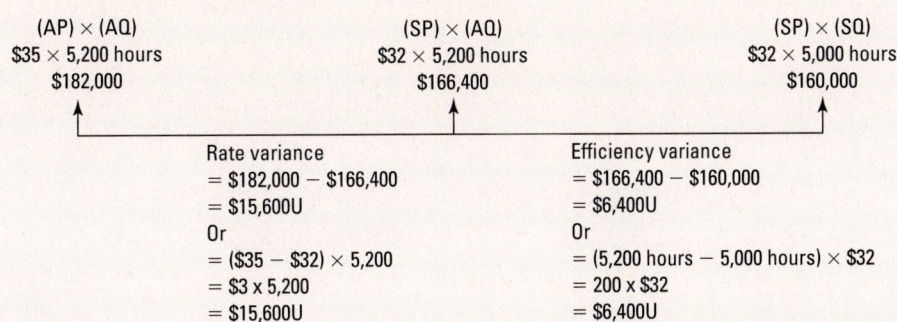

2. Journal Entries

Materials Inventory (3,000,000 × $0.08)   240,000
    Materials Purchase-Price Variance (3,000,000 × $0.005)   15,000
    Accounts Payable (3,000,000 × $0.075)   225,000
Purchased 3,000,000 pounds of XF–2000 at $0.075/per pound.

Work-in-Process Inventory ($0.08 × 2,500,000)   200,000
Materials Usage Variance (200,000 × $0.08)   16,000
    Materials Inventory (2,700,000 × $0.08)   216,000
Issued 2,700,000 pounds of XF–2000 for the production of
100,000 bags of Weed-Be-Doom.

Work-in-Process Inventory (5,000 × $32)   160,000
Labor Rate Variance (5,200 × $3)   15,600
Labor Efficiency Variance (200 × $32)   6,400
    Accrued Payroll (5,200 × $35)   182,000
Direct labor wages for the manufacturing of 100,000 bags
of Weed-Be-Doom for 5,200 hours at $35 per hour.

Operational Performance Measurement: Indirect-Cost Variances and Resource-Capacity Management

After studying this chapter, you should be able to . . .

1. Distinguish between the product-costing and control purposes of standard costs for manufacturing overhead
2. Calculate and properly interpret standard cost variances for manufacturing overhead using flexible budgets
3. Record overhead costs and associated standard cost variances
4. Apply standard costs to service organizations
5. Analyze overhead variances in an activity-based cost (ABC) system
6. Understand decision rules that can be used to guide the variance-investigation decision

"The third quarter was a difficult period for United. Revenue performance suffered significantly from the operational disruptions we experienced throughout the quarter," James Goodwin, United Airlines chairman and chief executive, said.[1] United (UAL) suffered from thousands of labor and weather-related flight cancellations and delays during the third quarter of 2000 while the airline negotiated a labor contract with its pilots. The earnings per share for the quarter decreased from a profit of $2.89 the previous year to a loss of $1.29.

UAL's operating results experienced this drastic change although the decrease in traffic was only a small percentage of total traffic during the third quarter of 2000. As it is for other companies with high fixed costs (i.e., high degrees of operating leverage), volume is a critical success factor for UAL. Fluctuations in traffic volume at UAL often explain the bulk of changes in operating results. UAL constantly monitors volume-variance data, which measures the effect on operating results of differences between actual volume (passenger miles) and budgeted volume.

Companies with high fixed costs experience wide variations in operating results in response to changes in output volume. Managers of these organizations monitor business volumes closely and attempt to reduce fluctuations in business activities. Continuing the discussion from Chapter 14, in this chapter we examine production volume and other indirect-cost variances that organizations use to monitor short-term financial performance. We expand the discussion of standard costs, flexible budgets, and variance analysis and apply these concepts to both traditional and ABC systems. Chapter 15 deals as well with recording standard overhead costs and with the end-of-period disposition of standard cost variances. We also consider in

---

[1] "UAL to Post Loss to 3rd Period, Probably for 4th," *The Wall Street Journal*, October 2, 2000, p. A12.

this chapter the use and importance of nonfinancial performance measures as part of a comprehensive management accounting and control system. Finally, we provide a discussion of resource-capacity management, an area of strategic importance to many organizations today.

Standard Overhead Costs: Planning versus Control

LEARNING OBJECTIVE 1

Distinguish between the product-costing and control purposes of standard costs for manufacturing overhead.

As pointed out in Chapter 14, standard costs can be used alone for control purposes, or they can be incorporated formally into the accounting records for both product-costing and control purposes. In Chapter 14 we used a flexible budget at the end of the period to calculate various revenue and cost variances, which helped explain why actual operating income for the period differed from operating income reflected in the master (static) budget. For *cost-control purposes,* we calculated a total flexible-budget variance and then proceeded to explain this total variance by calculating a selling price variance, fixed cost variances (for both manufacturing and nonmanufacturing costs), and a total flexible-budget variance for direct manufacturing costs.[2] We then subdivided the variance for direct labor and direct materials into price and efficiency components. The breakdown of the flexible-budget variance for factory overhead was left for Chapter 15. However, before looking at standard cost variances associated with manufacturing (factory) overhead, we need to differentiate the product-costing and cost-control purposes of standard costs used for factory overhead.

For *variable* factory overhead the underlying model for cost-control and product-costing purposes is the same, as illustrated in Exhibit 15.1. Recall that the Schmidt Machining Company uses direct labor hours as the activity variable for applying overhead costs. Other allocation bases, such as number of machine hours, could have been used by the company.

We reproduce as Exhibit 15.2 the manufacturing cost portion of the standard cost sheet for the Schmidt Machinery Company presented in Chapter 14. As you can see, the standard variable overhead rate per unit is $60 (5 standard direct labor hours/unit × $12 standard variable overhead cost per direct labor hour). It is this amount that is charged to production for the period (product-costing purpose) and that is used in the flexible budget (cost-control purpose) in Exhibit 14.7. In short, the graph depicted in Exhibit 15.1 for variable overhead cost is similar in form to what we could have prepared in Chapter 14 for either direct materials cost or direct labor cost. This makes sense because all three are variable costs.

The situation for fixed costs, however, is different, as reflected in the graph presented as Exhibit 15.3. For cost-control purposes, we see that budgeted (lump-sum) fixed overhead

EXHIBIT 15.1

Variable Manufacturing Overhead: Product-Costing versus Control Purposes

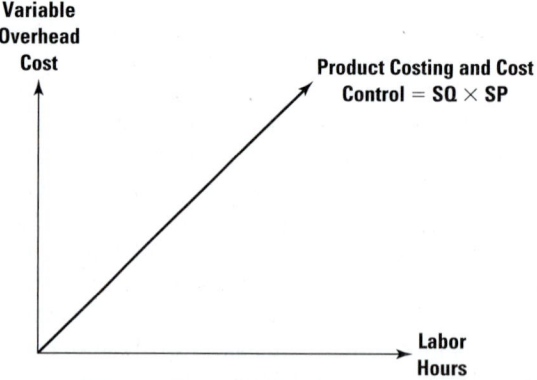

Legend: SQ = Standard allowed labor hours for units produced
SP = Standard variable overhead cost per labor hour

[2] As you recall, in order to explain the total operating-income variance for the period, we also calculated a sales-volume variance. Further analysis of this variance is covered in Chapter 16. Please refer back to Exhibit 14.15 for a summary of the variance-decomposition process used by Schmidt each period to explain the total operating-income variance for the period.

EXHIBIT 15.2
Standard Manufacturing Cost
Sheet (partial reproduction of
EXHIBIT 14.5)

SCHMIDT MACHINERY COMPANY				
Standard Manufacturing Cost Sheet				
Product: XV–1				
Descriptions	**Quantity**	**Unit Cost**	**Subtotal**	**Total**
Direct materials:				
Aluminum	4 pounds	$25	$100	
PVC	1 pound	40	40	
Direct labor	5 hours	40	200	
Variable factory overhead	5 hours	12	60	
Total variable manufacturing cost				$400
Fixed factory overhead	5 hours	24	120	180
Standard manufacturing cost per unit				$520

costs are used—see the horizontal line in Exhibit 15.3. At the end of the period, this budgeted amount is compared to the actual fixed overhead cost incurred. The resulting difference is called a *spending variance.* The spending variance for fixed overhead, along with the spending variance for nonmanufacturing fixed costs, is used to explain a portion of the total master budget variance for the period (see Exhibit 14.15).

For product-costing purposes, however, we must "unitize" fixed overhead costs.[3] As indicated in Exhibit 15.3, for product-costing purposes we treat fixed overhead costs *as if* they were variable costs. In the Schmidt Machinery Company case, the standard fixed overhead rate per unit produced is $120 (i.e., 5 standard direct labor hours per unit × $24 standard fixed overhead cost per hour). Thus, budgeted fixed overhead for the month was $120,000 (i.e., $120/unit × 1,000 units).

EXHIBIT 15.3
Fixed Manufacturing
Overhead Costs: Product
Costing versus Control

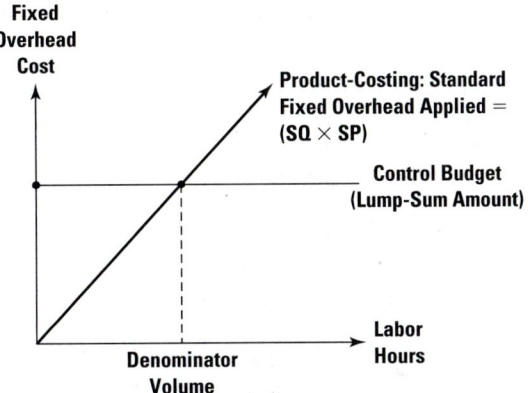

Legend: SQ = Standard allowed labor hours for units produced
       SP = Standard variable overhead cost per labor hour
       Denominator volume = Number of labor hours used to determine the fixed
              overhead application rate

[3] This holds for what is called the *absorption* or *full-cost approach* to product costing, which is currently required for external reporting, and for income-tax purposes in the United States. An alternative product-costing approach called *variable costing* treats fixed production costs as period costs. Variable costing is covered in Chapter 18. Income tax rules regarding inventory valuation are contained in IRC Section 263 ("Uniform Capitalization Rules"). Treasury Regulation 1.263 indicates that indirect (manufacturing) costs be "reasonably allocated" to outputs.

Variance Analysis for Manufacturing Overhead Costs

LEARNING OBJECTIVE 2
Calculate and properly interpret standard cost variances for manufacturing overhead using flexible budgets.

We assume that Schmidt Machinery Company uses a standard cost system. Thus, at the end of each period the accountant for the company prepares an analysis of the total standard cost variance for both variable and fixed overhead costs. In each case, the goal will be to explain the difference between the actual cost incurred and the cost charged to production (units produced) for the period. As shown later, these variances are recorded at the end of the period in separate variance accounts.

For product-costing purposes, the total overhead variance for the period (also called the total under/overapplied overhead) is equal to the difference between actual overhead cost incurred and the standard overhead cost applied to production. For Schmidt, the total overhead variance for October 2010 is $30,880U, as follows:

Total overhead variance = Total actual overhead − Total applied overhead

= (Total variable overhead + Total fixed overhead) − (Total overhead application rate ×
    Standard hours allowed for this period's production)

= ($40,630 + $130,650) − [$36/hour × (780 units × 5 hours/units)]

= $171,280 − $140,400 = $30,880U (i.e., $30,880 *under*applied overhead)

As explained below, the total overhead variance for the period can be subdivided into a set of variable overhead cost variances and a set of fixed overhead cost variances.

Variable Overhead Cost Analysis

The **total variable overhead variance** is the difference between actual variable overhead cost incurred and the standard variable overhead cost applied to production; also called *over- or underapplied variable overhead* for the period.

We provide in Exhibit 15.4 a graphical representation of the process used to decompose the **total variable overhead variance** for the period. As indicated in Exhibit 14.8, this variance for the Schmidt Machinery Company in October 2010 is $6,170F, which is the difference between actual variable overhead costs incurred ($40,630) and the standard variable overhead costs charged to production during October [$46,800 = (780 units × 5 standard labor hours per unit) × $12 standard variable overhead cost per labor hour]. Note that these figures are obtained from Exhibit 14.8. Note, too, that this total variance, from a product-costing standpoint, could be called *total over/underapplied variable overhead cost* for the period, a point consistent with Exhibit 15.1. Because in October the actual variable overhead costs were less than the variable overhead costs assigned to production, we call the $6,170 figure *over*applied variable overhead.

EXHIBIT 15.4
Schmidt Machinery Company
Variance Analysis: Variable
Manufacturing Overhead

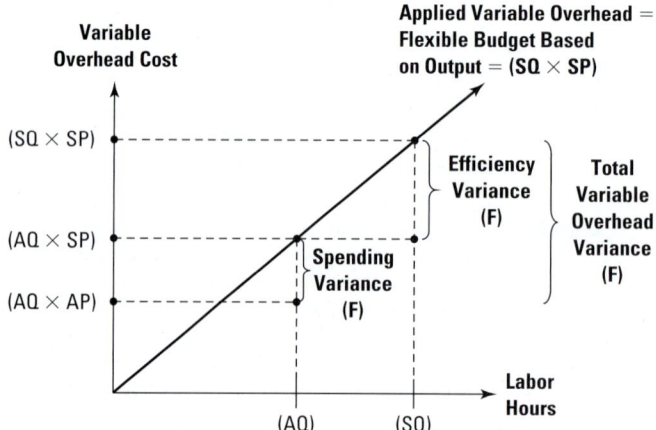

Legend: SQ = Standard direct labor hours allowed for units produced = 5 × 780 = 3,900 hours
SP = Standard variable overhead cost per labor hour = $12 (see Exhibit 15.2)
AQ = Actual labor hours worked = 3,510 hours
AP = Actual variable overhead cost per labor hour worked = $11.5755 (rounded)
Total variable overhead variance = Spending variance + Efficiency variance

Cost Control: Breakdown of the Total Variable Overhead Variance

Variable overhead spending variance
is the difference between actual variable overhead cost incurred and the flexible budget for variable overhead based on *inputs* for the period (e.g., actual labor hours worked).

We see from Exhibit 15.4 that the total variable overhead variance for a period ($6,170F in our example) can be broken down into a **variable overhead spending variance** and a **variable overhead efficiency variance,** as follows:

$$\text{Variable overhead spending variance} = \text{\textit{Actual} variable overhead} - \text{\textit{Budgeted} variable overhead based on inputs (e.g., actual labor hours worked)}$$
$$= (AQ \times AP) - (AQ \times SP)$$
$$= AQ \times (AP - SP)$$

From Exhibit 14.8 we see that Schmidt used 3,510 labor hours in October 2010 to produce 780 units; total variable overhead cost for the month was $40,630. Based on a standard variable overhead cost per direct labor hour of $12 and an actual variable overhead rate of $11.5755 per labor hour ($40,630/3,510 hours), the variable overhead spending variance is calculated as follows:

$$= \$40,630 - (3,510 \text{ hours} \times \$12/\text{hour})$$
$$= \$40,630 - \$42,120 = \$1,490F$$

Or

$$= 3,510 \text{ labor hours} \times (\$11.5755 - \$12)/\text{labor hour} = \$1,490F \text{ (rounded)}$$

Variable overhead efficiency variance
is the difference between the flexible budget for variable overhead based on *inputs* (e.g., actual labor hours worked) and the flexible budget for variable overhead based on *outputs* (i.e., standard allowed labor hours for units produced).

Next, we calculate the variable overhead efficiency variance, as follows:

$$\text{Variable overhead efficiency variance} = \text{\textit{Budgeted} variable overhead based on inputs} - \text{Standard variable overhead \textit{applied} to production}$$
$$= (AQ \times SP) - (SQ \times SP)$$
$$= SP \times (AQ - SQ)$$

As implied by the graph in Exhibit 15.1, the amount of standard overhead cost applied to production (product-costing purpose) and the flexible budget based on output (cost-control purpose) for variable overhead are always equal. Thus, the second term on the right-hand side of the above equation could have been expressed as "budgeted variable overhead based on outputs."

The standard for direct labor is 5 hours per unit. Thus, the variable overhead efficiency variance for October 2010 is:

$$= \$42,120 - [(780 \text{ units} \times 5 \text{ hours/unit}) \times \$12/\text{hour}]$$
$$= \$42,120 - \$46,800 = \$4,680F$$

Or

$$= \$12.00/\text{hour} \times (3,510 - 3,900) \text{ hours} = \$4,680F$$

Interpretation and Implications of Variable Overhead Variances

In traditional accounting systems, such as the system used by Schmidt Machinery Company, only a single activity variable (e.g., direct labor hours or machine hours) is used to assign manufacturing overhead costs to outputs. Further, as illustrated above, traditional systems use this single activity variable for cost-control purposes. That is, the flexible budget for such companies is based on a single, usually volume-related, activity variable. This simple approach requires careful interpretation of the resulting standard cost variances for variable overhead. While the formulas for these variances may look the same as those covered in Chapter 14 for direct labor and direct materials costs, the meaning and interpretation of these variances is not the same. In short, the imperfect relationship between variable factory overhead costs and the chosen activity variable (e.g., direct labor hours) that a company uses to allocate these costs to outputs requires careful interpretation of variable overhead variances.

Variable Overhead Spending Variance

This variance is attributable to actual spending for variable overhead items *per unit of the activity variable* being different from standard. In the Schmidt Machinery Company example for October 2010, the budgeted spending for variable overhead cost per direct labor hour is $12. The actual variable overhead cost per direct labor hour was approximately $11.5755 ($40,630/3,510 hours). Thus, spending for variable overhead during the period per direct labor hour worked was less than standard; for this reason the resulting variable overhead spending variance for the period ($1,490) is labeled *favorable*. The key to understanding this is to remember that the variable overhead application rate refers to the standard variable overhead cost per unit of the activity variable used for product-costing purposes and for constructing the flexible budget for cost-control purposes.

If the variable overhead spending variance is considered "material" or "significant," a follow-up analysis of individual variable overhead items is indicated. Essentially, managers of the Schmidt Machinery Company may want to know *why* spending for variable overhead items per labor hour worked during the period was different from expectations. To answer this question, a follow-up analysis of each variable overhead cost is required.

Perhaps the clearest example pertains to electricity costs for the factory. The electricity bill each month is a function of both *quantity* of kilowatt hours consumed and the *price* paid per kilowatt hour. Thus, if there is a spending variance for factory electric costs for the period, this variance could be broken down into *price* and *efficiency* components in exactly the same way in Chapter 14 where we subdivided the total direct labor or direct materials flexible-budget variance for the period into price (rate) and efficiency (quantity) components.

Variable Overhead Efficiency Variance

Care needs to be exercised when interpreting this variance. Simply put, the variable overhead efficiency variance reflects efficiency or inefficiency in the use of the activity variable used to apply variable overhead costs to products. In the case of Schmidt Machinery Company, this variable is direct labor hours. Thus, to the extent that the incurrence of variable overhead cost for Schmidt is related to the number of direct labor hours worked and the company during a given period uses a nonstandard amount of labor hours, it will incur both a direct labor efficiency variance (Chapter 14) and a variable overhead efficiency variance (Chapter 15). For October 2010, Schmidt used 3,510 direct labor hours to produce 780 units of output. The standard labor hours allowed for this level of output was 3,900 hours (780 units × 5 hours per unit). Thus, the company worked 390 fewer hours than standard for the period. *If* variable overhead is incurred at the rate of $12 per labor hour worked, then this 390-hour saving would translate to a savings of $4,680 of variable overhead costs.

The variable overhead efficiency variance is therefore related to efficiency or inefficiency in the use of whatever activity variable is used to apply variable overhead for product-costing purposes (and for constructing the flexible budget for cost-control purposes). This reinforces the need to choose the proper activity variable for allocating variable overhead costs. Also, whoever is responsible for controlling the use of this activity variable would be responsible for controlling the variable overhead efficiency variance. In the case of the Schmidt Machinery Company, this would most likely be the production supervisor.

Fixed Overhead Cost Analysis

The **total fixed overhead variance**

is the difference between the actual fixed overhead cost incurred and the fixed overhead cost applied to production based on a standard fixed overhead application rate; also called *over- or underapplied fixed overhead* for the period.

We provide in Exhibit 15.5 a graphical representation of the process used to decompose the **total fixed overhead variance** for the Schmidt Machinery Company, October 2010. For product-costing purposes, the total variance is $37,050U, which is the difference between actual fixed overhead costs incurred ($130,650, assumed) and the standard fixed overhead costs charged to production during October ($93,600 = 780 units × 5 standard labor hours per unit × $24 standard fixed overhead rate per labor hour—see Exhibit 15.2). Note, too, that this total variance, from a product-costing standpoint, could be called *total over- or underapplied fixed overhead cost* for the period. When the actual fixed overhead costs are greater than the fixed overhead costs assigned to production, as they were for the month of October, we call the $37,050 figure *under*applied fixed overhead.

The Production-Volume (Denominator) Variance

As noted earlier in footnote 3, for federal income tax and GAAP purposes, companies must report inventories on a full (absorption) cost basis. This means that each unit produced must absorb a share of fixed factory overhead costs in addition to variable manufacturing costs. In

EXHIBIT 15.5

Schmidt Machinery Company Variance Analysis: Fixed Manufacturing Overhead

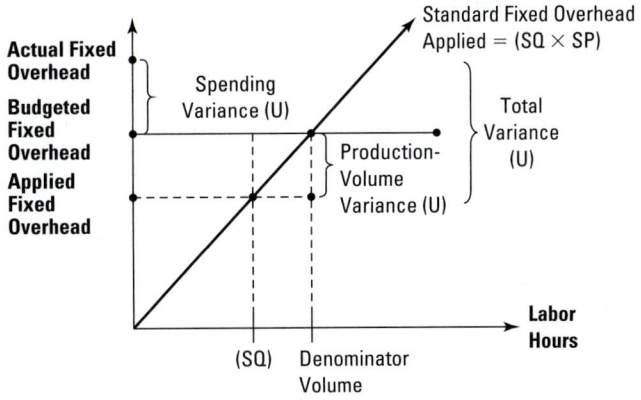

Legend: SQ = Standard labor hours allowed for units produced = 5 × 780 = 3,900 hours
SP = Standard fixed overhead cost per labor hour = $24 (see Exhibit 15.2)
Denominator volume = Number of labor hours used to determine the fixed overhead application rate = 5,000 (assumed)
Budgeted fixed overhead = $120,000 (assumed)
Total fixed overhead variance = Spending variance + Production-volume variance

turn, this requires that fixed overhead costs be "unitized" for product-costing purposes. The following four-step process can be used for this purpose.

Step 1: Determine budgeted total fixed factory overhead Fixed manufacturing overhead costs, by definition, do not vary in the short run in response to changes in output or activity. As such, these costs are often referred to as *capacity-related* manufacturing support costs. Thus, once an organization has determined its capacity for an upcoming period (e.g., one year), it constructs a budget for capacity-related costs. In the case of Schmidt Machinery Company, assume that the capacity-related manufacturing costs are estimated at $120,000 per month.

Step 2: Choose an appropriate activity measure for applying fixed factory overhead For product-costing purposes, capacity-related manufacturing costs are assigned to outputs based on one or more activity measures (machine hours, labor hours, etc.). Usually, this is the same activity measure used to apply variable overhead costs to outputs. The Schmidt Machinery Company uses direct labor hours as the activity measure for assigning fixed overhead costs to production (output).

Fixed overhead application rate
is a term used for product-costing purposes; the rate at which fixed overhead is charged to production per unit of activity (or output).

Denominator activity level (denominator volume)
is the output (activity) level used to establish the predetermined fixed overhead application rate; generally defined as *practical capacity*.

Theoretical capacity
is a measure of capacity (output or activity) that assumes 100% efficiency; maximum possible output (or activity).

Practical capacity
is theoretical capacity reduced by normal output losses due to personal time, normal maintenance, and so on.

Budgeted capacity utilization
represents planned (forecasted) output for the coming period, usually a year.

Normal capacity
represents expected average demand per year over an intermediate-term, for example, the upcoming three to five years.

Step 3: Choose a denominator activity level In order to unitize fixed overhead costs for product-costing purposes, we must choose some level of output (activity) over which the budgeted fixed costs for the period can be spread. The Schmidt Machinery Company uses 5,000 direct labor hours per month (i.e., 1,000 units × 5 direct labor hours per unit) for this purpose. The general term used to describe the level of output (activity) used to establish the standard **fixed overhead application rate** is **denominator activity level** or **denominator volume.** Several alternatives exist for defining the denominator activity level: two "supply-based" alternatives, and two "demand-based" alternatives.

Supply-Based Definitions of Capacity The denominator activity level can be defined in terms of output capacity supplied. In this regard it is useful to think in terms of two alternatives: **theoretical capacity** (the maximum level of activity or output based on available capacity), or **practical capacity** (theoretical capacity reduced by normal employee breaks, machine downtime for maintenance, and other "expected" loss of output). As a rough rule of thumb, you might think of practical capacity as somewhere in the neighborhood of 80 to 85 percent of theoretical capacity. Thus, the notion of practical capacity is not rigidly defined.

Demand-Based Definitions of Capacity It is also possible to define capacity in terms of the demand for the organization's output. For example, we could use **budgeted capacity utilization** (the expected level of activity or output for the upcoming period, usually a year), or **normal capacity** (the average level of demand for the company's product projected over an intermediate-level number of years into the future, say, three to five years).

Given these choices, which activity level should be chosen when determining the fixed overhead application rate? The answer is partly subjective. This is due largely to the fact that the resulting product-cost information can be used for different purposes, ranging from product-pricing decisions, to performance-evaluation purposes, to tax and external reporting requirements in accounting. In terms of the latter, Generally Accepted Accounting Principles (GAAP) (FASB ASC 330-10-30: Inventory-Overall-Initial Measurement [previously, *SFAS No. 151:* Inventory Costs—An Amendment of ARB No. 43, Chapter 4]) require that allocation of fixed production overhead to products be based on the *normal capacity* of the

FASB ASC 330-10-30
Provide financial-reporting guidance regarding the determination of overhead allocation rates and the treatment of abnormal idle-capacity variances.

production facilities. According to **FASB ASC 330-10-30,** normal capacity is the production expected to be achieved over a number of periods or seasons under normal circumstances, taking into account the loss of capacity resulting from planned maintenance. According to this financial-reporting standard, some variation in production levels from period to period is expected and establishes the range of normal capacity. As noted in footnote 3, current income-tax requirements specify only that methods used to allocate indirect costs to inventory should result in reasonable allocations across outputs. Additional guidance for income-tax purposes regarding the use of alternative denominator-volume levels for determining income under the absorption-costing approach is given in Treasury Regulation Section 1.471-11: Inventories of Manufacturers.

Note that different definitions of the denominator volume will result in different fixed overhead application rates, different amounts of fixed overhead costs charged to production, and therefore different amounts for the production-volume variance (discussed below). Depending on how variances are disposed of at the end of the year, the financial statements can be affected by the choice of denominator activity level.[4]

Our position is that *for internal reporting purposes practical capacity* be used as the denominator level for setting the fixed overhead allocation rate. We maintain this position for several reasons. One, though not necessarily controlling, the use of practical capacity is consistent with current Federal income tax requirements in the United States. Two, relative to budgeted output, the use of practical capacity volume provides more uniform data over time, which facilitates decision making on the part of management. (That is, managers do not have to continually reevaluate decisions based on changing product-cost data over time.) Third, the use of practical capacity in the denominator is logically consistent with the numerator in the fixed overhead rate calculation. That is, the numerator represents the costs of the capacity supplied and the denominator represents, in practical terms, the amount of capacity supplied.[5] Fourth, and perhaps most important, the use of practical capacity means that current customers and current production will not be burdened with the cost of unused capacity, which would be the case if budgeted output were used and budgeted output is less than practical capacity. From a pricing standpoint, this can help managers avoid the so-called death-spiral effect discussed in Chapter 5 (ABC and ABM). Finally, the resulting production-volume variance data (discussed below) can be interpreted, loosely, as the *cost of unused capacity* and therefore can be used for **resource-capacity planning** purposes. This information can facilitate decisions by management as to the appropriate *supply* of capacity-related resources (and associated costs).

Resource-capacity planning
refers to ensuring adequate but not excessive supply of capacity-related resources.

Step 4: Calculate the predetermined fixed overhead application rate The last step in the process is to divide budgeted fixed factory overhead for the period by the denominator activity level. For Schmidt, this calculation results in a rate of $24 per direct labor hour, as reported in Exhibit 15.2. Thus, for product-costing purposes each unit produced is assigned $120 of fixed factory overhead (i.e., $24/hour × 5 hours).

In summary, for product-costing purposes a company must choose an activity level over which it spreads budgeted fixed manufacturing costs for a given period. If the company actually operates at the level assumed when the application rate was determined, it will have assigned to production an amount exactly equal to the budgeted fixed overhead for the period. If, on the other hand, the company operates at any level of activity other than the denominator activity level, then it will have applied to production an amount greater or lesser than budgeted fixed overhead. It is this over- or underapplied budgeted fixed overhead that we call the **production-volume variance** for the period.

Fixed overhead production-volume variance
is the difference between budgeted fixed overhead for the period and the standard fixed overhead applied to production (using the fixed overhead allocation rate).

---

[4] As explained later in this chapter, there are different ways of disposing of standard cost variances at the end of the year. One of these methods is to restate cost of goods sold (CGS) and ending inventory amounts to actual costs by recalculating, at year-end, the actual fixed overhead cost per unit of output. Another approach is to allocate (prorate) variances to the ending inventory and CGS accounts. Under either of these approaches, the denominator activity level chosen at the beginning of the year for product-costing purposes during the year will have little or no effect on the financial statements for the year. The choice of denominator volume will, however, affect financial statements when standard cost variances are written off in their entirety to CGS. In short, in some cases the choice of denominator volume will affect an organization's financial statements for the year.

[5] We note that practical capacity can change over time due to changes in manufacturing layout, improvements in worker efficiencies, and so on.

Refer back to Exhibit 15.5. The line emanating from the origin represents the standard fixed overhead cost applied to production. The slope of this line is equal to the fixed overhead application rate, which in the case of Schmidt Machinery Company is $24 per hour (or, $120/unit). You will note that the only situation where the total fixed overhead applied exactly equals budgeted fixed overhead is when the output (activity) for the period is 5,000 standard allowed hours (or, equivalently, 1,000 units produced). The production-volume variance is therefore defined as the difference between budgeted fixed factory overhead cost and the standard fixed overhead cost applied to production. For October, this variance for the Schmidt Machinery Company is $26,400U, as follows:

$$\text{Production-volume variance} = \text{Budgeted fixed factory overhead cost} - \text{Standard}$$
$$\text{fixed overhead cost assigned to production}$$
$$= \$120,000 - [(780 \text{ units produced}$$
$$\times 5 \text{ hours/unit}) \times \$24 \text{ per hour}]$$
$$= \$120,000 - \$93,600 = \$26,400U$$

Or

$$= \text{SP} \times (\text{Denominator activity hours} - \text{SQ})$$
$$= \$24/\text{hour} \times [5,000 - (780 \text{ units} \times 5 \text{ hours/unit})]$$
$$= \$24 \times (5,000 - 3,900 \text{ hours}) = \$26,400U[6]$$

Fixed Overhead Spending (Budget) Variance

Fixed overhead spending (budget) variance
is the difference between budgeted and actual fixed factory overhead costs for a period.

Refer to Exhibit 15.5. We see that, in general, the **fixed overhead spending (budget) variance** is defined as the difference between budgeted and actual fixed factory overhead for the period. For Schmidt Machinery Company, the fixed overhead spending (budget) variance for October was $10,650U, as follows:

$$\text{Fixed overhead spending variance} = \text{Actual fixed overhead} - \text{Budgeted fixed overhead}$$
$$= \$130,650 - \$120,000$$
$$= \$10,650U$$

Note that this is the amount reported in the profit-variance report contained in Exhibits 14.15 and 15.7.

---

[6] Given the way costs are applied to outputs under a standard cost system, the production-volume variance can also be calculated as: Standard fixed overhead rate/unit × (Denominator volume, in units − Actual units produced). In the above example, we would have: $120/unit × (1,000 units − 780 units) = $26,400 underapplied. This approach to calculating the production-volume variance would, in fact, be the approach used by a company that produces a single product.

Interpretation of Fixed Overhead Variances

Production (Denominator) Volume Variance

This variance is an artifact of unitizing fixed overhead costs for product-costing purposes. As indicated in Exhibit 15.5, in and of itself this variance has no meaning for cost-control purposes. However, as we indicated earlier in this chapter, if practical capacity is used to establish the fixed overhead application rate, then the production-volume variance can be viewed as a rough measure of capacity utilization. This is because the variance reflects differences between available capacity and actual capacity usage. In short, the reporting of production-volume variances over time provides decision makers with information that can be used to manage *spending* on capacity-related resources. For example, consistently reported underapplied fixed overhead (i.e., unfavorable production-volume variances) may signal the need to reduce spending on capacity-related costs or motivate action to better utilize the capacity that does exist.

You will note that if the fixed overhead allocation rate were based on expected (budgeted) output, then the cost of unused capacity would be hidden, that is, charged to the units actually produced during the period. To the extent that selling prices are based on indicated costs and budgeted output is less than practical capacity, the use of budgeted output could lead to successively increasing charges (and, therefore, selling prices) over time, a situation referred to as the **death-spiral effect.** In this case, fixed overhead costs get allocated over successively lower outputs.

When practical capacity is used to calculate the fixed overhead application rate, the cost of unused capacity becomes visible to management through the amount and direction of the production-volume variance. To avoid misinterpretations, yet communicate information regarding capacity usage, some companies prefer to report the fixed overhead production-volume variance in physical terms only.

Finally, we note the importance of not placing too much emphasis on individual variances because of the interrelatedness of these performance indicators. For example, a production department in a manufacturing facility can generate a favorable production-volume variance by overproducing for the period, that is, producing more units than needed to meet sales and target ending inventory requirements. Such practice, of course, runs counter to the JIT philosophy. In this case, a financial performance indicator (production-volume variance) might be accompanied by one or more nonfinancial performance indicators (e.g., inventory turnover or spoilage/obsolescence rates).

The **death-spiral effect** is the continual raising of selling prices in an attempt to recover fixed costs, in spite of successive decreases in demand.

Fixed Overhead Spending (Budget) Variance

Fixed overhead spending variances typically arise when the budget procedure for the organization failed to anticipate or incorporate changes in spending for fixed overhead costs. For example, a budget that inadvertently neglected scheduled raises for factory managers, changes in property taxes on factory buildings and equipment, or purchases of new equipment create unfavorable spending variances.

EXHIBIT 15.6
General Model: Four-Way Analysis of Total Overhead Variance

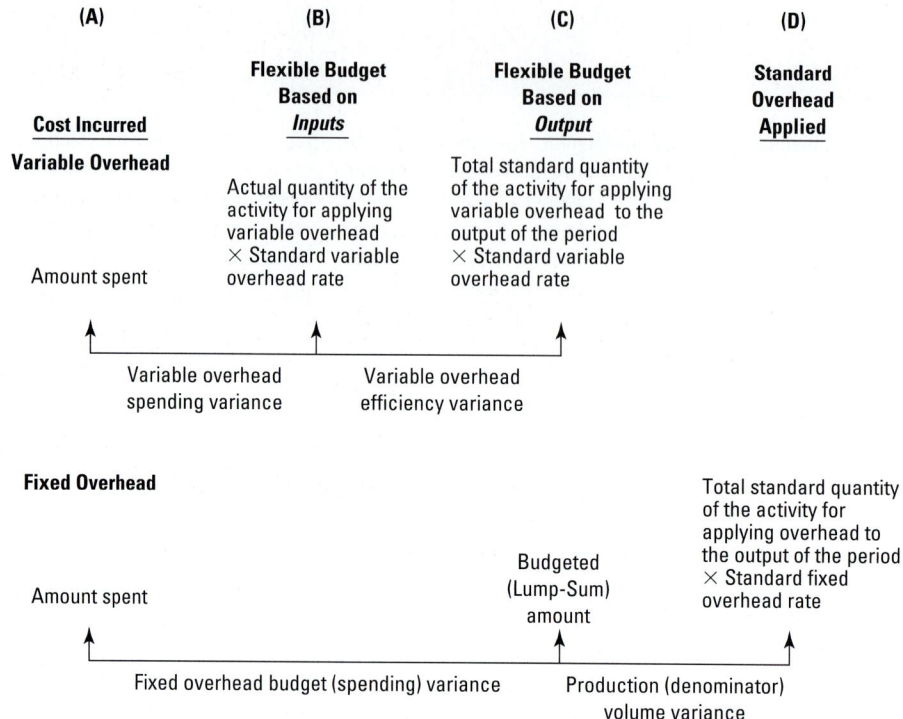

Unfavorable fixed overhead spending variances can also result from excessive spending due to improper or inadequate cost controls. Events such as emergency repairs, impromptu replacement of equipment, or the addition of production supervisors for an unscheduled second shift all would result in unfavorable fixed overhead spending variances for the period.

Alternative Analyses of Overhead Variances

In the discussion above, we separated the total variable overhead variance and the total fixed overhead variance each into two components. Such an analysis is referred to as a *four-variance analysis of factory overhead.* A general model for performing a four-variance analysis, which combines Exhibits 15.4 and 15.5, is given as Exhibit 15.6. Not all companies, however, want or need to analyze factory overhead costs in this level of detail. Furthermore, a company's chart of accounts may not separate total overhead into its fixed and variable components. In the following sections we discuss alternative, less-detailed, ways to analyze overhead variances.

Three-Variance Subdivision of the Total Overhead Variance

The three-variance analysis of manufacturing overhead separates the total overhead variance into three components: total spending variance, variable overhead efficiency variance, and fixed overhead production-volume variance. That is, in a three-variance analysis, the variable overhead spending variance and the fixed overhead spending variance are combined into a single overhead variance. Thus, the total overhead variance for the period, $30,880U, can be subdivided into a total spending variance, $9,160U ($10,650 unfavorable fixed overhead spending variance + $1,490 favorable variable overhead spending variance), a favorable variable overhead efficiency variance, $4,680, plus an unfavorable production-volume variance of $26,400.

Two-Variance Subdivision of the Total Overhead Variance

The **total flexible-budget variance for overhead** is equal to the difference between the actual factory overhead for a period and the flexible budget for overhead based on *output.*

Companies that do not separate fixed from variable overhead costs for product-costing purposes perform what is called a two-variance analysis of the total overhead variance. That is, the total overhead variance for the period is broken down into a **total flexible-budget variance for overhead** and a production-volume variance (which pertains only to the product-costing purpose of standard costing, as described above).

For the Schmidt Machinery Company, the total overhead variance in October, as before, is $30,880U. This variance is broken down as follows:

Flexible-budget variance
= Actual factory overhead − Flexible budget for factory overhead based on *output* (i.e., based on allowed hours for units produced)
= (Actual fixed overhead + Actual variable overhead) − [Budgeted fixed overhead + (Standard allowed hours × Standard variable overhead rate per hour)]
= ($130,650 + $40,630) − [$120,000 + ($12.00/hr. × 3,900 hrs.)]
= $171,280 − $166,800 = $4,480U

Note that $4,480 is the net amount of the two overhead flexible-budget variances contained in Exhibit 14.15: a total variable overhead variance of $6,170F, plus a total fixed overhead variance of $10,650U.

The second variance in a two-variance breakdown of the total overhead variance ($30,880U) is the production-volume variance, as follows:

$$\begin{matrix} \text{Production (denominator)} \\ \text{volume variance} \end{matrix} = \begin{matrix} \text{Flexible budget for} \\ \text{overhead based on } \textit{output} \end{matrix} - \begin{matrix} \text{Applied factory} \\ \text{overhead} \end{matrix}$$

$$= \$166,800 - (3,900 \text{ hrs.} \times \$36.00/\text{hr.}) = \$26,400U$$

Note that the production-volume variance is exactly the same as the amount calculated under the four-variance and the three-variance breakdown.

Summary of Overhead Variances

Exhibit 15.7 provides a summary of the various approaches to the analysis of overhead variances. In each case, the total variance to be explained for the Schmidt Machinery Company for October 2010 is $30,880U. The production-volume variance ($26,400U) relates to the product-costing use of standard costs. That is, this variance will occur only if a company uses a standard cost *system* and defines product cost as full manufacturing cost. The other variances can be calculated regardless of whether the firm uses a standard cost system. The degree of detail decreases as we go from the four-variance approach to the two-variance approach. None of these approaches is inherently good or bad: each has to be judged in terms of implementation cost versus perceived benefits associated with the resulting variance information.

Before leaving this discussion, it is important to point out some alternative terminology for the variances to which we referred in the preceding sections. When standard costs are incorporated formally into the accounting records (that is, when a standard cost *system* is used), we have already indicated that the total overhead variance for the period can also be referred to as *total over- or underapplied overhead.* Also, note that the production-volume variance is also referred to as the *capacity variance,* the *idle-capacity variance,* the *denominator-level variance,* the *output-level overhead variance,* or simply, the *denominator variance.* The spending variance for variable overhead is sometimes referred to as a *price variance* or a *budget variance.* The total flexible-budget variance for overhead (and by extension the total flexible-budget variance for fixed overhead and the total flexible-budget variance for variable overhead) is sometimes referred to as a *controllable variance.* This latter term is more descriptive of the use of standard costs and related variances for cost-control purposes. For this reason, the production-volume variance is sometimes referred to as the *noncontrollable overhead variance.* The important point is that, unfortunately, this is an area where the terminology is not standard. Therefore, you need to keep the above-listed alternatives in mind in any given situation.

EXHIBIT 15.7 **Schmidt Machinery Company, Overhead Variance Analyses, October 2010**

Panel 1: Four-Variance Analysis

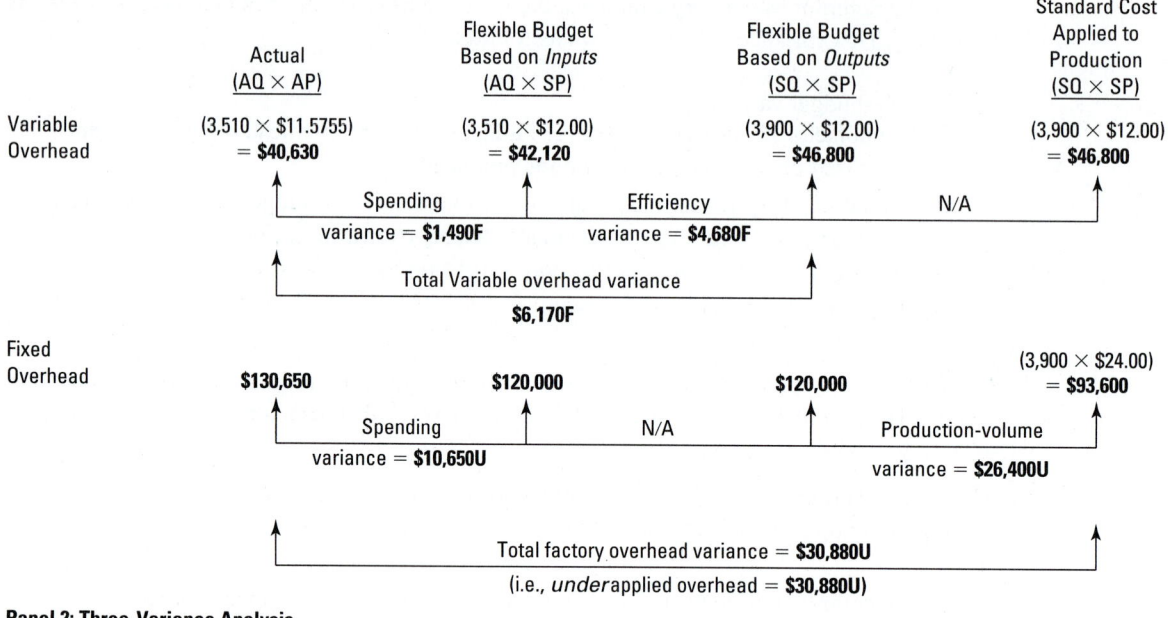

Panel 2: Three-Variance Analysis

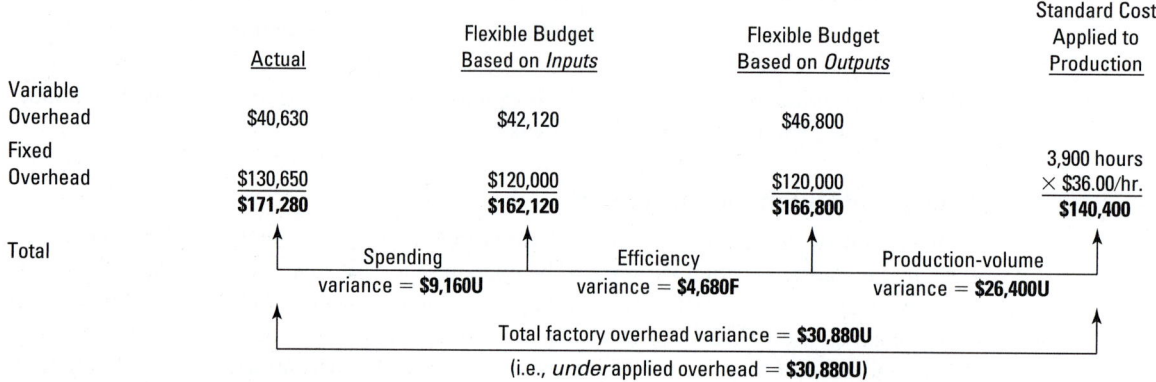

Panel 3: Two-Variance Analysis

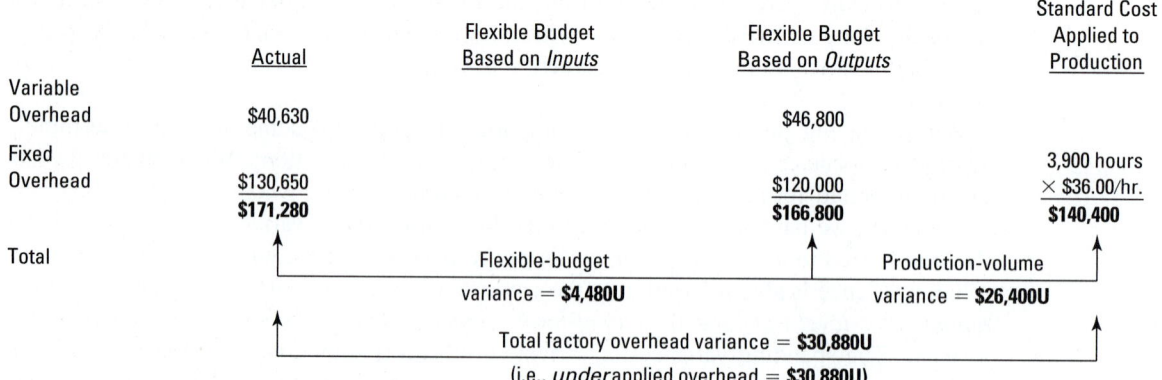

Recording Standard Overhead Costs

LEARNING OBJECTIVE 3

Record overhead costs and associated standard cost variances.

Journal Entries and Variances for Overhead Costs

As noted above and in Chapter 14, a standard cost *system* incorporates standard product costs in the formal accounting records (raw materials, WIP inventory, finished goods inventory, and cost of goods sold). As in the case of direct materials and direct labor, the standard overhead cost of the output of the period is charged to production, while actual overhead costs are recorded separately, in descriptive accounts such as Utilities Payable, Accumulated Depreciation, and Salaries Payable.

Assume that for October 2010, the Schmidt Machinery Company incurred the following variable overhead costs: utilities, $30,000, and indirect materials, $10,630. These actual overhead costs would be recorded as incurred, in entries such as the following:

Manufacturing Overhead	40,630	
Utilities Payable		30,000
Indirect Materials Inventory		10,630

At the end of the month (process cost system) or at the completion of one or more jobs (job-order cost system), the WIP inventory account must be charged for the standard variable overhead cost of the 780 units produced. The standard variable overhead rate is $12 per labor hour and the standard number of labor hours per unit is 5. Thus, for October 2010 the appropriate journal entry would be:

WIP Inventory [(780 units × 5 hrs./unit) × $12.00/hr.]	46,800	
Manufacturing Overhead		46,800

At this point, you can see that the balance in the Factory Overhead account ($46,800 cr. + $40,630 dr. = $6,170F) is the total variable overhead variance for the period.

Assume now, for simplicity, that the actual fixed overhead cost for October 2010 consisted of only two items: $100,000 supervisory salaries plus $30,650 of depreciation expense. The journal entry to record actual fixed overhead costs for the month would be:

Manufacturing Overhead	130,650	
Accumulated Depreciation		30,650
Salaries Payable		100,000

Recall that the standard fixed overhead rate is $24 per standard labor hour allowed, or equivalently, $120 per unit produced (since there are 5 standard labor hours per unit produced). The journal entry to charge production with standard fixed overhead cost would be:

WIP Inventory [(780 units × 5 hrs./unit) × $24/hr.]	93,600	
Manufacturing Overhead		93,600

Similar to entries we made in Chapter 14 for direct materials and direct labor, we would then use the following journal entry to transfer the standard overhead cost of completed production from WIP Inventory to Finished Goods Inventory:

Finished Goods Inventory ($180/unit × 780 units)	140,400	
WIP Inventory		140,400

After these entries are posted to the ledger, the Manufacturing Overhead account contains the net overhead balance for the period, $30,880 debit (i.e., net unfavorable variance). The component variances calculated using one of the approaches described above could be calculated and used to close out the $30,880 balance in the Manufacturing Overhead account. Assume that Schmidt Machinery Company uses the four-variance approach for overhead analysis. The appropriate journal entry to record the standard overhead cost variances for October 2010 would be as follows:

Production-Volume Variance	26,400	
Fixed Overhead Spending Variance	10,650	
Manufacturing Overhead		30,880
Variable Overhead Spending Variance		1,490
Variable Overhead Efficiency Variance		4,680

Variance Disposition

For interim purposes (e.g., preparation of monthly or quarterly financial statements), the standard cost variances calculated in this chapter and in Chapter 14 are typically not disposed of. That is, the variance accounts are carried forward on the balance sheet under the assumption that, over the course of the year, favorable and unfavorable interim variances will offset one another. If interim financial statements are prepared, the cost variances can be shown in a temporary (i.e., holding) account awaiting ultimate disposition at the end of the year.

At the end of the year, the appropriate treatment for standard cost variances depends on the size (materiality) of the net variance. Assume, for example, that variance data for Schmidt from Chapters 14 and 15 relate to the fiscal year, not just the month of October. These cost variances are as follows:

Variance	Source	Amount
DM purchase price variance	Exhibit 14.15	$ 4,350U
DM quantity variance	Exhibit 14.15	10,350U
DL rate variance	Exhibit 14.15	7,020U
DL efficiency variance	Exhibit 14.15	15,600F
Variable overhead spending variance	Exhibit 15.7, Panel 1	1,490F
Variable overhead efficiency variance	Exhibit 15.7, Panel 1	4,680F
Fixed overhead spending variance	Exhibit 15.7, Panel 1	10,650U
Fixed overhead volume variance	Exhibit 15.7, Panel 1	26,400U
Net standard manufacturing cost variance for the year		$37,000U

Net Variance Considered Immaterial

If the net manufacturing cost variance of $37,000U is not considered to be material, then an appropriate treatment at year-end would be to close all variances to Cost of Goods Sold. If the net variance is favorable, then it is closed out by crediting (i.e., reducing) Cost of Goods Sold. If, as in the present case, the net standard cost variance is unfavorable, the Cost of Goods Sold account is debited (i.e., increased) by the amount of the net variance. The following journal entry closes out the net unfavorable variance of $37,000:

Cost of Goods Sold	37,000	
Direct labor efficiency variance	15,600	
Variable overhead efficiency variance	4,680	
Variable overhead spending variance	1,490	
Direct materials purchase price variance		4,350
Direct materials quantity variance		10,350
Direct labor rate variance		7,020
Fixed overhead spending variance		10,650
Fixed overhead volume variance		26,400

EXHIBIT 15.8
Annual Income Statement with Write-Off of the Net Manufacturing Cost Variance

SCHMIDT MACHINERY COMPANY
Income Statement
For 2010

Sales (Exhibit 14.4), at standard selling price	$624,000	
Add: Selling price variance (Exhibit 14.4)	15,600F	
Net sales, at actual selling price		$639,600
Cost of goods sold (at standard: 780 units × $520/unit) (Exhibit.15.2)	$405,600	
Add: Net manufacturing cost variance	+ 37,000U[†]	
Total cost of goods sold		442,600
Gross margin		$197,000
Selling and administrative expenses ($39,000 variable + $30,000 fixed)		69,000
Operating income (before disposition of sales-volume variance)		$128,000

[†] $50F net variable cost variance (Exhibit 14.8) + $37,050U net fixed cost variance (Exhibit 15.7, Panel 1; $10,650U fixed overhead spending variance + $26,400U production-volume variance).

Under the assumption that the results for October represent annual results for the Schmidt Machinery Company, its condensed income statement for 2010 is reflected in Exhibit 15.8. As noted above, this treatment of the net variance for the period is appropriate when the amount involved is considered immaterial.

However, some accountants argue that any variance that results from inefficiencies that could in the judgment of management have been avoided, regardless of amount, should be written off against Cost of Goods Sold rather than carried forward on the balance sheet as is the case with the proration method discussed below. Not to do this implies that asset values reflected on the balance sheet (i.e., inventories) necessarily contain the cost of inefficiencies, a situation that some accountants would dismiss as improper.

Net Variance Considered Material in Amount

If the net manufacturing cost variance is considered material in amount, the net variance should be allocated to the Inventory and Cost of Goods Sold (CGS) accounts. *This allocation should be based on the relative amount of this period's standard cost in the end-of-period balance of each affected account.* This means that the direct materials price variance from Chapter 14 will be apportioned to five accounts—Materials Inventory, the Materials Quantity Variance, WIP Inventory, Finished Goods Inventory, and CGS—based on the amount of this period's standard cost in each account at the end of the period. The direct materials quantity variance would be allocated only to WIP Inventory, Finished Goods Inventory, and CGS. This is because the materials efficiency variance occurs *after* materials are issued to production.

Note that, as a practical matter, some companies allocate the price variance only to ending inventory and CGS accounts. This is, in fact, standard practice for problems on the Uniform CPA exam.

Any labor-cost variances and variable overhead variances would be allocated to WIP Inventory, Finished Goods Inventory, and CGS on the basis of this period's standard labor and standard variable overhead costs, respectively, in these accounts at year-end. The fixed overhead spending variance should be allocated to four accounts: WIP Inventory, Finished Goods Inventory, CGS, and the Production-Volume Variance. The Production-Volume Variance, if allocated, would be apportioned among WIP Inventory, Finished Goods Inventory, and CGS. Finally, we note that for external reporting purposes, accountants need to follow the provisions of Generally Accepted Accounting Principles, which specifies that "abnormal amounts" of idle facility expense should be recognized as current-period charges and not capitalized as part of inventory cost. One implication of this reporting requirement is that the amount of fixed overhead allocated to each unit of production is not increased as a consequence of abnormally low production or an idle plant.

Some companies take a simpler approach to the variance-allocation decision. For example, they may use the total end-of-period account balances, rather than this period's standard cost in each end-of-period account, to allocate the net manufacturing cost variance. Other companies, in particular those that have minimal ending inventories, choose to write off against CGS the net variance, regardless of its size, because most of the variance would be allocated to CGS anyway. Thus, the error of not allocating a portion of the variance to inventories, as well as CGS, is thought to be minimal.

The Effects on Absorption Costing Income of Denominator-Level Choice in Allocating Fixed Overhead

Managing earnings
refers to the manipulation of reported income.

Before leaving this section, we discuss one additional topic, principally because it deals with the issue of **managing earnings** through the selection of the denominator level used to establish the fixed-overhead application rate. We noted earlier in this chapter that alternative denominator-volume levels lead to different (fixed) overhead application rates, which in turn lead to different product costs, and ultimately to different levels of the production-volume variance. The accounting disposition of the production-volume variance essentially provides management with an opportunity to smooth, or manage, income as determined under absorption costing.

Under absorption (i.e., full) costing, a portion of fixed manufacturing overhead costs are either absorbed into or released from inventory, depending on the relationship between production volume and sales volume during the period. For example, for a given level of sales, the production of extra units shifts fixed overhead costs to the balance sheet (inventory) so that reported profit increases with increases in production. The opposite is true if inventory is decreasing. For a given level of sales, decreases in production requires not only this period's fixed overhead to be released as an expense on the income statement, it also implies the release of some previously capitalized fixed overhead costs (from inventory). Thus, for a given level of sales, absorption-costing income decreases as production decreases.

Note, however, a key point: the amount of fixed overhead costs absorbed or released is affected by the denominator level chosen for the predetermined overhead rate. Thus, the effect of a change in inventory can be intensified or reduced based on how the production-volume variance is disposed of at the end of the period. Specifically, this ability to affect reported income is confined to the situation where the production-volume variance is written off entirely to cost of goods sold (CGS), as follows:

- If inventory is *increasing,* choosing a *lower* denominator-volume level will *enhance* the increase in absorption costing income due to the deferral of fixed overhead in inventory.

- If inventory is *decreasing,* choosing a *higher* denominator level will *moderate* the decrease in absorption-costing income due to the release of fixed overhead into CGS.

Thus, it is through the interaction of how the fixed overhead rate is set and how the resulting production-volume variance is accounted for that provides management an opportunity to manage earnings under absorption costing. The above points suggest that managers can increase short-run operating income by: (1) choosing larger denominator levels if they expect inventory to decrease, or (2) choosing smaller denominator levels if they expect inventory to increase. Note, however, that if the production-volume variance is prorated based on the units creating the variance, then the denominator-level choice has no effect on absorption-costing income. This is because prorating this variance effectively changes the budgeted overhead application rate to the actual overhead application rate.

Standard Costs in Service Organizations

LEARNING OBJECTIVE 4

Apply standard costs to service organizations.

As noted in Chapter 14, a standard cost system facilitates planning (i.e., budget preparation) and financial control (through standard-cost variance analysis) and aids managers in making decisions such as product pricing and resource management. These benefits, however, are not limited to manufacturing companies. All organizations can potentially benefit from the use of a standard cost system.

Most costs in a service organization are short-term fixed (i.e., capacity-related) costs. The bulk of labor costs are for professional personnel who usually are paid a monthly salary. Variations from one period to the next for salaried personnel should be small or nonexistent. Other overhead costs for these organizations often consist of expenses related to facilities and equipment and are therefore fixed in the short run. Other service-sector companies have minimal labor relative to capacity-related costs. Examples include the airline industry, the shipping industry, and much of the telecommunications industry. The predominance of capacity-related costs for such companies increases the importance of monitoring fixed-cost spending variances and idle-capacity variances.

Furthermore, service organizations have varied measures of output. Exhibit 15.9 lists some measures of output often used by service organizations. As shown in Exhibit 15.10, hospitals use patient-days to measure output. Colleges and universities use credit-hour production to show their outputs. However, these output measures seldom are perfect indicators of the outputs of service organizations. Patients or their families are likely to place different values on the same number of patient-days, depending on the results of treatments. A patient

EXHIBIT 15.9

Output Measures for Selected Service Organizations

Organization	Output Measure
Airline	Revenue-producing passenger miles
Hospital	Patient days
Hotel	Occupancy rate or number of guests
Accounting, legal, and consulting firms	Professional staff hours
Colleges and universities	Credit hours
Primary and secondary schools	Number of students

REAL-WORLD FOCUS

Matching Capacity and Demand in the Services Industry—How Can IT Help?

The process of determining an appropriate level of capacity is one of the most strategically important decisions that managers must make. Unused capacity wastes resources; insufficient capacity incurs various costs, the most important of which are lost business (opportunity costs) and customer ill-will (and loss of future business). Capacity-related costs are important to service-sector entities, particularly those that compete on the basis of customer service.

One aspect of customer service relates to call centers, which customers (or potential customers) can access to get service-related information. The problem with call centers, however, is that incoming-call volumes fluctuate widely during the day and various times of the week. This complicates efforts to determine the appropriate supply of call-center capacity. Customers hate long waiting times, so it's important for companies to promptly pass calls to an appropriate agent. But that's hard to do in companies employing thousands of agents in different places.

However, new technologies, such as upgrades made to call-routing capabilities, are helping organizations make better capacity-related decisions. One major US airline found that, in spite of a large investment in call-distribution technology, agents in a Midwest call center sat idle while customers waited three minutes or more to speak to identically skilled agents on the West Coast.

This company has taken advantage of recent developments in Internet Protocol (IP) telephony and automated-call-distribution technology that radically improve the delivery of the right call to the right agent at the right time across a number of call centers. A $3 million investment in this new technology allowed the airline to manage calls more effectively and helped reduce operating costs by 5 percent, or $7 million a year, while improving service to meet their preexisting targets.

Source: Wayne E. Pietraszek and Adesh Ramchandran, "Using IT to Boost Call-Center Performance," *The McKinsey Quarterly* (www.mckinseyquarterly.com, accessed March 20, 2006). This article was first published in the Spring 2006 issue of *McKinsey on IT*.

who is cured of an illness is likely to be more pleased with the care received than is the family of a patient who died of the same disease, although the number of patient-days was identical for both. In addition, the amount and type of work performed by a service organization to complete an output unit often varies from one client to the next or from one patient-day to another. The amounts and types of work performed for two patients with identical heart diseases during their 10-day stays can be vastly different although the number of patient-days is identical and their illnesses are the same.

EXHIBIT 15.10

Standard Cost Sheet for a Hospital

Source: Based on Table 14 in *Managerial Cost Accounting for Hospitals* (Chicago: American Hospital Association, 1980), p. 97.

LANCASTER COUNTY HOSPITAL

Standard Cost Sheet for Pediatrics Floor

Direct Expenses	Rate/Price	Amount	Fixed
Salaries and wages:			
Supervisors			$9,000
RNs	$ 30.00 per hour	1.3 hours per patient-day	
LPNs	20.00 per hour	1.7 hours per patient-day	
Nursing assistants	13.00 per hour	0.9 hour per patient-day	
Supplies—Inventory	0.20 per unit	10 units per patient-day	
Supplies—noninventory			300
Pediatrician fees	$ 200 per hour	0.5 hour per patient-day	
Other direct expenses			250
Transferred Expenses			
Housekeeping	$ 10.00 per hour	48 hours + 0.4 hour per patient-day + 1.50 hours per patient discharge	
Laundry	$ 0.50 per pound	500 pounds + 15 pounds per patient-day + 30 pounds per discharge + 50 pounds per surgery	
Allocated Expenses			
Personnel	$ 0.16 per hour	242 hours + 3.9 hours per patient-day	
Other administrative and general	$ 6.00 per hour	118 hours + 0.05 hour per patient-day + 1.5 hours per patient discharge	

The differences in operating characteristics between service organizations and typical manufacturing companies make it a necessity to modify standard cost systems before applying them to service organizations.

Overhead Cost Variances in ABC Systems

LEARNING OBJECTIVE 5

Analyze overhead variances in an activity-based cost (ABC) system.

The manufacturing environment has evolved over the last few decades and many new management techniques have been developed during this period to emphasize continual improvement, total quality management, and managing activities rather than cost. These emphases have changed product costing, strategic and operational decisions, and cost-determination methods, as discussed in the preceding chapters. They also influence the ways in which many firms use standard cost systems as management tools, including the preparation of flexible budgets, the selection of performance-evaluation criteria, and the implication of reported variances.

ABC-Based Flexible Budgets for Control

Because a number of different activities influence factory overhead costs, the accountant needs to carefully select the activity measure, or measures, that will be used to construct the flexible budget for control purposes. The Schmidt Machinery Company, as illustrated thus far in the chapter, uses a single, volume-based activity measure (direct labor hours) for allocating overhead costs to outputs and for determining standard cost variances for control purposes.

As described in Chapter 5, more modern cost systems, such as activity-based costing (ABC) systems, apply manufacturing support (i.e., factory overhead) costs to outputs on the basis of activities performed for each product produced. That is, ABC attempts to assign manufacturing support costs to products on the basis of the resource demands, or resource consumption, of each output. To accomplish this, ABC systems use a broader set of activity measures, both volume-related and non-volume-related, in the cost-allocation process.

Cooper has developed a framework, in the form of a hierarchy, for classifying different types of activity measures used in ABC systems.[7] Cooper's framework classifies manufacturing support costs as unit-based, batch-level, product-level, or facilities-level. Unit-based measures are related to output volume and include machine hours, direct labor hours, units of output, and units of raw materials. Batch-level activity measures include the number of production setups, the number of times materials and parts are moved during the manufacturing process, and the number of receipts of materials. Product-level activity measures typically relate to engineering support activities and can include things such as number of products, number of processes, number of engineering change orders (ECOs), and number of schedule changes. At the top of the cost hierarchy are facilities-level costs, which are related to the capacity or ability to produce, not to the variety of outputs, the number of batches produced, or the volume of output.

Exhibit 15.11 illustrates a traditional flexible (control) budget prepared for a company that applies factory overhead cost to outputs on the basis of standard direct labor hours, similar in nature to the example discussed thus far in this chapter. The master budget in this exhibit is based on a planned output of 3,000 units for the period (1,500 standard labor hours). The flexible budget is based on the actual output of the period, 2,000 units (or, equivalently, 1,000 standard labor hours). The company in this example spent 1,200 direct labor hours to manufacture the 2,000 units. Exhibit 15.12 shows a typical financial report for manufacturing costs incurred during the period.

By contrast, Exhibit 15.13 illustrates a flexible budget for the period prepared under ABC. This representation specifies that manufacturing costs are assigned to outputs on the basis of multiple activity measures. In the present example, three different volume-related activity measures are used (units produced, direct labor hours, and machine hours) as well as one non-volume-related activity (number of production setups). Note that there is a single facility-level cost, insurance, that essentially has no well-defined activity variable. Because this cost is not related to volume of output, or number of batches, or number of products, it is allocated

---

[7] R. Cooper, "Cost Classification in Unit-Based and Activity-Based Manufacturing Cost Systems," *Journal of Cost Management for the Manufacturing Industry,* Fall 1990, pp. 4–14.

EXHIBIT 15.11 **Master Budget and Traditional Flexible Budget for Control**

Cost Elements			Flexible Budget for 2,000 Units (1,000 standard direct labor hours)	Master Budget for 3,000 Units (1,500 standard direct labor hours)
Variable	**Fixed**	**Cost Item**		
$20/unit		Direct materials	$ 40,000	$ 60,000
30/Direct labor hour		Direct labor	30,000	45,000
2/Direct labor hour		Indirect material	2,000	3,000
5/Direct labor hour		Repair and maintenance	5,000	7,500
	$ 5,000	Receiving	5,000	5,000
	30,000	Insurance	30,000	30,000
	75,000	Setup	75,000	75,000
		Total	$187,000	$225,500

EXHIBIT 15.12

Traditional Financial Performance Report

Generally Accepted Accounting Principles,	Actual Cost	Flexible Budget Based on Output	Flexible Budget Variance
Direct materials	$ 50,000	$ 40,000	$10,000U
Direct labor	36,000	30,000	6,000U
Indirect materials	3,000	2,000	1,000U
Repair and maintenance	6,500	5,000	1,500U
Receiving	3,000	5,000	2,000F
Insurance	30,000	30,000	—
Setup	50,000	75,000	25,000F
Total	$178,500	$187,000	$ 8,500F

to products using a systematic, but essentially arbitrary, method, such as square feet in the factory devoted to the production of each product.

Compared to the simpler control budget presented in Exhibit 15.11, the ABC-based flexible budget presented in Exhibit 15.13 provides more accurate representation of the manufacturing costs that should have been incurred for the production of 2,000 units. A financial-performance report for the period, based on the ABC flexible budget, is presented in Exhibit 15.14.

EXHIBIT 15.13 **Representation of Manufacturing Costs under an ABC System**

		Cost Function			
Data	**Activity Measure**	**Variable**	**Fixed**	**Flexible (Control) Budget**	**Master (Static) Budget**
Operating Data					
Output	Number of units			2,000 units	3,000 units
Standard Direct labor hours				1,000 hours	1,500 hours
Standard Machine hours				300,000 hours	450,000 hours
Number of setups				2 setups	3 setups
Cost Data					
Direct materials	Number of units	$20/unit	—	$ 40,000	$ 60,000
Direct labor	Direct labor hours	$30/hour, 0.5 hour/unit	—	30,000	45,000
Indirect materials	Direct labor hours	$2/direct labor hour	—	2,000	3,000
Repair and maintenance	Machine hours	$0.01/machine hour	$ 3,000	6,000	7,500
Receiving	Number of setups	$1,500/setup	500	3,500	5,000
Setup	Number of setups	$25,000/setup	—	50,000	75,000
Insurance	Facility-level		$30,000	30,000	30,000
Total				$161,500	$225,500

Destin Brass Products, Inc., located in Destin, Florida, has three product lines for fluid distribution systems: pumps, valves, and flow controllers. All products produced by the company are made of high-quality brass and are produced on the same manufacturing equipment. However, the products differ significantly in terms of their consumption of manufacturing support resources. The pump line consists of a more-or-less standardized product with no distinguishing characteristics. Pumps are produced in a single lot per month and are sold to a single customer; relatively small amounts of engineering support are needed for this product line. Flow controllers, on the other hand, are sold to a number of distributors, require high levels of engineering support, and have many more parts as compared to pumps. The company originally used a single volume-based activity measure (direct labor dollars) to apply manufacturing overhead costs to each of the three product lines.

The traditional cost system was replaced by a rudimentary ABC system and then a slightly more complex ABC system that applied manufacturing support (i.e., factory overhead) costs to products on the basis of a number of volume-based and non-volume-based activities. Indicated manufacturing costs for representative products in each of the three product lines under each of the three systems differed, and in some cases by a substantial amount.

One of the functions of the ABC system was to be able to predict cost incurrence at different activity and output levels. Managers found out that the cost of the more complex and resource-demanding product was seriously distorted under the traditional and under the simple ABC system. In fact, this product was being "subsidized" by the over-costing associated with the high-volume product line. Cost distortions under the old system were attributable to the fact that the system allocated manufacturing support costs using a volume-based activity measure. The ABC system was better able to budget manufacturing support costs based on the resource demands that each product line made on the organization. In turn, this information was used by management for pricing, process design, and cost-control purposes.

Source: William J. Bruns, Jr., *Destin Brass Products Co.,* Harvard Business School Case #9-190-089.

EXHIBIT 15.14 Financial-Performance Report Using ABC

	Cost Incurred	Flexible (Control) Budget	Flexible-Budget Variance
Direct materials	$ 50,000	$ 40,000 (2,000 units × $20 per unit)	$10,000U
Direct labor	36,000	30,000 (2,000 units × 0.5 hour per unit × $30 per hour)	6,000U
Indirect materials	3,000	2,000 (1,000 hours × $2 per hour)	1,000U
Repair and maintenance	6,500	6,000 [(300,000 machine hours × $0.01 per machine hour) + $3,000]	500U
Receiving	3,000	3,500 [(2 setups × $1,500 per setup) + $500]	500F
Insurance	30,000	30,000 ($30,000 per period)	—
Setup	50,000	50,000 (2 setups × $25,000 per setup)	—
Total	$178,500	$161,500	$17,000U

The total manufacturing cost flexible-budget variance for the period, based on a traditional costing system, is $8,500, favorable (Exhibit 15.12). In contrast, the ABC approach yields a $17,000 unfavorable variance for the same period (Exhibit 15.14). Exhibit 15.15 compares these short-run financial-performance reports.

Exhibit 15.15 demonstrates that cost variances identified using a traditional approach (single activity for applying factory overhead) can be misleading. Substantial differences are found in variances for repair and maintenance, receiving, and setups. The traditional

EXHIBIT 15.15

Financial Performance Reports: Comparison of Traditional and ABC Approaches

	Variance		
	Traditional	Activity-Based	Difference
Direct materials	$10,000U	$10,000U	—
Direct labor	6,000U	6,000U	—
Indirect materials	1,000U	1,000U	—
Repair and maintenance	1,500U	500U	$ 1,000
Receiving	2,000F	500F	1,500
Insurance	—	—	—
Setup	25,000F	—	25,000
Total	$ 8,500F	$17,000U	$25,500

approach in our example considers repair and maintenance a cost that varies with direct labor hours. In contrast, the ABC approach identifies repair and maintenance as a mixed cost with the variable portion of the cost varying with machine hours. As a result, the cost variance for repair and maintenance decreases from $1,500 unfavorable to $500 unfavorable. The traditional approach considers both receiving and setups as fixed costs while the ABC approach classifies these two overhead costs as variable, batch-related costs. As illustrated in Exhibit 15.15, the difference in the net variance between these two approaches is $25,500.

Flexible-Budget Analysis under ABC When There Is a Standard Batch Size for Production Activity

When production occurs in a standard (i.e., predetermined) batch size, the accountant can modify the preceding ABC analysis to provide more detailed information regarding the cause of any observed overhead cost variances. In the sections below we discuss these procedures within the context of production-related setup costs.

Fixed Setup Costs Under ABC

The short-term fixed cost component of setup costs is controlled using the same procedures discussed previously in this chapter. That is, the difference between actual fixed setup costs and budgeted fixed setup costs is called a *spending* (or, *flexible-budget*) *variance.* And, the difference between the fixed setup costs allocated to production and budgeted fixed setup costs is called a *production-volume variance.* The only complicating factor in terms of calculating the latter is the possible need to convert actual units produced to standard number of batches. This is necessary only when setup-related support costs are allocated on the basis of *setup hours* (not number of setups). We make this conversion by dividing actual output by the standard (i.e., budgeted or planned) batch size.

Variable Setup Costs Under ABC

If output is produced in a standard batch size, we must first convert (as we did above for fixed setup-related costs) the actual output of the period to number of standard batches allowed. We then convert this to the standard allowed setup hours. This latter figure, when multiplied by the standard variable setup cost per setup hour gives us the flexible budget for variable setup overhead costs. As we did earlier in the chapter, we then define the total flexible-budget variance for variable setup overhead as the difference between actual variable setup costs and the flexible budget for variable setup overhead costs. Finally, this total flexible-budget variance is decomposed into a *spending variance* and an *efficiency variance* using the procedures discussed earlier.

Interpretation of Setup-Related Standard Cost Variances

Management accountants can add value to their organization by accompanying cost-variance data with plausible explanations for these variances. This holds true regardless of whether the organization in question is using a traditional cost system or an ABC system. *Fixed-spending variances* for setup activities are likely to be relatively small but could arise if new setup equipment were leased or if the leasing charge actually incurred on setup equipment was different from the planned amount. They might also occur if salaries paid to supervisors or engineers allocated to setup activity are different from those planned. The production-volume variance for fixed setup costs can be viewed roughly as a measure of capacity utilization. One limitation of this interpretation, however, is the fact that it does not consider the income effect of reduced output. That is, lower-than-anticipated output volume could have been sold at a higher-than-budgeted selling price, thereby resulting in a net increase to short-term operating profit.

The *variable setup spending variance* exists because the actual variable cost per setup hour was different from the budgeted cost per setup hour. The interpretation of this variance follows the interpretation discussed earlier in this chapter. That is, this variance is partly due to the fact that the actual quantity of individual resources (e.g., energy) was different per setup hour than planned and/or the prices paid for these items were different from planned amounts. The *variable setup efficiency variance* is due to the actual number of setup hours, for the actual output of the period, being different from the standard setup hours allowed. This variance could be due to batch size being different from the planned size and/or a different number of setup hours per batch compared with standard.

Extension of ABC Analysis: GPK and RCA

GPK and **resource consumption accounting (RCA)** are two other sophisticated cost-management systems that are being proposed as extensions to ABC systems. Both GPK and RCA can be used to allocate indirect (i.e., support) costs across the value chain. Both of these systems rely on a significant number of cost centers and cost-allocation pools—far more than are typically found in an ABC system. As such, both GPK and RCA are usually paired with an enterprise resource planning (ERP) system that tracks and maintains detailed information regarding resources and activities associated with business processes.

GPK is a German cost-management system that attempts to establish a strong relationship between resources consumed and the appropriate cost driver. Notably, GPK distinguishes between flexible and short-term fixed (capacity-related) resources. In contrast, ABC systems typically embrace a long-term or strategic time horizon. Thus, GPK is proposed as a tool for managing short-run financial performance. RCA on the other hand, is a combination of ABC and GPK. Therefore, it is a mix of activity-based and direct assignment based on resource consumption. Proponents of RCA maintain that RCA provides increased product-cost accuracy because it only includes the cost of resources used.

Implementation results for RCA and GPK to date suggest that these systems are more effective in large organizations that have highly routine and repetitive operations. Such a context would seem conducive to the construction of the many resource cost pools characteristic of RCA and GPK. It will be interesting to see whether these systems for short-term planning and cost control will gain acceptance in the United States. As indicated in Chapter 5, some U.S. companies have been reluctant to implement an ABC system because of the perceived complexity. RCA and GPK systems would seem to be even more complex. Thus, additional experimentation in the United States is needed before we are able to draw a conclusion regarding the role of these systems. It may be the case that there is room for both ABC systems and more detailed systems such as RCA and GPK. The former may yield relevant information for strategic decision making, while the latter may be used for short-term financial control.

Supplementing Financial Results with Nonfinancial Performance Indicators

As is the case for the material presented in Chapter 14, the cost variances covered in this chapter are directed at what might be called *financial control*. These variances are calculated through the use of standard cost information and the use of flexible budgets. The overall intent of these variances is to tell management whether the organization is meeting its short-term financial goals. In the case of for-profit entities, financial control looks at the drivers of short-term profit, for example, the organization's ability to control costs for a given level of sales. Students of accounting should keep in mind, however, that financial control should be viewed as part of a larger and more comprehensive management accounting and control system.

The cost variances we cover in Chapters 14 and 15 are inherently limited because they relate only to *short-term* financial performance. As such, they are subject to the same criticisms as any other short-term performance measure. That is, the amount of variance can, at least to some extent, be manipulated in the short run. For example, production-volume variances can be decreased by increasing production (thereby absorbing more fixed overhead costs into inventory). Spending variances for fixed overhead items can be affected by managerial choice: cutting so-called discretionary spending on short-term fixed overhead will lead to favorable spending variances for fixed overhead costs.

GPK

is a detailed German cost accounting system, roughly translated as *flexible standard costing*.

Resource consumption accounting (RCA)

is a comprehensive cost-management system represented as a cross between GPK and ABC.

As indicated elsewhere in this chapter, the issue of capacity-resource management is important for a wide range of industries and companies. There are real and significant costs of having excess capacity (i.e., idle capacity and overspending on resources) and insufficient capacity (which results in opportunity costs). Because capacity-related costs tend to be fixed in the short term (and therefore not easily changed), the management of capacity-related spending is of strategic importance to many organizations. Recently, so-called German accounting (GPK) and resource-consumption accounting (RCA) have been proposed as alternatives to traditional cost-management systems used in the United States. Among other things, proponents of these systems maintain that such systems provide more decision-relevant information, including information regarding capacity management and resource spending. Both GPK and RCA include the use of a large number of resource cost centers (far more than the number used in conventional ABC systems), the breakdown of costs into (short-term) fixed and variable components, the use of replacement cost depreciation, a sophisticated ERP system for processing a large volume of data, and the use of practical (or even theoretical) capacity for setting cost-allocation rates. As a student of accounting you should be aware of these alternative cost-information systems.

Sources: Carl S. Smith, "Going for GPK—Stihl Moves toward This Costing System in the U.S.," *Strategic Finance,* April 2005, pp. 36–39; Brian Mackie, "Merging GPK and ABC on the Road to RCA," *Strategic Finance,* November 2006, pp. 33–39; B. Douglas Clinton and Sally A. Webber, "RCA at Clopay," *Management Accounting Quarterly,* October 2004, pp. 21–26; Kip R. Krumwiede, "Rewards and Realities of German Cost Accounting," *Strategic Finance* (April 2005), pp. 27–34; Anton van der Merwe and David E. Keyes, "The Case for Resource Consumption Accounting," *Strategic Finance,* April 2002, pp. 1–6.

We know, too, that financial measures (such as the cost variances discussed in this chapter and in Chapter 14) don't tell us what is wrong with a process or operation. They can tell us that perhaps something is wrong (because the financial results are not as expected), but we generally need to rely on an accompanying analysis of nonfinancial performance indicators to determine *why* operations are not proceeding as planned. For example, we might monitor quality, customer-response time, the ability to meet production schedules, employee motivation, employee safety, and the organization's commitment to ethical, social, and environmental commitments. In short, if a subunit of an organization is evaluated solely on the basis of its short-term financial performance (e.g., cost control), employees of that unit may ignore the unmeasured attributes of performance, such as quality and manufacturing cycle time. It is precisely for this reason that the notion of a balanced scorecard (BSC) as a strategic management system is of value. We discussed the BSC in Chapter 2 and will discuss it in greater detail in Chapter 18.

Finally, there is a question as to the appropriate role of financial-performance data for operating personnel. Certainly, managers of operating units require periodic financial-performance results. At the operational level, however, employees are probably better served with nonfinancial performance data, presumably on as close to a real-time basis as possible. These nonfinancial measures are likely predictors (i.e., leading indicators) of financial performance. As well, they are expressed in terms of that operating personnel can understand. Examples would include actual machine hours consumed per unit produced, actual energy consumption (e.g., kilowatt-hours) per machine hour, amount of indirect materials consumed per unit (or batch) of output, percentage of first-pass yields, and so on.

Investigation of Variances

LEARNING OBJECTIVE 6

Understand decision rules that can be used to guide the variance-investigation decision.

Identifying and reporting cost variances are the first steps in reducing variances and improving financial performance. Not all variances call for investigation and corrective action, however. In general, the proper response to a variance depends on the causes and degree of controllability of the variance.

In this and the preceding chapter, we abstracted from reality by assuming that production for a period equaled sales for the period, that is, that there was no change in inventory during the period. Although this is certainly possible, particularly for companies that embrace a JIT philosophy, the assumption is not reasonable for many other companies. We note, for example, that sales-related variances (discussed in Chapter 16) should logically be based on units *sold* while manufacturing-related variances (discussed in Chapters 14 and 15) should be based on *production volume*. So, this raises the question of how to account in the profit-variance model discussed in Chapters 14 and 15 for both planned and unplanned changes in inventory (i.e.,

for imbalances between production-volume and sales volume during a period). This issue has been addressed in the following article: R. Balakrishnan and G. B. Sprinkle, "Integrating Profit Variances and Capacity Costing to Provide Better Managerial Information," *Issues in Accounting Education* 17, no. 2 (May 2002), pp. 149–161.

Access the above reading and provide an explanation as to how the conventional profit-variance report can be expanded to include changes in inventory, both planned and unplanned. Also, discuss how the resulting variance information would be useful to managers.

(Refer to Comments on Cost Management in Action at end of Chapter.)

Causes and Controllability

Random variances
are variances beyond the control of management, either technically or financially, and often are considered as uncontrollable variances.

The causes of variances and the controllability of variances fall into two categories: random and systematic. **Random variances** are beyond the control of management, either technically or financially, and are often considered as *uncontrollable variances*. Many standards are point estimates of long-term average performance. Small variances in either direction occur in operations, and firms usually cannot benefit from investigating or responding to them. For example, prices of goods or services acquired in open markets fluctuate with, among other factors, supply and demand at the time of acquisition and the amount of time allowed to acquire the goods or services. These variances are essentially random and require no management action.

Systematic variances
are variances that, until corrected, are likely to continue.

Systematic variances, by contrast, are persistent and are likely to recur until corrected. They usually are controllable by management or can be eliminated or reduced through actions of management. Systematic variances that are material in amount require prompt corrective action. Among causes for systematic variances are errors in prediction, modeling, measurement, and implementation. Each of these factors has its own implications regarding the need for further investigation or proper managerial action to correct the variance. Exhibit 15.16 classifies variances according to controllability, causes, and actions to be taken.

A **prediction error**
is a deviation from the standard because of inaccurate estimations.

Prediction errors result from inaccurate estimation of the amounts of variables included in the standard-setting process. For example, management expected a 5 percent price increase for a direct material when the price increased 10 percent, or it expected to have adequate $15-per-hour workers available when a shortage forced the firm to hire workers at $25 per hour.

Modeling errors
are failures in not including all relevant variables or including wrong or irrelevant variables.

Modeling errors result from failing to include all relevant variables or from including wrong or irrelevant ones in the standard-setting process. For example, a modeling error occurs when a firm uses the production rate of experienced workers as a standard, although most of its workers are new hires with little or no experience. The unfavorable direct labor efficiency

EXHIBIT 15.16 Cause of Variance and Indicated Corrective Action

Controllability	Cause	Corrective Action	Example
Uncontrollable (random)	Random error	None	Overtime wages paid to make up time lost by employees ill with the flu Materials lost in a fire
Controllable (systematic)	Prediction error	Modify standard-setting processes	Increases in materials prices faster than expected
	Modeling error	Revise model or modeling process	Failure to consider learning-curve effect in estimating product costs Not allowing for normal materials lost
	Measurement error	Adjust accounting procedure	Bonus attributed to the period paid, not in the period earned Costs assigned to wrong jobs
	Implementation error	Take proper actions to correct the causes	Failure to provide proper training for the task

variance that the firm experiences is a result of modeling error, not of inefficient operations. The standard of making 100 gallons of output from every 100 gallons of input material is a modeling error when the manufacturing process has a 5 percent normal evaporation rate. Corrective actions for both prediction and modeling errors require the firm to change its standard and the standard-setting process.

Measurement errors
are uses of incorrect numbers because of improper or inaccurate accounting systems or procedures.

Measurement errors are uses of incorrect numbers because of improper or inaccurate accounting systems or procedures. Including bonuses for extraordinary productivity as a cost of the period in which the bonuses are paid rather than the period in which they are earned is a measurement error. Charging overhead incurred for setups based on direct production labor hours rather than the number of setups is a measurement error. Corrective actions for measurement errors include redesigning the firm's accounting system or procedures.

Implementation errors
are deviations from the standard due to operator errors.

Implementation errors are deviations from the standard due to operator errors. Unfavorable materials usage variances from using materials of lesser quality than those specified by the standard are implementation errors. The direct labor rate or efficiency variance in an operation that assigned workers with a different skill level than the one called for in the standard is an implementation error. Setting a cutting machine to cut tubes in lengths of 2 feet 9.7 inches, instead of 2 feet 10 inches as required, is an implementation error.

Some implementation errors are temporary and disappear in subsequent periods in the normal course of operations. Other implementation errors could be persistent and reappear until the firm takes proper corrective action. An incorrectly set cutting machine continues to manufacture products with wrong lengths until the problem is corrected. Use of wrong or excessive materials in production, on the other hand, might occur in one or only a few production runs.

Role of Control Chart

Managers and employees can use control charts to identify random versus systematic variances. A control chart plots measures of an activity or event over time; this widely used tool helps managers identify out-of-control variances. A control chart has a horizontal axis, a vertical axis, a horizontal line at the level of the desirable characteristic, and one or two additional horizontal lines for the allowable range of variation. The horizontal line represents time intervals, batch numbers, or production runs. The vertical line denotes scales for the characteristic of interest, such as the amount of the cost variance. Upper and lower limits indicate the allowable range of the variance. Variances within these limits are deemed random and no further action is needed unless a pattern emerges.

It is management's responsibility to set upper and lower control limits in control charts. When the control limits are established using a statistical procedure, the chart is called a

A **statistical control chart**
sets control limits using a statistical procedure.

statistical control chart. Please see Chapter 17 for a fuller discussion of the use of control charts.

The chapter Appendix examines a cost-benefit approach to the variance-investigation decision.

Summary

Establishing standard overhead application rates requires selection of appropriate activity measures. These rates can be determined using relatively simple procedures (e.g., a single, volume-related activity measure) or more sophisticated procedures, such as ABC. Recently, both GPK and RCA systems have been proposed as extensions to ABC systems. The resulting standard-cost data can be used both for product-costing purposes and, through their inclusion in flexible budgets, control purposes.

For control purposes, actual overhead costs (both variable and fixed) are compared to flexible-budget costs. A summary of the overhead cost variances realized by the Schmidt Machinery Company for October 2010 is presented in Exhibit 15.17. This exhibit is a variant of the model presented earlier in Exhibit 15.7. Both exhibits are general in nature and therefore can be used in a four-variance, a three-variance, and a two-variance approach to subdivide the total overhead variance for the period. Feel free to use whichever of the two models you find more appealing.

EXHIBIT 15.17
Overhead Variance Analysis
Summary: Schmidt Machinery
Company, October 2010

Variable Overhead: Standard Cost Variance Analysis—Alternative Format

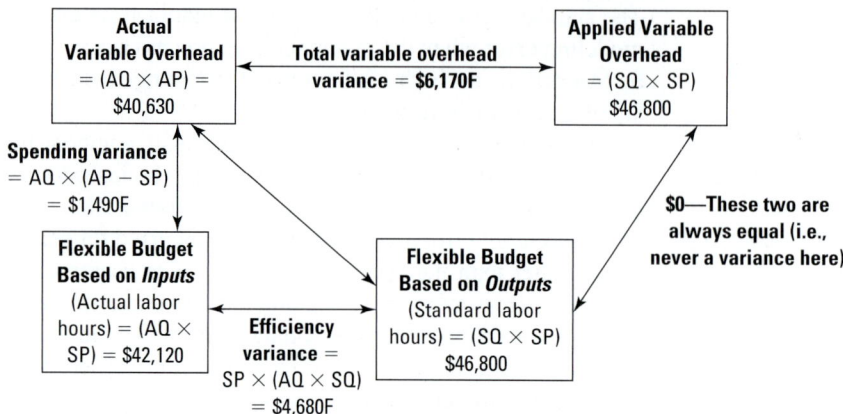

Legend: SQ = Standard labor hours allowed for units produced = 3,900
AQ = Actual labor hours worked during the period = 3,510
SP = Standard variable overhead cost = $12/hour
AP = Actual variable overhead cost per labor hour = $11.5755 (rounded)
Total variable overhead variance = Spending variance + Efficiency variance

Fixed Overhead: Standard Cost Variance Analysis—Alternative Format

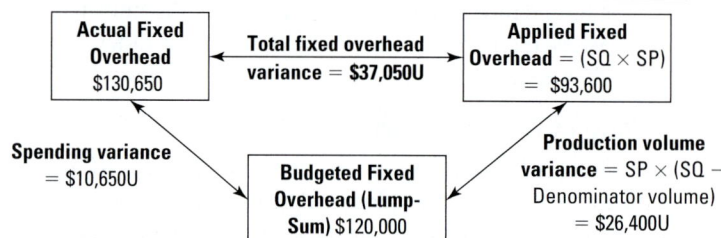

Legend: SQ = Standard labor hours allowed for units produced = 3,900 hours
SP = Standard fixed overhead cost = $24/hour
Denominator volume = Number of labor hours used to calculate the predetermined
  fixed overhead application rate = 1,000 units × 5 hours/unit = 5,000 hours
Total fixed overhead variance = Spending (budget) variance + Production-
  volume variance

As indicated in Exhibit 15.17, the *total variable overhead variance* (also referred to as the total *variable overhead flexible-budget variance* or the *total over- or underapplied variable overhead* for the period) is calculated as the difference between actual variable overhead cost for the period and the flexible budget for variable overhead based on *output* (i.e., based on allowed activity for the number of units manufactured during the period). Variable overhead spending and efficiency variances are components of the total variable overhead variance. The variable overhead efficiency variance reflects efficiency or inefficiency in the use of the activity measure used to construct the flexible budget; in the case of the Schmidt Machinery Company, this activity measure is direct labor hours. The spending variance for variable overhead reflects the fact that spending on variable overhead items, per direct labor hour, was different from planned spending. As such, this variance reflects both price effects and usage (efficiency) effects. The ability to disentangle these effects, however, requires detailed information about budgeted prices and budgeted quantities of individual variable overhead items.

Exhibit 15.17 also indicates a *total fixed overhead variance* for the period, which is also called the *total over- or underapplied fixed overhead for the period*. This variance can be decomposed into a fixed overhead spending variance and a production-volume variance. The former variance is defined as the difference between the actual fixed overhead costs and the budgeted (lump-sum) fixed overhead costs for the period. If management desires, this total variance can be broken down on a line-item basis. The production-volume variance exists only because of the product costing need to assign a share of fixed overhead costs to each unit produced. To do this, the accountant develops a fixed overhead allocation rate, which is defined as budgeted fixed overhead cost divided by an assumed level of activity, called the *denominator volume.* If the denominator volume is defined as *practical capacity,* then the resulting production-volume variance can be thought of as a rough (and admittedly incomplete) measure of the cost of unused capacity. Some organizations choose to report the production-volume variance in physical terms only.

You should remember that, in practice, different terms are used to describe the same overhead variance. Thus, you are advised in constructing any performance reports to clearly define the meaning of each variance contained in the report.

If a company uses a standard cost system, it records inventory and CGS amounts at standard cost. In such a system, variances from standard cost are recorded in separate accounts. At the end of the year, the company can dispose of standard-cost variances by charging them to CGS. Alternatively, the company can prorate the variances among the cost of goods sold, ending work-in-process inventory, and ending finished goods inventory. For materials price variances, the proration should include the materials ending inventory and materials usage variance. Generally Accepted Accounting Principles (viz., FASB ASC 330-10-30—available at www.asc.fasb.org) provide guidance for disposing of production-volume variances for external-reporting purposes.

Uses of standard cost systems are not limited to manufacturing operations; service firms and other organizations also can benefit from using them. Because operating characteristics of service firms often differ from those of manufacturing firms, modifications might be needed and emphases could be different when using standard costs in a service organization.

Changes in manufacturing environments in recent years have motivated changes in cost systems. Increasingly, companies are using systems with multiple activity measures, both volume-based and non-volume-based. Flexible budgets based on ABC systems provide more accurate data for cost-control purposes. The use of practical capacity for establishing ABC rates yields relevant information regarding the existence and cost of unused capacity. This information can be used over time for resource-capacity planning. For operational control purposes, financial results such as the cost variances reported in this chapter (and in Chapter 14), should be accompanied by relevant nonfinancial performance indicators.

Standard cost variances can be thought of as information signals. Whether to investigate a particular variance is a function of the assumed cause of the variance. Causes of variances can be random or systematic. The former generally require no follow-up, while the latter require some type of intervention on by managers. Control charts can be used to isolate random versus nonrandum variances. The Appendix discusses the variance-investigation decision under uncertainty.

APPENDIX

Variance Investigation Decisions under Uncertainty

Investigation of variances costs time and money. Managers must weigh the anticipated costs of investigation against the anticipated benefits in deciding whether to investigate a particular variance. The purpose of investigation is to determine the underlying cause of the variance in order to take appropriate corrective action.

As noted in the chapter, the states of nature underlying a variance can be either *random* or *systematic.* The alternative actions available to management when facing a variance are either to conduct an investigation or to take no action. With two possible states of nature and two courses of action, there are four combinations, each of which entails a different "cost" to the organization. These four combinations follow:

IR Investigate and conclude that the reported variance is a random fluctuation. No further action is needed.

IN Investigate and conclude that the reported variance is a result of systematic (i.e., non-random) causes. Management may need to take corrective action.

NR Do not investigate and the reported variance is a result of random variations.

NN Do not investigate and the reported variance is a result of systematic (i.e., non-random) causes.

PAYOFF TABLE

The cost to the firm for different courses of action and states of nature is likely to be different. Exhibit 15A.1 shows the consequences of alternative management actions under different states of nature. The cost of an investigation is represented as **I.** When the variance is the result of a nonrandom factor, the cost to the firm to correct the variance is **C.** The cost of correction includes the cost to correct the nonrandom factor that led to the variance and the cost of the process being out of control until the variance is corrected. If management decides not to investigate the reported variance and the variance is systematic and persistent, the firm suffers a total cost equal to **L** (the present value of all losses the firm will suffer before the next decision point).

The decision not to investigate is correct when the variance is a random occurrence. In this situation, the firm wastes no resources at all; it will, however, suffer a loss of *L* if the reported variance is the result of a nonrandom cause.

Management should also estimate the likelihood that the operation (e.g., raw material usage) is in control or out of control, based on its understanding of the state of nature of the operation. Being "in control" implies that the reported variance is in all likelihood a random phenomenon. Being "out of control" suggests that the reported variance is the result of one or more systematic causes. The estimated probabilities of the states of nature enable management to compute the expected costs for each alternative action. These expected costs then serve as the input to the variance-investigation decision.

Assume that upon receiving a variance report, management estimates the probability to be 90 percent that the reported variance is a random fluctuation. The cost to conduct an investigation is approximately $1,000. Corrective actions, if needed, will likely cost the firm approximately $5,000, including the loss realized from the process being out of control until the underlying problem is corrected. Assume that the firm will suffer losses with a present value of $30,000 if it conducts no investigation and if the variance stemmed from a nonrandom cause. Exhibit 15A.2 summarizes this information.

Management has a 90 percent chance of finding that the variance is merely a random fluctuation and that an investigation, if conducted, would be a waste of time and resources. However, there is a 10 percent chance that the variance results from one or more nonrandom factors that should be corrected to avoid further losses. With the cost of investigation, $1,000, and the cost of corrective action, $5,000, the firm's total cost will be $6,000 if the investigation finds that the cause of the variance is nonrandom. The expected value of investigation is, therefore, $1,500, as follows:

$$E(\text{Investigate}) = (\$1,000 \times 90\%) + (\$6,000 \times 10\%) = \$1,500$$

The states of nature in Exhibit 15A.2 suggest a 90 percent chance that the variance is random. The firm incurs no cost if it decides not to investigate. However, there is a

EXHIBIT 15A.1

Payoff Table for Variance-Investigation Decision

Management Action	States of Nature	
	Random	Nonrandom
Investigate	*I*	*I + C*
Do not investigate	none	*L*

EXHIBIT 15A.2

Payoff Table: Assumed Data

Management Action	States of Nature (probability)		Expected Value
	Random (90%)	Nonrandom (10%)	
Investigate	$1,000	$6,000	$1,500
Do not investigate	0	30,000	3,000

10 percent chance that the variance is a result of one or more nonrandom factors. The firm is likely to suffer a total loss of $30,000 if the variance is a result of one or more nonrandom factors and management allows the variance to continue by conducting no investigation. Thus, the expected cost of the decision to not investigate the cause of the variance is $3,000, as shown here:

$$E(\text{Do not investigate}) = (\$0 \times 90\%) + (\$30,000 \times 10\%) = \$3,000$$

The $1,500 expected cost of investigation is lower than the $3,000 cost of not investigating. Thus, according to the payoff table, the firm will incur a lower cost (on average) if it conducts an investigation to find the cause of the reported variance and then takes appropriate action based on the finding of the investigation.

INDIFFERENCE PROBABILITY

Indifference probability is the probability regarding States of Nature that makes management indifferent between courses of action.

In a form of sensitivity analysis, managers can use a payoff table to determine the maximum probability level for a nonrandom variance to occur. As long as the probability for a nonrandom variance is at or below the calculated probability, then according to the payoff table the preferred action is *not* to investigate the cause of the reported variance.

Let p be the probability for a nonrandom variance to occur. Then the probability of a random variance is $1 - p$. Exhibit 15A.3 shows the payoff table.

The expected costs of management actions can be represented as follows:

$$E(\text{Investigate}) = [I \times (1 - p)] + [(I + C) \times p]$$

and

$$E(\text{Do not investigate}) = L \times p$$

If the expected cost of each action is the same, it makes no difference to the firm which course of action is taken. That is, for management to be indifferent to either course of action (to investigate or not to investigate), the expected costs must be equal. Therefore, at the indifference point:

$$\left[I \times (1 - p)\right] + \left[(I + C) \times p\right] = L \times p$$

Simplifying the above equation, we get

$$I + (C \times p) = L \times p$$

Rewritten,

$$p = \frac{I}{L - C}$$

For data presented in Exhibit 15A.2, the indifference probability is 4 percent:

$$p = \frac{\$1,000}{\$30,000 - \$5,000} = 4\%$$

This result suggests that if the probability is 4 percent for the cause of variance to be one or more nonrandom factors, it makes no difference which course of action management takes. The expected final cost of taking either course of action will be the same. The optimal action is to conduct an investigation when the probability for nonrandom factors exceeds 4 percent. If the probability for a nonrandom cause is below 4 percent, the optimal action is not to investigate.

EXHIBIT 15A.3
Using a Payoff Table to Determine Indifference Probability

Management Action	States of Nature	
	Random (1 − p)	Nonrandom (p)
Investigate	I	I + C
Do not investigate	0	L

Key Terms

budgeted capacity
utilization, *652*
death-spiral effect, *655*
denominator activity level, *652*
denominator volume, *652*
expected value of perfect
information (EVPI), *678*
FASB ASC 330-10-30, 653
fixed overhead application
rate, *652*
fixed overhead production-
volume variance, *653*
fixed overhead spending
(budget) variance, *653*

GPK, *668*
implementation error, *671*
indifference probability, *675*
managing earnings, *661*
measurement error, *671*
modeling error, *670*
normal capacity, *652*
practical capacity, *652*
prediction error, *670*
random variances, *670*
resource-capacity planning, *653*
resource consumption
accounting (RCA), *668*
statistical control chart, *671*

systematic variances, *670*
theoretical capacity, *652*
total fixed overhead
variance, *650*
total flexible-budget
variance for overhead, *656*
total variable overhead
variance, *648*
variable overhead efficiency
variance, *649*
variable overhead spending
variance, *649*

Comments on Cost Management in Action

How Do We Account for Inventory Changes?

The authors of this paper provide a method to incorporate both planned and unplanned changes in inventory levels (essentially, capacity usage) into the profit-variance model discussed in Chapters 14 and 15 of the text. As such, their reporting framework overcomes an inherent limitation of the basic model, which assumes that inventory changes are zero (or, insignificant in amount so that, for analytical purposes, they can be ignored).

How does the revised model presented by Balakrishnan and Sprinkle work? Essentially, we need to make two changes to the model presented in the text: one, prepare a flexible budget based on output (actual sales volume and mix) and the *budgeted* change in inventory; and two, include in all columns of the profit-variance report the cost of planned unused capacity. The difference between the master (static) budget column and the new flexible-budget column is the sales-volume variance, the difference between the two flexible-budget columns is equal to the inventory change variance, and the difference between the actual column and the variance. In each of the four columns of the variance-analysis report, the cost of unused capacity is divided between planned and unplanned idle capacity. (For additional details, refer to the original article.)

What additional insight does the revised model provide to managers? The authors argue that the revised profit-variance analysis is superior for three reasons: (1) the framework highlights the profit effects of producing for inventory; (2) the framework helps management disentangle the effects on profit of planned versus unplanned (i.e., *a priori* unanticipated circumstances) changes in inventory; and (3) flexible budget cost variances are computed using *production* volume, not *sales* volume. As such, the revised format can better assist managers in managing capacity-related costs. Finally, the revised reporting format facilitates performance evaluation by separating the profit impact attributable to planned and unplanned changes in inventory, sales volume, and capacity utilization.

Source: R. Balakrishnan and G. B. Sprinkle, "Integrating Profit Variances and Capacity Costing to Provide Better Managerial Information," *Issues in Accounting Education*, no. 2 (May 2002), pp. 149–161.

Self-Study Problems
(For solutions, please turn to the end of the chapter.)

1. Analysis of the Total Overhead Variance

Simpson Manufacturing has the following standard cost sheet for one of its products:

		Total
Direct materials	5 pounds at $2 per pound	$ 10
Direct labor	2 hours at $25 per hour	50
Variable factory overhead	2 hours at $5 per hour	10
Fixed factory overhead	2 hours at $20 per hour	40
Cost per unit		$110

The company uses a standard cost system and applies factory overhead based on direct labor hours and determines the factory overhead rate based on a practical capacity of 400 units of the product.

Simpson has the following actual operating results for the year just completed:

Units manufactured	360	
Direct materials purchased and used	1,800 pounds	$19,800
Direct labor incurred	750 hours	20,250
Variable factory overhead incurred		4,800
Fixed factory overhead incurred		15,800

Before closing the periodic accounts, the (standard cost) entries in selected accounts follow:

Account	Debit (total)	Credit (total)
Work-in-process inventory	$153,000	$134,640
Finished goods inventory	134,640	111,690
Cost of goods sold	111,690	

Required

1. Determine for the period the following items:
   a. Flexible budget for variable overhead based on output for the period.
   b. Total variable overhead applied to production during the period.
   c. Total budgeted fixed overhead.
   d. Total fixed overhead applied to production during the period.
2. Compute the following variances using a four-variance analysis:
   a. Total variable overhead variance.
   b. Variable overhead spending variance.
   c. Variable overhead efficiency variance.
   d. Total underapplied or overapplied variable overhead.
   e. Fixed overhead spending variance.
   f. Production-volume variance.
   g. Total fixed overhead variance.
   h. Total underapplied or overapplied fixed overhead.
3. Compute the following variances using three-variance analysis:
   a. Overhead spending variance.
   b. Overhead efficiency variance.
   c. Production-volume variance.
4. Compute the total overhead flexible-budget variance and the production-volume variance using a two-variance analysis.
5. Using a single overhead account (e.g., Factory Overhead), make proper journal entries for:
   a. Incurrence of overhead costs.
   b. Application of overhead costs to production.
   c. Identification of overhead variances assuming that the firm uses the four-variance analysis identified in requirement 2.
   d. Close all overhead cost items and their variances of the period if:
      (1) The firm closes all variances to Cost of Goods Sold.
      (2) The firm prorates variances to the inventory accounts and the Cost of Goods Sold accounts.

2. Variance Investigation (Appendix)

David Smiley is the manager of Photobonics Manufacturing. He notices that the operation in the last four weeks has had an unfavorable materials usage variance of $25,000. He is trying to decide whether to investigate this variance. If he investigates and discovers that the process is out of control (i.e., not due to a random occurrence and therefore not likely to correct itself), corrective actions will likely cost the firm $5,000. The cost of investigation is expected to be $2,500. The company would suffer an estimated total loss (in present-value terms) of $55,000 if the out-of-control operation continues. Smiley estimates the probability the operation is out of control is 60 percent.

Required

1. What are the expected costs of investigating and of not investigating? Should the operation be investigated? Why or why not?

2. What is the indifference probability that the operation is out of control?

Expected value of perfect information
(EVPI) represents the maximum amount that a decision maker would be willing to pay for *perfect information*.

3. What is the **expected value of perfect information (EVPI)** in this case? EVPI is defined as the *maximum* value the manager would pay to have knowledge (i.e., certainty) of whether the process is in control or out of control. In this decision context, the EVPI can be thought of as the difference between the expected cost with perfect information and the expected cost without perfect information. To calculate the former, we need to choose for each possible state of nature the *best* course of action (decision) and then multiply the associated "cost" for this decision by the probability of that state of nature occurring. We then sum these resulting expected costs to get the *expected cost with perfect information.*

Thus, EVPI = Expected cost *with* perfect information − Expected cost *without* perfect information
= Expected cost *with* perfect information − Expected value of cost-minimizing choice under uncertainty
= Maximum amount manager would be willing to pay for perfect information

Questions

15-1 Verbatim Company budgeted $80,000 of factory overhead cost to manufacture 1,000 units in 2010. At the end of 2010, the company found out that it manufactured only 850 units. Verbatim spent $80,000 on factory overhead in 2010. Did the plant manager do a good job in controlling factory overhead cost if (a) the company had only fixed factory overhead, or (b) the budgeted factory overhead figure included $60,000 of variable factory overhead cost?

15-2 What is the relationship between the variable overhead efficiency variance and the direct labor efficiency variance for a company that uses direct labor hours to apply factory overhead?

15-3 What are the relationships among the total overhead spending variance, the variable overhead spending variance, the fixed factory overhead budget variance, and the variable overhead efficiency variance?

15-4 What is the overhead flexible-budget variance?

15-5 "The direction of a variance (favorable or unfavorable) is irrelevant in decisions on whether or not to investigate the variance." Do you agree? Why or why not?

15-6 "As long as the total actual factory overhead is not significantly different from the total standard applied factory overhead for the period, there is no need to conduct further analyses of the factory overhead variance." Do you agree? Why or why not?

15-7 Why do some firms choose to use a two-variance analysis instead of a three-variance or a four-variance analysis of the total overhead variance for the period?

15-8 What is the difference between the applied variable overhead and the total variable overhead in the flexible budget? What is the difference between the applied factory overhead and the total flexible budgeted fixed overhead?

15-9 Would the choice of denominator level affect the amount of the fixed factory overhead budget variance? Production-volume variance? Explain.

15-10 Can the total overhead variance for a period be separated into price and efficiency variances? Explain.

15-11 List causes that could lead to a variable overhead *spending* variance.

15-12 List causes that could lead to a variable overhead *efficiency* variance.

15-13 List causes that could lead to a fixed overhead *spending* variance.

15-14 List causes that could lead to a production-*volume* variance.

15-15 What are the justifications for using practical capacity as the denominator volume when calculating the fixed overhead application rate?

15-16 What provisions of GAAP (viz., FASB ASC 330-10-30, previously *SFAS No. 151*—available at www.asc.fasb.org) pertain to the issue of end-of-period disposition of overhead variances? Be specific.

15-17 Explain the general process of how an activity-based cost (ABC) system can be used to manage organizational spending on resource capacity.

15-18 How does the analysis of overhead variances differ for companies using a traditional cost system versus an ABC system?

15-19 Explain two available treatments for disposing of overhead variances at the end of a period.

15-20 What factors should be considered in determining whether or not to investigate a variance?

Brief Exercises

15-21   Sipple Furniture's master budget for the year includes $360,000 for fixed supervisory salaries. Practical capacity, which is used to set the fixed overhead allocation rate, is 500 units per month. Supervisory salaries are expected to be incurred uniformly throughout the year. During August, the company produced 250 units, incurred production supervisory salaries of $29,000, and reported underapplied fixed overhead of $14,000 for supervisory salaries. What is Sipple Furniture's supervisory salaries budget (spending) variance for August?

15-22   Baxter Corporation's master budget calls for the production of 5,000 units per month and $144,000 indirect labor costs for the year. Baxter considers indirect labor as a component of variable overhead cost. During April, the company produced 4,500 units and incurred indirect labor costs of $10,100. What amount would be reported in April as a flexible-budget variance for indirect labor?

15-23   Patel and Sons, Inc., uses a standard cost system to apply overhead costs to units produced. Practical capacity for the plant is defined as 50,000 machine hours per year, which represents 25,000 units of output. Annual budgeted fixed overhead costs are $250,000 and the budgeted variable overhead cost is $4 per unit. Factory overhead costs are applied on the basis of standard machine-hours allowed for units produced. Budgeted and actual output for the year was 20,000 units, which took 41,000 machine hours. Actual fixed overhead costs for the year amounted to $245,000 while the actual variable overhead cost per unit was $3.90. What was (a) the fixed overhead spending (budget) variance for the year, and (b) the overhead production-volume variance for the year?

15-24   Refer to the data in 15-23. Given this information, what was (a) the variable overhead spending variance for the year, and (b) the variable overhead efficiency variance for the year?

15-25   Refer to the data in 15-23. Provide the correct summary journal entries for actual and applied overhead costs (both variable and fixed) for the year. Assume that the company uses a single account, Factory Overhead, to record both actual and applied overhead. Also, assume that the only variable overhead cost was electricity and that actual fixed overhead consisted of depreciation of $150,000 and supervisory salaries of $95,000.

15-26   Refer to your answer to 15-23 and 15-24 and the journal entries made in conjunction with 15-25. Given this information, provide the appropriate journal entries: (a) to record the overhead variances for the period (thereby closing out the balance in the Factory Overhead account), and (b) to close the variance accounts to CGS at the end of the period.

15-27   As an extension of 15-26, assume that at the end of the year, management of Patel and Sons, Inc., decides that the overhead variances should be allocated to WIP Inventory, Finished Goods Inventory, and CGS using the following percentages: 10 percent, 20 percent, and 70 percent, respectively. Provide the proper journal entry to close out the manufacturing overhead variances for the year.

15-28   Refer to the information in 15-23. Calculate and label the following overhead variances for the year: (a) total overhead variance, (b) total flexible-budget variance, and (c) production-volume variance.

15-29   Refer to the variances you calculated in conjunction with 15-28 and to the information in 15-23 and 15-25. Give the appropriate journal entries to record: (a) the net overhead variance is actual and applied overhead costs for the year (both variable and fixed), and (b) the net overhead variance is the three manufacturing cost variances calculated in 15-28.

15-30   Refer to the journal entries made in 15-29. Provide an appropriate end-of-year closing entry for each of the following two independent situations: (a) the net overhead variance is closed entirely to Cost of Goods Sold, and (b) the net overhead variance is allocated among WIP Inventory, Finished Goods Inventory, and CGS using the following percentages: 10 percent, 20 percent, and 70 percent, respectively.

Exercises

15-31   **Variable Overhead Variances**   The Platter Valley factory of Bybee Industries manufactures field boots. The cost of each boot includes direct materials, direct labor, and manufacturing overhead. The firm traces all direct costs to products, and it assigns overhead based on direct labor hours.

   The company budgeted $15,000 variable overhead and 2,500 direct labor hours to manufacture 5,000 pairs of boots in March 2010.

   The factory spent 2,700 direct labor hours in March 2010 to manufacture 4,800 pairs of boots and spent $15,600 on variable overhead during the month.

Required

1.   Compute the flexible-budget variance, the spending variance, and the efficiency variance for variable overhead for March.

2.   Provide appropriate journal entries to record the variable overhead spending and efficiency variances.

3.   Comment on the factory's operation in March 2010 with regard to variable overhead.

15-32 **Fixed Overhead Variances** (Continuation of Exercise 15-31) For March 2010 the Platter Valley factory of Bybee Industries budgeted $90,000 of fixed overhead. Its practical capacity is 2,500 direct labor hours per month (to manufacture 5,000 pairs of boots).

The factory spent 2,700 direct labor hours in March 2010 to manufacture 4,800 pairs of boots. The actual fixed overhead incurred for the month was $92,000.

Required

1. Compute the spending (budget) variance and the production-volume variance for fixed overhead for March.

2. Compute the fixed overhead flexible-budget variance.

3. Provide appropriate journal entries to record the fixed overhead spending and fixed overhead production-volume variances for March.

4. Comment on the factory's results in March 2010 with regard to fixed overhead costs.

15-33 **Three-Variance and Four-Variance Analysis of Factory Overhead** (Continuation of Exercises 15-31 and 15-32) The Platter Valley factory of Bybee Industries uses a three-variance analysis of the total factory overhead variance.

Required

1. Use the data given in Exercises 15-31 and 15-32 to compute the total overhead spending variance, the efficiency variance, and the production-volume variance.

2. Use your answers for Requirement 1 of Exercises 15-31 and 15-32 to determine the spending variances (both variable and fixed), the efficiency variance, and the production-volume variance.

15-34 **Two-Variance Analysis of the Factory Overhead Variance** (Continuation of Exercises 15-31 and 15-32) The Platter Valley factory of Bybee Industries uses a two-variance analysis of the total factory overhead variance.

Required

1. Use the data given in Exercises 15-31 and 15-32 to compute the total flexible-budget variance and the production-volume variance for March.

2. Use your answers for Requirement 1 of Exercises 15-31 and 15-32 and determine the flexible-budget variance and the production-volume variance for March.

3. What information is contained in each of the variances in a two-variance breakdown of the total overhead variance?

15-35 **Factory Overhead Analysis—Two, Three, and Four Variances** Walkenhorst Company's machining department prepared its 2010 budget based on the following data:

Practical capacity	40,000 units
Machine hours per unit	2
Variable factory overhead	$3.00 per machine hour
Fixed factory overhead	$360,000

The department uses machine hours to apply factory overhead. In 2010, the department used 85,000 machine hours and $625,000 in total manufacturing overhead to manufacture 42,000 units. Actual fixed overhead for the year was $375,000.

Required Set up an Excel spreadsheet to determine for the year:

1. The variable, fixed, and total factory overhead application rates.

2. The flexible budget for overhead cost based on output achieved in 2010.

3. The production-volume variance.

4. The total overhead spending variance.

5. The overhead efficiency variance.

6. The variable and fixed overhead spending variances.

15-36 **Factory Overhead Flexible Budget and Variance Analyses** Lopez & Co. uses flexible budgets for cost control. During March, Lopez spent 2,850 machine hours to produce 10,800 units and incurred $13,000 in total factory overhead, of which $4,500 was for fixed factory overhead.

The master budget for the year called for production of 150,000 units using 37,500 machine hours and a total factory overhead of $180,000. The total fixed factory overhead in the annual budget was $60,000.

Required Compute the following for March:

1. Flexible budget for total overhead based on output (i.e., units produced).
2. Factory overhead flexible-budget variance.
3. All variances, including:
   a. Variable and fixed overhead spending variances.
   b. Variable overhead efficiency variance.
   c. Fixed overhead production-volume variance.
4. Reconcile your answers in Requirements 2 and 3 above.
5. What recommendation do you have regarding the manner in which the fixed-overhead application rate is determined?

15-37 **Three-Variance and Two-Variance Analyses** (Continuation of Exercise 15-36) Using data given in Exercise 15-36 for Lopez & Co.

Required

1. Use a three-way breakdown of the total overhead variance to determine the following variance components:
   a. Total overhead spending variance.
   b. Overhead efficiency variance.
   c. Production-volume variance.
2. Use a two-variance breakdown of the total overhead variance to determine the following variance components:
   a. Total overhead flexible-budget variance.
   b. Production-volume variance.
3. What is the total factory-overhead variance for the month of March?

15-38 **Flexible Budget and Variances for Depreciation** Somson SuperKlean Service's master budget includes $258,000 for equipment depreciation. The master budget was prepared for an annual volume of 103,200 chargeable hours. This volume is expected to occur uniformly throughout the year. During September, Somson performed 8,170 chargeable hours, and the firm recorded $20,500 of depreciation expense.

Required

1. Determine the flexible-budget amount for equipment depreciation in September.
2. Compute the spending variance for the depreciation expense on equipment.
3. Calculate the production-volume variance for the depreciation expense. What is the interpretation of this variance?
4. List possible reasons for the spending variance.

15-39 **Overhead: Four-Variance Analysis** The following information is available from Swinney Company for December:

Total factory overhead incurred	$40,000
Variable overhead expenses, incurred	$24,150
Fixed overhead expenses, budgeted	$18,000
Direct labor hours (DLH) worked	4,200
Standard direct labor hours allowed for the units manufactured	4,000
Practical capacity, in direct labor hours	4,500
Standard variable overhead rate per DLH	$5.00

Swinney uses direct labor hours to apply factory overhead.

Required Use the framework presented in Exhibit 15.7 to compute the following for the month of December:

1. Variable overhead spending variance.
2. Variable overhead efficiency variance.
3. Fixed overhead spending (budget) variance.
4. Fixed overhead production-volume variance.
5. Total overhead variance.

15-40 Graphical Analysis—Variable Overhead Variances You are in charge of making a presentation to operating managers regarding the meaning of the total overhead variance that appears each month on their performance reports. The controller suggested that a graphical presentation might be an effective way to communicate the essential points to your audience. As such, she provided you with this partially completed graph. This graph represents a situation where: (1) machine hours are used to apply variable overhead costs to products, and (2) there is both an unfavorable variable overhead spending variance and an unfavorable variable overhead efficiency variance for the period in question. The controller also indicated that she would like you to use the following notation for some of the items to be included in your chart: actual number of machine hours worked during the period = AQ; standard number of machine hours allowed for the output of the period = SQ; actual variable overhead cost per machine hour worked during the period = AP; and standard variable overhead cost per machine hour = SP.

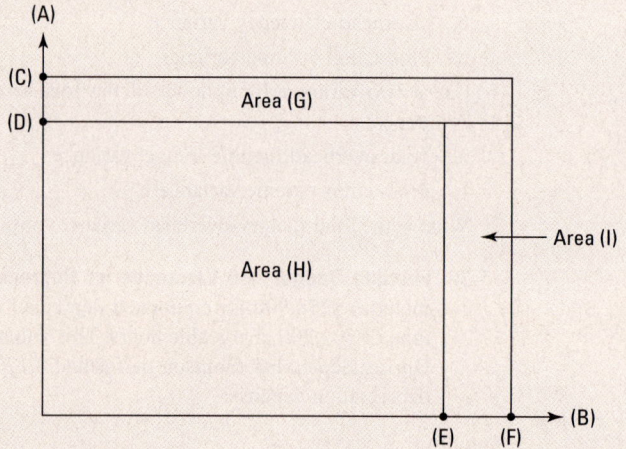

Required Based on the preceding assumptions and information, properly label the following components of the above graph:

1. (A) = ?
2. (B) = ?
3. (C) = ?
4. (D) = ?
5. (E) = ?
6. (F) = ?
7. Area (G) = ?
8. Area (H) = ?
9. Area (I) = ?
10. Sum of areas (G), (H), and (I) = ?

15-41 Graphical Analysis—Fixed Overhead Variances (Continuance of 15-40) The controller is satisfied with the graphical representation you prepared in conjunction with 15-40. She thinks this graphical representation of variable overhead variances will be well received by operating managers of the company. As such, she asks you to prepare an accompanying graph for fixed overhead variances. She indicates that you should assume the following in constructing your graph: (1) fixed overhead is applied to production on the basis of standard machine hours allowed for the output of the period (the standard total overhead cost per machine hour is $10, while the standard *variable* overhead cost per machine hour is $6); (2) during the example case, there was a favorable production-volume variance and an unfavorable spending (budget) variance for fixed overhead. Based on these assumptions, the controller has asked you to complete the following graph.

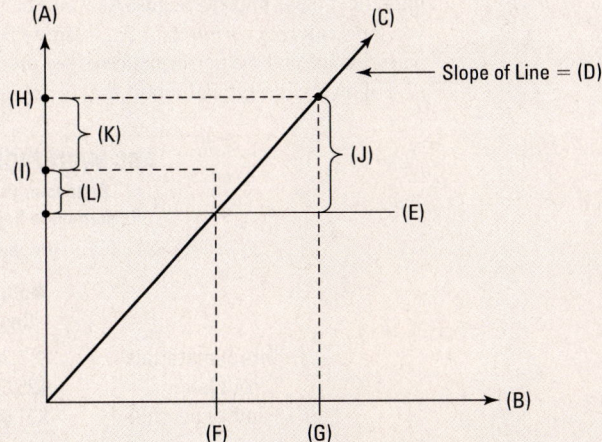

Required

1. (A) = ?
2. (B) = ?
3. (C) = ?
4. (D) = ?
5. (E) = ?
6. (F) = ?
7. (G) = ?
8. (H) = ?
9. (I) = ?
10. Vertical distance (J) = ?
11. Vertical distance (K) = ?
12. Vertical distance (L) = ?

15-42 **Fixed Overhead Rate, Denominator Level, and Two-Variance Analysis**   Overhead information for Danielson Company for October follows:

Total overhead incurred	$28,800
Budgeted fixed overhead	$7,200
Total standard overhead rate per machine hour (MH)	$4.50
Standard variable overhead rate per MH	$3.00
Standard MHs allowed for the units manufactured	3,500

Required

1. What is the standard fixed factory overhead rate per machine hour?
2. What is the denominator activity level that was used to establish the fixed overhead application note?
3. Prepare a diagram such as the one in Exhibit 15.7, Panel 3, to calculate the following overhead variances for October:
   a. Total flexible-budget variance for factory overhead.
   b. Factory overhead production-volume variance.
   c. Total factory overhead variance.

15-43 **Performance Reporting: The Use of Standard Cost Variance Information**   You have been hired recently as the cost accountant for the consumer products division of ABC Manufacturing Company. The production manager of one of the product lines in this division has expressed concern and dismay over the nature of the periodic reports used to evaluate her performance. In a recent conversation with you she stated: "I feel that the cost accounting reports used to evaluate the financial performance of my product line are misleading and unfair. I have been a line manager for over 15 years and, as such, know how to produce a good product! Because of competitive pressures, our line has even been able to cut raw material costs. It doesn't appear to me that the financial reports we get from accounting reflect these improvements. As well, the reports always contain only negative information—what you guys call *cost variances*. I am frustrated that the managers above use these reports to evaluate my performance and the performance of my product line."

Following is a typical report that is provided to the line manager in question:

ABC MANUFACTURING COMPANY
Consumer Products Division
Performance Report: Product Line X
December 2010

	Actual Cost	Master Budget	Cost Variance
Direct materials	$15,390	$14,000	$1,390U
Direct labor	$25,680	$24,500	$1,180U
Factory overhead	$21,500	$20,000	$1,500U
Totals	$62,570	$58,500	$4,070U

Note: U = unfavorable; F = favorable

Required Identify and discuss at least three changes to the monthly performance report that would make the information in the report more informative and less threatening to the operating managers.

(CMA Adapted)

15-44 **Overhead at Two Activity Levels and Four-Variance Versus Two-Variance Analysis** Greenhat Company applies factory overhead based on machine hours. The company had the following budget for its operation in 2009, which was at 80 percent level of theoretical capacity:

Standard machine hours (MH)	20,000
Variable factory overhead	$72,000
Total factory overhead rate per MH	$12.60

Greenhat budgeted its operation for 2010 at 90 percent of theoretical capacity. The standard calls for 2 machine hours per unit manufactured. During 2010 Greenhat used 23,000 machine-hours to manufacture 11,300 units. The company incurred $12,000 more factory overhead cost than the flexible-budget amount for the units manufactured, of which $5,000 was due to fixed factory overhead.

Required
1. What is the budgeted fixed factory overhead at an 80 percent level of operation? At a 100 percent level of operation?
2. What was the standard variable factory overhead rate and the standard fixed factory overhead rate in 2010? (Assume no change in the variable overhead rate.)
3. What is the total factory overhead flexible-budget amount for 2010? (Assume no cost change from 2009.)
4. Compute the following four overhead variances for the Greenhat Company:
   a. Variable overhead spending variance.
   b. Variable overhead efficiency variance.
   c. Fixed overhead spending variance.
   d. Production-volume variance.
5. Compute the following two overhead variances for the Greenhat Company:
   a. Total flexible-budget variance.
   b. Production-volume variance.

15-45 **Flexible-Overhead Budgets for Control** Johnny Lee, Inc., produces a line of small gasoline-powered engines that can be used in a variety of residential machines, ranging from different types of lawnmowers, to snowblowers, to garden tools (such as tillers and weed-whackers). The basic product line consists of three different models, each meant to fill the needs of a different market. Assume you are the cost accountant for this company and that you have been asked by the owner of the company to construct a flexible budget for manufacturing overhead costs, which seem to be growing for this company faster than revenues are growing. Currently, the company uses machine hours (MH) as the basis for assigning both variable and fixed factory overhead costs to products.

Within the relevant range of output, you determine that the following fixed overhead costs per month should occur: engineering support, $15,000; insurance on the manufacturing facility, $5,000; property taxes on the manufacturing facility, $12,000; depreciation on manufacturing equipment, $13,800; indirect labor costs: supervisory salaries, $14,800; set-up labor, $2,400; materials handling, $2,500. Variable overhead costs are budgeted at $21 per machine hour, as follows: electricity, $8; indirect materials: Material A = $1, Material B = $4; maintenance labor, $6; and, manufacturing supplies, $2.

Required

1. Use an Excel spreadsheet to prepare a flexible budget for Johnny Lee, Inc., for each of the following monthly levels of machine hours: 4,000; 5,000; and 6,000. (*Hint:* Provide in the spreadsheet a separate line for each of the overhead costs for the company.)

2. Generate an equation to represent, within the relevant range, the manufacturing overhead costs per month for Johnny Lee, Inc.

3. Generate a graphical representation of the monthly overhead cost function (within the relevant range) for Johnny Lee, Inc.

15-46 **Journal Entries for Factory Overhead Costs and Standard Cost Variances**   Refer to the information for Johnny Lee, Inc., in Exercise 15-45. Assume that in a given month the standard allowed machine hours for output produced were 5,500. Also, assume that the denominator activity level for setting the predetermined overhead rate is 6,550 machine hours per month.

Actual fixed overhead costs for the month were as follows: engineering support, $15,500 (salaries); factory insurance, $5,500; property taxes, $12,000; equipment depreciation, $13,800; supervisory salaries, $14,800; set-up labor, $2,200; materials-handling labor, $2,400. The actual variable overhead cost per machine hour worked was equal to the standard cost except for the following two items: electricity, $8.50 per machine hour; manufacturing supplies, $2.10 per machine hour. The company used 5,600 machine hours in December.

The company uses a single overhead account, Factory Overhead, and performs a two-way analysis of the total overhead variance each month.

Required

1. Calculate the (a) flexible-budget variance, and (b) the production-volume variance for the month. (*Hint:* The total overhead variance for the month is $16,660U.)

2. Provide summary journal entries to record actual overhead costs and standard overhead cost applied to production during the month.

3. Provide the journal entry to record the two overhead variances for the month.

4. Assume that the variances calculated above represent net variances for the year. Give the required journal entry to close these variances to the Cost of Goods Sold (CGS) account.

15-47 **Two-Variance Analysis and Direct Labor Variance**   Marilyn, Inc., uses a standard cost system and analyzes overhead using a two-variance analysis. The following information relates to its operations in April:

Actual total cost for direct labor	$86,800
Total direct labor hours worked	14,000
Total standard labor hours for the output in April	15,000
Direct labor rate variance—unfavorable	$2,800
Actual total overhead cost	$32,000
Budgeted fixed overhead cost	$9,000
Practical capacity, in hours	12,000
Total overhead application rate per standard direct labor hour	$2.25

Note: For the analysis of the total overhead variance, set up a model similar to the one presented in Exhibit 15.17.

Required

1. What was Marilyn's direct labor efficiency variance for April?
2. What was Marilyn's factory overhead flexible-budget variance for April?
3. What was Marilyn's production-volume variance for April?
4. What is the relationship between the direct labor efficiency variance and the variable overhead efficiency variance?

(CMA Adapted)

15-48 **Three-Variance Analysis** Use the data in Exercise 15-47 for Marilyn, Inc.

Required Use a model similar to the one presented in text Exhibit 15.17 to perform a three-way breakdown of the total overhead variance, as follows:

1. Overhead spending variance.
2. Variable overhead efficiency variance.
3. Production-volume variance
4. Prepare a reconciliation of results from the two-variance and three-variance approaches.

(CMA Adapted)

15-49 **Four-Variance Analysis** (Continuation of Exercise 15-47) Use the data given in Exercise 15-47 for Marilyn, Inc. In addition, the company has determined that actual variable overhead cost in April was $21,980.

Required Use the model presented in Exhibit 15.17 to Compute the following variances for April:

1. Variable overhead efficiency variance.
2. Variable overhead spending variance.
3. Fixed overhead spending (budget) variance.
4. Production-volume variance.

15-50 **Factory Overhead Variances** Shateau Job Shop had the following operating data for its operations in 2010:

Budgeted fixed overhead	$20,000
Standard variable overhead application rate	$3 per MH
Fixed overhead incurred	$21,400
Variable overhead incurred	$32,500
Practical capacity (5,000 units)	10,000 MH
Actual machine hours (MH) worked	9,500
Units produced	4,500

Required Build an Excel spreadsheet for the Shateau Job Shop that computes the following:

1. Variable overhead spending variance.
2. Variable overhead efficiency variance.
3. Fixed overhead spending (budget) variance.
4. Production-volume variance.
5. Overhead spending variance using a three-variance analysis.
6. Overhead flexible-budget (controllable) variance using a two-variance analysis.

15-51 **ABC Costing** Alden Company uses a two-variance analysis for overhead variances. Practical capacity is defined as 32 setups and 32,000 machine hours to manufacture 6,400 units for the year. Selected data for 2010 follow:

Budgeted fixed factory overhead:		
Setup	$ 64,000	
Other	200,000	$264,000
Total factory overhead incurred		$480,000
Variable factory overhead rate:		
Per setup		$600
Per machine hour		$5
Total standard machine hours allowed for the units manufactured		30,000 hours
Machine hours actually worked		35,000 hours
Actual total number of setups		28

Required

1. Compute (a) the total overhead spending variance, (b) the overhead efficiency variance, and (c) the total overhead flexible-budget variance for 2010.

2. Assume that the company includes all setup costs as variable factory overhead. The budgeted total fixed overhead, therefore, is $200,000, and the standard variable overhead rate per setup is $2,600. What are the (a) overhead spending, (b) efficiency, and (c) flexible-budget variances for the year?

3. Assume that the company uses only machine hours as the activity measure to apply both variable and fixed overhead, and that it includes all setup costs as variable factory overhead. What is the (a) overhead spending variance, (b) efficiency variance, and (c) flexible-budget variance for the year?

15-52 ABC and Practical Capacity   The ABC Manufacturing Company produces two products, S-101 and C-110. You have obtained the following information regarding the annual manufacturing support (i.e., factory overhead) costs associated with the manufacturing process used to produce these two products:

Cost Pools	Budgeted Costs	Activity Measure (Cost Driver)	Practical Capacity	Budgeted Activities for the Coming Year	
				S-101	C-110
Setup activity	$ 250,000	Setup hours	5,000	2,500	2,350
Packing and shipping	$ 50,000	Number of shipments	2,000	1,200	775
Inspection	$ 30,000	Number of batches	1,000	250	700
Machining	$ 750,000	Units produced	150,000	100,000	40,000
Purchase ordering	$ 40,000	Number of orders	300	50	110
Total	$1,120,000				

Estimated production for the coming year: S-101 = 100,000 units; C-110 = 40,000 units.

Required

1. Prepare an Excel spreadsheet that would provide ABC allocation rates based on budgeted activity units for the coming year. (a) What is the budgeted manufacturing support cost per unit of S-101? (b) What is the budgeted manufacturing support cost per unit of C-110?

2. Using your spreadsheet, recalculate the ABC allocation rates, this time based on practical capacity as the denominator activity level. (a) What is the budgeted manufacturing support cost per unit of S-101? (b) What is the budgeted manufacturing support cost per unit of C-110?

3. Compute, for each cost pool listed above, the difference between the budgeted cost for the year and the total cost allocated to production. How do you interpret these variances (differences)?

15-53 Flexible Budgets with ABC   The Cameron Corporation uses an ABC system, with the following manufacturing support (i.e., factory overhead) costs:

Unit-level support costs:	
Electricity	$1.00 per machine hour
Maintenance labor	$1.50 per machine hour
Batch-level support costs:	
Production set-ups	$300 per setup
Incoming Inspection	$100 per purchase order
Product-level support costs:	
Engineering support	$2,000 per engineering change order (ECO)
Facilities-level support costs:	
Depreciation—plant	$15,000 per month
Insurance and property taxes	$5,000 per month

The plant manager has asked you to prepare flexible (control) budgets for three levels of possible activity for the coming month: 4,000 machine hours, 5,000 machine hours, and 6,000 machine hours. Associated activity levels for manufacturing support costs are as follows:

	Level of Output (MH)		
	4,000	5,000	6,000
Production setups	20	24	28
Purchase orders	10	15	20
ECOs	12	15	18

Required

1. Use an Excel spreadsheet to prepare a flexible (control) budget for the following three output levels: (a) 4,000 machine hours, (b) 5,000 machine hours, and (c) 6,000 machine hours.

2. How do these flexible budgets differ from those prepared under a traditional approach (e.g., for the case where a single activity measure, machine hours, is used to construct the flexible (control) budget)?

15-54 ABC Data, Capacity-Resource Planning, Nonfinancial Performance Indicators National Computer (a fictitious company) competes at the retail level on the basis of customer service. It has invested significant resources in its Customer Service Department. Recently, the company has installed a traditional activity-based costing (ABC) system to provide better-quality cost information for pricing, decision making, and customer-profitability analysis. Most of the costs of running the Customer Service Department are considered committed (i.e., short-term fixed) costs (principally, personnel and equipment costs). The budgeted cost for the upcoming period is $1 million. Activity analysis, recently conducted when the ABC system was implemented, revealed the following information:

Activities	Percentage of Employee Time	Estimated (Budgeted) Cost-Driver Quantity
Handling customer orders	80%	8,000 customer orders
Processing customer complaints	10	400 customer complaints
Conducting customer credit checks	10	500 credit checks

Required

1. Based on the preceding information, calculate the activity-cost driver (ABC) rates for each of the three activities performed by the Customer Service Department. Assume that during the period actual cost-driver activity levels are exactly as planned. Under this situation, what is the total cost assigned to each of the three activities? For each activity, what is the cost of unused capacity?

2. Suppose that during the upcoming period, activities (i.e., cost-driver quantities) are exactly as budgeted. Suppose, too, that the practical capacity level for each of these activities is 10,000 customer orders, 500 customer complaints, and 500 credit checks. Using cost-driver rates based on practical capacity levels for each activity, what is the cost assigned to each of the three activities? Also, what is the unused capacity and the associated cost of unused capacity for each activity?

3. What actions might the management of National Computer take in response to the analysis conducted in response to (2) above?

4. What nonfinancial performance indicators do you recommend National Computer monitor in terms of its Customer Service Department? In general, how are these indicators chosen? (That is, how do you justify the items you are recommending?)

15-55 Use of Payoff Tables (Appendix): Past experience indicates an 85 percent probability that a reported overhead cost variance is not due to a specific cause (i.e., is attributable to random fluctuations). Past experience also shows that the average cost to investigate the underlying cause of a variance is $750 and that the cost to correct an out-of-control process is, on average, $3,000. If the underlying variance is systematic and management decides not to investigate the cause of the variance, the costs are thought to be significant: $25,000.

Required Set up an Excel spreadsheet to answer the following questions:

1. Given the preceding information, what is the expected value of investigating the reported variance?

2. Prepare a payoff table that summarizes the above information. (*Hint:* Your table should include cells for combinations of management actions (investigate vs. do not investigate) and states of nature (systematic cause vs. random event), plus cells to represent the expected cost of each management action.

3. Given the above information, what is the probability level, p, for nonrandom variance that makes management indifferent between the two courses of action: investigate versus do not investigate? (*Hint:* You can use the formula in the text to calculate p. You could also use the "goal-seek" function from the Tools menu in Excel to calculate this number.)

Problems **15-56 Four-Variance Analysis of Total Overhead Variance** Franklin Glass Works has the capacity to manufacture 200,000 units for the year ended November 30, 2010. The standard cost sheet specifies two direct labor hours (DLHs) for each unit manufactured. Total factory overhead was budgeted at $900,000 for the year with a fixed overhead rate of $3 per unit. Both fixed and variable overhead are assigned to products on the basis of standard DLHs. The actual data for the year ended November 30, 2010, follow:

Units manufactured	198,000
Direct labor hours worked	440,000
Variable factory overhead incurred	$352,000
Fixed factory overhead incurred	$575,000

Required

1. Determine the following for the year just completed:
   a. Total standard hours allowed for the units manufactured.
   b. Variable overhead efficiency variance.
   c. Variable overhead spending variance.
   d. Fixed overhead spending variance.
   e. Total fixed overhead cost applied to units manufactured.
   f. Production-volume variance.

2. Prepare appropriate journal entries for the four-variance analysis. Assume the company uses only two overhead accounts, one for variable overhead, the other for fixed overhead.

3. Provide a concise explanation of each of the four overhead variances you calculated.

15-57 **All Manufacturing Variances**   Eastern Company manufactures special electrical equipment and parts. The company uses a standard cost system with separate standards established for each product.

The transformer department manufactures a special transformer. This department measures production volume in terms of direct labor hours (DLHs) and uses a flexible-budget system to plan and control departmental overhead costs.

Standard costs for the special transformer are determined annually in September for the coming year. The standard cost of a transformer at its DeCatur plant for the year just completed is $67 per unit, as shown here:

Direct materials:		
Iron	5 sheets × $2	$10
Copper	3 spools × $3	9
Direct labor	4 hours × $7	28
Variable overhead	4 hours × $3	12
Fixed overhead	4 hours × $2	8
Total		$67

Overhead rates were based on practical capacity of 4,000 DLHs per month. Variable overhead costs are expected to vary with the number of DLHs actually used.

During October, the plant produced 800 transformers. This number was below expectations because a work stoppage occurred during labor contract negotiations. When the contract was settled, the department scheduled overtime in an attempt to reach expected production levels.

The following costs were incurred in October:

Direct Material	
Iron	Purchased 5,000 sheets at $2.00/sheet and used 3,900 sheets
Copper	Purchased 2,200 spools at $3.10/spool and used 2,600 spools

Direct Labor	
Regular time	2,000 hours at $7.00 and 1,400 hours at $7.20
Overtime	600 of the 1,400 hours were subject to overtime premium. The total overtime premium of $2,160 is included in variable overhead in accordance with company accounting practices.

Factory Overhead	
Variable	$12,000
Fixed	$8,800

Required

1. What is the most appropriate time to record any variance of actual materials prices from standard? Explain.
2. What is the total direct labor rate (price) variance for October?
3. What is the total direct labor efficiency variance for October?
4. What is the total direct materials purchase price variance for October?
5. What is the total direct materials usage variance for October?
6. What is the variable overhead spending variance for October?
7. What is the variable overhead efficiency variance for October?
8. What is the budget (spending) variance for fixed overhead for October?
9. What is the production-volume variance for October?

(CMA Adapted)

15-58 **Four-Variance Analysis**   Able Control Company, which manufactures electrical switches, uses a standard cost system and carries all inventory at standard cost. The standard factory overhead cost per switch is based on direct labor hours:

Variable overhead	(5 hours at $8/hour)	$ 40
Fixed overhead	(5 hours at $12*/hour)	60
Total standard overhead cost per unit produced		$100

*Based on a practical capacity of 300,000 direct labor hours per month.

The following information is for the month of October:

- The company produced 56,000 switches, although 60,000 switches were scheduled to be produced.
- The company worked 275,000 direct labor hours at a total cost of $2,550,000.
- Variable overhead costs were $2,340,000.
- Fixed overhead costs were $3,750,000.

The production manager argued during the last performance review that the company should use a more up-to-date base for charging factory overhead costs to production. She commented that her factory had been highly automated in the last two years and as a result now has hardly any direct labor. The factory hires only highly skilled workers to set up production runs and to do periodic adjustments of machinery whenever the need arises.

Required

1. Compute the following for Able Control Company:
   a. The fixed overhead spending variance for October.
   b. The production-volume variance for October.
   c. The variable overhead spending variance for October.
   d. The variable overhead efficiency variance for October.
2. Comment on the implications of the variances and suggest any action that the company should take to improve its operations.

(CMA Adapted)

15-59 **Comprehensive Variance Analysis**   Organet Stamping Company manufactures a variety of products made of plastic and aluminum components. During the winter months, substantially all production capacity is devoted to lawn sprinklers for the following spring and summer seasons. Other products are manufactured during the remainder of the year. Because a variety of products are manufactured throughout the year, factory volume is measured using production labor hours rather than units of production.

Production volume has grown steadily for the past several years, as the following schedule of production labor indicates:

This year	32,000 hours
1 year ago	30,000 hours
2 years ago	27,000 hours
3 years ago	28,000 hours
4 years ago	26,000 hours

The company has developed standard costs for its several products. It sets standard costs for each year in the preceding October. The standard cost of a sprinkler this year was $4.00, computed as follows:

Direct materials:		
Aluminum	0.2 pound × $0.40 per pound	$0.08
Plastic	1.0 pound × $0.38 per pound	0.38
Production labor	0.3 hour × $9.00 per hour	2.70
Overhead:		
Variable	0.3 hour × $1.60 per hour	0.48
Fixed*	0.3 hour × $1.20 per hour	0.36
Total		$4.00

* Calculated using 30,000 production labor-hours per year as practical capacity.

During February of this year, 8,500 good sprinklers were manufactured. The following costs were incurred and charged to production:

Materials requisitioned for production:		
Aluminum	(1,900 pounds × $0.40 per pound)	$ 760
Plastic: Regular	(6,000 pounds × $0.38 per pound)	2,280
Low grade†	(3,500 pounds × $0.38 per pound)	1,330
Production labor:		
Straight time	(2,300 hours × $10.00 per hour)	23,000
Overtime	(400 hours × $15.00 per hour)	6,000
Overhead:		
Variable	$5,200	
Fixed	3,100	8,300
Costs charged to production		$41,670

Materials price variations are charged to a materials price variation account at the time the invoice is entered. All materials are carried in inventory at standard prices. Materials purchases for February follow:

Aluminum	(1,800 pounds × $0.48 per pound)	$864
Plastic:		
Regular grade	(3,000 pounds × $0.50 per pound)	1,500
Low grade†	(6,000 pounds × $0.29 per pound)	1,740

† Plastic shortages forced the company to purchase lower-grade plastic than called for in the standards, which increased the number of sprinklers rejected on inspection.

Required   Compute the following for February:

1. The total variance from standard cost for the units produced this period.
2. The spending (budget) variance for the fixed portion of overhead costs.
3. The labor efficiency variance.
4. The labor rate variance.
5. The total variable manufacturing cost variance.
6. The variable overhead spending, efficiency, and flexible-budget variances.
7. The production-volume variance.
8. The materials variances (purchase-price and usage). Also comment on the effects of using materials of different grades.

(CMA Adapted)

15-60 **Standard Manufacturing Cost Per Unit**   Cain Company has an automated production process; consequently, it uses machine hours to describe production activity. The company employs a full absorption cost system. The annual profit plan for the coming fiscal year is finalized each April. The profit plan for the fiscal year ending May 31 called for production of 6,000 units, requiring 30,000 machine hours. The full absorption cost rate for the fiscal year was determined using 6,000 units of planned production. Cain develops flexible budgets for different levels of activity to use in evaluating performance. During the fiscal year, Cain produced 6,200 units requiring 32,000 machine hours. The following schedule compares Cain Company's actual costs for the fiscal year with the profit plan and the budgeted costs at two different activity levels:

CAIN COMPANY
Manufacturing Cost Report
For the Fiscal Year Ended May 31
(in thousands of dollars)

Item	Profit Plan (6,000 units)	Flexible Budget 31,000 Machine Hours	Flexible Budget 32,000 Machine Hours	Actual Costs
Direct material:				
G27 aluminum	$ 252.0	$ 260.4	$ 268.8	$ 270.0
M14 steel alloy	78.0	80.6	83.2	83.4
Direct labor:				
Assembler	273.0	282.1	291.2	287.0
Grinder	234.0	241.8	249.6	250.0
Manufacturing overhead:				
Maintenance	24.0	24.8	25.6	25.0
Supplies	129.0	133.3	137.6	130.0
Supervision	80.0	82.0	84.0	81.0
Inspectors	144.0	147.0	150.0	147.0
Insurance	50.0	50.0	50.0	50.0
Depreciation	200.0	200.0	200.0	200.0
Total cost	$1,464.0	$1,502.0	$1,540.0	$1,523.4

Required Compute these:

1. The actual cost of material used per unit of product produced this year.
2. The standard materials cost per machine hour.
3. The budgeted direct labor cost for each unit produced.
4. The standard variable overhead rate per machine hour.
5. The production-volume variance for the current year. Can you suggest an improved method for determining the fixed overhead allocation rate?
6. The total overhead spending variance for the year.
7. The total budgeted manufacturing cost for an output of 6,050 units.
8. Comment on how individual fixed overhead items are controlled on a day-to-day basis. How are individual variable overhead items controlled from day-to-day?

(CMA Adapted)

15-61 **Capacity Levels and Fixed Overhead Rates** At its Sutter City plant, Yuba Machine Company manufactures nut shellers, which it sells to nut processors throughout the world. Since its inception, the family-owned business has used actual factory overhead costs in costing factory output. On December 1, 2010, Yuba began using a predetermined factory overhead application rate to determine manufacturing costs on a more timely basis. The following information is from the 2010–2011 budget for the Sutter City plant:

Plant maximum (theoretical) capacity	100,000 DLHs
Variable overhead costs	$3.00 per DLH
Fixed overhead costs:	
Salaries	$ 80,000
Depreciation and amortization	50,000
Other expenses	30,000
Total fixed factory overhead	$160,000

Based on these data, the predetermined factory overhead application rate was established at $4.60 per DLH.

A variance report for the Sutter City plant for the six months ended May 31, 2011, follows. The plant incurred 40,000 DLHs, which represents one-half of the company's *practical capacity* level.

Variance Report

	Actual Costs	Applied*	Variance†
Total variable factory overhead	$120,220	$120,000	$ (220)
Fixed factory overhead:			
Salaries	$39,000	$32,000	$ (7,000)
Depreciation and amortization	25,000	20,000	(5,000)
Other expenses	15,300	12,000	(3,300)
Total fixed factory overhead	$ 79,300	$ 64,000	$(15,300)

* Based on 40,000 direct labor-hours (DLHs).
† Favorable (Unfavorable)

Yuba's controller, Sid Thorpe, knows from the inventory records that one-quarter of this period's applied fixed overhead costs remain in the work-in-process and finished goods inventory accounts. Based on this information, he has included $48,000 of fixed overhead (i.e., three-quarter's of the period's applied fixed overhead) as part of the cost of goods sold in the following interim income statement:

YUBA MACHINE COMPANY
Interim Income Statement
For Six Months Ended May 31, 2011

Sales	$625,000
Cost of goods sold	380,000
Gross profit	$245,000
Selling expense	44,000
Depreciation expense	58,000
Administrative expense	53,000
Operating income	$ 90,000

Required
1. Define the term *maximum (theoretical) capacity* and explain why it might not be a satisfactory basis for determining the fixed factory overhead application rate. What other capacity levels can be used to set the fixed overhead allocation rate? Explain.
2. Prepare a revised variance report for Yuba Machine Company using *practical capacity* as the basis for determining the fixed overhead application rate.
3. Determine the effect on Yuba's reported operating income of $90,000 at May 31, 2011, if the fixed factory overhead rate was based on practical capacity rather than on maximum capacity.
4. What capacity level should companies use to determine the factory overhead application rate? Why?

(CMA Adapted)

15-62 **Proration of Variances** Butrico Manufacturing Corporation uses a standard cost system, records materials price variances when raw materials are purchased, and prorates all variances at year-end. Variances associated with direct materials are prorated based on the balances of direct materials in the appropriate accounts, and variances associated with direct labor and manufacturing overhead are prorated to Finished Goods Inventory and CGS on the basis of the relative direct labor cost in these accounts at year-end.

The following Butrico information is for the year ended December 31:

Finished goods inventory at 12/31:	
Direct materials	$87,000
Direct labor	130,500
Applied manufacturing overhead	104,400
Raw materials inventory at 12/31	$65,000

(Continued)

Cost of goods sold for the year ended 12/31:	
Direct materials	$348,000
Direct labor	739,500
Applied manufacturing overhead	591,600
Direct materials price variance (unfavorable)	10,000
Direct materials usage variance (favorable)	15,000
Direct labor rate variance (unfavorable)	20,000
Direct labor efficiency variance (favorable)	5,000
Actual manufacturing overhead incurred	690,000

The company had no beginning inventories and no ending work-in-process (WIP) inventory. It applies manufacturing overhead at 80 percent of standard direct labor cost.

Required For (1) through (4), compute:

1. The amount of direct materials price variance to be prorated to finished goods inventory at December 31.

2. The total amount of direct materials cost in finished goods inventory at December 31, after all materials variances have been prorated. (*Hint:* The correct amount is $85,732.)

3. The total amount of direct labor cost in finished goods inventory at December 31, after all variances have been prorated. (*Hint:* The correct amount is $132,750.)

4. The total cost of goods sold for the year ended December 31, after all variances have been prorated. (*Hint:* The correct amount is $1,681,678.)

5. How, if at all, would the provisions of GAAP regarding inventory costing (i.e., FASB ASC 330-10-30, previously *SFAS No. 151*—available at www.asc.fasb.org) bear upon the end-of-period variance-disposition question?

6. Under absorption costing, explain how reported earnings can be managed by the method used to dispose of (fixed) overhead cost variances at the end of the period.

(CMA Adapted)

15-63 **Four-Variance Analysis and Journal Entries**   Edney Company employs a standard cost system for product costing. The standard cost of its product is

Raw materials	$14.50
Direct labor (2 direct labor hours × $8)	16.00
Manufacturing overhead (2 direct labor hours × $11)	22.00
Total standard cost	$52.50

The manufacturing overhead rate is based on a normal capacity level of 600,000 direct labor-hours. (Normal capacity is defined as the level of capacity needed to satisfy average customer demand over a period of two to four years. Operationally, this level of capacity would take into consideration sales trends, and both seasonal and cyclical factors affecting demand.) The firm has the following annual manufacturing overhead budget:

Variable	$3,600,000
Fixed	3,000,000
	$6,600,000

Edney spent $433,350 direct labor cost for 53,500 direct labor hours to manufacture 26,000 units in November. Costs incurred in November include $260,000 for fixed manufacturing overhead and $315,000 for variable manufacturing overhead.

Required

1. Determine each of the following for November:

   a. The variable overhead spending variance.

   b. The variable overhead efficiency variance.

   c. The fixed overhead spending (budget) variance.

   d. The production-volume variance.

   e. The total amount of under- or overapplied manufacturing overhead.

2. Provide appropriate journal entries to record actual overhead costs, standard overhead costs applied to production, and all four overhead variances.

3. Give the appropriate journal entry to close all overhead variances to the cost of goods sold (CGS) account. (Assume the variances you calculated above are for the year, not the month.)

4. How, if at all, would the provisions of GAAP regarding inventory costing (FASB ASC 330-10-30, previously *SFAS No. 151*—available at www.asc.fasb.org) bear upon the end-of-period variance-disposition question?

5. Explain how reported earnings under absorption costing can be managed by the method used to dispose of (fixed) overhead cost variances at the end of the period.

(CMA Adapted)

15-64 Variance Investigation under Uncertainty (Appendix)   The internal auditor of Transnational Company estimates the probability of its internal control procedure being in control to be 80 percent. She estimates the cost to conduct an investigation to find areas for improvement to be about $20,000 and the cost to revise and improve the internal control procedure to be approximately $50,000. The present value of savings from having the new procedure is expected to be $250,000.

Required

1. Construct a payoff table for the company to use in determining its best course of action.

2. What is the expected cost to the firm if it conducts an investigation? If it does not investigate? Should the firm investigate? Why or why not?

3. What is the expected value of perfect information? Note: The expected value of perfect information (EVPI) is defined as the *maximum* value the manager would pay to have knowledge (i.e., certainty) of whether the process is in control or out of control. In the present context, the EVPI can be thought of as the difference between the expected cost with perfect information and the expected cost without perfect information. (To calculate the former, we need to choose for each possible state of nature the best course of action [decision] and then multiply the associated "cost" by the probability of that state of nature occurring. We then sum these resulting expected costs to get the *expected cost with perfect information*.) (*Hint:* For this problem, the expected cost under perfect information is $14,000.)

15-65 Decision Making under Uncertainty (Appendix)   The manager of MMX Digital must decide whether to initiate an advertising campaign for the firm's newest multimedia computer chip. There has been some discussion among division managers about the chip's market condition. The marketing department assesses the probability of having a strong market to be 0.6.

The manager, with the help of the marketing staff, has estimated the profits she believes the firm could earn:

Profits with advertising:	
Strong market	$10 million
Weak market	4 million
Profits without advertising:	
Strong market	8 million
Weak market	5 million

Required

1. Should the firm undertake the advertising campaign? Why or why not?

2. What is the probability level regarding the state of the market that will render the manager indifferent as to the courses of action?

3. What is the maximum amount the firm should pay to obtain perfect information regarding the state of the market, assuming such information is available? (See the note appended to part 3 of problem 15-64.)

15-66 Two-Variance Analysis: Service Company Example   International Finance Incorporated issues letters of credit to importers for overseas purchases. The company charges a nonrefundable application fee of $3,000 and, on approval, an additional service fee of 2 percent of the amount of credit requested.

The firm's budget for the year just completed included fixed expenses for office salaries and wages of $500,000, leasing office space and equipment of $50,000, and utilities and other operating expenses of $10,000. In addition, the budget also included variable expenses for supplies and other variable overhead costs of $1,000,000. The company estimated these variable overhead costs to be $2,000 for each letter of credit approved and issued. The company approves, on average, 80 percent of the applications it receives.

During the year, the company received 600 requests and approved 75 percent of them. The total variable overhead was 10 percent higher than the standard amount applied; the total fixed expenses were 5 percent lower than the amount budgeted.

In addition to these expenses, the company paid a $270,000 insurance premium for the letters of credit issued. The insurance premium is 1 percent of the amount of credits issued in U.S. dollars. The actual amount of credit issued often differs from the amount requested due to fluctuations in exchange rates and variations in the amount shipped from the amount ordered by importers. The strength of the dollar during the year decreased the insurance premium by 10 percent.

Required

1. Calculate the (a) variable, and (b) fixed overhead rates for the year.

2. Prepare an analysis of the overhead variances for the year just completed. (a) What is the total controllable (i.e., flexible-budget) variance for the period? (b) What is the overhead volume variance for the period? (*Hint:* These two should sum to $88,000U.)

15-67 Ethics and Overhead Variance New Millennium Technologies uses a standard cost system and budgeted 50,000 machine hours to manufacture 100,000 units in 2010. The budgeted total fixed factory overhead was $9,000,000. The company manufactured and sold 80,000 units in 2010 and would report a loss of $9,600,000 after charging the production-volume variance to cost of goods sold (CGS) of the period.

Bob Evans, VP–Finance, believes that the denominator activity level of 50,000 machine hours is too low. The maximum capacity of the firm is between 5,000,000 and 6,000,000 machine hours. Bob considers a denominator level at half the low-end capacity to be reasonable. Furthermore, he believes that the unfavorable production-volume variance should be capitalized (rather than written off against current period's earnings) because the demand for the firm's products has been increasing rapidly. A conservative projection of the firm's sales places the total sales at a level that will require at least 5 million machine hours in less than 5 years. Bob was able to show a substantial improvement in operating income after revising the cost data. He used the revised operating result in briefing financial analysts.

Required

1. Compute the net effect on operating income of the two changes made regarding fixed factory overhead.

2. Is it ethical for Bob to make the changes? (Consult www.imanet.org.)

3. Do the provisions of GAAP regarding inventory costing (i.e., FASB ASC 330-10-30, previously *SFAS No. 151*—available at www.asc.fasb.org) bear upon the current issue? If so, how?

4. How does the choice of the denominator volume level in setting (fixed) overhead application rates provide managers with an opportunity to manage earnings?

15-68 ABC versus Traditional Approaches to Control of Batch-Related Overhead Costs The Bangor Manufacturing Company makes mechanical toy robots that are typically produced in batches of 250 units. Prior to the current year, the company's accountants used a standard cost system with a simplified method of assigning manufacturing support (i.e., overhead) costs to products: all such costs were allocated to outputs based on the standard machine hours allowed for output produced. You have recently joined the accounting team and are developing a proposal that the company adopt an ABC system for both product-costing and control purposes. To illustrate the benefit of such a system in terms of the latter, you decide to put together an analysis of batch-related overhead costs. You chose these costs because a previous investigation indicated that there is both a variable component to these costs (materials plus power) plus a fixed component (depreciation and salaries). Last year's budget indicated that the variable overhead cost per setup hour was $20 and that the fixed overhead production setup costs per year were $20,000. Output was budgeted at 10,000 units for the year. Typically a batch takes four hours of setup time. For cost-control purposes, assume that the flexible budget is based on the budgeted number of setup hours for the output of the period.

You have also collected data regarding actual results for the past year. Specifically, the company produced (and sold) 9,000 toy robots, which were produced in an average batch size of 200 units. The actual setup hours per batch last year turned out to be 4.25 hours and the actual variable overhead cost per setup hour was $19. Actual fixed setup-related overhead costs were $21,000 last year.

Your discussion with the company controller indicates that under the previous accounting system, all setup-related overhead costs were allocated to production based on machine hours. The standard machine hours allowed per unit produced was 1.50 hours. The denominator activity level assumed for applying fixed manufacturing support costs to units produced was 15,000 machine hours.

Required

1. Under the ABC approach, what was the (a) spending variance, and (b) production-volume variance last year for the *fixed* setup-related overhead costs described above? How would you explain these results to management?

2. Under the ABC approach, what was the (a) spending variance, and (b) efficiency variance last year for the *variable* setup-related overhead costs described above? How would you explain these results to management?

3. Write a brief statement outlining the projected costs and benefits of using an ABC approach for the day-to-day control of the overhead costs referred to above as compared to the use of a more traditional cost system.

4. The Bangor Manufacturing Company is currently experiencing severe cost-based pressure from foreign competitors. As such, top management of the company is interested in improving the existing financial-control system in the organization. What other recommendation might you have for management in this regard? That is, what do you recommend to accompany the type of financial analysis referred to above?

15-69   **Income Statement Effects of Alternative Denominator Activity Levels**   At a recent board meeting of the Grayson Manufacturing Company, several individuals in attendance expressed concern that they could not understand how the choice of an activity level for determining overhead application rates for the company could affect reported operating profits. The controller, Susanna Wu, who attended the meeting told members of the board that, in fact, companies have some latitude in how overhead application rates are set. For example, she told the board that companies can spread budgeted fixed overhead for the period over budgeted (forecasted) activity, over normal capacity, practical capacity, or even theoretical (maximum) capacity. All of this didn't resonate well with members of the board who basically saw the discussion as just another example of how accounting can be used to "manage income" (i.e., "cook the books"). The chair of the finance committee of the board asked Susanna to generate a concise report that would illustrate, in concrete terms, the issues involved. In turn, you have been asked to prepare this report, which will be distributed to attendees at the next meeting of the finance committee. These committee members are adept at using spreadsheets and therefore have requested that your report be distributed to them electronically.

Based on your subsequent discussions with the controller, you come up with the following information that is pertinent to your task:

a. Basis for applying overhead costs to units produced = standard machine hours.

b. Budgeted fixed overhead (total) = $350,000/year.

c. Standard number of machine hours per unit produced = 2.0.

d. Sales data: units sold = 11,500; unit selling price = $100.

e. Standard variable manufacturing cost per unit produced = $60.25.

f. Beginning inventory = $0 (0 units).

g. Budgeted operating costs: variable = $4.95/unit sold; fixed = $65,000/year.

h. Actual number of units produced during the year = 12,250.

i. Capacity levels (in machine hours): theoretical capacity = 30,000 hours; practical capacity = 27,000 hours; normal capacity = 25,000 hours; budgeted (forecasted) usage = 24,000 hours.

Required

1. Develop an Excel spreadsheet to calculate the amount of the production-volume variance under each of the following denominator activity levels that can be used to set the fixed overhead allocation rate: (a) theoretical capacity; (b) practical capacity; (c) normal capacity; and (d) budgeted capacity usage.

2. Determine the end-of-year balance in the Finished Goods Inventory account (at standard manufacturing cost) under each of the following denominator activity levels for establishing the fixed overhead allocation rate: (a) theoretical capacity; (b) practical capacity; (c) normal capacity; and, (d) budgeted capacity usage.

3. Assume that the practice of the company at the end of the year is to close any standard cost variances to cost of goods sold (CGS). What is the amount of operating profit that would be reported for each of the following choices for defining the denominator activity level for purposes of calculating the fixed overhead allocation rate: (a) theoretical capacity; (b) practical capacity; (c) normal capacity; and, (d) budgeted capacity usage?

4. What conclusions can be drawn based on the preceding analyses you conducted? That is, what is the bottom-line information you would like to convey to members of the finance committee?

5. How does GAAP regarding inventory costing (i.e., FASB ASC 330-10-30, previously *SFAS No. 151*) affect the decision as to how the production-volume variance (also known as the idle-capacity variance) is handled at the end of a period?

15-70 **Managing Resource Capacity through Activity-Based Costing (ABC)** This assignment deals with the application of a traditional ABC system to the problem of measuring and managing the cost of capacity. As controller for Zen Company, you've been asked to provide input regarding the appropriate level of resource capacity needed to support the strategic initiatives of the company, as indentified in the company's strategic planning system (e.g., its balanced scorecard system and associated strategy maps—see Chapter 18).

Because of the focus of the company on exceptional customer service, you've decided to run a pilot test by focusing on a single activity: *handling customer orders.* During the most recent year, total resource costs of this activity were $500,000. You've determined that, during the year, 7,000 customer orders were handled by the company. Observations of the process and your own interviews with knowledgeable personnel indicate that the current level of resource spending in this area provides the capacity to efficiently process approximately 10,000 customer orders. (That is, the practical capacity of resources supplied is 10,000 customer orders.) An analysis of past accounting data and the application of the cost-estimation techniques covered in Chapter 8 suggest that resource spending for this activity in the coming year will be approximately $560,000. The company expects to handle 8,000 customer orders during the coming year. Your basic task is to determine how the use of ABC data can facilitate decisions regarding the appropriate level of spending to support the customer-ordering process.

Required

1. Distinguish between short-term variable costs and short-term fixed (i.e., capacity-related) costs. For many organizations today, including the Zen Company, which type of costs characterize support costs, such as the cost of handling customer orders?

2. ABC fundamentally deals with the issue of assigning costs to activities, then activity-based costs to outputs such as products, services, or customers. From the start, however, you are a bit bewildered: which data at your disposal should be used to calculate the cost of handling a customer order? Show calculations. Include in your answer an explanation of the term *practical capacity* and a short discussion of what is referred to as the *death-spiral effect.*

3. How can the use of ABC data assist managers in managing spending on resource capacity? (*Hint:* be sure to address the issue of the *cost of unused capacity.*) Why is the management of resource capacity costs of strategic importance to companies such as Zen?

4. Assume that Zen, in an effort to improve the process of handling customer orders, implements a TQM or other initiative, the effect of which is to increase the number of orders that can be handled efficiently. As a result, the practical capacity of the process increases to approximately 14,000 orders per year. Has the cost of handling a customer order changed in response to the TQM initiative? (Assume a total cost, as before, of $560,000.) Assume, as before, that the company in the coming year expects to process 8,000 customer orders. After the TQM implementation, what is the estimated cost of unused capacity?

5. What strategies are available to managers for reducing or eliminating unused capacity?

6. What recommendation would you make to management regarding how the cost of unused capacity should be assigned?

15-71 **Activity-Based Costing (ABC) and Variance Analysis: Batch-Level Costs** As indicated in the chapter (and more fully in Chapter 5), ABC systems deal with the allocation of all support (i.e., indirect) costs of an organization. This assignment focuses on batch-related manufacturing support (i.e., overhead) costs allocated to outputs on the basis of an ABC system. ABC fundamentally views these support costs as variable costs in the long run. However, in the short run, these costs may have both fixed and variable components, a situation that has implications for short-term financial analysis. This assignment deals with the issue of short-term cost-variance analysis for batch-level costs in an ABC system.

XYZ Company produces a more-or-less standardized product, normally in batches of 50 units. Each batch requires six hours of setup time, on average. Setup resources are largely in the form of short-term fixed costs; the budget for these costs for the upcoming period is $50,000. Variable setup (i.e., batch-related) manufacturing support costs are budgeted at $10 per setup-hour. For the coming period, the company expects to produce 20,000 units of output. At the end of the current period, you collected the following information: actual production = 21,000 units; actual units per batch (average) = 47; average hours of setup time per batch = 6.4; actual variable setup support cost per setup hour = $9.50; and, actual fixed setup support costs incurred = $75,000.

Required

1. Distinguish between volume-related, batch-related, and product-sustaining manufacturing support costs. What time horizon under an ABC system is assumed in defining the behavior of these costs?

2. Give some examples of variable setup support costs and short-term fixed setup support costs.

3. Given planned output (units to be produced), what is the *budgeted* number of production setups for the current period?

4. Given actual output (units produced), what is the *actual* number of production setups during the period?

5. Given actual output (units produced), what is the *flexible budgeted* number of production setups for the period?

6. What is the budgeted (standard) allocation rate of short-term fixed setup support costs? (*Note:* your answer will be expressed in terms of a predetermined rate per setup *hour.*)

7. What is this period's fixed overhead spending variance and the production-volume variance for fixed setup support costs?

8. For variable setup support costs this period, what is the spending variance? What is the efficiency variance?

9. What recommendations can you offer the company as to how setup-related manufacturing support costs can be better controlled/managed?

15-72 **Managing Earnings, Denominator Capacity-Level, and Ethics** Any given cost-information system is a function of a number of design choices. For product-costing purposes, one such design choice relates to how overhead, particularly fixed manufacturing overhead, application rates are determined. As controller for your company, you have been asked to prepare a written presentation for an upcoming meeting of the board of directors of your company. In preparing this assignment, assume that board members are reasonably knowledgeable about financial-reporting issues, but not necessarily about the intricacies of cost accounting systems. As you construct your document, feel free to consult outside references in addition to the material in your text. You can assume that this document is meant as a formal presentation to members of the board. Thus, your writing should be concise, clear, and reflective of proper grammar and construction.

Required Prepare, in proper form, a memo for the board that addresses the following issues:

1. Explain how manufacturing overhead rates are constructed in conventional cost accounting systems. Speak separately about fixed versus variable overhead application rates. What key choices must be made in establishing these rates? In answering this question, you might want to discuss differences (if any) between current IRS (income tax) requirements and internal reporting purposes, and between financial reporting requirements (e.g., FASB ASC 330-10-30, previously *SFAS No. 151*—available at www.asc .fasb.org) and internal reporting purposes.

2. Your company uses a standard cost system. As such, at the end of each period it must "clean up" the accounts by disposing of any standard cost variances that occurred for the period. You need to educate members of the board about how the variances for fixed manufacturing overhead are disposed of at the end of the period. In your answer, pay particular attention to the following two financial-reporting issues: (a) the requirements of FASB ASC 330-10-30, and (b) how, under absorption costing, reported earnings can be "managed" by choice of the denominator volume used to establish the fixed overhead application rate.

3. Access the Institute of Management Accountant's *Statement of Ethical Professional Practice* (www. imanet.org/about_ethics_statement.asp). Which of the stated standards relate directly to the issue of setting (fixed) overhead application rates and the decision as to how any resulting production-volume variances are disposed of for financial-reporting purposes? Be specific.

15-73 **Research Assignment, Strategy, Resource Capacity Planning** Obtain from your library a copy of following article: Robert S. Kaplan and David P. Norton, "Mastering the Management System," *Harvard Business Review* (January 2008), pp. 63–77. The authors of this article propose a five-stage management system designed to balance strategy and operations, that is, short-term operational concerns with long-term (strategic) priorities. In general, stage three of the process deals with what the authors call *dynamic budgeting* to include resource and capacity planning. It is this issue that is the subject of the present research assignment. (**Note:** the following additional source, available for download from the Harvard Business Publishing Web site, may also be helpful: Robert S. Kaplan, "Resource Capacity Planning in the Strategy Execution System," *Balanced Scorecard Report,* Reprint No. B0809A [2008].)

Required After reading the above-referenced article(s), please respond to the following questions:

1. Provide an overview of the five-step cycle that comprises the management system proposed by the authors of this article.

2. Stage 3 of the proposed system focuses on "Planning Operations," a significant component of which deals with planning resource capacity. Describe the process of resource-capacity planning within the context of the five-stage management cycle proposed by the authors. For example, discuss the linkage of Stage 3 to both Stage 2 and Stage 4 of the management cycle.

3. The authors indicate that their preferred tool for resource-capacity planning is time-driven activity-based costing (TDABC). Provide a brief overview of TDABC including how this implementation differs from traditional ABC models. (*Hint:* in addition to the article, refer to Chapter 5 of the text.)

4. Refer to the Towerton Financial example presented on pages 70–71 of the article. How did this organization use TDABC results to determine the level of resource capacity (people and computing) needed to implement its strategy?

Solutions to Self-Study Problems

1. Analysis of the Total Overhead Variance

1. a.

Units manufactured during the period	360
Standard direct labor hours allowed per unit produced	× 2
Total standard direct labor hours allowed for the units manufactured	720
Standard variable factory overhead rate per direct labor hour	× $5.00
Flexible budget for variable factory overhead for the units produced	$3,600

b.

The total variable factory overhead applied to production (same as the flexible budget for variable overhead based on output)	$3,600

c.

Practical capacity (units)	400
Standard direct labor hours per unit	× 2
Total standard direct labor hours at practical capacity	800
Standard fixed factory overhead rate per direct labor hour (given)	× $20
Total budgeted fixed factory overhead for the period	$16,000

d.

Total standard direct labor hours for the units manufactured (from 1a)	720
Standard fixed factory overhead rate per direct labor hour	× $20
Total fixed factory overhead applied	$14,400

2. a, b, and c.

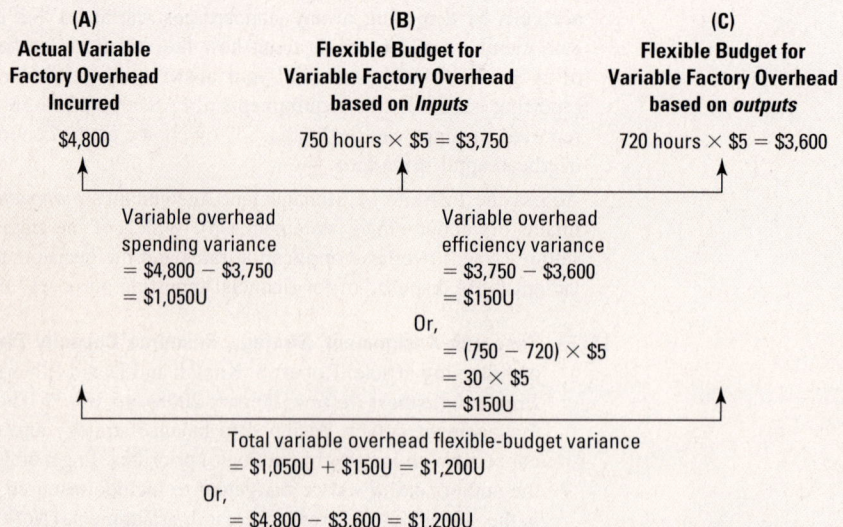

(A)	**(B)**	**(C)**
Actual Variable Factory Overhead Incurred	**Flexible Budget for Variable Factory Overhead based on *Inputs***	**Flexible Budget for Variable Factory Overhead based on *outputs***
$4,800	750 hours × $5 = $3,750	720 hours × $5 = $3,600

Variable overhead spending variance
= $4,800 − $3,750
= $1,050U

Variable overhead efficiency variance
= $3,750 − $3,600
= $150U

Or,
= (750 − 720) × $5
= 30 × $5
= $150U

Total variable overhead flexible-budget variance
= $1,050U + $150U = $1,200U

Or,
= $4,800 − $3,600 = $1,200U

d. Total underapplied variable factory overhead = total variable overhead flexible-budget variance = $1,200

e, f, and g.

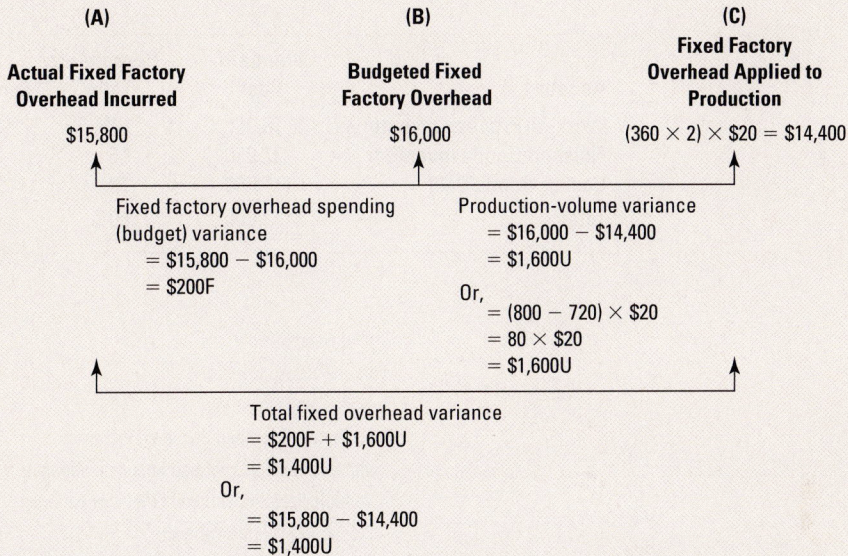

(A)	(B)	(C)
Actual Fixed Factory Overhead Incurred	**Budgeted Fixed Factory Overhead**	**Fixed Factory Overhead Applied to Production**
$15,800	$16,000	$(360 \times 2) \times \$20 = \$14,400$

Fixed factory overhead spending (budget) variance
= $15,800 − $16,000
= $200F

Production-volume variance
= $16,000 − $14,400
= $1,600U
Or,
= (800 − 720) × $20
= 80 × $20
= $1,600U

Total fixed overhead variance
= $200F + $1,600U
= $1,400U
Or,
= $15,800 − $14,400
= $1,400U

h. Total underapplied fixed factory overhead = Total fixed overhead variance = $1,400U

3. a. $\dfrac{\text{Factory overhead}}{\text{spending variance}} = \dfrac{\text{Variable factory overhead}}{\text{spending variance}} + \dfrac{\text{Fixed factory overhead}}{\text{spending variance}}$

= $1,050U + $200F

= $850U

b. $\dfrac{\text{Factory overhead}}{\text{efficiency variance}} = \dfrac{\text{Variable factory overhead}}{\text{efficiency variance}} = \$150U$

c. Production-volume variance = $1,600U

4. $\dfrac{\text{Factory overhead}}{\text{controllable (flexible-budget) variance}} = \dfrac{\text{Factory overhead}}{\text{spending variance}} + \dfrac{\text{Factory overhead}}{\text{efficiency variance}}$

= $850U + $150U

= $1,000U

Production-volume variance is $1,600U, the amount identified in both four-variance and three-variance analyses.

5. a.	Factory Overhead	20,600	
	Cash, Prepaid accounts, Accumulated depreciation; or sundry payable accounts		20,600
b.	Work-in-Process Inventory	18,000	
	Factory Overhead		18,000
c.			
	Variable Factory Overhead Spending Variance	1,050	
	Variable Factory Overhead Efficiency Variance	150	
	Production-Volume Variance	1,600	
	Factory Overhead		2,600
	Fixed Factory Overhead Spending Variance		200
d.(1)	Cost of Goods Sold	2,600	
	Fixed Factory Overhead Spending Variance	200	
	Variable Factory Overhead Spending Variance		1,050
	Variable Factory Overhead Efficiency Variance		150
	Production-Volume Variance		1,600

(2) Ending balances at standard cost:

Work-in-Process Inventory ($153,000 − $134,640)	$ 18,360
Finished Goods Inventory ($134,640 − $111,690)	22,950
Cost of Goods Sold (CGS)	$111,690
Total	$153,000

Account	Standard Cost	Percent of Total	Proration of Net Variance	Adjusted Cost
Work-in-Process Inventory	$ 18,360	12%	$2,600 × 0.12 = $ 312	$ 18,672
Finished Goods Inventory	22,950	15	2,600 × 0.15 = 390	23,340
Cost of Goods Sold	111,690	73	2,600 × 0.73 = 1,898	113,588
Total	$153,000	100%	$2,600	$155,600

Cost of Goods Sold	1,898	
Work-in-Process Inventory	312	
Finished Goods Inventory	390	
Fixed Factory Overhead Spending Variance	200	
Variable Factory Overhead Spending Variance		1,050
Variable Factory Overhead Efficiency Variance		150
Production-Volume Variance		1,600

2. Variance Investigation (Appendix)

Courses of Action

A_1: Investigate to determine the cause(s) of the efficiency variance.
A_2: Do not investigate.

States of Nature

S_1: The operation is in control (operates normally).
S_2: The operation is out of control.

Cost and Probability

I = Cost of investigation = $2,500
C = Cost of corrective action, if the process is found to be out-of-control = $5,000
L = Losses from being out of control with no corrective action taken = $55,000
P = Probability of the operation being in control = 40%

	Payoff Table	
	States of Nature	
Management Action	**In Control* (0.40)**	**Out of Control[†] (0.60)**
Investigate	$2,500	$2,500 + $5,000
Do not investigate	0	$55,000

* That is, the variance is due to random, not systematic, factors.
[†] That is, the variance is not due to random factors.

1. $E(\text{investigate})$ = (40% × $2,500) + (60% × $7,500) = $5,500
    $E(\text{do not investigate})$ = 60% × $55,000 = $33,000

    The expected total cost to the firm will be lower if Smiley investigates the variance and takes proper action to correct the cause of the variance, if the investigation finds the operation to be out of control.

2. Smiley is indifferent to the alternative courses of action if the probability of the process NOT being in control (p) is at a level that renders the expected cost of investigating and the expected cost of not investigating equal.

$$\mathrm{E}\left(\text{Investigate}\right) = \mathrm{E}\left(\text{Do Not Investigate}\right)$$
$$\left(\left[\mathrm{I} \times \left(1 - p\right)\right] + \left[\left(\mathrm{I} + \mathrm{C}\right) \times p\right]\right) = \mathrm{L} \times p$$
$$p = \mathrm{I}/\left(\mathrm{L} - \mathrm{C}\right)$$
$$p = \$2,500/\left(\$55,000 - \$5,000\right)$$
$$p = 0.05$$

Therefore, if the probability that the process is out of control is 5% (i.e., there is a 5% probability that the observed variance has a nonrandom cause), the company would be indifferent between conducting an investigation and not conducting an investigation. If the probability, p, of a nonrandom variance is less than 0.05, then the optimal action is NOT to conduct an investigation.

3. EVPI = [($0 × 0.40) + ($7,500 × 0.60)] − Expected cost without perfect information
   = $4,500 − $5,500 = $1,000

Thus, the manager would be willing to pay up to $1,000 for perfect information. This amount represents the long-run (or average) decrease in expected cost.

CHAPTER SIXTEEN

Operational Performance Measurement: Further Analysis of Productivity and Sales

After studying this chapter, you should be able to ...

1. Explain the strategic role of the flexible budget in analyzing sales and productivity
2. Calculate and interpret the measures for total productivity, partial operational productivity and partial financial productivity
3. Use the flexible budget to decompose partial financial productivity into input price and productivity, components
4. Use the flexible budget to calculate and interpret the sales quantity and sales mix variances
5. Use the flexible budget to calculate and interpret the market size and market share variances
6. Use the flexible budget to analyze sales performance over time

Toyota Motor Company, with sales increasing at 5 percent per year and productivity continuing its strong edge over U.S. automakers, is expected to increase its global presence in the coming years. One measure of productivity, the number of hours per vehicle assembled, in 2004 was 27.9 hours for Toyota, 37 for Ford, and 35.9 for Chrysler LLC; and while Ford, GM, and Chrysler improved productivity prior to 2004, Toyota's productivity increased at a faster rate. In contrast, the productivity gap has decreased since 2004, as recent productivity reports show that in 2007 Toyota required 29.9 hours per vehicle (a small increase over 2004) while the respective productivity numbers at Ford and Chrysler are 35 and 32.3 hours per vehicle, an improvement over 2004.

On the sales side, Toyota's share of sales in North America continues to increase relative to other auto manufacturers, as consumers' interest in full-size pickups and sport utility vehicles has fallen due to higher gas prices and economic recession. Measures of sales performance include those that look at sales growth and the profitability of sales. To illustrate, the average profit per vehicle in 2004 for Toyota was $1,742, while the North American manufacturers averaged a small loss on each sale. In 2007 the figures are lower for all auto companies: a profit of $922 at Toyota, and losses of $1,467 at Ford, $719 at GM, and $412 at Chrysler. The challenge of global competitiveness is very strong in the auto industry, where productivity and sales performance are two key performance measures. The competition is particularly strong in the current economic recession, as Chrysler and GM struggle for survival, and all major automakers are experiencing double digit sales declines.[1]

This chapter continues the focus on operational-level performance measures introduced in Chapters 14 and 15—standard costing and the flexible budget, nonfinancial operational

[1] Lee Hawkins, Jr., "U.S. Auto Makers Get Better Grades for Productivity," *The Wall Street Journal,* June 11, 2004, p. A3; Neal E. Boudette, "Detroit's Big 3 Make Productivity Strides," *The Wall Street Journal,* June 6, 2008, p B3.

performance measures, and resource-capacity planning. This chapter extends Chapters 14 and 15 through coverage of an extension of the flexible budget—productivity measures and additional sales variance measures. Other methods for improving efficiency and financial control are covered elsewhere in the text (see Chapter 1 for summary) including: target costing, benchmarking. business process improvement, and total quality management.

The Strategic Role of the Flexible Budget in Analyzing Sales and Productivity

LEARNING OBJECTIVE 1

Explain the strategic role of the flexible budget in analyzing sales and productivity.

The strategic role of sales analysis is to better understand the reasons behind an increase (or decrease) in total sales dollars over the budgeted amount, or an increase (decrease) over the prior year. The key questions for a competitive analysis is how the change in sales has affected the firm's profitability and growth in desired market areas. Is the firm meeting strategic sales goals? Are sales increasing in profitable or unprofitable product lines? To begin to answer these questions, the total amount of change in sales is decomposed into many components, each of which holds some answers about these strategic questions. For example, the total dollar change in sales over (or under) the budget can be explained in terms of changes in selling prices and changes in the volume of units sold. A change in prices or volume will affect total sales. The decomposition of total sales into these two variances, the selling price and volume variances, is illustrated using the flexible budget in Chapter 14. Chapter 16 now takes one of these two variances, the volume variance, and further decomposes it into elements that explain the effect of changes in product mix (the proportion of total sales for each of the products), the size of the markets for the firm's products, and the firm's share in these markets. The further analysis allows managers to see how changes in product mix and market size/share affect profits. The decomposition of the sales variances uses the flexible budget in two ways: (1) analyzing differences between actual sales and the master budget sales (as in the approach in Chapter 14) and (2) analyzing changes in sales over the prior year.

The strategic role of productivity analysis is to assist management in identifying the drivers of productivity and to implement methods that improve productivity and profitability. The good news is that in most countries productivity has been increasing in recent years. In the United States since 2001, productivity in the private, nonfarm business sector has increased an average of 2.7 percent per year in contrast to the average of 1.5 percent annual rate in the prior two decades. The current economic downturn is taking its toll, however, as the most recent figures for 2007 and 2008 show a decline to 1.4 percent in both of those years. Of course, productivity has differed substantially across industries, depending on the industry's ability to control waste, to control labor costs, and to develop product and manufacturing process innovations. For example, some of the industries that have been slow to innovate relative to other industries include furniture manufacturing, printing, and food manufacturing.[2]

The key determinants of productivity for most organizations are:

- Control of waste.
- Control of labor costs.
- Product and manufacturing process innovation.
- Fluctuations in demand due to changes in the business cycle or for other reasons.

The control of waste is achieved through efforts in work flow management and quality. A good example is the Toyota Production System (TPS) which has helped Toyota to become one of the most productive automakers in the world.[3] The main elements of TPS are (1) a long-term focus on relationships with suppliers and coordination with these suppliers; (2) an emphasis on balanced, continuous flow manufacturing with stable production levels; (3) continuous improvement in product design and manufacturing processes with the objective of eliminating waste (TPS defines waste as defects, overproduction, transportation, waiting time,

[2] James C. Cooper and Kathleen Madigan, "Can Productivity Keep Up the Good Work?" *BusinessWeek*, December 19, 2005, p. 25; David Huether, "The Case of the Missing Jobs," *BusinessWeek*, April 3, 2006, p. 136; James C. Cooper, "U.S.: The Double Whammy That Could Ignite Inflation," *BusinessWeek*, March 20, 2006, p. 25; "U.S. Factories Falling Behind," *BusinessWeek*, May 24, 2004, pp. 94–96.

[3] Taiichi Ohno, *Toyota Production System: Beyond Large Scale Production*, Productivity Inc, 1988.

inventory, and overprocessing); and (4) flexible manufacturing systems (FMS) in which different vehicles are produced on the same assembly line and employees are trained for a variety of tasks. The focus on waste and balanced production flows is also called *lean manufacturing.*

Product and process innovation is the third key determinant of competitiveness in productivity, often achieved through the implementation of information technology. Looking beyond these three determinants, it is important to understand that productivity in a firm or industry is greatly influenced by the business cycle. Higher productivity is usually seen when a firm is coming out of a low point in the business cycle, as the firm stretches existing resources to meet demand, and then productivity growth slows as resources are added. So it is always important to analyze productivity within the larger context of the competitive environment and business cycle in which the firm operates. While for simplicity many of the examples to follow are in the manufacturing context, the topic of productivity applies as well in service companies where labor costs are a high proportion of total costs. There are examples of productivity analysis in the service industries in the end-of-chapter problems.

Analyzing Productivity

LEARNING OBJECTIVE 2

Calculate and interpret the measures for total productivity, partial operational productivity, and partial financial productivity.

The single best measure of a country's average standard of living is productivity: the value of output of goods and services a country procures per worker. The more workers produce, the more income they receive, and the more they can consume. Higher productivity results in higher standards of living.

> *Martin Neil Baily and Matthew J. Slaughter*
> *Former Members of the U.S. President's*
> *Council of Economic Advisers*

Productivity
is the ratio of output to input.

Baily and Slaughter, writing in *The Wall Street Journal,* note that productivity is key to the success of a country, a company, and an individual worker.[4] **Productivity** is measured as the ratio of output to input.

$$\text{Productivity} = \frac{\text{Output}}{\text{Input}}$$

A firm that spends five days to manufacture 100 units has a productivity of 20 units per day. A social service worker who processes 75 cases over a four-week period has a productivity of 3.75 cases per day. A firm that uses 24.5 pounds of material for each unit manufactured is more productive than a firm that uses 25 pounds of the same materials to manufacture one unit of the same product. To improve productivity, firms need to know the productivity levels of their operations.

Operational productivity
is the ratio of output units to input units.

A measure of productivity can be either an operational or a financial productivity measure. **Operational productivity** is the ratio of output units to input units. Both the numerator and the denominator are physical measures. **Financial productivity** is also a ratio of output to input, except that either the numerator or the denominator is a dollar amount. For example, the number of tables made from a sheet of plywood involves operational productivity; the number of tables per dollar cost of plywood reflects financial productivity.

Financial productivity
is the ratio of output to input with either the numerator or the denominator a dollar amount.

Partial productivity
focuses on the relationship between input factors and output.

A productivity measure may include all production factors or focus on a single factor or part of the production factors that the firm uses in manufacturing. A productivity measure that focuses on the relationship between one input factor and the output attained is a **partial productivity** measure. The following are examples of partial productivity:

- Direct materials productivity (output/units of materials).
- Workforce productivity (output per labor-hour or output per person employed).
- Process productivity (output per machine-hour or output per kilowatt-hour).

Total productivity
includes all input resources in the computation of the ratio of output attained to input resources consumed.

A productivity measure that includes all input resources used in production is a **total productivity measure.** The number of tables manufactured per dollar of manufacturing costs is a

---

[4] Martin Neil Baily and Matthew J. Slaughter, "What's Behind the Recent Productivity Slowdown," *The Wall Street Journal,* December 13-14, 2008, p. A15.

Is corporate financial performance affected by the breadth of performance measures and whether such measures are aligned with strategy? A recent study examined this issue using a sample of 128 manufacturing firms. The authors collected survey data regarding (1) the diversity and extent of performance measures used (i.e., financial versus nonfinancial, subjective versus objective), (2) whether the firm was pursuing a quality-based strategy, and (3) self-assessments of performance of the respondent's department. Based on the responses, the authors concluded that regardless of the strategy pursued, companies with more extensive performance measurement systems had higher levels of self-reported performance. Also,

companies that embraced a quality-based manufacturing strategy had better self-reported performance when subjective nonfinancial measures were used (e.g., assessment of degree of cooperation or knowledge-sharing across departments). The results indicate the importance of using a wide range of financial and nonfinancial performance measures in order to both improve performance and better align performance with strategy.

Source: W.W. Van der Stede, C.W. Chow, and T. W. Lin, "Strategy, Choice of Performance Measures, and Performance," *Behavioral Research in Accounting* 18 (2006), pp. 185–205.

EXHIBIT 16.1 **Productivity Measures**

	Partial Productivity		Total Productivity	
	Operational	**Financial**	**Total Units of Output**	**Sales Value of Output**
Numerator (output)	Units of output	Units of output	Units of output	Sales value of output
Denominator (input)	Units of input	Dollar value of input	Dollar value of input	Dollar value of input
Productivity measure (output/input)	Units of output per unit of input	Units of output per dollar value of input	Units of output per dollar value of input	Dollar value of output per dollar value of input

total productivity measure because the denominator, manufacturing costs, includes all manufacturing costs incurred to make the tables. Exhibit 16.1 summarizes productivity measures.

Exhibit 16.2 presents selected production data of Erie Precision Tool Company in 2009 and 2010 for manufacturing drill bits. The manufacturing costs include total fixed factory overhead and other operating expenses of $300,000 per year and variable manufacturing costs consisting of metal alloy (direct materials) and direct labor-hours.

The firm earned $1,100,000 operating income in 2010, a 17 percent increase over the $940,000 earned in 2009. Without examining the operating data in detail, management would probably be happy with the improvement. The increase in operating income, however, compares unfavorably to the improvement in total sales. The total sales in 2010 are 120 percent of the total sales in 2009. With the fixed factory overhead and fixed operating expenses remaining unchanged at $300,000 each year, the increase in operating income should have been more than the 20 percent increase in total sales. The lower increase in operating income is a result of a higher-than-proportional increase in the firm's variable costs for direct materials and direct labor. The total variable costs increased 32 percent [($1,000,000 − $760,000)/$760,000] while the total sales increased only 20 percent.

Several factors could have contributed to the increase in direct materials and direct labor costs, including increases in the number of units manufactured and sold, changes in the amounts and/or the proportions of the inputs used in production; and increases in the unit cost of resources. The firm should identify factors that caused the changes so that management can decrease manufacturing costs and increase operating income.

Productivity measurements discussed in this chapter examine the effect of a firm's productivity on its operating income. Increased productivity decreases costs and increases operating income. Changes in the productivity of different resources, however, do not always occur in the same direction or at an equal rate. A firm's productivity or use of direct materials can improve while its direct labor productivity might deteriorate. For instance, a furniture manufacturer increased materials productivity by reducing waste due to improper cutting. However, to reduce improper cutting of materials, workers spent more labor-hours to cut the boards carefully. The labor-hour productivity decreased. Management needs to know the changes in productivities of individual production resources, which partial productivities provide.

EXHIBIT 16.2
Operating Data of Erie Precision Tool Company in 2009 and 2010

ERIE PRECISION TOOL COMPANY		
Operating Data		
	2010	**2009**
Units manufactured and sold	4,800	4,000
Total sales ($500 price per unit)	$2,400,000	$2,000,000
Direct materials (25,000 pounds at $24/pound in 2009 and 32,000 pounds at $25/pound in 2010)	800,000	600,000
Direct labor (4,000 hours at $40 per hour in 2009 and 4,000 hours at $50/hour in 2010)	200,000	160,000
Fixed factory overhead and fixed operating expenses	300,000	300,000
Operating income	$1,100,000	$ 940,000

Partial Productivity

A partial productivity measure depicts the relationship between output and one of the required input resources used in producing the output.

$$\text{Partial productivity} = \frac{\text{Number of units manufactured}}{\text{Number of units or cost of a single input resource}}$$

For example, partial productivity of the direct materials for the Erie Precision Tool Company in 2009 is 0.16 units of output per pound of material, as computed here:

$$\text{Partial productivity of direct materials in 2009} = \frac{4,000}{25,000} = 0.16 \text{ units/pound}$$

Partial Operational Productivity

Firms often use benchmarks in assessing productivity. Among benchmarks often used are past productivity measures of the firm, productivity of another firm in the same industry, the industry standard or average, or benchmarks established by the top management as the goal for the firm to attain. Sources of benchmarking information include industry and national associations focused on productivity and quality such as the American Production and Inventory Control Society (www.apics.org), the American Productivity & Quality Center (www.apqc.org), and the American Society for Quality (www.asq.org). In this example, we use Erie Precision Tool Company productivity level in 2009 as the benchmark to assess productivity in 2010.

A comparison of partial productivity from 2009 to 2010 shows that the partial productivity of direct materials decreased. The firm manufactured 0.16 units in 2009 but only 0.15 units in 2010 from 1 pound of direct materials, a 6.25 percent decrease in productivity [(0.16 − 0.15) ÷ 0.16 = 6.25%]. Partial productivity of direct labor, however, improved in 2010. The firm manufactured one unit for each direct labor-hour in 2009 and 1.2 units per hour in 2010, a 20 percent increase in productivity [(1.2 − 1) ÷ 1 = 20%]. See Exhibit 16.3.

Changes in productivity also can be examined by computing the amount of input resources that the firm would have used in 2010 had it maintained the 2009 partial productivity, as shown in Exhibit 16.4. In this case, the 4,800 units manufactured and sold in 2010 would have required only 30,000 pounds of direct materials (4,800 ÷ 0.16). The decreased partial productivity required the use of an additional 2,000 pounds in 2010 (32,000 − 30,000). Similarly, the firm would have used 4,800 direct labor-hours in 2010 had it had the same direct labor partial productivity in 2010 as in 2009. The firm saved the cost for 800 hours of direct labor (4,800 − 4,000) when its partial productivity in 2010 for direct labor increased from 1.0 to 1.2.

LEARNING OBJECTIVE 3

Use the flexible budget to decompose partial financial productivity into input price and productivity components.

Partial Financial Productivity

The bottom panel of Exhibit 16.3 reports the partial financial productivities of direct materials and direct labor. The partial financial productivity indicates the number of units of output manufactured for each dollar the firm spent on the input resource. The partial financial

EXHIBIT 16.3
Partial Productivity of Erie Precision Tool Company

ERIE PRECISION TOOL COMPANY		
Partial Productivity—Direct Materials and Direct Labor		
	Partial Operational Productivity	
	2010	**2009**
Direct materials	4,800/32,000 = 0.15	4,000/25,000 = 0.16
Direct labor	4,800/4,000 = 1.20	4,000/4,000 = 1.00
	Partial Financial Productivity	
	2010	**2009**
Direct materials	4,800/$800,000 = 0.006	4,000/$600,000 = 0.0067
Direct labor	4,800/$200,000 = 0.024	4,000/$160,000 = 0.025

EXHIBIT 16.4
Changes in Operational Partial Productivity of Erie Precision Tool Company

ERIE PRECISION TOOL COMPANY					
Effects of Changes in Operational Partial Productivity of Direct Materials and Direct Labor					
	(1)	(2) 2009 Partial Operational Productivity	(3) = (1) ÷ (2) 2010 Output at 2009 Productivity	(4) Input Used in 2010	(5) = (3) − (4) Savings (Loss) in Units of Input
Input Resource	**2010 Output**				
Direct materials	4,800	0.16	30,000	32,000	(2,000)
Direct labor	4,800	1.00	4,800	4,000	800

productivity for direct materials is determined by dividing the output (4,000 units in 2009 and 4,800 units in 2010) by the cost of the resource for the year (cost of direct materials: $600,000 in 2009 and $800,000 in 2010). The partial financial productivities are 0.0067 in 2009 and 0.006 in 2010. The partial financial productivity decreased from manufacturing 0.0067 units in 2009 to 0.006 units in 2010 for every dollar spent on direct materials, a decrease in productivity from 2009 to 2010 of 10 percent [(0.0067 − 0.006) ÷ 0.0067].

The direct labor partial *financial* productivity is 0.025 for 2009 and 0.024 for 2010, a decrease of 4 percent [(0.025 − 0.024) ÷ 0.025]. This result is in conflict with the direct labor partial *operational* productivity reported earlier (20 percent improvement). These results suggest that although employee productivity per hour increased, the cost increase due to higher hourly wages more than offset the gain in productivity per hour.

Factors that may contribute to the difference in manufacturing costs between two operations are differences in output level, input cost, or productivity. Panel 1 of Exhibit 16.5 shows how the flexible budget can be used for determining the effects of each of these factors. Point A is the actual operating results of 2010. The amounts for all three factors at point A are the actual 2010 figures: units of output, productivity, and input cost. Point B is the cost to manufacture the 2010 output at the *2009 productivity level* and 2010 input cost. The only difference between points A and B is in productivity. Thus, any difference between points A and B is attributable to changes in productivity between 2010 and 2009.

Point C is the cost to manufacture the 2010 output at the 2009 productivity level and *2009 input cost.* The only difference between points B and C is in the unit cost of the input resource in each of the years: point B uses the 2010 cost per unit for the input resource while point C uses the 2009 cost per unit for the input resource. The difference between the amounts in points B and C, if any, results from the difference in unit cost of the input resource.

Point D is the cost to manufacture the *2009 output* at 2009 productivity and 2009 unit cost of the input resource. Any difference in the costs between points C and D is because of different output levels between these two points. The output is then divided by the total cost of the required resource to manufacture the output. Because the total cost of the required resource in each of the years is determined using the same productivity level (2009 productivity) and the same unit cost of the input resource (2009 cost per unit of the input resource), the total

EXHIBIT 16.5 **Partitioning Partial Financial Productivity Using the Flexible Budget**

ERIE PRECISION TOOL COMPANY
Partitioning Partial Financial Productivity into Productivity Change and Input Price Change

Panel 1: Flexible Budget Framework

	A	B	C	D
Output	2010	2010	2010	2009
Productivity	2010	2009	2009	2009
Input Cost	2010	2010	2009	2009

Productivity Change   Input Price Change   Output Change

Panel 2: Operating Data for Partitioning Partial Financial Productivity

	Actual 2010 Operating Results	2010 Output at *2009 Productivity* and 2010 Input Cost	2010 Output at 2009 Productivity and *2009 Input Cost*	Actual 2009 Operating Results
Output units	4,800	4,800	4,800	4,000
Input units and costs				
Direct materials	32,000 × $25 = $ 800,000	30,000 × $25 = $750,000	30,000 × $24 = $720,000	25,000 × $24 = $600,000
Direct labor	4,000 × $50 = 200,000	4,800 × $50 = 240,000	4,800 × $40 = 192,000	4,000 × $40 = 160,000
Total	$1,000,000	$990,000	$912,000	$760,000

Panel 3: Partitioning Productivity and Input Price Changes

	2010 Operations			2009 Operations
	2010 output/ (2010 input × 2010 input costs)	2010 output/(2009 input for 2010 output × 2010 input costs)	2010 output/(2009 input for 2010 output × 2009 input costs)	2009 output/ (2009 input × 2009 input costs)
Direct materials	4,800/$800,000 = 0.006	4,800/$750,000 = 0.0064	4,800/$720,000 = 0.006667	4,000/$600,000 = 0.006667
Direct labor	4,800/$200,000 = 0.024	4,800/$240,000 = 0.0200	4,800/$192,000 = 0.025000	4,000/$160,000 = 0.025000

Productivity Change   Input Price Change   Output Change

Direct materials	0.0060 − 0.0064 = 0.0004U	0.006400 − 0.006667 = 0.000267U	0.006667 − 0.006667 = 0
Direct labor	0.0240 − 0.0200 = 0.0040F	0.02000 − 0.025000 = 0.005000U	0.025000 − 0.025000 = 0

Panel 4: Summary of Results

		Productivity Change from 2009 to 2010					
	Productivity Change		Input Price Change		Output Change		Total Change
Direct materials	0.0004U	+	0.000267U	+	0	=	0.000667U
Direct labor	0.0040F	+	0.005000U	+	0	=	0.001000U

		Change as Percent of 2009 Productivity					
	Productivity Change		Input Price Change		Output Change		Total Change
Direct materials	6%U	+	4%U	+	0%	=	10%U
Direct labor	16%F	+	20%U	+	0%	=	4%U

cost of the required resource in each of the years is in proportion to their respective output levels. As a result, the ratios of output to input (costs) at points C and D are always identical, and the change in productivity for output change from 2009 to 2010 is always equal to zero. The column for point D is included for completeness, to show the total change from the actual results of 2009 to the actual results of 2010; the change in productivity from 2009 to 2010 is the result of two changes only: the change in input prices and the change in materials or labor productivity.

The analysis shows that, of the 10 percent decrease in partial financial productivity of direct materials (from 0.0067 to 0.006, Exhibit 16.3), 6 percent (0.0004/0.0067, bottom of panel 4, Exhibit 16.5) is attributable to productivity change. The remaining 4 percent (bottom of panel 4, Exhibit 16.5) reflects the price change in the cost per pound of direct materials ($24 in 2009 to $25 in 2010).

The 2010 financial partial productivity of direct labor is 4 percent lower than that of 2009 (from 0.025 to 0.024, Exhibit 16.3). The lower partial financial productivity of direct labor in 2010 is not due to decreased productivity of direct labor in 2010, however. The partial productivity of direct labor increased by 16 percent (bottom of panel 4, Exhibit 16.5). The 25 percent increase in wages ($40 per hour in 2009 and $50 per hour in 2010) more than offsets the gain in labor productivity. As a result, total direct labor cost increased and the partial financial productivity decreased by 4 percent.

Partial Productivity: Operational versus Financial

Both the numerator and the denominator of a partial operational productivity measure are physical units. Using physical measures makes partial operational measures easy for operational personnel to understand and use in operations. The fact that an operational productivity measure is unaffected by price changes or other factors also makes it easier to benchmark.

Partial financial productivity has the advantage of considering the effects of both cost and quantity of an input resource on productivity. At the management level, the effect of cost, not merely the physical quantity, is the main concern. In addition, partial financial productivity can be used in operations that use more than one production factor. Partial operational productivity, on the other hand, measures only one input resource at a time.

Limitations of Partial Productivity Analysis

A partial productivity measure has several limitations. First, it measures only the relationship between an input resource and the output; it ignores any effect that changes in other manufacturing factors have on productivity. An improved partial productivity measure could have been obtained by decreasing the productivity of one or more other input resources. For example, Erie Precision Tool Company can improve its partial productivity of direct labor by speeding up labor usage, though waste of direct materials might increase. Or, it can boost direct materials partial productivity through reduction in direct materials waste by using more labor-hours to cut each piece of material carefully. Management accountants call this the cross-substitution of factors of input.

A second limitation is that partial productivity ignores any effect that changes in other production factors have on productivity. For example, increases in materials quality are likely to raise the partial productivity of direct materials as well as direct labor. Erie Precision Tool Company might have workers with more experience or higher skill in 2010 than those in 2009. As a result, the partial productivity of labor increased in 2010. The average hourly wage rate for workers with more experience or higher skill will be higher. Is it worthwhile for the firm to make the trade-off? Unfortunately, an analysis of operational partial productivity cannot provide an answer.

Third, partial productivity should include effects that changes in the firm's operating characteristics have on the productivity of the input resource. Installation of high-efficiency equipment improves direct labor partial operational productivity. The improvement in labor partial operational productivity can hardly be attributed to increased labor productivity.

Fourth, an improved partial productivity does not necessarily mean that the firm or division operates efficiently. No efficiency standard or benchmark is involved in the determinations of partial productivity measures, only comparison to the prior period.

Partial Productivity, the Flexible Budget, and Standard Costs (Review of Chapter 14)

It is common for productivity analysis as illustrated above to use the year-to-year analytical framework. The analysis could also be based upon a budget or standard, and then the analysis would be very much like the application of the flexible budget in Chapter 14. For example, in Exhibit 16.5, panel 2, the differences in total costs for each of the points A, B, C, and D represent differences in cost very much like the variances calculated in Chapter 14. The difference is that in Chapter 14 we compared actual performance to the master budget using the flexible budget to distinguish volume and flexible-budget variances. Note that the volume variance in dollars in Exhibit 16.5, panel 2 is $152,000 ($912,000 − $760,000); this is the increased cost for producing 800 more units at standard productivity and price. Now, look back to page 597 to review the calculation of the sales volume variance in Exhibit 14.4. The volume variance for variable expense of $99,000 in Exhibit 14.4 is calculated in the same way as the volume variance in Exhibit 16.5, panel 2; the only difference is that the benchmark in Exhibit 14.4 is the master budget, and the benchmark in Exhibit 16.5 is the prior year results. Similarly, the flexible-budget variances for labor and materials in Chapter 14 are computed in a way similar to the computation of the input price and productivity variances in Exhibit 16.5, panel 2.

In effect, the use of the flexible budget in Chapters 14 and 16 is quite similar, but there are different objectives. The flexible budget in Chapter 14 was used to identify the volume and flexible-budget variances for materials and labor, *for changes in volume relative to the master budget.* In contrast, the flexible budget is used in Exhibit 16.5 to identify changes in input prices and productivity *from year to year* (rather than to the master budget). The variances in Chapter 14 calculate the effect of differences in usage or price for a given level of good output, at a standard level of input. Chapter 14 works with the materials or labor standard of a certain number of materials units or labor-hours *per unit of output,* while productivity analysis looks at the inverse: the number of units of output *per unit or materials or labor input.*

Both standard cost analysis (Chapter 14) and productivity analysis (Chapter 16) are widely used and have different objectives. Standard cost analysis focuses on meeting standards of materials and labor usage, while productivity analysis analyzes changes in productivity over time.

Total Productivity

Total productivity is the ratio of output to the total cost of all input resources used to produce the output.

$$\text{Total productivity} = \frac{\text{Units or sales value of output}}{\text{Total cost of all input resources}}$$

Total productivity is a financial productivity measure. The numerator can be either the number of units or the sales value of the output attained. The denominator is the total dollar amount of all direct (variable cost) resources used in the production of the output.

The first panel of Exhibit 16.6 shows the computation of Erie Precision Tool Company's total productivity of variable manufacturing costs for 2009 and 2010. The computation of total productivity involves three steps: First, determine the output of each period: 4,000 units in 2009 and 4,800 units in 2010. Second, calculate the total variable costs incurred to produce

EXHIBIT 16.6

Total Productivity for Erie Precision Tool Company

ERIE PRECISION TOOL COMPANY		
Total Productivity		
Panel 1: Total Productivity in Units	**2010**	**2009**
(a) Total units manufactured	4,800	4,000
(b) Total variable manufacturing costs incurred	$1,000,000	$ 760,000
(c) Total productivity: (a) / (b)	0.004800	0.005263
(d) Decrease in productivity: 0.005263 − 0.004800 = 0.000463, or 8.8% (0.000463 ÷ 0.005263)		
Panel 2: Total Productivity in Sales Dollars		
(a) Total sales	$2,400,000	$2,000,000
(b) Total variable manufacturing costs incurred	$1,000,000	$ 760,000
(c) Total productivity: (a) / (b)	$ 2.4000	$ 2.6316
(d) Decrease in productivity: $2.6316 − $2.4000 = $0.2316, or 8.8% ($0.2316 ÷ $2.6316)		

As the auto industry goes, so does the auto parts industry. With domestic automakers losing market share, many of the U.S. auto parts makers are also in stress. Productivity problems plague the industry. For example, Delphi's labor costs are almost $70 per hour, nearly the highest of any manufacturing firm. The two largest parts manufacturers, Delphi and Visteon, are both facing job cuts, plant closings, reduction in retirement benefits for employees, and potential bankruptcy. Moreover, since January 1, 2005, three large auto parts manufacturers have filed for bankruptcy—Dana Corporation of Ohio, Tower Automotive of Novi, Michigan, and Collins & Aikman of Troy, Michigan; there are also a half-dozen smaller parts makers that have already filed for bankruptcy. Despite these failures, billionaire investor Wilbur Ross is looking to buy these failing companies. He has recently purchased some of Collins & Aikman's plants, a portion of Lear Corporation's automotive parts operations in Europe, and is seeking to buy part of the failing Delphi. What do you think his strategy is?

(Refer to Comments on Cost Management in Action at end of Chapter.)

the output: $760,000 in 2009 and $1,000,000 in 2010 (Exhibit 16.5, panel 2). Third, compute the total productivity by dividing the amount of output by the total cost of variable input resources: 0.005263 in 2009 and 0.004800 in 2010.

The total productivity indicates that for every thousand dollars of variable cost incurred in 2009, the firm manufactured 5.263 units of output. The total productivity in 2010 is 0.0048, indicating that the firm manufactures 4.8 units for every thousand dollars of variable cost.

The total productivity of all resources required to manufacture the output is often used in assessing production operations. Achieving higher productivity by making more units is an important first step for a successful firm.

Limitations of Total Productivity

Total productivity measures the combined productivity of all operating factors. As such, use of a total productivity measure in performance evaluations decreases the possibility of manipulating some of the manufacturing factors to improve the productivity measure of other manufacturing factors.

However, total productivity is a financial productivity measure. Personnel at the operational level may have difficulty linking financial productivity measures to their day-to-day operations. Furthermore, deterioration in total productivity can result from increased costs of resources that were beyond the manager's control, or decreased productivity of some of the input resources that were outside the control of the manager. Ambiguity in the relationship between the controllability of operations and a performance measure based on total productivity could defeat the purpose of having a productivity measurement.

In addition, productivity measures can ignore the effects of changes in demand for the product, changes in selling prices of the goods or services, and changes in special purchasing or selling arrangements on productivity. For example, a special arrangement to sell products at a discount price decreases the productivity in dollars of output per input unit. Alternatively, a special purchase of materials increases financial productivity. Neither of these actions can be attributed to a loss or gain in productivity.

Analyzing Sales: Comparison with the Master Budget

This section uses the flexible budget to help answer strategic questions about sales performance. Are sales increasing at the expected rate? Are sales as profitable as expected? How much success has the firm had at increasing its share of the market in its industry? What factors have contributed to the increase or decrease in sales growth and profitability? These questions can be answered by further analyzing the sales variances first introduced in Chapter 14. For a quick review, look at Exhibit 14.4 on page 597 and note that the comparison of actual sales with budgeted sales, using the flexible budget, identifies the two variances to explain the difference between actual and budgeted sales dollars. These two variances are the sales volume variance (measured in sales dollars rather than contribution) and the selling price variance. The sales volume variance is due to a change in units sold times budgeted selling price. The budgeted unit sales was 1,000 units in this example, budget price was $800, the actual sales in units was 780 units, and the total actual sales dollars was $639,600. The actual price received was

$639,600/780, or $820, a $20 improvement over the budgeted price. The sales volume variance of $176,000 (U) is computed in Exhibit 14.4 as follows:

$$\text{Sales volume variance} = \text{Budgeted sales price} \times \text{Change in sales volume}$$

$$\$176,000\ (U) = \$800 \times (1,000 - 780) = \$800,000 - \$624,000$$

We use the (U) after the variance to indicate it is unfavorable, because unit sales were below budget. The selling price variance is completed in a similar fashion. Note that it is favorable because of the $20 increase in price.

$$\text{Selling price variance} = \text{Actual sales units} \times \text{Change in price}$$

$$\$15,600\ (F) = 780 \times (\$820 - \$800) = \$15,600 = \$639,600 - \$624,000$$

The selling price variance reflects the positive effect on profits of an increase in selling price over the budget. For simplicity, this example has assumed a single product, so the sales price and sales volume variances are easy to interpret. The more common case is there are two or more products. The selling price variance could then be computed for each product in a manner similar to the above. Management would also investigate whether a change in the price of one product might be associated with or caused by a change in the price of another product. A more complete coverage of pricing issues is provided in Chapter 13.

When there are multiple products, the sales volume variance could also be computed for each product in a manner similar to the above. Also, the volume variance can be partitioned into two further parts, one that relates to the mix, or proportion, of products in total sales, and the other to the total quantity of sales. The further analysis allows managers to see how changes in product mix and total quantity affect profits. While the selling price variance is measured in sales dollars (as we have shown above), the volume, quantity, and mix variances are commonly measured in terms of *contribution margin,* as we will see below.

Sales Volume Variance Partitioned into Sales Quantity and Sales Mix Variances

Sales Quantity Variance

LEARNING OBJECTIVE 4

Use the flexible budget to calculate and interpret the sales quantity and sales mix variances.

One contributing factor to the sales volume variances of firms with multiple products is the difference between the budgeted and the actual sales units—sales quantity variance. The **sales quantity variance** measures the effect on contribution and income of deviations in the number of units sold from the number of units budgeted to be sold.

Sales quantity variance

measures the effect of deviation in the number of units sold from the number of units budgeted to be sold on operating results.

The sales quantity variance focuses on the effects of deviations of the actual sales quantity from the budgeted sales quantity. A product's sales quantity variance is the product of three elements:

1. The difference in *total units of all products* between the actual units sold and the units budgeted to be sold.
2. The budgeted sales mix ratio of the product.
3. The budgeted contribution margin per unit of the product.

With the focus of a sales quantity variance being the difference in total units between the actual units sold and the budgeted units, we use the budgeted amounts for the other two elements, sales mix and contribution margin per unit, to compute the sales quantity variance.

$$
\begin{array}{c}
\text{Sales} \\
\text{quantity} \\
\text{variance of} \\
\text{a product}
\end{array}
=
\left(
\begin{array}{c}
\text{Total units} \\
\text{of all} \\
\text{products} \\
\text{sold}
\end{array}
-
\begin{array}{c}
\text{Budgeted} \\
\text{total units} \\
\text{of all} \\
\text{products}
\end{array}
\right)
\times
\begin{array}{c}
\text{Budgeted} \\
\text{sales mix} \\
\text{of the} \\
\text{product}
\end{array}
\times
\begin{array}{c}
\text{Budgeted} \\
\text{contribution} \\
\text{margin per unit} \\
\text{of the product}
\end{array}
$$

Notice that the calculation of the sales quantity variance for a product uses the budgeted sales mix and the budgeted contribution margin per unit of the product. However, the difference in quantity is the difference between the total number of units sold and the total number of units budgeted to be sold for all of the firm's products.

Sales Mix Variance

Sales mix

is the relative proportion of sales of each product to total sales.

The second component of the volume variance is the sales mix variance. **Sales mix** is the relative proportion of a product's sales to total sales. A change in the sales mix can affect the

Sales mix variance
is the effect that changes in the relative proportions of products from the budgeted proportions have on the total contribution margin or operating income of the period.

firm's contribution margin. A product's **sales mix variance** is the effect that a change in the relative proportion of the product from the budgeted proportion has on the total contribution margin of the period. It is calculated by multiplying the difference in the sales mixes by the number of total units sold and the budgeted contribution margin per unit:

$$\begin{array}{c}\text{Sales mix} \\ \text{variance of} \\ \text{a product}\end{array} = \begin{bmatrix}\begin{array}{c}\text{Actual sales} \\ \text{mix of the} \\ \text{product}\end{array} - \begin{array}{c}\text{Budgeted sales} \\ \text{mix of the} \\ \text{product}\end{array}\end{bmatrix} \times \begin{array}{c}\text{Total} \\ \text{units} \\ \text{sold}\end{array} \times \begin{array}{c}\text{Budgeted contribution} \\ \text{margin per unit of} \\ \text{the product}\end{array}$$

Illustration of the Calculation of the Sales Quantity and Sales Mix Variances

The calculations for the sales quantity and sales mix variance can be illustrated using information from the Schmidt Manufacturing Company (used in Chapter 14). Assume that, as in Chapter 14, we have product XV-1 but that now in addition we have product FB-33. These are the only two products sold by Schmidt Machinery. In contrast to the results for the month of October 2010 used in Chapter 14, we are now considering budgeted and actual results for the month of December 2010; the budgeted information is shown in Exhibit 16.7 and the actual information is shown in Exhibit 16.8. Note in comparing Exhibits 16.7 and 16.8 that there is no difference in prices, variable costs or fixed costs; the only differences are in units sold. This allows us to focus strictly on the sales quantity and sales mix variances for these two products. To begin the analysis we calculate the budgeted and actual sales mix, as follows:

Product	Units Sold	Actual Sales Mix	Budgeted Sales Mix	Budgeted Sales
XV-1	1,600	32% = 1,600/5,000	25% = 1,000/4,000	1,000
FB-33	3,400	68% = 3,400/5,000	75% = 3,000/4,000	3,000
Total	5,000	100%	100%	4,000

The calculation of the mix and quantity variances for each product are illustrated in Exhibit 16.9, using the flexible budget. Panel 1 of Exhibit 16.9 shows the flexible budget framework that is used to calculate the variances. Note that the master budget is in the right-hand column C while column A has the actual sales mix, and B has the budgeted sales mix. The difference between columns B and C is the budgeted (column C) and actual (column B) total units sold. Panel 2 of Exhibit 16.9 shows the calculation of the mix and quantity variances for product XV-1, while panel 3 shows the calculations for product FB-33. Panel 4 shows the total for both products, and panel 5 shows the summary of the results for each product and in total. Note that the sales quantity variance plus the sales mix variance for each product equals the sales volume variance for that product. Also, the volume variance calculated here can be

EXHIBIT 16.7
Master Budget for Schmidt Machinery, December 2010

SCHMIDT MACHINERY COMPANY
Master Budget
For the Month Ended December 31, 2010

	XV-1 Total	XV-1 Per Unit	FB-33 Total	FB-33 Per Unit	Both Products Total
Units	1,000		3,000		4,000
Sales	$800,000	$800	$1,800,000	$600	$2,600,000
Variable costs	450,000	450	960,000	320	1,410,000
Contribution margin	$350,000	$350	$ 840,000	$280	$1,190,000
Fixed costs	150,000		450,000		600,000
Operating income	$200,000		$ 390,000		$ 590,000

EXHIBIT 16.8
Income Statements for Two Products

SCHMIDT MACHINERY COMPANY
Income Statement
For the Month Ended December 31, 2010

	XV-1	Per Unit	FB-33	Per Unit	Total
Units	1,600		3,400		5,000
Sales	$1,280,000	$800	$2,040,000	$600	$3,320,000
Variable costs	720,000	450	1,088,000	320	1,808,000
Contribution margin	$ 560,000	$350	$ 952,000	$280	$1,512,000
Fixed costs	150,000		450,000		600,000
Operating income	$ 410,000		$ 502,000		$ 912,000

EXHIBIT 16.9
Sales Mix and Quantity Variances

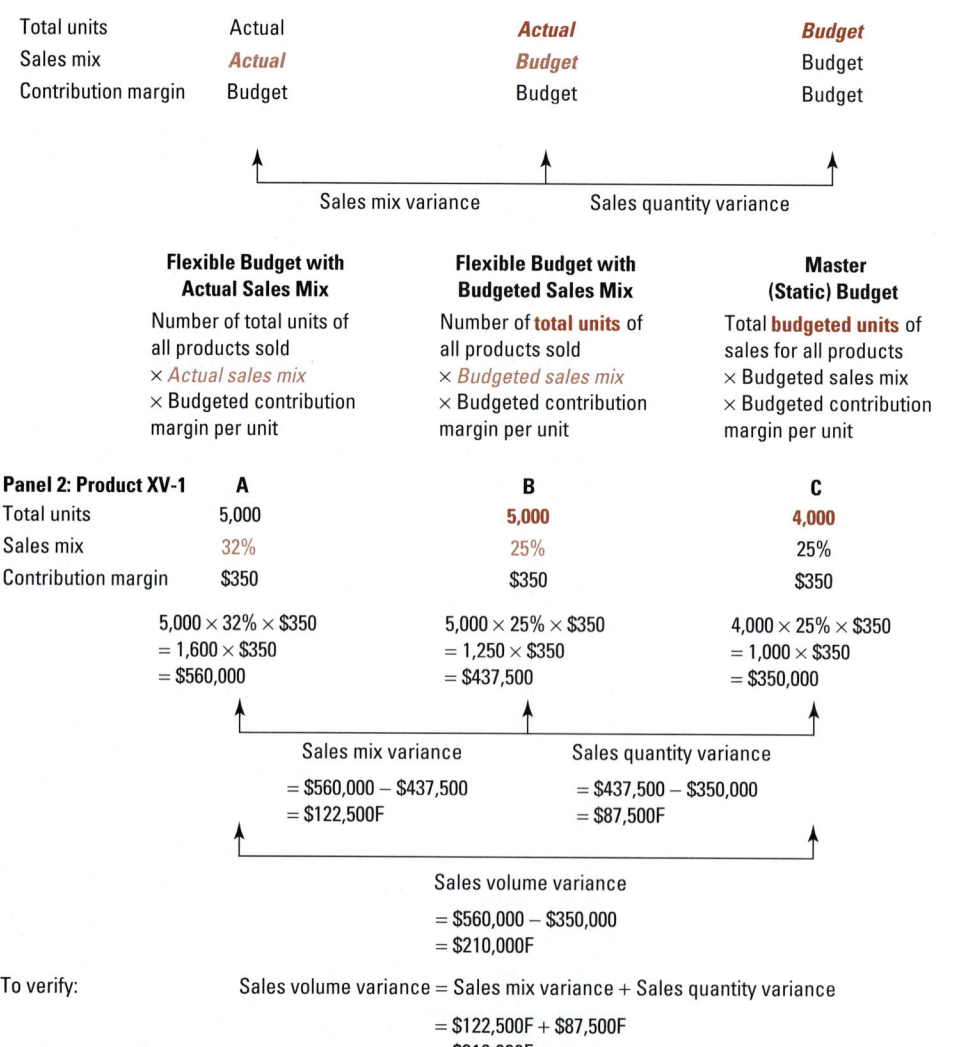

SCHMIDT MACHINERY COMPANY
Sales Mix and Quantity Variances
For December 2010

Panel 1: Flexible Budget Framework

	A	B	C
Total units	Actual	*Actual*	*Budget*
Sales mix	*Actual*	*Budget*	Budget
Contribution margin	Budget	Budget	Budget

Sales mix variance   Sales quantity variance

Flexible Budget with Actual Sales Mix	**Flexible Budget with Budgeted Sales Mix**	**Master (Static) Budget**
Number of total units of all products sold × *Actual sales mix* × Budgeted contribution margin per unit	Number of **total units** of all products sold × *Budgeted sales mix* × Budgeted contribution margin per unit	Total **budgeted units** of sales for all products × Budgeted sales mix × Budgeted contribution margin per unit

Panel 2: Product XV-1

	A	B	C
Total units	5,000	5,000	4,000
Sales mix	32%	25%	25%
Contribution margin	$350	$350	$350

5,000 × 32% × $350	5,000 × 25% × $350	4,000 × 25% × $350
= 1,600 × $350	= 1,250 × $350	= 1,000 × $350
= $560,000	= $437,500	= $350,000

Sales mix variance   Sales quantity variance
= $560,000 − $437,500   = $437,500 − $350,000
= $122,500F   = $87,500F

Sales volume variance
= $560,000 − $350,000
= $210,000F

To verify: Sales volume variance = Sales mix variance + Sales quantity variance

= $122,500F + $87,500F
= $210,000F

EXHIBIT 16.9
Continued

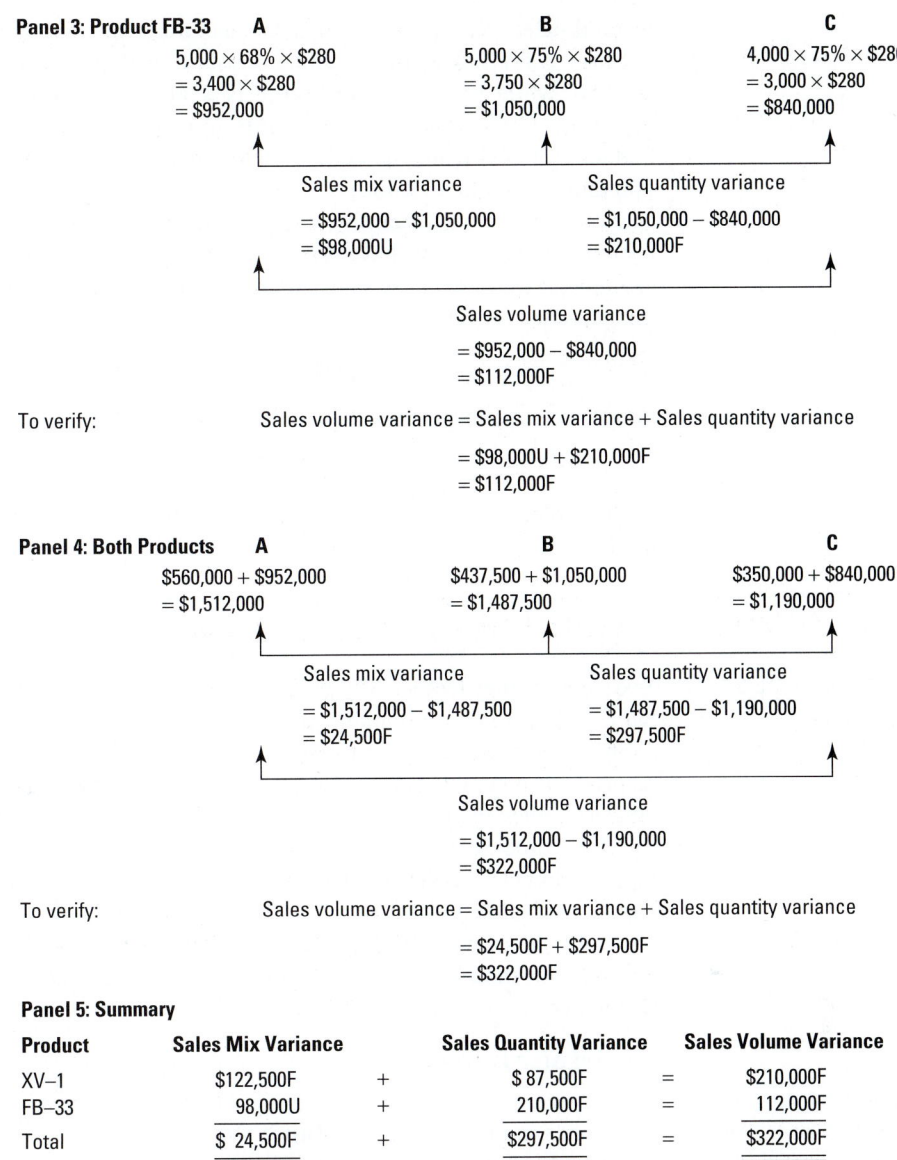

Panel 3: Product FB-33   **A**

$5,000 \times 68\% \times \$280$
$= 3,400 \times \$280$
$= \$952,000$

B

$5,000 \times 75\% \times \$280$
$= 3,750 \times \$280$
$= \$1,050,000$

C

$4,000 \times 75\% \times \$280$
$= 3,000 \times \$280$
$= \$840,000$

Sales mix variance
$= \$952,000 - \$1,050,000$
$= \$98,000U$

Sales quantity variance
$= \$1,050,000 - \$840,000$
$= \$210,000F$

Sales volume variance
$= \$952,000 - \$840,000$
$= \$112,000F$

To verify: Sales volume variance = Sales mix variance + Sales quantity variance
$= \$98,000U + \$210,000F$
$= \$112,000F$

Panel 4: Both Products   **A**

$\$560,000 + \$952,000$
$= \$1,512,000$

B

$\$437,500 + \$1,050,000$
$= \$1,487,500$

C

$\$350,000 + \$840,000$
$= \$1,190,000$

Sales mix variance
$= \$1,512,000 - \$1,487,500$
$= \$24,500F$

Sales quantity variance
$= \$1,487,500 - \$1,190,000$
$= \$297,500F$

Sales volume variance
$= \$1,512,000 - \$1,190,000$
$= \$322,000F$

To verify: Sales volume variance = Sales mix variance + Sales quantity variance
$= \$24,500F + \$297,500F$
$= \$322,000F$

Panel 5: Summary

Product	Sales Mix Variance		Sales Quantity Variance		Sales Volume Variance
XV–1	$122,500F	+	$ 87,500F	=	$210,000F
FB–33	98,000U	+	210,000F	=	112,000F
Total	$ 24,500F	+	$297,500F	=	$322,000F

reconciled to the volume variance as determined directly from the comparison of actual and budget results in Exhibits 16.8 and 16.7, respectively. Since actual sales price equals budget sales price in this example, the selling price variance equals zero, and since the volume variance plus the selling price variance is the total sales variance, the entire difference between actual and budget contribution margin is the volume variance ($1,512,000 − $1,190,000 = $322,000). See panel 4 of Exhibit 16.9.

	Actual (Exhibit 16.8)	Budget (Exhibit 16.7)	Sales Volume Variance
Sales	$3,320,000	$2,600,000	
Variable costs	1,808,000	1,410,000	
Contribution margin	$1,512,000	$1,190,000	$322,000

The analysis has partitioned the volume variance into meaningful components. For example, with the information in Exhibit 16.9, managers would note that the change in sales mix in favor of a higher proportion of sales of XV-1 (this product increased to 32%

of total sales over a budget of 25%) has a net positive effect on contribution and profit because XV-1 has a higher unit contribution than FB-33 (XV-1's contribution per unit is $350, while FB-33's contribution is $280, from Exhibit 16.8). The favorable quantity variance reflects that total sales units were greater than the number indicated in master budget (for XV-1, an increase of 600 units $= 1,600 - 1,000$; for FB-33, an increase of 400 units $= 3,400 - 3,000$).

Note that the mix, quantity, and volume variances can be calculated on the basis of contribution margin (as we have done above), or on the basis of total sales units or dollars. For example, if we were to use sales dollars to complete the analysis in Exhibit 16.9, then the sales mix variance for XV-1 would have been:

$$(1,600 - 1,250) \times \$800 = \$280,000$$

rather than as is currently calculated, based on contribution margin:

$$(1,600 - 1,250) \times \$350 = \$122,500$$

Both methods are used in practice, but the contribution margin method is more commonly used.

Sales Quantity Variance Partitioned into Market Size and Market Share Variances

LEARNING OBJECTIVE 5

Use the flexible budget to calculate and interpret the market size and market share variances.

Two contributing factors of the sales quantity variance are changes in the market size and the firm's share of the market. As the total global market for its products expands, a firm is likely to sell more units. Conversely, the firm is likely to sell fewer units when the market for its products contracts. Also, when a firm's share of the market increases, the firm sells more units and when market share decreases, sales fall.

At the time Schmidt prepared the budget for December 2010 the firm expected that the total worldwide market for both its products, XV-1 and FB-33, would be 40,000 units per month and that Schmidt would have 10 percent of the total market. The master budget data for December is shown in Exhibit 16.7. Exhibit 16.8 shows the actual operations of the month. Exhibit 16.9 shows that the firm had a favorable total sales quantity variance of $297,500 in December.

Market Size Variance

Market size variance
is the effect of changes in market size on a firm's total contribution margin.

Market size is the total units for the industry. The **market size variance** measures the effect of changes in market size on a firm's total contribution margin. As the market size expands, firms are likely to sell more units. Conversely, as the market size contracts, firms are likely to sell fewer units. In computing the market size variance, the focus is on the change in market size: the difference between the actual and budgeted market sizes (units). When determining the market size variance of a firm, we assume that the firm maintains the budgeted market share and the budgeted average contribution margin per unit. The equation for computing a market size variance follows:

$$\begin{array}{c}\text{Market} \\ \text{size} \\ \text{variance}\end{array} = \left(\begin{array}{c}\text{Actual} \\ \text{market size} \\ \text{(in units)}\end{array} - \begin{array}{c}\text{Budgeted} \\ \text{market size} \\ \text{(in units)}\end{array}\right) \times \begin{array}{c}\text{Budgeted} \\ \text{market} \\ \text{share}\end{array} \times \begin{array}{c}\text{Weighted-average} \\ \text{budgeted contribution} \\ \text{margin per unit}\end{array}$$

The first term on the right side of the equation is the focus of the variance: the difference in market size (in units) between the actual and the planned or budgeted market size. The second term is the budgeted market share. The product of the first two terms is the effect of the change in market size on unit sales if the firm maintains the budgeted market share. To estimate the effect on contribution of the change in sales units, we multiply the number of units by contribution margin per unit, the last term in the equation. Notice that the contribution margin per unit is the weighted-average budgeted contribution margin per unit of all of the firm's products in the same market, not the contribution margin per unit of an individual product. The weighted-average budgeted contribution margin per unit for a firm is determined by dividing the total units of the firm into the total contribution margin of the firm. Some managers refer to this contribution margin as the *composite contribution margin per unit.* Schmidt Company budgeted to sell 4,000 units of XV-1 and FB-33 to earn a total contribution margin of $1,190,000, as shown in Exhibit 16.7. Thus, the weighted-average budgeted contribution per unit is $297.50 ($1,190,000/4,000 units).

The firm budgeted to sell 4,000 units and expected the total market to be 40,000 units. The budgeted market share is 10 percent of the total market. The total market for December 2010 turned out to be 31,250 units; the total market size contracted. Panel 1 of Exhibit 16.10 shows the calculation of Schmidt's market size variance, which is $260,312.50 unfavorable.

The actual market size of the industry (31,250 units) is a decrease of 8,750 units from the budgeted market size of 40,000 units. If the firm maintained its budgeted market share of 10 percent, the 8,750 units decrease in market size would have decreased Schmidt's total sales by 875 units. With a weighted-average contribution margin of $297.50 per unit, the decrease in units (875) would have decreased Schmidt's total contribution margin and operating income by $260,312.50.

Market Share Variance

Market share is a firm's proportion of a particular market. The market share of a firm is a function of its core competitive competencies and competitive environment and reflects the firm's competitive position. A successful firm maintains or increases its market share. A firm experiencing continuous erosion in its market share would likely experience financial difficulties.

Market share variance

measures the effect of changes in market share on total contribution margin and operating income.

The **market share variance** compares a firm's actual market share to its budgeted market share and measures the effect of the difference in market shares on the firm's total contribution margin and operating income. Three items are involved in determining the market share variance: the difference between the firm's actual and budgeted market share, the total actual market size, and the weighted-average budgeted contribution margin per unit. Notice that the computation uses the *actual,* not budgeted, total market size and the *budgeted,* not actual, weighted-average contribution margin per unit. The product of these three factors—the difference in market shares, total actual market size, and weighted-average budgeted contribution margin per unit—is the market share variance. The equation is:

$$\begin{matrix} \text{Market} \\ \text{share} \\ \text{variance} \end{matrix} = \left(\begin{matrix} \text{Actual} \\ \text{market} \\ \text{share} \end{matrix} - \begin{matrix} \text{Budgeted} \\ \text{market} \\ \text{share} \end{matrix} \right) \times \begin{matrix} \text{Total actual} \\ \text{market size} \\ \text{(in units)} \end{matrix} \times \begin{matrix} \text{Weighted-average} \\ \text{budgeted contribution} \\ \text{margin per unit} \end{matrix}$$

EXHIBIT 16.10
Market Size and Market Share Variances

SCHMIDT MACHINERY COMPANY
Market Size and Share Variances
For December 2010

Panel 1: Market Size Variance
= Difference in market size × Budgeted market share × Weighted-average budgeted contribution margin per unit
= (31,250 − 40,000) × 10% × $297.50 = $260,312.50U

Panel 2: Market Share Variance
= Difference in market share × Actual market size × Weighted-average budgeted contribution margin per unit
= (16% − 10%) × 31,250 × $297.50 = $557,812.50F

Panel 3: Reconciliation

Market size variance	$260,312.50U
Market share variance	557,812.50F
Sales quantity variance	$297,500.00F

Panel 2 of Exhibit 16.10 shows the calculation of the market share variance for Schmidt Machinery Company's December 2010 operations.

Although the total market for the industry decreased to 31,250, Schmidt's total units sold are higher than the budgeted sales for the period. Its market share increased from the budgeted 10 percent to 16 percent (5,000 units ÷ 31,250 units = 16 percent)—an increase of 6 percent. With the actual total market size being 31,250 units, the 6 percent increase in the market share increased Schmidt's total sales by 1,875 units. At a budgeted weighted-average contribution margin of $297.50 per unit, the increase of 1,875 units increased its total contribution margin and operating income by $557,812.50.

Together, the market size variance and market share variance should equal the sales quantity variance of the period. Panel 3 of Exhibit 16.10 confirms this result. For December 2010, the total of these two variances is $297,500 favorable, which equals the sales quantity variance reported in Exhibit 16.9.

Exhibit 16.11 shows the calculation of the market size and market share variances using a flexible budget framework. The results are the same as in Exhibit 16.10. Remember that market share and market size variances explain the firm's sales quantity variance. The total variance in Exhibit 16.11, the difference between points A and C, is the total sales quantity variance for both products. Point A of Exhibit 16.11 is the budgeted total contribution margin that the firm would have earned from the actual number of units sold. Starting from the industry's total market size, the total number of units sold by the firm is the product of the industry's total actual market size and the firm's actual market share:

$$31,250 \text{ units} \times 16 \text{ percent} = 5,000 \text{ units}$$

The weighted-average budgeted contribution margin per unit is $297.50. Therefore, the total contribution margin from 5,000 units is $1,487,500, as shown at point A of panel 2.

Point B is the budgeted total contribution margin the firm would have earned, given the actual market size, had it maintained the budgeted market share. With the actual market size of 31,250, the firm would have sold 3,125 total units if it had maintained its budgeted market

EXHIBIT 16.11
Analyzing Market Size and Share Variances Using Columnar Form

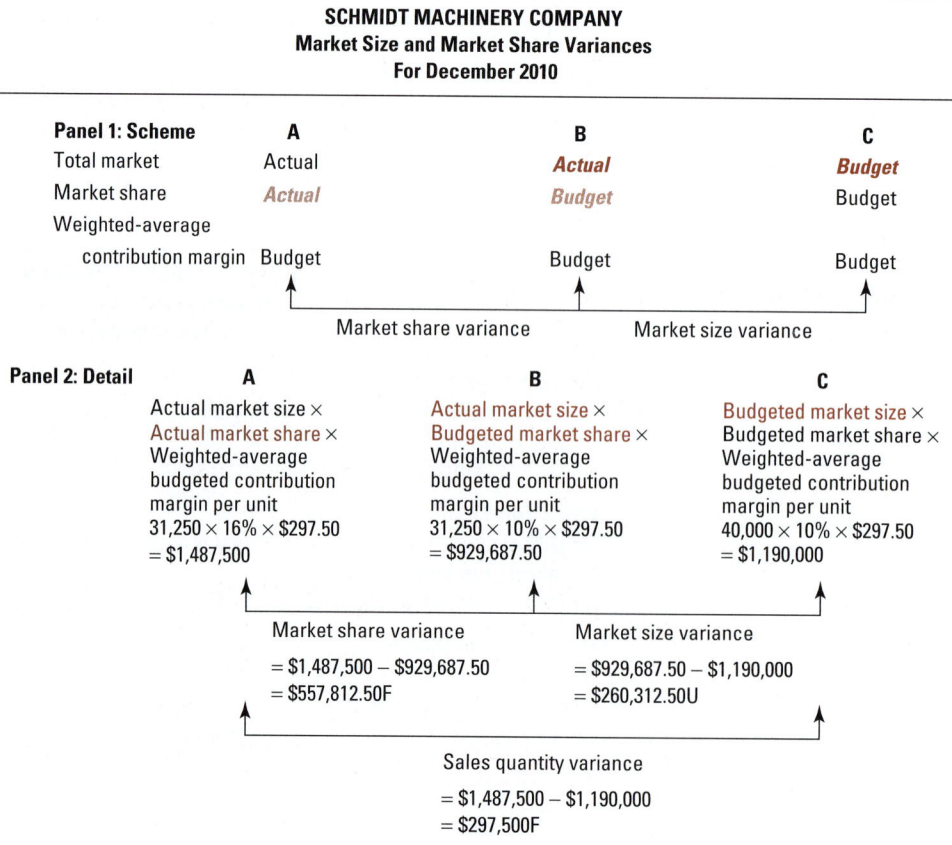

SCHMIDT MACHINERY COMPANY
Market Size and Market Share Variances
For December 2010

Panel 1: Scheme	A	B	C
Total market	Actual	*Actual*	*Budget*
Market share	*Actual*	*Budget*	Budget
Weighted-average contribution margin	Budget	Budget	Budget

Market share variance
Market size variance

Panel 2: Detail	A	B	C
	Actual market size × Actual market share × Weighted-average budgeted contribution margin per unit	Actual market size × Budgeted market share × Weighted-average budgeted contribution margin per unit	Budgeted market size × Budgeted market share × Weighted-average budgeted contribution margin per unit
	31,250 × 16% × $297.50 = $1,487,500	31,250 × 10% × $297.50 = $929,687.50	40,000 × 10% × $297.50 = $1,190,000

Market share variance
= $1,487,500 − $929,687.50
= $557,812.50F

Market size variance
= $929,687.50 − $1,190,000
= $260,312.50U

Sales quantity variance
= $1,487,500 − $1,190,000
= $297,500F

share of 10 percent. At the weighted-average budgeted contribution margin of $297.50 per unit the total contribution margin would be $929,687.50. The only difference between point A and point B is in market share. The $557,812.50 difference ($1,487,500 − $929,687.50) between these two points, therefore, is a market share variance. This variance is favorable because the actual market share is 16 percent, as opposed to the budgeted 10 percent.

Point C is the master budget. The budgeted total units of sales in the master budget is the product of the budgeted market size and the budgeted market share:

$$40,000 \times 10 \text{ percent } = 4,000 \text{ units}$$

At the weighted-average budgeted contribution margin of $297.50 per unit the total contribution margin in the master budget is

$$4,000 \text{ units} \times \$297.50 \text{ per unit } = \$1,190,000$$

The only difference between point B and point C is in the total market size: actual market size at Point B and budgeted market size at point C. The difference, therefore, is a market size variance, which is $260,312.50. The variance is unfavorable because the actual market size is smaller than the budgeted market size anticipated at the time when the firm prepared the master budget for December 2010.

The various components of sales performance are summarized in Exhibit 16.12.

Note that the market share and market size variances can be calculated on the basis of contribution margin (as we have done above) or on the basis of total sales units or sales dollars. All three methods are used in practice, but the contribution margin method is most common, and therefore is the one we use in this chapter.

The Five Steps of Strategic Decision Making for Schmidt Machinery

Schmidt Machinery is a well-established firm that produces very high-quality all-weather furniture which is used on patios and in decks and in sunrooms. Product XV-1 is a lightweight but durable lounge chair and FB-33 is a lightweight and durable table. Because of its very high quality and reputation for design innovation, Schmidt's products are sold largely by catalog, and over the firm's Web site; a few high-end retailers also carry the brand. The firm has few direct competitors in the United States, but there are a growing number of competitors from Europe and Asia. Also, the falling dollar has helped Schmidt maintain its domestic sales and to have some opportunities for foreign sales. However, a global economic recession and a recent rise in the dollar has reduced sales worldwide. While Schmidt's sales have increased, the company is concerned that the recession will deepen and that sales of its products will eventually be affected. Schmidt is facing questions such as which production lines to close and which product advertising to increase or decrease should that happen. Schmidt knows that the XV-1 product has a larger percentage of its sales overseas than FB-33 but Schmidt is not sure which of its two products should be supported at this difficult time.

1. **Determine the strategic issues surrounding the problem.** Schmidt is a differentiated manufacturer, selling a high-priced product to those who value its quality, design, and functionality. With the growth of foreign competition and the increased price competition, Schmidt is now looking for ways to maintain its profitability by determining an effective marketing strategy for its two products.

EXHIBIT 16.12
Components of Sales Variances

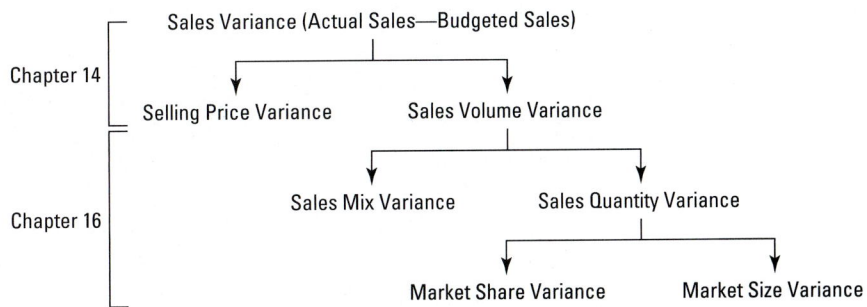

2. **Identify the alternative actions.** The question facing Schmidt is whether to scale back production and marketing of one or both of its products.

3. **Obtain information and conduct analyses of the alternatives.** Schmidt calculates the sales quantity and market share and market size variances as illustrated in Exhibits 16.10 and 16.11. Schmidt also conducts further economic analysis which shows that, in the coming years, the dollar will likely rise against other currencies and that the worldwide recession will continue to show lower and lower levels of consumer spending.

4. **Based on strategy and analysis, choose and implement the desired alternative.** Based on an analysis of the quantity, market share and market size variances for both products, which show an unfavorable market size variance, but a favorable market share variance and a favorable quantity variance, and with the negative news about the dollar and the global recession, Schmidt decides to make contingency plans for the possible reduction in the production and sales of the FB-33 product. One reason is the lower unit contribution of the FB-33 product. The second reason is that while the global recession will affect sales worldwide, and XV-1 has a greater share of worldwide sales, Schmidt expects that the recession will have the greatest negative impact on sales in the United States and thus a relatively greater impact on FB-33.

5. **Provide an ongoing evaluation of the effectiveness of implementation in step 4.** As the global economic environment becomes more predictable, including potential changes in the value of the dollar, management should continue to review its planning for the two products. Also, management should consider obtaining additional information about the market size for each product (for example, by country or region), so that the company can further partition the market share and market size variances for each product.

Analyzing Sales: Comparison with Prior Year Results

LEARNING OBJECTIVE 6

Use the flexible budget to analyze sales performance over time.

A common application of sales performance analysis is to partition the difference between current period's profit and prior years's profit. The analytical framework, based on the flexible budget, is the same as for the analysis of the master budget immediately above. For example, suppose that Schmidt Machinery has another month of operations to consider, the month of January. We use the actual data for December, as used in the prior section, and analyze the change in sales performance from December to January. The relevant information is shown in Exhibit 16.13. We assume that fixed costs do not change, and since unit variable costs have not changed, the only changes to analyze in this example are changes in units sold and prices for the two products.

Notice that the December 2010 data is the same as shown in Exhibit 16.8, with product contribution margins for XV-1 of \$350 (\$800 − \$450) and for FB-33, \$280 (\$600 − \$320). The contribution margins in January 2011 are \$355 and \$270 for XV-1 and FB-33, respectively. Our first step is to calculate the income statements for January and December, as shown in Exhibit 16.14.

EXHIBIT 16.13
Schmidt Machinery Company Actual Data

	January 2011	December 2010
Sales units	5,100	5,000
Sales mix for each product		
XV-1	30%	32%
FB-33	70%	68%
Price		
XV-1	\$805	\$800
FB-33	590	600
Variable cost per unit		
XV-1	450	450
FB-33	320	320

EXHIBIT 16.14
Comparative Income
Statements for Schmidt
Machinery Company

	January 2011	December 2010
Sales XV-1	$1,231,650	$1,280,000
Sales FB-33	2,106,300	2,040,000
Total sales	3,337,950	3,320,000
Less variable costs	1,830,900	1,808,000
Contribution margin	1,507,050	1,512,000
Less fixed costs	600,000	600,000
Operating income	$ 907,050	$ 912,000

Analysis of Selling Price and Volume Variances

The next step is to decompose the total difference in contribution (or difference in operating income) of $4,950 ($1,512,000 − $1,507,050; or also $912,000 − $907,050) by calculating the selling price and volume variances for January, as shown in Exhibit 16.15.

The selling price variance is a net unfavorable variance of $28,050, composed of a favorable selling price variance for XV-1 of $7,650 and an unfavorable selling price variance for FB-33 of $35,700. The selling price variance for XV-1 is due to the price increase of $5. $7,650 = 5,100 × .3 × $5. The selling price variance for FB-33 is due to the price decline of $10: $35,700 = 5,100 × .7 × $10.

The sales volume variance is a net favorable variance of $46,000. The volume for XV-1 fell by 70 units [(.32 × 5,000) − (.3 × 5,100)], at a price of $800 each, or $56,000 unfavorable. In contrast, the sales of FB-33 increased by 170 units [(.7 × 5,100) − (.68 × 5,000)], at a price of $600 each, or $102,000.

The flexible budget column in the center of Exhibit 16.15 is determined from January sales in units (including January sales mix), December prices, and December unit variable costs. For example, the flexible budget for sales of the two products is:

XV-1: $1,224,000 = 5,100 units × 30% mix × $800

FB-33: $2,142,000 = 5,100 units × 70% mix × $600

The flexible budget for variable costs for the two products is determined in a similar way:

XV-1: $688,500 = 5,100 units × 30% mix × $450

FB-33: $1,142,400 = 5,100 units × 70% mix × $320

EXHIBIT 16.15 Selling Price and Volume Variances for January

	January 2011	Sales Price Variance	Flexible Budget	Sales Volume Variance	December 2010
Sales					
XV-1	$1,231,650	$ 7,650	$1,224,000	$(56,000)	$1,280,000
FB-33	2,106,300	(35,700)	2,142,000	102,000	2,040,000
Total sales	3,337,950	(28,050)	3,366,000	46,000	3,320,000
Less variable costs					
XV-1	688,500	–	688,500	(31,500)	720,000
FB-33	1,142,400	–	1,142,400	54,400	1,088,000
Total variable costs	1,830,900		1,830,900	22,900	1,808,000
Contribution margin					
XV-1	543,150	7,650	535,500	(24,500)	560,000
FB-33	963,900	(35,700)	999,600	47,600	952,000
Total contribution margin	1,507,050	$ (28,050)	$1,535,100	$ 23,100	1,512,000
Less fixed costs	600,000				600,000
Operating income	$ 907,050				$ 912,000

In this case, since January unit variable costs are the same as December unit variable costs, the flexible budget for variable costs is the same as the total actual variable cost for January.

Overall, the analysis of sales data for January shows that the relatively small selling price changes are associated with significant changes in volume and selling price variances. For product XV-1, where price increased, there was a significant favorable selling price variance but a much larger unfavorable volume variance. The case for product FB-33 is somewhat different: the price decrease caused a significant unfavorable selling price variance, but a much larger favorable volume variance. Total sales increased by $17,950 ($46,000 − $28,050; or equivalently, $3,337,950 − $3,320,000) which is the net effect of the selling price and volume variances for both products. However, variable costs increased by $22,900 ($1,830,900 − $1,808,000) due to the increase in volume; that is, the increase in sales of 100 units caused an increase in total variable cost (170 units increase for FB-33 at $320 each, less 70 units reduction in volume for XV-1 at $450 each). The net effect is a relatively small reduction in total contribution and operating income of $4,950 ($912,000 − $907,050).

Analysis of Mix and Quantity Variances

The above analysis can be enhanced by computing the mix and quantity variances for each product, as illustrated in Exhibit 16.16.

The mix variances are determined as follows:

Change in mix × Units sold in January 2011 × December 2010 unit contribution

XV-1: $(.3 − .32) \times 5,100 \times \$350 = (\$35,700)$ unfavorable

FB-33: $(.7 − .68) \times 5,100 \times \$280 = 28,560$ favorable

The quantity variances are determined as follows:

Change in total units sold × December 2010 sales mix × December 2010 contribution margin

XV-1: $(5,100 − 5,000) \times .32 \times \$350 = \$11,200$ favorable

FB-33: $(5,100 − 5,000) \times .68 \times \$280 = \$19,040$ favorable

Note that the total of the mix and quantity variances equals the volume variance for each product, as expected. In effect the analysis of the change in operating income from December 2010 to January 2011 is very similar to the analysis for a comparison with the master budget, and the interpretation of the variances is also similar. In the period-to-period analysis, the

EXHIBIT 16.16
Sales Mix and Quantity Variances by Product Line

	Sales Mix Variance	Sales Quantity Variance	Volume Variance
XV-1	$(35,700)U	$11,200F	$(24,500)U
FB-33	28,560F	19,040F	47,600F
Contribution margin	$ (7,140)U	$30,240F	$ 23,100F

interpretation focuses on changes from the prior period, instead of on variances between performance and the master budget.

Analysis of Variable Cost Variances

The above approach can also be extended to analyze the changes in unit variable costs. This would involve calculating price and usage variances for materials and labor, much like the procedures used in Chapter 14. Again, the flexible budget based on actual output and prior year actual unit variable costs would provide the desired framework. For example, if the unit variable cost in January for product XV-1 was $460 rather than $450 as shown in Exhibit 16.13, and assuming that the unit variable cost for XV-1 was $450 in December, then we can calculate a variable cost variance as follows for January:

$$\text{Variable cost flexible-budget variance} = (\$460 - \$450) \times 5,100 \times .3 = \$15,300U$$

The variable cost flexible-budget variance could also then be partitioned into the six variances for usage and price of materials and labor, and usage and spending for variable overhead. The partition would be done in the same manner as explained and illustrated in Chapters 14 and 15.

Summary

Productivity is the ratio of output to input. Improvements in productivity enable firms to do more with fewer resources. A productivity measure is often compared to the performance of a prior period, another firm, the industry standard, or a benchmark in assessing a firm's productivity.

Partial productivity is the ratio of output level attained to the amount of an input resource used in the operation. The higher the ratio, the better. A partial operational productivity is the required physical amount of an input resource to produce one unit of output. The partial financial productivity of an input resource is the number of units or the value of output manufactured for each dollar spent on the input resource. A partial financial productivity measure can be separated into changes in productivity, input price, and output. The productivity change is the difference between the actual amount used and the expected amount of input resources to manufacture the output. The input price change accounts for the effects of the difference between the budgeted (or benchmark) and the actual prices for the input resource on the operating income of the period.

Total productivity measures the relationship between the output achieved and the total input costs and is usually a financial productivity measure.

Measures of productivity are applicable to all organizations including service firms and not-for-profit organizations. However, imprecise measures for output, or lack of definite relationships between output and input resources may limit the usefulness of productivity measures for some service or not-for-profit organizations.

Increasing global competition and rapid changes in technologies require management to be constantly alert to changes in resource productivity. Management must be aware of levels and changes in its productive factors, such as materials, labor, energy, and processes.

To effectively evaluate sales performance, management must be fully informed of the effects of changes in selling prices, sales volumes, sale mixes, market sizes, and market shares on the firm's sales.

The sales volume variance reflects the difference in contribution margin or operating income between a flexible budget and the master budget. The sales volume variance for a single product firm can be determined by multiplying the budgeted contribution margin per unit of the product times the difference in units between the number of units sold and the budgeted units to be sold. The sales volume variance of firms with multiple products can be separated into sales mix and sales quantity variances. The sales mix variance is the product of three components:

1. The difference between the actual sales mix (defined as the ratio of the units of the product to the total units of all products) and the budgeted sales mix
2. The total number of units of all products sold during the period
3. The product's budgeted contribution margin

A product's sales quantity variance has three elements: (1) the difference between the firm's total actual units sold and budgeted sales units, (2) the product's budgeted sales mix, and (3) the budgeted contribution margin. The product of these three elements is the product's sales quantity variance. A sales quantity variance assesses the effect of the difference between the units sold and budgeted sales on total contribution margin and operating income.

A sales quantity variance can be separated further into market size and market share variances. A market size variance assesses the effect of changes in the industry's total market size on the firm's total contribution margin and operating income. A market size variance is the product of three factors: (1) the difference between the actual and the budgeted total market size (in number of units), (2) the firm's budgeted market share, and (3) the weighted-average budgeted contribution margin per unit. The market size variance is favorable if the actual total market size is larger than the market size expected when the master budget was prepared. A market share variance measures the effect of changes in the firm's market share on its operating income. A market share variance is the product of three elements: (1) the actual total number of units in the market (actual market size), (2) the difference between the firm's actual and budgeted market share, and (3) the weighted average budgeted contribution margin per unit.

Sales performance can be analyzed from either of two benchmarks: the master budget or the prior period. The period-to-period analysis also uses the flexible budget, and the same variances are calculated, with similar interpretations.

Key Terms

financial productivity, *706*
market share variance, *719*
market size variance, *718*
operational productivity, *706*

partial productivity, *706*
productivity, *706*
sales mix, *714*
sales mix variance, *714*

sales quantity variance, *714*
total productivity, *706*

Comments on Cost Management in Action

The Auto Parts Business: Is It a Good Investment?

Because of the financial stress in the auto parts industry Ross is able to purchase the plants at very low cost. Ross has 20,000 auto parts employees in 17 countries. He intends to streamline the operations of the companies, to renegotiate labor contracts, and to return the companies to a narrow focus on low cost, high quality auto parts manufacturing. The auto parts industry began diversifying in the early 1990s, providing numerous services and types of parts. Much of this business has proven unprofitable. Ross plans to return the companies to a focus on parts manufacturing, and to reduce labor costs, in order to return the companies to their former levels of productivity.

Source: Monica Langley and Jeffrey McCracken, "Showdown on Auto Labor Costs Looms as Delphi Goes to Court," *The Wall Street Journal,* March 31, 2006, p. 1; Jeffrey McCracken, Jeanne Dugan, and Henry Sender, "Monied Investors Look for Gems in Auto Industry," *The Wall Street Journal,* October 26, 2006, p C1; "U.S. Automotive Parts Industry Annual Assessment," Office of Aerospace and Automotive Industries, U.S. Department of Commerce, March 2008 (www.trade.gov/static/auto_reports_parts_assessment.pdf).

Self-Study Problems
(For solutions, please turn to the end of the chapter.)

1. Productivity Variances

Carlson Automotive Company manufactures fuel-injection systems. It manufactured and sold 60,000 units in 2009 and 64,000 units in 2010 at $25 per unit. In 2009, the firm used 75,000 pounds of alloy TPX–45 at $7.20 per pound and used 10,000 direct labor-hours at an hourly wage rate of $30. In 2010, the firm used 89,600 pounds of alloy TPX–45 at $6.80 per pound and used 10,847 direct labor-hours at an hourly wage rate of $32. The total amount of all other expenses remains the same at $450,000 each year. Jerry Olson, CEO, was disappointed that although the total sales increased in 2010, operating income declined from $210,000 in 2009 to $193,616 in 2010.

Required   Analyze the following:

1. Partial operational productivity of direct material and direct labor for both 2009 and 2010.
2. Partial financial productivity of direct material and direct labor for both 2009 and 2010.
3. Detailed partition of partial financial productivity.
4. Total productivity for 2009 and 2010 as measured in both units and sales dollars.

2. Sales Variances

Springwater Brewery has two main products: premium and regular ale. Its operating results and master budget for 2010 (000s omitted) follow:

	Operating Results of 2010			Master Budget for 2010		
	Premium	**Regular**	**Total**	**Premium**	**Regular**	**Total**
Barrels	180	540	720	240	360	600
Sales	$28,800	$62,100	$90,900	$36,000	$43,200	$79,200
Variable expenses	16,200	40,500	56,700	21,600	27,000	48,600
Contribution margin	$12,600	$21,600	$34,200	$14,400	$16,200	$30,600
Fixed expenses	10,000	5,000	15,000	10,000	5,000	15,000
Operating income	$ 2,600	$16,600	$19,200	$ 4,400	$11,200	$15,600

Pam Kuder, CEO, expected the total industry sales to be 1,500,000 barrels during the period. After the year, Mark Goldfeder, the controller, reported that the total sales for the industry were 1,600,000 barrels.

Required   Calculate the following:

1. Selling price variances for the period for each product and for the firm.
2. Sales volume variances for the period for each product and for the firm.
3. Sales quantity variances for each product and the firm.
4. Sales mix variances for the period for each product and for the firm.
5. The sum of the sales quantity variance and sales mix variance and verify that this total equals the sales volume variance.
6. Market size variance.
7. Market share variance.
8. The sum of market size variance and market share variance and verify that this total equals the sales quantity variance.

Questions

16-1   What is productivity? What does it measure?

16-2   Discuss why improving productivity is important for a firm that competes on a cost leadership strategy.

16-3   List benchmarks or criteria often used in assessing productivity, and discuss their advantages and disadvantages.

16-4   What is operational productivity? Financial productivity?

16-5   What is partial productivity? Total productivity?

16-6   "A financial productivity measure contains more information than an operational productivity measure does." Do you agree?

16-7   "A total productivity measure encompasses all partial productivity measures." Do you agree?

16-8   "Partial productivity measures should be calculated only for high-value-added activities." Do you agree?

16-9   Why do manufacturing personnel prefer operational productivity measures to financial productivity measures?

16-10   "An activity productivity measure such as machine-hour productivity is more important in a JIT environment than in a non-JIT environment." Do you agree?

16-11   Which of the following statements is true? (a) The lower the partial productivity ratio, the greater the productivity, (b) productivity improves when partial productivity increases, (c) prices of inputs are incorporated in the partial productivity ratio, (d) the partial productivity ratio measures the number of outputs produced per multiple input, and (e) more than one of the above is true.

16-12   List important measures in assessing marketing effectiveness.

16-13   What are the components of the sales variance?

16-14   Distinguish between a selling price variance and a sales volume variance.

16-15   What is the difference between a sales quantity variance and a sales volume variance?

16-16   "As long as a firm sells more units than the units specified in the master budget, it will not have an unfavorable sales volume variance." Do you agree? Why?

16-17 What are the relationships among a selling price variance, a sales mix variance, a sales quantity variance, and a sales volume variance?

16-18 Distinguish between market size variance and market share variance.

16-19 "A favorable sales quantity variance indicates that the marketing manager has done a good job." Do you agree? Can you give an example in which a market size variance or market share variance is opposite to that of the sales quantity variance?

16-20 What are the relationships between market size variance, market share variance, sales quantity variance, and sales volume variance?

16-21 An improvement in earnings growth can be achieved at the expense of market share (an unfavorable market share variance). Do you agree?

Brief Exercises

Use the following information for brief exercises 16-22 through 16-24. CompuWorld sells two products, R66 and R100, and calculates sales variances using contribution margin. Pertinent data for the current year follow:

	Budgeted		Actual	
	R66	**R100**	**R66**	**R100**
Selling price	$ 50	$160	$ 55	$ 155
Variable cost per unit	40	90	43	95
Contribution margin	$ 10	$ 70	$ 12	$ 60
Fixed cost per unit	6	30	5	25
Operating income	$ 4	$ 40	$ 7	$ 35
Sales in units	1,200	400	1,000	1,000

16-22 What is the R66 sales quantity variance?

a. $400F
b. $1,000F
c. $1,200F

d. $3,000F
e. $3,600F

16-23 What is the R100 sales mix variance?

a. $20,000F
b. $30,000F
c. $35,000F

d. $40,000F
e. $70,000F

16-24 What is the total sales volume variance?

a. $10,000F
b. $12,400F
c. $13,000F

d. $22,000F
e. $40,000F

Use the following information for brief exercises 16-25 through 16-27. C. W. McCall sells a goldplated souvenir mug; McCall expects to sell 1,600 units for $45 each to earn a $25 contribution margin per unit. Janice McCall, president, expects the year's total market to be 32,000 units. For the year just completed, the local college won the national hockey championship, and the total market was 100,000 units. C. W. McCall sells 3,000 units and calculates sales variances using contribution margin.

16-25 What is the market share variance?

a. $8,000U
b. $11,200U
c. $40,000U

d. $50,000U
e. $70,000U

16-26 What is the market size variance?

a. $51,000F
b. $68,000F
c. $71,400F

d. $85,000F
e. $119,000F

16-27 What is the firm's sales volume variance?

   a. $35,000F   d. $85,000F

   b. $49,000F   e. $135,000F

   c. $51,000F

16-28 Darwin, Inc., provided the following information for a production factor:

Budgeted production	10,000 units
Actual production	9,500 units
Budgeted input	9,750 gallons
Actual input	8,950 gallons

Required What is the partial operational productivity ratio of the production factor?

a. 0.97 unit per gallon.

b. 1.02 units per gallon.

c. 1.06 units per gallon.

d. 1.12 units per gallon.

e. None of the above.

Exercises

16-29 **Partial Financial Productivity and Total Productivity**   RFD Corporation makes small parts from steel alloy sheets. Management has the flexibility to substitute direct materials for direct manufacturing labor. If workers cut the steel carefully, more parts can be manufactured from a metal sheet, but this requires additional direct manufacturing labor-hours. Alternatively, RFD can use fewer direct manufacturing labor-hours if it is willing to tolerate more waste of direct materials. RFD provides this information for the years 2009 and 2010:

	2009	2010
Output units	400,000	486,000
Direct manufacturing labor-hours	10,000	13,500
Wages per hour	$26	$25
Direct materials used	160 tons	180 tons
Direct materials cost per ton	$3,375	$3,125

Required Carry all computations to four digits after the decimal point.

1. Compute the partial financial productivity for both manufacturing factors for 2009 and 2010.

2. Calculate RFD's total productivity in units per dollar in 2009 and 2010.

3. Evaluate management's decision in 2010 to substitute one production factor for another.

16-30 **Partial Operational and Financial Productivity**   Software Solution (SOS) helps subscribers solve software problems. All transactions are made over the telephone. For the year 2009, 10 engineers, most of whom are recent graduates, handled 100,000 calls. The average yearly salary for software engineers was $45,000. Starting in 2010, the firm retained and hired only software engineers with at least two years of experience. SOS raised the engineers' salary to $60,000 per year. In 2010, eight engineers handled 108,000 calls.

Required

1. Calculate the partial operational productivity ratio for both years.

2. Calculate the partial financial productivity ratio for both years.

3. Did the firm make the right decision to hire only software engineers with at least two years' experience?

4. List other factors that should be considered in making the decision.

16-31 **Sales Performance at Hewlett-Packard**   In early 2006, the new CEO of Hewlett-Packard (H-P), Mark Hurd, became aware of a number of customer complaints about the accessibility of sales support at the company. The complaints referred to a confusing management structure and lack of contact with sales support personnel from H-P. There were 17,000 people working in H-P sales, and customers, particularly the large corporate customers, were frustrated dealing with the complexity of the H-P sales system.

Required What would you propose to Mark Hurd, the CEO at H-P, regarding an overhaul of the sales support systems at H-P?

16-32 **Productivity: Which Way to Lean?** Lean manufacturing is what a lot of manufacturing firms are after these days. This means a renewed focus on productivity and profitability, particularly for firms that compete on a cost leadership strategy and are facing increased global low-cost competition. Adopting the right accounting approach to facilitate improvements in productivity is critical for these companies. Companies like Whirlpool, Pratt-Whitney (a unit of United Technologies), General Electric, and many other manufacturers are adopting the methods of lean manufacturing.

Required

1. How can productivity measures described in this chapter help a company to achieve lean manufacturing?

2. The founding principles of lean manufacturing are based in part on the Toyota Production System. Explain the Toyota Production System and list its four main elements.

16-33 **Sales Volume, Sales Quantity, and Sales Mix Variances** The Varner Performing Arts Center has a total capacity of 7,500 seats: 2,000 center seats, 2,500 side seats, and 3,000 balcony seats. The budgeted and actual tickets sold for a Broadway musical show are as follows:

		Percentage	
	Ticket Price	Budgeted Seats	Actual Seats
Center	$60	80%	95%
Side	50	90	85
Balcony	40	85	75

The actual ticket prices are the same as those budgeted. Once a show has been booked, the total cost does not vary with the total attendance.

Required Compute the following for the show (round the variances to the nearest whole dollar):

1. The budgeted and actual sales mix percentages for different types of seats.
2. The budgeted average contribution margin per seat.
3. The total sales quantity variance and the total sales mix variance.
4. The total sales volume variance.

16-34 **Quality and Productivity** Each summer the Harbour Report (www.oliverwyman.com/ow/automotive.htm) rates the productivity of the major automakers, including the Detroit Big 3, Toyota, Honda, and many other brands. The report is closely watched as a barometer of the future profitability of the firms. However, some have argued that the productivity reports are insufficient. For example, a company can temporarily raise its productivity by laying off or "buying out" employees. Also, some would argue that the focus on productivity fails to draw attention to other key strategic factors such as quality, design, and customer service. For example, the J.D. Power organization (www.jdpower.com/autos) rates the initial quality of many new cars.

Required What do you think are the priorities for the auto companies: quality, productivity, customer service, design, or some other key strategic success factor? Briefly explain your answer.

16-35 **Productivity and the Economy** The U.S. Bureau of Labor Statistics (www.bls.gov) provides quarterly data for productivity in business, nonfarm business, and manufacturing industries. The Bureau also breaks down this data into industry segments. The data for the annual percentage change in productivity for the recent decade is as follows, for the category of business productivity. Preliminary data show that the productivity rate for 2008 will be similar to that for 2007.

Year	Percentage Change
1997	1.6
1998	2.8
1999	2.9
2000	2.8
2001	2.5
2002	4.1
2003	3.7
2004	3.0
2005	2.3
2006	2.1
2007	1.4

Required Economists argue that the changes in productivity are influenced by changes in the economy, for example, the economic downturn of 2000–2001 as well as the current recession which started in 2007. Others argue that productivity is most affected by advances in and adoption of information technology, investments in research and development, and capital investment in new plant and equipment—more highly automated and efficient manufacturing facilities. The data above show that productivity appears to be on the decline in the period 2005–2008. In 2008, capital investment was sluggish as was the pace of innovation and adoption of information technology. What do you forecast the productivity rate will be for 2008 and the following couple of years?

16-36 Alternative Measures of Productivity A common measure of productivity, as explained in this chapter and as used by many business and trade organizations including the U.S. Bureau of Labor Statistics, is the ratio of output to input, where input is typically measured in units of materials, labor hours, or related measures. An alternative is to use the ratio of capacity available to capacity utilized. For example, the amount of capacity in the U.S. manufacturing industries has continued to increase over the last two decades (an 88 percent increase from 1980 to 2006). However, the rate of capacity utilization (output/capacity available) has fallen slightly over this period of time. Some would say that this measure gives a better picture of productivity than the one we have used in the chapter.

Required Compare the measure of productivity based on capacity utilization with the measure used in the chapter. Which measure do you think is most useful for assessing the state of the manufacturing sector of the economy? Explain briefly.

16-37 Productivity Measures for Call Centers Our examples in the chapter have focused on manufacturing, where the output is units of product and the inputs are manufacturing activities or costs. The concept of productivity can be applied in a variety of settings, wherever there are inputs and outputs. For example, consider the call center for a cell phone company. Suppose the call center operates 24 hours a day every day of the week to respond to user problems and questions. To calculate productivity for the call center, we could divide the total number of calls over a period of time by the number of hours or the number of employees in the call center during that period.

Required Evaluate the productivity measure identified above for the call center. Identify some alternative measures of productivity for the call center and explain your choices.

16-38 Sales Variances; Year to Year Hathaway Products, Inc., produces an innovative lighting system used in restaurants and high-end retail stores to provide a pleasing, warm atmosphere. Hathaway produces two versions of the product, called Starlight and Moonlight. Sales management at

Hathaway wants to complete a sales performance analysis and has collected the following information for 2009 and 2010.

	2010	2009
Sales units	12,000	10,000
Sales mix for each product		
Starlight	20%	25%
Moonlight	80%	75%
Price		
Starlight	$ 35.00	$ 35.00
Moonlight	$ 85.00	$ 90.00
Variable cost per unit		
Starlight	$ 22.00	$ 22.00
Moonlight	$ 48.00	$ 48.00
Fixed cost	$150,000	$150,000

Required

1. Calculate a flexible budget contribution income statement for 2010, showing the 2010 results, the 2009 results, and the flexible budget. Use Exhibit 16.15 as a guide.

2. Calculate the volume variances for each product based both on sales dollars and contribution margin.

3. Determine the sales volume variance, the sales mix variance, and the sales quantity variance for each product, based on contribution margin.

Problems

16-39 Partial Operational Productivity Frisen Communication Inc. manufactures a scrambling device for cellular telephones. The device's main component is a delicate part, CSU10. CSU10 is easily damaged and requires careful handling. Once damaged, it must be discarded. The firm hires only skilled laborers to manufacture and install CSU10; however, some are still damaged. Robotic instruments process all other parts. Frisen's operating data for 2009 and 2010 follow:

	2010	2009
Units manufactured	500,000	600,000
Number of CSU10 used	800,000	825,000
Number of direct labor-hours spent	150,000	200,000
Cost of CSU10 per unit	$156	$135
Direct labor wage rate per hour	$56	$63

Required

1. Compute the partial operational productivity for 2009 and 2010.

2. On the basis of the partial operational productivity that you computed, what conclusions can you draw about the firm's productivity in 2010 relative to 2009?

16-40 Partial Financial Productivity Use the data for Frisen Communication Inc. in problem 16-39 to complete the requirements.

Required

1. Compute the partial financial productivity ratios for 2009 and 2010.

2. On the basis of the partial financial productivity ratios you computed, what conclusions can you draw about the firm's productivity in 2010 relative to 2009?

3. Separate the change of the partial financial productivity ratio from 2009 to 2010 into productivity changes, input price changes, and output changes.

4. Does the detailed information provided by separating the change of the partial financial production ratio offer any additional insight into the relative productivity for 2009 and 2010?

16-41 Total Productivity Use the data for Frisen Communication Inc. in problem 16-39 for the following.

Required

1. Compute the total productivity ratios for 2009 and 2010.

2. On the basis of the total productivity that you computed, what conclusions can you draw about the firm's productivity in 2010 relative to 2009?

16-42 **Partial Operational and Financial Productivity**   In the fourth quarter of 2009 Simpson Company embarked on a major effort to improve productivity. It redesigned products, reengineered manufacturing processes, and offered productivity improvement courses. The effort was completed in the last quarter of 2009. The controller's office has gathered the following year-end data to assess the results of this effort.

	2010	2009
Units manufactured and sold	18,000	15,000
Selling price of the product	$40	$40
Materials used (pounds)	12,600	12,000
Cost per pound of materials	$10	$8
Labor-hours	5,000	6,000
Hourly wage rate	$25	$20
Power (kwh)	2,000	1,000
Cost of power per kwh	$2	$2

Required

1. Prepare a summary contribution approach income statement for each of the two years and calculate the change in operating income.

2. Compute the partial operational productivity ratios for each production factor in 2009 and 2010.

3. Compute the partial financial productivity ratios for each production factor in 2009 and 2010.

4. On the basis of the partial operational and financial productivity you computed, what conclusions can you make about the firm's productivity in 2009 relative to 2010?

5. Separate the changes in the partial financial productivity ratio from 2009 to 2010 into productivity changes, input price changes, and output changes.

6. Discuss additional insight on the relative productivity between 2009 and 2010 from the detailed information provided by separating the change in the financial partial productivity ratios.

16-43 **Comparative Income Statements and Sales Performance Variances; Current to Prior Year**   Clippers Inc. (CI) manufactures two types of garden clippers, a light duty model called the "half-inch" which is intended for clipping branches and stems up to one-half inch thick. The "one-inch" model is designed for heavier stems and branches. To boost sales, CI decided at the beginning of 2010 to reduce the price of the half-inch model to better position its price relative to some key competitors. On the other hand, CI felt that the one-inch model was technically superior to competitors' models and decided that a small price increase was appropriate. The data for the current and prior year are as follows:

	2010	2009
Sales units	7,200	6,500
Sales mix for each product		
Half-inch model	50%	30%
One-inch model	50%	70%
Price		
Half-inch model	$ 12.00	$ 14.00
One-inch model	$ 36.00	$ 32.00
Variable cost per unit		
Half-inch model	$ 6.00	$ 6.00
One-inch model	$ 8.00	$ 8.00
Fixed cost	$35,000	$35,000

Required

1. Calculate a comparative contribution income statement for CI for 2010 that shows the volume and selling price variances for each product based on contribution margin. (Hint: Use Exhibit 16.15 as an example)

2. Determine the sales mix variance and the sales quantity variance for each product, based on contribution margin.

3. Did the price change have the expected results? Why or why not?

16-44 **Partial Operational and Financial Productivity** Varceles Design has decided to experiment with two alternative manufacturing approaches, identified as MF and LI, for producing men's fashions. The firm expects the total demand to be 20,000 suits. Management estimates the required input resources using different manufacturing approaches are:

	Materials (yds.)	Labor (hrs.)
MF	300,000	100,000
LI	200,000	120,000

The cost of materials is $8 per yard; the cost of labor is $25 per hour.

Required

1. Compute the partial operational productivity ratios for each of the production approaches. Which approach would you select based on the partial operational productivity ratios?

2. Calculate the partial financial productivity ratios for each of the production approaches. Which approach would you select based on the partial financial productivity ratios?

3. Compute the total productivity ratios for each of the production approaches. Which approach would you select based on the total productivity ratios?

16-45 **Direct Labor Rate and Efficiency Variances; Productivity Measures; Review of Chapter 14** Textron Manufacturing Inc. assembles industrial testing instruments in two departments, assembly and testing. Operating data for 2009 and 2010 follow:

	2010	2009
Assembly department		
Actual direct labor-hours per instrument	20	25
Actual wage rate per hour	$36	$30
Standard direct labor-hours per instrument	21	24
Standard wage rate per hour	$35	$28
Testing department		
Actual direct labor-hours per instrument	10	12
Actual wage rate per hour	$24	$20
Standard direct labor-hours per instrument	11	14
Standard wage rate per hour	$25	$21

The firm assembled and tested 20,000 instruments in both 2009 and 2010.

Required

1. Calculate the direct labor rate and the efficiency variances for both departments in both years.

2. Calculate the direct labor partial operational productivity ratio for both departments in both years.

3. Calculate the partial financial productivity for both departments in both years.

4. Compare your answers for requirements 2 and 3. Comment on the results.

5. Do productivity measures offer different perspectives for the firm's strategic decisions from those of variance analysis?

16-46 **Comparative Income Statements and Sales Performance Variances; Current to Prior Year** Lawn Master manufactures riding lawn mowers that it sells to the large discount stores such as Wal-Mart, Lowes, and Home Depot. The mowers are marketed as a "value" product, with good quality at a very good price. The company's two products are the Quality mower, which in 2009 sold for $1,000 (the discounters retailed it for $1,500), and the Heavy Duty model which Lawn Master sold for $1,500 (and was retailed for $2,200). At the end of 2009, the company has come under increased price competition from other manufacturers. The company believes it must reduce its price in 2010 on both products to keep its current market share with sales of 3,300 units. The unit variable costs for the Quality product are $800 and $950 for the Heavy Duty product. Management does not believe it can reduce these variable costs for the coming year but will begin to study ways to do so for 2011. In the meantime, the company management believes it can maintain its total market share by increasing its advertising expenses by $150,000 and cutting the price on both models by 10 percent. Fixed costs were $550,000 in 2009 and are not expected to change in 2010, with the exception of the increase in advertising. In 2009 the sales mix was one-third for Quality and two-thirds for Heavy Duty, respectively. In 2010, the sales mix was 40 percent for Quality and 60 percent for Heavy Duty, respectively.

Required

1. Calculate a comparative contribution income statement for Lawn Master for 2010 that shows the volume and selling price variances for each product based on contribution margin. (Hint: Use Exhibit 16.15 as an example.)

2. Determine the sales mix variance and the sales quantity variance for each product, based on contribution margin.

3. Did the price change and increase in advertising have the expected results? Why or why not?

4. What methods should Lawn Master adopt to become more competitive in 2010 and 2011?

16-47 **Productivity and Market Share in the Auto Industry; Internet Exercise**   The following data is obtained from the recent financial statements for two U.S. automakers (in $millions).

	Ford	GM
Sales	$154,379	$178,199
Cost of goods sold	142,589	166,239

Required

1. Calculate and interpret total productivity in dollars for the two automakers. Assume that total variable manufacturing costs are 80 percent of cost of goods sold for each automaker.

2. Go to the Internet for these companies and look under investor information to find the financial statements for each company. Review the sections on management's discussion and analysis and related financial statements and footnotes, and find the market size and market share information provided by these firms.

   Ford: www.ford.com

   GM: www.gm.com

16-48 **Productivity and Ethics**   Janice Interiors installs custom interiors for luxury mobile homes. In its most recent negotiation with the union, the firm proposed to share productivity gains in direct labor equally with the union. In return, the union agreed not to demand wage increases. Most union members, however, are skeptical about management's honesty in calculating productivity measures. Nevertheless, union members voted to try the program. Kim Tomas, the management accountant responsible for determining productivity measures, collected these data at the end of 2010:

	2010	2009
Number of installations	560	500
Direct labor-hours	112,000	99,000

Steve Janice, the CEO, is very anxious to demonstrate the firm's good intentions by showing the labor union a positive result. He suggests to Kim that some of the direct labor-hours are actually indirect. For example, some of the labor-hours are indirect because these hours cannot be allocated to specific types of work. Following his suggestion, Kim reclassifies 12,000 hours as indirect labor.

Required

1. Evaluate whether Steve's suggestion to reclassify some of the direct labor-hours as indirect labor is ethical.

2. Would it be ethical for Kim to modify her calculations?

16-49 **Market Size, Market Share, Working Backward**   Triple Delight is a foodstand located on a busy corner in the local business district. On average it sells three cheeseburgers and one fishwich for every four hamburgers sold. The following data were culled from its operation for 2010:

Total operating income variance	
Hamburger	$18,000 Unfavorable
Cheeseburger	50,000 Favorable
Fishwich	10,000 Unfavorable
Sales quantity variance	
Hamburger	14,000 Favorable
Cheeseburger	15,000 Favorable
Fishwich	1,000 Favorable
Sales mix variance	
Hamburger	2,240 Unfavorable
Cheeseburger	4,800 Unfavorable
Fishwich	1,600 Favorable
Fixed costs variances	0
Market share variance	$96,000 Unfavorable
Market size variance	126,000 Favorable
Change in market share	4%
Fixed cost flexible budget variance	0

The estimated total volume for the foodstands in the region was 2,500,000 units. Consistent good weather pushed the total volume for the year to 4,000,000.

Required   Determine the following:
1. Budgeted weighted-average contribution margin.
2. Budgeted and actual market shares.
3. Budget and actual total units sold.
4. Sales quantity variances for fishwich.
5. Budgeted contribution margin of each product.
6. Actual sales mix of each product.
7. Budget and actual units sold for each product.

16-50 **Sales Variances; Flexible-Budget Variance; Review of Chapter 14**   Robinson Company has two products, A and B. Robinson's budget for August follows:

	Master Budget	
	Product A	**Product B**
Sales	$240,000	$300,000
Variable cost	140,000	180,000
Contribution margin	$100,000	$120,000
Fixed cost	80,000	40,000
Operating income	$ 20,000	$ 80,000
Selling price	$ 120	$ 50

On September 1, these operating results for August were reported:

	Operating Results	
	Product A	**Product B**
Sales	$180,400	$341,120
Variable cost	106,600	216,480
Contribution margin	$ 73,800	$124,640
Fixed cost	80,000	40,000
Operating income	$ (6,200)	$ 84,640
Units sold	1,640	6,560

Required

1. For each product determine the following variances measured in contribution margin:
   a. Flexible budget variance.
   b. Sales volume variance.
   c. Sales quantity variance.
   d. Sales mix variance.
2. Explain the flexible budget variance using selling price and variable cost variances.

16-51   **Sales Variances; Flexible-Budget Variance; Review of Chapter 14**   Jerry Tanner, CEO and a major stockholder of Tanner Company, was unhappy with its operating results in 2010. The company manufactures two environmentally friendly industrial cleaning machines used primarily in automobile repair shops, gas stations, and auto dealerships. The master budget and operating results of the year (000s omitted except for the selling price per unit) follow:

	Actual		Budget	
	G80	**H20**	**G80**	**H20**
Sales	$85,500	$56,700	$100,000	$40,000
Variable cost	45,900	31,050	50,000	25,000
Contribution	$39,600	$25,650	$ 50,000	$15,000
Fixed cost	10,000	10,000	10,000	10,000
Operating income	$29,600	$15,650	$ 40,000	$ 5,000
Units sold	900	1,350		
Unit selling price			$ 100	$ 40

Required

1. Compute the contribution margin flexible-budget variance, contribution margin sales volume variance, contribution margin sales quantity variance, and contribution margin sales mix variance for each product and for the firm.
2. Write a memo to Jerry Tanner about the implications of the variances that you just computed on planning and operational control.

16-52   **Sales Variances; Flexible-Budget Variance; Review of Chapter 14**   Lau & Lau, Ltd., of Hong Kong manufacture two products for the same market. Its budget and operating results for the year just completed follow:

	Budget	Actual
Unit of sales		
Product A	30,000	35,000
Product B	60,000	65,000
Contribution margin per unit		
Product A	$4.00	$3.00
Product B	10.00	12.00
Selling price per unit		
Product A	$10.00	$12.00
Product B	25.00	24.00

At the time of budget preparation, the budgeting department and sales department agreed that the industry volume for the year would likely be 1,500,000 units. Actual industry volume turned out to be 2,000,000 units.

Required (you may round fractions to three decimal places)

1. What is the average budgeted contribution margin per unit?
2. What is the sales volume contribution margin variance for each product?
3. What is the sales mix contribution margin variance for each product?
4. What is the sales quantity contribution margin variance for each product?
5. What is the market size contribution margin variance?

6. What is the market share contribution margin variance?

7. What is the total flexible budget contribution margin variance?

8. What is the total variable cost price variance if the total contribution margin price variance is $50,000 favorable?

9. What is the total variable cost efficiency variance if the total contribution margin price variance is $50,000 favorable?

16-53 Sales Volume, Sales Quantity, and Sales Mix Variances   Classic Ice Cream operates several stores in a major metropolitan city and its suburbs. Its budget and operating data for 2010 follow:

	Budgeted Data			Actual Operating Results		
Flavor	**Gallons**	**Selling Price per Gallon**	**Variable Costs per Gallon**	**Gallons**	**Selling Price per Gallon**	**Variable Costs per Gallon**
Vanilla	250,000	$1.20	$0.50	180,000	$1.00	$0.45
Chocolate	300,000	1.50	0.60	270,000	1.35	0.50
Strawberry	200,000	1.80	0.70	330,000	2.00	0.75
Anchovy	50,000	2.50	1.00	180,000	3.00	1.20

Required

1. Compute these variances for the individual flavors and total sold:

    a. Sales volume.

    b. Sales mix. Extend mix calculation to five decimal places.

    c. Sales quantity.

2. Assess sales in of 2010 based on your analyses.

16-54 Sales Volume, Sales Quantity, and Sales Mix Variances; Working Backward   DOA Alive is a group of aspiring musicians and actors who perform in theaters and dinner clubs. It has a matinee and evening show. These operating data pertain to the month of July:

Master budget data	
Total operating income	$10,000
Total monthly fixed cost	$39,200
Total number of shows	100
Contribution margin per show: Matinee	$ 240
Evening	$ 600
Actual operating results	
Total sales quantity variance	$ 4,920U
The actual matinees were 150 percent of the evening shows.	

Required

1. Calculate for each type of show and the total:

    a. Sales mix variances.

    b. Sales quantity variances.

    c. Sales volume variances.

2. What strategic implications can you draw from the variances?

16-55 Market Size and Share Variances   Transpacific Airlines (TPA) budgeted 80 million passenger-miles, or 5 percent of the total market for the year just completed at a contribution margin of 40 cents per mile. The budgeted variable cost is 12 cents per mile.

The operating data for the year show that TPA flew 69.12 million passenger-miles with an average price of 48 cents per passenger-mile. The terrorist activity in the early part of the year in several countries in the region decreased the total miles flown by all airlines for the year by 10 percent. There is no flexible-budget variance for all costs.

Required   Assess the effects of the price, sales volume, market size, and market share on the firm's operating results for the year.

16-56 **Market Size and Market Share Variances for Small Business**   Diane's Designs is a small business run out of its owner's house. For the past six months, the company has been selling two products, a welcome sign and a birdhouse. The owner has been concerned about the company's marketing effectiveness. The master budget and actual results for March of this year follow:

	Master Budget		
	Welcome Sign	**Birdhouse**	**Total**
Units	50	25	75
Sales	$1,000	$250	$1,250
Variable costs	890	120	1,010
Contribution margin	$ 110	$130	$ 240
Fixed costs	75	75	150
Operating income	$ 35	$ 55	$ 90

	Actual Results		
	Welcome Signs	**Birdhouses**	**Total**
Units	45	35	80
Sales	$675	$420	$1,095
Variable costs	580	270	850
Contribution margin	$ 95	$150	$ 245
Fixed costs	75	75	150
Operating income	$ 20	$ 75	$ 95

The total market for welcome signs for the last six months are 3,000 budgeted and 3,000 actual. Diane expected the total market for birdhouses to be 200 units per month; the actual volume for the entire market, however, turned out to be only 175 units per month.

Required (rounding differences are acceptable)

1. Compare Diane's Designs' market share for welcome signs and birdhouses.
2. What is the market share contribution margin variance?
3. What is the market size contribution margin variance?
4. Explain possible reasons for these variances.

16-57 **Sales and Variable Cost Variances; Current to Prior Year; Review of Chapter 14**   Ross Product, Inc., manufactures a single product with the following information for the years 2009 and 2010.

	2010	2009
Sales units	25,000	22,000
Price	$41.00	$40.00
Materials cost per unit of materials	$18.00	$16.00
Materials usage (materials required per/unit of output)	0.75	1.00
Labor usage (labor-hours required/unit)	2.25	2.00
Wage rate ($/hour)	$ 9.00	$10.00

Required

1. Determine the selling price variance for 2010 based on sales dollars. Determine the volume variance based on both (a) sales and (b) contribution margin.
2. Determine the variable cost variances (review of Chapter 14, where year 2009 is used for the budget):
   a. The usage and price variances for materials (assume there is no change in inventory).
   b. The usage and rate variances for labor.
3. Analyze your findings in parts 1 and 2 above.

16-58 **Partial Operational and Financial Productivity; Medical Practice** Comprehensive Medical Care (CMC) is a family medical practice with 6 physicians and a nursing staff of 8 to 10 nurses and an administrative staff that varies from 4 to 7 personnel. Jay Kloger, the chief physician at CMC, is interested in studying the efficiency of the practice as a basis to set some benchmarks for further improvement, for rewarding his staff, and for comparing the efficiency of the CMC practice to other family medical practices. He is able to get comparable data for other practices from industry sources. So that the data is consistent with the industry sources, Jay has asked Marin & Associates, his accounting firm, to develop a set of productivity measures that would satisfy this requirement. Upon investigation, Joseph Marin finds that the measures to be used are the partial financial and operational productivity measures as defined in the chapter. The following information is for the last two years for the CMC practice:

	2010	2009
Patient visits	30,000	27,600
Nursing hours used	18,675	18,600
Administrative hours used	12,225	12,500
Cost of nursing support per hour	$39.00	$37.50
Cost of administration per hour	$25.56	$23.50
Industry average financial productivity		
Nursing	.035	.034
Administrative	1.120	1.140

Required

1. Compute the partial financial productivity ratios for nursing and administrative support for 2009 and 2010.

2. Separate the change of the partial financial productivity ratio from 2009 to 2010 into productivity changes, input price changes, and output changes.

3. Write a brief memo from Joseph Marin to Jay Kloger interpreting the findings above.

16-59 **Market Size and Market Share Variances; Foreign Currency Fluctuations** Big Spring Brewery (BSB) makes two specialty beers in its micro-brewery: Big Springs Ale and Dark Springs, BSB's dark beer. Both beers sell for the same price per case in the U.S. market and in the export market. The latter market is primarily European countries. Both beers also have the same variable production costs, though the export product has slightly higher variable costs due to shipping and other distribution costs associated with the export beers. The price, cost, and market information for the two beers are shown below.

	Budget	Actual	Budgeted Wt Avg CM
Sales units (cases)			
Domestic	22,000	21,575	
Export	12,000	15,225	
Total	34,000	36,800	
Price per case			
Domestic	$ 88	$ 87	
Export	90	92	
Variable cost per case			
Domestic	62	62	
Export	68	68	
Contribution margin per case			
Domestic	26	25	
Export	22	24	
Total contribution margin			
Domestic	$572,000	$539,375	$24.588
Export	$264,000	$365,400	

	Industry Budget	Industry Actual
Sales units		
Domestic	915,250	924,550
Export	659,500	645,750

The budget was prepared with the expectation that the currency exchange rate would be $1.29 per Euro. The actual average exchange rate for the period reflected the falling dollar, at $1.42 per Euro.

Required

1. What is the market share variance?
2. What is the market size variance?
3. Explain possible reasons for these variances, including a consideration of the effect of the change in the currency exchange rate for the dollar and the Euro.

16-60 **Sales and Variable Cost Variances; Current to Prior Year; Review of Chapter 14**   RJM Enterprises is a manufacturer of consumer electronics products. The industry is very competitive and RJM has seen its profits fall in recent years, including an operating loss of $18,585 in 2009. RJM was able to turn that around in 2010 by aggressively cutting costs. The summarized financial results for RJM are shown below.

	2010	2009
Gross sales:	$934,920	$1,273,545
Less variable costs		
Materials	$550,368	$ 746,200
Labor	329,280	511,875
Total contribution margin	$ 55,272	$ 15,470
Fixed costs	33,509	34,055
Operating income	$ 21,763	$ (18,585)

Jim Green, the management accountant at RJM, is analyzing the company's performance for 2010, in order explain to management the specific aspects that drove the company to success. Some of the information Jim obtained is:

	2010	2009
Sales units	39,200	45,500
Price	$23.85	$27.99
Materials cost per unit of material	$ 7.80	$ 8.20
Materials required/unit	1.80	2.00
Labor required/unit	0.60	0.75
Wage rate ($/hour)	$14.00	$15.00

Assume that RJM, for efficiency and to reduce cost, maintains little or no materials or work in process inventory.

Required

1. Determine the selling price variance for 2010 based on sales dollars. Determine the volume variance based on contribution margin.
2. Determine the variable cost variances:
   a. The usage and price variances for materials.
   b. The usage and rate variances for labor.
3. Interpret your findings in parts 1 and 2 above.

Solutions to Self-Study Problems

1. Productivity Variances

1. Operational partial productivity

	2009				2010			
	Output	÷	Input Resource Used	=	Partial Productivity	Output	÷	Input Resource Used	=	Partial Productivity
TPX–45	60,000	÷	75,000	=	0.8	64,000	÷	89,600	=	0.7143
Direct labor	60,000	÷	10,000	=	6.0	64,000	÷	10,847	=	5.9002

2. Financial partial productivity

	2009			2010		
	Units of Output	Cost of Input Resource Used	Partial Productivity	Units of Output	Cost of Input Resource Used	Partial Productivity
TPX–45	60,000 ÷	$540,000 =	0.1111	64,000 ÷	$609,280 =	0.1050
Direct labor	60,000 ÷	$300,000 =	0.2000	64,000 ÷	$347,104 =	0.1844

3. Separation of financial partial productivity

	(A) 2010 Output with **2010 Productivity** at 2010 Input Costs	(B) 2010 Output with **2009 Productivity** *at 2010 Input Costs*	(C) **2010 Output with** 2009 Productivity *at 2009 Input Costs*	(D) **2009 Output with** 2009 Productivity at 2009 Input Costs
Direct materials	64,000/$609,280 = 0.1050	64,000/$544,000 = 0.1176	64,000/$576,000 = 0.1111	60,000/$540,000 = 0.1111
Direct labor	64,000/$347,104 = 0.1844	64,000/$341,333 = 0.1875	64,000/$320,000 = 0.2000	60,000/$300,000 = 0.2000

	Productivity change	Input price change	Output change
Direct materials	0.1050 − 0.1176 = 0.0126U	0.1176 − 0.1111 = 0.0065F	0.1111 − 0.1111 = 0
Direct labor	0.1844 − 0.1875 = 0.0031U	0.1875 − 0.2000 = 0.0125U	0.2000 − 0.2000 = 0

Summary of Results:

	Productivity Change	Input Price Change	Total Change	Change as Percent of 2009 Productivity* Productivity Change	Input Price Change	Total Change
Direct materials						
TPX–45	0.0126U	0.0065F	0.0061U	11.34%U	5.85%F	5.49%U
Direct labor	0.0031U	0.0125U	0.0156U	1.55%U	6.25%U	7.8%U

* 2009 productivity: Direct materials − TPX–45   60,000 units ÷ (75,000 pounds × $7.20 per pound) = 0.111111
            Direct labor   60,000 units ÷ (10,000 hours × $30 per hour) = 0.2

Change as percent of 2009 productivity:

	Productivity Change	Input Price Change	Total Change
DM − TPX–45	0.0126 ÷ 0.111111 = 11.34%	0.0065 ÷ 0.111111 = 5.85%	0.0061 ÷ 0.111111 = 5.49%
Direct labor	0.0031 ÷ 0.2 = 1.55%	0.0125 ÷ 0.2 = 6.25%	0.0156 ÷ 0.2 = 7.8%

4. Total productivity

Total productivity in units	2009	2010
(a) Total units manufactured	60,000	64,000
(b) Total variable manufacturing costs incurred	$840,000	$956,384
(c) Total productivity (a) / (b)	0.071429	0.066919
(d) Decrease in productivity	0.071429 − 0.066919 = 0.00451	

Total productivity in sales dollars	2009	2010
(a) Total sales	$1,500,000	$1,600,000
(b) Total variable manufacturing costs incurred	$840,000	$956,384
(c) Total productivity (a) / (b)	$1.7857	$1.6730
(d) Decrease in productivity	$1.7857 − $1.6730 = $0.1127	

2. Sales Variances

1. Selling price variances (in 000s)

Flexible budget sales:

| | Master Budget for 2010 | | | Budgeted Selling | | Total Units | | Flexible |
	Total Sales	Units		Price per Unit		Sold in 2010		Budget Sales
Premium	$36,000	÷	240	=	$150	×	180	=	$27,000
Regular	43,200	÷	360	=	120	×	540	=	64,800

Selling price variances:

| | Premium | | | Regular | | |
	Actual	Flexible Budget	Selling Price Variance	Actual	Flexible Budget	Selling Price Variance
Barrels	180	180		540	540	
Sales	$28,800	$27,000	$1,800F	$62,100	$64,800	$2,700U

2. Sales volume variances (in 000s) for the period for each product and for the firm.

Flexible budget variable expenses:

| | Master Budget for 2010 | | | Budgeted | | Total Units | | Flexible |
	Total Variable Expenses	Number of Units		Variable Expenses per Unit		Sold in 2010		Budget Variable Expenses
Premium	$ 21,600	÷	240	=	$90	×	180	=	$16,200
Regular	27,000	÷	360	=	75	×	540	=	40,500

Sales volume variances:

| | Premium | | | Regular | | |
	Flexible Budget	Master Budget	Sales Volume Variance	Flexible Budget	Master Budget	Sales Volume Variance
Barrels	180	240	60U	540	360	180F
Sales	$27,000	$36,000	$9,000U	$64,800	$43,200	$21,600F
Variable expenses	16,200	21,600	5,400F	40,500	27,000	13,500U
Contribution margin	$10,800	$14,400	$3,600U	$24,300	$16,200	$ 8,100F
Fixed expenses	10,000	10,000	—	5,000	5,000	—
Operating income	$ 800	$ 4,400	$3,600U	$19,300	$11,200	$ 8,100F

3. Sales quantity variances for the firm and for each product. (See the solution for 4.)
4. Sales mix variances for the period for each product and for the firm (000s omitted).

Sales mixes:

| | Budgeted | | Actual | |
	Total Sales in Units	Sales Mix	Total Sales in Units	Sales Mix
Premium	240	0.40	180	0.25
Regular	360	0.60	540	0.75
Total	600	1.00	720	1.00

Budgeted contribution margin per unit =
Budgeted selling price per unit (item 1 above) − Budgeted variable
cost per unit (item 2 above)

Premium = $150 − $90 = $60
Regular   = $120 − $75 = $45

Sales mix and sales quantity variances:

Flexible Budget	*Total units of all products*	Master Budget
Total units of all products sold × **Actual sales mix** × Budgeted (standard) contribution margin per unit	*sold × Budgeted sales mix × Budgeted (standard) contribution margin per unit*	*Total budgeted units of all products to be sold ×* Budgeted sales mix × Budgeted (standard) contribution margin per unit

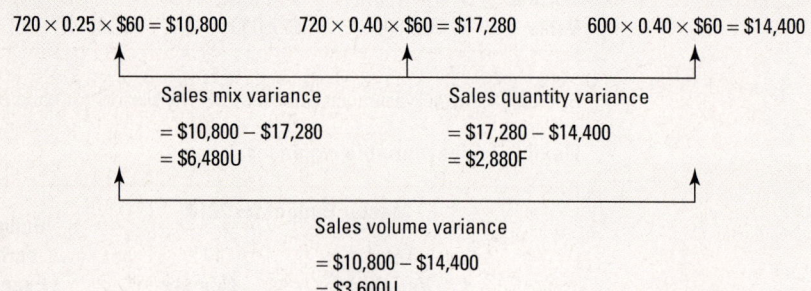

Premium

$$720 \times 0.25 \times \$60 = \$10,800 \qquad 720 \times 0.40 \times \$60 = \$17,280 \qquad 600 \times 0.40 \times \$60 = \$14,400$$

Sales mix variance
= $10,800 − $17,280
= $6,480U

Sales quantity variance
= $17,280 − $14,400
= $2,880F

Sales volume variance
= $10,800 − $14,400
= $3,600U

To verify: Sales volume variance = Sales mix variance + Sales quantity variance

= $6,480U + $2,880F
= $3,600U

Regular

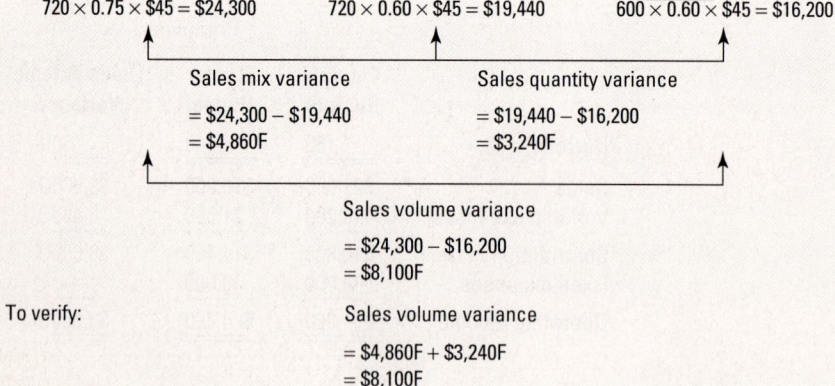

$$720 \times 0.75 \times \$45 = \$24,300 \qquad 720 \times 0.60 \times \$45 = \$19,440 \qquad 600 \times 0.60 \times \$45 = \$16,200$$

Sales mix variance
= $24,300 − $19,440
= $4,860F

Sales quantity variance
= $19,440 − $16,200
= $3,240F

Sales volume variance
= $24,300 − $16,200
= $8,100F

To verify: Sales volume variance

= $4,860F + $3,240F
= $8,100F

Total (both premium and regular)

Sales mix variance = $6,480U + $4,860F = $1,620U
Sales quantity variance = $2,880F = $3,240F = $6,120F

5. Verification

Sales mix variance + Sales quantity variance = Sales volume variance

Premium	$6,480U	+	$2,880F	=	$3,600U
Regular	4,860F	+	3,240F	=	8,100F
Total	$1,620U	+	$6,120F	=	$4,500F

6. Market size variance. (See the solution for 7.)

7. Market share variance (000s omitted).

Weighted-Average Budgeted Contribution Margin Per Unit

Master budget total contribution margin	$30,600
Master budget total sales units	÷ 600
Total	$ 51

Market Shares:

Budgeted: Total sales in units 600 ÷ Total sales of the industry 1,500 = 0.40
Actual: Total sales in units 720 ÷ Total sales of the industry 1,600 = 0.45

Market Share and Size Variances:

Actual total market size × **Actual market share** × Average budgeted contribution margin per unit	*Actual total market size* × **Budgeted market share** × Average budgeted contribution margin per unit	**Budgeted total market size** × Budgeted market share × Average budgeted contribution margin per unit

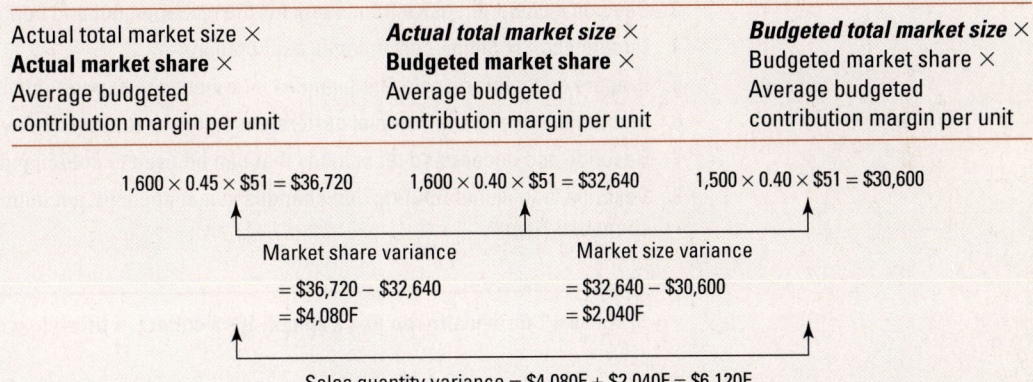

1,600 × 0.45 × $51 = $36,720   1,600 × 0.40 × $51 = $32,640   1,500 × 0.40 × $51 = $30,600

Market share variance   Market size variance

= $36,720 − $32,640   = $32,640 − $30,600
= $4,080F   = $2,040F

Sales quantity variance = $4,080F + $2,040F = $6,120F

8. The sum of market size variance and market share variance follows. It verifies that this total equals the sales quantity variance.

Total market size variance + Total market share variance = Total quantity variance
$2,040F   + $4,080F   = $6,120F

CHAPTER SEVENTEEN

The Management and Control of Quality

After studying this chapter, you should be able to . . .

1. Discuss the strategic importance of quality
2. Define accounting's role in the management and control of quality
3. Develop a comprehensive framework for the management and control of quality
4. Understand Six Sigma performance expectations
5. Prepare and interpret relevant financial information to support quality-related initiatives
6. Discuss the use of nonfinancial performance data to support quality-related initiatives
7. Describe and understand techniques that can be used to detect and correct quality problems
8. Describe lean manufacturing and changes in management accounting systems to support a change to "lean"

You can't turn quality on like a spigot. It's a culture, a lifestyle within a company.

A Ford Engineer

The competitive landscape of the world has changed dramatically. Today, high quality of products and services is a non-negotiable given. Global competition gives consumers abundant choices, and consumers today are much more cost conscious and value conscious. Most organizations, to varying degrees, have responded with quality-related management programs, with names such as total quality management (TQM), Six Sigma, and lean management (or lean manufacturing). Organizations that fail to embrace such initiatives may find themselves at a competitive disadvantage.

This chapter attempts to answer the following question: how can cost-management systems be configured to support managerial initiatives related to quality? We derive a framework (Exhibit 17.2) that can be used to guide the development of a comprehensive approach to the management and control of quality. We then divide the discussion into three primary sections: setting quality expectations (including a Six Sigma approach); financial and nonfinancial data related to the management and control of quality; and accounting for lean. In all cases our task is to demonstrate how accounting can add value to the organization by providing managers with information that supports quality-related initiatives embraced by the organization.

LEARNING OBJECTIVE 1

Discuss the strategic importance of quality

The Strategic Importance of Quality

Total quality management (TQM) is the unyielding and continuous effort by everyone in the firm to understand, meet, and exceed the expectations of customers.

Many firms in the United States have engaged in relentless efforts to improve the quality of their products and services. In this text, we refer to such efforts collectively as **total quality management (TQM)**, that is, the unyielding and continuous effort by everyone in the organization to understand, meet, and exceed the expectations of customers. In fact, continuous improvement has become a way of life for many firms and organizations, both in the United States and abroad, as evidenced by the quality standards and awards discussed below.

For decades, five-star hotels and restaurants have had consumers lining up to get in. Now comes a new consumer rating: five-star child-care. Just as if they were restaurants or hotels, child-care facilities (both child-care centers and family child-care homes) are being assigned star ratings by state regulators. These ratings are fast becoming the linchpin of states' drive to raise child-care quality. The ratings systems evaluate facilities on such criteria as low child–adult ratios, teacher credentials, curriculum, group size, and the safety and richness of the environment. Some of these criteria have in research studies been associated with better outcomes in children. There is some preliminary evidence that the ratings systems are improving quality. For example, in Oklahoma (the first state to set up a rating system) close to 60 percent of all child-care slots in the state are in facilities rated in the top two tiers, up from 30 percent in 2003. In Tennessee, where provider participation in star ratings is mandatory, 50 percent of facilities have earned a top rating, up from 30 percent in 2002.

Source: S. Shellenbarger, "Finding Five-Star Child-Care: States Rate Facilities in Effort to Boost Quality," *The Wall Street Journal*, March 23, 2006, p. D1.

Baldrige Quality Award

In 1987, Congress established the Malcolm Baldrige National Quality Award to enhance the competitiveness of U.S. businesses by promoting quality awareness, recognizing quality and performance achievements, and publicizing successful performance strategies of U.S. organizations in the areas of manufacturing, service, small business, and—added in 1999—education and health care. Seven broad categories make up the criteria: leadership, strategic planning, customer and market focus, information and analysis, human resource focus, process management, and business results. The fierce competition to win the award is evidence of the importance U.S. organizations place on being recognized for the quality of their operations.

ISO 9000 and ISO 14000

ISO 9000: 2000 is a set of guidelines for quality management and quality standards developed by the International Organization for Standardization, located in Geneva, Switzerland.

In 1947, to standardize practices for quality management, a specialized agency (the International Organization for Standardization) was formed. In 1987 this body adopted a set of quality standards, which were revised in 1994 and again in 2000. Thus, the current set of quality-management standards is referred to as **ISO 9000:2000**. Worldwide, ISO 9000 has become a certification sought after by global companies to gain the stamp of approval on the quality of their products and services.

The ISO 9000:2000 standards focus on developing, documenting, and implementing effective procedures for ensuring consistency of operations and performance in production and service delivery processes, with an overall goal of continual improvement. Note that the set of ISO 9000 standards relates to *processes* in place to ensure that outputs of the organization satisfy customer quality requirements. In the supply chain, trading partners of suppliers have all but eliminated their receiving department inspections because they expect zero-defect products to be delivered. Being ISO certified has become an entry ticket to participate in trade and commerce.

ISO 14000 is a set of quality standards designed to minimize environmental effects of an organization's outputs.

ISO 14000 is a set of standards that relate to environmental management, that is, what an organization does to minimize harmful effects to the environment. As with ISO 9000, ISO 14000 is concerned with quality management, that is, processes in place that ensure a product will have the least harmful impact on the environment, at any stage of its life cycle, either by pollution or by depleting natural resources. As of this writing, more than 700,000 organizations in 154 countries have implemented ISO 9000 and ISO 14000 standards (see www.iso.ch).

Quality and Profitability: Conceptual Linkage

Whether a company competes through a strategy of cost leadership or product differentiation, quality issues permeate every aspect of operations. A company choosing to compete through low prices is not necessarily choosing to produce low-quality products. Its low-priced products must still meet customer expectations. Similarly, a differentiation strategy will not be successful, or at least will not be as successful as it could be, if the company fails to build quality into its products. Thus, from top management's perspective, a key question is how best to manage and control quality and quality-related costs.

Exhibit 17.1 shows that a firm with improved quality can achieve competitive advantage and enjoy higher profitability and a higher return on investment. Improved quality decreases product returns. Lower returns decrease warranty costs and repair expenses. Improved quality lowers inventory levels for raw materials, components, and finished products because the firm has more reliable manufacturing processes and schedules. Improved product quality also lowers manufacturing costs as the firm reduces or eliminates rework costs and increases productivity. Customers are likely to perceive quality products as having higher values, which allows the firm to command higher prices and enjoy a larger market share. Higher prices and greater market shares increase revenues and profits. Improved quality also decreases cycle time. Faster cycle times speed deliveries, and prompt delivery makes

EXHIBIT 17.1
Conceptual Relationship between Improved Quality and Financial Performance

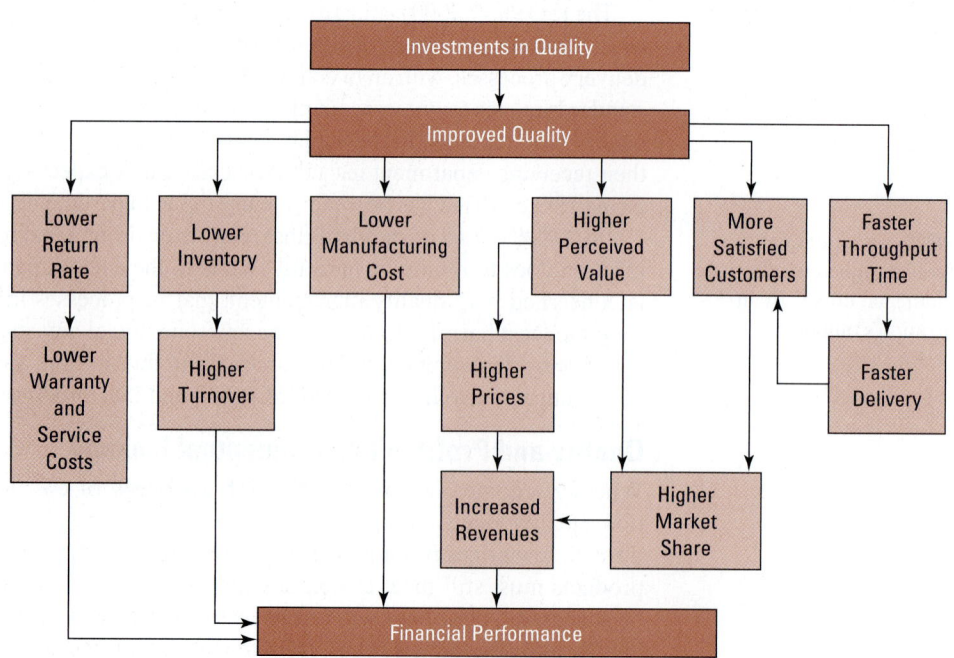

happy customers, creates new demand, and increases market shares. Higher revenues and lower costs boost net income and increase the firm's return on investment (ROI).

Accounting's Role in the Management and Control of Quality

LEARNING OBJECTIVE 2

Define accounting's role in the management and control of quality.

The preceding discussion should have conveyed to you that quality initiatives, such as TQM, are management, not accounting, initiatives or prerogatives. Thus, an appropriate question to ask at this point is how accounting can add value to, or support, quality-related initiatives of management. An inspection of Exhibit 17.1 suggests that accountants can add value to the process by providing managers with relevant and timely information, of both a financial and nonfinancial nature, that supports the quality-oriented initiatives of an organization. The following example provides an overview of the process that was used to develop internal accounting procedures for measuring and managing quality in the pharmaceutical industry.

The Five Steps of Strategic Decision Making: Improving Quality in Pharmaceutical and Medical-Product Companies[1]

Many world-class manufacturers, including producers of semiconductors and goods for the aerospace and electronics industries, have implemented effective systems for measuring and managing product quality. However, the situation in the pharmaceutical and medical-products sectors is different: historically, quality control was superseded in importance by a focus on product innovation and compelling marketing.

1. **Determine the strategic issues surrounding the problem.**   Lack of effective systems for monitoring and controlling quality in the pharmaceutical and medical-products industry ("pharma" for short) is becoming costly for these firms. Over the period 2001–2007, the industry incurred more than $700 million in fines and, it is thought, suffered billions more in lost revenues. Thus, for some firms in this industry, adopting world-class manufacturing processes can create a competitive advantage—both by reducing regulatory risk and by reducing production costs. One such process is the movement to lean manufacturing coupled with Six Sigma quality-performance expectations.

2. **Identify the alternative actions.**   At one level, corporate management may feel that strict regulation in the industry obviates the need for investing in a new quality-management system. At another level, executives may feel that a new quality-management and compliance-management system is needed to secure competitive advantage and reduce regulatory risk. In terms of a new system, choices need to be made as to (a) what data should be collected (e.g., qualitative vs. quantitative, including financial data regarding product quality), (b) to whom such data should be reported, (c) how often the data should be reported, and (d) how targeted performance in terms of quality (e.g., Six Sigma) should be specified. Finally, a decision needs to be made as to the methods that should be used to isolate and correct quality-related problems.

3. **Obtain information and conduct analyses of the alternatives.**   Corporate management would have to estimate the required investment outlay for the new monitoring and control system, as well as ongoing operating costs associated with the system. Benefits of the new quality-management and compliance system would have to be quantified and reported over time. These costs would be compared to anticipated benefits of the new system, both financial and nonfinancial in nature (e.g., improved relationship with regulators). Financial benefits would include opportunity costs as well as out-of-pocket costs, a point we made in Chapter 11.

---

[1] Background information for this example is taken from Anil G. D'souza, David J. Keeling, and Richard D. Phillips, "Improving Quality in 'Pharma' Manufacturing," *The McKinsey Quarterly*, September 2007.

4. **Based on strategy and analysis, choose and implement the desired alternative.** The company in question can choose to implement a comprehensive system for managing and controlling quality. This system might consist of a cost-of-quality (COQ) reporting framework that would report, on a time-series basis using activity-based costing data, both out-of-pocket and opportunity cost information. Such data could be benchmarked against best-in-class performers (either within or external to the company). Nonfinancial performance indicators would be derived from an explicit statement of strategy and would be analyzed statistically to justify their continued use. If lean production methods are adopted, then the company must consider whether and how to change its internal reporting system to support this change in production philosophy.

5. **Provide an ongoing evaluation of the effectiveness of implementation in step 4.** Assuming the investment in the new system is made, management could institute a post-audit review of the decision, to see how close the actual results were to the projected costs and benefits of the new system. (The topic of conducting post-audits in conjunction with long-term investment analysis was introduced in Chapter 12.)

Chapter Preview

In this chapter, we discuss ways in which accounting systems can be reconfigured to support quality-related initiatives of top management. We first define the term *quality* and then proceed to develop a framework for managing and controlling quality-related costs. As you will see, this framework integrates many of the ideas and concepts covered earlier in the text. This should reinforce in your mind the notion that accounting systems are dynamic in nature and need to evolve over time to meet the information needs and requirements of top management.

Comprehensive Framework for Managing and Controlling Quality

LEARNING OBJECTIVE 3

Develop a comprehensive framework for the management and control of quality.

Quality is defined as customer satisfaction with the total experience of a product or service, that is, the difference between customer expectations and actual performance of the product or service.

Design quality is the difference between customer expectations (for attributes, services, functionality, etc.) and product design.

Performance quality is the difference between the design specifications of the product and the actual performance of the product.

The Meaning of Quality

For purposes of discussion we define the term **quality** to mean the total level of customer satisfaction with the organization's product or service. Defined in this manner, we can decompose quality into two broad components: *features* and *performance*. The former component refers to the extent to which product/service design is consistent with customer expectations (in terms of product/service characteristics, attributes, or functionality)—in short, **design quality.** Outputs that fail to meet such expectations result in quality-of-design failure costs. Conceptually, you can think of design failure as the difference between the actual features of the product (or service) and the features that the customer wants. Such failures represent one component of total quality cost. One way to manage (i.e., reduce) design failure is through the use of target-costing procedures, as discussed in Chapter 13.

In this chapter, we are concerned with the management and control of the other broad component of quality, **performance quality,** which is defined as the difference between the design specifications of the product and the actual performance of the product. Thus, a personal computer whose electronic mouse consistently malfunctions or whose operating system constantly locks up relates to what can be called *performance-quality failures*. We define performance-quality costs as those related to providing a customer's required level of product or service performance.

Exhibit 17.1 provides broad guidance for the development of a comprehensive framework (or system) for the management and control of quality. One possible framework is presented in Exhibit 17.2. This exhibit serves as the focal point around which the discussion in the rest of the chapter is built. We now provide an overview of the primary elements of the framework.

Knowledge of Business Processes

Because the framework presented in Exhibit 17.2 is comprehensive, it presumes knowledge of key business processes. Thus, the development and implementation of a comprehensive

As noted earlier, some organizations have a quality orientation and embrace managerial initiatives such as TQM to support this competitive strategy. For each of the following examples, consider (1) which nonfinancial performance indicators, or controls, might be instituted to help control quality, and (2) what kinds of quality-related costs might be involved by failing to control quality:

- A study published in the November 15, 2005, issue of *Cancer* (a journal of the American Cancer Society) underscores the difficulty of improving screening rates to detect colon cancer, the third leading cause of cancer deaths.[*] Based on a review of patient charts from individuals associated with a California HMO, fewer than 30 percent of eligible patients over age 50 received any of the three types of colon-cancer tests. According to the National Committee for Quality Assurance, a Washington-based nonprofit organization that promotes health-care quality, Tufts Health Plan (Waltham, MA) achieved the highest score in the nation, 72 percent, for colorectal cancer screening.

- UnumProvident Corporation, a disability-income insurer, paid an $8 million civil penalty and $600,000 court costs to settle a suit brought against the company by the California Department of Insurance, to resolve allegations that it cheated policyholders by improperly denying claims.[†] This settlement followed an earlier fine of $15 million paid by the company to the U.S. Labor Department in a multistate settlement.

- Boston Scientific Corporation recently reached an agreement with the U.S. Food and Drug Administration (FDA) in which the company committed itself to an "aggressive timeline" for resolving quality-control problems.[‡] Prior to this agreement, the FDA had announced that it would withhold approval of some new products until the company resolved these issues. The FDA alleged that the company had failed to report, or delayed reporting, potential safety problems associated with its products.

- PeopleSoft, Incorporated, prior to their acquisition by Oracle, reached an agreement to pay Cleveland State University $4.25 million to settle a lawsuit over computer problems that delayed financial aid to thousands of students.[§] The university claimed that students often waited months for financial aid because of computer problems that also hindered other services for more than two years.

Sources:
[*] R. L. Rundle, "Colon-Cancer Screening Rates Rise Only Slightly, Study Says," *The Wall Street Journal* (October 11, 2005), p. B1.
[†] D. Gullapalli, "UnumProvident Is Set to Pay $8 Million Penalty in California," *The Wall Street Journal* (October 3, 2005), p. C3.
[‡] "Boston Scientific Sets to Fix Quality Issues," *The Wall Street Journal* (February 4, 2006), p. A2.
[§] "Software Firm Will Pay CSU $4.25M Settlement," *The Wall Street Journal* (February 4, 2006), p. A2.

framework for managing and controlling quality is best thought of as a cross-functional effort, with input of managers from across the firm's internal value chain. Because of their record-keeping and reporting responsibilities, accountants can be viewed as the key point of contact across various subunits and managers within the organization. Thus, the development of such

EXHIBIT 17.2
Comprehensive Framework for Managing and Controlling Quality

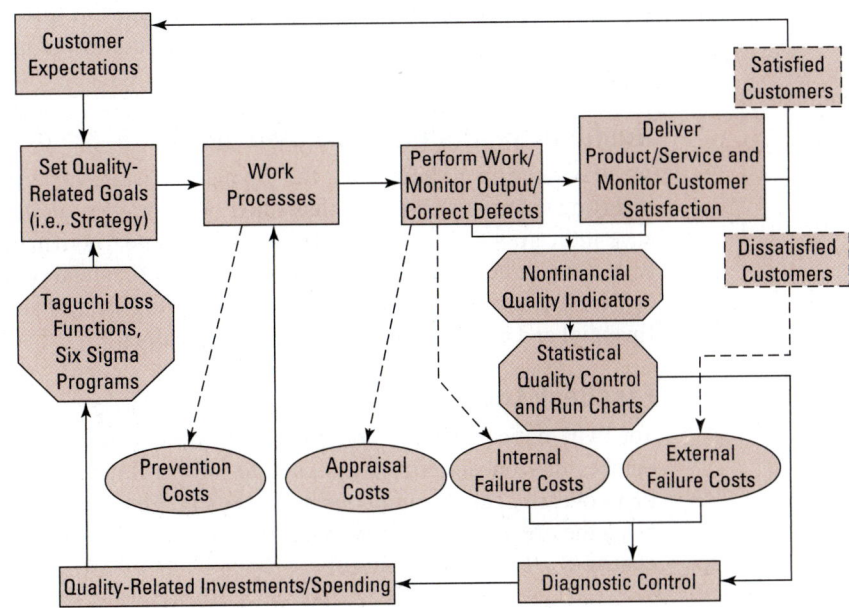

a comprehensive system requires the accountant to have broad business knowledge, including knowledge of fundamental business processes.

Role of the Customer

In the past, most quality-control reporting systems had a decidedly inward focus. That is, measures and techniques were developed and used based on what the organization felt were appropriate to the situation. More recently, however, organizations have begun to realize a fundamental flaw in system design: failure to embrace an outward (i.e., customer-based) viewpoint. Thus, in the comprehensive model shown in Exhibit 17.2, we depict consumer expectations as the cornerstone of the entire framework. In this sense, then, the model can be viewed as customer-based. As well, the model attempts to capture (as "external failure costs") various costs associated with dissatisfied customers.

Financial Component

You will notice that the reporting of quality *cost* information is a key element of the comprehensive framework shown in Exhibit 17.2. In fact, we depict cost information in four separate categories to give prominence to the different types of quality costs that organizations incur. This financial approach to the management and control of quality, known as *cost of quality,* is dealt with in greater detail later in the chapter.

Nonfinancial Performance Indicators

As illustrated in Exhibit 17.2, the financial performance indicators of our comprehensive reporting framework are complemented by both internal and external nonfinancial performance indicators. As we explain later in the chapter, nonfinancial performance indicators can be leading indicators (i.e., predictors) of future financial performance. As such, any comprehensive framework for managing and controlling quality should have a combination of both financial and nonfinancial performance indicators.

Feedback Loops

You will notice that the comprehensive framework illustrated in Exhibit 17.2 contains a number of feedback loops, designed to inform future decisions and to support an organization's overall goal of continuous improvement. Thus, for example, the entire model continually helps the organization better understand "customer expectations" and, in turn, set appropriate quality goals for the organization.

Pharmaceutical Companies Use Six Sigma across the Value Chain to Speed Time to Market, Reduce Costs, and Address Manufacturing Inefficiencies

In recent years, many major pharmaceutical companies have discovered the benefits of using Six Sigma principles to eliminate manufacturing process variation, defects, and inefficiencies. A smaller number of such companies are applying Six Sigma to Research and Development (R&D), in addition to the manufacturing function. Some aggressive companies, however, are applying the concept to functions across the entire value chain of activities. Among the benefits cited by pharmaceutical companies regarding Six Sigma are the following:

- Changing economics of the industry: the Medicare Modernization Act (January 2006) will likely motivate increased use of generic equivalents. For companies that have a thin pipeline of new drugs or major drugs going off patent, the only way to enhance profitability (at least in the short run) is to focus on cost controls and process efficiencies, both of which are supported by the use of Six Sigma.
- Maximizing employee value: the biggest asset for knowledge-based organizations, such as pharmaceutical companies, is people. The cultural shift to Six Sigma allows companies to get their employees more engaged. Tying rewards to accomplishments is particularly important to instituting such a culture change.
- Competitive advantage: early adopters of Six Sigma in the pharmaceutical industry stand to gain competitive advantage. Traditionally, cost-cutting and eliminating process variation (two targets of Six Sigma) have not been widely embraced in the industry. Thus, early adopters of this approach can gain at least temporary competitive advantage in an increasingly competitive environment.

For Six Sigma to work, most consultants believe that top management support and commitment are key. To change the culture of an organization to support Six Sigma, significant personnel training costs are likely. Still the financial return of such implementations can be significant. For example, Eli Lilly estimates that its cumulative benefit to date from the use of Six Sigma, over 160 projects, is approximately $250 million.

Source: N. D'Amore, "Six Sigma Adds Up for Pharma," *MedAdNews* 25, no. 2 (February 1, 2006), p. 18.

Relevant Cost Analysis

As indicated in Exhibit 17.2, management accountants can provide relevant financial information that can be used by managers for evaluating quality-related spending and investment decisions. Thus, the framework presented in Exhibit 17.2 draws directly from the material covered in Chapters 11 and 12 of the text.

Link to Operations Management

The framework presented in Exhibit 17.2 provides a good example of cross-disciplinary inputs to a management process. As noted above, accounting has primary reporting responsibility for relevant financial and nonfinancial performance measures. The question arises, then, as to how managers, after using such information, identify and analyze quality-related problems. For this, we draw from the field of operations management techniques such as control charts, Pareto diagrams, and cause-and-effect diagrams. Management accountants should have at least cursory knowledge of these techniques.

Breadth of the System

In the past, for many organizations (particularly manufacturers), quality was assumed to be the responsibility of production (i.e., the manufacturing process). Thus, as discussed earlier in this text, companies can calculate and report production-related failure costs, such as the cost of normal spoilage, the cost of abnormal spoilage, and so on. However, as indicated at the beginning of this chapter, many organizations today are embracing a broader responsibility for quality—across all elements of the value chain. Any comprehensive framework developed to support a TQM strategy should therefore have a broad reporting perspective. You will note that the performance measures reflected in Exhibit 17.2 cut across the entire value chain.

In the remaining sections of this chapter, we discuss in greater detail the elements of the conceptual framework illustrated in Exhibit 17.2.

Setting Quality-Related Expectations: The Role of Six Sigma

LEARNING OBJECTIVE 4
Understand Six Sigma performance expectations.

As seen from Exhibit 17.2, the actual quality goals embraced by the organization are affected principally by customer demands—that is, the level of quality (including product functionality) customers are willing to pay for. In this section we discuss the Six Sigma approach to setting quality-related performance standards. This is followed by a discussion of an alternative approach: the use of "goalpost" versus absolute conformance standards.

Setting Quality Expectations: A Six Sigma Approach

Six Sigma is an overall strategy to accelerate improvements and achieve unprecedented performance levels by focusing on characteristics that are critical to customers and identifying and eliminating causes of errors or defects in processes.

Six Sigma[2] has been embraced by many organizations as the guiding principle that drives improvements in products, services, and processes (e.g., product development, logistics, sales, marketing, and distribution). **Six Sigma** can perhaps best be defined as a business process-improvement approach that seeks to find and eliminate causes of defects and errors, reduce cycle times and manufacturing costs, improve productivity, better meet customer expectations, and achieve higher asset utilization and returns on investment in both manufacturing and service operations.[3]

Rudisill and Clary[4] offer the following actual examples of improvements realized by the move to Six Sigma:

- Reduction of scrap in a ball-bearing manufacturing plant and capacity assembly plant.
- Identification and reduction of unnecessary spare parts inventory for a paper cup plant.
- Reduction of defects and product variation in a textile finishing plant.
- Reduction of lead-times for product development and scale-up in a pharmaceutical company.
- Reduction of wait-time for loan approval notification (from the bank).

Six Sigma is based on a simple problem-solving methodology, **DMAIC**—**D**efine, **M**easure, **A**nalyze, **I**mprove, and **C**ontrol. Typically, the application of Six Sigma is done using cross-functional teams, more or less on a consulting project basis. In the design stage of the project, the Six Sigma team *defines* the problem and specifies the deliverables of the project. In the *measure* stage, the team collects relevant process performance data. In the *analyze* stage, the team tries to uncover root causes of an underlying quality problem. This is followed by the *improve* stage, in which proposed solutions to the underlying problem(s) are generated and then implemented. Finally, in the *control* stage of the project, appropriate controls are put in place to ensure that the identified problem does not recur.

Motorola, Inc. pioneered the concept of Six Sigma as a structured approach for assessing and improving both product and service quality. Today, this approach has gained notoriety and credibility because of its adoption by firms such as Allied Signal and General Electric. The term Six Sigma actually comes from statistics: in a normal distribution, the area outside of $+/-$ six standard deviations from the mean is very, very small. From a control standpoint, we can express this area in terms of relative number of defects. One interpretation of a Six Sigma quality expectation is approximately 3.4 defects per million items produced.[5]

The move from, say, a 3-sigma to a 6-sigma quality level is dramatic. For example, suppose your bank tracks the number of errors associated with checks written on the bank by its customers. If the bank finds, say, 12 errors per 1,000 checks processed, this is equivalent to an error rate of 12,000 per million—somewhere between 3.5 and 4 sigma levels! As Evans and Lindsay point out,[6] a change from 3 to 4 sigma represents a 10-fold

---

[2] Six Sigma is a federally registered trademark and service mark of Motorola, Inc.

[3] J. R. Evans and W. M. Lindsay, *An Introduction to Six Sigma and Process Improvement* (Mason, OH: South-Western, 2005), p. 3.

[4] F. Rudisill and D. Clary, "The Management Accountant's Role in Six Sigma," *Strategic Finance*, November 2004, pp. 35–39.

[5] As Evans and Lindsay (2005, pp. 36–38) show, this is a loose interpretation of the statistical basis for Six Sigma. That is, they show that the general specification for a k-sigma quality level is as follows: $k \times$ Process standard deviation = Tolerance/2.

[6] Ibid., p. 39.

Six Sigma is best characterized as a "business-improvement" methodology, the overall objective of which is to deliver high performance, reliability, and value to the end customer by identifying, analyzing, and improving work processes and by eliminating waste. Although highly touted by many companies as a strategy for increasing competitiveness, there are questions regarding the relationship between adoption of Six Sigma and stock-market performance. Case in point is The Home Depot. QualPro Inc., a company that markets a competing process-management technique, has issued a study comparing the stock performance of companies that adopted Six Sigma with the performance of the Standard & Poor's 500-stock index. Of the 58 companies reviewed in the QualPro report, 52 underperformed the S&P 500 index from the time they launched their Six Sigma programs through December 5, 2006.

In addition to The Home Depot, other underperformers include Lockheed Martin Corp., Ford Motor Co., and Xerox Corp. Six Sigma companies that beat the S&P 500 include Caterpillar Inc., Federated Department Stores, Inc., Starwood Hotels & Resorts Worldwide, Inc., Target Corp., and Whirlpool Corp. Further research would seem needed to test the empirical relationship between financial returns (such as stock price) and the adoption of Six Sigma, and the conditions under which the implementation of Six Sigma leads to increased financial returns.

Source: Karen Richardson (karen.richardson@awsj.com), "The 'Six Sigma' Factor for Home Depot; Departure of CEO Nardelli Brings into Focus A Management Technique He Championed," *The Wall Street Journal,* January 4, 2007, p. C3. Also available at *The WSJ Online* (online.wsj.com/article/SB116787666577566679-email.html).

improvement in quality; a change from 4 to 5 sigma, a 30-fold improvement; and a change from 5 to 6 sigma, a 70-fold improvement. For this reason, Six Sigma is not likely the goal for all processes and operations. The appropriate quality expectation is a function of the strategic importance of the process and the anticipated costs of taking the process to a higher level of quality.

Implementation Tips: Six Sigma[7]

Following are steps management can take to ensure the success of Six Sigma projects.

- First and foremost, *provide necessary leadership and resources.* As with many other strategic initiatives, the CEO and top-management team must exhibit strong support for the Six Sigma program. Such support can come in the form of employee training and making sure that there is appropriate buy-in for the concept on the part of key managers in the organization.

- *Implement a reward system.* Bonus and incentive schemes for the organization might have to be amended to accommodate rewards associated with reaching Six Sigma goals.

- *Provide ongoing training.* Since Six Sigma is a *process* (think of the DMAIC approach as iterative in nature), employee training should be ongoing, reinforcing the strategic importance of the process and the need for continual improvement.

- *Judiciously select early projects.* As noted above, Six Sigma principles can be applied to processes throughout the entire value chain of the organization. It is recommended, however, that top management starts with easy, nonpolitical, and noncontroversial projects that support the strategic goals of the organization. Given success with these projects, Six Sigma can then be rolled out to other more complicated and difficult projects.

- *Break up difficult projects.* Top management should try to parse complicated projects into smaller, short-term segments, each of which has its own milestone. This allows individuals to experience success along the way and to be recognized for their efforts to help the organization succeed.

- *Avoid employee lay-offs.* From a motivational standpoint, it is crucial that improvements based on Six Sigma should not jeopardize the jobs of those who helped accomplish the goal. Judicious job reassignment is one strategy for dealing with this situation; layoffs should be viewed as a last resort.

---

[7] This discussion is adapted from P. C. Brewer and J. E. Eighme, "Using Six Sigma to Improve the Finance Function: Here Are Some Tips for Success," *Strategic Finance* (May 2005), pp. 27–33.

Many organizations today are using Six Sigma principles to improve manufacturing efficiency and to lower costs. Others are using Six Sigma to improve service processes. Sodhi and Sodhi (2005) provide a recent example of a global manufacturer of industrial equipment that applied Six Sigma rigor to increase revenues.

The company in question offers a diverse product line, with many products manufactured to customer specification. Each sale, therefore, has its own individually approved discount and hence its own invoice price. With tens of thousands of sales transactions per year, the task of making sure that each invoice accords with the list and approved prices is indeed daunting.

The company had already experienced success in applying Six Sigma principles to its manufacturing operations. In fact, several individuals within the company had earned Six Sigma certifications (Green Belt, Black Belt). The company then decided to apply, on a pilot basis, a Six Sigma approach to its price-setting process.

The project in question involved a cross-disciplinary team (IT, sales, pricing, finance, and marketing) and five Six Sigma steps, referred to as DMAIC: **D**efine (the team decided that a defect should be defined as a transaction invoiced at a price lower than the one Pricing had approved); **M**easure (the team developed a map of the pricing process, which included six sequential steps; in theory, the process was straightforward, but in practice shortcuts were often taken and the quality of information available at various steps was deemed deficient); **A**nalyze (the team used a cause-and-effect matrix at each of the six steps to depict possible causes for lack of control); **I**mprove (the goal here was to decrease the number of unapproved prices without creating an onerous approval process); and, **C**ontrol (in the present case, the company set up a monthly review process to ensure that the company was experiencing higher transaction prices, fewer pricing exceptions, and no loss of market share).

The overall result? The original goal was to increase sales revenues by $500,000 for the year. In just six months, however, revenues had increased by a whopping $5.8 million, most of which went directly to the bottom line. As such, the company is now rolling out Six Sigma pricing across the entire organization.

Source: M. S. Sodhi and N. S. Sodhi, "Six Sigma Pricing," *Harvard Business Review,* May 2005, pp. 135–142.

Setting Quality Expectations: Goalpost versus Absolute Conformance Standards

Tolerance refers to an acceptable range of a quality characteristic, such as thickness (measured, for example, in centimeters).

An alternative approach to defining quality expectations, or product **tolerances,** is to choose between goalpost and absolute conformance standards. One advantage of the latter is that it is consistent with the use of Taguchi loss functions for control purposes, a subject dealt with in the Appendix to this chapter.

Goalpost Conformance

Goalpost conformance is conformance to a quality specification expressed as a specified range around the target.

Goalpost conformance is conformance to a quality specification expressed as a specified range around the target. The target is the ideal or desirable outcome of the operation. The range around the target is referred to as the *quality tolerance.*

For example, the target for a production process to manufacture 0.5-inch sheet metal is 0.5-inch thickness for all sheet metal manufactured. Recognizing that meeting the target every time in manufacturing is difficult, a firm often specifies a tolerance range. A firm that specifies a tolerance of ± 0.05 inch meets the stated quality standard when the thickness of its products is between 0.55 inch and 0.45 inch.

This approach assumes that the customer would accept any value within the tolerance range. As such, the approach assumes that quality-related costs do not depend on the actual value of the quality characteristic, as long as this value falls within the specified range. Exhibit 17.3 depicts the goalpost conformance specifications for the sheet metal example.

EXHIBIT 17.3
Goalpost Conformance

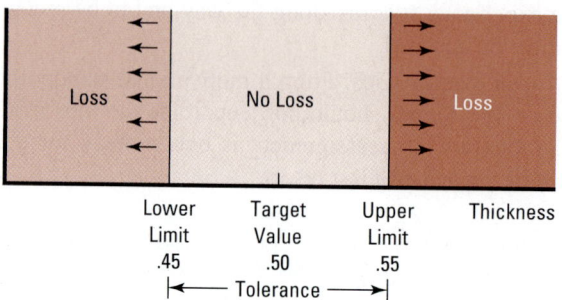

Absolute Quality Conformance

Absolute quality conformance (robust quality approach) requires all products or services to meet the target value exactly with no variation.

Absolute quality conformance or the **robust quality approach** aims for all products or services to meet the target value *exactly* with no variation. An absolute conformance requires all sheet metal to have a thickness of 0.5 inch, not 0.5 inch $\pm$ 0.05 inch or even 0.5 inch $\pm$ 0.0005 inch. Exhibit 17.4 depicts the robust quality approach. This approach assumes that the smaller the departure from the target value, the better the quality.

Variations from the target value are assumed to have negative economic consequences. As discussed in the Appendix (and, as indicated in Exhibit 17.4), the "cost" of deviating from the target value is assumed to be nonlinear in nature. Thus, robustness in quality comes with meeting the exact target consistently. Any deviation from the target is viewed as a quality failure and weakens the overall quality of the product or service.

Goalpost or Absolute Conformance?

Goalpost conformance assumes that a firm incurs no quality or failure cost or loss if all quality measures fall within the specified limits. That is, the firm suffers quality costs or losses only when the measure is outside the limits. No such quality tolerance exists in absolute conformance, which views quality costs or losses as a continuously increasing function starting from the target value. Quality costs, hidden or out-of-pocket, occur whenever the quality measure deviates from its target value.

Which of these two approaches, goalpost or absolute conformance, is better? Perhaps we can find an answer in the experience Sony had in two of its plants that manufacture color televisions.[8]

The two Sony plants manufacture the same television sets and follow the same specification for color density. The two plants, however, adopt different types of quality conformance. The San Diego plant uses goalpost conformance, and the Tokyo plant adopts absolute conformance. On examining the operating data over the same period, Sony found that all the units produced at the San Diego plant fell within the specifications (zero defects), but some of those manufactured at the Japanese plant did not. The quality of the Japanese units, however, was more uniform around the target value, while the quality of the San Diego units was uniformly distributed between the lower and upper limits of the specification, the goalpost, as depicted in Exhibit 17.5.

The average quality cost (loss) per unit of the San Diego plant, however, was $0.89 higher than that of the Japanese plant. One reason for the higher quality cost for units produced at the San Diego plant was the need for more frequent field service. Customers are more likely to complain when the density is farther away from the target value. Although the plant in Tokyo had a higher rejection rate, it experienced lower warranty and repair costs for its products. For firms desiring to attain long-term profitability and customer satisfaction, absolute conformance may be the better approach.

The extension of absolute performance standards to estimate Taguchi quality loss functions is covered in the Appendix to this chapter.

EXHIBIT 17.4
Absolute Conformance (Robust Quality Approach)

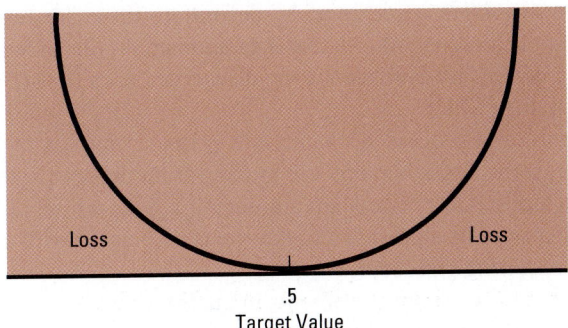

[8] Evans and Lindsay, *The Management and Control of Quality*, pp. 112–113.

EXHIBIT 17.5

Color Density of Sony TV Sets Manufactured in the San Diego Plant and a Japanese Plant

Source: J. R. Evans and W. M. Lindsay, *The Management and Control of Quality*, 6th ed. (Mason, OH: South-Western, 2005), p. 113.

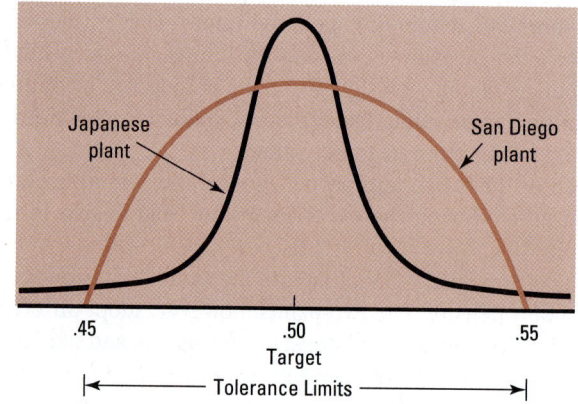

Financial Measures and Cost of Quality (COQ)

LEARNING OBJECTIVE 5

Prepare and interpret relevant financial information to support quality-related initiatives.

As indicated in Exhibit 17.2, there are two major situations in which accountants can provide relevant financial information as part of a comprehensive framework for managing and controlling quality: relevant cost (and revenue) data for decision-making purposes, and cost-of-quality (COQ) reports.

Relevant Cost Analysis

Quality-related spending (investment) affects the target level of quality and ultimately work processes and outputs—as depicted in Exhibit 17.2. In terms of spending on quality-related initiatives, we can employ the same decision framework that we presented in Chapter 11. That is, financial information relevant to quality-related decisions consists of future costs (and revenues) that differ between decision alternatives. In terms of relevant costs, we can also use the term *avoidable costs* since, by definition, these are future costs that can be avoided by choosing one decision alternative over another. As discussed in Chapter 12, long-term investments in quality are evaluated using discounted cash flow (DCF) decision models, such as net present value (NPV).

Activity and process decisions are prime examples of quality-related investments. For example, some manufacturers are moving from process layouts (batch processing) to cellular manufacturing. Other firms are embracing a just-in-time (JIT) production philosophy. Obviously, there can be significant outlay costs associated with a plant-layout change or a change in manufacturing philosophy.

At the same time, improvements in quality provide an opportunity for increasing revenues and for significant cost savings. The managerial accountant can provide decision makers with accurate estimates of costs and benefits associated with quality-related spending, such as a move to JIT. Benefits could include the contribution margin associated with increased sales (because of decreased cycle times associated with JIT production or the use of cellular manufacturing). Benefits could also include reduced spending on rework/scrap costs, lower financing costs associated with inventory reductions, reduced inventory obsolescence costs, reduced spending on inventory-recording costs, and reduced inventory-handling and storage-activity costs. Note that, as in Chapter 11, *relevant costs* include both *opportunity costs* and *out-of-pocket costs*.

Cost-of-Quality (COQ) Reporting

Quality costs for many companies are essentially buried in the company's financial statements. For example, in the case of a manufacturer some costs appear in manufacturing (factory) overhead accounts (e.g., product testing, materials inspection, normal spoilage costs), while other quality costs are included as part of general and administrative expenses. When warranted, traditional cost accounting systems—both job-order and process—report separately the cost of abnormal spoilage.

However, as indicated in Exhibit 17.2, quality costs are associated with activities across the value chain—from the design of work processes, to production of outputs (goods and services), to delivery of outputs to customers. Thus, quality costs also include costs associated with support functions such as product design, purchasing, public relations, and customer services.

The traditional general ledger is an effective instrument for what it is designed to do: post and summarize transactions into specific account balances. But the expense data in this format (e.g., salaries, supplies, depreciation) are structurally deficient for decision support, including measuring the total **cost of quality (COQ)** for the organization. They disclose what was spent but not why or for what or for whom. Expense data must be transformed into the costs of the activities within processes that traverse across the departmental cost centers reported in a general ledger system—and ultimately transformed into the cost of products, services, and customers.

Thus, an expansive view would define *cost of quality* as the cost of activities associated with the prevention, identification, repair, and rectification of poor quality, as well as opportunity costs from lost production and lost sales as a result of poor quality. For interpretive purposes, we might subdivide total COQ into the following four categories: prevention cost, appraisal cost, internal failure cost, and external failure cost. These terms are defined below. Exhibit 17.6 provides examples of the components of COQ. Consistent

Cost of quality (COQ) is a comprehensive reporting framework for classifying quality-related costs.

EXHIBIT 17.6

Examples of Quality Costs, by Category

Prevention Costs	Appraisal Costs
Training	Raw materials inspection
Instructor fees	Work-in-process inspection
Testing equipment	Finished goods inspection
Tuition for external training	Test equipment
Wages and salaries for time spent	Depreciation
on training and education	Salaries and wages
Planning and execution of a quality program	Maintenance
Salaries	Software
Cost of meetings/Quality circles	**External Failure Costs**
Investments	Sales returns and allowances
Product redesign	Warranty cost/field service
Process improvement	Contribution margin of cancelled sales orders
Equipment maintenance	Contribution margin of lost sales orders*
Internal Failure Costs	Product recalls
Scrap disposal (net cost)	Product liability lawsuits
Rework (materials, labor, overhead)	
Loss due to downgrades*	
Reinspection costs	
Loss due to work interruptions*	

*Opportunity costs

with the discussion in Chapter 11, we include both out-of-pocket as well as opportunity costs in the analysis of COQ.

Prevention Costs

Prevention costs are costs incurred to keep quality defects from occurring.

Prevention costs are incurred to keep quality defects from occurring. Prevention costs include the following:

- **Quality training costs.** Costs incurred to conduct internal training programs and for employees to participate in external programs to ensure proper manufacturing, delivering, and servicing of products and services, and to improve quality. These costs include salaries and wages for time spent in training, instruction costs, clerical staff expenses and miscellaneous supplies, and costs expended to prepare handbooks and instructional manuals.
- **Equipment maintenance costs.** Costs incurred to install, calibrate, maintain, repair, and inspect production equipment.
- **Supplier-assurance costs.** Costs incurred to ensure that materials, components, and services received meet the firm's quality standards. These costs include costs of selection, evaluation, and training of suppliers to conform with the requirements of total quality management (TQM).
- **Information systems costs.** Costs expended for developing data requirements and measuring, auditing, and reporting of data on quality.
- **Product redesign and process improvement.** Costs incurred to evaluate and improve product designs and operating processes to simplify manufacturing processes or to reduce or eliminate quality problems.
- **Quality circles.** Costs incurred to establish and operate quality control circles to identify quality problems and to offer solutions to improve the quality of products and services.

Quality circle
is a small group of employees from the same work area that meet regularly to identify and solve work-related problems and to implement and monitor solutions to the problems.

Appraisal Costs

Appraisal (detection) costs
are expenditures devoted to the measurement and analysis of data to determine conformity of outputs to specifications.

Appraisal (detection) costs are costs devoted to the measurement and analysis of data to determine conformity of outputs to specifications. These costs are incurred during production and prior to deliveries to customers. Through measurement, analysis, and monitoring of manufacturing processes and inspection of products and services prior to delivery, firms identify defective items and ensure that all units meet or exceed customer requirements. Appraisal costs include the following:

- **Test and inspection cost.** Costs incurred to test and inspect incoming materials, work in process, and finished goods, and the cost incurred to inspect machinery; also, costs associated with field-testing of products at the site of the consumer.
- **Test equipment and instruments.** Expenditures incurred to acquire, operate, or maintain facilities, software, machinery, and instruments for testing or appraising the quality of products, services, or processes.

Internal Failure Costs

Internal failure costs
are associated with defective processes or defective products detected before delivery to customers.

Internal failure costs are associated with defective processes or defective products found prior to delivery to customers. These costs include:

- **Costs of corrective action.** Costs for time spent to find the cause of failure and to correct the problem.
- **Rework and (net) scrap costs.** Materials, labor, and overhead costs for scrap, rework, and reinspection.
- **Process costs.** Costs expended to redesign the product or processes, unplanned machine downtime for adjustment, and lost production due to process interruption for repair or rework.

- **Expediting costs.** Costs incurred to expedite manufacturing operations due to time spent for repair or rework.
- **Reinspection and retest costs.** Salaries, wages, and expenses incurred during reinspection or retesting of reworked or repaired items.
- **Lost contributions due to increased demand on constrained resources.** Constrained resources spent on defective units increase cycle time and reduce total output. Contributions lost from units not produced because of the unavailability of the constrained resources reduce the operating income of the firm.

External Failure Costs

External failure costs
are associated with defective/ poor-quality outputs detected after being delivered to customers.

External failure costs are costs related to quality defects detected after unacceptable products or services reach the customer. External failure costs include the following:

- **Repair or replacement costs.** Repair or replacement of returned products.
- **Costs to handle customer complaints and returns.** Salaries and administrative overhead of the customer service department; allowances or discounts granted for poor quality; and, freight charges for returned products.
- **Product recall and product liability costs.** Administrative costs to handle product recalls, repairs, or replacements; legal costs; and settlements resulting from legal actions.
- **Lost sales and customer ill-will due to defective outputs.** Lost contribution margins on canceled orders, lost sales, and decreased market shares.
- **Costs to restore reputation.** Costs of marketing activities to minimize damages from a tarnished reputation and to restore the firm's image and reputation.

Conformance and Nonconformance Costs

Costs of conformance
are prevention costs and appraisal costs.

Costs of nonconformance
are internal failure costs and external failure costs.

Conceptually, the total cost of quality (COQ) can also be categorized into conformance costs and nonconformance costs. Prevention and appraisal costs are **costs of conformance** because they are incurred to ensure that products or services meet customers' expectations. Internal failure costs and external failure costs are **costs of nonconformance.** They are costs incurred, including opportunity costs, because of poor-quality products or services. The total cost of quality (COQ) is the sum of conformance and nonconformance costs.

Prevention costs are usually the least expensive and the easiest among the four costs of quality for management to control. Internal and external failure costs are among the most expensive costs of quality, especially external failure costs. In a typical scenario, the cost of prevention may be $0.10 per unit, the cost of testing and replacing poor quality parts or components during production may be $5, the cost of reworking or reassembling may be $50, and the cost of field repair and other external costs may be $5,000 or higher.

Better prevention of poor quality reduces all other costs of quality. With fewer problems in quality, less appraisal is needed because the products are made right the first time. Fewer defective units also reduce internal and external failure costs as repairs, rework, and recalls decrease. By spending more on prevention and appraisal, companies spend less on internal or external failure costs. The savings alone can be substantial. Meanwhile, the firm enjoys higher perceived values of its products, increased sales and market share, and improved earnings and return on investment, as depicted earlier in Exhibit 17.1.

COQ Reports

The purpose of reporting quality costs is to make management aware of the magnitude of these costs, to motivate continuous improvement in COQ, and to provide a baseline against which the impact of quality-improvement investments can be measured.

Ford Motor Company unveiled the 2001 model of its best-selling sport-utility vehicle, the Ford Explorer, in late 2000. The 2001 model added a host of new safety features that enhanced the most popular SUV on the market since its introduction a few years earlier. Ford expected the new model to increase the firm's market share and to add substantial amounts to its bottom line. Yet, three months after the redesigned Explorer began rolling off the assembly line not a single one of the 5,000 built was in dealer showrooms. Instead, they were parked outside factories in St. Louis and Louisville while Ford engineers pored over them looking for defects. Jacques Nasser, CEO of the Ford Motor Company at that time, ordered factory managers to hold off on shipping the new Explorer until engineers had the opportunity to correct quality problems.

When asked by financial analysts to comment on the cost of delay and repairing defects, Nasser responded, "Pick a number. It is over $1 billion." The delay was expensive, but Ford executives said the cost of fixing warranty claims later would have been far higher. One defect caught by engineers was an internal steering-column switch that might have led motorists to start the engine in the "drive" position. Left uncorrected, this problem had the potential of resulting in big-time safety recalls. What was the root cause of the problem? It was traced to a supplier who used too much solder on a $1 circuit board. "When you get to the bottom of it, they are that trivial," says a company official of such glitches. "But when you let them escape, they are just huge."

Source: N. Muller, "Putting the Explorer under the Microscope," *Business-Week,* February 12, 2001, p. 40.

Report Format

A COQ report is useful only if its recipients understand, accept, and can use the content of the report. Each organization should select and design a reporting system that (1) can be integrated into its information system, and (2) promotes the quality initiatives specified by top management. To facilitate assessment of the magnitude of quality costs and their impact, the organization should express its COQ component costs relative to net sales (or total operating costs) for the period.

A cost-of-quality matrix, as illustrated in Exhibit 17.7, is a convenient and useful tool in reporting quality costs. With columns identifying functions or departments across the value chain, and rows delineating COQ categories, a cost-of-quality matrix enables each department,

EXHIBIT 17.7   **Cost-of-Quality Matrix**

Source: J. R. Evans and W. M. Lindsay, *The Management and Control of Quality,* 6th ed. (Mason, OH: South-Western, 2005), p. 400.

	Design Engineering	Purchasing	Production	Finance	Accounting	Other	Totals	% of Sales
Prevention costs Quality planning Training Other								
Appraisal costs Test and Inspect Instruments Other								
Internal failure costs Scrap Rework Other								
External failure costs Returns Recalls Other								
Totals								

function, process, or product line to identify and recognize the effects of its actions on the total cost of quality and to pinpoint areas of improvement.

Illustration of a COQ Report

Exhibit 17.8 illustrates a COQ report.[9] Bally Company is a small midwestern manufacturing company with annual sales of around $9 million. The company operates in a highly competitive environment and has been experiencing increasing pressures from new and existing competitors to raise quality and lower cost. The report shows that the external failure costs for items such as warranty claims, customer dissatisfaction, and loss of market share accounted for 75 percent of the total COQ in year 0 ($1,770,000 ÷ $2,360,000, or 22.13% ÷ 29.5%).

To be more competitive and to increase market share, Bally began a corporatewide three-year TQM process. The firm started with substantial increases in prevention and appraisal expenditures. The investment started to pay off in year 2. Internal failure, external failure, and total quality costs have all decreased. COQ reports over time can help document these improvements.

Exhibit 17.8 compares the current year's quality costs to those of a base year. Alternative bases for comparisons can be the budgeted amounts, flexible budget costs, or long-range goals.

To better communicate results, the accountant can transform time-series data, such as the data presented in Exhibit 17.8, into one or more histograms. Based on before-and-after

EXHIBIT 17.8

Cost-of-Quality (COQ) Report for Bally Company

	Year 2	% of Sales	Year 0	% of Sales	Percent Change in Cost
Prevention Costs					
Training	$ 90,000		$ 20,000		350%
Quality planning	86,000		20,000		330
Other quality improvement	60,000		40,000		50
Supplier evaluation	40,000		30,000		33
Total	$ 276,000	3.07%	$ 110,000	1.38%	151
Appraisal Costs					
Testing	120,000		100,000		20
Quality performance measurement	100,000		80,000		25
Supplier monitoring	60,000		10,000		500
Customer surveys	30,000		10,000		200
Total	$ 310,000	3.44%	$ 200,000	2.50%	55
Internal Failure Costs					
Rework and reject	55,000		150,000		(63)
Reinspection and testing	35,000		30,000		16
Equipment failure	30,000		50,000		(40)
Downtime	20,000		50,000		(60)
Total	$ 140,000	1.56%	$ 280,000	3.50%	(50)
External Failure Costs					
Product liability insurance	70,000		250,000		(72)
Warranty repairs	100,000		120,000		(17)
Customer losses (estimated)	600,000		1,400,000		(57)
Total	$ 770,000	8.55%	$1,770,000	22.12%	(56)
Total Quality Costs	**$1,496,000**	**16.62%**	**$2,360,000**	**29.50%**	(37)
Total sales	$9,000,000	100.00%	$8,000,000	100.00%	

[9] Adapted from "Managing Quality Improvements," *Statement of Management Accounting No. 4-R* (Montvale, NJ: Institute of Management Accountants, 1993).

histograms, managers are more able to see improvement in overall COQ spending that has occurred over time. The visual representation of the histograms also enables managers to better evaluate trade-offs, such as increased spending in prevention and appraisal with the expectation of reductions in failure costs. This process of feedback and evaluation makes COQ more than just an accounting scheme—it becomes a financial investment justification tool.

COQ and Activity-Based Costing (ABC)

An ABC system is ideally suited to the preparation of COQ reports. An ABC system identifies cost with activities and thus increases the visibility of costs of quality. Costs of activities that are the result of poor quality become clear to the organization. Traditional costing systems, in contrast, focus the cost reporting on organizational functions such as production, sales, and administration. An organization with a good ABC system in place needs only to identify costs and activities relating to COQ and classify these costs according to the COQ categories that the firm chooses to use.

Nonfinancial Quality Indicators

LEARNING OBJECTIVE 6

Discuss the use of nonfinancial performance data to support quality-related initiatives.

As seen from the preceding discussion, relevant financial data are needed to guide investment decision making and in planning and controlling quality-related costs. However, as indicated in Exhibit 17.2, *nonfinancial* performance data also play an important role in a comprehensive framework for managing and controlling quality.

Internal Nonfinancial Quality Metrics

Organizations strive to specify internal dimensions of quality on which they must focus in order to meet customer expectations. Thus, we find the following examples of internal nonfinancial quality measures:

- Process yield (i.e., good output/total output).
- Productivity (i.e., ratio of acceptable outputs—goods or services—to resource inputs).
- Percentage of first-pass yields (i.e., percentage of initial output meeting quality standards).
- Number of defective parts produced (e.g., parts-per-million, *ppm*).
- Machine up-time (or, machine down-time).
- Trend in dollar amount of inventory held.
- Employee turnover (e.g., number of employees who voluntarily leave the company/total number of employees).
- Safety record (e.g., number of accidents per month, number of days since last accident).
- Throughput (i.e., outputs—goods or services—produced and delivered to customers).
- Production (manufacturing) lead time (i.e., difference between when an order is received by manufacturing and when that order is completed).
- Cycle-time efficiency (i.e., ratio of time spent on value-added activities to the sum of time spent on value-added and non-value-added activities; also known as *throughput time ratio* or *process cycle efficiency*).
- Throughput efficiency (i.e., the ratio of throughput to resources used).
- New product (or service) development time.

You will notice that many of the preceding metrics relate to process efficiency. Improving quality should improve many if not most of these measures. In actual practice, responsibility for implementing process changes designed to improve these measures is assigned to cross-functional teams. Further, some type of benchmark, either internal or external, is generally used as the standard against which actual performance is gauged.

External (Customer Satisfaction) Quality Metrics

A comprehensive framework for managing and controlling quality will include a set of external, as well as internal, quality measures. These metrics are customer-based, as shown by the following examples:

- Number of defective units shipped to customers as a percentage of total units shipped.
- Number of customer complaints.
- Percentage of products that experience early or excessive failure.
- Delivery delays (e.g., difference between scheduled delivery date and date requested by the customer).
- On-time delivery rate (e.g., percentage of shipments made on or before the scheduled delivery date).
- Market research information on customer preferences and satisfaction with specific product features.
- Customer response time (CRT) i.e., the total lapse of time between when a customer places an order and when the customer actually receives the completed goods; this total time can be broken down into three components: receipt time; manufacturing lead time; and, delivery time. (See Exhibit 14.14.)

The preceding list is meant to be illustrative, not exhaustive. In practice, the actual metrics used are based on an organization's strategy. As is the case with internal quality measures, the preceding metrics require some benchmark (standard) against which actual performance for a period can be compared.

Role of Nonfinancial Performance Measures

Internal and external nonfinancial measures of quality are important components of the framework presented in Exhibit 17.2 for a number of reasons:

- They are, for the most part, readily available (compared, for example, to the generation of activity-based costs, the preceding list of nonfinancial quality performance data are much less costly to obtain).

- Such information is relevant to operating personnel (production employees, salespersons, etc.)—that is, operating personnel understand these metrics and therefore can use them as the basis for improving operations.

- Because these measures relate to physical processes, they focus attention on precise problem areas that need attention.

- Such information is more timely than financial measures of quality—in the extreme, these measures of quality can be reported on a real-time basis (i.e., instantaneously as operations occur). Thus, nonfinancial quality indicators provide immediate short-run feedback on whether quality-improvement efforts have, in fact, succeeded in improving quality.

- These nonfinancial performance measures can be useful predictors (i.e., leading indicators) of future *financial* performance.

Detecting and Correcting Poor Quality

LEARNING OBJECTIVE 7

Describe and understand techniques that can be used to detect and correct quality problems.

As indicated in Exhibit 17.2, a comprehensive framework for managing and controlling quality relies on the use of a number of techniques for detecting poor quality and then taking appropriate corrective action. These techniques come principally from the field of operations management. In general, you can think of these techniques as embracing a single, overall goal: improving underlying business processes.

Detecting Poor Quality

Once an appropriate set of financial and nonfinancial performance indicators has been specified, management needs to determine how to analyze the data it collects. The overall goal is to determine when the underlying process is not in control and, therefore, is in need of correction. One way to accomplish this is through the use of control charts.

A **control chart** plots successive observations of an operation taken at constant intervals.

A **control chart** plots successive observations of an operation (or cost), taken at constant intervals, to help determine whether a process is in control or not. The operation can be a machine, workstation, individual worker, work cell, part, process, or department. Costs can include labor, materials, energy, or any of the costs of quality discussed earlier in this chapter. Intervals can be time periods, batches, production runs, or other demarcations of the operation.

A typical control chart has a horizontal axis representing units, time intervals, batch numbers, or production runs, and a vertical axis denoting a financial or nonfinancial performance measure. The vertical measure has a specified allowable range of variations, which are referred to as *upper* and *lower limits,* respectively. Exhibit 17.9 contains control charts for manufacturing 1/8-inch drill bits in three workstations.

Assume that a firm has determined all drill bits must be within 0.0005 inch of the specified diameter. All units from workstation A are within the specified range ($\pm$ 0.0005″), and no further investigation is necessary. Three units from workstation B are outside the specified range—an indication that the process in Workstation B may not be in proper control. Management may want to investigate the cause of the aberration to prevent further quality failures. Although all units manufactured by workstation C are within the specified range acceptable to the firm, the control chart reveals that quality characteristics of workstation C are drifting upward. (Used in this manner, the control chart is often referred to as a **run chart.** A run chart shows the trend of observations over time.) Management may want to launch an investigation

A **run chart** shows trends in quality measures over time.

EXHIBIT 17.9
Control Charts for 1/8-Inch Drill Bit

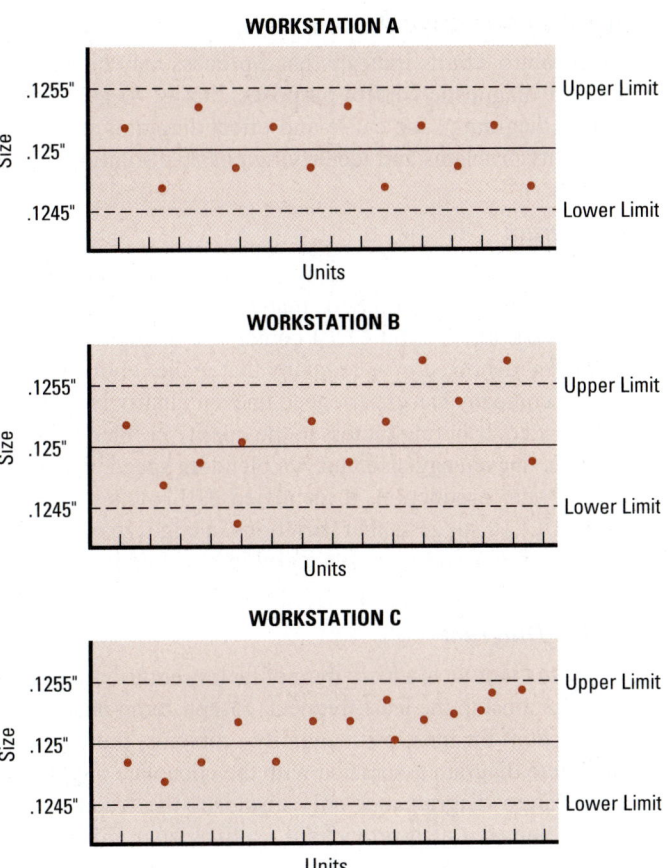

WORKSTATION A

WORKSTATION B

WORKSTATION C

because the trend suggests that in the near future the operation may produce drill bits outside the control limits.

When the central line and the limits in a control chart are determined through a statistical process, the control chart is a *statistical quality control* (SQC) *chart* or *statistical process control* (SPC) *chart*. The control charts presented in Exhibit 17.9 are SQC (or SPC) charts if the line in the center, 0.125″, is determined by calculating the arithmetic mean (μ, read mu) of the observations and the limits, 0.1255″ and 0.1245″, are determined based on the standard deviation (σ, read sigma) of the observations. For example, the standard deviation of the drill bits is, say, 0.00025″ and the firm has determined that variations within two standard deviations are acceptable. Thus the limits are $\mu \pm 2\sigma$, or 0.125″ $\pm$ 2 $\times$ 0.00025″, which are 0.1255″ and 0.1245″ for upper and lower limits, respectively.

A firm sets the upper and lower control limits based on experience, technology, and customer expectations. The purpose of a control chart is to distinguish between random and nonrandom variations. A process (or operation, or cost) is considered to be in *statistical control* if no sample observation is outside the established limits. Variations that fall within the established limits are deemed *random* variations so that no further investigation is needed. Observations outside the limits may signal quality failures.

However, for observations within the established limits to be considered random, the observations should show no apparent patterns or runs, with an approximately equal number of observations above and below the center line and most points nearing the center line. A process may be out of control if the observations show trends, cycles, clusters, or sudden shifts hugging the center line or the control limits. Posting control charts in a common area facilitates early detection of quality problems, promotes awareness of workers on the quality status of their products or services, and encourages active participation in efforts to raise quality.

Taking Corrective Action

Once control charts indicate that a process may be out of control, what techniques are available for diagnostic control purposes, that is, to guide corrective action? Histograms, Pareto charts (diagrams), and cause-and-effect diagrams are useful techniques for diagnosing causes of quality problems and identifying possible solutions to these problems.

Histogram

A **histogram**
is a graphical representation of the frequency of attributes or events in a given set of data.

A **histogram** is a graphical representation of the frequency of attributes or events in a given set of data. Patterns or variations that are often difficult to see in a set of numbers become clear in a histogram. Exhibit 17.10 contains a histogram of factors that contribute to the quality problems identified by a company that makes chocolate mousse.

The company has experienced uneven quality in one of its product. The company has identified six contributing factors to the quality problem: substandard chocolate, improper liqueur mixture, uneven egg size, uneven blending speed, variant blending time, and improper refrigeration after production. It identified 210 batches as having poor quality. The histogram in Exhibit 17.10 suggests that variations in egg size may be the largest contributor to the quality problem, followed by uneven speed in blending ingredients.

Pareto Diagram

A **Pareto diagram**
is a histogram of the frequency of factors contributing to a quality problem, ordered from the most to the least frequent.

A **Pareto diagram** is a histogram of factors contributing to a specified quality problem, ordered from the most to the least frequent. Joseph Juran observed in the 1950s that a few causes usually account for most of the quality problems, thus the name Pareto.[10] See Exhibit 17.11 for the Pareto diagram associated with the chocolate mousse quality problem.

A Pareto diagram not only discloses the frequency of factors associated with a quality problem but also provides a useful visual aid. A Pareto diagram includes a curve that shows the cumulative number of causes, as shown in Exhibit 17.11. Using a Pareto diagram,

EXHIBIT 17.10

Histogram of Quality Problem: Contributing Factors

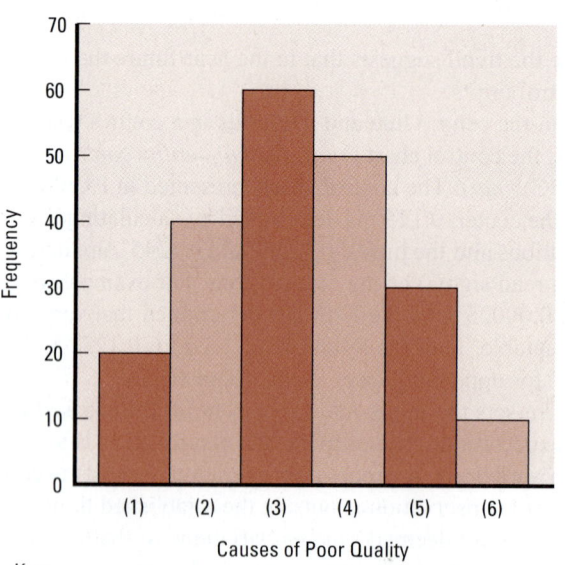

Key:
(1) Quality of chocolate
(2) Liqueur
(3) Egg size
(4) Blending speed
(5) Blending duration
(6) Improper refrigeration

Causes of Poor Quality

---

[10] V. Pareto, a nineteenth-century Italian economist, observed that 80 percent of the wealth in Milan was owned by 20 percent of its residents.

EXHIBIT 17.11
Pareto Diagram of Quality Problem: Ranking of Contributing Factors

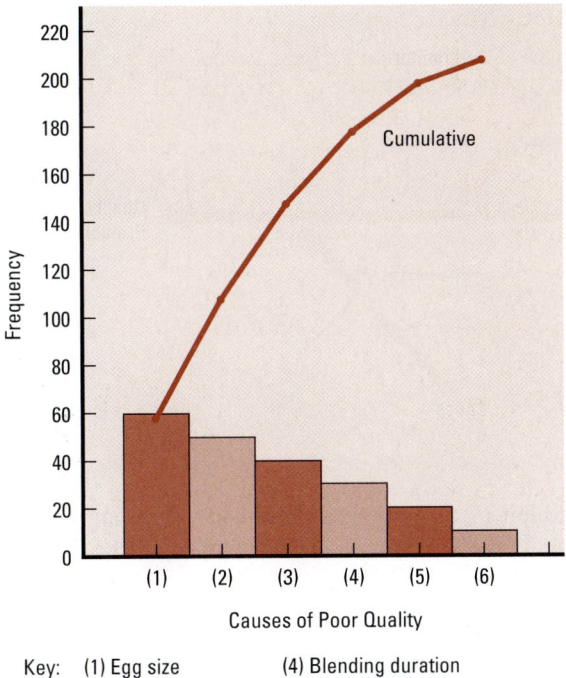

Key: (1) Egg size   (4) Blending duration
       (2) Blending speed (5) Quality of chocolate
       (3) Liqueur   (6) Improper refrigeration

management can separate the few major causes of quality problems from the many trivial ones and identify areas that contribute most to poor quality. Thus, management can focus its efforts on areas that are likely to have the greatest impact on quality improvement. For example, the cumulative line in Exhibit 17.11 shows that improper egg size and erratic blending speed account for 110 quality problems in manufacturing chocolate mousse. To improve quality, management would most likely demand that all suppliers deliver eggs uniform in size and that operating personnel regulate the speed of blenders.

Cause-and-Effect Diagram

A **cause-and-effect diagram** organizes a chain of cases and effects to sort out root causes of an identified quality problem.

The **cause-and-effect,** or "fish-bone," **diagram** organizes a chain of causes and effects to sort out root causes of an identified quality problem. Karou Ishikawa discovered that for situations with myriad factors the number of factors that influenced a process or contributed to a quality problem were often overwhelming. He developed cause-and-effect diagrams as an organizing aid.[11]

A cause-and-effect diagram consists of a spine, ribs, and bones. At the right end of the horizontal spine is the quality problem at hand. The spine connects causes to the effect, the quality problem. Each branch or rib pointing into the spine describes a main cause of the problem. Bones pointing to each rib are contributing factors to the cause. In Exhibit 17.12 we illustrate the general structure of a cause-and-effect diagram.

Typical main causes for quality problems in manufacturing operations are

- Machines
- Materials
- Methods
- Manpower

Some users refer to the four main categories as *4M.*

[11] K. Ishikawa, *Guides to Quality Control,* 2nd ed. (Tokyo: Asian Productivity Organization, 1986).

EXHIBIT 17.12
Basic Cause-and-Effect ("Fish-Bone") Diagram

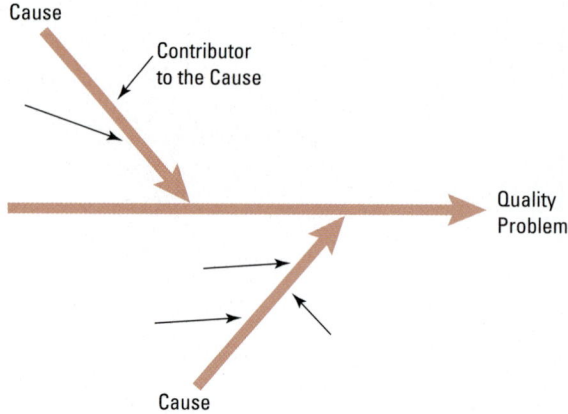

In Exhibit 17.13 we show a cause-and-effect diagram for the quality problems in the manufacturing of chocolate mousse. The company identified these main causes for the 20 percent rejection rate:

- Machines
  Equipment not properly calibrated
  Timer functions erratically
- Materials
  Suppliers delivered wrong or irregular-size eggs
  Low-quality chocolate
  Wrong liqueur used
- Methods
  Improper refrigeration of ingredients
  Ingredients not added at proper time or in prescribed sequence
  Inappropriate preheating
- Manpower
  Hiring of new workers without proper experience and not giving adequate training
  Workers failed to follow instructions

Many organizations have found brainstorming an effective technique in constructing cause-and-effect diagrams similar to the one presented in Exhibit 17.13.

EXHIBIT 17.13
Cause-and-Effect Diagram for the Chocolate Mousse Quality Problem

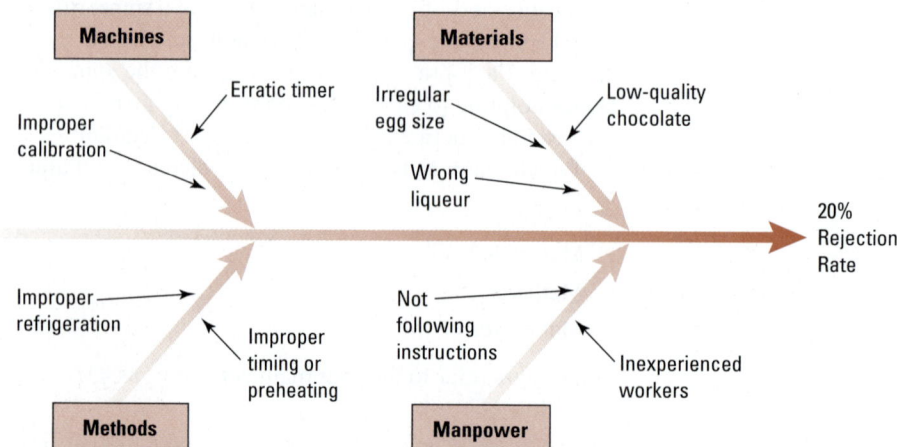

Lean Manufacturing and Accounting for Lean

LEARNING OBJECTIVE 8

Describe lean manufacturing and changes in management accounting systems needed to support a change to "lean."

Lean Manufacturing

The practice of total quality management (TQM), when combined with a strategic focus on productivity (Chapter 18) and an emphasis on increasing the speed of product flow and reducing inventory levels and customer lead times (the theory of constraints, Chapter 13), has led a number of companies to adopt what is called *lean manufacturing*. The goal of lean manufacturing ("lean," for short) is to increase product flow and product quality, reduce inventory, improve decision making, and increase profitability. Organizations adopting lean usually also adopt lean accounting, a new approach to costing and performance measurement that helps the organization show the financial benefits of the lean manufacturing initiative. Chapter 13 explains how lean manufacturing is related to productivity goals and measures. In Chapters 9 and 11, we show how lean accounting can play a role in the application of cost-volume-profit (CVP) analysis and short-term decision making, respectively. And in Chapter 18, we show how lean accounting plays a role in performance measurement. The objective of the discussion of lean in this chapter is to outline the strategic role of lean manufacturing and lean accounting and to illustrate the methods used to implement them. As such, the material in this section can be considered an extension of the topics covered earlier in this chapter. The primary conceptual lesson is the need to reexamine and redesign cost-management systems as the underlying environment changes.

At the heart of lean manufacturing is the Toyota Production System (TPS) which has helped Toyota to become one of the most productive automakers in the world.[12] The main elements of TPS are: (1) a long-term focus on relationships with suppliers and coordination with these suppliers; (2) an emphasis on balanced, continuous-flow manufacturing with stable production levels; (3) continuous improvement in product design and manufacturing processes, with the objective of eliminating waste; and (4) flexible manufacturing systems in which different vehicles are produced on the same assembly line and employees are trained for a variety of tasks. Lean manufacturing is an approach to operations that has similar goals. The five principles of lean manufacturing are:[13]

1. *Value*   Lean starts with what is of value to the customer; rather than focus on internal standards of performance, lean measures success in terms of providing value to the customer.

2. *Value Stream*   The value stream consists of all the activities required to create customer value for a family, or group, of related products or services. Lean organizations do not

---

[12] Taiichi Ohno, *Toyota Production System: Beyond Large Scale Production,* Productivity Inc, 1988.

[13] Institute of Management Accountants (IMA), Statements on Management Accounting, "Accounting for the Lean Enterprise: Major Changes to the Accounting Paradigm," and "Lean Enterprise Fundamentals" (www.imanet.org/publications_statements.asp).

	Traditional Production	Lean Manufacturing
Key focus points	Reduce cost Reduce idle time	Meet customer demand with short lead time Reduce overproduction and inventory level
Manufacturing scheduling	Meet forecasted demand (push); production in batches	Meet a customer order received (pull); production is driven by the receipt of customer orders
Batch production	Reduce *number* of setups to reduce setup costs	Reduce setup *time* to maximize manufacturing flexibility and to reduce inventory; maximize the ability to meet diverse customer needs; the principle of one-piece flow

focus on the cost of individual products but on the costs and profitability of the value stream. As such, the cost accounting system is greatly simplified, which gives rise to the notion of lean accounting.

3. *Pull and Flow* A lean production process is scheduled to satisfy customer orders as they arrive at the company; this is the concept of *pull* production. The emphasis is on reducing lead time—the time it takes to process a customer's order. The company does not produce to meet a production forecast or budget (this is called the *push* approach), an approach that can result in excess inventory—especially when the inventory does not satisfy changed customer needs.

4. *Empowerment* The lean manufacturing system has measures of performance, both financial and nonfinancial, that help the employee achieve the organization's lean goals. In the lean system these measures are collected in what is called a *box score,* which is similar to the balanced scorecard. The lean approach produces these measures frequently (daily or weekly) so that operating and management personnel have real-time information on progress to goals.

5. *Perfection* The lean approach emphasizes Six Sigma, continuous improvement, and elimination of non-value-added transactions (processes).

The key concepts of lean manufacturing as compared to traditional production systems are summarized in Exhibit 17.14.

Accounting for Lean

Accounting for lean (lean accounting, for short) uses value streams to measure the financial benefits of a firm's progress in implementing lean manufacturing. Lean accounting places the firm's product and services into value streams, each of which is a group of related products or services. For example, a company manufacturing consumer electronics might have two groups of products (and two value streams)—digital cameras and video cameras—with several models in each group. Accounting for value streams significantly reduces the need for cost allocations (since the products are aggregated into value streams), which can help the firm to better understand the profitability of its process improvements and product groups.[14]

A second motivation for value stream accounting arises from the fact that organizations implementing lean may see the operating improvements rather quickly, but traditional financial statements will not show these improvements for some time. The organization's commitment to lean manufacturing may take several months or years to complete, so that the failure to see these improvements in the financial statements for a long period could undermine the commitment and success of the effort.

There are three reasons why the improvements in financial results typically appear later than the operating improvements from implementing lean manufacturing.[15]

---

[14] For a reference on the value-stream income statement see the Institute of Management Accountants, Statements on Management Accounting: "Accounting for the Lean Enterprise: Major Changes to the Accounting Paradigm," and Frances A. Kennedy and Peter C. Brewer, "Lean Accounting: What's It All About," *Strategic Finance,* November 2005, pp. 27–34.

[15] Robin Cooper and Brian Maskell, "How to Manage Through Worse-Before-Better," *MIT Sloan Management Review* (Summer 2008), pp. 58–65.

1. Customers will benefit from the improved manufacturing flexibility by ordering in smaller, more diverse quantities. In the short term, this means that total sales may fall, as will financial results. In the longer term, the increased value added to the customers will increase sales and the overall volume of customer demand should increase.

2. Improvements in productivity will create excess capacity; as equipment and facilities are used more efficiently, some will become idle. The result is no improvement in short-term financial results. When the excess capacity is reduced over time, or redeployed, the financial results will show the improvement from the cost savings.

3. Because full-cost accounting methods include all manufacturing costs as part of product cost, fixed manufacturing costs are included in the balance sheet as part of inventory until the product is sold. The decrease in inventory that results from lean means that, using full-cost accounting, the fixed costs incurred in prior periods (when inventory was increasing) flow through the income statement when inventory is decreasing. This effect is explained more fully in Chapter 18, in the section "Variable Costing versus Full Costing."

Value-stream income statements can be adapted to separate from operating income the effects of each of the above items. An example of a value-stream income statement that addresses the third item above (viz., the effect of inventory reduction) is shown in Exhibit 17.15. Rimmer Company has two value streams, digital cameras and video cameras. Assume that the operating costs and other value-stream costs are directly traceable to the two value streams, so no cost allocation is involved; the costs that cannot be traced to a value stream ($209,000 in total) are assigned only to the total company level. Note also that the recent implementation of lean has resulted in the decline in inventory, and that the prior period fixed manufacturing cost flowing through the current income statement are shown separately: $10,000 for the Digital Cameras stream, and $20,000 for the Video Cameras stream. The temporary total effect on income, $30,000, is set apart; lean managers would argue that, taking a long-term view, total operating income should be interpreted as $85,200 ($55,200 + $30,000).

The Strategic Role of Lean Accounting

Lean manufacturing and lean accounting can play a key role in an organization's success. Lean is particularly appropriate for firms in dynamic and competitive environments, where there is product complexity and changing customer expectations. These are the types of firms that Robin Cooper describes in his study of lean enterprises—firms like Toyota, Nissan, and Sony.[16] These companies have long embraced the principles of lean, just-in-time, and

---

[16] Robin Cooper describes a type of competition that differs from cost leadership and differentiation, as described by Michael Porter and explained in Chapter 1. Cooper studied firms that compete on both cost and product leadership, in very competitive environments. See *When Lean Enterprises Collide: Competing through Confrontation,* Harvard Business School Press, 1995.

As noted in the text, traditional accounting may not accurately measure the results that lean manufacturing delivers. Some commentators maintain that traditional accounting provides hard-to-understand financial reports and measurements that drive managers to make wasteful decisions, such as the unnecessary and wasteful build-up of inventory. Jusko (2007) notes that some big-name companies (e.g., Ariens, Parker Hannifin, Buck Knives, and Textron) have implemented lean accounting successfully.

Buck Knives is, in fact, a leader in lean-accounting implementation. First, the company reorganized itself into a number of value streams. Next, the company replaced its performance metrics with new ones that, it thinks, better reflects its lean goals. As with any

cultural change, the change to lean manufacturing and lean accounting is likely to engender some opposition. This was actually the case with Buck Knives. When creating value streams, Buck Knives met resistance from operators who wanted to cling to their traditional functional roles. This resistance was understandable, given the fact that the company was attempting to change the way things had been done at the company for over 45 years.

Sources: Jill Jusko, "Accounting for Lean Tastes," *Industry Week* (September 1, 2007). Accessed online at www.industryweek.com/ReadArticle .aspx?ArticleID=14766 (December 2, 2008); Tonya Vinas, "Knife Company Hones Competitiveness by Bucking the Status Quo," Lean Enterprise Institute (www.lean.org, accessed November 12, 2008).

continuous improvement. A commodity-based firm (agribusiness, building products, etc.) with a few homogeneous products and integrated manufacturing processes would probably focus on efficiency and many of the lean manufacturing principles but have little need for the value-stream income statement. Similarly, firms such as Coach and Tiffany that succeed on the basis of a strong differentiated brand would likely focus on performance measures that advanced its brand, rather than emphasize the principles of lean. Exhibit 17.16 provides a summary of the strategic role that can be played by the lean approach relative to full-cost accounting.

EXHIBIT 17.15   Sample Value-Stream Income Statement

	RIMMER COMPANY Value Stream Income Statement				
	Digital Cameras		**Video Cameras**		**Total**
Sales		$585,000		$540,000	$1,125,000
Operating costs:					
Materials	$ 25,200		$ 12,800		
Labor	168,000		88,000		
Equipment related costs	92,400		48,400		
Occupancy costs	11,200		4,800		
Total operating costs		296,800		154,000	$ 450,800
Less other value stream costs:					
Manufacturing	120,000		240,000		
Selling and administration	10,000	130,000	10,000	250,000	380,000
Value stream profit before inventory change		158,200		136,000	294,200
Less: Cost of decrease in inventory		(10,000)		(20,000)	(30,000)
Value stream profit		$148,200		$116,000	$ 264,200
Less nontraceable costs					
Manufacturing					155,000
Selling and administration					54,000
Total nontraceable fixed costs					209,000
Operating income					$ 55,200

EXHIBIT 17.16   **Summary Comparison: Traditional (Absorption) Costing vs. Lean Accounting**

	Full-Cost Accounting	**Lean Accounting**
Key focus points	Causality; linking resources, cost drivers, and cost objects Obtain accurate product costs	Process flow and throughput; speed up product throughput Facilitate the five principles of lean manufacturing Support just-in-time (JIT) and theory-of-constraints efforts; reduce inventory and customer lead time
Strategy implementation	Full-cost based; can be used to support long-term decisions	Short-term focus on reducing lead times, inventory levels, and value stream income; value stream goals can be linked to company strategy Focus on day-to-day decisions
Cost allocation	Trace direct costs and use cost drivers for indirect costs	The goal is to avoid cost allocation; the use of the value stream, by aggregating products into product families, means that many costs can be traced directly to the value stream and allocation is not needed.
Nonfinancial information included?	Can be a supplement, as in a balanced scorecard	Included in the box score report that includes operational, capacity usage, and financial measures
Product cost detail and product-mix analysis	Individual product; product mix at the detail level	Aggregation of products; product cost at the value stream level; analysis of average product cost within value stream
Reflects the financial benefits of lean manufacturing?	Only in the long term	Directly shows the financial benefits of lean efforts, through value-stream accounting and through the recognition of the cost of decreasing inventory levels
Product costs for pricing	Product costs may or may not play a role in pricing	Assumes that the firm is a price-taker; costs are not used in pricing
Reporting interval	Often monthly	Frequent; often weekly or daily

Summary

In today's global competition, with short product life-cycles and rapidly changing technologies and consumer tastes, organizations can sustain long-term survival and profitability only by manufacturing quality products and rendering quality services.

A quality product or service meets or exceeds customer expectations at a price customers are willing to pay. To achieve quality products or services, many firms adopt *total quality management,* which requires continuous efforts by everyone in an organization to understand, meet, and exceed the expectations of both internal and external customers.

How can accounting add value to the organization by supporting quality-related initiatives of management? We propose, in Exhibit 17.2, a comprehensive framework that can be used to manage and control quality for a business. This framework begins, and ends, with the goal of meeting customer expectations. That is, the framework implies an iterative or continuous process. One primary role in this process for accounting is to provide relevant financial information. We identify two such examples: relevant cost (and revenue) data for evaluating spending and investments in quality, and the preparation of cost-of-quality (COQ) reports. Such financial information regarding quality is supplemented with internal and external nonfinancial measures of quality. To detect poor quality (i.e., out-of-control processes), these data can be analyzed using run or control charts. Histograms, Pareto diagrams, and cause-and-effect diagrams can then be used for diagnostic control purposes, that is, to identify the source of quality problems in order to inform appropriate corrective action.

Management accountants, with training and expertise in analyzing, measuring, and reporting information, can help design and implement the type of comprehensive control system depicted in Exhibit 17.2.

Recently, some companies have embraced lean manufacturing initiatives. In response, the management accounting and control systems for these organizations may have to be revised to better reflect and support such initiatives. The use of value-stream income statements was illustrated in the chapter as one possible revision. The primary conceptual lesson is the organic nature of cost-management systems: they need to change in response to changes in business strategy—a lesson that has been a primary theme throughout this text.

Appendix

Taguchi Quality Loss Function

Genichi Taguchi and Y. Wu proposed the absolute quality conformance approach as an *off-line* quality control.[17] Taguchi and Wu hypothesize that any variation from the exact specifications entails a cost or loss to the firm. This cost or loss can be depicted by a quadratic function similar to the one shown in Exhibit 17.4.

Taguchi quality loss function depicts the relationship between quality costs and level of deviation from target quality.

The **Taguchi quality loss function** depicts the cost function associated with deviation from target quality. The loss grows larger as the variation increases (a quadratic function): the total loss increases as the magnitude of a quality characteristic of the product or service moves farther away from the target value. In a quadratic function the loss quadruples when the deviation from the target value doubles. For instance, if the loss is $4 when the deviation is 0.1 from the target value, the loss will be $16 when the deviation doubles, or is 0.2 from the target value.

The total cost of deviations from the quality target includes direct costs in manufacturing and service, and hidden quality costs. Direct costs are costs such as rework, warranty repair or replacement, additional production costs, and loss on disposal. The hidden quality losses include customer dissatisfaction, loss of future business, loss of market share, additional engineering costs, additional management costs, and additional inventory.

QUALITY LOSS FUNCTION

Taguchi and Wu show that a quadratic function provides a good approximation of quality losses. For a quality characteristic with the target value T, the loss from having a quality characteristic x can be estimated by this quadratic function:

$$L(x) = k(x - T)^2$$

where

x = the observed value of the quality characteristic
T = the target value of the quality characteristic
k = the cost coefficient, determined by the firm's costs of failure

k is a constant estimated for the quality characteristic based on the total production and service costs and hidden costs to the firm due to deviation of the quality characteristic from the target value. The value of k for a particular quality characteristic can be estimated as follows:

$$k = \frac{\text{Total quality cost}}{(\text{Tolerance allowed})^2}$$

For example, assume that a company has determined that no customer will accept sheet metal deviating more than 0.05 inch from the target value in thickness, that the target thickness is 0.5 inch, and that the estimated cost to the firm is $5,000 for each rejection by a customer. The $5,000 estimated cost to the firm includes repair or replacement, processing, service costs, and other costs due to customer dissatisfaction. Then

$$k = \frac{\$5,000}{0.05^2}$$
$$k = \$2,000,000$$

---

[17] Taguchi and Wu, *Introduction to Off-Line Quality Control.* See also Evans and Lindsay, *The Management and Control of Quality*, pp. 594–597, and T. L. Albright and H. P. Roth, "The Measurement of Quality Costs: An Alternative Paradigm," *Accounting Horizons*, June 1992, pp. 15–27.

EXHIBIT 17A.1
Total Estimated Quality Losses
Using a Taguchi Loss Function

(1)	(2)	(3)	(4) = (2) × (3)	(5)	(6) = (2) × (5)
x	*L(x)*	Plant A		Plant B	
Measured Thickness	Quality Cost (or Loss)	Probability	Weighted Loss	Probability	Weighted Loss
0.43	$9,800	0	$ 0	0.02	$196
0.46	3,200	0.20	640	0.03	96
0.48	800	0.20	160	0.15	120
0.50	0	0.20	0	0.60	0
0.52	800	0.20	160	0.15	120
0.54	3,200	0.20	640	0.03	96
0.57	9,800	0	0	0.02	196
Expected loss			$1,600		$824

If the actual thickness of a unit is 0.47, then the estimated quality cost (or loss) for the unit is

$$L(0.47) = \$2,000,000(0.47 - 0.5)^2 = \$1,800$$

If, however, the thickness is 0.46, then the estimated total loss from the deviation increases to $3,200, as follows:

$$L(0.46) = \$2,000,000(0.46 - 0.5)^2 = \$3,200$$

TOTAL LOSS AND AVERAGE LOSS

The loss just calculated is the estimated loss from having one unit with the observed quality characteristic. The total loss for all the units manufactured during a period is the sum of the losses from all units whose observed value of the quality characteristic deviated from the target value.

Alternatively, the total loss due to variations in the quality characteristic can be determined by multiplying the average loss per unit by the total number of units manufactured. The average loss per unit is the expected loss due to variations in the quality characteristic. Exhibit 17A.1 shows the calculations of the expected total losses in two plants identified as A and B. These two plants have different probability distributions of deviations from the target value, as noted in columns (3) and (5).

The output from plant A spreads evenly over the range from 0.46 to 0.54, with no unit falling outside the tolerance limits. In contrast, the output from plant B concentrates near the specified target value, but not all units lie within the tolerance limits.

Albright and Roth show that the expected, or average, loss per unit can be determined using variance and the square of the mean deviation from the target value, as follows:[18]

$$EL(x) = k(\sigma^2 + D^2)$$

where

$EL(x)$ = expected (average) loss from having quality characteristic x
σ^2 = variance of the quality characteristic about the target value[19]
D = the deviation of the mean value of the quality characteristic from the target value
   = $\bar{x} - T$

[18] Albright and Roth, "The Measurement of Quality Costs," p. 23.

[19] Variance, σ^2, is computed as follows:

$$\sigma^2 = \Sigma(x - \bar{x})^2 f(x)$$

where, x = quality characteristic, e.g. measured thickness, as in Exhibit 17A.1

$\bar{x}$ = mean value of quality characteristic, $\bar{x} = \Sigma x f(x)$

$f(x)$ = probability of observing quality characteristic, x; each value of $f(x)$ lies between 0 and 1, and all values of $f(x)$ sum to 1.

Assume that the variance is 0.0008 for plant A[20] and 0.000412 for plant B and that the value of D is 0 for both plants.[21] Thus,

Plant A: $EL(x)$	$= \$2,000,000(0.0008 + 0) = \$1,600$
Plant B: $EL(x)$	$= \$2,000,000(0.000412 + 0) = \$824$

Notice the similarity in the quality characteristic between plant A and that observed in the Sony plant at San Diego (as depicted in Exhibit 17.5): all units are within and spread evenly over the specified tolerance limits. The quality characteristic of plant B is similar to that observed in the Sony plant in Japan: not all units lie within the tolerance limits, but most units cluster around the target value. Some units, however, fall outside the tolerance limits. Plant B, like the Sony plant in Japan, incurs a smaller average cost per unit. Even though all units of plant A fall within the tolerance limits while some units of plant B are outside the limits, plant B has a lower expected loss than that of plant A.

USING QUALITY LOSS FUNCTION (QLF) FOR TOLERANCE DETERMINATION

The Taguchi quality loss function (QLF) can also be used to set tolerances for an operation. A firm can repair rejected units that exceed the tolerance level. Even though repairs cost money, repairs that correct defects save downstream quality costs such as field repairs, warranty costs, and loss of goodwill. By contrasting the cost of repair with the quality cost of not detecting and repairing defects, firms can determine acceptable tolerance levels. Rewriting the equation for estimating the value of k:

$$\text{Total quality cost} = k \times (\text{Tolerance})^2$$

Assume that in the sheet metal example, the cost to the firm is \$300 if the firm repairs the product before shipping. The firm repairs all units that exceed the tolerance level for thickness. Then, the firm can determine the tolerance as follows:

$$\$300 = \$2,000,000(\text{Tolerance})^2$$

Solve the equation,

$$\text{Tolerance} = 0.0122$$

Alternatively, the tolerance can be determined as shown below.

$$\text{Tolerance} = T_0\sqrt{C_1/C_2}$$

where

T_0 = current (or customer) tolerance
C_2 = manufacturer's quality cost when the product fails to meet customer's specification
C_1 = manufacturer's cost to rework or scrap the unit before shipping

In the example above, the firm expects the external failure cost, C_2, to be \$5,000; the cost to the firm to be \$300 if the firm repairs, reworks, or scraps the defective unit before shipping (C_1); and the customer's tolerance to be 0.05. The firm would then set the tolerance at 0.0122, as follows:

$$\text{Tolerance} = 0.05\sqrt{\$300/\$5,000} = 0.0122$$

---

[20] For plant A,

$\bar{x} = \text{column}(1) \times \text{column}(3) = \Sigma xf(x) = (0.46 \times 0.20) + (0.48 \times 0.20) + (0.50 \times 0.20) + (0.52 \times 0.20) + (0.54 \times 0.20) = 0.50$

and, $\sigma^2 = [(0.46 - 0.50)^2 \times 0.20] + [(0.48 - 0.50)^2 \times 0.20] + [(0.50 - 0.50)^2 \times 0.20] + [(0.52 - 0.50)^2 \times 0.20] + [(0.54 - 0.50)^2 \times 0.20]$

$= 0.0008$

[21] The mean value of the quality characteristic is 0.50 for plant A, as calculated in footnote 20. The target value of the quality characteristic is also 0.50. Therefore $D = 0.50 - 0.50 = 0$. Verify that the value of D is also zero for plant B by carrying out the same procedure.

Key Terms

absolute quality conformance, 757
appraisal (detection) costs, 760
cause-and-effect diagram, 769
control chart, 766
costs of conformance, 761
costs of nonconformance, 761
cost of quality (COQ), 759
design quality, 750
external failure costs, 761

goalpost conformance, 756
histogram, 768
internal failure costs, 760
ISO 9000, 747
ISO 14000, 747
Pareto diagram, 768
performance quality, 750
prevention costs, 760
quality, 750
quality circle, 760

robust quality approach, 757
run chart, 766
Six Sigma, 754
Taguchi quality loss function, 776
tolerance, 756
total quality management (TQM), 746

Self-Study Problems

(For solutions, please turn to the end of the chapter.)

1. Relevant Cost Analysis: Quality Improvement

An automobile manufacturer plans to spend $1 billion to improve the quality of a new model. The manufacturer expects the quality-improvement program to eliminate the need for recall and reduce the costs for other warranty repairs. The firm's experience had been, on average, 1.5 recalls for each new model at a cost of $300 per vehicle per recall. The average cost per recall, if one is needed, is expected to increase by 10 percent for the new model. Costs for other warranty repairs are expected to decrease from $200 to $80 per unit sold. Sales of the new model were expected to be 500,000 units without the quality-improvement program. The company believes that the well-publicized quality-improvement program will increase total sales to 650,000 units. If there is a profit of $5,000 per unit on any incremental sales attributable to the quality-improvement program, is the $1 billion expenditure justified?

2. Taguchi Quality Loss Function (Appendix)

Marlon Audio Company manufactures cassette tapes. The desired speed of its model SF2000 is 2 inches per second. Any deviation from this value distorts pitch and tempo resulting in poor sound quality. The company sets the quality specification to 2 ± 0.25 inches per second because an average customer is likely to complain and return the tape if the speed is off by more than 0.25 inch per second. The cost per return is $36. The repair cost before the tape is shipped, however, is only $3 per tape.

Required

1. Compute $L(x)$ if x is 2.12 inches per second.
2. Estimate the tolerance for the firm to minimize its quality-related cost (loss).

3. Cost-of-Quality (COQ) Report

Precision Electric Instruments manufacturers fans for mini and micro computers. As a first step to focus on quality improvements, the firm has compiled the following operating data for 2011 (in thousands):

Line inspection	$ 55
Training	120
Returns	100
Warranty repairs	68
Preventive equipment maintenance	20
Recalls	157
Design engineering	67
Scrap (net of salvage value)	30
Downtime	40
Product-testing equipment	88
Product liability insurance	20
Supplier evaluation	15
Rework	35
Inspection and testing of incoming materials	25
Litigation costs to defend allegation of defective products	240

Required Prepare a cost-of-quality (COQ) report and classify the costs as prevention, appraisal, internal failure, and external failure. Express each category subtotal as a percentage of total COQ.

Questions

17-1 Define *quality*. For management and control purposes, define the two primary components of quality.

17-2 What are the reasons that the cost of poor quality reached an epidemic level before U.S. companies were motivated to do something about the problem in the 1980s?

17-3 What is TQM? At what point can a firm consider its effort to achieve total quality management complete?

17-4 What is the Malcolm Baldrige National Quality Award and the ISO 9000 certificate? Why do many firms in the United States seek them?

17-5 In what respect are traditional accounting systems deficient in terms of the goal of managing and controlling quality?

17-6 Why is continuous quality improvement kaizen essential to achieve TQM and critical to an organization's success and competitive position?

17-7 Describe the major elements of a comprehensive framework for managing and controlling quality, such as the framework presented in Exhibit 17.2.

17-8 What are the purposes of conducting a quality audit?

17-9 What is meant by Six Sigma? What five steps are usually associated with Six Sigma applications?

17-10 What implementation guidelines can you offer for ensuring the success of a Six Sigma program?

17-11 Describe goalpost conformance.

17-12 Discuss the difference between goalpost conformance and absolute quality conformance.

17-13 Taguchi argues that being within specification limits is not enough to be competitive in today's global economy. Do you agree? Why?

17-14 As indicated in Exhibit 17.2 and the accompanying discussion, a comprehensive framework for the management and control of quality will likely include both financial and nonfinancial data. Explain the primary role of each in terms of the overall quality-management process. For example, is financial information likely to be more relevant to managers or operating personnel?

17-15 Name three costs associated with each of the following COQ categories:
  a. Prevention
  b. Appraisal
  c. Internal failure
  d. External failure

17-16 Which of the following cost categories tend to increase during the early years of TQM? Which of them tend to decrease over the years due to successful total quality management? Why?
  a. Prevention
  b. Appraisal
  c. Internal failure
  d. External failure

17-17 What is cost of conformance? Nonconformance?

17-18 Many organizations have found that investments in prevention and appraisal usually result in major cost savings in other areas. Explain this phenomenon.

17-19 What functions does a cost-of-quality (COQ) report play in a quality-improvement program?

17-20 Name and briefly describe three methods that companies can use to either identify or correct quality problems.

17-21 What is a cause-and-effect diagram? What is its primary purpose?

17-22 What are the main causes of quality problems depicted in a typical cause-and-effect diagram for manufacturing operations?

17-23 What is a Pareto chart? What is its function?

17-24 Define the terms *customer-response time, manufacturing-lead (manufacturing cycle) time,* and *cycle time efficiency* (also known as *throughput time ratio* or *process cycle efficiency*).

17-25 As explained in the chapter, many organizations today are embracing the notion of total quality management (TQM), that is, they are attempting to secure competitive advantage through quality across all areas of the value chain. Discuss the role that management accounting can play to support the goal of TQM. *(Hint:* Use Exhibit 17.2 as a reference point.)

17-26 Define what is meant by the term *relevant financial information* (for decision-making purposes). Within the context of quality-related spending and investments, list some of the more important benefits (cost savings and revenue gains) that organizations can anticipate.

17-27 From a design standpoint, what are some desirable characteristics of a cost of quality (COQ) reporting system? That is, if you were to design such a system from scratch, what would the key attributes of the system be?

17-28 Of the four categories in a COQ report, which category of quality cost is the most damaging to the organization? Why is this the case?

17-29 Provide a brief explanation of the conceptual relationship between improvements in quality and improvements in financial performance.

17-30 How are process and product variations from standard lead indicators (predictors) of quality?

Brief Exercises

17-31 A customer places an order on January 1, 2011. Ten days later that order is received by the manufacturing department. Fifteen days later, the order is put into production. Processing (manufacturing) time is 20 days for this order. The completed order was then shipped ten days later. For this order, what was the total customer response time (CRT)?

17-32 On average, the manufacturing (processing) time spent per order is approximately four days. In addition, a typical order spends four days moving from process to process, three days in storage, and two days in inspection. For an average order, what is the manufacturing cycle efficiency?

17-33 For a typical order, assume the following times (in hours): storage time (in between processes), 5.0; inspection time, 1.0; move time (from process to process), 2.0; and manufacturing (processing) time, 8.0. Given this information, what is the manufacturing cycle efficiency?

17-34 (Appendix): Solidtronic, Inc., an OEM manufacturer, has a product specification of 75 +/− 5. The cost for warranty services is estimated as $500 per unit. What is the value of k, the cost coefficient, in the Taguchi loss function?

17-35 (Appendix): Refer to the information in 17-34. Calculate the estimated total cost when the measured quality characteristic, x (e.g., inches, pounds, units), is 78.

17-36 (Appendix): Refer to the information in 17-34. What is the expected loss (cost) per unit if the manufacturing process is centered on the target specification with a standard deviation of 2?

17-37 Listed below are selected items from the cost-of-quality (COQ) report for Watson Products for last month.

Category	Amount
Rework	$ 725
Equipment maintenance	1,154
Product testing	786
Field-service costs	560
Spoilage	459
Product liability insurance	780
Product repair	695

What is Watson's total prevention and appraisal cost for the month?

17-38 A customer's order is delivered (received by the customer) on December 1, 2011. This order was placed with the company on September 1, 2011, and received by the manufacturing department on September 15, 2011. Actual production on the order began on October 15, 2011, and was completed November 15, 2011. Based on this information, calculate the following for this order: total customer response time (CRT); order receipt time; manufacturing lead time (processing time); manufacturing wait time; manufacturing time; and delivery time. (*Hint*: Refer to Exhibit 14.14.) Prepare your answers in days.

17-39 In 2011 a manufacturing company instituted a total quality management (TQM) program producing the report shown below:

Summary COQ Report
(in thousands)

	2011	2012	% Change
Prevention costs	$ 200	$ 300	+50
Appraisal costs	210	315	+50
Internal failure costs	190	114	−40
External failure costs	1,200	621	−48
Total COQ	$1,800	$1,350	−25

On the basis of this report, which one of the following statements is *most* likely correct?

a. An increase in conformance costs resulted in a higher-quality product and, therefore, a decrease in nonconformance costs.

b. An increase in inspection costs was solely responsible for the decrease in quality.

c. Quality costs such as scrap and rework decreased by 48 percent.

d. Quality costs such as returns and repairs under warranty decreased by 40 percent.

e. Nonconformance costs increased by 50 percent and conformance costs decreased by approximately 47 percent.

17-40 Assume that a plasma TV company is working at a three-sigma level of quality in terms of each of 100 component parts in each TV it manufactures. Because of the high price associated with these TV sets, the company defines a product defect as any unit with one or more defective components. (That is, a good-quality output is defined as a TV set with zero defective parts.) On average, what is the probability of producing a unit with zero defects? (Show calculations.)

Exercises

17-41 **Cost-of-Quality (COQ) Reporting—Multiple-Choice** Circle the letter corresponding to the *best* answer to each of the following items.

1. All of the following would generally be included in a cost-of-quality (COQ) report except
   a. Warranty claims.
   b. Design engineering.
   c. Supplier evaluations/certifications.
   d. Sales commission expense.
   e. Transportation cost related to product recalls.

2. An example of an internal failure cost is
   a. Maintenance.
   b. Inspection.
   c. Rework.
   d. Product recalls.
   e. Loss of customer goodwill.

3. Product quality-related costs are part of a total quality control program. A product quality-related cost incurred in detecting individual products that do not conform to specifications is an example of a(n)
   a. Prevention cost.
   b. Appraisal cost.
   c. Internal failure cost.
   d. External failure cost.
   e. Opportunity cost.
   f. Both b and e are correct.

4. In recent years, much attention has been placed on product quality and total quality control. Which one of the following items would not normally be considered a cost of quality (COQ)?
   a. Costs incurred in preventing production of defective units.
   b. Costs incurred in detecting defective products during production.
   c. Cost incurred in detecting defective products produced before they are shipped to customers.
   d. Cost incurred after defective products have been shipped to customers.
   e. All of the above are likely considered a cost of quality (COQ).

5. The four categories of cost associated with a cost-of-quality (COQ) report are
   a. External failure, internal failure, prevention, and carrying.
   b. External failure, internal failure, prevention, and appraisal.
   c. External failure, internal failure, conformance, and appraisal.
   d. Warranty, internal failure, appraisal, and product liability.
   e. Warranty, product liability, prevention, and appraisal.

6. In a cost-of-quality (COQ) report, the ongoing cost of using a statistical quality control (SQC) process is classified as a(n)
   a. External failure cost.
   b. Internal failure cost.

    c. Training cost.

    d. Appraisal cost.

    e. Prevention cost.

7. In a cost-of-quality (COQ) report, the cost of scrap, rework, and excess maintenance would be classified as a(n)

    a. External failure cost.

    b. Internal failure cost.

    c. Training cost.

    d. Appraisal cost.

    e. Prevention cost.

8. Which of the following can be used for diagnostic control (i.e., to diagnose the cause(s) and possible solutions to identified quality problems)?

    a. Linear regression analysis

    b. Flexible budgets and standard costs

    c. Cause-and-effect ("fish-bone") diagrams

    d. Cost estimation analysis

    e. Taguchi loss functions

17-42   Six Sigma Interpretation   To what probabilities do each of the following sigma levels correspond, based on a standard normal curve: 3 sigma, 4 sigma, 5 sigma, and 6 sigma? (*Hint:* Use the NORMSDIST function in Excel. Note that this function returns the standard normal *cumulative* distribution function. The distribution has a mean of 0 (zero) and a standard deviation of one.) **Check figures:** for three sigma, the two-tailed probability equals 0.27%; for six sigma, the two-tailed probability level is 0.0000002%. To what level of defects per million do each of the two-tailed probabilities correspond to? What is the point of these calculations?

17-43   Quality Ratings—Graduate Business Programs   You can see from the discussion in the text that quality-ratings, and quality-award programs, exist for various types of businesses and organizations. Some of you may be contemplating enrolling in an MBA program upon completion of your undergraduate studies. It might interest you, therefore, that graduate business programs in this country and abroad are ranked by a number of publications, including *The Wall Street Journal, BusinessWeek,* the *Financial Times,* the *Economist,* and *U.S. News & World Report.* To some extent, these sources use different measures to determine their quality rankings. Develop a list of criteria that could be used to generate quality rankings of graduate business programs.

17-44   Spotting Quality in Business Programs   Through its accreditation function, AACSB International (www.aacsb.edu) seeks continuous quality improvement in the content, delivery, and administration of management education. The AACSB in fact accredits business programs, at both the undergraduate and graduate levels, based on an overall assessment of the quality of these programs. As a student, you may have formed some thoughts regarding how to spot quality in a business-degree program. If you were in charge of developing accreditation standards for business-degree programs, what specific measures of quality would you include? That is, how would you spot quality in terms of a business-degree program?

17-45   Management Accounting's Role in Six Sigma   This chapter contains an overview of the Six Sigma process that many organizations are using today to improve services and products. One could get the impression from the discussion that this topic is more properly a management or an operations management issue. Respond to this position by speculating as to the appropriate role of the management accountant in the Six Sigma process. (*Hint:* Use as the basis of structuring your response the DMAIC implementation approach that is commonly associated with Six Sigma.)

17-46   Applying Six Sigma Principles to the Accounting Function   Brewer and Eighme (2005) report the results of an actual case study of applying Six Sigma principles to improve the accounting function, specifically, to improve the speed with which a subsidiary communicated quarterly financial results to its parent company (to allow preparation of consolidated financial statements). Assume you are in charge of a Six-Sigma project designed to address this problem. Discuss steps you would take as project manager to address the problem, including the five steps in the *DMAIC* (design, measure, analyze, improve, and control) framework discussed in the text. (P. C. Brewer and J. E. Eighme, "Using Six Sigma to Improve the Finance Function," *Strategic Finance* (May 2005), pp. 27–33.)

17-47 **Cost of Environmental Quality Reporting** This chapter includes an overview of a cost-of-quality (COQ) reporting system. Such a system has, in fact, been applied in practice by a number of companies. This exercise pertains to the application of a COQ reporting framework to environmental management.

1. What motivation is there to implement an environmental accounting and control system?

2. Construct a sample environmental cost-of-quality report using the four categories that comprise a traditional COQ report (i.e., prevention costs, appraisal/detection costs, internal failure costs, and external failure costs).

3. Do you think firms would be motivated to provide to shareholders information contained in the environmental COQ report you propose above in (2)? Why or why not?

17-48 **Cost of Environmental Quality Report** You are given the following environmental quality-related costs:

Employee training	$100,000
Product design	140,000
Supplier certification	40,000
Process inspection	320,000
Depreciation—pollution-control equipment	400,000
Maintaining pollution-control equipment	200,000
Cleaning up polluted lake	500,000
Restoring land after use	700,000
Property damage claim	600,000

Required

1. Prepare a cost of environmental quality report for the year. Determine subtotals for each of the four reporting categories and express each subtotal as a percentage of total operating expenses ($10,000,000) for the year.

2. Based on the report you prepare, what conclusions can you draw regarding the company's environmental quality performance for the year?

3. Can you offer management suggestions for the design of an effective cost of environmental quality reporting system? (That is, what would make for a good reporting system?)

17-49 **Nonfinancial (Operational) Control Measures: Environmental Performance** Assume that the company for which you are working is interested in implementing a comprehensive monitoring and control system regarding environmental performance. The company is convinced that improved performance in this area will lead to reduced costs, an improved corporate image, greater market share, and ultimately to greater financial returns. To supplement a number of financial-performance indicators in the area of environmental quality, the company is interested in developing a set of nonfinancial performance indicators, which (it is hoped) will motivate better environmental quality. In this regard, the company has embraced five strategic objectives: minimize hazardous materials; minimize raw/virgin materials usage; minimize energy requirements; minimize release of residues into the environment; and maximize opportunities to recycle. For each of these five strategic objectives, provide at least two relevant nonfinancial performance indicators that could lead to improved environmental performance.

17-50 **Graphical Depiction: Is There an Optimal Level of Spending on Quality, or Is Quality "Free"?** Some proponents of TQM assert that quality is free, that is, that quality is a never-ending quest and that improving product/service quality will reduce a firm's total spending on quality. Others believe that after a point there are diminishing returns to additional expenditures on quality. Provide a graphical representation of each of these arguments. (*Hint*: Let the vertical axis of your graph represent $ (e.g., revenues or costs), and let the horizontal axis represent the level of quality—the higher the value, on the x-axis, the greater the indicated quality level.) Supplement your graphs with appropriate explanations/interpretations.

17-51 **Pareto Diagram (Chart)** The following causes of absenteeism for a fellow student are for the year just completed:

Cause of Absenteeism	Occurrences
Personal illness	12
Child's illness	26
Car broke down	8
Personal emergency	32
Overslept	9
Unexpected visitor	11

Required   Construct a Pareto diagram (chart). In conjunction with the framework presented in Exhibit 17.2 what role is played by the use of these diagrams?

17-52   **COQ Histogram**   Genova Company classifies its costs of quality into four categories. The costs of quality (COQ) as a percentage of cost of goods sold for the last three years are as follows:

	2010	2011	2012
Prevention costs	1.00%	4.00%	2.00%
Appraisal costs	3.00	2.50	1.50
Internal failure costs	27.00	23.00	14.00
External failure costs	31.00	18.00	12.00

Required

1. Use a spreadsheet to prepare a histogram that shows the costs of quality (COQ) trends as a percentage of costs of goods sold.

2. Comment on the trends in cost of quality (COQ) over the three-year period from 2010 to 2012.

3. What cost of quality can the company expect as a percentage of its cost of goods sold in 2013? Explain.

17-53   **Quality Cost Classification**

Required   Classify each of the following costs into one of the four quality cost (i.e., COQ) categories:

1. Materials, labor, and overhead costs of scrapped units.

2. Engineering time spent to determine the causes of failures to meet product specification.

3. Wages and salaries for the time spent by workers to gather quality measurements.

4. Information systems costs expended to develop data requirements.

5. Clerical staff expenses to coordinate training programs.

6. Salaries for members of problem-solving teams.

7. Payment to settle a product-liability lawsuit.

17-54   **Benefits and Challenges of Lean**   Much discussion at your organization recently has centered on the notion of lean. In preparation for an upcoming meeting of senior managers, across business functions, you have been asked to prepare an explanatory memo. Your memo should address, at a minimum, the following issues: (1) the definition of lean, (2) strategic value of adopting lean principles for your organization, (3) anticipated costs of moving to lean, (4) implications for cost-system design, and (5) sources for additional information regarding these issues.

Required   Prepare, in good form, a memo for management that addresses the preceding issues. In responding to this assignment, please access and read the following Statement of Management Accounting: *Accounting for the Lean Enterprise: Major Changes to the Accounting Paradigm.* Montvale, NJ: Institute of Management Accountants, 2006. (Accessible on the Web at the following address: www.imanet.org/publications_statements.asp#C.)

17-55   **Cost-of-Quality Improvement—Relevant Cost Analysis**   PIM Industries, Inc., manufactures electronics components. Each unit costs $30 before the final test. The final test rejects, on average, 5 percent of the 50,000 units manufactured per year. The average rejection rate of the industry is 3 percent. A consultant has determined that poor lighting is the most likely cause of this high rejection rate. It would cost $100,000 to install adequate lighting in the assembly department, which would be useful for 5 years. With adequate lighting that will cost an additional $5,000 in operating cost each year, the firm expects to reduce its rejection rate to no higher than the industry average.

Required

1. Should the firm install the lighting? (show calculations)

2. What other considerations might affect this decision?

3. What is the primary role of the management accountant in this decision context?

17-56   **Assessing the Use and Role of Nonfinancial Performance Indicators**   This question pertains to the use of nonfinancial performance indicators as part of a comprehensive management accounting and control system. You are asked to think critically about the value and challenges of using such data for performance-evaluation purposes. The following source should be accessed and read prior to answering the questions that appear below: Christopher D. Ittner and David F. Larker, "Coming Up Short on Nonfinancial Performance Measurement," *Harvard Business Review* (November 2003), pp. 88–95.

Required

1. What are the primary benefits of incorporating nonfinancial performance indicators as part of an overall management accounting and control system?
2. Why do the authors of this above-referenced article believe that many companies fail to realize the kinds of benefits listed above in (1)?
3. The Institute of Management Accountants (IMA) recently revised its definition of "management accounting" (see www.imanet.org/pdf/definition.pdf). After accessing this statement, comment on an appropriate role of the management accountant as regards the development and use of nonfinancial performance indicators.

17-57 **Taguchi Loss Function Analysis (Appendix)**   Flextronchip, an OEM manufacturer, has a fifth-generation chip for cell phones, with chip specification of 0.2 ± 0.0002 mm for the distance between two adjacent pins. The loss due to a defective chip has been estimated as $20.

Required

1. Compute the value of k in the Taguchi loss function.
2. Assume that the quality control manager takes a sample of 100 chips from the production process. The results are as follows:

Measurement	Frequency
0.1996	2
0.1997	5
0.1998	12
0.1999	11
0.2000	45
0.2001	10
0.2002	8
0.2003	5
0.2004	2

  a. Calculate the estimated quality loss for each of the observed measurements.
  b. Calculate the expected (i.e., average) loss for the production process as a whole.
3. Using the data from (2) above:
  a. Determine the variance in the measured distance between two pins.
  b. Calculate the expected loss of the process using the calculated variance, per the method presented by Albrecht and Roth, "The Measurement of Quality Costs: An Alternative Paradigm," *Accounting Horizons* (June 1992), pp. 15–27.

17-58 **Using Taguchi Loss Function to Determine Tolerance (Appendix)**   The desired distance for Flextronchip customers is 0.2 mm between two adjacent pins. Any deviation from this value causes interference. The process of handling complaints costs the firm at least $40 per chip. The engineers of the firm expect the average customer will be likely to complain when the distance is off target by at least 0.0001. At the factory, the adjustment can be made at a cost of $1.60, which includes the labor to make the adjustment and additional testing.

Required   What should the tolerance be before an adjustment is made at the factory?

17-59 **Relevant Cost Analysis—Conversion to JIT**   As part of its commitment to quality, the J. J. Borden manufacturing company is proposing to introduce just-in-time (JIT) production methods. Managers of the company have an intuitive feel regarding the financial benefits associated with a change to JIT, but they would like to have some data to inform their decision making in this regard. You are provided with the following data:

Item	Existing Situation	After Adopting JIT
Manufacturing Costs as Percentage of Sales:		
Product-level support costs	12%	5%
Variable manufacturing overhead	28%	10%
Direct materials	30%	20%
Direct manufacturing labor	22%	15%

(Continued)

Other Financial Data:

Sales revenue	$1,350,000	$1,650,000
Inventory of WIP	$180,000	$30,000

Other Data:

Manufacturing cycle time	60 days	30 days
Inventory financing cost (per annum)	10%	10%

Required You have been asked, in conjunction with your position as the management accountant for the company, to construct an Excel spreadsheet that can be used to estimate the financial benefits associated with the adoption of JIT.

17-60 **Relevant Cost Analysis—Quality Improvements** Destin Company produces water control valves, made of brass, which they sell primarily to builders for use in commercial real estate construction. These valves must meet rigid specifications (i.e., the quality tolerance is small). Valves that, upon inspection, get rejected are returned to the Casting Department, i.e., to stage one of the four-stage manufacturing process. Rejected items are melted and then recast. As such, no new materials in Casting are required to rework these items. However, new materials must be added in the Finishing Department for all reworked valves. As the cost accountant for the company, you have prepared the following cost data regarding the production of a typical valve:

Cost	Casting	Finishing	Inspection	Packing	Total
Direct materials	$200	$12	$-0-	$8	$220
Direct labor	110	120	20	20	270
Variable manufacturing overhead	100	150	20	20	290
Allocated fixed overhead	70	80	40	10	200
	$480	$362	$80	$58	$980

The company, spurred by intense price pressures from foreign manufacturers, recently initiated a number of quality programs. As a result, the rejection rate for valves has decreased from 5.0 percent to 3.5 percent of annual output (equal in total to 15,000 units). The reduction in reject rates has enabled the company to reduce its inventory holdings from $400,000 to $250,000. Destin estimates that the annual financing cost associated with inventory holdings is 12 percent.

Required Provide a dollar estimate of the annual cost savings associated with the recently enacted quality improvements. Show calculations.

17-61 **Control Charts** Refer to the background information in Exercise 17-60 for the Destin Company. One of the quality improvements management instituted recently was the use of statistical control charts. Over the most recent 12-week period, you have obtained the following average cycle-time data regarding the valve-production process:

Week	Average Manufacturing Cycle Time (minutes)
1	12.5
2	18.0
3	15.0
4	10.0
5	15.5
6	12.8
7	23.5
8	16.5
9	17.5
10	11.0
11	14.5
12	16.0

Required
1. Use Excel to prepare a control chart from the weekly, sequential observations given above. Management has determined that the target performance level for cycle time is 14.0 minutes, and that the upper and lower control limits should be set, respectively, at 16.0 and 12.0 minutes.

2. What is the mean and what is the standard deviation of the 12 manufacturing cycle-time observations?

3. What conclusions can you draw about the process, based on the cycle-time data contained in your spreadsheet?

4. What is the primary difference between the control chart you produced and what is called a *statistical control chart*?

17-62 Using Run Charts to Examine Process Stability   All processes illustrate some variation (in quality, conformance to specification, etc.). One hallmark of a quality process is stability. As noted in the text, both control charts and run charts (as well as histograms) can be used to examine process stability. In this exercise you are provided with some information regarding loan processing times at a bank (for an individual loan officer) over a 20-day period. In sequential order, these data are as follows: 90, 73, 62, 88, 47, 68, 87, 68, 50, 69, 26, 78, 80, 30, 32, 73, 60, 50, 36, and 89.

Required

1. Use Excel to plot the above data, in time-series fashion.

2. What is meant by the term *process stability?*

3. What techniques might you use to support a conclusion as to whether or not this process is stable?

17-63 Implementation of Lean Accounting   Watlow Electric Manufacturing Company introduced lean principles in 2005 and reported a successful implementation in 2008. Watlow began with the implementation of lean principles and then adopted value stream management (VSM) using the value stream income statement. As expected, the use of VSM achieved better decision making (previously the firm had treated direct labor as a pure variable cost that varied with volume; after VSM it was clear that the behavior of labor costs was far more complex), reduced inventory, reduced cycle times, and improved communication and coordination among employees. It was this latter result, better communication, that surprised Watlow management, as employees began to work as teams that focused on the key success factors for the firm. The steps taken by Watlow to implement lean included:

- Identify the main value streams of the company (Watlow selected value streams consisting of 25-150 employees each; more than 90% of the company's employees were assigned to a value stream)
- Determine the key measures for achieving the company's strategic goals (these included measures of quality, safety, on-time delivery, and cost)
- The accounting system was adapted to VSM, including changes in the accounting for materials, labor and overhead

Required   Given the implementation of lean as described above, what do you see as the challenges ahead for Watlow? What features of lean accounting have yet to be implemented?

17-64 Toyota: Keeping It Lean   Toyota has grown to become the largest auto manufacturer in the world, with plants located around the world. In 2005–2007 the company hired 40,000 new employees to keep up with this growth. A challenge for Toyota during times of growth is to make sure that the new hires effectively become part of the company's culture, including the Toyota Production System which guides the flow of product through Toyota's plants. The new hires must also learn the Toyota Way, an eight-step method for decision making. Toyota's new managers go through extensive training at the Toyota Institute in Japan. Even veteran Toyota managers are required to go back to the Institute for training when they get a promotion. Concerned about the decline in quality in recent years, Toyota has redoubled its efforts in training and has begun to hire back some retired workers in Japan. New entry-level employees are trained at Toyota Technical Institutes located around the world.

Required   Why is training so important for Toyota?

17-65 Value-Stream Income Statement   The Marshall Company is a large manufacturer of office furniture. The company has recently adopted lean accounting and has identified two value streams—office chairs and office tables. Total sales in the most recent period for the two streams are $245 and $310 million, respectively.

In the most recent accounting period, Marshall had the following operating costs, which were traced to the two value streams as follows (in thousands).

	Chairs	Tables
Operating costs:		
Materials	$ 16,500	$14,500
Labor	123,000	96,500
Equipment-related costs	44,500	62,800
Occupancy costs	11,350	12,600

In addition to the traceable operating costs, the company had manufacturing costs of $116,750,000 and selling and administrative costs of $25 million that could not be traced to either value stream. Due to the implementation of lean methods, the firm has been able to reduce inventory in both value streams significantly and has calculated the fixed cost of prior period inventory that is included in the current income statement to be $5.5 million for the office chair stream and $22.5 million for the office table stream.

Required   Prepare the value stream income statement for Marshall Company.

17-66   **Taguchi Loss Function Analysis (Appendix)**   Duramold specializes in manufacturing molded plastic panels to be fitted on car doors. The blueprint specification for the thickness of a high-demand model calls for 0.1875 ± 0.0025 inch. It costs $120 to manufacture and $150 to scrap a part that does not meet these specifications. The thickness measure for the unit just completed is 0.1893 inch.

Required

1. Use the Taguchi Loss Function, $L(x)$, to determine:
   a. The value of the cost coefficient, k
   b. The amount of loss for the unit, $L(x = 0.1893)$

2. Assume that Duramold can eliminate the uneven thickness by adding a production worker, at the critical production point, for $6 per unit. Under this assumption:
   a. At what tolerance should the panels be manufactured? Show calculations.
   b. What should be the production specification for these panels?

Problems   17-67   **Cost-of-Quality (COQ) Analysis**   The Duncan Materials Company manufactures and sells synthetic coatings that can withstand high temperatures. Its primary customers are aviation manufacturers and maintenance companies. The following table contains financial information pertaining to cost of quality (COQ) in 2010 and 2011 in thousands of dollars:

	2010	2011
Sales	$15,000	$18,750
Materials inspection	300	60
Production inspection	160	125
Finished product inspection	225	70
Preventive equipment maintenance	20	60
Scrap (net)	500	300
Warranty repairs	700	400
Product design engineering	150	270
Vendor certification	10	60
Direct costs of returned goods	250	80
Training of factory workers	40	140
Product testing—equipment maintenance	60	60
Product testing labor	210	90
Field repairs	70	30
Rework before shipment	240	180
Product-liability settlement	360	60
Emergency repair and maintenance	190	60

Required

1. Classify the cost items in the table into cost-of-quality (COQ) categories.

2. Calculate the ratio of each COQ category to revenues in each of the two years.

3. Comment on the results.

4. In addition to the financial measures listed in the table, what nonfinancial measures might Duncan Materials Company monitor in its effort to achieve overall improvements in quality?

5. Are financial or nonfinancial quality measures likely of more use to: (a) managers? (b) operating personnel? Why?

17-68   **Spreadsheet Application**   Use the data in Problem 17-67 and a spreadsheet to complete this problem. Use the spreadsheet functions to carry out all calculations. Do not hard-code or carry out calculations elsewhere and type in the calculated amounts.

1. Determine the information you'll need to generate cost-of-quality (COQ) report and set up a spreadsheet for this information. Among the items to be included in the COQ report are proper headings of the report, revenue and cost items (cost items should be in the cost-of-quality category), and cost as a percentage of revenues for each of the two years.

2. Input the data provided in 17-67 into the spreadsheet by COQ category.

3. Enter functions or steps to calculate the total amount for each COQ category and the total COQ. Do not hard-code or type in the amounts.

4. Enter functions or steps to calculate the total cost of each COQ category as a percentage of revenues for each of the years. Use two digits after the decimal point for the percentages. Do the same for the total COQ. Do not hard-code or type in the amounts.

5. Move to another area of the spreadsheet or use a fresh sheet and title the area "Cost of Quality Trend Analysis." Enter functions or steps for the percentages; do not hard-code or type in the amounts.

6. Create a bar chart to compare the percentages of each of the COQ categories and the total COQ in 2010 and 2011.

7. Do a sensitivity analysis by making the following changes to the 2011 amounts:
   - Increase the total sales by 5 percent.
   - Increase total prevention cost by 6 percent.
   - Decrease total internal failure cost by 60 percent.
   - Decrease total external failure cost by 50 percent.

Required   What is the total COQ as a percentage of total sales?

17-69   Ethics   Jan Williams was recently hired as assistant controller of GroChem, Inc., which processes chemicals for use in fertilizers. Williams was selected for this position because of her past experience in the chemical processing field. During her first month on the job, Williams made a point of getting to know the people responsible for the plant operations and learning how things are done at GroChem.

During a conversation with the plant supervisor, Williams asked about the company procedures for handling toxic waste materials. The plant supervisor replied that he was not involved with the disposal of wastes and suggested that Williams might be wise to simply ignore the issue. This response strengthened the resolve of Williams to probe the area further, to be sure that the company was not vulnerable to litigation.

Upon further investigation, Williams discovered evidence that GroChem was suing a nearby residential landfill to dump toxic wastes. It appeared that some members of GroChem's management team were aware of this situation and, in fact, may have been involved in arranging for this dumping; however, Williams was unable to determine whether her superior, the controller, was involved.

Uncertain as to how she should proceed, Williams began to consider her options by outlining the following three alternative courses of action:

1. Seek the advice of her superior, the controller.

2. Anonymously release the information to the local newspaper.

3. Discuss the situation with an outside member of the board of directors, with whom Williams is acquainted.

Required

1. Explain how the use of a cost-of-quality (COQ) reporting framework can facilitate better managerial control and decision making regarding environmental costs and potential liabilities.

2. Discuss why Jan Williams has an ethical responsibility to take some action in the matter of GroChem, Inc., and the dumping of toxic wastes. Refer to the specific ethical standards contained in the IMA's *Statement of Ethical Professional Practice* (www.imanet.org) to support your answer.

3. For each of the three alternative courses of action that Jan Williams has outlined, explain whether or not the action is consistent with the ethical standards referred to above.

4. Without prejudice to your answer to (3), assume that Jan Williams sought the advice of her superior, the controller, and discovered that the controller was involved in the decision to dump the toxic waste produced by the company. Refer to the IMA's *Statement of Ethical Professional Practice* and describe steps that Williams should take to resolve the situation.

(CMA Adapted)

17-70   Cost-of-Quality (COQ) Reporting   Carrie Lee, the president of Lee Enterprises, was concerned about the results of her company's new quality control efforts. "Maybe the emphasis we've placed on upgrading our quality control system will pay off in the long run, but it doesn't seem to be helping us much right now. I thought improved quality would give a real boost to sales, but sales have remained flat at about $10,000,000 for the last two years."

Lee Enterprises has seen its market share decline in recent years because of increased foreign competition. An intensive effort to strengthen the quality control system was initiated a year ago (on January 1, 2011) in the hope that better quality would strengthen the company's competitive position and reduce warranty and servicing costs. The following costs (in thousands) relate to quality and quality control over the last two years:

	2010	2011
Warranty repairs	$420	$140
Rework labor	140	200
Supplies used in testing	4	6
Depreciation of testing equipment	22	34
Warranty replacements	60	18
Field servicing	180	120
Inspection	76	120
Systems development	64	106
Disposal of defective products	54	76
Net cost of scrap	86	124
Product recalls	340	82
Product testing	98	160
Statistical process control	—	74
Quality engineering	56	80

Required

1. Prepare a spreadsheet that produces a cost-of-quality (COQ) report for both 2010 and 2011. Carry percentage computations to two decimal places.

2. Use your spreadsheet to prepare a histogram showing the distribution of the various quality costs by category. (Note: Your histogram should include results for both 2010 and 2011.)

3. Prepare a written evaluation to accompany the reports you have prepared in requirements 1 and 2. This evaluation should discuss the distribution of quality costs in the company, changes in this distribution that you detect have taken place over the last year, and any other information you believe would be useful to management.

4. A member of the management team believes that employees will be more conscientious in their work if they are held responsible for mistakes. He suggests that workers should do rework on their own time and that they also should pay for disposal of defective units and the cost of scraps. The proposal estimates that the firm can save another $400,000 in quality costs and the employees are less likely to make as many errors. Should the firm implement the proposal? Why or why not?

(CMA Adapted)

17-71   **Ethics**   Keystone Electronics Corporation (KEC) is an eight-year-old company that has developed a process to produce highly reliable electronic components at a cost well below the established competition. In seeking to expand its overall components business KEC decided to enter the facsimile equipment business as there was a niche for lower-priced facsimile machines in a vigorously growing marketplace. The market KEC pursued consisted of small regional businesses not yet approached by the larger vendors. KEC sells its machines with a one-year warranty and has established a maintenance force to handle machine breakdowns.

As KEC customers learned of the benefits of fax transmissions, some increased their usage significantly. After six months, large-volume users began experiencing breakdowns, and the field technicians' portable test equipment was not sophisticated enough to detect hairline breaks in the electronic circuitry caused by the heavier-than-expected usage. Consequently, field technicians were required to replace the damaged components and return the defective ones to the company for further testing.

This situation caused an increase in maintenance costs, which added to the cost of the product. Unfortunately, there was no way to determine how many of the businesses would become heavy users and be subject to breakdowns. Some of the heavier-volume users began switching to the more expensive machines available from the larger competitors. Although new sales orders masked the loss of heavier-volume customers, the increased maintenance costs had an unfavorable impact on earnings. In her recent report prepared for the quarterly meeting of the board of directors, Mary Stein, KEC's assistant controller, summarized this situation and its anticipated affect on earnings.

Jim March, vice president of manufacturing, is concerned that the report does not provide any solutions to the problem. He asked Maria Sanchez, the controller, to have the matter deferred so that his engineering staff could work on the problem. He believes that the electronic components can be redesigned. This redesigned model, while more costly, could be an appropriate solution for the heavier-volume users, who should not expect a low-cost model to serve their anticipated needs. March expects that the board could decide to discontinue the product line if no immediate solution is available, and the company could miss a potentially profitable opportunity. March further believes that the tone of the report places his organization in an unfavorable light.

The controller called Stein into her office and asked her to suppress the part of the formal report related to the component failures. Sanchez asked Stein to just cover it orally at the meeting, noting that "engineering is working with marketing on the situation to reach a satisfactory solution." Stein feels strongly that the board will be misinformed about a potentially serious impact on earnings if she follows the advice of Sanchez.

Required

1. Refer to the IMA's *Statement of Ethical Professional Practice* (www.imanet.org). Explain why the request from Maria Sanchez to Mary Stein is unethical. Cite both actions and nonactions on the part of Sanchez that result in an unethical situation.

2. Identify steps that Mary Stein should follow to resolve the situation.

(CMA Adapted)

17-72 Relevant Costs and Quality Improvement Lightening Bulk Company is a moving company specializing in transporting large items worldwide. The firm has an 85 percent on-time delivery rate. Twelve percent of the items are misplaced and the remaining 3 percent are lost in shipping. On average, the firm incurs an additional $60 per item to track down and deliver misplaced items. Lost items cost the firm about $300 per item. Last year the firm shipped 5,000 items with an average freight bill of $200 per item shipped.

The firm's manager is considering investing in a new scheduling and tracking system costing $150,000 per year. The new system is expected to reduce misplaced items to 1 percent and lost items to 0.5 percent. Furthermore, the firm expects total sales to increase by 10 percent with the improved service. The average contribution margin on any increased sales volume is expected to be 40%.

Required

1. Based on a relevant-cost analysis, should the firm install the new tracking system? Show calculations.

2. What other factors does the firm's manager need to consider in making the decision?

3. Upon further investigation, the manager discovered that 80 percent of the misplaced or lost items either originated in or were delivered to the same country. What is the maximum amount the firm should spend to reduce the problems in that country by 90 percent?

17-73 Quality Improvement, Relevant Cost Analysis Worrix Corporation manufactures and sells each year 3,000 premium-quality multimedia projectors at $12,000 per unit. At the current production level, the firm's manufacturing costs include variable costs of $2,500 per unit and annual fixed costs of $6,000,000. Additional selling, administrative, and other expenses, not including 15 percent sales commissions, are $10,000,000 per year.

The new model, introduced a year ago, has experienced a flickering problem. On average the firm reworks 40 percent of the completed units and still has to repair under warranty 15 percent of the units shipped. The additional work required for rework and repair causes the firm to add additional capacity with annual fixed costs of $1,800,000. The variable costs per unit are $2,000 for rework and $2,500, including transportation cost, for repair.

The chief engineer, Patti Mehandra, has proposed a modified manufacturing process that will almost entirely eliminate the flickering problem. The new process will require $12,000,000 for new equipment and installation and $3,000,000 for training. Patti believes that current appraisal costs of $600,000 per year and $50 per unit can be eliminated within one year after the installation of the new process. The firm currently inspects all units before shipment. Furthermore, warranty repair cost per unit will be only $1,000, for no more than 5 percent of the units shipped.

Worrix believes that none of the fixed costs of rework or repair can be saved and that a new model will be introduced in three years. The new technology will most likely render the current equipment obsolete.

The accountant estimates that repairs cost the firm 20 percent of its business.

Required
1. What is the net investment cost associated with the new process?
2. What is the net financial benefit (over the next three years) from using the new process?
3. Based on financial information, should Worrix use the new process?
4. What additional factors should be considered before making the final decision?
5. A member of the board is very concerned about the substantial amount of additional funds needed for the new process. Because the current model will be replaced in about three years, the board member suggests that the firm should take no action and the problem will go away in three years. Do you agree?

17-74 **Taguchi Loss Function Analysis (Appendix)** North Platt Machinery Company manufactures a shaft that must fit inside a sleeve. The firm has just received an order of 50,000 units from Southernstar Exploration Company for $80 per unit. North Platt can manufacture the shaft at $50 per unit. Southernstar desires the diameter of the shaft to be 1.275 cm. The diameter of the shaft must not be less than 1.25 cm, in order to fit properly inside the sleeve. To be able to insert the shaft into a sleeve without the use of force, the diameter cannot be larger than 1.30 cm. A defective shaft is discarded and a replacement has to be shipped via express freight to locations around the world. North Platt estimates that the average cost of handling and shipping a replacement shaft will be approximately $70. Shown below are the diameters from a sample of 80 shafts manufactured during a trial run.

Diameter	Number of Units	Diameter	Number of Units	Diameter	Number of Units
1.232	1	1.273	6	1.292	2
1.240	2	1.274	7	1.293	1
1.250	3	1.275	18	1.294	4
1.258	2	1.276	8	1.298	2
1.262	2	1.277	5	1.300	2
1.270	3	1.280	2	1.304	1
1.272	6	1.288	2	1.320	1

Required Set up an Excel spreadsheet that uses a Taguchi loss function to determine:
1. The expected loss from this process.
2. The diameter tolerance that should be set for the manufacture of the shaft.

17-75 **Analyzing Cost-of-Quality (COQ) Reports** Bergen Inc. produces telephone equipment at its Georgia plant. In recent years, the company's market share has been eroded by stiff competition from Asian and European competitors. Price and product quality are the two key areas in which companies compete in this market.

Jerry Holman, Bergen's president, decided to devote more resources to the improvement of product quality after learning that, in a 2008 survey of telephone equipment users, his company's products had been ranked fourth in product quality. He believed that Bergen could no longer afford to ignore the importance of product quality. Jerry set up a task force (that he headed) to implement a formal quality-improvement program. Included on the task force were representatives from engineering, sales, customer service, production, and accounting because Jerry believed that this is a companywide program and that all employees should share the responsibility for its success.

After the first task-force meeting, Sheila Haynes, manager of sales, asked Tony Reese, production manager, what he thought of the proposed program. Tony replied, "I have reservations. Quality is too abstract to be attaching costs to it and then to be holding you and me responsible for cost improvements. I like to work with goals that I can see and count! I don't like my annual bonus to be based on a decrease in quality costs; there are too many variables that we have no control over!"

Bergen's quality-improvement program has been in operation for 18 months, and the following cost report was recently issued.

As they were reviewing the report, Sheila asked Tony what he thought of the quality program now. "The work is really moving through the production department," replied Reese. "We used to spend time helping the customer service department solve its problems, but they are leaving us alone these days. I have no complaints so far. I'll be anxious to see how much the program increases our bonuses."

Cost-of-Quality (COQ) Report by Quarter
(in thousands)

	June 30, 2010	September 30, 2010	December 31, 2010	March 31, 2011	June 30, 2011	September 30, 2011
Prevention costs:						
Machine maintenance	$ 215	$ 215	$ 202	$ 190	$ 170	$ 160
Training suppliers	5	45	25	20	20	15
Design reviews	20	102	111	100	104	95
	$ 240	$ 362	$ 338	$ 310	$ 294	$ 270
Appraisal costs:						
Incoming inspection	$ 45	$ 53	$ 57	$ 36	$ 34	$ 22
Final testing	160	160	154	140	115	94
	$ 205	$ 213	$ 211	$ 176	$ 149	$ 116
Internal failure costs:						
Rework	$ 120	$ 106	$ 114	$ 88	$ 78	$ 62
Scrap (net)	68	64	53	42	40	40
	$ 188	$ 170	$ 167	$ 130	$ 118	$ 102
External failure costs:						
Warranty repairs	$ 69	$31	$ 24	$ 25	$ 23	$ 23
Customer returns	262	251	122	116	87	80
	$ 331	$ 282	$ 146	$ 141	$ 110	$ 103
Total COQ	$ 964	$1,027	$ 862	$ 757	$ 671	$ 591
Total production cost	$4,120	$4,540	$4,380	$4,650	$4,580	$4,510

Required

1. Identify at least three factors that should be present for an organization to successfully implement a quality-improvement program.

2. By analyzing the cost-of-quality (COQ) report presented, determine whether Bergen's quality-improvement program has been successful. (*Hint:* You might want to focus on the oldest quarter and on the most recent quarter.) List specific evidence to support your answer.

3. Discuss why Tony Reese's current reaction to the quality-improvement program is more favorable than his initial reaction.

4. Jerry Holman believed that the quality-improvement program was essential and that Bergen could no longer afford to ignore the importance of product quality. Discuss how Bergen could measure the opportunity cost of not implementing the quality-improvement program.

5. Comment on the following statement: "COQ reports allow an organization to focus on the reduction or elimination of non-value-added costs of quality."

(CMA Adapted)

17-76 **Expected Quality Cost, Confidence Interval, and Sample Size (Requires Chapter 8)** Paragon Manufacturing produces small motors for assembly in handheld tools such as chain saws and circular saws. The company recently began manufacturing a new motor, model EZ3, and forecasts an annual demand of 200,000 units for this model.

Each model EZ3 requires a housing manufactured to precise engineering specifications. Paragon purchases these housings, which are not subject to quality control inspection before entering the production process; however, Paragon performance-tests the entire motor after final assembly. During pilot production runs of the new motor, several of the housings had wrong sizes and were rejected. If the housings were too shallow, they could not be assembled correctly; if they were too deep, the motor would not operate properly.

Ross Webster, Paragon's production manager, gathered the following information during the pilot production runs:

• When housings were rejected during assembly because they were too shallow, they were replaced with new housings. This change in housings required nine minutes of additional direct labor for each affected unit.

- The units that were rejected during performance testing because the housings were too deep had to be torn down and reassembled with new housings. This operation required 1 hour and 15 minutes of additional direct labor for each affected unit.

- The supplier of the housings is willing to take back the defective housings but will refund only one-half of the price. In the future, if Paragon inspects the housings before they enter the assembly process, the supplier will refund the full price of all rejected housings.

- The costs of model EZ3 follow:

Materials*	$ 44
Direct labor (3 hrs. @ $12/hr.)	36
Variable overhead (@ $18/hr.)	54
Total costs	$134

* Includes $7.00 for housing.

- The majority of the rejections experienced during the pilot runs were related to the housings. Ross's estimate of the probability of rejections for a lot of 800 housings follows:

Rejection during Assembly		Rejection during Performance Testing	
Quantity	Probability	Quantity	Probability
90	0.40	50	0.50
70	0.30	40	0.15
50	0.20	20	0.15
30	0.10	10	0.20

If Paragon decides to inspect the housings prior to assembly, Ross must select the appropriate sample size by using the following two formulas. The estimated sample size (formula 1) must be modified by the second formula (final sample size) because Ross will be sampling without replacement.

Formula 1	Formula 2
$nc = C^2 pq/a^2$	$nf = \dfrac{nc}{1 + \dfrac{nc}{N}}$

where:

nc = first estimate of sample size

nf = final sample size

C = confidence coefficient

p = maximum rejection rate

$q = 1 - p$

a = precision level

N = number of items in the population

Required

1. Determine the maximum amount that Paragon Manufacturing would be willing to spend annually to implement quality control inspection of the housings before assembly begins. (Check figure: $509,000.)

2. For the purpose of quality control inspection, determine the sample size that Ross should select from a lot of 800 housings if the desired level is 95.5 percent (confidence coefficient 2.00) with a precision of 1 percent and rejections not to exceed 1 percent. (Check figure: 265 Units.)

3. Without prejudice to your answer in requirement 2, for quality control inspection purposes, assume that the sample size is 240 housings and the desired level is 95.5 percent (confidence coefficient 2.00) with a precision of 1 percent and rejections not to exceed 1 percent. Determine whether Ross should accept or reject a lot if there are:

    a. Two defective housings in the sample.

    b. Three defective housings in the sample.

    Explain your answer in each situation.

(CMA Adapted)

17-77   **Benefits of Switching to JIT**   You have recently been hired as the management accountant for ABC Manufacturing Technologies, Inc. The company produces a broad line of subassemblies that are used in the production of flat-screen TVs and other electronic equipment. Competitive pressures, principally from abroad, have caused the company to reexamine its competitive strategy and associated management accounting and control systems. More to the point, the company feels a pressing need to adopt JIT manufacturing, to improve the quality of its outputs (in response to ever-increasing demands by consumers of electronic products), and to better manage its cost structure.

A year ago ABC acquired, via a five-year lease, new manufacturing equipment, the annual cost of which is $500,000. To support the move to JIT, however, ABC would have to acquire new, computer-controlled manufacturing equipment, the leasing cost of which is estimated at $2 million per year for four years. If the company were to break its existing lease it would incur a one-time penalty of $240,000.

The replacement equipment is expected to provide significant decreases in variable manufacturing cost per unit, from $50 to $35. This reduction is attributed to faster set-up times with the new machine, faster processing speed, a reduction in material waste, and a reduction in direct labor expenses (because of increased automation). In addition, improvements in manufacturing cycle time and improvements in product quality are expected to increase annual sales (in units) by approximately 30 percent (based on a current volume of 40,000 units).

Additional financial information regarding each decision alternative (existing equipment versus replacement equipment) is as follows:

Item	Pre-JIT	Post-JIT
Selling cost per unit	$ 5.00	$ 5.00
Average per-unit cost of raw materials inventory	$15.00	$12.00
Average per-unit cost of WIP inventory	$25.00	$20.00
Average per-unit cost of finished goods inventory	$40.00	$30.00
Selling price per unit	$65.00	$65.00

The increased automation, including computer-based manufacturing controls, associated with the replacement equipment will greatly reduce the need for inventory holdings. The annual inventory-holding cost, based on the company's weighted-average cost of capital, is 15 percent. Based on engineering estimates provided to ABC by the lessor company, all inventory holdings (raw materials, WIP, and finished goods) can safely be cut in half from current levels. Currently, ABC holds, on average, four months of raw materials inventory, three months of WIP inventory, and two months of finished goods inventory—all of which are based on production requirements.

Required

1. Essentially, how is a JIT manufacturing system different from a conventional system?

2. What is an appropriate role for management accounting regarding the adoption by a company of a JIT manufacturing system?

3. Based on the information presented above, determine the annual financial benefit (including reduction in inventory carrying costs) associated with the proposed move by the company to JIT.

4. Based on an analysis of financial considerations alone, should the company in this situation make the switch to JIT? Why or why not?

5. What qualitative factors might bear on the decision at hand?

17-78   **Research Assignment, Strategy**   Obtain from your library a copy of following article: John H. Flemming, Curt Coffman, and James K. Harter, "Manage Your Human Sigma," *Harvard Business Review* (July-August, 2005), pp. 107–114. The authors of this article state (p. 114): "Ask any CEO to list his or her most pressing business challenges, and you will no doubt hear concerns about customer and employee retention, authentic and sustainable growth, eroding margins, and cost efficiencies. . . . We are confident that measuring and managing two simple factors—employee and customer engagement—can lead to breakthrough improvements in all aspects of your business."

Required   After reading the above-referenced article, answer the following questions:

1. What is the general issue addressed by the authors of this article? That is, what managerial problem are they discussing?

2. How, conceptually, is the Human Sigma approach developed by the authors of this article similar to or distinct from Six Sigma?

3. How do the authors propose to measure the effectiveness of the employee-customer encounter? What evidence do they offer regarding the predictive value of the performance metric they are proposing?

4. According to the authors, what strategies can an organization use to improve the quality of the employee-customer encounter?

17-79   Environmental Performance: Meeting Stakeholder Expectations   How important to stakeholders is environmental performance (e.g., management of greenhouse gas emissions) of publicly listed companies? This issue is addressed in the following short piece: D. C. Esty, "What Stakeholders Demand," *Harvard Business Review* (October 2007), pp. 30, 34, which can be accessed as background reading for the following set of questions.

Required

1. What are the primary stakeholders that would be interested in corporate disclosures regarding environmental performance?

2. Go to the following Web site (www.climatecounts.org/scorecard_overview.php) and obtain information regarding the "scorecard" that this organization has developed to rate environmental performance. What are the 22 criteria used by Climate Counts to rate corporate environmental performance?

3. In the electronics industry group, what distinguishes the environmental performance of IBM versus Apple Computer according to the scorecard used by Climate Counts?

4. Provide arguments as to likely consequences of companies that fail to meet stakeholder expectations regarding environmental performance.

5. What strategic role can the management accountant assume as regards corporate environmental performance?

17-80   Constructing and Interpreting a Control Chart   As indicated in the text, various tools from operations management and statistics are used to help support Six Sigma goals and process improvements in a lean environment. One such tool is a control chart—a key element used to assess statistical process control (SPC). You are given the following error rates for a loan-processing activity at a bank: 2.8, 2.4, 2.4, 4.2, 1.8, 2.8, 3.8, 3.4, 3.2, 3.2, 2.2, 1.6, 1.4, 1.4, 2.4, 1.8, 2.6, 2.0, 2.4, 2.4, 2.2, 2.8, and 2.4.

Required

1. Define the term *control chart*. What is the difference between a control chart and a run chart? What do these charts have in common?

2. Use the data on error rates to construct a control chart for the loan-processing operation. Although there are various ways to construct the chart (see any text on Operations Management or Quality Control for details), define the upper-control limit (UCL) of your chart as the mean plus 2 standard deviations; define the lower-control limit (LCL) of your chart as the mean less 2 standard deviations. (In each case, use the sample standard deviation for the data set at hand.)

3. Supply an interpretation of the control limits you established above in (2).

4. What techniques can be used to judge, using a control chart, whether a process is in *statistical* control?

5. Control charts were developed many years ago for application in the manufacturing sector. However, these charts can be used in other contexts as well. What quality measure might you collect, for use in a control chart, for each of the following nonmanufacturing settings: hospital, insurance company, hotel, and local police department?

Solutions to Self-Study Problems

1. Relevant Cost Analysis: Quality Improvement

Cost of the quality-improvement program		$1,000,000,000
Savings from eliminating recalls	$300 × 110% × 1.5 × 500,000 = $247,500,000	
Decrease in warranty-repair cost	($200 – $80) × 500,000 = 60,000,000	
Profit from increased sales	(650,000 – 500,000) × $5,000 = 750,000,000	1,057,500,000
Increase in Profit from the Quality-Improvement Program		$ 57,500,000

Yes, the increase in profit from the additional sales and decrease in costs of warranty repairs and recalls exceed the $1 billion cost of quality improvements.

2. Taguchi Quality Loss Function (Appendix)

1. $\$36 = k(0.25)^2$
   $k = \$576$
   $L(x = 2.12) = \$576(2.12 - 2.0)^2 = \$8.2944$
2. $\$3 = \$576(\text{tolerance})^2$
   Tolerance $= 0.0722$
   Therefore, the specification should be set at 2 inches $\pm$ 0.0722 inch.

3. Cost-of-Quality (COQ) Report

PRECISION ELECTRIC INSTRUMENTS
Cost-of-Quality Report
For the Year 2011

		% of total
Prevention costs:		
Training	$ 120	
Design engineering	67	
Preventive equipment maintenance	20	
Supplier evaluation	15	
Total prevention costs	$ 222	20.6
Appraisal costs:		
Line inspection	$ 55	
Product-testing equipment	88	
Inspection and testing of incoming materials	25	
Total appraisal costs	$ 168	15.5
Internal failure costs:		
Scrap (net)	$ 30	
Downtime	40	
Rework	35	
Total internal failure costs	$ 105	9.7
External failure costs:		
Returns	$ 100	
Warranty repairs	68	
Recalls	157	
Product liability insurance	20	
Litigation costs	240	
Total external failure costs	$ 585	54.2
Total cost of quality (COQ)	$1,080	100.0

PART FOUR

Management-Level Control

A common element of Parts Three and Four is the focus on control (performance evaluation)—that is, the methods, procedures, and systems used to monitor performance to ensure that the organization is implementing its strategic goals. As part of a comprehensive management and accounting and control system, we discuss incentives and rewards for individuals and managers to work most effectively in implementing the organization's strategy. Part Three focuses on the level of operations (*operational control*) while Part Four focuses on the higher level, that is, *management control*.

The objective of the three chapters in Part Four is to present a variety of tools that top managers (such as CFOs) use to evaluate mid-level managers and the organization as a whole. Mid-level managers include plant managers, product-line managers, heads of research and development (R&D) departments, and regional sales managers. They all have significant responsibility in helping the organization achieve its strategic goals.

In **Chapters 18 and 19** we introduce the concept of responsibility accounting and a performance evaluation framework that consists of the following organizational subunits: cost centers, revenue centers, profit centers, and investment centers. Tied to the concept of controllability, different mechanisms are used to evaluate the short-term financial performance of each of these subunits of the organization. The coverage in Part Four of the text has a strong strategic focus since mid-level managers have a significant responsibility for achieving strategic goals, and it is critical that the performance evaluation be aligned with these strategic goals.

The comparison of variable costing with full costing (**Chapter 18**) is included as part of the coverage of assessing profit centers. We cover this topic in Part Four because of its importance in performance evaluation; variable costing is also extensively covered in Part Three, Planning and Decision Making, while full costing is covered throughout Part One.

Transfer pricing, covered in **Chapter 19,** is an important topic for the assessment of both profit centers and investment centers. When buying and selling exist between units within the organization, the determination of the transfer price will affect the performance evaluation of both the buying unit and the selling unit. Therefore, we cover the topic of transfer pricing both as an *incentive issue* (having the right incentive for the unit managers to choose to trade inside or outside the firm in a manner that achieves the firm's strategic and financial goals) and as a *motivation issue* (the choice of a transfer price should result in a fair measure of performance for both units).

Management compensation, covered in **Chapter 20,** discusses the link from performance to rewards, and the motivation that is needed for managers to achieve strategic goals. Going one step further, one can evaluate the performance of the firm as a whole, that is, of its top managers collectively. **Chapter 20** provides different ways to develop this assessment.

CHAPTER EIGHTEEN

Strategic Performance Measurement:
Cost Centers, Profit Centers, and the Balanced Scorecard

After studying this chapter, you should be able to . . .

1. Identify the objectives of management control

2. Identify the types of management control systems

3. Define strategic performance measurement and show how centralized, decentralized, and team-oriented organizations can apply it

4. Explain the objectives and applications of strategic performance measurement in three common strategic business units: cost centers, revenue centers, and profit centers

5. Explain the role of the balanced scorecard in strategic performance measurement

6. Explain the role of strategic performance measurement in service firms and not-for-profit organizations

---

It is not enough to do your best: you must know what to do, then do your best.

W. Edwards Deming

Deming, the influential business consultant and innovator, understood the importance of performance measurement in strategy implementation. He also understood the importance of aligning managers' incentives with the organization's strategic goals. When incentives are aligned, managers are evaluated and rewarded for achieving the critical success factors that contribute to the organization's success. Many of the most successful companies use this approach, often with the help of the balanced scorecard (BSC), a key tool for aligning performance and strategic goals. The BSC has helped many organizations achieve strategic goals, including United Parcel Service (UPS) and Duke Children's Hospital (DCH), an academic children's hospital within the Duke University Health System in Durham, North Carolina.[1] At DCH, the implementation of the BSC resulted in a nearly $30 million reduction in cost and a

---

[1] Robert S. Kaplan and David P. Norton, *The Strategy-Focused Organization: How Balanced Scorecard Companies Thrive in the New Business Environment* (Boston: Harvard Business School Press, 2001); Robert S. Kaplan and David P. Norton, *Strategy Maps,* (Boston: Harvard Business School Press, 2004); and Robert S. Kaplan and David P. Norton, "How to Implement a New Strategy Without Disrupting Your Organization," *Harvard Business Review,* March 2006, pp. 100–109.

$50 million increase in net margin. The BSC helped UPS significantly increase its revenues. As Kaplan and Norton note:

> The Balanced Scorecard made the difference. Each organization executed strategies using the same physical and human resources that had previously produced failing performance. The strategies were executed with the same products, the same facilities, the same employees, and the same customers. The difference was a new senior management team using the Balanced Scorecard to focus all organizational resources on a new strategy. The scorecard allowed these successful organizations to build a new kind of management system—one designed to manage strategy.

The BSC is particularly important in difficult economic times, when traditional profit-based measures are distorted and difficult to benchmark against established benchmarks such as prior year earnings, industry earnings, and competitors' earnings. Moreover, the manager's attention during difficult times is to look for long-term actions taken currently which are expected to lead to profit growth in the future. This means a refocus on nonfinancial measures that define the organization's competitive advantage—the critical success factors. Additionally, in difficult economic times, a company may need to change strategic direction, to move from a focus on product development and innovation to cost control, or to make another type of strategic change. In the recent economic decline, the firms with a strong ability to reduce costs and meet customer expectations will be more successful. At the end of 2008, the only two firms in the Dow Jones Industrial Index to experience increasing stock prices were Wal-Mart and McDonalds; these firms are uniquely positioned to meet the needs of the new consumer, the economic-slump consumer.

This chapter covers the measures used to evaluate management performance. These measures include topics introduced in previous chapters, such as the balanced scorecard, the contribution income statement, cost allocation, the flexible budget, and outsourcing. These topics are covered here in the important role they play in management performance evaluation. For example, an understanding of the difference between the contribution income statement and the full-cost income statement is important in an effective analysis of performance. We begin with an explanation of the broad concepts underlying performance evaluation.

Performance Measurement and Control

LEARNING OBJECTIVE 1

Identify the objectives of management control.

Performance measurement is the process by which managers at all levels gain information about the performance of tasks within the firm and judge that performance against preestablished criteria as set out in budgets, plans, and goals.

Management control refers to the evaluation by upper-level managers of the performance of mid-level managers.

Operational control means the evaluation of operating level employees by mid-level managers.

Performance measurement (also called *performance evaluation*) is the process by which managers at all levels gain information about the performance of tasks within the firm and judge that performance against preestablished criteria as set out in budgets, plans, and goals.

Performance is evaluated at many different levels in the firm: top management, mid-management, and the operating level of individual production and sales employees. In operations, the performance of individual production supervisors at the *operating level* are evaluated by plant managers, who in turn are evaluated by executives at the *management level*. Similarly, individual salespersons are evaluated by sales managers who are evaluated in turn by upper-level sales management.

Management control refers to the evaluation by upper-level managers of the performance of mid-level managers. **Operational control** means the evaluation of operating-level employees by mid-level managers. Part Three covered operational control. Part Four, which begins with this chapter, covers management control. Since upper-level managers are more directly responsible for implementing the organization's strategy, we call control at this level *strategic performance measurement*. In contrast, control at the operating level is called *operational performance measurement*.

Operational Control versus Management Control

In contrast to operational control, which focuses on detailed short-term performance measures, management control focuses on higher-level managers and long-term, strategic issues. Operational control has a management-by-exception approach; that is, it identifies units or individuals whose performance does not comply with expectations so that the problem can be promptly corrected. In contrast, management control is more consistent with the management-by-objectives approach, in which long-term objectives such as growth and profitability are determined and performance is periodically measured against these goals.

Management control also has a broader and more strategic objective: to evaluate the unit's overall profitability as well as the performance of its manager, to decide whether the unit should be retained or closed, and to motivate the manager to achieve top management's goals. Because of this broader focus, various objectives for management control generally have multiple measures of performance rather than a single financial or operating measure, as is sometimes true in operational control. Exhibit 18.1 is an organization chart that illustrates the different roles of management control and operational control.

Objectives of Management Control

In a management-by-objectives approach, top management assigns a set of responsibilities to each mid-level manager. The nature of these responsibilities and, therefore, the precise nature of top management's objectives depends on the functional area involved (operations, marketing, etc.) and on the scope of authority of the mid-level manager (the extent of the resources under the manager's command).

These areas of responsibility are often called *strategic business units* (SBUs). The concept of a strategic business unit is particularly useful for diversified firms that need performance measures to rationalize and manage the different business units. General Electric Company (GE) is widely cited as pioneering the concept.

A **strategic business unit** consists of a well-defined set of controllable operating activities over which the SBU manager is responsible. Generally, managers have autonomy for making decisions and for managing the SBU's human and physical resources. In practice, a variety of terms are used for the SBU: business unit, center, division, or simply unit. For consistency throughout this text we will use the concept of *SBU* when referring to strategic performance measurement in a general sense, and the term *center* when referring to the four types of SBUs covered in this chapter and the following chapter: cost centers, profit centers, revenue centers, and investment centers. Each of these centers is a type of SBU.

The objectives of management control are to:

1. *Motivate* managers to exert a high level of effort to achieve the goals set by top management.
2. Provide the right *incentive* for managers to make decisions consistent with the goals set by top management, that is, to align managers' efforts with desired strategic goals. The alignment of managers' goals with those of top management is also referred to as *goal congruence.*

> A **strategic business unit (SBU)** consists of a well-defined set of controllable operating activities over which an SBU manager is responsible.

EXHIBIT 18.1
Organization Chart: Operational and Management Control

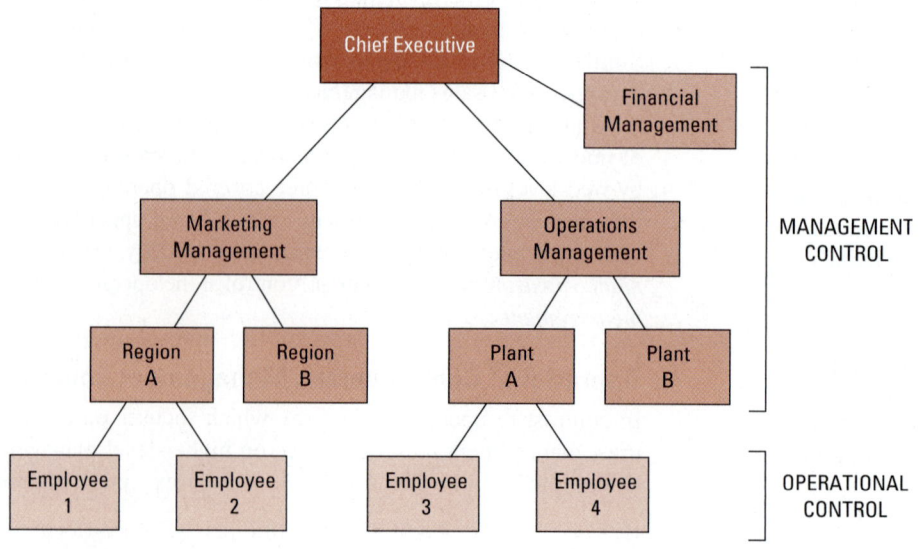

3. *Determine fairly the rewards* earned by managers for their effort and skill and the effectiveness of their decision making.

A concise summary of top management's objectives is to provide fair compensation to the manager for working hard and making the right decisions, all within the context of autonomous action by the SBU manager. A common mechanism for achieving these multiple objectives is to develop an **employment contract** between the manager and top management that covers each of these points. Assuming that managers act in autonomous self-interest, the contract is designed to provide incentives for them to act independently while achieving top management's objectives and earning the desired compensation. This is called goal congruence. The contract specifies the manager's desired behaviors and the compensation to be awarded for achieving specific outcomes by using these behaviors. The contract can be written or unwritten, explicit or implied; some contracts are legal and enforceable by the courts. For clarity and effectiveness, organizations often use explicit written contracts.

Employment Contracts

An economic model called the **principal-agent model** is a prototype that contains the key elements that contracts must have to achieve the desired objectives. The model sets out three important aspects of management performance that affect the contracting relationship, uncertainty, risk aversion, and lack of observability.

Uncertainty

Each manager operates in an environment that is influenced by factors beyond the manager's control—operating factors such as unexpected and unpreventable machine breakdowns and external factors such as fluctuations in market prices and demands. The manager's lack of control means that there is some degree of *uncertainty* about the effectiveness of the manager's actions, independent of the efforts and abilities the manager brings to the job.

Risk, gentlemen! That's why we're aboard her.

Captain James T. Kirk, U.S.S. Enterprise

Risk Aversion

The presence of uncertainty in the manager's environment means that it is important to also consider the manager's tolerance for risk. A manager's risk preferences are important in management and control because they can have unexpected and undesirable effects on the manager's behavior. Risk preferences describe the way individuals view decision options because they place a weight on certain outcomes that is different from the weight on uncertain outcomes. The risk associated with uncertain outcomes may be undesirable (or desirable) to the decision maker, irrespective of the value of the outcome itself. It is necessary to separate the value of the outcome from the positive or negative weight associated with the risk due to uncertainty. For example, it is common for managers to be averse to risk and thus to prefer a certain $50 over a 50-50 chance of winning $100. A risk-neutral manager would see these options as equivalent. One who prefers risk would prefer to have the chance at winning the $100, but this type of risk-prone behavior is less common among managers.

There are implications for performance evaluation. For example, the risk-averse manager is most likely to be motivated by supervision and rewards that reduce risk. Moreover, risk preferences can interfere with proper decision making. For example, a risk-averse manager may choose not to take a risky action that top management would take (for example, to install a costly new machine that would probably reduce operating costs) because of the personal consequences to the manager of a potential unfavorable outcome. For proper motivation and decision making, management control systems should be designed to reduce the negative effects of risk preferences.

Lack of Observability

The efforts and decisions made by the manager are *not observable to top management*. The manager generally possesses information not accessible to top management. Because of the manager's independent and unobservable actions, top management is able to observe only

An **employment contract** is an agreement between the manager and top management designed to provide incentives for the manager to act independently to achieve top management's objectives.

The **principal-agent model** is a conceptual model that contains the key elements that contracts must have to achieve the desired objectives.

the observable outcomes of those actions, not the efforts that led to these outcomes. We assume that the manager, in addition to being risk-averse, is typically also effort-averse.

The presence of uncertainty in the job environment and the lack of observability and the existence of private information for the manager complicate the contracting relationship. Ideally, with no uncertainty and perfect observability, the manager and top management would base their contract on the amount of effort the manager is to supply. An observable effort would assure both parties of the desired effort. However, the presence of uncertainty, risk aversion, and the lack of observability mean that the contract between the manager and top management must rely on effective incentives that specifically incorporate both uncertainty and the lack of observability. This can be accomplished by understanding and applying the three principles of employment contracts:

1. Because of uncertainty in the manager's environment, the contract should recognize that other factors inside and outside the firm also influence the outcomes of the manager's efforts and abilities. Therefore, the contract should separate the outcome of the manager's actions from the effort and decision-making skills employed by the manager; that is, separate the performance of the manager from the performance of the SBU.

2. The contract must include only factors that the manager controls. This principle is similar to the first principle, which separates the manager from the SBU; this second principle excludes *known* uncontrollable factors from the contract.

3. Because of uncertainty and lack of observability, the interests of the risk-averse manager are not aligned with those of top management. The risk-averse manager might make decisions to avoid risk, when top management (because of its ability to diversify risk over the entire organization) might prefer the risky choices.

In effect, the contract between top management and the manager should recognize the manager's risk aversion and the role of uncertainty: the need to understand and to apply the three principles of contracting.

In the principal-agent model illustrated in Exhibit 18.2, top management supplies compensation to the manager who operates in an environment of uncertainty. The manager supplies effort and decision-making skills as well as a degree of risk aversion. The effect of the effort and decision-making skills on the factors in the environment produces the outcomes. The outcomes are multifaceted, including financial and nonfinancial results: earnings, customer

EXHIBIT 18.2
The Principal-Agent Model

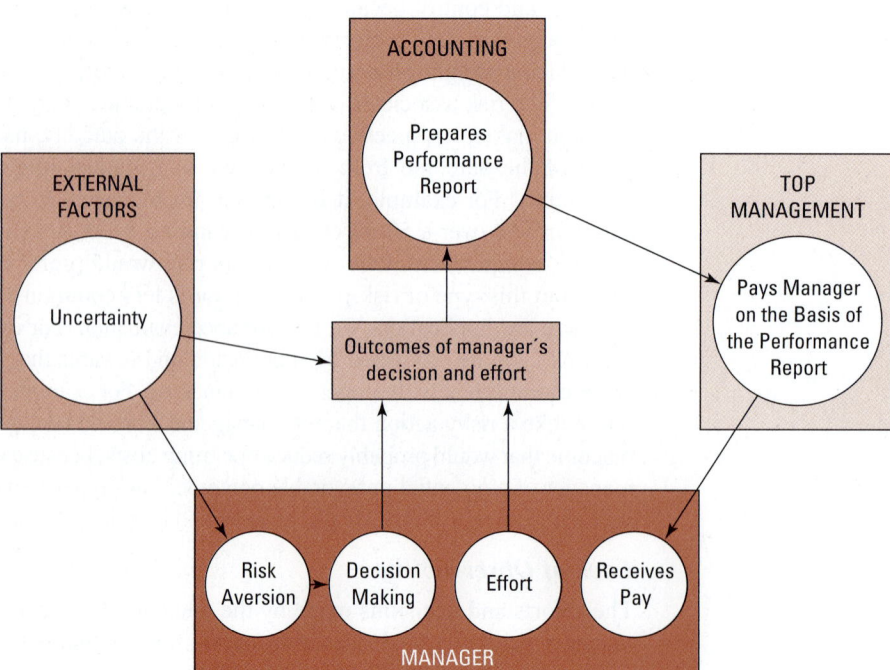

satisfaction, operating efficiency, and so on. The accountant prepares a performance report consisting of financial and nonfinancial measures of the outcomes of the manager's decisions and efforts; the performance report goes to top management, which uses it to determine the manager's pay. In this way, the principal-agent model shows the relationships among the key factors that affect the manager's performance and compensation.[2]

Design of Management Control Systems for Motivation and Evaluation

LEARNING OBJECTIVE 2

Identify the types of management control systems.

Developing a management control system involves clearly identifying the *who, what,* and *when* for the evaluation. We start with the *who,* that is, who is interested in evaluating the organization's performance? The four recipients of performance reports are: (1) the firm's owners, directors, or shareholders, (2) its creditors, (3) the community or governmental units affected by its operations, and (4) its employees. Each has a different view about what performance is desired.

The second aspect of management control is *what* is being evaluated. Commonly the evaluation is of the individual manager, to assess the effectiveness and efficiency of the manager's performance. Alternatively, the focus of the evaluation might be the SBU under the manager's control for the purpose of determining whether or not to expand or to divest the SBU. Rather than focusing on the individual manager, the evaluation might be directed to a team of managers. A manager's performance can be compared either with that of other managers or with the manager's own previous performance. Comparison to other managers is common, but comparison to the manager's previous performance is preferable when comparison to others is inappropriate or unfair in some way.

The third aspect of management control is *when* the performance evaluation is conducted. There are two considerations. First, the evaluation can be done on the basis of either *resources input* to the manager or *outputs* of the manager's efforts. The first approach uses the master budget (Chapter 10), while the second uses the flexible budget (Chapter 14). The focus is on inputs when measuring the outputs of the manager's efforts is difficult or the nature and extent of the manager's control over the outputs is not clear. Then the manager's evaluation is performed *ex ante,* that is, before the manager's efforts and decisions have been made. In effect, the manager negotiates with top management for the amount of resources needed. This approach is common in service and not-for-profit organizations for which the outputs are often difficult to measure. In contrast, in manufacturing, where the inputs and outputs are often relatively easy to measure, the *ex post* approach based on actual outputs is more commonly used.

Another timing option is to tie the evaluation to the product life cycle. The life cycle of a product or service is the time from its introduction to its removal from the market. In the early stages of a product's sales life cycle, management focuses primarily on nonfinancial factors such as market penetration and success in developing certain customers. The appropriate performance measures at this time include revenue according to customer class and area, the number of back orders, the number of new customers, and customer satisfaction. As the product achieves market acceptance, profitability and asset management become more important, and the performance measures change. Finally, when the product is in its mature phase—when the nature of the competition is established and the future of the market is clear—the focus on profitability continues with the addition of interest in strategic issues such as customer satisfaction, information regarding product modifications, and potential new markets. Top management must choose the types of performance measures that are appropriate for the sales life cycle stage of the product or service, as illustrated in Exhibit 18.3.

EXHIBIT 18.3
Sales Life Cycle of Management Control

Stage of Product's Sales Life Cycle	Appropriate Performance Evaluation Measures
Early	Revenue, market penetration
Growth	Profitability, asset management
Mature	Profitability, strategy

[2] The principal-agent model illustrates the concept of what is called *moral hazard*—the risk that the manager might take advantage of the firm's lack of observability to claim and receive rewards that are not earned under the employment contract.

EXHIBIT 18.4
Systems for Management Control

	INFORMAL SYSTEMS	FORMAL SYSTEMS
INDIVIDUAL	Aspiration Level Personal Drives	Hiring Practices Promotion Policies Strategic Performance Measurement
TEAMS	Peer Norms Organization Culture	Keiretsu Shared Responsibility

The systems for management control are of two types, formal and informal. Formal systems are developed with explicit management guidance while informal systems arise from the unmanaged, and sometimes unintended, behavior of managers and employees. Informal systems reflect the managers' and employees' reactions and feelings that result from the positive and negative aspects of the work environment. An example is the positive feelings of security and acceptance held by an employee in a company that has a successful product and offers generous employee benefits.

Informal Control Systems

Informal systems are used in firms at both the individual and the team levels. At the individual level, employees' performance is influenced by the individual drives and aspirations they bring to the workplace; these are separate from any incentives and guidance provided by management. Such individual motivators explain performance differences between employees.

When informal systems exist at the work group or team level, shared team norms, such as a positive attitude to help the firm achieve quality goals or to improve sales, influence the performance of team members. At a broader level, organization-level norms can influence the behavior of teams and of individual employees. For example, some firms have a culture of commitment to customer service (IBM and the retailer Nordstrom); others have a culture devoted to quality (Toyota, FedEx) or innovation (3M, Hewlett-Packard). Management accountants must consider these informal systems to properly develop control systems that have the desired impact on employees' performance.

Formal Control Systems

The three important formal management control systems at the individual employee level are (1) hiring practices, (2) promotion policies, and (3) strategic performance measurement systems. In each system, management sets expectations for desired employee performance. Hiring and promotion policies are critical in all companies and supplement strategic performance measurement systems. Strategic performance measurement systems are the most common method for evaluating managers.

LEARNING OBJECTIVE 3

Define strategic performance measurement and show how centralized, decentralized, and team-oriented organizations can apply it.

Little is known about formal systems for management control at the team or group level, although the increased emphasis on teamwork in recent years is likely to produce demand for such systems. Some U.S. companies have adopted the *keiretsu* system of shared responsibility prevalent in Japanese companies, and it is a likely starting place for such a development. The four management control systems are summarized in Exhibit 18.4.

Strategic Performance Measurement

Strategic performance measurement
is a system used by top management to evaluate SBU managers.

Strategic performance measurement is a system used by top management to evaluate SBU managers. It is used when responsibility can be effectively delegated to SBU managers and adequate measures for evaluating the performance of the managers exist. Before designing strategic performance measurement systems, top managers determine when delegation of responsibility (called *decentralization*) is desirable.

Decentralization

A firm is **decentralized** if it has chosen to delegate a significant amount of responsibility to SBU managers.

A firm is **decentralized** if it has chosen to delegate a significant amount of responsibility to SBU managers. In contrast, a centralized firm reserves much of the decision making at the top management level. For example, in a centralized multistore retail firm, all pricing decisions, product purchasing, and advertising decisions are made at the top management level, typically by top-level marketing and operations executives. In contrast, a decentralized retail firm allows local store managers to decide which products to purchase and the type and amount of advertising to use.

The strategic benefit of the centralized approach is that top management retains control over key business functions, ensuring a desired level of performance. Additionally, with top management involvement in most decisions, the expertise of top management can be effectively utilized, and the activities of the different units within the firm can be effectively coordinated. For many firms, however, a decentralized approach is preferable. The main reason is that top management cannot effectively manage the operations at a very detailed level; it lacks the necessary local knowledge. Decisions at lower levels in the firm must be made on a timely basis using the information at hand to make the firm more responsive to the customer. For example, the retail store manager must often make quick changes in inventory, pricing, and advertising to respond to local competition and changing customer buying habits and tastes.

Although the main reason for decentralization is the use of local or specialized knowledge by SBU managers, other important incentives exist. First, many managers would say that decentralized strategic performance measurement is more motivating because it provides them the opportunity to demonstrate their skill and their desire to achieve as well as to receive recognition and compensation for doing so. Second, because of the direct responsibility assumed by SBU managers, the decentralized approach provides a type of training for future top-level managers. Finally, most managers would agree that the decentralized approach is a better basis for performance evaluation. It is perceived to be more objective and to provide more opportunity for the advancement of hard-working, effective managers.

As shown in Exhibit 18.5, decentralization has a downside as well. It can hinder coordination within the firm. The increased focus on competition also could cause increased conflict among managers, which can lead to counterproductive actions and reduced overall performance.

Types of Strategic Business Units

Cost centers are a firm's production or support SBUs that provide the best quality product or service at the lowest cost.

The four types of strategic business units (SBUs) are cost centers, revenue centers, profit centers, and investment centers.

Cost centers are a firm's production or support SBUs that provide the best quality product or service at the lowest cost. Examples include a plant's assembly department, data processing department, and shipping and receiving department. When the focus is on the selling function, centers are called **revenue centers** and are defined either by product line or by geographical area. When an SBU both generates revenues and incurs the major portion of the cost for producing these revenues, it is a **profit center.** Profit center managers are responsible for both revenues and costs and therefore seek to achieve a desired operating profit. The use of profit centers is an improvement over cost and revenue centers in many firms because they align the manager's goals more directly with top management's goal to make the firm profitable.

A **revenue center** is defined either by product line or by geographical area and focuses on the selling function.

A **profit center** both generates revenues and incurs the major portion of the cost for producing these revenues.

EXHIBIT 18.5
Advantages and Disadvantages of Decentralization

Advantages of Decentralization	Disadvantages of Decentralization
• Uses local knowledge	• Can hinder coordination among SBUs
• Allows timely and effective response to customers	• Can cause potential conflict among SBUs
• Trains managers	
• Motivates managers	
• Offers objective method of performance evaluation	

The choice of a profit, cost, or revenue center depends on the nature of the production and selling environment in the firm. Products that have little need for coordination between the manufacturing and selling functions are good candidates for cost centers. These include many commodity products such as food and paper products. For such products, the production manager rarely needs to adjust the functionality of the product or the production schedule to suit a particular customer. For this reason, production managers should focus on reducing cost while sales managers focus on sales; this is what cost and revenue centers accomplish.

In contrast, sometimes close coordination is needed between the production and selling functions. For example, high-fashion and consumer products require close coordination so that consumer information coming into the selling function promptly reaches the design and manufacturing functions. Cost and revenue centers could fail to provide the incentive for coordination; in this case, production managers would be focusing on cost and not listening to the ever-changing demands coming from the selling function. A preferred option is to use the profit center for both the revenue and production managers so that both coordinate efforts to achieve the highest overall profit for the firm.

When a firm has many different profit centers because it has many different product lines, comparing their performance could be difficult because they vary greatly in size and in the nature of their products and services. A preferred approach is to use **investment centers,** which include assets employed by the center as well as profits in the performance evaluation. Investment centers are covered in Chapter 19.

An **investment center** includes assets employed by the SBU as well as profits in performance evaluation.

The Balanced Scorecard

Each of the four types of centers described above focuses on a critical financial measure of performance. Rather than focus on financial performance only, most firms use multiple measures of performance to evaluate centers, often in the form of a balanced scorecard. The balanced scorecard provides a more comprehensive performance evaluation, and therefore an evaluation that can be more effective in meeting the evaluation objectives of motivation, fairness and proper incentives for the alignment of managers' performance with strategic goals.

Cost Centers

LEARNING OBJECTIVE 4

Explain the objectives and applications of strategic performance measurement in three common strategic business units: cost centers, revenue centers, and profit centers.

Cost SBUs include manufacturing plants or direct manufacturing departments such as assembly or finishing and manufacturing support departments such as materials handling, maintenance, or engineering. The direct manufacturing and manufacturing support departments are often evaluated as cost centers since these managers have significant direct control over costs but little control over revenues or decision making for investment in facilities.

Strategic Issues Related to Implementing Cost Centers

Three strategic issues arise when implementing cost centers. One is cost shifting, the second is excessively focusing on short-term objectives, and the third is the tendency of managers and top management to miscommunicate because of the pervasive problem of budget slack.

Cost Shifting

Cost shifting occurs when a department replaces its controllable costs with noncontrollable costs. For example, the manager of a production cost center that is evaluated on controllable costs has the incentive to replace variable costs with fixed costs. The reason for this is that the manager generally is not held responsible for increases in noncontrollable fixed costs. The net effect might be higher overall costs for the firm, although controllable costs in the manager's department might decrease. Fixed costs go up while variable costs go down. The effective use of cost centers requires top management to anticipate and prevent cost shifting by requiring an analysis and justification of equipment upgrades and any changes in work patterns that affect other departments.

Cost-shifting issues also arise in not-for-profit organizations. For example, many governmental units do not distinguish between direct and indirect costs in their performance reporting. This can lead to poor decision making, as illustrated by the U.S. Forest Service:

> Inappropriate accounting measures allegedly caused the United States Forest Service to cut down trees that an ordinary business would have left standing . . . the Forest Service is not charged for the cost of constructing roads into remote areas to reach the lumber. The Forest Service's response to these measures of its performance is to cut down a great deal of lumber and to construct costly, intricate roads to reach it. The Service already has 342,000 miles of logging roads and plans to build yet another 262,000 by 2040. Critics contend that these roads are constructed to reach increasingly poor quality timber and that they inflict considerable environmental damage. They recommend new measures of its performance that account for the full cost of logging, including the cost of raising the timber, building the roads to reach it, and replacing it.[3]

The Forest Service's failure to identify the full cost of the logging, including the costs of the roads as well as the logging of the trees, can cause poor decision making.

Another incentive for cost shifting in not-for-profit entities is that certain services are reimbursed on a cost-plus basis while others are charged as fixed fees. Cost shifting in this context means allocating joint costs (see Chapter 7) from the fixed-charge to the cost-plus services. The cost shifting can be done in a variety of ways. A number of hospitals, for example, have shifted the costs of Medicare and Medicaid (fixed-fee) patients to private (cost-plus) patients.[4] Cost shifting undermines the motivation and fairness of the performance evaluation systems within these hospitals.

Excessive Short-Term Focus

A second strategic issue is the broad concern that many performance measurement systems focus excessively on annual cost figures; this motivates managers to attend only to short-term costs and to neglect long-term strategic issues. This concern is an important reason why cost centers should use nonfinancial strategic considerations as well as financial information on costs.

Role of Budget Slack

Budget slack is the difference between budgeted performance and expected performance.

A third strategic issue in implementing cost-based SBUs is to recognize both the negative and the positive roles of budget slack. **Budget slack** is the difference between budgeted and expected performance. The majority of SBUs have some amount of slack, evidenced by a budgeted cost target that is somewhat easier to attain than is reasonably expected. Managers often plan for a certain amount of slack in their performance budgets to allow for unexpected unfavorable events. However, a significant amount of slack might result from SBU managers' attempts to simply make their performance goals easier to achieve.

The positive view of slack is that it effectively addresses the decision-making and fairness objectives of performance evaluation. By limiting managers' exposure to environmental uncertainty, it reduces their relative risk aversion. The resulting evaluation therefore satisfies fairness, and the reduced risk helps the managers make decisions that are more nearly congruent with the goals of top management.

Implementing Cost Centers in Departments

Production and Support Departments

The two methods for implementing cost centers for production and support departments are the discretionary-cost method and the engineered-cost method. These two methods have different underlying cost behavior and a different focus: inputs or outputs, respectively. When costs are predominantly fixed, an input-oriented planning focus is appropriate because fixed costs are

---

[3] Regina E. Herzlinger and Denise Nitterhouse, *Financial Accounting and Managerial Control for Nonprofit Organizations* (Cincinnati: South Western Publishing, 1994), p. 419; also, Cox et al., "Responsibility Accounting and Operational Control for Governmental Units," *Accounting Horizons*, June 1989, pp. 38–48, show the results of a survey of 830 governmental units in the United States and Canada with a principal finding that the strategic performance measurement systems in three-fourths of these units did not distinguish between controllable and uncontrollable costs.

[4] See Leslie Eldenburg and Sanjay Kallapur, "Changes in Hospital Service Mix and Cost Allocations in Response to Changes in Medicare Reimbursement Schemes," *Journal of Accounting and Economics*, May 1997, pp. 31–51.

The **discretionary-cost method** considers costs largely uncontrollable and applies discretion at the planning stage; it is an input-oriented approach.

The **engineered-cost method** considers costs to be variable and therefore engineered, or controllable; it is an output-oriented approach.

not controllable in the short term. The planning approach is taken so that top management can effectively budget for expected costs in each discretionary-cost center; the focus is on beginning-of-period planning for expected costs rather than end-of-period evaluation of the amount of costs expended. In contrast, if costs are primarily variable and therefore controllable, an output-oriented approach, based on end-of-period evaluation of controllable costs, is appropriate. The input-oriented approach is called the **discretionary-cost method** because costs are considered to be largely uncontrollable and discretion is applied at the planning stage. The output-oriented approach is called the **engineered-cost method** since costs are variable and therefore "engineered," or controllable.

Another factor in choosing between discretionary-cost and engineered-cost costs is the complexity of the work environment. Cost centers that have relatively ill-defined outputs (for instance, research and development) or have less well-defined goals are therefore more likely to be evaluated as discretionary-cost centers; costs for which the operations are well defined and the output goals are more clearly determined will have engineered-cost costs. See Exhibit 18.6.

Cost behavior in a production department is therefore important in choosing the cost department method. As explained in Chapter 5, the behavior of an activity measure depends on the level of analysis: the facility, the product, the batch of production, or the unit of production. Similarly, when studying a cost center, we must know on which level of analysis it operates. For example, costs in the engineering department are driven primarily by product-level activity measures: the number of new products or product changes. Also, costs in the inspection department are caused primarily by batch-level activity measures: the number of production runs or setups.

Relatively few cost drivers exist at the facility level because most of its costs are fixed and do not fluctuate with changes in production level, production mix, or product. Therefore, most departments at this level are evaluated as discretionary-cost centers.

For cost departments at the unit, batch, and product levels, managers commonly implement the engineered-cost method based on the appropriate cost driver for that production activity. For example, for the engineering department where the cost driver is at the product level, the engineered-cost method uses the number of engineering changes to new and existing products as the cost driver and evaluates the performance of the engineering department on its costs for each engineering change completed. Similarly, for the inspection department where the cost driver is at the batch level (inspection is done for each batch), the appropriate cost center method is again the engineered-cost method, in which management reviews the cost incurred versus the number of batches inspected.

Some production departments are more difficult to classify as batch, product, or facility level. For example, the maintenance department can be viewed as a facility-level activity because much of the demand for maintenance is for plant and equipment that is not influenced by production level (units or batches). However, because the wear on equipment is greater at a higher level of production or for a larger number of batches, batch and unit cost drivers also can be appropriate. The choice of method depends in part on management's objectives. If management wants to motivate a reduction in maintenance use (because of rising maintenance costs or of overall budget constraints), the engineered-cost method is appropriate since it rewards cost reduction.[5] In contrast, if management is concerned about the low overall serviceability of plant and equipment (due perhaps to a prior lack of maintenance), the discretionary-cost method provides the proper incentive by reducing the maintenance manager's risk aversion and thereby motivating proper additional expenditures on maintenance.

Another option for management control of the engineering department or maintenance department is to treat each of them as profit centers and to charge users a price for their services. The effects of using a profit center method are added emphasis on cost control and an incentive for the center to provide quality service and perhaps seek markets outside the firm.

[5] Note, however, that Robin Cooper and Robert S. Kaplan, in "Activity-Based Systems: Measuring the Costs of Resource Usage," *Accounting Horizons,* September 1992, explain that methods such as the engineered-cost method do not necessarily achieve a reduction in costs unless the supply of resources is reduced following a reduction in the usage of resources.

EXHIBIT 18.6
Cost Centers for Production and Support Departments

Discretionary-Cost Approach	Engineered-Cost Approach
Costs are mainly fixed, uncontrollable	Costs are mainly variable, controllable
Firms use an input-oriented planning focus	Firms use an output-oriented evaluation focus
Outputs are ill-defined	Outputs are well-defined
The focus is on planning	The focus is on evaluation

Administrative Support Departments

Administrative support departments such as human resources, research and development, information technology services, and printing and duplicating are also commonly evaluated as cost centers. They seldom have a source of revenue, but the department managers control most of the costs, so the cost center method is appropriate. The choice of a discretionary-cost or engineered-cost method for these departments depends on the cost behavior in the department and on management's objectives, as explained earlier. The proper choice of method might change over time. For example, when cost reduction is a key objective, the human resources department might be treated as an engineered-cost center for a time. Later it might be changed to a discretionary-cost SBU to motivate managers to focus on long-term goals such as the design of new employee bonus systems.

Cost behavior in administrative support departments is often a step-cost, as illustrated in Exhibit 18.7. As clerical and/or service support personnel are added, labor costs increase in a step-cost pattern. Suppose that one clerk is required to process 100 new employee applications per month and that each clerk is paid $1,200 per month. If the firm processes 250 applications per month, it needs three clerks at a total cost of $3,600 per month. If the discretionary-cost method is used, the supervisor of personnel management is likely to have negotiated for three clerks *at the beginning of the year,* and therefore the budget is $3,600 and there is no meaningful *ex post* evaluation. The discretionary-cost method is represented by the horizontal line in Exhibit 18.7.

Recognizing that processing each application in effect costs $12 ($1,200/100), management might choose to use an engineered-cost method that evaluates the personnel department manager by comparing the budget of $3,000 (250 applications times $12 per application) to the actual expenditure of $3,600. Because slack or overcapacity can exist due to the nature of the step-cost, an unfavorable cost variance is likely; only when the operation is exactly at one of the full-capacity points (100, 200, 300 . . .) will there be no variance. Therefore, the interpretation of the cost variances must include both the productivity of labor and the underutilization of labor due to excess capacity.

Outsourcing or Consolidating Cost Centers

Outsourcing is the term used to describe a firm's decision to have a service or product currently provided by a support department supplied by an outside firm. Many firms have found that the

EXHIBIT 18.7
Step-Cost Administrative Support Costs: Discretionary Cost versus Engineered Cost

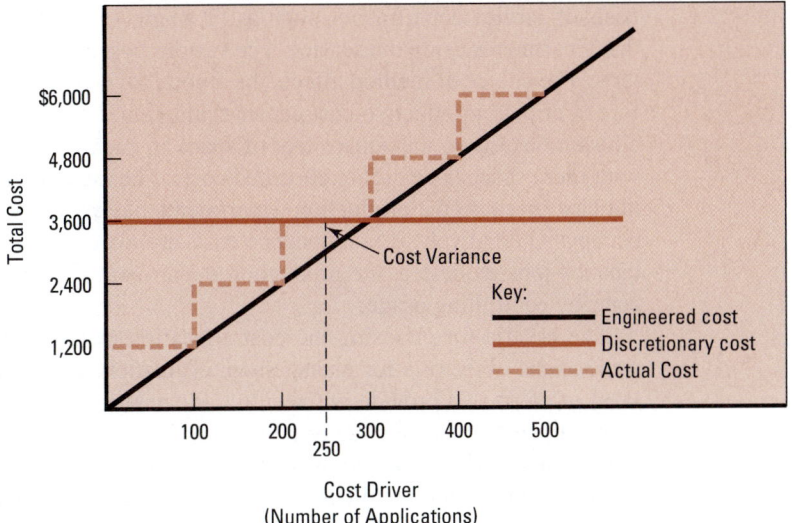

THE PLUS SIDE

As noted in Chapter 1 and following Thomas L. Friedman's observation in his recent book, *The World Is Flat,* many of today's products and services are becoming commodities, provided by the lowest-cost global supplier. The reasons include cost savings, but often there are strategic reasons as well. The outsourcing relationship provides assistance in product innovation and product and service quality and can even save a multinational company on its global tax burden. But most important, companies say that the outsourcing relationships allow them to focus on key business processes, to enhance the firm's most competitive value-adding processes, products, and services. A recent survey of 226 global customers of outsourcing showed that 76 percent indicated that the top reason was costs savings, while 70 percent indicated that the top reason was to gain access to talent for innovation and competitive advantage.

ON THE MINUS SIDE

Outsourcers also note that sometimes problems arise. Quality problems can develop if the projects are not planned and managed carefully. Also, security problems can arise as data and technologies are dispersed into other countries. Critical innovations and technologies can be at risk of unwanted exposure. But most important, the cost savings may not be realized as expected, because the outsourcing activity creates requirements for additional management supervision, the cost of increased security measures, wages increase in the host country, or unexpected additional operating costs arise. The recent survey of 226 global users of outsourcing indicated that top obstacles to outsourcing were establishing the cost savings (48%), lack of experience in selecting an outsourcing partner (48%), and conflict between outsourcing and company values (45%). Apparently because these were *global* companies, only 22 percent saw the "ethics of moving jobs offshore" as an obstacle to outsourcing.

Source: Thomas L. Friedman, *The World Is Flat: A Brief History of the Twenty-First Century* (New York: Farrar, Straus, and Giroux, 2005); Pricewaterhouse-Coopers Global Outsourcing Survey, 2007; Scott Thurm, "Behind Outsourcing: Promise and Pitfalls," *The Wall Street Journal,* February 26, 2007, p. B3; Niraj Sheth and Nathan Koppel, "With Times Tight, Even Lawyers Get Outsourced," *The Wall Street Journal,* November 26, 2008, p. B1; Stanley Holmes, "Danger in the Repair Shop: FAA Investors Are Warning about the Risks of Outsourcing Maintenance," *BusinessWeek,* July 30, 2007, p. 36; Pui-Wing Tam and Jackie Range, "Some in Silicon Valley Begin to Sour on India," *The Wall Street Journal*, July 3, 2007, p. 1; Ben Worthen, "Outsourcers Brace for a Hit," *The Wall Street Journal,* December 30, 2008, p. B4; Sarah Johnson, "Offshoring's Uncertain Future in 2009," CFO.com, January 8, 2009.

use of an outside source is an effective way to obtain reliable product or service at a reasonable cost without the risk of obsolescence and other potential management problems. It can also enable a firm to gain access to new technologies. The cost of outsourcing is that the firm loses control over a potentially strategic resource and must rely on the outside firm's competence and continued performance. For this reason, firms analyze this decision thoroughly, select the vendors carefully, and develop precisely worded contracts. Outsourcing is an option increasingly used by many firms for their manufacturing, customer service, engineering, and other services.

Another option often used by companies is to consolidate decentralized cost centers into one or a few centralized cost centers. The goals are to reduce overall costs and to increase the overall quality of the services provided. Accounting and human resource service departments are often consolidated for these reasons.

Cost Allocation

When the cost center is centralized, an important issue is how to allocate the jointly incurred costs of service departments, such as IT, engineering, human resources, or maintenance, to the departments using the service. The various cost allocation methods are explained in Chapter 7. The choice of method affects the amount of cost allocated to each cost center and therefore is critical in effective cost center evaluation. For example, if the cost of maintenance is allocated based on the square feet of space in each production department, the departments with more space have higher allocated costs. The incentives of such an allocation method are not clear because the production departments likely cannot control the amount of space they occupy. Alternatively, if maintenance costs are allocated on the basis of the number of maintenance jobs requested, the production departments can control their allocated maintenance costs by controlling usage.

The criteria for choosing the cost allocation method, as explained in Chapter 7, are the same as the objectives for management evaluation: to (1) motivate managers to exert a high level of effort, (2) provide an incentive for managers to make decisions consistent with top management's goals, and (3) provide a basis for a fair evaluation of managers' performance. For example, when management wants to encourage production departments to reduce the amount of maintenance, allocation based on usage provides the desired incentive. In contrast,

A number of large firms, including Eastman Kodak, Xerox, and governmental units such as the U.S. Marine Corps and the State of Connecticut are outsourcing significant parts of their information technology (IT) operations. Approximately 20 percent of the largest U.S. firms have already outsourced this operation, according to current estimates, and the trend is for that percentage to increase. Some of the outsourcing is to application service providers (ASPs), which provide a wide range of IT services (e-mail, transaction processing, and more), often over the Internet. In other cases, the IT tasks have been taken over by large consulting firms such as Accenture, IBM, Electronic Data Systems, and Computer Science Corp. Why are these firms outsourcing their IT function? How does outsourcing IT make the firm more competitive?

(Refer to Comments on Cost Management in Action at end of Chapter.)

if management wants the departments to increase the use of maintenance to improve the serviceability of the equipment, the most effective incentive might be not to allocate the maintenance cost or perhaps to subsidize it in some way.

Dual allocation

is a cost allocation method that separates fixed and variable costs. Variable costs are directly traced to user departments, and fixed costs are allocated on some logical basis.

A useful approach to achieving the three criteria just explained is to use dual allocation. **Dual allocation** is a cost allocation method that separates fixed and variable costs. Variable costs are directly traced to user departments, and fixed costs are allocated on some logical basis. For example, the variable costs of maintenance, such as supplies, labor, and parts, can be traced to each maintenance job and charged directly to the user department. This approach is both fair and positively motivating. In contrast, the fixed costs of the maintenance department (training, manuals, equipment, etc.) that cannot be traced to each maintenance job should be allocated to the user departments using a basis that fairly reflects each department's use of the service. For example, those departments for which maintenance jobs require more expensive equipment might be allocated a higher proportion of the maintenance department's fixed costs.

To improve dual allocation, indirect costs could be traced to cost centers using activity-based costing (Chapter 5). This approach tends to produce the most accurate cost assignment and therefore would be the most motivating and fairest to the SBU managers.

Revenue Centers

Revenue drivers

are the factors that affect sales volume, such as price changes, promotions, discounts, customer service, changes in product features, delivery dates, and other value-added factors.

Management commonly uses revenue drivers in evaluating the performance of revenue centers. **Revenue drivers** in manufacturing firms are the factors that affect sales volume, such as price changes, promotions, discounts, customer service, changes in product features, delivery dates, and other value-added factors. In service firms, the revenue drivers focus on many of the same factors, with a special emphasis on the quality of the service—is it courteous, helpful, and timely?

The marketing and sales departments can be viewed as both revenue and cost centers. The revenue center responsibility stems from the fact that these departments manage the revenue-generating process. These managers must therefore report revenues, typically by product line, and sometimes by sales area and salesperson. Top management uses the revenue reports to assess performance in achieving desired sales goals. Often this analysis is performed at a detailed level to determine the separate effects of changes in price, quantity, and sales mix on overall sales dollars.[6]

The marketing and sales departments also can be cost centers. In the pharmaceuticals, cosmetics, software, games and toys, and specialized electrical equipment industries, the cost of advertising and promotion is a significant portion of the total cost of producing and selling the product. The marketing and sales departments incur two types of costs: order-getting and order-filling costs. **Order-getting costs** are expenditures to advertise and promote the product. They include samples, demonstrations, advertising and promotion, travel and entertainment expenses, commissions, and marketing research. Because showing how these costs have directly affected sales is often difficult, managers frequently view order-getting costs as

Order-getting costs

are expenditures to advertise and promote the product.

[6] Sales variances are explained in Chapter 16. Also, some marketing managers have a relatively broad view of the responsibility of the marketing function, which includes responsibility for sales and cost of sales. This is suggested, for example, by the Institute of Marketing's definition: "Marketing is the management process for identifying, anticipating, and satisfying customer requirements profitably."

a discretionary-cost center and focus on planning these expenditures rather than evaluating their effectiveness. In contrast, other firms have developed extensive analyses of order-getting costs to identify the most effective activities for improving sales. Such additional analyses might consist of statistical analyses of general economic data and the firm's sales and operating data, with operational analyses consisting of ratios of sales per salesperson, sales per number of follow-ups on inquiries, and returns and allowances per product and salesperson.

Order-filling costs include freight, warehousing, packing and shipping, and collections.

A second category of marketing costs is **order-filling costs,** which include freight, warehousing, packing and shipping, and collections. These costs have a relatively clear relationship to sales volume and as a result, they can often be effectively managed as an engineered-cost center. The engineered-cost method could be implemented by using customer cost analysis as explained in Chapter 5 or by developing appropriate operating ratios—average shipping cost per item, average freight cost per sales dollar, and so on.

Profit Centers

The profit center manager's goal is to earn profits. A key advantage of the profit center is that it brings the manager's incentives into congruence with those of top management: to improve the firm's profitability. Moreover, the profit center should also motivate individual managers because by earning profits, the managers are contributing directly to the firm's success. For these reasons, the profit center meets the management control objectives of motivation and decision making explained earlier.

Strategic Role of Profit Centers

Three strategic issues cause firms to choose profit centers rather than cost or revenue centers. First, profit centers provide the incentive for the desired coordination among the marketing, production, and support functions. The handling of rush orders is a good example. A cost center would view a rush order unfavorably because of the potential added cost associated with the disruption of the production process, but a revenue center would view it favorably. If they are in separate cost and revenue centers, the production manager has little incentive to meet with the marketing manager to coordinate the rush order. In contrast, if the production unit is a profit unit, its manager accepts the order if it improves the center's profit, a decision consistent with the goals of both the production unit and top management.

This idea is illustrated in Exhibit 18.8. Panel A of Exhibit 18.8 shows a cost leadership firm in which a commodity is manufactured to certain standard quality and functionality specifications. These standards are common in the industry and firms compete primarily on price. In this case, the manufacturing plant's role is to provide product for sale at the lowest price; this can be visualized as filling the warehouse, as shown in the exhibit. The warehouse might be small if the firm's supply chain management system is effective. The function of the sales organization is to sell product from the warehouse. In effect, the sales and manufacturing units

EXHIBIT 18.8
Cost Leadership, Differentiation, and SBUs

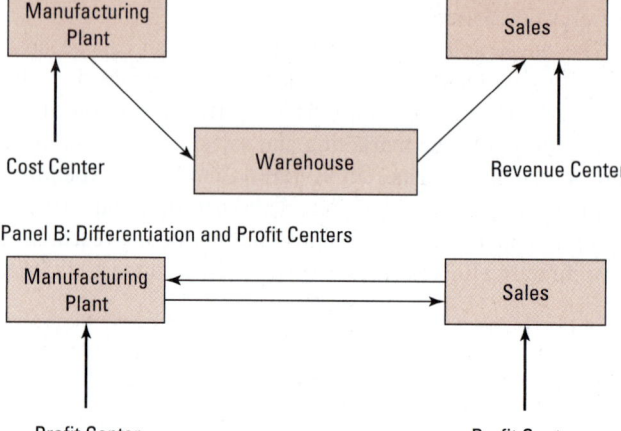

Panel A: Cost Leadership: Cost Centers and Revenue Centers

Manufacturing Plant

Sales

Cost Center

Warehouse

Revenue Center

Panel B: Differentiation and Profit Centers

Manufacturing Plant

Sales

Profit Center

Profit Center

are logically separate and can be evaluated simply: the plant as a cost center and the sales organization as a revenue center. These performance measures align very well with the objectives of the plant and the sales organization in this case.

In contrast, see panel B of Exhibit 18.8, which reflects a firm that competes on differentiation. The arrows shown going in both directions between the plant and the sales organization indicate that this product requires extensive coordination between manufacturing and sales. An example is fashion apparel. The design and manufacturing of the apparel must be closely coordinated with sales, since styles may change frequently, and the new style preferences must be communicated from sales to the plant in a closely coordinated way. Profit centers for both the plant and the sales organization provide the right incentive in this case, as it requires both the plant and sales management to attend to both customer preferences and manufacturing costs. An alternative approach is to organize responsibility to the product lines (responsible for both manufacturing and sales) and evaluate the product lines as profit centers, rather than to separate the manufacturing and sales functions.

A second reason that firms use profit centers rather than cost centers is to motivate managers to consider their product or service as marketable to outside customers. Production departments that provide products and services primarily for other internal departments might find that they can market their products or services profitably outside the firm, or that the firm might be able to purchase the product or service at a lower price outside the firm.

The third reason for choosing profit centers is to motivate managers to develop new ways to make profit from their products and services. For example, an increasing number of companies find that service contracts (for home entertainment equipment, business equipment, appliances, and so on) provide a significant source of profit in addition to the sale of the product. In the software industry, revenues from providing service and upgrades can be as important as the software's original sales price. Coordination between marketing, production, and design is critical for the success of these efforts, and since many of these contracts are for three years or more, the expected future costs of the service must be carefully analyzed. In a profit center, managers have the incentive to develop creative new products and services because the profit center evaluation rewards the incremental profits.

The Contribution Income Statement

The **contribution income statement** is based on the contribution margin developed for each profit center and for each relevant group of profit centers.

A common form of profit center evaluation is the **contribution income statement,** which is based on the contribution margin developed for each profit center and for each relevant group of profit centers. The contribution income statement is illustrated in Exhibit 18.9 for Machine Tools Inc. (MTI). MTI has two operating divisions, A and B, each of which is considered a profit center. The level of detail at which the contribution income statement is developed varies depending on management's needs. For a firm with a limited number of products, the level of detail in Exhibit 18.9 is common. For a firm with several products, a

EXHIBIT 18.9 Machine Tools Inc. Contribution Income Statement (000s omitted)

	Company as a Whole	Company Breakdown into Profit Centers		Breakdown of Division B to Product-Level Profit Centers			
		Division A	Division B	Not Traceable	Product 1	Product 2	Product 3
Net revenues	$2,000	$600	$1,400		$400	$700	$300
Variable costs	900	200	700		100	350	250
Contribution margin	$1,100	$400	$ 700		$300	$350	$ 50
Controllable fixed costs	250	100	150	$ 25	25	100	0
Controllable margin	$ 850	$300	$ 550	(25)	$275	$250	$ 50
Noncontrollable fixed costs	400	120	280	20	10	130	120
Contribution by profit center (CPC)	$ 450	$180	$ 270	$(45)	$265	$120	$ (70)
Untraceable costs	200						
Operating income	$ 250						

more extensive contribution income statement would be required to provide sufficient detail for management analysis.

This contribution income statement is an extension of the income statement illustrated in Exhibits 11.14 through 11.16 of Chapter 11. Chapter 11 introduces the idea of traceable fixed costs; that is, fixed costs can be traced directly to a product line or production unit. Exhibit 18.9 shows both contribution margin and contribution margin less traceable fixed costs, **contribution by profit center (CPC)**. The concept of CPC is important because it measures profit after all traceable costs and is therefore controllable by the profit center manager. CPC is a more complete and fair measure of performance than either contribution margin or operating income.

This chapter expands the contribution income statement by distinguishing controllable and noncontrollable fixed costs. **Controllable fixed costs** are fixed costs that the profit SBU manager can influence in approximately a year or less. That is, the manager typically budgets these costs in the annual budget; some of them involve contractual relationships for a year or less. Examples include advertising; sales promotion; certain engineering, data processing, and research projects; and management consulting. In contrast, **noncontrollable fixed costs** are those that are not controllable within a year's time; usually they include facilities-related costs such as depreciation, taxes, and insurance.

As illustrated in Exhibit 18.9, the firm develops a useful measure of the profit SBU manager's short-term performance by subtracting controllable fixed costs from the contribution margin to determine the **controllable margin.** In contrast, to measure the manager's performance in managing both short- and long-term costs, the CPC measure is most appropriate since it includes both short-term and long-term fixed costs.

One complication in completing the contribution income statement is that some costs that are not traceable at a detailed level are traceable at a higher level of aggregation. The untraceable costs column in the income statement represents costs traceable to division B but not traceable to any of the product lines. For example, the $25,000 controllable fixed costs might consist of the cost of advertising that was arranged at the division level to benefit all three products, so it is not traceable to any one product.

In addition to providing useful measures of the manager's performance in managing costs, the contribution income statement can be used to determine whether a profit center should be dropped or retained, much like the contribution margin analysis in Exhibit 11.16. The analysis is now enhanced because of our ability to distinguish controllable and noncontrollable fixed costs. For example, using the analysis in Exhibit 18.9, MTI can determine that if it drops product 3, the short-term effect will be to reduce profit by $50,000, the amount of the controllable margin. All costs involved in the determination of the controllable margin are avoidable within a period of one year. Taking the longer-term view, suppose that MTI could ultimately save an additional $120,000 of noncontrollable fixed costs by dropping product 3. Then, in the long term, MTI can save a net of $70,000 by dropping product 3, the amount of the contribution by CPC for product 3. The above analysis has assumed that the sales of the products are independent, that a change in sales for one product will not affect the level of sales for another product. Sales interdependencies between products must also be included in the analysis when they occur.

Variable Costing versus Full Costing

The use of the contribution income statement often is called *variable costing* because it separates variable and fixed costs. Only variable costs are included in determining the cost of sales and the contribution margin. In contrast, full costing is a cost system that includes fixed cost in product cost and cost of sales. Full costing is the conventional costing system because it is required by financial reporting standards (generally accepted accounting principles) and by the Internal Revenue Service for determining taxable income. A key reason full costing is preferred for financial reporting is that it satisfies the matching principle; that is, in determining cost of goods sold it matches the revenues of the period with the full cost of the product. The details of full-costing systems are explained in Chapters 3 through 7.

The advantage of variable costing is that it meets the three objectives of management control systems by showing separately those costs that can be traced to, and controlled by, each profit center. In this section, we see an additional reason for using variable costing. Although income

---

The **contribution by profit center (CPC)** measures *all* costs traceable to, and therefore controllable by, the individual profit centers.

Controllable fixed costs are those fixed costs that the profit center manager can influence in approximately a year or less.

Noncontrollable fixed costs are those that are not controllable within a year's time, usually including facilities-related costs such as depreciation, taxes, and insurance.

Controllable margin is determined by subtracting short-term controllable fixed costs from the contribution margin.

determined using full costing is affected by changes in inventory levels, income using variable costing is not affected. Exhibits 18.10A and B show how using full costing affects income.

Panel 1 in Exhibit 18.10A shows the data used in the illustration, including units produced and sold and costs for two periods. Panel 2 shows both the full- and variable-cost income statements for the first of two periods. Two periods are used to show the differences for both possible cases, increasing or decreasing inventory. In the first period, inventory increases; in the second period, it decreases. Exhibit 18.10B shows the comparison of the two income statements for period 2.

In period 1, inventory increases by 40 units because production of 100 units exceeds sales of 60 units. Inventory decreases by the same amount in period 2. Using full costing, the unit product cost is $30 variable plus $40 fixed, or $70 per unit in both periods. The $70 unit cost is used to calculate the cost of goods sold on the income statements in periods 1 and 2 for full costing. The selling and administrative costs ($5 variable and $1,200 fixed) are deducted after gross margin to determine the income of $300 in period 1 and $2,300 in period 2.

The variable-costing income statement uses only variable cost to determine product cost. The cost of sales and inventory figures are determined using a variable manufacturing cost of $30 per unit. To calculate the total contribution margin, the variable selling and administrative

EXHIBIT 18.10A

Comparison of Full and Variable Costing–Period 1

Panel 1 Data Summary	Period 1	Period 2	
Units			
Beginning inventory	0	40	
Price	$100	$100	
Sold	60	140	
Produced	100	100	
Unit variable costs			
Manufacturing	$30	$30	
Selling and administrative costs	$5	$5	
Fixed costs			Per unit
Manufacturing	$4,000	$4,000	$40
Selling and administrative costs	$1,200	$1,200	

Panel 2				
Period 1 Income Statement	**Full Costing**		**Variable Costing**	
Sales (60 × $100)		$6,000		$ 6,000
Less: Cost of goods sold				
Beginning inventory	$ 0		$ 0	
+ Cost of goods produced	7,000		3,000	
	(= 100 × $70)		(= 100 × $30)	
= Cost of goods available for sale	7,000		3,000	
− Ending inventory ($1,600 difference)	2,800		1,200	
	(= 40 × $70)		(= 40 × $30)	
= Cost of goods sold		4,200		1,800
Less: Variable selling and administrative costs		N/A		300
Gross margin		**$1,800**		
Contribution margin				**$ 3,900**
Less: Fixed manufacturing costs	N/A		$4,000	
Less: Selling and administrative costs				
Variable	$ 300		N/A	
Fixed	1,200		1,200	
Total other costs		1,500		5,200
Operating income ($1,600 difference)		$ 300		$(1,300)
Recap				
Difference in income = $300 − $(1,300) = $1,600				
Difference in ending inventory = $2,800 − $1,200 = $1,600 (or 40 units × $40/unit = $1,600)				

N/A = not applicable.

EXHIBIT 18.10B

Comparison of Full and Variable Costing–Period 2

Period 2 Income Statement			
Sales (140 × $100)		$14,000	$14,000
Less: Cost of goods sold			
Beginning inventory ($1,600 difference)	$2,800		$1,200
+ Cost of goods produced (for 100 units, same as period 1)	7,000		3,000
= Cost of goods available for sale	9,800		4,200
− Ending inventory	0		0
= Cost of goods sold		9,800	4,200
Less: Variable selling and administrative		N/A	700
Gross margin		**$ 4,200**	
Contribution margin			**$ 9,100**
Less: Fixed manufacturing costs	N/A		$4,000
Less: Selling and administrative costs			
Variable	$ 700		N/A
Fixed	1,200		1,200
Total other costs		1,900	5,200
Operating income ($1,600 difference)		$ 2,300	$ 3,900
Recap			
Difference in income = $3,900 − $2,300 = $1,600			
Difference in beginning inventory = $2,800 − $1,200 = $1,600			

costs of $5 per unit sold are deducted along with the $30 variable cost of sales per unit. The result is a total contribution margin of $3,900 in period 1 and $9,100 in period 2. In variable costing, all fixed costs (both manufacturing fixed cost of $4,000 and selling and administration fixed costs of $1,200) are deducted from the contribution margin, to get a $1,300 loss in period 1 and $3,900 income in period 2.

The difference in income in period 1 for full and variable costing is $1,600 ($300 income compared to a $1,300 loss), which is exactly the amount of fixed cost put into the increase in inventory under full costing ($1,600 = 40 units × $40 per unit fixed cost). Note that the amount of ending inventory in period 1 differs by $1,600 ($2,800 for full cost versus $1,200 for variable costing). This amount is also the difference in income for variable and full costing for both periods 1 and 2, when inventory decreases by 40 units. Note the shaded areas in Exhibit 18.10 which show the difference of $1,600 in operating income for each period is due to the difference in the value of inventory (ending inventory for period 1 and beginning inventory for period 2, since the two periods start and end with no inventory). A useful guide then is that *full-costing income exceeds variable-costing income (by the amount of fixed cost in the inventory change) when inventory increases, and variable-costing income is higher than full-costing income when inventory decreases.*

The important point is that variable costing is not affected by the change in inventory because all fixed costs are deducted from income in the period in which they occur; fixed costs are not included in inventory so that inventory changes do not affect income. For this reason, variable-costing income can be considered a more reliable measure and is preferable for use in strategic performance measurement. When full costing is used (as is required for financial reporting), the management accountant must use special caution in interpreting the amount of income and attempt to determine what portion of income, if any, might be due to inventory changes. This is especially important if income is used as a basis for performance evaluation, as it is in profit centers. A survey of senior financial executives showed that a majority (76 percent) use full costing for both financial reporting and for internal purpose such as performance evaluation and decision making; the remaining 24 percent used variable costing for internal purposes.[7]

[7] Ashish Garg, Debashis Ghosh, James Hudick, and Chuen Nowacki, "Roles and Practices in Management Accounting Today," *Strategic Finance,* July 2003, pp. 31–35.

The Contribution Income Statement and Value Streams

In applications of lean accounting, products and services are grouped in families called *value streams*. The value-stream income statement shows the contribution of each of the organization's value streams in much the same way as the contribution income statement illustrated in Exhibit 18.9; each value stream is a profit center. Moreover, a unique feature of the value-stream income statement is that it shows separately the increase or decrease in profit due to a change in inventory; in effect, the value-stream income statement adjusts the full-cost income statement to contribution-based variable costing. The ability to see the inventory effect as a separate item on the income statement provides significant additional information for managers, one of the contributions of value streams in lean accounting.[8]

Strategic Performance Measurement and the Balanced Scorecard

LEARNING OBJECTIVE 5

Explain the role of the balanced scorecard in strategic performance measurement.

The sacred obligation of senior leadership:
Vision: What will it be?
Goals: What four or five things must we do to get there?
Alignment: Translate the work of each person into an alignment with the goals.

Soichiro Honda, Founder of Honda Motor Company

Cost, revenue, and profit centers are widely used methods to achieve strategic performance measurement. A common characteristic of these SBUs in practice is that they use little or no nonfinancial information. However, a complete strategic performance evaluation necessarily attends to all critical success factors of the business, including many nonfinancial factors. A useful approach for a complete strategic performance evaluation is to include both financial and nonfinancial factors for the SBU using the balanced scorecard. The balanced scorecard measures the SBU's performance in four key perspectives: (1) customer satisfaction, (2) financial performance, (3) internal business processes, and (4) learning and innovation. Cost, revenue, and profit centers focus on the financial dimension. The main concept of the balanced scorecard is that no single measure can properly evaluate the SBU's progress to strategic success. Rather, multiple measures typically grouped in the four key perspectives provide the desired comprehensive evaluation of the SBU's performance. Moreover, by attending directly to the firm's critical success factors, the balanced scorecard effectively aligns the performance measurement/evaluation process to the firm's strategy.

Implementing the Balanced Scorecard and the Strategy Map for Performance Evaluation

Several issues are of concern in effectively implementing the BSC and strategy map for performance evaluation.

- The BSC and strategy map are more likely to be used in an evaluation of performance over time rather than for performance of a SBU relative to other SBUs. The reason is that the scorecard measures for one unit may not be appropriate for another and, therefore, it is difficult to compare them.

- Many studies have shown that the BSC is widely used for strategic planning and often also for performance evaluation, but less often in management compensation. To effectively tie performance to strategic objectives, the BSC should be tied to management compensation.

- The successful implementation of a balanced scorecard requires the validation of the links between measures that are assumed to improve performance throughout the scorecard. Without validation, the company cannot be sure that attention to the measures will produce the desired results. Validation involves using a causal model to test the effects of

[8] For more information on the value-stream income statement see Frances A. Kennedy and Peter C. Brewer, "Lean Accounting: What's It All About," *Strategic Finance*, November 2005, pp. 27–34, and Statement on Management Accounting, "Accounting for the Lean Enterprise: Major Changes to the Accounting Paradigm" (www.imanet.org/publications_statements.asp).

the measures on desired performance. In one study, 23 percent of the firms participating used the causal model approach to validate the links in the scorecard, and these companies had on the average 2.95 percent higher return on assets and 5.14 percent higher return on equity than the other companies in the study.[9]

- Managers must be provided information on the strategic linkages in the scorecard. One study has shown that those evaluating the performance of a business relied more on the strategically linked measures than other measures when they were provided information on the strategically relevant measures. In contrast, the nonstrategically linked measures were most commonly used when the strategic linkage information was not provided.[10]

- Many large firms have installed extensive computer systems called *enterprise resource planning* systems (ERPs). They provide an information system base that stores the detailed information for the balanced scorecard. Firms without an ERP might have difficulty developing and maintaining the data needed for the scorecard.

- In contrast to financial data that are subject to financial audit and control systems, much of the nonfinancial information used in the scorecard is not subject to control or audit. Thus, the reliability and accuracy of some of the nonfinancial data could be questionable.

- The performance reviews of managers occur at regular intervals—usually every quarter or every year—which fits well with the typical firm's preparation of financial information quarterly and annually. In contrast, the nonfinancial information is often prepared on a weekly or daily basis for effective use in operations and decision making. This variance in preparation cycles can complicate the nature and timing of reviews.

- Typically, all financial data used by the cost or profit SBUs are developed internally, using well-developed information systems. In contrast, some of the most valuable nonfinancial information, such as customer surveys, are developed external to the firm, which creates additional issues regarding the timeliness and the reliability of this nonfinancial information.

Implementing Strategy Using the BSC: Six Steps to Maximize the Value of Nonfinancial Measures

In 2004, Deloitte & Touche, in collaboration with *The Economist,* surveyed 250 executives and board members of large companies in North America, Europe, and Asia.[11] The findings were that many executives (73%) felt that their companies were under increasing pressure to measure and report nonfinancial indicators, including customer satisfaction, innovation, sustainability, and employee commitment. However, while 86 percent said their companies are good to excellent at measuring financial performance, only 34 percent responded favorably about measuring nonfinancial performance. Ittner and Larcker, writing a year earlier, found similar results, which they explained as failed implementation due to:

- Not linking the nonfinancial measures to strategy.
- Not validating the assumptions behind the links of performance measures to desired outcomes.
- Setting the wrong performance targets.
- Measuring the results incorrectly.

To address the need for more effective implementation of nonfinancial measures, Ittner and Larcker suggest the following six steps.

1. **Develop a causal model** to show the links of measures to performance and desired outcomes.

---

[9] Christopher D. Ittner and David F. Larcker, "Coming up Short on Nonfinancial Performance Measures," *Harvard Business Review,* November 2003, pp. 88–95.

[10] Rajiv D. Banker, Hsihui Chang, and Mina J. Pizzini, "The Balanced Scorecard: Judgmental Effects of Performance Measures Linked to Strategy," *The Accounting Review,* January 2004, pp. 1–23.

[11] Based on information from the Deloitte & Touche 2004 survey (in collaboration with *The Economist*), "In the Dark: What Boards and Executives Don't Know about the Health of Their Businesses." See also Christopher D. Ittner and David F. Larcker, "Coming Up Short on Nonfinancial Performance Measurement," *Harvard Business Review,* November 2003, pp. 88–95.

2. **Gather data** to find out who maintains the nonfinancial data in the firm, with the objective of improving the consistency and accuracy and accessibility of the data to decision makers.

3. **Turn the data into Information** by using regression analysis and other statistical tools, including forecasting and other analytical tools, to test the validity of the model developed in part 1 above.

4. **Continually refine the model** by monitoring internal and external events and by rebuilding the model on a timely basis.

5. **Base actions on findings.** Have the confidence in the model to follow where it leads.

6. **Assess outcomes.** Continuously assess the effectiveness of the model and of the actions taken in step 5 to produce the desired outcomes; does the model work?

Management Control in Service Firms and Not-for-Profit Organizations

LEARNING OBJECTIVE 6

Explain the role of strategic performance measurement in service firms and not-for-profit organizations.

Management control in service firms and not-for-profit organizations is commonly implemented in the form of a cost center or a profit center. As do manufacturing and retail firms, these organizations choose a cost center when the manager's critical mission is to control costs; a profit center is preferred when the department manager must manage both costs and revenues or, alternatively (in a not-for-profit organization), manage costs without exceeding budgeted revenues.

The most common type of SBU in service firms and not-for-profit organizations is the cost center. For example, the performance of a bank's consumer loan department often is monitored as a cost center, as illustrated in Exhibit 18.11. Note that the structure of the performance report is much like that of the profit center analysis in Exhibit 18.9. The difference is that the focus in Exhibit 18.11 is on costs, which are separated into variable costs such as labor and supplies, controllable fixed costs such as supervision salaries, and noncontrollable fixed costs such as data processing and facilities management. In addition, Exhibit 18.11 includes information regarding certain operating measures critical to the department's success: the number of new accounts, number of closed accounts, number of transactions processed, and number of inquiries handled. This information is used to evaluate the department's performance over time and perhaps to compare its performance to that of related departments such as the mortgage loan department. Note that the report does not include the cost of funds provided for the loans since it is assumed that the department manager cannot control either the supply or the cost of those funds.

EXHIBIT 18.11

Performance Report for the Consumer Loan Department

Variable costs	
Direct labor	$23,446
Supplies	3,836
Controllable fixed costs	
Supervision salaries	15,339
Advertising	6,500
Fees and services	4,226
Other	766
Noncontrollable fixed costs	
Facilities	650
Data processing	2,200
Other	899
Total costs	$57,862
Operating performance	
Number of accounts at end of month	1,334
Number of new accounts	54
Number of closed accounts	22
Number of transactions processed	1,994
Number of inquiries processed	334

Is the Use of Scorecards in Performance Measurement Systems Largely Confined to the U.S.? Recent Survey Evidence Suggests Not

A recent survey of companies from 44 countries around the globe provides evidence of the widespread use of scorecard systems. While initially developed and implemented as a North American strategic tool, the balanced scorecard and other scorecarding systems are now being used around the world. As the table below shows, of the 382 respondents to a recent survey, more than half use scorecarding systems, with the highest rate of usage among South American respondents and the lowest rate among European respondents.

The five most-cited reasons for implementing a scorecarding system, in order of frequency, are: (1) need to track progress toward achieving organizational goals; (2) need to align employee behavior with an organization's strategic objectives; (3) need to communicate strategy to everyone in a clear and simple manner; (4) need to measure performance at different levels in an organization; and (5) ability to measure people, projects, and strategies.

Use of Scorecarding Systems by Region

Region	Total Respondents	Percentage Using Scorecarding System
Africa (primarily South Africa)	19	68%
Asia (including the Middle East)	62	50
Europe	137	39
U.S. and Canada	135	55
South and Central America	28	79
Total	382	51

Source: R. Lawson, W. Stratton, and T. Hatch, "Scorecarding Goes Global: Companies around the World Are Deriving Benefits from Performance Management Tools," *Strategic Finance,* March 2008, pp. 35–41.

Summary

The principal focus of management control systems is strategic performance measurement. The goal of top management in using strategic performance measurement is to *motivate the managers* to provide a high level of effort, to *guide them to make decisions that are congruent with the goals of top management,* and to provide a basis for determining *fair compensation for the managers.*

A large number of management control systems are used in practice, including both formal and informal systems and individual or team-based systems. The chapter focuses on one type of formal control system at the individual level, the strategic performance measurement system.

Strategic performance measurement systems are implemented in four different forms, depending on the nature of the manager's responsibilities: the revenue center, cost center, profit center, and investment center.

The four types of SBUs are employed in manufacturing firms as well as service firms, not-for-profit, and governmental organizations. Typical cost centers in manufacturing firms are production and production-support departments. Cost centers often are evaluated as either engineered-cost centers or discretionary-cost centers. Discretionary-cost centers focus on planning desired cost levels; the engineered-cost centers focus on evaluation of achieved cost levels.

The marketing and sales departments may be evaluated as revenue centers or cost centers. As a revenue center, these departments have the goal of sales growth; as a cost center, there are goals for managing order-getting and order-filling costs.

The profit center is used when the manager is responsible for both costs and revenues and when coordination between the marketing and production areas is needed: for example, in handling special orders or rush orders. Evaluation on profit provides the incentive for the departments to work together. Profit centers are also used to set a desirable competitive tone. All departments have the profit incentive to compete with other providers of the product or service, inside or outside the firm. The contribution income statement is an effective method for evaluating profit centers because it identifies each profit center's controllable costs.

The contribution income statement is used for profit centers. It has the benefit of not being affected by changes in finished goods inventory. In contrast, income as determined by the conventional income statement based on full costing is affected by inventory changes.

A key issue in the effective use of strategic performance measurement systems is the integration of strategic considerations into the evaluation. This requires an identification of the firm's critical success factors, and use of appropriate measurement and reporting of these factors, commonly in the form of a balanced scorecard. In many cases, a substantial portion of these factors is nonfinancial, including operating and economic data from sources external to the firm.

Key Terms

budget slack, *809*

contribution by profit center (CPC), *816*

contribution income statement, *815*

controllable fixed costs, *816*

controllable margin, *816*

cost center, *807*

decentralized, *807*

discretionary-cost method, *810*

dual allocation, *813*

employment contract, *803*

engineered-cost method, *810*

investment center, *808*

management control, *801*

noncontrollable fixed costs, *816*

operational control, *801*

order-filling costs, *814*

order-getting costs, *813*

performance measurement, *801*

principal-agent model, *803*

profit center, *807*

revenue center, *807*

revenue drivers, *813*

strategic business unit (SBU), *802*

strategic performance measurement, *806*

Comments on Cost Management in Action

Outsourcing Information Technology

In a recent survey of CFOs, 57 percent reported that their firms were outsourcing a portion or all of their information technology (IT) needs. The motivation for outsourcing IT is twofold. First, it can help to dramatically reduce the firm's overall cost of IT. Second, and perhaps most important, it helps the firm to keep up with advancing technology by partnering with an application service provider or consulting firm with a high level of expertise.

How does IT make the firm more competitive? Consultants and analysts disagree on this point. Some argue that IT is a strategic resource in most industries and should be supported within the firm to achieve the desired integration of IT and business strategy. They point to Wal-Mart that has used IT to improve its strategic goal of low cost and low price. Similarly, ADP, Inc., and Levi Strauss have used IT to improve their competitive position through enhancements in customer service.

Others argue that the question is not *whether* to outsource but *which* of the IT activities to choose to outsource and *where* to outsource. For example, Xerox has an outsourcing arrangement with Electronic Data Systems (EDS) to handle its operational IT tasks while it maintains a partnership with the software developer Oracle to develop Xerox's strategic goals for IT. Also, IT outsourcing has gone global. Software engineers and database managers in India and the Philippines are less costly than in other areas of the world.

N. Venkatraman, a leading author on IT outsourcing, argues that IT should be viewed as a strategic SBU in either a cost, profit, investment, or service form (for Venkatraman, a "service" SBU puts customer service as top priority). Venkatraman proposes a simple formula for choosing the type of SBU based on two factors: (1) the degree to which the firm needs either operational efficiency or business capability from IT and (2) the degree of risk the firm is willing to bear. A low-risk firm that requires operational efficiency should choose the cost center; a low-risk firm that requires business capability should use a service provider. In contrast, a firm willing to accept risk and requiring business capability should choose an investment center because it will provide the desired long-term perspective for IT.

Sources: Based on "Outsourcing Comes of Age: The Rise of Collaborative Partnering," PricewaterhouseCoopers, 2007; Pete Engardio and Arlene Weintraub, "Outsourcing the Drug Industry," *BusinessWeek,* September 15, 2008, pp. 49–50; "In a Pinch: How the Financial Crisis Will Affect the Outsourcing Industry," *The Economist,* October 11, 2008, p. 86; Sarah Johnson, "Nobody Doesn't Like Outsourcing," *CFO.com,* December 11, 2008. N. Venkatraman, "Beyond Outsourcing: Managing IT Resources as a Value Center," *Sloan Management Review,* Spring 1997, pp. 51–64; Pete Engardio, Aaron Bernstein, and Manjeet Kripalani, "Is Your Job Next," *BusinessWeek,* February 3, 2003, pp. 48–60; "Beyond Blue," *BusinessWeek,* April 18, 2005, pp. 68–76. For further information view the Outsourcing Institute's Web site at http://outsourcing.com/.

Self-Study Problem

(For solution, please turn to the end of the chapter.)

Discretionary-Cost and Engineered-Cost Methods

C. B. (Chuck) Davis is the manager of the claims processing department for Liberty Life Insurance Co. He has 12 clerks working for him to process approximately 900 claims per month. Each clerk earns a monthly salary of $2,400, including benefits. The number of claims varies somewhat, and, in recent years, it has been as low as 810 and as high as 1,020 per month. Chuck has argued with Liberty officials that his 12 clerks are not enough to handle 1,000 or more claims; he knows from a recent study of his department that it takes a well-trained clerk an average of 121 minutes to process a claim (processing time also varies widely, from as little as a few minutes to as much as several hours, depending on the claim's complexity). While Liberty management agrees that 12 clerks are not sufficient for a month with 1,000 claims, it notes that most months require that only 800 claims be processed. Management concludes, therefore, that 12 clerks are about right. Assume that each clerk works an eight-hour day except for 40 minutes of break time and that each month has an average of 22 working days. In the most recent month, January, the department processed 915 claims.

Required

1. What type of SBU does Liberty management appear to use for the claims processing department?

2. Assuming that Liberty uses the discretionary-cost method to implement cost centers, what is the budgeted cost in the claims department for January?

3. Assuming that Liberty uses the engineered-cost method to implement cost centers, what is the budgeted cost in the claims department for January?

4. If you were Chuck Davis, what would you use as a more effective argument to top management in requesting additional clerks?

Questions

18-1 What is the difference between management control, performance evaluation, and operational control?

18-2 What is strategic performance measurement, and why is it important for effective management?

18-3 Does an effective performance evaluation focus on individual or team performance?

18-4 Explain the difference between informal and formal control systems. What type of control system is strategic performance measurement?

18-5 Name two types of organizational design and explain how they differ.

18-6 What are four types of SBUs, and what are the goals of each?

18-7 Since full costing is accepted for financial reporting purposes and variable costing is not, why should we be concerned about the difference between them? What is the difference, and why is it important?

18-8 What are some important behavioral and implementation issues in strategic performance measurement? How does the management accountant deal with these issues?

18-9 What is the role of cost allocation in strategic performance measurement?

18-10 Can strategic performance measurement be used for service firms and not-for-profit organizations? How?

18-11 In what situations is a cost center most appropriate? A profit center? A revenue center?

18-12 How do centralized and decentralized firms differ? What are the advantages of each?

18-13 Can the marketing department be both a revenue center and a cost center? Explain.

Brief Exercises

18-14 Which type of cost center has a planning focus, and which type has an evaluation focus?

18-15 What is the role of risk preference in performance evaluation?

18-16 Pepper's Automotive produces auto parts for various automotive retailers. Peppers is evaluating the exhaust system division of the company and has come up with the following data for the year: net revenues are $1,000,000, variable costs are $300,000, and fixed costs are $400,000. Of the fixed costs, controllable fixed costs are $100,000 and noncontrollable fixed costs are $300,000. What is the controllable margin and total contribution by profit center (CPC)?

18-17 Pepper's Automotive has further analyzed the exhaust division into three products, exhaust pipes, intake valves, and intake pipes. The income statement is available below. What is the change in profit in both the short run and long run by dropping intake valves from their product line?

	Exhaust Pipes	Intake Valves	Intake Pipes
Net revenues	$500,000	$300,000	$200,000
Variable costs	50,000	150,000	100,000
Contribution margin	450,000	150,000	100,000
Controllable fixed costs	50,000	50,000	0
Controllable margin	400,000	100,000	100,000
Noncontrollable fixed costs	100,000	150,000	50,000
Contribution by profit center	$300,000	$ (50,000)	$ 50,000

18-18 Meargia Plastics is evaluating its plastic bottles division. The accounting manager has come up with the following data for the year: contribution margin of $500,000, controllable fixed costs of $200,000, and noncontrollable fixed costs of $50,000. What is the controllable margin and total contribution by profit center?

18-19 Explain the difference between the engineered-cost and discretionary-cost approaches to evaluating support departments.

18-20 Manuel Inc. produces textiles in many different forms. After recording lower than anticipated profits last year, Manuel has decided to shut down one of its divisions that is not performing well. The accounting manager has compiled the following data on the two divisions being considered for closing and asked you to evaluate the short-term and long-term effects on profits of closing each division. Which division should be closed and why?

	Winter Outerwear	High End Suits
Net revenues	$1,000,000	$5,000,000
Variable costs	500,000	2,000,000
Contribution margin	500,000	3,000,000
Controllable fixed costs	0	2,000,000
Controllable margin	500,000	1,000,000
Noncontrollable fixed costs	750,000	1,500,000
Contribution by SBU	$ (250,000)	$ (500,000)

18-21 Calabria Healthcare supplies prescription drugs to pharmacies. As the management accountant, you are required to analyze the financial statements for this quarter. You already have analyzed the company's two divisions, Name Brand and Generic, and your supervisor wants an analysis of the comparable profitability of the SBUs. The contribution margins are $500,000 and $200,000, respectively; the controllable fixed costs are $200,000 and $50,000; and the noncontrollable fixed costs are $50,000 and $100,000. What are the total contributions by profit center (CPC) for these divisions and operating income for the company? Assume there are no untraceable fixed costs.

18-22 Phelps Glass Inc. has reported the following financial data: net revenues of $10 million, variable costs of $5 million, controllable fixed costs of $2 million, noncontrollable fixed costs of $1 million, and untraceable costs of $500,000. The accounting manager has supplied you with this data and asked you to come up with the controllable margin, total contribution, CPC, and operating income.

Exercises

18-23 **Departmental Cost Allocation in Profit centers**   Elvis Wilbur owns two restaurants, the Beef Barn and the Fish Bowl. Each restaurant is treated as a profit center for performance evaluation. Although the restaurants have separate kitchens, they share a central baking facility. The principal costs of the baking area include depreciation and maintenance on the equipment, materials, supplies, and labor.

Required

1. Elvis allocates the monthly costs of the baking facility to the two restaurants based on the number of tables served in each restaurant during the month. In April the costs were $24,000, of which $12,000 is fixed cost. The Beef Barn and the Fish Bowl each served 3,000 tables. How much of the joint cost should be allocated to each restaurant?

2. In May total fixed and unit variable costs remained the same, but the Beef Barn served 2,000 tables and the Fish Bowl served 3,000. How much should be allocated to each restaurant? Explain your reasoning.

18-24 **Allocation of Marketing and Administrative Costs; Profit SBUs**   Tilton Academy allocates marketing and administrative costs to its three schools based on total annual tuition revenue for the schools. In 2009 the allocations (000s omitted) were as follows:

	Lower School	Middle School	Upper School	Total
Tuition revenue	$1,500	$500	$2,000	$4,000
Marketing and administration	375	125	500	$1,000

In 2010, the middle and upper schools experienced no change in revenues, but the lower school's tuition revenue increased to $1.9 million. Marketing and administrative costs rose to $1,250,000.

Required

1. Using revenue as an allocation base, how should the costs be allocated for 2010?
2. What are the shortcomings of this allocation formula?

18-25 **Allocation of Administrative Costs**   Wical Rental Management Services manages four apartment buildings, each with a different owner. Wical's top management has observed that the apartment buildings with more expensive rental rates tend to require more of her time and also the time of her staff. The four apartment buildings incur a total monthly operating expense of $7,345,733, and these operating expenses are traced directly to the apartments buildings for the purpose of determining the profit earned by the building owners. The management fee that Wical earns is based on a percentage of total operating expenses and is negotiated each year. For the current year the fee rate is 6 percent, and Wical has the following information for the month of November, including average rental rates and occupancy rates.

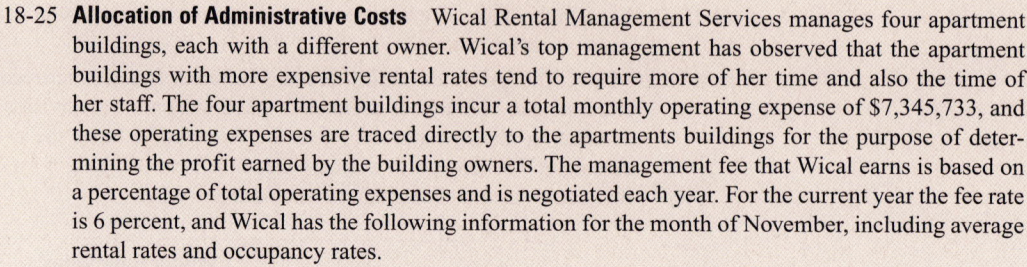

Apartment Complex	Number of Units	Average Occupancy	Average Rent
Cape Point	100	88.0%	$1,895
Whispering Woods	250	77.0	1,295
Hanging Rock	200	72.0	995
College Manor	350	82.0	895
Total	900		

Required

1. Assuming November is a representative month for the year, how should the annual management fee be allocated to the four apartment buildings? Explain your choice of method and show how much of the management fee would be allocated to each apartment building using your method.
2. What ethical issues, if any, are involved in the choice of method in part 1 above?

18-26 **Responsibility for Inefficiency; Ethics**   General Hospital leases its diagnostic equipment from Normed Leasing, which is also responsible for maintaining the equipment. Recently the hospital's MRI machine needed repair and physicians were required to order expensive nonemergency laboratory tests for their patients to diagnose conditions that could have been diagnosed more easily (and less expensively) using the MRI machine. Rather than bill its patients for the entire costs of these tests, the hospital billed the patients for the cost of an MRI and billed the difference to Normed. Normed disputes the charge, claiming that the physicians should have postponed diagnosis of the patients' conditions until the MRI machine could be repaired.

Required   What issues should be addressed to determine how the charge should be handled properly? How can this situation be prevented? If appropriate, include ethical issues in your response.

18-27 **Assigning Responsibility**   Kristen Langdon, the sales manager at a large bicycle manufacturer, has secured an order from a major department store that is due to ship on November 1. She is eager to please the department store in the hope of getting more future business. She asks Bryan Collins, the company's purchasing agent, to procure all necessary parts in time for production to begin on October 10. Bryan orders the parts from reputable suppliers, and most of them arrive by October 7. George Watkins, the production manager, begins production as scheduled on October 10, although the gears that Bryan ordered were delayed because of quality control problems at the manufacturer. Bryan assures George that the gear shipment will arrive before October 16 when those parts are scheduled to be attached to the bicycles. The shipment finally arrives on October 18 after production has been delayed for two days.

Required   Which department should bear the responsibility for the two days' downtime? How can similar problems be avoided in the future?

18-28 **Risk Aversion and Decision Making**   John Smith is the production manager of Elmo's Glue Company. Because of limited capacity, the company can produce only one of two possible products. The two products are:

a. A space-age bonding formula that has a 15 percent probability of making a profit of $1,000,000 for the company and an 85 percent chance of generating $200,000 in profit.
b. A reformulated household glue that has a 100 percent chance of making a profit of $310,000.

John gets a bonus of 20 percent of the profit from his department. John has the responsibility to choose between the two products. Assume John is more risk-averse than the top management of Elmo's Glue Company.

Required

1. Which product will John choose? Why?

2. Is this the product Elmo's would choose? Why or why not? Assume the company is risk-neutral.

3. How can Elmo's change its reward system to have John consistently make decisions which are consistent with top management's wishes?

18-29   **Risk Aversion; Strategy**   John Holt is the production supervisor for ITEXX, a manufacturer of plastic parts with customers in the automobile and consumer products industries. On a Tuesday morning, one of ITEXX's sales managers has just asked John to reschedule his manufacturing jobs for the rest of the week to accommodate a special order from a new customer. The catch is that getting the customer requires fast turn-around on the order and would mean not only delaying the current production schedule, but in addition running the production equipment all three shifts for the remainder of the week. This would make it impossible to complete the regularly scheduled maintenance on the equipment that John had planned for midweek. The sales manager is keen on getting the new customer, which could mean an important increase in overall sales and output at the plant. However, John is worried not only about the delay of the current jobs, but the chance that the delay in maintenance will cause one of the machines to fail, which would back up the orders in the plant for at least a week, meaning a substantial delay for the new order as well as those currently scheduled.

Required   Explain how you think John should resolve this problem. What would be a good policy for handling issues like this in the future?

18-30   **Profit centers: Full and Variable Costing**   Fitzpatrick Inc. planned and manufactured 500,000 units of its single product in 2010, its first year of operations. Variable manufacturing cost were $40 per unit of production. Planned fixed manufacturing costs were $1,200,000. Marketing and administrative costs (all fixed) were $500,000 in 2010. Fitzpatrick sold 450,000 units of products in 2010 at $50 per unit.

Required

1. Determine Fitzpatrick Inc.'s operating income using full costing.

2. Determine Fitzpatrick Inc.'s operating income using variable costing.

3. Explain the difference between the operating incomes in requirements 1 and 2.

18-31   **Centralization versus Decentralization; Health Care**   Doctors Health Care System has integrated health networks in three different regions: northern California, southern Florida, and Oklahoma. These three markets have vast regional differences. Because of the increasing penetration of the U.S. health-care market by managed care companies, Doctors Health Care System must create a system that offers continuity of care across the continuum for a set price in order to remain competitive. Its board of directors set the system's goal as being a leader in developing and maintaining integrated health networks that improve the health status of their communities.

Required   To meet this goal in the three regions, should the health system's management structure be decentralized or centralized? What are the advantages and disadvantages of each option?

18-32   **Cost Allocation; Sharing Cab Fare**   Suppose there are three passengers sharing a single cab ride and that passenger A's usual fare to his destination would be $12, passenger B's usual fare to her destination would be $18, and passenger C's fare would be $30. Since they are sharing the cab, and assuming no surcharge, the total cab fare is $30, rather than the $60 they would have pay in total individually. So there is a $30 saving to sharing the cab.

Required   How would you split up the total cost of the cab fare among A, B, and C?

18-33   **Intangibles; Validating the Balanced Scorecard**   Today intangibles, such as customer relationships, account for more than half of total assets of firms in the United States. The importance of nonfinancial measures is one of the motivations for the increased use of the balanced scorecard, which includes a perspective on customer relationships. However, according to recent research, data on intangibles such as customer satisfaction can yield significant forecasts of earnings only when the data are analyzed in conjunction with financial statistics and only when tied to corporate strategy. This result is based on a wide range of customer relationship data (e.g., customer satisfaction, employee turnover, the speed of loan processing, and the average number of products and services purchased) from 115 retail banks and represents potentially useful guidance for managers wanting to know how to use nonfinancial measures effectively.

Required Comment on the implications of the study for the use of the balanced scorecard. We have noted in the text that it is important to validate the balanced scorecard. What does it mean to validate the scorecard in the context of the retail bank example above?

18-34 **Managing the Research and Development Department** Effective use of research and development (R&D) is an important part of any firm's competitive strategy. Some firms take an "incrementalist" approach to R&D, continually striving to add value to their products and services. Other firms take a quite different approach by looking only for "breakthrough" results from R&D. The breakthrough results are those that fundamentally change the nature of the products, the services, and the competition in the industry. An example of a breakthrough result is General Electric's digital X-ray technology, first sold in 1996, which uses digital imaging to replace the conventional film-based technology. Other examples include Apple's iPhone and Toyota's hybrid vehicles.

Many firms employ both strategies: one R&D department uses the incrementalist approach that focuses on continually improving existing products and another R&D department uses the breakthrough approach that develops fundamental changes. The incrementalist R&D projects help to keep the current product lines competitive while the breakthrough projects hold the promise of a successful future.

Required What type of SBU would you recommend for each of the two types of research and development departments and explain why?

18-35 **Financial Reporting and SBU Performance** Samentech Inc. operates in the highly competitive agribusiness industry. Recently, rising fuel costs have added a significant financial burden to day-to-day operations, and top management has become increasingly concerned about the financial performance of several of its business units. Business unit performance and the performance of the unit managers is evaluated using the financial information in the "Segment Reporting" section of Samentech's annual report. Samentech uses this approach to evaluation because it knows that the information is audited and therefore accurate.

Some key executives have noticed that many business unit leaders seem unwilling to cooperate and coordinate with other business units; difficulties have arisen for example in convincing unit managers to share certain services when the result would be to reduce total costs to the company. A recent example is the failure of the unit managers to agree to share the services of an insurance firm that offered lower rates if all units used the same insurance policy; some unit managers wanted to maintain individual insurance coverage for their units so that they had maximum flexibility in choosing the terms of the coverage.

Moreover, the financial performance of many units and for Samentech overall has been behind industry averages, and the firm's stock price has been declining as well. These issues were largely ignored in recent years because there were "more important issues" at hand. But the pace of decline in stock price has alarmed Frank Ramirez, the CFO of Samentech Inc., who believes that the lackluster performance of many of the business units may be due to inadequacies in the company's performance measurement system.

Required Mr. Ramirez asks you to help him prepare a report for top management in which you

1. Explain why Samentech Inc. should or should not use information from the company's annual financial report to evaluate leaders of business units.
2. Provide a proposed new evaluation plan for business unit leaders.
3. Explain the long-term benefits Samentech Inc. could gain if it adopts a more effective evaluation strategy for its business unit leaders.

18-36 **Financial Incentives and Auto Repair/Inspections Companies** Some states in the United States are finding increased pressure from citizen groups and other organizations to increase efforts to reduce carbon emissions. One of the key producers of carbon emissions is the automobile, so that some states have become more strict in implementing auto inspection procedures that include compliance with emissions standards. The goal is to reduce emissions overall in the vehicles operating in the state. Some environmental groups that support the emissions tests have suggested that the financial incentive for those inspecting vehicles is to be strict with the testing because any failed tests would require some repair that could then be performed by the inspector. However, recent research shows the unexpected—the Environmental Protection Agency (EPA) estimates that approximately 50 percent of inspections for which the vehicle fails to comply with state-level emission standards are allowed to pass the inspection without the repair needed for compliance. In most states, vehicle inspections are performed by auto mechanics, auto dealers, and other companies that repair autos.

Required Develop a brief explanation of the finding that many inspections were not in compliance with state standards. What incentives are necessary to improve the rate of compliance? Are there ethical issues you identify in developing your answer?

Problems

18-37 Allocation of Central Costs; Profit centers Holiday Resorts, Inc. operates four resort hotels in the heavily wooded areas of eastern Texas. The resorts are named after the predominant trees at the resort: Oak Glen, Birch Glen, Mimosa, and Walnut Arbor. Holiday allocates its central office costs to each of the four hotels according to the annual revenue it generated. For the current year, these costs (000s omitted) were as follows:

Front office personnel (desk, clerks, etc.)	$ 6,000
Administrative and executive salaries	4,000
Interest on resort purchase	2,000
Advertising	600
Housekeeping	1,000
Depreciation on reservations computer	80
Room maintenance	800
Carpet-cleaning contract	50
Contract to repaint rooms	400
	$14,930

	Oak Glen	Walnut Arbor	Birch Glen	Mimosa	Total
Revenue (000s)	$ 4,550	$ 8,975	$ 9,678	$ 6,220	$ 29,423
Square feet	65,122	77,375	38,655	82,556	263,708
Rooms	88	125	64	175	452
Assets (000s)	$88,125	$132,775	$68,545	$55,883	$345,328

Required

1. Based on annual revenue, what amount of the central office costs are allocated to each hotel? What are the shortcomings of this allocation method?

2. Suppose that the current method were replaced with a system of four separate cost pools with costs collected in the four pools allocated on the basis of revenues, assets invested in each hotel, square footage, and number of rooms, respectively. Which costs should be collected in each of the four pools?

3. Using the cost pool system in requirement 2, how much of the central office costs would be allocated to each hotel? Is this system preferable to the single-allocation base system used in requirement 1? Why or why not?

18-38 Profit Centers: Comparison of Variable and Full Costing Yale Company manufactures hair brushes that sell at wholesale for $3 per unit. The company had no beginning inventory in 2009. These data summarize the 2009 and 2010 operations:

	2009	2010
Sales	1,800 units	2,200 units
Production:	2,000 units	2,000 units
Production cost		
Factory—variable (per unit)	$0.60	$0.60
—fixed	$1,000	$1,000
Marketing—variable	$.40	$.40
Administrative—fixed	$500	$500

Required   Prepare the following, using a spreadsheet.

1. An income statement for each year based on full costing.

2. An income statement for each year based on variable costing.

3. A reconciliation and explanation of the differences in the operating income resulting from using the full-costing method and variable-costing method.

18-39   Full versus Variable Costing   Jackson Jones Corp. (JJC) is a manufacturer of an electronic control system used in the manufacture of certain special-duty auto transmissions used primarily for police and military applications. The part sells for $45 per unit and had sales of 3,600 units in the current year, 2009. JJC has 400 units available for sale at the end of 2009 and is projecting sales of 4,400 units in 2010. JJC is planning the same production level for 2010 as in 2009, 4,000 units. The variable manufacturing costs for JJC are $16 and the variable selling costs are only $.50 per unit. The fixed manufacturing costs are $100,000 per year and the fixed selling costs are $500 per year.

Required   Prepare the following, using a spreadsheet:

1. An income statement for 2009 and 2010 using full costing.

2. An income statement for 2009 and 2010 using variable costing.

3. A reconciliation and explanation of the difference in the operating income resulting from the full- and variable-costing methods.

18-40   Profit Centers: Comparison of Variable and Full Costing (Underapplied Overhead)   Mark Hancock, Inc. manufactures a specialized surgical instrument called the HAN-20. The firm has grown rapidly in recent years because of the product's low price and high quality. However, sales have declined this year due primarily to increased competition and a decrease in the surgical procedures for which the HAN-20 is used. The firm is concerned about the decline in sales, and has hired a consultant to analyze the firm's profitability. The consultant has provided the following information:

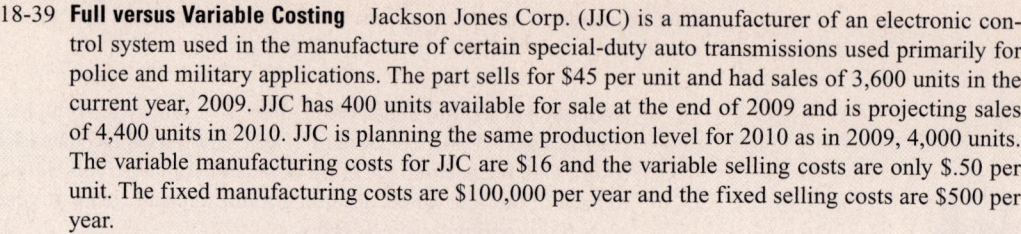

	2009	2010
Sales (units)	3,200	2,800
Production	3,800	2,300
Budgeted production and sales	4,000	3,400
Beginning inventory	800	1,400
Data per unit (all variable)		
Price	$2,095	$1,995
Direct materials and labor	1,200	1,200
Selling costs	125	125
Period cost (all fixed)		
Manufacturing overhead	$700,000	$595,000
Selling and administrative	120,000	120,000

Hancock explained to the consultant that the unfavorable economic climate in 2009 and 2010 had caused the firm to reduce its price and production levels and reduce its fixed manufacturing costs in response to the decline in sales. Even with the price reduction there was a decline in sales in both 2009 and 2010. This led to an increase in inventory in 2009, which the firm was able to reduce in 2010 by further reducing the level of production. In both years Hancock's actual production was less than the budgeted level so that the overhead rate for fixed overhead, calculated from budgeted production levels, was too low and a production volume variance was calculated to adjust cost of goods sold for the underapplied fixed overhead (the calculation of the production-volume variance is explained fully in Chapter 15, and reviewed briefly below).

The production-volume variance for 2009 was determined from the fixed overhead rate of $175 per unit ($700,000/4,000 budgeted units). Since the actual production level was 200 units short of the budgeted level in 2009 (4,000-3,800), the amount of the production-volume variance in 2009 was 200 × $175 = $35,000. The production-volume variance is underapplied (since actual production level is less than budgeted) and is therefore added back to cost of goods sold to determine the amount of cost of goods sold in the full-cost income statement. The full-cost income statement for 2009 is shown below:

Sales		$6,704,000
Cost of goods sold:		
Beginning inventory	$1,100,000	
Cost of goods produced	5,225,000	
Cost of goods available for sale	$6,325,000	
Less ending inventory	1,925,000	
Cost of goods sold:		$4,400,000
Plus underapplied production-volume variance		35,000
Adjusted cost of goods sold		$4,435,000
Gross margin		$2,269,000
Less selling and administrative costs		
Variable	$ 400,000	
Fixed	120,000	520,000
Net income		$1,749,000

Required

1. Using the full-cost method, prepare the income statements for 2010.

2. Using variable costing, prepare an income statement for each period, and explain the difference in income from that obtained in requirement 1.

3. Write a brief memo to the firm to explain the difference in operating income between variable costing and full costing.

18-41 **Full versus Variable Costing** Stultz Manufacturing has the following information for the years ended December 31, 2009, and December 31, 2010:

	2009	2010
Units		
Beginning inventory (units)	400	
Price	$90	$90
Units sold	1,000	1,900
Actual production (units)	1,200	1,500
Budgeted production (units)	1,200	1,500
Unit variable costs		
Manufacturing	$30	$30
Selling and administrative	$5	$5
Fixed costs		
Manufacturing	$24,000	$30,000
Selling and administrative	$10,000	$10,000

Required

1. Prepare the variable-cost and full-cost income statements for 2009 and 2010.

2. Prepare a reconciliation and explanation for the differences between full-cost and variable-cost operating income for both years.

18-42 **Balanced Scorecard**

Required Prepare problem 2-31.

18-43 **Balanced Scorecard**

Required Prepare problem 2-35.

18-44 **Balanced Scorecard**

Required Prepare problem 2-39.

18-45 **Contribution Income Statement for Profit Centers**   Glamour, Inc., is an upscale clothing store in New York City and London. Each store has two main departments, Men's Apparel and Women's Apparel. Marie Phelps, Glamour's CFO, wants to use strategic performance measurement to better understand the company's financial results. She has decided to use the profit centers method to measure performance and has gathered the following information about the two stores and the two departments of the New York City store:

Total net sales	$2,250,000
Fixed costs	
Partly traceable and controllable	200,000
Partly traceable but noncontrollable	160,000
Nontraceable costs	55,000
Total net sales (percent)	
London Store	40%
New York—Men's Apparel	30
New York—Women's Apparel	70
Cost of goods sold—variable (percent of sales)	
London	55%
New York—Men's Apparel	60
New York—Women's Apparel	40
Variable operating costs (percent of sales)	
London	34%
New York—Men's Apparel	24
New York—Women's Apparel	30
Fixed controllable costs—partly traceable (percent of total)	
London	40%
New York total	40
Men's Apparel	45
Women's Apparel	40
Could not be traced to Men's or Women's apparel	15
Could not be traced to New York or London	20
Fixed noncontrollable costs—partly traceable (percent of total)	
London	50%
New York total	40
Men's Apparel	30
Women's Apparel	10
Could not be traced to Men's or Women's apparel	60
Could not be traced to London or New York	10

Required

1. Using this information and a spreadsheet system, prepare a contribution income statement for Glamour, showing contribution margin, controllable margin, and contribution by profit center (CPC) for both the London and New York stores and for both departments of the New York store.

2. What are the global issues that are an important part of the profit center evaluation for Glamour Inc.?

18-46 **Allocating the Costs of the Legal Department**   Most large companies have an in-house legal staff that helps the company deal with current and pending legal matters. Often the legal staff's efforts are assisted by outside counsel, especially when specialized technical issues are involved. The legal department is growing in importance for some firms, as the firms attempt to deal with new government regulations. For management accountants, the regulatory changes have been dramatic, as a result of the Sarbanes-Oxley Act of 2002 which increased the responsibilities of financial managers in publicly held firms. One portion of the act, for example, requires a company to maintain a code of ethics.

Required   Most companies allocate the cost of legal services to their SBUs on the basis of some measure of size, such as the total assets or total revenues of the SBU. What is the likely effect of this allocation approach on the desired motivation and behavior within the SBUs? What approach would you propose for allocating legal costs, and why?

18-47 **Validating the Balanced Scorecard**   Bernard Daisy Inc. is a chain of home supply and gardening product stores. In 2010, Daisy adopted the balanced scorecard (BSC) for evaluation of store and store manager performance. The BSC has helped Daisy to identify the critical success factors for sales and profitability. In particular, it has helped Daisy better understand its competitive environment and the drivers of success in that environment. On the advice of its chief financial officer, Daisy's board has requested the company president to conduct a study to validate the balanced scorecard. The objective of the study is to make sure that the scorecard measures being used are in fact the key measures associated with success. The following data has been obtained for the most recent quarter's results for each of the company's 30 stores, listed in order of when the store was opened (most recent is store 30). There are five district managers, each of which is responsible for six of the stores. In this study a store manager's success is measured by increase in sales of each store for the current quarter over the same quarter last year. The data below include the percentage change in sales and four of the measures included in the customer perspective of the company's BSC. The scorecard measures include:

1. A survey of customers; this measure is taken from a survey form that is handed to customers on a random basis as they leave the store. The customers rate the store's performance on a scale of 0 to 100, where 100 is the highest score.

2. Each district manager evaluates each store once a quarter, using also a scale from 0 to 100, where 100 is the highest score.

3. The district managers have a staff that on a random basis measures the wait time in the check-out line for customers in each store. The figures shown here are the average wait times, in seconds, for the samples taken in the most recent quarter.

4. Average number of store employees who have had one or more of the company's in-house training courses in the past quarter, as a proportion of total employees at the store.

Required   Use regression and correlation analysis in Excel to analyze the validity of the four scorecard measures in the customer perspective of the BSC; here validity means that the BSC measure contributes to an increase in sales over the prior quarter. What conclusions can you draw from your analysis?

Store Number	Sales	Survey	Manager Review	Average Wait Time	Employee Training
1	−18.1%	65	33	95	56
2	−13.3%	54	54	92	30
3	0.5%	72	86	81	45
4	−9.8%	50	94	89	60
5	−4.5%	53	40	85	75
6	0.0%	57	86	81	50
7	7.5%	61	80	75	45
8	15.5%	67	74	69	88
9	20.6%	70	70	80	90
10	31.5%	79	61	71	60
11	35.0%	81	88	68	30
12	12.5%	64	76	80	18
13	−2.6%	54	38	83	33
14	3.5%	59	27	78	48
15	20.6%	71	70	65	63
16	7.8%	62	80	75	78
17	14.5%	66	43	69	93
18	20.0%	71	70	65	55
19	29.4%	77	63	58	39
20	39.4%	84	55	50	67
21	45.7%	88	49	59	34
22	59.4%	84	87	49	78
23	63.8%	89	56	45	48
24	35.6%	81	58	62	36
25	5.2%	60	82	77	51
26	11.8%	64	77	72	66
27	30.7%	77	62	57	81
28	7.8%	77	73	68	96
29	15.1%	73	67	62	57
30	24.8%	77	62	57	36

18-48 **Contribution Income Statement for Profit Centers; Strategy, International**   Stratford Corporation is a diversified company whose products are marketed both domestically and internationally. Its major product lines are pharmaceutical products, sports equipment, and household appliances. At a recent meeting, Stratford's board of directors had a lengthy discussion on ways to improve overall corporate profitability without new acquisitions. New acquisitions are problematic because the company already has a lot of debt. The board members decided that they needed additional financial information about individual corporate operations to target areas for improvement. Dave Murphy, Stratford's controller, has been asked to provide additional data to assist the board in its investigation. Stratford is not a public company and, therefore, has not prepared complete income statements by product line. Dave has regularly prepared an income statement by product line through contribution margin. However, he now believes that income statements prepared through operating income along both product lines and geographic areas would provide the directors with the required insight into corporate operations. Dave has the following data available:

| | Product Lines | | | |
	Pharmaceutical	Sports	Appliances	Total
Production/Sales in units	160,000	180,000	160,000	500,000
Average selling price per unit	$8.00	$20.00	$15.00	
Average variable manufacturing cost per unit	4.00	9.50	8.25	
Average variable selling expense per unit	2.00	2.50	2.25	
Fixed factory overhead excluding depreciation				$500,000
Depreciation of plant and equipment				400,000
Administrative and selling expense				1,160,000

Dave had several discussions with the division managers from each product line and compiled this information:

- The division managers concluded that Dave should allocate fixed factory overhead on the basis of the ratio of the variable costs per product line or per geographic area to total variable costs.

- Each division manager agreed that a reasonable basis for the allocation of depreciation on plant and equipment would be the ratio of units produced per product line or per geographic area to the total number of units produced.

- There was little agreement on the allocation of administrative and selling expenses, so Dave decided to allocate only those expenses that were directly traceable to the SBU that is, manufacturing staff salaries to product lines and sales staff salaries to geographic areas. He used these data for this allocation:

Manufacturing Staff		**Sales Staff**	
Pharmaceutical	$120,000	United States	$ 60,000
Sports	140,000	Canada	100,000
Appliances	80,000	Europe	250,000

- The division managers provided reliable sales percentages for their product lines by geographic area:

| | Percentage of Unit Sales | | |
	United States	Canada	Europe
Pharmaceutical	40%	10%	50%
Sports	40	40	20
Appliances	20	20	60

Dave prepared this product-line income statement:

STRATFORD CORPORATION
Statement of Income by Product Lines
For the Fiscal Year Ended April 30, 2010

	Product Lines				
	Pharmaceutical	Sports	Appliances	Unallocated	Total
Sales in units	160,000	180,000	160,000		500,000
Sales	$1,280,000	$3,600,000	$2,400,000	—	$7,280,000
Variable manufacturing and selling costs	960,000	2,160,000	1,680,000	—	4,800,000
Contribution margin	$ 320,000	$1,440,000	$ 720,000	—	$2,480,000
Fixed costs					
Fixed factory overhead	$ 100,000	$ 225,000	$ 175,000	—	$500,000
Depreciation	128,000	144,000	128,000	—	400,000
Administrative and selling expense	120,000	140,000	80,000	$ 820,000	1,160,000
Total fixed costs	$ 348,000	$ 509,000	$ 383,000	$ 820,000	$2,060,000
Operating income (loss)	$ (28,000)	$ 931,000	$ 337,000	$(820,000)	$ 420,000

Required

1. Prepare a contribution income statement for Stratford Corporation based on the company's geographic areas of sales.

2. As a result of the information disclosed by both income statements (by product line and by geographic area), recommend areas on which Stratford Corporation should focus its attention to improve corporate profitability.

3. What changes would you make to Stratford's strategic performance measurement system? Include the role, if any, of the firm's international business operations in your response.

(CMA Adapted)

18-49   **Centralization versus Decentralization: Banking**   RNB is a bank holding company for a statewide group of retail consumer-oriented banks. RNB was formed in the early 1960s by investors who believed in a high level of consumer services. The number of banks owned by the holding company expanded rapidly. These banks gained visibility because of their experimentation with innovations such as free-standing 24-hour automated teller machines, automated funds transfer systems, and other advances in banking services.

RNB's earnings performance has been better than that of most other banks in the state. The founders organized RNB and continue to operate it on a highly decentralized basis. As the number of banks owned has increased, RNB's executive management has delegated more responsibility and authority to individual bank presidents, who are considered to be representatives of executive management. Although certain aspects of each bank's operations are standardized (such as procedures for account and loan applications and salary rates), bank presidents have significant autonomy in determining how each bank will operate.

The decentralization has led each bank to develop individual marketing campaigns. Several of them have introduced unique "packaged" accounts that include a combination of banking services; however, they sometimes fail to notify the other banks in the group as well as the executive office of these campaigns. One result has been interbank competition for customers where the market overlaps. The corporate marketing officer had also recently begun a statewide advertising campaign that conflicted with some of the individual banks' advertising. Consequently, customers and tellers have occasionally experienced both confusion and frustration, particularly when the customers attempt to receive services at a bank other than their "home" bank.

RNB's executive management is concerned that earnings will decline for the first time in its history. The decline appears to be attributable to reduced customer satisfaction and higher operating costs. The competition among the banks in the state is keen. Bank location and consistent high-quality customer service are important. RNB's 18 banks are well located, and the three new bank acquisitions planned for next year are considered to be in prime locations. The increase in operating costs appears to be directly related to the individual banks' aggressive marketing efforts and new programs. Specifically, expenditures increased for advertising and for the special materials and added personnel related to the "packaged" accounts.

For the past three months RNB's executive management has been meeting with the individual bank presidents to review RNB's recent performance and seek ways to improve it. One recommendation that appeals to executive management is to make the organization's structure more centralized. The specific proposal calls for reducing individual bank autonomy and creating a centralized individual bank management committee of all bank presidents to be chaired by a newly created position, vice president of bank operations. The individual banks' policies would be set by consensus of the committee to conform to overall RNB plans.

Required

1. Discuss the advantages of a decentralized organizational structure.

2. Identify disadvantages of a decentralized structure. Support each disadvantage with an example from RNB's situation.

3. Do you think the proposed more centralized structure is in the strategic best interests of RNB? Why or why not?

(CMA Adapted)

18-50 **Performance Measurement; Cost Accounting Standards; Ethics** Callum Corporation is a diversified manufacturing company with corporate headquarters in St. Louis. The three operating divisions are the aerospace division, the ceramic products division, and the glass products division.

Much of the manufacturing activity of the aerospace division is related to work performed for the National Aeronautics and Space Administration (NASA) under negotiated contracts. The contracts provide that cost shall be allocated to the contracts in accordance with the federal government's Cost Accounting Standards (as promulgated by the Cost Accounting Standards Board and administered by the General Accounting Office).

Callum Corporation headquarters provide general administrative support and computer services to each of the three operating divisions. The Cost Accounting Standards provide that the cost of general administration may be allocated to negotiated defense contracts. Further, the standards provide that in institutions where computer services are provided by corporate headquarters, the actual costs (fixed and variable) of operating the computer department may be allocated to the defense division based on a reasonable measure of computer usage.

Another provision of the Cost Accounting Standards deals with the situation in which a defense division acquires noncommercial components from a sister division. The standards provide that when there is no established market price for the component, the component must be transferred to the defense division at cost without a markup for profit. This provision of the standards applies to Callum Corporation because the aerospace division purchases custom designed ceramic components from the ceramic products division. There is no established market price for these custom components.

The general managers of the three divisions are evaluated as profit center managers based on the before-tax profit of the division. The November 2010 performance evaluation reports for each of the divisions (in millions of dollars) are shown in the following table:

	Aerospace Division	Ceramic Products Division	Glass Products Division
Sales	$23.0	$15.0*	$55.0
Cost of goods sold	13.0	7.0	38.0
Gross profit	$10.0	$ 8.0	$17.0
Selling and administration:			
Division selling and administration	$ 5.0	$ 5.0	$ 8.0
Corporate—general administration	1.0	—	—
Corporate—computing	1.0	—	—
Total selling and administration	$ 7.0	$ 5.0	$ 8.0
Profit before taxes	$ 3.0	$ 3.0	$ 9.0

* Includes $3,000,000 of custom ceramic products sold to aerospace division at cost and the remainder ($12,000,000) sold to the glass products division and outside customers at established market prices.

Required

1. Review the November performance evaluation reports for the three operating divisions of Callum Corporation.
   a. Identify specific instances where the federal government's Cost Accounting Standards have influenced Callum's divisional performance reporting.
   b. For each specific instance identified, discuss whether the use of accounting practices based on Cost Accounting Standards is desirable for internal reporting and performance evaluation.

2. Considering the accounting practices and reporting methods currently employed by Callum Corporation, describe the improper decision making that could result for the company as a whole if the demand for commercial (nondefense related) ceramic products is equal to or greater than the productive capacity of the ceramic products division.

3. Without a charge for computing services, the operating divisions may not make the most cost-effective use of the resources of the computer systems department of Callum Corporation. Outline and discuss methods for charging the operating divisions for the use of computer services that would promote cost consciousness by the operating divisions and operating efficiency by the computer systems department.

18-51 **Balanced Scorecard; Strategic Business Units; Ethics** Pittsburgh-Walsh Company, Inc. (PWC), manufactures lighting fixtures and electronic timing devices. The lighting fixtures division assembles units for the upscale and mid-range markets. The trend in recent years as the economy has been expanding is for sales in the upscale market to increase while those in the mid-range market have been relatively flat. Over the years, PWC has tried to maintain strong positions in both markets, believing it is best to offer customers a broad range of products to protect the company against a sharp decline in either market. PWC has never been the first to introduce new products but watches its competitors closely and quickly follows their lead with comparable products. PWC is proud of its customer service functions, which have been able to maintain profitable relationships with several large customers over the years.

   The electronic timing devices division manufactures instrument panels that allow electronic systems to be activated and deactivated at scheduled times for both efficiency and safety purposes. Both divisions operate in the same manufacturing facilities and share production equipment.

   PWC's budget for the year ending December 31, 2010, follows; it was prepared on a business unit basis under the following guidelines:

   - Variable expenses are directly assigned to the division that incurs them.
   - Fixed overhead expenses are directly assigned to the division that incurs them.
   - Common fixed expenses are allocated to the divisions on the basis of units produced, which bears a close relationship to direct labor. Included in common fixed expenses are costs of the corporate staff, legal expenses, taxes, marketing staff, and advertising.
   - The company plans to manufacture 8,000 upscale fixtures, 22,000 mid-range fixtures, and 20,000 electronic timing devices during 2010.

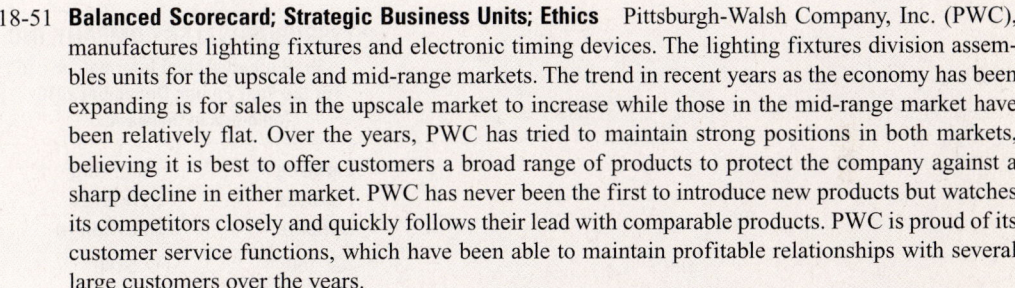

PITTSBURGH-WALSH COMPANY
Budget
For the Year Ending December 31, 2010
(amounts in thousands)

	Lighting Fixtures Upscale	Lighting Fixtures Mid-Range	Electronic Timing Devices	Totals
Sales	$1,440	$770	$800	$3,010
Variable expenses				
Cost of goods sold	720	439	320	1,479
Selling and admin.	170	60	60	290
Contribution margin	$ 550	$271	$420	$1,241
Fixed overhead	140	80	80	300
Divisional contribution	$ 410	$191	$340	$ 941
Common fixed expenses				
Overhead	48	132	120	300
Selling and admin.	11	31	28	70
Operating Income	$ 351	$ 28	$192	$ 571

PWC established a bonus plan for division management that provides a bonus for the manager if the division exceeds the planned product line income by 10 percent or more.

Shortly before the year began, Jack Parkow, the CEO, suffered a heart attack and retired. After reviewing the 2010 budget, Joe Kelly, the new CEO, decided to close the lighting fixtures mid-range product line by the end of the first quarter and use the available production capacity to grow the remaining two product lines. The marketing staff advised that electronic timing devices could grow by 40 percent with increased direct sales support. Increasing sales above that level and of upscale lighting fixtures would require expanded advertising expenditures to increase consumer awareness of PWC as an electronics and upscale lighting fixture company. Joe approved the increased sales support and advertising expenditures to achieve the revised plan. He advised the divisions that for bonus purposes, the original product-line income objectives must be met and that the lighting fixtures division could combine the income objectives for both product lines for bonus purposes.

Prior to the close of the fiscal year, the division controllers were given the following preliminary actual information to review and adjust as appropriate. These preliminary year-end data reflect the revised units of production amounting to 12,000 upscale fixtures, 4,000 mid-range fixtures, and 30,000 electronic timing devices.

PITTSBURGH-WALSH COMPANY, INC.
Preliminary Actual Information
For the Year Ending December 2010
(amounts in thousands)

	Lighting Fixtures Upscale	Lighting Fixtures Mid-Range	Electronic Timing Devices	Totals
Sales	$2,160	$140	$1,200	$3,500
Variable expenses				
Cost of goods sold	1,080	80	480	1,640
Selling and admin.	260	11	96	367
Contribution margin	$ 820	$ 49	$ 624	$1,493
Fixed overhead	140	14	80	234
Divisional contribution	$ 680	$ 35	$ 544	$1,259
Common fixed expenses				
Overhead	78	27	195	300
Selling and admin.	60	20	150	230
Operating Income (loss)	$ 542	$(12)	$ 199	$ 729

The controller of the lighting fixtures division, anticipating a similar bonus plan for 2011, is contemplating deferring some revenue into the next year on the pretext that the sales are not yet final and accruing, in the current year, expenditures that will be applicable to the first quarter of 2011. The corporation would meet its annual plan, and the division would exceed the 10 percent incremental bonus plateau in 2010 despite the deferred revenues and accrued expenses contemplated.

Required

1. Did the new CEO make the correct decision? Why or why not?

2. Outline the benefits that an organization realizes from profit center reporting, and evaluate profit center reporting on a variable-cost basis versus a full-cost basis.

3. Why would the management of the electronics timing devices division be unhappy with the current reporting? Should the current performance measurement system be revised?

4. Explain why the adjustments contemplated by the controller of the lighting fixtures division are unethical by citing specific standards in the Institute of Management Accountants' Standards of Ethical Conduct.

5. Develop a balanced scorecard for PWC, providing three to five perspectives and four to six measures of each perspective. Make sure your measures are quantifiable.

18-52 **Profit Centers** Charleston Manufacturing Company, a maker of building products for commercial and industrial construction, has four divisions: bathroom fixtures; roofing products; adhesives, paints, and other chemicals; and flooring. Each division is evaluated on its profit as determined by the annual financial report, and the profit figure is used to determine the division managers' compensation. The firm has continued to grow in both sales and profits over the recent years, but top management has observed that it is not growing as fast as other firms in the industry. Moreover, the building products business is experiencing strong overall growth due in part to the rapid increase in construction in the mid-atlantic states where Charleston competes. The firm's CEO is concerned that it is losing ground in the industry at a time of improving opportunities. The CEO believes that the problem might be in the firm's performance measurement system and sets up a task force to determine how the firm should proceed.

Required You are assigned to lead the task force. What are your suggestions for the CEO regarding Charleston's performance measurement system?

18-53 **Choice of Strategic Business Unit** Hamilton-Jones, a large consulting firm in Los Angeles, has experienced rapid growth over the last five years. To better serve its clients and to better manage its practice, the firm decided two years ago to organize into five strategic business units, each of which serves a significant base of clients: accounting systems, executive recruitment and compensation, client-server office information systems, manufacturing information systems, and real-estate consulting. Each client SBU is served by a variety of administrative services within the firm, including payroll and accounting, printing and duplicating, report preparation, and secretarial support. Hamilton-Jones management closely watches the trend in the total costs for each administrative support area on a month-to-month basis. Management has noted that the costs in the printing and duplicating area have risen 40 percent over the last two years, a rate that is twice that of any other support area.

Required Should Hamilton-Jones evaluate the five strategic business units as cost or profit centers? Why? How should the administrative support areas be evaluated?

18-54 **Choice of Strategic Business Unit** Martinsville Manufacturing Company develops parts for the automobile industry. The main product line is interior systems, especially seats and carpets. Martinsville operates in a single large plant that has 30 manufacturing units: carpet dyeing, seat frame fabrication, fabric cutting, and so on. In addition to the 30 manufacturing units, there are six manufacturing support departments: maintenance, engineering, janitorial, scheduling, materials receiving and handling, and information systems. The costs of the support departments are allocated to the 30 manufacturing units on the basis of direct labor cost, materials costs, or the square feet of floor space in the plant occupied by the unit. In the case of the maintenance department, the cost is allocated on the basis of square feet. Maintenance costs have been relatively stable in recent years, but the firm's accountant advises that the amount of maintenance cost is a little high relative to the industry average.

Required What are the incentive effects on the manufacturing units of the current basis for allocating maintenance costs? What would be a more desirable way, if any, for allocating these costs? Explain your answer.

18-55 **Design of Strategic Business Unit** MetroBank is a fast-growing bank that serves the region around Jacksonville, Florida. The bank provides commercial and individual banking services, including investment and mortgage banking services. The firm's strategy is to continue to grow by acquiring smaller banks in the area to broaden the base and variety of services it can offer. The bank now has 87 strategic business units, which represent different areas of service in different locations. To support its growth, MetroBank has invested several million dollars in upgrading its information services function. The number of networked computers and of support personnel has more than doubled in the last four years and now accounts for 13 percent of total operating expenses. Two years ago, MetroBank decided to charge information services to the SBUs based on the head count (number of employees) in each SBU. Recently, some of the larger SBUs have complained that this method overcharges them and that some of the smaller SBUs are actually using a larger share of the total information services resources. MetroBank's controller has decided to investigate these complaints. His inquiry of the director of the information services department revealed that the larger departments generally use more services, but some small departments in fact kept him pretty busy. Based on this response, the controller is considering changing the charges for information services to the basis of actual service calls in each SBU rather than the head count.

Required Is the information services department at MetroBank a profit center or a cost center? Which type of unit should it be, and why? Also, evaluate the controller's decision regarding the basis for charging information services costs to the SBUs.

18-56 **Profit Centers: Hospitals** Suburban General Hospital owns and operates several community hospitals in North Carolina. One of its hospitals, Cordona Community Hospital, is a not-for-profit institution that has not met its financial targets in the past several years because of decreasing volume. It has been losing market share largely because of the entrance of a new competitor, Jefferson Memorial Hospital. Jefferson has successfully promoted itself as the premier provider of quality care; its slogan is "Patients Come First." To compete with Jefferson, Cordona has developed a new department, guest services, to improve patient relations and overall customer service. Guest services personnel will be positioned throughout the hospital and at major entrances to help patients and their families get where they are going. Guest services will also be visible in the waiting rooms of high-volume areas such as cardiovascular services and women's services to help guide the patients throughout their visit. Cordona's management is wrestling with how to charge guest services to the various profit centers in the hospital.

Required What are some different ways to allocate the guest service costs, and what would be the effect of each on the behavior of the managers of the different profit centers?

18-57 **Strategy: Balanced Scorecard** WaveCrest Boats, Inc., located in Kinston, North Carolina, is a large manufacturer of sailboats. The company was founded by brothers Tom and Bill Green, who started it to combine their work and hobby, sailing. The Greens's boats are intended primarily for the first-time boat buyer and accordingly include a number of design features for ease of use. Some of WaveCrest's innovative designs have received the attention of other manufacturers in the industry and of sailing magazine editors. The intended market for the boats is the recreational boating enthusiast and sailing camps and clubs that are looking for a durable and easy-to-use boat.

The sailboat industry can be described as a very cyclical business and depends a great deal on overall economic conditions. Because most customers view sailing as a rather expensive recreational hobby, sales increase when the economy is at its best. The adoption of a boat for racing in a given area and the requirement that competitors use that particular boat to compete have dramatically affected sales.

WaveCrest's plant occupies a single large building plus three smaller buildings for supplies, administration, and other manufacturing uses. The plant has two key manufacturing departments, each with a supervisor. The molding department develops the molds for the boats and produces the fiberglass hull for each boat. The assembly department installs the fittings, rub-rail and other hardware, and packs the mast, sails, lines, and other items for shipment.

WaveCrest is currently manufacturing two boat designs, a 14-foot cat-rigged boat and a 16-foot sloop-rigged boat. The wholesale price of these boats is $4,500 and $8,950, respectively. The plant manufactures an average of 100 of the 14-foot boats and 50 of the 16-foot boats per month. The plant is staffed by six highly skilled workers in the molding department, and five additional employees in the assembly department. Tom and Bill work on marketing and customer relations in addition to boat design and testing. Tom is principally responsible for design and production and has been able to create two promising new designs that the firm is market testing and considering for production, as well as some new ideas for streamlining the production process. Bill is primarily responsible for marketing and customer relations and is on the road much of the time attending boat shows and visiting sailing camps and clubs.

Required

1. Develop what you think is or should be WaveCrest's competitive strategy.

2. The Green brothers are interested in evaluating their performance other than using the financial report. In particular, they want to be able to evaluate their progress toward specific goals in each business area. Because they do not see much of each other as a result of Bill's travel, they also want a way to be more aware of what the other is doing and accomplishing. Someone has suggested the use of a balanced scorecard for this purpose. Based on the firm's strategy, develop three to five perspectives of a potential balanced scorecard and four to six measures for each perspective. Do you think the balanced scorecard will provide the information the brothers are seeking?

18-58 **Performance Measurement; Balanced Scorecard; Hospital** Bridgeport Hospital and Health Care Services (BHHS) in Bridgeport, Connecticut, is a part of the Yale University Health System. BHHS is a 450-bed community-teaching hospital with the following mission: "In 2001, Bridgeport Hospital and Health Care Services, as an integral part of the Yale New Haven Health System, will be the system patients choose, the system to which physicians and payers refer, and the employer of choice for health-care personnel."

To transform this mission to reality, BHHS adopted the balanced scorecard for performance measurement, and a plan to implement it by the end of 2005. In the first year of the scorecard, 1999,

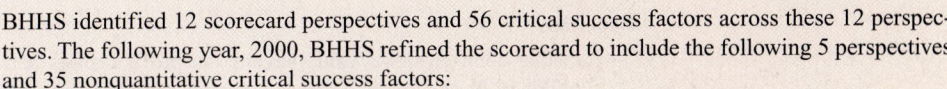

BHHS identified 12 scorecard perspectives and 56 critical success factors across these 12 perspectives. The following year, 2000, BHHS refined the scorecard to include the following 5 perspectives and 35 nonquantitative critical success factors:

1. **Organizational health** (teamwork, leadership development, communications, facilities . . .).
2. **Process improvement** (reducing delays, streamlining processes, and maximizing the effective use of technology . . .).
3. **Quality improvement** (patient satisfaction, improving patient outcomes, external recognition for patient care . . .).
4. **Volume and market share growth** (expanded clinical services . . .).
5. **Financial health** (financial returns, system efficiencies . . .).

Required

1. Why did BHHS reduce the number of scorecard perspectives and critical success factors in 2000? The number of perspectives was further reduced to four in 2001; state which you think are the remaining four perspectives and explain why.
2. For the five perspectives in the 2000 plan, develop two to five possible measurable critical success factors that the hospital might use to measure performance toward the goals of each perspective.
3. Will the scorecard as described in the 2000 plan be effective in helping BHHS achieve its mission?
4. Develop a strategy map for BHHS, incorporating each of the five perspectives of the 2000 plan. Explain why you have developed the map in this way.

18-59 **Value Streams and Profit Centers** Johnson Company is a manufacturer of very inexpensive DVD players and television sets. The company uses recycled parts and a highly structured manufacturing process to keep costs low so that it can sell at very low prices. The company uses lean accounting procedures to help keep costs low and to examine financial performance. Johnson uses value streams to study the profitability of its two main product groups, DVD players and TVs. Information about finished goods inventory, sales, production, and average sales price follows.

	DVD Group	TV Group
Units		
Beginning inventory	400	800
Price	$ 65	$ 45
Sold	10,500	15,500
Budgeted and Actual production	12,000	15,000

Johnson's costs for the current quarter are as follows. Note that some of the company's manufacturing and selling costs are traceable directly to the two value streams, while other costs are not traceable. Johnson considers all fixed costs to be controllable by the manager of each group. Also, Johnson's value stream shows operating income determined by the full cost method; the difference from the traditional full cost income statement is that the effect on income from a change in inventory is shown as a separate item on the value stream income statement.

	DVD Group	TV Group	Total
Unit variable costs			
Manufacturing	$ 28	$ 16	
Selling and administrative	5	3	
Traceable fixed costs			
Manufacturing	120,000	240,000	$ 360,000
Selling and administrative	10,000	10,000	20,000
Nontraceable fixed costs			
Manufacturing			130,000
Selling and administrative			80,000

Required

1. Consider Johnson's two value streams as profit centers and use the contribution income statement (Exhibit 18.9) as a guide to develop a value stream income statement for the company. In your solution, replace the term *controllable margin* (in Exhibit 18.9) with *value-stream income*. Be sure to include the inventory effect on profit as a separate line item in your value stream income statement.

2. Interpret the findings of the analysis you completed in part 1.

3. What is the benefit of the use of value streams for evaluating profit centers relative to the use of the contribution income statement for individual product lines?

18-60 Cost Centers; The Finance Function; Global The consulting firm A. T. Kearney analyzes and ranks the top offshore outsourcing locations for companies seeking to outsource the finance function. Kearney provides three measures of the attractiveness of the country as a location for outsourcing: financial attractiveness (low cost), skills availability, and business environment (that supports investment in the country). For each measure, a larger score is a better score; financial attractiveness is scored in the range from 0 to 4, while skills availability and business environment are scored from 0 to 3. Twenty countries selected from the top of the 2007 Kearny list are shown below, together with the measures for the year 2007.

The A.T. Kearney measures are useful to a firm that is considering outsourcing its finance function and is also considering outsourcing this function to a foreign country. A firm that considers the finance function as a cost center may wish to find a location where the work can be done reliably at the lowest possible cost. Note that outsourcing would not be considered if for any reason the finance function is considered strategically critical to the company; in that case the finance function would be retained close to top management. For example, a company with a stable and cost leadership type of operation would be more likely to offshore the finance function than a company that operates in a dynamic competitive environment where financial skills are needed for many day-to-day decisions. Note: The countries below are listed in alphabetical order. You can review the Cost Management in Action section of the chapter for more information on outsourcing.

	Financial Attractiveness	Skills Availability	Business Environment
Brazil	2.64	1.78	1.47
Bulgaria	3.16	1.04	1.56
Chile	2.65	1.18	1.93
China	2.93	2.25	1.38
Czech Republic	2.43	1.10	2.05
Egypt	3.22	1.14	1.25
Estonia	2.44	0.96	2.20
India	3.22	2.34	1.44
Indonesia	3.29	1.47	1.06
Jordan	3.09	0.98	1.54
Latvia	2.64	0.91	2.00
Malaysia	2.84	1.26	2.02
Mexico	2.63	1.49	1.61
Philippines	3.26	1.23	1.26
Poland	2.59	1.17	1.79
Singapore	1.65	1.51	2.53
Slovakia	2.79	1.04	1.79
Thailand	3.19	1.21	1.62
United Arab Emirates	2.93	0.86	1.92
Vietnam	3.33	0.99	1.22

Required

1. Using Excel, analyze the above measures for these 20 countries and develop a ranking of the countries for choosing the best country for the location for offshoring the finance function. Explain briefly how you developed your ranking.

2. What are some of the strategic and global issues to consider in outsourcing the finance function?

18-61 Contribution Income Statement for Profit Centers Outdoor World Inc. (OWI) is a sporting goods retailer that specializes in bicycles, running shoes, and related clothing. The firm has become successful by careful attention to trends in cycling, running, and changes in the technology and fashion of sport clothing. In recent years however, the profit margins have begun to fall, and OWI has decided to employ a contribution income statement to further analyze the company's profitability. The company has two stores, one in Hartford, Connecticut, and the other in Boston, Massachusetts. The total sales for the two stores for the most recent year are $6,875,000 and $5,625,000 for the Hartford and Boston stores respectively. Both stores are considered profit centers, and within each store are two profit centers: one for clothing and the other for cycles and running shoes. The breakdown of sales within the two stores is approximately 50 percent clothing and 50 percent cycles/shoes for Boston but is estimated to be 60 percent/40 percent for Hartford, due to the greater interest in cycling in the Boston area. OWI is interested in finding the profit contribution of clothing and cycling/shoes at the Hartford store but not at the Boston store.

Cost of purchases for resale averages 60 percent of retail value at Boston, and at Hartford the cost is 70 percent for clothing and 50 percent for cycles/shoes. Variable operating costs at each store are similar—30 percent of retail sales at Boston, and at Hartford operating costs are 25 percent of retail sales for the clothing unit and 35 percent for the cycle/shoes unit. OWI estimates it has a total of $1,075,000 fixed cost, of which $325,000 could not be traced to either store; of the remaining $750,000, $400,000 was traceable to the stores and controllable by store managers and $350,000 could be traced to the stores but could not be controlled in the short term by the store managers. These fixed costs are estimated to be traceable to the stores as follows.

Fixed Controllable Costs	Percent of Total Cost
Boston	45%
Hartford total	40
Clothing	50
Cycle&Run	30
Could not be traced to clothing or cycling at Hartford	20
Could not be traced to Boston or Hartford	15

Fixed Noncontrollable Costs	Percent of Total Cost
Boston	40%
Hartford total	50
Clothing	55
Cycle&Run	35
Could not be traced to clothing or cycling at Hartford	10
Could not be traced to Boston or Hartford	10

Required

1. Prepare a contribution income statement for OWI showing the contribution margin, controllable margin, and contribution by profit center for both the Boston and Hartford stores, and also for the clothing and cycles/shoes units of the Hartford store.

2. Interpret the contribution income statement you prepared in (1) above. What recommendations do you have for the management of OWI?

18-62 Choice of Strategic Business Unit

Required For each of the following cases, determine whether the business unit should be evaluated as a cost center or a profit center and explain why. If you choose cost center, then explain which type of cost center, the discretionary-cost center or the engineered-cost center.

1. A trucking firm has experienced a rapid increase in fuel costs and has only been partly successful in passing along the increased costs to customers. In recent months, fuel prices have come back down, but the firm's management knows to expect a continued volatility in the cost of fuel. To secure the firm's profits when fuel costs are rising, the company has established an Office of Sustainability to develop and implement a strategy for reducing costs and reducing the firm's overall carbon footprint.

2. To more effectively compete in a dynamic market for consumer electronics, a manufacturer of consumer electronics products has established a new department for Innovation and Refinement that reports directly to the chief operating officer (COO). The role of the new department is to develop new products and to refine existing products that keep the firm on the leading edge of innovation in the industry. A

key tool of the new department is to use predictive analytics, a type of statistical analysis that is used to analyze market trends, consumer data, and economics forecasts, to best identify the products that consumers want and what types of innovation are most likely to be valued.

3. The recent economic downturn has convinced Marshall Clothing Stores Inc. to initiate risk management practices and to locate this activity in a new department that reports directly to the chief financial officer (CFO). The objectives of risk management are to identify significant new risks that could potentially affect the company in the coming one to five years and to develop plans for adapting to the risk. For example, the company is concerned about the rapidly increasing inventories in certain departments of its stores, due to unexpected decrease in demand in these areas. The company faces losses on selling these items at a discount.

18-63 **Research and Development: Risk Aversion and Performance Measurement**   As the economic outlook in many countries becomes uncertain, some managers look to cut costs in research and development to provide a short-term boost to profits. The problem with this strategy is that it reduces the opportunities for new products and product improvements in the coming years, which are necessary for the long-term competitiveness of the firm. As Intel Chairman Craig Barrett says, "You cut off your future if you do not invest."

Required

1. What role does risk aversion play in determining the amount to invest in research and development on an ongoing basis? How would a firm manage risk aversion so as to continue the desired level of spending on research and development?

2. What type of strategic business unit would you choose to evaluate the performance of the research and development department? Explain your choice briefly.

Solution to Self–Study Problem

Discretionary-Cost and Engineered-Cost Methods

1. Liberty management is apparently using a cost center for its claims department because it generates no revenues. Since management has chosen not to adjust the number of clerks for the changing number of claims each month, it appears to be using a discretionary-cost method to budget these costs. That is, management has determined it is more effective to provide a reasonable resource (12 clerks) for the claims processing area and not to be concerned directly with the clerks' efficiency, the slack during slow times, or the hectic pace at peak load times. Management's view is that the work averages out over time.

2. If Liberty uses the discretionary-cost method, the budget would be the same each month and would not depend on the level of claims to be processed. The budget would include the costs to provide the number of clerks that management judges to be adequate for the job (12 clerks × $2,400 per month), or $28,800 per month.

3. If Liberty uses the engineered-cost method, each claim that is processed has a budgeted cost based on the average time used as determined by a work flow study. Assume that each clerk works an eight-hour day except for 40 minutes of break time; the number of claims a clerk can process each month (assuming 22 working days) is

$$\frac{[(8 \text{ hours} \times 60 \text{ minutes}) - 40] \times 22 \text{ days}}{121 \text{ minutes}} = 80 \text{ claims per month}$$

The cost per claim is thus

$$\$2,400/80 = \$30 \text{ per claim}$$

The engineered-cost budget for January is

$$915 \text{ claims} \times \$30 \text{ per claim} = \$27,450$$

The unfavorable variance for January using the engineered-cost method is $1,350 ($28,800 actual expenditure less $27,450 budgeted expenditure). This unfavorable variance is best interpreted as the cost of unused capacity for processing claims. Since the capacity for processing claims is 80 × 12 = 960 claims, the department has unused capacity of 45 claims (960 − 915 = 45 claims), or approximately one-half of one clerk.

4. Chuck could make the strategic argument that the claims processing department should be staffed for peak capacity rather than for average capacity to ensure promptness and accuracy during the busy months and to provide a better basis for employee morale, which is an important factor in performance during the low-volume months as well.

CHAPTER NINETEEN

Strategic Performance Measurement:
Investment Centers

After studying this chapter, you should be able to . . .

1. Explain the use and limitations of return on investment (ROI) for evaluating investment centers
2. Explain the use and limitations of residual income (RI) for evaluating investment centers
3. Explain the use and limitations of economic value added (EVA®) for evaluating investment centers
4. Explain the objectives of transfer pricing and the advantages and disadvantages of various transfer-pricing alternatives
5. Discuss important international issues that arise in transfer pricing

As indicated in the preceding chapter, when an organization decentralizes it does so to achieve certain objectives, including maximization of shareholder value. From top management's viewpoint, one of the costs of decentralization is the need to implement an effective performance-measurement system. The traditional approach to the design of such a system is to focus on the tenet of controllability: subunits of a decentralized organization (and their managers) should, as much as possible, be evaluated only on factors they can control, or at least influence, by their actions. In previous chapters, we've looked at how top management can evaluate the financial performance of lower-level units of the organization (viz., cost centers and profit centers). This chapter covers issues related to the performance of investment centers—the highest subunit level of an organization. By definition, managers of these units exercise control over revenues, costs, and level of investment. Thus, the evaluation of financial performance of these units should logically incorporate a measure of invested capital. Such measures allow top management to compare the financial performance of different investment centers within the organization. As indicated in the vignette that follows, the task of evaluating the performance of investment units is complicated when these units exchange goods and services with one another. That is, in such situations a "transfer price" between units must be chosen to evaluate the financial performance of both the buying unit and the selling unit. Setting an appropriate transfer price is especially challenging in an international context.

Five Steps in the Evaluation of the Financial Performance of Strategic Investment Units in an Organization

Global Electronics, Inc. (a fictitious company) was started five years ago by a small group of entrepreneurial students. The company produces innovative electronics products that appeal to young, educated individuals. Global is pursuing a low-cost, high-volume strategy. In fact, the company has from its inception grown rapidly and now does business in all 50 states as well as selected countries abroad. Its incentive to go abroad is to reduce cost and to facilitate growth in foreign sales. The company is decentralized and organized into a series of cost centers, profit centers, and investment centers. Recently, to take advantage of income-tax opportunities, Global has established several foreign subsidiaries, which both produce and distribute the company's products. Initially, the company felt little need for a comprehensive performance-evaluation system. However, with recent growth and development, the owners of the company are looking at alternative models for evaluating the performance of the various units into which the company is divided. Business consultants with whom the owners met recently recommended the following five-step process for developing a performance-measurement system for Global.

1. **Determine the strategic issues surrounding the problem.** Global Electronics, Inc., has organized itself into a number of decentralized units, including strategic investment units where the managers have broad responsibility over operating decisions and level of investment in the unit. The owners of the company want to institute a performance-measurement system that would allow the owners to evaluate the financial performance of each of the investment centers it has created.

2. **Identify the alternative actions.** The primary task is to choose one or more financial-performance indicators that incorporate in the measure the level of investment in each unit. Proposed alternative indicators include return on investment (ROI), residual income (RI), or economic value added (EVA®).[1] Global must also choose the time period over which financial performance will be evaluated (i.e., one year versus time-series basis). For interdivisional transfers of products and services, Global must choose an appropriate transfer-pricing system from among the following alternatives: variable cost, full cost, market price, or negotiated price. Further, the company must determine whether transfer prices will be recorded at actual, at budgeted, or at standard cost.[2] Finally, Global must decide whether to use a single or a dual transfer-pricing system.

3. **Obtain information and conduct analyses of the alternatives.** The choice of a performance-evaluation system for decentralized units, such as investment centers, has important behavioral consequences. For example, to a greater or lesser extent the aforementioned choices maintain or decrease managerial autonomy, increase or decrease managerial motivation, and to a greater or lesser extent result in goal congruency. Further, some choices as to system design are simpler (administratively) to implement and maintain. In terms of selecting the appropriate transfer-pricing method, there are significant income-tax considerations, particularly given the (now) international scope of the company's operations. To protect itself, the company is considering entering into an advance pricing agreement (APA) with the IRS regarding its transfer-pricing method to be used for both domestic and international purposes. Finally, the company is concurrently considering the introduction of a balanced scorecard (BSC) (see Chapter 18) and so management needs to consider choice of performance metric(s) in conjunction with the design of its BSC.

4. **Based on strategy and analysis, choose and implement the desired alternative.** After discussion of these issues with its consultants, the company chooses a mix of financial-performance indicators and a specific transfer-pricing system that attempts to balance implementation costs against behavioral benefits and income-tax considerations. The high-level financial-performance indicators should be linked strategically to the company's BSC. Overall, the proposed performance-evaluation system for its investment centers will help Global implement its growth strategy and determine where growth is most profitable.

5. **Provide an ongoing evaluation of the effectiveness of the step 4 implementation.** The financial performance of all strategic investment centers of the company is evaluated quarterly, in conjunction with both subunit and corporate scorecards. Further, the financial-performance metrics are benchmarked to best-in-class performance of Global's competitors. Changes to the way financial performance is evaluated, as well as potential changes to the transfer-pricing system used by the company, are discussed during quarterly meetings with the owners of the company.

The rest of this chapter is divided into two parts. In part one we discuss alternatives for evaluating the financial performance of investment centers. In part two we discuss the issue of transfer pricing. In both cases, our approach is to discuss both the advantages and limitations of various alternatives that exist. As you will see, evaluation of the *financial performance* of

---

[1] EVA® is a registered trademark of Stern Stewart & Co.

[2] As noted in Chapter 14, standard costs are *normative*—they represent the costs that *should be* incurred under relatively efficient operating conditions.

investment centers is important, but incomplete. Thus, a strategic analysis of the performance of an investment center must also include *nonfinancial-performance indicators,* such as those included in an entity's balanced scorecard. In fact, all of these points were considered by the management of Global in its attempt to implement a performance-evaluation system for its investment centers.

Part One: Financial-Performance Indicators for Investment Centers

Under the notion of *controllability,* it is appropriate for top management to evaluate the profitability of each investment center in relation to the amount of capital invested in the subunit. In practice, top management can use one or a combination of the following metrics: return on investment (ROI), residual income (RI), or economic value added (EVA®). Each of these measures is discussed in this part of the chapter. In general, we evaluate each of these alternatives on the basis of the following criteria:

- Extent to which the measure motivates a high level of effort on the part of subunit managers.
- Extent to which the use of the measure results in goal congruency (consistency between decisions made by managers and the goals of top management).
- Extent to which the measure rewards managers fairly for their effort and skill, and for the effectiveness of the decisions they make.

Please keep the preceding criteria in mind as you study the rest of this chapter.

Return on Investment

LEARNING OBJECTIVE 1

Explain the use and limitations of return on investment (ROI) for evaluating investment centers.

Return on investment (ROI)
is some measure of profit divided by some measure of investment in the business unit.

The most commonly used measure of short-term financial performance of an investment center is **return on investment (ROI)**, which is defined as some measure of profit divided by some measure of investment in the business unit. ROI is a percentage, and the larger the percentage, the better the ROI. The achieved level of ROI depends on many factors, including general economic conditions, and, in particular, the current economic conditions of the company's industry. For example, cyclical industries such as airlines and home construction have ROIs that vary significantly under differing economic conditions. In calculating ROI, "profit" (i.e., the numerator of the ratio) for an investment center (compared to the firm as a whole) is typically defined as divisional operating income. The amount of "investment" (i.e., the denominator of the ratio) is often determined by the assets of the business unit.

ROI Equals Return on Sales Times Asset Turnover[3]

ROI is the product of two components, return on sales and asset turnover. Since sales and profits relate to a period of time, for consistency the amount of assets used to calculate ROI usually is determined from the simple average of the value of assets at the start of the period and the value of assets at the end of the period.

$$\text{ROI} = \text{Return on sales} \times \text{Asset turnover}$$
$$\text{ROI} = \frac{\text{Profit}}{\text{Sales}} \times \frac{\text{Sales}}{\text{Assets}}$$

Return on sales (ROS),
or profit per sales dollar,
measures the manager's ability
to control expenses and increase
revenues to improve profitability.

Asset turnover (AT),
amount of dollar sales achieved
per dollar of investment,
measures the manager's ability to
increase sales from a given level
of investment.

Return on sales (ROS), or profit per sales dollar, measures the manager's ability to control expenses and increase revenues to improve profitability. Return on sales is also called *profit margin.* **Asset turnover (AT)**, the amount of dollar sales achieved per dollar of investment, measures the manager's ability to increase sales from a given level of investment. Together, the two components of ROI tell a more complete story of the manager's performance and enhance

[3] ROI based on asset turnover and return on sales is often referred to as the *DuPont approach* since it was originated by Donaldson Brown, chief financial officer of DuPont Corporation early in the 1900s.

Industries Differ in the Relationship of Return on Sales and Asset Turnover

The figure to the right shows the relationship between asset turnover (AT) and return on sales (ROS) for a return on investment of 10 percent. Any point falling above the line would represent an ROI of greater than 10 percent; a point falling below this line would be an ROI of less than 10 percent. The curve shows that there are lots of different combinations of AT and ROS that will produce an ROI of 10 percent. Also, it is common that different industries will fall at different points of the figure. For example, restaurants typically have low ROS and higher AT so they will appear to the upper left of the figure (for example in 2008 Einstein Noah Restaurant Group, Inc. had an ROS of 5% and AT of 2.57, for an ROI of 13%). In contrast, utilities typically have lower AT and higher ROS (for example, Duke Energy in 2008 had an ROS of 10.3% and AT of 0.26, for an ROI of 2.7%).

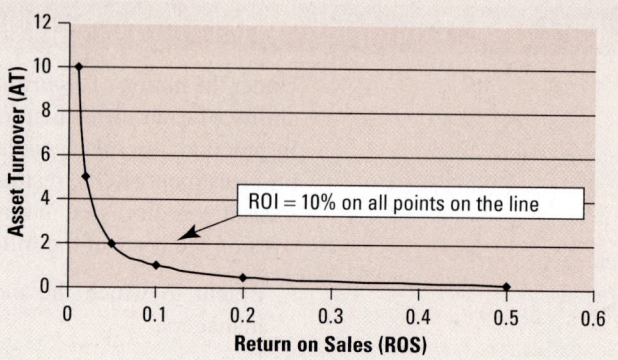

ROI = 10% on all points on the line

top management's ability to evaluate and compare different units within the organization. For example, research has shown that firms with different operating strategies tend also to have a different mix of return on sales versus asset turnover. Firms with high operating leverage (see Chapter 9) tend to have low asset turnover and high return on sales; those with low operating leverage and commodity-like products tend to have the highest asset turnover and the lowest return on sales. Please see the above RWF item for an elaboration on these points.

Illustration of Evaluation Using ROI

Assume that CompuCity is a retailer with three product lines, computers, software, and computer help books. The company has stores in three regions, the Boston area, South Florida, and the Midwest. Each store sells only books, computers, and software. CompuCity's profits for the Midwest declined last year, due in part to increased price competition in the computer unit.

Because of this decline in profits, top management uses ROI to study the performance of the Midwest region. Each product line is considered an investment center for evaluation purposes. CompuCity knows that the markups are highest in software and lowest for computers because of price competition. Investment in each unit consists of the inventory for sale and the value of the real estate and improvements of the retail stores. Inventory is relatively low in the computer unit since merchandise is restocked quickly from the manufacturers. Inventory is also low in the book unit because about 40 percent of CompuCity's books are on consignment from publishers.

The current book value (recorded cost) of the real estate and store improvements is allocated to each of the three units on the basis of square feet of floor space used. The software unit occupies the largest amount of floor space, followed by computers and books. Panel 1 of Exhibit 19.1 shows the operating income, sales, and investment information for the Midwest region of CompuCity in 2009 and 2010. Panel 2 shows the calculation of ROI, including ROS and asset turnover, for the Midwest region for both 2009 and 2010.

The data in Exhibit 19.1 indicate that Midwest region's ROI has fallen (from 14.4 percent in 2009 to 13.5 percent in 2010) due mainly to a decline in overall ROS (from 6.1 percent in 2009 to 5.1 percent in 2010). Further analysis shows that the drop in ROS is due to the sharp decline in ROS for the computer product line (from 4 percent in 2009 to 2 percent in 2010). The computer unit's decline in ROS is likely the result of the increased price competition.

The analysis also shows that software is the most profitable business unit (based on an ROI of 20 percent in 2010); this is so primarily because of the relatively high ROS (highest at

EXHIBIT 19.1 ROI, Return on Sales (ROS), and Asset Turnover for CompuCity *(Midwest Region)*

Panel 1: Operating Income, Investment, and Sales

	Operating Income		Investment (Assets)		Sales	
	2009	**2010**	**2009**	**2010**	**2009**	**2010**
Computers	$ 8,000	$ 5,000	$ 50,000	$ 62,500	$200,000	$250,000
Software	15,000	16,000	100,000	80,000	150,000	160,000
Books	3,200	5,000	32,000	50,000	80,000	100,000
Total	$26,200	$26,000	$182,000	$192,500	$430,000	$510,000

Panel 2: Return on Sales, Asset Turnover, and ROI

	Return on Sales (ROS)		Asset Turnover (AT)		ROI	
	2009	**2010**	**2009**	**2010**	**2009**	**2010**
Computers	4% = 8,000/200,000	2% = 5,000/250,000	4.00 = 200,000/50,000	4.00 = 250,000/62,500	16% = 8,000/50,000	8% = 5,000/62,500
Software	10% = 15,000/150,000	10% = 16,000/160,000	1.50 = 150,000/100,000	2.00 = 160,000/80,000	15% = 15,000/100,000	20% = 16,000/80,000
Books	4% = 3,200/80,000	5% = 5,000/100,000	2.50 = 80,000/32,000	2.00 = 100,000/50,000	10% = 3,200/32,000	10% = 5,000/50,000
Total	6.10% = 26,200/430,000	5.10% = 26,000/510,000	2.36 = 430,000/182,000	2.65 = 510,000/192,500	14.40% = 26,200/182,000	13.50% = 26,000/192,500

The cost of training employees can be 15 percent or more of total payroll costs in some firms. These significant expenditures are incurred because of the importance of investing in the job-related abilities of the firm's employees. Since employee training costs are not included on the balance sheet as assets according to generally accepted accounting principles, the training function within a firm is often not viewed as an investment center. In contrast, other firms consider training to be one of the most strategically important investments they make and, accordingly, determine an ROI value for it. Software vendors and consultants assist firms in developing the proper measurements.

Source: Based on Ann P. Bartel, "Measuring the Employer's Return on Investments in Training: Evidence from the Literature," *Industrial Relations,* July 2000, pp. 502–24; and Felix Barber and Rainer Strack, "The Surprising Economics of the People Business," *Harvard Business Review,* June 2005, pp. 81–90.

10 percent since the markup on software products is relatively high). In contrast, the computer and book units have higher asset turnovers due to the lower required levels of inventory and floor space than the computer unit, and the large percentage of consignment inventory for the book unit. ROI has also improved significantly for the software unit because of the decline in investment, due either to a reduction in inventory or a decrease in floor space for software (recall that investment is allocated to the units on the basis of floor space).

Strategic Analysis Using ROI

Use of ROI enables CompuCity to evaluate the short-term financial performance of each of the three units. CompuCity can set performance goals for each unit in terms of both return on sales (ROS) and asset turnover (AT). The unit managers then have very clear goals to increase sales and reduce costs, reduce inventory, and use floor space effectively. To be effective, the goals should recognize differences in the competitive factors among the units. For example, a lower ROS should be expected of the computer unit because of competitive pricing that affects that unit.

Exhibit 19.1 data also reflect the way that competitive factors in the computer unit and business relationships regarding inventory in the computer and book units affect profitability. This provides a useful basis for an improved analysis, that is, for determining how the firm should position itself strategically. How should CompuCity's competitive approach be changed in view of recent and expected changes in the competitive environment? Perhaps the computer unit should be reduced and the software unit expanded. Which stores in the Midwest are successful, and why? A value-chain analysis might provide insight into strategic competitive advantage and opportunity. For example, CompuCity might find it more profitable to reduce its computer unit and replace it with products that are potentially more profitable, such as printers, pagers, cell phones, fax machines, supplies, and computer accessories.

Return on Investment: Measurement Issues

If ROI is used to evaluate the relative performance of business units, then income and investment should be determined consistently and fairly across these units.

1. Income and investment, to the extent possible, be measured in the same way for each unit. For example, all units to be evaluated should use the same inventory cost-flow assumption (FIFO or LIFO) and the same depreciation method.[4]
2. The measurement method must be reasonable and fair for all units. For example, if some units have much older assets than other units have, the use of net book value (NBV) for assets can significantly bias the ROI measures in favor of the older units.

---

[4] Each of the policies also has the effect of either simultaneously increasing income and increasing investment or simultaneously decreasing income and decreasing investment. Since ROI is a ratio that normally is between zero and 1, an increase in income increases ROI although investment also has increased by the same amount, and vice versa.

EXHIBIT 19.2
Effect on ROI of Capitalizing Certain Costs: CompuCity
(Midwest Region)

Panel 1: ROI Prior to Capitalizing Display Materials (same as Exhibit 19.1, 2010)		
	Computer Unit	**Book Unit**
Assets	$62,500	$50,000
Income	$5,000	$5,000
ROI	8%	10%

Panel 2: Year-One Results—Book Unit Expenses Display Costs While the Computer Unit Capitalizes These Costs

Assets	$64,000 = $62,500 + $1,500	$50,000
Income	$6,500 = $5,000 + $1,500	$5,000
ROI	10.16% = $6,500/$64,000	10%

To illustrate the effect of an accounting policy on divisional ROIs, assume that all units of CompuCity expense all furniture and other items used to display products; these items cost $2,000 per year. Suppose the computer unit decides to capitalize these expenses. What is the short-term effect on ROI if depreciation is $500 per year on these items? The increase in the NBV of assets for the Computer Unit is $1,500, and the net effect on income for this unit is $1,500. Exhibit 19.2 compares the Computer Unit to the Book Unit before the change (Panel 1) and after the change (Panel 2).

The illustration shows that the decision to capitalize the display costs in the short run increased the Computer Unit's assets, income, and ROI. Although the Book Unit has the higher ROI when both units expense display costs, the Computer Unit's decision to capitalize these costs while the Book Unit does not has caused the Computer Unit to at least temporarily have the higher ROI.

Which Assets to Include in the ROI Calculation

A common method for calculating ROI is to define investment as the net cost of long-lived assets plus working capital (i.e., current assets minus current liabilities). A key criterion for including an asset in ROI is the degree to which the unit controls it. For example, if the unit's cash balance is controlled at the firmwide level, only a portion (or perhaps none) of the cash balance should be included in the investment amount for calculating divisional ROI. Similarly, receivables and inventory should include only those controllable at the unit level.

Long-lived assets commonly are included in investment if they are traceable to the unit (for shared assets, see the next section). Management problems arise, however, if the long-lived assets are leased or if some significant portion of them is idle. Leasing requires a clear firmwide policy regarding how to treat leases in determining ROI so that unit managers are properly motivated to lease or not to lease, as is the firm's policy. In general, the leased assets should be included as investments since they represent assets used to generate income, and the failure to include them can cause a significant overstatement of ROI.

For idle assets, the main issue is again controllability. If the idle assets have an alternative use or are readily saleable, they should be included in the investment amount for ROI. Also, if top management wants to encourage the divestment of idle assets, including idle assets in ROI would motivate the desired action since divestment would reduce investment and increase ROI. Alternatively, if top management sees a potential strategic advantage to holding the idle assets, excluding idle assets from ROI would provide the most effective motivation since holding idle assets would not affect the ROI calculation.

Measuring Investment: Allocating Shared Assets

When shared facilities, such as a common maintenance facility, are involved, management must determine a fair sharing arrangement. As in joint cost allocation (Chapter 7), top management should trace the assets to the business units that used them and allocate the assets that cannot be traced on a basis that is as close to actual usage as possible. For example, the investment in a vehicle maintenance facility might be allocated on the basis of the number of vehicles in each unit or on the total value of these vehicles.

Alternatively, the required capacity and therefore the investment in the joint facility are sometimes large because the user units require high levels of service at periods of high demand. In this case, the assets should be allocated according to the *peak demand* by each individual unit; units with higher peak-load requirements would be allocated a relatively larger portion of the total investment cost. For example, a computer services department might require a high level of computer capacity because certain units within the company require a large amount of service at certain times.

Measuring Investment: Current Values

Historical cost of divisional assets
is the book value of current assets plus the net book value (NBV) of long-lived assets.

Net book value (NBV)
is the original cost of a depreciable asset less accumulated depreciation to date on that asset.

The amount of investment is typically the **historical cost of divisional assets**, which is defined as the book value of current assets plus the net book value (NBV) of long-lived assets. **Net book value (NBV)** for a depreciable asset is the difference between original cost of the asset and accumulated depreciation on that asset. A problem arises when the long-lived assets are a significant portion of total investment because most long-lived assets are stated at historical-cost, and price changes since their purchase can make the historical-cost figures irrelevant and misleading.

If the relatively small historical-cost value is used for investment in ROI, the result is that *ROI can be significantly overstated* relative to ROI determined with the current value of the assets. The consequence is that the use of historical-cost ROI can mislead strategic decision makers, since the inflated ROI figures can create an illusion of profitability. The illusion is removed when the assets are replaced later at their current value.

For example, a division that enjoys a relatively high ROI of 20 percent based on NBV (e.g., income of $200,000 and NBV of assets of $1,000,000) would find that *if* replacement cost of the assets were four times book value ($4 \times \$1,000,000 = \$4,000,000$), the ROI after replacement would become a relatively low 5 percent ($200,000/$4,000,000). Strategically, the firm should have identified the low profitability of this business unit in a timely manner, but use of historical-cost ROI can delay this recognition. Thus, instead of measuring assets at historical cost (for purposes of calculating ROI) an organization may choose some measure of current value of these assets. Presumably, the resulting ROIs better inform management about the true profitability of its various business units. Note, however, that if current-cost data are not currently being reported (for example, for financial accounting purposes) the organization in this case will incur additional information-gathering costs.

In addition to its strategic value, the use of current value helps to reduce the unfairness of historical-cost NBV when comparing among business units with *different aged assets.* Units with older assets under the NBV method have significantly higher ROIs than units with newer assets because of the effect of price changes and of accumulating depreciation over the life of

EXHIBIT 19.3
Investment Data and ROI
for CompuCity in Its Three
Marketing Regions (000s
omitted)

| | | Measure of Assets | | | |
Region	Income	Net Book Value	Gross Book Value	Replacement Cost	Liquidation Value
Financial data:					
Midwest	$26,000	$192,500	$250,500	$388,000	$ 332,000
Boston area	38,500	212,000	445,000	650,000	1,254,600
South Florida	16,850	133,000	155,450	225,500	195,000
Return on investment:					
Midwest		13.5%	10.4%	6.70%	7.8%
Boston area		18.2	8.7	5.9	3.1
South Florida		12.7	10.8	7.5	8.6

the assets. If the old and new assets are contributing equivalent service, the bias in favor of the unit with older assets is unfair to the manager of a unit with newer assets.

Measures of Current Value The three methods for developing or estimating the current values of assets are (1) gross book value, (2) replacement cost, and (3) liquidation value. **Gross book value (GBV)** is historical cost without the reduction for accumulated depreciation. It is a rough estimate of the current value of the assets. GBV improves on NBV because it removes the bias due to differences in the age of assets and differences in depreciation methods used across different business units. However, it does not address potential price changes in the assets since the time of original purchase.

Gross book value (GBV)
is historical cost without the
reduction for accumulated
depreciation.

Replacement cost represents the current cost to replace the assets at the current level of service and functionality. In contrast, **liquidation value** is the estimated price that could be received from sale of the assets of a business unit. In effect, replacement cost is a purchase price and liquidation value is a sales price. Generally, replacement cost is higher than liquidation value.

Replacement cost
represents the current cost to
replace the assets at the current
level of service and functionality.

Liquidation value
is the estimated price that could
be received from the sale of the
assets of a business unit.

GBV is preferred by those who value the objectivity of a historical-cost number; original purchase cost is a reliable, verifiable number. In contrast, replacement cost is preferred when ROI is used to evaluate the manager or the unit as a continuing enterprise because the use of replacement cost is consistent with the idea that the assets will be replaced at the current cost and the business will continue. On the other hand, liquidation value is most useful when top management is using ROI to evaluate the business unit for potential disposal, and the relevant current cost is the sales (i.e., liquidation) value of the assets.

To illustrate, consider CompuCity's three marketing regions. CompuCity has 15 stores in the Midwest, 18 in the Boston area, and 13 in South Florida. CompuCity owns and manages each store. Exhibit 19.3 shows the NBV, GBV, estimated replacement cost, and estimated liquidation value for 2010 for the stores in each region.[5]

The stores in the Boston area, where CompuCity began, are among the oldest and are located in areas where real estate values have risen considerably. The newer stores (in the Midwest and Florida) are also experiencing significant appreciation in real estate values. ROI based on NBV shows the Boston area to be the most profitable. Additional analysis based on GBV, however, shows that when considering that the Boston area stores are somewhat older, the ROI figures for all three regions are comparable, illustrating the potentially misleading information from ROI based on NBV.

Replacement cost is useful in evaluating managers' performance because it best measures the investment in the continuing business: the ROI figures show that all three regions are somewhat comparable, with South Florida slightly in the lead.

Liquidation value provides a somewhat different picture. The ROI based on liquidation value for the Boston area is very low relative to the other two areas. Because of the significant appreciation in real estate values at the Boston area stores, the liquidation value for the Boston region

---

[5] The values for net book value (NBV) and gross book value in Exhibit 19.3 represent the simple average of beginning-of-year and end-of-year values (beginning and ending values are not shown). Replacement cost and liquidation value are estimated as of the point when ROI is calculated.

is quite high. The replacement cost figure is lower than liquidation cost because of the assumption that if CompuCity replaces its stores in the Boston area, these stores would be located where the real estate values are lower. The analysis of liquidation-based ROIs is useful for showing CompuCity management that the real estate value of these stores could now exceed their value as CompuCity retail locations. Perhaps the company should sell these stores and relocate elsewhere in areas whose values are near those suggested by the replacement-cost figures.

Strategic Issues Regarding the Use of ROI

The use of ROI for performance-evaluation purposes is well entrenched in business practice. However, management accountants should be aware of some of the limitations or deficiencies of using ROI to evaluate the performance of investment centers. We address four such issues: applicability of ROI as a performance indicator in the knowledge-based economy; goal-congruency problems associated with the use of any short-term financial-performance indicator, such as ROI; behavioral consequences associated with using different models (e.g., NPV and ROI) for investment decision making and subsequent performance evaluation; and, incentive effects regarding new investment by the most profitable units of the organization.

Value Creation in the New Economy

As indicated in footnote 3, the ROI metric was developed for use by industrial-age companies (DuPont, General Motors, etc.). For such companies, the ROI performance indicator served its purpose well: its use allowed top management to effectively allocate capital across organizational subunits, such as investment centers. In short, companies in that era competed by how effectively they managed their physical assets (plant, property, and equipment). It was entirely appropriate, therefore, to evaluate these units on the basis of the amount of profit generated by the use of these physical assets.

Today's business environment is drastically different. Value creation for many companies competing in what can be called the *knowledge-based economy* consists of managing intangible, as well as tangible, assets. Examples of such assets are: the skills level of the organization's employees (i.e., human capital); distinctive processes, including supply chains; loyal customers; and, innovative products and services. Thus, in today's competitive environment a broader performance-measurement and control system is demanded, such as the use of a balanced scorecard (BSC), covered in this text in Chapters 2 and 18. Although including high-level financial goals such as ROI, an entity's BSC is broader in that it includes the drivers of that financial performance, many of which are nonfinancial in nature. Chapter 18 discusses a food-ingredients company's use of the BSC in strategic performance measurement. Selected Real-World Focus items in the present chapter provide examples of alternative approaches to implementing ROI in the knowledge-based economy.

Short-Term Focus of the Metric

Somewhat related to the above, we note that ROI (and, as we shall see, RI as well) are short-term measures of profitability and as such are subject to manipulation on the part of managers. ROI is a ratio. Thus, managers, particularly those whose bonuses are tied to realized ROI figures, are motivated to do whatever it takes to increase the numerator of the calculation or to decrease the denominator, or both. Some actions border on the unethical, if not illegal. Other actions (e.g., delaying needed repairs and maintenance, reducing spending on critical research and development activities or on productivity-improvement programs) can be myopic in nature. That is, they can provide a short-term boost to reported profits (i.e., to the numerator of the ROI metric), but at the expense of the long-term competitive position of the business.

On the denominator side, the use of ROI can provide further goal-congruency problems: it can discourage managers from making investments that increase the value of the organization. There are two dimensions to this problem: (1) there can be a disconnect between the method used to make capital-budgeting decisions (e.g., discounted cash flow [DCF] decision models, as discussed in Chapter 12) and the method used subsequently to evaluate managerial performance, and (2) the disincentive effects on short-term ROI associated with new investment opportunities. We explore these issues in the following two sections. Both situations can motivate suboptimal decision-making on the part of divisional managers.

Long-Term versus Short-Term Performance Measurement: Intangible Assets

A useful way to consider the issue of short- versus long-term performance evaluation is to consider, as the balanced scorecard does, financial versus nonfinancial factors. Using only financial factors such as ROI tends to produce a short-term focus as managers seek to maximize current revenues and reduce current costs. In contrast, the use of nonfinancial measures such as employee training, product development, and customer satisfaction can cause managers to focus on these measures, which will build the base for profitability and strategic success in the long term.

Another way to consider short-term versus long-term performance measurement is to look beyond only physical and monetary assets to intangible assets, which are very real but difficult to measure. For example, employee training is not an asset on the balance sheet, yet it has real value. How is its value measured in dollars, as is the case for other assets? Although expenditures on research and development (R&D) likely bring future benefits, what dollar value can we now place on these benefits? R&D is not typically included in the assets used to measure ROI, nor are training expenses, or advertising and marketing expenses.

Sources: Based on Alan M. Webber, "New Math for a New Economy," *Fast Company,* January–February 2000, pp. 214–24; Baruch Lev, *Intangibles: Management, Measurement, and Reporting* (Washington, DC: Brookings Institution Press, 2001); and, Felix Barber and Rainer Strack, "The Surprising Economics of the People Business," *Harvard Business Review,* June 2005, pp. 81–90.

Decision Model and Performance Model Inconsistency

As we demonstrated in Chapter 12, long-term investment projects should be evaluated using a discounted cash flow (DCF) decision model, such as net present value (NPV). Such a model compares the present value of expected after-tax cash flows from a project to the present value of cash outflows (investment outlays) for the project. If the NPV is positive, the project in question should be accepted because the expectation is that the project will increase the value of the organization.

In practice, the divisional manager's financial performance may be judged using an accounting-based metric such as ROI. The use of two different metrics, one for making the investment decision (NPV) and the other for evaluating subsequent financial performance (ROI) creates an inherent and significant incentive problem: it may discourage managers from making investment decisions that add value to the organization (i.e., NPV > 0) yet have unfavorable short-term effects on ROI. One solution to this problem is to calculate depreciation, for ROI purposes, on a present-value basis. (This issue is explored in end-of-chapter assignment 19-43.) The end result is that the use of present-value depreciation aligns the decision-making model with the model used subsequently to evaluate divisional performance.

As demonstrated in the following section, investment disincentive effects can exist even when ROI, rather than NPV, is used to evaluate long-term investment proposals.

ROI: Disincentive for New Investment by the Most Profitable Units

Business units evaluated on ROI have an important disincentive that conflicts with the goals of the firm: ROI encourages units to invest only in projects that earn *higher than the unit's current ROI* so that the addition of the investment improves the unit's overall ROI. Thus, the most profitable units have a corresponding disincentive to invest in any project that does not exceed their current ROI, even those projects that, on a present-value basis, are attractive to the organization as a whole.[6]

The disincentive for new investment hurts the firm strategically in two ways. First, it rejects investment projects that would be beneficial. Second, to take advantage of a unit's apparent management skill, ROI evaluation provides a disincentive for the best units to grow. In contrast, the units with the lowest ROI have an incentive to invest in new projects to improve their ROI. Management skills could be lacking in the low-ROI units, however.

The disincentive can be illustrated if we assume that CompuCity's Boston region has an option to purchase for $22,500 a telephone switch that can increase the capacity of its toll-free service number and reduce operating costs by $10,000 per year. The switch is expected to last for three years and have no salvage value. Exhibit 19.4 shows the determination of ROI for the

---

[6] As we demonstrated in Chapter 12, an attractive project is one that has a positive estimated net present value (NPV).

EXHIBIT 19.4 **ROI for Boston Region's Proposed Investment**

	First Year	Second Year	Third Year
Depreciation expense (straight-line method)	$7,500 = $22,500/3	$7,500	$7,500
NBV at year-end	$15,000 = $22,500 − $7,500	$7,500 = $15,000 − $7,500	$ 0 = $7,500 − $7,500
Average NBV for the year	$18,750 = ($22,500 + $15,000)/2	$11,250 = ($15,000 + $7,500)/2	$3,750 = ($7,500 + $0)/2
ROI	$13.33\% = \dfrac{\$10,000 - \$7,500}{\$18,750}$	$22.22\% = \dfrac{\$10,000 - \$7,500}{\$11,250}$	$66.67\% = \dfrac{\$10,000 - \$7,500}{\$3,750}$

purchase of the switch using the straight-line method of depreciation. The ROI for its purchase is expected to be 13.33 percent in the first year, and 22.22 percent and 66.67 percent in the second and third years, respectively.[7]

Using NBV, the Boston region's ROI is currently 18.2 percent (Exhibit 19.3). Consequently, the division might not purchase the switch because the first year's return of 13.33 percent is less than the division's current ROI. Buying the switch would reduce Boston's ROI from 18.16 percent to 17.77 percent [($38,500 + $10,000 − $7,500)/($212,000 + $18,750)] in the first year. In later years, the ROI from the switch would substantially exceed Boston's current ROI, but the manager might not be able (or willing) to wait for that improvement if strong pressure for current profits exists.

Moreover, from a firmwide perspective, since the rate of return on the switch in each year exceeds the firm's threshold rate of return of 12 percent, the Boston region should purchase it. Thus, a significant limitation of ROI is that it can cause investment center managers to decline some investments, in conflict with firmwide interests. This situation is an excellent example of a goal-congruency problem: the use of ROI to evaluate the short-term financial performance of subunit managers may not motivate decisions that increase the value of the business. One way to address this limitation is to use an alternative measure of investment center profitability, called *residual income.*

Residual Income

LEARNING OBJECTIVE 2

Explain the use and limitations of residual income for evaluating investment centers.

Residual income (RI)

is a dollar amount equal to the income of a business unit less a charge for the level of investment in the diviision.

In contrast to ROI, which is a percentage, **residual income (RI)** is a dollar amount equal to the income of a business unit less an imputed charge for the level of investment in the unit. The charge is determined by multiplying a desired minimum rate of return by the the level of investment in the division.[8] Residual income can be interpreted as the income earned after the division has "paid" a charge for the funds invested by top management in the division.

The RI calculation for CompuCity is illustrated in Exhibit 19.5 using a minimum rate of return of 12 percent. Note that since all three subunits have an ROI higher than 12 percent, all also have a positive RI. Note, too, that in this case each unit's ranking on ROI is the same as its ranking based on RI: the Boston area unit has the highest ROI and residual income. However, this will not always be the case.

The issues regarding the measurement of investment and income for RI are the same as those discussed earlier for ROI. However, RI does have the advantage of motivating a subunit to pursue an investment opportunity as long as the investment's expected return exceeds the minimum return set by the firm. For example, using RI, the Boston region would accept the opportunity to purchase the telephone switch described in Exhibit 19.4 because this investment would increase the unit's residual income. The RI in the first year after the investment in the switch would be

$$\$13,310 = (\$38,500 + \$10,000 - \$7,500) - [0.12 \times (\$212,000 + \$18,750)]$$

This amounts to a $250 improvement over the unit's current RI ($13,060, from Exhibit 19.5).

[7] Using the discounted cash flow methods explained in Chapter 12, the purchase of the switch has an internal rate of return (IRR) of approximately 16 percent ($22,500/$10,000 = 2.250; the PV annuity factor for 16 percent and three years is 2.246).

[8] Conceptually, the minimum desired rate of return is defined as an entity's weighted-average cost of capital. However, we are speaking here about the evaluation of an investment center, not firmwide performance. Thus, adjustments to the firm's WACC are likely appropriate when evaluating *subunit* performance.

In a knowledge-based economy, people are the most important asset. Managing human capital is therefore of strategic concern for many organizations today, as indicated by the discussion in the text and various other Real-Word Focus boxes in this chapter. PricewaterhouseCoopers Saratoga, part of the Human Resource Services Advisory Practice of the firm, maintains a global database on human capital performance metrics and provides benchmark data for industry sectors (banking, insurance, finance, etc.) and geographic locations (U.K., U.S., Western Europe, etc.). PwC Saratoga uses a unique metric, the HR ROI, to estimate the value added per FTE (full-time equivalent) employee. HC ROI is calculated as the ratio of pretax profit, prior to employment costs, to employee investment (total compensation), as follows:

$$HC\ ROI = \frac{Revenue - Nonwage\ costs}{Number\ of\ FTEs \times Average\ remuneration}$$

Because the metric is in ratio form, it is useful for making comparisons across commercial sectors, regions, and nations. This metric covers all of the following: revenue production, cost incurrence, employment level, and amount invested in employees. As such, it provides direction for improving the return on human capital for a given organization.

Source: *PricewaterhouseCoopers, "Managing People in a Changing World—Key Trends in Human Capital: A Global Perspective, 2008."*

EXHIBIT 19.5
Illustration of Residual Income Calculations for CompuCity Divisions

	Income	Net Book Value
Financial data (from Exhibit 19.3):		
Midwest	$26,000	$192,500
Boston area	38,500	212,000
South Florida	16,850	133,000
Return on investment (ROI):		
Midwest	13.51%	
Boston area	18.16%	
South Florida	12.67%	
Residual income (RI):		
Midwest	$2,900 = $26,000 − (0.12 × $192,500)	
Boston area	$13,060 = $38,500 − (0.12 × $212,000)	
South Florida	$890 = $16,850 − (0.12 × $133,000)	

An additional advantage of RI is that a firm can adjust the required rates of return for differences in risk. For example, units with higher business risk can be evaluated at a higher minimum rate of return. The increased risk might be due to obsolete products, increased competition in the industry, or other economic factors affecting the business unit. In Exhibit 19.5 we used the same minimum rate of return when calculating the RI of each business division of CompuCity. However, this is not required or perhaps even desirable. We could have used different rates of return for each division, in order to capture risk differences across the three divisions of the company.

Another advantage is that it is possible to calculate a different investment charge for different types of assets. For example, a higher minimum rate of return could be used for long-lived assets that are more likely to be specialized in use and thus not so readily saleable.

Time Period of Analysis

Both ROI and RI are *short-term* indicators of financial performance. That is, they both generally reflect one-year performance. Because of this, some organizations choose to evaluate these performance indicators over multiple years. Trend analysis, perhaps combined with competitive benchmarking, would yield more informative indications of an investment center's financial performance. By including multiple years in the evaluation window, there may be less incentive to engage in short-term behaviors that are dysfunctional in terms of long-term profitability. Finally, in the discussion of ROI we pointed out that the use of present-value depreciation is one mechanism for achieving compatibility between the model used for long-term investment decision making and the model used subsequently to evaluate managerial performance. The use of multiyear residual income figures is thought to accomplish the same objective. Why? Because the NPV of residual incomes over the life of a project, if cash flows are exactly as predicted, will be exactly equal to the NPV of net after-tax cash flows. In short, the use of multiyear RI figures helps to achieve goal congruency.

Limitations of Residual Income (RI)

Although the residual income measure deals effectively with the disincentive problem of ROI, it has its own limitations. A key issue is that because RI is not a percentage, it is not useful for comparing units of significantly different sizes. RI favors larger units that would be expected to have larger residual incomes, even with relatively poor performance. Moreover, relatively small changes in the minimum rate of return can dramatically affect the RI for units of different size, as illustrated in Exhibit 19.6. Although both units A and B have the same ROI of 15 percent, the RI amount differs significantly: $300,000 for unit A, but only $22,500 for unit B. The difference would be greater for a smaller minimum return.

ROI and RI can complement each other in the evaluation of investment centers. The advantages and limitations of each measure are summarized in Exhibit 19.7.

EXHIBIT 19.6   **The Effect of Unit Size and Minimum Desired Rate of Return on Residual Income (RI)**

	Business Unit A	Business Unit B
Investment	$10,000,000	$750,000
Income	$1,500,000	$112,500
ROI	15% = $1,500,000/$10,000,000	15% = $112,500/$750,000
Residual income, at a minimum desired return of 12 percent	$300,000 = $1,500,000 − (0.12 × $10,000,000)	$22,500 = $112,500 − (0.12 × $750,000)

EXHIBIT 19.7   **Advantages and Limitations of ROI and Residual Income (RI)**

	Advantages	Limitations
ROI	• Easily understood by managers • Comparable to interest rates and to rates of return on alternative investments • Widely used	• Disincentive for high-ROI units to invest in projects with ROI higher than the minimum rate of return but lower than the unit's current ROI • Can lead to goal-congruency problems (e.g., suboptimal investment decision making)
Residual income	• Supports incentive to accept all projects with ROI above the minimum rate of return • Can use the minimum rate of return to adjust for differences in risk • Can use a different minimum rate of return for different types of assets	• Favors large units • Can be difficult to determine a minimum rate of return for organizational subunits
Both ROI and residual income	• *Comprehensive financial measure;* includes key elements important to top management: revenues, costs, and level of investment • *Comparability;* expands top management's span of control by allowing comparison of business units	• *Can mislead strategic decision making;* not as comprehensive as the balanced scorecard, which includes customer satisfaction, business processes, and learning, as well as financial measures; the balanced scorecard is linked to strategy • *Measurement issues;* variations in the measurement of inventory and long-lived assets and in the treatment of nonrecurring items, income taxes, foreign exchange effects, and the use/cost of shared assets • *Short-term focus;* investments with long-term benefits might be neglected; captures financial performance for only a single year ; may cause goal-congruency problems within the organization • Failure to capture value-creating activities (i.e., managing an organization's intangible assets)

Economic Value Added

LEARNING OBJECTIVE 3

Explain the use and limitation of economic value added (EVA®) for evaluating investment centers.

Economic value added (EVA®) is an estimate of a business unit's economic profit generated during a given period.

Economic value added (EVA®) is an estimate of a business's *economic profit* generated during a given period. In its simplest form, EVA® can be defined as profit less an imputed charge for the use of assets (capital) during the period. We might depict this measure of earnings as follows:

Sales
Less: Operating expenses (including taxes)
Less: Financing expense (cost of capital × amount of invested capital)
EVA®

As with RI and ROI, EVA® is a potentially useful metric for evaluating the financial performance of investment units because it explicitly incorporates the level of invested capital in the measure. That is, similar to residual income (RI), no measure of return *on* investment is indicated until there is a recovery of the cost *of* capital. Similar to RI, EVA® motivates managers to increase investment as long as such investments return at least $1 beyond the cost of capital. In this sense, this use of EVA® is thought to better align the interests of shareholders and managers of a company.

On the surface, RI and EVA® look confusingly similar. There is a major difference, however. Residual income (RI) is calculated entirely using reported (i.e., GAAP-based) accounting data. As such, the resulting measure of profitability suffers from all of the limitations associated with historical-based accounting statements. By contrast, EVA® attempts to approximate economic, rather than accounting, earnings and level of invested capital.

Thus, RI and EVA® are similar in form but strikingly different in terms of measurement. The overall objective of EVA® is to provide an estimate of the *value added* to (or destroyed by) each division of an organization (or the entire organization itself) during a given period. As such, EVA® is one approach to what we call *value-based management.*

Estimating EVA®

The equation listed above for EVA® can be expanded as follows:

$$EVA® = NOPAT - (k \times \text{Average invested capital})$$

where NOPAT = After-tax *cash* operating income, after depreciation (that is, "the total pool

of cash funds available to suppliers of capital")

= Revenues − Cash operating costs − Depreciation − Cash taxes on

operating income

It is precisely because of the deduction for depreciation that the earnings figure in the computation of EVA® is referred to as *net* operating profit after tax (i.e., as NOPAT). In the above formulation, capital = economic capital = cash contributed by suppliers of funds to the business (or business unit).

Finally, note that in determining the imputed charge for invested capital, k represents the weighted-average cost of capital (WACC).[9]

An alternative specification of EVA® is:

$$\text{EVA}® = (r - k) \times \text{capital}$$

where r = Rate of return on capital (what economists might call *cash on cash return*)

= NOPAT/Invested capital

and k = WACC.

The primary advantage of the preceding formulation is its associated interpretation:

If $r > k$ during a period, then shareholder value was increased during that period (i.e., EVA® was positive).

As seen from the above, in order to calculate EVA® for a period, we need to estimate both NOPAT and capital. Stewart, in the seminal work in the area, lists 164 possible adjustments to reported accounting data to estimate NOPAT and capital.[10] In the EVA® literature, adjustments to the capital figures reported in financial statements are referred to as *equity-equivalent (EE)* adjustments.

The actual number of adjustments in practice is typically much less than 164. Note that if no adjustments to reported accounting data were made, then the EVA® reduces to RI. The following table lists some common adjustments that analysts can make when estimating EVA®.

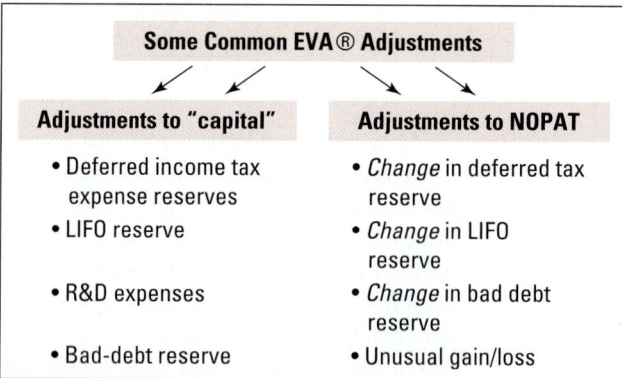

Some Common EVA® Adjustments	
Adjustments to "capital"	**Adjustments to NOPAT**
• Deferred income tax expense reserves	• *Change* in deferred tax reserve
• LIFO reserve	• *Change* in LIFO reserve
• R&D expenses	• *Change* in bad debt reserve
• Bad-debt reserve	• Unusual gain/loss

Alternative Approaches to Estimating EVA® NOPAT and EVA® Capital

Stewart provides two alternative ways for estimating an entity's EVA®: the *operating approach*, and the *financing approach*. Which of the two methods you use is simply a matter of personal preference. If applied correctly, both yield the same estimate of EVA®.

Financing Approach

In the financing approach, NOPAT is estimated by building up to the rate of return on capital from the standard return on equity (ROE) calculation in three steps:

1. Eliminate financial leverage (i.e., the effect of debt financing).
2. Eliminate so-called financial distortions.
3. Eliminate so-called accounting distortions.

[9] See Chapter 12 for a discussion of the calculation of the weighted-average cost of capital (WACC) for a company as a whole. As indicated in footnote 8, supra, adjustments to the firmwide WACC may be needed when estimating *divisional* discount rates.

[10] G. Bennett Stewart III, *The Quest for Value*, New York: Harper Collins, 1995.

As a result of the first two adjustments above, NOPAT will represent the total returns available to *all* providers of capital to the company. The NOPAT return therefore represents the productivity of capital employed in the business, irrespective of how investments in that capital were financed.

To calculate EVA® capital using the financing approach, you would first determine the total of interest-bearing debt plus capitalized leases. To this figure, you would add the book value of common equity (par value of stock, capital in excess of par, and retained earnings), the book value of preferred stock, and noncontrolling interests (if any). Finally, we must account for equity equivalents, such as the estimated present value of noncapitalized leases, the balance sheet amount of deferred taxes, and the LIFO reserve (if any). The resulting figure represents an estimate of EVA® capital.

Operating Approach

The operating approach to estimating NOPAT essentially consists of starting with (cash) sales and then subtracting depreciation and recurring cash economic expenses. Next, we deduct the amount of cash operating taxes, after which time we are left with EVA® NOPAT. In estimating the amount of cash taxes paid, we adjust reported income tax expense by the change in the deferred tax account during the period. Note that interest expense, because it is a financing charge, is ignored in the determination of EVA® NOPAT. What this means, therefore, is that we must remove (that is, add back to income tax expense) the assumed income tax benefit associated with the deductibility of interest expense. Finally, to estimate EVA® NOPAT we make a number of "EE" adjustments (e.g., the effect of a change in the LIFO reserve account, and imputed interest on noncapitalized leases). The resulting profit figure should be the same as the NOPAT figure calculated under the financing approach.

Under the operating approach, EVA® capital is estimated basically by looking at the left-hand side of the entity's balance sheet. We define EVA® capital as net working capital (NWC) plus net fixed assets (NFA), where NWC is defined as (adjusted) current assets less NIBCLS (noninterest-bearing current liabilities). Typical EE adjustments that are made to reported balance sheet data include adjustments for the LIFO reserve and for the present value of non-capitalized leases. In effect, we capitalize these leases and therefore put them on par with capitalized leases, if any, that already appear on the company's balance sheet.

Problems 19-46 and 19-47 at the end of the chapter explore the issue of estimating EVA® using the operating approach and financing approach, respectively.[11]

Using Average Total Assets

For purposes of calculating ROI, RI, and EVA®, at what point in the accounting period are assets measured? In practice, accountants use the average of the beginning and ending balances of the year for total assets in these performance metrics. The reason is that since income is applicable to the entire year, then using a simple average of the amount of total assets for the year is consistent with the period covered by the income. For example, CompuCity's ROI for 2010 (using information from Exhibit 19.1 and assuming the investment amounts shown in the exhibit are for the year-end) would be calculated as 13.89%:

$$\text{ROI} = \frac{\$26,000}{(\$182,000 + \$192,500)/2} = 13.89\%$$

Part Two: Transfer Pricing

Transfer pricing
is the determination of an exchange price for a product or service when different business units within a firm exchange it.

Transfer pricing is the determination of an exchange price for a product or service when different business units within a firm exchange it. The products can be final products sold to outside customers or intermediate products provided to other internal units. Regardless of whether subunits of an organization are considered profit centers (Chapter 18) or investment centers, transfer prices are needed for performance-evaluation purposes. For example, without

---

[11] Additional guidance for estimating EVA® NOPAT and EVA® capital are provided in the following sources: G. Bennett Stewart III, *The Quest for Value* (New York: Harper Collins, 1995), and D. S. Young and S. F. O'Byrne, *EVA® and Value-Based Management: A Practical Guide to Implementation* (New York: McGraw-Hill, 2001).

transfer prices it would not be possible to implement the performance metrics discussed in part one of this chapter (i.e., ROI, RI, and EVA®).

When Is Transfer Pricing Important?

Transfers of products and services between business units is most common in firms with a high degree of vertical integration. Such firms engage in a number of different value-creating activities in the value chain. Wood product, food product, and consumer product firms are examples. For instance, a computer manufacturer must determine transfer prices if it prepares the chips, boards, and other components and assembles the computer itself. (See Exhibit 2.3 in Chapter 2: Value Chain for the Computer-Manufacturing Industry.) A useful way to visualize the transfer-pricing context is to create a graphic such as the one in Exhibit 19.8 that illustrates the business units involved in the transfer of products and services and identifies them as inside or outside the firm, international or domestic. Exhibit 19.8 shows the transfers for a hypothetical computer manufacturer, High Value Computer (HVC), that purchases a key component, the x-chip, from both internal and external suppliers and purchases other components from international sources. The internal unit that manufactures x-chips sells them both internally and externally. Where it is known, the transfer price is shown in Exhibit 19.8.

The management accountant's role is to help determine the proper transfer price for the internal sales of the x-chip. We begin by considering the objectives of transfer pricing.

Objectives of Transfer Pricing

LEARNING OBJECTIVE 4

Explain the objectives of transfer pricing, and the advantages and disadvantages of various transfer-pricing alternatives.

Transfer prices are used to accomplish certain objectives. It is against these objectives that alternative transfer-price options can be evaluated. As is the case with the financial-performance metrics discussed in part one of this chapter, we can identify three primary objectives for transfer prices:

1. Motivate a high level of effort on the part of subunit managers (i.e., extent to which a particular transfer-pricing method maintains divisional autonomy).
2. Goal congruency (i.e., achieve consistency between decisions made by managers and the goals of top management); for example, one important goal of transfer pricing is to minimize, within allowable limits, income-tax consequences of intradivisional transfers of goods and services.
3. Reward managers fairly for their effort and skill, and for the effectiveness of the decisions they make.

EXHIBIT 19.8

Transfer Pricing Context for High Value Computer (HVC)

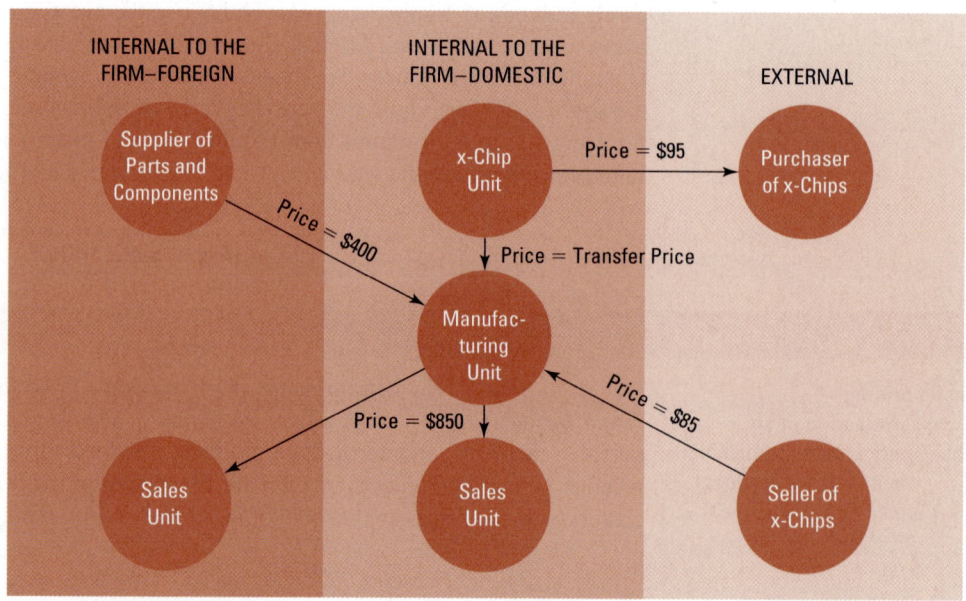

From a practical standpoint, specific transfer-pricing alternatives can also be evaluated in terms of implementation/administrative costs. In the next section we discuss several transfer-pricing methods, including advantages and disadvantages of each of these methods.

Transfer-Pricing Methods

The **variable-cost method** sets the transfer price equal to the variable cost of the selling unit.

The **full-cost method** sets the transfer price equal to the variable cost plus allocated fixed cost for the selling unit.

The **market-price method** sets the transfer price as the current price of the product in the external market.

The **negotiated-price method** involves a negotiation process and sometimes arbitration between units to determine the transfer price.

Dual pricing involves the use of multiple prices for an internal transfer.

The four available methods for determining the transfer price are: variable cost, full cost, market price, and negotiated price.

The **variable-cost method** sets the transfer price equal to the selling unit's variable cost, with or without a mark-up. This method is desirable when the selling unit has excess capacity and the transfer price's chief objective is to satisfy the internal demand for the goods. The relatively low transfer price encourages buying internally. To motivate an internal transfer and because of equity considerations, some companies add a mark-up to variable cost when determining the transfer price. One alternative in this regard is to add a lump-sum amount to variable costs. Also, variable costs can be defined either as actual or as standard costs.

The **full-cost method** sets the transfer price equal to variable costs plus an allocated share of the selling unit's fixed costs, with or without a markup for profit. Advantages of this approach are that it is well understood and that the information is readily available in the accounting records. A key disadvantage is that it includes fixed costs, which can cause improper decision making (Chapter 11). To improve on the full-cost method, firms can use the activity-based cost method described in Chapter 5.[12] Again, costs can be defined either as actual or as standard costs.

The **market-price method** sets the transfer price as the current price of the product in the external market. Its key advantage is objectivity; it best satisfies the arm's-length criterion desired for both management and tax purposes. A key disadvantage is that the market price, especially for intermediate products, is often not available.

The **negotiated-price method** involves a negotiation process and sometimes arbitration between units to determine the transfer price. This method is desirable when the units have a history of significant conflict and negotiation can result in an agreed-upon price. The primary limitation is that the method can reduce the desired autonomy of the units. Further, this method may be costly and time-consuming to implement.

Firms can also use two or more methods, called **dual pricing**. For example, when numerous conflicts exist between two units, standard full cost might be used as the buyer's transfer price, while the seller might use market price.[13]

The advantages and limitations of each of the four methods are summarized in Exhibit 19.9.

Choosing the Right Transfer-Pricing Method: The Firmwide Perspective

One aspect of transfer pricing is whether the transfer price will lead to actions that benefit the organization as a whole. Looked at differently, we might ask whether the transfer price motivates an internal transfer when this benefits the firm, and whether it motivates an external sale when such a sale is warranted (from the an organization-wide perspective). To guide such a decision, three questions must be addressed:

1. Is there an outside supplier?
2. Is the seller's variable cost less than the market price?
3. Is the selling unit operating at full capacity?

Exhibit 19.10 shows the influence of each of these three factors on the choice of a transfer price and on the decision to purchase inside or out.

First: Is there an outside supplier? If not, there is no market price, and the best transfer price is based on cost or negotiated price. If there is an outside supplier, we must consider the relationship of the inside seller's variable cost to the market price of the outside supplier by answering the second question.

[12] For an explanation of the use of activity-based costing in transfer pricing, see Robert S. Kaplan, Dan Weiss, and Eyal Desheh, "Transfer Pricing with ABC," *Management Accounting,* May 1997, pp. 20–28, and Gary J. Colbert and Barry H. Spicer, "Linking Activity-Based Costing and Transfer Pricing for Improved Decisions and Behavior," *Journal of Cost Management,* May–June 1998, pp. 20–26.

[13] For an illustration of dual allocation in transfer pricing, see David W. Young, "Two-Part Transfer Pricing Improves IDS Financial Control," *Healthcare Financial Management,* August 1998, pp. 56–65.

EXHIBIT 19.9   **Advantages and Limitations of Alternative Transfer-Pricing Methods**

Method	Advantages	Limitations
Variable cost	• Provides the proper motivation for the manager to make the correct *short-term decision*, in which the seller's fixed costs are not expected to change. When the seller's variable cost is less than the buyer's outside price, the variable cost transfer price will cause internal sourcing, the correct decision	• Inappropriate for long-term decision making in which fixed costs are relevant, and prices must cover fixed as well as variable costs • Unfair to seller if seller is profit or investment center (i.e., no profit recognized on the transfer)
Full cost	• Easy to implement • Intuitive and easily understood • Preferred by tax authorities over variable cost • Appropriate for long-term decision making in which fixed costs are relevant, and prices must cover fixed as well as variable costs	• Irrelevance of fixed cost in short-term decision making; fixed costs should be ignored in the buyer's choice of whether to buy inside or outside the firm • If used, should be standard rather than actual cost (allows buyer to know cost in advance and prevents seller from passing along inefficiencies)
Market price	• Helps to preserve unit autonomy • Provides incentive for the selling unit to be competitive with outside suppliers • Has arm's-length standard desired by taxing authorities	• Intermediate products often have no market price • Should be adjusted for any cost savings associated with an internal transfer, such as reduced selling costs
Negotiated price	• Can be the most practical approach when significant conflict exists • Is consistent with the theory of decentralization	• Need negotiation rule and/or arbitration procedure, which can reduce autonomy • Potential tax problems; might not be considered arm's length • Can be costly and time-consuming to implement • Resulting profitability measures (e.g., ROI or RI) are partly a function of the negotiating skills of the manager, rather than the operational performance of the business unit

EXHIBIT 19.10   **Choosing the Right Transfer Price**

	Decision to Transfer	Transfer Price
First: Is there an outside supplier? If there is *no* outside supply; ⟶	Buy inside	Cost or negotiated price
If there is an outside supply, answer the second question;		
Second: Is the seller's variable cost less than the outside price?		
If it is greater than the outside price, the seller must look for ways to reduce cost ⟶	Buy outside	No transfer price
If seller's variable costs are less than the outside price, answer the third question;		
Third: Is the selling unit operating at full capacity?		
If seller has excess capacity, then ⟶	Buy inside	**Low**: variable cost **High**: market price
If the seller is at full capacity ⟶ And if the contribution of the outside sales to the entire firm is **greater than** the savings of the inside purchase ⟶	Buy outside	No transfer price
Or if the contribution of the outside sales to the entire firm is **less than** the savings of the inside purchase ⟶	Buy inside	Market price

Second: Is the seller's variable cost less than the market price? If not, the seller's costs are likely far too high, and from the standpoint of the organization as a whole the buyer should buy outside. On the other hand, if the seller's variable costs are less than the market price, we must consider the capacity in the selling unit by answering the third question. (Note: We focus on variable costs in this second step because commonly the transfer-pricing issue is addressed as a short-term decision in which fixed costs are not expected to differ whether the internal transfer is made or is not made. In this case, the analysis is very much like the make-or-buy decision problem covered in Chapter 11—the fixed costs of the seller are irrelevant since they will not change in the short run.)

Third: Is the selling unit operating at full capacity? That is, will the order from the internal buyer cause the selling unit to deny other sales opportunities? If not, the selling division should provide the order to the internal buyer at a transfer price somewhere between variable cost and market price. In contrast, if the selling unit is at full capacity, we must determine and compare the cost savings of internal sales versus the selling division's opportunity cost of lost sales. If the cost savings to the inside buyer are higher than the cost of lost sales to the seller, then from the standpoint of the organization as a whole, the buying unit should buy inside, and the proper transfer price should be the market price.

Determining the correct transfer price and correct transfer decision can be illustrated using the High Value Computer (HVC) case (Exhibit 19.8). HVC has the option to purchase the x-chip outside the firm for $85 or to manufacture it. Note that if the manufacturing unit of HVC purchases the x-chip from the outside suppler, it must add a component to the x-chip at a variable cost of $5 to make the x-chip function as desired; this additional step would not be necessary if the x-chip is purchased internally. Also, note that the x-chip production unit can sell its chip outside for $95 but there is a variable selling cost of $2 per unit; there is no selling cost for internal transfer. The relevant information is presented in the top portion of Exhibit 19.11. The lower portion of Exhibit 19.11 shows the calculation of the relevant costs for each option.

EXHIBIT 19.11

Transfer-Pricing Example: The High Value Computer Company

Key assumptions:
  The manufacturing unit can buy the x-chip inside or outside the firm.
  The x-chip unit can sell inside or outside the firm.
  The x-chip unit is at full capacity (150,000 units).
  One x-chip is needed for each computer manufactured by High Value.
Other information:

Sales price of computer for HVC's computer unit	$850
Variable manufacturing cost of the computer unit (excluding x-chip) ($400 parts and $250 labor)	650
Variable x-chip manufacturing cost for HVC's x-chip unit	60
Price of x-chip from outside supplier, to HVC computer unit	85
Variable cost to computer unit to add needed component to outside supplier's x-chip	5
Price of x-chip from HVC's x-chip unit to outside buyer	95
Variable selling cost to the x-chip unit for outside sales	2

Option 1: X-Chip Unit Sells Outside

High Value manufactures 150,000 computers, using x-chips purchased for $85 from outside supplier; High Value's x-chip unit sells 150,000 units for $95 each to outside buyer.

Contribution Income Statement[*]
(000s omitted)

	Computer Manufacturing Unit	X-Chip Unit	Total
Sales (price = $850, $95)	$127,500	$14,250	$141,750
Less: Variable costs			
x-chip ($85 + $5)	13,500		13,500
Other costs ($650, $60 + $2)	97,500	9,300	106,800
Contribution margin	$ 16,500	$ 4,950	$ 21,450

Option 2: X-Chip Unit Sells Inside

High Value manufactures 150,000 computers, using x-chips purchased for $60 (variable cost) from the inside supplier.

	Computer Manufacturing Unit	X-Chip Unit	Total
Sales (price = $850, $60)	$127,500	$9,000	$136,500
Less: Variable costs			
x-chip ($60)	9,000		9,000
Other costs ($650, $60)	97,500	9,000	106,500
Contribution margin	$ 21,000	—	$ 21,000

[*]It is assumed that fixed costs will not differ for the two options; thus, these costs are excluded from the analysis.

The decline in value of Southeast Asian currencies (the Indonesian rupiah, Thai baht, Malaysian ringgit, and Sri Lanka rupee) relative to the U.S. dollar in the early 2000s appeared to be an opportunity for some Southeast Asian manufacturers to increase their exports to U.S. retailers and manufacturers. The idea is that the falling currency prices would make the Asian goods less expensive in U.S. dollars, which would increase their appeal in the United States relative to other products and thus increase demand. Nike, which has a number of manufacturing plants in Southeast Asia, says, however, that these currency changes will not have much effect on U.S. prices. Is Nike likely to miss the potential to lower prices and increase U.S. sales? (Refer to Comments on Cost Management in Action at end of Chapter.)

A comparison of options 1 and 2 in Exhibit 19.11 shows that the firm as a whole benefits under option 1 when the manufacturing unit purchases the x-chip outside, and the x-chip unit also sells outside. The reason is that the computer manufacturing unit's savings of $30 from internal transfer ($30 = $85 outside price plus $5 for additional variable cost to add a component to the x-chip less $60 variable cost of the internal x-chip unit) is less than the x-chip unit's opportunity cost of lost sales, $33 ($95 less $60 manufacturing cost less $2 selling cost). The opportunity cost of the x-chip unit is important since the unit is at full capacity. The $450,000 difference between the two options is due to the net difference identified above, ($33 − $30) × 150,000 = $450,000. In summary, we can answer the same three questions for HVC in the following way:

First: Is there an outside supplier? High Value has an outside supplier, so we must compare the inside seller's variable costs to the outside seller's price.

Second: Is the seller's variable cost less than the market price? For High Value, it is, so we must consider the utilization of capacity in the inside selling unit.

Third: Is the selling unit operating at full capacity? For High Value, it is, so we must consider the contribution of the selling unit's outside sales relative to the savings from selling inside. Again, for High Value the contribution of the selling unit's outside sales is $33 per unit, which is higher than the savings from selling inside ($30). Therefore, High Value's selling unit should choose outside sales and make no internal transfers.

General Transfer-Pricing Rule

The preceding discussion, and accompanying summary (Exhibit 19.10), may seem overwhelming to you in terms of detail and complexity. It may also seem as if the transfer-pricing decision can be mechanized according to a set of rules. This is certainly not the case because as we stated at the beginning of this section of the chapter, the ultimate transfer-pricing decision is a function of several considerations. One of these is the extent to which the transfer price motivates the "correct" decision from the standpoint of the firm as a whole. Thus, in interpreting Exhibit 19.10 you should understand that the stated rules relate to this issue.

In Chapter 11 we introduced you to the notion of relevant costs for decision making. One definition of such costs is the sum of out-of-pocket costs plus opportunity costs (if any). We can appeal to this same notion in the context of setting an appropriate transfer price. Thus, the essence of Exhibit 19.10 can be summarized by the following General Transfer-Pricing Rule:

$$\frac{\text{Minimum}}{\text{transfer price}} = \frac{\text{Incremental (i.e., out-of-pocket) cost of the producing division} + \text{Opportunity}}{\text{cost to the organization (if any) by making an internal transfer}}$$

From the standpoint of the firm as a whole, the preceding rule will generally ensure that the optimum decision (transfer internally or not) will be motivated by the transfer price. At the same time, we should correctly view the amount indicated by the general rule as a minimum amount that the selling division should accept. In Chapter 11, we essentially saw the same thing: in deciding whether a business should accept a special (i.e., one-time) order, the minimum specified price was the sum of out-of-pocket costs plus opportunity cost (if any). (Recall the notion of *opportunity cost:* benefit forgone by taking a particular course of action.) *Minimum* within the context of the special sales order means the *floor* below which the firm would

Effective transfer pricing can enhance a company's overall profitability, but there is a delicate balance between smart business and smart government as businesses seek to minimize tax payments and countries seek to maximize tax revenue. For those businesses without adequate transfer-planning the risk of staggering penalties imposed by the IRS is very real, as the following two examples illustrate.

- In a recent case, Symantec Corporation found itself in a $1 billion transfer-pricing dispute with the IRS after the company acquired software maker Veritas in 2005. According to the IRS, licensing fees Veritas received from an Irish subsidiary were too low, and the company accounting records credited U.S. operations with too much of the cost of creating certain technologies. This approach increased income at the Irish subsidiary, which operated in a lower-tax environment and therefore allowed the company to lower its U.S. tax liability.

- In September 2006, GlaxoSmithKline agreed to pay the U.S. government $3.4 billion to settle a 17-year dispute with the IRS over the company's transfers between the U.K. parent company and its American subsidiary. This was the largest settlement of a tax dispute in U.S. history. The investigations carried out by IRS found that the American subsidiary of GlaxoSmithKline overpaid its U.K. parent company for drug supplies during 1989–2005 period, mainly for its blockbuster drug, Zantac. These overpayments were meant to reduce the company's profit in the United States and thereby its tax bill. Other items under dispute included the value of marketing

in the United States, and trademarks and other intangible assets that were developed and owned by the U.K. parent company. The IRS charged the company for engaging in what is viewed as manipulative transfer pricing.

All kinds of transactions within related entities are subject to transfer-pricing rules, including raw material; finished products; and payments such as management fees, intellectual property royalties, loans, interest on loans, payments for technical assistance and know-how, and other transactions. These rules generally require intrafirm transactions to be recorded at an "arm's length" basis, which means that any transaction between two entities of the same company should be priced as if the transaction were conducted between two unrelated parties.

As the above two examples show, the penalties for not adhering to transfer-pricing rules can be very significant. In the United States, transfer-pricing rules are contained in Internal Revenue Code Section 482. Companies that violate these rules may be responsible for additional tax and interest, and depending on circumstances uncovered in an audit, the IRS can impose penalties of 20 percent or 40 percent of the underpaid tax. Furthermore, there is the chance that both countries involved in a transfer-pricing dispute would assess taxes on the same profits, effectively doubling the amount of tax owed.

Sources: "How to Minimize Risks of an IRS Transfer Pricing Review," *RSM Advantage* 3, no. 6 (October 2006); and, "Transfer Pricing Studies Can Lead to Planning Opportunities," RSM McGladrey, October 2006.

not normally consummate the deal. The same logic would apply in the transfer-pricing case. Here, opportunity cost is the contribution margin the organization forgoes, if any, by transferring internally rather than making the sale to an external party.

We conclude here by noting that estimating opportunity costs may not be an easy task, or even possible in some situations. For example, unless the product in question is traded in a purely competitive market (e.g., commodity-type products), then selling price, and therefore opportunity cost, are partly a function of the amount of internal versus external sales by the producer. These interactions complicate efforts to determine an opportunity cost associated with internal transfers. As another example, the product in question may be in the form of an intermediate product for which no organized external market exists. In such cases, the organization would have to rely on the use of one of the other transfer-pricing options.

International Issues in Transfer Pricing

LEARNING OBJECTIVE 5

Discuss important international issues that arise in transfer pricing.

Two surveys have found that more than 80 percent of multinational firms (MNCs) see transfer pricing as a major international tax issue, and more than half these firms said it was the most important issue.[14] Most countries now accept the Organization of Economic Cooperation and Development's model treaty, which calls for transfer prices to be adjusted using the arm's-length standard, that is, to a price that unrelated parties would have set. The model treaty is widely accepted, but the way countries apply it can differ. However, worldwide support is

[14] Based on information from two surveys: (1) the Ernst & Young Transfer Pricing Global Survey of 400 MNCs, as reported in the *Ernst & Young Business UpShot,* October 1997; and (2) a survey of 210 companies in the United States, United Kingdom, Japan, Australia, the Netherlands, France, and Germany, as reported in *Accounting Today,* August 21–September 10, 1995.

The **arm's-length standard** says that transfer prices should be set so they reflect the price that unrelated parties acting independently would have set.

The **comparable-price method** establishes an arm's-length price by using the sales prices of similar products made by unrelated firms.

The **resale-price method** is based on determining an appropriate markup based on gross profits of unrelated firms selling similar products.

The **cost-plus method** determines the transfer price based on the seller's cost plus a gross profit percentage determined by comparing the seller's sales to those of unrelated parties.

strong for an approach to limit attempts by MNCs to reduce tax liability by setting transfer prices that differ from the arm's-length standard.[15]

The **arm's-length standard** calls for setting transfer prices to reflect the price that unrelated parties acting independently would have set. The arm's-length standard is applied in many ways, but the three most widely used methods are (1) the comparable-price method, (2) the resale-price method, and (3) the cost-plus method. The **comparable-price method** is the most commonly used and the most preferred by tax authorities. It establishes an arm's-length price by using the sales prices of similar products made by unrelated firms.[16]

The **resale-price method** is used for distributors and marketing units when little value is added and no significant manufacturing operations exist. In this method, the transfer price is based on an appropriate markup using gross profits of unrelated firms selling similar products.

The **cost-plus method** determines the transfer price based on the seller's costs plus a gross profit percentage determined by comparing the seller's sales to those of unrelated parties or to unrelated parties' sales to those of other unrelated parties.

By keeping detailed records of the determination of cost, the management accountant can assist in determining the appropriate transfer price for international transfers of goods and services. The application of modern costing techniques, such as ABC (Chapter 5), would be particularly useful in terms of justifying a particular transfer price. While it is true that there are limits to the transfer price charged in multinational transactions, it is also true that minimizing worldwide tax is a legitimate business objective. By setting a (legitimate) high transfer price for goods or services transferred to a unit operating in a relatively high-tax country, a company can reduce its tax liability. Such a transfer price would increase the cost and thus reduce the income of the purchasing unit, thereby minimizing taxes for this unit. At the same time, the higher profits shown by the selling unit (as a result of the high transfer price) would be taxed at lower rates in the seller's home country.

Other International Considerations

In addition to income tax, there are other considerations that bear upon the transfer-price decision in an international context. These include minimizing customs charges, using trans-fer prices to deal with currency restrictions of foreign countries, and dealing with the risk of expropriation of assets.

Risk of Expropriation

Expropriation occurs when a government takes ownership and control of assets that a foreign investor has invested in that country.

Expropriation occurs when a government takes ownership and control of assets that a foreign investor has invested in that country. In managing the relationship with any one country, the

[15] For further information on international taxation and transfer pricing, see B. J. Arnold and M. J. McIntyre, *International Tax Primer*, 2nd ed. (Boston: Kluwer Law International, 2002).

[16] In this context, *unrelated* indicates that the firm has no common ownership interest.

management accountant attempts to find a strategic balance among these sometimes conflicting objectives. When a significant risk of expropriation exists, the firm can take appropriate actions such as limiting new investment or developing improved relationships with the foreign government (e.g., by actually paying higher taxes to that government via the transfer-pricing decision).

Minimization of Customs Charges

The transfer price amount can affect the overall cost, including the customs charges, of goods imported from a foreign unit. For example, if customs charges on the parts and components imported by the domestic manufacturing unit are significant in amount, High Value Computer's relatively low transfer price on these imports would be beneficial in terms of reducing the amount of customs charges.

Currency Restrictions

As a foreign unit accumulates profits, a problem arises in some countries that limits the amount and/or timing of repatriation of these profits to the parent company. One way to deal with these restrictions is to set the transfer price so that profits accumulate at a relatively low rate. This issue therefore provides managers and the management accountant with additional planning opportunities in certain circumstances.

Advance Pricing Agreements

An **advance pricing agreement (APA)**
is an agreement between the
Internal Revenue Service (IRS)
and a firm that establishes an
agreed-upon transfer price.

An **advance pricing agreement (APA)** is an agreement between the Internal Revenue Service (IRS) and a firm that establishes an agreed-upon transfer price. The APA usually is obtained before the firm engages in the transfer. The APA program's goal is to resolve transfer-pricing disputes in a timely manner and to avoid costly litigation. The program supplements the dispute resolution methods already in place: administrative (IRS), judicial, and treaty mechanisms. Two-thirds of the MNCs in a recent survey indicated that they expected to use APAs in determining their transfer prices.[17]

Summary

Return on investment (ROI) and residual income (RI) are two of the most commonly used and well-understood measures for evaluating the financial performance of investment centers.

ROI, which is defined as the ratio of operating income generated by the investment center to the level of investment in the investment center, has several disadvantages: a short-term focus, the difficulty in determining a unique measure for earnings and investment, and investment-disincentive effects.

RI is computed as the investment center's earnings less a capital charge based on a minimum desired rate of return. RI solves some, but not all, of ROI's problems. For example, both have a short-term focus, both rely on accrual-based accounting numbers, and both focus solely on financial performance.

The increased interest in the balanced scorecard (BSC) and in economic value added (EVA®) suggests that firms are adapting performance-appraisal systems for investment centers to include a long-term strategic focus.

When an organization's business units exchange goods or services internally and management desires to assess the financial performance of these units, a transfer price must be associated with the internal transfers. The management accountant can serve an important role by overseeing many objectives of transfer pricing: performance evaluation (of management and business units), tax minimization, management of foreign currencies and risks, and other strategic objectives. Common transfer-pricing methods include variable cost, full cost, market value, and negotiated price. Cost-based transfer prices can be set either at actual or at standard cost (see Chapter 14). In setting the transfer price, management considers the availability and quality of outside supply, the internal selling unit's capacity utilization, and the firm's strategic objectives in determining the proper

---

[17] For a recent survey of advance pricing agreements in 27 different countries, see Susan C. Borkowski, "Transfer Pricing Advance Pricing Agreements: Current Status by Country," *The International Tax Journal,* Spring 2000, pp. 1–16. For U.S. APA procedures, see Steven C. Wrappe, Ken Milani, and Julie Joy, "The Transfer Price Is Right," *Strategic Finance,* July 1999, pp. 39–43.

transfer price. A general transfer-pricing guideline specifies that the minimum transfer price to the selling division is the sum of out-of-pocket costs plus opportunity costs to the seller (if any). Some companies use dual pricing in which two separate transfer prices are used to price an internal transfer.

Perhaps the most important aspect in determining a transfer price for international transfers is minimizing international taxes. With the efforts of various international groups, each country monitors transfer prices used in international trade. The most common transfer-pricing methods used for international trade include the comparable-price method, the resale-price method, and the cost-plus method. A firm can determine the acceptability (to various countries) of its transfer-pricing method by requesting what is called an *advance pricing agreement* (APA).

Key Terms

advance pricing agreements (APAs), *869*
arm's-length standard, *868*
asset turnover (AT), *847*
comparable-price method, *868*
cost-plus method, *868*
economic value added, (EVA®), *859*
dual pricing, *863*

expropriation, *868*
full-cost method, *863*
gross book value (GBV), *853*
historical cost of divisional assets, *852*
liquidation value, *853*
market-price method, *863*
negotiated-price method, *863*
net book value, *852*

replacement cost, *853*
resale-price method, *868*
residual income (RI), *856*
return on investment (ROI), *847*
return on sales (ROS), *847*
transfer pricing, *861*
variable-cost method, *863*

Comments on Cost Management in Action

Foreign Currency Translation, Transfer Pricing, and Profits

Nike is probably correct that U.S. prices for its products and those of its competitors will not change much. The reason is that the cost elements of its products from Southeast Asia affected by the falling local currencies, primarily labor costs, represent only a modest portion of the total product cost. Most of the cost of these manufactured products is for materials, which are imported from the United States and elsewhere outside Southeast Asia. Thus, the effect of the falling Southeast Asian currencies on *total* product cost is likely to be small; Nike estimates it to be 10 percent or less although some currencies have fallen to less than half of their previous value to the dollar.

Moreover, Southeast Asian manufacturers find that they have increased financing costs and sometimes reduced financing availability when the local currency falls and the raw materials from the United States and elsewhere become more expensive. For some of these manufacturers, the total operating and financing cost (in U.S. dollars) might even increase.

From a transfer-pricing perspective, the dramatic change in currency value presents real problems in performance evaluation. Should the local manufacturing unit be responsible for costs in U.S. currency or in terms of the local currency? Are the currency fluctuations controllable by the local managers? The answers to these questions are difficult and complex, but many companies expect their local managers to take steps to mitigate the negative effects of currency fluctuations by buying or selling options or other financial instruments, for example.

Source: Based on Jonathan Moore and Moon Ihlwan, "Cheaper Exports? Not So Fast," *BusinessWeek*, February 2, 1998, pp. 48–49.

Self-Study Problems

(For solutions, please turn to the end of the chapter.)

1. Return on Investment (ROI) and Residual Income (RI)

Selected data from an investment center of IROL, INC. follow:

Sales	$8,000,000
Net book value of assets, beginning	2,500,000
Net book value of assets, end	2,600,000
Net operating income	640,000
Minimum rate of return	12%

Required

1. Calculate return on sales (ROS), asset turnover (AT), and return on investment (ROI).

2. Calculate residual income.

2. Transfer Pricing

Johnston Chemical Company manufactures a wide variety of industrial chemicals and adhesives. It purchases much of its raw material in bulk from other chemical companies. One chemical, T-Bar, is prepared in one of Johnston's own plants. T-Bar is shipped to other Johnston plants at a specified internal price.

The Johnston adhesive plant requires 10,000 barrels of T-Bar per month and can purchase it from an outside supplier for $150 per barrel. Johnston's T-Bar unit has a capacity of 20,000 barrels per month and is presently selling that amount to outside buyers at $165 per barrel. The difference between the T-Bar unit's price of $165 and the outside firm's T-Bar price of $150 is due to short-term pricing strategy only; the materials are equivalent in quality and functionality. The T-Bar unit's selling cost is $5 per barrel, and its variable cost of manufacturing is $90 per barrel.

Required

1. From the standpoint of the company as a whole, should the adhesive unit purchase T-Bar inside or outside the firm? Show calculations to support your answer.

2. Based on your answer in requirement 1, what is T-Bar's proper transfer price?

3. How would your answer to requirements 1 and 2 change if the T-Bar unit had a capacity of 30,000 barrels per month?

Questions

19-1 What is meant by the term *investment center?* How is the financial performance of investment centers measured?

19-2 What are the three financial-performance measures for investment centers?

19-3 What is return on investment, and how is it calculated?

19-4 What are the measurement issues to consider when using return on investment (ROI)?

19-5 What are the advantages and limitations of return on investment (ROI) as a performance measure?

19-6 What is meant by the *arm's-length standard,* and for what is it used?

19-7 What are the components of residual income (RI)?

19-8 What are the advantages and limitations of residual income (RI) as a performance measure?

19-9 What are the objectives of measures used to evaluate the financial performance of investment centers?

19-10 What is return on equity, how is it calculated, and how is it interpreted?

19-11 What are the three methods most commonly used in international taxation to determine a transfer price acceptable to tax authorities? Explain each method briefly.

19-12 What does *expropriation* mean, and what is the role of transfer pricing in this regard?

19-13 How does the concept of economic value added EVA® compare, as a measure of financial performance, to return on investment and residual income?

Brief Exercises

19-14 Smith Branded Apparel designs t-shirts for businesses and corporations. The accounting manager has presented the latest quarter's return on sales of 10 percent and asset turnover of 1.5. What is the company's current return on investment (ROI)?

19-15 Williams Manufacturing uses scrap metal to produce various tools, such as drill bits, hammer heads, saw blades, and nails. The CEO has asked you to analyze the saw blades division to determine asset turnover for last quarter. You find that the saw blades division had an ROI of 20 percent, sales of $10 million, and operating profits of $1 million. What was the asset turnover rate for last quarter?

19-16 Scott Healthcare provides a walk-in clinic for its patients and a pharmacy for any medication prescribed by the doctor. Last year Scott generated total sales of $500,000 and $100,000 in profits. Scott also had average assets of $250,000 for the year. What are Scott Healthcare's return on sales, asset turnover, and return on investment?

19-17 Matthews Produce harvests and sells Florida oranges. Matthews has hired you to determine its return on investment (ROI) based on both net book value and on gross book value. You are given that profits are $2 million, the net book value (NBV) of operating assets is $10 million, and the gross book value (GBV) of these assets is $40 million. What is ROI based on NBV and based on GBV?

19-18 Foreman Publishing Company's income for the most recent quarter was $500,000, and the average net book value of assets during the quarter was $1.5 million. If the company has a required rate of return of 15 percent on investment, what was residual income for the quarter?

19-19   Tinsley Plastics manufactures plastic bottles used for beverages and household cleaners. The average net book value (NBV) of assets during the quarter is estimated as $500,000. If the required rate of return is 10 percent on average assets, and the firm wants to have residual income (RI) of $100,000 for this quarter, what must its profits be?

19-20   Moore Money is a financial services firm specializing in fixed-income investments. You have been asked by the accounting manager to analyze the company's financial data from last quarter. You find the firm had return on investment (ROI) of 15 percent and asset turnover of 0.5. What was the firm's return on sales?

19-21   King Mattresses sells both mattress sets and bed frames. Last quarter total sales were $50,000 for mattress sets and $25,000 for bed frames. ROI was 10 percent for both divisions, while asset turnover was 5 for mattress sets and 2 for bed frames. What was the amount of operating profit for each division?

19-22   Using the data from 19-21 above, compute King Mattresses' total return on sales (ROS).

19-23   Felton Co. produces rubber bands for commercial and home use. Felton reported $1 million residual income (RI) with $20 million net book value (NBV) of assets and $5 million in income for the year. What was the required rate of return?

19-24   Chacon Enterprises manufactures energy-efficient glass for commercial and residential use. Last year Chacon reported sales of $10 million, profits of $2 million, and an asset turnover of 2. What was Chacon's return on investment (ROI)?

19-25   Cano Inc. sells retail apparel. You have been asked to compute ROI using average assets for last quarter. Profits were $50,000, beginning-of-quarter assets were $150,000, and end-of-quarter assets were $190,000. What was the ROI?

Exercises

19-26   **Investment Centers; The Sales Life Cycle (Review of Chapter 18)**   The sales life cycle is used to describe the phases a product goes through from introduction to withdrawal from the market. The four phases are: (a) introduction, (b) growth, (c) maturity, and (d) decline and withdrawal.

  In the introduction phase, the firm relies on product differentiation to attract new customers to the product. In the growth phase, the product attracts competition, although differentiation is still an advantage for the firm. In the maturity phase, competition is keen, and cost control and quality considerations become important. In the final phase, differentiation again becomes important as do cost control and quality (see Chapter 13 and Chapter 18 for more detail).

Required   At which phases of the sales life cycle, if any, should investment-center evaluation methods be used, and why?

19-27   **Investment Centers; The Cost Life Cycle**   As explained in Chapter 13, the cost life cycle consists of the phases a product goes through within a firm to prepare the product for distribution and service. The five phases of the cost life cycle are: (a) research and development, (b) design, (c) production, (d) marketing and distribution, and (e) customer service.

  The early phases of the cost life cycle are particularly important in that a relatively high percentage (some say as high as 80 percent or more) of the product's life-cycle costs are determined at these phases. That is, the downstream costs of manufacturing, service, and repair are a direct consequence of the quality of the design.

Required   At which phases of the cost life cycle, if any, should investment-center evaluation methods be used, and why?

19-28   **Return on Investment (ROI) and Residual Income (RI)**   Consider the following data (in millions) from Midwest Financial, Inc., which has two main divisions: mortgage loans, and consumer loans:

	Mortgage Loans	Consumer Loans
Average total assets	$2,000	$20,000
Operating income	$400	$2,500
ROI	20%	12.5%

Required

1. Based on ROI, which division is more successful? Why?

2. Midwest uses RI as a measure of the financial performance of its divisions. What is the residual income (RI) for each division if the minimum desired rate of return is: (a) 10 percent, (b) 15 percent, and (c) 20 percent? Which division is more successful under each of these rates?

19-29 **Return On Investment (ROI); Comparisons of Three Investment Centers (Divisions)**

Required Fill in the blanks:

	Division		
	X	**Y**	**Z**
Sales	$1,500,000	$750,000	$ _____
Operating Income	150,000	75,000	_____
Investment (assets)	600,000	_____	2,500,000
Return on sales			0.5%
Asset turnover	_____	_____	1.5
Return on investment	_____	1%	_____

19-30 **ROI, Residual Income, and EVA®** Jean Cooper Cosmetics (JCC) manufactures a variety of products and is organized into three divisions (investment centers): soap products, skin lotions, and hair products. Information about the most recent year's operations follows. The information includes the value of intangible assets including research and development, patents, and other innovations that are not included on JCC's balance sheet. Were these intangibles to be included in the financial statements (as they are for EVA®), the increase in the balance sheet and the increase in after-tax operating income are as given below.

Division	Operating Income	Average Total Assets	Value of Intangibles	Intangibles' Effect on Income
Soap products	$3,250,000	$60,000,000	$1,500,000	$1,000,000
Skin lotions	2,750,000	33,000,000	8,000,000	6,000,000
Hair products	5,000,000	55,000,000	1,000,000	700,000
Minimum desired rate of return	5.00%			
Cost of capital	4.00%			

Required

1. Calculate the ROI for each division.
2. Calculate the residual income (RI) for each division.
3. Calculate EVA® for each division and comment on your answers for ROI, RI, and EVA®.

19-31 **ROI, Residual Income, and EVA®** Gordon Distributors has three operating divisions that are defined by geographical regions. The financial results for the most recent year are shown below. The firm's total assets using generally accepted accounting principles (GAAP) are shown at net book value (NBV). Gordon uses a minimum desired rate of return of 12 percent for selecting new projects and for evaluating the three divisions using residual income (RI). The firm's weighted-average cost of capital is 8 percent.

Region	Net Operating Income	Net Book Value (NBV)	NBV Plus Intangibles
Eastern	$35,440	$195,500	$225,600
Central	41,000	212,000	233,000
Western	23,600	133,000	135,000
(All figures in thousands)			

Required

1. Calculate the ROI for each division.
2. Calculate the RI for each division.
3. Gordon has estimated the amount of intangibles that are not recorded on the firm's financial statements using generally accepted accounting principles and has included that additional information above. Assume that adjusting for the unrecorded intangibles would increase net operating income of the Eastern,

Central, and Western divisions by $22,000, $15,000, and $1,500, respectively, after tax. Determine the EVA® for each division.

4. Compare and interpret the differences between your answers in parts 1, 2, and 3.

19-32 **ROI, Goal-Congruency Issues** As indicated in the chapter, ROI is well entrenched in business practice. However, its use can have negative incentive effects on managerial behavior. For example, assume you are the manager of an investment center and that your annual bonus is a function of achieved ROI for your division. You have the opportunity to invest in a project that would cost $250,000 and that would increase annual operating income of your division by $25,000. (This level of return is considered acceptable from top management's standpoint.) Currently, your division generates annual operating profits of approximately $300,000, on an asset base (i.e., level of investment) of $2,000,000.

Required

1. What is the current return on investment (ROI) being realized by your division (i.e., before considering the new investment)?

2. What would happen to the near-term ROI of your division after adding the effect of the new investment?

3. As manager of this division, given your incentive-compensation plan, would you be motivated to make the new investment? Why or why not?

4. Can you offer any recommendations for improving the design of the incentive-compensation plan under which you are working? That is, can you think of a plan that would result in increased goal congruency between your incentives and the goals of the company?

19-33 **Transfer Pricing; Decision Making** Daniels Inc., which manufactures sports equipment, consists of several operating divisions. Division A has decided to go outside the company to buy materials since division B informed it that the division's selling price for the same materials would increase to $200. Information for division A and division B follows:

Outside price for materials	$150
Division A's annual purchases	10,000 units
Division B's variable costs per unit	$140
Division B's fixed costs, per year	$1,250,000
Division B's capacity utilization	100%

Required

1. Will the company benefit if division A purchases outside the company? Assume that division B cannot sell its materials to outside buyers.

2. Assume that division B can save $200,000 in fixed costs if it does not manufacture the material for division A. Should division A purchase from the outside market?

3. Assume the situation in requirement 1. If the outside market value for the materials drops $20, should A buy from the outside? Explain.

19-34 **Transfer Pricing; Decision Making** Using the information from requirement 1 of exercise 19-33, assume that division B could sell 10,000 units outside for $210 per unit with variable marketing costs of $8. Should division B sell outside or to division A? Explain.

19-35 **Target Sales Price; Return On Investment (ROI)** Preferred Products, a bicycle manufacturer, uses normal volume as the basis for setting prices. That is, it sets prices on the basis of long-term volume predictions and then adjusts these prices only for large changes in pay rates or material prices. You are given the following information:

Materials, wages, and other variable costs	$300 per unit
Fixed costs	$200,000 per year
Target return on investment (ROI)	20%
Normal volume	1,500 units per year
Investment (average total assets)	$800,000

Required
1. What sales price is needed to attain the 20 percent target ROI?
2. What ROI rate will be earned at sales volumes of 2,000 and 1,000 units, respectively, using the sales price you determined in requirement 1?

19-36 **ROI, Return On Sales, and Asset Turnover** Roberts, Inc., has the following financial results for the years 2010 through 2012 for its three regional divisions:

	2010	2011	2012
Revenue			
Southwest	$15,000	$22,000	$26,000
Midwest	6,600	7,200	7,000
Southeast	12,500	12,800	13,300
Total	$34,100	$42,000	$46,300
Net Operating Income			
Southwest	$ 1,100	$ 1,200	$ 1,400
Midwest	1,250	1,500	1,550
Southeast	900	1,200	1,600
Total	$ 3,250	$ 3,900	$ 4,560
Average Total Assets			
Southwest	$14,000	$14,000	$16,500
Midwest	4,200	4,200	4,200
Southeast	5,300	5,600	5,600
Total	$23,500	$23,800	$26,300

Required Calculate return on sales (ROS), asset turnover (AT) and return on investment (ROI) for each division and for the firm as a whole for each of the three years 2010, 2011, and 2012.

19-37 **ROI; Different Measures for Total Assets** Benjamin Joseph, Inc., has the following financial data for 2010 for its three regional divisions:

		Historical Cost		Current Cost	
Region	Operating Income	Net Book Value	Gross Book Value	Replacement Cost	Liquidation Value
North Atlantic	$55,000	$225,000	$450,000	$990,000	$350,000
Mid Atlantic	44,000	289,000	310,000	380,000	445,000
South Atlantic	33,000	115,000	166,000	650,000	980,000

Required Calculate return on sales (ROS) for each division for 2010. The sales in the North, Mid, and South Atlantic regions are $2,350,000, $1,450,000, and $500,000, respectively. Calculate investment (asset) turnover and ROI for each of the four measures of investment.

19-38 **Economic Profit and Employee Productivity; Service Industries** A recent *Harvard Business Review* article points out a new way to calculate economic profit that could be more appropriate for service firms and other "people-intensive" companies. Instead of focusing on investment and return on investment, the focus is on employee productivity, both in terms of generating revenues and reducing costs.

The approach is to first determine economic profit in the conventional way, except that we ignore taxes, so that economic profit is before tax, as follows:

$$\text{Economic profit} = \text{Operating profit} - \text{Capital charge}$$

Assume the following information for a hotel chain that wishes to adopt the new method. The firm has $100 million in operating profit, $1 billion in investment, and uses a cost of capital rate of 5 percent, so the capital charge is $50 million and the economic profit is $50 million. Relevant calculations are contained in Part 1 of the following schedule.

Part 1: Economic Profit (in thousands, except cost of capital rate)

Revenue	$500,000
Operating costs	
Personnel costs	300,000
Other costs	100,000
Operating profit	$100,000
Operating profit before personnel costs (OPBP)	$400,000
Investment (capital)	$1,000,000
Cost of capital, rate	0.05
Capital charge	$ 50,000
Economic profit = Operating profit − Capital charge	$ 50,000

Part 2: Economic Profit Calculated Using Employee Productivity

Number of employees	10,000
Employee productivity	
Operating profit before personnel cost per employee ($400,000/10,000)	$40
Capital charge per employee ($50,000/10,000)	5
Employee productivity	$35
Less personnel cost per employee	30
Economic profit per employee = Productivity − Cost	$ 5
Total economic profit, all employees	$50,000

Note: All numbers in thousands except for number of employees

---

The next step is to decompose economic profit using employee productivity. To do this we first determine operating profit before personnel costs (OPBP):

$$OPBP = Operating\ profit + Personnel\ costs$$
$$\$400,000 = \$100,000 + \$300,000$$

Employee productivity can be determined by calculating OPBP less capital charge, per employee. For this example, since there are 10,000 employees, OPBP is $40,000 per employee and the capital charge is $5,000 per employee, so that productivity is $35,000 per employee. The next step is to determine personnel cost per employee, $30,000, and subtract that from employee productivity to obtain economic profit per employee, $5,000 (i.e., $35,000 − $30,000). Total economic profit for all employees is thus $5,000 × 10,000, or $50 million, the same amount as determined in the conventional way. The value of the decomposition of economic profit into employee productivity and personnel costs per employee is that it provides measures that the hotel chain can benchmark to other hotel chains. It also provides a direct measure of the profit that is being generated per employee relative to the average personnel cost for each employee. Measures of revenue per employee and personnel cost per employee are widely used in the hospital, health and human services, and other people-oriented service industries.

Source: Felix Barber and Rainer Strack, "The Surprising Economics of the People Business," *Harvard Business Review,* June 2005, pp. 81–90.

Required   Use the above approach and assume a chain of residential care facilities that employs 15,000 people, has a cost of capital of 6 percent, and has the following information (000s).

Revenue	$600,000
Operating costs	
Personnel costs	360,000
Other costs	150,000
Operating profit	$ 90,000
Investment	$1,000,000

Determine the productivity per employee, personnel costs per employee, and economic profit per employee.

19-39 **General Transfer-Pricing Rule**   Glendale Manufacturing is organized into two divisions: Fabrication and Assembly. Components transferred between the two divisions are recorded at a predetermined transfer price. Standard variable manufacturing cost per unit in the Fabrication Division is $500. At the present time, this division is working to capacity. Fabrication estimates that the units it produces could be sold on the external market for $650. The product under consideration is viewed as a commodity-type product, with no differentiating features or characteristics.

Required

1. What roles are played by transfer prices? That is, why are transfer prices needed?

2. Use the general transfer-pricing rule presented in the chapter to determine an appropriate transfer price. Why (or in what sense) is the amount you calculated considered an appropriate transfer price?

3. What if the Fabrication Division had excess capacity? How would this change the indicated transfer price? Why is the amount you determined considered an appropriate transfer price?

4. Are there any downsides of using the general transfer-pricing rule to determine the transfer price for internal transfers?

Problems 19-40 **ROI; Different Measures for Assets** Ready Products, Inc., operates two divisions, each with its own manufacturing facility. The accounting system reports the following data for 2010:

HEALTH CARE PRODUCTS DIVISION
Income Statement for the Year
Ended December 31, 2010 (000s)

Revenues	$600
Operating costs	470
Operating income	$130

COSMETICS DIVISION
Income Statement for the Year
Ended December 31, 2010 (000s)

Revenues	$600
Operating costs	400
Operating income	$200

Ready estimates the useful life of each manufacturing facility to be 15 years. As of the end of 2010, the plant for the health-care division is four years old, while the manufacturing plant for the cosmetics division is six years old. Each plant had the same cost at the time of purchase, and both have useful lives of 15 years with no salvage value. The company uses straight-line depreciation and the depreciation charge is $70,000 per year for each division. The manufacturing facility is the only long-lived asset of either division. Current assets are $300,000 in each division.

An index of construction costs, replacement cost, and liquidation values for manufacturing facilities for the period that Ready has been operating is as follows:

			Liquidation Value	
Year	Cost Index	Replacement Cost	Health-care	Cosmetics
2004	80	$1,000,000	$800,000	$ 800,000
2005	82	1,000,000	800,000	800,000
2006	84	1,100,000	700,000	700,000
2007	89	1,150,000	600,000	700,000
2008	94	1,200,000	600,000	800,000
2009	96	1,250,000	600,000	900,000
2010	100	1,300,000	500,000	1,000,000

Required

1. Compute ROI for each division using the historical cost of divisional assets (including current assets) as the investment base. Interpret the results.

2. Compute ROI for each division, incorporating current-cost estimates as follows:

   a. Gross book value (GBV) of long-lived assets, plus book value of current assets.

   b. GBV of long-lived assets restated to current cost using the index of construction costs, plus book value of current assets.

   c. Net book value of long-lived assets restated to current cost using the index of construction costs, plus book value of current assets.

   d. Current replacement cost of long-lived assets, plus book value of current assets.

   e. Current liquidation value of long-lived assets, plus book value of current assets.

3. Which of the measures calculated in requirement 2 would you choose to (a) evaluate the performance of each division manager, and (b) decide which division is most profitable for the overall firm. What are the strategic advantages and disadvantages to the firm of each measure for both (a) and (b)?

19-41 **Calculating ROI & RI and Comparing Results**   Blackwood Industries manufactures die machinery. To meet its expansion needs, it recently (2008) acquired one of its suppliers, Delta Steel. To maintain Delta's separate identity, Blackwood reports Delta's operations as an investment center. Blackwood monitors all of its investment centers on the basis of return on investment (ROI). Management bonuses are based on ROI, and all investment centers are expected to earn a minimum 10 percent return before income taxes.

Delta's ROI has ranged from 14 percent to 18 percent since 2008. The company recently had the opportunity for a new investment that would have yielded a 13 percent ROI. However, division management decided against the investment because it believed that the investment would decrease the division's overall ROI.

The 2010 operating statement for Delta follows. The division's operating assets were $15,000,000 at the end of 2010, a 5 percent increase over the 2009 year-end balance.

DELTA DIVISION		
Operating Statement for Year Ended		
December 31, 2010 (000s omitted)		
Sales		$25,000
Cost of goods sold		16,600
Gross profit		8,400
Operating expenses:		
Administration	$2,340	
Selling	3,610	5,950
Operating income		$ 2,450

Required

1. Calculate the following performance measures for 2010 for the Delta division:
   a. Return on average investment in operating assets.
   b. Residual Income (RI) calculated on the basis of average operating assets.
2. Which performance measure (ROI or RI) should Blackwood Industries use to provide the proper incentive for each division to act autonomously in the firm's best interests? Would Delta's management have been more likely to accept the capital investment opportunity if RI had been used as a performance measure instead of ROI? Explain.
3. What type of strategic performance measurement do you recommend for the Delta division? Explain.

19-42 **ROI and Incentive/Goal-Congruency Issues**   Assume the purchase of new equipment (e.g., delivery trucks) used in a product-delivery service (such as UPS or FedEx). This equipment is needed to improve delivery service and respond to recent environmental goals embraced by the company. The cost of the new equipment is $1 million; the expected useful life of these assets is five years. Estimated salvage value at the end of five years is $0. The company in question will depreciate these assets over a five-year period using straight-line depreciation. The anticipated increase in operating income (before depreciation deductions) attributable to the use of the new equipment is $300,000. Ignore taxes.

Required

1. Generate a schedule of the year-by-year ROIs associated with this investment opportunity. For purposes of these calculations, define the investment base (denominator of the ROI ratio) as average net book value (NBV) of the assets during the year.
2. Generate a second schedule showing the year-by-year ROIs for this investment opportunity under the assumption that the denominator in the ROI calculation is defined as the gross book value of the assets to be acquired.
3. Why do the results differ in (1) and (2) above? What behavioral issue is associated with the use of (1) versus (2) above?
4. What impact would the use of an accelerated depreciation method have on the conclusions above in (1) and (2)? For example, prepare a new schedule of annual ROIs under the assumption that the double-declining-balance depreciation method is used. (Assume a switch to straight-line depreciation in year 4. Thus, the total depreciation charge over the five-year period should be $1 million.)

5. Would the use of the residual income (RI) measure of financial performance eliminate the behavioral issue raised above? Why or why not? For the options specified above in parts 1,2, and 4, show the year-by-year RIs for this investment, based on a weighted-average cost of capital (WACC) of 10 percent. For each of the four options, base the imputed interest charge each year on a simple average of beginning-of-year and end-of-year asset values.

19-43 **ROI, Present-Value Depreciation**   As indicated in the chapter, there are goal-congruency problems associated with the use of ROI as an indicator of investment-center financial performance. One such problem relates to the bias against accepting new investments because of the adverse effect on a center's ROI metric. Assume, for example, that a manager of an investment center can invest in a new, depreciable asset costing $30,000, and that this asset has a three-year life with no salvage value. Cash inflows associated with this investment are projected to be as follows: $12,000, $14,400, and $17,280. (Ignore taxes.) This scenario leads to an estimated internal rate of return (IRR) of 20 percent. Assume that the minimum required rate of return is 15 percent.

Required
1. Demonstrate, using the IRR function in Excel, that the IRR on this proposed investment is indeed 20 percent.
2. Calculate the year-by-year ROI (accounting rate of return) on this proposed investment, using each year as the denominator of your calculation the beginning-of-year book value of the asset. Assume the asset will be depreciated using the straight-line method. What incentive effects can you anticipate based on the data you generated?
3. Recalculate the year-by-year ROI (accounting rate of return) on this proposed investment, this time using "present value" depreciation (defined as the change in the present value of the asset during the period). Use the project's anticipated IRR (20 percent) as the discount factor in your calculations. As in (2) above, define the denominator of your calculation as the beginning-of-year book value of the investment. (*Hint:* Your depreciation figures should be $6,000, $9,600, and $14,400, respectively, for years 1, 2, and 3.) What incentive effects do you anticipate based on your calculations?
4. Calculate for each of three years the residual income (RI) for this proposed investment. RI is defined as income after (present-value) depreciation and after a capital charge assessed on beginning-of-year book value of the asset. For purposes of these calculations assume a 10 percent cost of capital (discount rate). Use the built-in function in Excel to estimate the NPV of the proposed investment. (*Hint:* Your answer should be approximately $5,800.) At a discount rate of 10 percent, determine the net present value (NPV) of the residual income (RI) figures you estimated. What is the potential value of using multiyear RI figures determined with present-value depreciation?

19-44 **Residual Income (RI), Performance Evaluation Time Horizon**   As referenced in the five-step process presented at the beginning of this chapter, one issue that confronts top management is selection of an appropriate time period for evaluating the financial performance of the company's investment centers. This exercise demonstrates why, in conjunction with residual income (RI), it is desirable to evaluate financial performance over a multiyear period. The primary point is that, by doing so, top management is better able to align manager goals and incentives with organizational goals.

Assume, as covered in Chapter 12, that your company uses the net present value (NPV) method to evaluate capital investment opportunities. Generally speaking, this means that a long-term investment project will be undertaken if the present value of future net cash flows (after-tax) is positive when discounted at the firm's weighted-average cost of capital (WACC). The following facts pertain to an investment opportunity that is available to the manager of one of the investment centers in your company. Investment outlay cost, time period 0, equals $800,000. This amount relates to an asset with a five-year life, and no salvage value, that will be depreciated using the straight-line (SL) method. The investment is expected to increase cash inflows by $300,000 per year. Assume a discount rate of 10 percent, both for purposes of calculating NPV and for calculating annual residual income (RI) figures.

Required
1. Prepare a schedule that contains annual cash-flow data, annual operating income amounts, and annual residual income (RI) figures. What is the estimated NPV of the proposed investment? What is the present value (PV) of the stream of expected residual incomes (RIs) from this investment?
2. From a behavioral perspective, what is the primary implication of the analysis you conducted above in (1)?

19-45 **Transfer Pricing; Decision Making**   Phoenix Inc., a cellular communication company, has multiple divisions. Each division's management is compensated based on the division's operating income. Division A currently purchases cellular equipment from outside markets and uses it to produce communication systems. Division B produces similar cellular equipment that it sells to outside customers but not to division A at this time. Division A's manager approaches division B's manager with a proposal to buy the equipment from division B. If it produces the cellular equipment that division A desires, division B would incur variable manufacturing costs of $60 per unit.

Relevant Information about Division B

Sells 50,000 units of equipment to outside customers at $130 per unit.
Operating capacity is currently 80 percent; the division can operate at 100 percent.
Variable manufacturing costs are $70 per unit.
Variable marketing costs are $8 per unit.
Fixed manufacturing costs are $580,000.

Income per Unit for Division A (assuming parts purchased outside, not from division B)

Sales revenue		$320
Manufacturing costs:		
Cellular equipment	80	
Other materials	10	
Fixed costs	40	
Total manufacturing costs		130
Gross margin		190
Marketing costs:		
Variable	35	
Fixed	15	
Total marketing costs		50
Operating income per unit		$140

Required

1. Division A wants to buy all 25,000 units from division B at $75 per unit. Should division B accept or reject the proposal? How would your answer differ if (a) Division A requires all 25,000 units in the order to be shipped by the same supplier, or (b) Division A would accept partial shipment from Division B?

2. What is the range of transfer prices over which the divisional managers might negotiate a final transfer price? Provide a rationale for the range you provide.

19-46 **EVA® NOPAT and EVA® Capital: Operating Approach** You are provided with the following financial statement information from Astro, Inc. for its most recent fiscal year.

Statement of Financial Position (Balance Sheet)
End of Year (000s)

Assets	
Cash	$ 35
Net Accounts Receivable (A/R)	190
Inventory	190
Other current assets	95
Total current assets	$ 510
Property, plant, and equipment (net)	605
Other long-term assets	120
Total assets	$1,235
Liabilities and Stockholders' Equity	
Short-term debt (@10%)	$ 100
Accounts payable	150
Income taxes payable	20
Other current liabilities	200
Total current liabilities	$ 470

Long-term debt (8%)	150
Other long-term liabilities	120
Total liabilities	$ 740
Deferred income taxes	70
Common equity	425
Total liabilities and shareholders' equity	$1,235

The statement of income for the company for the year just ended is as follows:

Statement of Income
Most Recent Year (000s)

Net sales	$2,000
Cost of goods sold (CGS)	1,670
Gross margin	330
Less: SG&A costs	185
Depreciation	35
Other operating expenses	50
Total expenses	270
Net operating profit	60
Less: Interest expense	22
Plus: Other income	12
Income before tax	50
Less: Income tax (@ 40%)	20
Net profit after tax	$ 30

Assume a weighted-average cost of capital (WACC) of 10.7% and an income tax rate of 40%.

Required

1. Prepare, using the *operating approach*, an estimate of EVA® NOPAT. In addition to the above data, you discovered the following: increase during the year of the LIFO reserve, $2; imputed interest expense on noncapitalized leases, $4; and increase in deferred tax liability during the year, $5. (*Hint:* The correct answer is $53; the amount of cash taxes paid on operating profit during the year is $25.) What is the rationale for the various adjustments you made to the company's reported income statement?

2. Prepare, using the *operating approach*, an estimate of EVA® capital. (*Hint:* The correct answer is $925.) In addition to the above information, you note the following: end-of-year value of the LIFO reserve, $10; and present value of noncapitalized leases, $50. What is the rationale for the adjustments you made to reported balance sheet amounts in order to estimate EVA® capital?

3. Given the company's WACC, what is the estimated EVA® for the year? How do you interpret this figure?

19-47 EVA® NOPAT and EVA® Capital: Financing Approach Refer to the preceding problem for reported financial statement data for Astro, Inc.

Required

1. Prepare, using the *financing approach*, an estimate of EVA® NOPAT. In addition to the above data, you've discovered the following: increase during the year of the LIFO reserve, $2; imputed interest expense on noncapitalized leases, $4; and increase in deferred tax liability during the year, $5. (*Hint:* The correct answer is $53.) What is the rationale for the various adjustments you made to the company's reported income statement?

2. Prepare, using the *financing approach*, an estimate of EVA® capital. (*Hint:* The correct answer is $925.) In addition to the above information, you note the following: end-of-year value of the LIFO reserve, $10; and present value of noncapitalized leases, $50. What is the rationale for the adjustments you made to reported balance sheet amounts in order to estimate EVA® capital?

3. Given the company's WACC, what is the estimated EVA® for the year? How do you interpret this figure?

19-48 **Return on Investment; Residual Income** Raddington Industries is a diversified manufacturer with several divisions, including the Reigis Division. Raddington monitors its divisions on the basis of both unit contribution and return on investment (ROI), with investment defined as average operating assets employed. All investments in operating assets are expected to earn a minimum return of 9 percent before income taxes.

Reigis's cost of goods sold is considered to be entirely variable; however, its administrative expenses do not depend on volume. Selling expenses are a mixed cost with 40 percent attributed to sales volume. The 2010 operating statement for Reigis follows. The division's operating assets employed were $80,750,000 at November 30, 2010, unchanged from the year before.

REIGIS STEEL DIVISION
Operating Statement
For the Year Ended November 30, 2010
(000s omitted)

Sales revenue		$35,000
Less expenses:		
Cost of goods sold	$18,500	
Administrative expenses	3,955	
Selling expenses	2,700	25,155
Income from operations, before tax		$ 9,845

Required

1. Calculate Reigis Steel Division's unit contribution if it produced and sold 1,484,000 units during the year ended November 30, 2010.
2. Calculate the following performance measures for 2010 for Reigis:
   a. Pretax ROI, based on average operating assets employed.
   b. Residual income (RI), calculated on the basis of average operating assets employed.
3. Reigis management is presented the opportunity to invest in a project that would earn an ROI of 10 percent. Is Reigis likely to accept the project? Why or why not?
4. Identify several items that Reigis should control if it is to be fairly evaluated as a separate investment center within Raddington Industries using either ROI or RI performance measures.

(CMA Adapted)

19-49 **Divisional Performance Evaluation** Darmen Corporation is one of the major producers of prefabricated homes in the home building industry. The corporation consists of two divisions: (1) Bell Division, which acquires the raw materials to manufacture the basic house components and assembles them into kits, and (2) Cornish Division, which takes the kits and constructs the homes for final home buyers. The corporation is decentralized and the management of each division is measured by its income and return on investment.

Bell Division assembles seven separate home kits using raw materials purchased at the prevailing market prices. The seven kits are sold to Cornish for prices ranging from $45,000 to $98,000. The prices are set by corporate management of Darmen using prices paid by Cornish when it buys comparable units from outside sources. The smaller kits with the lower prices have become a large portion of the units sold because the final home buyer is faced with prices that are increasing more rapidly than personal income. The kits are manufactured and assembled in a new plant just purchased by Bell this year. The division had been located in a leased plant for the past four years.

All kits are assembled upon receipt of an order from Cornish Division. When the kit is completely assembled, it is loaded immediately on a Cornish truck. Thus, Bell Division has no finished goods inventory.

The Bell Division's accounts and reports are prepared on an actual cost basis. There is no budget and no product standards have been developed. A factory overhead rate is calculated at the beginning of each year. The rate is designed to charge all overhead to the product each year. Any under- or over-applied overhead is allocated to the cost of goods sold account and work in process inventories.

Bell Division's performance report follows. This report forms the basis of the evaluation of the division and its management by the corporate CFO. Additional information regarding corporate and division practices is as follows:

- The corporate office does all the personnel and accounting work for each division.
- The corporate personnel costs are allocated on the basis of number of employees in the division.

- The corporate accounting costs are allocated to the division on the basis of total costs excluding corporate charges.
- The division administration costs are included in factory overhead.
- The financing charges include a corporate imputed interest charge on division assets and any divisional lease payments.
- The division investment for the return on investment (ROI) calculation includes division inventory and plant and equipment at gross book value.

BELL DIVISION
Performance Report
For the Year Ended December 31, 2010

	2010	2009	Increase or (Decrease) from 2009 to 2010	
			Amount	Percent Change
Summary Data				
Division income ($000 omitted)	$ 34,222	$ 31,573	$ 2,649	8.4%
Return on investment (ROI)	37%	43%		
Production Data (in units)				
Kits started	2,400	1,600	800	50.0
Kits shipped	2,000	2,100	(100)	(4.8)
Kits in process at year-end	700	300	400	133.3
Financial Data ($000 omitted)				
Sales	$138,000	$162,800	($24,800)	(15.2)
Production costs of units sold				
Raw material	$ 32,000	$ 40,000	$ (8,000)	(20.0)
Labor	41,700	53,000	(11,300)	(21.3)
Factory overhead	29,000	37,000	(8,000)	(21.6)
Cost of units sold	$102,700	$130,000	$(27,300)	(21.0)
Other costs				
Corporate charges for				
Personnel services	$ 228	$ 210	$ 18	8.6
Accounting services	425	440	(15)	(3.4)
Financing costs	300	525	(225)	(42.9)
Total other costs	$ 953	$ 1,175	$ (222)	(18.9)

	2010	2009	Increase or (Decrease) from 2009 to 2010	
			Amount	Percent Change
Adjustments to income				
Unreimbursed fire loss	—	$ 52	$ (52)	(100.00)
Raw material losses due to improper storage	$ 125	—	$ 125	—
Total adjustments	$ 125	$ 52	$ 73	140.4
Total deductions	$103,778	$131,227	$(27,449)	(20.9)
Division income	$ 34,222	$ 31,573	$ 2,649	8.4
Division Investment	$ 92,000	$ 73,000	$ 19,000	26.0
Return on Investment	37%	43%		

Required

1. What performance-evaluation system does Darmen Corporation use? Discuss the value of the system in evaluating the Bell Division and its management.

2. Present specific recommendations to the management of Darmen Corporation to improve its performance-evaluation system.

(CMA Adapted)

19-50 **Performance Evaluation; Strategy Map; Review of Chapter 18; Correlation Analysis**   Maydew Manufacturing Inc. is a large manufacturer of lawn and garden equipment including mowers, edgers, tillers, related equipment, and accessories. The firm has been very successful in recent years, and sales have grown more than 10 percent in each of the last five years. The firm is organized into 15 investment centers based on product-line groups. Return on investment (ROI) and residual income (RI) calculations have been made for each of the last four years and used in management compensation for the last two years. Recently Maydew's top management has contracted with MM&PC, a large consulting firm to review the performance-measurement process at the firm. One of MM&PC's key recommendations has been to consider the implementation of the balanced scorecard (BSC) both for performance measurement and for strategic management. As a step in this direction, MM&PC has asked Maydew for some data on ROI and other measures being considered for the BSC to analyze the relationships among these data. It is hoped that the analysis will help MM&PC develop a strategy map for the firm. The following data show the most recent year's ROI for each investment center and the average for the last three years for training hours per employee in the center, customer retention rate in the unit (customers are primarily large department store chains and other distributors of lawn and garden equipment), the QSV score, and the defect rate (per thousand products). The QSV score is a measure of the Quality-Service-Value of the investment center made by an analysis of a variety of operating data including the results of on-site inspection of each unit by key operating executives and other measures of operating performance (the highest score is 10, and the lowest is 0).

Manager	ROI	Training Hours per Employee	Customer Retention	QSV Score	Defect Rate
1	21.3	98	99.3	7	3.3
2	15.4	122	98.2	8	4.7
3	9.6	67	86.7	6	11.2
4	12.4	88	84.5	9	13.7
5	18.6	92	91.4	8	2.1
6	4.5	33	90.7	4	28.9
7	8.8	49	88.9	6	1.2
8	22.6	77	93.5	10	12.4
9	11.8	102	95.5	9	8.0
10	14.6	95	91.1	6	7.4
11	16.5	87	92.7	6	2.8
12	12.1	80	86.4	8	4.9
13	6.2	66	80.2	4	15.3
14	1.3	50	78.0	4	22.8
15	9.7	78	85.5	7	30.5

Required

1. Using the concept of the strategy map, consider how the nonfinancial factors (training hours, customer retention, QSV, and defect rate) affect ROI. Which of these variables has the greatest influence on ROI? Use regression and correlation analysis to address this requirement.

2. Explain which two managers you would rate as the best overall and which you would rate as the worst overall, and give reasons why.

19-51 **General Transfer-Pricing Rule; Goal Congruence**   American Motors, Inc., is divided, for performance-evaluation purposes, into several investment centers. The Automobile Division of American Motors purchases most of its transmission systems from another unit of the company. The Transmission Division's incremental cost for manufacturing a standard transmission is approximately $900 per unit. This division is currently working at 75 percent of capacity. The current market price for a standard transmission is approximately $1,250.

Required

1. Using the general guideline equation presented in the chapter, what is the minimum price at which the Transmission Division would sell its output to the Automobile Division?

2. Suppose now that American Motors requires that whenever divisions with excess capacity sell their output internally to other divisions of the company, they must do so at the incremental cost of the supplying (producing) division. Evaluate this transfer-pricing rule vis-à-vis each of the following objectives: autonomy, goal congruency, performance evaluation of the divisions, and motivation/incentive effects.

3. If the two divisions of American Motors were to negotiate a transfer price, what is the likely range of possible prices? Evaluate the use of a negotiated transfer price using the same objectives listed above in (2).

4. Which, in your opinion, is the preferable transfer-pricing method—(2) or (3) above? Why?

(CMA Adapted)

19-52 **Transfer Pricing—International Example**   A subsidiary company located in country A purchases $100 worth of goods. It then repackages, exports, and sells those goods to the parent company, located in country B, for $200. The parent company sells the goods for $300. Therefore, both entities have a $100 profit. Assume that the income tax rate in country A is 20 percent, while the tax rate in country B is 60 percent.

Required
1. Given the above facts and assumptions, what is the company's combined (i.e., worldwide) after-tax income for this transaction? (Show calculations.)

2. Consider now a transfer-pricing approach in which the subsidiary sells the goods to the parent company for $280, and the parent company then sells the goods for $300. What is the revised worldwide (i.e., combined) after-tax profit for this transaction? (Show calculations.)

3. What is the effect of the transfer-pricing decision when the income-tax rates for the two countries in question are equal?

4. What limitations exist regarding the setting of transfer prices for multinational transfers?

19-53 **Transfer Pricing, International Considerations, and Strategy**   As indicated in the chapter, determining the appropriate transfer price in a multinational setting is a very complex problem, with multiple strategic considerations. Consider as an example a U.S. company with a subsidiary in Italy and a subsidiary in Ireland. The Italian subsidiary produces a product at a cost of $1,000 per unit. This unit is then sold to the Irish subsidiary, which adds $100 of cost to each unit. The unit is then shipped to the U.S. parent company, which adds an additional $100 of cost to each unit. The unit is then sold to a U.S. customer for $2,000. Assume that the tax rate in Italy is 30 percent, the tax rate in Ireland is 15 percent, and the tax rate in the United States is 35 percent.

Required
1. Define the term *transfer price*. Why is the issue of transfer pricing of strategic concern to organizations?

2. Fundamentally, what creates income tax planning opportunities as regards the determination of transfer pricing in a multinational setting? Where could one go to obtain information regarding stated income-tax rates for various countries?

3. Assume that the transfer price associated with the sale to the Irish subsidiary is $1,200, and that the transfer price for the sale to the U.S. parent company is $1,600. Under this situation, what is the income tax paid by each of the following: (a) the Italian subsidiary, (b) the Irish subsidiary, (c) the U.S. parent company, and (d) the consolidated entity (i.e., worldwide tax paid)?

4. Assume now that the transfer price associated with the sale to the Irish subsidiary is $1,100, and that the transfer price for the sale to the U.S. parent company is $1,800. Under this situation, what is the income tax paid by each of the following: (a) the Italian subsidiary, (b) the Irish subsidiary, (c) the U.S. parent company, and (d) the consolidated entity (i.e., worldwide tax paid)?

5. What considerations, including qualitative factors, bear on the transfer-pricing decision in a multinational context?

19-54 **Transfer-Pricing Methods**   Lynsar Corporation started as a single plant to produce its major components and then assembled its main product into electric motors. Lynsar later expanded by developing outside markets for some components used in its motors. Eventually, the company reorganized into four manufacturing divisions: bearing, casing, switch, and motor. Each manufacturing division operates as an autonomous unit, and divisional performance is the basis for year-end bonuses.

Lynsar's transfer-pricing policy permits the manufacturing divisions to sell either externally or internally. The price for goods transferred between divisions is negotiated between the buying and selling divisions without any interference from top management.

Lynsar's profits for the current year have dropped although sales have increased, and the decreased profits can be traced almost entirely to the motor division. Jere Feldon, Lynsar's chief financial officer, has learned that the motor division purchased switches for its motors from an outside supplier during the current year rather than buying them from the switch division, which is at capacity and has refused to sell to the motor division. It can sell them to outside customers at a price higher than the actual full (absorption) manufacturing cost that has always been negotiated in the past with the motor division. When the motor division refused to meet the price that the switch division was receiving from its outside buyer, the motor division had to purchase the switches from an outside supplier at an even higher price.

Jere is reviewing Lynsar's transfer-pricing policy because he believes that suboptimization has occurred. Although the switch division made the correct decision to maximize its division profit by not transferring the switches at actual full manufacturing cost, this was not necessarily in Lynsar's best interest because of the price the motor division paid for them. The motor division has always been Lynsar's largest division and has tended to dominate the smaller divisions. Jere has learned that the casing and bearing divisions are also resisting the motor division's expectation to use the actual full manufacturing cost as the negotiated price.

Jere has requested that the corporate accounting department study alternative transfer-pricing methods to promote overall goal congruence, motivate divisional management performance, and optimize overall company performance. Three transfer-pricing methods being considered follow. The one selected will be applied uniformly across all divisions.

- Standard full manufacturing costs plus markup.
- Market selling price of the products being transferred.
- Outlay (out-of-pocket) costs incurred to the point of transfer plus opportunity cost to the seller, per unit.

Required

1. Discuss the following:

   a. The positive and negative motivational implications of employing a negotiated transfer price system for goods exchange between divisions.

   b. The motivational problems that can result from using actual full (absorption) manufacturing costs as a transfer price.

2. Discuss the motivational issues that could arise if Lynsar Corporation decides to change from its current policy of covering the transfer of goods between divisions to a revised transfer-pricing policy that would apply uniformly to all divisions.

3. Discuss the likely behavior of both buying and selling divisional managers for each transfer-pricing method listed earlier, if it were adopted by Lynsar.

(CMA Adapted)

19-55 Transfer-Pricing Issues   When transfer prices are based on actual cost, a supplying division often has no incentive to reduce cost. For example, a design change that would reduce the supplying division's manufacturing cost would benefit only downstream divisions if the transfer price is based on a markup over cost.

Required   What can or should be done to provide the supplying division an incentive to reduce manufacturing costs when the transfer price is cost-based?

19-56 Transfer Pricing; International Taxation   Harris Company has a manufacturing subsidiary in Singapore that produces high-end exercise equipment for U.S. consumers. The manufacturing subsidiary has total manufacturing costs of $1,500,000, plus general and administrative expenses of $350,000. The manufacturing unit sells the equipment for $2,500,000 to the U.S. marketing subsidiary, which sells it to the final consumer for an aggregate of $3,500,000. The sales subsidiary has total marketing, general, and administrative costs of $200,000. Assume that Singapore has a corporate tax rate of 33 percent and that the U.S. tax rate is 46 percent. Assume that no tax treaties or other special tax treatments apply.

Required   What is the effect on Harris Company's total corporate-level taxes if the manufacturing subsidiary raises its price by 20 percent to the sales subsidiary?

19-57 Transfer Pricing; Strategy   Advanced Manufacturing Inc. (AMI) produces electronic components in three divisions: industrial, commercial, and consumer products. The commercial products division annually purchases 10,000 units of part 23–6711, which the industrial division produces for use in manufacturing one of its own products. The commercial division is growing rapidly. The commercial division is expanding its production and now wants to increase its purchases of part 23–6711 to 15,000 units per year. The problem is that the industrial division is at full capacity. No new investment in the industrial division has been made for some years because top management sees little future growth in its products, so its capacity is unlikely to increase soon.

The commercial division can buy part 23–6711 from HighTech Inc. or from Britton Electric, a customer of the industrial division, now purchasing 650 units of part 88–461. The industrial division's sales to Britton would not be affected by the commercial division's decision about part 23–6711.

Industrial division

Data on part 23–6711:

Price to commercial division	$185
Variable manufacturing costs	155
Price to outside buyers	205

Data on part 88–461:

Variable manufacturing costs	$ 65
Sales price	95

Other suppliers of part 23–6711:

HighTech Inc., price	$200
Britton Electric, price	210

Required

1. What is the proper decision regarding where the commercial division should purchase the additional 5,000 parts and what is the correct transfer price?

2. Assume that the industrial division's sales to Britton would be cancelled if the commercial division does not buy from Britton. What would be the unit cost to AMI in this case, and would the desired transfer price change?

3. What are the strategic implications of your answer to requirement 1? How can AMI become more competitive in one or more of its divisions?

19-58 **Return on Investment (ROI); Residual Income (RI)** Jump-Start Co. (JSC), a subsidiary of Mason Industries, manufactures go-carts and other recreational vehicles. Family recreational centers that feature go-cart tracks as well as miniature golf courses, batting cages, and arcade games have increased in popularity. As a result, Mason management has been pressuring JSC to diversify into some of these other recreational areas. Recreational Leasing Inc. (RLI), one of the largest firms that leases arcade games to these family recreational centers, is looking for a buyer. Mason's top management believes that RLI's assets could be acquired for an investment of $3.2 million and has strongly urged Bill Grieco, JSC's division manager, to consider the acquisition.

Bill has reviewed RLI's financial statements with his controller, Marie Donnelly; they believe that the acquisition may not be in JSC's best interest. "If we decide not to do this, the Mason people are not going to be happy," Bill said. "If we could convince them to base our bonuses on something other than ROI, maybe this acquisition would look more attractive. How would we do if the bonuses were based on RI using the company's 15 percent cost of capital?"

Mason has traditionally evaluated all divisions on the basis of ROI, which is the ratio of operating income to total assets. The desired rate of return for each division is 20 percent. The management team of any division reporting an annual increase in ROI is automatically eligible for a bonus. To be eligible for a bonus, the management of divisions reporting a decline in ROI must provide convincing explanations for the decline. The bonus for divisions with a declining ROI is limited to 50 percent of the amount of the bonus paid to divisions reporting an increase.

The following are the condensed financial statements of JSC and RLI for the fiscal year ended May 31, 2010.

	JSC	RLI
Sales revenue	$10,500,000	—
Leasing revenue	—	$2,800,000
Variable expenses	7,000,000	1,000,000
Fixed expenses	1,500,000	1,200,000
Operating income	$ 2,000,000	$ 600,000
Current assets	$ 2,300,000	$1,900,000
Long-term assets	5,700,000	1,100,000
Total assets	$ 8,000,000	$3,000,000
Current liabilities	$ 1,400,000	$ 850,000
Long-term liabilities	3,800,000	1,200,000
Shareholders' equity	2,800,000	950,000
Total liabilities and shareholders' equity	$ 8,000,000	$3,000,000

Required

1. If Mason Industries continues to use ROI as the sole measure of divisional performance, explain why JSC would be reluctant to acquire RLI. Support your answer with appropriate calculations.

2. If Mason Industries could be persuaded to use RI to measure JSC's performance, explain why JSC would be more willing to acquire RLI. Support your answer with appropriate calculations.

3. Discuss how the behavior of division managers is likely to be affected by the use of:

   a. ROI as a performance measure.

   b. RI as a performance measure.

(CMA Adapted)

19-59 **Return on Investment (ROI)**   Videonet Company manufactures highly specialized products for networking video-conferencing equipment. Production of specialized units are, to a large extent, performed under contract, with standard units manufactured according to marketing projections. Maintenance of customer equipment is an important area of customer satisfaction. With the recent downturn in the computer industry, the video-conferencing equipment segment has suffered, causing a slide in Videonet's financial performance. Its income statement for the fiscal year ended October 31, 2010, follows.

VIDEONET COMPANY
Income Statement
For the Year Ended October 31, 2010
(000s omitted)

Net sales:	
Equipment	$6,500
Maintenance contracts	1,800
Net sales	$8,300
Expenses:	
Cost of goods sold	4,600
Customer maintenance	1,000
Selling expense	600
Administrative expense	900
Interest expense	150
Total expenses	$7,250
Income before tax	1,050
Income tax	420
Net income	$ 630

Videonet's return on sales before interest and income tax was 14.5 percent in fiscal 2010 when the industry average was 18 percent. Its total asset turnover was two times, and its return on average assets before interest and income tax was 29 percent, both well below the industry average. To improve performance and raise these ratios closer to, or above, industry averages, Bill Hunt, Videonet's president, established the following goals for fiscal 2011:

Return on sales, before interest and income tax	15%
Total asset turnover	3 times
Return on average assets, before interest and income tax	35%

To achieve Hunt's goals, Videonet's management team considered the growth in the international video-conferencing market and proposed the following actions for fiscal 2011:

- Increase equipment sales prices by 10 percent.

- Increase the cost of each unit sold by 3 percent for needed technology, and quality improvements and for increased variable costs.

- Increase maintenance inventory by $250,000 at the beginning of the year and add two maintenance technicians at total cost of $130,000 to cover wages and related travel expenses. These revisions are intended to improve customer service and response time. The increased inventory will be financed at an annual interest rate of 12 percent; no other borrowings or loan reductions are contemplated during fiscal 2011. All other assets will be held to fiscal 2010 levels.

(continued)

- Increase selling expenses by $250,000, but hold administrative expenses at 2010 levels.
- The effective combined federal and state income tax rate for 2011 is expected to be 40 percent, the same as it was in 2010.

These actions were taken to increase equipment unit sales by 8 percent, with a corresponding 8 percent growth in maintenance contracts.

Required

1. Prepare a budgeted income statement for Videonet for the fiscal year ending October 31, 2011, on the assumption that the proposed actions are implemented as planned and that the increased sales objectives will be met.

2. Calculate the following ratios for Videonet for fiscal year 2011 and determine whether Bill Hunt's goals will be achieved:

   a. Return on sales (ROS), before interest and income tax.

   b. Total asset turnover.

   c. Return on average assets, before interest and income tax.

3. Discuss the limitations and difficulties that can be encountered in using the ratios in requirement 2, particularly when making comparisons to industry averages.

(CMA Adapted)

19-60 **Strategy; Strategic Performance Measurement; Transfer Pricing**   Ajax Consolidated has several divisions; however, only two transfer products to other divisions. The mining division refines toldine, which it transfers to the metals division where toldine is processed into an alloy and is sold to customers for $150 per unit. Ajax currently requires the mining division to transfer its total annual output of 400,000 units of toldine to the metals division at total (actual) manufacturing cost plus 10 percent. Unlimited quantities of toldine can be purchased and sold on the open market at $90 per unit. The mining division could sell all the toldine it produces at $90 per unit on the open market, but it would incur a variable selling cost of $5 per unit.

Brian Jones, the mining division's manager, is unhappy transferring the entire output of toldine to the metals division at 110 percent of cost. In a meeting with Ajax management, he said, "Why should my division be required to sell toldine to the metals division at less than market price? For the year just ended in May, the contribution margin on metals was more than $19 million on sales of 400,000 units while the mining division's contribution was just over $5 million on the transfer of the same number of units. My division is subsidizing the profitability of the metals division. We should be allowed to charge the market price for toldine when we transfer it to the metals division."

The following is the detailed unit cost structure for both the mining and metals divisions for the fiscal year ended May 31, 2010:

	Cost per Unit	
	Mining Division	**Metals Division**
Transfer price from mining division	—	$66
Direct material	$12	6
Direct labor	16	20
Manufacturing overhead	32*	25[†]
Total cost per unit	$60	$117

* Manufacturing overhead in the mining division is 25 percent fixed and 75 percent variable.
[†] Manufacturing overhead in the metals division is 60 percent fixed and 40 percent variable.

Required

1. Explain whether transfer prices based on cost are appropriate as a divisional performance measure and why.

2. Using the market price as the transfer price, determine the contribution margin for both divisions for the year ended May 31, 2010.

3. If Ajax were to institute the use of negotiated transfer prices and allow divisions to buy and sell on the open market, determine the price range for toldine that both divisions would accept. Explain your answer.

4. Identify which of the three types of transfer prices—cost-based, market-based, or negotiated—is most likely to elicit desirable management behavior at Ajax and thus benefit overall operations. Explain your answer.

19-61 Transfer Pricing; Strategy   Better Life Products (BLP), Inc., is a large U.S.–based manufacturer of health-care products; it specializes in cushions, braces, and other remedies for a variety of health problems experienced by elderly and disabled persons. BLP knows that its industry is price-competitive and hopes to compete through rapid growth, primarily within the United States, where it has a well-established brand image. Because of the competitive industry conditions, BLF is focusing on cost and price reductions as a principal way to attract customers. Because of rising domestic production costs, lower production costs in other countries, and a modest increase in global demand for its products, BLP manufactures some of these products outside the United States. Much of the materials for use by foreign manufacturers is shipped from the United States to the foreign manufacturer, which assembles the final product. In this way, BLP takes advantage of the foreign country's lower labor costs. For this purpose, BLP has formed three divisions, one in the United States to purchase and perform limited assembly of the raw materials; one a foreign division to complete the manufacturing, especially of the labor-intensive components of manufacturing; and one a marketing and sales division in the United States. Sales of BLP's products are approximately 80 percent in the United States, 10 percent in Canada, and 10 percent worldwide. The foreign divisions tend to focus only on manufacturing because of the specialized nature of the products and because of BLP's desire to have the U.S. sales division coordinate all sales activities. BLP now has 18 U.S. divisions and 23 foreign divisions operating in this manner.

Foreign divisions' shipments to the United States are subject to customs duties according to the U.S. Tariff Code, which adds to BLP's cost of the foreign-based manufacturing. However, the code requires U.S. companies to pay duty on only the value added in foreign countries. For example, a product imported from an Argentine company to BLP pays customs on only the amount of the product's cost resulting from labor incurred in Argentina. To illustrate, a product with $10 of materials shipped from the United States to Argentina that incurs $10 of labor costs in Argentina is charged a tariff based on the $10 of labor costs, not the $20 of total product cost. Thus, for tariff purposes, having as small a portion of total product cost from the foreign country as possible is advantageous to BLP.

BLP division managers, including those of the foreign manufacturing facilities, are evaluated on the basis of profit. Jorge Martinez is the manager of the manufacturing plant in Argentina; his compensation from BLP is based on meeting profit targets.

BLP uses a transfer-pricing approach common in the industry to allow each of the company's divisions to determine the transfer pricing autonomously through interdivision negotiations. In recent years, however, top management has played an increased role in such negotiations. In particular, when the divisions determine a transfer price that can lead to increased taxes, foreign exchange exposure, or tariffs, the corporate financial function becomes involved. This has meant that the transfer prices charged by foreign divisions to U.S. sales divisions have fallen to reduce the value added by the foreign country and thereby reduce the tariffs. To avoid problems with U.S. and Argentine government agencies, the transfer prices have been reduced slowly over time.

One effect of this transfer-pricing strategy has been the continued decline of the foreign divisions' profitability. Jorge and others have difficulty meeting their profit targets and personal compensation goals because of the continually declining transfer prices.

Required

1. Assess BLP's manufacturing and marketing strategies. Are they consistent with each other and with what you consider to be the firm's overall business strategy?

2. Assess BLP's performance-measurement system. What changes would you suggest and why?

19-62 Transfer Pricing; Ethics   Target Manufacturing, Inc., is a multinational firm with sales and manufacturing units in 15 countries. One of its manufacturing units, in country X, sells its product to a retail unit in country Y for $200,000. The unit in Country X has manufacturing costs of $100,000 for these products. The retail unit in country Y sells the product to final customers for $300,000. Target is considering adjusting its transfer prices to reduce overall corporate tax liability.

Required

1. Assume that both country X and country Y have corporate income tax rates of 40 percent and that no special tax treaties or benefits apply to Target. What would be the effect on Target's total tax burden if the manufacturing unit raises its price from $200,000 to $240,000?

2. What would be the effect on Target's total taxes if the manufacturing unit raised its price from $200,000 to $240,000 and the tax rate in country X is 20 percent and in country Y is 40 percent?

3. Comment on the ethical issues you observe, if any, in this case.

19-63 Strategic Performance Measurement   With the multinational company (MNC) becoming a significant business structure throughout the world, a growing problem is developing in the analysis of the MNC's financial results. When the incidents in this problem occurred, the U.S. dollar was strengthening considerably relative to other currencies. Besides causing economic problems in many developing countries, it also created a problem in the proper evaluation of a multinational's subsidiaries and their contribution to its total results.

Security System Corporation provides financial services for dealers and consumers in a variety of construction and consumer product areas. The firm is searching for the proper method to evaluate its subsidiaries. Of concern is each subsidiary's contribution to the company's overall earnings and how to evaluate whether the specific goals developed by the subsidiary's management have been met.

In search of answers, the company is concerned with the following concepts:

- Analysis of results: In local currency or U.S. dollars?
- Management's explanation of variances: In local currency or U.S. dollars?
- What should the time frames be for comparative data: Plan or forecast?

The company has six distinctive business segments in the new-residential-housing market: consumer appliance market, commercial nonresidential construction, consumer aftermarket, home furnishings market, automotive market, and capital goods markets. Last year the company achieved 30 percent of its revenues and 35 percent of its earnings from its international subsidiaries. However, years ago, when one British pound sterling equaled US$2.33 (whereas now it's one pound = US$1.62), the company achieved 35 percent of its revenue—but more significantly, 47 percent of its earnings—from its international subsidiaries. During the past five years, although the U.S. dollar equivalent of earnings from the international subsidiaries has declined from 47 percent of the total to 35 percent, most operations have reported significant, steady year-to-year gains when expressed in the local currency.

All operations report their monthly financial data to the company's world headquarters in U.S. dollars. They use the existing exchange rate at the close of business on the last day of the month. The company reports the exchange based on accounting guidelines (except for one or two special situations). The comparisons of the monthly financial data are made against a financial plan that uses a predetermined exchange rate for the various months of the year.

Over the past five years, as the U.S. dollar has fluctuated against foreign currencies, the company has analyzed the financial results of its operations totally in U.S. dollars. It then compares these results to a fixed-plan exchange rate.

The company establishes exchange rates to be used each year, many times optimistically, and then sets an earnings per share (EPS) target on that basis. If the dollar strengthens even more, the company misses its targets and prepares statements showing that a particular group missed its planned targets when, in fact, all of the group's operations could have exceeded their local currency plans but are losing on the comparison because of unfavorable exchange-rate effects.

Required   How should the firm measure its results to enhance its competitive position? How can it safeguard its overall EPS target if it uses local currencies in the reporting system? Where does the responsibility for the U.S.-dollar-denominated goals lie?

(CMA Adapted)

19-64 **Transfer Pricing; Decision Making**   Bramwell Adhesives, Inc, manufactures chemicals and adhesives for commercial and industrial use. Division A is currently purchasing 300 barrels per year of a required chemical (PB4) from an outside supplier for $550 per barrel. The $550 price is a competitive, fair price, but Division A is not satisfied with the service and reliability of the supplier. Fortunately, Division A has discovered that another Bramwell division, Division B, has the technology to manufacture PB4. Division B would have to purchase some new equipment to produce PB4, but the equipment is readily available and can be installed in a timely manner for $90,000. With the purchase of the machine, Division B would have the capacity to produce up to 1,000 barrels of the chemical per year. Division A would be willing to commit to a three-year contract for 300 barrels per year if the divisions could agree on a transfer price.

Division B projects the following costs per barrel for PB4.

Variable manufacturing cost	$200
Fixed costs per barrel*	300
Profit margin for Division B (20% of total cost)	100
Total projected price of PB4 to Div A	$600

* Allocation of the cost of purchased equipment over three years, based on an assumed production of 300 barrels in each of the three years.

Required

1. Is the purchase of the new equipment for $90,000 relevant to the decision to transfer internally and/or the determination of the transfer price?

2. Should Division B sell PB4 to Division A and, if so, at what price?

19-65 **Return on Customer; Review of Chapter 5**   The concept of return on investment (ROI) has been adapted widely for a variety of uses. One recent development is to extend customer profitability analysis to include the concept of "return on customer." In Chapter 5, we presented an approach for using ABC to determine the full cost of serving a customer, including product and service, thereby determining the net profit from serving that customer. The analysis was further extended in Chapter 5 to calculate a measure of the expected value of the customer based on expected future sales. That value was called *customer lifetime value (CLV),* which is the net present value of all estimated future profits from the customer. For example, assume a customer is expected to produce profits of $20,000 per year for each of the next three years. Using a discount rate of 6 percent, the CLV for this customer is 2.673 × $20,000 = $53,460. (The PV annuity factor, 2.673, is obtained from Appendix C, Chapter 12.)

Return on customer (ROC) can be measured as the increase in customer value plus the current year profit on the customer, relative to the prior year value of the customer. The first step in calculating ROC is to determine the customer lifetime value (CLV) at the end of each year. CLV can rise or fall, as our projections of future profits from the customer increase or decrease. Suppose we have the following information for customer Y:

Customer Lifetime Value at the end of 2009 = $2,000,000
Customer Lifetime Value at the end of 2010 = $2,500,000
Profit on sales to customer Y during 2010 = $250,000

ROC for customer Y for 2010 is determined as follows:

$$ROC = \frac{\text{Profit from customer Y in 2010} + \text{Change in CLV from 2009 to 2010}}{\text{CLV for customer Y in 2009}}$$

$$ROC \text{ for customer Y} = \frac{\$250,000 + (\$2,500,000 - \$2,000,000)}{\$2,000,000}$$

$$= 37.5\%$$

ROC gives management a way to further analyze the profitability of a given customer. The goal is to attract and retain high-ROC customers.

Required   Assume Customer X has a CLV at the beginning of the year of $150,000, a CLV at the end of the year of $75,000, and that profits from sales to X were $25,000 during the year. Customer Z has a CLV at the end of the year of $100,000, a CLV at the beginning of the year of $50,000, and profits from sales this year of $10,000. Determine the ROC for each customer and interpret the results for these two customers.

19-66 **Return on Investment (ROI) for Innovative Companies**   A survey by *BusinessWeek* and the Boston Consulting Group identified the world's 25 most innovative companies, looking at three dimensions of innovation: process innovation, product innovation, and business model innovation. The top-five companies were Apple, Google, 3M, Toyota, and Microsoft. The top-25 companies were great performers over the 10-year period 1995–2005. The 25 companies had an average return on sales of 3.4 percent in comparison to 0.40 percent for the Standard & Poor's 1200 Global Stock Index. The top 25 stock returns, based on increase in stock price and dividends over this 10-year period, averaged a 14.3 percent annual return, in contrast to the 11.1 percent return for the S&P Global 1200. These companies are surpassing the Global 1200 companies in part because of superior innovation.

Required   What are the issues to consider in calculating the return on investment (ROI), residual income (RI), and EVA® for a highly innovative company?

19-67 **Research Assignment, Strategy**   Obtain from your library a copy of following article: Laurie Bassie and Daniel McMurrer, "Maximizing Your Return on People," *Harvard Business Review* (March 2007), pp. 115–123. The authors of this article state (p. 123): "Globalization has left only one true path to profitability for firms operating in high-wage, developed nations: to base their competitive strategy on exceptional human capital management (HCM) . . . managing human capital by instinct and intuition becomes not only inadequate, but reckless. The most competitive companies will be those that manage their employees like the assets they are."

Required After reading the above-referenced article, answer the following questions:

1. What is the general issue addressed by the authors of this article? That is, what managerial problem are they discussing?

2. The authors develop a framework that, they assert, can be useful for increasing the long-term value of investments in human capital. What are the two major factors in the authors' framework? How can the framework be used by managers as part of a comprehensive management accounting and control system?

3. The authors provide three examples of how their evaluation/assessment framework was used in practice to assess the quality of an organization's HCM. For each example, indicate how organizational performance was defined, and how the evaluation framework proposed by the authors was used to improve that performance. (That is, what principal results were achieved?)

Solutions to Self–Study Problems

1. Return on Investment (ROI) and Residual Income (RI)

1. ROS = Operating income/Sales

   $$= \$640,000/\$8,000,000$$

   $$= 0.08$$

   Asset turnover = Sales/Average investment

   $$= \$8,000,000/(\$2,500,000 + \$2,600,000)/2$$

   $$= 3.137 \text{ times}$$

   ROI = ROS × Asset turnover

   $$= 0.08 \times 3.137$$

   $$= 25.1\%$$

2. Residual income = Operating income − (Average investment × Minimum rate of return)

   $$= \$640,000 - ([(\$2,500,000 + \$2,600,000)/2] \times 0.12)$$

   $$= \$334,000$$

2. Determining the Proper Transfer Price

1. Since the T-Bar unit is at full capacity and the contribution on outside sales of $70 (= $165 − $5 − $90) is higher than the $60 cost saving of inside production (= $150 − $90), the T-Bar unit should sell outside and the adhesive unit should purchase T-Bar for $150 outside the firm.

2. From the standpoint of the company as a whole, the correct decision is induced if we appeal to the general transfer-pricing rule. The minimum transfer price, from the firm's standpoint, is the sum of out-of-pocket costs of the T-Bar division ($90) plus the opportunity cost, if any, incurred because of an internal transfer ($70 = $165 − $90 − $5), or a total of $160. At this amount, the adhesive division will be motivated to purchase externally (at $150/unit) and the T-Bar unit will be indifferent between selling internally (contribution margin per unit = $160 − $90 = $70) and selling externally (contribution margin per unit = $165 − $90 − $5 = $70). Because of the latter, we say that $160 represents a minimum transfer price.

3. If the T-Bar unit has excess capacity, it can sell T-Bar both internally and externally. The correct transfer price is then the price that will cause the adhesive unit to purchase internally; that is, any price between variable cost of the seller ($90) and the outside market price to the adhesive unit ($150). The units might agree on a price by considering what is a fair return to each unit and in effect split the profit on the sale between them. The actual outcome of the negotiations for the transfer price depends on a number of factors, including the negotiation skills of the two managers.

CHAPTER TWENTY

Management Compensation, Business Analysis, and Business Valuation

After studying this chapter, you should be able to . . .

1. Identify and explain the types of management compensation
2. Identify the strategic role of management compensation and the different types of compensation used in practice
3. Explain the three characteristics of a bonus plan: the base for determining performance, the compensation pool from which the bonus is funded, and the bonus payment options
4. Describe the role of tax planning and financial reporting in management compensation planning
5. Explain how management compensation plans are used in service firms
6. Apply the different methods for business analysis and business valuation

---

There's no praise to beat the sort you can put in your pocket.

Moliére

The goals of this chapter are to determine how to compensate managers, how to analyze a firm's overall performance, and how to estimate the economic value of the firm. We have emphasized strategy throughout the book. How do we quantitatively assess the firm's success in achieving its strategy and fairly compensate management for this success? Fundamentally, all measures of the firm's value are predictions of future performance—an assessment of the future value of the current ownership in the firm. Choosing a method for predicting future value is a difficult task, as Bill Barker, a writer for the Motley Fool says: "I don't think there is any method that anyone will think is the perfect one. If you ask 10 investors what the Holy Grail method would be, you'd get 10 different answers." In this spirit, we consider a number of different valuation methods in this chapter.[1]

Part One: Management Compensation

LEARNING OBJECTIVE 1

Identify and explain the types of management compensation.

Recruiting, motivating, rewarding, and retaining effective managers are critical to the success of all firms. Effective management compensation plans are an important and integral part of the determination of a strategic competitive advantage and are important concerns of the management accountant.

---

[1] The Motley Fool (*www.fool.com*) is an organization that provides education and information for investors.

TRENDS IN CEO PAY

CEO pay has increased significantly over the last decade. For example, the total compensation of the top five executives of 1,500 of the largest U.S. companies increased from an average of 4.8 percent of the firm's earnings in 1993 to 12.1 percent of the firm's earnings in 2000–2002. After a substantial fall in 2001–2003, CEO pay began to increase again in 2004–2005, by 3.7 percent in 2004 and 2005 and 5 percent in 2007. The rate of growth in 2004–2007 is significantly less than the double-digit increases of the 1990s. However, CEO pay fell in 2008 as a consequence of the recession, and is expected to fall again in 2009. Also, the Federal Reserve Bank and U.S. Treasury are considering new regulations (for financial service firms) that are intended to ". . . align compensation with sound risk management and long-term value creation." Other reasons for the decrease in CEO pay: (1) increased oversight of CEO compensation by corporate boards and federal agencies (oversight especially for those firms receiving federal assistance), and (2) new disclosure rules by the SEC.

NEW SEC DISCLOSURE RULES

New SEC rules require increased disclosure of executive compensation. The SEC requires a company to disclose:

- A total compensation amount for executives.
- A breakdown of compensation to include stock options, both the number of shares and the value of the shares involved in these options.

- Exactly what payments an executive would receive if there is a change in the executives' role in the company.
- The above information for each executive.

The objective of the new disclosures is to provide investors with a clearer and more complete understanding of the compensation of the firm's key executives. On the other hand, some have pointed out that firms' compensation disclosures are so complex that many investors are left confused and frustrated.

Source: PricewaterhouseCoopers, "2007 Global Equity Incentives Survey," (www.pwc.com/extweb/pwcpublications.nsf/docid/eeace28ff7a0b05e852573b700758d02); Claudia Deutsch, "A Brighter Spotlight, Yet the Pay Rises," *The New York Times,* April 6, 2008, Business Section, p. 1; Jane Sasseen, "A Better Look at the Bosses Pay: New SEC Rule Rules Require Greater Disclosure, but Don't Expect the CEOs to Take a Hit," *BusinessWeek,* February 26, 2007, pp. 44–45; Phred Dvorak, "Firms Disclose Formulas Behind Executive Pay, Leaving Many Baffled," *The Wall Street Journal,* March 21, 2008, p. 1; Joann S. Lublin, "Adding it Up," *The Wall Street Journal,* April 10, 2006, p. R1; Deborah Solomon and Damian Paletta, "U.S. Eyes Bank Pay Overhaul," *The Wall Street Journal,* May 13, 2009, p1; David Dvorak, "Executive Salaries May Fall More Sharply in 2009," *The Wall Street Journal,* April 3, 2009, p. B4; Kara Scannell, " SEC Ready to Require More Pay Disclosures," *The Wall Street Journal,* June 3, 2009, p. C1.

Types of Management Compensation

Management compensation plans
are policies and procedures for compensating managers.

A salary
is a fixed payment.

A bonus
is based on the achievement of performance goals for the period.

Benefits
include special travel, membership in a fitness club, tickets to entertainment events, and other extras paid for by the firm.

Management compensation plans are policies and procedures for compensating managers. Compensation includes one or more of the following: salary, bonus, and benefits. **Salary** is a fixed payment; a **bonus** is based on the achievement of performance goals for the period. **Benefits** include travel, membership in a fitness club, life insurance, medical benefits, tickets to entertainment events, and other extras paid for by the firm. Benefits are often also referred to as *perks.*

Compensation can be paid currently (usually an annual amount paid monthly, twice a month, or weekly) or deferred to future years. Salary and benefits are typically awarded currently; bonuses are either paid currently or deferred, though a wide variety of plans is found in practice.

The compensation plans for high-level managers are generally explained in the firm's proxy statements and must be approved by the shareholders. Base salary usually is an annual amount paid throughout the year, although it can also include predetermined future cash payments and/or stock awards. Perks are commonly awarded on an annual basis, although they can include future payments or benefits. Base salary and perks are negotiated when the manager is hired and when compensation contracts are reviewed and renewed. They are not commonly influenced by the manager's current performance, as is bonus pay. A recent study of top executives at public companies showed that bonus pay is the fastest growing part of total compensation: firms are moving to linking executive pay to performance. The median bonus was more than salary for the sampled firms.[2]

---

[2] Joann S. Lublin, "Adding it Up," *The Wall Street Journal,* April 10, 2006, p. R1; Jesse Eisinger, " Lavish Pay Put a Bite on Profits," *The Wall Street Journal,* January 11, 2006, p. C1. A public company is required to send each shareholder a proxy statement prior to shareholder votes; the statement includes background information about the company's directors, executive compensation, and other information.

Strategic Role and Objectives of Management Compensation

LEARNING OBJECTIVE 2

Identify the strategic role of management compensation and the different types of compensation used in practice.

The strategic role of management compensation has three aspects: (1) the strategic conditions facing the firm, (2) the effect of risk aversion on managers' decision making, and (3) certain ethical issues.

Design the Compensation Plan for Existing Strategic Conditions

The compensation plan should be grounded in the strategic analysis of the firm: its competitive strengths and weaknesses and critical success factors. As the strategic conditions facing the firm change over time, the compensation plan should also change. For example, the firm's strategy changes as its products move through the different phases of the sales life cycle: product introduction, growth, maturity, and decline (Chapter 13). As a firm's product moves from the growth phase to the maturity phase, the firm's strategy also moves from product differentiation to cost leadership. When this happens, the compensation plan should change in response to the new strategy. Exhibit 20.1 illustrates how the mix of salary, bonus, and perks might change as the firm and its products move through different phases of the sales life cycle.

Note in Exhibit 20.1 that the mix of the three parts of total compensation changes as strategic conditions change. For example, in the mature phase of the product's life cycle, when competition is likely to be the highest and the firm is interested in maintaining an established market and controlling costs, a balanced compensation plan of competitive salary, bonus, and benefits is needed to attract, motivate, and retain the best managers. In contrast, during the growth phase when the need for innovation and leadership is the greatest, the emphasis is on relatively large bonuses to effectively motivate managers. In effect, top management considers the specific strategic conditions facing the firm as a basic consideration in developing the compensation plan and making changes as strategic conditions change.

Risk Aversion and Management Compensation

The manager's relative risk aversion can have an important effect on decision making (see Chapter 18, "Employment Contracts"). Risk aversion is the tendency to prefer decisions with predictable outcomes over those that are uncertain. It is a relatively common decision-making characteristic of managers. A risk-averse manager is biased against decisions that have an uncertain outcome, even if the expected outcome is favorable.

For example, a risk-averse manager might cancel a planned investment in new equipment that would reduce operating costs if there is a chance that nonoperating costs from installation problems, employee training needs, or other reasons might increase. In contrast, the firm's top management and shareholders might not see the risk of additional nonoperating costs as significant relative to the potential for a long-term reduction in operating costs. The difference in perspective comes about because the outcome of the decision, while likely to have a relatively small impact on the firm and therefore on top management and shareholders, is likely to directly and significantly impact the manager's current bonus.

Compensation plans can manage risk aversion effectively by carefully choosing the mix of salary and bonus in total compensation. The higher the proportion of bonus in total compensation, the higher the incentive for the manager to avoid risky outcomes. To reduce the effect of risk aversion, a relatively large proportion of salary should be in total compensation, with a smaller portion in bonus. Determining the proper balance between salary and bonus must consider all three compensation objectives.

EXHIBIT 20.1

Compensation Plans Tailored for Different Strategic Conditions

Product Sales Life Cycle Phase	Salary	Bonus	Benefits
Product introduction	High	Low	Low
Growth	Low	High	Competitive
Maturity	Competitive	Competitive	Competitive
Decline	High	Low	Competitive

Ethical Issues

There is a common concern that executive pay is too high and that lower-level employees are not properly compensated relative to the very high salaries and bonuses of top executives, particularly during periods of corporate downsizing and falling earnings. High executive compensation is unjust, some argue, and compensation plans are unethical. Others point out that most executives are worth their high compensation because they bring far greater value to the firm than the cost of their compensation. Shareholders and bondholders who see their investments appreciate and attribute this to the executive are likely to see the compensation plans as just and ethical. For example, when a key manager left Wal-Mart the firm's stock price fell 4 percent on the day of the announcement, indicating the very high importance investors placed on this executive.[3]

Sometimes the management compensation plan provides an incentive for unethical action. Recent examples include Kenneth Lay, CEO of Enron; Andrew Fastow, CFO of Enron; Scott Sullivan, CFO of WorldCom; and Dennis Kozlowski, CEO of Tyco International. Each of these executives has been convicted of or admitted to illegal activities that have harmed their companies and the companies' shareholders. In all these cases, the incentive to increase cash or stock option-based compensation was present. Also, a recent study of 1,200 corporations found evidence that private inside information of top executives was used to time the exercise of their stock options, because of a significant pattern of rising stock prices prior to the exercise of the options followed by a pattern of falling stock prices following the exercise of the stock options.[4]

Objectives of Management Compensation

The firm's key objective is to develop management compensation plans that support its strategic objectives, as set forth by management and the owners. The objectives of management compensation are therefore consistent with the three objectives of management control as defined in Chapter 18:

1. To motivate managers to exert a high level of effort to achieve the goals set by top management.
2. To provide the incentive for managers, acting autonomously, to make decisions consistent with the goals set by top management.
3. To determine fairly the rewards earned by managers for their effort and skill and the effectiveness of their decision making.

In Chapters 18 and 19, these objectives were used to develop performance measurement systems (e.g., cost, profit, and investment centers). In this chapter, the objectives are used to develop effective management compensation plans.

The first objective is to motivate managers to exert a high level of effort to achieve the firm's goals. A performance-based compensation plan is best for this purpose. For example, a bonus plan that rewards the manager for achieving particular goals is appropriate. The goals could be financial or nonfinancial, current or long term.

The second objective is to provide the appropriate incentive for managers to make decisions that are consistent with the firm's objectives. The firm's objectives are identified in the strategic competitive analysis from which its critical success factors (CSFs) are derived. CSFs include customer satisfaction, quality, service, product development, and innovation in production and distribution. Firms attend to CSFs by making them part of the manager's compensation.

For example, McDonald's rewards managers who develop its CSFs—quality, service, cleanliness, and value—in addition to the conventional financial performance measures (earnings,

---

[3] *The Wall Street Journal,* March 29, 1996. Bill Fields, a 25-year veteran of Wal-Mart, left his position as chief of the main discount store business department to accept a similar position at Viacom, Inc. A similar case is reported for Black & Decker, whose stock fell by 8 percent the day Joseph Galli, its chief executive, departed; see "Power Drain," *BusinessWeek,* May 17, 1999, p. 50. See also, Robert B. Reich, "CEOs Deserve Their Pay," *The Wall Street Journal,* September 14, 2007, p. A13. Reich makes the point that those with the skills necessary to be a successful CEO, to deliver competitive advantage for the company, are very hard to find.

[4] Eli Bartov and Partha Mahanram, "Private Information, Earnings Manipulations, and Executive Stock-Option Exercises," *The Accounting Review,* October 2004, pp. 889–920. See also, Scott Patterson and Serena Ng, "Executives' Stock Deals Preceded Price Drops," *The Wall Street Journal,* June 4, 2009, p. C1.

growth in sales). International Paper Company includes nonfinancial factors such as quality, safety, and minority employee development as factors in management compensation plans. Research has shown that successful firms with clear strategic goals specified in CSFs include these factors in their compensation plans.[5]

In developing compensation plans, the management accountant works with other financial professionals to achieve fairness by making the plan simple, clear, and consistent. Fairness also means that the plan focuses only on the controllable aspects of the manager's performance. For example, compensation should not be affected by expenses that cannot be tied directly to the manager's unit. Similarly, the manager's performance evaluation should be separate from that of the unit because economic factors beyond the manager's control are likely to affect the unit's performance. Fairness in this sense is often achieved by basing the manager's compensation on performance relative to prior years or to agreed-upon goals rather than on comparison to the performance of other managers.

Bonus Plans

> As a general view, remuneration by fixed salaries does not in any class of functionaries produce the maximum amount of zeal.
>
> *John Stuart Mill, English philosopher and economist, 1806–1873*

As stated earlier, bonus compensation is the fastest growing element of total compensation and often the largest part. A wide variety of bonus pay plans can be categorized according to three key aspects:

- The **base of the compensation,** that is, how the bonus pay is determined. The three most common bases are (1) stock price, (2) cost, revenue, profit, or investment center–based performance, and (3) the balanced scorecard.
- **Compensation pools,** that is, the source from which the bonus pay is funded. The two most common compensation pools are earnings in the manager's own SBU and a firmwide pool based on the firm's total earnings.
- **Payment options,** that is, how the bonus is to be awarded. The two common options are cash and stock (typically common shares). The cash or stock can either be awarded currently or deferred to future years. Stock can either be awarded directly or granted in the form of stock options.

Bases for Bonus Compensation

LEARNING OBJECTIVE 3

Explain the three characteristics of a bonus plan: the base for determining performance, the compensation pool from which the bonus is funded, and the bonus payment options.

The key objective in determining the base for compensation is to align managers' incentives with the strategic goals of the company. Bonus compensation can be determined on the basis of stock price, strategic performance measures (cost, revenue, profit, or investment center), or the balanced scorecard (critical success factors). For example, when the manager's unit is publicly held, its stock price is a relevant base. When stock price is used, the amount of the bonus could depend on the amount of the increase in stock price or on whether the stock price reaches a certain predetermined goal. When an accounting measure or CSF is used, the amount of the bonus can be determined in any one of three ways: (1) by comparison of current performance to that of prior years, (2) comparison of performance to a predetermined budget, or (3) comparison of the manager's performance to that of other managers. A limitation of the first two methods, comparison to prior years or to budget, is that the economic

[5] C. Ittner and D. Larcker, "Total Quality Management and the Choice of Information and Reward Systems," *Journal of Accounting Research* (1995 Supplement), pp. 1–34; R. Bushman, R. Indjejikian, and A. Smith, "CEO Compensation: The Role of Individual Performance Evaluation," *Journal of Accounting and Economics,* April 1996; and Antonio Davila and Mahan Venkatachalam, "The Relevance of Non-Financial Performance Measures for CEO Compensation: Evidence from the Airline Industry," *Review of Accounting Studies* 9, 2004, pp. 443–464.

situation of the manager's unit may have changed significantly from the prior year or from the time the budget target was set, thereby making the budget or prior year amount an unfair basis for evaluation and compensation. A problem with the third method is that it does not take into account the different economic circumstances of the different managers, some of whom may be in units that are in favorable economic times while others are not. The firm chooses its compensation plan to achieve the best balance of motivation and fairness from these options.

The choice of a base comes from a consideration of the compensation objectives, as outlined in Exhibit 20.2. A common choice is to use cost, revenue, profit, or investment centers because they are often a good measure of economic performance; therefore, they are motivating and perceived to be fair. As many firms move to a more strategic approach to cost management, however, the use of CSFs and scorecard-based measures in compensation is likely to increase.

Once the base is chosen the firm also must choose a method for calculating the amount of the bonus based on the actual level of performance relative to the target. The most common approach is a simple linear calculation, that is, the greater the amount that performance exceeds the target (prior year, budget, or that of other managers) the greater the amount of the bonus. For example, if the bonus formula is 10 percent of profit over budget, and actual and budgeted profit are $200,000 and $100,000 respectively, then the amount of the bonus would be 10 percent $\times$ ($200,000 $-$ $100,000) = $10,000.

The base for the bonus is likely to have multiple targets. As noted in the section on "Objectives of Management Control" above, it is common to have management control systems with the balanced scorecard or some combination of financial and operating measures. In this case there are multiple bases for the performance measurement. The issue then is to determine a weighting for the multiple measures—which measures have the greatest priority? A common solution is to provide a numerical weight (as illustrated in many of the books and cases on the balanced scorecard), while a popular alternative is to have top management state the priorities in a ranking or general way at the beginning of the period and then, at the end of the period (at the time of the performance evaluation), assess the overall performance of the manager by considering all of the performance measures simultaneously, without quantitative weights. This more subjective approach is favored by some who feel that top management needs the flexibility to apply their judgment to aggregate and assess the overall performance of the manager based upon the multiple measures.

Some firms may further complicate the performance assessment by using a nonlinear compensation of one or more of the performance measures. Nonlinear plans make sense in that the drivers of a firm's profitability are likely to be nonlinear with profits. For example, Chrysler has used a nonlinear system for dealer bonuses, based on the understanding that increases in

EXHIBIT 20.2 **Advantages and Disadvantages of Different Bonus Compensation Bases Relative to Compensation Objectives**

	Motivation	Right Decision	Fairness
Stock price	(+/−) Depends on whether stock and stock options are included in base pay and bonus (+) Aligns management compensation with shareholder interests	(+) Consistent with shareholder's interests.	(−) Lack of controllability
Strategic performance measures (cost, revenue, profit, and investment centers)	(+) Strongly motivating if noncontrollable factors are excluded	(+) Generally a good measure of economic performance (−) Typically has only a short-term focus (−) If bonus is very high, creates an incentive for inaccurate reporting	(+) Intuitive, clear, and easily understood (−) Measurement issues: differences in accounting conventions, cost allocation methods, and financing methods
Balanced scorecard (critical success factors)	(+) Strongly motivating if noncontrollable factors are excluded (+) Aligns management compensation with shareholder interests	(+) Consistent with management's strategy (−) Can be subject to inaccurate reporting of nonfinancial factors	(+) If carefully defined and measured, CSFs are likely to be perceived as fair (−) Potential measurement issues, as above

Key: (+) means the base has a positive effect on the objective.
      (−) means the base has a negative effect on the objective.

customer satisfaction or customer service are likely to increase profits at less than a linear rate, at least in the short term.[6]

Bonus Compensation Pools

A **unit-based pool**
is a basis for determining
a bonus according to the
performance of the manager's
unit.

A manager's bonus can be determined by the so-called **unit-based pool** that is based on the performance of the manager's unit. For example, the bonus pool might be determined as the amount of the unit's earnings that are more than 5 percent of the investment in the unit. The appeal of the unit-based pool is the strong motivation for effective managers to perform and to receive rewards for their effort; the upside potential to the individual manager is very motivating.

A **firmwide pool**
is a basis for determining the
bonus available to all managers
through an amount set aside for
this purpose.

Alternatively, the amount of bonus available to all managers is often a **firmwide pool** set aside for this purpose. A firmwide pool, for example, might be the amount of firmwide earnings that are more than 5 percent of firmwide investment. Each unit manager's bonus is then drawn from this common pool. General Electric Corporation's bonus compensation plan includes the following in its 2007 Proxy Statement regarding the firm's pool:

> Each December the CEO reviews with the (Board's) Management Development Compensation Committee the company's estimated full-year financial results against the financial, strategic and operational goals established for the year, and the company's financial performance in prior periods. Based on that review, the management development compensation committee determines on a preliminary basis, and as compared to the prior year, an estimated appropriation to provide for the payment of cash bonuses to employees.

When the bonus pool is unit-based, the amount of the bonus for any one manager is independent of the performance of the other managers. In contrast, when a firmwide pool is used,

[6] Gerald K. DeBusk and Aaron D Crabtree, "Does the Balanced Scorecard Improve Performance, *Management Accounting Quarterly*, Fall 2006, pp. 44–48; Kate Plourd, "Setting Bonus Targets with Hindsight," *CFO.com*, March 31, 2008; Michael C. Jensen, "Corporate Budgeting Is Broken—Let's Fix It," *Harvard Business Review*, November 2001, pp. 95–101.

each manager's bonus depends in some predetermined way on the firm's performance as a whole. The sharing arrangements vary widely, although a common arrangement is for all managers to share equally in the firmwide bonus pool. Generally, the firmwide pool provides an important incentive for coordination and cooperation among units within the firm since all managers share in the higher overall firm profits that result from cross-unit efforts. Moreover, those who think executive pay is too high often argue that pay linked to overall firm performance is preferable since all managers share in this success. We summarize the advantages and disadvantages of each approach to bonus pools in Exhibit 20.3.

Bonus Payment Options

In recent years, the use of different payment options for bonus compensation plans has greatly increased. In the competition for top executives, firms are developing innovative ways to attract and retain the best.

We look at the four most common payment options:

1. **Current bonus** (cash and/or stock) based on current (usually annual) performance, the most common bonus form.
2. **Deferred bonus** (cash and/or stock) earned currently but not paid for two or more years. Deferred plans are used to avoid or delay taxes or to affect the manager's future total income stream in some desired way. This type of plan can also be used to retain key managers because the deferred compensation is paid only if the manager stays with the firm.
3. **Stock options** confer the right to purchase stock at some future date at a predetermined price. Stock options are used to motivate managers to increase stock price for the benefit of the shareholders. Some firms require executives to own a significant amount of stock in the company. The problem with stock options for the firms awarding them is that they must be valued and the expense taken as a reduction in income.
4. **Performance shares** grant stock for achieving certain performance goals over two years or more.

The current and deferred bonus plans generally focus the manager's attention on short-term performance measures, most commonly on accounting earnings. In contrast, stock options and performance shares focus attention directly on shareholder value. See the advantages and disadvantages of the four plans in Exhibit 20.4 (page 902).

EXHIBIT 20.3   **Advantages and Disadvantages of Different Bonus Pools Relative to Compensation Objectives**

	Motivation	Right Decision	Fairness
Unit-based	(+) Strong motivation for an effective manager—the upside potential (−) Unmotivating for manager of economically weaker units	(−) Provides the incentive for individual managers *not* to cooperate with and support other units when needed for the good of the firm	(−) Does not separate the performance of the unit from the manager's performance
Firmwide	(+) Helps to attract and retain good managers throughout the firm, even in economically weaker units (−) Not as strongly motivating as the unit-based pool	(+) Effort for the good of the overall firm is rewarded—motivates teamwork and sharing of assets among units	(+) Separates the performance of the manager from that of the unit (+) Can appear to be fairer to shareholders and others who are concerned that executive pay is too high

Key: (+) means the pool has a positive effect on the objective.
    (−) means the pool has a negative effect on the objective.

All public companies must determine the expense of stock options that have been granted to executives and employees, and must show this expense in the income statement.

WHY STOCK OPTIONS?

Stock options are favored as a method that helps to align the interests of top executives with those of shareholders—the improvement of shareholder value. Also, many firms, particularly in the technology industries, have used stock options as a relatively low-cost way to attract and retain key employees. At their height in 2002, it is estimated that 10 million U.S. employees had stock options.

HOW IS THE EXPENSE CALCULATED?

Most firms are expected to use an option pricing model, such as the Black-Scholes model, for valuing the options and the expense. The model is an equation that involves the following components: current stock price, option exercise price, expected option life, the risk-free interest rate, dividend yield, and the expected volatility of the stock price.

HOW ARE FIRMS RESPONDING?

Some firms (GE, IBM, Microsoft, and FedEx, among others) have reduced the granting of stock options to executives and instead use stock grants or cash. Other firms are looking for ways to reduce the amount of the expense:

- Some firms made changes in the components of the Black-Scholes model. For example, it is estimated that in the period 2002–2005, 66 percent of technology companies reduced the stock volatility estimate used in the model, thereby reducing the amount of the expense. Other changes in the model include shortening the option life by awarding options that expire sooner.

- A recent survey of 152 multinational companies from 15 countries shows that these companies, while sharply reducing the amount of compensation in the form of stock options (50 percent fewer companies used stock options in 2007 relative to 2003), still rely significantly upon equity-based compensation, and stock options continue to be the most popular form of equity-based compensation for these firms.

Source: PricewaterhouseCoopers, "2007 Global Equity Incentives Survey," (www.pwc.com/extweb/pwcpublications.nsf/docid/eeace28ff7a0b05e852573b700758d02); Jane Sasseen, "Stock Options: Old Game, New Tricks," *BusinessWeek,* December 19, 2005, pp. 35–36; FASB Statement 123 (www.fasb.org/pdf/fas123r.pdf).

EXHIBIT 20.4 **Advantages and Disadvantages of Bonus Payment Options Relative to Compensation Objectives**

	Motivation	Right Decision	Fairness
Current bonus	(+) Strong motivation for current performance; stronger motivation than for deferred plans	(−) Short-term focus (−) Risk-averse manager avoids risky but potentially beneficial projects	(+/−) Depends on the clarity of the bonus arrangement and the consistency with which it is applied
Deferred bonus	(+) Strong motivation for current performance, but not as strong as for the current bonus plan since the reward is delayed	Same as for current bonus	Same as for current bonus
Stock options	(+) Unlimited upside potential is highly motivating (−) Delay and uncertainty in reward reduces motivation	(+) Incentive to consider longer-term issues (+) Provides better risk incentives than for current or deferred bonus plans (+) Consistent with shareholder interests	(−) Uncontrollable factors affect stock price Also, same as for current bonus
Performance shares	Same as for stock options	(+) Incentive to consider long-term factors that affect stock price (+) Consistent with the firm's strategy, when critical success factors are used (+) Consistent with shareholder interests when earnings per share is used	(+/−) Depends on the clarity of the bonus arrangements and the consistency with which it is applied

Key: (+) means the payment option has a positive effect.
  (−) means the payment option has a negative effect.

Tax Planning and Financial Reporting

LEARNING OBJECTIVE 4

Describe the role of tax planning and financial reporting in management compensation planning.

In addition to achieving the three main objectives of compensation plans, firms attempt to choose plans that reduce or avoid taxes for both the firm and the manager. By combining salary, bonus, and perks, accountants can maximize potential tax savings for the firm, and delay or avoid taxes for the manager. For example, many perks (club memberships, company car, entertainment) are deductible to reduce the firm's tax liability but are not considered income to the manager (and therefore not taxed).

In contrast, although salary is a deductible business expense for the firm, it is taxable income for the manager. Bonus plans have a variety of tax effects as outlined in Exhibit 20.5. Tax planning is complex and dynamic, an integral part of compensation planning. Exhibit 20.5 suggests general relationships; a thorough coverage of tax planning is beyond the scope of this text.

Firms also attempt to design compensation plans that have a favorable effect on the firm's financial report. For example, present accounting rules do not require current recognition of certain types of compensation, such as deferred compensation. A thorough coverage of financial reporting rules regarding management compensation is not attempted here. Exhibit 20.5 provides an overview of the issues.

EXHIBIT 20.5   **Tax and Financial Report Effects of Compensation Plans**

		Financial Statement Effect	Tax Effect*	
			On the Firm	**On the Manager**
Salary		Current expense	Current deduction	Currently taxed
Bonus	Current	Current expense	Current deduction	Currently taxed
	Deferred	Deferred expense	Deferred deduction	Deferred tax
	Stock options—nonqualified plans	Stock options must be valued (e.g., using an options pricing model) and the expense taken against current income	Deduction when expensed	Taxed as ordinary income when exercised
	Stock options—qualified plans	As above	No deduction	Taxed as capital gains when stock is sold if held 18 months from exercise date
	Performance shares	As above	Deferred deduction	Deferred tax
Perks	Certain retirement plans	Current expense	Current deduction	Deferred tax
	Other perks	Current expense	Current deduction	Never taxed

* The tax law regarding deferred compensation has changed as a result of the American Jobs Creation Act of 2004. The new law places restrictions on the deferral of taxes under these compensation plans. See for example, Anne Tergesen, "Rethink that Deferred Comp Plan Now," *BusinessWeek,* June 30, 2008, pp. 66–67.

Management Compensation in Service Firms

LEARNING OBJECTIVE 5

Explain how management compensation plans are used in service firms.

Although most compensation plans are used by manufacturing or merchandising firms, an increasing number of service firms, especially financial and professional service firms, are using these plans. A good example is the compensation plan for the architectural and engineering design firm, Short-Elliott-Hendrickson, Inc. (SEH).[7] SEH provides professional services in a variety of markets, each of which is organized as a profit center: airport planning,

[7] Mark Pederson and Gary A. Lidgerding, "Pay-for-Performance in a Service Firm," *Management Accounting,* November 1995, pp. 40–43. A similar balanced scorecard-based system, designed for public accounting firms, is described by Michael Hayes in "Pay for Performance," *Journal of Accountancy,* June 2002, pp. 24–28.

water resources, waste management, municipal services, structural engineering, architecture, and others. SEH has developed a compensation plan for managers of each profit center. The plan uses a balanced scorecard approach that focuses on three areas: (1) financial results, (2) client satisfaction, and (3) improvement in the process of developing and providing the services. Management considers the financial results area to be the most important and has developed the following three criteria for evaluating managers and each profit center: profitability, efficiency, and collections of accounts receivable.

1. **Profitability** is measured by the *profit multiplier,* the ratio of net revenues to direct labor dollars.

2. **Efficiency** is measured by *staff utilization,* which is determined from the ratio of direct labor-hours chargeable (to clients) to total hours worked less vacation and holiday time.

3. **Collection of accounts** as measured by two ratios:

   a. The percentage of accounts receivable over 90 days, a measure of the ability to collect customer accounts.

   b. Average days of unbilled work outstanding, a measure of the ability to complete assignments and bill promptly for them.

As shown in Exhibit 20.6, SEH's compensation plan is based on three criteria and four measures (two measures for collection of accounts). Note that the water resources group fell short of

EXHIBIT 20.6   Management Compensation Plan for the Water Resources Group of SEH Inc.

	1. Profit Multiplier (ratio: net revenues to direct labor dollars)		2. Staff Utilization (ratio: chargeable time to total time)		3. Collection of Accounts			
					Percentage of Accounts Receivable > 90 Days		Days Revenue Unbilled	
Actual	88%		Actual	79%	Actual	14%	Actual	50 days
Goal	95%		Goal	83%	Goal	10%	Goal	45 days
Variance	7%		Variance	4%	Variance	4%	Variance	5 days
Multiply by weight of	3		Multiply by weight of	3	Multiply by weight of	2	Divide by goal	45 days
Weighted variance	21%		Weighted variance	12%	Weighted variance	8%	Percent variance	11%
Less	100%		Less	100%	Less	100%	Less	100%
Score	**79%**			**88%**		**92%**		**89%**

What does a company do when its stock price falls and its executive stock options are no longer attractive? If the firm does not move quickly, it can lose key executives to other employers that offer a more attractive compensation package. With the inevitable ups and downs of the stock market, firms are likely to face this problem at one point or another.

(Refer to Comments on Cost Management in Action at end of Chapter.)

its target in each of the three areas with scores of 79 percent for the profit multiplier, 88 percent for staff utilization, and 92 percent and 89 percent, respectively, for each of the two measures of collections of accounts. The advantage of this compensation plan is that it clearly places responsibility for results on the three criteria that are important to SEH's strategy and is therefore consistent with the objectives of management compensation. The objectives of motivation and correct decision making are achieved since the managers of SEH's profit centers have clear, attainable goals consistent with the firm's strategy. The objective of fairness is achieved by focusing on ratios rather than total profits, which increases comparability among managers.

Part Two: Business Analysis and Business Valuation

LEARNING OBJECTIVE 6

Apply the different methods for business analysis and business valuation.

Business analysis

uses the balanced scorecard, financial ratio analysis and economic value added to evaluate the firm's overall performance.

Business valuation

values the firm by estimating its total market value, which can then be compared to the market value for prior periods or for comparable firms.

In this second part of the chapter, we examine the evaluation of the firm as a whole. The goal of strategic cost management is the success of the firm in maintaining competitive advantage, so we evaluate the firm's overall performance as well as the performance of individual managers. Business valuation is particularly important in difficult economic times, when failing companies are acquired by stronger companies, and analysts must value the acquired company—the price paid in the acquisition. Also, as some companies fall short of meeting their financial goals due to the weakening economy and the market value of the company falls, business valuation provides top management a means to assess the risk of takeover by a venture capital firm or other set of investors. In response, the Institute of Management Accountants provides an updated (2009) *Statement on Management Accounting,* "Business Valuation" (www.imanet.org/smas).

We take a broad approach that includes both the process of evaluating a firm's overall performance and the process of determining an overall value for the firm; ultimately, the objective of the firm's managers is to improve the overall value of the firm.

Business analysis uses the balanced scorecard, financial ratio analysis, and economic value added as benchmarks to evaluate the firm's overall performance. In contrast, **business valuation** values the firm by estimating its total market value, which can then be compared to the market value for prior periods or for comparable firms.[8]

Business Analysis

Business analysis includes a set of tools used to evaluate the firm's competitiveness and financial performance. The objective is a comprehensive evaluation. Business analysis begins with a careful strategic and competitive analysis of the firm, including SWOT analysis and strategic positioning analysis, tools that are explained in Chapters 1 and 2. Then we consider tools used to implement strategy, including the balanced scorecard. Finally, we move to ratios and other measures, including some that were used in Chapter 19 to measure the performance of individual SBU managers. We put all these tools together to complete a comprehensive business analysis of the firm.

Because business analysis for any company is comprehensive and extensive, we can only present a summary of some of the highlights of the analysis. We use an example of a firm that manufactures cleaning products, EasyKleen; summarized information for the firm is shown in Exhibit 20.7. The information includes the firm's balance sheet and income statement,

[8] A thorough presentation of business analysis and valuation goes beyond the scope of this text. Excellent references include the following texts: Krishna G. Palepu and Paul M. Healy. *Business Analysis and Valuation: Using Financial Statements,* 4th ed. (Mason, OH: South-Western, 2007), and John J. Wild, K.R. Subramanyam, and Robert F. Halsey, *Financial Statement Analysis,* 9th ed. (New York: McGraw Hill, 2007).

EXHIBIT 20.7

Selected Financial Information

EASYKLEEN COMPANY
Summary of Selected Financial Information
For the Year Ended December 31,

Financial Statements	2010	2009
Current assets		
Cash	$ 50,000	$ 70,000
Accounts receivable	100,000	80,000
Inventory	50,000	60,000
Total current assets	$ 200,000	$210,000
Long-lived assets	200,000	180,000
Total assets	$ 400,000	$390,000
Current liabilities	$ 50,000	$ 60,000
Long-term debt	150,000	200,000
Total liabilities	$ 200,000	$260,000
Shareholders' equity	200,000	130,000
Total liabilities and equity	$ 400,000	$390,000
Sales	$1,000,000 (50% are credit sales)	
Cost of sales	500,000	
Gross margin	$ 500,000	
Operating expense	300,000	
Operating income	$ 200,000	
Income tax (50%)	100,000	
Net income	$ 100,000	

Additional Financial Information	
Depreciation expense	$30,000
Capital expenditures	$50,000
Dividends	$30,000
Year-end share price	$ 16.25
Number of outstanding shares	50,000
Interest expense	$10,000 ($5,000 after tax)
Training expenses	$30,000 ($15,000 after tax; 26 hours per employee)
Quality defects	350 ppm (parts per million)
Weighted-average cost of capital (WACC)	6%

Cash Flow from Operations	
Net income	$100,000
Depreciation expense	30,000
Decrease (increase) in accounts receivable	(20,000)
Decrease (increase) in inventory	10,000
Increase (decrease) in current liabilities	(10,000)
Total cash flow from operations	$110,000

Free Cash Flow	
Cash flow from operations	$110,000
Less: Capital expenditures	50,000
Less: Dividends	30,000
Free cash flow	$ 30,000

additional financial information, the statement of operating cash flows, and calculation of free cash flow. The following shows a brief example of how the balanced scorecard, financial ratio analysis, and EVA® can be used for a business analysis of EasyKleen.

The Balanced Scorecard

The use of the balanced scorecard to evaluate the firm is similar to the use of critical success factors in evaluating and compensating the individual manager. When evaluating the firm using CSFs, the management accountant uses benchmarks from industry information and considers how the CSFs have changed from prior years. A favorable evaluation results when the CSFs are superior to the benchmarks and to prior years' performance. For example, assume that EasyKleen has three CSFs, one each from the three key performance categories:

1. Return on total assets (financial performance).
2. Number of quality defects (business processes).
3. Number of training hours for plant workers (human resources).

A target level of performance is set for each CSF based on a study of the performance of the best firms in the industry. The benchmark is set at 90 percent of the best performance in the industry, and EasyKleen is evaluated on its overall performance, as illustrated in Exhibit 20.8.

EasyKleen management sees from the balanced scorecard that the firm met its goal in the financial area but fell short in both the operations and human resources areas. The scorecard is a guide for directing attention to achieving desired goals.

Financial Ratio Analysis

Financial ratio analysis uses financial statement ratios to evaluate the firm's performance. Two common measures of performance are liquidity and profitability. *Liquidity* refers to the firm's ability to pay its current operating expenses (usually for a year or less) and maturing debt. The six key measures of liquidity are the accounts receivable turnover, the inventory turnover, the current ratio, the quick ratio, and two cash flow ratios. The higher these ratios the better and the higher the evaluation of the firm's liquidity. The four key profitability ratios are gross margin percent, return on assets, return on equity, and earnings per share. The six liquidity ratios and four profitability ratios are explained in other finance and accounting texts and are not covered here. Instead, we show how each of the ratios is calculated for EasyKleen Company in Exhibit 20.9. The information is taken from Exhibit 20.7 and assumes that the benchmark level of performance is 90 percent of the best in the industry.

As Exhibit 20.9 indicates, EasyKleen had a very good year financially. It met seven of its ten goals. Profitability is the strongest area; it exceeded three of four ratios substantially; only the earnings per share target was unmet by a small margin. The liquidity goals were largely met, although receivables turnover and cash flow from operations fell short. This points to the need to improve the collection of receivables, which would improve all three of these ratios. Overall, the financial ratio analysis shows that EasyKleen performed quite well.

Economic Value Added

Economic value added (EVA®) is a business unit's income after taxes and after deducting the cost of capital. The cost of capital is usually obtained by calculating a weighted average of the cost of the firm's two sources of funds, borrowing and selling stock. EVA® focuses managers' attention on creating value for shareholders. By earning higher profits than the firm's cost of capital, the firm increases its internal resources available for dividends and/or to finance its continued growth, which increases stock price and adds shareholder value.

The calculation of EVA® is described fully in Chapter 19. Here we take a simple example such that the only adjustments to income are training expenses and interest expense and the

EXHIBIT 20.8   **Balanced Scorecard**

EASYKLEEN COMPANY Balanced Scorecard For the Year Ended December 31, 2010				
Category	**CSF**	**Target Performance**	**Actual Performance***	**Variance**
Financial Operations	Return on total assets	22%	25.3%	3.3% (exceeded)
Operations	Quality defects	300 ppm	350 ppm	50 ppm (unmet)
Human Resources	Training hours	32 hours per employee	26 hours per employee	6 hours (unmet)

* See Exhibit 20.9 for return on assets and Exhibit 20.7 for quality defects and training hours.

EXHIBIT 20.9 **Financial Ratio Analysis**

EASYKLEEN COMPANY
Financial Ratio Analysis
For the Year Ended December 31, 2010

Ratio	Benchmark	Actual	Percent Achievement
Liquidity Ratios			
Accounts receivable turnover (Credit sales/Average receivables)	7	5.56 = $500,000/($100,000 + $80,000)/2	79% (unmet)
Inventory turnover (Cost of sales/Average inventory)	8	9.09 = $500,000/($50,000 + $60,000)/2	114% (met)
Current ratio (Current assets/Current liabilities)	2	4 = $200,000/$50,000	200% (met)
Quick ratio (Cash and receivables/Current liabilities)	1	3 = ($50,000 + $100,000)/$50,000	300% (met)
Liquidity: Cash Flow Ratios			
Cash flow ratio (Cash flow from operations/Current liabilities)	2.5	2.2 = $110,000/$50,000	88% (unmet)
Free cash flow ratio (Free cash flow/Current liabilities)	.5	.6 = $30,000/$50,000	120% (met)
Profitability Ratios			
Gross margin percent (Gross profit/Net sales)	35%	50% = $500,000/$1,000,000	143% (met)
Return on assets (Net income/Average total assets)	22%	25.3% = $100,000/[($400,000 + $390,000)/2]	115% (met)
Return on equity (Net income/Average shareholders' equity)	44%	60.6% = $100,000/[($200,000 + $130,000)/2]	138% (met)
Earnings per share (Net income/Weighted—average number of shares outstanding)	$2.15	$2.00 = $100,000/50,000	93% (unmet)

only adjustment to invested capital is training expense. In effect, we are assuming for simplicity that there are no "equity equivalents" such as noncapitalized leases or deferred taxes, the firm uses FIFO for inventory, cost of goods sold equals the cash paid for inventory, and all operating expenses and taxes are paid in cash.

$$
\begin{aligned}
\text{EVA}^{\circledR} &= \text{EVA}^{\circledR} \text{ net income} - (\text{Cost of capital} \times \text{EVA}^{\circledR} \text{ Invested capital}) \\
&= \text{Net income} + \text{training expenses after tax} + \text{interest expense after tax} \\
&\quad - 0.06 \times (\text{Average Total assets} + \text{Training expenses} - \text{Current liabilities}) \\
&= (\$100,000 + \$15,000 + \$5,000) - 0.06 \times [(\$400,000 + \$390,000)/2 \\
&\quad + \$30,000 - \$50,000] \\
&= \$97,500
\end{aligned}
$$

The EVA$^{\circledR}$ of $97,500 for EasyKleen is a very positive value relative to net income and invested capital. It indicates the firm's strong profitability and, in particular, its significant contribution to shareholder value.[9]

Business Valuation

This section examines how to value the company, to come up with a single dollar figure for the company. Some might argue the value of the company and changes in its value are the most useful measures of the firm's success. Certainly these measures are relevant for the owners of the firm and interested investors.

Initially we take the approach of the owner, shareholder, or interested investor and calculate the value of the firm's shareholder equity. Later, we consider the broader question of what one would pay to purchase the entire company-debt, equity, and assets.

[9] If the EVA$^{\circledR}$ for future periods is projected and then the discounted value of each of these future EVA$^{\circledR}$ values is taken, the sum is what is called market value added (MVA). MVA is an estimate of the difference between the market value of a company and the amount of invested capital. It is interpreted just as EVA$^{\circledR}$; the difference is that it aggregates the net present value of all future projected EVA$^{\circledR}$ amounts. MVA helps to understand a company's market performance (and value) by linking it to projected returns on capital.

There are four approaches to measuring the value of shareholders' equity: the book value method, the market value method, the discounted cash flow method, and the multiples-based method. A fifth measure, enterprise value, estimates the acquisition value of a firm. The first and easiest is to obtain the book value of the firm's shareholder equity from the balance sheet. For EasyKleen, the book value of equity is $200,000 in 2010. An advantage of the book value measure is its clarity, accessibility, and objectivity. A limitation is that it reflects book values only, and therefore does not reflect the market value of the firm's assets or liabilities, and may not include key intangible assets. In many cases the book value of the firm's equity is relatively small and undervalues the firm's equity.

A second approach is to obtain the market value of the firm's common equity, directly from the current market value of the firm's shares. Here for simplicity we assume that all of EasyKleen's shareholders are common shareholders; there is no preferred stock.

The firm's market value is determined by multiplying the number of outstanding shares by the current market price of the shares. For the EasyKleen Company, the value is:

$$\text{Number of shares} \times \text{Share price}$$
$$= 50,000 \times \$16.25 = \$812,500$$

The market value method has the advantage of providing a clear and objective measure of equity which reflects the current value of the company. This measure is often called the firm's *market capitalization.*

For nonpublic firms a relevant stock price is not available, and one of the other methods is needed to evaluate the firm.[10]

The third method for obtaining the value of the firm is to obtain the present value of the firm's cash flows, and is called the *discounted cash flow (DCF) method.* It is one of the most commonly used methods in equity valuation. Economic and accounting theory say that the equity value of an investment should be the present value of future dividends from the investment, and the DCF method is the most consistent with that.

The Discounted Cash Flow Method

The discounted cash flow (DCF) method measures the firm's equity value as the discounted present value of its net cash flows. The DCF method is based on the same concepts used in Chapter 12 for capital-budgeting decisions. Cash flows a year or more into the future are discounted to consider the time value of money; cash flows in recent periods are more valuable than cash flows in distant periods.

There are four steps in the application of the DCF method.[11]

1. **Forecast free cash flows over a finite horizon (usually five years).** Free cash flow is cash flows available for investing and financing activities of the company and is calculated as operating cash flow less capital expenditures and less dividends paid. For EasyKleen, free cash flow in 2010 is equal to $30,000. For this illustration, we assume that free cash flows will also be $30,000 in 2011 and will increase by $10,000 in each of the next four years. These cash flow assumptions are shown in Exhibit 20.10.

2. **Forecast free cash flows beyond the finite horizon, using some simplifying assumption.** For EasyKleen, we make the conservative forecast that free cash flows after 2015 will continue at the rate of $70,000 per year (the same as year 2015), and we also assume that these cash flows will continue indefinitely.

3. **Discount free cash flows at the weighted-average cost of capital (WACC), the firm's cost of capital weighted for both debt and equity.** The weighted-average cost of capital (WACC) for EasyKleen is given as 6 percent. The derivation of WACC is explained in Chapter 12 and is not duplicated here. The present value of free cash flows is determined using the WACC of 6 percent, as illustrated in Exhibit 20.10. The sum of the present values for the first five years is $205,700.

[10] The valuation of privately held businesses is examined in David S Jenkins and Gregory Kane, "A Contextual Analysis of Income- and Asset-Based Approaches to Private Equity Valuation," *The Accounting Review,* March 2006, pp. 19–35.

[11] The steps shown here are guided by the steps illustrated in the text by Krishna G. Palepu and Paul M. Healy, *Business Analysis and Valuation: Using Financial Statements,* 4th ed. (Mason, OH: South-Western, 2007).

EXHIBIT 20.10
DCF Valuation of the EasyKleen Company

Years	Free Cash Flow	Present Value Factor (for 6%)	Present Value of Cash Flows
2011	$30,000	0.943	$ 28,290
2012	40,000	0.890	35,600
2013	50,000	0.840	42,000
2014	60,000	0.792	47,520
2015	70,000	0.747	52,290
Total present value of cash flows in the planning period		→	$ 205,700 (A)
2016+	$70,000	16.667	$1,166,690 (B)
Total present value of 2016+ years' cash flows 0.747			871,517 (C) = (B) × 0.747
Plus: Marketable securities and investments			0 (D)
Less: Market value of debt (assumed = book value)			150,000 (E)
Value of the firm's equity			$ 927,217 = (A) + (C) + (D) − (E)

The present value of the cash flows from 2016 on are determined using the discount factor for an annuity with a continuing life, which is the inverse of the discount rate $(1/0.06 = 16.667)$.[12] This gives a discounted value for these six-year-plus cash flows of $1,166,690. To discount this amount back from the beginning of 2016 to the present, we discount $1,166,690 by the fifth year discount factor (0.747) to arrive at the discounted value of the continuing (six-year-plus) cash flows, $871,517.

4. **Calculate the value of equity.** To determine the firm's *net valuation,* we now add the discounted value of the planning period cash flows and the discounted value of six-year-plus cash flows to the value of current nonoperating investments such as marketable securities, and we subtract the market value of long-term debt. The net valuation for the firm's equity is then $927,217. If the cash flow estimates are reliable, the DCF method provides a useful measure in determining the firm's value.

---

[12] Typically, the firm's cash flows are assumed to continue indefinitely, and thus the discount factor for an annuity is used in perpetuity (continuing life). This assumption is consistent with the idea that the firm is an ongoing entity with little or no likelihood of bankruptcy. If a shorter period is desired, the appropriate discount factor from the annuity table can be used for the desired number of years. For example, if the desired period, after the planning period, is from the 6th year to the 20th year, the discount factor is found in the annuity table for 15 years (6 through 20), or 9.712. The factor 9.712 is then used in place of the factor 16.667 in the analysis in Exhibit 20.10.

Multiples-Based Valuation

A common and easy-to-apply approach to valuing a business is to use the ratio of stock price to some financial measure—usually sales, earnings, or cash flow. For example, the earnings-based multiple computes value as the product of expected annual accounting earnings times a multiplier (stock price/earnings). The earnings multiple is also called the price-to-earnings ratio. The earnings multiplier has important limitations. The accounting treatment of inventory, depreciation, and other important components of earnings might not be comparable to that of other firms in the industry. Also, there can be large fluctuations in the multiplier as the economy moves in and out of recession. When earnings are not comparable for these reasons, determining a relevant and useful multiplier is difficult.

The price-to-earnings ratio measures the amount the investor is willing to pay for a dollar of the firm's earnings per share. If the price-to-earnings ratio is not available for a given firm, an average or representative value is taken from the price-to-earnings ratios of other firms in the industry. This ratio can then be adjusted upward to recognize a firm with future profit potential not recognized in current earnings or vice versa. Assume that the relevant price-to-earnings multiple for EasyKleen is 8.5. Then the value of EasyKleen using this method is determined as follows:

$$\text{Earnings multiplier} \times \text{Earnings}$$
$$= 8.5 \times \$100,000 = \$850,000$$

The earnings multiplier is easy to apply and can provide a useful evaluation of the firm, subject to the limitations noted. The sales-based multiple and the cash flow-based multiples are applied in a similar fashion.

In practice, the management accountant and analyst commonly use two or more of the valuation techniques and evaluate the assumptions in each to arrive at an overall valuation. In the case of EasyKleen, a valuation of approximately $900,000 is reasonable, given the range of measures obtained.

Enterprise Value

The methods we have considered thus far determine the value of the firm's equity. Enterprise value (EV) is another measure of what the market says the company is worth, but this time in an acquisition. In an acquisition, an acquirer would "buy" not only the firm's equity, but also the firm's debt, cash, and cash equivalents. So EV is measured as the market value of the firm's equity (market capitalization) plus debt, and less cash (cash is subtracted because it is available after the acquisition to pay off debt or for other uses):

$$EV = \text{Market capitalization} + \text{Debt} - \text{Cash}$$

EV is used by investors and shareholders when an acquisition is being considered.

An Illustration of the Five Steps of Strategic Decision Making in the Valuation of a Fashion Retailer

Arizona Sunrise Inc (ASI) is a retailer of women's fashion clothing with 455 stores in the United States and 55 in Canada, an increase of 62 stores over the prior year. The company is growing fast because of its unique fashion styles and the quality of its clothing. ASI products are priced at levels slightly higher than competitive brands, but production and selling costs are somewhat higher as well, thus sales have grown very fast, but earnings and cash flows have trailed behind. In some recent quarterly periods, cash flow from operations has been low and in some cases even negative. Bettman, PLC, a similar retailer located in London, is also known for its fashion-wise designs and product quality. Bettman has expressed an interest in buying ASI, both because of ASI's recent success and because the fall in the dollar relative to the British pound in recent years has effectively reduced the purchase cost in U.K. currency. Bettman would maintain the ASI brand name for at least a few years and at least initially would maintain the local store management. In the longer term, Bettman's plan is to integrate the two products lines into a single global brand. Bettman plans to purchase ASI in a cash transaction, but is not sure what value to place on ASI.[13]

[13] For a discussion of the effect of the falling dollar on non-U.S-based retailers, see Jennifer Saranow and Kris Hudson, "Apparel Retailers from Overseas Are Hitting the Mall in the U.S.," *The Wall Street Journal*, July 29, 2008, p. B1.

The Five Steps of Strategic Decision Making for Arizona Sunrise Inc.

1. **Determine the strategic issues surrounding the problem.** Both firms involved in the case are differentiators based on quality and style. The key business issue is how the combined firms will be more or less competitive than the separate firms. Bettman's plan to move the two firms to a larger, global brand, could help the firm establish a presence globally, thereby improving its opportunity for further growth. The immediate issue is to determine the purchase price of ASI.

2. **Identify the alternative actions.** Bettman can use a variety of methods to value ASI, as described above: discounted cash flows, multiples of earnings, and enterprise value, among other methods.

3. **Obtain information and conduct analyses of the alternatives.** Bettman performs a discounted cash flow analysis based on ASI's projected free cash flow for the next five years and projects a value of $24 billion. A valuation based on the earnings multiple yielded a smaller value of $14 billion, the current market value of ASI's equity was $16 billion, and the enterprise value was calculated to be $15 billion.

4. **Based on strategy and analysis, choose and implement the desired alternative.** The analysis produced a wide range of valuations, but a cluster of them was around $15 billion. Moreover, enterprise value is particularly appropriate for valuing a purchase because it takes into account ASI's debt and cash equivalents available to the purchaser. Bettman also considers the strategic advantages and disadvantages of the purchase and is persuaded to make an offer of $15 billion because the acquisition of ASI could help Bettman establish a stronger brand globally, thereby improving its opportunity for further growth and profitability.

5. **Provide an ongoing evaluation of the effectiveness of implementation in step 4.** If Bettman purchases ASI, it will need to complete the implementation through a plan for integrating the two businesses operationally, financially, and strategically. This will be a key management goal for the first few years after the acquisition. Bettman is required by international financial accounting standards to regularly assess the value of the acquisition, and if the value of the acquisition should fall, Bettman must write the asset down to the new fair market value.

If the purchase is not completed, Bettman should continue to look for firms like ASI that would help Bettman obtain the global presence that is central to its strategy.

Summary

In this chapter we discussed management compensation and the evaluation of a business. The first part introduces the objectives and methods for compensating managers. The three principal objectives for management compensation, which follow directly from the objectives for management control, are the *motivation* of the manager, the *incentive* for proper decision making, and *fairness* to the manager.

The three main types of compensation are *salary, bonus,* and *benefits.* The bonus is the fastest growing part of total compensation and often the largest part. The three important factors in the development of a bonus plan are the base for computing the bonus (strategic performance measures, stock price, and critical success factors), the source of funding for the bonus (the business unit or the entire firm), and the payment options (current and deferred bonus, stock options, and performance shares). The development of an executive compensation plan is a complex process involving these three factors and the three types of compensation, as well as the objectives of management control.

Tax planning and financial reporting concerns are important in compensation planning because of management's desire to reduce taxes and report financial results favorably. Thus, accountants must consider taxes and financial reporting issues when they develop a compensation plan for managers.

Management compensation plans are used in service and not-for-profit organizations as well. The chapter illustrates an actual example for a professional services firm.

The second part of the chapter considers the evaluation of the entire firm in contrast to the previous two chapters and the first part of this chapter that focused on the individual manager. The evaluation of the firm is important for investors and as one part of an overall assessment of the performance of top management. The common evaluation methods include the balanced scorecard, financial ratio analysis, and economic value added. Methods used to directly value a business include the market value method, the discounted cash flow method, the multiples-based method, and enterprise value.

Key Terms

benefits, *895*
bonus, *895*
business analysis, *905*
business valuation, *905*

firmwide pool, *900*
management compensation
  plans, *895*

salary, *895*
unit-based pool, *900*

Comments on Cost Management in Action

When Good Options Go Bad

When a company's stock price falls and its executive stock options no longer look attractive, it has a number of choices. One is to simply reprice the options to a lower price that is more in keeping with the lower market price of the firm's stock. Another choice is to grant new options that have a lower exercise price to replace the old.

Another approach is for the executive to hedge his or her own stockholding or stock options by buying "put" (right-to-sell) options on the firm's stock in the open market. If the stock price falls dramatically, the executive can still sell the stock or exercise the options at the relatively favorable ("put") price. This practice is very much like that engaged in by global firms to hedge their exposure to foreign exchange fluctuations.

The problem with executives hedging their stock holdings and options is that it undermines the principle of pay for performance. Through hedging, the executive can effectively protect against a fall in the stock. Hedging reduces the risk of stock ownership and therefore reduces the incentive for executives to take steps to sustain stock price.

Source: Brian J. Hall and Thomas A. Knox, "Underwater Options and the Dynamics of Executive Pay-to-Performance Sensitivities," *Journal of Accounting Research,* May 2004, p. 365; and "GE: When Execs Outperform the Stock," *BusinessWeek,* April 17, 2006, p. 74.

Self-Study Problem

(For solution, please turn to the end of the chapter.)

Management Compensation Plan

Davis-Thompson-Howard & Associates (DTH) is a large consulting firm that specializes in the evaluation of governmental programs. The lawyers, accountants, engineers, and other specialists at DTH evaluate both the performance of existing programs and the success of potential new government programs. DTH obtains most of its consulting engagements by completing proposals in open bidding for the services desired by governmental agencies. The competition for these proposals has increased in recent years, and as a result DTH's yield (the number of new engagements divided by proposals) has fallen from 49 percent a few years ago to only 26 percent in the most recent year. The firm's profitability has fallen as well. DTH has decided to study its management compensation plan as one step among the many it will take in attempting to return the firm to its previous level of profitability.

DTH has six regional offices, two located near Washington, D.C., and the others near large metropolitan areas where most of their clients are located. Each office is headed by an office manager who is one of the firm's professional associates. The firm's services in these offices are classified into financial and operational audit services, educational evaluation, engineering consulting, and financial systems. The Washington offices tend to provide most of the financial and audit services, and the other offices offer their own mix of professional services. No two offices are alike since each has adapted to the needs of its regional client base. DTH's objective is to be among the three most competitive firms in its areas of service and to increase its revenues by at least 10 percent per year.

DTH's compensation plan awards each office a bonus based on (1) the increase in billings over the prior year and (2) the number of net new clients acquired in the current year. The office manager has the authority to divide the office bonus as appropriate, although these same two criteria are generally used to allocate it to the office professionals. Top management is not aware of any problems with the compensation plan; there have been no significant complaints.

One observation by the CEO might suggest a reason for the firm's decline in yield of proposals. It has been losing out particularly on large new contract proposals that require a large number of staff and a significant professional travel commitment. These are jobs for which it would be necessary to coordinate two or more DTH offices. The CEO notes that DTH has as many regional offices as most of its competitors, which now seem to be winning a larger share of these contracts.

Required Discuss the pros and cons of DTH's compensation plan. Is it consistent with the company's objectives and competitive environment?

Business Valuation

WebSmart is a relatively new Internet company that sells educational products on the Web. The firm focuses on students preparing for college entrance exams. The key competitive advantage at WebSmart is its highly regarded publication, *Guide to Competitive Colleges,* which is sold widely in bookstores and on Amazon.com. The firm has grown rapidly and now is seeking additional venture capital investment to allow it to improve its operations and provide additional advertising and promotion. One of the venture capital firms that WebSmart approached has asked WebSmart to provide an estimate of the firm's value. Relevant financial information about WebSmart from the most recent financial statement follows. WebSmart owns no significant fixed assets, but operates out of leased space. WebSmart management knows that the median stock price-to-sales multiple in the industry is approximately 7.

Total assets per most recent financial statement	$1,450,000
Total book value of equity, per most recent financial statements	1,200,000
Estimated market value of *Guide to Competitive Colleges*	1,350,000
Net income	(85,000)
Cash flow from operations	(165,000)
Total revenues	$600,000

Required Develop an estimate of the value of WebSmart and explain your reasoning.

Questions

20-1 Identify and explain the three objectives of management compensation.

20-2 Explain the three types of management compensation.

20-3 Explain how a manager's risk aversion can affect decision making and how compensation plans should be designed to deal with risk aversion.

20-4 Explain how management compensation can provide an incentive to unethical behavior. What methods can be used to reduce the chance of unethical activities resulting from compensation plans?

20-5 From a financial reporting standpoint, what form of compensation is most desirable for the firm?

20-6 From a tax-planning standpoint, what form of compensation is least desirable for the manager? For the firm?

20-7 List the three bases for bonus incentive plans; explain how they differ and how each achieves or does not achieve the three objectives of management compensation.

20-8 Identify and explain the six financial ratios used to evaluate liquidity as part of the firm's business analysis.

20-9 What are the two types of bonus pools for bonus incentive plans? How do they differ, and how does each achieve or not achieve the three objectives of management compensation?

20-10 List the four types of bonus payment options and explain how they differ. How does each achieve or not achieve the three objectives of management compensation?

20-11 Develop arguments to support your view as to whether executive pay in the United States is too high.

20-12 Explain the different business valuation methods. Which do you think is superior and why?

20-13 What type of management compensation is the fastest growing part of total compensation? Why do you think this is the case?

20-14 Why do you think it is important for a management accountant to be able to complete an evaluation of the firm separate from an evaluation of individual managers?

20-15 How does the firm's management compensation plan change over the life cycle of the firm's products?

Brief Exercises

20-16 Sticky Fingers Inc. produces scotch tape and masking tape. Last year's annual report has been compiled, and you are in charge of business analysis for the year. The company had a goal for inventory turnover of 6, cost of goods sold of $400,000, beginning inventory of $50,000, and ending inventory of $70,000. What was the actual inventory turnover, and at what percent did the firm achieve its goal?

20-17   Tinsley Inc. is an industry-leading cardboard manufacturer. You have been asked to determine a market value for the firm's equity. The firm has 100,000 shares outstanding, earnings per share of $2.50 last year, and a stock price of $25. What is the market value?

20-18   Jamison Auto Parts produces replacement parts for automobiles. Last year Jamison had EVA® net income of $200,000, cost of capital of 10 percent, and EVA® capital of $750,000. Determine the firm's economic value added.

20-19   Moore Heel is a shoe manufacturing company. Moore has hired you to value the company based on the discounted cash flow method. You have determined that the present value of the company's cash flows is $400,000, marketable securities total $150,000, and the market value of debt is $250,000. What is the value of the firm?

20-20   Smith Co. is a firm specializing in financial advice for retired individuals. After some analysis, you have determined that an earnings multiplier of 7 is appropriate for this type of business. Smith's most recent earnings totaled $250,000. What is the value of the firm based on the earnings multiplier?

20-21   Johnson Healthcare is a health-care firm specializing in products for the disabled. Johnson plans to maintain a 10 percent gross profit margin. After analyzing last year's data, you found that Johnson had gross profit of $250,000 and net sales of $1,500,000. What was the gross profit margin, and by what percentage did the firm achieve its goal?

Exercises

20-22   **Compensation, Strategy, and Market Value**   Jackson Supply Company is a publicly owned firm that serves the medical supply needs of hospitals and large medical practices in six southeastern states. The firm has grown significantly in recent years, as the areas it serves have grown. Jackson has focused on customer service and has developed an excellent reputation for speed of delivery and overall quality of service. The company ensures that customer service is each manager's main focus by making it count for 50 percent of the management bonus. The firm measures specific indicators of customer service monthly; progress toward these measures as well as others is used to determine each manager's bonus. In the past several months, top management has noticed that although most managers are meeting or exceeding their customer service goals and receiving bonuses accordingly, the firm's stock price has been lagging while competitive firms' stock prices have been rising steadily.

Required   What modification, if any, should Jackson Supply Company make to its management compensation plan?

20-23   **Performance Evaluation and Risk Aversion**   Jill Lewis is the office manager of PureBreds, Inc. Her office has 30 employees whose collective job is to process applications by dog owners who want to register their pets with the firm. There is never a shortage of applications waiting to be processed, but random events beyond Lewis's control (e.g., employees out sick) cause fluctuations in the number of applications that her office can process. Jill is aware that it is important that the applications be processed quickly and accurately.

Alex Zale, the district manager to whom Jill reports, bases his evaluation of Jill on the number of applications that are processed.

Required

1. If Jill is risk-averse, how should Alex compensate her? Why?
2. What is a disadvantage of an evaluation method that is based only on the number of processed applications?
3. List at least two ways that Alex could measure how accurately Jill's office is processing the applications.

20-24   **Performance Evaluation and Risk Aversion**   Heartwood Furniture Corporation has a line of sofas marketed under the name NightTime Sleepers. Heartwood management is considering several compensation packages for Amy Johnson, NightTime's general manager. Amy's duties include making all investing and operating decisions for NightTime.

Required

1. Amy is risk-neutral and prefers to receive the maximum reward for her hard work. Do you recommend compensation based on flat salary, an ROI-based bonus, or a combination of both? Why?
2. If Amy does not make investing decisions for NightTime, is ROI still a good performance measure? If so, then explain why. If not, suggest an alternative.

3. Heartwood Furniture plans to evaluate Amy by comparing NightTime's ROI to the ROI of Stiles Furniture, which operates in a business environment similar to that of NightTime. Both companies have the same capabilities, but Stiles uses a significantly different manufacturing strategy than NightTime.

    a. Would evaluating Amy with this benchmark be fair?

    b. Would using residual income instead of ROI offer any advantages for Heartwood?

20-25 Evaluating an Incentive Pay Plan; Strategy   Anne-Marie Fox is the manager of a new and used boat dealership. She has decided to reevaluate the compensation plan offered to her sales representatives to determine whether the plan encourages the dealership's success. The representatives are paid no salary, but they receive 20 percent of the sales price of every boat sold, and they have the authority to negotiate the boats' prices as far down as their wholesale cost if necessary.

Required   Is this plan in the dealership's strategic best interest? Why or why not?

20-26 Alternative Compensation Plans   ADM, Inc., an electronics manufacturer, uses growth in earnings per share (EPS) as a guideline for evaluating executive performance. ADM executives receive a bonus of $5,000 for every penny increase in EPS for the year. This bonus is paid in addition to fixed salaries ranging from $500,000 to $900,000 annually.

Cygnus Corporation, a computer components manufacturer, also uses EPS as an evaluation tool. Its executives receive a bonus equal to 40 percent of their salary for the year if the firm's EPS is in the top third of a list ranking the EPS for Cygnus and its 12 competitors.

Required

1. Why are companies such as ADM, Inc., and Cygnus Corporation switching from stock option incentives to programs more like the ones described? What does the use of these plans by the two firms say about each firm's competitive strategy?

2. What are the weaknesses of incentive plans based on EPS?

20-27 Business Analysis   Somerfeld Company is a manufacturer of auto parts having the following financial statements for 2009–2010.

Balance Sheet December 31, 2010 and 2009		
	2010	**2009**
Cash	$ 395,000	$ 125,000
Accounts receivable	350,000	275,000
Inventory	200,000	175,000
Total current assets	945,000	575,000
Long-lived assets	1,440,000	1,500,000
Total assets	$2,385,000	$2,075,000
Current liabilities	$ 200,000	$ 250,000
Long-term debt	900,000	800,000
Shareholders' Equity	1,285,000	1,025,000
Total liabilities and equity	$2,385,000	$2,075,000

Income Statement For years ended December 31, 2010 and 2009		
	2010	**2009**
Sales	$3,500,000	$3,600,000
Cost of sales	2,500,000	2,600,000
Gross margin	1,000,000	1,000,000
Operating expense*	500,000	450,000
Operating income	500,000	550,000
Tax expense (40%)	200,000	220,000
Net income	$ 300,000	$ 330,000

* Operating expense includes depreciation expense.

(Continued)

Cash Flow from Operations

	2010	2009
Net income	$300,000	$330,000
Plus depreciation expense	60,000	50,000
+Decrease (-inc) in Accounts receivable and Inventory	(100,000)	—
+Increase (-dec) in Current Liabilities	(50,000)	—
Cash flow from operations	$210,000	$380,000

Additional financial information, including industry averages for 2010, where appropriate:

	2010	2009	Industry 2010
Income tax rate	40%	40%	40.0%
Capital expenditures	$0	$0	
Dividends	$40,000	—	
Year-end stock price	$2.25	$2.75	

	2010	2009	Industry 2010
Number of outstanding shares	1,800,000	1,800,000	
Sales multiplier			1.5
Free cash flow multiplier			18.00
Earnings multiplier			9.00
Cost of capital	6.0%	6.0%	
Accounts receivable turnover			11.1
Inventory turnover			11.30
Current ratio			2.80
Quick ratio			2.00
Cash flow from operations ratio			1.20
Free cash flow ratio			1.10
Gross margin percentage			30.0%
Return on assets (net book value)			20.0%
Return on equity			30.0%

Required   Calculate and interpret the financial ratios (per Exhibit 20.9) for Somerfeld for 2009 and 2010. Since the calculation of many ratios requires the average balance in an account (e.g., average receivables is required in calculating receivables turnover) you may assume that the balances in these accounts in 2009 are the same as those in 2008.

20-28 **Business Valuation**   Refer to the information in exercise 20-27.

Required   Develop a business valuation for Somerfeld Company for 2010 using the following methods: (1) book value of equity, (2) market value of equity, (3) discounted cash flow (DCF), (4) enterprise value, and (5) all the multiples-based valuations for which there is an industry average multiplier. For the calculation of the DCF valuation, you may use the simplifying assumption that free cash flows will continue indefinitely at the amount in 2010.

20-29 **Business Valuation**   Ruth's Chris Steak House (RCSH) is a chain of restaurants that began 43 years ago as a single location in New Orleans and has grown to more than 90 restaurants. RCSH went public, with an initial public offering of stock (IPO) in August 2005. A question at the time of the IPO was how to value the company, given available information. Ruth's had sales of $192.2 million in 2004, earnings of $23.3 million, and net debt less cash of $117 million. One analyst chose to use the enterprise value of comparable companies, noting that Smith and Wollensky Restaurant Group (another chain of steak restaurants) had a ratio of enterprise value to sales of 70 percent. Another restaurant chain, Morton's, had recently gone private and, in the last year as a public company, had an enterprise ratio to sales of 80 percent.

Required   Develop an estimate of the market value of equity of RCSH in August 2005 and explain your reasoning.

20-30 Business Valuation Five different analysts have submitted valuations for a private technology firm that is the subject of a possible acquisition. The valuations are as follows:

Analyst	Valuation
1	$26,331,000
2	38,803,000
3	65,000,000
4	27,000,000
5	17,000,000

Required The value of having multiple analyst reports is that one can develop a range of possible valuations, and select a final valuation that seems appropriate. What valuation would you choose for this technology company? Explain your reasoning.

20-31 Compensation; Strategy Corona is a privately held high-end luxury retailer that operates stores in the wealthiest cities and suburbs in the United States. The corporate headquarters is located in New York City. The company has a long history of profitability and a strong national image as the pinnacle of luxury. However, in the past two years Corona's profitability has begun to drop off and many of the top executives fear that the company's most important asset, its brand image, might come into jeopardy if it cannot regain its past profitability.

Bernard Starnes, Corona's long-time CEO, wonders if the company's aged compensation plan might be at least partially responsible for Corona's tough times. He remembers a time when the company was rapidly expanding by creating several new divisions and aggressively promoting its brand image. It seemed like he was attending a new store opening every week. During those times divisional managers worked hard for their bonuses. It was almost as if there was a competition between divisions as to which could beat their sales plans by the widest margin because that would mean the largest bonuses. This was due to the fact that a significant portion of the managers' compensation was tied to their bonuses. Now the company is not expanding as rapidly and its focus has shifted to promoting current products and growing same-store sales.

Furthermore, Mr. Starnes has noticed several troubling trends within the company. First, he has noticed a steady decline in cross-divisional cooperation and coordination. Second, there have been several recent occasions where Mr. Starnes had to become personally involved in situations where divisional managers were making decisions that were beneficial to their individual divisions but not strategically aligned with the firm as a whole. Finally, management turnover is becoming somewhat of a problem, especially right after bonuses are awarded at the end of each fiscal year.

Required Suggest a new compensation plan that would help solve the problems Mr. Starnes has noticed at Corona. Show how your answer effectively addresses the strategic goals of the company.

20-32 Ways to Create Shareholder Value A leading author in accounting and finance, Alfred Rappaport focuses in his work on the importance of a firm's management continually taking steps that increase shareholder value. In a recent article he set out his "Ten Ways to Create Shareholder Value:"

1. Do not manage earnings or provide earnings guidance; do not focus on earnings as it reflect neither the company's value or the change in value over the reporting period.

2. Make the strategic decisions that maximize expected value, even at the expense of lowering near-term earnings; this may mean divesting units that do not contribute to the company's long-term strategic goals though they do contribute to current profits.

3. Make acquisitions that maximize expected value, even at the expense of lowering near-term earnings; do not make acquisitions that improve only current earnings per share, but those that are expected to contribute to long-term value.

4. Carry only assets that maximize value; continually review assets and be prepared to sell units, brands, real estate, or other assets that can be sold for a price that is greater than their value to the company.

5. Return cash to shareholders when there are no credible value-creating opportunities to invest in the business; through cash dividends and stock buybacks.

6. Reward CEOs and other senior executives for delivering superior long-term returns.

7. Reward operating unit managers for adding superior multiyear value.

8. Reward middle managers and frontline employees for delivering superior performance on the key value drivers that they influence directly.

9. Require senior executives to bear risks of ownership just as shareholders do.

10. Provide investors with value relevant information.

Required   A key topic in management accounting is the valuation of a company. Focusing on public companies, Rappaport explains how to increase business value to shareholders. Consider each of his 10 recommendations and show how they can be related to cost management, management compensation, and business valuation.

20-33 **Compensation at Nonpublic Companies**   The executive compensation programs of the largest public companies often include the types of equity-based compensation such as stock options and performance shares as described in this chapter. Smaller nonpublic companies often have the same types of strategic goals and want to provide the same types of compensation plans as do the larger public companies but do not have the equity types of compensation to offer since the firms do not have publicly-traded stock.

Required:

1. What are the advantages of equity-based compensation such as stock options and performance shares?
2. What types of compensation can nonpublic companies offer that would provide the desired incentives that equity-based compensation offers?

20-34 **Compensation for Operational-Level Managers and Employees**   Retailers and restaurants such as McDonald's and Wal-Mart have a very large number of stores and store managers. These two firms have been very successful and have continued to grow during the 2008–2009 recession even though many other firms have suffered. McDonald's and Wal-Mart's success depends to a great deal on the energy, hard work, and effectiveness of these store managers. It is critical for these two firms and for firms in these two industries to provide effective compensation plans for the store managers.

Required   What type of compensation plan would you develop for managers of stores such as Wal-Mart and McDonald's, and why?

20-35 **Compensation in Tough Economic Times**   During an economic recession companies are under pressure to reduce costs, and a significant part of total cost for most companies is salaries and wages, including both executive compensation and employee compensation.

Required   Review the types of compensation we have covered in this chapter and explain which types of compensation you would reduce if needed to help a company through difficult economic times.

Problems   20-36 **Compensation; Net Present Value**   Choco-Lots Candy Co. makes chewy chocolate candies at a plant in Winston-Salem, North Carolina. Brian Main, the production manager at this facility, installed a packaging machine last year at a cost of $400,000. This machine is expected to last for 10 more years with no residual value. Operating costs for the projected levels of production are $80,000 annually.

Brian has just learned of a new packaging machine that would work much more efficiently in Choco-Lots' production line. This machine would cost $420,000 installed, but the annual operating costs would be only $30,000. This machine would be depreciated over 10 years with no residual value. He could sell the current packaging machine this year for $150,000.

Brian has worked for Choco-Lots for seven years. He plans to remain with the firm for about two more years, when he expects to become a vice president of operations at his father-in-law's company. Choco-Lots pays Brian a fixed salary with an annual bonus of 1 percent of net income for the year.

Assume that Choco-Lots uses straight-line depreciation and has a 10 percent required rate of return. Ignore income tax effects.

Required

1. As the owner of Choco-Lots, would you want Brian to keep the current machine or purchase the new one?
2. Why might Brian not prefer to make the decision that the owner of Choco-Lots desires?

20-37 **Compensation; Benefits; Ethics**   DuMelon Publishing Inc. is a nationwide company headquartered in Boston, Massachusetts. The firm's benefits are a significant element of employee compensation. All professional employees at DuMelon receive company-paid benefits including medical insurance, term life insurance, and paid vacations and holidays. They also receive a set reimbursement amount of $250 per day maximum for travel expenses when they conduct business for DuMelon. DuMelon offers a 25 percent match for money the professionals deposit in the company-sponsored 401(k) plan.

These benefits vary, depending on the employee's salary and level in the company. For example, the amount of vacation days increases as a professional is promoted to higher levels. The maximum amount that can be contributed to the 401(k) plan also increases as the employee's salary increases, subject to an overall limitation provided by tax laws.

When a DuMelon employee attains the position of vice president of a function, such as operations or sales, that person qualifies for a special class of additional benefits: a company car, a larger office with decoration allowances, and access to the executive suite at the Boston office. (The executive suite features a dining room and lounge for the executives' use.) The perks also include total reimbursement for all business travel expenses.

Required

1. Explain the implications for employee behavior and performance of DuMelon's two levels of benefits for professional employees, including ethical issues.

2. Suppose that the policy for benefits is not applied strictly at DuMelon. As a result, the following instances have occurred:

   a. The company has occasionally paid the travel expenses of VPs' spouses. Company policy is unclear as to whether this is allowed.

   b. Some VPs have special-ordered their company-provided vehicles, which on average costs the company an additional $23,000 for each car.

   c. Passes to the executive suite have been lent to other DuMelon professionals.

   d. Some of the vice presidents have offices that are much larger than those of other vice presidents. No apparent factors determine who gets the larger offices.

   How might this situation affect the behavior of vice presidents and other professionals at DuMelon? What are the underlying implications for cost control of benefits? Use specific examples when applicable.

20-38 **Incentive Pay in The Hotel Industry**   Ramon Martinez is the general manager of Classic Inn, a local mid-priced hotel with 100 rooms. His job objectives include providing resourceful and friendly service to the hotel's guests, maintaining an 80 percent occupancy rate, improving the average rate received per room to $88 from the current $85, and achieving a savings of 5 percent on all hotel costs. The hotel's owner, a partnership of seven people who own several hotels in the region, want to structure Ramon's future compensation to objectively reward him for achieving these goals. In the past, he has been paid an annual salary of $72,000 with no incentive pay. The incentive plan the partners developed has each of the goals weighted as follows:

Measure	Percent of Total Responsibility
Occupancy rate (also reflects guest service quality)	40%
Operating within 95 percent of expense budget	25
Average room rate	35
	100%

If Ramon achieves all of these goals, the partners determined that his performance should merit a bonus of $23,000. The partners also agreed that his salary would be reduced to $60,000 because of the addition of the bonus.

The goal measures used to compensate Ramon are as follows:

Occupancy goal:	29,200 room-nights = 80 percent occupancy rate × 100 rooms × 365 days
Compensation:	40 percent weight × $23,000 target reward = $9,200 $9,200/29,200 = $0.315 per room-night
Expense goal:	5 percent savings
Compensation:	25 percent weight × $23,000 target reward = $5,750 $5,750/5 = $1,150 for each percentage point saved
Room rate goal:	$3 rate increase
Compensation:	35 percent weight × $23,000 target reward = $8,050 $8,050/300 = $26.83 per each cent increase

Ramon's new compensation plan will thus pay him a $60,000 salary plus 31.5 cents per room-night sold plus $1,150 for each percentage point saved in the expense budget plus $26.83 per each cent increase in average room rate.

Required

1. Based on this plan, what will Ramon's total compensation be if his performance results are

   a. 30,000 room-nights, 5 percent saved, $3.00 rate increase?

   b. 25,000 room-nights, 3 percent saved, $1.15 rate increase?

   c. 28,000 room-nights, 0 saved, $1.00 rate increase?

2. Comment on the expected effectiveness of this plan.

20-39 Incentive Pay Formula Development Use the concepts in problem 20-38 to complete the following requirements.

Required

1. Design an incentive pay plan for a restaurant manager whose goals are to serve 300 customers per day at an average price per customer of $6.88. The restaurant is open 365 days per year. These two goals are equally important. The incentive pay should be $12,800 if the manager achieves all goals. Assume the manager's salary is $68,000.

2. Calculate the manager's total compensation if the restaurant serves 280 customers per day at an average price of $6.75.

20-40 Compensation Pools; Residual Income; Review of Chapter 19 Great Brands Inc. (GBI) is a retailer of consumer products. The company made two acquisitions in previous years to diversify its product lines. In 2008, GBI acquired a consumer electronics firm producing computers. GBI now (2010) has three divisions: consumer electronics, cameras, and computers. The following information (in thousands) presents operating revenue, operating income, and invested assets of the company over the last three years.

	Revenue	Income	Assets
Consumer Electronics			
2008	$115,400	$14,560	$66,356
2009	110,450	8,900	45,750
2010	123,500	11,200	51,250
Cameras			
2008	45,600	1,950	22,500
2009	38,500	1,350	22,400
2010	49,800	2,100	22,200
Computers			
2008	98,900	2,350	11,250
2009	92,500	1,650	10,800
2010	106,450	2,675	11,200

The number of executives covered by GBI's current compensation package follows:

	2008	2009	2010
Consumer Electronics	300	350	375
Cameras	40	40	37
Computers	120	140	175

The current compensation package is an annual bonus award. Senior executives share in the bonus pool, which is calculated as 10 percent of the company's annual residual income. *Residual income* is defined as operating income minus an interest charge of 8 percent of invested assets.

Required

1. Use asset turnover, return on sales, and ROI to explain the differences in profitability of the three divisions.

2. Compute the bonus amount to be paid during each year; also compute individual executive bonus amounts.

3. If the bonuses were calculated by divisional residual income, what would the individual bonus amounts be?

4. Discuss the advantages and disadvantages of basing the bonus on GBI's residual income compared to divisional residual income.

20-41 **Compensation; Strategic Issues** Mobile Business Incorporated (MBI) is a worldwide manufacturing company that specializes in high technology products for the aerospace, automotive, and plastics industries. State-of-the-art technology and business innovation have been key to the firm's success over the last several years. MBI has 10 manufacturing plants in six foreign countries. Its products are sold worldwide through sales representatives and sales offices in 23 countries. Performance information from these plants and offices is received weekly and is summarized monthly at the Toronto headquarters.

The company's current bonus compensation package focuses on giving rewards based on the utilization of capital within the company (i.e., management of inventory, collection of receivables, and use of physical assets). The board of directors is concerned, however, with the short-term focus of this plan.

Some employees believe that the company's current compensation plan does not reflect its stated goals of maintaining and enhancing its global position through innovative products.

Required Develop a bonus package that considers MBI's strategic goals and the global environment in which it operates.

20-42 **Executive Compensation; Teams; Ethics** Universal Air Inc. supplies instrumentation components to airplane manufacturers. Although only a few competitors are in this market, the competition is fierce.

Universal uses a traditional performance incentive plan to award middle-management bonuses on the basis of divisional profit. Recently, Charles Gross, chief executive officer, concluded that these objectives might be better served with new performance measures. On January 1, 2010, he assigned his executive team of top-level managers to develop these new measures.

The executive team conducted a customer survey. Although Universal has always prided itself on being on the technological forefront, the survey results indicated technology to be a low priority for customers, who were more concerned with product quality and customer service. As a result, the executive team developed 30 new criteria to measure middle-management performance and directed the controller to develop the necessary monthly reports and graphs to report on these new measures. Then the executive team announced to middle managers that these new indicators would be used to evaluate their performance. The managers were not enthusiastic and complained that some measures were influenced by the performance of other departments that they could not control. Over the next few months, customer complaints increased, and a major customer chose a competitor over Universal.

Upon seeing these results, Charles decided to review the new process. In a meeting with executive and middle managers, he emphasized that the new measures should help balance the company's performance between increased customer value and improved operating process efficiency. He set up two cross-functional teams of executives and middle managers to develop a second set of new measures: one to evaluate new product development and the other to evaluate the customer order and fulfillment process. Both teams are to focus on cost, quality, and scheduling time.

Richard Strong, quality inspection manager, is the brother-in-law of John Brogan, cost accounting manager. On June 1, John telephoned Sara Wiley, the purchasing manager at Magic Aircraft Manufacturing Inc., one of Universal's major customers. Brogan said, "Listen Sara, we're jumping through all these hoops over here to measure performance, and management seems to be changing the measures every day. It was so easy before, getting a bonus based on the bottom line; now we have to worry about things out of our control based on how the customer perceives our performance. Would you do me a favor? If you have any complaints, please have your people call me directly so I can forward the complaint to the right person. All that really matters is for all of us to make money." In actuality, Richard was the only person to whom John reported the customer complaints that Sara offered.

Required

1. For Universal Air Inc. to remain competitive, should it implement the second set of new performance measures? Identify for the company:

   a. At least three customer value-added measures.

   b. At least three process-efficiency measures.

2. Identify at least three types of employee behaviors that Universal can expect by having middle management participate in the development of the second set of new performance measures.

3. Describe what executive management at Universal should do to ensure the effectiveness of the cross-functional teams.

4. Referring to the specific standards for ethical conduct by a management accountant (Chapter 1), consider whether John Brogan's behavior is unethical.

(CMA Adapted)

20-43 Executive Compensation Jensen Corporation is a holding company with several diversified divisions operating throughout the United States. Jensen's management allows the divisions to operate on an autonomous basis in most areas; however, the corporate office becomes involved in determining some division strategies related to capital budgeting, development of marketing campaigns, and implementation of incentive plans. The area of incentive plans has often been a problem to Jensen because many of the companies it has acquired already had such plans in place. These plans are not easily changed without causing discontent among the managers. Jensen has striven for consistency among its divisions with regard to bonus and incentive plans, but this has not always been achievable.

The restaurant division operates a chain of vegetarian restaurants, Hobbit Hole, in the eastern United States. Jensen acquired it approximately three years ago and has made very few changes to it. The restaurant's reputation was well established and, aside from nominal changes in marketing strategy, the chain has been allowed to operate in much the same manner as it did before its acquisition. In addition to a base salary, Hobbit Hole unit managers participate in the restaurant's profits. This incentive plan was in place when Jensen acquired the chain; although the profit percentage might vary among restaurant units, the overall plans are basically the same. The unit managers are satisfied with this incentive strategy, and Jensen's management does not believe that changes are necessary.

Jensen's motel division was formed 15 years ago when Jensen purchased a small group of motels in the Midwest. Since that time, the division has grown significantly as the company has acquired motels throughout the country using the name Cruise and Snooze Inns. Since its initial motel purchase, Jensen has implemented its own incentive program for unit managers in the individual motels. The incentive program provides annual bonuses based on the achievement of specific goals that are not necessarily finance oriented but pertain to areas such as improved quality control and customer service. This program requires administrative time, but Jensen believes that the results have been satisfactory.

Required

1. Hobbit Hole's restaurant unit managers are covered by a profit participation incentive plan. Discuss the following for this incentive plan:
   a. Its benefits to Jensen Corporation.
   b. The incentive effects that it could cause, if any.

2. The Cruise and Snooze Inns' motel unit managers participate in an incentive program based on goal attainment. Discuss the following for this type of incentive plan:
   a. Advantages to Jensen Corporation.
   b. Disadvantages to Jensen Corporation.

3. Having two different types of incentive plans for two operating divisions of the same company raises questions.
   a. Describe the potential negative incentive effects of having different types of incentive plans for Hobbit Hole and Cruise and Snooze Inns.
   b. Present the rationale that Jensen Corporation can give to the unit managers of Hobbit Hole and Cruise and Snooze Inns to justify having different incentive plans for two operating divisions of the same company.

(CMA Adapted)

20-44 Business Analysis Blue Water Yachts is a small company founded by two businesspeople who are friends and avid sailors. At present, they are interested in expanding the business and have asked you to review its financial statements.

Blue Water Yachts sells approximately 100 to 150 sailboats each year, ranging from 14-foot dinghies to 20-foot sailboats. Their sales prices range from $2,000 to more than $10,000. The company has a limited inventory of boats consisting primarily of one or two boats from each of the four manufacturers that supply Blue Water. The company also sells a variety of supplies and parts and performs different types of service. Most sales are on credit.

The company operates from a large building that has offices, storage, and sales for some of the smaller sailboats. The larger sailboats are kept in a fenced area adjacent to the main building, and an ample parking area is nearby. This year Blue Water purchased a boat lift to haul boats. The lift has brought in revenues for boat repairs, hull painting, and related services, as well as the boat hauls.

The balance sheet and income statement for Blue Water Yachts for 2005 through 2009 and for the first eleven months of 2010 follow. The increase in net fixed assets in the recent two years is due to improvements in the building, paving of the parking area, and the purchase of the lift.

The company obtains its debt financing from two sources: a small savings and loan for its short-term funds, and a larger commercial bank, also for short-term loans, but principally for long-term financing. The terms of the loan agreement with the bank include a restriction that its current ratio must remain higher than 1.5.

Required   Evaluate the liquidity and profitability of Blue Water Yachts using selected financial ratios. Assess the company's overall profitability, liquidity, and desirability as an investment. Use a spreadsheet to improve the speed and accuracy of your analysis.

BLUE WATER YACHTS COMPANY
Comparative Balance Sheet
For the Years Ended December 31,

	2005	2006	2007	2008	2009	2010 (11 months)
Cash	$ 23,260	$ 21,966	$ 18,735	$ 28,426	$ 43,692	$ 31,264
Accounts receivable	99,465	102,834	112,903	125,663	104,388	142,009
Allowance for bad debts	(9,304)	(8,786)	(8,824)	(11,266)	(7,282)	(12,506)
Inventory	35,009	56,784	61,792	67,884	58,994	95,774
Other current assets	11,894	12,894	9,024	11,006	18,923	22,903
Total current assets	$160,324	$185,692	$193,630	$221,713	$218,715	$279,444
Property and equipment	262,195	282,008	299,380	368,565	405,269	498,626
Accumulated depreciation	(65,984)	(93,442)	(122,892)	(158,099)	(187,227)	(226,307)
Total assets	$356,535	$374,258	$370,118	$432,179	$436,757	$551,763
Accounts payable	82,635	78,127	63,346	56,256	40,189	49,544
Taxes payable	11,630	10,983	11,780	14,083	3,738	15,632
Short-term loans	59,876	56,980	37,583	41,093	49,594	76,962
Accrued payroll payable	5,227	4,598	3,649	4,224	4,774	4,779
Total current liabilities	$159,368	$150,688	$116,358	$115,656	$98,295	$146,917
Long-term debt	158,173	172,388	179,490	214,997	229,471	262,258
Equity	38,994	51,182	74,270	101,526	108,991	142,588
Total liabilities and equity	$356,535	$374,258	$370,118	$432,179	$436,757	$551,763

BLUE WATER YACHTS COMPANY
Comparative Statement of Income and Operating Cash Flow
For the Years Ended December 31,

	2005	2006	2007	2008	2009	2010 (11 months)
Sales	$767,580	$724,878	$777,480	$929,478	$764,610	$938,857
Returns and allowances	38,379	35,645	40,334	45,998	32,887	46,380
Cost of sales	473,908	441,298	458,015	545,778	453,669	530,597
Gross margin	$255,293	$247,935	$279,131	$337,702	$278,054	$361,880
Depreciation expense	$ 29,075	$27,458	$ 29,450	$ 35,208	$ 29,128	$ 35,563
Interest expense	18,597	19,557	20,998	21,475	24,889	28,993
Salaries and wages	81,923	73,664	77,846	95,764	92,903	99,447
Accounting and legal	9,304	8,786	9,323	11,834	13,108	11,380
Administration expense	79,666	75,234	80,693	96,469	87,995	97,441
Other expense	12,630	18,927	15,763	22,903	18,934	22,662
Total expense	$231,195	$223,626	$234,073	$283,653	$266,957	$295,486
Net income	$ 24,098	$ 24,309	$ 45,058	$ 54,049	$ 11,097	$ 66,394
Cash flow from operations						
Depreciation		$ 27,458	$ 29,450	$ 35,208	$ 29,128	$ 35,563
Decrease (increase) in receivables		(3,887)	(10,031)	(10,318)	17,291	(32,397)
Decrease (increase) in inventory		(21,775)	(5,008)	(6,092)	8,890	(36,780)
Decrease (increase) in other current assets		(1,000)	3,870	(1,982)	(7,917)	(3,980)
Increase (decrease) in current liabilities		(8,680)	(34,330)	(702)	(17,361)	48,622
		$ 16,425	$ 29,009	$ 70,163	$ 41,128	$ 77,422

20-45 **Business Valuation** Refer to the information in problem 20-44 for the Blue Water Yachts Company.

Required Develop a business valuation for Blue Water Yachts Company for 2010 using the book value of equity method and the multiples-based method. Assume that the industry average earnings multiple is 8 and the industry average multiple on operating cash flow is 12. Which of the methods would you use and why?

20-46 **Business Analysis** Johnson Home Products, Inc. (JHP) manufactures plumbing fixtures and other home improvement products that are sold in Home Depot and Wal-Mart as well as hardware stores. JHP has a solid reputation for providing value products, good quality, and a good price. The company has been approached by an investment banking firm representing a third company, Garden Specialties Inc. (GSI) that is interested in acquiring JHP. The acquiring firm (GSI) is a retailer of garden supplies; it sees the potential synergies of the combined firm and is willing to pay JHP shareholders $25 cash per share for their stock which is greater than the current stock price; the stock has traded at about $23.45 in recent months. Summary financial information about JHP follows.

Required Evaluate JHP as a company using financial ratio analysis. Since the calculation of some ratios requires the averaging of balances, you may assume that the balances in 2008 are the same as those in 2009.

JOHNSON HOME PRODUCTS, INC.
Selected Financial Information

	2010	2009	2010 Industry Average
Cash	$ 81,516,171	$ 2,546,000	
Accounts receivable	56,778,465	84,776,336	
Inventory	39,665,416	49,886,736	
Long-lived assets:			
Gross book value	168,163,461	145,663,461	
Net book value	104,172,967	98,447,620	
Replacement cost	175,483,000	175,483,000	
Liquidation value	67,430,000	78,366,000	
Current liabilities	122,365,299	101,667,355	
Long-term debt	34,567,445	34,577,653	
Capital expenditures	22,500,000	11,234,000	
Sales	645,339,000	589,645,335	
Cost of sales	498,657,788	453,887,390	
Operating expense*	102,667,355	122,654,888	
Income tax rate	38%	38%	38.0%
Depreciation expense	$ 16,774,653	$ 14,662,893	
Dividends	$ 1,500,000	$ 1,000,000	
Year-end stock price	$ 23.45	$ 17.22	
Number of outstanding shares	22,587,336	22,847,559	
Sales multiplier			1.40
Free cash flow multiplier			8.80

* Operating expense includes depreciation expense

(Continued)

	2010	2009	2010 Industry Average
Earnings multiplier			13.50
Cost of capital	6.1%	6.1%	
Accounts receivable turnover			5.50
Inventory turnover			8.60
Current ratio			1.90
Quick ratio			1.10
Cash flow from operations ratio			1.40
Free cash flow ratio			1.10
Gross margin percentage			33.0%
Return on assets (net book value)			19.0%
Return on equity			28.0%
Earnings per share			$2.33

20-47 Business Valuation   Refer to the information in Problem 20-46.

Required

1. Develop a business valuation for 2010 using the market value method, the book value method, and the multiples-based methods.
2. Determine an estimated value for JHP using the discounted free cash flow method, assuming that the 2010 amount of free cash flow continues indefinitely.
3. Which of the methods would you use and why?
4. Is the GSI offer a good one? Why or why not?

20-48 Business Analysis and Business Valuation   Gordon Supply Company manufactures high quality gardening supplies for sale primarily to nursery and landscaping companies. Gordon Supply is a business that has continued to grow because of its commitment to quality and service to a relatively small number of large, loyal customers. The financial statements for Gordon for the most recent two years are shown below, together with selected industry information.

Balance Sheet, Dec 31,		
	2010	**2009**
Cash	$ 382,000	$ 200,000
Accounts receivable	90,000	120,000
Inventory	90,000	100,000
Total current assets	562,000	420,000
Long-lived assets	1,840,000	1,900,000
Total assets	$2,402,000	$2,320,000
Current liabilities	$ 200,000	$ 250,000
Long-term debt	650,000	650,000
Shareholders' equity	1,552,000	1,420,000
Total debt and equity	$2,402,000	$2,320,000

(Continued)

Income Statement, for year ended Dec 31,

	2010	2009
Sales	$2,000,000	$1,800,000
Cost of sales	1,400,000	1,300,000
Gross margin	600,000	500,000
Operating expense	400,000	350,000
Operating income	200,000	150,000
Tax expense	68,000	51,000
Net income	$ 132,000	$ 99,000

Cash Flow from Operations

	2010	2009
Net income	$132,000	$ 99,000
Plus depreciation expense	60,000	50,000
+Decrease (-inc) in accounts receivable and inventory	40,000	—
+Increase (-dec) in current liabilities	(50,000)	—
Cash Flow from Operations	$182,000	$149,000

Industry Benchmark Information 2010

Sales multiplier	2.50
Free cash flow multiplier	15.00
Earnings multiplier	22.00
Accounts receivable turnover	10.00
Inventory turnover	12.00
Current ratio	2.00
Quick ratio	1.50
Cash flow from operations ratio	1.20
Free cash flow ratio	1.10
Gross margin percentage	30.0%
Return on assets (net book value)	10.0%
Return on equity	15.0%

Number of outstanding shares in both 2009 and 2010 is 1,650,000
Weighted average cost of capital for Gordon's Supply is 5%
Year-end stock price, $3.00

Required

1. Calculate and interpret the liquidity, cash flow, and profitability ratios for Gordon's Supply for 2009 and 2010. For simplicity, you may calculate the 2009 ratios with the assumption that receivables, inventory, and total assets are the same in 2009 as 2008.

2. Develop a business valuation for Gordon Supply Company for 2010 using the following methods: (a) book value of equity, (b) market value of equity, (c) discounted cash flow (DCF), (d) enterprise value, and (e) all the multiples-based valuations for which there is an industry average multiplier. For the calculation of the DCF valuation, you may use the simplifying assumption that free cash flows will continue indefinitely at the amount in 2010.

20-49 **Executive Compensation; Regression Analysis** A recent study of the airline industry examined whether a performance for a selected nonfinancial measure was a significant predictor of CEO compensation. A sample of 35 firms was taken and regression obtained to determine the potential relationship between selected financial and nonfinancial independent variables and three dependent variables: (a) CEO cash compensation, (b) CEO compensation in the form of options granted during the year, and (c) total CEO compensation (a + b).

The independent variables were:

- Passenger load (PL), the proportion of seats filled to the seats available.
- Stock price return (RT), the increase in stock price plus dividends over the year relative to beginning of year.
- Return on assets (ROA), income over total assets.
- Sales.
- Stock price volatility (V), the standard deviation of daily stock price changes in the company's stock price.
- CEO ownership (CEO), the percentage of the company's outstanding shares owned by the CEO.
- CEO tenure(CEO-T), the number of years the CEO has been on the job.
- Ratio of book value of the company to the market value of the company (BM), a measure of the market value of the company.

The table below shows the three dependent variables, the eight independent variables, and the significance (p-value) of the independent variable in each equation. For example, in the regression with the dependent variable, cash compensation (Regression One), the PL variable is significant at the .01 level, RT is significant at the .01 level, and the ROA variable is not significant. The authors of the study hypothesized that there would be a positive significant relationship between CEO compensation and the one nonfinancial variable, passenger load.

	Regression One*	Regression Two*	Regression Three*
Passenger load (PL)	0.01	NS	NS
Stock return (RT)*	0.01	0.01	0.01
Return on assets (ROA)	NS	NS	NS
Sales*	0.01	0.01	0.01
Stock price volatility (V)	NS	NS	0.05
CEO ownership % (CEO)[†]	0.01	0.01	0.01
CEO tenure (CEO-T)	0.01	NS	0.05
Book value to Market Value (BM)	NS	0.05	NS
R squared	69.3%	11.0%	50.0%

* Dependent variables were transformed using the natural logarithm.
[†] This variable had a significant negative coefficient, indicating an inverse relationship with the dependent variable.

Required   Review the three regressions above and develop a brief explanation for each of the following:

1. Which of the three regressions would you most rely on, and why?
2. What do the regression results tell you about the relationships of the independent variables to the three dependent variables?
3. Were the authors of the study correct about their expectation regarding the PL variable?
4. How would you use this information in designing compensation plans for executives in the airline industry?

20-50 **Business Analysis and Business Valuation**   JJP Autoparts, Inc., a manufacturer of auto parts, experienced a decline in earnings in the recent year and has consulted its accounting firm for an analysis of the firm's financial statements. Additionally, the company knows that its market value has fallen from the prior year, since the share price has fallen from $5.50 at the end of 2009 to $2.34 at the end of 2010. So, JJP also want an analysis of the firm's change in value. The comparative balance sheet and income statement for 2010 follows:

Balance Sheet	2010	2009
Cash	$ 453,680	$ 455,675
Accounts receivable	38,756	34,885
Inventory	156,754	134,665
Total current assets	649,190	625,225
Long-lived assets	452,541	445,287
Total assets	$1,101,731	$1,070,512

(Continued)

Current liabilities	$ 219,884	$ 265,448
Long-term debt	350,000	350,000
Shareholders' equity	531,847	455,064
Total debt and equity	$1,101,731	$1,070,512
Income Statement		
Sales	$1,588,364	$1,455,634
Cost of sales	1,289,665	1,109,886
Gross margin	298,699	345,748
Operating expenses	174,855	133,874
Operating income	123,844	211,874
Tax expense	47,061	80,512
Net income	$ 76,783	$ 131,362

Note: The amounts for operating expense above include depreciation expense of $43,997 in 2009 and $42,746 in 2010.

Additional relevant information about JJP is that it uses a cost of capital rate of 5.7 percent. Also it incurred capital expenditures of $100,000 in 2009 and $50,000 in 2010; there were no cash dividends in either year. The number of outstanding shares is 653,554, the same in both years.

Industry data, the average values for firms in the autoparts industry, follow:

Sales multiplier:	2.20
Free cash flow multiplier	8.80
Earnings multiplier	21.00
Accounts receivable turnover	8.80
Inventory turnover	7.00
Current ratio	2.00
Quick ratio	1.10
Cash flow from operations ratio	1.40
Free cash flow ratio	1.10
Gross margin percentage	30.0%
Return on assets (net book value)	18.0%
Return on equity	24.0%
Earnings per share	$ 1.15

Required:

1. Calculate and interpret the liquidity, cash flow, and profitability ratios for JJP for 2009 and 2010. In your calculations, you may assume that the balance sheet values for 2009 are the same as for the prior year, 2008.

2. Develop and interpret a business valuation for JJP for 2009 and 2010 using the methods you think appropriate.

Solution to Self-Study Problem

Management Compensation Plan

DTH's goal is to increase its business by at least 10 percent a year in a very competitive environment. The compensation plan is consistent with this goal because it rewards increases in revenues and new clients. It is likely, however, that under the current plan, each office is focusing only on the client base in its own region.

A problem occurs when DTH must make proposals that require joint cooperation and participation among two or more offices. The compensation plan does not have an incentive for cooperation. In fact, it could be a distraction and reduce the potential for a substantial bonus for any given office to develop a proposal for a large contract in which other offices might benefit. The cost of the proposal would be borne by the office, and the benefits would accrue to other offices as well as the originating office. The cost of the proposal for large contracts must therefore be shared among the offices in some way, or any one office will not have the incentive to spend the time and money necessary to develop a large proposal.

In addition to sharing the cost of the proposal, DTH should consider having a firmwide proposal development group for these large projects. The individual offices would then be charged for the cost of this group, perhaps in proportion to the fees received from large contracts in that office. Clearly, the firm is losing the larger contracts, and the compensation and proposal development plans must provide the needed incentive for each office to go after them aggressively.

Another alternative is to go to a firmwide compensation pool that would provide a direct and strong incentive for each office to cooperate in developing new business. A disadvantage of this approach is that it would reduce the motivation for each office to seek business in its own region because the revenues from these individual efforts would be shared firmwide.

Another issue concerning the current compensation plan is the office manager's discretion to divide the office bonus among the professionals in the office. Although no one has complained, a lower-level professional is unlikely to complain about the office manager's bonus decisions. The equity of this system should be reviewed to ensure that each office manager is using this discretion in a fair and appropriate way.

Business Valuation

Since WebSmart is a relatively new company currently showing losses and negative cash flows, the earnings-multiple and discounted cash flow approaches are not suitable. Moreover, since the company is not public, there is no current stock price. This leaves two possibilities: the book value of equity method and the revenues-multiple method. The book value of equity is given at $1,200,000. In contrast, the revenue multiple would estimate value at $4,200,000 = 7 \times $600,000$. Alternatively, WebSmart could use projected revenues in the multiple calculation. Moreover, it could use projected cash flows in a cash flow multiple or discounted cash flow calculation, since cash flow would presumably be positive in the coming years.

Also, the firm has an asset, the Guide, which has a market value of $1,350,000, so any valuation would have to be higher than that figure. Overall, this is a difficult firm to value; the range from $1,350,000 to $4,200,000 is a very wide range. Also, there is significant uncertainty about future cash flows, which are critical to the overall valuation.

A

abnormal spoilage An unacceptable unit that should not arise under efficient operating conditions

absolute quality conformance (robust quality approach) Conformance that requires all products or services to meet the target value exactly with no variation

accounting (book) rate of return Equals the ratio of some measure of accounting profit to some measure of investment in the project

activity A specific task or action of work done

activity analysis The development of a detailed description of the specific activities performed in the firm's operations

activity-based budgeting (ABB) A budgeting process that is based on activities and associated activity costs to support production and sales

activity-based costing (ABC) A costing approach that assigns resource costs to cost objects based on activities performed for the cost objects

activity-based management (ABM) Uses activity analysis and activity-based costing to help managers identify the value of activities and to make strategic performance management decisions—adding and deleting products, adjusting process capacities, adjusting prices, removing costs and complexities, and more

activity consumption cost driver Measures how much of an activity a cost object uses

actual costing system A costing process that uses actual costs incurred for direct materials, direct labor, and factory overhead

actual factory overhead Costs incurred in an accounting period for indirect materials, indirect labor, and other indirect factory costs, including factory rent, insurance, property tax, depreciation, repairs and maintenance, power, light, heat, and employer payroll taxes for factory personnel

additional processing costs or separable costs Costs that occur after the split-off point and can be identified directly with individual products

advance pricing agreement (APA) An agreement between the Internal Revenue Service (IRS) and a firm that establishes an agreed-upon transfer price

allocation bases The cost drivers used to allocate costs

analysis of variance table A table that separates the total variance of the dependent variable into both error and explained variance components

analytic hierarchy process (AHP) A multicriteria decision technique that can combine qualitative and quantitative factors in the overall evaluation of decision alternatives

appraisal (detection) costs Expenditures devoted to the measurement and analysis of data to determine conformity of outputs to specifications

arm's-length standard A transfer price set to reflect the price that unrelated parties acting independently would have set

asset turnover The amount of sales dollars achieved per dollar of investment; measures the manager's ability to increase sales from a given level of investment

authoritative standard A standard determined solely or primarily by management

average cost The total of manufacturing cost (materials, labor, and overhead) divided by the number of units of output

average cost method A method that uses units of output to allocate joint costs to joint products

average-risk projects Projects that approximate the risk of the firm's existing assets and operations; the WACC is used in DCF models to evaluate average-risk investment projects

B

backflush costing A method that charges current production costs (using standard costs) directly to finished goods inventory without accounting for the flows in and out of work-in-process

balanced scorecard (BSC) An accounting report that includes the firm's critical success factors in four areas: (1) financial performance, (2) customer satisfaction, (3) internal processes, and (4) learning and growth

batch-level activity An activity performed for each batch of products or services

benchmarking A process by which a firm identifies its critical success factors, studies the best practices of other firms (or other business units within a firm) for achieving these critical success factors, and then implements improvements in the firm's processes to match or beat the performance of those competitors

benefits Special benefits for the employee, such as travel, membership in a fitness club, tickets to entertainment events, and other extras paid for by the firm

beta coefficient (β) A measure of the sensitivity of a given stock's return to fluctuations in the overall market; the average beta of all stocks is 1.0; betas greater than 1 imply greater sensitivity to market fluctuations

bill of materials A detailed list of the components of the manufactured product

bonus Compensation based on the achievement of performance goals for the period

book rate of return The average net income from an investment as a percentage of the investment's book value

breakeven after-tax cash flow The minimum annual after-tax cash inflows needed for an investment project to be acceptable

breakeven point The point at which revenues equal total costs and profit is zero

budget A detailed plan for the acquisition and use of financial and other resources over a specified period of time—typically a fiscal year

budgeted capacity utilization The planned (forecasted) output for the coming period, usually a year

budgeting The process of projecting continuing operations and projects and then reflecting their financial impact

budgetary slack The "cushion" managers intentionally build into budgets to help ensure success in meeting the budget

business analysis   Evaluates the firm's overall performance by using the balanced scorecard, financial ratio analysis and economic value added

business intelligence   An approach to strategy implementation in which the management accountant uses data to understand and analyze business performance

business process improvement   A management method by which managers and workers commit to a program of continuous improvement in quality and other critical success factors

business valuation   Values the firm by estimating its total market value, which can be compared to the market value for prior periods or for comparable firms

by-products   Products in a joint production process whose total sales values are minor in comparison with the sales value of the joint products

C

capital asset pricing model (CAPM)   Model that depicts the risk-return relationship for equity securities and that can be used to estimate the required rate of return on equity for a given company; equal to the risk-free rate of return plus a risk premium measured as the product of β and the market-risk premium

capital budget   A listing of approved investment projects for a given accounting period

capital budgeting   A process of identifying, evaluating, selecting, and controlling an organization's capital (long-term) investments

capital investment   A project that involves a large expenditure of funds and expected future benefits over a number of years

capital rationing   The case where investment capital for a given accounting period is limited—hence the need for these funds to be "rationed"

capital structure   The means by which a company is financed; the mix between debt and equity capital

cash budget   A schedule depicting the effects on cash of all budgeted activities

cause-and-effect diagram   A diagram that organizes a chain of cases and effects to sort out root causes of an identified quality problem

comparable price method   Establishes an arm's-length price by using the sales prices of similar products made by unrelated firms

concurrent engineering   An engineering method that integrates product design with manufacturing and marketing throughout the product's life cycle; also called simultaneous engineering

confidence interval (CI)   In regression analysis, the CI refers to a range around the regression line within which the management accountant can be confident the actual value of the predicted cost will likely fall

constraints   Those activities that slow the product's total cycle time

continuous improvement   (The Japanese word is *kaizen*.)   A management technique in which managers and workers commit to a program of continuous improvement in quality and other critical success factors

continuous-improvement standard   A standard that gets progressively tighter over time

contract manufacturing   The practice of having another manufacturer (sometimes a direct competitor) manufacture a portion of the firm's products

contribution by profit center (CPC)   measures profit after traceable costs and is therefore a performance measure that is controllable by the profit center manager

contribution income statement   Focuses on variable costs and fixed costs, in contrast to the conventional income statement, which focuses on product costs and nonproduct costs

contribution margin income statement   An income statement based on contribution margin that is developed for each profit center and for each relevant group of profit centers

contribution margin ratio   The ratio of the unit contribution margin to unit sales price, $(p - v)/p$

control   The set of procedures, tools, and systems that organizations use to reach their goals

control chart   A graph that depicts successive observations of an operation taken at constant intervals

controllable cost   A cost that a manager or employee has discretion in choosing to incur or can significantly influence the amount of within a given, usually short, period of time

controllable fixed costs   Fixed costs that the profit center manager can influence in approximately a year or less

controllable margin   A margin determined by subtracting short-term controllable fixed costs from the contribution margin

conversion cost   Direct labor and overhead combined into a single amount

core competencies   Skills or competencies that the firm employs especially well

correlation   A given variable tends to change predictably in the same or opposite direction for a given change in the other, correlated variable

cost   Incurred when a resource is used for some purpose

cost allocation   The process of assigning indirect costs to cost pools and cost objects

cost assignment   The process of assigning costs to cost pools or from cost pools to cost objects

cost center   A firm's production or support unit that provides the best quality product or service at the lowest cost

cost driver   Any factor that causes a change in the cost of an activity

cost driver analysis   The examination, quantification, and explanation of the effects of cost drivers

cost element   An amount paid for a resource consumed by an activity and included in a cost pool

cost estimation   The development of a well-defined relationship between a cost object and its cost drivers for the purpose of predicting the cost

costing   The process of accumulating, classifying, and assigning direct materials, direct labor, and factory overhead costs to products, services, or projects

cost leadership   A strategy in which a firm outperforms competitors by producing products or services at the lowest cost

cost life cycle   The sequence of activities within the firm that begins with research and development, followed by design, manufacturing, marketing/distribution, and customer service

cost management   the development and use of cost management information

cost management information   The information developed and used to implement the organization's strategy. It consists of financial information about costs and revenues, and nonfinancial information about customer retention, productivity, quality, and other key success factors for the organization

cost object   Any product, service, customer, activity, or organizational unit to which costs are accumulated for some management purpose

cost of capital   A composite of the cost of various sources of funds comprising a firm's capital structure

cost of goods manufactured   The cost of goods that were finished and transferred out of Work-in-Process Inventory account during a given period

cost of goods sold   The cost of the product transferred to the income statement when inventory is sold

cost of quality (COQ)   A comprehensive reporting framework for classification of quality-related costs

cost of quality (COQ) report   A report that shows the costs of prevention, appraisal, internal, and external failures. An important type of cost of quality report is the quality matrix, which shows the different quality costs for each operating and support function

cost-plus method   A method that determines the transfer price based on the seller's costs plus a gross profit percentage determined by comparing the seller's sales to unrelated parties

cost pools   The meaningful groups into which costs are collected

costs of conformance   Prevention and appraisal costs

costs of nonconformance   Internal failure costs and external failure costs

cost tables   Computer-based databases that include comprehensive information about the firm's cost drivers

cost-volume-profit (CVP) analysis   A method for analyzing how various operating decisions and marketing decisions will affect net income

critical success factors (CSFs)   Measures of those aspects of the firm's performance that are essential to its competitive advantage and therefore to its success

cross-sectional regression   Estimates costs for a particular cost object based on information on other cost objects and variables, where the information for all variables is taken from the same period of time

currently attainable standard   A level of performance that workers with proper training and experience can attain most of the time without extraordinary effort

customer cost analysis   Identifies cost activities and cost drivers to service customers

customer equity   The sum of the CLVs for all the firm's customers

customer lifetime value (CLV)   The net present value of all estimated future profits from the customer

customer profitability analysis   Identifies customer service activities, cost drivers, and the profitability of individual customers or groups of customers

customer-response time   A measure of operating performance defined as the elapsed time between the time the customer places an order and the time the customer receives the order

CVP graph   Illustrates how the levels of revenues and total costs change over different levels of output

cycle time   The amount of time between receipt of a customer order and shipment of the order

D

death-spiral effect   Continual raising of selling prices in an attempt to recover fixed costs, in spite of successive decreases in demand; generally described as one of the dangers of cost-plus pricing

decentralized   A firm that has chosen to delegate a significant amount of responsibility to SBU managers.

degrees of freedom   Represents the number of independent choices that can be made for each component of variance

denominator activity level   The output (activity) level used to establish the predetermined fixed overhead application rate; generally defined as *practical capacity;* also called the denominator volume

denominator volume   The output (activity) level used to calculate the predetermined fixed overhead application rate; generally defined as *practical capacity;* also called the denominator activity level

departmental overhead rate   An overhead rate calculated for a single production department

dependent variable   The cost to be estimated

design analysis   A common form of value engineering in which the design team prepares several possible designs of the product, each having similar features with different levels of performance and different costs

design quality   The difference between customer expectations (for attributes, services, functionality, etc.) and actual product design

desired rate of return   The minimum rate of return the investing firm requires for an investment

differential cost   A cost that differs for each decision option and is therefore relevant

differentiation   A competitive strategy in which a firm succeeds by developing and maintaining a unique value for the product (or service) as perceived by consumers

direct cost   A cost conveniently and economically traced directly to a cost pool or a cost object

direct labor cost   The labor used to manufacture the product or to provide the service

direct labor efficiency variance   The difference between the actual hours worked and the standard hours allowed for the units manufactured, multiplied by the standard wage rate

direct labor rate variance   The difference between the actual and standard hourly wage rate multiplied by the actual direct hours worked during the period

direct materials cost   The cost of the materials in the product and a reasonable allowance for scrap and defective units

direct materials flexible-budget variance   For each material, the difference between total direct materials cost incurred and the flexible-budget amount for the units manufactured during the period

direct materials price variance   For each direct material, the difference between the actual and standard unit price of the material multiplied by the actual quantity used

direct materials purchases budget   A plan that shows the physical amount and cost of planned purchases of direct materials

direct materials usage budget   A plan that shows the amount and budgeted cost of direct materials required for production

direct materials usage variance   For each material, the difference between the actual units used during the period and the number of standard units that should have been used for the output of the period, multiplied by the standard cost per unit of the direct material

direct method   Service department cost allocation accomplished by using the service flows *only to production departments* and determining each production department's share of that service

discounted cash flow (DCF) models   Represent capital-budgeting decision models that incorporate the present value of future after-tax cash flows

discount rate   A generic term that refers to the rate used in capital budgeting for converting future cash flows to a present-value basis

discretionary-cost method   Used when costs are considered largely uncontrollable; apply discretion at the planning stage; an input-oriented approach

dual allocation   A cost allocation method that separates fixed and variable costs and traces variable service department costs to the user departments; fixed costs are allocated based on either equal shares among departments or a predetermined budgeted proportion

dual pricing   involves the use of multiple prices for an internal transfer or cost allocation, one based on variable cost and one based on fixed cost

dummy variable   Used to represent the presence or absence of a condition in a regression model

Durbin-Watson statistic   A measure of the extent of nonlinearity in the regression

E

economic value added (EVA®)   A measure of financial performance designed to approximate an entity's economic profit; calculated most often as net operating profit after-taxes (adjusted for accounting "distortions") less an imputed charge based on the level of invested capital

effective operation   The attainment of the goal set for the operation

employment contract   An agreement between the manager and top management, designed to provide incentives for the manager to act autonomously to achieve top management's objectives

engineered-cost method   An output-oriented method that considers costs to be variable and therefore controllable

enterprise risk management   A framework and process that firms use to manage the risks that could negatively or positively affect the company's competitiveness and success

enterprise sustainability   The balancing of the company's short- and long-term goals in all three dimensions of performance—social, environmental, and financial

equivalent units   The number of the same or similar completed units that could have been produced given the amount of work actually performed on both completed and partially completed units

executional cost drivers   Factors that the firm can manage in the short term to reduce costs such as workforce involvement, design of the production process, and supplier relationships

expected value of perfect information (EVPI)   The maximum amount that a rational decision maker would be willing to pay for "perfect information"

expropriation   A situation in which a government takes ownership and control of assets that a foreign investor has invested in that country

external failure costs   Costs associated with defective/poor-quality outputs detected after being delivered to customers

F

facility-level activity   An activity performed to support operations of products in general

factory overhead   All the indirect manufacturing costs commonly combined into a single cost pool in a manufacturing firm

factory overhead applied   The amount of overhead assigned to a cost object using a predetermined factory overhead rate

FIFO method   A process costing method for calculating the unit cost that includes only costs incurred and work performed during the current period

financial budgets   A plan that identifies sources and uses of funds for budgeted operations and capital expenditures for the coming period

financial control   The comparison between actual and budgeted financial results

financial productivity   The ratio of output to the dollar amount of one or more input factors

finished goods inventory   The cost of goods that are ready for sale

firmwide pool   A basis for determining the bonus available to all managers through an amount set aside for this purpose

fixed cost   The portion of the total cost that does not change with a change in the quantity of the cost driver, within the relevant range and a given time period (e.g., one year)

fixed overhead application rate   A term used for product-costing purposes; the rate at which fixed overhead is charged to production per unit of activity (or output)

fixed overhead production volume variance   The difference between budgeted fixed overhead and the standard fixed overhead applied to production (using the fixed overhead allocation rate); also called the production volume variance

fixed overhead spending (budget) variance   The difference between budgeted and actual fixed factory overhead costs for a period

fixed performance contract   An incentive compensation plan whereby compensation is a function of actual performance compared to a fixed (budgeted) target

flexible budget   A budget that adjusts revenues and costs to the actual output level achieved

flexible-budget (FB) variance   The difference between actual and flexible-budget amounts on the income statement

flow diagram   A flowchart of the work done that shows the sequence of processes and the amount of time required for each

***F*-statistic**   A useful measure of the statistical reliability of a regression model

full-cost method   A transfer price set equal to the variable cost plus allocated fixed cost for the selling unit

functional analysis   A common type of value engineering in which the performance and cost of each major function or feature of the product is examined

G

gaming the performance measure   Non-value-adding actions taken by managers to improve indicated performance

goal congruence   The consistency between the goals of the firm and the goals of its employees. It is achieved when the manager acts independently in such a way as to simultaneously achieve top management's objectives

goalpost conformance   Conformance to a quality specification expressed as a specified range around a target value

GPK (Grenzplankostenregnung)   Detailed German cost accounting system, roughly translated as *flexible-standard costing;* an extension of ABC

gross book value (GBV)   An asset's historical cost without the reduction for accumulated depreciation

group technology   A method of identifying similarities in the parts of products manufactured so the same part can be used in two or more products, thereby reducing costs

H

high-low method   A method using algebra to determine a *unique* estimation line between representative high and low points in a given data set

high-value-added activity   Increases the value of the product or service to the customer

histogram   A graphical representation of the frequency of attributes or events in a given set of data

historical cost   The book value of current assets plus the net book value of long-lived assets

hurdle rate   The minimum acceptable rate of return on an investment for capital-budgeting purposes, also referred to as the *required rate of return*

I

ideal standard   A standard that reflects perfect implementation and maximum efficiency in every aspect of the operation

implementation error   A deviation from standard due to operator errors

independent variable   The cost driver used to estimate the value of the dependent variable

indifference probability   The probability regarding states of nature that makes management indifferent between courses of action

indirect cost   A cost that is not conveniently or economically traceable to a specific cost pool or cost object

indirect labor cost   Supervision, quality control, inspection, purchasing and receiving, and other labor-related manufacturing support costs

indirect materials cost   The cost of materials used in manufacturing that are not easily or economically traceable to the finished product

internal accounting controls   A set of policies and procedures that restrict and guide activities in the processing of financial data with the objective of preventing or detecting errors and fraudulent acts

internal failure costs   Costs associated with defective processes or defective products detected before delivery to customers

internal rate of return (IRR)   An estimate of the true (i.e., economic) rate of return on an investment

investment center   A business unit that includes in its financial-performance metric the level assets (capital) employed by the unit as well as profit generated by that unit

ISO 9000   A set of guidelines for quality management and quality standards developed by the International Organization for Standardization, located in Geneva, Switzerland

ISO 14000   A set of quality standards designed to minimize environmental effects of an organization's outputs

J

job costing   A product costing system that accumulates and assigns costs to a specific job

job cost sheet   A cost sheet that records and summarizes the costs of direct materials, direct labor, and factory overhead for a particular job

joint products   Products from the same production process that have relatively substantial sales values

just-in-time (JIT) system   A comprehensive production and inventory system that purchases or produces materials and parts only as needed and just in time to be used at each stage of the production process

K

kaizen budgeting   A budgeting approach that incorporates continuous improvement expectations in the budget

kanban   A set of control cards used to signal the need for materials and products to move from one operation to the next in an assembly line

L

lean accounting   The accounting technique that uses value streams to measure the financial benefits of a firm's progress in implementing lean manufacturing

learning curve analysis   A systematic method for estimating costs when learning is present

learning rate   The percentage by which average time (or total time) falls from previous levels, as output doubles

least squares regression   One of the most effective methods for estimating costs, found by minimizing the sum of the squares of the estimation errors

life-cycle costing   A method used to identify and monitor the costs of a product throughout its life cycle

linear programming   A mathematical technique that can be used to solve for the best product mix

liquidation value   The estimated price that could be received from the sale of the assets of a business unit

long-range plan   A plan that identifies actions required during the 5- to 10-year period covered by the plan to attain the firm's strategic goals

low-value-added activity   Consumes time, resources, or space, but adds little to satisfying customer needs

M

management accounting   A profession that involves partnering in management decision making, devising planning and performance management systems, and providing expertise in financial reporting and control to assist management in the formulation and implementation of an organization's strategy

management accounting and control system   An organization's core performance-measurement system

management compensation plans   Policies and procedures for compensating managers

management control   The evaluation of mid-level managers by upper-level managers

managing earnings   The manipulation of reported income

manufacturing cycle efficiency (MCE)   The ratio of processing time to total cycle time

margin of safety   The excess of forecasted sales over breakeven sales

margin of safety ratio   A useful measure for comparing the risk of two or more alternative products

market-price method   A transfer price set as the current price of the product in the external market

market risk premium   The spread between the expected rate of return on a market portfolio of securities and the risk-free rate of return; represented as $(r_m - r_f)$, where r_m = return on a market portfolio of securities and r_f = risk-free rate of return

market share variance   A comparison of the firm's actual market share to its budgeted market share and measurement of the effect of changes in the firm's market share on its total contribution margin and operating income

market size variance   A measure of the effect of changes in the total market size on the firm's total contribution margin and operating income

master budget   A comprehensive plan of operations for the upcoming period; it translates short-term objectives into action steps; set of financial and operational budgets

master (static) budget variance   The difference between actual operating income and the master budget operating income for a period; also called the **operating-income variance**

materials inventory   Materials used in the manufacturing process or to provide the service

materials requisition   A department supervisor uses this to request materials for production

materials usage ratio   The ratio of the quantity used to the quantity purchased

mean absolute percentage error (MAPE)   Calculated by taking the absolute value of each prediction error, averaging these errors, and converting the result to a percentage of the actual value

mean squared variance   The ratio of the amount of variance of a component to the number of degrees of freedom for that component

measurement errors   Incorrect numbers resulting from improper or inaccurate accounting systems or procedures

merchandise purchases budget   A plan that shows the amount of merchandise the firm needs to purchase during the budget period

mixed cost   A cost that includes both variable and fixed cost components

modeling error   A deviation from the standard because of the failure to include all relevant variables or because of the inclusion of wrong or irrelevant variables in the standard-setting process

modified internal rate of return (MIRR)   The internal rate of return (IRR) of a capital investment adjusted to account for an assumed rate of return associated with interim project cash inflows

Monte Carlo simulation   An extension to scenario analysis in which a computer provides a distribution of possible outcomes, for example, project NPVs, based on repeated sampling from a distribution associated with each input variable in a decision model

multicollinearity   The condition when two or more independent variables are highly correlated with each other

multicriteria decision model   A model that includes more than one decision criterion

multiple linear regression   Used to describe regression applications having two or more independent variables

multistage ABC   The assignment of resource costs to certain activities which in turn are assigned to other activities before being assigned to the final cost objects

mutually exclusive projects   An extreme form of project interdependence: the acceptance of one investment alternative precludes the acceptance of one or more other alternatives

N

negotiated-price method   The determination of a transfer price through a negotiation process and sometimes arbitration between units

net book value (NBV)   An asset's historical cost less accumulated depreciation

net present value (NPV)   Equals the difference between the present value of future cash inflows and the present value of future cash outflows of an investment project

net realizable value (NRV)   The estimated sales value of the product at the split-off point is determined by subtracting the additional processing and selling costs beyond the split-off point from the ultimate sales value of the product

network diagram   A flowchart of the work done that shows the sequence of processes and the amount of time required for each

nonconstant variance   The condition when the variance of the errors is not constant over the range of the independent variable

noncontrollable fixed costs   Costs that are not controllable within a year's time, usually including facilities-related costs such as depreciation, taxes, and insurance

non-DCF models   Capital-budgeting models that are not based on the present value of future cash flows

non-value-added activity   An activity that does not contribute to customer value or to the organization's needs

normal capacity   The expected average demand per year over an intermediate term, for example, the upcoming three to five years

normal costing system   A costing process that uses actual costs for direct materials and direct labor and applies factory overhead to various jobs using a predetermined basis

normal spoilage   An unacceptable unit that occurs under efficient operating conditions; spoilage that is inherent in the manufacturing process

O

operating budgets   Plans that identify resources needed to support operating activities and the acquisition of these resources

operating-income variance   The difference between the actual operating income of the period and the master budget operating income projected for the period; also referred to as the **master (static) budget variance** for the period

operating leverage   The ratio of the contribution margin to operating profit at a given level of output. Also called the degree of operating leverage (DOL).

operational control   The monitoring of short-term operating performance; takes place when mid-level managers monitor the activities of operating-level managers and employees

operational productivity   The ratio of output to the number of units of an input factor

operation costing   A hybrid costing system that uses job costing to assign direct materials costs to jobs and process costing to assign conversion costs to products or services

opportunity cost   The benefit lost when choosing one option precludes receiving the benefits from an alternative option

order-filling costs   Expenditures for freight, warehousing, packing and shipping, and collections

order-getting costs   Expenditures to advertise and promote the product

outliers   Unusual data points that strongly influence a regression analysis

overapplied overhead   The amount of factory overhead applied that exceeds the actual factory overhead cost

overhead   All the indirect costs commonly combined into a single cost pool

overhead application or allocation   A process of allocating overhead costs to cost objects

overtime premium   The *excess* wage rate over the standard hourly wage rate

P

Pareto analysis   A management tool that shows 20 percent of a set of important cost drivers are responsible for 80 percent of the total cost incurred

Pareto diagram   A histogram of the frequency of factors contributing to a quality problem, ordered from the most to the least frequent

partial productivity   A productivity measure that focuses only on the relationship between one of the inputs and the output attained

participative standards   Active participation throughout the standard-setting process by employees affected by the standards

payback period   The length of time required for the cumulative after-tax cash inflows from an investment to recover the initial investment outlay

performance evaluation   The process by which managers at all levels gain information about the performance of tasks within the firm and judge that performance against preestablished criteria as set out in budgets, plans, and goals

performance measurement   A measurement that identifies items that indicate the work performed and the results achieved by an activity, process, or organizational unit

performance quality   The difference between the design specifications of the product and the actual performance of the product

period costs   All nonproduct expenditures for managing the firm and selling the product

physical measure method   A method that uses a physical measure such as pounds, gallons, yards, or units of volume produced at the split-off point to allocate the joint costs to joint products

planning and decision making   Budgeting and profit planning, cash flow management, and other decisions related to operations

plantwide overhead rate   A single overhead rate used throughout the entire production facility

post-audit   An in-depth review of a completed capital-investment project

practical capacity   Theoretical capacity reduced by normal output losses due to personal time, normal maintenance, and so on; the measure of capacity used to estimate cost-driver rates under ABC and TDABC systems

predatory pricing   Exists when a company has set prices below average variable cost and plans to raise prices later to recover the losses from the lower prices

predetermined factory overhead rate   An estimated rate used to apply factory overhead cost to a cost object

prediction error   A deviation from a standard because of an inaccurate estimation of the amounts for variables used in the standard-setting process

preparation of financial statements   Requires management to comply with the financial reporting requirements of regulatory agencies

present value   Equals future cash flows expressed in terms of current purchasing power; also referred to as time-adjusted value

present value payback period   The length of time required for the cumulative *present value* of after-tax cash inflows to recover the initial outlay for an investment

prevention costs   Costs incurred to keep quality defects from occurring

prime costs   The sum of direct materials and direct labor

principal-agent model   A conceptual model that contains the key elements that contracts must have to achieve the desired objectives

process costing   A costing system that accumulates product or service costs by process or department and then assigns them to a large number of nearly identical products

processing cycle efficiency (PCE) A measure of operating performance defined as the ratio of processing time to total manufacturing time (or, the ratio of value-added time to total time)

product costs Under GAAP, the costs necessary to complete the product (direct materials, direct labor, and factory overhead)

production budget A budget showing planned output (production) for an upcoming period

production cost report A report that summarizes the physical units and equivalent units of a department, the costs incurred during the period, and the costs assigned to units completed and to units in ending work-in-process inventories

production volume variance Represents the over- or under-applied budgeted fixed overhead for the period, that is, the difference between the fixed overhead costs applied to production and the (lump-sum) budgeted fixed overhead for the period; also called fixed overhead production volume variance

productivity The ratio of output to input

product-level activity An activity performed to support the production of a specific product or service

profit center A business unit whose manager is responsible for revenues and expenses, but not the level of invested capital, in the unit

profitability index (PI) A rate-of-return measure, defined as the ratio of the NPV of a project to the original investment outlay for the project

profit-volume graph Illustrates how the level of profits changes over different levels of output

p-value Measures the risk that a particular independent variable has only a chance relationship to the dependent variable

Q

quality Defined as customer satisfaction with the total experience of a product or service, that is, the difference between customer expectations and actual performance of the product or service

quality circle A small group of employees from the same work area that meets regularly to identify and solve work-related problems, and to implement and monitor solutions to these problems

quality function deployment (QFD) The integration of value engineering, marketing analysis, and target costing to assist in determining which components of the product should be targeted for re-design

R

random variances Variances beyond the control of management, either technically or financially, that often are considered as uncontrollable variances

rank-order correlation A statistic that measures the degree to which two sets of numbers tend to have the same order or rank

real assets Investments in both tangible property (e.g., a manufacturing facility) and intangible property (e.g., a new information system); can be contrasted with real options

real options Flexibilities and/or growth opportunities embedded in capital-investment projects; can be contrasted with financial options, which are traded on an organized exchange

reciprocal flows The flow of services back and forth between service departments

reciprocal method A cost allocation method that considers all reciprocal flows between service departments through simultaneous equations

regression analysis A statistical method for obtaining the unique cost-estimating equation that best fits a set of data points

relative performance contracts Assessment of performance based on comparison of actual results with specified benchmarks, not budgeted targets; contrast with fixed-performance contracts

relevant cost A cost with two properties: it differs for each decision option and it will be incurred in the future

relevant range The range of the cost driver in which the actual value of the cost driver is expected to fall, and for which the relationship is assumed to be approximately linear

replacement cost The current cost to replace the assets at the current level of service and functionality

resale-price method A transfer-pricing method based on determining an appropriate markup based on gross profits of unrelated firms selling similar products

residual income (RI) A dollar amount equal to the income of a business unit less a charge for the level of investment in the division

resource An economic element applied or used to perform activities

resource-capacity planning Procedures used to ensure adequate but not excessive supply of capacity-related resources

resource consumption accounting (RCA) An adaptation of ABC that emphasizes resource consumption by greatly increasing the number of resource cost pools, which allows more direct tracing of resource costs to cost objects than does an ABC system with fewer cost centers; a comprehensive cost-management system represented as a cross between GPK and ABC

resource consumption cost driver An activity or characteristic that consumes resources

return on investment (ROI) Some measure of profit divided by some measure of investment in a business unit

return on sales (ROS) A firm's profit per sales dollar; measures the manager's ability to control expenses and increase revenues to improve profitability

revenue center A business unit with responsibility for sales, defined either by product line or by geographical area and focuses on the selling function

revenue drivers The factors that affect sales volume, such as price changes, promotions, discounts, customer service, changes in product features, delivery dates, and other value-added factors

rework A produced unit that must be reworked into a good unit that can be sold in regular channels

risk preferences The way individuals differentially view decision options, because they place a weight on *certain* outcomes that differs from the weight they place on *uncertain* outcomes

robot A computer-programmed and controlled machine that performs repetitive activities

rolling financial forecast A constant planning horizon with the use of regularly updated forecasts

R-squared A number between zero and one. Often it is described as a measure of the explanatory power of the regression;

that is, the degree to which changes in the dependent variable can be predicted by changes in the independent variable

run chart A chart that shows trends in quality measures over time

S

salary A fixed payment

sales budget A schedule showing forecasted sales in units and at expected selling prices

sales life cycle The sequence of phases in a product's or service's life in the market—from the introduction of the product or service to the market, to growth in sales, and finally maturity, decline, and withdrawal from the market

sales mix The proportion of units (or dollars) of each product or service to the total of all products or services

sales mix variance The product of the difference between the actual and budgeted sales mix multiplied by the actual total number of units of all products sold, and by the budgeted contribution margin per unit of the product

sales quantity variance The product of three elements: (1) the difference between the budgeted and actual total sales quantity, (2) the budgeted sales mix of the product, and (3) the budgeted contribution margin per unit of the product. It measures the effect of the change in the number of units sold from the number of units budgeted to be sold

sales value at split-off method A method that allocates joint costs to joint products on the basis of their relative sales values at the split-off point

sales volume variance The difference between the flexible-budget amount for that item and the amount for that item reflected in the master budget for the period for each income statement item

schedule of cost of goods manufactured and sold A schedule that shows the manufacturing costs incurred, the change in the work-in-process inventory, the cost of goods sold, and the change in finished goods inventory during the period

scenario analysis Represents an attempt to look at how a proposed investment project would fare under different combinations of variables, called *scenarios;* a special form of sensitivity analysis that is appropriate when the variables in a decision model are interrelated

scrap Residual output that has little or no value

selling price variance The difference between the total actual sales revenue and the total flexible-budget sales revenue for the units sold during a period

sensitivity analysis The process of selectively varying a key input variable, for example, the discount rate, to identify the range over which a capital-budgeting decision is valid

simple linear regression Used to describe regression applications having a single independent variable

Six Sigma An overall strategy to accelerate improvements and achieve unprecedented performance levels by focusing on characteristics that are critical to customers and identifying and eliminating causes of errors or defects in processes

Solver An analytical tool available on the Data Tab in Excel which can be used to solve linear programming problems

split-off point The first point in a joint production process at which individual products can be identified

spoilage An unaccepted unit that is discarded or sold for disposal value

standard cost The cost a firm should incur for an operation

standard cost sheet A listing of the standard price and quantity of each manufacturing cost element for the production of one unit of a product

standard cost system One in which standard, not actual, costs flow through the formal accounting records

standard error of the estimate (SE) A measure of the accuracy of the regression's estimates

static budget variance (See **master budget variance**)

statistical control charts Charts that set control limits using a statistical procedure

step cost A cost that varies with the cost driver, but in discrete steps; also called semi-fixed cost

step method A cost allocation method that uses a sequence of steps in allocating service department costs to production departments

strategic budget expenditures Planned spending on projects and initiatives that lead to long-term value and competitive advantage

strategic business unit (SBU) A well-defined set of controllable operating activities over which an SBU manager is responsible

strategic control system The processes and procedures organizations use to monitor progress toward strategic goals of the organization

strategic cost management The development of cost management information to facilitate the principal management function, strategic management

strategic management The development and implementation of a sustainable competitive position

strategic performance measurement An accounting system used by top management for the evaluation of SBU managers

strategy A plan for using resources to achieve sustainable goals within a competitive environment

strategy map A graphical representation of the organization's value proposition; used to depict the series of cause-and-effects embodied in the four perspectives of an organization's balanced scorecard

structural cost drivers Strategic plans and decisions that have a long-term effect with regard to issues such as scale, experience, technology, and complexity

sunk costs Costs that have been incurred in the past or committed for the future, and are therefore irrelevant for decision-making purposes

sustainability The balancing of short- and long-term goals in all three dimensions of the company's performance—social, economic, and environmental

SWOT analysis A systematic procedure for identifying a firm's critical success factors: its internal strengths and weaknesses, and its external opportunities and threats

systematic (controllable) variances Variances that, until corrected, are likely to recur; also called nonrandom variances

T

Taguchi quality loss function Depicts the relationship between quality costs and level of deviation from target quality

Takt time   The speed at which units must be manufactured to meet customer demand

target costing   The desired cost for a product as determined on the basis of a given competitive price, so the product will earn a desired profit

theoretical capacity   A measure of capacity (output or activity) that assumes 100 percent efficiency; maximum possible output (or activity)

theory of constraints (TOC)   An analysis of operations that improves profitability and cycle time by identifying the bottleneck in the operation and determining the most profitable product mix given the bottleneck

throughput margin   A TOC measure of product profitability; it equals price less materials cost, including all purchased components and materials handling costs

time-driven activity-based budgeting   An approach to budgeting wherein budgets are prepared in conjunction with a time-driven activity-based cost (TDABC) system

time-driven activity-based costing (TDABC)   The assignment of resource costs directly to cost objects using the cost per time unit of supplying the resource, rather than first assigning costs to activities and then from activities to cost objects

time-series regression   The application of regression analysis to predict future amounts, using prior periods' data

time ticket   A sheet showing the time an employee worked on each job, the pay rate, and the total cost chargeable to each job

tolerance   An acceptable range of a quality characteristic, such as thickness (measured, for example, in centimeters)

total contribution margin   The unit contribution margin multiplied by the number of units sold

total fixed overhead variance   The difference between actual fixed overhead costs for the period and the standard fixed overhead costs charged to production for the period; this variance can be broken down into a fixed overhead spending variance and a fixed overhead production volume variance

total flexible-budget (FB) variance   The difference between the flexible-budget operating income and the actual operating income for the period

total manufacturing cost   The sum of materials used, labor, and overhead for the period

total flexible-budget variance for overhead   The difference between the actual overhead for a period and the flexible budget for overhead based on *output*

total productivity   A measure including all input resources in computing the ratio of the output attained and the input used to attain the output

total quality management (TQM)   The unyielding and continuous effort by everyone in the organization to understand, meet, and exceed customer expectations

total variable cost flexible-budget (FB) variance   The difference between variable costs incurred and the total variable costs in the flexible budget for the period

total variable overhead variance   The difference between actual variable overhead cost incurred and the standard variable overhead cost applied to production; also called "over- or underapplied variable overhead" for the period

transfer pricing   The determination of an exchange price for a product or service when different business units within a firm exchange it

transferred-in costs   The costs of work performed in the earlier department that are transferred into the present department

trend variable   A variable that takes on values of 1, 2, 3, . . . for each period in sequence

***t*-value**   A measure of the reliability of each of the independent variables; that is, the degree to which an independent variable has a valid, stable, long-term relationship with the dependent variable

two-stage cost allocation   A procedure that assigns a firm's resource costs, namely resource costs, to cost pools and then to cost objects

U

underapplied overhead   The amount that actual factory overhead exceeds the factory overhead applied

unit-based pool   A basis for determining a bonus according to the performance of the manager's unit

unit contribution margin   The difference between unit sales price and unit variable cost; it is a measure of the change in profit for a unit change in sales

unit cost   The total manufacturing cost (materials, labor, and overhead) divided by the number of units of output

unit-level activity   An activity performed for each unit of the cost object

units accounted for   The sum of the units transferred out and ending inventory units

units to account for   The sum of the beginning inventory units and the number of units started during the period

V

value activities   Firms in an industry perform activities to design, manufacture, and provide customer service.

value-added activity   An activity that contributes to customer value and satisfaction or satisfies an organizational need

value chain   An analytic tool firms use to identify the specific steps required to provide a product or service to the customer

value-chain analysis   A strategic analysis tool used to identify where value to customers can be increased or costs reduced, and to better understand the firm's linkages with suppliers, customers, and other firms in the industry

value engineering   Used in target costing to reduce product cost by analyzing the trade-offs between different types of product functionality and total product cost

value stream   A group of related products; useful for preparing profitability reports as part of lean accounting

variable cost   The change in total cost associated with each change in the quantity of the cost driver

variable-cost method   In transfer pricing, the transfer price equals the variable cost of the selling unit

variable expense flexible-budget variance   The difference between the actual variable expenses incurred and the total standard variable expenses in the flexible budget for the units sold during the period

variable overhead efficiency variance   The difference between the flexible budget for variable overhead based on *inputs* (e.g., actual labor hours worked) and the flexible budget for variable overhead based on *outputs* (i.e., standard allowed labor hours for units produced)

variable overhead spending variance   The difference between actual variable overhead cost incurred and the flexible budget for variable overhead based on *inputs* for the period (e.g., actual labor hours worked)

variances   The differences between budgeted and actual amounts, for either financial or nonfinancial measures

W

weighted-average cost of capital (WACC)   An average of the (after-tax) cost of debt and equity capital for a firm; in general, the WACC is the appropriate discount rate to use for future cash flows associated with "average risk" projects

weighted-average method   A method for calculating unit cost that includes all costs, both those incurred during the current period and those incurred in the prior period that are shown as the beginning work-in-process inventory of the current period

what-if analysis   The calculation of an amount given different levels for a factor that influences that amount

work cells   Small groups of related manufacturing processes organized in clusters to assemble parts of finished products

work-in-process inventory   Contains all costs put into the manufacture of products that are started but not complete at the financial statement date

Y

yield-to-maturity   A long-term bond yield (rate of return) expressed as an annual rate; the calculation takes into account the current market price of the bond, its par value, the coupon interest rate, and the time-to-maturity; the total performance of a bond, coupon payments as well as capital gain or loss, from the time of purchase until maturity

Z

zero-base budgeting (ZBB)   A budgeting process that requires managers to prepare budgets each period from a base of zero

INDEX

Page numbers followed by n refer to notes.

A